First Philosophy

First Philosophy

Fundamental Problems and Readings in Philosophy

SECOND EDITION

Knowing and Being

Edited by

ANDREW BAILEY

with

ROBERT M. MARTIN

broadview press

Library and Archives Canada Cataloguing in Publication

    First philosophy : fundamental problems and readings in philosophy : knowing and being / general editor Andrew Bailey ; contributing editor Robert M. Martin.

Second edition.
Includes bibliographical references.
ISBN 978-1-55481-181-6

    1. Knowledge, Theory of. 2. Metaphysics. I. Bailey, Andrew, 1969-, editor of compilation II. Martin, Robert M., editor of compilation.

B29.F573 2013   110   C2013-901048-3

Broadview Press is an independent, international publishing house, incorporated in 1985.

We welcome comments and suggestions regarding any aspect of our publications—please feel free to contact us at the addresses below or at broadview@broadviewpress.com.

North America   PO Box 1243, Peterborough, Ontario, Canada K9J 7H5
2215 Kenmore Ave., Buffalo, New York, USA 14207
Tel: (705) 743-8990; Fax: (705) 743-8353
email: customerservice@broadviewpress.com

UK, Europe, Central Asia,   Eurospan Group, 3 Henrietta St., London WC2E 8LU, United Kingdom
Middle East, Africa, India,   Tel: 44 (0) 1767 604972; Fax: 44 (0) 1767 601640
and Southeast Asia   email: eurospan@turpin-distribution.com

Australia and   NewSouth Books
New Zealand   c/o TL Distribution, 15-23 Helles Ave., Moorebank, NSW, Australia 2170
Tel: (02) 8778 9999; Fax: (02) 8778 9944
email: orders@tldistribution.com.au

www.broadviewpress.com

Broadview Press acknowledges the financial support of the Government of Canada through the Canada Book Fund for our publishing activities.

This book is printed on paper containing 50% postconsumer fibre.

PRINTED IN CANADA

CONTENTS

HOW TO USE THIS BOOK

This book is an introduction to epistemology and metaphysics. Within these areas, it is intended to be a reasonably representative—though very far from exhaustive—sampling of important philosophical questions, major philosophers and their most important works, periods of philosophical history, and styles of philosophical thought.[1] Nearly half of the included readings, however, were published since 1950, and another important aim of the book is to provide some background for *current* philosophical debates, to give the interested reader a springboard for the plunge into the exciting world of contemporary philosophy (debates about the nature of consciousness, say, or quantum theories of free will, or the status of scientific knowledge, or …).

The aim of this book is to introduce philosophy through philosophy itself: it is not a book *about* philosophy but a book *of* philosophy, in which dozens of great philosophers speak for themselves. Each of the readings is prefaced by a set of notes, but these notes make no attempt to explain or summarize the reading. Instead, the goal of the notes is to provide *background information* helpful for understanding the reading—to remove as many of the unnecessary barriers to comprehension as possible, and to encourage a deeper and more sophisticated encounter with great pieces of philosophy. The notes to selections, therefore, do not stand alone and *certainly* are not a substitute for the reading itself: they are meant to be consulted in combination with the reading. (The philosophical selections are also quite heavily annotated throughout by the editor, again in an effort to get merely contingent difficulties for comprehension out of the way and allow the reader to devote all his or her effort to understanding the philosophy itself.)

The reader can of course take or leave these notes as they choose, and read them (or not) in any order. One good way of proceeding, however, would be the following. First, read the selection (so that nothing said in the notes inadvertently taints your first impression of the piece). Then, go back and read some of the notes—the biographical sketch, information on the author's philosophical project, structural and background information—and with these things in mind read the selection again. Spend some time *thinking* about the reading: ask yourself if you really feel you have a good grasp on what the author is trying to say, and then—no less importantly—ask yourself whether the author gives good reasons to believe that their position is *true*. (Chapter 1 tries to give some helpful suggestions for this process of critical reflection.) After this, it should be worthwhile going back to the notes, checking your impressions against any 'common misconceptions,' and then running through at least some of the suggestions for critical reflection. Finally, you might want to go on and read more material by the philosopher in question, or examine what other philosophers have said about his or her ideas: the suggestions for further reading will point you in the right direction.

A word of explanation about the 'Suggestions for Critical Reflection' section: although the notes to the readings contain no philosophical critique of the selection, the questions in this section are largely intended to help the reader generate his or her own critique. As such, they are supposed to be thought-provoking, rather than straightforwardly easy to answer. They try to suggest fruitful avenues for critical thought (though they do not cover every possible angle of questioning, or even all the important ones), and only very rarely is there some particular 'right an-

---

1 There are two major exceptions to this. First, this book focuses exclusively on 'Western' philosophy—that is, roughly, on the philosophical traditions of Europe and of the descendents of European settlers in North America and Australasia. In particular, it does not attempt to encompass the rich philosophical heritage of Asia or Africa. Second, this collection generally ignores an important strain of twentieth-century philosophy, so-called 'Continental' philosophy, which includes thinkers such as Husserl, Heidegger, Sartre, Foucault, Derrida, and Habermas, and is characterized by such movements as existentialism, hermeneutics, structuralism, and deconstructionism.

swer' to the question. Thus, these questions should not be considered a kind of 'self-test' to see if you understand the material: even people with a very good grasp of the material will typically be puzzled by the questions—because they are *supposed* to be puzzling questions.

The readings and their accompanying notes are designed to be 'modular'; that is, in general, one reading can be understood without the benefit of having read any of the other selections. This means that the selections can be read in any order. The current arrangement of the readings groups them by topic, and then orders them so that they follow a reasonably natural progression through a particular philosophical problem. However, quite different courses of study could be plotted through this book, emphasizing, say, philosophers grouped by nationality, by historical period, by philosophical approach, and so on. Furthermore, often readings from one section can quite naturally be brought into another (e.g., Descartes's *Meditations* into the Philosophy of Mind section). One natural way of doing the readings is chronologically; here is a list of the contents of the book arranged according to the date of the first 'publication' of the work in its original language:

The readings in this anthology are, so far as is practicable, 'complete': that is, they are entire articles, chapters, or sections of books. The editors feel it is important for students to be able to see an argument in the context in which it was originally presented; also, the fact that the readings are not edited to include only what is relevant to one particular philosophical concern means that they can be used in a variety of different ways following a variety of different lines of thought across the ages. Some instructors will wish to assign for their students shorter excerpts of some of these readings, rather than having them read all of the work included: the fact that complete, or almost complete, pieces of philosophy are included in this anthology gives the instructor the freedom to pick the excerpts that best fit their pedagogical aims. We have also included an alternative table of contents giving suggestions for abridgement corresponding to the shortened pieces most commonly found in other introductory philosophy anthologies.

The notes to the readings in this anthology are almost entirely a work of synthesis, and a large number of books and articles were consulted in their preparation; it is impossible—without adding an immense apparatus of notes and references—to acknowledge them in detail, but all my main sources have been included as suggestions for further reading. This is, I believe, appropriate for a textbook, but it is not intended to model good referencing practices for student essays. All the material and annotations accompanying the readings was written by the editors, and none of it (unless otherwise noted) was copied from other sources. Typically, the notes for each reading amalgamate information from a dozen or so sources; in a few instances, especially for biographical information on still-living philosophers, the notes rely heavily on a smaller number of sources (and I tried to indicate this in the text when it occurred). These sources are not footnoted in the body of the text, as they should be in a student (or professional) essay. However, citations are provided at the back of the book for all direct quotations. All of the books, articles and websites that I referred to and found useful are also listed in bibliographies: Chapter 1 lists general works of reference, and the introductory material for each selection includes suggestions for further reading which include the works I looked at (when I found them helpful).

Students should make sure they are aware of the citation system that their instructor prefers them to use in their class work.

Thanks to Alan Belk, Lance Hickey, Peter Loptson, and Mark Migotti for pointing out errors and omissions in earlier editions. In case of new editions but also, more importantly, for the general good of his soul, the editor would warmly welcome further corrections or suggestions for improvement:

Andrew Bailey
Department of Philosophy
The University of Guelph
Guelph, Ontario N1G 2W1
Canada
abailey@uoguelph.ca

SUGGESTIONS FOR ABRIDGEMENT

The following version of the table of contents identifies shorter excerpts of the readings—often those selections most frequently reprinted in other introductory philosophy anthologies—as suggestions for instructors who wish to assign briefer readings for their students.

CHAPTER 1

Philosophy

WHAT IS PHILOSOPHY?

Philosophy, at least according to the origin of the word in classical Greek, is the "love of wisdom"—philosophers are lovers of wisdom. The first philosophers of the Western tradition lived on the shores of the Mediterranean in the sixth century BCE (that is, more than 2,500 years ago);[1] thinkers such as Thales, Xenophanes, Pythagoras, Heraclitus, and Protagoras tried systematically to answer questions about the ultimate nature of the universe, the standards of knowledge, the objectivity of moral claims, and the existence and nature of God. Questions like these are still at the core of the discipline today.

So what is philosophy? It can be characterized either as a particular sort of *method*, or in terms of its *subject matter*, or as a kind of intellectual *attitude*.

Philosophy as a Method

One view is that philosophy studies the same things—the same world—as, for example, scientists do, but that they do so in a different, and complementary, way. In particular, it is often claimed that while scientists draw conclusions from empirical *observations* of the world, philosophers use *rational arguments* to justify claims about the world. For instance, both scientists and philosophers are involved in contemporary studies of the human mind. Neuroscientists and psychologists are busily mapping out correlations between brain states and mental states—finding which parts of the visual

cortex play a role in dreaming, for example—and building computer models of intelligent information processing (such as chess-playing programs). Philosophers are also involved in cognitive science, trying to discover just what would *count* as discovering that dreaming is really nothing more than certain electro-chemical events in the brain, or would count as building a computer which feels pain or genuinely has beliefs. These second kinds of questions are crucial to the whole project of cognitive science, but they are not empirical, scientific questions: there simply is no fact about the brain that a scientist could observe to answer them. And so these questions—which are part of cognitive science—are dealt with by philosophers.

Here are two more examples. Economists study the distribution of wealth in society, and develop theories about how wealth and other goods can come to be distributed one way rather than another (e.g., concentrated in a small proportion of the population, as in Brazil, or spread more evenly across society, as in Sweden). However, questions about which kind of distribution is more *just*, which kind of society is best to live in, are not answered within economic theory—these are philosophical questions. Medical professionals are concerned with facts about sickness and death, and often have to make decisions about the severity of an illness or weigh the risk of death from a certain procedure. Philosophers also examine the phenomenon of death, but ask different questions: for example, they ask whether people can survive their own deaths (i.e., if there is a soul), whether death is really a harm for the person who dies, under what conditions—if any—we should assist people in committing suicide, and so on.

---

1   In the East, Lao-Tzu, the founder of Taoism, probably lived at about the same time in China. Buddha and Confucius were born a few decades later. In India, an oral literature called the *Veda* had been asking philosophical questions since at least 1500 BCE.

One reason why philosophers deal differently with phenomena than scientists do is that philosophers are using different techniques of investigation. The core of the philosophical method is the application of *rational thought* to problems. There are (arguably) two main aspects to this: the use of conceptual or linguistic *analysis* to clarify ideas and questions; and the use of formal or informal *logic* to argue for certain answers to those questions.

For example, questions about the morality of abortion often pivot on the following question: is a foetus a *person* or not? A person is, roughly, someone who has similar moral status to a normal adult human being. Being a person is not simply *the same thing* as being a member of the human species, however, since it is at least possible that some human beings are not persons (brain-dead individuals in permanent comas, for example?) and some persons might not be human beings (intelligent life from other planets, or gorillas, perhaps?). If it turns out that a foetus *is* a person, abortion will be morally problematic—it may even be a kind of murder. On the other hand, if a foetus is no more a person than, say, one of my kidneys, abortion may be as morally permissible as a transplant. So *is* a foetus a person? How would one even go about discovering the answer to this question? Philosophers proceed by using *conceptual analysis*. What we need to find out, first of all, is what makes something a person—what the essential difference is between persons and non-persons—and then we can apply this general account to human foetuses to see if they satisfy the definition. Put another way, we need to discover precisely what the word "person" means.

Since different conceptual analyses will provide importantly different answers to questions about the morality of abortion, we need to *justify* our definition: we need to give reasons to believe that one particular analysis of personhood is correct. This is where logic comes in: logic is the study of arguments, and its techniques are designed to distinguish between good arguments—by which we should be persuaded—and bad arguments, which we should not find persuasive. (The next main section of this chapter will tell you a little more about logic.)

Philosophy as a Subject Matter

Another way of understanding philosophy is to say that philosophers study a special set of issues, and that it is this subject matter which defines the subject. Philosophical questions fit three major characteristics:

1. They are of deep and lasting interest to human beings;
2. They have answers, but the answers have not yet been settled on;
3. The answers cannot be decided by science, faith, or common sense.

Philosophers try to give the best possible answers to such questions. That is, they seek the one answer which is more justified than any other possible answer. There are lots of questions which count as philosophical, according to these criteria. All can be classified as versions of one of three basic philosophical questions.

The first foundational philosophical question is *What exists?* For example: Does God exist? Are quarks really real, or are they just fictional postulates of a particular scientific theory? Are numbers real? Do persons exist, and what is the difference between a person and her physical body, or between a person and a 'mere animal'? The various questions of existence are studied by the branch of philosophy called Metaphysics, and by its various sub-fields such as Philosophy of Mind and Philosophy of Religion.

The second fundamental philosophical question is *What do we know?* For example, can we be sure that a scientific theory is actually true, or is it merely the currently dominant simplification of reality? The world appears to us to be full of colors and smells, but can we ever find out whether it really is colored or smelly (i.e., even if no one is perceiving it)? Everyone believes that 5+6=11, but what makes us so sure of this—could we be wrong, and if not, why not? The branch of philosophy which deals with these kinds of questions is called Epistemology. Philosophy of Science examines the special claims to knowledge made by the natural sciences, and Logic is the study of the nature of rational justification.

The third major philosophical question is *What should we do?* If I make a million dollars selling widgets or playing basketball, is it okay for me to keep all of that money and do what I want with it, or do I have some kind of moral obligation to give a portion of my income to the less well off? If I could get out of trouble by telling a lie, and no one else will really be harmed by my lie, is it alright to do so? Is Mozart's *Requiem* more or less artistically valuable than The Beatles' *Sergeant Pepper's Lonely Hearts Club Band*? Questions like these are addressed by Value Theory, which includes such philosophical areas as Ethics, Aesthetics, Political Philosophy, and Philosophy of Law.

Philosophy as an Attitude

A third view is that philosophy is a state of being—a kind of intellectual independence. Philosophy is a reflective activity, an attitude of critical and systematic thoughtfulness. To be philosophical is to continue to question the assumptions behind every claim until we come to our most basic beliefs about reality, and then to critically examine those beliefs. For example, most of us assume that criminals are responsible for their actions, and that this is at least partly why we punish them. But *are* they responsible for what they do? We know that social pressures are very powerful in affecting our behavior. Is it unfair to make individuals entirely responsible for society's effects on them when those effects are negative? How much of our personal identity is bound up with the kind of community we belong to, and how far are we free to choose our own personalities and values? Furthermore, it is common to believe that the brain is the physical cause of all our behavior, that the brain is an entirely physical organ, and that all physical objects are subject to deterministic causal laws. If all of this is right, then presumably all human behavior is just the result of complex causal laws affecting our brain and body, and we could no more choose our actions than a falling rock could choose to take a different route down the mountainside. If this is true, then can we even make sense of the notion of moral responsibility? If it is not true, then where does free will come from and how (if at all) does it allow us to escape the laws of physics? Here, a questioning attitude towards our assumptions about criminals has shown that we might not have properly considered the bases of our assumptions. This ultimately leads us to fundamental questions about the place of human beings in the world.

Here are three quotes from famous philosophers which give the flavor of this view of philosophy as a critical attitude:

Socrates, one of the earliest Western philosophers, who lived in Greece around 400 BCE, is said to have declared that "it is the greatest good for a man to discuss virtue every day and those other things about which you hear me conversing and testing myself and others, for the unexamined life is not worth living."

Immanuel Kant—the most important thinker of the late eighteenth century—called this philosophical state of being "Enlightenment."

> Enlightenment is the emergence of man from the immaturity for which he is himself responsible. Immaturity is the inability to use one's understanding without the guidance of another. Man is responsible for his own immaturity, when it is caused, by lack not of understanding, but of the resolution and the courage to use it without the guidance of another. *Sapere aude!* Have the courage to use your own reason! is the slogan of Enlightenment.

Finally, in the twentieth century, Bertrand Russell wrote the following assessment of the value of philosophy:

> Philosophy is to be studied, not for the sake of any definite answers to its questions, since no definite answers can, as a rule, be known to be true, but rather for the sake of the questions themselves; because these questions enlarge our conception of what is possible, enrich our intellectual imagination and diminish the dogmatic assurance which closes the mind against speculation; but above all because, through the greatness of the universe which philosophy contemplates, the mind also is rendered great, and becomes capable of that union with the universe which constitutes its highest good.

Questions for Further Thought:

1. Here are some more examples of phenomena which are studied by both scientists and philosophers: color, sense perception, medical

practices like abortion and euthanasia, human languages, mathematics, quantum mechanics, the evolution of species, democracy, taxation. What contribution (if any) might philosophers make to the study of these topics?

2. How well does *mathematics* fit into the division between science and philosophy described above? How does *religion* fit into this classification?

3. Here are a few simple candidate definitions of "person": a person is anything which is capable of making rational decisions; a person is any creature who can feel pain; a person is any creature with a soul; a person is any creature which has the appropriate place in a human community. Which of these, if any, do you think are plausible? What are the consequences of these definitions for moral issues like abortion or vegetarianism? Try to come up with a more sophisticated conceptual analysis of personhood.

4. Do you think criminals are responsible for their actions?

5. Should society support philosophy, and to what degree (e.g., should tax dollars be spent paying philosophers to teach at public universities? Why (not)?)?

Suggestions for Further Reading

As a general rule, it is far better to read philosophy than to read *about* philosophy. A brief but moving work often anthologized in the "what is philosophy" section of introductory textbooks is Plato's *Apology*, which features a speech by Socrates defending the practice of philosophy in the face of his fourth-century BCE Athenian contemporaries, who are about to condemn him to death for it. Two more modern works, which are introductions to philosophy but also significant pieces of philosophy in their own right, are Bertrand Russell's *The Problems of Philosophy* (Oxford University Press, 1912) and *The Central Questions of Philosophy* by A.J. Ayer (Penguin, 1973).

Two aging, slightly idiosyncratic, but nevertheless well-respected histories of western philosophy are Bertrand Russell's *A History of Western Philosophy* (George Allen & Unwin, 1961) and the massive *History of Philosophy* by Frederick Copleston, originally published between 1946 and 1968 and recently re-issued in nine garish volumes by Image Books. Two shorter and more recent histories are *A Brief History of Western Philosophy* by Anthony Kenny (Blackwell, 1998) and *The Oxford Illustrated History of Western Philosophy*, edited by Anthony Kenny (Oxford University Press, 1994).

Finally, there are a number of useful philosophical reference works. The major encyclopedia of philosophy is now the ten-volume *Routledge Encyclopedia of Philosophy*, published in 1998. This replaced the old standby—which is still a useful work, consisting of eight volumes—*The Encyclopedia of Philosophy* edited by Paul Edwards (Macmillan, 1967). Shorter philosophy reference works include *The Concise Routledge Encyclopedia of Philosophy* (Routledge, 2000); *The Cambridge Dictionary of Philosophy*, edited by Robert Audi (Cambridge University Press, 1999); the *Oxford Dictionary of Philosophy*, by Simon Blackburn (Oxford University Press, 1996); *The Blackwell Companion to Philosophy*, edited by Nicholas Bunnin and E.P. Tsui-James (Blackwell, 1996); *The Oxford Companion to Philosophy*, edited by Ted Honderich (Oxford University Press, 1995); *The Philosopher's Dictionary*, by Robert Martin (Broadview, 1994); and the *Penguin Dictionary of Philosophy*, edited by Thomas Mautner (Penguin, 1997). Online philosophy is not always very reliable and should be treated with caution, but two websites which are dependable and likely to be around for a while are the *Stanford Encyclopedia of Philosophy* (http://plato.stanford.edu/) and *The Internet Encyclopedia of Philosophy* (http://www. utm.edu/research/iep/).

A BRIEF INTRODUCTION TO ARGUMENTS

Evaluating Arguments

The main tool of philosophy is the *argument*. An argument is any sequence of statements intended to establish—or at least to make plausible—some particular claim. For example, if I say that Vancouver is a better place to live than Toronto because it has a beautiful setting between the mountains and the ocean, is less congested, and has a lower cost of living, then I am making an argument. The claim which is being defended is called the *conclusion*, and the statements which together are supposed to show that the conclusion is (likely to be) true are called the *premises*. Often arguments will be strung together in a sequence, with the conclusions of earlier arguments featuring as premises of the later ones. For example, I might go on to argue that since Vancouver is a better place to live than Toronto, and since one's living conditions are a big part of what determines one's happiness, then the people who live in Vancouver must, in general, be happier than those living in Toronto. Usually, a piece of philosophy is primarily made up of chains of argumentation: good philosophy consists of good arguments; bad philosophy contains bad arguments.

What makes the difference between a good and a bad argument? It's important to notice, first of all, that the difference is *not* that good arguments have true conclusions and bad arguments have false ones. A perfectly good argument might, unluckily, happen to have a conclusion that is false. For example, you might argue that you know this rope will bear my weight because you know that the rope's rating is greater than my weight, you know that the rope's manufacturer is a reliable one, you have a good understanding of the safety standards which are imposed on rope makers and vendors, and you have carefully inspected this rope for flaws. Nevertheless, it still might be the case that this rope is the one in 50 million which has a hidden defect causing it to snap. If so, that makes me unlucky, but it doesn't suddenly make your argument a bad one—we were still being quite reasonable when we trusted the rope. On the other hand, it is very easy to give appallingly bad arguments for true conclusions: Every sentence beginning with the letter "c" is true; "Chickens lay eggs" begins with the letter "c"; Therefore, chickens lay eggs.

But there is a deeper reason why the evaluation of arguments doesn't begin by assessing the truth of the conclusion. The whole point of making arguments is to establish *whether or not* some particular claim is true or false. An argument works by starting from some claims which, ideally, everyone is willing to accept as true—the premises—and then showing that something interesting—something *new*—follows from them: i.e., an argument tells you that *if* you believe these premises, *then* you should also believe this conclusion. In general, it would be unfair, therefore, to simply reject the conclusion and suppose that the argument must be a bad one—in fact, it would often be intellectually dishonest. If the argument *were* a good one, then it would show you that you might be *wrong* in supposing its conclusion to be false; and to refuse to accept this is not to respond to the argument but simply to ignore it.[2]

It follows that there are exactly two reasonable ways to criticize an argument: the first is to question the truth of the *premises*; and the second is to question the claim that if the premises are true then the conclusion is true as well—that is, one can critique the *strength* of the argument. Querying the truth of

---

2   Of course, occasionally, you might legitimately know *for sure* that the conclusion is false, and then you could safely ignore arguments which try to show it is true: for example, *after* the rope breaks, I could dismiss your argument that it is safe (again, though, this would not show that your argument was *bad*, just that I need not be persuaded that the conclusion is true). However, this will not do for philosophical arguments: all interesting philosophy deals with issues where, though we may have firm opinions, we cannot just insist that we know all the answers and can therefore afford to ignore relevant arguments.

the premises (i.e., asking whether it's really true that Vancouver is less congested or cheaper than Toronto) is fairly straightforward. The thing to bear in mind is that you will usually be working backwards down a chain of argumentation: that is, each premise of a philosopher's main argument will often be supported by sub-arguments, and the controversial premises in these sub-arguments might be defended by further arguments, and so on. Normally it is not enough to merely demand to know whether some particular premise is true: one must look for *why* the arguer thinks it is true, and then engage with *that* argument.

Understanding and critiquing the strength of an argument (either your own or someone else's) is somewhat more complex. In fact, this is the main subject of most books and courses in introductory logic. When dealing with the strength of an argument, it is usual to divide arguments into two classes: *deductive* arguments and *inductive* arguments. Good deductive arguments are the strongest possible kind of argument: if their premises are true, then their conclusion *must necessarily* be true. For example, if all bandicoots are rat-like marsupials, and if Billy is a bandicoot, then it cannot possibly be false that Billy is a rat-like marsupial. On the other hand, good inductive arguments establish that, if the premises are true, then the conclusion is *highly likely* (but not absolutely certain) to be true as well. For example, I may notice that the first bandicoot I see is rat-like, and the second one is, and the third, and so on; eventually, I might reasonably conclude that all bandicoots are rat-like. This is a good argument for a probable conclusion, but nevertheless the conclusion can never be shown to be *necessarily* true. Perhaps a non-rat-like bandicoot once existed before I was born, or perhaps there is one living now in an obscure corner of New Guinea, or perhaps no bandicoot so far has ever been non-rat-like but at some point, in the future, a mutant bandicoot will be born that in no way resembles a rat, and so on.

Deductive Arguments and Validity

The strength of deductive arguments is an on/off affair, rather than a matter of degree. Either these arguments are such that if the premises are true

then the conclusion necessarily must be, or they are not. Strong deductive arguments are called *valid*; otherwise, they are called *invalid*. The main thing to notice about validity is that its definition is an *if… then…* statement: *if* the premises *were* true, then the conclusion *would* be. For example, an argument can be valid even if its premises and its conclusion are not true: all that matters is that if the premises *had* been true, the conclusion necessarily would have been as well. This is an example of a valid argument:

1. Either bees are rodents or they are birds.
2. Bees are not birds.
3. Therefore bees are rodents.

If the first premise were true, then (since the second premise is already true), the conclusion would *have* to be true—that's what makes this argument valid. This example makes it clear that validity, though a highly desirable property in an argument, is not enough all by itself to make a good argument: good deductive arguments are both valid *and* have true premises. When arguments are good in this way they are called *sound*: sound arguments have the attractive feature that they necessarily have true conclusions. To show that an argument is unsound, it is enough to show that it is either invalid or has a false premise.

It bears emphasizing that even arguments which have true premises and a true conclusion can be unsound. For example:

1. Only US citizens can become the President of America.
2. George W. Bush is a US citizen.
3. Therefore, George W. Bush was elected President of America.

This argument is not valid, and therefore it should not convince anyone who does not already believe the conclusion to start believing it. It is not valid because the conclusion could have been false even though the premises were true: Bush could have lost to Gore in 2000, for example. The question to ask, in thinking about the validity of arguments is this: Is there a coherent possible world, which I can even *imagine*, in which the premises are true and the conclusion false? If there is, then the argument is invalid.

When assessing the deductive arguments that you encounter in philosophical work, it is often useful to try to lay out, as clearly as possible, their *structure*. A standard and fairly simple way to do this is simply to pull out the logical connecting phrases and to replace, with letters, the sentences they connect. Five of the most common and important 'logical operators' are *and, or, it is not the case that, if … then …*, and *if and only if.…* For example, consider the following argument: "If God is perfectly powerful (omnipotent) and perfectly good, then no evil would exist. But evil does exist. Therefore, God cannot be both omnipotent and perfectly good, so either God is not all-powerful or he is not perfectly good." The structure of this argument could be laid bare as follows:

1. If (O and G) then not-E.
2. E.
3. Therefore not-(O and G).
4. Therefore either not-O or not-G.

Revealing the structure in this way can make it easier to see whether or not the argument is valid. And in this case, it is valid. In fact, no matter what O, G, and E stand for—no matter how we fill in the blanks—*any* argument of this form must be valid. You could try it yourself—invent random sentences to fill in for O, G, and E, and no matter how hard you try, you will never produce an argument with all true premises and a false conclusion.[3] What this shows is that validity is often a property of the *form* or structure of an argument. (This is why deductive logic is known as "formal logic." It is not formal in the sense that it is stiff and ceremonious, but because it has to do with argument forms.)

Using this kind of shorthand, therefore, it is possible to describe certain general argument forms which are *invariably* valid and which—since they are often used in philosophical writing—it can be handy to look out for. For example, a very common and valuable form of argument looks like this: if P then Q; P; therefore Q. This

form is often called *modus ponens*. Another—which appears in the previous argument about God and evil—is *modus tollens*: if P then Q; not-Q; therefore not-P. A *disjunctive syllogism* works as follows: either P or Q; not-P; therefore Q. A *hypothetical syllogism* has the structure: if P then Q; if Q then R; therefore if P then R. Finally, a slightly more complicated but still common argument structure is sometimes called a *constructive dilemma*: either P or Q; if P then R; if Q then R; therefore R.

Inductive Arguments and Inductive Strength

I noted above that the validity of deductive arguments is a yes/no affair—that a deductive argument is either extremely strong or it is hopelessly weak. This is not true for inductive arguments. The strength of an inductive argument—the amount of support the premises give to the conclusion—is a matter of degree, and there is no clear dividing line between the 'strong' inductive arguments and the 'weak' ones. Nevertheless, some inductive arguments are obviously much stronger than others, and it is useful to think a little bit about what factors make a difference.

There are lots of different types and structures of inductive arguments; here I will briefly describe four which are fairly representative and commonly encountered in philosophy. The first is *inductive generalization*. This type of argument is the prototype inductive argument—indeed, it is often what people mean when they use the term "induction"—and it has the following form:

1. *x* per cent of observed Fs are G.
2. Therefore *x* per cent of all Fs are G.

That is, inductive generalizations work by inferring a claim about an entire *population* of objects from data about a *sample* of those objects. For example:

(a) Every swan I have ever seen is white, so all swans (in the past and future, and on every part of the planet) are white.
(b) Every swan I have ever seen is white, so probably all the swans around here are white.
(c) 800 of the 1,000 rocks we have taken from the Moon contain silicon, so probably around 80% of the Moon's surface contains silicon.

---

3   Since the argument about God and evil is valid, then we are left with only two possibilities. Either all its premises are true, and then it is sound and its conclusion *must* inescapably be true. Or one of its premises is false, in which case the conclusion *might* be false (though we would still not have shown that it *is* false). The only way to effectively critique this argument, therefore, is to argue against one of the claims 1 and 2.

(d) We have tested two very pure samples of copper in the lab and found that each sample has a boiling point of 2,567°C; we conclude that 2,567°C is the boiling point for copper.

(e) Every intricate system I have seen created (such as houses and watches) has been the product of intelligent design, so therefore all intricate systems (including, for example, frogs and volcanoes) must be the product of intelligent design.

The two main considerations when assessing the strength of inductive generalizations are the following. First, ask how *representative* is the sample? How likely is it that whatever is true of the sample will also be true of the population as a whole? For instance, although the sample size in argument (c) is much larger than that in argument (d), it is much more likely to be biased: we know that pure copper is very uniform, so a small sample will do; but the surface of the Moon might well be highly variable, and so data about the areas around moon landings may not be representative of the surface as a whole. Second, it is important to gauge how cautious and *accurate* the conclusion is, given the data—how far beyond the evidence does it go? The conclusion to argument (a) is a much more radical inference from the data than that in argument (b); consequently, though less exciting, the conclusion of argument (b) is much better supported by the premise.

A second type of inductive argument is an *argument from analogy*. It most commonly has the following form:

1. Object (or objects) A and object (or objects) B are alike in having features F, G, H, …
2. B has feature X.
3. Therefore A has feature X as well.

These examples illustrate arguments from analogy:

(a) Human brains and dolphin brains are large, compared to body size. Humans are capable of planning for the future. So, dolphins must also be capable of planning for the future.

(b) Humans and dolphins are both mammals and often grow to more than five feet long. Humans are capable of planning for the future. So, dolphins must also be capable of planning for the future.

(c) Eagles and robins are alike in having wings, feathers, claws, and beaks. Eagles kill and eat sheep. Therefore, robins kill and eat sheep.

(d) Anselm's ontological argument has the same argumentative form as Gaunilo's "perfect island" argument. But Gaunilo's argument is a patently bad argument. So there must be something wrong with the ontological argument.

(e) An eye and a watch are both complex systems in which all of the parts are inter-dependent and where any small mis-adjustment could lead to a complete failure of the whole. A watch is the product of intelligent design. Therefore, the eye must also be the product of intelligent design (i.e., God exists).

The strength of an argument from analogy depends mostly on two things: first, the degree of *positive relevance* that the noted similarities (F, G, H …) have to the target property X; and second, the absence of *relevant dissimilarities*—properties which A has but B does not, which make it *less* likely that A is X. For example, the similarity (brain size) between humans and dolphins cited in argument (a) is much more relevant to the target property (planning) than are the similarities cited in argument (b). This, of course, makes (a) a much stronger argument than (b). The primary problem with argument (c), on the other hand, is that we know that robins are much smaller and weaker than eagles and this dissimilarity makes it far less likely that they kill sheep.

A third form of inductive argument is often called *inference to the best explanation* or sometimes *abduction*. This kind of argument works in the following way. Suppose we have a certain quantity of data to explain (such as the behavior of light in various media, or facts about the complexity of biological organisms, or a set of ethical claims). Suppose also that we have a number of theories which account for this data in different ways (e.g., the theory that light is a particle, or the theory that light is a wave, or the theory that it is somehow both). One way of arguing for the truth of one of these theories, over the others, is to show that one theory provides a much *better explanation* of the data than the others. What counts as making a theory a better explanation can be a bit tricky, but some basic criteria would be:

1. The theory predicts all the data we know to be true.
2. The theory explains all this data in the most economical and theoretically satisfying way (scientists and mathematicians often call this the most *beautiful* theory).
3. The theory predicts some *new* phenomena which turn out to exist and which would be a big surprise if one of the competing theories were true. (For example, one of the clinchers for Einstein's theory of relativity was the observation that starlight is bent by the sun's gravity. This would have been a big surprise under the older Newtonian theory, but was predicted by Einstein's theory.)

Here are some examples of inferences to the best explanation:

(a) When I inter-breed my pea plants, I observe certain patterns in the properties of the plants produced (e.g., in the proportion of tall plants, or of plants which produce wrinkled peas). If the properties of pea plants were generated randomly, these patterns would be highly surprising. However, if plants pass on packets of information (genes) to their offspring, the patterns I have observed would be neatly explained. Therefore, genes exist.

(b) The biological world is a highly complex and inter-dependent system. It is highly unlikely that such a system would have come about (and would continue to hang together) from the purely random motions of particles. It would be much less surprising if it were the result of conscious design from a super-intelligent creator. Therefore, the biological world was deliberately created (and therefore, God exists).

(c) The biological world is a highly complex and inter-dependent system. It is highly unlikely that such a system would have come about (and would continue to hang together) from the purely random motions of particles. It would be much less surprising if it were the result of an evolutionary process of natural selection which mechanically preserves order and eliminates randomness, and which (if it existed) would produce a world much like the one we see around us. Therefore, the theory of evolution is true.

The final type of inductive argument that I want to mention here is usually called *reductio ad absurdum*, which means "reduction to absurdity." It is always a negative argument, and has this structure:

1. Suppose (for the sake of argument) that position *p* were true.
2. If *p* were true then something else, *q*, would also have to be true.
3. However *q* is absurd—it can't possibly be true.
4. Therefore *p* can't be true either.

In fact, this argument style can be either inductive or deductive, depending on how rigorous the premises 2 and 3 are. If *p* logically implies *q*, and if *q* is a logical contradiction, then it is deductively certain that *p* can't be true (at least, assuming the classical laws of logic). On the other hand, if *q* is merely absurd but not literally *impossible*, then the argument is inductive: it makes it highly likely that *p* is false, but does not prove it beyond all doubt.

Here are a few examples of *reductio* arguments:

(a) Suppose that gun control were a good idea. That would mean it's a good idea for the government to gather information on anything we own which, in the wrong hands could be a lethal weapon, such as kitchen knives and baseball bats. But that would be ridiculous. This shows gun control cannot be a good idea.

(b) If you think that foetuses have a right to life because they have hearts and fingers and toes, then you must believe that *anything* with a heart, fingers, and toes has a right to life. But that would be absurd. Therefore, a claim like this about foetuses cannot be a good argument against abortion.

(c) Suppose, for the sake of argument, that this is not the best possible world. But that would mean God had either deliberately chosen to create a sub-standard world or had failed to notice that this was not the best of all possible worlds, and either of these options is absurd. Therefore, it must be true that this is the best of all possible worlds.

(d) "The anti-vitalist says that there is no such thing as vital spirit. But this claim is self-refuting. The speaker can be taken seriously only if his claim cannot. For if the claim is true, then the speaker does not have vital spirit and must be *dead*. But if he is dead, then his statement is a meaningless string of noises, devoid of reason and truth." (If you want more information, see Paul Churchland's "Eliminative Materialism and the Propositional Attitudes," *Journal of Philosophy* 78 [1981].)

The critical questions to ask about *reductio* arguments are simply: *Does* the supposedly absurd consequence follow from the position being attacked? and Is it *really* absurd?

A Few Common Fallacies

Just as it can be useful to look for common patterns of reasoning in philosophical writing, it can also be helpful to be on guard for a few recurring fallacies—and, equally importantly, to take care not to commit them in your own philosophical writing. Here are four common ones:

Begging the question does not mean, as the media would have us believe, stimulating one to ask a further question; instead, it means to assume as true (as one of your premises) the very same thing which you are supposedly attempting to prove. This fallacy is sometimes called *circular reasoning* or even (the old Latin name) *petitio principii*. To argue, for example, that God exists because (a) it says in the Bible that God exists, (b) God wrote the Bible, and (c) God would not lie, is to commit a blatant case of begging the question. In this case, of course, one would have no reason to accept the premises as true unless one *already* believed the conclusion. Usually, however, arguments that beg the question are a little more disguised. For example, "Adultery is immoral, since sexual relations outside marriage violate ethical principles," or "Terrorism is bad, because it encourages further acts of terrorism," are both instances of circular reasoning.

Arguing *ad hominem* means attacking or rejecting a position not because the arguments for it are poor, but because the person presenting those arguments is unattractive in some way: i.e., an attack is directed at the person (*ad hominem*) rather than at their argument. The following are implicit *ad hominem* arguments: "You say you want to close down the church? Well, Hitler and Stalin would agree with you!" and "We shouldn't trust the claim, by philosophers such as Anselm, Aquinas, and Leibniz, that God exists, since they were all Christian philosophers and so of course they were biased." Such attacks are fallacious because they have nothing at all to do with how reasonable a claim is: even if the claim is false, *ad hominem* attacks do nothing to show this.

Straw man arguments are particularly devious, and this fallacy can be hard to spot (or to avoid committing) unless great care is taken. The *straw man* fallacy consists in misrepresenting someone else's position so that it can be more easily criticized. It is like attacking a dummy stuffed with straw instead of a real opponent. For example, it's not uncommon to see attacks on "pro-choice" activists for thinking that abortion is a good thing. However, whatever the merits of either position, this objection is clearly unfair—no serious abortion advocates think it is a positively *good thing* to have an abortion; at most they claim that (at least in some circumstances) it is a lesser evil than the alternative. Here's an even more familiar example, containing two straw men, one after the other: "We should clean out the closets. They're getting a bit messy." "Why, we just went through those closets last year. Do we have to clean them out every day?" "I never said anything about cleaning them out every day. You just want to keep all your junk forever, which is simply ridiculous."

Arguments from ignorance, finally, are based on the assumption that lack of evidence *for* something is evidence that it is false, or that lack of evidence *against* something is evidence for its truth. Generally, neither of these assumptions are reliable. For example, even if we could find no good proof to show that God exists, this would not, all by itself, suffice to show that God does *not* exist: it would still be possible, for example, that God exists but transcends our limited human reason. Consider the following 'argument' by Senator Joseph McCarthy, about some poor official in the State Department: "I do not have much information on this except the general statement of the agency that there is nothing in the files to disprove his Communist connections."

Suggestions for Critical Reflection

1. Suppose some deductive argument has a premise which is necessarily false. Is it a valid argument?
2. Suppose some deductive argument has a conclusion which is necessarily true. Is it a valid argument? From this information alone, can you tell whether it is sound?
3. Is the following argument form valid: if P then Q; Q; therefore P? How about: if P then Q; not-P; so not-Q?
4. No inductive argument is strong enough to *prove* that its conclusion is true: the best it can do is to show that the conclusion is highly probable. Does this make inductive arguments bad or less useful? Why don't we restrict ourselves to using only deductive arguments?
5. Formal logic provides mechanical and reliable methods for assessing the validity of deductive arguments. Do you think there might be some similar system for evaluating the strength of inductive arguments?
6. I have listed four important fallacies; can you identify any other common patterns of poor reasoning?

Suggestions for Further Reading

An entertaining, thought-provoking and brief introduction to logic can be found in Graham Priest's *Logic: A Very Short Introduction* (Oxford University Press, 2000); an equally brief but highly practical primer on arguing is Anthony Weston's *A Rulebook for Arguments* (Hackett, 2008). There are many books which competently lay out the nuts and bolts of formal logic: Richard Jeffrey's *Formal Logic: Its Scope and Limits* (McGraw-Hill, 1991) is short but rigorous and clear; *The Logic Book* by Bergmann, Moor, and Nelson (McGraw-Hill, 2013), on the other hand, is rather painstaking but is one of the most complete texts. An interesting book which explains not only classical formal logic but also makes accessible some more recently developed logical languages, such as modal logic and intuitionistic logic, is Bell, DeVidi, and Solomon's *Logical Options* (Broadview Press, 2001). Two somewhat older texts, which were used to teach many of the current generation of professional philosophers and are still much used today, are Wilfrid Hodges's *Logic* (Penguin, 1977) and E.J. Lemmon's *Beginning Logic* (Hackett, 1978).

One of the best introductory texts on inductive logic is Brian Skyrms's *Choice & Chance* (Wadsworth, 2000). Other good texts include Copi and Burgess-Jackson's *Informal Logic* (Prentice Hall, 1995), Fogelin and Sinnott-Armstrong's *Understanding Arguments* (Harcourt, 2009), and Douglas Walton's *Informal Logic: A Handbook for Critical Argumentation* (Cambridge University Press, 1989). Quite a good book on fallacies is *Attacking Faulty Reasoning* by T. Edward Damer (Wadsworth, 2012), while Darrell Huff's *How to Lie with Statistics* (W.W. Norton, 1954) is an entertaining guide to the tricks that can be played with bad inductive arguments in, for example, advertising.

INTRODUCTORY TIPS ON READING AND WRITING PHILOSOPHY

Reading Philosophy

As you will soon find out, if you haven't already, it is not easy to read philosophy. It can be exhilarating, stimulating, life-changing, or even annoying, but it isn't easy. There are no real shortcuts for engaging with philosophy (though the notes accompanying the readings in this book are intended to remove a few of the more unnecessary barriers); however, there are two things to remember which will help you get the most out of reading philosophy—*read it several times*, and *read it actively*.

Philosophical writing is not like a novel, a historical narrative, or even a textbook: it is typically dense, compressed, and written to contribute to an ongoing debate with which you may not yet be fully familiar. This means, no matter how smart you are, it is highly unlikely that you will get an adequate understanding of any halfway interesting piece of philosophy the first time through, and it may even take two or three more readings before it really becomes clear. Furthermore, even after that point, repeated readings of good philosophy will usually reveal new and interesting nuances to the writer's position, and occasionally you will notice some small point that seems to open a mental door and show you what the author is trying to say in a whole new way. As they say, if a piece of philosophy isn't worth reading at least twice, it isn't worth reading once. Every selection in this book, I guarantee, is well worth reading once.

As you go through a piece of philosophy, it is very important to engage with it: instead of just letting the words wash over you, you should make a positive effort, first, to understand and then, to critically assess the ideas you encounter. On your first read-through it is a good idea to try to formulate a high-level understanding of what the philosopher is attempting: What are the main claims? What is the overall structure of the arguments behind them? At this stage, it can be useful to pay explicit attention to section headings and introductory paragraphs.

Ideally during a second reading, you should try to reconstruct the author's arguments and sub-arguments in more detail. To help yourself understand them, consider jotting down their outlines on a sheet of paper. At this point, it can be extremely fruitful to pay attention to special definitions or distinctions used by the author in the arguments. It is also helpful to consider the historical context in which the philosopher wrote, and to look for connections to ideas found in other philosophical works.

Finally, on third and subsequent readings, it is valuable to expressly look for *objections* to the writer's argument (Are the premises true? Is the argument strong?), *unclarities* in position statements, or *assumptions* they depend upon, but do not argue for. I make these suggestions partly because the process of critical assessment is helpful in coming to understand a philosopher's work; but more importantly for the reason that—perhaps contrary to popular opinion—philosophers are typically playing for very high stakes. When philosophers write about whether God exists, whether science is a rational enterprise, or whether unfettered capitalism creates a just society, they are seriously interested in discovering the *answers* to these questions. The arguments they make, if they are good enough, will be strong reasons to believe one thing rather than another. If you are reading philosophy properly, you must sincerely join the debate and be honestly prepared to be persuaded—but it is also important not to let yourself be persuaded too easily.

Writing Philosophy

Writing philosophy consists, in roughly equal measures, of *thinking* about philosophy and then of trying to express your ideas *clearly and precisely*. This makes it somewhat unlike other writing: the point of writing philosophy is not, alas, to entertain, nor to explain some chunk of knowledge, nor to trick or cajole the reader into accepting a certain thesis. The point of philosophical writing is, really, to *do* philosophy. This means that, since philosophy is based on arguments, most philosophical essays will have the underlying structure of an argument. They will seek to defend some particular philosophical claim by developing one or more good arguments for that claim.[4]

There is no particular template to follow for philosophical writing (there are lots of different kinds of good philosophical writing—lots of different ways of arguing well), but here are seven suggestions you might find useful:

1. Take your time. Spend time thinking, and then leave yourself enough time to get the writing right.

2. After you've thought for a while, begin by making an outline of the points you want to make (rather than immediately launching into prose). Then write several drafts, preferably allowing some cooling-off time between drafts so you can come back refreshed and with a more objective eye. Be prepared for the fact that writing a second draft doesn't mean merely tinkering with what you've already got, but starting at the beginning and writing it again.

3. Strive to be clear. Avoid unnecessary jargon, and use plain, simple words whenever possible; concrete examples can be extremely useful in explaining what you mean. It's also worth remembering that the clarity of a piece of writing has a lot to do with its structure. Ideally, the argumentative structure of your essay should be obvious to the reader, and it is a good idea to use your introduction to give the reader a 'road map' of the argument to follow.

4. Aim for precision. Make sure the *thesis* of your essay is spelled out in sufficient detail that the reader is left in no doubt about what you are arguing for (and therefore, what the implications will be, if your arguments are strong ones). Also, take care to define important terms so the reader knows exactly what you mean by them. Terms should normally be defined under any of the following three conditions: (a) the word is a technical term which a layperson probably won't know the meaning of (e.g., "intrinsic value"); (b) it is an ordinary word whose meaning is not sufficiently clear or precise for philosophical purposes (e.g., "abortion"); or (c) it is an ordinary word that you are going to use to mean something other than what it normally means (e.g., "person").

5. Focus. Everything you write should directly contribute to establishing your thesis. Anything which is unnecessary for your arguments should be eliminated. Make every word count. Also, don't be over-ambitious; properly done, philosophy moves at a fairly slow pace—it is unlikely that anyone could show adequately that, for example, there is no such thing as matter in three or fewer pages.

6. Argue as well and as carefully as you can. Defend your position using reason and not rhetoric; critically assess the strength of your arguments, and consider the plausibility of your premises. It's important to consider alternatives to your own position and possible counter-arguments; don't be afraid to raise and attempt to reply to objections to your position. (If you make a serious objection, one which you cannot answer, perhaps you should change your position.)

7. When you think you are finished, read the essay out loud and/or give it to someone else to read—at a minimum, this is a good way of checking for ease of reading, and it may reveal problems with your essay or argument that hadn't previously occurred to you.

---

4   The conclusion of a philosophical essay, however, need not always be something like: "God exists," or "Physical objects are not colored." It could just as legitimately be something like: "Philosopher A's third argument is flawed," or "When the arguments of philosopher A and those of philosopher B are compared, B wins," or "No one has yet given a good argument to show either P or not-P," or even "Philosopher A's argument is not, as is widely thought, X but instead it is Y." Though these kinds of claims are, perhaps, less immediately exciting than the first two examples, they are still philosophical claims, they still need to be argued for, and they can be extremely important in an overall debate about, say, the existence of God.

Suggestions for Further Reading

There are several short books devoted to helping students do well in philosophy courses. Perhaps the best of the bunch is Jay Rosenberg's *The Practice of Philosophy: A Handbook for Beginners* (Prentice Hall, 1995); A.P. Martinich's *Philosophical Writing* (Blackwell, 2005) is also very good. Also useful are: Anne M. Edwards, *Writing to Learn: An Introduction to Writing Philosophical Essays* (McGraw-Hill, 1999); Graybosch, Scott, and Garrison, *The Philosophy Student Writer's Manual* (Prentice Hall, 2002); and Zachery Seech, *Writing Philosophy Papers* (fifth edition, Wadsworth, 2008).

CHAPTER 2

Epistemology—Is the External World the Way It Appears to Be?

INTRODUCTION TO THE QUESTION

'Epistemology' is the theory of knowledge (the word comes from the Greek *epistēmē*, meaning knowledge). Epistemology can be thought of as arranged around three fundamental questions:

i) *What is knowledge?* For example, what is the difference between believing something that happens to be true and actually *knowing* it to be true? How much justification or proof do we need (if any) before we can be said to know something? Or does knowledge have more to do with, say, the *reliability* of our beliefs than our arguments for them? What is the difference between the conclusions of good science and those of, say, astrology? Or between astrology and religion?

ii) *What can we know?* What are the scope and limits of our knowledge? Can we ever really *know* about the real, underlying nature of the universe? Can we aspire to religious knowledge (e.g., of the true nature of God), or to ethical knowledge (as opposed to mere ethical belief or opinion), or to reliable knowledge of the historical past or the future? Can I ever know what you are thinking, or even *that* you are thinking? Do I even really know what *I* am thinking: e.g., might I have beliefs and desires that I am unaware of, perhaps because they are repressed or simply non-conscious?

iii) *How do we know that we know?* That is, how can we *justify* our claims to know things? What counts as 'enough' justification for a belief? Where does our knowledge—if we have any at all—come from in the first place? Do we acquire knowledge only through sense-experience, or can we also come to know important things through the power of our own naked reason? Do we have some beliefs which are especially 'basic'—which can be so reliably known that they can form a foundation for all our other beliefs? Or, by contrast, do all our pieces of knowledge fit together like the answers in a giant crossword puzzle, with each belief potentially up for grabs if the rest of the puzzle changes?

The epistemological question that is the focus of this chapter is sometimes called 'the problem of the external world.' In its starkest form, it is simply this: are *any* of our beliefs about the world outside our own heads justified? Can we be sure that any of them at all are *true*? For example, I currently believe that there is a laptop computer in front of me, and a soft-drink can on the table to my left, and a window to my right out of which I can see trees and grass and other houses. Furthermore, I not only believe that these objects exist but I also believe that they have a certain nature: that the pop can is colored red; that the trees outside are further away from me in space than the window I am looking through; that the houses are three-dimensional objects with solid walls, and that they continue to exist even when I close my eyes or turn away; that my computer will continue to behave in a (relatively!) predictable way in accordance with the laws of physics and of computing. But are any of these beliefs of mine justified: do any of them cross the threshold into being *knowledge*, as opposed to mere conjecture? And if some of them are known and not others, *which* are the ones I really know? Which are the beliefs to which a rational person should be committed, and which are the ones a rational person should jettison?

It may seem that these kinds of questions should be fairly straightforward to answer. *Of course* I know that my pop can exists and is really red; it should be pretty easy just to think for a while and give my compelling reasons for having this belief—the reasons which make this belief much more likely to be true than, say, the belief that the can is a figment of my imagination, or is really colorless. However, it turns out, the problem of the external world is a very challenging problem indeed, and one which has been an important philosophical issue since at least the seventeenth century.

The first five readings in this chapter explore different aspects of the problem of the external world. First, we might ask, does the external world exist *at all*—is there any such thing as a world outside my own head, or might reality be just a dream? Descartes is the classic source for the formulation of this problem, which he raises and then tries to answer. However, in 'solving' this problem, Descartes comes to the conclusion that only some of the things we commonsensically believe about the real nature of the external world are true or justifiable. The Locke reading can be thought of as extending this insight and making it more precise through his discussion of the distinction between 'primary qualities' (which resemble our ideas of them) and 'secondary qualities' (which do not). Locke also raises a somewhat different question: what can we know about the sort of 'stuff' that the external world is made of—if it is 'matter,' then what can we say about the kind of *substance* which is matter? Berkeley seizes upon this problem and uses it as a reason to abandon the whole notion of matter: though he does not deny that an 'external' world exists, nor that most of what we normally believe about it is true, Berkeley does deny that our materialist *theory* of the external world is true: he holds that the 'external' world is really a collection of ideas in the mind of God.

Kant, faced with what by this time seemed the intractable problem of proving that mind-independent material objects exist and resemble our ideas of them, attempted to make a radical break with the philosophical assumptions which he thought had generated the puzzle in the first place. Instead of assuming that our mental representations of the world are passive pictures of reality (which, like a portrait, could either be a good likeness or misleadingly inaccurate), he argued that our minds actually *interact* with data from the external world to *create* 'empirical reality.' For example, he claims, we cannot be mistaken in believing that external objects are three-dimensional, persist through time, and interact causally with each other, since all these features of reality are essential features of empirical experience: it is impossible, according to Kant, that anyone could experience an external reality which was not arranged in this way.

Russell represents a twentieth-century approach to the problem of the external world. He suggests that our belief in the existence of a material external world is justified since it is the simplest hypothesis which could explain the behavior of our 'sense-data.' However, he points out that science tells us that the real nature of this external world is radically different than the way it appears to us.

The final two readings in this section introduce two key epistemological innovations of the twentieth century. Gettier's article "Is Justified True Belief Knowledge?" presents a deep problem for the basic philosophical intuition—which in some form goes all the way back to Plato—that any belief that is both true and properly justified counts as an instance of knowledge. Meanwhile, Lorraine Code challenges another generally historically-unquestioned assumption: that the ideal knower should be as objective as possible, such that any item of knowledge should be equally justifiable no matter what standpoint one occupies. Instead, Code argues, knowers are *situated*, and what they (can) know reflects their particular perspectives (as, for example, a woman rather than a man).

There are several good introductory epistemology textbooks currently available if you want more background information. For example: Robert Audi, *Epistemology* (Routledge, 2010); Ralph Baergen, *Contemporary Epistemology* (Harcourt Brace, 1995); Jonathan Dancy, *Introduction to Contemporary Epistemology* (Blackwell, 1985); Everitt and Fisher, *Modern Epistemology* (McGraw-Hill, 1995); Richard Feldman, *Epistemology* (Prentice Hall, 2002); Keith Lehrer, *Theory of Knowledge* (Westview, 1990); Adam Morton,

A Guide Through the Theory of Knowledge (Blackwell, 2002); Pollock and Cruz, *Contemporary Theories of Knowledge* (Rowman & Littlefield, 1999); Matthias Steup, *An Introduction to Contemporary Epistemology* (Prentice Hall, 1996); Steup and Sosa (eds.), *Contemporary Debates in Epistemology* (Blackwell, 2005); and Michael Williams, *Problems of Knowledge* (Oxford Uni-

versity Press, 2001). There are also a couple of useful reference works on epistemology: Dancy, Sosa, and Steup (eds.), *A Companion to Epistemology* (Blackwell, 2010); Paul K. Moser, *The Oxford Handbook of Epistemology* (Oxford University Press, 2005); and Greco and Sosa (eds.), *The Blackwell Guide to Epistemology* (Blackwell, 1999).

RENÉ DESCARTES
Meditations on First Philosophy

Who Was René Descartes?

René Descartes was born in 1596 in a small town nestled below the vineyards of the Loire in western France; at that time the town was called La Haye, but it was later renamed Descartes in his honor. His early life was probably unhappy: he suffered from ill health, his mother had died a year after he was born, and he didn't get on well with his father. (When René sent his father a copy of his first published book, his father's only reported reaction was that he was displeased to have a son "idiotic enough to have himself bound in vellum."[1]) At the age of about ten he went to the newly-founded college of La Flèche to be educated by the Jesuits. Descartes later called this college "one of the best schools in Europe," and it was there that he learned the medieval "scholastic" science and philosophy that he was later decisively to reject. Descartes took a law degree at the University of Poitiers and studied mathematics and mechanics; then, at 21, he joined first the Dutch army of Prince Maurice of Nassau and then the forces of Maximilian of Bavaria. As a soldier he saw little action, traveling around Europe supported by his family's wealth. During this period, he had resolved "to seek no knowledge other than

that which could be found either in myself or in the great book of the world," developing an intense interest in mathematics, which stayed with him for the rest of his life. In fact, Descartes was one of the most important figures in the development of algebra, which is the branch of mathematics that allows abstract relations to be described without using specific numbers, and which is therefore capable of unifying arithmetic and geometry:

> I came to see that the exclusive concern of mathematics is with questions of order or method, and that it is irrelevant whether the measure in question involves numbers, shapes, stars, sounds, or any other object whatsoever. This made me realize that there must be a general science which explains all the points that can be raised concerning order and measure irrespective of subject matter. (from *Rules for the Direction of Our Native Intelligence* [1628])

This insight led Descartes directly to one of the most significant intellectual innovations of the modern age: the conception of science as the exploration of abstract mathematical descriptions of the world.

It was also during this time—in 1619—that Descartes had the experience said to have inspired him to take up the life of a philosopher, and which, perhaps, eventually resulted in the form of the *Medita-*

---

1   Vellum is the parchment made from animal skin that was used to make books.

tions. Stranded by bad weather near Ulm on the river Danube, Descartes spent the day in a *poêle* (a stove-heated room[2]) engaged in intense philosophical speculations. That night he had three vivid dreams which he later described as giving him his mission in life. In the first dream Descartes felt himself attacked by phantoms and then a great wind; he was then greeted by a friend who gave him a message about a gift. On awaking after this first dream, Descartes felt a sharp pain which made him fear that the dream was the work of some deceitful evil demon. Descartes eventually fell back asleep and immediately had the second dream: a loud thunderclap, which woke him in terror believing that the room was filled with fiery sparks. The third and last dream was a pleasant one, in which he found an encyclopedia on a table next to a poetry anthology, open to a poem which begins with the line "Which road in life shall I follow?" A man then appeared and said "*Est et non*"—"it is and is not." While still asleep, Descartes apparently began to speculate about the meaning of his dreams, and decided, among other things, that the gift of which his friend spoke in the first dream was the gift of solitude, the dictionary represented systematic knowledge, and "*Est et non*" spoke of the distinction between truth and falsity as revealed by the correct scientific method. Descartes concluded that he had a divine mission to found a new philosophical system to underpin all human knowledge.

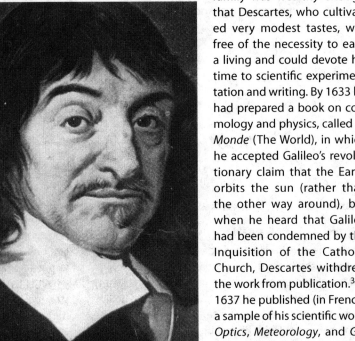

In 1628, at the age of thirty-two, Descartes settled in Holland (at the time the most intellectually vibrant nation in Europe), where he lived for most of his remaining life. It was only then that he began sustained work in metaphysics and mathematical physics. His family was wealthy enough that Descartes, who cultivated very modest tastes, was free of the necessity to earn a living and could devote his time to scientific experimentation and writing. By 1633 he had prepared a book on cosmology and physics, called *Le Monde* (The World), in which he accepted Galileo's revolutionary claim that the Earth orbits the sun (rather than the other way around), but when he heard that Galileo had been condemned by the Inquisition of the Catholic Church, Descartes withdrew the work from publication.[3] In 1637 he published (in French) a sample of his scientific work, *Optics, Meteorology,* and *Geometry,* together with an introduction called *Discourse on the Method of Rightly Conducting One's Reason and Reaching the Truth in the Sciences.* Criticisms of this methodology led Descartes to compose his philosophical masterpiece, *Meditations on First Philosophy,* first published in Latin in 1641. (A French translation, prepared with Descartes's supervision and incorporating his changes, was published in 1647.) In 1644 he published a summary of his scientific and philosophical views, the *Principles of Philosophy,* which he hoped would become a standard university textbook, replacing the medieval texts

---

2   Sometimes Descartes's words are taken in what might be their literal meaning, that he spent time in a stove. But although there is other evidence of his eccentricity, this seems an uncharitable translation.

3   Descartes was very aware of the Catholic authorities' opposition to his ideas, and afraid of it. After his death, all his works were placed on the Index of Prohibited Works by the Church, with the note that they would remain there "until corrected." (This Index, with Descartes's works still listed, was abolished in 1966.)

used at the time. His last work, published in 1649, was *The Passions of the Soul*, which attempted to extend his scientific methodology to ethics and psychology.

Descartes never married, but in 1635 he had a daughter, Francine, with a serving woman called Hélène Jans. He made arrangements to care for and educate the girl but she died of scarlet fever at the age of five, a devastating shock for Descartes.

In 1649 Descartes accepted an invitation to visit Stockholm and give philosophical instruction to Queen Kristina of Sweden. He was required to give tutorials at the royal palace at five o'clock in the morning; ever since he was a sickly schoolboy, he stayed in bed till 11 am, and it is said that the strain of this sudden break in his habits caused him to catch pneumonia; he died in February, 1650. His dying words are said to have been, "*ça mon âme; il faut partir*"—so, my soul, it's time to part. His body was returned to France but, apparently, his head was secretly kept in Sweden; in the 1820s a skull bearing the faded inscription "René Descartes" was discovered in Stockholm and is now on display in the Museum of Natural History in Paris.

What Was Descartes's Overall Philosophical Project?

Descartes lived at a time when the accumulated beliefs of centuries—assumptions based on religious doctrine, straightforward observation, and common sense—were being gradually but remorselessly stripped away by exciting new discoveries. (The most striking example of this was the evidence mounting against the centuries-old belief that an unmoving Earth is the center of the universe, orbited by the moon, sun, stars, and all the other planets.) In this intellectual climate, Descartes became obsessed by the thought that no lasting scientific progress was possible without a systematic method for sifting through our preconceived assumptions and distinguishing between those that are reliable and those that are false. Descartes's central intellectual goal was to develop just such a reliable scientific method, and then to construct a coherent and unified theory of the world and of humankind's place within it. This theory, he hoped, would replace scholasticism, the deeply-

flawed medieval system of thought based on the science of Aristotle and Christian theology.

A key feature of Descartes's system is that all knowledge should be based on utterly reliable foundations, discovered through the systematic rejection of any assumptions that can possibly be called into doubt. Then, as in mathematics, complex conclusions could be reliably derived from these foundations by chains of valid reasoning—of simple and certain inferences. The human faculty of *reason* was therefore of the greatest importance. Furthermore, Descartes urged that scientific knowledge of the external world should be rooted, not in the deceptive and variable testimony of the senses, but in the concepts of pure mathematics. That is, Cartesian science tries to reduce all physics to "what the geometers call *quantity*, and take as the object of their demonstrations, i.e., that to which every kind of division shape and motion is applicable" (*Principles of Philosophy* [1644]). (There is, however, for Descartes, a place for empirical investigation in science—not as a tool for producing general understanding, but rather to determine the real external existences of particular things.)

These ideas (though they have never been uncritically and uniformly accepted) have come to permeate the modern conception of science, including Descartes's influential metaphor of a unified "tree of knowledge," with metaphysics as the roots, physics as the trunk, and the special sciences (like biology, anthropology, or ethics) as the branches. His most important and lasting influence on scientific thought is his idea that the physical world is a unified whole, governed by very basic universal mathematical and physical laws, and that finding these is the most basic job of science. One much less familiar, and less lasting, aspect of Descartes's method for the production of knowledge is the central role played by God in his system. For Descartes, all human knowledge of the world around us essentially relies upon our prior knowledge that a non-deceiving God exists. Science, properly understood, not only does not conflict with religion but actually *depends* on religion, he believed.

Finally, one of the best-known results of Descartes's metaphysical reflections is "Cartesian dualism." This doctrine states that mind and body are two completely different substances—that the mind is a nonphysical self in which all the operations of thought take place, and which can be wholly separated from the body after death. Like much of Descartes's work, this theory came to have the status of a more or less standard view for some three hundred years after his death, but at the time it was a radical philosophical innovation, breaking with the traditional Aristotelian conception of mental activity as a kind of *attribute* of the physical body (rather than as something entirely separable from the body).

What Is the Structure of This Reading?

The *Meditations* is not intended to be merely an exposition of philosophical arguments and conclusions, but is supposed to be an exercise in philosophical reflection for the reader—as Bernard Williams has put it, "the 'I' that appears throughout them from the first sentence on does not specifically represent [Descartes]: it represents anyone who will step into the position it marks, the position of the thinker who is prepared to reconsider and recast his or her beliefs, as Descartes supposed we might, from the ground up."[4] Descartes aims to convince us of the truth of his conclusions by making us conduct the arguments ourselves. (It is interesting to note that the structure of the *Meditations* was modeled on the "spiritual exercises" that students at Jesuit schools, such as the one Descartes attended, were required to undertake in order to learn to move away from the world of the senses and to focus on God.)

In the First Meditation (after introductory letters from Descartes to a theology faculty and to the reader) the thinker applies a series of progressively more radical doubts to his or her preconceived opinions, which leaves her unsure whether she knows anything at all. But then in the Second Meditation the thinker finds a secure foundational belief in her indubitable awareness of her own existence. The rest of this meditation is a reflection on the thinker's own nature as a "thinking thing." In the Third Meditation the thinker realizes that final certainty can only be achieved through the existence of a non-deceiving God, and argues from the idea of God found in her own mind to the conclusion that God must really exist and be the cause of this idea (this is sometimes nicknamed the "Trademark Argument," from the notion that our possession of the idea of God is God's "trademark" on his creation). The Fourth Meditation urges that the way to avoid error in our judgments is to restrict our beliefs to things of which we are clearly and distinctly certain. The Fifth Meditation introduces Cartesian science by discussing the mathematical nature of our knowledge of matter, and also includes a second proof for God's existence which resembles the eleventh-century "ontological argument" of St. Anselm. Finally, in the Sixth Meditation, the thinker re-establishes our knowledge of the real existence of the external world, argues that mind and body are two distinct substances, and reflects on how mind and body are related.

Some Useful Background Information

1. Descartes makes frequent use of the terms "substance," "essence," and "accident." A substance is, roughly, a bearer of attributes, i.e., a thing that has properties. The essence of a substance is its fundamental intrinsic nature, a property without which that thing, of that sort, could not exist. Descartes held that for every substance there is exactly one property which is its essence. A substance's "accidents"[5] are all the rest of its properties, the ones which are not part of its essence.

   Take, for example, a red ball: its redness, the spherical shape, the rubbery feel, and so on, are all properties—accidents—of the ball, and the ball's substance is the "stuff" that underlies and possesses these properties. According to Descartes, the fundamental nature of this stuff—its essence—is that it is extended in three dimensions, that it fills space.

---

4   This appears in his introductory essay to the Cambridge University Press edition of the *Meditations* (1996).

5   Strictly speaking, Descartes thought of accidents as being 'modes' of the one essential property of the substance (rather than being really separate properties): shape, for example, is a mode of being extended in space.

For Descartes and his contemporaries there is also another important aspect to the idea of substance. Unlike an instance of a property, which cannot exist all by itself (there can't be an occurrence of redness without there being something which is red—some bit of substance which is the bearer of that property), substances are not dependent for their existence on something else. In fact, for Descartes, this is actually the *definition* of a substance: "By 'substance' we can understand nothing other than a thing which exists in such a way as to depend on no other things for its existence" (*Principles of Philosophy*). So, for instance, a tree is not really a substance, since trees do depend for their existence on other things (such as soil, light, past trees, and so on). On the other hand, according to Descartes, matter itself—all matter, taken as a whole—is a substance. Matter cannot be destroyed or created (except by God), it can only change its local form, gradually moving from the form of a tree to the form of a rotting tree trunk to the form of soil, for example.

2. Descartes relies quite heavily in the *Meditations* on a three-fold contrast between intellect (or understanding), the will, and sensation and imagination. He explains this distinction in some detail in the Sixth Meditation, but the basic distinction is as follows: Sensation and imagination involve the presentation of ideas, especially mental images. "Imagination" is thought of in a more particular sense than the modern one, which includes any sort of speculation or invention; Descartes's notion is an earlier one, involving the having of mental images—pictures in the mind's eye, so to speak. The understanding is our intellectual apprehension of ideas, the faculty by which the mind considers the contents of thoughts (indeed, without understanding, mere sensations have no content at all). The will is our ability to either assent or dissent to these ideas—it is our faculty of judgment. An act of will (assent) is necessary for there to be a belief at all, according to Descartes—a mere idea by itself can be neither accurate nor erroneous.

Two key details are worth bearing in mind for a fuller appreciation of Descartes's arguments in the *Meditations*. First, although the understanding/imagination distinction would have been quite familiar at the time, Descartes departs from the intellectual tradition of Aristotle in holding that sensation and imagination, though they certainly intimately involve the body, are modes of the mind. (Aristotle and his followers held that only the intellect is properly mental.) Furthermore, Descartes emphasized that our sensations, by themselves, tell us nothing about the world—only our understanding generates judgments. This is arguably the central point of the famous wax example, in Meditation Two.

Second, Descartes believed that the understanding is a passive, rather than an active, mental faculty: it takes in the deliveries of sensation, for example, and produces thoughts almost automatically, according to the way in which God has created us. By contrast, the will (also given to us by God) is an active mental faculty. We cannot choose how the world appears to us, but we can choose whether or not to certify those judgments as accurate. In this way, for Descartes, error is almost a moral failing—a failure of the will. Our mistakes are not God's fault, but our own.

3. A related phrase frequently used by Descartes in the *Meditations* is the "natural light." Descartes has in mind here what in earlier writings he calls "the light of reason"—the pure inner light of the intellect, a faculty given to us by God, which allows us to see the truth of the world much more clearly than we can with the confused and fluctuating testimony of the senses.

4. Descartes, following the scholastic jargon of the time, calls the representational content of an idea its "objective reality" (he uses this term in his attempted proof of the existence of God in the Third Meditation). Confusingly, according to this terminology, for something to have merely objective reality in this sense is for it to belong to the mental world of ideas, and not to the mind-independent external world at all.

For example, if I imagine Santa Claus as being fat and jolly, then Descartes would say that fatness is "objectively" present in my idea—an idea of fatness forms part of my idea of Santa Claus. By contrast, the baby beluga at the Chicago aquarium is fat, but its fatness is not merely the *idea* of fatness but an actual property of the beluga. In general, for any idea I that represents a thing X which has the property of being F, F-ness will be present formally in X but objectively in I.

What Descartes and his contemporaries call "formal reality," then, is just the reality something has simply in virtue of existing. Since ideas exist (they are modes of a thinking substance), they have both formal reality—the idea itself—and objective reality—the content of the idea.

5. Although Descartes's talk of a non-physical "soul" was in accord with contemporary Christian theology, his reasons for holding that the mind is immortal and non-material (largely in Meditations Two and Six) were not primarily religious ones. Descartes does not think of the soul as being especially "spiritual" or as being identical with our "better nature," for example. For Descartes the word "soul" simply means the same as the word "mind," and encompasses the whole range of conscious mental activity, including the sensations of sight, touch, sound, taste, and smell; emotions (such as joy or jealousy); and cognitive activities like believing, planning, desiring, or doubting. For Descartes the mind, or soul, is also to be distinguished from the brain: our brains, since they are extended material things, are part of our body and not our mind.

6. Descartes's metaphysics was a radical departure from the then-prevailing Aristotelian view of nature. In very brief summary, Aristotelians saw natural bodies as being composed of both form and matter. Matter cannot exist without form, and a thing's form determines its nature: that is, a thing's form makes it what it is—a horse, a tree, a cloud—by determining its characteristic development and behavior.

There are four basic substances—earth, air, fire, and water—and four basic qualities—hot, cold, wet, and dry. Most natural bodies are made up of mixtures of elements, and each belongs to different kinds (such as species or types of minerals) defined by their forms. In this way, Aristotelian science made no distinction between biological processes, such as growth or nutrition, and other natural phenomena such as burning or gravity: they are all the playing out of essential forms, principles of growth and change, that are 'built in' to the entities involved. For the Aristotelian, then, scientific explanation will be a matter of identifying the multifarious forms—the essential natures—of all the different items in the natural world. Furthermore, the objects that we encounter in nature really have the properties they appear to have to our senses—color, texture, taste, odor and so on—and what it is for us to perceive the world is a transfer of these qualities from external objects to our sense organs (where they are received in our sensory soul as a "form without matter"). One final important aspect of Aristotelian science: the changing, natural realm in which we live is located at the center of the universe (due to the tendency of earth and water, because of their natures, to seek the center and thus collect there), but there is a radical discontinuity between this world and the heavenly spheres—literally, crystalline spheres in which the moon, sun, planets, and stars were thought to be embedded—which are unchanging, and not even made of the familiar four elements but of a completely different fifth element (called quintessence).

One of the interpretive tasks in reading the *Meditations* (which Descartes secretly thought of as being designed to present his new and, for his audience highly counter-intuitive, physics) is to discover the differences between the Aristotelian tradition and Descartes's own account. Some of the Cartesian departures to look for are: that different natural kinds differ only in the sizes, shapes, and motions of the particles that make them up; that matter does not contain within it its own principle of motion and change but is 'passive' and subject to external forces; that the qualities we encounter in sense experience do not resemble the causes of those experiences; and that the whole material world, including the heliocentric solar system, is governed by the same small set of laws of motion.

Some Common Misconceptions

1. The *Meditations* describe a process, in which the thinker moves from pre-reflective starting points towards a clearer understanding of knowledge. As a consequence, not everything that Descartes writes—especially in the earlier meditations—is something that he, or the thinker, will agree with by the time they have completed the process. (For example, he begins by saying that "[u]p to this point, what I have accepted as very true I have derived either from the senses or through the senses," which is a principle he later rejects.)

2. Descartes is not a skeptic. Although he is famous for the skeptical arguments put forward in the First Meditation, he uses these only in order to go beyond them.[6] It is a bit misleading, however, to think of Descartes as setting out in the *Meditations* to defeat skepticism: his main interest is probably not in proving the skeptic wrong, but in discovering the first principles upon which a proper science can be built. He uses skepticism, surprisingly, in order to create knowledge—to show that a properly constituted science would have nothing to fear from even the most radical doubts of the skeptic. Thus, for example, Descartes does not at any point argue that we should actually believe that

the external world does not exist—instead, he suspends his belief in external objects until he has a chance to properly build a foundation for this belief (and by the end of the *Meditations* he is quite certain that the external world exists).

3. The "method of doubt" which Descartes uses in the *Meditations* is not an everyday method—it is not supposed to be an appropriate technique for making day-to-day decisions, or even for doing science or mathematics. Most of the time it would be hugely impractical for us to call into question everything that we might possibly doubt, to question all our presuppositions, before we make a judgment. Instead the method of the *Meditations* is supposed to be a once-in-a-lifetime exercise, by which we discover and justify the basic "first principles" that we rely on in everyday knowledge. In short, we always have to rely on certain assumptions when we make decisions or do science, and this is unavoidable but dangerous; the exercise of the *Meditations* can ensure that the assumptions we rely upon are absolutely secure.

4. Although "I think therefore I am" (or "I am, I exist") is the first step in Descartes's reconstruction of human knowledge in the *Meditations*, it is nevertheless not the first piece of *knowledge* that he recognizes—it does not arise out of a complete knowledge vacuum. Before the thinker can come to know that "I think therefore I am" is true, Descartes elsewhere admits that she must know, for example, what is meant by thinking, and that doubting is a kind of thought, and that in order to think one must first exist. Therefore, it is best to think of "I think therefore I am," not as the first item of knowledge, but as the first *non-trivial* piece of secure knowledge about the world that a thinker can have. It's a piece of information not just about concepts or logic but actually about the world—but, according to Descartes, it's information we can only get if we *already* (somehow) possess a certain set of concepts.

5. It is sometimes supposed that Descartes thought that all knowledge could be mathematically deduced from the foundational

---

6   In one of his letters, Descartes noted that, when ancient medical authorities such as Galen or Hippocrates wrote about the causes of disease, no one accused them of telling people how to get sick; in the same way, Descartes complained, "I put forward these reasons for doubting not to convince people of them but, on the contrary, in order to refute them."

beliefs that remain after he has applied his method of doubt. But this is not quite right. He thought that the proper *concepts and terms*, which science must use to describe the world, were purely mathematical and were deducible through pure rational reflection. But he also recognized that only through empirical investigation can we discover which scientific descriptions, expressed in the proper mathematical terms, are actually *true* of the world. For example, reason tells us (according to Descartes—and this was a radically new idea at the time) that matter can be defined simply in terms of extension in three dimensions, and that the laws which guide the movements of particles can be understood mathematically. However, only experience can tell us how the bits of matter in, for example, the human body are actually arranged.

6. Descartes does not conclude that error is impossible, even for those who adopt the proper intellectual methods of science. He argues only that *radical and systematic* error is impossible for the conscientious thinker. For example, even after completing Descartes's course of meditations we might still occasionally be tricked by perceptual illusions, or think we are awake when in fact we are dreaming; what Descartes thinks he has blocked, however, is the possibility that such errors show that our entire picture of reality might be wrong.

7. Descartes's project is to show how, by setting our knowledge of the world on firm foundations, we can overcome any skeptical doubts and have confidence in the conception of reality that results. It is less widely appreciated, however, that the common-sense picture of the world, as it is apparently revealed to our senses, with which Descartes begins is very different from the worldview with which we are left at the end of the *Meditations*. Descartes does not merely rescue common sense from skepticism; instead, he replaces a naïve view of the world with a more modern, scientific one.

8. Descartes is sometimes portrayed as making the following (bad) argument to establish that mind is distinct from body: I can doubt that my body exists; I cannot doubt that my mind exists; there is therefore at least one property that my mind has which my body lacks (i.e., being doubtable); and therefore mind and body are not identical. Descartes does seem to make an argument which resembles this (in the Second Meditation), but he later denied that this is really what he meant, and he formulates much stronger—though perhaps still flawed—arguments for dualism in the Sixth Meditation.

How Important and Influential Is This Text?

Descartes is one of the most widely studied of any of the Western philosophers, and his *Meditations on First Philosophy* is his philosophical masterpiece and most important work. John Cottingham, an expert on Descartes, has written of the *Meditations* that:

> The radical critique of preconceived opinions or prejudices which begins that work seems to symbolize the very essence of philosophical inquiry. And the task of finding secure foundations for human knowledge, a reliable basis for science and ethics, encapsulates, for many, what makes philosophy worth doing.[7]

"I think therefore I am" ("*cogito ergo sum*" in Latin) is the most famous dictum in the history of philosophy. Note that this is not what it is often popularly taken to be: praise of the intellectual life as the real source of human identity. It's rather Descartes's foundational claim beginning his reconstruction of indubitable truth. These exact words, by the way, never appear in the *Meditations*—they are found in other writings by Descartes, including *Discourse on the Method* and the *Principles of Philosophy*; the *Meditations*, however, contains Descartes's most complete account of how this principle, today simply called "the Cogito," is established.

The importance of Descartes's work to the history of thought is profound. He is commonly considered

---

7   This appears in his Introduction to the *Cambridge Companion to Descartes* (1992).

the first great philosopher of the modern era, since his work was central in sweeping away medieval scholasticism based on Aristotelian science and Christian theology and replacing it with the methods and questions that dominated philosophy until the twentieth century.[8] This change from scholastic to modern modes of thought was also crucial to the phenomenal growth of natural science and mathematics beginning in the seventeenth century. In recent years, however, it has been fashionable to blame Descartes for what have been seen as philosophical dead ends, and many of the assumptions which he built into philosophy have been questioned (this is one of the reasons why the philosophy of the second half of the twentieth century and beyond has been so exciting).

Suggestions for Critical Reflection

1. Descartes, in the *Meditations*, has traditionally been seen as raising and then trying to deal with the problem of radical skepticism: that is, according to this interpretation, he raises the possibility that (almost) all our beliefs might be radically mistaken and then argues that this is, in fact, impossible. A more recent line of interpretation, though, sees Descartes not as attempting to answer the skeptic, but as trying to replace naïve empirical assumptions about science with a more modern, mathematical view—in particular, that Descartes is trying to show our most fundamental pieces of knowledge about mind, God, and the world come not from sensory experience, but directly from the intellect. Which interpretation do you think is more plausible? Could they both be right? If Descartes does want to refute skepticism, is he successful in doing so? If his goal is to overturn naïve scholastic empiricism, do you think he manages to do that?

2. Descartes's foundational claim "I think therefore I am" is usually called the Cogito, from the Latin *cogito ergo sum*. How does Descartes justify this claim? Does he have, or need, an *argument* for it? Is an argument that justifies this claim even possible?

3. Descartes says, in the Third Meditation, "[t]here cannot be another faculty [in me] as trustworthy as natural light, one which could teach me that the ideas [derived from natural light] are not true." What do you think he means by this? Is he right? How important to his arguments is it that he be right about this?

4. Eighteenth-century Scottish philosopher David Hume dryly said, of the *Meditations*, "To have recourse to the veracity of the supreme Being, in order to prove the veracity of our senses, is surely making a very unexpected circuit" (Section XII of *An Enquiry Concerning Human Understanding*, 1748). What do you think? Does Descartes establish the existence of God?

5. On Descartes's picture, do you think an atheist can have any knowledge? Why or why not?

6. It seems to be crucial to Descartes's arguments (especially those in Meditation Four) that God is not responsible for our errors, that what we believe—and, indeed, whether we believe or simply suspend our belief—is something that is under our direct control: that we can freely will to believe or not. Does this seem plausible to you? (Could you really decide not to believe that, say, your body exists?) How might Descartes argue for this position? If it cannot be defended, how problematic would this be for the project of the *Meditations*?

7. A famous objection to Descartes's conclusions in the *Meditations* (raised for the first time by some of his contemporaries) is today known as the problem of the Cartesian Circle. Descartes says in the Third Meditation, "Whatever

---

8   Alan Gewirth went so far as to write, in 1970, "the history of twentieth-century philosophy … consists in a series of reactions to Descartes's metaphysics. Examples of these reactions are Ryle's castigations of the Cartesian mind-body dualism, Sartre's and Hare's attacks on Cartesian intellectualism and intuitionism, Chomsky's support of Cartesian innatism, and the opposed views taken on Cartesian doubt by Russell and Husserl on the one hand and by Moore, Dewey, Austin, and the later Wittgenstein on the other" ("The Cartesian Circle Reconsidered," *The Journal of Philosophy* 67, 668–685).

I perceive very clearly and distinctly is true." Call this the CDP Principle. It is this principle that he thinks will allow him to reconstruct a body of reliable scientific knowledge on the foundations of the Cogito. However, he immediately admits, the CDP Principle will only work if we cannot ever make mistakes about what we clearly and distinctly perceive; to show this, Descartes tries to prove that God exists and has created human beings such that what we clearly and distinctly see to be evidently true really is true. But how does Descartes prove God exists? Apparently, by arguing that we have a clear and distinct idea of God, and so it must be true that God exists. That is, the objection runs, Descartes relies upon the CDP Principle to prove that the CDP Principle is reliable—and this argument just goes in a big circle and doesn't prove anything. What do you think of this objection?

8. "How do I know that I am not ten thinkers thinking in unison?" (Elizabeth Anscombe, "The First Person" (1975)). What, if anything, do you think Descartes has proved about the nature of the self?

9. How adequate are Descartes's arguments for mind-body dualism? If mind and body are two different substances, do you think this might cause other philosophical problems to arise? For example, how might mind and body interact if they are radically different and have no properties in common? How could we come to know things about other people's minds? How could we be sure whether animals have minds or not, and if they do what they might be like?

10. Descartes recognized no physical properties but size, shape, and motion. Where do you think Descartes would say colors, tastes, smells, and so on come from?

Suggestions for Further Reading

Meditations on First Philosophy was originally published with an extensive set of objections from contemporary thinkers and replies by Descartes. Cambridge University Press has published Descartes's collected philosophical writings and letters in three volumes, translated by John Cottingham, Robert Stoothoff, Dugald Murdoch, and Anthony Kenny. (Volume II, which includes the *Meditations* and the complete *Objections and Replies*, was published in 1984; Volume I was published in 1985 and the letters in 1991.)

The secondary literature on Descartes is vast, but here are a few starting points. An entertaining recent biography of Descartes is from A.C. Grayling, *Descartes: The Life and Times of a Genius* (Walker & Company, 2006); an even more thorough biography is *Descartes: An Intellectual Biography* by Stephen Gaukroger (Oxford University Press, 1995). Useful general introductions to Descartes's thought are John Cottingham's *Descartes* (Blackwell, 1991), Anthony Kenny's *Descartes: A Study of His Philosophy* (Random House, 1968), Bernard Williams's *Descartes: The Project of Pure Enquiry* (Penguin, 1978, reissued by Taylor & Francis in 2007), and Margaret Dauler Wilson's *Descartes* (Routledge, 1978); a second edition of Georges Dicker's *Descartes: An Analytical and Historical Introduction* (Oxford University Press) is due to be released in 2013. There is a *Blackwell Guide to Descartes' Meditations* (Wiley-Blackwell, 2006), edited by Stephen Gaukroger, and Gary Hatfield has written a Routledge GuideBook to *Descartes and the Meditations* (Taylor and Francis, 2007). *The Cambridge Companion to Descartes* edited by John Cottingham (Cambridge University Press, 1992) is very helpful, and there is also a Blackwell *Companion to Descartes* (2010) edited by Janet Broughton and John Carriero. Two good collections of articles on the *Meditations* are A.O. Rorty's *Essays on Descartes's Meditations* (University of California Press, 1986) and Vere Chappell's *Descartes's Meditations: Critical Essays* (Rowman and Littlefield, 1997). Several important essays are also contained in Willis Doney (ed.), *Descartes: A Collection of Critical Essays* (University of Notre Dame Press, 1967).

A few of the more influential (and sometimes controversial) recent books on Descartes are Harry Frankfurt's *Demons, Dreamers, and Madmen* (Bobbs-Merrill, 1970), E.M. Curley's *Descartes Against the Sceptics* (Harvard University Press, 1978), Peter J. Markie's *Descartes's Gambit* (Cornell University Press, 1986), Richard Watson's *The Breakdown of Cartesian Metaphysics* (Humanities Press, 1987), Daniel Garber's *Des-*

cartes's *Metaphysical Physics* (University of Chicago Press, 1992), Janet Broughton, *Descartes's Method of Doubt* (Princeton University Press, 2002), Marleen Rozemond's *Descartes's Dualism* (Harvard University Press, 2002), Desmond Clarke's *Descartes's Theory of Mind* (Oxford University Press, 2005), Tom Sorrell's *Descartes Reinvented* (Cambridge University Press, 2005), and Deborah Brown's *Descartes and the Passionate Mind* (Cambridge University Press, 2008). A well-known book that is tangentially about Descartes is *Descartes' Error: Emotion, Reason, and the Human Brain*, by Antonio Damasio (Penguin, 2005), while Richard Rorty's *Philosophy and the Mirror of Nature* (Princeton University Press, 1979) attributes a wide swath of modern intellectual failings to the pernicious influence of Descartes.

A representative handful of the papers published on Descartes (excluding those in the collections already mentioned) are: Elizabeth Anscombe, "The First Person," in Anscombe, *Metaphysics and the Philosophy of Mind* (Blackwell, 1981), 21–36; O.K. Bouwsma, "Descartes' Evil Genius," *Philosophical Review*, 58 (1949), 141–151; John Cottingham, "Cartesian Trialism," *Mind* 94 (1985), 218–230; Alan Gewirth, "The Cartesian Circle," *Philosophical Review* 50 (1941), 368–395; Jaako Hintikka, "Cogito ergo sum: Inference or Performative?" *Philosophical Review* 71 (1962), 3–32; Anthony Kenny, "Descartes the Dualist," *Ratio* 12 (1999), 114–127; Louis Loeb, "The Priority of Reason in Descartes," *Philosophical Review* 99 (1990), 3–43; Norman Malcolm, "Descartes' Proof that He Is Essentially a Non-Material Thing," in Malcolm, *Thought and Knowledge* (Cornell University Press, 1977), 58–84; Dugald Murdoch, "The Cartesian Circle," *Philosophical Review* 108 (1999), 221–244; Stephen Schiffer, "Descartes on His Essence," *Philosophical Review* 85 (1976), 21–43; and James Van Cleve, "Foundationalism, Epistemic Principles, and the Cartesian Circle," *Philosophical Review* 88 (1979), 55–91.

Meditations on First Philosophy

In which the existence of God and the difference between the human soul and body are demonstrated[9]

Synopsis of the Six Following Meditations

In the First Meditation I set down the reasons which enable us to place everything in doubt, especially material things, at least as long as we do not have foundations for the sciences different from those we have had up to now. Although at first glance the usefulness of such a widespread doubt is not apparent, it is, in fact, very great, because it frees us from all prejudices, sets down the easiest route by which we can detach our minds from our senses, and finally makes it impossible for us to doubt anymore those things which we later discover to be true.

In the Second Meditation, the mind, using its own unique freedom, assumes that all those things about whose existence it can entertain the least doubt do not exist, and recognizes that during this time it is impossible that it itself does not exist. And that is also extremely useful, because in this way the mind can easily differentiate between those things pertaining to it, that is, to its intellectual nature, and those pertaining to the body. However, since at this point some people may perhaps expect an argument [proving] the immortality of the soul, I think I should

---

9   Translated by Ian Johnston, Vancouver Island University, 2012. *Translator's Note:* This translation is based upon the first Latin edition of Descartes's *Meditations* (1641). I have incorporated most of the relatively few corrections made to that text in the second Latin edition (1642), none of which is particularly important. I have also inserted a number of additions made to the Latin text in the first French edition (1647), which was supervised by Descartes, who approved of the result. These additions from the French edition are inserted here only where they help to clarify the meaning of the original Latin (for example, by clarifying Descartes's Latin pronouns). Other changes in the French text I have ignored. Words in square brackets are insertions and additions from the first French edition.

warn them that I have tried to avoid writing anything which I could not accurately demonstrate and that, therefore, I was unable to follow any sequence of reasoning other than the one used by geometers. That means I start by setting down everything on which the proposition we are looking into depends, before I reach any conclusions about it. Now, the first and most important prerequisite for understanding the immortality of the soul is to form a conception of the soul that is as clear as possible, one entirely distinct from every conception [we have] of the body. And that I have done in this section. After that, it is essential also for us to know that all those things we understand clearly and distinctly are true in a way which matches precisely how we think of them. This I was unable to prove before the Fourth Meditation. We also need to have a distinct conception of corporeal[10] nature. I deal with that point partly in this Second Meditation and partly in the Fifth and Sixth Meditations, as well. And from these we necessarily infer that all those things we conceive clearly and distinctly as different substances, in the same way we think of the mind and the body, are, in fact, truly different substances, distinct from one another, a conclusion I have drawn in the Sixth Meditation. This conclusion is also confirmed in the same meditation from the fact that we cannot think of the body as anything other than something divisible, and, by contrast, [cannot think of] the mind as anything other than something indivisible. For we cannot conceive of half a mind, in the same way we can with a body, no matter how small. Hence, we realize that their natures are not only different but even, in some respects, opposites. However, I have not pursued the matter any further in this treatise for two reasons: (1) because these points are enough to show that the annihilation of the mind does not follow from the corruption of the body, so we mortals thus ought to entertain hopes of another life; and (2) because the premises on the basis of which we can infer the immortality of the mind depend upon an explanation of all the principles of physics. For (2), first of all, we would have to know that all substances without exception—or those things which, in order to exist,

must be created by God—are by their very nature incorruptible and can never cease to exist, unless God, by denying them his concurrence,[11] reduces them to nothing, and then, second, we would have to understand that a body, considered generally, is a substance and thus it, too, never dies. But the human body, to the extent that it differs from other bodies, consists merely of a certain arrangement of parts, with other similar accidental[12] properties; whereas, the human mind is not made up of any accidental properties in this way, but is a pure substance. For even if all the accidental properties of the mind were changed—if, for example, it were to think of different things or have different desires and perceptions, and so on—that would not mean it had turned into a different mind. But the human body becomes something different from the mere fact that the shape of some of its parts has changed. From this it follows that the [human] body does, in fact, perish very easily, but that the mind, thanks to its nature, is immortal.

In the Third Meditation I have set out what seems to me a sufficiently detailed account of my main argument to demonstrate the existence of God. However, in order to lead the minds of the readers as far as possible from the senses, in this section I was unwilling to use any comparisons drawn from corporeal things, and thus many obscurities may still remain. But these, I hope, have later been entirely removed in the replies [I have made] to the objections.[13] For instance, among all the others, there is the issue of how the idea of a supremely perfect being, which is present within us, could have so much objective reality that it is impossible for it not to originate from a supremely perfect cause. This is illustrated [in the replies] by the comparison with a wholly perfect machine, the idea of which exists in the mind of some craftsman. For just as the objective ingenuity of this idea must have some cause, that is, the technical skill of this craftsman or of

---

10   Bodily, physical

11   The continuous divine action which many Christians think necessary to maintain things in existence.

12   See the section in the Introduction, "Some Useful Background Information," 1., for explanation of "accidental" here.

13   Descartes refers to the set of objections and replies he published at the end of *Meditations,* not reprinted here.

someone else from whom he got the idea, so the idea of God, which is in us, cannot have any cause other than God Himself.

In the Fourth Meditation, I establish that all the things which we perceive clearly and distinctly are true, and at the same time I explain what constitutes the nature of falsity; these are things that we have to know both to confirm what has gone before and to understand what still remains. (However, in the meantime I must observe that in this part I do not deal in any way with sin, that is, with errors committed in pursuit of good and evil, but only with those which are relevant to judgments of what is true and false. Nor do I consider matters relevant to our faith or to the conduct of our lives, but merely those speculative truths we can know only with the assistance of our natural light.)

In the Fifth Meditation, I offer a general explanation of corporeal nature and, in addition, also demonstrate the existence of God in a new argument, in which, however, several difficulties may, once again, arise. These I have resolved later in my replies to the objections. And finally, I point out in what sense it is true that the certainty of geometrical demonstrations depends upon a knowledge of God.

Finally, in the Sixth Meditation, I differentiate between the understanding and the imagination and describe the principles of this distinction. I establish that the mind is truly distinct from the body, and I point out how, in spite of that, it is so closely joined to the body that they form, as it were, a single thing. I review all the errors which customarily arise through the senses and explain the ways in which such errors can be avoided. And then finally, I set down all the reasons which enable us to infer the existence of material things. I believe these are useful not because they demonstrate the truth of what they prove—for example, that there truly is a world, that human beings have bodies, and things like that, which no one of sound mind ever seriously doubted—but rather because, when we examine these reasons, we see that they are neither as firm or as evident as those by which we arrive at a knowledge of our own minds and of God, so that the latter are the most certain and most evident of all things which can be known by the human intellect. The proof of this one point was the goal I set out to attain in these *Mediations*. For that reason I am not reviewing here, as they arise [in this treatise], various [other] questions I have dealt with elsewhere.

First Meditation
Concerning Those Things Which Can Be Called into Doubt

It is now several years since I noticed how from the time of my early youth I had accepted many false claims as true, how everything I had later constructed on top of those [falsehoods] was doubtful, and thus how at some point in my life I needed to tear everything down completely and begin again from the most basic foundations, if I wished to establish something firm and lasting in the sciences. But this seemed an immense undertaking, and I kept waiting until I would be old enough and sufficiently mature to know that no later period of my life would come [in which I was] better equipped to undertake this disciplined enquiry. This reason made me delay the project for so long that I would now be at fault if, by [further] deliberation, I wasted the time still left to carry it out. And so today, when I have conveniently rid my mind of all worries and have managed to find myself secure leisure in solitary withdrawal, I will at last find the time for an earnest and unfettered general demolition of my [former] opinions.

Now, for this task it will not be necessary to show that every opinion I hold is false, something which I might well be incapable of ever carrying out. But reason now convinces me that I should withhold my assent from opinions which are not entirely certain and indubitable, no less than from those which are plainly false; so if I uncover any reason for doubt in each of them, that will be enough to reject them all. For that I will not need to run through them separately, a task that would take forever, because once the foundations are destroyed, whatever is built above them will collapse on its own. Thus, I shall at once assault the very principles upon which all my earlier beliefs rested.

Up to this point, what I have accepted as true I have derived either from the senses or through the senses. However, sometimes I have discovered that these are mistaken, and it is prudent never to place one's entire trust in things which have deceived us even once.

However, although from time to time the senses deceive us about minuscule things or those further away, it could well be that there are still many other matters about which we cannot entertain the slightest doubt, even though we derive [our knowledge] of them from sense experience—for example, the fact that I am now here, seated by the fire, wearing a winter robe, holding this paper in my hands, and so on. And, in fact, how could I deny that these very hands and this whole body are mine, unless perhaps I were to compare myself with certain insane people whose brains are so troubled by the stubborn vapors of black bile[14] that they constantly claim that they are kings, when, in fact, they are very poor, or that they are dressed in purple, when they are nude, or that they have earthenware heads, or are complete pumpkins, or made of glass? But these people are mad, and I myself would appear no less demented if I took something from them and applied it to myself as an example.

A brilliant piece of reasoning! But nevertheless I am a person who sleeps at night and experiences in my dreams all the things these [mad] people do when wide awake, sometimes even less probable ones. How often have I had an experience like this: while sleeping at night, I am convinced that I am here, dressed in a robe and seated by the fire, when, in fact, I am lying between the covers with my clothes off! At the moment, my eyes are certainly wide open and I am looking at this piece of paper, this head which I am moving is not asleep, and I am aware of this hand as I move it consciously and purposefully. None of what happens while I am asleep is so distinct. Yes, of course—but nevertheless I recall other times when I have been deceived by similar thoughts in my sleep. As I reflect on this matter carefully, it becomes completely clear to me that there are no certain indicators which ever enable us to differentiate between being awake and being asleep, and this is astounding; in my confusion I am almost convinced that I may be sleeping.

So then, let us suppose that I am asleep and that these particular details—that my eyes are open, that I am moving my head, that I am stretching out my hand—are not true, and that perhaps I do not even have hands like these or a whole body like this. We must, of course, still concede that the things we see while asleep are like painted images, which could only have been made as representations of real things. And so these general things—these eyes, this head, this hand, and this entire body—at least are not imaginary things but really do exist. For even when painters themselves take great care to form sirens and satyrs with the most unusual shapes, they cannot, in fact, give them natures which are entirely new. Instead, they simply mix up the limbs of various animals or, if they happen to come up with something so new that nothing at all like it has been seen before and thus [what they have made] is completely fictitious and false, nonetheless, at least the colors which make up the picture certainly have to be real. For similar reasons, although these general things—eyes, head, hand, and so on—could also be imaginary, still we are at least forced to concede the reality of certain even simpler and more universal objects, out of which, just as with real colors, all those images of things that are in our thoughts, whether true or false, are formed.

Corporeal nature appears, in general, to belong to this class [of things], as well as its extension,[15] the shape of extended things, their quantity or their size and number, the place where they exist, the time which measures how long they last, and things like that.

Thus, from these facts perhaps we are not reaching an erroneous conclusion [by claiming] that physics, astronomy, medicine, and all the other disciplines which rely upon a consideration of composite objects are indeed doubtful, but that arithmetic, geometry, and the other [sciences] like them, which deal with only the simplest and most general matters and have little concern whether or not they exist in the nature of things, contain something certain and indubitable. For whether I am awake or asleep, two and three always add up to five, a square does not have more than four sides, and it does not seem possible to suspect that such manifest truths could be false.

Nevertheless, a certain opinion has for a long time been fixed in my mind—that there is an all-powerful God who created me and [made me] just as I am. But

---

14 One of the four basic bodily fluids then thought to be associated with disease when in imbalance.

15 Something's extension is its spatial magnitude—the volume of space it occupies.

how do I know He has not arranged things so that there is no earth at all, no sky, no extended thing, no shape, no magnitude, no place, and yet seen to it that all these things appear to me to exist just as they do now? Besides, given that I sometimes judge that other people make mistakes with the things about which they believe they have the most perfect knowledge, might I not in the same way be wrong every time I add two and three together, or count the sides of a square, or do something simpler, if that can be imagined? Perhaps God is unwilling to deceive me in this way, for He is said to be supremely good. But if it is contrary to the goodness of God to have created me in such a way that I am always deceived, it would also seem foreign to His goodness to allow me to be occasionally deceived. The latter claim, however, is not one that I can make.

Perhaps there may really be some people who prefer to deny [the existence of] such a powerful God, rather than to believe that all other things are uncertain. But let us not seek to refute these people, and [let us concede] that everything [I have said] here about God is a fiction. No matter how they assume I reached where I am now, whether by fate, or chance, or a continuous series of events, or in some other way, given that being deceived and making mistakes would seem to be something of an imperfection, the less power they attribute to the author of my being, the greater the probability that I will be so imperfect that I will always be deceived. I really do not have a reply to these arguments. Instead, I am finally compelled to admit that there is nothing in the beliefs which I formerly held to be true about which one cannot raise doubts. And this is not a reckless or frivolous opinion, but the product of strong and well-considered reasoning. And therefore, if I desire to discover something certain, in future I should also withhold my assent from those former opinions of mine, no less than [I do] from opinions which are obviously false.

But it is not sufficient to have called attention to this point. I must [also] be careful to remember it. For these habitual opinions constantly recur, and I have made use of them for so long and they are so familiar that they have, as it were, acquired the right to seize hold of my belief and subjugate it, even against my wishes, and I will never give up the habit of defer-

ring to and relying on them, as long as I continue to assume that they are what they truly are: opinions which are to some extent doubtful, as I have already pointed out, but still very probable, so that it is much more reasonable to believe them than to deny them. For that reason, I will not go wrong, in my view, if I deliberately turn my inclination into its complete opposite and deceive myself, [by assuming] for a certain period that these earlier opinions are entirely false and imaginary, until I have, as it were, finally brought the weight of both my [old and my new] prejudices into an equal balance, so that corrupting habits will no longer twist my judgment away from the correct perception of things. For I know that doing this will not, for the time being, lead to danger or error and that it is impossible for me to indulge in excessive distrust, since I am not concerned with actions at this point, but only with knowledge.

Therefore, I will assume that it is not God, who is supremely good and the fountain of truth, but some malicious demon, at once omnipotent and supremely cunning, who has been using all the energy he possesses to deceive me. I will suppose that sky, air, earth, colors, shapes, sounds, and all other external things are nothing but the illusions of my dreams, set by this spirit as traps for my credulity. I will think of myself as if I had no hands, no eyes, no flesh, no blood, nor any senses, and yet as if I still falsely believed I had all these things. I shall continue to concentrate resolutely on this meditation, and if, in doing so, I am, in fact, unable to learn anything true, I will at least do what is in my power and with a resolute mind take care not to agree to what is false or to enable the deceiver to impose anything on me, no matter how powerful and cunning [he may be]. But this task is onerous, and laziness brings me back to my customary way of life. I am like a prisoner who in his sleep may happen to enjoy an imaginary liberty and who, when he later begins to suspect that he is asleep, fears to wake up and willingly cooperates with the pleasing illusions [in order to prolong them]. In this way, I unconsciously slip back into my old opinions and am afraid to wake up, in case from now on I would have to spend the period of challenging wakefulness that follows this peaceful relaxation not in the light, but in the inextricable darkness of the difficulties I have just raised.

Second Meditation
Concerning the Nature of the Human Mind and the Fact that It Is Easier to Know than the Body

Yesterday's meditation threw me into so many doubts that I can no longer forget them or even see how they might be resolved. Just as if I had suddenly fallen into a deep eddying current, I am hurled into such confusion that I am unable to set my feet on the bottom or swim to the surface. However, I will struggle along and try once again [to follow] the same path I started on yesterday—that is, I will reject everything which admits of the slightest doubt, just as if I had discovered it was completely false, and I will proceed further in this way, until I find something certain, or at least, if I do nothing else, until I know for certain that there is nothing certain. In order to shift the entire earth from its location, Archimedes asked for nothing but a fixed and immovable point. So I, too, ought to hope for great things if I can discover something, no matter how small, which is certain and immovable.

Therefore, I assume that everything I see is false. I believe that none of those things my lying memory represents has ever existed, that I have no senses at all, and that body, shape, extension, motion, and location are chimeras.[16] What, then, will be true? Perhaps this one thing: there is nothing certain.

But how do I know that there exists nothing other than the items I just listed, about which one could not entertain the slightest momentary doubt? Is there not some God, by whatever name I call him, who places these very thoughts inside me? But why would I think this, since I myself could perhaps have produced them? So am I then not at least something? But I have already denied that I have senses and a body. Still, I am puzzled, for what follows from this? Am I so bound up with my body and my senses that I cannot exist without them? But I have convinced myself that there is nothing at all in the universe—no sky, no earth, no minds, no bodies. So then, is it the case that I, too, do not exist? No, not at all: if I persuaded myself of something, then I certainly existed. But there is

some kind of deceiver, supremely powerful and supremely cunning, who is constantly and intentionally deceiving me. But then, if he is deceiving me, there again is no doubt that I exist—for that very reason. Let him trick me as much as he can, he will never succeed in making me nothing, as long as I am aware that I am something. And so, after thinking all these things through in great detail, I must finally settle on this proposition: the statement *I am, I exist* is necessarily true every time I say it or conceive of it in my mind.

But I do not yet understand enough about what this *I* is, which now necessarily exists. Thus, I must be careful I do not perhaps unconsciously substitute something else in place of this *I* and in that way make a mistake even here, in the conception which I assert is the most certain and most evident of all. For that reason, I will now reconsider what I once believed myself to be, before I fell into this [present] way of thinking. Then I will remove from that whatever could, in the slightest way, be weakened by the reasoning I have [just] brought to bear, so that, in doing this, by the end I will be left only with what is absolutely certain and immovable.

What then did I believe I was before? Naturally, I thought I was a human being. But what is a human being? Shall I say a *rational animal*? No. For then I would have to ask what an *animal* is and what *rational* means, and thus from a single question I would fall into several greater difficulties. And at the moment I do not have so much leisure time that I wish to squander it with subtleties of this sort. Instead I would prefer here to attend to what used to come into my mind quite naturally and spontaneously in earlier days every time I thought about what I was. The first thought, of course, was that I had a face, hands, arms, and this entire mechanism of limbs, the kind one sees on a corpse, and this I designated by the name *body*. Then it occurred to me that I ate and drank, walked, felt, and thought. These actions I assigned to the *soul*. But I did not reflect on what this *soul* might be, or else I imagined it as some kind of attenuated substance, like wind, or fire, or aether,[17]

---

16   In Greek mythology, a female fire-breathing monster with a lion's head, a goat's body, and a serpent's tail; more generally, an absurd or horrible idea or wild fancy.

---

17   Aether is the fifth element of medieval alchemy, and the idea has its origins in the classical Greek notion of the pure atmosphere beyond the sky in which the gods

spread all through my denser parts. However, I had no doubts at all about my body—I thought I had a clear knowledge of its nature. Perhaps if I had attempted to describe it using the mental conception I used to hold, I would have explained it as follows: By a *body* I understand everything that is appropriately bound together in a certain form and confined to a place; it fills a certain space in such a way as to exclude from that space every other body; it can be perceived by touch, sight, hearing, taste, or smell, and can also be moved in various ways, not, indeed, by itself, but by something else which makes contact with it. For I judged that possessing the power of self-movement, like the ability to perceive things or to think, did not pertain at all to the nature of body. Quite the opposite in fact, so that when I found out that faculties rather similar to these were present in certain bodies, I was astonished.

But what [am I] now, when I assume that there is some extremely powerful and, if I may be permitted to speak like this, malevolent and deceiving being who is deliberately using all his power to trick me? Can I affirm that I possess even the least of all those things which I have just described as pertaining to the nature of body? I direct my attention [to this], think [about it], and turn [the question] over in my mind. Nothing comes to me. It is tedious and useless to go over the same things once again. What, then, of those things I used to attribute to the soul, like eating, drinking, or walking? But given that now I do not possess a body, these are nothing but imaginary figments. What about sense perception? This, too, surely does not occur without the body. And in sleep I have apparently sensed many objects which I later noticed I had not [truly] perceived. What about thinking? Here I discover something: thinking does exist. This is the only thing which cannot be detached from me. *I am, I exist*—that is certain. But for how long? Surely for as long as I am thinking. For it could perhaps be the case that, if I were to abandon thinking altogether, then in that moment I would completely cease to be. At this point I am not agreeing to anything except what is

necessarily true. Therefore, strictly speaking, I am merely a thinking thing, that is, a mind or spirit, or understanding, or reason—words whose significance I did not realize before. However, I am something real, and I truly exist. But what kind of thing? As I have said, a thing that thinks.

And what else besides? I will let my imagination roam. I am not that interconnection of limbs we call a human body. Nor am I even some attenuated air which filters through those limbs—wind, or fire, or vapor, or breath, or anything I picture to myself. For I have assumed those things were nothing. Let this assumption hold. Nonetheless, I am still something. Perhaps it could be the case that these very things which I assume are nothing, because they are unknown to me, are truly no different from that *I* which I do recognize. I am not sure, and I will not dispute this point right now. I can render judgment only on those things which are known to me: I know that I exist. I am asking what this *I* is—the thing I know. It is very certain that knowledge of this *I*, precisely defined like this, does not depend on things whose existence I as yet know nothing about and therefore on any of those things I conjure up in my imagination. And this phrase *conjure up* warns me of my mistake, for I would truly be conjuring something up if I imagined myself to be something, since imagining is nothing other than contemplating the form or the image of a physical thing. But now I know for certain that I exist and, at the same time, that it is possible for all those images and, in general, whatever relates to the nature of body to be nothing but dreams [or chimeras]. Having noticed this, it seems no less foolish for me to say "I will let my imagination work, so that I may recognize more clearly what I am" than if I were to state, "Now I am indeed awake, and I see some truth, but because I do yet not see it with sufficient clarity, I will quite deliberately go to sleep, so that in my dreams I will get a truer and more distinct picture of it." Therefore, I realize that none of those things which I can understand with the aid of my imagination is pertinent to this idea I possess about myself and that I must be extremely careful to summon my mind back from such things, so that it may perceive its own nature with the utmost clarity, on its own.

---

were thought to live, and which they breathed, analogous to (but different from) the air of the terrestrial atmosphere.

But what then am I? A thinking thing. What is this? It is surely something that doubts, understands, affirms, denies, is willing, is unwilling, and also imagines and perceives.

This is certainly not an insubstantial list, if all [these] things belong to me. But why should they not? Surely I am the same *I* who now doubts almost everything, yet understands some things, who affirms that this one thing is true, denies all the rest, desires to know more, does not wish to be deceived, imagines many things, even against its will, and also notices many things which seem to come from the senses? Even if I am always asleep and even if the one who created me is also doing all he can to deceive me, what is there among all these things which is not just as true as the fact that I exist? Is there something there that I could say is separate from me? For it is so evident that I am the one who doubts, understands, and wills, that I cannot think of anything which might explain the matter more clearly. But obviously it is the same *I* that imagines, for although it may well be the case, as I have earlier assumed, that nothing I directly imagine is true, nevertheless, the power of imagining really exists and forms part of my thinking. Finally, it is the same *I* that feels, or notices corporeal things, apparently through the senses: for example, I now see light, hear noise, and feel heat. But these are false, for I am asleep. Still, I certainly seem to see, hear, and grow warm—and this cannot be false. Strictly speaking, this is what in me is called sense perception and, taken in this precise meaning, it is nothing other than thinking.

From these thoughts, I begin to understand somewhat better what I am. However, it still appears that I cannot prevent myself from thinking that corporeal things, whose images are formed by thought and which the senses themselves investigate, are much more distinctly known than that obscure part of me, the *I*, which is not something I can imagine, even though it is really strange that I have a clearer sense of those things whose existence I know is doubtful, unknown, and alien to me than I do of something which is true and known, in a word, of my own self. But I realize what the trouble is. My mind loves to wander and is not yet allowing itself to be confined within the limits of the truth. All right, then, let us at this point for once give it completely free rein, so that

a little later on, when the time comes to pull back, it will consent to be controlled more easily.

Let us consider those things we commonly believe we understand most distinctly of all, that is, the bodies we touch and see—not, indeed, bodies in general, for those general perceptions tend to be somewhat more confusing, but rather one body in particular. For example, let us take this [piece of] beeswax. It was collected from the hive very recently and has not yet lost all the sweetness of its honey. It [still] retains some of the scent of the flowers from which it was gathered. Its color, shape, and size are evident. It is hard, cold, and easy to handle. If you strike it with your finger, it will give off a sound. In short, everything we require to be able to recognize a body as distinctly as possible appears to be present. But watch. While I am speaking, I bring the wax over to the fire. What is left of its taste is removed, its smell disappears, its color changes, its shape is destroyed, its size increases, it turns to liquid, and it gets hot. I can hardly touch it. And now, if you strike it, it emits no sound. After [these changes], is what remains the same wax? We must concede that it is. No one denies this; no one thinks otherwise. What then was in [this piece of wax] that I understood so distinctly? Certainly nothing I apprehended with my senses, since all [those things] associated with taste, odor, vision, touch, and sound have now changed. [But] the wax remains.

Perhaps what I now think is as follows: the wax itself was not really that sweetness of honey, that fragrance of flowers, that white color, or that shape and sound, but a body which a little earlier was perceptible to me in those forms, but which is now [perceptible] in different ones. But what exactly is it that I am imagining in this way? Let us consider that point and, by removing those things which do not belong to the wax, see what is left over. It is clear that nothing [remains], other than something extended, flexible, and changeable. But what, in fact, do *flexible* and *changeable* mean? Do these words mean that I imagine that this wax can change from a round shape to a square one or from [something square] to something triangular? No, that is not it at all. For I understand that the wax has the capacity for innumerable changes of this kind, and yet I am not able to run through these innumerable changes by using my imagination. Therefore, this conception [I have of the wax] is not produced by the faculty of imagination. What about extension? Is not the extension of the wax also unknown? For it becomes greater when the wax melts, greater [still] when it boils, and once again [even] greater, if the heat is increased. And I would not be judging correctly what wax is if I did not believe that it could also be extended in various other ways, more than I could ever grasp in my imagination. Therefore, I am forced to admit that my imagination has no idea at all what this wax is and that I perceive it only with my mind. I am talking about this [piece of] wax in particular, for the point is even clearer about wax in general. But what is this wax which can be perceived only by the mind? It must be the same as the wax I see, touch, and imagine—in short, the same wax I thought it was from the beginning. But we should note that the perception of it is not a matter of sight, or touch, or imagination, and never was, even though that seemed to be the case earlier, but simply of mental inspection, which could be either imperfect and confused as it was before, or clear and distinct as it is now, depending on the lesser or greater degree of attention I bring to bear on those things out of which the wax is composed.

However, now I am amazed at how my mind is [weak and] prone to error. For although I am considering these things silently within myself, without speaking aloud, I still get stuck on the words themselves and am almost deceived by the very nature of the way we speak. For if the wax is there [in front of us], we say that we see the wax itself, not that we judge it to be there from the color or shape. From that I could immediately conclude that I recognized the wax thanks to the vision in my eyes, and not simply by mental inspection. But by analogy, suppose I happen to glance out of the window at people crossing the street; in normal speech I also say I see the people themselves, just as I do with the wax. But what am I really seeing other than hats and coats, which could be concealing automatons[18] underneath? However, I judge that they are people. And thus what I thought I was seeing with my eyes I understand only with my faculty of judgment, which is in my mind.

But someone who wishes [to elevate] his knowledge above the common level should be ashamed to have based his doubts in the forms of speech which ordinary people use, and so we should move on to consider next whether my perception of what wax is was more perfect and more evident when I first perceived it and believed I knew it by my external senses, or at least by my so-called *common sense*,[19] in other words, by the power of imagination, or whether it is more perfect now, after I have investigated more carefully both what wax is and how it can be known. To entertain doubts about this matter would certainly be silly. For in my first perception of the wax what was distinct? What did I notice there that any animal might not be capable of capturing? But when I distinguish the wax from its external forms and look at it as something naked, as if I had stripped off its clothing, even though there could still be some error in my judgment, it is certain that I could not perceive it in this way without a human mind.

But what am I to say about this mind itself, in other words, about myself? For up to this point I am not admitting there is anything in me except mind. What, I say, is the *I* that seems to perceive this wax so distinctly? Do I not know myself not only much more truly and certainly, but also much more distinctly and clearly than I know the wax? For if I judge that the wax exists from the fact that I see it, then from the very fact that I see the wax it certainly follows much more clearly that I myself also exist. For it could be that what I see is not really wax. It could be the case that I do not have eyes at all with which to see anything. But when I see or think I see (at the moment I am not differentiating between these two), it is completely impossible that I, the one doing the thinking, am not something. For similar reasons, if I judge that the wax exists from the fact that I am touching it, the same conclusion follows once again, namely, that I exist. The result is clearly the same if [my judgment rests] on the fact that I imagine the

---

18 Mechanical person-imitations; robots.

19 This is the supposed mental faculty which unites the data from the five external senses—sight, smell, sound, touch, and taste—into a single sensory experience. The notion goes back to Aristotle, and is different from what we call "common sense" today.

wax or on any other reason at all. But these observations I have made about the wax can be applied to all other things located outside of me. Furthermore, if my perception of the wax seemed more distinct after it was drawn to my attention, not merely by sight or touch, but by several [other] causes, I must concede that I now understand myself much more distinctly, since all of those same reasons capable of assisting my perception either of the wax or of any other body whatsoever are even better proofs of the nature of my mind! However, over and above this, there are so many other things in the mind itself which can provide a more distinct conception of its [nature] that it hardly seems worthwhile to review those features of corporeal things which might contribute to it.

And behold—I have all on my own finally returned to the place where I wanted to be. For since I am now aware that bodies themselves are not properly perceived by the senses or by the faculty of imagination, but only by the intellect, and are not perceived because they are touched or seen, but only because they are understood, I realize this obvious point: there is nothing I can perceive more easily or more clearly than my own mind. But because it is impossible to rid oneself so quickly of an opinion one has long been accustomed to hold, I would like to pause here, in order to impress this new knowledge more deeply on my memory with a prolonged meditation.

Third Meditation
Concerning God and the Fact that He Exists

Now I will close my eyes, stop up my ears, and withdraw all my senses. I will even blot out from my thinking all images of corporeal things, or else, since this is hardly possible, I will dismiss them as empty and false images of nothing at all, and by talking only to myself and looking more deeply within, I will attempt, little by little, to acquire a greater knowledge of and more familiarity with myself. I am a thinking thing—in other words, something that doubts, affirms, denies, knows a few things, is ignorant of many things, wills, refuses, and also imagines and feels. For, as I have pointed out earlier, although those things which I sense or imagine outside of myself are perhaps nothing, nevertheless, I am certain that the thought processes I call sense experience and

imagination, given that they are only certain modes of thinking, do exist within me.

In these few words, I have reviewed everything I truly know, or at least [everything] that, up to this point, I was aware I knew. Now I will look around more diligently, in case there are perhaps other things in me that I have not yet considered. I am certain that I am a thinking thing. But if that is the case, do I not then also know what is required for me to be certain about something? There is, to be sure, nothing in this first knowledge other than a certain clear and distinct perception of what I am affirming, and obviously this would not be enough for me to be certain about the truth of the matter, if it could ever happen that something I perceived just as clearly and distinctly was false. And now it seems to me that now I can propose the following general rule: all those things I perceive very clearly and very distinctly are true.

However, before now I have accepted as totally certain and evident many things that I have later discovered to be doubtful. What, then, were these things? [They were], of course, the earth, the sky, the stars, and all the other things I used to grasp with my senses. But what did I clearly perceive in them? Obviously I was observing in my mind ideas or thoughts of such things. And even now I do not deny that those ideas exist within me. However, there was something else which I held to be true and which, because I was in the habit of believing it, I also thought I perceived clearly, although I really was not perceiving it at all, namely, that certain things existed outside of me from which those ideas proceeded and which were like them in every way. And here was where I went wrong, or, if anyway I was judging truthfully, that certainly was not the result of the strength of my perception.

What [then was] true? When I was thinking about something very simple and easy in arithmetic or geometry—for example, that two and three added together make five, and things of that sort—was I not recognizing these with sufficient clarity at least to affirm that they were true? Later on, to be sure, I did judge that such things could be doubted, but the only reason I did so was that it crossed my mind that some God could perhaps have placed within me a certain kind of nature, so that I deceived myself even about those things which appeared most obvious. And every time this preconceived opinion about the supreme power of God occurs to me, I cannot but confess that if He wished, it would be easy for Him to see to it that I go astray, even in those matters which I think I see as clearly as possible with my mind's eye. But whenever I turn my attention to those very things which I think I perceive with great clarity, I am so completely persuaded by them, that I spontaneously burst out with the following words: Let whoever can deceive me, do so; he will still never succeed in making me nothing, not while I think I am something, or in making it true someday that I never existed, since it is true that I exist now, or perhaps even in making two and three, when added together, more or less than five, or anything like that, in which I clearly recognize a manifest contradiction. And since I have no reason to think that some God exists who is a deceiver and since, up to this point, I do not know enough to state whether there is a God at all, it is clear that the reason for any doubt which rests on this supposition alone is very tenuous and, if I may say so, metaphysical. However, to remove even that doubt, as soon as the occasion presents itself, I ought to examine whether God exists and, if He does, whether He can be a deceiver. For as long as this point remains obscure, it seems to me that I can never be completely certain about anything else.

But now an orderly arrangement would seem to require that I first divide all of my thoughts into certain kinds and look into which of these [kinds], strictly speaking, contain truth or error. Some of my thoughts are, so to speak, images of things, and for these alone the name *idea* is appropriate, for example, when I think of a man, or a chimera, or the sky, or an angel, or God. But other thoughts, in addition to these, possess certain other forms. For example, when I will, when I fear, when I affirm, and when I deny, I always apprehend something as the object of my thinking, but in my thought I also grasp something more than the representation of that thing. In this [group of thoughts], some are called volitions[20] or feelings, and others judgments.

Now, where ideas are concerned, if I consider these only in and of themselves, not considering whether they refer to anything else, they cannot, strictly speaking, be false. For whether I imagine a goat or a chimera, it is no less true that I imagine one than it is that I imagine the other. And we also need have no fear of error in willing or in feeling, for although I can desire something evil or even things which have never existed, that still does not make the fact that I desire them untrue. And thus, all that remains are judgments, in which I must take care not to be deceived. But the most important and most frequent error I can discover in judgments consists of the fact that I judge the ideas within me are similar to or conform to certain things located outside myself. For obviously, if I considered ideas themselves only as certain modes of my thinking, without considering their reference to anything else, they would hardly furnish me any material for making a mistake.

Of these ideas, some, it seems to me, are innate,[21] others come from outside, and still others I have myself made up. For the fact that I understand what a thing is, what truth is, and what thinking is I seem to possess from no source other than my own nature. But if I now hear a noise, see the sun, or feel heat, I have up to now judged that [these sensations] come from certain things placed outside of me. And, finally, sirens, hippogriffs,[22] and such like are things I myself dream up. But perhaps I could also believe that all [these ideas] come from outside, or else are all innate, or else are all made up, for I have not yet clearly perceived their true origin.

However, the most important point I have to explore here concerns those ideas which I think of as being derived from objects existing outside me: What reason leads me to suppose that these ideas are similar to those objects? It certainly seems that I am taught to think this way by nature. Furthermore, I know by experience that these [ideas] do not depend on my will and therefore not on me myself, for they often present themselves to me even against my will. For example, whether I will it or not, I now feel heat, and thus I believe that the feeling or the idea of heat

---

20 Acts of decision-making.

21 Inborn—an idea that is already inside me.

22 In Greek mythology, sirens are half woman, half bird; hippogriffs are combinations of horse and griffin (which is part eagle, part lion).

reaches me from some object apart from me, that is, from [the heat] of the fire I am sitting beside. And nothing is more obvious than my judgment that this object is sending its own likeness into me rather than something else.

I will now see whether these reasons are sufficiently strong. When I say here that I have been taught to think this way by nature, I understand only that I have been carried by a certain spontaneous impulse to believe it, not that some natural light has revealed its truth to me. There is an important difference between these two things. For whatever natural light reveals to me—for example, that from the fact that I am doubting it follows that I exist, and things like that—cannot admit of any possible doubt, because there cannot be another faculty [in me] as trustworthy as natural light, one which could teach me that the ideas [derived from natural light] are not true. But where natural impulses are concerned, in the past, when there was an issue of choosing the good thing to do, I often judged that such impulses were pushing me in the direction of something worse, and I do not see why I should place more trust in them in any other matters.

Moreover, although those ideas do not depend on my will, it is not therefore the case that they must come from objects located outside of me. For just as those impulses I have been talking about above are within me and yet seem to be different from my will, so perhaps there is also some other faculty in me, one I do not yet understand sufficiently, which produces those ideas, in the same way they have always appeared to be formed in me up to now while I sleep, without the help of any external objects [which they represent].

Finally, even if these ideas did come from things different from me, it does not therefore follow that they have to be like those things. Quite the contrary, for in numerous cases I seem to have often observed a great difference [between the object and the idea]. So, for example, I find in my mind two different ideas of the sun. One, which is apparently derived from the senses and should certainly be included among what I consider ideas coming from outside, makes the sun appear very small to me. However, the other, which is derived from astronomical reasoning, that is, elicited by certain notions innate in me or else produced by me in some other manner, makes the sun appear many times larger than the earth. Clearly, these two [ideas] cannot both resemble the sun which exists outside of me, and reason convinces [me] that the one which seems to have emanated most immediately from the sun itself is the least like it.

All these points offer me sufficient proof that previously, when I believed that certain things existed apart from me that conveyed ideas or images of themselves, whether by my organs of sense or by some other means, my judgment was not based on anything certain but only on some blind impulse.

However, it crosses my mind that there is still another way of exploring whether certain things of which I have ideas within me exist outside of me. To the extent that those ideas are [considered] merely certain ways of thinking, of course, I do not recognize any inequality among them, and they all appear to proceed from me in the same way. But to the extent that one idea represents one thing, while another idea represents something else, it is clear that they are very different from each other. For undoubtedly those that represent substances to me and contain in themselves more objective reality, so to speak, are something more than those that simply represent modes or accidents.[23] And, once again, that idea thanks to which I am aware of a supreme God—eternal, infinite, omniscient, omnipotent, the Creator of all things that exist outside of Him—certainly has more objective reality in it than those ideas through which finite substances are represented.

Now, it is surely evident by natural light that there must be at least as much [reality] in the efficient and total cause as there is in the effect of this cause. For from where, I would like to know, can the effect receive its reality if not from its cause? And how can the cause provide this reality to the effect, unless the cause also possesses it? But from this it follows that something cannot be made from nothing and also that what is more perfect, that is, contains more reality in itself, cannot be produced from what is less perfect. This is obviously true not only of those effects whose reality

---

23   See the introduction for background information on "substance," "accident," "objective reality," and "formal reality."

is [what the philosophers call] actual or formal, but also of those ideas in which we consider only [what they call] objective reality. For example, some stone which has not previously existed cannot now begin to exist, unless it is produced by something which has in it, either formally or eminently, everything that goes into the stone,[24] and heat cannot be brought into an object which was not warm previously, except by something which is of an order at least as perfect as heat, and so on with all the other examples. But beyond this, even the idea of heat or of the stone cannot exist within me, unless it is placed in me by some cause containing at least as much reality as I understand to be in the heat or in the stone. For although that cause does not transfer anything of its own reality, either actual or formal, into my idea, one should not therefore assume that [this cause] must be less real. Instead, [we should consider] that the nature of the idea itself is such that it requires from itself no formal reality other than what it derives from my own thinking, of which it is a mode [that is, a way or style of thinking]. But for the idea to possess this objective reality rather than another, it must surely obtain it from some cause in which there is at least as much formal reality as the objective reality contained in the idea itself. For if we assume that something can be discovered in the idea which was not present in its cause, then it must have obtained this from nothing. But no matter how imperfect the mode of being may be by which a thing is objectively present in the understanding through its idea, that mode is certainly not nothing, and therefore [this idea] cannot come from nothing.

And although the reality which I am considering in my ideas is only objective, I must not imagine that it is unnecessary for the same reality to exist formally in the causes of those ideas, that it is sufficient if [the reality] in them is objective as well. For just as that mode of existing objectively belongs to ideas by their very nature, so the mode of existing formally belongs to the causes of [these] ideas, at least to the

first and most important causes, by their nature. And although it may well be possible for one idea to be born from another, still this regress cannot continue on *ad infinitum*,[25] for we must finally come to some first [idea], whose cause is, as it were, the archetype [or original idea], which formally contains the entire reality that exists only objectively in the idea. And thus natural light makes it clear to me that ideas exist within me as certain images that can, in fact, easily fall short of the perfection of the things from which they were derived but that cannot contain anything greater or more perfect than those things do.

And the more time and care I take examining these things, the more clearly and distinctly I recognize their truth. But what am I finally to conclude from them? It is clear that if the objective reality of any of my ideas is so great that I am certain that the same reality is not in me either formally or eminently and that therefore I myself cannot be the cause of that idea, it necessarily follows that I am not alone in the world but that some other thing also exists which is the cause of that idea. But if I do not find any such idea within me, then I will obviously have no argument that confirms for me the existence of anything beyond myself. For I have been searching very diligently and have not been able to find any other argument up to now.

But of these ideas of mine, apart from the one which reveals my own self to me, about which there can be no difficulty, there is another [that represents] God [to me], and there are others which represent corporeal and inanimate things, as well as others representing angels, animals, and finally other men who resemble me.

As far as concerns those ideas which display other human beings or animals or angels, I understand readily enough that I could have put these together from ideas I have of myself, of corporeal things, and of God, even though there might be no people apart from me, or animals or angels in the world.

Where the ideas of corporeal things are concerned, I see nothing in them so great that it seems as if it could not have originated within me. For if I inspect these ideas thoroughly and examine them individually in the same way I did yesterday with the idea

---

24 That is, it has either the same properties as the stone (e.g., a certain hardness) or possesses even more perfect or pronounced versions of those properties (e.g., perfect hardness). An effect is "eminently" in a cause when the cause is more perfect than the effect.

---

25 Forever (to infinity).

of the wax, I notice that there are only a very few things I perceive in them clearly and distinctly—for example, magnitude or extension in length, breadth, and depth; shape, which emerges from the limits of that extension; position, which different forms derive from their relation to each other; and motion or a change of location. To these one can add substance, duration, and number. However, with the other things, like light, colors, sounds, odors, tastes, heat, cold, and other tactile qualities, my thoughts of them involve so much confusion and obscurity, that I still do not know whether they are true or false—in other words, whether the ideas I have of these [qualities] are ideas of things or of non-things. For although I observed a little earlier that falsehood (or, strictly speaking, formal falsehood) could occur only in judgments, nonetheless there is, in fact, a certain other material falsehood in ideas, when they represent a non-thing as if it were a thing. Thus, for example, ideas which I have of heat and cold are so unclear and indistinct that I am not able to learn from them whether cold is merely a lack of heat, or heat a lack of cold, or whether both of these are real qualities, or whether neither [of them is]. And because there can be no ideas which are not, as it were, ideas of things, if it is indeed true that cold is nothing other than a lack of heat, the idea which represents cold to me as if it were something positive and real will not improperly be called false, and that will also hold for all other ideas [like this].

To such ideas I obviously do not have to assign any author other than myself, for, if they are, in fact, false, that is, if they represent things which do not exist, my natural light informs me that they proceed from nothing—in other words, that they are in me only because there is something lacking in my nature, which is not wholly perfect. If, on the other hand, they are true, given that the reality they present to me is so slight that I cannot distinguish the object from something which does not exist, then I do not see why I could not have come up with them myself.

As for those details which are clear and distinct in my ideas of corporeal things, some of them, it seems to me, I surely could have borrowed from the idea of myself, namely, substance, duration, number, and other things like that. I conceive of myself as a thinking and non-extended thing, but of the stone as an extended thing which does not think; so there is a great difference between the two; but nevertheless, I think of both as *substance*, something equipped to exist on its own. In the same way, when I perceive that I now exist and also remember that I have existed for some time earlier, and when I have various thoughts whose number I recognize, I acquire ideas of *duration* and *number*, which I can then transfer to any other things I choose. As for all the other qualities from which I put together my ideas of corporeal things, that is, extension, shape, location, and motion, they are, it is true, not formally contained in me, since I am nothing other than a thinking thing, but because they are merely certain modes of a substance and I, too, am a substance, it seems that they could be contained in me eminently.

And so the only thing remaining is the idea of God. I must consider whether there is anything in this idea for which I myself could not have been the origin. By the name *God* I understand a certain infinite, [eternal, immutable,] independent, supremely intelligent, and supremely powerful substance by which I myself was created, along with everything else that exists (if, [in fact], anything else does exist). All of these [properties] are clearly [so great] that the more diligently I focus on them, the less it seems that I could have brought them into being by myself alone. And thus, from what I have said earlier, I logically have to conclude that God necessarily exists.

For although the idea of a substance is, indeed, in me—because I am a substance—that still does not mean [that I possess] the idea of an infinite substance, since I am finite, unless it originates in some other substance which is truly infinite.

And I should not think that my perception of the infinite comes, not from a true idea, but merely from a negation of the finite, in [the same] way I perceive rest and darkness by a negation of motion and light. For, on the contrary, I understand clearly that there is more reality in an infinite substance than in a finite one and that therefore my perception of the infinite is somehow in me before my perception of the finite— in other words, my perception of God comes before my perception of myself. For how would I know that I am doubting or desiring, or, in other words, that something is lacking in me and that I am not entirely perfect, unless some idea of a perfect being was in me and I recognized my defects by a comparison?

And one cannot claim that this idea of God might well be materially false and thus could have come from nothing, the way I observed a little earlier with the ideas of heat and cold and things like that. Quite the reverse: for [this idea] is extremely clear and distinct and contains more objective reality than any other, and thus no idea will be found which is more inherently true and in which there is less suspicion of falsehood. This idea, I say, of a supremely perfect and infinite being is utterly true, for although it may well be possible to imagine that such a being does not exist, it is still impossible to imagine that the idea of Him does not reveal anything real to me, in the way I talked above about the idea of cold. This idea of a perfect Being is also entirely clear and distinct, for whatever I see clearly and distinctly which is real and true and which introduces some perfection is totally contained within [this idea]. The fact that I cannot comprehend the infinite or that there are innumerable other things in God that I do not understand or even perhaps have any way of contacting in my thoughts—all this is irrelevant. For something finite, like myself, cannot comprehend the nature of the infinite, and it is sufficient that I understand this very point and judge that all things which I perceive clearly and which I know convey some perfection, as well as innumerable others perhaps which I know nothing about, are in God, either formally or eminently, so that the idea I have of Him is the truest, clearest, and most distinct of all the ideas within me.

But perhaps I am something more than I myself understand, and all those perfections which I attribute to God are potentially in me somehow, even though they are not yet evident and are not manifesting themselves in action. For I already know by experience that my knowledge is gradually increasing, and I do not see anything which could prevent it from increasing more and more to infinity. Nor do I even know of any reasons why, with my knowledge augmented in this way, I could not, with its help, acquire all the other perfections of God or, finally, why, if the power [to acquire] those perfections is already in me, it would not be sufficient to produce the idea of those perfections.

And yet none of these things is possible. For, in the first place, although it is true that my knowledge is gradually increasing and that there are potentially many things within me which have not yet been realized, still none of these is relevant to the idea of God, in which, of course, nothing at all exists potentially. For the very fact that my knowledge is increasing little by little is the most certain argument for its imperfection. Beyond that, even if my knowledge is always growing more and more, nonetheless, that does not convince me that it will ever be truly infinite, since it can never reach a stage where it is not capable of increasing any further. But I judge that God is actually infinite, so that nothing can possibly be added to His perfection. And lastly, I perceive that the objective existence of an idea cannot be produced from a being that is merely potential, which, strictly speaking, is nothing, but only from something which actually or formally exists.

Obviously everything in all these thoughts is evident to the natural light in anyone who reflects carefully [on the matter]. But when I pay less attention and when images of sensible[26] things obscure the vision in my mind, I do not so readily remember why the idea of a being more perfect than myself must necessarily proceed from some entity that is truly more perfect than me. Therefore, I would like to enquire further whether I, who possess this idea [of God], could exist if such a being did not exist.

If that were the case, then from whom would I derive my existence? Clearly from myself or from my parents or from some other source less perfect than God. For we cannot think of or imagine anything more perfect than God or even anything equally perfect.

However, if I originated from myself, then I would not doubt or hope, and I would lack nothing at all, for I would have given myself all the perfections of which I have any idea within me, and thus I myself would be God. I must not assume that those things which I lack might be more difficult to acquire than those now within me. On the contrary, it clearly would have been much more difficult for me—that is, a thinking thing or substance—to emerge from nothing than to

---

26   I.e., things that can be perceived with the physical senses.

acquire a knowledge of the many things about which I am ignorant, for knowing such things is merely an accident of that thinking substance. And surely if I had obtained from myself that greater perfection [of being the author of my own existence], then I could hardly have denied myself the perfections which are easier to acquire, or, indeed, any of those I perceive contained in the idea of God, since, it seems to me, none of them is more difficult to produce. But if there were some perfections more difficult to acquire, they would certainly appear more difficult to me, too, if, indeed, everything else I possessed was derived from myself, because from them I would learn by experience that my power was limited.

And I will not escape the force of these arguments by assuming that I might perhaps have always been the way I am now, as if it followed from that assumption that I would not have to seek out any author for my own existence. For since the entire period of my life can be divided into innumerable parts each one of which is in no way dependent on the others, therefore, just because I existed a little while ago, it does not follow that I must exist now, unless at this very moment some cause is, at it were, creating me once again—in other words, preserving me. For it is clear to anyone who directs attention to the nature of time that, in order for the existence of anything at all to be preserved in each particular moment it lasts, that thing surely needs the same force and action which would be necessary to create it anew if it did not yet exist. Thus, one of the things natural light reveals is that preservation and creation are different only in the ways we think of them.

Consequently, I now ought to ask myself whether I have any power which enables me to bring it about that I, who am now existing, will also exist a little later on, for since I am nothing other than a thinking thing—or at least since my precise concern at the moment is only with that part of me which is a thinking thing—if such a power is in me, I would undoubtedly be conscious of it. But I experience nothing [of that sort], and from this fact alone I recognize with the utmost clarity that I depend upon some being different from myself.

But perhaps that being is not God, and I have been produced by my parents or by some other causes less perfect than God. But [that is impossible]. As I have already said before, it is clear that there must be at least as much [reality] in the cause as in the effect and that thus, since I am a thinking thing and have a certain idea of God within me, I must concede that whatever I finally designate as my own cause is also a thinking substance containing the idea of all the perfections I attribute to God. It is possible once again to ask whether that cause originates from itself or from something else. If it comes from itself, then, given what I have said, it is obvious that the cause itself is God. For clearly, if it derives its power of existing from itself, it also undoubtedly has the power of actually possessing all the perfections whose idea it contains within itself, that is, all those that I think of as existing in God. But if it is produced from some other cause, then I ask once again in the same way whether this cause comes from itself or from some other cause, until I finally reach a final cause, which will be God.

For it is clear enough that this questioning cannot produce an infinite regress, particularly because the issue I am dealing with here is a matter not only of the cause which once produced me but also—and most importantly—of the cause which preserves me at the present time.

And I cannot assume that perhaps a number of partial causes came together to produce me and that from one of them I received the idea of one of the perfections I attribute to God and from another the idea of another perfection, so that all those perfections are indeed found somewhere in the universe, but they are not all joined together in a single being who is God. Quite the contrary, [for] the unity and simplicity—or the inseparability of all those things present in God—is one of the principal perfections which I recognize in Him. And surely the idea of this unity of all His perfections could not have been placed in me by any cause from which I did not acquire ideas of the other perfections as well, for no single cause could have made it possible for me to understand that those perfections were joined together and inseparable, unless at the same time it enabled me to recognize what those perfections were.

And finally, concerning my parents, even if everything I have ever believed about them is true, it is perfectly clear that they are not the ones who preserve me and that, to the extent that I am a thinking thing, there is no way they could have even made me. Instead they merely produced certain arrangements in the material substance which, as I have judged the matter, contains me—that is, contains my mind, for that is all I assume I am at the moment. And thus the fact that my parents contributed to my existence provides no problem for my argument. Given all this, however, from the mere fact that I exist and that I have the idea of a supremely perfect being, or God, I must conclude that I have provided an extremely clear proof that God does, indeed, exist.

All that is left now is to examine how I have received that idea from God. For I have not derived it from the senses, and it has never come to me unexpectedly, as habitually occurs with the ideas of things I perceive with the senses, when those ideas of external substances impinge, or seem to impinge, on my sense organs. Nor is it something I just made up, for I am completely unable to remove anything from it or add anything to it. Thus, all that remains is that the idea is innate in me, just as the idea of myself is also innate in me.

And obviously it is not strange that God, when He created me, placed that idea within me, so that it would be, as it were, the mark of the master craftsman impressed in his own work—not that it is at all necessary for this mark to be different from the work itself. But the fact that God created me makes it highly believable that He made me in some way in His image and likeness, and that I perceive this likeness, which contains the idea of God, by the same faculty with which I perceive myself. In other words, when I turn my mind's eye onto myself, I not only understand that I am an incomplete thing, dependent on something else, and one that aspires [constantly] to greater and better things without limit, but at the same time I also realize that the one I depend on contains within Himself all those greater things [to which I aspire], not merely indefinitely and potentially, but actually and infinitely, and thus that He is God. The entire force of my argument rests on the fact that I recognize I could not possibly exist with the sort of nature I possess, namely, having the idea of God within me, unless God truly existed as well—that God, I say, whose idea is in me—the Being having all those perfections which I do not grasp but which I am somehow capable of touching in my thoughts, and who is entirely free of any defect. These reasons are enough to show that He cannot be a deceiver, for natural light clearly demonstrates that every fraud and deception depends upon some defect.

But before I examine this matter more carefully and at the same time look into other truths I could derive from it, I wish to pause here for a while to contemplate God himself, to ponder His attributes, and to consider, admire, and adore the beauty of His immense light, to the extent that the eyes of my darkened intellect can bear it. For just as we believe through faith that the supreme happiness of our life hereafter consists only in this contemplation of the Divine Majesty, so we know from experience that the same [contemplation] now, though far less perfect, is the greatest joy we are capable of in this life.

Fourth Meditation
Concerning Truth and Falsity

In these last few days, I have grown accustomed to detaching my mind from my senses, and I have clearly noticed that, in fact, I perceive very little with any certainty about corporeal things and that I know a great deal more about the human mind and even more about God. As a result, I now have no difficulty directing my thoughts away from things I [perceive with the senses or] imagine, and onto those purely intellectual matters divorced from all material substance. And clearly the idea I have of the human mind, to the extent that it is a thinking thing that has no extension in length, breadth, and depth and possesses nothing else which the body has, is much more distinct than my idea of any corporeal substance. Now, when I direct my attention to the fact that I have doubts, in other words, that [I am] something incomplete and dependent, the really clear and distinct idea of an independent and complete being, that is, of God, presents itself to me. From this one fact—that there is an idea like this in me—or else because of the fact that I, who possess this idea, exist, I draw the clear conclusion that God also exists and that my entire existence depends on Him every single moment [of my life]. Thus, I believe that the human intellect can know nothing with greater clarity and greater certainty. And now it seems to me I see a way by which I can go from this contemplation of the true God, in whom all the treasures of science and wisdom are hidden, to an understanding of everything else.

First of all, I recognize that it is impossible that God would ever deceive me, for one discovers some sort of imperfection in everything false or deceptive. And although it may appear that the ability to deceive is evidence of a certain cleverness or power, the wish to deceive undoubtedly demonstrates either malice or mental weakness, and is therefore not found in God.

Then, I know from experience that there is in me a certain faculty of judgment, which I certainly received from God, like all the other things within me. Since He is unwilling to deceive me, He obviously did not give me the kind of faculty that could ever lead me into error, if I used it correctly.

There would remain no doubt about this, if it did not seem to lead to the conclusion that I could never make mistakes. For if whatever is within me I have from God and if He did not give me any power to commit errors, it would appear that I could never make a mistake. Now, it is true that as long as I am thinking only about God and directing myself totally to Him, I detect no reason for errors or falsity. But after a while, when I turn back to myself, I know by experience that I am still subject to innumerable errors. When I seek out their cause, I notice that I can picture not only a certain real and positive [idea] of God, or of a supremely perfect being, but also, so to speak, a certain negative idea of nothingness, or of something removed as far as possible from every perfection, and [I recognize] that I am, as it were, something intermediate between God and nothingness—that is, that I am situated between a supreme being and non-being in such a way that, insofar as I was created by a supreme being, there is, in fact, nothing in me which would deceive me or lead me into error, but insofar as I also participate, to a certain extent, in nothingness or non-being—in other words, given that I myself am not a supreme being—I lack a great many things. Therefore, it is not strange that I am deceived. From this I understand that error, to the extent that it is error, is not something real which depends on God, but is merely a defect. Thus, for me to fall into error, it is not necessary that I have been given a specific power to do this by God. Instead, I happen to make mistakes because the power I have of judging what is true [and what is false], which I do have from God, is not infinite within me.

However, this is not yet entirely satisfactory, for error is not pure negation, but rather the privation or lack of a certain knowledge that somehow ought to be within me. But to anyone who thinks about the nature of God, it does not seem possible that He would place within me any power that is not a perfect example of its kind or that lacks some perfection it ought to have. For [if it is true] that the greater the skill of the craftsman, the more perfect the works he produces, what could the supreme maker of all things create which was not perfect in all its parts? And there is no doubt that God could have created me in such a way that I was never deceived, and, similarly, there is no doubt that He always wills what is best. So then, is it better for me to make mistakes or not to make them?

As I weigh these matters more attentively, it occurs to me, first, that I should not find it strange if I do not understand the reasons for some of the things God does; thus I should not entertain doubts about His existence just because I happen to learn from experience about certain other things and do not grasp why or how He has created them. For given the fact that I already know my nature is extremely infirm and limited and that, by contrast, the nature of God is immense, incomprehensible, and infinite, I understand sufficiently well that He is capable of innumerable things about whose causes I am ignorant. For that reason alone, I believe that the entire class of causes we are in the habit of searching out as *final causes*[27] is completely useless in matters of physics, for I do not think I am capable of investigating the final purposes of God without appearing foolhardy.

---

27 The final cause of something is (roughly) the purpose or reason for that thing's existence: e.g., the final cause of a statue might be an original idea or artistic goal in the sculptor's head which prompted her to make that particular statue. This terminology goes back to Aristotle, and involves a contrast between final causes and three other sorts of cause—material causes (the marble out of which the statue is hewn), formal causes (the shape—the form—of the statue), and efficient causes (the sculptor's craft in making the statue).

It also occurs to me that, whenever we look into whether the works of God are perfect, we should not examine one particular creature by itself, but rather the universal totality of things. For something which may well justly appear, by itself, very imperfect, is utterly perfect [if we think of it] as part of the [entire] universe. And although, given my wish to doubt everything, I have up to now recognized nothing as certain, other than the existence of myself and God, nonetheless, since I have observed the immense power of God, I cannot deny that He may have created many other things or at least is capable of creating them and therefore that I may occupy a place in a universe of things.

After that, by examining myself more closely and looking into the nature of my errors (the only things testifying to some imperfection in me), I observe that they proceed from two causes working together simultaneously, namely, from the faculty of knowing, which I possess, and from the faculty of choosing, or from my freedom to choose—in other words from both the intellect and the will together. For through my intellect alone I [do not affirm or deny anything, but] simply grasp the ideas of things about which I can make a judgment, and, if I consider my intellect in precisely this way, I find nothing there which is, strictly speaking, an error. For although countless things may well exist of which I have no idea at all within me, I still should not assert that I am deprived of them, in the proper sense of that word, [as if that knowledge were something my understanding was entitled to thanks to its nature]. I can only make the negative claim that I do not have them, for obviously I can produce no reason which enables me to prove that God ought to have given me a greater power of understanding than He has provided. And although I know that a craftsman is an expert, still I do not assume that he must therefore place in each of his works all the perfections he is capable of placing in some. Moreover, I certainly cannot complain that I have received from God a will or a freedom to choose that is insufficiently ample and perfect. For I clearly know from experience that my will is not circumscribed by any limits. And what seems to me particularly worthy of notice is the fact that, apart from my will, there is nothing in me so perfect or so great that I do not recognize that it could be still more perfect or even greater. For, to consider an example: if I think about the power of understanding, I see at once that in me it is very small and extremely limited. At the same time, I form an idea of another understanding which is much greater, even totally great and infinite, and from the mere fact that I can form this idea, I see that it pertains to the nature of God. By the same reasoning, if I examine my faculty of memory or of imagination or any other faculty, I find none at all which I do not recognize as tenuous and confined in me and immense in God. It is only my will or my freedom to choose which I experience as so great in me that I do not apprehend the idea of anything greater. Thus, through my will, more than through anything else, I understand that I bear a certain image of and resemblance to God. For although the will is incomparably greater in God than in myself—because the knowledge and power linked to it make it much stronger and more efficacious and because, with respect to its object, His will extends to more things—nonetheless, if I think of the will formally and precisely in and of itself, His does not appear greater than mine. For the power of will consists only in the ability to do or not to do [something] (that is, to affirm or to deny, to follow or to avoid)—or rather in this one thing alone, that whether we affirm or deny, follow or avoid [something] which our understanding has set before us, we act in such a way that we do not feel that any external force is determining what we do. For to be free, I do not have to be inclined in two [different] directions. On the contrary, the more I am inclined to one—whether that is because I understand that principles of the true and the good are manifestly in it or because that is the way God has arranged the inner core of my thinking—the more freely I choose it. Clearly divine grace and natural knowledge never diminish liberty, but rather increase and strengthen it. However, the indifference I experience when there is no reason urging me to one side more than to the other is the lowest degree of liberty. It does not demonstrate any perfection in [the will], but rather a defect in my understanding or else a certain negation. For if I always clearly perceived what is true and good, I would never need to deliberate about what I ought to be judging or choosing, and thus, although I would be entirely free, I could never be indifferent.

For these reasons, however, I perceive that the power of willing, which I have from God, considered in itself, is not the source of my errors. For it is extremely ample and perfect. And the source is not my power of understanding. For when I understand something, I undoubtedly do so correctly, since my [power of] understanding comes from God, and thus it is impossible for it to deceive me. So from where do my errors arise? Surely from the single fact that my will ranges more widely than my intellect, and I do not keep it within the same limits but extend it even to those things which I do not understand. Since the will does not discriminate among these things, it easily turns away from the true and the good, and, in this way, I make mistakes and transgress.

For example, in the past few days, when I was examining whether anything in the world existed and I observed that, from the very fact that I was exploring this [question], it clearly followed that I existed, I was not able [to prevent myself] from judging that what I understood so clearly was true, not because I was forced to that conclusion by any external force, but because a great light in my understanding was followed by a great inclination in my will, and thus the less I was indifferent to the issue, the more spontaneous and free was my belief. For example: now I know that I exist, to the extent I am a thinking thing; but I am in doubt about whether this thinking nature within me (rather, which I myself *am*) is of that corporeal nature also revealed to me. I assume that up to this point no reason has offered itself to my understanding which might convince me that I am, or am not, of corporeal nature. From this single fact it is clear that I am indifferent as to which of the two I should affirm or deny, or whether I should even make any judgment in the matter.

Furthermore, this indifference extends not merely to those things about which the understanding knows nothing at all, but also, in general, to everything which it does not recognize with sufficient clarity at the time when the will is deliberating about them. For, however probable the conjectures [may be] which draw me in one direction, the mere knowledge that they are only conjectures and not certain and indubitable reasons is enough to urge me to assent to the opposite view. In the past few days I have learned this well enough by experience, once I assumed that all those things I had previously accepted as absolutely true were utterly false, because of the single fact that I discovered they could in some way be doubted.

But when I do not perceive that something is true with sufficient clarity and distinctness, if, in fact, I abstain from rendering judgment, I am obviously acting correctly and am not deceived. But if at that time I affirm or deny, [then] I am not using my freedom to choose properly. If I make up my mind [and affirm] something false, then, of course I will be deceived. On the other hand, if I embrace the alternative, then I may, indeed, hit upon the truth by chance, but that would not free me from blame, since natural light makes it clear that a perception of the understanding must always precede a determination of the will. And it is in this incorrect use of the freedom of the will that one finds the privation which constitutes the nature of error. Privation, I say, inheres in this act of the will, to the extent that it proceeds from me, but not in the faculty I have received from God, nor even in the act, insofar as it depends upon Him.

For I have no cause to complain at all about the fact that God has not given me a greater power of understanding or a more powerful natural light than He has, because it is in the nature of a finite intellect not to understand many things and it is in the nature of a created intellect to be finite. Instead, I should thank Him, who has never owed me anything, for His generosity, rather than thinking that He has deprived me of something He did not provide or else has taken it away.

And I also have no reason to complain on the ground that He gave me a will more extensive than my understanding. For since the will consists of only a single thing and is, so to speak, indivisible, it does not seem that its nature is such that anything could be removed [without destroying it]. And, of course, the more extensive my will, the more I ought to show gratitude to the one who gave it to me.

And finally I also ought not to complain because God concurs with me in bringing out those acts of will or those judgments in which I am deceived. For those actions are true and good in every way, to the extent that they depend on God, and in a certain way there is more perfection in me because I am capable of eliciting these actions than if I were not. But privation, in which one finds the only formal reason for falsity and failure, has no need of God's concurrence, because it is not a thing, and if one links it to Him as its cause, one should not call it privation but merely negation. For obviously it is not an imperfection in God that He has given me freedom to assent or not to assent to certain things, when He has not placed a clear and distinct perception of them in my understanding. However, it is undoubtedly an imperfection in me that I do not use that liberty well and that I bring my judgment to bear on things which I do not properly understand. Nonetheless, I see that God could easily have created me so that I never made mistakes, even though I remained free and had a limited understanding. For example, He could have placed in my intellect a clear and distinct perception of everything about which I would ever deliberate, or He could have impressed on my memory that I should never make judgments about things which I did not understand clearly and distinctly, and done that so firmly that it would be impossible for me ever to forget. And I readily understand that, if God had made me that way, insofar as I have an idea of this totality, I would have been more perfect than I am now. But I cannot therefore deny that there may somehow be more perfection in this whole universe of things because some of its parts are not immune to errors and others are—more perfection than if all things were entirely alike. And I have no right to complain just because the part God wanted me to play in the universe is not the most important and most perfect of all.

Besides, even if I am unable to avoid errors in the first way [mentioned above], which depends upon a clear perception of all those things about which I need to deliberate, I can still use that other [method], which requires me only to remember to abstain from rendering judgment every time the truth of something is not evident. For although experience teaches me that I have a weakness which renders me incapable of keeping [my mind] always focused on one and the same thought, I can still see to it that by attentive and frequently repeated meditation I remember that fact every time the occasion demands. In this way I will acquire the habit of not making mistakes.

Since the greatest and preeminent perfection of human beings consists in this ability to avoid mistakes, I think that with the discovery in today's meditation of the cause of error and falsity I have gained a considerable gift. Clearly the source of mistakes can be nothing other than what I have identified. For as long as I keep my will restrained when I deliver judgments, so that it extends itself only to those things which reveal themselves clearly and distinctly to my understanding, I will surely be incapable of making mistakes, because every clear and distinct perception is undoubtedly something [real]. Therefore, it cannot exist from nothing but necessarily has God as its author—God, I say, that supremely perfect being, who would contradict His nature if He were deceitful. And thus, [such a perception] is unquestionably true. I have learned today not only what I must avoid in order to ensure that I am never deceived, but also at the same time what I must do in order to reach the truth. For I will assuredly reach that if I only pay sufficient attention to all the things I understand perfectly and distinguish these from all the other things which I apprehend confusedly and obscurely. In future, I will pay careful attention to this matter.

Fifth Meditation
Concerning the Essence of Material Things, and, Once Again, Concerning the Fact that God Exists

Many other [issues] concerning the attributes of God are still left for me to examine, [as well as] many things about myself, that is, about the nature of my mind. However, I will perhaps return to those at another time. Now (after I have taken note of what I must avoid and what I must do to arrive at the truth) nothing seems to be more pressing than for me to attempt to emerge from the doubts into which I have fallen in the last few days and to see whether I can know anything certain about material things.

But before I look into whether any such substances exist outside of me, I ought to consider the ideas of them, insofar as they are in my thinking, and see which of them are distinct and which confused.

For example, I distinctly imagine quantity (which philosophers commonly refer to as 'continuous' quantity)—that is, the length, breadth, and depth of the quantity, or rather, of the object being quantified.

Further, I enumerate the various parts of the object, and assign to those parts all sorts of sizes, shapes, locations, and local movements, and to those movements all sorts of durations.

And in this way I not only clearly observe and acquire knowledge of those things when I examine them in general, but later, by devoting my attention to them, I also perceive innumerable particular details about their shapes, number, motion, and so on, whose truth is so evident and so well suited to my nature, that when I discover them for the first time, it seems that I am remembering what I used to know, rather than learning anything new, or else noticing for the first time things which were truly within me earlier, although I had not previously directed my mental gaze on them.

I believe that the most important issue for me to consider here is that I find within me countless ideas of certain things which, even if they perhaps do not exist outside of me at all, still cannot be called nothing. Although in a certain sense I can think of them whenever I wish, still I do not create them. They have their own true and immutable natures. For example, when I imagine a triangle whose particular shape perhaps does not exist and has never existed outside my thinking, it nevertheless has, in fact, a certain determinate nature or essence or form which is immutable and eternal, which I did not produce, and which does not depend upon my mind; this is clearly shown in the fact that I can demonstrate the various properties of that triangle, namely, that the sum of its three angles is equal to two right angles, that the triangle's longest side has its endpoints on the lines made by the triangle's largest angle, and so on. These properties I now recognize clearly whether I wish to or not, although earlier, when I imagined the triangle [for the first time], I was not thinking of them at all and therefore did not invent them.

In this case it is irrelevant if I tell [myself] that perhaps this idea of a triangle came to me from external things through my sense organs, on the ground that I have certainly now and then seen objects possessing a triangular shape. For I am able to think up countless other shapes about which there can be no suspicion that they ever flowed into me through my senses, and yet [I can] demonstrate various properties about

them, no less than I can about the triangle. All these properties are *something* and not pure nothingness, since I conceive of them clearly and distinctly, and, as I have shown above, thus they must be true. Besides, even if I had not proved this, the nature of my mind is certainly such that I cannot refuse to assent to them, at least for as long as I am perceiving them clearly. And I remember that, even in those earlier days, when I was attracted as strongly as possible to objects of sense experience, I always maintained that the most certain things of all were those kinds of truth which I recognized clearly as shapes, numbers, or other things pertinent to arithmetic or geometry or to pure and abstract mathematics generally.

But if it follows from the mere fact that I can draw the idea of some object from my thinking that all things which I perceive clearly and distinctly as pertaining to that object really do belong to it, can I not also derive from this an argument which proves that God exists? For clearly I find the idea of Him, that is, of a supremely perfect being, within me just as much as I do the idea of some shape or number. I know that [actual and] eternal existence belongs to His nature just as clearly and distinctly as [I know] that what I prove about some shape or number also belongs to the nature of that shape or number. And therefore, even if all the things I have meditated on in the preceding days were not true, for me the existence of God ought to have at least the same degree of certainty as [I have recognized] up to this point in the truths of mathematics.

At first glance, however, this argument does not look entirely logical but [appears to] contain some sort of sophistry.[28] For, since in all other matters I have been accustomed to distinguish existence from essence, I can easily persuade myself that [existence] can also be separated from the essence of God and thus that I [can] think of God as not actually existing. However, when I think about this more carefully, it becomes clear that one cannot separate existence from the essence of God, any more than one can separate the fact that the sum of the three angles in a triangle is equal to two right angles from the essence of a triangle, or separate the idea of a valley from the idea of

---

28   That is, clever-sounding but deceptive reasoning.

a mountain. Thus, it is no less contradictory to think of a God (that is, of a supremely perfect being) who lacks existence (that is, who lacks a certain perfection) than it is to think of a mountain without a valley.[29]

Nonetheless, although I cannot conceive of God other than as something with existence, any more than I can of a mountain without a valley, the truth is that just because I think of a mountain with a valley, it does not therefore follow that there is any mountain in the world. In the same way, just because I think of God as having existence, it does not seem to follow that God therefore exists. For my thinking imposes no necessity on things, and in the same way as I can imagine a horse with wings, even though no horse has wings, so I could perhaps attribute existence to God, even though no God exists.

But this [objection] conceals a fallacy. For from the fact that I cannot think of a mountain without a valley, it does not follow that a mountain and valley exist anywhere, but merely that the mountain and valley, whether they exist or not, cannot be separated from each other. However, from the fact that I cannot think of God without existence, it does follow that existence is inseparable from God, and thus that He truly does exist. Not that my thought brings this about or imposes any necessity on anything, but rather, by contrast, because the necessity of the thing itself, that is, of the existence of God, determines that I must think this way. For I am not free to think of God without existence (that is, of a supremely perfect being lacking a supreme perfection) in the same way that I am free to imagine a horse with wings or without them.

Suppose somebody objects: Agreed that once one has assumed that God has every perfection it is in fact necessary to admit that He exists (because existence is part of perfection), but it is not necessary to make that assumption, just as it is unnecessary to assume that all quadrilaterals [can] be inscribed in a circle. For if one assumed that, one would have to conclude that any rhombus could be inscribed in a circle—but this is clearly false.[30] But this objection is invalid.

For although it may not be necessary for me ever to entertain any thought of God, nevertheless, whenever I do happen to think of a first and supreme being, and, as it were, to derive an idea of Him from the storehouse of my mind, I have to attribute to Him all perfections, even though I do not enumerate them all at that time or attend to each one of them individually. And this necessity is obviously sufficient to make me conclude correctly, once I have recognized that existence is a perfection, that a first and supreme being exists. In the same way, it is not necessary that I ever imagine any triangle, but every time I wish to consider a rectilinear[31] figure with only three angles, I have to attribute to it those [properties] from which I correctly infer that its three angles are no greater than two right angles, although at that time I may not notice this. But when I think about which figures [are capable of being] inscribed in a circle, it is not at all necessary that I believe every quadrilateral is included in their number. On the contrary, I cannot even imagine anything like that, as long as I do not wish to admit anything unless I understand it clearly and distinctly. Thus, there is a great difference between false assumptions of this kind and the true ideas which are innate in me, of which the first and most important is the idea of God. For, in fact, I understand in many ways that this [idea] is not something made up which depends upon my thought but [is] the image of a true and immutable nature: first, because I cannot think of any other thing whose essence includes existence, other than God alone; second, because I am unable to conceive of two or more Gods of this sort, and because, given that I have already assumed that one God exists, I see clearly that it is necessary that He has previously existed from [all] eternity and will continue [to exist] for all eternity; and finally because I perceive many other things in God, none of which I can remove or change.

But, in fact, no matter what reasoning I finally use by way of proof, I always come back to the point that the only things I find entirely persuasive are those I

---

29 That is, an upslope without a downslope.

30 Quadrilaterals are four-sided figures. A figure can be inscribed in a circle when a circle can be drawn that passes through each corner. Rhombuses are figures

with four sides of equal length. Squares (a type of rhombus) can be inscribed in a circle, but rhombuses not containing four right angles cannot.

31 Formed by straight lines.

perceive clearly and distinctly. Among the things I perceive in this way, some are obvious to everyone, while others reveal themselves only to those who look into them more closely and investigate more diligently, but nevertheless once the latter have been discovered, they are considered no less certain than the former. For example, even though the fact that the hypotenuse of a right triangle is opposite the largest angle of the triangle is more apparent than the fact that the square of the hypotenuse is equal to the sum of the squares of the other two sides, nonetheless, after we have initially recognized the second fact, we are no less certain of its truth [than we are of the other]. But where God is concerned, if I were not overwhelmed with prejudices, and if images of perceptible things were not laying siege to my thinking on all sides, there is certainly nothing I would recognize sooner or more easily than Him. For what is more inherently evident than that there is a supreme being; in other words, that God exists, for existence [necessarily and eternally] belongs to His essence alone?

And although it required careful reflection on my part to perceive this [truth], nonetheless I am now not only as sure about it as I am about all the other things which seem [to me] most certain, but also, I see that the certainty of everything else is so dependent on this very truth that without it nothing could ever be perfectly known.

For although my nature is such that, as long as I perceive something really clearly and distinctly, I am unable to deny that it is true, nevertheless, because I am also by nature incapable of always fixing my mental gaze on the same thing in order to perceive it clearly, [and because] my memory may often return to a judgment I have previously made at a time when I am not paying full attention to the reasons why I made such a judgment, other arguments can present themselves which, if I knew nothing about God, might easily drive me to abandon that opinion. Thus, I would never have any true and certain knowledge, but merely vague and changeable opinions. For example, when I consider the nature of a triangle, it is, in fact, very evident to me (given that I am well versed in the principles of geometry) that its three angles are equal to two right angles, and, as long as I focus on

the proof of this fact, it is impossible for me not to believe that it is true. But as soon as I turn my mental gaze away from that, although I still remember I perceived it very clearly, it could still easily happen that I doubt whether it is true, if, in fact, I had no knowledge of God. For I can convince myself that nature created me in such a way that I am sometimes deceived by those things I think I perceive as clearly as possible, especially when I remember that I have often considered many things true and certain that I later judged to be false, once other reasons had persuaded me.

However, after I perceived that God exists, because at the same time I also realized that all other things depend on Him and that He is not a deceiver, I therefore concluded that everything I perceive clearly and distinctly is necessarily true. Thus, even if I am not fully attending to the reasons why I have judged that something is true, if I only remember that I have perceived it clearly and distinctly, no opposing argument can present itself that would force me to have doubts. Instead, I possess true and certain knowledge about it—and not just about that, but about all other matters which I remember having demonstrated at any time, for example, [about the truths] of geometry and the like. For what argument could I now bring against them? What about the fact that I am created in such a manner that I often make mistakes? But now I know that I cannot be deceived about those things which I understand clearly. What about the fact that I used to consider many other things true and certain which I later discovered to be false? But I was not perceiving any of these [things] clearly and distinctly, and, in my ignorance of this rule [for confirming] the truth, I happened to believe them for other reasons which I later discovered to be less firm. What then will I say? Perhaps I am dreaming (an objection I recently made to myself), or else everything I am now thinking is no more true than what happens when I am asleep? But even this does not change anything: for surely even though I am asleep, if what is in my intellect is clear, then it is absolutely true.

In this way I fully recognize that all certainty and truth in science depend only on a knowledge of the true God, so much so that, before I knew Him, I could have no perfect knowledge of anything else.

But now I am able to understand innumerable things completely and clearly, about both God Himself and other intellectual matters, as well as about all those things in corporeal nature that are objects of study in pure mathematics.

Sixth Meditation
Concerning the Existence of Material Things and the Real Distinction Between Mind and Body

It remains for me to examine whether material things exist. At the moment, I do, in fact, know that they *could* exist, at least insofar as they are objects of pure mathematics, since I perceive them clearly and distinctly. For there is no doubt that God is capable of producing everything which I am capable of perceiving in this way, and I have never judged that there is anything He cannot create, except in those cases where there might be a contradiction in my clear perception of it. Moreover, from my faculty of imagination, which I have learned by experience I use when I turn my attention to material substances, it seems to follow that they exist. For when I consider carefully what the imagination is, it seems nothing other than a certain application of my cognitive faculty to an object which is immediately present to it and which therefore exists.

In order to clarify this matter fully, I will first examine the difference between imagination and pure understanding. For example, when I imagine a triangle, not only do I understand that it is a shape composed of three lines, but at the same time I also see those three lines as if they were, so to speak, present to my mind's eye. This is what I call imagining. However, if I wish to think about a chiliagon, even though I understand that it is a figure consisting of one thousand sides just as well as I understand that a triangle is a figure consisting of three sides, I do not imagine those thousand sides in the same way, nor do I see [them], as it were, in front of me. And although, thanks to my habit of always imagining something whenever I think of a corporeal substance, it may happen that [in thinking of a chiliagon] I create for myself a confused picture of some shape, nevertheless, it is obviously not a chiliagon, because it is no different from the shape I would also picture to myself if I were thinking of a myriagon[32] or of any other figure with many sides. And that shape is no help at all in recognizing those properties which distinguish the chiliagon from other polygons. However, if it is a question of a pentagon, I can certainly understand its shape just as [well as] I can the shape of a chiliagon, without the assistance of my imagination. But, of course, I can also imagine the pentagon by applying my mind's eye to its five sides and to the area they contain. From this I clearly recognize that, in order to imagine things, I need a certain special mental effort that I do not use to understand them, and this new mental effort reveals clearly the difference between imagination and pure understanding.

Furthermore, I notice that this power of imagining, which exists within me, insofar as it differs from the power of understanding, is not a necessary part of my own essence, that is, of my mind. For even if I did not have it, I would still undoubtedly remain the same person I am now. From this it would seem to follow that my imagination depends upon something different from [my mind]. I understand the following easily enough: If a certain body—my body—exists, and my mind is connected to it in such a way that whenever my mind so wishes it can direct itself (so to speak) to examine that body, then thanks to this particular body it would be possible for me to imagine corporeal things. Thus, the only difference between imagination and pure understanding would be this: the mind, while it is understanding, in some way turns its attention to itself and considers one of the ideas present in itself, but when it is imagining, it turns its attention to the body and sees something in it which conforms to an idea which it has either conceived by itself or perceived with the senses. I readily understand, as I have said, that the imagination *could* be formed in this way, if the body exists, and because I can think of no other equally convenient way of explaining it, I infer from this that the body probably exists—but only probably—and although I am looking into everything carefully, I still do not yet see how from this distinct idea of corporeal nature which I find in my imagination I can derive any argument which necessarily concludes that anything corporeal exists.

---

32 A myriagon is a 10,000-sided polygon.

However, I am in the habit of imagining many things apart from the corporeal nature which is the object of study in pure mathematics, such as colors, sounds, smells, pain, and things like that, although not so distinctly. And since I perceive these better with my senses, through which, with the help of my memory, they appear to have reached my imagination, then in order to deal with them in a more appropriate manner, I ought to consider the senses at the same time as well and see whether those things which I perceive by this method of thinking, which I call sensation, will enable me to establish some credible argument to prove the existence of corporeal things.

First of all, I will review in my mind the things that I previously believed to be true, because I perceived them with my senses, along with the reasons for those beliefs. Then I will also assess the reasons why I later called them into doubt. And finally I will consider what I ought to believe about them now.

To begin with, then, I sensed that I had a head, hands, feet, and other limbs making up that body which I looked on as if it were a part of me or perhaps even my totality. I sensed that this body moved around among many other bodies which could affect it in different ways, either agreeably or disagreeably. I judged which ones were agreeable by a certain feeling of pleasure and which ones were disagreeable by a feeling of pain. Apart from pain and pleasure, I also felt inside me sensations of hunger, thirst, and other appetites of this kind, as well as certain physical inclinations towards joy, sadness, anger, and other similar emotions. And outside myself, besides the extension, shapes, and motions of bodies, I also had sensations of their hardness, heat, and other tactile qualities and, in addition, of light, colors, smells, tastes, and sounds. From the variety of these, I distinguished sky, land, sea, and other bodies, one after another. And because of the ideas of all those qualities which presented themselves to my thinking, although I kept sensing these as merely my own personal and immediate ideas, I reasonably believed that I was perceiving certain objects entirely different from my thinking, that is, bodies from which these ideas proceeded. For experience taught me that these ideas reached me without my consent, so that I was unable to sense any object, even if I wanted to, un-less it was present to my organs of sense, and I was unable not to sense it when it was present. And since the ideas I perceived with my senses were much more vivid, lively, and sharp, and even, in their own way, more distinct than any of those which I myself intentionally and deliberately shaped by meditation or which I noticed impressed on my memory, it did not seem possible that they could have proceeded from myself. Thus, the only conclusion left was that they had come from some other things. Because I had no conception of these objects other than what I derived from those ideas themselves, the only thought my mind could entertain was that [the objects] were similar to [the ideas they produced]. And since I also remembered that earlier I had used my senses rather than my reason and realized that the ideas which I myself formed were not as vivid, lively, and sharp as those which I perceived with my senses and that most of the former were composed of parts of the latter, I easily convinced myself that I had nothing at all in my intellect which I had not previously had in my senses. I also maintained, not without reason, that this body, which, by some special right, I called my own, belonged to me more than any other object, for I could never separate myself from it, as I could from other [bodies], I felt every appetite and emotion in it and because of it, and finally, I noticed pain and the titillation of pleasure in its parts, but not in any objects placed outside it. But why a certain strange sadness of spirit follows a sensation of pain and a certain joy follows from a sensation of [pleasurable] titillation, or why some sort of twitching in the stomach, which I call hunger, is urging me to eat food, while the dryness of my throat [is urging me] to drink, and so on—for that I had no logical explanation, other than that these were things I had learned from nature. For there is clearly no relationship (at least, none I can understand) between that twitching [in the stomach] and the desire to consume food, or between the sensation of something causing pain and the awareness of sorrow arising from that feeling. But it seemed to me that all the other judgments I made about objects of sense experience I had learned from nature. For I had convinced myself that that was how things happened, before I thought about any arguments which might prove it.

However, many later experiences have gradually weakened the entire faith I used to have in the senses. For, now and then, towers which seemed round from a distance appeared square from near at hand, immense statues standing on the tower summits did not seem large when I viewed them from the ground, and in countless other cases like these I discovered that my judgments were deceived in matters dealing with external senses. And not just with external [senses], but also with internal ones as well. For what could be more internal than pain? And yet I heard that people whose legs or arms had been cut off sometimes still seemed to feel pain in the part of their body which they lacked. Thus, even though I were to feel pain in one of my limbs, I did not think I could be completely certain that it was the limb which caused my pain. To these reasons for doubting sense experience, I recently added two extremely general ones. First, there was nothing I ever thought I was sensing while awake that I could not also think I was sensing now and then while asleep, and since I do not believe that those things I appear to sense in my sleep come to me from objects placed outside me, I did not see why I should give more credit to those I appear to sense when I am awake. Second, because I was still ignorant—or at least was assuming I was ignorant—of the author of my being, there seemed to be nothing to prevent nature from constituting me in such a way that I would make mistakes, even in those matters which seemed to me most true. As for the reasons which had previously convinced me of the truth of what I apprehended with my senses, I had no difficulty refuting them. For since nature seemed to push me to accept many things which my reason opposed, I believed I should not place much trust in those things nature taught. And although perceptions of the senses did not depend upon my will, I did not believe that was reason enough for me to conclude that they must come from things different from myself, because there could well be some other faculty in me, even one I did not yet know, which produced them.

But now that I am starting to gain a better understanding of myself and of the author of my being, I do not, in fact, believe that I should rashly accept all those things I appear to possess from my senses, but, at the same time, [I do not think] I should call everything into doubt.

First, since I know that all those things I understand clearly and distinctly could have been created by God in a way that matches my conception of them, the fact that I can clearly and distinctly understand one thing, distinguishing it from something else, is sufficient to convince me that the two of them are different, because they can be separated from each other, at least by God. The power by which this [separation] takes place is irrelevant to my judgment that they are distinct. And therefore, given the mere fact that I know I exist and that, at the moment, I look upon my nature or essence as absolutely nothing other than that I am a thinking thing, I reasonably conclude that my essence consists of this single fact: I am a thinking thing. And although I may well possess (or rather, as I will state later, although I certainly do possess) a body which is very closely joined to me, nonetheless, because, on the one hand, I have a clear and distinct idea of myself, insofar as I am merely a thinking thing, without extension, and, on the other hand, [I have] a distinct idea of body, insofar as it is merely an extended thing which does not think, it is certain that my mind is completely distinct from my body and can exist without it.

Moreover, I discover in myself faculties for certain special forms of thinking, namely, the faculties of imagining and feeling. I can conceive of myself clearly and distinctly as a complete being without these, but I cannot do the reverse and think of these faculties without me, that is, without an intelligent substance to which they belong. For the formal conception of them includes some act of intellection by which I perceive that they are different from me, just as [shapes, movement, and the other] modes [or accidents of bodies are different] from the object [to which they belong]. I also recognize certain other faculties [in me], like changing position, assuming various postures, and so on, which certainly cannot be conceived, any more than those previously mentioned, apart from some substance to which they belong, and therefore they, too, cannot exist without it. However, it is evident that these [faculties], if indeed they [truly] exist, must belong to some corporeal or extended substance, and not to any intelligent substance, since the clear and distinct conception of them obviously contains some [form of] extension, but no intellectual activity whatsoever. Now, it is, in fact, true that I do have a certain passive faculty of perception, that is, of receiving and recognizing ideas of sensible things. But I would be unable to use this power unless some active faculty existed, as well, either in me or in some other substance capable of producing or forming these ideas. But this [active faculty] clearly cannot exist within me, because it presupposes no intellectual activity at all, and because, without my cooperation and often even against my will, it produces those ideas. Therefore I am left to conclude that it exists in some substance different from me that must contain, either formally or eminently, all the reality objectively present in the ideas produced by that faculty (as I have just observed above).[33] This substance is either a body, that is, something with a corporeal nature which obviously contains formally everything objectively present in the ideas, or it must be God, or some other creature nobler than the body, one that contains [those same things] eminently. But since God is not a deceiver, it is very evident that He does not transmit these ideas to me from Himself directly or even through the intervention of some other creature in which their objective reality is contained, not formally but only eminently. For since he has given me no faculty whatsoever for recognizing such a source, but by contrast, has endowed me with a powerful tendency to believe that these ideas are sent out from corporeal things, I do not see how it would be possible not to think of Him as a deceiver, if these [ideas] were sent from any source other than corporeal things. And therefore corporeal things exist. However, perhaps they do not all exist precisely in the ways I grasp them with my senses, since what I comprehend with my senses is very obscure and confused in many things. But at least [I should accept as true] all those things in them which I understand clearly and distinctly, that is, generally speaking, everything which is included as an object in pure mathematics.

---

33 See the introduction for an explanation of the distinction between formally and objectively present, and note 24 in the Third Meditation for what it is to be eminently present.

But regarding other material things which are either merely particular, for example that the sun is of such and such a magnitude and shape, and so on, or less clearly understood, for example light, sound, pain, and things like that, although these may be extremely doubtful and uncertain, nonetheless, because of the very fact that God is not a deceiver and thus it is impossible for there to be any falsity in my opinions which I cannot correct with another faculty God has given me, I have the sure hope that I can reach the truth even in these matters. And clearly there is no doubt that all those things I learn from nature contain some truth. For by the term *nature*, generally speaking, I understand nothing other than either God himself or the coordinated structure of created things established by God, and by the term *my nature*, in particular, nothing other than the combination of all those things I have been endowed with by God.

However, there is nothing that nature teaches me more emphatically than the fact that I have a body, which does badly when I feel pain, which needs food or drink when I suffer from hunger or thirst, and so on. And therefore I should not doubt that there is some truth in this.

For through these feelings of pain, hunger, thirst, and so on, nature teaches me that I am not merely present in my body in the same way a sailor is present onboard a ship, but that I am bound up very closely and, so to speak, mixed in with it, so that my body and I form a certain unity. For if that were not the case, then when my body was injured, I, who am merely a thinking thing, would not feel any pain because of it; instead, I would perceive the wound purely with my intellect, just as a sailor notices with his eyes if something is broken on his ship. And when my body needed food or drink, I would understand that clearly and not have confused feelings of hunger and thirst. For those sensations of thirst, hunger, pain, and so on are really nothing other than certain confused ways of thinking, which arise from the union and, as it were, the mixture of the mind with the body.

Moreover, nature also teaches me that various other bodies exist around my own and that I should pursue some of these and stay away from others. And certainly from the fact that I sense a wide diversity of colors, sounds, odors, tastes, heat, hardness, and similar things, I reasonably conclude that in the bodies from which these different sense perceptions come there are certain variations which correspond to these perceptions, even if they are perhaps not like them. And given the fact that I find some of these sense perceptions pleasant and others unpleasant, it is entirely certain that my body, or rather my totality, since I am composed of body and mind, can be affected by various agreeable and disagreeable bodies surrounding it.

However, many other things which I seemed to have learned from nature I have not really received from her, but rather from a certain habit I have of accepting careless judgments [about things]. And thus it could easily be the case that these judgments are false—for example, [the opinion I have] that all space in which nothing at all happens to stimulate my senses is a vacuum, that in a warm substance there is something completely similar to the idea of heat which is in me, that in a white or green [substance] there is the same whiteness or greenness which I sense, that in [something] bitter or sweet there is the same taste as I sense, and so on, that stars and towers and anything else some distance away have bodies with the same size and shape as the ones they present to my senses, and things of that sort. But in order to ensure that what I perceive in this matter is sufficiently distinct, I should define more accurately what it is precisely that I mean when I say I have learned something from nature. For here I am taking the word *nature* in a more restricted sense than *the combination of all those things which have been bestowed on me by God.* For this combination contains many things which pertain only to the mind, such as the fact that I perceive that what has been done cannot be undone, and all the other things I grasp by my natural light [without the help of the body]. Such things are not under discussion here. This combination also refers to many things which concern only the body, like its tendency to move downward, and so on, which I am also not dealing with [here]. Instead, I am considering only those things which God has given me as a combination of mind and body. And so nature, in this sense, certainly teaches me to avoid those things which bring a sensation of pain and to pursue those which [bring] a sensation of pleasure, and such like, but, beyond that, it is not clear that with those sense perceptions nature teaches us that we can conclude anything about things placed outside of us without a previous examination by the understanding, because to know the truth about them seems to belong only to the mind and not to that combination [of body and mind]. And so, although a star does not make an impression on my eyes any greater than the flame of a small candle, nonetheless, that fact does not incline me, in any real or positive way, to believe that the star is not larger [than the flame], but from the time of my youth I have made this judgment without any reason [to support it]. And although I feel heat when I come near the fire, and even pain if I get too close to it, that is really no reason to believe that there is something in the fire similar to that heat I feel, any more than there is something similar to the pain. The only thing [I can conclude] is that there is something in the fire, whatever it might be, which brings out in us those sensations of heat or pain. So, too, although in some space there is nothing which stimulates my senses, it does not therefore follow that the space contains no substances. But I see that in these and in a great many other matters, I have grown accustomed to undermine the order of nature, because, of course, these sense perceptions are, strictly speaking, given to me by nature merely to indicate to my mind which things are agreeable or disagreeable to that combination of which it is a part, and for that purpose they are sufficiently clear and distinct. But then I use them as if they were dependable rules for immediately recognizing the essence of bodies placed outside me. However, about such bodies they reveal nothing except what is confusing and obscure.

In an earlier section, I have already examined sufficiently why my judgments may happen to be defective, in spite of the goodness of God. However, a new difficulty crops up here concerning those very things which nature reveals to me as objects I should seek out or avoid, and also concerning the internal sensations, in which I appear to have discovered errors: for example, when someone, deceived by the pleasant taste of a certain food, eats a poison hidden within it [and thus makes a mistake]. Of course, in this situation, the person's nature urges him only to eat food which has a pleasant taste and not the poison, of which he has no knowledge at all. And from this, the only conclusion I can draw is that my nature does not know everything. There is nothing astonishing about that, because a human being is a finite substance and thus is capable of only limited perfection.

However, we are frequently wrong even in those things which nature urges [us to seek]. For example, sick people are eager for drink or food which will harm them soon afterwards. One could perhaps claim that such people make mistakes because their nature has been corrupted. But this does not remove the difficulty, for a sick person is no less a true creature of God than a healthy one, and thus it seems no less contradictory that God has given the person a nature which deceives him. And just as a clock made out of wheels and weights observes all the laws of nature with the same accuracy when it is badly made and does not indicate the hours correctly as it does when it completely satisfies the wishes of the person who made it, in the same way, if I look on the human body as some kind of machine composed of bones, nerves, muscles, veins, blood, and skin, as if no mind existed in it, the body would still have all the same motions it now has in those movements that are not under the control of the will and that, therefore, do not proceed from the mind [but merely from the disposition of its organs]. I can readily acknowledge, for example, that in the case of a body sick with dropsy,[34] it would be quite natural for it to suffer from a parched throat, which usually conveys a sensation of thirst to the mind, and for its nerves and other parts also to move in such a way that it takes a drink and thus aggravates the illness. And when nothing like this is harming the body, it is equally natural for it to be stimulated by a similar dryness in the throat and to take a drink to benefit itself. Now, when I consider the intended purpose of the clock, I could say that, since it does not indicate the time correctly, it is deviating from its own nature, and, in the same way, when I think of the machine of the human body as something formed for the motions which usually take place in it, I might believe that it, too, is deviating from its own nature, if its throat is dry when a drink does not benefit its own preservation. However, I am fully aware that this second meaning

of the word *nature* is very different from the first. For it is merely a term that depends on my own thought, a designation with which I compare a sick person and a badly constructed clock with the idea of a healthy person and a properly constructed clock, and thus, the term is extrinsic to these objects. But by that [other use of the term *nature*] I understand something that is really found in things and that therefore contains a certain measure of the truth.

Now, when I consider a body suffering from dropsy, even though I say that its nature has been corrupted, because it has a dry throat and yet does not need to drink, clearly the word *nature* is merely an extraneous term. However, when I consider the composite, that is, the mind united with such a body, I am not dealing with what is simply a term but with a true error of nature, because this composite is thirsty when drinking will do it harm. And thus I still have to enquire here why the goodness of God does not prevent its nature, taken in this sense, from being deceitful.

At this point, then, my initial observation is that there is a great difference between the mind and the body, given that the body is, by its very nature, always divisible, whereas the mind is completely indivisible. For, in fact, when I think of [my mind], that is, when I think of myself as purely a thinking thing, I cannot distinguish any parts within me. Instead, I understand that I am something completely individual and unified. And although my entire mind seems to be united with my entire body, nonetheless, I know that if a foot or arm or any other part of the body is sliced off, that loss will not take anything from my mind. And I cannot call the faculties of willing, feeling, understanding, and so on parts of the mind because it is the same single mind that wishes, feels, and understands. By contrast, I cannot think of any corporeal or extended substance that my thought is not capable of dividing easily into parts. From this very fact, I understand that the substance is divisible. (This point alone would be enough to teach me that the mind is completely different from the body, if I did not already know that well enough from other sources.)

Furthermore, I notice that the mind is not immediately affected by all parts of the body, but only by the brain, or perhaps even by just one small part of it,

---

34 An abnormal accumulation of watery fluid in the body (now called edema).

namely, the one in which our *common sense*[35] is said to exist. Whenever this part is arranged in the same particular way, it delivers the same perception to the mind, even though the other parts of the body may be arranged quite differently at the time. This point has been demonstrated in countless experiments, which I need not review here.

In addition, I notice that the nature of my body is such that no part of it can be moved by any other part some distance away which cannot also be moved in the same manner by any other part lying between them, even though the more distant part does nothing. So, for example, in a rope ABCD [which is taut throughout], if I pull on part D at the end, then the movement of the first part, A, will be no different than it would be if I pulled at one of the intermediate points, B or C, while the last part, D, remained motionless. And for a similar reason, when I feel pain in my foot, physics teaches me that this sensation occurs thanks to nerves spread throughout the foot. These nerves stretch from there to the brain, like cords, and when they are pulled in my foot, they also pull the inner parts of the brain, where they originate, and stimulate in them a certain motion which nature has established to influence the mind with a sense of pain apparently present in the foot. However, since these nerves have to pass through the shin, the thigh, the loins, the back, and the neck in order to reach the brain from the foot, it can happen that, even if that portion of the nerves which is in the foot is not affected, but only one of the intermediate portions, the motion created in the brain is exactly the same as the one created there by an injured foot. As a result, the mind will necessarily feel the identical pain. And we should assume that the same is true with any other sensation whatsoever.

Finally, I notice that, since each of those motions created in that part of the brain which immediately affects the mind introduces into it only one particular

---

35   See note 19, Second Meditation. Descartes is probably thinking of the pineal gland here, a tiny structure located between the two hemispheres of the brain; this is because he knew it to be the only anatomical structure of the brain which existed as a single part, rather than one half of a pair.

sensation, we can, given this fact, come up with no better explanation than that this sensation, out of all the ones which could be introduced, is the one which serves to protect human health as effectively and frequently as possible [when a person is completely healthy]. But experience testifies to the fact that all sensations nature has given us are like this, and thus we can discover nothing at all in them which does not bear witness to the power and benevolence of God. Thus, for example, when the nerves in the foot are moved violently and more than usual, their motion, passing through the spinal cord to the inner core of the brain, gives a signal there to the mind which makes it feel something—that is, it feels as if there is a pain in the foot. And that stimulates [the mind] to do everything it can to remove the cause of the pain as something injurious to the foot. Of course, God could have constituted the nature of human beings in such a way that this same motion in the brain communicated something else to the mind, for example, a sense of its own movements, either in the brain, or in the foot, or in any of the places in between—in short, of anything you wish. But nothing else would have served so well for the preservation of the body. In the same way, when we need a drink, a certain dryness arises in the throat which moves its nerves and, with their assistance, the inner parts of the brain. And this motion incites in the mind a sensation of thirst, because in this whole situation nothing is more useful for us to know than that we need a drink to preserve our health. The same is true for the other sensations.

From this it is clearly evident that, notwithstanding the immense goodness of God, human nature, given that it is composed of mind and body, cannot be anything other than something that occasionally deceives us. For if some cause, not in the foot, but in some other part through which the nerves stretch between the foot and the brain, or even in the brain itself, stimulates exactly the same motion as that which is normally aroused when a foot is injured, then pain will be felt as if it were in the foot, and the sensation will naturally be deceiving. Since that same motion in the brain is never capable of transmitting to the mind anything other than the identical sensation and since [the sensation] is habitually aroused much more frequently from an injury in the foot than from anything else in another place, it is quite reasonable that it should always transmit to the mind a pain in the foot rather than a pain in any other part of the body. And if sometimes dryness in the throat does not arise, as it usually does, from the fact that a drink is necessary for the health of the body, but from some different cause, as occurs in a patient suffering from dropsy, it is much better that it should deceive us in a case like that than if it were, by contrast, always deceiving us when the body is quite healthy. The same holds true with the other sensations.

This reflection is the greatest help, for it enables me not only to detect all the errors to which my nature is prone, but also to correct or to avoid them easily. For since I know that, in matters concerning what is beneficial to the body, all my senses show [me] what is true much more frequently than they deceive me, and since I can almost always use several of them to examine the same matter and, in addition, [can use] my memory, which connects present events with earlier ones, as well as my understanding, which has now ascertained all the causes of my errors, I should no longer fear that those things which present themselves to me every day through my senses are false. And I ought to dismiss all those exaggerated doubts of the past few days as ridiculous, particularly that most important [doubt] about sleep, which I did not distinguish from being awake. For now I notice a significant distinction between the two of them, given that our memory never links our dreams to all the other actions of our lives, as it [usually] does with those things which take place when we are awake. For clearly, if someone suddenly appears to me when I am awake and then immediately afterwards disappears, as happens in my dreams, so that I have no idea where he came from or where he went, I would reasonably judge that I had seen some apparition or phantom created in my brain [similar to the ones created when I am asleep], rather than a real person. But when certain things occur and I notice distinctly the place from which they came, where they are, and when they appeared to me, and when I can link my perception of them to the rest of my life as a totality, without a break, then I am completely certain that this is taking place while I am awake and not in my sleep. And I should not have the slightest doubt about the truth of these perceptions if, after I have called upon all my senses, my memory, and my understanding to examine them, I find nothing in any of them which contradicts any of the others. For since God is not a deceiver, it must follow that in such cases I am not deceived. But because, in dealing with what we need to do, we cannot always take the time for such a scrupulous examination, we must concede that human life is often prone to error concerning particular things and that we need to acknowledge the frailty of our nature.

JOHN LOCKE

An Essay Concerning Human Understanding

Who Was John Locke?

John Locke was born in the Somerset countryside, near the town of Bristol, in 1632. His parents were small landowners—minor gentry—who subjected the young Locke to a strict Protestant upbringing. Thanks to the influence of one of his father's friends Locke was able to gain a place at Westminster School, at the time the best school in England, where he studied Greek, Latin, and Hebrew. He went on to Christ Church College, Oxford, and graduated with a BA in 1656. Shortly afterwards he was made a senior student of his college—a kind of teaching position— which he was to remain until 1684, when the king of England, Charles II, personally (and illegally) demanded his expulsion.

During the 1650s and early '60s Locke lectured on Greek and rhetoric at Oxford but he was idle and unhappy, and became increasingly bored by the traditional philosophy of his day. He developed an interest in medicine and physical science (in 1675 he tried and failed to gain the degree of Doctor of Medicine), and in 1665 Locke left the confines of the academic world, and began to make his way into the world of politics and science. In the winter of 1665–66 he was ambassador to the German state of Brandenburg, where his first-hand observation of religious toleration between Calvinists, Lutherans, Catholics, and Anabaptists made a big impression on him.

A chance encounter in 1666 was the decisive turning-point in Locke's life: he met a nobleman called Lord Ashley, then the Chancellor of the Exchequer, and soon went to live at Ashley's London house as his confidant and medical advisor. In 1668, Locke was responsible for a life-saving surgical operation on Ashley, implanting a small silver spigot to drain off fluid from a cyst on his liver; the lord never forgot his gratitude (and wore the small tap in his side for the rest of his life). Under Ashley's patronage, Locke had both the leisure to spend several years working on his *Essay Concerning Human Understanding*, and a sequence of lucrative and interesting government positions, including one as part of a group drafting the constitution of the new colony of Carolina in the Americas.

Ashley's support was also essential in giving Locke— an introverted and hypersensitive soul, who suffered for most of his life from bad asthma and general poor health—the confidence to do original philosophy. Locke never married, was a life-long celibate, shied away from drinking parties and a hectic social life, but enjoyed the attentions of lady admirers, and throughout his life he had many loyal friends and got on especially well with some of his friends' children.

Locke spent the years from 1675 until 1679 traveling in France (where he expected to die of tuberculosis, but survived—Locke spent a large portion of his life confidently expecting an early death), and when he returned to England it was to a very unsettled political situation. The heir to the British throne, Charles II's younger brother James, was a Catholic, and his succession was feared by many politicians, including Ashley—who was, by this time, the Earl of Shaftesbury—and his political party, the Whigs. Their greatest worry was that the return of a Catholic monarchy would mean the return of religious oppression to England, as was happening in parts of Europe. Charles, however, stood by his brother and in 1681 Shaftesbury was sent to prison in the Tower of London, charged with high treason. Shaftesbury was acquitted by a grand jury, but he fled to Holland and died a few months later (spending his last few hours, the story goes, discussing a draft of Locke's *Essay* with his friends). Locke, in danger as a known associate of Shaftesbury's, followed his example in 1683 and secretly moved to the Netherlands, where he had to spend a year underground evading arrest by the Dutch government's agents on King Charles's behalf. While in Holland he rewrote material for the *Essay*, molding it towards its final state, and published an abridgement of the book in a French scholarly periodical which immediately attracted international attention.

In 1689 the political tumult in England had subsided enough for Locke to return—James's brief reign (as James II) had been toppled by the Protestant William of Orange and his queen Mary—and he moved as a permanent house-guest to an estate called Oates about twenty five miles from London. He returned to political life (though he refused the post of ambassador to Brandenburg, on grounds of ill health), and played a significant role in loosening restrictions on publishers and authors.

It was in this year, when Locke was 57, that the results of his thirty years of thinking and writing were suddenly published in a flood. First, published anonymously, came the *Letter on Toleration*, then *Two Treatises on Government*. In the *Two Treatises*—which was influential in the liberal movements of the next century that culminated in the French and Ameri-

can revolutions—Locke argued that the authority of monarchs is limited by individuals' rights and the public good. Finally, *An Essay Concerning Human Understanding* was published under his own name, to almost instant acclaim: the publication of this book catapulted Locke overnight to what we would now think of as international superstardom.

These three were his most important works, but Locke—by now one of the most famous men in England—continued to write and publish until his death fifteen years later. He wrote, for example, works on the proper control of the currency for the English government; *Some Thoughts Concerning Education* (which, apparently, was historically important in shaping the toilet-training practices of the English educated classes); a work on the proper care and cultivation of fruit trees; and a careful commentary on the *Epistles* of St. Paul. He died quietly, reading in his study, in October 1704.

What Was Locke's Overall Philosophical Project?

Locke is the leading proponent of a school of philosophy now often called "British empiricism." Some of the central platforms of this doctrine are as follows: First, human beings are born like a blank, white sheet of paper—a *tabula rasa*—without any innate knowledge but with certain natural powers, and we use these powers to adapt ourselves to the social and physical environment into which we are born. Two especially important natural powers are the capacity for conscious sense experience and for feeling pleasure and pain, and it is from the interaction of these capacities with the environment that we acquire all of our ideas, knowledge, and habits of mind. All meaningful language must be connected to the ideas that we thus acquire, and the abuse of language to talk about things of which we have no idea is a serious source of intellectual errors—errors that can have harmful consequences for social and moral life, as well as the growth of the sciences. British empiricism—whose other main exponents were Thomas Hobbes (1588–1679), George Berkeley (1685–1753), and David Hume (1711–1776)—was generally opposed to religious fervor and sectarian strife, and cautious about the human capacity for attaining absolute knowledge about things that go beyond immediate experience.

An Essay Concerning Human Understanding is Locke's attempt to present a systematic and detailed empiricist account of the human mind and human knowledge. It also includes an account of the nature of language, and touches on philosophical issues to do with logic, religion, metaphysics, and ethics. Locke was also consciously interested in defending a certain modern way of thinking against the habits of the past: instead of relatively uncritical and conservative acceptance of Greek and Roman history, literature and philosophy, and of Christian theology, Locke defended independent thought, secular values, and the power of modern ideas and social change to produce useful results.

Locke was optimistic about the power and accuracy of his own theory of human understanding—and thus about the powers of human beings to come to know the world—but he nevertheless thought it was a *limited* power. There are some things human beings just cannot ever come to know with certainty, Locke thought, and we should be humble in our attempts to describe reality. Thus, there are some domains in which, according to Locke, our human capacities are sufficient to produce certain knowledge: mathematics, morality, the existence of God, and the existence of things in the world corresponding to our 'simple ideas' (i.e., roughly, the things we perceive). However, there are other areas where the best we can do is to make skillful guesses: these more difficult questions have to do with the underlying nature and workings of nature—that is, with scientific theory—and with the details of religious doctrine. God has given us the capacity to effectively get by in the world by making these careful guesses, according to Locke, but he has not given us the capacity to ever know for sure whether our guesses are correct or not. (This is one reason why Locke believed we should be tolerant of other people's religious beliefs.)

What Is the Structure of This Reading?

An Essay Concerning Human Understanding is split into four Books, each of which is further divided into chapters, which in turn are divided into sections. The first Book is primarily an attack on the notion, which Locke found especially in Descartes, that human beings are born with certain "innate ideas"—concepts and knowledge which are not the product of experience but which are, perhaps, implanted in us by God. Book II develops Locke's alternative empiricist theory of ideas: here he describes the different sorts of ideas human beings have (such as our ideas of external objects, space, time, number, cause and effect, and so on), and tries to show how these ideas all derive ultimately from reflection on our own sense-experience. In Book III Locke describes the workings of language, and in particular defends the thesis that all meaningful language derives that meaning from its connections to our ideas. Finally, Book IV is where Locke considers the question of human knowledge and asks how much justification there is for our beliefs about God and nature, concluding that, although limited, the scope of our knowledge is more than enough for practical purposes.

The first two selections collected here come from Book II (and so are about ideas), and the third from Book IV (and so is about knowledge). The first selection asks how much our ideas resemble those things in the world that cause them and, among other things, describes and defends an important distinction between "primary" and "secondary" qualities. The second extract deals with the topic of "substance," the 'stuff' of the material world. The third approaches head-on the issue of the extent and limits of our knowledge of the external world.

Some Useful Background Information

1. Locke writes in a very straightforward and clear style—he deliberately set out to write informally, for a general educated readership—but his language is the English of the seventeenth century and some readers might find this a little distracting. Here is a short glossary of the words which might be either unfamiliar or used in an unfamiliar way.
   Admit of: accept
   Apprehension: understanding, perception
   Bare/barely: mere/merely

Corpuscles: small particles

Denominate: apply a name to something

Doth: does

Evidences: shows

Experiment: experience

Extravagant: odd, peculiar

Fain: gladly, happily

Figure: shape

Hath: has

Impulse: causal impact

Manna: the sweet dried juice of the Mediterranean ash tree and other plants, which can be used as a mild laxative (also, a substance miraculously supplied as food to the Israelites in the wilderness, according to the Bible)

Peculiar: particular, specific

Sensible/insensible: able to be sensed/invisible to the senses

Superficies: outside surfaces

V.g.: for example

Viz.: in other words, that is

Without: outside (us)

2. Locke's notion of an *idea* is central to his philosophy—which is even sometimes called "the way of ideas"—and he uses the word in his own special and carefully worked out way. For Locke, ideas are not activities of the mind but instead are the *contents* of the mind—they are the things we think about, the objects of our thought. (In fact, for Locke, thought consists entirely in the succession of ideas through consciousness.) Thus, for example, the things we believe, know, remember, or imagine are what Locke would call ideas.

As the term suggests, Locke probably assumes ideas are mental entities—they are things that exist in our minds rather than in the external world. Certainly, there are no ideas floating around that are not part of someone's consciousness; every idea is necessarily the object of some act of thinking. Furthermore, ideas are the *only* things we directly think about—our thought and our mental experience, for Locke, is internally rather than externally directed: it is an experience of our ideas and the operations of our mind, not directly of the world. When Locke uses the word "perception," for example, he often means the mind's perception (awareness) of its own ideas, not, as we would usually mean, perception of objects outside our own minds.

However, this is not to say that we don't think about or perceive the external world; Locke commonsensically thought that we saw trees, tasted oranges, heard the speech of other human beings, and so on. But it does mean that all our thought and perception is mediated by ideas, which intervene between us and external reality. The ideas we have before our minds are the "immediate objects of perception," and the things those ideas represent are the "indirect objects of perception." Yet it is important to remember that, for Locke, ideas *do* naturally and evidently represent things beyond themselves (although not necessarily the whole, or even the most important aspects, of the nature of those things)—Locke does not believe for a moment that we are locked inside our own heads.

Locke distinguishes between lots of different types of ideas, but one especially important contrast is between simple and complex ideas. A simple idea is "nothing but one uniform appearance, or conception in the mind, and is not distinguishable into different ideas," whereas complex ideas are compounded out of more than one simple idea. For example, redness is a simple idea, while the idea of a London double-decker bus is a complex idea. For Locke, all simple ideas are acquired from experience, either through sense perception or through the perception of our own thoughts (often called "introspection"): we are not free to simply invent or ignore such ideas, as they are physically caused by the things they represent. However, we are free to construct complex ideas out of this raw material as we like, and we can do so in various ways: we can add simple ideas together into a single idea (e.g., the idea of a horse), or we can compare two ideas and perceive the relation that holds between them (e.g., the idea of being taller than), or we can generalize about simple ideas to form abstract ideas (e.g., the idea of time or infinity).

3. Locke held the modern (at the time) "corpuscular" theory of matter, which was developed by Pierre Gassendi (1592–1655) and Robert Boyle (1627–1691) and which, though a "mechanical philosophy," contradicted some important elements of Descartes's physical theory. As a corpuscularian, Locke thought that the physical world was made up of tiny indestructible particles, invisible to the human eye, moving around in empty space, and having only the following properties: solidity, extension in three dimensions, shape (or "figure"), motion or rest, number, location ("situation"), volume ("bulk"), and texture. All the phenomena of the material world are built out of or caused by these particles and their properties and powers. Thus, collections of particles big enough to be visible have certain properties (which Locke called "qualities"), e.g., the shape and size of a gold nugget, its color, malleability, luster, chemical inertness, and so on. Our perception of the world—that is to say, our experience of these qualities—is brought about by invisible streams of tiny particles emanating from the objects in our environment and striking our sense-receptors (our eyes, ears, skin, and so on). Locke and his contemporaries thought this stimulation of our senses causes complex reactions in our "animal spirits," and this is what gives rise to our ideas. Animal spirits were supposed to be a fine fluid (itself made up of tiny particles) flowing through our nervous system and carrying signals from one place to another—ultimately to our brain.

Some Common Misconceptions

1. In reading Locke, it is important not to confuse ideas with qualities. Ideas are mental entities; they constitute our *experience* of the world. Qualities are non-mental attributes of chunks of matter in the world; they are the things ideas are *about*. Thus, in Locke's view, our idea of color should not be confused with the property of color itself. The distinction between primary and secondary qualities, then, is mainly a distinction between types of physical property (though it does have implications for the taxonomy of our ideas).

2. The secondary qualities do not only include colors, tastes, smells, sounds, and feels; they also include properties like solubility, brittleness, flammability, being nutritious, being a pain-killer, and so on.

3. It is sometimes thought Locke argued that secondary qualities do not really exist, and that color, smell, taste, and so on are only ideas in our mind. But this is not so. Locke does think that material objects in the world really have secondary qualities, but he argues that we have misunderstood the *nature* of these qualities in a particular way.

4. In thinking about the nature of the secondary qualities it is helpful to consider the nature of their connection with our ideas of them. In this context, two concepts are useful but are sometimes confused with each other. The first notion is that of *perceiver-relativity*: this is the idea that how something *seems* depends on who is perceiving it. To say that "beauty is in the eye of the beholder" is to make a claim about perceiver-relativity; more interestingly, being poisonous is an example of a perceiver-relative property, since substances that are poisonous to one kind of perceiver might not be poisonous to others (e.g., chemicals called avermectins are lethal to many invertebrates but harmless to mammals). The second, different, notion is of *perceiver-dependence*: this is the idea that the very existence of something depends upon being perceived or thought about. An example of this would be a conscious visual image—there can be no such thing as a conscious image that is not in anybody's consciousness, and so mental images must be mind-dependent.

5. In the third selection below, when Locke is writing about substance, his main topic is the *idea* of substance, not substance itself. That is, he does not ask (directly) whether substance really exists; instead, his question is, do we have

an idea of substance? And whatever his conclusions about the idea of substance, Locke denied being skeptical about the actual existence of substance.

How Important and Influential Is This Passage?

"The *Essay* has long been recognized as one of the great works of English literature of the seventeenth century, and one of the epoch-making works in the history of philosophy. It has been one of the most repeatedly reprinted, widely disseminated and read, and profoundly influential books of the past three centuries." So writes Peter Nidditch, an expert on Locke's philosophy. Locke's *Essay* is often credited with being the most thorough and plausible formulation and defense of empiricism ever written, and it has exercised a huge influence on, especially, English-speaking philosophers right up until the present day (though with a period in the philosophical wilderness during the 1800s). In the eighteenth century Locke was widely considered as important for philosophy, and what we would today call psychology, as Newton was for physics.

Although the distinction between primary and secondary qualities was certainly not invented by Locke, his account of it was very influential and was taken as the standard line in subsequent discussions of this important idea. Furthermore, the problem Locke raised about the coherence of our idea of material substance has been an important metaphysical problem since he formulated it, and was an important motivator for Berkeley's idealism (which we consider in the next section).

Suggestions for Critical Reflection

1. It is relatively easy to see roughly how Locke's distinction between primary and secondary qualities is supposed to go, but harder to see what Locke's *argument* for this distinction is. Do you think Locke backs up his claims with arguments? If so, how strong do you think they are? In the end, how plausible is the primary/secondary quality distinction?

2. Similarly, while it is relatively easy to see roughly how Locke's distinction between primary and secondary qualities is supposed to go, it is harder to see *precisely* how the distinction works. For example, what might Locke mean by saying that our ideas of primary qualities resemble their causes while our ideas of secondary qualities do not? Does this really make any sense? If it doesn't, then what other criterion should we use to help us make the distinction?

3. There has recently been some controversy about Locke's position on substance. The traditional view is that Locke defended substance, but was wrong to do so since his own arguments had effectively shown that we could have no such idea. The notion of substance in question here is that of a "bare particular" or "substratum"—that which underlies properties, as opposed to any of the properties themselves. A more recent interpretation holds that Locke did indeed defend some notion of substance, but one which is more defensible. This is the idea of substance as the "real essence" of something: roughly, for Locke, something's real essence is supposed to be the (unknown) set of properties that forms the causal basis for the observable properties of that thing (just as the atomic structure of gold is responsible for its color, softness, shininess, and so on). Which of these two conceptions of substance do you find the more plausible? (Can you see why philosophers have typically found the notion of a substratum difficult to make sense of?) Which of these notions of substance do you think fits better with what Locke actually says? Do you perhaps prefer a third interpretation?

4. What do you make of Locke's response to skepticism about the existence of the external world? Does it convince you? Do you find plausible the way Locke carefully divides up different types of knowledge about the external world and gives different answers for them?

5. What kind of entity might a Lockean idea be? What, if anything, is it made of? How determinate must it be? For example, if I clearly perceive the idea of a speckled hen, must we say that I

perceive (have the idea of) a particular number of speckles, say 12,372? If not, does that mean the idea does not *have* a determinate number of speckles (even though it's a perfectly clear idea and not blurry at all)? What kind of object could *that* be? Some recent commentators, such as John Yolton, have tried to defend Locke from these kinds of puzzles by suggesting that Locke never meant ideas to be mental *things* at all: what, then, could they be instead?

6. How could an idea, in Locke's sense, really be *caused* by material objects in the external world? What could the last few steps of this causal chain be like?

7. If ideas are the objects of our thought—the things we "perceive" in thought—then what is it that does the perceiving, do you think? Can we distinguish it from the succession of ideas?

Suggestions for Further Reading

The standard edition of Locke's *An Essay Concerning Human Understanding* is edited by Peter H. Nidditch and was published by Oxford University Press in 1975. Several abridgements are also available, such as one by John Yolton in the Everyman Classics series. The standard biography of Locke is Maurice Cranston's *John Locke: A Biography* (Oxford University Press, 1985), though it is now a little out of date. Two good recent collections of essays about Locke are *Locke* (Oxford University Press, 1998) and *A Cambridge Companion to Locke* (Cambridge University Press, 1994), both edited by Vere Chappell. Finally, here are a few useful books on Locke: Michael Ayers, *Locke: Epistemology and Ontology* (Routledge, 1991); Nicholas Jolley, *Locke: His Philosophical Thought* (Oxford University Press, 1999); J.L. Mackie, *Problems from Locke*, (Oxford University Press, 1976); and John Yolton, *Locke: An Introduction* (Blackwell, 1985).

from *An Essay Concerning Human Understanding*[1]

Book II, Chapter VIII: Some Farther Considerations Concerning Our Simple Ideas.

§1. Concerning the simple ideas of Sensation, it is to be considered, that whatsoever is so constituted in nature as to be able, by affecting our senses, to cause any perception in the mind, doth thereby produce in the understanding a simple idea, which, whatever be the external cause of it, when it comes to be taken notice of by our discerning faculty, it is by the mind looked on and considered there to be a real positive idea in the understanding, as much as any other whatsoever; though, perhaps, the cause of it be but a privation[2] of the subject.

§2. Thus the ideas of heat and cold, light and darkness, white and black, motion and rest, are equally clear and positive ideas in the mind, though, perhaps, some of the causes which produce them are barely privations in subjects, from whence our senses derive those ideas. These the understanding, in its view of them, considers all as distinct positive ideas, without taking notice of the causes that produce them; which is an inquiry not belonging to the idea, as it is in the understanding, but to the nature of the things existing without us. These are two very different things, and carefully to be distinguished; it being one thing to perceive and know the idea of white or black, and quite another to examine what kind of particles they must be, and how ranged in the superficies, to make any object appear white or black.

§3. A painter or dyer, who never inquired into their causes, hath the ideas of white and black, and other colours, as clearly, perfectly, and distinctly in his understanding, and perhaps more distinctly, than the philosopher, who hath busied himself in considering their natures, and thinks he knows how far either of

---

1 Locke's *An Essay Concerning Human Understanding* was first published in 1690. The excerpts given here are from the sixth edition of 1710, reprinted from Locke's ten-volume *Collected Works* (first published in 1714 and reprinted with corrections in 1823).

2 A privation is a loss or absence of something.

them is in its cause positive or privative; and the idea of black is no less positive in his mind than that of white, however the cause of that colour in the external object may be only a privation.

§4. If it were the design of my present undertaking to inquire into the natural causes and manner of perception, I should offer this as a reason why a privative cause might, in some cases at least, produce a positive idea, viz. that all sensation being produced in us only by different degrees and modes of motion in our animal spirits, variously agitated by external objects, the abatement of any former motion must as necessarily produce a new sensation as the variation or increase of it; and so introduce a new idea, which depends only on a different motion of the animal spirits in that organ.

§5. But whether this be so or not I will not here determine, but appeal to every one's own experience, whether the shadow of a man, though it consists of nothing but the absence of light (and the more the absence of light is, the more discernible is the shadow) does not, when a man looks on it, cause as clear and positive idea in his mind as a man himself, though covered over with clear sunshine? And the picture of a shadow is a positive thing. Indeed, we have negative names, which stand not directly for positive ideas, but for their absence, such as insipid, silence, nihil, &c. which words denote positive ideas; v.g. taste, sound, being, with a signification of their absence.

§6. And thus one may truly be said to see darkness. For supposing a hole perfectly dark, from whence no light is reflected, it is certain one may see the figure of it, or it may be painted; or whether the ink I write with makes any other idea, is a question. The privative causes I have here assigned of positive ideas are according to the common opinion; but, in truth, it will be hard to determine whether there be really any ideas from a privative cause, till it be determined, whether rest be any more a privation than motion.

§7. To discover the nature of our ideas the better, and to discourse of them intelligibly, it will be convenient to distinguish them as they are ideas or perceptions in our minds; and as they are modifications of matter in the bodies that cause such perceptions in us: that so we may not think (as perhaps usually is done) that they are exactly the images and resemblances of something inherent in the subject; most of those of sensation being in the mind no more the likeness of something existing without us, than the names that stand for them are the likeness of our ideas, which yet upon hearing they are apt to excite in us.

§8. Whatsoever the mind perceives in itself, or is the immediate object of perception, thought, or understanding, that I call idea; and the power to produce any idea in our mind, I call quality of the subject wherein that power is. Thus a snow-ball having the power to produce in us the ideas of white, cold, and round, the powers to produce those ideas in us, as they are in the snow-ball, I call qualities; and as they are sensations or perceptions in our understandings, I call them ideas; which ideas, if I speak of sometimes as in the things themselves, I would be understood to mean those qualities in the objects which produce them in us.

§9. Qualities thus considered in bodies are, first, such as are utterly inseparable from the body, in what state soever it be; such as in all the alterations and changes it suffers, all the force can be used upon it, it constantly keeps; and such as sense constantly finds in every particle of matter which has bulk enough to be perceived; and the mind finds inseparable from every particle of matter, though less than to make itself singly be perceived by our senses: v.g. take a grain of wheat, divide it into two parts; each part has still solidity, extension, figure, and mobility; divide it again, and it retains still the same qualities, and so divide it on, till the parts become insensible, they must retain still each of them all those qualities. For division (which is all that a mill, or pestle, or any other body, does upon another, in reducing it to insensible parts) can never take away either solidity, extension, figure, or mobility from any body, but only makes two or more distinct separate masses of matter, of that which was but one before; all which distinct masses, reckoned as so many distinct bodies, after division make a certain number. These I call original or primary qualities of body, which I think we may observe to produce simple ideas in us, viz. solidity, extension, figure, motion or rest, and number.

§10. Secondly, such qualities which in truth are nothing in the objects themselves, but powers to produce various sensations in us by their primary qualities, i.e., by the bulk, figure, texture, and motion of their insensible parts, as colours, sounds, tastes, &c. these I call secondary qualities. To these might be added a third sort, which are allowed to be barely powers; though they are as much real qualities in the subject as those which I, to comply with the common way of speaking, call qualities, but for distinction, secondary qualities. For the power in fire to produce a new colour, or consistency, in wax or clay, by its primary qualities, is as much a quality in fire, as the power it has to produce in me a new idea or sensation of warmth or burning, which I felt not before, by the same primary qualities, viz. the bulk, texture, and motion of its insensible parts.

§11. The next thing to be considered is, how bodies produce ideas in us; and that is manifestly by impulse, the only way which we can conceive bodies to operate in.

§12. If then external objects be not united to our minds, when they produce ideas therein, and yet we perceive these original qualities in such of them as singly fall under our senses, it is evident that some motion must be thence continued by our nerves, or animal spirits, by some parts of our bodies, to the brains or the seat of sensation, there to produce in our minds the particular ideas we have of them. And since the extension, figure, number, and motion of bodies, of an observable bigness, may be perceived at a distance by the sight, it is evident some singly imperceptible bodies must come from them to the eyes, and thereby convey to the brain some motion, which produces these ideas which we have of them in us.

§13. After the same manner, that the ideas of these original qualities are produced in us, we may conceive that the ideas of secondary qualities are also produced, viz. by the operation of insensible particles on our senses. For it being manifest that there are bodies, and good store of bodies, each whereof are so small that we cannot, by any of our senses, discover either their bulk, figure, or motion, as is evident in the particles of the air and water, and others extremely smaller than those; perhaps as much smaller than the particles of air and water as the particles of air and water are smaller than peas or hail-stones: let us suppose at present, that the different motions and figures, bulk and number

of such particles, affecting the several organs of our senses, produce in us those different sensations, which we have from the colours and smells of bodies; v.g. that a violet, by the impulse of such insensible particles of matter of peculiar figures and bulks, and in different degrees and modifications of their motions, causes the ideas of the blue colour and sweet scent of that flower to be produced in our minds, it being no more impossible to conceive that God should annex such ideas to such motions, with which they have no similitude, than that he should annex the idea of pain to the motion of a piece of steel dividing our flesh, with which that idea hath no resemblance.

§14. What I have said concerning colours and smells may be understood also of tastes and sounds, and other the like sensible qualities; which, whatever reality we by mistake attribute to them, are in truth nothing in the objects themselves, but powers to produce various sensations in us, and depend on those primary qualities, viz. bulk, figure, texture, and motion of parts as I have said.

§15. From whence I think it easy to draw this observation, that the ideas of primary qualities of bodies are resemblances of them, and their patterns do really exist in the bodies themselves, but the ideas produced in us by these secondary qualities have no resemblance of them at all. There is nothing like our ideas, existing in the bodies themselves. They are, in the bodies we denominate from them, only a power to produce those sensations in us; and what is sweet, blue, or warm in idea, is but the certain bulk, figure, and motion of the insensible parts, in the bodies themselves, which we call so.

§16. Flame is denominated hot and light; snow white and cold; and manna white and sweet, from the ideas they produce in us: which qualities are commonly thought to be the same in those bodies that those ideas are in us, the one the perfect resemblance of the other, as they are in a mirror; and it would by most men be judged very extravagant if one should say otherwise. And yet he that will consider that the same fire, that at one distance produces in us the sensation of warmth, does at a nearer approach produce in us the far different sensation of pain, ought to bethink himself what reason he has to say, that his idea of warmth, which was produced in him by the fire, is actually in the fire; and his idea of pain, which the same fire produced in him the same way, is not in the fire. Why are whiteness and coldness in snow, and pain not, when it produces the one and the other idea in us, and can do neither but by the bulk, figure, number, and motion of its solid parts?

§17. The particular bulk, number, figure, and motion of the parts of fire, or snow, are really in them, whether any one's senses perceive them or no; and therefore they may be called real qualities, because they really exist in those bodies: but light, heat, whiteness, or coldness, are no more really in them than sickness or pain is in manna. Take away the sensation of them; let not the eyes see light or colours, nor the ears hear sounds; let the palate not taste, nor the nose smell; and all colours, tastes, odours, and sounds, as they are such particular ideas, vanish and cease, and are reduced to their causes, i.e., bulk, figure, and motion of parts.

§18. A piece of manna of a sensible bulk is able to produce in us the idea of a round or square figure, and, by being removed from one place to another, the idea of motion. This idea of motion represents it as it really is in manna moving: a circle or square are the same, whether in idea or existence, in the mind or in the manna; and this, both motion and figure, are really in the manna, whether we take notice of them or no: this every body is ready to agree to. Besides, manna, by the bulk, figure, texture, and motion of its parts, has a power to produce the sensations of sickness, and sometimes of acute pains or gripings in us. That these ideas of sickness and pain are not in the manna, but effects of its operations on us, and are nowhere when we feel them not: this also every one readily agrees to. And yet men are hardly to be brought to think, that sweetness and whiteness are not really in manna; which are but the effects of the operations of manna, by the motion, size, and figure of its particles on the eyes and palate; as the pain and sickness caused by manna are confessedly nothing but the effects of its operations on the stomach and guts, by the size, motion, and figure of its insensible parts, (for by nothing else can a body operate, as has been proved); as if it could not operate on the eyes and palate, and thereby produce in the mind particular distinct ideas, which in itself it has not, as well as we allow it can operate

on the guts and stomach, and thereby produce distinct ideas, which in itself it has not. These ideas being all effects of the operations of manna, on several parts of our bodies, by the size, figure, number, and motion of its parts; why those produced by the eyes and palate should rather be thought to be really in the manna than those produced by the stomach and guts; or why the pain and sickness, ideas that are the effect of manna, should be thought to be nowhere when they are not felt: and yet the sweetness and whiteness, effects of the same manna on other parts of the body, by ways equally as unknown, should be thought to exist in the manna, when they are not seen or tasted, would need some reason to explain.

§19. Let us consider the red and white colours in porphyry:[3] hinder light from striking on it, and its colours vanish, it no longer produces any such ideas in us; upon the return of light it produces these appearances on us again. Can any one think any real alterations are made in the porphyry by the presence or absence of light; and that those ideas of whiteness and redness are really in porphyry in the light, when it is plain it has no colour in the dark? It has, indeed, such a configuration of particles, both night and day, as are apt, by the rays of light rebounding from some parts of that hard stone, to produce in us the idea of redness, and from others the idea of whiteness; but whiteness or redness are not in it at any time, but such a texture that hath the power to produce such a sensation in us.

§20. Pound an almond, and the clear white colour will be altered into a dirty one, and the sweet taste into an oily one. What real alteration can the beating of the pestle make in any body, but an alteration of the texture of it?

§21. Ideas being thus distinguished and understood, we may be able to give an account how the same water, at the same time, may produce the idea of cold by one hand and of heat by the other; whereas it is impossible that the same water, if those ideas were really in it, should at the same time be both hot and cold: for if we imagine warmth, as it is in our hands, to be nothing but a certain sort and degree of motion in the minute particles of our nerves or animal spirits,

---

3   A hard red rock filled with large red or white crystals.

we may understand how it is possible that the same water may, at the same time, produce the sensations of heat in one hand, and cold in the other; which yet figure never does, that never producing the idea of a square by one hand, which has produced the idea of a globe by another. But if the sensation of heat and cold be nothing but the increase or diminution of the motion of the minute parts of our bodies, caused by the corpuscles of any other body, it is easy to be understood, that if that motion be greater in one hand than in the other; if a body be applied to the two hands, which has in its minute particles a greater motion, than in those of one of the hands, and a less than in those of the other; it will increase the motion of the one hand and lessen it in the other, and so cause the different sensations of heat and cold that depend thereon.

§22. I have in what just goes before been engaged in physical inquiries a little further than perhaps I intended. But it being necessary to make the nature of sensation a little understood, and to make the difference between the qualities in bodies, and the ideas produced by them in the mind, to be distinctly conceived, without which it were impossible to discourse intelligibly of them, I hope I shall be pardoned this little excursion into natural philosophy, it being necessary in our present inquiry to distinguish the primary and real qualities of bodies, which are always in them (viz. solidity, extension, figure, number, and motion, or rest; and are sometimes perceived by us, viz. when the bodies they are in are big enough singly to be discerned), from those secondary and imputed qualities, which are but the powers of several combinations of those primary ones, when they operate, without being distinctly discerned; whereby we may also come to know what ideas are, and what are not, resemblances of something really existing in the bodies we denominate from them.

§23. The qualities, then, that are in bodies, rightly considered, are of three sorts. First, The bulk, figure, number, situation, and motion, or rest of their solid parts; those are in them, whether we perceive them or no; and when they are of that size that we can discover them, we have by these an idea of the thing, as it is in itself, as is plain in artificial things. These I call primary qualities.

Secondly, The power that is in any body, by reason of its insensible primary qualities, to operate after a peculiar manner on any of our senses, and thereby produce in us the different ideas of several colours, sounds, smells, tastes, &c. These are usually called sensible qualities.

Thirdly, The power that is in any body, by reason of the particular constitution of its primary qualities, to make such a change in the bulk, figure, texture, and motion of another body, as to make it operate on our senses, differently from what it did before. Thus the sun has a power to make wax white, and fire to make lead fluid. These are usually called powers.

The first of these, as has been said, I think may be properly called real, original, or primary qualities; because they are in the things themselves, whether they are perceived or no; and upon their different modifications it is that the secondary qualities depend.

The other two are only powers to act differently upon other things, which powers result from the different modifications of those primary qualities.

§24. But, though the two latter sorts of qualities are powers barely, and nothing but powers, relating to several other bodies, and resulting from the different modifications of the original qualities, yet they are generally otherwise thought of: for the second sort, viz. the powers to produce several ideas in us by our senses, are looked upon as real qualities in the things thus affecting us; but the third sort are called and esteemed barely powers, v.g. the idea of heat, or light, which we receive by our eyes or touch from the sun, are commonly thought real qualities, existing in the sun, and something more than mere powers in it. But when we consider the sun in reference to wax, which it melts or blanches, we look on the whiteness and softness produced in the wax, not as qualities in the sun, but effects produced by powers in it: whereas, if rightly considered, these qualities of light and warmth, which are perceptions in me when I am warmed or enlightened by the sun, are no otherwise in the sun, than the changes made in the wax, when it is blanched or melted, are in the sun. They are all of them equally powers in the sun, depending on its primary qualities; whereby it is able, in the one case, so to alter the bulk, figure, texture, or motion of some of the insensible parts of my eyes or hands, as thereby to produce in me the idea of light or heat; and in the other, it is able so to alter the bulk, figure, texture, or motion of the insensible parts of the wax, as to make them fit to produce in me the distinct ideas of white and fluid.

§25. The reason why the one are ordinarily taken for real qualities, and the other only for bare powers, seems to be, because the ideas we have of distinct colours, sounds, &c., containing nothing at all in them of bulk, figure, or motion, we are not apt to think them the effects of these primary qualities, which appear not, to our senses, to operate in their production, and with which they have not any apparent congruity or conceivable connection. Hence it is that we are so forward to imagine, that those ideas are the resemblances of something really existing in the objects themselves: since sensation discovers nothing of bulk, figure, or motion of parts in their production; nor can reason show how bodies, by their bulk, figure, and motion, should produce in the mind the ideas of blue or yellow, &c. But, in the other case, in the operations of bodies changing the qualities one of another, we plainly discover, that the quality produced hath commonly no resemblance with anything in the thing producing it; wherefore we look on it as a bare effect of power. For, through receiving the idea of heat or light from the sun, we are apt to think it is a perception and resemblance of such a quality in the sun; yet when we see wax, or a fair face, receive change of colour from the sun, we cannot imagine that to be the reception or resemblance of anything in the sun, because we find not those different colours in the sun itself. For our senses being able to observe a likeness or unlikeness of sensible qualities in two different external objects, we forwardly enough conclude the production of any sensible quality in any subject to be an effect of bare power, and not the communication of any quality, which was really in the efficient, when we find no such sensible quality in the thing that produced it. But our senses not being able to discover any unlikeness between the idea produced in us, and the quality of the object producing it, we are apt to imagine, that our ideas are resemblances of something in the objects, and not the effects of certain powers placed in the modification of their primary qualities, with which primary qualities the ideas produced in us have no resemblance.

§26. To conclude, beside those before-mentioned primary qualities in bodies, viz. bulk, figure, extension, number, and motion of their solid parts; all the rest whereby we take notice of bodies, and distinguish them one from another, are nothing else but several powers in them, depending on those primary qualities; whereby they are fitted, either by immediately operating on our bodies to produce several different ideas in us; or else, by operating on other bodies, so to change their primary qualities, as to render them capable of producing ideas in us different from what before they did. The former of these, I think, may be called secondary qualities, immediately perceivable: the latter, secondary qualities, mediately perceivable.

Book II, Chapter XXIII: Of Our Complex Ideas of Substances [§§1–6].

§1. The mind being, as I have declared, furnished with a great number of the simple ideas, conveyed in by the senses, as they are found in exterior things, or by reflection on its own operations, takes notice also, that a certain number of these simple ideas go constantly together; which being presumed to belong to one thing, and words being suited to common apprehensions, and made use of for quick dispatch, are called, so united in one subject, by one name; which, by inadvertency, we are apt afterward to talk of and consider as one simple idea, which indeed is a complication of many ideas together; because, as I have said, not imagining how these simple ideas can subsist by themselves, we accustom ourselves to suppose some substratum wherein they do subsist, and from which they do result; which therefore we call substance.

§2. So that if any one will examine himself concerning his notion of pure substance in general, he will find he has no other idea of it at all, but only a supposition of he knows not what support of such qualities, which are capable of producing simple ideas in us; which qualities are commonly called accidents. If any one should be asked, what is the subject wherein colour or weight inheres, he would have nothing to say, but the solid extended parts: and if he were demanded, what is it that solidity and extension adhere in, he would not be in a much better case than the Indian[4] before mentioned who, saying that the world was supported by a great elephant, was asked what the elephant rested on; to which his answer was a great tortoise. But being again pressed to know what gave support to the broad-backed tortoise, replied, something, he knew not what. And thus here, as in all other cases where we use words without having clear and distinct ideas, we talk like children; who, being questioned what such a thing is, which they know not, readily give this satisfactory answer, that it is something: which in truth signifies no more, when so used, either by children or men, but that they know not what; and that the thing they pretend to know, and talk of, is what they have no distinct idea of at all, and so are perfectly ignorant of it, and in the dark. The idea then we have, to which we give the general name substance, being nothing but the supposed, but unknown support of those qualities we find existing, which we imagine cannot subsist, "*sine re substante*," without something to support them, we call that support *substantia*; which, according to the true import of the word, is, in plain English, standing under or upholding.

§3. An obscure and relative idea of substance in general being thus made, we come to have the ideas of particular sorts of substances, by collecting such combinations of simple ideas as are, by experience and observation of men's senses taken notice of to exist together, and are therefore supposed to flow from the particular internal constitution, or unknown essence of that substance. Thus we come to have the ideas of a man, horse, gold, water, &c. of which substances, whether any one has any other clear idea, farther than of certain simple ideas co-existent together, I appeal to every one's own experience. It is the ordinary qualities observable in iron, or a diamond, put together, that make the true complex idea of those substances, which a smith or a jeweller commonly knows better than a philosopher; who, whatever substantial forms he may talk of, has no other idea of those substances, than what is framed by a collection of those simple ideas which are to be found in them: only we must take notice, that our complex ideas of substances,

besides all those simple ideas they are made up of, have always the confused idea of something to which they belong, and in which they subsist. And therefore when we speak of any sort of substance, we say it is a thing having such or such qualities; as body is a thing that is extended, figured, and capable of motion; spirit, a thing capable of thinking; and so hardness, friability,[5] and power to draw iron, we say, are qualities to be found in a loadstone.[6] These, and the like fashions of speaking, intimate, that the substance is supposed always something besides the extension, figure, solidity, motion, thinking, or other observable ideas, though we know not what it is.

§4. Hence, when we talk or think of any particular sort of corporeal substances, as horse, stone, &c., though the idea we have of either of them be but the complication or collection of those several simple ideas of sensible qualities, which we used to find united in the thing called horse or stone; yet, because we cannot conceive how they should subsist alone, nor one in another, we suppose them existing in and supported by some common subject; which support we denote by the name substance, though it be certain we have no clear or distinct idea of that thing we suppose a support.

§5. The same thing happens concerning the operations of the mind, viz. thinking, reasoning, fearing, &c., which we concluding not to subsist of themselves, nor apprehending how they can belong to body, or be produced by it, we are apt to think these the actions of some other substance, which we call spirit: whereby yet it is evident, that having no other idea or notion of matter, but something wherein those many sensible qualities which affect our senses do subsist; by supposing a substance wherein thinking, knowing, doubting, and a power of moving, &c. do subsist, we have as clear a notion of the substance of spirit, as we have of body; the one being supposed to be (without knowing what it is) the substratum to those simple ideas we have from without; and the other supposed (with a like ignorance of what it is) to be the substratum to those operations we experiment

---

4   A person from the subcontinent of India (rather than a native of North America).

5   Brittleness, crumbliness.

6   A piece of magnetite (iron oxide) that has magnetic properties.

in ourselves within. It is plain then, that the idea of corporeal substance in matter is as remote from our conceptions and apprehensions, as that of spiritual substance, or spirit: and therefore, from our not having any notion of the substance of spirit, we can no more conclude its non-existence, than we can for the same reason deny the existence of body; it being as rational to affirm there is no body, because we have no clear and distinct idea of the substance of matter, as to say there is no spirit, because we have no clear and distinct idea of the substance of a spirit.

§6. Whatever therefore be the secret, abstract nature of substance in general, all the ideas we have of particular distinct sorts of substances are nothing but several combinations of simple ideas co-existing in such, though unknown, cause of their union, as make the whole subsist of itself. It is by such combinations of simple ideas, and nothing else, that we represent particular sorts of substances to ourselves; such are the ideas we have of their several species in our minds; and such only do we, by their specific names, signify to others, v.g. man, horse, sun, water, iron: upon hearing which words, every one who understands the language, frames in his mind a combination of those several simple ideas, which he has usually observed, or fancied to exist together under that denomination; all which he supposes to rest in, and be as it were, adherent to that unknown common subject, which inheres not in anything else. Though, in the mean time it be manifest, and every one upon inquiry into his own thoughts will find, that he has no other idea of any substance, v.g. let it be gold, horse, iron, man, vitriol,[7] bread, but what he has barely of those sensible qualities, which he supposes to inhere, with a supposition of such a substratum, as gives, as it were, a support to those qualities or simple ideas, which he has observed to exist united together. Thus the idea of the sun, what is it but an aggregate of those several simple ideas, bright, hot, roundish, having a constant regular motion, at a certain distance from us, and perhaps some other? As he who thinks and discourses of the sun has been more or less accurate in observing those sensible qualities, ideas, or properties, which are in that thing which he calls the sun.

---

7   Sulphuric acid.

Book IV, Chapter XI: Of Our Knowledge of the Existence of Other Things.

§1. The knowledge of our own being we have by intuition. The existence of a God, reason clearly makes known to us, as has been shown.[8]

The knowledge of the existence of any other thing we can have only by sensation: for there being no necessary connection of real existence with any idea a man hath in his memory, nor of any other existence but that of God, with the existence of any particular man; no particular man can know the existence of any other being, but only when, by actual operating upon him, it makes itself perceived by him. For, the having the idea of anything in our mind no more proves the existence of that thing, than the picture of a man evidences his being in the world, or the visions of a dream make thereby a true history.

§2. It is therefore the actual receiving of ideas from without, that gives us notice of the existence of other things, and makes us know that something doth exist at that time without us, which causes that idea in us, though perhaps we neither know nor consider how it does it: for it takes not from the certainty of our senses, and the ideas we receive by them, that we know not the manner wherein they are produced: v.g. whilst I write this, I have, by the paper affecting my eyes, that idea produced in my mind, which, whatever object causes, I call white; by which I know that that quality or accident (i.e., whose appearance before my eyes always causes that idea) doth really exist, and hath a being without me. And of this, the greatest assurance I can possibly have, and to which my faculties can attain, is the testimony of my eyes, which are the proper and sole judges of this thing, whose testimony I have reason to rely on as so certain, that I can no more doubt, whilst I write this, that I see white and black, and that something really exists, that causes that sensation in me, than that I write or move my hand; which is a certainty as great as human nature is

---

8   These two claims were argued for in his previous two chapters (IX and X). Intuition, for Locke, is roughly direct knowledge—something we can directly see to be true—and is to be contrasted with the indirect knowledge we get from sensation, memory, or reason.

capable of, concerning the existence of anything but a man's self alone, and of God.

§3. The notice we have by our senses of the existing of things without us, though it be not altogether so certain as our intuitive knowledge, or the deductions of our reason, employed about the clear abstract ideas of our own minds; yet it is an assurance that deserves the name of knowledge. If we persuade ourselves that our faculties act and inform us right, concerning the existence of those objects that affect them, it cannot pass for an ill-grounded confidence: for I think nobody can, in earnest, be so sceptical as to be uncertain of the existence of those things which he sees and feels. At least, he that can doubt so far (whatever he may have with his own thoughts) will never have any controversy with me; since he can never be sure I say anything contrary to his own opinion. As to myself, I think God has given me assurance enough of the existence of things without me; since by their different application I can produce in myself both pleasure and pain, which is one great concernment of my present state. This is certain, the confidence that our faculties do not herein deceive us, is the greatest assurance we are capable of concerning the existence of material beings. For we cannot act anything, but by our faculties; nor talk of knowledge itself, but by the helps of those faculties, which are fitted to apprehend even what knowledge is. But besides the assurance we have from our senses themselves, that they do not err in the information they give us, of the existence of things without us, when they are affected by them, we are further confirmed in this assurance by other concurrent reasons.

§4. First, it is plain those perceptions are produced in us by exterior causes affecting our senses; because those that want the organs of any sense never can have the ideas belonging to that sense produced in their minds. This is too evident to be doubted: and therefore we cannot but be assured that they come in by the organs of that sense, and no other way. The organs themselves, it is plain, do not produce them; for then the eyes of a man in the dark would produce colours, and his nose smell roses in the winter: but we see nobody gets the relish of a pine-apple till he goes to the Indies, where it is, and tastes it.

§5. Secondly, because sometimes I find that I cannot avoid the having those ideas produced in my mind. For though when my eyes are shut, or windows fast, I can at pleasure recall to my mind the ideas of light, or the sun, which former sensations had lodged in my memory; so I can at pleasure lay by that idea, and take into my view that of the smell of a rose, or taste of sugar. But, if I turn my eyes at noon towards the sun, I cannot avoid the ideas, which the light, or sun, then produces in me. So that there is a manifest difference between the ideas laid up in my memory (over which, if they were there only, I should have constantly the same power to dispose of them, and lay them by at pleasure) and those which force themselves upon me, and I cannot avoid having. And therefore it must needs be some exterior cause, and the brisk acting of some objects without me, whose efficacy I cannot resist, that produces those ideas in my mind, whether I will or no. Besides, there is nobody who doth not perceive the difference in himself between contemplating the sun, as he hath the idea of it in his memory, and actually looking upon it; of which two his perception is so distinct, that few of his ideas are more distinguishable one from another. And therefore he hath certain knowledge, that they are not both memory, or the actions of his mind, and fancies only within him; but that actual seeing hath a cause without.

§6. Thirdly, add to this, that many of those ideas are produced in us with pain, which afterwards we remember without the least offence. Thus, the pain of heat or cold, when the idea of it is revived in our minds, gives us no disturbance; which, when felt, was very troublesome, and is again, when actually repeated; which is occasioned by the disorder the external object causes in our bodies when applied to it. And we remember the pains of hunger, thirst, or the head-ache, without any pain at all; which would either never disturb us, or else constantly do it, as often as we thought of it, were there nothing more but ideas floating in our minds, and appearances entertaining our fancies, without the real existence of things affecting us from abroad. The same may be said of pleasure, accompanying several actual sensations: and though mathematical demonstration depends not upon sense, yet the examining them by diagrams gives great credit to the evidence of our sight, and seems to give it a certainty approaching to that of demonstration itself. For it would be very strange that a man should allow it for an undeniable truth, that two angles of a figure, which he measures by lines and angles of a diagram, should be bigger one than the other; and yet doubt of the existence of those lines and angles, which by looking on he makes use of to measure that by.

§7. Fourthly, our senses in many cases bear witness to the truth of each other's report, concerning the existence of sensible things without us. He that sees a fire may, if he doubt whether it be anything more than a bare fancy, feel it too; and be convinced, by putting his hand in it: which certainly could never be put into such exquisite pain by a bare idea or phantom, unless that the pain be a fancy too; which yet he cannot, when the burn is well, by raising the idea of it, bring upon himself again.

Thus I see, whilst I write this, I can change the appearance of the paper: and by designing the letters, tell beforehand what new idea it shall exhibit the very next moment, by barely drawing my pen over it: which will neither appear (let me fancy as much as I will) if my hands stand still; or though I move my pen, if my eyes be shut: nor, when those characters are once made on the paper, can I choose afterwards but see them as they are; that is, have the ideas of such letters as I have made. Whence it is manifest, that they are not barely the sport and play of my own imagination, when I find that the characters, that were made at the pleasure of my own thought, do not obey them; nor yet cease to be, whenever I shall fancy it; but continue to affect my senses constantly and regularly, according to the figures I made them. To which if we will add, that the sight of those shall, from another man, draw such sounds as I beforehand design they shall stand for; there will be little reason left to doubt that those words I write do really exist without me, when they cause a long series of regular sounds to affect my ears, which could not be the effect of my imagination, nor could my memory retain them in that order.

§8. But yet, if after all this any one will be so sceptical as to distrust his senses, and to affirm that all we see and hear, feel and taste, think and do, during our whole being, is but the series and deluding appearances of a long dream, whereof there is no reality; and therefore will question the existence of all things, or our knowledge of any thing; I must desire him to consider, that, if all be a dream, then he doth but dream that he makes the question; and so it is not much matter that a waking man should answer him. But yet, if he pleases, he may dream that I make him this answer, that the certainty of things existing *in rerum natura*,[9] when we have the testimony of our senses for it, is not only as great as our frame can attain to, but as our condition needs. For, our faculties being suited not to the full extent of being, nor to a perfect, clear, comprehensive knowledge of things free from all doubt and scruple; but to the preservation of us, in whom they are, and accommodated to the use of life; they serve to our purpose well enough, if they will but give us certain notice of those things which are convenient or inconvenient to us. For he that sees a candle burning, and hath experimented the force of its flame, by putting his finger in it, will little doubt that this is something existing without him, which does him harm, and puts him to great pain: which is assurance enough, when no man requires greater certainty to govern his actions by than what is as certain as his actions themselves. And if our dreamer pleases to try whether the glowing heat of a glass furnace be barely a wandering imagination in a drowsy man's fancy; by putting his hand into it he may perhaps be wakened into a certainty greater than he could wish, that it is something more than bare imagination. So that this evidence is as great as we can desire, being as certain to us as our pleasure or pain, i.e., happiness or misery; beyond which we have no concernment, either of knowing or being. Such an assurance of the existence of things without us is sufficient to direct us in the attaining the good, and avoiding the evil, which is caused by them; which is the important concernment we have of being made acquainted with them.

§9. In fine, then, when our senses do actually convey into our understandings any idea, we cannot but be satisfied that there doth something at that time really exist without us, which doth affect our senses, and by them give notice of itself to our apprehensive faculties, and actually produce that idea which we then perceive: and we cannot so far distrust their

---

9   "In the nature of things," or sometimes, more specifically "in physical reality."

testimony, as to doubt that such collections of simple ideas as we have observed by our senses to be united together, do really exist together. But this knowledge extends as far as the present testimony of our senses, employed about particular objects that do then affect them, and no further. For if I saw such a collection of simple ideas, as is wont to be called man, existing together one minute since, and am now alone, I cannot be certain that the same man exists now, since there is no necessary connection of his existence a minute since with his existence now: by a thousand ways he may cease to be, since I had the testimony of my senses for his existence. And if I cannot be certain that the man I saw last to-day is now in being, I can less be certain that he is so who hath been longer removed from my senses, and I have not seen since yesterday, or since the last year: and much less can I be certain of the existence of men that I never saw. And, therefore, though it be highly probable that millions of men do now exist, yet, whilst I am alone writing this, I have not that certainty of it which we strictly call knowledge; though the great likelihood of it puts me past doubt, and it be reasonable for me to do several things upon the confidence that there are men (and men also of my acquaintance, with whom I have to do) now in the world: but this is but probability, not knowledge.

§10. Whereby yet we may observe how foolish and vain a thing it is for a man of a narrow knowledge, who having reason given him to judge of the different evidence and probability of things, and to be swayed accordingly,—how vain, I say, it is to expect demonstration and certainty in things not capable of it, and refuse assent to very rational propositions, and act contrary to very plain and clear truths, because they cannot be made out so evident, as to surmount every the least (I will not say reason but) pretence of doubting. He that, in the ordinary affairs of life would admit of nothing but direct plain demonstration, would be sure of nothing in this world, but of perishing quickly. The wholesomeness of his meat or drink would not give him reason to venture on it: and I would fain know, what it is he could do upon such grounds as are capable of no doubt, no objection.

§11. As when our senses are actually employed about any object, we do know that it does exist; so by our memory we may be assured, that heretofore things that affected our senses have existed. And thus we have knowledge of the past existence of several things whereof, our senses having informed us, our memories still retain the ideas; and of this we are past all doubt, so long as we remember well. But this knowledge also reaches no further than our senses have formerly assured us. Thus, seeing water at this instant, it is an unquestionable truth to me that water doth exist: and remembering that I saw it yesterday, it will also be always true, and as long as my memory retains it, always an undoubted proposition to me, that water did exist the 10th of July, 1688, as it will also be equally true that a certain number of very fine colours did exist, which at the same time I saw upon a bubble of that water: but, being now quite out of sight both of the water and bubbles too, it is no more certainly known to me that the water doth now exist, than that the bubbles or colours therein do so; it being no more necessary that water should exist to-day, because it existed yesterday, than that the colours or bubbles exist to-day, because they existed yesterday; though it be exceedingly much more probable, because water hath been observed to continue long in existence but bubbles and the colours on them, quickly cease to be.

§12. What ideas we have of spirits,[10] and how we come by them, I have already shown. But though we have those ideas in our minds, and know we have them there, the having the ideas of spirits does not make us know that any such things do exist without us, or that there are any finite spirits, or any other spiritual beings but the eternal God. We have ground from revelation, and several other reasons, to believe with assurance that there are such creatures: but our senses not being able to discover them, we want the means of knowing their particular existences. For we can no more know, that there are finite spirits really existing, by the idea we have of such beings in our minds, than by the ideas any one has of fairies, or centaurs, he can come to know that things answering those ideas do really exist.

And therefore concerning the existence of finite spirits, as well as several other things, we must content ourselves with the evidence of faith; but universal

---

10   Spiritual beings such as angels.

certain propositions concerning this matter are beyond our reach. For however true it may be, *v.g.* that all the intelligent spirits that God ever created do still exist; yet it can never make a part of our certain knowledge. These and the like propositions we may assent to as highly probable, but are not, I fear, in this state capable of knowing. We are not then to put others upon demonstrating, nor ourselves upon search of universal certainty, in all those matters, wherein we are not capable of any other knowledge, but what our senses give us in this or that particular.

§13. By which it appears that there are two sorts of propositions: 1. There is one sort of propositions concerning the existence of any thing answerable to such an idea: as having the idea of an elephant, phoenix, motion, or an angel, in my mind, the first and natural inquiry is, Whether such a thing does anywhere exist? And this knowledge is only of particulars. No existence of anything without us, but only of God, can certainly be known farther than our senses inform us. 2. There is another sort of propositions, wherein is expressed the agreement or disagreement of our abstract ideas, and their dependence on one another. Such propositions may be universal and certain. So having the idea of God and myself, of fear and obedience, I cannot but be sure that God is to be feared and obeyed by me: and this proposition will be certain, concerning man in general, if I have made an abstract idea of such a species, whereof I am one particular. But yet this proposition, how certain soever, that men ought to fear and obey God proves not to me the existence of men in the world, but will be true of all such creatures, whenever they do exist: which certainty of such general propositions depends on the agreement or disagreement to be discovered in those abstract ideas.

§14. In the former case, our knowledge is the consequence of the existence of things producing ideas in our minds by our senses: in the latter, knowledge is the consequence of the ideas (be they what they will) that are in our minds, producing there general certain propositions. Many of these are called *aeternae veritates*,[11] and all of them indeed are so; not from being written all or any of them in the minds of all men; or that they were any of them propositions in any one's mind till he, having got the abstract ideas, joined or separated them by affirmation or negation. But wheresoever we can suppose such a creature as man is, endowed with such faculties, and thereby furnished with such ideas as we have, we must conclude, he must needs, when he applies his thoughts to the consideration of his ideas, know the truth of certain propositions that will arise from the agreement or disagreement which he will perceive in his own ideas. Such propositions are therefore called eternal truths, not because they are eternal propositions actually formed, and antecedent to the understanding, that at any time makes them; nor because they are imprinted on the mind from any patterns, that are anywhere out of the mind, and existed before: but because being once made about abstract ideas, so as to be true, they will, whenever they can be supposed to be made again at any time past or to come, by a mind having those ideas, always actually be true. For names being supposed to stand perpetually for the same ideas, and the same ideas having immutably the same habitudes one to another; propositions concerning any abstract ideas that are once true, must needs be eternal verities.

---

11 "Eternal verities"—things that are eternally true.

GEORGE BERKELEY

Three Dialogues Between Hylas and Philonous

Who Was George Berkeley?

George Berkeley was born in 1685 near Kilkenny, an attractive medieval town in the southern part of Ireland which, in the 1640s, had briefly been the center of Irish resistance to the British. He was the son of a gentleman farmer and went to one of Ireland's leading schools, Kilkenny College, at the age of 11. At the early age of 15 Berkeley entered Trinity College, Dublin (the pre-eminent Irish university), and in 1707 became a Fellow of the College. Two years later he published *An Essay Towards a New Theory of Vision*, an influential scientific work which remained the standard theory of vision until the mid-nineteenth century, but which Berkeley intended, from the outset, to solve a problem for his developing "immaterialist" theories.[1] In fact, Berkeley probably arrived at his main philosophical views in his early twenties, and never wavered from them thereafter.

In 1710 Berkeley was ordained a priest in the protestant Church of Ireland and, in the same year, published *A Treatise Concerning the Principles of Human Knowledge*, in which he put forward his theory, today called "subjective idealism." In a nutshell, he claimed matter does not exist. The book met with a cool reception, and Berkeley felt he was merely dismissed as an eccentric: indeed, a London doctor theorized that Berkeley must be insane, and a bishop publicly expressed pity for Berkeley's need to seek notoriety. Gamely, therefore, he set out to represent his ideas in a more acceptable form; *Three Dialogues Between Hylas and Philonous*, published in London in 1713, was the result. This book was much more successful, and though it persuaded few to agree with his conclusions it made him something of a literary celebrity in London social circles.

Berkeley, who had moved to London in 1713, spent much of the next decade traveling in France and Italy, first as chaplain to the Earl of Peterborough and then as tutor to the son of a bishop. There is a story (probably untrue) that a fit of apoplexy brought on by arguing with Berkeley caused the death of the important Cartesian philosopher Nicolas Malebranche in 1715.

In 1721 Berkeley published *De Motu* ("On Motion"), attacking Newton's philosophy of space on the basis of Berkeley's own philosophical system (despite his great admiration for Newton's work in general). In the same year he published *An Essay Towards Preventing the Ruin of Great Britain,* which diagnosed Britain's economic problems (the result of a huge stock market crash in 1720, known as the collapse of the South

---

1   The problem that Berkeley needed to solve was the apparent fact that we seem to just 'see' things as being three-dimensional solids located outside of ourselves; he solved it by arguing that vision itself merely provides us with information about a sequence of color patches in our visual field, and we have to learn to make *inferences* about spatial location on the basis of this data and its correlation with the sensations of touch. In other words, he argued that we don't just 'see' that there is a material world located outside of our heads.

Sea Bubble) as being caused by a general decline in religion, morality, and sense of duty to the public good. Berkeley himself, however, attained economic security just two years later when he was made Dean of Derry, a church position which carried with it a very sizeable income.

In 1724 Berkeley enthusiastically embarked on a project for establishing a college in Bermuda to provide Christian education to both colonial and indigenous North Americans. He raised £6,000 in private donations, managed to convince five Fellows of Trinity to give up their secure academic positions in Dublin and commit themselves to becoming teachers in Bermuda, and with his new wife Anne Forster he set sail for the New World in 1728. He settled in Newport, Rhode Island, and bought a farm to provide extra income for his college. Unfortunately, the £20,000 in funding promised by the British government for the college never materialized and in 1731 Berkeley was forced to abandon the project and return to London, hoping instead for advancement in the church. In 1734 he was duly made Bishop of Cloyne (near Cork, in Ireland), and moved there immediately. He devoted most of his energies for the rest of his life to looking after the spiritual and practical interests of the people of the see of Cloyne. His last publication was the strange *Siris: A Chain of Philosophical Reflections and Inquiries*, in which, among other things, he expounded the medicinal benefits of tar-water (a concoction, served cold, made by boiling pine resin in water). Berkeley died suddenly in Oxford in 1753 whilst visiting his second son, George, who was at university there. He was buried a week later (since, out of fear of being buried alive, he had left instructions that he was not to be buried until his body showed signs of decay) in the nave of Christ Church cathedral.

What Was Berkeley's Overall Philosophical Project?

Berkeley is best known as the inventor of the philosophical theory today called "subjective idealism" (and which he called "immaterialism"). This is the theory that the physical world exists only in the experiences that minds have of it—in other words, that the world consists of nothing more than a set of mental experiences. As it is often put, for Berkeley *esse est percipi*: "to exist is to be perceived."[2]

Berkeley's main philosophical project was to attack the prevailing mechanical philosophy, a general world-outlook given early form by the work of Descartes (1596–1650), embodied in the science of Robert Boyle (1627–1691) and Isaac Newton (1642–1727), and provided with its most influential philosophical defender in Locke (1632–1704). What Berkeley saw in the mechanical philosophy was a complete split between mind and matter as two radically different types of thing, combined with the comfortable assumption that our minds can nevertheless interact with and come to know a great deal about the world of matter. He argued throughout his life that these two claims are mutually inconsistent: that to adopt a mechanical view of the external world inevitably commits us to radical skepticism. Furthermore, the new mechanical philosophy, Berkeley felt, tempts us towards materialism (i.e., the denial of the existence of immaterial spirits) and atheism (since Newton's deterministic physics seems to leave little role in the universe for an active God).

Berkeley's way out of what he saw as a deep conceptual confusion was to deny the reality of any non-mental stuff called "matter." That is, Berkeley tries to save us from skepticism by showing that reality is entirely mental, and pointing out that we have extremely close acquaintance with—and so highly reliable knowledge of—our own ideas and their relations with each other. (For most subsequent philosophers, however, this cure has seemed worse than the disease.)

What Is the Structure of This Reading?

Set in a garden, this reading is a dialogue between Hylas and Philonous. Hylas, whose name is derived from *hyle*, the Greek word for matter, defends the mechanistic, scientific account of the material world as existing independently of the mind. Philonous, whose name means "lover of mind," speaks for Berkeley, and defends idealism.

---

2   Actually, the full version of the maxim is *esse est percipi vel percipere*: "to exist is either to be perceived or to perceive."

The *Three Dialogues* have the following scheme. In the First Dialogue, Berkeley lays out most of his arguments for the non-existence of matter. Then, in the Second Dialogue, he tries to show that his conclusions are neither skeptical nor atheistic, and that they in fact refute skepticism and give God a crucial role in the running of the universe. He goes on to argue that the existence of matter is not only unsupported by argument but actually inconceivable. In the Third Dialogue, Berkeley has Philonous defend subjective idealism against a sequence of over twenty objections from Hylas, and especially against the objection that Berkeley's theory is shocking, strange, skeptical, and generally just as indefensible as materialism has turned out to be.

The First Dialogue, the selection reprinted here, pursues several rather complex lines of argument but can be seen as falling into three parts. After an initial exchange on the dangers of skepticism, Philonous argues against the externality of secondary qualities (see the reading from Locke, above, for the classic account of the primary-secondary qualities distinction). Berkeley presents at least three distinct arguments for this conclusion, which today are often called the argument from illusion, the causal argument, and (what Howard Robinson has called) the "assimilation argument." This last works by trying to show that all sensory states essentially contain an irreducibly subjective component, like pain or pleasure.

In the second part of the argument of the First Dialogue, Philonous argues against the externality of the primary qualities. He starts by using similar arguments to those just applied to the secondary qualities, but then comes a fairly long digression in which Hylas raises two interesting suggestions. First, Hylas tries to defend the mind-independence of reality by distinguishing between the *act* of perception and its *object* (i.e., the thing it is a perception of), and arguing that only the first of these is subjective. After Philonous responds to this argument, Hylas then tries appealing to the notion of a material "substratum" or "substance" underlying the qualities we perceive, and Philonous argues that such a notion is meaningless. Finally, Hylas returns to the question of the mind-independence of the primary qualities and tries to defend a view sometimes called the "representative theory of perception" (which can be found in Locke). This theory treats our ideas or sensations not as

being mind-independent themselves but as *representing* or *resembling* mind-independent qualities in the world. Philonous argues that, if this were the case, we could never know anything about the material causes of our ideas.

In the third and final stage of Berkeley's argument, Philonous continues his critique of the representative theory of perception by making two new points. First, he claims in a small section sometimes called his "Master Argument" (since he says he will let everything rest on this argument alone), it is incoherent even to assert that we can conceive of something existing unconceived. It follows that it is incoherent to talk about objects that are not themselves perceived but that cause our perceptions. Second, Berkeley argues that nothing but an idea can be anything like an idea (this is often called Berkeley's "Likeness Principle"). That is, he criticizes the coherence of the view that some of our ideas resemble their material causes.

Some Useful Background Information

1. Berkeley's use of the term "idea," which is crucial to his philosophical system, is taken from Locke; see the background information notes on Locke for an explanation of this usage.
2. Berkeley's metaphysical system contains the following elements. First, Berkeley claims that the only things that exist are minds, and he restricts the list of minds or "spirits" to something like the usual suspects: humans, animals, angels and so on, and God. So humans and animals do exist, but they have no bodies or brains: they are "pure spirit." These minds are each populated by mental entities which Berkeley calls, following Locke, ideas; so now we have two kinds of thing in the universe (and only two): selves and their ideas.[3]

---

3   Another way of putting this is to say there is just one sort of *substance*—mind—and its *modes* or attributes, which include the ideas. This opposes the dualism of Descartes and Locke, where we have *two* substances, mind and matter. (See the background information section on Descartes for more information about the notion of a substance and its modes.)

In humans, these ideas are related to each other in the ways that are familiar from experience: for example, the visual image of a rose is often shortly followed by the sensation of a certain scent, and the sound of horses on the street outside gives rise to the idea of a carriage passing by. Some of our ideas are within our control, such as when we are using our imagination to invent new mythical animals, but others are not, such as when we feel the pain of frostbite. Those ideas not controlled by us are placed in our minds directly by God: it is God, according to Berkeley, who is constantly bringing about our sensory experiences of sight, taste, touch, etc. In other words, instead of causing our experience by the complicated route of creating a mind-independent world which then causes our sensations, God simply produces sensations directly in our minds. These ideas constitute "the real world"—which we can perfectly well call "the physical world" if we want to—and so there is no barrier between us and physical reality: skepticism and atheism are no longer a temptation.

3. Although Berkeley admitted that his theory makes reality mind-dependent (that is, nothing at all can exist without some mind to perceive or contain it, unless it is itself a mind), he denied that our reality—the physical world—was dependent on our *individual* minds. The difference between reality and illusion and hallucination, for Berkeley, is precisely that hallucinations are experienced privately by only one mind, whereas real objects are publicly available to a range of observers. Reality is mind-dependent, but it is dependent on God's mind, not ours.

Some clear terminology might be helpful here. Berkeley defends the existence of "physical reality," but denies that it has "absolute existence." He calls the sort of physical object supposedly capable of absolute existence a "material" thing or "matter"—hence, he denies that matter exists. The kind of "real existence" for physical objects that he does endorse is one where those objects are independent of their perceivers (us), but are not capable of existing independently of any mind at all. That is, they are ideas in the mind of God.

This problem, of the continued existence of sensible objects even when we are not looking at them, and Berkeley's solution to it, has been summed up in two well-known limericks:

There was a young man who said "God
Must think it exceedingly odd
If he finds that this tree
Continues to be
When there's no one about in the Quad."

(A Quad, short for quadrangle, is the courtyard of an Oxford college.) The reply runs as follows:

Dear Sir:
    Your astonishment's odd;
I am always about in the Quad.
And that's why the tree
Will continue to be,
Since observed by
    Yours faithfully,
    GOD.

4. There is one important aspect of his metaphysical system about which Berkeley seems to be careful to sit on the fence (or unable to give a definite answer). He holds that "sensible things"—that is, things we perceive or sense—are independent of our minds since they can continue to exist even when we cease to perceive them; this is because they continue to be ideas in the mind of God. This raises the following question, which Berkeley never really answers clearly: in perceiving a sensible thing, is what I perceive an idea in my mind which is a *copy* of an 'archetypal' idea in the mind of God, or (alternatively) do I perceive the very idea in *God's* mind?[4]

---

4 Think of it this way. When I dream about clocks, those clocks are ideas in my mind only; if you also dream of clocks, even if your dream clocks are just like mine, your clock images are in your mind and not in mine. Now consider my sensory image of a tree, and ask: is my tree-image actually, somehow, an idea in *another* mind (God's), or is it just a *copy* of a tree-image in

Some Common Misconceptions

1. Berkeley was emphatic that he did not deny the *reality* of the physical world. He believed in the existence of rocks and trees, other people and animals, cities, and paintings just as fervently as everyone else; we can trip over them, look at them, talk to them, live in them, buy and sell them, and so on, just as we always thought we could. In fact, rightly or wrongly, Berkeley would have said he had a much clearer and more commonsensical view of the real existence of trees and stars than philosophers like Locke and Descartes. (When the contemporary essayist Samuel Johnson kicked a pebble and declared, of Berkeley, "I refute him thus," Johnson was simply missing Berkeley's point.) What Berkeley was denying, then, is not the existence of trees but a particular account of the *nature* of so-called physical objects and their existence. One can put it this way: Berkeley denies that 'trees,' as defined by the philosophers, exist; but he does not want to deny that trees, as understood by pre-theoretical common sense, exist and are independent of our minds.

2. Berkeley was not a skeptic, an (intentional) enemy of common sense, nor a purveyor of paradoxes. His main concern was to defend the solidity and truth of the very reality we see, hear, taste, and touch, against a picture that treats this reality as a flimsy and deceptive veil behind which operates a mysterious, mechanical machinery of which we can never have direct knowledge.

3. Berkeley was not anti-science. Berkeley, like Locke, was an empiricist, and believed that all knowledge comes ultimately from experience. He had an intense and genuine admiration for Newton and his scientific achievements, and he believed his immaterialism was not only compatible with most of the data and laws of empirical science, but improved it by removing unnecessary metaphysical baggage.

God's mind? This is analogous to asking: is my dream-clock actually part of your dream, or is it instead a copy of the one in your dream?

How Important and Influential Is This Passage?

Berkeley's subjective idealism won very few converts during his lifetime, and has continued to be a very unpopular philosophical position since then: Berkeley is the only major philosopher to ever seriously adopt it.[5] Ironically, far from saving religion and common sense from the depredations of atheism and skepticism, Berkeley's philosophy is usually seen as an important stepping stone on the way to David Hume's skeptical atheism. The philosophical value of this selection from Berkeley's *Three Dialogues*, then, is not so much the plausibility of Berkeley's conclusions as his brilliant challenge to the apparent consistency of our common-sense assumptions about the external world and its relation with our mind: it is not enough, Berkeley shows, to just vaguely hope that our notions of substance, perception, causation, representation, knowledge, mind, and so on will all fit together satisfactorily, but instead we must give careful thought to what we believe and be prepared to adjust our assumptions, possibly in some quite radical ways.

Suggestions for Critical Reflection

1. Do you think Berkeley proves that "colors, sounds, tastes, in a word all those termed *secondary qualities*, have certainly no existence without the mind"? What exactly would it be to show such a thing? Would, for example, Locke accept this claim about secondary qualities?

2. What do you make of Berkeley's Likeness Principle, that only an idea can be like another idea? Does it seem plausible? If so how, if at all, does it help to show that there can be no such thing as matter?

3. Berkeley denies that matter exists, but he holds that minds do exist, and minds are not themselves ideas (they are conscious spiritual

---

5   Though, to be fair, some philosophical theories that have had periods of popularity owe quite a lot to Berkeley's influence, such as the British neo-Hegelian theories of the late nineteenth century and the scientific phenomenalism of the early twentieth century.

agents which perceive ideas). Is Berkeley being consistent here? Do his arguments against matter work just as well against spirit? In thinking about this question, you should be aware that Berkeley himself considers it in the Third Dialogue so you might want to go and find out what he has to say there.

4. Berkeley wants us to accept that the physical world really exists, independently of us, since it consists of ideas in the mind of God. How satisfactory do you find this notion? What could the relationship be between our sensations of the external world and God's ideas? Is it any clearer than the relation between our sensations and material objects would be?

5. Berkeley recognized the existence of only two sorts of things: minds and ideas. Ideas, for Berkeley, are entirely passive, and the only active agencies in the world are minds. It follows that there can be no causation, as we would normally understand it. One idea cannot cause another, they can only be somehow connected together by a mind. In other words, (an idea of) fire cannot bring about (an idea of) heat, which in turn cannot cause (an idea of) the expansion of metal: all that can happen is that some mind decides the first idea is followed by the second, the second by the third, and so on. Given all this, could we possibly continue to do science if we accepted Berkeley's metaphysics? If so, what might this new science look like?

6. Locke and Berkeley can be seen as presenting two opposed philosophical world-views: which of them is right? If you think that neither is, then what third position is available? Would it help to abandon some of the presuppositions shared by Locke and Berkeley, such as their notion of an *idea*?

Suggestions for Further Reading

The standard edition of Berkeley's works continues to be *Works of George Berkeley, Bishop of Cloyne*, edited by Luce and Jessop and published in nine volumes between 1948 and 1957 by Nelson & Sons. A good student edition of the *Three Dialogues* was published

by Oxford University Press in 1998, with lots of useful supplementary material from Jonathan Dancy. In the same year Oxford published a similar edition of Berkeley's *The Principles of Human Knowledge*. Any serious student of Berkeley's *Three Dialogues* should begin by reading his *Principles*.

The standard biography of Berkeley is by A.A. Luce, *The Life of George Berkeley, Bishop of Cloyne* (Nelson, 1949). There are various useful books about Berkeley's philosophy, including the short *Berkeley*, by J.O. Urmson (Oxford University Press, 1982), the somewhat longer *Berkeley*, by G.J. Warnock (Pelican, 1953), and the even more substantial *Berkeley: An Introduction*, by Jonathan Dancy (Blackwell, 1987). Also available are *Berkeley: The Central Arguments*, by A.C. Grayling (Duckworth, 1986), *Berkeley*, by George Pitcher (Routledge & Kegan Paul, 1977), and *Berkeley: An Interpretation*, by Kenneth Winkler (Oxford University Press, 1989). A collection of essays can be found in *Essays on Berkeley*, ed. Foster and Robinson (Oxford University Press, 1985), and in *Locke and Berkeley*, ed. Martin and Armstrong (Doubleday, 1968). Finally, Jonathan Bennett's *Locke, Berkeley, Hume: Central Themes* (Oxford, 1971) is well worth consulting.

Three Dialogues Between Hylas and Philonous[6]

First Dialogue

Three dialogues between Hylas and Philonous, the design of which is plainly to demonstrate the reality and perfection of human knowledge, the incorporeal nature of the soul, and the immediate providence of a deity: in opposition to sceptics and atheists; also to open a method for rendering the sciences more easy, useful, and compendious.

---

6 Berkeley's *Three Dialogues* was first published in 1713, reissued in 1725, and then revised for a third edition in 1734. The text reprinted here is from the third edition (with mostly modernized spelling, punctuation, and capitalization).

The First Dialogue

PHILONOUS. Good morrow, Hylas: I did not expect to find you abroad so early.

HYLAS. It is indeed something unusual; but my thoughts were so taken up with a subject I was discoursing of last night, that finding I could not sleep, I resolved to rise and take a turn in the garden.

PHILONOUS. It happened well, to let you see what innocent and agreeable pleasures you lose every morning. Can there be a pleasanter time of the day, or a more delightful season of the year? That purple sky, those wild but sweet notes of birds, the fragrant bloom upon the trees and flowers, the gentle influence of the rising sun, these and a thousand nameless beauties of nature inspire the soul with secret transports; its faculties too being at this time fresh and lively, are fit for those meditations, which the solitude of a garden and tranquillity of the morning naturally dispose us to. But I am afraid I interrupt your thoughts: for you seemed very intent on something.

HYLAS. It is true, I was, and shall be obliged to you if you will permit me to go on in the same vein; not that I would by any means deprive myself of your company, for my thoughts always flow more easily in conversation with a friend, than when I am alone: but my request is, that you would suffer me to impart my reflexions to you.

PHILONOUS. With all my heart, it is what I should have requested myself if you had not prevented me.

HYLAS. I was considering the odd fate of those men who have in all ages, through an affectation of being distinguished from the vulgar,[7] or some unaccountable turn of thought, pretended either to believe nothing at all, or to believe the most extravagant things in the world. This however might be borne, if their paradoxes and scepticism did not draw after them some consequences of general disadvantage to mankind. But the mischief lieth here; that when men of less leisure see them who are supposed to have spent their whole time in the pursuits of knowledge professing an entire ignorance of all things, or advancing such notions as are repugnant to plain and commonly received principles, they will be tempted to entertain suspicions concerning the most important truths, which they had hitherto held sacred and unquestionable.

PHILONOUS. I entirely agree with you, as to the ill tendency of the affected doubts of some philosophers, and fantastical conceits of others. I am even so far gone of late in this way of thinking, that I have quitted several of the sublime notions I had got in their schools for vulgar opinions. And I give it you on my word, since this revolt from metaphysical notions to the plain dictates of nature and common sense, I find my understanding strangely enlightened, so that I can now easily comprehend a great many things which before were all mystery and riddle.

HYLAS. I am glad to find there was nothing in the accounts I heard of you.

PHILONOUS. Pray, what were those?

HYLAS. You were represented, in last night's conversation, as one who maintained the most extravagant opinion that ever entered into the mind of man, to wit, that there is no such thing as *material substance* in the world.

PHILONOUS. That there is no such thing as what *philosophers call material substance*, I am seriously persuaded: but if I were made to see anything absurd or sceptical in this, I should then have the same reason to renounce this that I imagine I have now to reject the contrary opinion.

HYLAS. What! Can anything be more fantastical, more repugnant to common sense, or a more manifest piece of scepticism, than to believe there is no such thing as *matter*?

PHILONOUS. Softly, good Hylas. What if it should prove that you, who hold there is, are by virtue of that opinion a greater sceptic, and maintain more paradoxes and repugnances to common sense, than I who believe no such thing?

HYLAS. You may as soon persuade me the part is greater than the whole, as that, in order to avoid absurdity and scepticism, I should ever be obliged to give up my opinion in this point.

PHILONOUS. Well then, are you content to admit that opinion for true, which upon examination shall appear most agreeable to common sense, and remote from scepticism?

HYLAS. With all my heart. Since you are for raising disputes about the plainest things in nature, I am content for once to hear what you have to say.

---

7   The common people and their beliefs.

PHILONOUS. Pray, Hylas, what do you mean by a *sceptic*?

HYLAS. I mean what all men mean—one that doubts of everything.

PHILONOUS. He then who entertains no doubts concerning some particular point, with regard to that point cannot be thought a sceptic.

HYLAS. I agree with you.

PHILONOUS. Whether doth doubting consist in embracing the affirmative or negative side of a question?

HYLAS. In neither; for whoever understands English cannot but know that *doubting* signifies a suspense between both.

PHILONOUS. He then that denies any point, can no more be said to doubt of it, than he who affirmeth it with the same degree of assurance.

HYLAS. True.

PHILONOUS. And, consequently, for such his denial is no more to be esteemed a sceptic than the other.

HYLAS. I acknowledge it.

PHILONOUS. How cometh it to pass then, Hylas, that you pronounce me *a sceptic*, because I deny what you affirm, to wit, the existence of matter? Since, for aught you can tell, I am as peremptory[8] in my denial, as you in your affirmation.

HYLAS. Hold, Philonous, I have been a little out in my definition; but every false step a man makes in discourse is not to be insisted on. I said indeed that a *sceptic* was one who doubted of everything; but I should have added, or who denies the reality and truth of things.

PHILONOUS. What things? Do you mean the principles and theorems of sciences? But these you know are universal intellectual notions, and consequently independent of matter. The denial therefore of this doth not imply the denying them.

HYLAS. I grant it. But are there no other things? What think you of distrusting the senses, of denying the real existence of sensible things, or pretending to know nothing of them. Is not this sufficient to denominate a man a *sceptic*?

PHILONOUS. Shall we therefore examine which of us it is that denies the reality of sensible things, or pro-

fesses the greatest ignorance of them; since, if I take you rightly, he is to be esteemed the greatest *sceptic*?

HYLAS. That is what I desire.

PHILONOUS. What mean you by sensible things?

HYLAS. Those things which are perceived by the senses. Can you imagine that I mean anything else?

PHILONOUS. Pardon me, Hylas, if I am desirous clearly to apprehend your notions, since this may much shorten our inquiry. Suffer me then to ask you this farther question. Are those things only perceived by the senses which are perceived immediately? Or, may those things properly be said to be *sensible* which are perceived mediately, or not without the intervention of others?

HYLAS. I do not sufficiently understand you.

PHILONOUS. In reading a book, what I immediately perceive are the letters; but mediately, or by means of these, are suggested to my mind the notions of God, virtue, truth, &c. Now, that the letters are truly sensible things, or perceived by sense, there is no doubt: but I would know whether you take the things suggested by them to be so too.

HYLAS. No, certainly: it were absurd to think *God* or *virtue* sensible things; though they may be signified and suggested to the mind by sensible marks, with which they have an arbitrary connexion.

PHILONOUS. It seems then, that by *sensible things* you mean those only which can be perceived *immediately* by sense?

HYLAS. Right.

PHILONOUS. Doth it not follow from this, that though I see one part of the sky red, and another blue, and that my reason doth thence evidently conclude there must be some cause of that diversity of colours, yet that cause cannot be said to be a sensible thing, or perceived by the sense of seeing?

HYLAS. It doth.

PHILONOUS. In like manner, though I hear variety of sounds, yet I cannot be said to hear the causes of those sounds?

HYLAS. You cannot.

PHILONOUS. And when by my touch I perceive a thing to be hot and heavy, I cannot say, with any truth or propriety, that I feel the cause of its heat or weight?

HYLAS. To prevent any more questions of this kind, I tell you once for all, that by *sensible things* I mean

---

8   Decisive, final, confident.

those only which are perceived by sense; and that in truth the senses perceive nothing which they do not perceive *immediately*: for they make no inferences. The deducing therefore of causes or occasions from effects and appearances, which alone are perceived by sense, entirely relates to reason.

PHILONOUS. This point then is agreed between us— That *sensible things are those only which are immediately perceived by sense.* You will farther inform me, whether we immediately perceive by sight anything beside light, and colours, and figures;[9] or by hearing, anything but sounds; by the palate, anything beside tastes; by the smell, beside odours; or by the touch, more than tangible qualities.

HYLAS. We do not.

PHILONOUS. It seems, therefore, that if you take away all sensible qualities, there remains nothing sensible?

HYLAS. I grant it.

PHILONOUS. Sensible things therefore are nothing else but so many sensible qualities, or combinations of sensible qualities?

HYLAS. Nothing else.

PHILONOUS. *Heat* then is a sensible thing?

HYLAS. Certainly.

PHILONOUS. Doth the *reality* of sensible things consist in being perceived? or, is it something distinct from their being perceived, and that bears no relation to the mind?

HYLAS. To *exist* is one thing, and to be *perceived* is another.

PHILONOUS. I speak with regard to sensible things only. And of these I ask, whether by their real existence you mean a subsistence exterior to the mind, and distinct from their being perceived?

HYLAS. I mean a real absolute being, distinct from, and without any relation to, their being perceived.

PHILONOUS. Heat therefore, if it be allowed a real being, must exist without the mind?

HYLAS. It must.

PHILONOUS. Tell me, Hylas, is this real existence equally compatible to all degrees of heat, which we perceive; or is there any reason why we should attribute it to some, and deny it to others? And if there be, pray let me know that reason.

_____

9   Shapes.

HYLAS. Whatever degree of heat we perceive by sense, we may be sure the same exists in the object that occasions it.

PHILONOUS. What! the greatest as well as the least?

HYLAS. I tell you, the reason is plainly the same in respect of both. They are both perceived by sense; nay, the greater degree of heat is more sensibly perceived; and consequently, if there is any difference, we are more certain of its real existence than we can be of the reality of a lesser degree.

PHILONOUS. But is not the most vehement and intense degree of heat a very great pain?

HYLAS. No one can deny it.

PHILONOUS. And is any unperceiving thing capable of pain or pleasure?

HYLAS. No, certainly.

PHILONOUS. Is your material substance a senseless being, or a being endowed with sense and perception?

HYLAS. It is senseless without doubt.

PHILONOUS. It cannot therefore be the subject of pain?

HYLAS. By no means.

PHILONOUS. Nor consequently of the greatest heat perceived by sense, since you acknowledge this to be no small pain?

HYLAS. I grant it.

PHILONOUS. What shall we say then of your external object; is it a material substance, or no?

HYLAS. It is a material substance with the sensible qualities inhering in it.

PHILONOUS. How then can a great heat exist in it, since you own it cannot in a material substance? I desire you would clear this point.

HYLAS. Hold, Philonous, I fear I was out in yielding intense heat to be a pain. It should seem rather, that pain is something distinct from heat, and the consequence or effect of it.

PHILONOUS. Upon putting your hand near the fire, do you perceive one simple uniform sensation, or two distinct sensations?

HYLAS. But one simple sensation.

PHILONOUS. Is not the heat immediately perceived?

HYLAS. It is.

PHILONOUS. And the pain?

HYLAS. True.

PHILONOUS. Seeing therefore they are both immediately perceived at the same time, and the fire affects you only with one simple or uncompounded idea, it follows that this same simple idea is both the intense heat immediately perceived, and the pain; and, consequently, that the intense heat immediately perceived is nothing distinct from a particular sort of pain.

HYLAS. It seems so.

PHILONOUS. Again, try in your thoughts, Hylas, if you can conceive a vehement sensation to be without pain or pleasure.

HYLAS. I cannot.

PHILONOUS. Or can you frame to yourself an idea of sensible pain or pleasure in general, abstracted from every particular idea of heat, cold, tastes, smells? &c.

HYLAS. I do not find that I can.

PHILONOUS. Doth it not therefore follow, that sensible pain is nothing distinct from those sensations or ideas, in an intense degree?

HYLAS. It is undeniable; and, to speak the truth, I begin to suspect a very great heat cannot exist but in a mind perceiving it.

PHILONOUS. What! are you then in that sceptical state of suspense, between affirming and denying?

HYLAS. I think I may be positive in the point. A very violent and painful heat cannot exist without the mind.

PHILONOUS. It hath not therefore according to you, any *real* being?

HYLAS. I own it.

PHILONOUS. Is it therefore certain, that there is no body in nature really hot?

HYLAS. I have not denied there is any real heat in bodies. I only say, there is no such thing as an intense real heat.

PHILONOUS. But, did you not say before that all degrees of heat were equally real; or, if there was any difference, that the greater were more undoubtedly real than the lesser?

HYLAS. True: but it was because I did not then consider the ground there is for distinguishing between them, which I now plainly see. And it is this: because intense heat is nothing else but a particular kind of painful sensation; and pain cannot exist but in a perceiving being; it follows that no intense heat can really exist in an unperceiving corporeal substance. But this is no reason why we should deny heat in an inferior degree to exist in such a substance.

PHILONOUS. But how shall we be able to discern those degrees of heat which exist only in the mind from those which exist without it?

HYLAS. That is no difficult matter. You know the least pain cannot exist unperceived; whatever, therefore, degree of heat is a pain exists only in the mind. But, as for all other degrees of heat, nothing obliges us to think the same of them.

PHILONOUS. I think you granted before that no unperceiving being was capable of pleasure, any more than of pain.

HYLAS. I did.

PHILONOUS. And is not warmth, or a more gentle degree of heat than what causes uneasiness, a pleasure?

HYLAS. What then?

PHILONOUS. Consequently, it cannot exist without[10] the mind in an unperceiving substance, or body.

HYLAS. So it seems.

PHILONOUS. Since, therefore, as well those degrees of heat that are not painful, as those that are, can exist only in a thinking substance; may we not conclude that external bodies are absolutely incapable of any degree of heat whatsoever?

HYLAS. On second thoughts, I do not think it so evident that warmth is a pleasure as that a great degree of heat is a pain.

PHILONOUS. I do not pretend that warmth is as great a pleasure as heat is a pain. But, if you grant it to be even a small pleasure, it serves to make good my conclusion.

HYLAS. I could rather call it an *indolence*. It seems to be nothing more than a privation of both pain and pleasure. And that such a quality or state as this may agree to an unthinking substance, I hope you will not deny.

PHILONOUS. If you are resolved to maintain that warmth, or a gentle degree of heat, is no pleasure, I know not how to convince you otherwise than by appealing to your own sense. But what think you of cold?

HYLAS. The same that I do of heat. An intense degree of cold is a pain; for to feel a very great cold, is to perceive a great uneasiness: it cannot therefore exist

---

10 "Without," here and elsewhere in this selection, means "outside" (rather than "not having").

without the mind; but a lesser degree of cold may, as well as a lesser degree of heat.

PHILONOUS. Those bodies, therefore, upon whose application to our own, we perceive a moderate degree of heat, must be concluded to have a moderate degree of heat or warmth in them; and those, upon whose application we feel a like degree of cold, must be thought to have cold in them.

HYLAS. They must.

PHILONOUS. Can any doctrine be true that necessarily leads a man into an absurdity?

HYLAS. Without doubt it cannot.

PHILONOUS. Is it not an absurdity to think that the same thing should be at the same time both cold and warm?

HYLAS. It is.

PHILONOUS. Suppose now one of your hands hot, and the other cold, and that they are both at once put into the same vessel of water, in an intermediate state; will not the water seem cold to one hand, and warm to the other?

HYLAS. It will.

PHILONOUS. Ought we not therefore, by your principles, to conclude it is really both cold and warm at the same time, that is, according to your own concession, to believe an absurdity?

HYLAS. I confess it seems so.

PHILONOUS. Consequently, the principles themselves are false, since you have granted that no true principle leads to an absurdity.

HYLAS. But, after all, can anything be more absurd than to say, *there is no heat in the fire*?

PHILONOUS. To make the point still clearer; tell me whether, in two cases exactly alike, we ought not to make the same judgment?

HYLAS. We ought.

PHILONOUS. When a pin pricks your finger, doth it not rend and divide the fibres of your flesh?

HYLAS. It doth.

PHILONOUS. And when a coal burns your finger, doth it any more?

HYLAS. It doth not.

PHILONOUS. Since, therefore, you neither judge the sensation itself occasioned by the pin, nor anything like it to be in the pin; you should not, conformably to what you have now granted, judge the sensation occasioned by the fire, or anything like it, to be in the fire.

HYLAS. Well, since it must be so, I am content to yield this point, and acknowledge that heat and cold are only sensations existing in our minds. But there still remain qualities enough to secure the reality of external things.

PHILONOUS. But what will you say, Hylas, if it shall appear that the case is the same with regard to all other sensible qualities, and that they can no more be supposed to exist without the mind, than heat and cold?

HYLAS. Then indeed you will have done something to the purpose; but that is what I despair of seeing proved.

PHILONOUS. Let us examine them in order. What think you of *tastes*, do they exist without the mind, or no?

HYLAS. Can any man in his senses doubt whether sugar is sweet, or wormwood[11] bitter?

PHILONOUS. Inform me, Hylas. Is a sweet taste a particular kind of pleasure or pleasant sensation, or is it not?

HYLAS. It is.

PHILONOUS. And is not bitterness some kind of uneasiness or pain?

HYLAS. I grant it.

PHILONOUS. If therefore sugar and wormwood are unthinking corporeal substances existing without the mind, how can sweetness and bitterness, that is, pleasure and pain, agree to them?

HYLAS. Hold, Philonous, I now see what it was deluded me all this time. You asked whether heat and cold, sweetness and bitterness, were not particular sorts of pleasure and pain; to which I answered simply, that they were. Whereas I should have thus distinguished: those qualities, as perceived by us, are pleasures or pains, but not as existing in the external objects. We must not therefore conclude absolutely, that there is no heat in the fire, or sweetness in the sugar, but only that heat or sweetness, as perceived by us, are not in the fire or sugar. What say you to this?

PHILONOUS. I say it is nothing to the purpose. Our discourse proceeded altogether concerning sensible things, which you defined to be, *the things we immediately perceive by our senses*. Whatever other qualities, therefore, you speak of as distinct from these, I know nothing of them, neither do they at all belong

---

11 A bitter extract of aromatic herbs and shrubs, used for making absinthe and flavoring certain wines.

to the point in dispute. You may, indeed, pretend to have discovered certain qualities which you do not perceive, and assert those insensible qualities exist in fire and sugar. But what use can be made of this to your present purpose, I am at a loss to conceive. Tell me then once more, do you acknowledge that heat and cold, sweetness and bitterness (meaning those qualities which are perceived by the senses), do not exist without the mind?

HYLAS. I see it is to no purpose to hold out, so I give up the cause as to those mentioned qualities. Though I profess it sounds oddly, to say that sugar is not sweet.

PHILONOUS. But, for your farther satisfaction, take this along with you: that which at other times seems sweet, shall, to a distempered palate, appear bitter. And, nothing can be plainer than that divers persons perceive different tastes in the same food; since that which one man delights in, another abhors. And how could this be, if the taste was something really inherent in the food?

HYLAS. I acknowledge I know not how.

PHILONOUS. In the next place, *odours* are to be considered. And, with regard to these, I would fain know whether what hath been said of tastes doth not exactly agree to them? Are they not so many pleasing or displeasing sensations?

HYLAS. They are.

PHILONOUS. Can you then conceive it possible that they should exist in an unperceiving thing?

HYLAS. I cannot.

PHILONOUS. Or, can you imagine that filth and ordure[12] affect those brute animals that feed on them out of choice, with the same smells which we perceive in them?

HYLAS. By no means.

PHILONOUS. May we not therefore conclude of smells, as of the other forementioned qualities, that they cannot exist in any but a perceiving substance or mind?

HYLAS. I think so.

PHILONOUS. Then as to *sounds*, what must we think of them: are they accidents[13] really inherent in external bodies, or not?

HYLAS. That they inhere not in the sonorous bodies is plain from hence: because a bell struck in the exhausted receiver of an air-pump[14] sends forth no sound. The air, therefore, must be thought the subject of sound.

PHILONOUS. What reason is there for that, Hylas?

HYLAS. Because, when any motion is raised in the air, we perceive a sound greater or lesser, according to the air's motion; but without some motion in the air, we never hear any sound at all.

PHILONOUS. And granting that we never hear a sound but when some motion is produced in the air, yet I do not see how you can infer from thence, that the sound itself is in the air.

HYLAS. It is this very motion in the external air that produces in the mind the sensation of *sound*. For, striking on the drum of the ear, it causeth a vibration, which by the auditory nerves being communicated to the brain, the soul is thereupon affected with the sensation called *sound*.

PHILONOUS. What! is sound then a sensation?

HYLAS. I tell you, as perceived by us, it is a particular sensation in the mind.

PHILONOUS. And can any sensation exist without the mind?

HYLAS. No, certainly.

PHILONOUS. How then can sound, being a sensation, exist in the air, if by the *air* you mean a senseless substance existing without the mind?

HYLAS. You must distinguish, Philonous, between sound as it is perceived by us, and as it is in itself; or (which is the same thing) between the sound we immediately perceive, and that which exists without us. The former, indeed, is a particular kind of sensation, but the latter is merely a vibrative or undulatory motion of the air.

PHILONOUS. I thought I had already obviated that distinction, by the answer I gave when you were applying it in a like case before. But, to say no more of that, are you sure then that sound is really nothing but motion?

HYLAS. I am.

PHILONOUS. Whatever therefore agrees to real sound, may with truth be attributed to motion?

HYLAS. It may.

---

12   Excrement, dung.

13   (Non-essential) properties.

14   A near-vacuum. This experiment was first performed by Otto von Guericke in the 1650s.

PHILONOUS. It is then good sense to speak of *motion* as of a thing that is *loud, sweet, acute,* or *grave*.[15]

HYLAS. I see you are resolved not to understand me. Is it not evident those accidents or modes belong only to sensible sound, or sound in the common acceptation of the word, but not to *sound* in the real and philosophic sense; which, as I just now told you, is nothing but a certain motion of the air?

PHILONOUS. It seems then there are two sorts of sound—the one vulgar, or that which is heard, the other philosophical and real?

HYLAS. Even so.

PHILONOUS. And the latter consists in motion?

HYLAS. I told you so before.

PHILONOUS. Tell me, Hylas, to which of the senses, think you, the idea of motion belongs? to the hearing?

HYLAS. No, certainly; but to the sight and touch.

PHILONOUS. It should follow then, that, according to you, real sounds may possibly be *seen* or *felt*, but never *heard*.

HYLAS. Look you, Philonous, you may, if you please, make a jest of my opinion, but that will not alter the truth of things. I own, indeed, the inferences you draw me into sound something oddly; but common language, you know, is framed by, and for the use of the vulgar: we must not therefore wonder if expressions adapted to exact philosophic notions seem uncouth and out of the way.

PHILONOUS. Is it come to that? I assure you, I imagine myself to have gained no small point, since you make so light of departing from common phrases and opinions; it being a main part of our inquiry, to examine whose notions are widest of the common road, and most repugnant to the general sense of the world. But, can you think it no more than a philosophical paradox, to say that *real sounds are never heard*, and that the idea of them is obtained by some other sense? And is there nothing in this contrary to nature and the truth of things?

HYLAS. To deal ingenuously,[16] I do not like it. And, after the concessions already made, I had as well grant that sounds too have no real being without the mind.

---

15 "Acute" means high-pitched or shrill, and "grave" low-pitched.

16 Openly, honestly.

PHILONOUS. And I hope you will make no difficulty to acknowledge the same of *colours*.

HYLAS. Pardon me: the case of colours is very different. Can anything be plainer than that we see them on the objects?

PHILONOUS. The objects you speak of are, I suppose, corporeal substances existing without the mind?

HYLAS. They are.

PHILONOUS. And have true and real colours inhering in them?

HYLAS. Each visible object hath that colour which we see in it.

PHILONOUS. How! is there anything visible but what we perceive by sight?

HYLAS. There is not.

PHILONOUS. And, do we perceive anything by sense which we do not perceive immediately?

HYLAS. How often must I be obliged to repeat the same thing? I tell you, we do not.

PHILONOUS. Have patience, good Hylas; and tell me once more, whether there is anything immediately perceived by the senses, except sensible qualities. I know you asserted there was not; but I would now be informed, whether you still persist in the same opinion.

HYLAS. I do.

PHILONOUS. Pray, is your corporeal substance either a sensible quality, or made up of sensible qualities?

HYLAS. What a question that is! who ever thought it was?

PHILONOUS. My reason for asking was, because in saying, *each visible object hath that colour which we see in it*, you make visible objects to be corporeal substances; which implies either that corporeal substances are sensible qualities, or else that there is something besides sensible qualities perceived by sight: but, as this point was formerly agreed between us, and is still maintained by you, it is a clear consequence, that your *corporeal substance* is nothing distinct from *sensible qualities*.

HYLAS. You may draw as many absurd consequences as you please, and endeavour to perplex the plainest things; but you shall never persuade me out of my senses. I clearly understand my own meaning.

PHILONOUS. I wish you would make me understand it too. But, since you are unwilling to have your notion of corporeal substance examined, I shall urge that point no farther. Only be pleased to let me know, whether the same colours which we see exist in external bodies, or some other.

HYLAS. The very same.

PHILONOUS. What! are then the beautiful red and purple we see on yonder clouds really in them? Or do you imagine they have in themselves any other form than that of a dark mist or vapour?

HYLAS. I must own, Philonous, those colours are not really in the clouds as they seem to be at this distance. They are only apparent colours.

PHILONOUS. *Apparent* call you them? How shall we distinguish these apparent colours from real?

HYLAS. Very easily. Those are to be thought apparent which, appearing only at a distance, vanish upon a nearer approach.

PHILONOUS. And those, I suppose, are to be thought real which are discovered by the most near and exact survey.

HYLAS. Right.

PHILONOUS. Is the nearest and exactest survey made by the help of a microscope, or by the naked eye?

HYLAS. By a microscope, doubtless.

PHILONOUS. But a microscope often discovers colours in an object different from those perceived by the unassisted sight. And, in case we had microscopes magnifying to any assigned degree, it is certain that no object whatsoever, viewed through them, would appear in the same colour which it exhibits to the naked eye.

HYLAS. And what will you conclude from all this? You cannot argue that there are really and naturally no colours on objects: because by artificial managements they may be altered, or made to vanish.

PHILONOUS. I think it may evidently be concluded from your own concessions, that all the colours we see with our naked eyes are only apparent as those on the clouds, since they vanish upon a more close and accurate inspection which is afforded us by a microscope. Then as to what you say by way of prevention: I ask you whether the real and natural state of an object is better discovered by a very sharp and piercing sight, or by one which is less sharp?

HYLAS. By the former without doubt.

PHILONOUS. Is it not plain from *dioptrics*[17] that microscopes make the sight more penetrating, and represent objects as they would appear to the eye in case it were naturally endowed with a most exquisite sharpness?

HYLAS. It is.

PHILONOUS. Consequently the microscopical representation is to be thought that which best sets forth the real nature of the thing, or what it is in itself. The colours, therefore, by it perceived are more genuine and real than those perceived otherwise.

HYLAS. I confess there is something in what you say.

PHILONOUS. Besides, it is not only possible but manifest, that there actually are animals whose eyes are by nature framed to perceive those things which by reason of their minuteness escape our sight. What think you of those inconceivably small animals perceived by glasses?[18] Must we suppose they are all stark blind? Or, in case they see, can it be imagined their sight hath not the same use in preserving their bodies from injuries, which appears in that of all other animals? And if it hath, is it not evident they must see particles less than their own bodies; which will present them with a far different view in each object from that which strikes our senses? Even our own eyes do not always represent objects to us after the same manner. In the jaundice[19] every one knows that all things seem yellow. Is it not therefore highly probable those animals in whose eyes we discern a very different texture from that of ours, and whose bodies abound with different humours,[20] do not see the same colours in every object that we do? From all which, should it not seem to follow that all colours are equally apparent, and that none of those which we perceive are really inherent in any outward object?

HYLAS. It should.

PHILONOUS. The point will be past all doubt, if you consider that, in case colours were real properties or affections inherent in external bodies, they could admit of no alteration without some change wrought in the very bodies themselves: but, is it not evident from what hath

---

17　The part of optics dealing with the study of refraction.

18　By magnifying lenses (e.g., in a microscope).

19　A yellowing of the skin and the eyes, often caused by liver disease.

20　Bodily fluids.

been said that, upon the use of microscopes, upon a change happening in the humours of the eye, or a variation of distance, without any manner of real alteration in the thing itself, the colours of any object are either changed, or totally disappear? Nay, all other circumstances remaining the same, change but the situation of some objects, and they shall present different colours to the eye. The same thing happens upon viewing an object in various degrees of light. And what is more known than that the same bodies appear differently coloured by candle-light from what they do in the open day? Add to these the experiment of a prism which, separating the heterogeneous rays of light, alters the colour of any object, and will cause the whitest to appear of a deep blue or red to the naked eye. And now tell me whether you are still of opinion that every body hath its true real colour inhering in it; and, if you think it hath, I would fain know farther from you, what certain distance and position of the object, what peculiar texture and formation of the eye, what degree or kind of light is necessary for ascertaining that true colour, and distinguishing it from apparent ones.

HYLAS. I own myself entirely satisfied, that they are all equally apparent, and that there is no such thing as colour really inhering in external bodies, but that it is altogether in the light. And what confirms me in this opinion is, that in proportion to the light colours are still more or less vivid; and if there be no light, then are there no colours perceived. Besides, allowing there are colours on external objects, yet, how is it possible for us to perceive them? For no external body affects the mind, unless it acts first on our organs of sense. But the only action of bodies is motion; and motion cannot be communicated otherwise than by impulse. A distant object therefore cannot act on the eye; nor consequently make itself or its properties perceivable to the soul. Whence it plainly follows that it is immediately some contiguous[21] substance, which, operating on the eye, occasions a perception of colours: and such is light.

PHILONOUS. How! is light then a substance?

HYLAS. I tell you, Philonous, external light is nothing but a thin fluid substance, whose minute particles being agitated with a brisk motion, and in various man-

ners reflected from the different surfaces of outward objects to the eyes, communicate different motions to the optic nerves; which, being propagated to the brain, cause therein various impressions; and these are attended with the sensations of red, blue, yellow, &c.

PHILONOUS. It seems then the light doth no more than shake the optic nerves.

HYLAS. Nothing else.

PHILONOUS. And consequent to each particular motion of the nerves, the mind is affected with a sensation, which is some particular colour.

HYLAS. Right.

PHILONOUS. And these sensations have no existence without the mind.

HYLAS. They have not.

PHILONOUS. How then do you affirm that colours are in the light; since by *light* you understand a corporeal substance external to the mind?

HYLAS. Light and colours, as immediately perceived by us, I grant cannot exist without the mind. But in themselves they are only the motions and configurations of certain insensible particles of matter.

PHILONOUS. Colours then, in the vulgar sense, or taken for the immediate objects of sight, cannot agree to any but a perceiving substance.

HYLAS. That is what I say.

PHILONOUS. Well then, since you give up the point as to those sensible qualities which are alone thought colours by all mankind beside, you may hold what you please with regard to those invisible ones of the philosophers. It is not my business to dispute about *them*; only I would advise you to bethink yourself, whether, considering the inquiry we are upon, it be prudent for you to affirm—*the red and blue which we see are not real colours, but certain unknown motions and figures which no man ever did or can see are truly so.* Are not these shocking notions, and are not they subject to as many ridiculous inferences, as those you were obliged to renounce before in the case of sounds?

HYLAS. I frankly own, Philonous, that it is in vain to stand out any longer. Colours, sounds, tastes, in a word all those termed *secondary qualities*, have certainly no existence without the mind. But by this acknowledgment I must not be supposed to derogate the reality of matter, or external objects; seeing it is no more than several philosophers maintain, who

---

21   Immediately next to, touching.

nevertheless are the farthest imaginable from denying matter. For the clearer understanding of this, you must know sensible qualities are by philosophers divided into *primary* and *secondary*. The former are extension, figure, solidity, gravity, motion, and rest; and these they hold exist really in bodies. The latter are those above enumerated; or, briefly, *all sensible qualities beside the primary*; which they assert are only so many sensations or ideas existing nowhere but in the mind. But all this, I doubt not, you are apprised of. For my part, I have been a long time sensible there was such an opinion current among philosophers, but was never thoroughly convinced of its truth until now.

PHILONOUS. You are still then of opinion that *extension* and *figures* are inherent in external unthinking substances?

HYLAS. I am.

PHILONOUS. But what if the same arguments which are brought against secondary qualities will hold good against these also?

HYLAS. Why then I shall be obliged to think, they too exist only in the mind.

PHILONOUS. Is it your opinion the very figure and extension which you perceive by sense exist in the outward object or material substance?

HYLAS. It is.

PHILONOUS. Have all other animals as good grounds to think the same of the figure and extension which they see and feel?

HYLAS. Without doubt, if they have any thought at all.

PHILONOUS. Answer me, Hylas. Think you the senses were bestowed upon all animals for their preservation and well-being in life? or were they given to men alone for this end?

HYLAS. I make no question but they have the same use in all other animals.

PHILONOUS. If so, is it not necessary they should be enabled by them to perceive their own limbs, and those bodies which are capable of harming them?

HYLAS. Certainly.

PHILONOUS. A mite[22] therefore must be supposed to see his own foot, and things equal or even less than it, as bodies of some considerable dimension; though at the same time they appear to you scarce discernible, or at best as so many visible points?

HYLAS. I cannot deny it.

PHILONOUS. And to creatures less than the mite they will seem yet larger?

HYLAS. They will.

PHILONOUS. Insomuch that what you can hardly discern will to another extremely minute animal appear as some huge mountain?

HYLAS. All this I grant.

PHILONOUS. Can one and the same thing be at the same time in itself of different dimensions?

HYLAS. That were absurd to imagine.

PHILONOUS. But, from what you have laid down it follows that both the extension by you perceived, and that perceived by the mite itself, as likewise all those perceived by lesser animals, are each of them the true extension of the mite's foot; that is to say, by your own principles you are led into an absurdity.

HYLAS. There seems to be some difficulty in the point.

PHILONOUS. Again, have you not acknowledged that no real inherent property of any object can be changed without some change in the thing itself?

HYLAS. I have.

PHILONOUS. But, as we approach to or recede from an object, the visible extension varies, being at one distance ten or a hundred times greater than another. Doth it not therefore follow from hence likewise that it is not really inherent in the object?

HYLAS. I own I am at a loss what to think.

PHILONOUS. Your judgement will soon be determined, if you will venture to think as freely concerning this quality as you have done concerning the rest. Was it not admitted as a good argument, that neither heat nor cold was in the water, because it seemed warm to one hand and cold to the other?

HYLAS. It was.

PHILONOUS. Is it not the very same reasoning to conclude, there is no extension or figure in an object, because to one eye it shall seem little, smooth, and round, when at the same time it appears to the other, great, uneven, and regular?

HYLAS. The very same. But does this latter fact ever happen?

---

22 Any of a large number of species of tiny arachnids, often parasites, some of which are so small that they cannot be seen by the naked eye.

PHILONOUS. You may at any time make the experiment, by looking with one eye bare, and with the other through a microscope.

HYLAS. I know not how to maintain it; and yet I am loath to give up *extension*, I see so many odd consequences following upon such a concession.

PHILONOUS. Odd, say you? After the concessions already made, I hope you will stick at nothing for its oddness. But, on the other hand, should it not seem very odd, if the general reasoning which includes all other sensible qualities did not also include extension? If it be allowed that no idea, nor anything like an idea, can exist in an unperceiving substance, then surely it follows that no figure, or mode of extension, which we can either perceive, or imagine, or have any idea of, can be really inherent in matter; not to mention the peculiar difficulty there must be in conceiving a material substance, prior to and distinct from extension, to be the *substratum* of extension. Be the sensible quality what it will—figure, or sound, or colour, it seems alike impossible it should subsist in that which doth not perceive it.

HYLAS. I give up the point for the present, reserving still a right to retract my opinion, in case I shall hereafter discover any false step in my progress to it.

PHILONOUS. That is a right you cannot be denied. Figures and extension being despatched, we proceed next to *motion*. Can a real motion in any external body be at the same time very swift and very slow?

HYLAS. It cannot.

PHILONOUS. Is not the motion of a body swift in a reciprocal proportion to the time it takes up in describing[23] any given space? Thus a body that describes a mile in an hour moves three times faster than it would in case it described only a mile in three hours.

HYLAS. I agree with you.

PHILONOUS. And is not time measured by the succession of ideas in our minds?

HYLAS. It is.

PHILONOUS. And is it not possible ideas should succeed one another twice as fast in your mind as they do in mine, or in that of some spirit of another kind?

HYLAS. I own it.

_____

23   Crossing.

PHILONOUS. Consequently the same body may to another seem to perform its motion over any space in half the time that it doth to you. And the same reasoning will hold as to any other proportion: that is to say, according to your principles (since the motions perceived are both really in the object) it is possible one and the same body shall be really moved the same way at once, both very swift and very slow. How is this consistent either with common sense, or with what you just now granted?

HYLAS. I have nothing to say to it.

PHILONOUS. Then as for *solidity*; either you do not mean any sensible quality by that word, and so it is beside our inquiry: or if you do, it must be either hardness or resistance. But both the one and the other are plainly relative to our senses: it being evident that what seems hard to one animal may appear soft to another, who hath greater force and firmness of limbs. Nor is it less plain that the resistance I feel is not in the body.

HYLAS. I own the very *sensation* of resistance, which is all you immediately perceive, is not in the body; but the *cause* of that sensation is.

PHILONOUS. But the causes of our sensations are not things immediately perceived, and therefore are not sensible. This point I thought had been already determined.

HYLAS. I own it was; but you will pardon me if I seem a little embarrassed: I know not how to quit my old notions.

PHILONOUS. To help you out, do but consider that if *extension* be once acknowledged to have no existence without the mind, the same must necessarily be granted of motion, solidity, and gravity; since they all evidently suppose extension. It is therefore superfluous to inquire particularly concerning each of them. In denying extension, you have denied them all to have any real existence.

HYLAS. I wonder, Philonous, if what you say be true, why those philosophers who deny the secondary qualities any real existence should yet attribute it to the primary. If there is no difference between them, how can this be accounted for?

PHILONOUS. It is not my business to account for every opinion of the philosophers. But, among other reasons which may be assigned for this, it seems probable that pleasure and pain being rather annexed to the former than the latter may be one. Heat and cold, tastes and smells, have something more vividly pleasing or disagreeable than the ideas of extension, figure, and motion affect us with. And, it being too visibly absurd to hold that pain or pleasure can be in an unperceiving substance, men are more easily weaned from believing the external existence of the secondary than the primary qualities. You will be satisfied there is something in this, if you recollect the difference you made between an intense and more moderate degree of heat; allowing the one a real existence, while you denied it to the other. But, after all, there is no rational ground for that distinction; for, surely an indifferent sensation is as truly *a sensation* as one more pleasing or painful; and consequently should not any more than they be supposed to exist in an unthinking subject.

HYLAS. It is just come into my head, Philonous, that I have somewhere heard of a distinction between absolute and sensible extension. Now, though it be acknowledged that *great* and *small*, consisting merely in the relation which other extended beings have to the parts of our own bodies, do not really inhere in the substances themselves; yet nothing obliges us to hold the same with regard to *absolute extension*, which is something abstracted from *great* and *small*, from this or that particular magnitude or figure. So likewise as to motion; *swift* and *slow* are altogether relative to the succession of ideas in our own minds. But, it doth not follow, because those modifications of motion exist not without the mind, that therefore absolute motion abstracted from them doth not.

PHILONOUS. Pray what is it that distinguishes one motion, or one part of extension, from another? Is it not something sensible, as some degree of swiftness or slowness, some certain magnitude or figure peculiar to each?

HYLAS. I think so.

PHILONOUS. These qualities, therefore, stripped of all sensible properties, are without all specific and numerical differences, as the schools call them.

HYLAS. They are.

PHILONOUS. That is to say, they are extension in general, and motion in general.

HYLAS. Let it be so.

PHILONOUS. But it is a universally received maxim that *everything which exists is particular*. How then can motion in general, or extension in general, exist in any corporeal substance?

HYLAS. It will take time to solve your difficulty.

PHILONOUS. But I think the point may be speedily decided. Without doubt you can tell whether you are able to frame this or that idea. Now I am content to put our dispute on this issue. If you can frame in your thoughts a distinct *abstract idea* of motion or extension, divested of all those sensible modes, as swift and slow, great and small, round and square, and the like, which are acknowledged to exist only in the mind, I will then yield the point you contend for. But if you cannot, it will be unreasonable on your side to insist any longer upon what you have no notion of.

HYLAS. To confess ingenuously, I cannot.

PHILONOUS. Can you even separate the ideas of extension and motion from the ideas of all those qualities which they who make the distinction term *secondary*?

HYLAS. What! is it not an easy matter to consider extension and motion by themselves, abstracted from all other sensible qualities? Pray how do the mathematicians treat of them?

PHILONOUS. I acknowledge, Hylas, it is not difficult to form general propositions and reasonings about those qualities, without mentioning any other; and, in this sense, to consider or treat of them abstractedly. But, how doth it follow that, because I can pronounce the word *motion* by itself, I can form the idea of it in my mind exclusive of body? or, because theorems may be made of extension and figures, without any mention of *great* or *small*, or any other sensible mode or quality, that therefore it is possible such an abstract idea of extension, without any particular size or figure, or sensible quality, should be distinctly formed, and apprehended by the mind? Mathematicians treat of quantity, without regarding what other sensible qualities it is attended with, as being altogether indifferent to their demonstrations. But, when laying aside the words, they contemplate the bare ideas, I believe you will find, they are not the pure abstracted ideas of extension.

HYLAS. But what say you to *pure intellect*? May not abstracted ideas be framed by that faculty?

PHILONOUS. Since I cannot frame abstract ideas at all, it is plain I cannot frame them by the help of pure *intellect*, whatsoever faculty you understand by those words. Besides, not to inquire into the nature of pure intellect and its spiritual objects, as *virtue, reason, God*, or the like, thus much seems manifest—that sensible things are only to be perceived by sense, or represented by the imagination. Figures, therefore, and extension, being originally perceived by sense, do not belong to pure intellect: but, for your farther satisfaction, try if you can frame the idea of any figure, abstracted from all particularities of size, or even from other sensible qualities.

HYLAS. Let me think a little—I do not find that I can.

PHILONOUS. And can you think it possible that should really exist in nature which implies a repugnancy in its conception?

HYLAS. By no means.

PHILONOUS. Since therefore it is impossible even for the mind to disunite the ideas of extension and motion from all other sensible qualities, doth it not follow, that where the one exist there necessarily the other exist likewise?

HYLAS. It should seem so.

PHILONOUS. Consequently, the very same arguments which you admitted as conclusive against the secondary qualities are, without any farther application of force, against the primary too. Besides, if you will trust your senses, is it not plain all sensible qualities coexist, or to them, appear as being in the same place? Do they ever represent a motion, or figure, as being divested of all other visible and tangible qualities?

HYLAS. You need say no more on this head. I am free to own, if there be no secret error or oversight in our proceedings hitherto, that all sensible qualities are alike to be denied existence without the mind. But, my fear is that I have been too liberal in my former concessions, or overlooked some fallacy or other. In short, I did not take time to think.

PHILONOUS. For that matter, Hylas, you may take what time you please in reviewing the progress of our inquiry. You are at liberty to recover any slips you might have made, or offer whatever you have omitted which makes for your first opinion.

HYLAS. One great oversight I take to be this—that I did not sufficiently distinguish the *object* from the *sensation*. Now, though this latter may not exist without the mind, yet it will not thence follow that the former cannot.

PHILONOUS. What object do you mean? the object of the senses?

HYLAS. The same.

PHILONOUS. It is then immediately perceived?

HYLAS. Right.

PHILONOUS. Make me to understand the difference between what is immediately perceived and a sensation.

HYLAS. The sensation I take to be an act of the mind perceiving; besides which, there is something perceived; and this I call the *object*. For example, there is red and yellow on that tulip. But then the act of perceiving those colours is in me only, and not in the tulip.

PHILONOUS. What tulip do you speak of? Is it that which you see?

HYLAS. The same.

PHILONOUS. And what do you see beside colour, figure, and extension?

HYLAS. Nothing.

PHILONOUS. What you would say then is that the red and yellow are coexistent with the extension; is it not?

HYLAS. That is not all; I would say they have a real existence without the mind, in some unthinking substance.

PHILONOUS. That the colours are really in the tulip which I see is manifest. Neither can it be denied that this tulip may exist independent of your mind or mine; but, that any immediate object of the senses—that is, any idea, or combination of ideas—should exist in an unthinking substance, or exterior to *all* minds, is in itself an evident contradiction. Nor can I imagine how this follows from what you said just now, to wit, that the red and yellow were on the tulip *you saw*, since you do not pretend to *see* that unthinking substance.

HYLAS. You have an artful way, Philonous, of diverting our inquiry from the subject.

PHILONOUS. I see you have no mind to be pressed that way. To return then to your distinction between *sensation* and *object*; if I take you right, you distinguish in every perception two things, the one an action of the mind, the other not.

HYLAS. True.

PHILONOUS. And this action cannot exist in, or belong to, any unthinking thing; but whatever beside is implied in a perception may?

HYLAS. That is my meaning.

PHILONOUS. So that if there was a perception without any act of the mind, it were possible such a perception should exist in an unthinking substance?

HYLAS. I grant it. But it is impossible there should be such a perception.

PHILONOUS. When is the mind said to be active?

HYLAS. When it produces, puts an end to, or changes, anything.

PHILONOUS. Can the mind produce, discontinue, or change anything, but by an act of the will?

HYLAS. It cannot.

PHILONOUS. The mind therefore is to be accounted *active* in its perceptions so far forth as *volition* is included in them?

HYLAS. It is.

PHILONOUS. In plucking this flower I am active, because I do it by the motion of my hand, which was consequent upon my volition; so likewise in applying it to my nose. But is either of these smelling?

HYLAS. No.

PHILONOUS. I act too in drawing the air through my nose; because my breathing so rather than otherwise is the effect of my volition. But neither can this be called *smelling*: for, if it were, I should smell every time I breathed in that manner?

HYLAS. True.

PHILONOUS. Smelling then is somewhat consequent to all this?

HYLAS. It is.

PHILONOUS. But I do not find my will concerned any farther. Whatever more there is—as that I perceive such a particular smell, or any smell at all—this is independent of my will, and therein I am altogether passive. Do you find it otherwise with you, Hylas?

HYLAS. No, the very same.

PHILONOUS. Then, as to seeing, is it not in your power to open your eyes, or keep them shut; to turn them this or that way?

HYLAS. Without doubt.

PHILONOUS. But, doth it in like manner depend on *your* will that in looking on this flower you perceive *white* rather than any other colour? Or, directing your open eyes towards yonder part of the heaven, can you avoid seeing the sun? Or is light or darkness the effect of your volition?

HYLAS. No, certainly.

PHILONOUS. You are then in these respects altogether passive?

HYLAS. I am.

PHILONOUS. Tell me now, whether *seeing* consists in perceiving light and colours, or in opening and turning the eyes?

HYLAS. Without doubt, in the former.

PHILONOUS. Since therefore you are in the very perception of light and colours altogether passive, what is become of that action you were speaking of as an ingredient in every sensation? And, doth it not follow from your own concessions, that the perception of light and colours, including no action in it, may exist in an unperceiving substance? And is not this a plain contradiction?

HYLAS. I know not what to think of it.

PHILONOUS. Besides, since you distinguish the *active* and *passive* in every perception, you must do it in that of pain. But how is it possible that pain, be it as little active as you please, should exist in an unperceiving substance? In short, do but consider the point, and then confess ingenuously, whether light and colours, tastes, sounds, &c. are not all equally passions or sensations in the soul. You may indeed call them *external objects*, and give them in words what subsistence you please. But, examine your own thoughts, and then tell me whether it be not as I say?

HYLAS. I acknowledge, Philonous, that, upon a fair observation of what passes in my mind, I can discover nothing else but that I am a thinking being, affected with variety of sensations; neither is it possible to conceive how a sensation should exist in an unperceiving substance. But then, on the other hand, when I look on sensible things in a different view, considering them as so many modes and qualities, I find it necessary to suppose a *material substratum*, without which they cannot be conceived to exist.

PHILONOUS. *Material substratum* call you it? Pray, by which of your senses came you acquainted with that being?

HYLAS. It is not itself sensible; its modes and qualities only being perceived by the senses.

PHILONOUS. I presume then it was by reflexion and reason you obtained the idea of it?

HYLAS. I do not pretend to any proper positive *idea* of it. However, I conclude it exists, because qualities cannot be conceived to exist without a support.

PHILONOUS. It seems then you have only a relative *notion* of it, or that you conceive it not otherwise than by conceiving the relation it bears to sensible qualities?

HYLAS. Right.

PHILONOUS. Be pleased therefore to let me know wherein that relation consists.

HYLAS. Is it not sufficiently expressed in the term *substratum*, or *substance*?

PHILONOUS. If so, the word *substratum* should import that it is spread under the sensible qualities or accidents?

HYLAS. True.

PHILONOUS. And consequently under extension?

HYLAS. I own it.

PHILONOUS. It is therefore somewhat in its own nature entirely distinct from extension?

HYLAS. I tell you, extension is only a mode, and matter is something that supports modes.[24] And is it not evident the thing supported is different from the thing supporting?

PHILONOUS. So that something distinct from, and exclusive of, extension is supposed to be the *substratum* of extension?

HYLAS. Just so.

PHILONOUS. Answer me, Hylas. Can a thing be spread without extension? or is not the idea of extension necessarily included in *spreading*?

HYLAS. It is.

PHILONOUS. Whatsoever therefore you suppose spread under anything must have in itself an extension distinct from the extension of that thing under which it is spread?

HYLAS. It must.

PHILONOUS. Consequently, every corporeal substance, being the *substratum* of extension, must have in itself another extension, by which it is qualified to be a *substratum*: and so on to infinity. And I ask whether this be not absurd in itself, and

---

24 For Berkeley (as opposed to Locke) a mode is simply a quality, a kind of property.

repugnant to what you granted just now, to wit, that the *substratum* was something distinct from and exclusive of extension?

HYLAS. Aye but, Philonous, you take me wrong. I do not mean that matter is *spread* in a gross literal sense under extension. The word *substratum* is used only to express in general the same thing with *substance*.

PHILONOUS. Well then, let us examine the relation implied in the term *substance*. Is it not that it stands under accidents?

HYLAS. The very same.

PHILONOUS. But, that one thing may stand under or support another, must it not be extended?

HYLAS. It must.

PHILONOUS. Is not therefore this supposition liable to the same absurdity with the former?

HYLAS. You still take things in a strict literal sense. That is not fair, Philonous.

PHILONOUS. I am not for imposing any sense on your words: you are at liberty to explain them as you please. Only, I beseech you, make me understand something by them. You tell me matter supports or stands under accidents. How! is it as your legs support your body?

HYLAS. No; that is the literal sense.

PHILONOUS. Pray let me know any sense, literal or not literal, that you understand it in.—How long must I wait for an answer, Hylas?

HYLAS. I declare I know not what to say. I once thought I understood well enough what was meant by matter's supporting accidents. But now, the more I think on it the less can I comprehend it: in short I find that I know nothing of it.

PHILONOUS. It seems then you have no idea at all, neither relative nor positive, of matter; you know neither what it is in itself, nor what relation it bears to accidents?

HYLAS. I acknowledge it.

PHILONOUS. And yet you asserted that you could not conceive how qualities or accidents should really exist, without conceiving at the same time a material support of them?

HYLAS. I did.

PHILONOUS. That is to say, when you conceive the real existence of qualities, you do withal conceive something which you cannot conceive?

HYLAS. It was wrong, I own. But still I fear there is some fallacy or other. Pray what think you of this? It is just come into my head that the ground of all our mistake lies in your treating of each quality by itself. Now, I grant that each quality cannot singly subsist without the mind. Colour cannot without extension, neither can figure without some other sensible quality. But, as the several qualities united or blended together form entire sensible things, nothing hinders why such things may not be supposed to exist without the mind.

PHILONOUS. Either, Hylas, you are jesting, or have a very bad memory. Though indeed we went through all the qualities by name one after another, yet my arguments or rather your concessions, nowhere tended to prove that the secondary qualities did not subsist each alone by itself; but, that they were not *at all* without the mind. Indeed, in treating of figure and motion we concluded they could not exist without the mind, because it was impossible even in thought to separate them from all secondary qualities, so as to conceive them existing by themselves. But then this was not the only argument made use of upon that occasion. But (to pass by all that hath been hitherto said, and reckon it for nothing, if you will have it so) I am content to put the whole upon this issue. If you can conceive it possible for any mixture or combination of qualities, or any sensible object whatever, to exist without the mind, then I will grant it actually to be so.

HYLAS. If it comes to that the point will soon be decided. What more easy than to conceive a tree or house existing by itself, independent of, and unperceived by, any mind whatsoever? I do at this present time conceive them existing after that manner.

PHILONOUS. How say you, Hylas; can you see a thing which is at the same time unseen?

HYLAS. No, that were a contradiction.

PHILONOUS. Is it not as great a contradiction to talk of *conceiving* a thing which is *unconceived*?

HYLAS. It is.

PHILONOUS. The tree or house therefore which you think of is conceived by you?

HYLAS. How should it be otherwise?

PHILONOUS. And what is conceived is surely in the mind?

HYLAS. Without question, that which is conceived is in the mind.

PHILONOUS. How then came you to say, you conceived a house or tree existing independent and out of all minds whatsoever?

HYLAS. That was I own an oversight; but stay, let me consider what led me into it.—It is a pleasant[25] mistake enough. As I was thinking of a tree in a solitary place, where no one was present to see it, methought that was to conceive a tree as existing unperceived or unthought of; not considering that I myself conceived it all the while. But now I plainly see that all I can do is to frame ideas in my own mind. I may indeed conceive in my own thoughts the idea of a tree, or a house, or a mountain, but that is all. And this is far from proving that I can conceive them *existing out of the minds of all spirits*.

PHILONOUS. You acknowledge then that you cannot possibly conceive how any one corporeal sensible thing should exist otherwise than in the mind?

HYLAS. I do.

PHILONOUS. And yet you will earnestly contend for the truth of that which you cannot so much as conceive?

HYLAS. I profess I know not what to think; but still there are some scruples remain with me. Is it not certain I see things at a distance? Do we not perceive the stars and moon, for example, to be a great way off? Is not this, I say, manifest to the senses?

PHILONOUS. Do you not in a dream too perceive those or the like objects?

HYLAS. I do.

PHILONOUS. And have they not then the same appearance of being distant?

HYLAS. They have.

PHILONOUS. But you do not thence conclude the apparitions in a dream to be without the mind?

HYLAS. By no means.

PHILONOUS. You ought not therefore to conclude that sensible objects are without the mind, from their appearance, or manner wherein they are perceived.

HYLAS. I acknowledge it. But doth not my sense deceive me in those cases?

PHILONOUS. By no means. The idea or thing which you immediately perceive, neither sense nor reason informs you that it actually exists without the mind. By sense you only know that you are affected with

---

25 Amusing.

such certain sensations of light and colours, &c. And these you will not say are without the mind.

HYLAS. True: but, beside all that, do you not think the sight suggests something of *outness* or *distance*?

PHILONOUS. Upon approaching a distant object, do the visible size and figure change perpetually, or do they appear the same at all distances?

HYLAS. They are in a continual change.

PHILONOUS. Sight therefore doth not suggest, or any way inform you, that the visible object you immediately perceive exists at a distance, or will be perceived when you advance farther onward; there being a continued series of visible objects succeeding each other during the whole time of your approach.

HYLAS. It doth not; but still I know, upon seeing an object, what object I shall perceive after having passed over a certain distance: no matter whether it be exactly the same or no: there is still something of distance suggested in the case.

PHILONOUS. Good Hylas, do but reflect a little on the point, and then tell me whether there be any more in it than this: from the ideas you actually perceive by sight, you have by experience learned to collect what other ideas you will (according to the standing order of nature) be affected with, after such a certain succession of time and motion.

HYLAS. Upon the whole, I take it to be nothing else.

PHILONOUS. Now, is it not plain that if we suppose a man born blind was on a sudden made to see, he could at first have no experience of what may be suggested by sight?

HYLAS. It is.

PHILONOUS. He would not then, according to you, have any notion of distance annexed to the things he saw; but would take them for a new set of sensations, existing only in his mind?

HYLAS. It is undeniable.

PHILONOUS. But, to make it still more plain: is not *distance* a line turned endwise to the eye?

HYLAS. It is.

PHILONOUS. And can a line so situated be perceived by sight?

HYLAS. It cannot.

PHILONOUS. Doth it not therefore follow that distance is not properly and immediately perceived by sight?

HYLAS. It should seem so.

PHILONOUS. Again, is it your opinion that colours are at a distance?

HYLAS. It must be acknowledged they are only in the mind.

PHILONOUS. But do not colours appear to the eye as coexisting in the same place with extension and figures?

HYLAS. They do.

PHILONOUS. How can you then conclude from sight that figures exist without, when you acknowledge colours do not; the sensible appearance being the very same with regard to both?

HYLAS. I know not what to answer.

PHILONOUS. But, allowing that distance was truly and immediately perceived by the mind, yet it would not thence follow it existed out of the mind. For, whatever is immediately perceived is an idea: and can any idea exist out of the mind?

HYLAS. To suppose that were absurd: but, inform me, Philonous, can we perceive or know nothing beside our ideas?

PHILONOUS. As for the rational deducing of causes from effects, that is beside our inquiry. And, by the senses you can best tell whether you perceive anything which is not immediately perceived. And I ask you, whether the things immediately perceived are other than your own sensations or ideas? You have indeed more than once, in the course of this conversation, declared yourself on those points; but you seem, by this last question, to have departed from what you then thought.

HYLAS. To speak the truth, Philonous, I think there are two kinds of objects:—the one perceived immediately, which are likewise called *ideas*; the other are real things or external objects, perceived by the mediation of ideas, which are their images and representations. Now, I own ideas do not exist without the mind; but the latter sort of objects do. I am sorry I did not think of this distinction sooner; it would probably have cut short your discourse.

PHILONOUS. Are those external objects perceived by sense or by some other faculty?

HYLAS. They are perceived by sense.

PHILONOUS. How! is there any thing perceived by sense which is not immediately perceived?

HYLAS. Yes, Philonous, in some sort there is. For example, when I look on a picture or statue of Julius

Caesar, I may be said after a manner to perceive him (though not immediately) by my senses.

PHILONOUS. It seems then you will have our ideas, which alone are immediately perceived, to be pictures of external things: and that these also are perceived by sense, inasmuch as they have a conformity or resemblance to our ideas?

HYLAS. That is my meaning.

PHILONOUS. And, in the same way that Julius Caesar, in himself invisible, is nevertheless perceived by sight; real things, in themselves imperceptible, are perceived by sense.

HYLAS. In the very same.

PHILONOUS. Tell me, Hylas, when you behold the picture of Julius Caesar, do you see with your eyes any more than some colours and figures, with a certain symmetry and composition of the whole?

HYLAS. Nothing else.

PHILONOUS. And would not a man who had never known anything of Julius Caesar see as much?

HYLAS. He would.

PHILONOUS. Consequently he hath his sight, and the use of it, in as perfect a degree as you?

HYLAS. I agree with you.

PHILONOUS. Whence comes it then that your thoughts are directed to the Roman emperor, and his are not? This cannot proceed from the sensations or ideas of sense by you then perceived; since you acknowledge you have no advantage over him in that respect. It should seem therefore to proceed from reason and memory: should it not?

HYLAS. It should.

PHILONOUS. Consequently, it will not follow from that instance that anything is perceived by sense which is not immediately perceived. Though I grant we may, in one acceptation,[26] be said to perceive sensible things mediately by sense: that is, when, from a frequently perceived connexion, the immediate perception of ideas by one sense *suggests* to the mind others, perhaps belonging to another sense, which are wont to be connected with them. For instance, when I hear a coach drive along the streets, immediately I perceive only the sound; but, from the experience I have had that such a sound is connected with a coach, I am said to

---

26   In one way of using the word.

hear the coach. It is nevertheless evident that, in truth and strictness, nothing can be *heard* but *sound*; and the coach is not then properly perceived by sense, but suggested from experience. So likewise when we are said to see a red-hot bar of iron; the solidity and heat of the iron are not the objects of sight, but suggested to the imagination by the colour and figure which are properly perceived by that sense. In short, those things alone are actually and strictly perceived by any sense, which would have been perceived in case that same sense had then been first conferred on us. As for other things, it is plain they are only suggested to the mind by experience, grounded on former perceptions. But, to return to your comparison of Caesar's picture, it is plain, if you keep to that, you must hold the real things, or archetypes of our ideas, are not perceived by sense, but by some internal faculty of the soul, as reason or memory. I would therefore fain know what arguments you can draw from reason for the existence of what you call *real things* or *material objects*. Or, whether you remember to have seen them formerly as they are in themselves; or, if you have heard or read of any one that did.

HYLAS. I see, Philonous, you are disposed to raillery; but that will never convince me.

PHILONOUS. My aim is only to learn from you the way to come at the knowledge of *material beings*. Whatever we perceive is perceived immediately or mediately: by sense, or by reason and reflexion. But, as you have excluded sense, pray shew me what reason you have to believe their existence; or what *medium* you can possibly make use of to prove it, either to mine or your own understanding.

HYLAS. To deal ingenuously, Philonous, now I consider the point, I do not find I can give you any good reason for it. But, thus much seems pretty plain, that it is at least possible such things may really exist. And, as long as there is no absurdity in supposing them, I am resolved to believe as I did, till you bring good reasons to the contrary.

PHILONOUS. What! Is it come to this, that you only *believe* the existence of material objects, and that your belief is founded barely on the possibility of its being true? Then you will have me bring reasons against it: though another would think it reasonable the proof should lie on him who holds the affirmative. And, after all, this very point which you are now resolved to maintain, without any reason, is in effect what you have more than once during this discourse seen good reason to give up. But, to pass over all this; if I understand you rightly, you say our ideas do not exist without the mind, but that they are copies, images, or representations, of certain originals that do?

HYLAS. You take me right.

PHILONOUS. They are then like external things?

HYLAS. They are.

PHILONOUS. Have those things a stable and permanent nature, independent of our senses; or are they in a perpetual change, upon our producing any motions in our bodies—suspending, exerting, or altering, our faculties or organs of sense?

HYLAS. Real things, it is plain, have a fixed and real nature, which remains the same notwithstanding any change in our senses, or in the posture and motion of our bodies; which indeed may affect the ideas in our minds, but it were absurd to think they had the same effect on things existing without the mind.

PHILONOUS. How then is it possible that things perpetually fleeting and variable as our ideas should be copies or images of anything fixed and constant? Or, in other words, since all sensible qualities, as size, figure, colour, &c., that is, our ideas, are continually changing, upon every alteration in the distance, medium, or instruments of sensation; how can any determinate material objects be properly represented or painted forth by several distinct things, each of which is so different from and unlike the rest? Or, if you say it resembles some one only of our ideas, how shall we be able to distinguish the true copy from all the false ones?

HYLAS. I profess, Philonous, I am at a loss. I know not what to say to this.

PHILONOUS. But neither is this all. Which are material objects in themselves—perceptible or imperceptible?

HYLAS. Properly and immediately nothing can be perceived but ideas. All material things, therefore, are in themselves insensible, and to be perceived only by our ideas.

PHILONOUS. Ideas then are sensible, and their archetypes or originals insensible?

HYLAS. Right.

PHILONOUS. But how can that which is sensible be like that which is insensible? Can a real thing, in itself *invisible*, be like a *colour*; or a real thing, which is not *audible*, be like a *sound*? In a word, can anything be like a sensation or idea, but another sensation or idea?

HYLAS. I must own, I think not.

PHILONOUS. Is it possible there should be any doubt on the point? Do you not perfectly know your own ideas?

HYLAS. I know them perfectly; since what I do not perceive or know can be no part of my idea.

PHILONOUS. Consider, therefore, and examine them, and then tell me if there be anything in them which can exist without the mind: or if you can conceive anything like them existing without the mind.

HYLAS. Upon inquiry, I find it is impossible for me to conceive or understand how anything but an idea can be like an idea. And it is most evident that *no idea can exist without the mind.*

PHILONOUS. You are therefore, by your principles, forced to deny the *reality* of sensible things; since you made it to consist in an absolute existence exterior to the mind. That is to say, you are a downright sceptic. So I have gained my point, which was to shew your principles led to scepticism.

HYLAS. For the present I am, if not entirely convinced, at least silenced.

PHILONOUS. I would fain know what more you would require in order to a perfect conviction. Have you not had the liberty of explaining yourself all manner of ways? Were any little slips in discourse laid hold and insisted on? Or were you not allowed to retract or reinforce anything you had offered, as best served your purpose? Hath not everything you could say been heard and examined with all the fairness imaginable? In a word have you not in every point been convinced out of your own mouth? And, if you can at present discover any flaw in any of your former concessions, or think of any remaining subterfuge, any new distinction, colour, or comment whatsoever, why do you not produce it?

HYLAS. A little patience, Philonous. I am at present so amazed to see myself ensnared, and as it were imprisoned in the labyrinths you have drawn me into, that on the sudden it cannot be expected I should find my way out. You must give me time to look about me and recollect myself.

PHILONOUS. Hark; is not this the college bell?

HYLAS. It rings for prayers.

PHILONOUS. We will go in then, if you please, and meet here again tomorrow morning. In the meantime, you may employ your thoughts on this morning's discourse, and try if you can find any fallacy in it, or invent any new means to extricate yourself.

HYLAS. Agreed.

IMMANUEL KANT
Critique of Pure Reason

Who Was Immanuel Kant?

Immanuel Kant—by common consent the most important philosopher of the past 300 years, and arguably the most important of the past 2,300—was born in 1724 on the coast of the Baltic Sea, in Königsberg, a regionally important harbor city in East Prussia.[1] Kant spent his whole life living in this town, and never ventured outside its region. His family were devout members of an evangelical Protestant sect (rather like the Quakers or early Methodists) called the Pietists, and Pietism's strong emphasis on moral responsibility, hard work, and distrust of religious dogma had a deep effect on Kant's character. Kant's father was a craftsman (making harnesses and saddles for horses) and his family was fairly poor; Kant's mother, whom he loved deeply, died when he was 13.

Kant's life is notorious for its outward uneventfulness. He was educated at a strict Lutheran school in Königsberg, and after graduating from the University of Königsberg in 1746 (where he supported himself by some tutoring but also by his skill at billiards and card games) he served as a private tutor to various local families until he became a lecturer at the university in 1755. However his position—that of *Privatdozent*—carried no salary, and Kant was expected to support himself by the income from his lecturing; financial need caused Kant to lecture for thirty or more hours a week on a huge range of subjects (including mathematics, physics, geography, anthropology, ethics, and law). During this period Kant published several scientific works and his reputation as a scholar grew; he turned down opportunities for professorships in other towns (Erlangen and Jena), having his heart set on a professorship in Königsberg. Finally, at the age of 46, Kant became professor of logic and metaphysics at the University of Königsberg, a position he held until his retirement twenty-six years later in 1796. After a tragic period of senility he died in 1804, and was buried with pomp and circumstance in the "professors' vault" at the Königsberg cathedral.[2]

Kant's days were structured by a rigorous and unvarying routine—indeed, it is often said that the housewives of Königsberg were able to set their clocks by the regularity of his afternoon walk. He never married (though twice he nearly did), had very few close friends, and lived by all accounts an austere and outwardly unemotional life. He was something of a hypochondriac, hated noise, and disliked all mu-

---

1 Prussia is a historical region which included what is today northern Germany, Poland, and the western fringes of Russia. It became a kingdom in 1701, and then a dominant part of the newly unified Germany in 1871. Greatly reduced after World War I, the state of Prussia was formally abolished after World War II, and Königsberg—renamed Kaliningrad during the Soviet era, after one of Stalin's henchmen—now sits on the western rump of Russia (between Poland and Lithuania).

2 His body no longer remains there: in 1950 his sarcophagus was broken open by unknown vandals and his corpse was stolen and never recovered.

sic except for military marches. Nevertheless, anecdotes by those who knew him give the impression of a warm, impressive, rather noble human being, capable of great kindness and dignity and sparkling conversation. He did not shun society, and in fact his regular daily routine included an extended lunchtime gathering at which he and his guests—drawn from the cosmopolitan stratum of Königsberg society—would discuss politics, science, philosophy, and poetry.

Kant's philosophical life is often divided into three phases: his "pre-Critical" period, his "silent" period, and his "Critical" period. His pre-Critical period began in 1747 when he published his first work (*Thoughts on the True Estimation of Living Forces*) and ended in 1770 when he wrote his Inaugural Dissertation—*Concerning the Form and Principles of the Sensible and Intelligible World*—and became a professor. Between 1770 and 1780, Kant published almost nothing. In 1781, however, at the age of 57, Kant made his first major contribution to philosophy with his monumental *Critique of Pure Reason* (written, Kant said, over the course of a few months "as if in flight"). He spent the next twenty years in unrelenting intellectual labor, trying to develop and answer the new problems laid out in this masterwork. First, in order to clarify and simplify the system of the *Critique* for the educated public, Kant published the much shorter *Prolegomena to Any Future Metaphysics* in 1783. In 1785 came Kant's *Foundations of the Metaphysics of Morals*, and in 1788 he published what is now known as his "second Critique": the *Critique of Practical Reason*. His third and final Critique, the *Critique of Judgement*, was published in 1790—an amazing body of work produced in less than ten years.

By the time he died, Kant had already become known as a great philosopher, with a permanent place in history. Over his grave was inscribed a quote from the *Critique of Practical Reason*, which sums up the impulse for his philosophy: "Two things fill the

mind with ever new and increasing admiration and reverence, the more often and more steadily one reflects on them: the starry heavens above me and the moral law within me."

What Was Kant's Overall Philosophical Project?

Kant began his philosophical career as a follower of rationalism. Rationalism was an important seventeenth- and eighteenth-century intellectual movement begun by Descartes and developed by Leibniz and his follower Christian Wolff, which held that all knowledge was capable of being part of a single, complete "science": that is, all knowledge can be slotted into a total, unified system of *a priori*, and certainly true, claims capable of encompassing everything that exists in the world, whether we have experience of it or not. In other words, for the German rationalists of Kant's day, metaphysical philosophy—which then included theoretical science—was thought of as being very similar to pure mathematics. Rationalism was also, in Kantian terminology, "dogmatic" as opposed to "critical": that is, it sought to construct systems of knowledge without first attempting a careful examination of the scope and limits of possible knowledge. (This is why Kant's rationalist period is usually called his pre-Critical phase.)

In 1781, after ten years of hard thought, Kant rejected this rationalistic view of philosophy: he came to the view that metaphysics, as traditionally understood, is so far from being a rational science that it is not even a body of knowledge at all. Three major stimuli provoked Kant into being "awakened from his dogmatic slumber," as he put it. First, in about 1769, Kant came to the conclusion that he had discovered several "antinomies"—sets of contradictory propositions *each* of which can apparently be *rationally proven* to be true of reality (if we assume that our intellectual concepts apply to reality at all) and yet which can't both be true. For example, Kant argued that rational arguments are available to prove both that reality is finite but also that it is infinite, and that it is composed of indivisible atoms yet also infinitely divisible. Since both halves of these two pairs can't possibly be true at the same time, Kant argued that this casts serious doubt on the power of pure reason to draw metaphysical conclusions.

Second, Kant was worried about the conflict between free will and natural causality (this is a theme that appears throughout Kant's Critical works). He was convinced that genuine morality must be based on *freely* choosing—or "willing"—to do what is right. To be worthy of moral praise, in Kant's view, one must choose to do *X* rather than *Y*, not because some law of nature causes you to do so, but because your rational self is convinced that it is the right thing to do. Yet he also thought that the rational understanding of reality sought by the metaphysicians could only be founded on universally extending the laws we find in the scientific study of nature—and this includes universal causal determination, the principle that nothing (including choosing *X* over *Y*) happens without a cause. This, for Kant, produces an antinomy: some actions are free (i.e., *not* bound by the laws of nature) and yet everything that happens *is* determined by a law of nature.

Kant resolved this paradox by arguing that the scientific view of reality (including that pursued by the rationalists) must in principle be *incomplete*. Roughly, he held that although we can only rationally understand reality by thinking of it as causally deterministic and governed by scientific laws, our intellectual reason can never encompass *all* of reality. According to Kant, there must be a level of ultimate reality which is beyond the scope of pure reason, and which allows for the free activity of what Kant calls "practical reason" (which therefore holds open the possibility of genuine morality).

The third alarm bell to rouse Kant from his pre-Critical dogmatism was his reading of the Scottish philosopher David Hume (see Chapter 4). Hume was not a rationalist but instead represented the culmination of the other main seventeenth- and eighteenth-century stream of philosophical thought, usually called empiricism. Instead of thinking of

knowledge as a unified, systematic, *a priori* whole, as the rationalists did, empiricists like Locke and Hume saw knowledge as being a piecemeal accumulation of claims derived primarily, not from pure logic, but from *sensation*—from our experience of the world. Science, for Hume, is thus not *a priori* but *a posteriori*: for example, we cannot just *deduce* from first principles that heavy objects tend to fall to the ground, as the rationalists supposed we could; we can only learn this by observing it to happen in our experience. The trouble was that Hume appeared to Kant (and to many others) to have shown that experience is simply *inadequate* for establishing the kind of metaphysical principles that philosophers have traditionally defended: no amount of sense-experience could ever either prove or disprove that God exists, that substance is imperishable, that we have an immortal soul, or even that there exist mind-independent "physical" objects which interact with each other according to causal laws of nature. Not just what we now think of as "philosophy" but theoretical science itself seemed to be called into question by Hume's "skeptical" philosophy. Since Kant was quite sure that mathematics and the natural sciences were genuine bodies of knowledge, he needed to show how such knowledge was possible despite Hume's skepticism: that is, as well as combating the excessive claims of rationalism, he needed to show how empiricism went wrong in the other direction.

Prior to Kant, seventeenth- and eighteenth-century philosophers divided knowledge into exactly two camps: "truths of reason" (or "relations of ideas") on the one hand, and "truths of fact" (or "matters of fact") on the other. Rationalism was characterized by the doctrine that all final, complete knowledge was a truth of reason: that is, it was made up entirely of claims that could be proven *a priori* as being necessarily true, as a matter of logic, since it would be self-contradictory for them to be false. Empiricists, on the other hand, believed that all genuinely *informative* claims were truths of fact: if we wanted to find out about the world itself, rather than merely the logical relations between our own concepts, we had to rely upon the (*a posteriori*) data of sensory experience.

Kant, however, reshaped this distinction in a new framework which, he argued, cast a vital new light upon the nature of metaphysics. Instead of merely drawing a distinction between truths of reason and truths of fact, Kant replaced this with *two* separate distinctions: that between "*a priori*" and "*a posteriori*" propositions, and that between "analytic" and "synthetic" judgments. On this more complex scheme, the rationalists' truths of reason turn out to be "analytic *a priori*" knowledge, while empirical truths of fact are "synthetic *a posteriori*" propositions. But, Kant pointed out, this leaves open the possibility that there is at least a *third* type of knowledge: *synthetic a priori* judgments. These are judgments which we know *a priori* and thus do not need to learn from experience, but which nevertheless go beyond merely "analytic" claims about our own concepts. Kant's central claim in the *Critique of Pure Reason* is that he is the first philosopher in history to understand that the traditional claims of metaphysics—questions about God, the soul, free will, the underlying nature of space, time, and matter—consist entirely of synthetic *a priori* propositions. (He also argues that pure mathematics is synthetic *a priori* as well.)

Kant's question therefore becomes: *How is synthetic a priori knowledge possible?* After all, the source of this knowledge can be neither experience (since it is *a priori*) nor the logical relations of ideas (since it is synthetic), so where could this kind of knowledge possibly come from? Once we have discovered the conditions of synthetic *a priori* knowledge, we can ask what its limits are: in particular, we can ask whether the traditional claims of speculative metaphysics meet those conditions, and thus whether they can be known to be true.

In bald (and massively simplified) summary, Kant's answer to these questions in the *Critique of Pure Reason* is the following. Synthetic *a priori* knowledge is possible insofar as it is knowledge of the *conditions of our experience of the world* (or indeed, of any *possible* experience). For example, for Kant, our judgments about the fundamental nature of space and time are not claims about our experiences themselves, nor are they the results of logic: instead, the forms of space and time are the conditions under which we are capable of having experience *at all*—we *can* only undergo sensations (either perceived or imaginary) that are arranged in space, and spread out in time; anything

else is just impossible for us. So we can know *a priori*, but not analytically, that space and time must have a certain nature, since they are the forms of (the very possibility of) our experience.

Kant, famously, described this insight as constituting a kind of "Copernican revolution" in philosophy: just as Copernicus set cosmology on a totally new path by suggesting (in 1543) that the Earth orbits the Sun and not the other way around, so Kant wanted to breathe new life into philosophy by suggesting that, rather than assuming that "all our knowledge must conform to objects," we might instead "suppose that objects must conform to our knowledge." That is, rather than merely passively representing mind-independent objects in a "real" world, Kant held that the mind actively *constitutes* its objects—by *imposing* the categories of time, space, and causation onto our sensory experience, the subject actually *creates* the only kind of reality to which it has access. (This is why Kant's philosophy is often called "transcendental idealism." However, Kant is not a full-out idealist in the way that, say, Berkeley is. He does not claim that the *existence* of objects is mind-dependent— only God's mind is capable of this kind of creation, according to Kant. Instead, the *a priori properties* of objects are what we constitute, by the structures of our cognition.)

When we turn to speculative metaphysics, however, we try to go beyond experience and its conditions—we attempt to move beyond what Kant called the "phenomena" of experience, and to make judgments about the nature of a reality that lies behind our sensory experience, what Kant called the "noumenal" realm. And here pure reason reaches its limits. If we ask about the nature of "things in themselves," independently of our experience of them, or if we try to show whether a supra-sensible God really exists, then our faculty of reason is powerless to demonstrate that these synthetic *a priori* judgments are either true or false—these metaphysical questions are neither empirical, nor logical, nor about the basic categories of our experience, so there is simply no way to answer them. The questions are meaningful ones (human beings crave answers to them) but they are beyond the scope of our faculty of reason. In short, we can have knowledge only of things that can be objects of possible experience, and cannot know anything that transcends the phenomenal realm.

This result, according to Kant, finally lets philosophy cease its constant oscillation between dogmatism and skepticism. It sets out the area in which human cognition is capable of attaining lasting truth (theoretical science—the metaphysics of experience—and mathematics), and that in which reason leads to self-contradiction and illusion (speculative metaphysics). Importantly, for Kant, this Copernican revolution provides *morality* with all the metaphysical support it needs, by clearing an area for free will.

What Is the Structure of This Reading?

Kant begins by conceding to the empiricists that, as a matter of psychological fact, we acquire a lot of knowledge through our experience of the world. But, he claims, this does not by itself show that all our knowledge is really *empirical*, and in Section I he draws a distinction between "pure" and "empirical" knowledge in order to make this issue clearer. In the next section he lays out two criteria for distinguishing between pure and empirical knowledge and uses these criteria to argue that we do in fact have a quantity of important pure *a priori* knowledge. However, in Section III, Kant claims that a lot of what we think can be known *a priori* is actually mere fabrication: what is needed, therefore, is a way of accurately *telling the difference* between reliable and unreliable *a priori* judgments. The first step in doing this, according to Kant, is to draw a distinction between analytic and synthetic judgments. He proceeds to do this in Section IV. He then argues, in Section V, that all our interesting *a priori* knowledge—mathematics, the principles of natural science, metaphysics—is synthetic. The "general problem of pure reason," therefore (Section VI) is to develop an account of how synthetic *a priori* judgments are possible, which will in turn tell us when they are reliable and when they are not. According to Kant, we must replace dogmatic philosophy with *critical* and *transcendental* philosophy: i.e., we must undertake a critique of pure reason, as Kant explains in Section VII.

Some Useful Background Information

1. *A priori* is Latin for "what is earlier" and *a posteriori* means "what comes after." These terms were used as early as the fourteenth century to mark a distinction (which dates back to Aristotle) between two different directions of *reasoning*: in this usage, now out of date, an *a priori* argument reasons from a ground to its consequence, while to argue *a posteriori* is to argue backwards from a consequence to its ground. For example, Descartes's "Trademark" argument for the existence of God in the Third Meditation is *a posteriori* in this archaic sense since it starts from his idea of God and moves to the 'only' possible cause of that idea, which is God himself. By contrast, St. Anselm of Canterbury's ontological argument is *a priori* in the medieval sense since, while it also begins with the idea of God, it does not argue 'backwards' to the cause of the idea but 'forwards' to the idea's (alleged) logical consequence, which is the necessary existence of God.

The *modern* usage of *a priori* and *a posteriori*, however, was formulated in the late seventeenth and eighteenth century, primarily by Leibniz and Kant, and has now wholly replaced the older meanings. The selection from Kant reprinted here includes the classic statement of the distinction (though the new usage first appeared much earlier—see, for example, section eight of Leibniz's *Discourse on Metaphysics*, published in 1686). One thing to notice is that the distinction is no longer one between two different directions of reasoning but instead distinguishes primarily between two different types of *knowledge*: the standard example of *a priori* knowledge is the truths of mathematics, and of *a posteriori* knowledge, the results of the natural sciences. This distinction between kinds of knowledge then motivates a similar distinction between two kinds of proposition, two kinds of concept, and two kinds of justification.

Kant himself prefers to use the words "pure" and "empirical" for *a priori* and *a posteriori* knowledge themselves, and usually reserves the terms "*a priori*" and "*a posteriori*" to describe the sources of this knowledge—the way in which it is acquired.

2. At the end of the Introduction to the *Critique*, Kant says that there are "two stems of human knowledge": sensibility and understanding. This is an important assumption of Kant's, and is reflected throughout the reading given here (in, for example, Kant's distinction between intuitions and concepts). Furthermore, it structures the way in which Kant proceeds with his critique of pure reason after the introduction: he deals first with what he calls the Transcendental Aesthetic,[3] which has to do with the faculty of sensibility, and secondly with the Transcendental Analytic, which applies to the faculty of understanding. The faculty of sensibility, according to Kant, is our capacity to passively receive objects into our mental world; this is achieved primarily through sensation, but these sensations are possible only if the objects are *intuited*: that is, roughly, represented as concretely existing in space and time. The faculty of understanding, on the other hand, is our capacity to actively produce knowledge through the application of *concepts*. When concepts are compared with each other, we produce logical knowledge; when concepts (such as space, time, and causation) are combined with intuitions we get empirical knowledge. (However, when concepts that arise out of our knowledge of the empirical world are applied to a realm beyond experience we do not get *any* kind of knowledge, according to Kant: he calls these metaphysical concepts *ideas*, the three most important of which are God, freedom, and immortality.)

A Common Misconception

Some people, on reading Kant for the first time, are thrown off by the word "transcendental." For Kant,

transcendental knowledge is knowledge about the necessary conditions for the possibility of experience (for example, "every event has a cause" is a transcendental claim, according to Kant). Thus, transcendental knowledge is *not*, as would be easy to assume, knowledge of *things which are transcendent* (i.e., of things which lie beyond the empirical world, such as God and other spirits). Therefore Kant's "transcendental philosophy" has nothing to do with, say, Transcendental Meditation.

How Important and Influential Is This Passage?

Within just a few years of the publication of the *Critique of Pure Reason*, Kant was recognized by many of his intellectual contemporaries as one of the great philosophers of all time. The first *Critique* is a candidate for being the single most important philosophical book ever written, and can be thought of as decisively changing the path of Western philosophy. In particular, it did away with the assumption that knowledge is a fixed and stable thing which can be more or less passively received into the mind through either experience or reason, and replaced it with a picture that sees human beings as active *participants* in the construction of our representations of the world. That is, the mind is not a passive receptacle of data but is instead an active *filter* and *creator* of our reality. The implications of this view are still being explored by professional philosophers, such as Hilary Putnam and Richard Rorty, today.

The distinction between analytic and synthetic propositions which Kant formulates in the selection reprinted here, as well as being foundational to his new philosophical system, has also had a great impact on philosophy. From the end of the eighteenth century until the 1950s it was generally accepted as marking a fundamental and important difference between kinds of knowledge. Today, however, the distinction has been thrown into question by philosophers who doubt that we can really make good sense of one concept "containing" or being "synonymous" with another.

---

3   When Kant uses the word "aesthetic"—as in "the transcendental aesthetic"—he means generally "having to do with sense-perception" rather than merely "beautiful."

Suggestions for Critical Reflection

1. Kant's two distinctions—between *a priori* and *a posteriori* propositions, and between analytic and synthetic propositions—allow him to distinguish between *four* different types of knowledge. However, he only entertains the possibility of *three* of those classes of proposition: the analytic *a priori*, synthetic *a priori*, and synthetic *a posteriori*. What is it about the notion of *analytic a posteriori* knowledge which causes Kant to dismiss it as incoherent? Is Kant right about this?

2. There is another distinction between types of propositions which Kant was clearly aware of, and which is often listed along with the *a priori/a posteriori* and analytic/synthetic contrasts: this is the distinction between propositions which are *necessarily* true, and those which are only *contingently* true. (A proposition is necessarily true if it is true no matter what—if no change you could possibly make to the world would make it false. A proposition is contingent if it is possibly, but not necessarily, true.) How, if at all, might this necessary/contingent distinction complicate Kant's classification of knowledge? For example, could some synthetic *a posteriori* propositions be necessary and others be contingent?

3. How adequate is Kant's criterion for the distinction between analytic and synthetic propositions? If you try out this distinction on a number of examples, do you find you can easily tell which are analytic and which synthetic? (How about, for example, "nothing is red all over and green all over at the same time," "water is H_2O," "all tigers are mammals," "2 is less than 3," "contradictions are impossible," or "every event has a cause"?)

4. Kant argues that mathematical knowledge is synthetic rather than analytic. Do you think he is right, or do you think it is more plausible to say that mathematics deals entirely with the *analytic* relations between our mathematical *concepts*? If Kant is wrong about mathematics being synthetic, how much harm do you think this causes to his overall philosophical framework—for example, would he then be in danger of turning into just a German Hume?

5. Kant claims that some of the principles of natural science are synthetic *a priori*: that is, they are not learned from experience but are in some sense *prior* to experience. (As he hints at the beginning of the reading, Kant's view is that although all our knowledge *begins* with experience it does not all *arise* out of experience.) How plausible do you find this claim? How radical is it—what implications might it have for the way we think of the relationship between our minds and external reality?

6. Do you share Kant's skepticism about speculative metaphysics? If so, do you agree with his reasons for rejecting it? If not, where does Kant go wrong?

7. Are there really any such things as synthetic *a priori* propositions, or are all *a priori* propositions really analytic and all synthetic propositions really *a posteriori*?

Suggestions for Further Reading

Three translations into English of the *Critique of Pure Reason* are currently available: the old standard by Norman Kemp Smith (Macmillan, 1933), the relatively student-friendly version by Werner Pluhar (Hackett, 1997), and the new scholarly edition by Paul Guyer and Allen Wood (Cambridge University Press, 1998). The *Critique of Pure Reason* is notoriously difficult to read, partly because of its philosophical difficulty but also because of its relatively unattractive prose style and complex structure (the German poet Heinrich Heine accused it of having a "colorless, dry, packing-paper style" with a "stiff, abstract form"). Kant himself was aware of this problem, and his *Prolegomena to Any Future Metaphysics* was intended to be a shorter and more lively summary of the main themes of the *Critique*. Cambridge University Press published a good edition translated by Gary Hatfield in 1997; a well-used older translation is by Lewis White Beck, originally published in 1950 by Bobbs-Merrill.

Kant's Life and Thought, by Ernst Cassirer (translated by James Haden and published by Yale University Press in 1981) is a well-respected intellectual biography of Kant, while perhaps the best single, short introduction to the *Critique* itself is Sebastian Gardner's *Kant and the Critique of Pure Reason* (Routledge, 1999). A.C. Ewing's *Short Commentary on Kant's Critique of Pure Reason* (University of Chicago Press, 1938) is an older but still well-respected brief introduction to this work. Two detailed running commentaries on the *Critique* are by Norman Kemp Smith, *A Commentary to Kant's "Critique of Pure Reason"* (revised and enlarged second edition from Humanities Press, 1992) and H.J. Paton, *A Commentary on the First Half of the "Kritik der reinen Vernunft"* (Allen & Unwin, 1936).

Recent critical commentaries on the *Critique* can be divided into two camps depending, roughly, on whether their authors see Kant as primarily an epistemologist, analyzing the limits of our experience, or primarily a metaphysician, showing how the objects that we experience are *constituted* by the knower; that is, it depends on how seriously the authors take Kant's transcendental idealism. Prominent members of the former group are Peter Strawson, with his *The Bounds of Sense* (Methuen, 1966), and Paul Guyer in *Kant and the Claims of Knowledge* (Cambridge University Press, 1987). The idealists have been particularly active and influential in the past few years, and recent important books on Kant and his first Critique from this side include: Henry Allison, *Kant's Transcendental Idealism* (Yale University Press, 1983); Karl Ameriks, *Kant's Theory of Mind* (Oxford University Press, 1982); Robert Pippin, *Kant's Theory of Form* (Yale University Press, 1982); and Ralph Walker, *Kant* (Routledge, 1978).

A seminal modern article which attacks the viability of the distinction between analytic and synthetic propositions is W.V. Quine's "Two Dogmas of Empiricism," which can be found in *From a Logical Point of View* (Harvard University Press, 1953); H.P. Grice and P.F. Strawson replied to Quine in "In Defense of a Dogma," *Philosophical Review* 65 (1956).

There is an old but still useful anthology of essays about Kant's philosophy called *Kant: A Collection of Critical Essays*, edited by Robert Paul Wolff (Doubleday, 1967). Finally, Paul Guyer has edited a collection of articles on Kant designed to summarize the high points of his philosophy: *The Cambridge Companion to Kant* (Cambridge University Press, 1992).

Critique of Pure Reason

Introduction[4]

I. The Distinction between Pure and Empirical Knowledge

There can be no doubt that all our knowledge begins with experience. For how should our faculty[5] of knowledge be awakened into action did not objects affecting our senses partly of themselves produce representations, partly arouse the activity of our understanding to compare these representations, and, by combining or separating them, work up the raw material of the sensible impressions[6] into that knowledge of objects which is entitled experience? In the order of time, therefore, we have no knowledge antecedent to experience, and with experience all our knowledge begins.

But though all our knowledge begins with experience, it does not follow that it all arises out of experience. For it may well be that even our empirical knowledge is made up of what we receive through impressions and of what our own faculty of knowledge (sensible impressions serving merely as the occasion) supplies from itself. If our faculty of knowledge makes any such addition, it may be that we are not in a position to distinguish it from the raw material,

---

4   Kant's *Critique of Pure Reason,* as first published in German in 1781, is usually called the "A" edition. A significantly different second edition, the "B" edition, was published in 1787. The translation used here, of the Introduction to the "B" edition, was made in 1929 by Norman Kemp Smith (Basingstoke, Hants: Palgrave. Copyright © 1929; revised edition 1933). Reproduced with permission of Palgrave Macmillan.

5   A "faculty," in this sense, is an inherent mental power or capacity, such as the faculty of speech or the faculty of memory.

6   A "sensible impression" is an effect produced on the mind which is received by the faculty of sensory perception. Sensible impressions are, roughly, the data we receive from the world (such as, perhaps, colors, sounds, pains, and so on) out of which our conscious perceptual experience (say the experience of being bitten by a squirrel) is constructed.

until with long practice of attention we have become skilled in separating it.

This, then, is a question which at least calls for closer examination, and does not allow of any off-hand answer:—whether there is any knowledge that is thus independent of experience and even of all impressions of the senses. Such knowledge is entitled *a priori*, and distinguished from the *empirical*, which has its sources *a posteriori*, that is, in experience.

The expression '*a priori*' does not, however, indicate with sufficient precision the full meaning of our question. For it has been customary to say, even of much knowledge that is derived from empirical sources, that we have it or are capable of having it *a priori*, meaning thereby that we do not derive it immediately from experience, but from a universal rule—a rule which is itself, however, borrowed by us from experience. Thus we would say of a man who undermined the foundations of his house, that he might have known *a priori* that it would fall, that is, that he need not have waited for the experience of its actual falling. But still he could not know this completely *a priori*. For he had first to learn through experience that bodies are heavy, and therefore fall when their supports are withdrawn.

In what follows, therefore, we shall understand by *a priori* knowledge, not knowledge independent of this or that experience, but knowledge absolutely independent of all experience. Opposed to it is empirical knowledge, which is knowledge possible only *a posteriori*, that is, through experience. *A priori* modes of knowledge are entitled pure when there is no admixture of anything empirical. Thus, for instance, the proposition, 'every alteration has its cause', while an *a priori* proposition, is not a pure proposition, because alteration is a concept which can be derived only from experience.

II. We Are in Possession of Certain Modes of *a priori* Knowledge, and Even the Common Understanding Is Never Without Them

What we here require is a criterion by which to distinguish with certainty between pure and empirical knowledge. Experience teaches us that a thing is so and so, but not that it cannot be otherwise. First, then, if we have a proposition which in being thought is

thought as *necessary*, it is an *a priori* judgment; and if, besides, it is not derived from any proposition except one which also has the validity of a necessary judgment, it is an absolutely *a priori* judgment. Secondly, experience never confers on its judgments true or strict but only assumed and comparative *universality*, through induction.[7] We can properly only say, therefore, that so far as we have hitherto observed, there is no exception to this or that rule. If, then, a judgment is thought with strict universality, that is, in such manner that no exception is allowed as possible, it is not derived from experience, but is valid absolutely *a priori*. Empirical universality is only an arbitrary extension of a validity holding in most cases to one which holds in all, for instance, in the proposition, 'all bodies are heavy'. When, on the other hand, strict universality is essential to a judgment, this indicates a special source of knowledge, namely, a faculty of *a priori* knowledge. Necessity and strict universality are thus sure criteria of *a priori* knowledge, and are inseparable from one another. But since in the employment of these criteria the contingency of judgments is sometimes more easily shown than their empirical limitation, or, as sometimes also happens, their unlimited universality can be more convincingly proved than their necessity, it is advisable to use the two criteria separately, each by itself being infallible.

Now it is easy to show that there actually are in human knowledge judgments which are necessary and in the strictest sense universal, and which are therefore pure *a priori* judgments. If an example from the sciences be desired, we have only to look to any of the propositions of mathematics; if we seek an example from the understanding in its quite ordinary employment, the proposition, 'every alteration must have a cause', will serve our purpose. In the latter case, indeed, the very concept of a cause so manifestly contains the concept of a necessity of connection with an effect and of the strict universality of the rule, that

---

7 Induction is the inference of a general law from particular instances. For example, if you see that one chickadee is chirpy, and you see that the next chickadee is chirpy, and so on, eventually you might conclude that all chickadees are chirpy. See Chapter 3 for more discussion of induction.

the concept would be altogether lost if we attempted to derive it, as Hume has done,[8] from a repeated association of that which happens with that which precedes, and from a custom of connecting representations, a custom originating in this repeated association, and constituting therefore a merely subjective necessity. Even without appealing to such examples, it is possible to show that pure *a priori* principles are indispensable for the possibility of experience, and so to prove their existence *a priori*. For whence could experience derive its certainty, if all the rules, according to which it proceeds, were always themselves empirical, and therefore contingent? Such rules could hardly be regarded as first principles. At present, however, we may be content to have established the fact that our faculty of knowledge does have a pure employment, and to have shown what are the criteria of such an employment.

Such *a priori* origin is manifest in certain concepts, no less than in judgments. If we remove from our empirical concept of a body, one by one, every feature in it which is [merely] empirical, the colour, the hardness or softness, the weight, even the impenetrability, there still remains the space which the body (now entirely vanished) occupied, and this cannot be removed. Again, if we remove from our empirical concept of any object, corporeal or incorporeal, all properties which experience has taught us, we yet cannot take away that property through which the object is thought as substance or as inhering in a substance (although this concept of substance is more determinate than that of an object in general). Owing, therefore, to the necessity with which this concept of substance forces itself upon us, we have no option save to admit that it has its seat in our faculty of *a priori* knowledge.

---

8   Kant is referring to Hume's *An Enquiry Concerning Human Understanding*, which was published in 1748 and translated into German by 1755. (Hume's earlier book, the *Treatise of Human Nature*, was not translated into German until 1791, and Kant probably had no first-hand acquaintance with most of it.) See the Hume reading in Chapter 3 for more information on this philosopher and his views, and especially for some of his views on causation.

III. Philosophy Stands in Need of a Science Which Shall Determine the Possibility, the Principles, and the Extent of All *a priori* Knowledge

But what is still more extraordinary than all the preceding is this, that certain modes of knowledge leave the field of all possible experiences and have the appearance of extending the scope of our judgments beyond all limits of experience, and this by means of concepts to which no corresponding object can ever be given in experience.

It is precisely by means of the latter modes of knowledge, in a realm beyond the world of the senses, where experience can yield neither guidance nor correction, that our reason carries on those enquiries which owing to their importance we consider to be far more excellent, and in their purpose far more lofty, than all that the understanding can learn in the field of appearances. Indeed we prefer to run every risk of error rather than desist from such urgent enquiries, on the ground of their dubious character, or from disdain and indifference. These unavoidable problems set by pure reason itself are *God, freedom,* and *immortality*. The science which, with all its preparations, is in its final intention directed solely to their solution is metaphysics; and its procedure is at first dogmatic, that is, it confidently sets itself to this task without any previous examination of the capacity or incapacity of reason for so great an undertaking.

Now it does indeed seem natural that, as soon as we have left the ground of experience, we should, through careful enquiries, assure ourselves as to the foundations of any building that we propose to erect, not making use of any knowledge that we possess without first determining whence it has come, and not trusting to principles without knowing their origin. It is natural, that is to say, that the question should first be considered, how the understanding can arrive at all this knowledge *a priori*, and what extent, validity, and worth it may have. Nothing, indeed, could be more natural, if by the term 'natural' we signify what fittingly and reasonably ought to happen. But if we mean by 'natural' what ordinarily happens, then on the contrary nothing is more natural and more intelligible than the fact that this enquiry has been so long neglected. For one part of this knowledge, the mathematical, has long been of established reliability, and so gives rise to a favourable presumption as regards the other part,[9] which may yet be of quite different nature. Besides, once we are outside the circle of experience, we can be sure of not being *contradicted* by experience. The charm of extending our knowledge is so great that nothing short of encountering a direct contradiction can suffice to arrest us in our course; and this can be avoided, if we are careful in our fabrications—which none the less will still remain fabrications. Mathematics gives us a shining example of how far, independently of experience, we can progress in *a priori* knowledge. It does, indeed, occupy itself with objects and with knowledge solely in so far as they allow of being exhibited in intuition.[10] But this circumstance is easily overlooked, since the intuition, in being thought, can itself be given *a priori*, and is therefore hardly to be distinguished from a bare and pure concept. Misled by such a proof of the power of reason, the demand for the extension of knowledge recognises no limits. The light dove, cleaving the air in her free flight, and feeling its resistance, might imagine that its flight would be still easier in empty space. It was thus that Plato left the world of the senses, as setting too narrow limits to the understanding, and ventured out beyond it on the wings of the ideas, in the empty space of the pure understanding. He did not observe that with all his efforts he made no advance—meeting no resistance that might, as it were, serve as a support upon which he could take a stand, to which he could apply his powers, and so set his understanding in motion. It is, indeed, the common fate of human reason to complete its speculative

structures as speedily as may be, and only afterwards to enquire whether the foundations are reliable. All sorts of excuses will then be appealed to, in order to reassure us of their solidity, or rather indeed to enable us to dispense altogether with so late and so dangerous an enquiry. But what keeps us, during the actual building, free from all apprehension and suspicion, and flatters us with a seeming thoroughness, is this other circumstance, namely, that a great, perhaps the greatest, part of the business of our reason consists in analysis of the concepts which we already have of objects. This analysis supplies us with a considerable body of knowledge, which, while nothing but explanation or elucidation of what has already been thought in our concepts, though in a confused manner, is yet prized as being, at least as regards its form, new insight. But so far as the matter or content is concerned, there has been no extension of our previously possessed concepts, but only an analysis of them. Since this procedure yields real knowledge *a priori*, which progresses in an assured and useful fashion, reason is so far misled as surreptitiously to introduce, without itself being aware of so doing, assertions of an entirely different order, in which it attaches to given concepts others completely foreign to them, and moreover attaches them *a priori*. And yet it is not known how reason can be in position to do this. Such a question is never so much as thought of. I shall therefore at once proceed to deal with the difference between these two kinds of knowledge.

IV. The Distinction between Analytic and Synthetic Judgments

In all judgments in which the relation of a subject to the predicate[11] is thought (I take into consideration affirmative judgments only, the subsequent application to negative judgments being easily made), this

---

9   Metaphysics.

10   By "intuition" (*Anschauung*) Kant means the direct perception of an object. An intuition is a mental representation that is *particular* and *concrete*, rather like an image. The main contrast, for Kant, is with *concepts*, which he thinks of as abstract and general representations. For example, the concept of redness is an idea that can apply to many things at once (lots of different things can be red all at the same time); by contrast, an intuition of redness is a sensory impression of some particular instance of red—it is an apprehension of *this* redness.

---

11   A predicate is a describing-phrase, and the subject of a sentence is the thing being described. An affirmative judgment says that some predicate is true of (or "satisfied by") a subject, while a negative judgment says that a subject does not satisfy that predicate. For example, "this nectarine is ripe" is an affirmative judgment (where the nectarine is the subject and '____ is ripe' is the predicate); "this nectarine is not juicy" is a negative judgment.

relation is possible in two different ways. Either the predicate B belongs to the subject A, as something which is (covertly) contained in this concept A; or outside the concept A, although it does indeed stand in connection with it. In the one case I entitle the judgment analytic, in the other synthetic. Analytic judgments (affirmative) are therefore those in which the connection of the predicate with the subject is thought through identity;[12] those in which this connection is thought without identity should be entitled synthetic. The former, as adding nothing through the predicate to the concept of the subject, but merely breaking it up into those constituent concepts that have all along been thought in it, although confusedly, can also be entitled explicative. The latter, on the other hand, add to the concept of the subject a predicate which has not been in any wise thought in it, and which no analysis could possibly extract from it; and they may therefore be entitled ampliative. If I say, for instance, 'All bodies are extended', this is an analytic judgment. For I do not require to go beyond the concept which I connect with 'body' in order to find extension as bound up with it. To meet with this predicate, I have merely to analyse the concept, that is, to become conscious to myself of the manifold which I always think in that concept. The judgment is therefore analytic. But when I say, 'All bodies are heavy', the predicate is something quite different from anything that I think in the mere concept of body in general; and the addition of such a predicate therefore yields a synthetic judgment.

Judgments of experience, as such, are one and all synthetic. For it would be absurd to found an analytic judgment on experience. Since, in framing the judgment, I must not go outside my concept, there is no need to appeal to the testimony of experience in its support. That a body is extended is a proposition that holds *a priori* and is not empirical. For, before appealing to experience, I have already in the concept of body all the conditions required for my judgment. I have only to extract from it, in accordance with the principle of contradiction,[13] the required predicate, and in so doing can at the same time become conscious of the necessity of the judgment—and that is what experience could never have taught me. On the other hand, though I do not include in the concept of a body in general the predicate 'weight', none the less this concept indicates an object of experience through one of its parts, and I can add to that part other parts of this same experience, as in this way belonging together with the concept. From the start I can apprehend the concept of body analytically through the characters of extension, impenetrability, figure, etc., all of which are thought in the concept. Now, however, looking back on the experience from which I have derived this concept of body, and finding weight to be invariably connected with the above characters, I attach it as a predicate to the concept; and in doing so I attach it synthetically, and am therefore extending my knowledge. The possibility of the synthesis of the predicate 'weight' with the concept of 'body' thus rests upon experience. While the one concept is not contained in the other, they yet belong to one another, though only contingently, as parts of a whole, namely, of an experience which is itself a synthetic combination of intuitions.

But in *a priori* synthetic judgments this help is entirely lacking. [I do not here have the advantage of looking around in the field of experience.] Upon what, then, am I to rely, when I seek to go beyond the concept A, and to know that another concept B is connected with it? Through what is the synthesis made possible? Let us take the proposition, 'Everything which happens has its cause'. In the concept

---

12 By "identity" here Kant means self-identity: for example, to say that rapper Eminem *is identical with* Slim Shady (or that Garth Brooks is identical with Chris Gaines, or even that Cicero is identical with Tully) is to say that they are not two different people but are one and the same person being named in different ways. Another example, more relevant to Kant's concerns in this passage, is that being a vixen *is identical with* being a female fox: these are just two different ways of describing one and the same property.

13 The principle of contradiction states that a proposition and its negation cannot both be true. For example it can't *both* be true that it is now Sunday *and* true that it is not now Sunday; if it is true that the spiny anteater lays eggs then it is not true that it is false that the spiny anteater lays eggs. As Aristotle once pithily put it, "nothing can both be and not be at the same time in the same respect."

of 'something which happens', I do indeed think an existence which is preceded by a time, etc., and from this concept analytic judgments may be obtained. But the concept of a 'cause' lies entirely outside the other concept, and signifies something different from 'that which happens', and is not therefore in any way contained in this latter representation. How come I then to predicate of that which happens something quite different, and to apprehend that the concept of cause, though not contained in it, yet belongs, and indeed necessarily belongs to it? What is here the unknown = X which gives support to the understanding when it believes that it can discover outside the concept A a predicate B foreign to this concept, which it yet at the same time considers to be connected with it? It cannot be experience, because the suggested principle has connected the second representation with the first, not only with greater universality, but also with the character of necessity, and therefore completely *a priori* and on the basis of mere concepts. Upon such synthetic, that is, ampliative principles, all our *a priori* speculative knowledge must ultimately rest; analytic judgments are very important, and indeed necessary, but only for obtaining that clearness in the concepts which is requisite for such a sure and wide synthesis as will lead to a genuinely new addition to all previous knowledge.

V. In All Theoretical Sciences of Reason Synthetic *a priori* Judgments Are Contained as Principles

1. *All mathematical judgments, without exception, are synthetic.* This fact, though incontestably certain and in its consequences very important, has hitherto escaped the notice of those who are engaged in the analysis of human reason, and is, indeed, directly opposed to all their conjectures. For as it was found that all mathematical inferences proceed in accordance with the principle of contradiction[14] (which the nature of all apodeictic[15] certainty requires), it was supposed

that the fundamental propositions of the science can themselves be known to be true through that principle. This is an erroneous view. For though a synthetic proposition can indeed be discerned in accordance with the principle of contradiction, this can only be if another synthetic proposition is presupposed, and if it can then be apprehended as following from this other proposition; it can never be so discerned in and by itself. First of all, it has to be noted that mathematical propositions, strictly so called, are always judgments *a priori*, not empirical; because they carry with them necessity, which cannot be derived from experience. If this be demurred to, I am willing to limit my statement to *pure* mathematics, the very concept of which implies that it does not contain empirical, but only pure *a priori* knowledge.

We might, indeed, at first suppose that the proposition $7 + 5 = 12$ is a merely analytic proposition, and follows by the principle of contradiction from the concept of a sum of 7 and 5. But if we look more closely we find that the concept of the sum of 7 and 5 contains nothing save the union of the two numbers into one, and in this no thought is being taken as to what that single number may be which combines both. The concept of 12 is by no means already thought in merely thinking this union of 7 and 5; and I may analyse my concept of such a possible sum as long as I please, still I shall never find the 12 in it. We have to go outside these concepts, and call in the aid of the intuition which corresponds to one of them, our five fingers, for instance, or, as Segner does in his *Arithmetic*,[16] five points, adding to the concept of 7, unit by unit, the five given in intuition. For starting with the number 7, and for the concept of 5 calling in the aid of the fingers of my hand as intuition, I now add one by one to the number 7 the units which I previously took together to form the number 5, and with the aid of that figure [the hand] see the number

---

14 By showing that they must be true, since if they were false this would lead to a contradiction.

15 For Kant, an apodeictic proposition states what *must* be the case, i.e., what is necessary. (By contrast, in Kant's terminology, an "assertoric" proposition says what *is* the case—i.e., what is actual—and a "problematic" proposition asserts what *can* be the case, i.e., what is possible.)

16 The book Kant refers to is *Anfangsgründe der Arithmetik*, translated from the original Latin, the second edition of which was published in 1773.

12 come into being. That 5 should be added to 7, I have indeed already thought in the concept of a sum = 7 + 5, but not that this sum is equivalent to the number 12. Arithmetical propositions are therefore always synthetic. This is still more evident if we take larger numbers. For it is then obvious that, however we might turn and twist our concepts, we could never, by the mere analysis of them, and without the aid of intuition, discover what [the number is that] is the sum.

Just as little is any fundamental proposition of pure geometry analytic. That the straight line between two points is the shortest, is a synthetic proposition. For my concept of *straight* contains nothing of quantity, but only of quality. The concept of the shortest is wholly an addition, and cannot be derived, through any process of analysis, from the concept of the straight line. Intuition, therefore, must here be called in; only by its aid is the synthesis possible. What here causes us commonly to believe that the predicate of such apodeictic judgments is already contained in our concept, and that the judgment is therefore analytic, is merely the ambiguous character of the terms used. We are required to join in thought a certain predicate to a given concept, and this necessity is inherent in the concepts themselves. But the question is not what we *ought* to join in thought to the given concept, but what we *actually* think in it, even if only obscurely; and it is then manifest that, while the predicate is indeed attached necessarily to the concept, it is so in virtue of an intuition which must be added to the concept, not as thought in the concept itself.

Some few fundamental propositions, presupposed by the geometrician, are, indeed, really analytic, and rest on the principle of contradiction. But, as identical propositions,[17] they serve only as links in the chain of method and not as principles; for instance, $a = a$; the whole is equal to itself; or $(a + b) > a$, that is, the whole is greater than its part. And even these propositions, though they are valid according to pure concepts, are only admitted in mathematics because they can be exhibited in intuition.

2. *Natural science (physics) contains* a priori *synthetic judgments as principles.* I need cite only

---

17   As assertions of identities (or non-identities).

two such judgments: that in all changes of the material world the quantity of matter remains unchanged; and that in all communication of motion, action and reaction must always be equal. Both propositions, it is evident, are not only necessary, and therefore in their origin *a priori*, but also synthetic. For in the concept of matter I do not think its permanence, but only its presence in the space which it occupies. I go outside and beyond the concept of matter, joining to it *a priori* in thought something which I have not thought *in* it. The proposition is not, therefore, analytic, but synthetic, and yet is thought *a priori*; and so likewise are the other propositions of the pure part of natural science.

3. *Metaphysics*, even if we look upon it as having hitherto failed in all its endeavours, is yet, owing to the nature of human reason, a quite indispensable science, and *ought to contain* a priori *synthetic knowledge*. For its business is not merely to analyse concepts which we make for ourselves *a priori* of things, and thereby to clarify them analytically, but to extend our *a priori* knowledge. And for this purpose we must employ principles which add to the given concept something that was not contained in it, and through *a priori* synthetic judgments venture out so far that experience is quite unable to follow us, as, for instance, in the proposition, that the world must have a first beginning, and such like. Thus metaphysics consists, at least *in intention*, entirely of *a priori* synthetic propositions.

VI. The General Problem of Pure Reason

Much is already gained if we can bring a number of investigations under the formula of a single problem. For we not only lighten our own task, by defining it accurately, but make it easier for others, who would test our results, to judge whether or not we have succeeded in what we set out to do. Now the proper problem of pure reason is contained in the question: How are *a priori* synthetic judgments possible?

That metaphysics has hitherto remained in so vacillating a state of uncertainty and contradiction, is entirely due to the fact that this problem, and perhaps even the distinction between analytic and synthetic judgments, has never previously been considered. Upon the solution of this problem, or upon a sufficient proof that the possibility which it desires to have explained does in fact not exist at all, depends the success or failure of metaphysics. Among philosophers, David Hume came nearest to envisaging this problem, but still was very far from conceiving it with sufficient definiteness and universality. He occupied himself exclusively with the synthetic proposition regarding the connection of an effect with its cause (*principium causalitatis*[18]), and he believed himself to have shown that such an *a priori* proposition is entirely impossible. If we accept his conclusions, then all that we call metaphysics is a mere delusion whereby we fancy ourselves to have rational insight into what, in actual fact, is borrowed solely from experience, and under the influence of custom has taken the illusory semblance of necessity. If he had envisaged our problem in all its universality, he would never have been guilty of this statement, so destructive of all pure philosophy. For he would then have recognised that, according to his own argument, pure mathematics, as certainly containing *a priori* synthetic propositions, would also not be possible; and from such an assertion his good sense would have saved him.

In the solution of the above problem, we are at the same time deciding as to the possibility of the employment of pure reason in establishing and developing all those sciences which contain a theoretical *a priori* knowledge of objects, and have therefore to answer the questions:

> How is pure mathematics possible?
> How is pure science of nature possible?

Since these sciences actually exist, it is quite proper to ask *how* they are possible; for that they must be possible is proved by the fact that they exist.[19] But the

poor progress which has hitherto been made in metaphysics, and the fact that no system yet propounded can, in view of the essential purpose of metaphysics, be said really to exist, leaves everyone sufficient ground for doubting as to its possibility.

Yet, in a certain sense, this *kind of knowledge* is to be looked upon as given; that is to say, metaphysics actually exists, if not as a science, yet still as natural disposition (*metaphysica naturalis*[20]). For human reason, without being moved merely by the idle desire for extent and variety of knowledge, proceeds impetuously, driven on by an inward need, to questions such as cannot be answered by any empirical employment of reason, or by principles thence derived. Thus in all men, as soon as their reason has become ripe for speculation, there has always existed and will always continue to exist some kind of metaphysics. And so we have the question:

> How is metaphysics, as natural disposition, possible?

that is, how from the nature of universal human reason do those questions arise which pure reason propounds to itself, and which it is impelled by its own need to answer as best it can?

But since all attempts which have hitherto been made to answer these natural questions—for instance, whether the world has a beginning or is from eternity—have always met with unavoidable contradictions, we cannot rest satisfied with the mere natural disposition to metaphysics, that is, with the pure faculty of reason itself, from which, indeed, some sort of metaphysics (be it what it may) always arises. It must be possible for reason to attain to certainty whether we know or do not know the objects of metaphysics, that is, to come to a decision either in regard to the objects of its enquiries or in regard to the capacity or incapacity of reason to pass any judgment upon them, so that we may either with confidence extend our pure reason or set to it sure and determinate limits. This last question, which arises out of the previous general problem, may, rightly stated, take the form:

> How is metaphysics, as science, possible?

18 "The origin of causation."

19 [Author's note] Many may still have doubts as regards pure natural science. We have only, however, to consider the various propositions that are to be found at the beginning of (empirical) physics, properly so called, those, for instance, relating to the permanence in the quantity of matter, to inertia, to the equality of action and reaction, etc., in order to be soon convinced that they constitute a *physica pura*, or *rationalis*, which well deserves, as an independent science, to be separately dealt with in its whole extent, be that narrow or

wide.

20 "Natural metaphysics."

Thus the critique of reason, in the end, necessarily leads to scientific knowledge; while its dogmatic employment, on the other hand, lands us in dogmatic assertions to which other assertions, equally specious,[21] can always be opposed—that is, in *scepticism*.

This science cannot be of any very formidable prolixity,[22] since it has to deal not with the objects of reason, the variety of which is inexhaustible, but only with itself and the problems which arise entirely from within itself, and which are imposed upon it by its own nature, not by the nature of things which are distinct from it. When once reason has learnt completely to understand its own power in respect of objects which can be presented to it in experience, it should easily be able to determine, with completeness and certainty, the extent and the limits of its attempted employment beyond the bounds of all experience.

We may, then, and indeed we must, regard as abortive all attempts, hitherto made, to establish a metaphysic *dogmatically*. For the analytic part in any such attempted system, namely, the mere analysis of the concepts that inhere in our reason *a priori*, is by no means the aim of, but only a preparation for, metaphysics proper, that is, the extension of its *a priori* synthetic knowledge. For such a purpose, the analysis of concepts is useless, since it merely shows what is contained in these concepts, not how we arrive at them *a priori*. A solution of this latter problem is required, that we may be able to determine the valid employment of such concepts in regard to the objects of all knowledge in general. Nor is much self-denial needed to give up these claims, seeing that the undeniable, and in the dogmatic procedure of reason also unavoidable, contradictions of reason with itself have long since undermined the authority of every metaphysical system yet propounded. Greater firmness will be required if we are not to be deterred by inward difficulties and outward opposition from endeavouring, through application of a method entirely different from any hitherto employed, at last to bring to a prosperous and fruitful growth a science indispensable to human reason—a science whose every branch may be cut away but whose root cannot be destroyed.

VII. The Idea and Division of a Special Science, under the Title "Critique of Pure Reason"

In view of all these considerations, we arrive at the idea of a special science which can be entitled the Critique of Pure Reason. For reason is the faculty which supplies the principles of *a priori* knowledge. Pure reason is, therefore, that which contains the principles whereby we know anything absolutely *a priori*. An organon[23] of pure reason would be the sum-total of those principles according to which all modes of pure *a priori* knowledge can be acquired and actually brought into being. The exhaustive application of such an organon would give rise to a system of pure reason. But as this would be asking rather much, and as it is still doubtful whether, and in what cases, any extension of our knowledge be here possible, we can regard a science of the mere examination of pure reason, of its sources and limits, as the *propaedeutic*[24] to the system of pure reason. As such, it should be called a critique, not a doctrine, of pure reason. Its utility, in speculation, ought properly to be only negative, not to extend, but only to clarify our reason, and keep it free from errors—which is already a very great gain. I entitle *transcendental* all knowledge which is occupied not so much with objects as with the mode of our knowledge of objects in so far as this mode of knowledge is to be possible *a priori*. A system of such concepts might be entitled transcendental philosophy. But that is still, at this stage, too large an undertaking. For since such a science must contain, with completeness, both kinds of *a priori* knowledge, the analytic no less than the synthetic, it is, so far as our present purpose is concerned, much too comprehensive. We have to carry the analysis so far only as is indispensably necessary in order to comprehend, in their whole extent, the principles of *a priori* synthesis, with which alone we are called upon to deal. It is upon this enquiry, which should be entitled not a doctrine,

---

21 Superficially plausible, but actually false.
22 Tedious length.

23 An instrument of thought, especially a system of logic or a method for reasoning. (Aristotle's logical writings were historically grouped together as the *Organon*, and Francis Bacon's influential 1620 book on the scientific method was called the *Novum* (new) *Organon*.)
24 Preliminary or introductory instruction (from the Greek, meaning "to teach beforehand").

but only a transcendental critique, that we are now engaged. Its purpose is not to extend knowledge, but only to correct it, and to supply a touchstone of the value, or lack of value, of all *a priori* knowledge. Such a critique is therefore a preparation, so far as may be possible, for an organon; and should this turn out not to be possible, then at least for a canon,[25] according to which, in due course, the complete system of the philosophy of pure reason—be it in extension or merely in limitation of its knowledge—may be carried into execution, analytically as well as synthetically. That such a system is possible, and indeed that it may not be of such great extent as to cut us off from the hope of entirely completing it, may already be gathered from the fact that what here constitutes our subject-matter is not the nature of things, which is inexhaustible, but the understanding which passes judgment upon the nature of things; and this understanding, again, only in respect of its *a priori* knowledge. These *a priori* possessions of the understanding, since they have not to be sought for without, cannot remain hidden from us, and in all probability are sufficiently small in extent to allow of our apprehending them in their completeness, of judging as to their value or lack of value, and so of rightly appraising them. Still less may the reader here expect a critique of books and systems of pure reason; we are concerned only with the critique of the faculty of pure reason itself. Only in so far as we build upon this foundation do we have a reliable touchstone for estimating the philosophical value of old and new works in this field. Otherwise the unqualified historian or critic is passing judgments upon the groundless assertions of others by means of his own, which are equally groundless.

Transcendental philosophy is only the idea of a science, for which the critique of pure reason has to lay down the complete architectonic[26] plan. That is to say, it has to guarantee, as following from principles, the completeness and certainty of the structure in all its parts. It is the system of all principles of pure reason. And if this critique is not itself to be entitled a transcendental philosophy, it is solely because, to

be a complete system, it would also have to contain an exhaustive analysis of the whole of *a priori* human knowledge. Our critique must, indeed, supply a complete enumeration of all the fundamental concepts that go to constitute such pure knowledge. But it is not required to give an exhaustive analysis of these concepts, nor a complete review of those that can be derived from them. Such a demand would be unreasonable, partly because this analysis would not be appropriate to our main purpose, inasmuch as there is no such uncertainty in regard to analysis as we encounter in the case of synthesis, for the sake of which alone our whole critique is undertaken; and partly because it would be inconsistent with the unity of our plan to assume responsibility for the completeness of such an analysis and derivation, when in view of our purpose we can be excused from doing so. The analysis of these *a priori* concepts, which later we shall have to enumerate, and the derivation of other concepts from them, can easily, however, be made complete when once they have been established as exhausting the principles of synthesis, and if in this essential respect nothing be lacking in them.

The critique of pure reason therefore will contain all that is essential in transcendental philosophy. While it is the complete idea of transcendental philosophy, it is not equivalent to that latter science; for it carries the analysis only so far as is requisite for the complete examination of knowledge which is *a priori* and synthetic.

What has chiefly to be kept in view in the division of such a science, is that no concepts be allowed to enter which contain in themselves anything empirical, or, in other words, that it consist in knowledge wholly *a priori*. Accordingly, although the highest principles and fundamental concepts of morality are *a priori* knowledge, they have no place in transcendental philosophy, because, although they do not lay at the foundation of their precepts the concepts of pleasure and pain, of the desires and inclinations, etc., all of which are of empirical origin, yet in the construction of a system of pure morality these empirical concepts must necessarily be brought into the concept of duty, as representing either a hindrance, which we have to overcome, or an allurement, which must not be made into a

---

25   A general principle or criterion.

26   Having to do with the scientific systematization of knowledge.

motive. Transcendental philosophy is therefore a philosophy of pure and merely speculative reason. All that is practical, so far as it contains motives, relates to feelings, and these belong to the empirical sources of knowledge.

If we are to make a systematic division of the science which we are engaged in presenting, it must have first a *doctrine of the elements*,[27] and secondly, a *doctrine of the method of pure reason*. Each of these chief divisions will have its subdivisions, but the grounds of these we are not yet in a position to explain. By way of introduction or anticipation we need only say that

there are two stems of human knowledge, namely, *sensibility*[28] and *understanding*, which perhaps spring from a common, but to us unknown, root. Through the former, objects are given to us; through the latter, they are thought. Now in so far as sensibility may be found to contain *a priori* representations constituting the condition under which objects are given to us, it will belong to transcendental philosophy. And since the conditions under which alone the objects of human knowledge are given must precede those under which they are thought, the transcendental doctrine of sensibility will constitute the first part of the science of the elements.

---

27   The "elements" are the constituents of cognition, which for Kant are intuitions and concepts.

28   The power of sensation.

BERTRAND RUSSELL
The Problems of Philosophy

I heard the beat of centaur's hoofs over the hard turf
As his dry and passionate talk devoured the afternoon.
"He is a charming man"—"But after all what did he
*   mean?" —*
"His pointed ears.... He must be unbalanced," —
"There was something he said that I might have
*   challenged."*
      (from a poem by T.S. Eliot about
      Bertrand Russell called "Mr. Apollinax")

Who Was Bertrand Russell?

Bertrand Arthur William, 3rd Earl Russell was, with G.E. Moore, the founder of modern analytic philosophy in Britain, and one of the most important logicians of the twentieth century. He had a long and checkered career as an academic, a pacifist, a political activist and social reformer, an educational theorist, and a moral "free-thinker."

Born in 1872, Russell was orphaned at the age of 4 and brought up by his aristocratic grandmother, who

educated him at home with the help of tutors. Russell's interest in philosophical problems began early. His older brother introduced him at the age of 11 to Euclidian geometry (which shows how a large swathe of mathematics can be derived from a few apparently self-evident assumptions, or "axioms"). "This was one of the great events of my life, as dazzling as first love," Russell later wrote; however, when he demanded of his brother to be told how the axioms themselves were justified, he was informed that the axioms must simply be accepted as given. This Russell found a deeply unsatisfying answer.

In 1890 Russell went to study mathematics at Trinity College, Cambridge, but three years later he switched to philosophy. After a rather unhappy and lonely childhood, Russell wrote that "Cambridge opened up for me a new world of infinite delight." In 1895 he was elected to a six-year Fellowship at Trinity on the basis of a dissertation on the foundations of geometry. The intellectual turning-point in Russell's life occurred five years later, at the International Congress of Philosophy in Paris, where Russell met the Italian logician and mathematician Giuseppe Peano, who appeared to have done for arithmetic what Euclid had done for geometry: that is, shown how it could be derived from a small number of axioms. Russell set out to master Peano's notation and results and to use them for the general project of setting mathematics on solid foundations:

> The time was one of intellectual intoxication. My sensations resembled those one has after climbing a mountain in a mist, when, on reaching the summit, the mist suddenly clears, and the country becomes visible for forty miles in every direction…. Suddenly, in the space of a few weeks, I discovered what appeared to be definitive answers to the problems which had baffled me for years. (Russell's *Autobiography*)

This period of intellectual joy for Russell was quickly followed by one of emotional unhappiness as he "suddenly" realized he no longer loved his first wife Alys Pearsall Smith, whom he had married in 1894, and also began to see the cracks emerging in his meta-mathematical theory, showing that his answers might be less definitive than he had hoped.

In 1907 he stood unsuccessfully for Parliament as the candidate for the National Union of Women's Suffrage Societies, and in 1910 he tried to be adopted as the Liberal candidate for a London borough. He was rejected, however, because of his public atheism; Russell later called this rejection a lucky escape since it enabled him to accept a Lectureship at Trinity College, Cambridge, which he was offered that year. Between 1910 and 1916 he was a university lecturer at Cambridge, but was dismissed because of his pacifist opposition to World War I. In 1918 he was imprisoned for six months for having written that the US Army used intimidation tactics with strikers.

In 1921 Russell married again—to Dora Black—and had his first child. Since he had already given away most of his inherited money and lost his job at Cambridge, he now needed to find some way of making an income. As a result, most of his writings from this point until the mid-1930s were intended for a popular audience, and he went on several well-paid lecture tours of America. Many of his writings were considered scandalous for their liberal attitude towards sex and marriage—the best known of them are *Marriage and Morals* (1929) and *The Conquest of Happiness* (1930)—but they made him a lot of money. On the other hand, the progressive Beacon Hill School he founded with his wife in 1927, which aimed to provide a less authoritarian education than was then generally available, suffered large losses.

In 1936, after another divorce, Russell married his third wife, Patricia ('Peter') Spence, and two years later went to the United States to take up one-year appointments at the University of Chicago and then the University of California at Los Angeles. In 1939 he was offered a professorship at the College of the City of New York; however, there was a public outcry against the appointment on the grounds that Russell's lifestyle was immoral and his writings "lecherous, libidinous, lustful, venerous, erotomaniac, aphrodisiac, irreverent, narrow-minded, untruthful, and bereft of moral fibre." A lawsuit by some outraged taxpayers against the Municipality of New York led to Russell's appointment being revoked. This caused Russell financial problems but he was rescued by a lecturing job at the Barnes Foundation; it was here that he began his monumental book *A History of Western Philosophy*, which was published in 1945 and won him the 1950 Nobel prize for literature.

In 1944 Russell returned to Trinity College, Cambridge, as a Fellow, and in 1952, after the break-up of his third marriage, wed Edith Finch. In 1958 he became president of the Campaign for Nuclear Disarmament and wrote two books on the dangers of nuclear war: *Common Sense and Nuclear Warfare* (1959) and *Has Man a Future?* (1961). He was jailed for a week in 1961, even though he was then 89 years old, for inciting civil disobedience. He was instrumental in founding the Pugwash Conference, at which distinguished scientists from around the world meet to discuss international issues,[1] and in 1963 he became president of the British wing of the Who Killed Kennedy Committee. In 1964 he founded the Bertrand Russell Peace Foundation and in 1967 he set up an International War Crimes Tribunal which, together with his book *War Crimes in Vietnam*, condemned the foreign policy of the United States. Russell died in 1970 at the age of 97.

What Was Russell's Overall Philosophical Project?

Russell's earliest work, and probably his most lasting contribution to philosophy, was in mathematical logic. His project—which today might seem almost unnecessary but which was an extremely important contribution to mathematical thought at the beginning of the twentieth century—was to place all of pure mathematics on a sound footing by showing that it is reducible to a demonstrably sound logical system. This program was called 'logicism,' and its culmination for Russell was the massive *Principia Mathematica*, co-written with Alfred North Whitehead and published between 1910 and 1913. In the process, Russell created essentially the standard formulation of modern classical logic. (The project ran into dif-

ficulties, however, with the discovery of several very deep paradoxes which threaten any sufficiently powerful logical system which makes use of the notion of a class or set;[2] Russell's solution—called the "theory of types"—is generally considered a rather problematic treatment of these paradoxes.) The best introduction to Russell's logicism is his *Introduction to Mathematical Philosophy*, written while he was in prison in 1918.

Lying behind this early work, as well as many of his other philosophical writings, was the dictum that "all sound philosophy should begin with an analysis of propositions": that is, Russell thought, good philosophy starts by examining a particular feature or type of language—such as mathematics—and looking for its underlying logic. This kind of analysis can be seen at work in two of Russell's most seminal papers, "On Denoting" (1905) and "Knowledge by Acquaintance and Knowledge by Description" (1910). The ultimate aim of this philosophical project is to construct an ideal logically correct language to solve or dissolve many, if not all, of our philosophical problems. Such a system, Russell thought, would reveal how mathematical and scientific reality is a "logical construction" of basic data, such as numbers and sense-data.

This philosophical project gave rise to Russell's second important contribution to philosophy: a theory called "logical atomism."[3] This is a metaphysical

---

1   It is named after the village in Nova Scotia where the first meeting was held in 1957. Pugwash conferences still continue, and the organization received the Nobel peace prize in 1995.

2   The most fundamental of these paradoxes is usually called "Russell's paradox," and goes as follows. Some sets are members of themselves and others are not. For example, the set of chimpanzees is not itself a chimp, but the set of sets is itself a set. Now, consider the following (apparently perfectly legitimate) set: the set of all sets that are not members of themselves. Call this set R. The problematic question is: is R a member of itself or not? It can't be true that R *is* a member of itself, since all the members of R are not members of themselves. On the other hand, it can't be true that R is *not* a member of itself, because then it would be a member of itself. Yet it must surely be one or the other. This is a paradox which seems to arise directly out of the notion of a set itself, and it has big implications for logic and mathematics.

3   Ludwig Wittgenstein's book *Tractatus Logico-Philosophicus* (1922) is the other main source for this theory.

doctrine which is simultaneously about the nature of language, knowledge, and the world. Its central claim is that reality is ultimately composed of atomic facts and that these facts are connected together by certain fundamental relations (such as 'and,' 'or,' or 'if … then …') which can be pictured in formal logic. Language, according to this theory, represents the world by sharing its logical structure: that is, *language* (just like reality) is ultimately composed of 'atomic' units which are joined together by logical rules into more complex compounds (i.e., into phrases and sentences). The business of philosophy, according to logical atomism, is to purify our language until it properly reflects the structure of reality, and this goal is achieved through logical analysis. For example, we want the atomic units of our perfect logical language to include the *names* of the atomic individuals and their basic properties, and the grammatical rules for the construction of compound sentences should be the same as the logical relations by which reality is constructed. Finally, human knowledge of the world, according to logical atomism, turns out to have two different components: our acquaintance with the basic elements of reality (which Russell for a long time thought of as sense-data), and our understanding of how these elements can be and are combined (which Russell labeled "knowledge by description").

Three of Russell's works that describe and develop his logical atomism are *Our Knowledge of the External World* (1914), the lectures "The Philosophy of Logical Atomism" (1918), and *The Analysis of Matter* (1927).

After 1938 Russell switched the main focus of his philosophical research to epistemology, the study of the nature of human knowledge. He began by searching for a method that would guarantee the certainty of our beliefs (for example, our scientific beliefs), but he was forced gradually to the conclusion that "all human knowledge is uncertain, inexact, and partial. To this doctrine we have not found any limitation whatever." Part of the reason for Russell's increasing lack of confidence in scientific knowledge was his growing appreciation of "the problem of induction." His work in epistemology can be found in *An Inquiry into Meaning and Truth* (1940) and his last significant philosophical work, *Human Knowledge: Its Scope and Limits* (1948).

Russell's short book *The Problems of Philosophy* (1912), from which our reading is taken, has become one of the most popular introductions to philosophy ever written. In its day it was also important for drawing attention to the previously underrated work of the British empiricists, especially Berkeley and Hume. The book was written while Russell was still developing his logical atomism: in his later work (for a time) he abandoned the notion that matter is *inferred* from our knowledge of sense-data and replaced it with the idea that matter is simply a *logical construction* of actual and possible sense-data. That is, he moved from the theory that matter is the best explanation for what causes our experiences of the world, to the theory that statements about 'matter' are just shorthand statements about past and future experiences themselves.

What Is the Structure of This Reading?

Russell's *Problems of Philosophy* contains fifteen chapters, and the first three are reprinted here. Russell begins his introduction to philosophy by treating it as the search for *certainty*—for knowledge that no "reasonable man" could doubt. In the first chapter he argues that most everyday knowledge about the world we live in fails sadly to live up to this standard and, as the title of the first chapter suggests, he uses simple examples from daily life to draw a distinction between appearance and reality. Russell then distinguishes between two different sorts of questions about the nature of reality: (1) Is there a real table at all? (2) If so, what sort of object can it be? Chapter 2 addresses the first of these questions (and Russell argues that physical tables do exist); Chapter 3 is about the second (where Russell argues that matter cannot resemble our sense-data).

Suggestions for Critical Reflection

1. Do you think philosophy is best thought of as the search for certainty? Does Russell think of it in that way? Judging from the reading, for example, does he require *certainty* in his philosophical arguments?

2. Do you agree that Russell's appearance/reality distinction is a serious blow to our common-sense beliefs about the world? Why, or why not?

3. Do you agree with Russell that "the supposition that the whole of life is a dream ... [is] a less simple hypothesis, viewed as a means of accounting for the facts of our own life, than the common-sense hypothesis that there really are objects independent of us"?

4. How adequate do you find Russell's proof that physical tables exist? What does he mean by "physical" (e.g., does he mean something like "made of sub-atomic particles"?) in this context?

5. What kind of knowledge do you think Russell would be willing to grant us of the real nature of matter? That is, as well as knowing what matter is *not*, how much might we be able to find out (on Russell's picture) about what matter *is*?

Suggestions for Further Reading

After reading the rest of *The Problems of Philosophy* (Oxford University Press, 1912), the best places to start with Russell's philosophy are his *Introduction to Mathematical Philosophy* (George Allen & Unwin, 1919) and the collection of essays edited by R.C. Marsh called *Logic and Knowledge* (George Allen & Unwin, 1956). The latter includes his "The Philosophy of Logical Atomism." Every student of philosophy should at some point read Russell's *A History of Western Philosophy* (George Allen & Unwin, 1945). Probably still the best book about Russell's life is his *Autobiography*, published in three volumes between 1967 and 1969 by George Allen & Unwin. Apart from that, the standard biography continues to be Ronald William Clark's *The Life of Bertrand Russell* (Cape, 1972).

Two useful books about Russell's philosophy are *Bertrand Russell*, by John Slater (Thoemmes Press, 1994) and *Russell*, by R.M. Sainsbury (Routledge & Kegan Paul, 1979). Perhaps the most comprehensive book on Russell's thought is by Ronald Jager, *The Development of Bertrand Russell's Philosophy* (Allen & Unwin, 1972). Essays about Russell's philosophy are collected in David Pears (ed.), *Bertrand Russell: A Collection of Critical Essays* (Anchor Books, 1972).

The Problems of Philosophy

Chapters 1–3[4]

Chapter 1: Appearance and Reality

Is there any knowledge in the world which is so certain that no reasonable man could doubt it? This question, which at first sight might not seem difficult, is really one of the most difficult that can be asked. When we have realized the obstacles in the way of a straightforward and confident answer, we shall be well launched on the study of philosophy—for philosophy is merely the attempt to answer such ultimate questions, not carelessly and dogmatically, as we do in ordinary life and even in the sciences, but critically, after exploring all that makes such questions puzzling, and after realizing all the vagueness and confusion that underlie our ordinary ideas.

In daily life, we assume as certain many things which, on a closer scrutiny, are found to be so full of apparent contradictions that only a great amount of thought enables us to know what it is that we really may believe. In the search for certainty, it is natural to begin with our present experiences, and in some sense, no doubt, knowledge is to be derived from them. But any statement as to what it is that our immediate experiences make us know is very likely to be wrong. It seems to me that I am now sitting in a chair, at a table of a certain shape, on which I see sheets of paper with writing or print. By turning my head I see out of the window buildings and clouds and the sun. I believe that the sun is about ninety-three million miles from the earth; that it is a hot globe many times bigger than the earth; that, owing to the earth's rotation, it rises every morning, and will continue to do so for an indefinite time in the future. I believe that, if any other normal person comes into my room, he will see the same chairs and tables and books and papers as I see, and that the table which I see is the same as the table which I feel pressing against my arm. All this seems to be so evident as to

_____

4 Chapters 1-3 of *The Problems of Philosophy*, The Home University Library Series, Williams and Norgate, 1912. Reprinted with the permission of Oxford University Press.

be hardly worth stating, except in answer to a man who doubts whether I know anything. Yet all this may be reasonably doubted, and all of it requires much careful discussion before we can be sure that we have stated it in a form that is wholly true.

To make our difficulties plain, let us concentrate attention on the table. To the eye it is oblong, brown and shiny, to the touch it is smooth and cool and hard; when I tap it, it gives out a wooden sound. Any one else who sees and feels and hears the table will agree with this description, so that it might seem as if no difficulty would arise; but as soon as we try to be more precise our troubles begin. Although I believe that the table is 'really' of the same colour all over, the parts that reflect the light look much brighter than the other parts, and some parts look white because of reflected light. I know that, if I move, the parts that reflect the light will be different, so that the apparent distribution of colours on the table will change. It follows that if several people are looking at the table at the same moment, no two of them will see exactly the same distribution of colours, because no two can see it from exactly the same point of view, and any change in the point of view makes some change in the way the light is reflected.

For most practical purposes these differences are unimportant, but to the painter they are all-important: the painter has to unlearn the habit of thinking that things seem to have the colour which common sense says they 'really' have, and to learn the habit of seeing things as they appear. Here we have already the beginning of one of the distinctions that cause most trouble in philosophy—the distinction between 'appearance' and 'reality', between what things seem to be and what they are. The painter wants to know what things seem to be, the practical man and the philosopher want to know what they are; but the philosopher's wish to know this is stronger than the practical man's, and is more troubled by knowledge as to the difficulties of answering the question.

To return to the table. It is evident from what we have found, that there is no colour which pre-eminently appears to be *the* colour of the table, or even of any one particular part of the table—it appears to be of different colours from different points of view, and there is no reason for regarding some of these as more really its colour than others. And we know that even from a given point of view the colour will seem different by artificial light, or to a colour-blind man, or to a man wearing blue spectacles, while in the dark there will be no colour at all, though to touch and hearing the table will be unchanged. This colour is not something which is inherent in the table, but something depending upon the table and the spectator and the way the light falls on the table. When, in ordinary life, we speak of *the* colour of the table, we only mean the sort of colour which it will seem to have to a normal spectator from an ordinary point of view under usual conditions of light. But the other colours which appear under other conditions have just as good a right to be considered real; and therefore, to avoid favouritism, we are compelled to deny that, in itself, the table has any one particular colour.

The same thing applies to the texture. With the naked eye one can see the grain, but otherwise the table looks smooth and even. If we looked at it through a microscope, we should see roughnesses and hills and valleys, and all sorts of differences that are imperceptible to the naked eye. Which of these is the 'real' table? We are naturally tempted to say that what we see through the microscope is more real, but that in turn would be changed by a still more powerful microscope. If, then, we cannot trust what we see with the naked eye, why should we trust what we see through a microscope? Thus, again, the confidence in our senses with which we began deserts us.

The *shape* of the table is no better. We are all in the habit of judging as to the 'real' shapes of things, and we do this so unreflectingly that we come to think we actually see the real shapes. But, in fact, as we all have to learn if we try to draw, a given thing looks different in shape from every different point of view. If our table is 'really' rectangular, it will look, from almost all points of view, as if it had two acute angles and two obtuse angles. If opposite sides are parallel, they will look as if they converged to a point away from the spectator; if they are of equal length, they will look as if the nearer side were longer. All these things are not commonly noticed in looking at a table, because experience has taught us to construct the 'real' shape from the apparent shape, and the 'real' shape is what interests us as practical men. But the 'real' shape is not what we see; it is something inferred from what we see. And what we see is constantly changing in shape as we move about the room; so that here again the senses seem not to give us the truth about the table itself, but only about the appearance of the table.

Similar difficulties arise when we consider the sense of touch. It is true that the table always gives us a sensation of hardness, and we feel that it resists pressure. But the sensation we obtain depends upon how hard we press the table and also upon what part of the body we press with; thus the various sensations due to various pressures or various parts of the body cannot be supposed to reveal *directly* any definite property of the table, but at most to be *signs* of some property which perhaps *causes* all the sensations, but is not actually apparent in any of them. And the same applies still more obviously to the sounds which can be elicited by rapping the table.

Thus it becomes evident that the real table, if there is one, is not the same as what we immediately experience by sight or touch or hearing. The real table, if there is one, is not *immediately* known to us at all, but must be an inference from what is immediately known. Hence, two very difficult questions at once arise; namely, (1) Is there a real table at all? (2) If so, what sort of object can it be?

It will help us in considering these questions to have a few simple terms of which the meaning is definite and clear. Let us give the name of 'sense-data' to the things that are immediately known in sensation: such things as colours, sounds, smells, hardnesses, roughnesses, and so on. We shall give the name 'sensation' to the experience of being immediately aware of these things. Thus, whenever we see a colour, we have a sensation *of* the colour, but the colour itself is a sense-datum, not a sensation. The colour is that *of* which we are immediately aware, and the awareness itself is the sensation. It is plain that if we are to know anything about the table, it must be by means of the sense-data—brown colour, oblong shape, smoothness, etc.—which we associate with the table; but, for the reasons which have been given, we cannot say that the table is the sense-data, or even that the sense-data are directly properties of the table. Thus a problem arises as to the relation of the sense-data to the real table, supposing there is such a thing.

The real table, if it exists, we will call a 'physical object'. Thus we have to consider the relation of sense-data to physical objects. The collection of all physical objects is called 'matter'. Thus our two questions may be re-stated as follows: (1) Is there any such thing as matter? (2) If so, what is its nature?

The philosopher who first brought prominently forward the reasons for regarding the immediate objects of our senses as not existing independently of us was Bishop Berkeley (1685–1753). His *Three Dialogues between Hylas and Philonous, in Opposition to Sceptics and Atheists*,[5] undertake to prove that there is no such thing as matter at all, and that the world consists of nothing but minds and their ideas. Hylas has hitherto believed in matter, but he is no match for Philonous, who mercilessly drives him into contradictions and paradoxes, and makes his own denial of matter seem, in the end, as if it were almost common sense. The arguments employed are of very different value: some are important and sound, others are confused or quibbling. But Berkeley retains the merit of having shown that the existence of matter is capable of being denied without absurdity, and that if there are any things that exist independently of us they cannot be the immediate objects of our sensations.

There are two different questions involved when we ask whether matter exists, and it is important to keep them clear. We commonly mean by 'matter' something which is opposed to 'mind', something which we think of as occupying space and as radically incapable of any sort of thought or consciousness. It is chiefly in this sense that Berkeley denies matter; that is to say, he does not deny that the sense-data which we commonly take as signs of the existence of the table are really signs of the existence of *something* independent of us, but he does deny that this something is non-mental, that it is neither mind nor ideas entertained by some mind. He admits that there must be something which continues to exist when we go out of the room or shut our eyes, and that what we call seeing the table does really give us reason for believing in something which persists even when we are not seeing it. But he thinks that this something cannot be radically

_____

5   See the Berkeley selection in this chapter.

different in nature from what we see, and cannot be independent of seeing altogether, though it must be independent of *our* seeing. He is thus led to regard the 'real' table as an idea in the mind of God. Such an idea has the required permanence and independence of ourselves, without being—as matter would otherwise be—something quite unknowable, in the sense that we can only infer it, and can never be directly and immediately aware of it.

Other philosophers since Berkeley have also held that, although the table does not depend for its existence upon being seen by me, it does depend upon being seen (or otherwise apprehended in sensation) by *some* mind—not necessarily the mind of God, but more often the whole collective mind of the universe. This they hold, as Berkeley does, chiefly because they think there can be nothing real—or at any rate nothing known to be real—except minds and their thoughts and feelings. We might state the argument by which they support their view in some such way as this: 'Whatever can be thought of is an idea in the mind of the person thinking of it; therefore nothing can be thought of except ideas in minds; therefore anything else is inconceivable, and what is inconceivable cannot exist.'

Such an argument, in my opinion, is fallacious; and of course those who advance it do not put it so shortly or so crudely. But whether valid or not, the argument has been very widely advanced in one form or another; and very many philosophers, perhaps a majority, have held that there is nothing real except minds and their ideas. Such philosophers are called 'idealists'. When they come to explaining matter, they either say, like Berkeley, that matter is really nothing but a collection of ideas, or they say, like Leibniz (1646–1716), that what appears as matter is really a collection of more or less rudimentary minds.

But these philosophers, though they deny matter as opposed to mind, nevertheless, in another sense, admit matter. It will be remembered that we asked two questions; namely, (1) Is there a real table at all? (2) If so, what sort of object can it be? Now both Berkeley and Leibniz admit that there is a real table, but Berkeley says it is certain ideas in the mind of God, and Leibniz says it is a colony of souls. Thus both of them answer our first question in the affirmative, and only diverge from the views of ordinary mortals in their answer to our second question. In fact, almost all philosophers seem to be agreed that there is a real table: they almost all agree that, however much our sense-data—colour, shape, smoothness, etc.—may depend upon us, yet their occurrence is a sign of something existing independently of us, something differing, perhaps, completely from our sense-data whenever we are in a suitable relation to the real table.

Now obviously this point in which the philosophers are agreed—the view that there *is* a real table, whatever its nature may be—is vitally important, and it will be worth while to consider what reasons there are for accepting this view before we go on to the further question as to the nature of the real table. Our next chapter, therefore, will be concerned with the reasons for supposing that there is a real table at all.

Before we go farther it will be well to consider for a moment what it is that we have discovered so far. It has appeared that, if we take any common object of the sort that is supposed to be known by the senses, what the senses *immediately*[6] tell us is not the truth about the object as it is apart from us, but only the truth about certain sense-data which, so far as we can see, depend upon the relations between us and the object. Thus what we directly see and feel is merely 'appearance', which we believe to be a sign of some 'reality' behind. But if the reality is not what appears, have we any means of knowing whether there is any reality at all? And if so, have we any means of finding out what it is like?

Such questions are bewildering, and it is difficult to know that even the strangest hypotheses may not be true. Thus our familiar table, which has roused but the slightest thoughts in us hitherto, has become a problem full of surprising possibilities. The one thing we know about it is that it is not what it seems. Beyond this modest result, so far, we have the most complete liberty of conjecture. Leibniz tells us it is a community of souls: Berkeley tells us it is an idea in the mind of God; sober science, scarcely less wonderful, tells us it is a vast collection of electric charges in violent motion.

---

6   Without an intermediary (as opposed to "straight away").

Among these surprising possibilities, doubt suggests that perhaps there is no table at all. Philosophy, if it cannot *answer* so many questions as we could wish, has at least the power of *asking* questions which increase the interest of the world, and show the strangeness and wonder lying just below the surface even in the commonest things of daily life.

Chapter 2: The Existence of Matter

In this chapter we have to ask ourselves whether, in any sense at all, there is such a thing as matter. Is there a table which has a certain intrinsic nature, and continues to exist when I am not looking, or is the table merely a product of my imagination, a dream-table in a very prolonged dream? This question is of the greatest importance. For if we cannot be sure of the independent existence of objects, we cannot be sure of the independent existence of other people's bodies, and therefore still less of other people's minds, since we have no grounds for believing in their minds except such as are derived from observing their bodies. Thus if we cannot be sure of the independent existence of objects, we shall be left alone in a desert—it may be that the whole outer world is nothing but a dream, and that we alone exist. This is an uncomfortable possibility; but although it cannot be strictly *proved* to be false, there is not the slightest reason to suppose that it is true. In this chapter we have to see why this is the case.

Before we embark upon doubtful matters, let us try to find some more or less fixed point from which to start. Although we are doubting the physical existence of the table, we are not doubting the existence of the sense-data which made us think there was a table; we are not doubting that, while we look, a certain colour and shape appear to us, and while we press, a certain sensation of hardness is experienced by us. All this, which is psychological, we are not calling in question. In fact, whatever else may be doubtful, some at least of our immediate experiences seem absolutely certain.

Descartes (1596–1650), the founder of modern philosophy, invented a method which may still be used with profit—the method of systematic doubt. He determined that he would believe nothing which he did not see quite clearly and distinctly to be true. Whatever he could bring himself to doubt, he would

doubt, until he saw reason for not doubting it. By applying this method he gradually became convinced that the only existence of which he could be *quite* certain was his own. He imagined a deceitful demon, who presented unreal things to his senses in a perpetual phantasmagoria; it might be very improbable that such a demon existed, but still it was possible, and therefore doubt concerning things perceived by the senses was possible.

But doubt concerning his own existence was not possible, for if he did not exist, no demon could deceive him. If he doubted, he must exist; if he had any experiences whatever, he must exist. Thus his own existence was an absolute certainty to him. 'I think, therefore I am,' he said (*Cogito, ergo sum*); and on the basis of this certainty he set to work to build up again the world of knowledge which his doubt had laid in ruins. By inventing the method of doubt, and by showing that subjective things are the most certain, Descartes performed a great service to philosophy, and one which makes him still useful to all students of the subject.

But some care is needed in using Descartes's argument. '*I* think, therefore *I* am' says rather more than is strictly certain. It might seem as though we were quite sure of being the same person to-day as we were yesterday, and this is no doubt true in some sense. But the real Self is as hard to arrive at as the real table and does not seem to have that absolute, convincing certainty that belongs to particular experiences. When I look at my table and see a certain brown colour, what is quite certain at once is not '*I* am seeing a brown colour', but rather, 'a brown colour is being seen'. This of course involves something (or somebody) which (or who) sees the brown colour; but it does not of itself involve that more or less permanent person whom we call 'I'. So far as immediate certainty goes, it might be that the something which sees the brown colour is quite momentary, and not the same as the something which has some different experience the next moment.

Thus it is our particular thoughts and feelings that have primitive certainty. And this applies to dreams and hallucinations as well as to normal perceptions: when we dream or see a ghost, we certainly do have the sensations we think we have, but for various reasons it is held that no physical object corresponds to these sensations. Thus the certainty of our knowledge of our own experiences does not have to be limited in any way to allow for exceptional cases. Here, therefore, we have, for what it is worth, a solid basis from which to begin our pursuit of knowledge.

The problem we have to consider is this: Granted that we are certain of our own sense-data, have we any reason for regarding them as signs of the existence of something else, which we can call the physical object? When we have enumerated all the sense-data which we should naturally regard as connected with the table have we said all there is to say about the table, or is there still something else—something not a sense-datum, something which persists when we go out of the room? Common sense unhesitatingly answers that there is. What can be bought and sold and pushed about and have a cloth laid on it, and so on, cannot be a *mere* collection of sense-data. If the cloth completely hides the table, we shall derive no sense-data from the table, and therefore, if the table were merely sense-data, it would have ceased to exist, and the cloth would be suspended in empty air, resting, by a miracle, in the place where the table formerly was. This seems plainly absurd; but whoever wishes to become a philosopher must learn not to be frightened by absurdities.

One great reason why it is felt that we must secure a physical object in addition to the sense-data, is that we want the same object for different people. When ten people are sitting round a dinner-table, it seems preposterous to maintain that they are not seeing the same tablecloth, the same knives and forks and spoons and glasses. But the sense-data are private to each separate person; what is immediately present to the sight of one is not immediately present to the sight of another: they all see things from slightly different points of view, and therefore see them slightly differently. Thus, if there are to be public neutral objects, which can be in some sense known to many different people, there must be something over and above the private and particular sense-data which appear to various people. What reason, then, have we for believing that there are such public neutral objects?

The first answer that naturally occurs to one is that, although different people may see the table slightly differently, still they all see more or less similar things

when they look at the table, and the variations in what they see follow the laws of perspective and reflection of light, so that it is easy to arrive at a permanent object underlying all the different people's sense-data. I bought my table from the former occupant of my room; I could not buy *his* sense-data, which died when he went away, but I could and did buy the confident expectation of more or less similar sense-data. Thus it is the fact that different people have similar sense-data, and that one person in a given place at different times has similar sense-data, which makes us suppose that over and above the sense-data there is a permanent public object which underlies or causes the sense-data of various people at various times.

Now in so far as the above considerations depend upon supposing that there are other people besides ourselves, they beg the very question at issue.[7] Other people are represented to me by certain sense-data, such as the sight of them or the sound of their voices, and if I had no reason to believe that there were physical objects independent of my sense-data, I should have no reason to believe that other people exist except as part of my dream. Thus, when we are trying to show that there must be objects independent of our own sense-data, we cannot appeal to the testimony of other people, since this testimony itself consists of sense-data, and does not reveal other people's experiences unless our own sense-data are signs of things existing independently of us. We must therefore, if possible, find, in our own purely private experiences, characteristics which show, or tend to show, that there are in the world things other than ourselves and our private experiences.

In one sense it must be admitted that we can never *prove* the existence of things other than ourselves and our experiences. No logical absurdity results from the hypothesis that the world consists of myself and my thoughts and feelings and sensations, and that everything else is mere fancy. In dreams a very complicated world may seem to be present, and yet on waking we find it was a delusion; that is to say, we find that the sense-data in the dream do not appear to have corresponded with such physical objects as we should natu-

---

7   Presuppose the truth of the very thing they are trying to prove.

rally infer from our sense-data. (It is true that, when the physical world is assumed, it is possible to find physical causes for the sense-data in dreams: a door banging, for instance, may cause us to dream of a naval engagement. But although, in this case, there is a physical *cause* for the sense-data, there is not a physical object *corresponding* to the sense-data in the way in which an actual naval battle would correspond.) There is no logical impossibility in the supposition that the whole of life is a dream, in which we ourselves create all the objects that come before us. But although this is not logically impossible, there is no reason whatever to suppose that it is true; and it is, in fact, a less simple hypothesis, viewed as a means of accounting for the facts of our own life, than the common-sense hypothesis that there really are objects independent of us, whose action on us causes our sensations.

The way in which simplicity comes in from supposing that there really are physical objects is easily seen. If the cat appears at one moment in one part of the room, and at another in another part, it is natural to suppose that it has moved from the one to the other, passing over a series of intermediate positions. But if it is merely a set of sense-data, it cannot have ever been in any place where I did not see it; thus we shall have to suppose that it did not exist at all while I was not looking, but suddenly sprang into being in a new place. If the cat exists whether I see it or not, we can understand from our own experience how it gets hungry between one meal and the next; but if it does not exist when I am not seeing it, it seems odd that appetite should grow during non-existence as fast as during existence. And if the cat consists only of sense-data, it cannot be *hungry*, since no hunger but my own can be a sense-datum to me. Thus the behaviour of the sense-data which represent the cat to me, though it seems quite natural when regarded as an expression of hunger, becomes utterly inexplicable when regarded as mere movements and changes of patches of colour, which are as incapable of hunger as a triangle is of playing football.

But the difficulty in the case of the cat is nothing compared to the difficulty in the case of human beings. When human beings speak—that is, when we hear certain noises which we associate with ideas, and simultaneously see certain motions of lips and expressions of face—it is very difficult to suppose that what we hear is not the expression of a thought, as we know it would be if we emitted the same sounds. Of course similar things happen in dreams, where we are mistaken as to the existence of other people. But dreams are more or less suggested by what we call waking life, and are capable of being more or less accounted for on scientific principles if we assume that there really is a physical world. Thus every principle of simplicity urges us to adopt the natural view, that there really are objects other than ourselves and our sense-data which have an existence not dependent upon our perceiving them.

Of course it is not by argument that we originally come by our belief in an independent external world. We find this belief ready in ourselves as soon as we begin to reflect: it is what may be called an *instinctive* belief. We should never have been led to question this belief but for the fact that, at any rate in the case of sight, it seems as if the sense-datum itself were instinctively believed to be the independent object, whereas argument shows that the object cannot be identical with the sense-datum. This discovery, however—which is not at all paradoxical in the case of taste and smell and sound, and only slightly so in the case of touch—leaves undiminished our instinctive belief that there *are* objects *corresponding* to our sense-data. Since this belief does not lead to any difficulties, but on the contrary tends to simplify and systematize our account of our experiences, there seems no good reason for rejecting it. We may therefore admit—though with a slight doubt derived from dreams—that the external world does really exist, and is not wholly dependent for its existence upon our continuing to perceive it.

The argument which has led us to this conclusion is doubtless less strong than we could wish, but it is typical of many philosophical arguments, and it is therefore worth while to consider briefly its general character and validity. All knowledge, we find, must be built up upon our instinctive beliefs, and if these are rejected, nothing is left. But among our instinctive beliefs some are much stronger than others, while many have, by habit and association, become entangled with other beliefs, not really instinctive, but falsely supposed to be part of what is believed instinctively.

Philosophy should show us the hierarchy of our instinctive beliefs, beginning with those we hold most strongly, and presenting each as much isolated and as free from irrelevant additions as possible. It should take care to show that, in the form in which they are finally set forth, our instinctive beliefs do not clash, but form a harmonious system. There can never be any reason for rejecting one instinctive belief except that it clashes with others; thus, if they are found to harmonize, the whole system becomes worthy of acceptance.

It is of course *possible* that all or any of our beliefs may be mistaken, and therefore all ought to be held with at least some slight element of doubt. But we cannot have *reason* to reject a belief except on the ground of some other belief. Hence, by organizing our instinctive beliefs and their consequences, by considering which among them is most possible, if necessary, to modify or abandon, we can arrive, on the basis of accepting as our sole data what we instinctively believe, at an orderly systematic organization of our knowledge, in which, though the *possibility* of error remains, its likelihood is diminished by the interrelation of the parts and by the critical scrutiny which has preceded acquiescence.

This function, at least, philosophy can perform. Most philosophers, rightly or wrongly, believe that philosophy can do much more than this—that it can give us knowledge, not otherwise attainable, concerning the universe as a whole, and concerning the nature of ultimate reality. Whether this be the case or not, the more modest function we have spoken of can certainly be performed by philosophy, and certainly suffices, for those who have once begun to doubt the adequacy of common sense, to justify the arduous and difficult labours that philosophical problems involve.

Chapter 3: The Nature of Matter

In the preceding chapter we agreed, though without being able to find demonstrative reasons, that it is rational to believe that our sense-data—for example, those which we regard as associated with my table—are really signs of the existence of something independent of us and our perceptions. That is to say, over and above the sensations of colour, hardness, noise, and so on, which make up the appearance of the table to me, I assume that there is something else, *of* which these things are appearances. The colour ceases to exist if I shut my eyes, the sensation of hardness ceases to exist if I remove my arm from contact with the table, the sound ceases to exist if I cease to rap the table with my knuckles. But I do not believe that when all these things cease the table ceases. On the contrary, I believe that it is because the table exists continuously that all these sense-data will reappear when I open my eyes, replace my arm, and begin again to rap with my knuckles. The question we have to consider in this chapter is: What is the nature of this real table, which persists independently of my perception of it?

To this question physical science gives an answer, somewhat incomplete it is true, and in part still very hypothetical, but yet deserving of respect so far as it goes. Physical science, more or less unconsciously, has drifted into the view that all natural phenomena ought to be reduced to motions. Light and heat and sound are all due to wave-motions, which travel from the body emitting them to the person who sees light or feels heat or hears sound. That which has the wave-motion is either aether[8] or 'gross matter', but in either case is what the philosopher would call matter. The only properties which science assigns to it are position in space, and the power of motion according to the laws of motion. Science does not deny that it *may* have other properties; but if so, such other properties are not useful to the man of science, and in no way assist him in explaining the phenomena.

It is sometimes said that 'light *is* a form of wave-motion', but this is misleading, for the light which we immediately see, which we know directly by means of

---

8   This is the invisible, all-pervasive substance assumed by classical physics to fill up all the 'empty' space in the universe and to be the medium through which light waves are propagated (just as water is the medium for watery waves). The hypothesis was rendered obsolete by Einstein's theory of special relativity in 1905. (In a foreword to the German edition of 1926, Russell admitted that when *The Problems of Philosophy* was written in 1911 he had not yet sufficiently understood the importance of Einstein's theories. Later Russell became a well-known popularizer of relativity theory, for example, in his *ABC of Relativity* [1925].)

our senses, is *not* a form of wave-motion, but something quite different—something which we all know if we are not blind, though we cannot describe it so as to convey our knowledge to a man who is blind. A wave-motion, on the contrary, could quite well be described to a blind man, since he can acquire a knowledge of space by the sense of touch; and he can experience a wave-motion by a sea voyage almost as well as we can. But this, which a blind man can understand, is not what we mean by *light*: we mean by *light* just that which a blind man can never understand, and which we can never describe to him.

Now this something, which all of us who are not blind know, is not, according to science, really to be found in the outer world: it is something caused by the action of certain waves upon the eyes and nerves and brain of the person who sees the light. When it is said that light *is* waves, what is really meant is that waves are the physical cause of our sensations of light. But light itself, the thing which seeing people experience and blind people do not, is not supposed by science to form any part of the world that is independent of us and our senses. And very similar remarks would apply to other kinds of sensations.

It is not only colours and sounds and so on that are absent from the scientific world of matter, but also *space* as we get it through sight or touch. It is essential to science that its matter should be in *a* space, but the space in which it is cannot be exactly the space we see or feel. To begin with, space as we see it is not the same as space as we get it by the sense of touch; it is only by experience in infancy that we learn how to touch things we see, or how to get a sight of things which we feel touching us. But the space of science is neutral as between touch and sight; thus it cannot be either the space of touch or the space of sight.

Again, different people see the same object as of different shapes, according to their point of view. A circular coin, for example, though we should always *judge* it to be circular, will *look* oval unless we are straight in front of it. When we judge that it *is* circular, we are judging that it has a real shape which is not its apparent shape, but belongs to it intrinsically apart from its appearance. But this real shape, which is what concerns science, must be in a real space, not the same as anybody's apparent space. The real space is public,

the *apparent* space is private to the percipient. In different people's *private* spaces the same object seems to have different shapes; thus the real space, in which it has its real shape, must be different from the private spaces. The space of science, therefore, though *connected* with the spaces we see and feel, is not identical with them, and the manner of its connexion requires investigation.

We agreed provisionally that physical objects cannot be quite like our sense-data, but may be regarded as *causing* our sensations. These physical objects are in the space of science, which we may call 'physical' space. It is important to notice that, if our sensations are to be caused by physical objects, there must be a physical space containing these objects and our sense-organs and nerves and brain. We get a sensation of touch from an object when we are in contact with it; that is to say, when some part of our body occupies a place in physical space quite close to the space occupied by the object. We see an object (roughly speaking) when no opaque body is between the object and our eyes in physical space. Similarly, we only hear or smell or taste an object when we are sufficiently near to it, or when it touches the tongue, or has some suitable position in physical space relatively to our body. We cannot begin to state what different sensations we shall derive from a given object under different circumstances unless we regard the object and our body as both in one physical space, for it is mainly the relative positions of the object and our body that determine what sensations we shall derive from the object.

Now our sense-data are situated in our private spaces, either the space of sight or the space of touch or such vaguer spaces as other senses may give us. If, as science and common sense assume, there is one public all-embracing physical space in which physical objects are, the relative positions of physical objects in physical space must more or less correspond to the relative positions of sense-data in our private spaces. There is no difficulty in supposing this to be the case. If we see on a road one house nearer to us than another, our other senses will bear out the view that it is nearer; for example, it will be reached sooner if we walk along the road. Other people will agree that the house which looks nearer to us is nearer; the ordnance map[9] will take the same view; and thus everything points to a spatial relation between the houses corresponding to the relation between the sense-data which we see when we look at the houses. Thus we may assume that there is a physical space in which physical objects have spatial relations corresponding to those which the corresponding sense-data have in our private spaces. It is this physical space which is dealt with in geometry and assumed in physics and astronomy.

Assuming that there is physical space, and that it does thus correspond to private spaces, what can we know about it? We can know *only* what is required in order to secure the correspondence. That is to say, we can know nothing of what it is like in itself, but we can know the sort of arrangement of physical objects which results from their spatial relations. We can know, for example, that the earth and moon and sun are in one straight line during an eclipse, though we cannot know what a physical straight line is in itself, as we know the look of a straight line in our visual space. Thus we come to know much more about the *relations* of distances in physical space than about the distances themselves; we may know that one distance is greater than another, or that it is along the same straight line as the other, but we cannot have that immediate acquaintance with physical distances that we have with distances in our private spaces, or with colours or sounds or other sense-data. We can know all those things about physical space which a man born blind might know through other people about the space of sight; but the kind of things which a man born blind could never know about the space of sight we also cannot know about physical space. We can know the properties of the relations required to preserve the correspondence with sense-data, but we cannot know the nature of the terms between which the relations hold.

With regard to time, our *feeling* of duration or of the lapse of time is notoriously an unsafe guide as to the time that has elapsed by the clock. Times when we are bored or suffering pain pass slowly, times when we are agreeably occupied pass quickly, and times when we are sleeping pass almost as if they did not exist. Thus, in so far as time is constituted by duration, there is the same necessity for distinguishing a public and a private time as there was in the case of space. But in so far as time consists in an *order* of before and after, there is no need to make such a distinction; the time-order which events seem to have is, so far as we can see, the same as the time-order which they do have. At any rate no reason can be given for supposing that the two orders are not the same. The same is usually true of space: if a regiment of men are marching along a road, the *shape* of the regiment will look different from different points of view, but the men will appear arranged in the same *order* from all points of view. Hence we regard the *order* as true also in physical space, whereas the shape is only supposed to correspond to the physical space so far as is required for the preservation of the order.

In saying that the time-order which events *seem to have* is the same as the time-order which they *really have*, it is necessary to guard against a possible misunderstanding. It must not be supposed that the various states of different physical objects have the same time-order as the sense-data which constitute the perceptions of those objects. Considered as physical objects, the thunder and lightning are simultaneous; that is to say, the lightning is simultaneous with the disturbance of the air in the place where the disturbance begins, namely, where the lightning is. But the sense-datum which we call hearing the thunder does not take place until the disturbance of the air has travelled as far as to where we are. Similarly, it takes about eight minutes for the sun's light to reach us; thus, when we see the sun we are seeing the sun of eight minutes ago. So far as our sense-data afford evidence as to the physical sun they afford evidence as to the physical sun of eight minutes ago; if the physical sun had ceased to exist within the last eight minutes, that would make no difference to the sense-data which we call 'seeing the sun'. This affords a fresh illustration of the necessity of distinguishing between sense-data and physical objects.

What we have found as regards space is much the same as what we find in relation to the correspondence of the sense-data with their physical

---

9   A reference to the standard large-scale maps of Britain made by the Ordnance Survey (originally maps made for the military during the Napoleonic wars).

counterparts. If one object looks blue and another red, we may reasonably presume that there is some corresponding difference between the physical objects; if two objects both look blue, we may presume a corresponding similarity. But we cannot hope to be acquainted directly with the quality in the physical object which makes it look blue or red. Science tells us that this quality is a certain sort of wave-motion, and this sounds familiar, because we think of wave-motions in the space we see. But the wave-motions must really be in physical space, with which we have no direct acquaintance; thus the real wave-motions have not that familiarity which we might have supposed them to have. And what holds for colours is closely similar to what holds for other sense-data. Thus we find that, although the *relations* of physical objects have all sorts of knowable properties, derived from their correspondence with the relations of sense-data, the physical objects themselves remain unknown in their intrinsic nature, so far at least as can be discovered by means of the senses. The question remains whether there is any other method of discovering the intrinsic nature of physical objects.

The most natural, though not ultimately the most defensible, hypothesis to adopt in the first instance, at any rate as regards visual sense-data, would be that, though physical objects cannot, for the reasons we have been considering, be *exactly* like sense-data, yet they may be more or less like. According to this view, physical objects will, for example, really have colours, and we might, by good luck, see an object as of the colour it really is. The colour which an object seems to have at any given moment will in general be very similar, though not quite the same, from many different points of view; we might thus suppose the 'real' colour to be a sort of medium colour, intermediate between the various shades which appear from the different points of view.

Such a theory is perhaps not capable of being definitely refuted, but it can be shown to be groundless. To begin with, it is plain that the colour we see depends only upon the nature of the light-waves that strike the eye, and is therefore modified by the medium intervening between us and the object, as well as by the manner in which light is reflected from the object in the direction of the eye. The intervening air alters colours unless it is perfectly clear, and any strong reflection will alter them completely. Thus the colour we see is a result of the ray as it reaches the eye, and not simply a property of the object from which the ray comes. Hence, also, provided certain waves reach the eye, we shall see a certain colour, whether the object from which the waves start has any colour or not. Thus it is quite gratuitous to suppose that physical objects have colours, and therefore there is no justification for making such a supposition. Exactly similar arguments will apply to other sense-data.

It remains to ask whether there are any general philosophical arguments enabling us to say that, if matter is real, it *must* be of such and such a nature. As explained above, very many philosophers, perhaps most, have held that whatever is real must be in some sense mental, or at any rate that whatever we can know anything about must be in some sense mental. Such philosophers are called 'idealists'. Idealists tell us that what appears as matter is really something mental; namely, either (as Leibniz held) more or less rudimentary minds, or (as Berkeley contended) ideas in the minds which, as we should commonly say, 'perceive' the matter. Thus idealists deny the existence of matter as something intrinsically different from mind, though they do not deny that our sense-data are signs of something which exists independently of our private sensations. In the following chapter we shall consider briefly the reasons—in my opinion fallacious—which idealists advance in favour of their theory.

EDMUND L. GETTIER
"Is Justified True Belief Knowledge?"

Who Is Edmund Gettier?

Edmund Gettier's career has been one of the most unusual in contemporary academic philosophy. His first teaching job was at Wayne State University, in Detroit, Michigan. During the early sixties, the chair of his department suggested that, as tenure consideration approached, some publication might help. The result was "Is Justified True Belief Knowledge?" This article took up all of three pages of a 1963 issue of *Analysis*, but it's the best-known article ever published in epistemology. All Gettier did there was to present two examples, but these two showed that the most basic assumption of epistemology since Plato was wrong. David Lewis cited Gettier (and Gödel) as maybe the only philosophers ever who conclusively refuted a philosophical theory.[1]

Opinions differ on the extent of the remainder of Gettier's publication dossier. One of his friends thinks there's a second article in print; the other believes there are two others.[2] The Philosopher's Index lists only two others, both translations; the title listed for one of these, clearly translated into Hungarian and back, is "If Knowledge Is a Justified True Belief?"[3]

But Gettier has not been relaxing since his career began in the late 1950s. His friends agree that, coupled with his "massive indifference to the usual trappings of an academic career," Gettier has shown an "abiding, deep commitment to philosophy."[4] Colleagues and students have enjoyed decades of energetic, creative philosophical interchange. In 1967 Gettier moved to the University of Massachusetts, Amherst, where he is now Professor Emeritus.

What Was Gettier's Overall Philosophical Project?

Gettier attacks a widely-accepted analysis of the concept of *knowledge*. The analysis of knowledge Gettier attacks is the claim that the necessary and sufficient conditions for S knows that P are that (a) P is true; (b) S believes P; (c) S has justification for this belief.

What Is the Structure of This Reading?

Gettier begins with two assumptions. The first is that one can have justification for believing something that's false.

1   *Philosophical Papers*, Vol I (London: Oxford University Press, 1983), p. x.
2   The first opinion from Robert C. Sleigh, Jr., "Knowing Edmund Gettier," *Philosophical Analysis: A Defense by Example*, ed. by David F. Austin (Dordrecht: Kluwer, 1987), p. xiv; the second from Austin's Preface to that book, p. xii.

3   *Magyar Filozofiai Szemle*, no. 1–2, pp. 231–233 (1995).
4   Sleigh, p. xiii.

A tiny bit of background in logic is necessary for understanding the second. Logicians say that a statement P is *entailed* by another statement Q when it's logically impossible for P to be false given the truth of Q. So, for example, *The picnic is off* is entailed by *It's raining; and if it's raining, the picnic is off.*

Gettier's second assumption is that whenever P is entailed by Q, and a person believes Q, and is justified in this belief, and deduces P from Q, and accepts P on this basis, then that person is justified in believing P. Suppose, for example, you believe, with good justification, that it's raining and if it's raining, the picnic is off. And so you deduce from this, and accordingly believe, that the picnic is off. According to Gettier's second assumption, you're justified in believing that the picnic is off.

The second assumption seems quite reasonable. After all, the fact that one's belief that Q is justified means that you'd count Q as likely to be true; and the fact that Q entails P means that P is likely to be true also; so you'd also be justified in believing P.

Applying these reasonable assumptions to Smith's belief in each of Gettier's two examples, we'd conclude that Smith is justified in his belief in both cases. Since both beliefs are true, they should count as knowledge, under the traditional analysis of knowledge as justified true belief; but in neither case would we agree that Smith's true beliefs are knowledge.

There has been an enormous amount of discussion in print concerning what to do about Gettier's examples (and other similar sorts of examples, known as Gettier-type cases). Some philosophers have tried to propose an account of justification that would account better for our judgments about the beliefs of Smith (and the believers in other Gettier-type cases). Others have argued that what's needed is that an additional condition (beside justified true belief) should be added for the correct analysis of knowledge.

Some Useful Background Information

1. In Gettier's time, but less frequently nowadays, philosophers took it that their job (or one of them) was to provide analyses of concepts; an analysis, in this sense, provides the conditions for the concept's application, and it was generally thought that the ideal analysis of any concept would provide a list of *necessary* and *sufficient* application conditions.

   The *necessary conditions* for application of a concept are those such that if something doesn't meet those conditions, the concept doesn't apply to it. Thus, for example, one of the necessary conditions for being someone's brother is being male. You can't be anyone's brother unless you're male. The sufficient conditions are those such that if something does meet these conditions, the concept does apply to it. Thus, being someone's male sibling is sufficient for the application of the concept *brother*. In this case, being someone's male sibling is also necessary. So it's necessary and sufficient; and the successful analysis of the concept *brother* is given by providing this list of conditions which are each necessary and together sufficient: (a) male; (b) somebody's sibling.

2. It's clear, and hardly needs argument, that believing P is necessary for knowing P. If you don't believe it, you wouldn't be said to know it. And the truth of P is another obvious necessary condition; your beliefs that are in fact false aren't knowledge, even though you think they are. The third necessary condition—that P be justified—needs a bit more explanation. This is added to distinguish between genuine knowledge and just a lucky guess. If S believes some true P merely because of a hunch, S's belief has no firm grounding, no justification, so it doesn't merit being called knowledge. When Fred wins the lottery, and says he *knew* he'd win, what he says is false. He may have been firmly convinced he'd win, but he had no justification for this, so he didn't know it. (Note that one may sometimes have justification for a false belief, when a large preponderance of evidence points toward it. But then it's not knowledge either.)

3. The places in Plato's writing Gettier mentions in a footnote, where Plato appears to suggest that knowledge is justified true belief, are these:

From Plato, *Theaetetus*

SOCRATES: But, my friend, if true opinion and knowledge were the same thing in law courts, the best of judges could never have true opinion without knowledge; in fact, however, it appears that the two are different.

THEAETETUS: Oh yes, I remember now, Socrates, having heard someone make the distinction, but I had forgotten it. He said that knowledge was true opinion accompanied by reason, but that unreasoning true opinion was outside of the sphere of knowledge; and matters of which there is not a rational explanation are unknowable—yes, that is what he called them—and those of which there is are knowable.

From Plato, *Meno*

SOCRATES: Well, and a person who had a right opinion as to which was the way, but had never been there and did not really know, might give right guidance, might he not?

MENO: Certainly.

SOCRATES: And so long, I presume, as he has right opinion about that which the other man really knows, he will be just as good a guide—if he thinks the truth instead of knowing it—as the man who has the knowledge.

MENO: Just as good.

SOCRATES: Hence true opinion is as good a guide to rightness of action as knowledge; and this is a point we omitted just now in our consideration of the nature of virtue, when we stated that knowledge is the only guide of right action; whereas we find there is also true opinion.

MENO: So it seems.

SOCRATES: Then right opinion is just as useful as knowledge.

MENO: With this difference, Socrates, that he who has knowledge will always hit on the right way, whereas he who has right opinion will sometimes do so, but sometimes not.

SOCRATES: How do you mean? Will not he who always has right opinion be always right, so long as he opines rightly?

MENO: It appears to me that he must; and therefore I wonder, Socrates, this being the case, that knowledge should ever be more prized than right opinion, and why they should be two distinct and separate things.

SOCRATES: Well, do you know why it is that you wonder, or shall I tell you?

MENO: Please tell me.

SOCRATES: It is because you have not observed with attention the images of Daedalus.[5] But perhaps there are none in your country.

MENO: What is the point of your remark?

SOCRATES: That if they are not fastened up they play truant and run away; but, if fastened, they stay where they are.

MENO: Well, what of that?

SOCRATES: To possess one of his works which is let loose does not count for much in value; it will not stay with you any more than a runaway slave: but when fastened up it is worth a great deal, for his productions are very fine things. And to what am I referring in all this? To true opinion. For these, so long as they stay with us, are a fine possession, and effect all that is good; but they do not care to stay for long, and run away out of the human soul, and thus are of no great value until one makes them fast with causal reasoning. And this process, friend Meno, is recollection,[6] as in our previous talk we have agreed. But when once they are fastened, in the first place they turn into knowledge, and in the second, are abiding. And this is why knowledge is more prized than right opinion: the one transcends the other by its trammels.

MENO: Upon my word, Socrates, it seems to be very much as you say.

[Both translations by Jowett.]

---

5   Socrates refers here to the legend that the first sculptor, Daedalus, put mechanisms inside his works that made them move.

6   Socrates argues earlier in this dialogue that real knowledge comes from recollection of the general Forms of things encountered before birth.

Suggestions for Critical Reflection

1. Sometimes you say, "I just know that ..." when what you're saying is merely that you feel certain. But most philosophers would say that feeling certain that P is not a sufficient condition for knowing that P. Do you agree? Why / why not? Perhaps a more likely claim is that feeling certain that P is a necessary condition for knowing that P. Do you agree? Why / why not?

2. One suggestion to deal with Gettier-type cases is to add an additional necessary condition to the traditional analysis: that S's belief not be the result of S's inference from a false belief. But consider this example: S believes that there are sheep in the field, and this is true; but what S in fact has seen is really a large furry dog. So S doesn't know there are sheep there. It's sometimes thought that there's no inference from a false belief in this case—why might this be, and do you agree? If so, why might this show the inadequacy of the current proposal?

3. Another suggestion is that S's belief has to have been arrived at by a generally reliable method. But consider this example: S's watch has kept perfect time for years, so looking at her watch is a generally reliable way of finding out what time it is. Today, S looks at her watch at exactly 1 pm, and the watch shows 1:00. S believes correctly that it's 1 pm. But the watch stopped the previous night at 1 am. So S doesn't know that it's 1 pm. This is sometimes taken to show the inadequacy of this proposal—does it?

4. Here's a third troublesome Gettier-type case. S knows a barn when she sees one. But today, unbeknownst to her, she's traveling in an area where they're making a movie, and have built a large number of barn-facades that look just like real barns from the road. By fortunate coincidence, S sees, however, what is the only real barn in the area, and believes (correctly) that there's a real barn there. Does S know that there's a (real) barn there? Is this true belief justified, given that S is an excellent barn-detector?

Suggestions for Further Reading

These articles survey the problem and its main responses: "An Introduction to the Analysis of Knowledge" by Jack Crumley, in *Introduction to Epistemology* by Jack Crumley (Broadview Press, 2009); "Gettier problem" by Paul K. Moser, in *A Companion to Epistemology* (Blackwell, 1992); "Conditions and Analyses of Knowing" by Robert Shope, in *The Oxford Handbook of Epistemology*, Paul K. Moser, ed. (Oxford University Press, 2002); "Knowledge" by Jonathan Dancy, Chapter 2 of *An Introduction to Contemporary Epistemology* by Jonathan Dancy (Blackwell, 1985); "Gettier Problems" by Stephen Hetherington and "Epistemology" by David A. Truncellito, Part 2d, both online in the *Internet Encyclopedia of Philosophy*; "Epistemology" by Matthias Steup, Part 1.2, online in the *Stanford Encyclopedia of Philosophy*.

These articles argue for important positions responding to Gettier. "Knowledge: Undefeated Justified True Belief" by Keith Lehrer and Thomas D. Paxson, Jr., *Journal of Philosophy*, 66, pp. 225–237. Reprinted in *Epistemology: Contemporary Readings*, Michael Huemer, ed. (Routledge, 2002), and in *Readings in Contemporary Epistemology*, Sven Bernecker and Fred Dretske, eds. (Oxford University Press, 2000), and in *Justification and Knowledge*, G. Pappas and M. Swain, eds. (Cornell University Press, 1978). "A Causal Theory of Knowing" by Alvin I. Goldman, *Journal of Philosophy* 64, pp. 355–372. Reprinted in *Justification and Knowledge*, G. Pappas and M. Swain, eds. (Cornell University Press, 1978). "Epistemic Defeasibility" by Marshal Swain, *American Philosophical Quarterly*, 11, pp. 15–25. Reprinted in *Justification and Knowledge*, G. Pappas and M. Swain, eds. (Cornell University Press, 1978). "Knowledge and Grounds: A Comment on Mr. Gettier's Paper" by Michael Clark, *Analysis* 24 (2) (December, 1963), pp. 46–48. Reprinted in *Epistemology: Contemporary Readings*, Michael Huemer, ed. (Routledge, 2002). "An Alleged Defect in Gettier Counter-Examples" by Richard Feldman, *Australasian Journal of Philosophy* 52 (1), pp. 68–69. Reprinted in *Knowledge: Readings in Contemporary Epistemology*, Sven Bernecker and Fred Dretske, eds. (Oxford University Press, 2000). "Conclusive Reasons" by Fred Dretske, *Australasian Journal of Philosophy* 49, pp. 1–22. Reprinted in *Justification and Knowledge*, G. Pappas and M. Swain, eds. (Cornell University Press, 1978).

"Is Justified True Belief Knowledge?"[7]

Various attempts have been made in recent years to state necessary and sufficient conditions for someone's knowing a given proposition. The attempts have often been such that they can be stated in a form similar to the following:[8]

(a) S knows that P   IFF[9]
   (i)   P is true,
   (ii) S believes that P, and
   (iii) S is justified in believing that P.

For example, Chisholm has held that the following gives the necessary and sufficient conditions for knowledge:[10]

(b) S knows that P   IFF
   (i)   S accepts P,
   (ii) S has adequate evidence for P, and
   (iii) P is true.

Ayer has stated the necessary and sufficient conditions for knowledge as follows:[11]

(c) S knows that P   IFF
   (i)   P is true,
   (ii) S is sure that P is true, and
   (iii) S has the right to be sure that P is true.

I shall argue that (a) is false in that the conditions stated therein do not constitute a *sufficient* condition for the truth of the proposition that S knows that P. The same argument will show that (b) and (c) fail if 'has adequate evidence for' or 'has the right to be sure that' is substituted for 'is justified in believing that' throughout.

I shall begin by noting two points. First, in that sense of 'justified' in which S's being justified in believing P is a necessary condition of S's knowing that P, it is possible for a person to be justified in believing a proposition that is in fact false. Secondly, for any proposition P, if S is justified in believing P, and P entails Q, and S deduces Q from P and accepts Q as a result of this deduction, then S is justified in believing Q. Keeping these two points in mind, I shall now present two cases in which the conditions stated in (a) are true for some proposition, though it is at the same time false that the person in question knows that proposition.

Case I

Suppose that Smith and Jones have applied for a certain job. And suppose that Smith has strong evidence for the following conjunctive proposition:[12]

(d) Jones is the man who will get the job, and Jones has ten coins in his pocket.

Smith's evidence for (d) might be that the president of the company assured him that Jones would in the end be selected, and that he, Smith, had counted the coins in Jones's pocket ten minutes ago. Proposition (d) entails:

(e) The man who will get the job has ten coins in his pocket.

Let us suppose that Smith sees the entailment from (d) to (e), and accepts (e) on the grounds of (d), for

---

7   "Is Justified True Belief Knowledge?" *Analysis* 23, June 1963, pp. 121–123. By permission of Oxford University Press.

8   [Author's footnote] Plato seems to be considering some such definition at *Theaetetus* 201, and perhaps accepting one at *Meno* 98. [See "Some Useful Background Information" in Introduction to this reading.]

9   'IFF' is an abbreviation for 'If and only if.' 'X if and only if Y' means if X then Y, and if Y then X.

10 [Author's footnote] Roderick M. Chisholm, *Perceiving: A Philosophical Study*, Cornell University Press (Ithaca, New York, 1957), p. 16.

11 [Author's footnote] A.J. Ayer, *The Problem of Knowledge*, Macmillan (London, 1956), p. 34.

12 A conjunctive proposition is a statement composed of two propositions connected by 'and.' 'It's raining and it's Tuesday' is an example. A conjunctive proposition is true when both of its components are true; otherwise, it's false.

which he has strong evidence. In this case, Smith is clearly justified in believing that (e) is true.

But imagine, further, that unknown to Smith, he himself, not Jones, will get the job. And, also, unknown to Smith, he himself has ten coins in his pocket. Proposition (e) is then true, though proposition (d), from which Smith inferred (e), is false. In our example, then, all of the following are true: (*i*) (e) is true, (*ii*) Smith believes that (e) is true, and (*iii*) Smith is justified in believing that (e) is true. But it is equally clear that Smith does not *know* that (e) is true; for (e) is true in virtue of the number of coins in Smith's pocket, while Smith does not know how many coins are in Smith's pocket, and bases his belief in (e) on a count of the coins in Jones's pocket, whom he falsely believes to be the man who will get the job.

Case II

Let us suppose that Smith has strong evidence for the following proposition:

(f) Jones owns a Ford.

Smith's evidence might be that Jones has at all times in the past within Smith's memory owned a car, and always a Ford, and that Jones has just offered Smith a ride while driving a Ford. Let us imagine, now, that Smith has another friend, Brown, of whose whereabouts he is totally ignorant. Smith selects three place-names quite at random, and constructs the following three propositions:

(g) Either Jones owns a Ford, or Brown is in Boston;

(h) Either Jones owns a Ford, or Brown is in Barcelona;

(i) Either Jones owns a Ford, or Brown is in Brest-Litovsk.

Each of these propositions is entailed by (f).[13] Imagine that Smith realizes the entailment of each of these propositions he has constructed by (f), and proceeds to accept (g), (h), and (i) on the basis of (f). Smith has correctly inferred (g), (h), and (i) from a proposition for which he has strong evidence. Smith is therefore completely justified in believing each of these three propositions. Smith, of course, has no idea where Brown is.

But imagine now that two further conditions hold. First, Jones does *not* own a Ford, but is at present driving a rented car. And secondly, by the sheerest coincidence, and entirely unknown to Smith, the place mentioned in proposition (h) happens really to be the place where Brown is. If these two conditions hold then Smith does *not* know that (h) is true, even though (*i*) (h) *is* true, (*ii*) Smith does believe that (h) is true, and (*iii*) Smith is justified in believing that (h) is true.

These two examples show that definition (a) does not state a *sufficient* condition for someone's knowing a given proposition. The same cases, with appropriate changes, will suffice to show that neither definition (b) nor definition (c) do so either.

---

13   Note that a statement 'P' entails 'P or Q,' where 'Q' is any proposition at all. That's because a disjunctive proposition—one composed by connecting two component propositions with 'or'—is true when (at least) one of its components is true. So assuming that P is true, then it follows that P or anything-at-all must also be true.

LORRAINE CODE

"Is the Sex of the Knower Epistemologically Significant?"

Who Is Lorraine Code?

Lorraine Code (1937–) is Distinguished Research Professor of Philosophy at York University, Toronto, Canada. She received her undergraduate degree from Queen's University and her PhD from the University of Guelph, both in Ontario. Her main areas of interest are epistemology, ethics, feminist philosophy, and the politics of knowledge. She was named the Distinguished Woman Philosopher for 2009 by the US Society for Women in Philosophy.

How Important and Influential Is This Passage?

An idea which has moved from the fringes to the mainstream of philosophical ethics and social/political theory in the past few decades is *feminism*. The notion that women have, throughout history, been systematically subordinated and disparaged by male-dominated society—and that this immoral situation must be changed not only through the reform of social structures but also by adjustments to some of our most basic philosophical concepts and assumptions—was once controversial but is now widely accepted by the philosophical community. Thus, there are today a range of feminist projects to critique traditional ways of doing philosophy, and the present article illustrates one of these.

Feminist epistemology examines the assumptions which lie at the basis of traditional epistemology—such as that the ideal knower is perfectly rational and objective, or that the paradigm model for knowledge-acquisition is the scientific method—and subjects them to critical assessment from a feminist point of view. The central concept of feminist epistemology is that of a *situated knower*—and thus of situated knowledge: knowledge that reflects the particular perspectives of the subject—and a central feminist argument is that gender is a particularly important way of being situated. Code lays out these ideas in a clear and careful way.

Suggestions for Critical Reflection

1. Code contrasts the traditional idea that knowledge claims should be assessed "on their own merits" with the claim that "the circumstances of knowledge acquisition" are relevant to their evaluation. Which of these two stances do you think is the most plausible—or epistemically responsible—on the face of it? After reading Code's article carefully, does she change your views?

2. Exactly *how* do "the circumstances of knowledge acquisition," and especially who the knower is, affect the evaluation of knowledge claims, on Code's view? For example, can some factual claim be true or justified if it is asserted by one knower but not if it is asserted by another? (Does Code in fact think that the circumstances of the knower are relevant to the *justification* of knowledge claims at all?) Are all types of knowledge claims equally relative to their knower, or are there differences between kinds of knowledge (e.g., between ethical knowledge and geographical knowledge)?

3. What is the significance of Code's claim that most pieces of knowledge are not 'all or nothing' but are a matter of *degree*?

4. Do you agree with Code—if this is indeed her view—that "there is no universal, unchanging framework or scheme for rational adjudication among competing knowledge claims"? How

radical do you think this claim is? Is the kind of relativism that Code adopts, as she claims, an 'enabling' rather than a problematic position?

5. Code suggests that the nature and circumstances of the knower have not been ignored or treated neutrally in traditional epistemology. Rather, traditional epistemology—such as that of Descartes—has been shaped by tacit, often concealed, and sexist assumptions about the nature of the knower. What do you make of this claim? What is its significance for Code's project?

6. Why does Code reject essentialism about female nature? Is she pragmatically or theoretically right to do so? What is the significance of this stance for her version of feminist epistemology?

ledge, 1996); Carol Gilligan, *In a Different Voice* (Harvard University Press, 1982); Sandra Harding, *Whose Science? Whose Knowledge?* (Cornell University Press, 1991); Evelyn Fox Keller, *Reflections on Gender and Science* (Yale University Press, 1985); Kathleen Lennon and Margaret Whitford, eds., *Knowing the Difference: Feminist Perspectives in Epistemology* (Routledge, 1994); Helen Longino, *Science as Social Knowledge* (Princeton University Press, 1990); Genevieve Lloyd, *The Man of Reason: 'Male' and 'Female' in Western Philosophy* (2nd edition, University of Minnesota Press, 1993); and Alessandra Tanesini, *An Introduction to Feminist Epistemologies* (Blackwell, 1999). There is also *The Cambridge Companion to Feminism in Philosophy*, edited by Miranda Fricker and Jennifer Hornsby (Cambridge University Press, 2000).

Suggestions for Further Reading

Among Lorraine Code's books are *What Can She Know? Feminist Theory and the Construction of Knowledge* (Cornell University Press, 1991), *Rhetorical Spaces: Essays on (Gendered) Locations* (Routledge, 1995), and *Ecological Thinking: The Politics of Epistemic Location* (Oxford University Press, 2006); she has also edited several collections, including the *Encyclopedia of Feminist Theories* (Routledge, 2000) and, with Sandra Burt, *Changing Methods: Feminists Transforming Practice* (Broadview Press, 1995). Some other central readings in feminist epistemology are: Linda Alcoff and Elizabeth Potter, eds., *Feminist Epistemologies* (Routledge, 1993); Louise Antony and Charlotte Witt, eds., *A Mind of One's Own: Feminist Essays on Reason and Objectivity* (Westview Press, 1993); Ann Garry and Marilyn Pearsall, eds., *Women, Knowledge and Reality* (2nd edition, Rout-

"Is the Sex of the Knower Epistemologically Significant?"[1]

The Question

A question that focuses on the knower, as the title of this chapter does, claims that there are good reasons for asking who that knower is.[2] Uncontroversial as

---

1 This is Chapter 1 of Lorraine Code's *What Can She Know? Feminist Theory and the Construction of Knowledge* (Ithaca: Cornell University Press, 1991), pp. 1–26. Copyright © 1991 by Cornell University. Used by permission of the publisher, Cornell University Press.

2 [Author's note] This question is the title of my paper published in *Metaphilosophy* 12 (July–October 1981): pp. 267–276. In this early essay I endorse an essentialism with respect to masculinity and femininity, and

such a suggestion would be in ordinary conversations about knowledge, academic philosophers commonly treat 'the knower' as a featureless abstraction. Sometimes, indeed, she or he is merely a place holder in the proposition 'S knows that p'. Epistemological analyses of the proposition tend to focus on the 'knowing that', to determine conditions under which a knowledge claim can legitimately be made. Once discerned, it is believed, such conditions will hold across all possible utterances of the proposition. Indeed, throughout the history of modern philosophy the central 'problem of knowledge' has been to determine necessary and sufficient conditions for the possibility and justification of knowledge claims. Philosophers have sought ways of establishing a relation of correspondence between knowledge and 'reality' and/or ways of establishing the coherence of particular knowledge claims within systems of already-established truths. They have proposed methodologies for arriving at truth, and criteria for determining the validity of claims to the effect that 'S knows that p'. Such endeavors are guided by the putatively self-evident principle that truth once discerned, knowledge once established, claim their status as truth and knowledge by virtue of a grounding in or coherence within a permanent, objective, ahistorical, and circumstantially neutral framework or set of standards.

The question 'Who is S?' is regarded neither as legitimate nor as relevant in these endeavors. As inquirers into the nature and conditions of human knowledge, epistemologists commonly work from the assumption that they need concern themselves only with knowledge claims that meet certain standards of *purity*. Questions about the circumstances of knowledge acquisition serve merely to clutter and confuse the issue with contingencies and other impurities. The question 'Who is S?' is undoubtedly such a question. If it matters who S is, then it must follow that something peculiar to S's character or nature could bear on the validity of the knowledge she or he claims: that S's *identity* might count among the conditions that make that knowledge claim possible. For many

convey the impression that 'positive thinking' can bring an end to gender imbalances. I would no longer make these claims.

philosophers, such a suggestion would undermine the cherished assumption that knowledge can—and should—be evaluated on its own merits. More seriously still, a proposal that it matters who the knower is looks suspiciously like a move in the direction of epistemological relativism. For many philosophers, an endorsement of relativism signals the end of knowledge and of epistemology.

Broadly described, epistemological relativists hold that knowledge, truth, or even 'reality' can be understood only in relation to particular sets of cultural or social circumstances, to a theoretical framework, a specifiable range of perspectives, a conceptual scheme, or a form of life. Conditions of justification, criteria of truth and falsity, and standards of rationality are likewise relative: there is no universal, unchanging framework or scheme for rational adjudication among competing knowledge claims.

Critics of relativism often argue that relativism entails incommensurability: that a relativist cannot evaluate knowledge claims comparatively. This argument is based on the contention that epistemological relativism entails conceptual relativism: that it contextualizes language just as it contextualizes knowledge, so that there remains no 'common' or neutral linguistic framework for discussion, agreement, *or* disagreement. Other critics maintain that the very concept 'knowledge' is rendered meaningless by relativism: that the only honest—and logical—move a relativist can make is once and for all to declare her or his skepticism. Where there are no universal standards, the argument goes, there can be no knowledge worthy of the name. Opponents often contend that relativism is simply incoherent because of its inescapable self-referentiality. Relativism, they argue, is subject to the same constraints as every other claim to knowledge and truth. Any claim for the truth of relativism must itself be relative to the circumstances of the claimant; hence relativism itself has no claim to objective or universal truth. In short, relativism is often perceived as a denial of the very possibility of epistemology.[3]

3   [Author's note] I consider some of these objections to relativism at greater length in "The Importance of Historicism for a Theory of Knowledge," *International Philosophical Quarterly* 22 (June 1982): pp. 157–174.

Now posing the question 'Who is S?'—that is, 'Who is the knowing subject?'—does indeed count as a move in the direction of relativism, and my intention in posing it is to suggest that the answer has epistemological import. But I shall invoke certain caveats[4] to demonstrate that such a move is not the epistemological disaster that many theorists of knowledge believe it to be.

It is true that, on its starkest construal, relativism may threaten to slide into subjectivism, into a position for which knowledge claims are indistinguishable from expressions of personal opinion, taste, or bias. But relativism need not be construed so starkly, nor do its *limitations* warrant exclusive emphasis. There are advantages to endorsing a measure of epistemological relativism that make of it an enabling rather than a constraining position. By no means the least of these advantages is the fact that relativism is one of the more obvious means of avoiding reductive explanations, in terms of drastically simplified paradigms of knowledge, monolithic explanatory modes, or privileged, decontextualized positions. For a relativist, who contends that there can be many valid ways of knowing any phenomenon, there is the possibility of taking several constructions, many perspectives into account. Hence relativism keeps open a range of interpretive possibilities. At the same time, because of the epistemic choices it affirms, it creates stringent accountability requirements of which knowers have to be cognizant. Thus it introduces a moral-political component into the heart of epistemological enquiry.[5]

There probably is no absolute authority, no practice of all practices or scheme of all schemes. Yet it does not follow that conceptual schemes, practices, and paradigms are radically idiosyncratic or purely subjective. Schemes, practices, and paradigms evolve out of communal projects of inquiry. To sustain viability and authority, they must demonstrate their adequacy in enabling people to negotiate the everyday world and to cope with the decisions, problems, and puzzles they encounter daily. From the claim that no single scheme has absolute explanatory power, it does not follow that all schemes are equally valid. Knowledge is qualitatively variable: some knowledge is *better* than other knowledge. Relativists are in a good position to take such qualitative variations into account and to analyze their implications.

Even if these points are granted, though, it would be a mistake to believe that posing the 'Who is S?' question indicates that the circumstances of the knower are *all* that counts in knowledge evaluation. The point is, rather, that understanding the circumstances of the knower makes possible a more *discerning* evaluation. The claim that certain of those circumstances are epistemologically significant—the sex of the knower, in this instance—by no means implies that they are definitive, capable of bearing the entire burden of justification and evaluation. This point requires special emphasis. Claiming epistemological significance for the sex of the knower might seem tantamount to a dismissal, to a contention that S made such a claim only because of his or her sex. Dismissals of this sort, both of women's knowledge *and* of their claims to be knowers in any sense of the word, are only too common throughout the history of western thought. But claiming that the circumstances of the knower are not epistemologically definitive is quite different from claiming that they are of no epistemological consequence. The position I take in this book is that the sex of the knower is one of a cluster of *subjective* factors (i.e., factors that pertain to the circumstances of cognitive agents) constitutive of received conceptions of knowledge and of what it means to be a knower. I maintain that subjectivity and the specificities of cognitive agency can and must be accorded central epistemological significance, yet that so doing does not commit an inquirer to outright subjectivism. Specificities count, and they require a place in epistemological evaluation, but they cannot tell the whole story.

Knowers and the Known

The only thing that is clear about S from the standard proposition 'S knows that p' is that S is a (would-be) knower. Although the question 'Who is S?' rarely arises, certain assumptions about S as knower perme-

---

4   A caveat is a warning or a reservation.

5   [Author's note] I discuss some of these accountability requirements, and the normative realism from which they derive, in my *Epistemic Responsibility* (Hanover, NH: University Press of New England, 1987).

ate epistemological inquiry. Of special importance for my argument is the assumption that knowers are self-sufficient and solitary individuals, at least in their knowledge-seeking activities. This belief derives from a long and venerable heritage, with its roots in Descartes's quest for a basis of perfect certainty on which to establish his knowledge. The central aim of Descartes's endeavors is captured in this claim: "I shall have the right to conceive high hopes if I am happy enough to discover one thing only which is certain and indubitable."[6] That "one thing," Descartes believed, would stand as the fixed, pivotal, Archimedean point on which all the rest of his knowledge would turn. Because of its systematic relation to that point, his knowledge would be certain and indubitable.

Most significant for this discussion is Descartes's conviction that his quest will be conducted in a private, introspective examination of the contents of his own mind. It is true that, in the last section of the *Discourse on the Method*, Descartes acknowledges the benefit "others may receive from the communication of [his] reflection," and he states his belief that combining "the lives and labours of many"[7] is essential to progress in scientific knowledge. It is also true that this individualistically described act of knowing exercises the aspect of the soul that is common to and alike in all knowers: namely, the faculty of reason. Yet his claim that knowledge seeking is an introspective activity of an individual mind accords no relevance either to a knower's embodiment or to his (or her) intersubjective relations. For each knower, the Cartesian route to knowledge is through private, abstract thought, through the efforts of reason unaided either by the senses or by consultation with other knowers. It is this individualistic, self-reliant, private aspect of Descartes's philosophy that has been influential in shaping subsequent epistemological ideals.

---

6   [Author's note] René Descartes, *Meditations*, in *The Philosophical Works of Descartes*, trans. Elizabeth S. Haldane and G.R.T. Ross (Cambridge: Cambridge University Press, 1969), 1:149.

7   [Author's note] René Descartes, *Discourse on the Method of Rightly Conducting the Reason and Seeking for Truth in the Sciences*, in ibid., pp. 124, 120.

Reason is conceived as autonomous in the Cartesian project in two ways, then. Not only is the quest for certain knowledge an independent one, undertaken separately by each rational being, but it is a journey of reason alone, unassisted by the senses. For Descartes believed that sensory experiences had the effect of distracting reason from its proper course.

The custom of formulating knowledge claims in the 'S knows that p' formula is not itself of Cartesian origin. The point of claiming Cartesian inspiration for an assumption implicit in the formulation is that the knower who is commonly presumed to be the subject of that proposition is modeled, in significant respects, on the Cartesian pure inquirer. For epistemological purposes, all knowers are believed to be alike with respect both to their cognitive capacities and to their methods of achieving knowledge. In the empiricist tradition this assumption is apparent in the belief that simple, basic observational data can provide the foundation of knowledge just because perception is invariant from observer to observer, in standard observation conditions. In fact, a common way of filling the places in the 'S knows that p' proposition is with substitutions such as "Peter knows that the door is open" or "John knows that the book is red." It does not matter who John or Peter is.

Such knowledge claims carry implicit beliefs not only about would-be knowers but also about the knowledge that is amenable to philosophical analysis. Although (Cartesian) rationalists and empiricists differ with respect to what kinds of claim count as foundational, they endorse similar assumptions about the relation of foundational claims to the rest of a body of knowledge. With 'S knows that p' propositions, the belief is that such propositions stand as paradigms for knowledge in general. Epistemologists assume that knowledge is analyzable into propositional 'simples' whose truth can be demonstrated by establishing relations of correspondence to reality, or coherence within a system of known truths. These relatively simple knowledge claims (i.e., John knows that the book is red) could indeed be made by most 'normal' people who know the language and are familiar with the objects named. Knowers would seem to be quite self-sufficient in acquiring such knowledge. Moreover, no one would claim to know "a little" that the book is red or to be in the process of acquiring knowledge about the openness of the door. Nor would anyone be likely to maintain that S knows better than W does that the door is open or that the book is red. Granting such examples paradigmatic status creates the mistaken assumption that all knowledge worthy of the name will be like this.

In some recent epistemological discussion, emphasis has shifted away from simple perceptual claims toward processes of evaluating the 'warranted assertability' of more complex knowledge claims. In such contexts it does make sense to analyze the degree or extent of the knowledge claimed. Yet claims of the simple, perceptual sort are still most commonly cited as exemplary. They are assumed to have an all-or-nothing character; hence they seem not to admit of qualitative assessment. Granting them exemplary status implies that, for knowledge in general, it is appropriate to ask about neither the circumstances of the knowing process nor who the knower is. There would be no point to the suggestion that her or his identity might bear on the *quality* of the knowledge under discussion.

Proposing that the sex of the knower is significant casts doubt both on the autonomy of reason and on the (residual) exemplary status of simple observational knowledge claims. The suggestion that reason might function differently according to whose it is and in what circumstances its capacities are exercised implies that the manner of its functioning is dependent, in some way, on those circumstances, not independent from them. Simple perceptual examples are rendered contestable for their tendency to give a misleading impression of how knowledge is constructed and established and to suppress diversities in knowledge acquisition that derive from the varied circumstances—for example, the sex—of different knowers.

Just what am I asking, then, with this question about the epistemological *significance* of the sex of the knower? First, I do not expect that the question will elicit the answer that the sex of the knower is pertinent among conditions for the existence of knowledge, in the sense that taking it into account will make it possible to avoid skepticism. Again, it is unlikely that information about the sex of the knower could count among criteria of evidence or means of

justifying knowledge claims. Nor is it prima facie obvious that the sex of the knower will have a legitimate bearing on the qualitative judgments that could be made about certain claims to know. Comparative judgments of the following kind are not what I expect to elicit: that if the knower is female, her knowledge is likely to be better grounded; if the knower is male, his knowledge will likely be more coherent.

In proposing that the sex of the knower is epistemologically significant, I am claiming that the scope of epistemological inquiry has been too narrowly defined. My point is not to denigrate projects of establishing the best foundations possible or of developing workable criteria of coherence. I am proposing that even if it is not possible (or not *yet* possible) to establish an unassailable foundationalist or coherentist position, there are numerous questions to be asked about knowledge whose answers matter to people who are concerned to know well. Among them are questions that bear not just on criteria of evidence, justification, and warrantability, but on the 'nature' of cognitive agents: questions about their character; their material, historical, cultural circumstances; their interests in the inquiry at issue. These are questions about how credibility is established, about connections between knowledge and power, about the place of knowledge in ethical and aesthetic judgments, and about political agendas and the responsibilities of knowers. I am claiming that all of these questions are epistemologically significant.

The Sex of the Knower

What, then, of the sex of the knower? In the rest of this chapter—and this book—I examine some attempts to give content to the claim that the sex of the knower *is* epistemologically significant.[8] Many of these en-

---

8 [Author's note] In this chapter I discuss the sex of the knower in a way that may seem to conflate biological sex differences with their cultural elaborations and manifestations as gender differences. I retain the older term—albeit inconsistently—for two reasons. The first, personally historical, reason connects this text with my first thoughts on these matters, published in my *Metaphilosophy* paper (see note [2], above). The second, philosophically historical, reason reflects the

deavors have been less than satisfactory. Nonetheless, I argue that the claim itself is accurate.

Although it has rarely been spelled out prior to the development of feminist critiques, it has long been tacitly assumed that S is male. Nor could S be just any man, the apparently infinite substitutability of the 'S' term notwithstanding. The S who could count as a model, paradigmatic knower has most commonly—if always tacitly—been an adult (but not old), white, reasonably affluent (latterly middle-class) educated man of status, property, and publicly acceptable accomplishments. In theory of knowledge he has been allowed to stand for all men.[9] This assumption does not merely derive from habit or coincidence, but is a manifestation of engrained philosophical convictions. Not only has it been taken for granted that knowers properly so-called are male, but when male philosophers have paused to note this fact, as some indeed have done, they have argued that things are as they should be. Reason may be alike in all men, but it would be a mistake to believe that 'man', in this respect, 'embraces woman'. Women have been judged incapable, for many reasons, of achieving knowledge worthy of the name. It is no exaggeration to say that anyone who wanted to *count* as a knower has commonly had to be male.

In the *Politics*, Aristotle observes: "The freeman rules over the slave after another manner from that in which the male rules over the female, or the man over the child; although the parts of the soul are present in all of them, they are present in different degrees. For the slave has no deliberative faculty at all; the woman has, but it is without authority, and the child has, but it is immature."[10] Aristotle's assumption that a woman will naturally be ruled by a man connects directly with his contention that a woman's deliberative faculty is "without authority." Even if a woman could, in her sequestered, domestic position, acquire deliberative skills, she would remain reliant on her husband for her sources of knowledge and information. She must be ruled by a man because, in the social structure of the *polis*, she enjoys neither the autonomy nor the freedom to put into visible practice the results of the deliberations she may engage in, in private. If she can claim no authority for her rational, deliberative endeavors, then her chances of gaining recognition as a knowledgeable citizen are seriously limited, whatever she may do.[11]

Aristotle is just one of a long line of western thinkers to declare the limitations of women's cognitive capacities.[12] Rousseau maintains that young men and women should be educated quite differently

---

relatively recent appearance of 'gender' as a theoretical term of art. In the history of 'the epistemological project', which I discuss in these early chapters, 'sex' would have been the term used, had these questions been raised.

9   [Author's note] To cite just one example: in *The Theory of Epistemic Rationality* (Cambridge: Harvard University Press, 1987), Richard Foley appeals repeatedly to the epistemic judgments of people who are "like the rest of us" (p. 108). He contrasts their beliefs with beliefs that seem "crazy or bizarre or outlandish ... beliefs to most of the rest of us" (p. 114), and argues that an account of rational belief is plausible only if it can be presented from "some nonweird perspective" (p. 140). Foley contends that "an individual has to be at least minimally like us in order for charges of irrationality even to make sense" (p. 240). Nowhere does he address the question of who 'we' are. (I take this point up again in Chapter 7 [of *What Can She Know?*].)

10 [Author's note] Aristotle, *Politics*, trans. Benjamin Jowett, in *The Basic Works of Aristotle*, ed. Richard McKeon (New York: Random House, 1941), 1260b.

11 [Author's note] I discuss the implications of this lack of authority more fully in Chapters 9 and 6. See Elizabeth V. Spelman, *Inessential Woman: Problems of Exclusion in Feminist Thought* (Boston: Beacon, 1988), for an interesting discussion of some more complex exclusions effected by Aristotle's analysis.

12 [Author's note] It would be inaccurate, however, to argue that this line is unbroken. Londa Schiebinger demonstrates that in the history of science—and, by implication, the history of the achievement of epistemic authority—there were many periods when women's intellectual achievements were not only recognized but respected. The "long line" I refer to is the dominant, historically most visible one. Schiebinger, *The Mind Has No Sex? Women in the Origins of Modern Science* (Cambridge: Harvard University Press, 1989).

because of women's inferiority in reason and their propensity to be dragged down by their sensual natures. For Kierkegaard, women are merely aesthetic beings: men alone can attain the (higher) ethical and religious levels of existence. And for Nietzsche, the Apollonian (intellectual) domain is the male preserve, whereas women are Dionysian (sensuous) creatures. Nineteenth-century philosopher and linguist Wilhelm von Humboldt, who writes at length about women's knowledge, sums up the central features of this line of thought as follows: "A sense of truth exists in [women] quite literally as a sense: ... their nature also contains a lack or a failing of analytic capacity which draws a strict line of demarcation between ego and world; therefore, they will not come as close to the ultimate investigation of truth as man."[13] The implication is that women's knowledge, if ever the products of their projects deserve that label, is inherently and inevitably *subjective*—in the most idiosyncratic sense—by contrast with the best of men's knowledge.

Objectivity, quite precisely construed, is commonly regarded as a defining feature of knowledge per se.[14] So if women's knowledge is declared to be *naturally* subjective, then a clear answer emerges to my question. The answer is that if the would-be knower is female, then her sex is indeed epistemologically significant, for it disqualifies her as a knower in the fullest sense of that term. Such disqualifications will operate differently for women of different classes, races, ages, and allegiances, but in every circumstance they will operate asymmetrically for women and for men. Just what is to be made of these points—how their epistemological significance is to be construed—is the subject of this book.

The presuppositions I have just cited claim more than the rather simple fact that many kinds of knowledge and skill have, historically, been inaccessible to women on a purely practical level. It is true, historically speaking, that even women who were the racial and social 'equals' of standard male knowers were only rarely able to become learned. The thinkers I have cited (and others like them) claim to find a rationale for this state of affairs through appeals to dubious 'facts' about women's natural incapacity for rational thought. Yet deeper questions still need to be asked: Is there knowledge that is, quite simply, inaccessible to members of the female, or the male, sex? Are there kinds of knowledge that only men, or only women, can acquire? Is the sex of the knower crucially determining in this respect, across all other specificities? The answers to these questions should not address only the *practical* possibilities that have existed for members of either sex. Such practical possibilities are the constructs of complex social arrangements that are themselves constructed out of historically specific choices, and are, as such, open to challenge and change.

Knowledge, as it achieves credence and authoritative status at any point in the history of the male-dominated mainstream, is commonly held to be a product of the individual efforts of human knowers. References to Pythagoras's theorem, Copernicus's revolution, and Newtonian and Einsteinian physics signal an epistemic community's attribution of pathbreaking contributions to certain of its individual members. The implication is that *that* person, single-handedly, has effected a leap of progress in a particular field of inquiry. In less publicly spectacular ways, other cognitive agents are represented as contributors to the growth and stability of public knowledge.

Now any contention that such contributions are the results of independent endeavor is highly contestable. As I argue elsewhere,[15] a complex of historical and other sociocultural factors produces the conditions that make 'individual' achievement possible, and 'individuals' themselves are socially constituted.[16] The claim that individual *men* are the creators of the authoritative (often Kuhn[17]-paradigm-establishing)

---

13   [Author's note] *Humanist without Portfolio: An Anthology of the Writings of Wilhelm von Humboldt,* trans. with intro. by Marianne Cowan (Detroit: Wayne State University Press, 1963), p. 349.

14   [Author's note] I analyze this precise construal of objectivity in Chapter 2.

15   [Author's note] See chap. 7, "Epistemic Community," of my *Epistemic Responsibility.*

16   [Author's note] I discuss the implications of these points for analyses of subjectivity in Chapter 3.

17   Philosopher of science Thomas Kuhn, who is most associated with the notion that paradigms—roughly,

landmarks of western intellectual life is particularly interesting for the fact that the contributions—both practical and substantive—of their lovers, wives, children, servants, neighbors, friends, and colleagues rarely figure in analyses of their work.[18]

The historical attribution of such achievements to specific cognitive agents does, nonetheless, accord a significance to individual efforts which raises questions pertinent to my project. It poses the problem, in another guise, of whether aspects of human specificity could, in fact, constitute conditions for the existence of knowledge or determine the kinds of knowledge that a knower can achieve. It would seem that such incidental physical attributes as height, weight, or hair color would not count among factors that would determine a person's capacities to know (though the arguments that skin color *does* count are too familiar). It is not necessary to consider how much Archimedes weighed when he made his famous discovery,[19] nor is there any doubt that a thinner or a fatter person could have reached the same conclusion. But in cultures in which sex differences figure prominently in virtually every mode of human interaction,[20] being female or male is far more fundamental to the construction of subjectivity than are such attributes as size or hair color. So the question is whether femaleness or maleness are the kinds of subjective factor (i.e., factors about the circumstances of a knowing subject) that are constitutive of the form and content of knowledge. Attempts to answer this question are complicated by the fact that sex/gender does not function uniformly and universally, even in western societies. Its implications vary across class, race, age, ability, and numerous other interwoven specificities. A separated analysis of sex/gender, then, always risks abstraction and is limited in its scope by the abstracting process. Further, the question seems to imply that sex and gender are themselves constants, thus obscuring the processes of *their* sociocultural construction. Hence the formulation of adequately nuanced answers is problematic and necessarily partial.

Even if it should emerge that gender-related factors play a crucial role in the construction of knowledge, then, the inquiry into the epistemological significance of the sex of the knower would not be complete. The task would remain of considering whether a distinction between 'natural' and socialized capacity can retain any validity. The equally pressing question as to how the hitherto devalued products of *women's* cognitive projects can gain acknowledgment as 'knowledge' would need to be addressed so as to uproot entrenched prejudices about knowledge, epistemology, and women. 'The epistemological project' will look quite different once its tacit underpinnings are revealed.

Reclaiming 'the Feminine'

Whether this project could or should emerge in a *feminist epistemology* is quite another question. Investigations that start from the conviction that the sex of the knower is epistemologically significant will surely question received conceptions of the nature of knowledge and challenge the hegemony[21] of mainstream epistemologies. Some feminist theorists have maintained that there are distinctively female—or feminine—ways of knowing: neglected ways, from which the label 'knowledge', traditionally, is withheld. Many claim that a recognition of these 'ways of knowing' should prompt the development of new, rival, or even separate epistemologies. Others have adopted Mary

---

sets of key experimental concepts and results—govern scientific research.

18 [Author's note] I owe this point—and the list—to Polly Young-Eisendrath, "The Female Person and How We Talk about Her," in Mary M. Gergen, ed., *Feminist Thought and the Structure of Knowledge* (New York: New York University Press, 1988).

19 The principle, which Archimedes is said to have discovered in his bath, that the apparent loss of weight of a body when immersed in a liquid is equal to the weight of the liquid displaced.

20 [Author's note] Marilyn Frye points out: "Sex-identification intrudes into every moment of our lives and discourse, no matter what the supposedly primary focus or topic of the moment is. Elaborate, systematic, ubiquitous and redundant marking of a distinction between two sexes of humans and most animals is customary and obligatory. One *never* can ignore it." Frye, *The Politics of Reality: Essays in Feminist Theory* (Trumansburg, NY: Crossing Press, 1983), p. 19.

---

21 Domination, especially political or social domination.

O'Brien's brilliant characterization of mainstream epistemology as "malestream,"[22] claiming that one of the principal manifestations of its hegemony is its suppression of female—or 'feminine'—knowledge. In this section I sketch some classic and more recent arguments in favor of feminine 'ways of knowing' and offer a preliminary analysis of their strengths and shortcomings.

Claims that there are specifically female or feminine ways of knowing often find support in the contention that women's significantly different experiences (different, that is, from men's experiences) lead them to know 'the world' differently (i.e., from the ways men do). A putatively different female consciousness, in turn, generates different theories of knowledge, politics, metaphysics, morality, and aesthetics. Features of women's experiences commonly cited are a concern with the concrete, everyday world; a connection with objects of experience rather than an objective distance from them; a marked affective tone; a respect for the environment; and a readiness to listen perceptively and responsibly to a variety of 'voices' in the environment, both animate and inanimate, manifested in a tolerance of diversity.

Many of these features are continuous with the attributes with which the dominant discourse of affluent western societies characterizes a good mother. Indeed, one of the best-known advocates of a caring, maternal approach both to knowledge and to a morality based on that knowledge is Sara Ruddick, in her now-classic article "Maternal Thinking." Maternal thinking, Ruddick believes, grows out of the *practice* of caring for and establishing an intimate connection with another being—a growing child. That practice is marked by a "unity of reflection, judgment and emotion ... [which is] ... no more relative to its particular reality (the growing child) than the thinking that arises from scientific, religious, or other practice"[23]

is relevant to scientific or religious matters alone. Just as scientific or religious thought can structure a knower's characteristic approach to experiences and knowledge in general, Ruddick believes that attitudes and skills developed in the attentive and painstaking practices of caring for infants and small children are generalizable across cognitive domains.

Ruddick's celebration of values traditionally associated with mothering and femininity is not the first such in the history of feminist thought. Among nineteenth-century American feminists, both Margaret Fuller and Matilda Gage praised women's intuition as a peculiarly insightful capacity. Fuller, for example, believed that women have an intuitive perception that enables them to "seize and delineate with unerring discrimination" the connections and links among the various life forms that surround them.[24] In this respect, she maintains, women are superior to men. And Gage believed that women have unique intellectual capacities, manifested especially in an intuitive faculty that does not "need a long process of ratiocination" for its operations.[25] Both Fuller and Gage, albeit in quite different contexts, advocate legitimizing this suppressed and undervalued faculty whose deliverances, they believe, are attuned to and hence better able to reveal the secrets of nature and (for Gage) of spirituality, than masculine ratiocinative practices.[26]

This nineteenth-century belief in the powers of female intuition is echoed in the work of two of the best-known twentieth-century radical feminists, Shulamith Firestone and Mary Daly. For Firestone, there are two sharply contrasting modes or styles of response to experience: an "aesthetic response," which she links to femaleness and characterizes as "subjective, intuitive, introverted, wishful, dreamy or fantastic, concerned with the subconscious (the id), emotional, even tem-

---

22   [Author's note] See Mary O'Brien, *The Politics of Reproduction* (London: Routledge & Kegan Paul, 1980).

23   [Author's note] Sara Ruddick, "Maternal Thinking," *Feminist Studies* 6 (1980): p. 348. I develop a critical analysis of Ruddick's position in Chapter 3. It should be noted that in Ruddick's 1989 book, *Maternal Thinking: Toward a Politics of Peace* (Boston: Beacon,

1989), she addresses some of the issues I raise about the essentialism of this earlier article.

24   [Author's note] Margaret Fuller, *Woman in the Nineteenth Century* (1845; New York: Norton, 1971), p. 103.

25   [Author's note] Matilda Jocelyn Gage, *Women, Church, and State* (1893; Watertown, Mass.: Persephone, 1980), p. 238.

26   Practices having to do with reasoning.

peramental (hysterical)"; and a technological response, which she describes as masculine: "objective, logical, extroverted, realistic, concerned with the conscious mind (the ego), rational, mechanical, pragmatic and down-to-earth, stable."[27] Firestone's claim is not that the aesthetic (= the feminine) should dominate, but that there should be a fusion between the two modes. To overcome patriarchal domination, she believes, it is vital for the aesthetic principle to manifest itself in all cultural and cognitive activity and for technology to cease operating to exclude affectivity.

Daly's concern with spirituality and with the celebration of witchcraft places her closer to Gage than to Fuller. Daly invokes the metaphor of spinning to describe the creation of knowledge and to connect the process with women's traditional creative activities. She claims that "Gyn/Ecology Spins around, past, and through the established fields, opening the coffers/coffins in which 'knowledge' has been stored, re-stored, re-covered ... [where] its meaning will be hidden from the Grave Keepers of tradition." These "Grave Keepers" are the arbiters of knowledge in patriarchal culture: the men who determine the legitimacy of knowledge claims. In consequence of their forced adherence to masculine epistemic norms, Daly contends, "women are encouraged, that is, dis-couraged, to adapt to a maintenance level of cognition and behavior by all the myth-masters and enforcers." Gyn/Ecology is a process of breaking the "spell of patriarchal myth"—by which Daly means all 'received' knowledge in patriarchal cultures— "bounding into freedom"; weaving "the tapestries of [one's] own creation."[28] Once freed from patriarchal myth, women will acquire the knowledge they need to validate their pleasures and powers as marks of their own authority and to unmask patriarchy. Daly's is a vision of female empowerment.

Some theorists maintain that research into the lateralization of brain function reveals 'natural' female-male cognitive differences. The findings of this research are frequently interpreted to indicate that in men, "left-brain" functions predominate, whereas "right-brain" functioning is better developed in women. Evidence that women have better verbal skills and fine motor coordination, whereas men are more adept at spatial skills, mathematics, and abstract thinking, is cited as proof of the existence of female and male cognitive differences. Depending on the political orientation of the inquirer, such findings are read either as confirmations of male supremacy and female inferiority or as indications of a need to revalue 'the feminine'. Among the celebratory interpretations are Gina Covina's claim that women, whom she describes as more "rightbrained" than men, deal with experience "in a diffuse non-sequential way, assimilating many different phenomena simultaneously, finding connections between separate bits of information." By contrast, men, whom she labels "leftbrained," engage typically in thinking that is "focused narrowly enough to squeeze out human or emotional considerations ... [and to enable] ... men to kill (people, animals, plants, natural processes) with free consciousnesses."[29] For Covina, there are 'natural' female-male differences. They are marked not just descriptively but evaluatively.

If brain-lateralization studies, or theories like Daly's and Firestone's, can be read as demonstrations of women's and men's necessarily different cognitive capacities, then my title question requires an affirmative answer. But it is not clear that such conclusions follow unequivocally. Consider the fact that allegedly sex-specific differences are not observable in examinations of the structure of the brain itself, and that in small children "both hemispheres appear to be equally proficient."[30] At most, then, it would seem,

27   [Author's note] Shulamith Firestone, *The Dialectic of Sex: The Case for Feminine Revolution* (New York: Bantam, 1971), p. 175.

28   [Author's note] Mary Daly, *Gyn/Ecology: The Metaethics of Radical Feminism* (Boston: Beacon, 1978), pp. xiii, 53, 57, 320.

29   [Author's note] Gina Covina, "Rosy Rightbrain's Exorcism/Invocation," in G. Covina and Laurel Galana, eds., *The Lesbian Reader* (Oakland, Calif.: Amazon, 1975), p. 96.

30   [Author's note] See Gordon Rattray Taylor, *The Natural History of the Mind* (London: Granada, 1979), p. 127. In an earlier article Taylor points out that "if the eyelids of an animal are sewn up at birth, and freed at maturity, it cannot see and will never learn to do so. The brain has failed to develop the necessary connections at

the brain may come to control certain processes in sexually differentiated ways. Evidence suggests that the brain *develops* its powers through training and practice.[31] Brains of creatures presented with a wide variety of tasks and stimuli develop strikingly greater performance capacities than brains of creatures kept in impoverished environments. As Ruth Bleier points out, "the biology of the brain itself is shaped by the individual's environment and experiences."[32]

Bleier notes the difficulty of assessing the implications of lateralization research. She observes that there are just as many studies that find no sex differences as there are studies that do, and that variability within each sex is greater than variability between them.[33] Janet Sayers suggests that it is as plausible to argue that sex differences in the results of tests to measure spatial ability are the results of sex-specific strategies that subjects adopt to deal with the tests themselves as it is to attribute them to differences in brain organization. She points out that there is no conclusive demonstration that differences in brain organization actually "*cause* sex differences in spatial

ability."[34] It is not easy to see, then, how these studies can plausibly support arguments about general differences in male and female cognitive abilities or about women's incapacity to enter such specific domains as engineering and architecture, where spatial abilities figure largely.

These are just some of the considerations that recommend caution in interpreting brain-lateralization studies. Differences in female and male brain functioning are just as plausibly attributable to sociocultural factors such as the sex-stereotyping of children's activities or to differing parental attitudes to children of different sexes, even from earliest infancy. It would be a mistake to rely on the research in developing a position about the epistemological significance of the sex of the knower, especially as its results are often elaborated and interpreted to serve political ends.[35]

Now Fuller, Gage, Ruddick, Firestone, Daly, and Covina evidently believe—albeit variously—in the effectiveness of *evaluative reversals* of alleged differences as a fundamental revolutionary move. Philosophers should acknowledge the superiority of feminine ideals in knowledge acquisition as much as in social life and institutions, and masculine ways of thought should give way, more generally, to feminine ways. These recommendations apply to theoretical content and to methodology, to rules for the conduct of inquiry, and to principles of justification and legitimation.

The general thesis that inspires these recommendations is that women have an edge in the development and exercise of just those attributes that merit celebration as feminine: in care, sensitivity, responsiveness and responsibility, intuition and trust. There is no

the period when it was able to do so." Taylor, "A New View of the Brain," *Encounter* 36, 2 (1971): 30.

31 [Author's note] In this connection Oliver Sacks recounts an illuminating story of a fifty-nine-year-old, congenitally blind woman with cerebral palsy, whose manual sensory capacities, he determined, were intact and quite normal. But when he met her, she had no use of her hands, referring to them as "useless lumps of dough." It became apparent that her hands were functionless because she had never used them: "being 'protected', 'looked after', 'babied' since birth [had] prevented her from the normal exploratory use of the hands which all infants learn in the first months of life." This woman first learned to use her hands in her sixtieth year. Oliver Sacks, "Hands," in *The Man Who Mistook His Wife for a Hat and Other Clinical Tales* (New York: Summit, 1985), p. 57.

32 [Author's note] Ruth Bleier, "Lab Coat: Robe of Innocence or Klansman's Sheet?" in Teresa de Lauretis, ed., *Feminist Studies / Critical Studies* (Bloomington: Indiana University Press, 1986), p. 65.

33 [Author's note] Ibid., pp. 58–59.

34 [Author's note] Janet Sayers, *Biological Politics* (London: Tavistock, 1982), p. 103.

35 [Author's note] Sayers notes: "So germane do ... findings about sex differences in brain organization appear to the current political debate about the justice of continuing sexual inequalities in professional life that they are now regularly singled out for coverage in newspaper reports of scientific meetings." Ibid., p. 101. See Lynda Birke's elaboration of this point in her *Women, Feminism, and Biology* (Brighton: Harvester, 1986), p. 29.

doubt that these traits are commonly represented as constitutive of femininity. Nor is there much doubt that a society that valued them might be a better society than one that denigrates and discourages them. But these very traits are as problematic, both theoretically and practically, as they are attractive. It is not easy to separate their appeal from the fact that women—at least women of prosperous classes and privileged races—have been encouraged to cultivate them throughout so long a history of oppression and exploitation that they have become marks of acquiescence in powerlessness. Hence there is a persistent tension in feminist thought between a laudable wish to celebrate 'feminine' values as tools for the creation of a better social order and a fear of endorsing those same values as instruments of women's continued oppression.

My recurring critique, throughout this book, of theoretical appeals to an *essential* femininity is one I engage in from a position sensitive to the pull of both sides in this tension. By 'essentialism' I mean a belief in an essence, an inherent, natural, eternal female nature that manifests itself in such characteristics as gentleness, goodness, nurturance, and sensitivity. These are some of women's more positive attributes. Women are also represented, in essentialist thought, as naturally less intelligent, more dependent, less objective, more irrational, less competent, more scatterbrained than men: indeed, essential femaleness is commonly defined against a masculine standard of putatively *human* essence.

Essentialist attributions work both normatively and descriptively. Not only do they purport to describe how women essentially *are*, they are commonly enlisted in the perpetuation of women's (usually inferior) social status. Yet essentialist claims are highly contestable. Their diverse manifestations across class, race, and ethnicity attest to their having a sociocultural rather than a 'natural' source. Their deployment as instruments for keeping women in their place means that caution is always required in appealing to them— even though they often appear to designate women's *strengths*. Claims about masculine essence need also to be treated with caution, though it is worth noting that they are less commonly used to oppress men. Essential masculine aggressiveness, sexual needs, and ego-enhancing requirements are often added, rather, to reasons why women should remain subservient. Perhaps there are some essential female or male characteristics, but claims that there are always need to be evaluated and analyzed. The burden of proof falls on theorists who appeal to essences, rather than on those who resist them.

As I have noted, some of the thinkers I have cited advocate an evaluative reversal, in a tacit acceptance of stereotypical, essentialist conceptions of masculinity and femininity. To understand the import of the tension in feminist thought, these stereotypes need careful analysis. The issues of power and theoretical hegemony that are inextricably implicated in their maintenance need likewise to be analyzed. As an initial step toward embarking on this task I offer, in the remainder of this section, a critical analysis of three landmark articles that engage with mainstream epistemology with the intention of revealing grounds for feminist opposition to its traditional structures.

(i) In her early piece, "Methodocracy, Misogyny and Bad Faith: Sexism in the Philosophic Establishment," Sheila Ruth characterizes mainstream philosophy in its content, methodology, and practice as male, masculine, and masculinist. Noting, correctly, that most philosophers—even more in the late 1970s than in the 1990s—are men, Ruth maintains that the content of their philosophy reflects masculine interests and that their standard methodologies reflect imperialist masculine values, values whose normative status derives from their association with maleness. Ruth writes that "philosophical sexism, metasexism ... is epistemological, permeating philosophy to its roots—the structure of its methods and the logic of its criticism." She argues that "what should not be is the raising of ... male [intellectual] constructs to the status of universals—the identification of male constructs with allowable constructs so that women cannot 'legitimately' think, perceive, select, argue, etc. from their unique stance."[36] For Ruth, the sex of the knower *is* epistemologically significant at a fundamental level, with all-pervasive implications.

---

36 [Author's note] Sheila Ruth, "Methodocracy, Misogyny, and Bad Faith: Sexism in the Philosophic Establishment," *Metaphilosophy* 10, 1 (1979): pp. 50, 56.

This essay attests to the surprise and anger occasioned by early 'second wave' feminist realizations that theories that had posed, for centuries, as universal, neutral, and impartial were, in fact, deeply invested in furthering the self-interest of a small segment of the human population. Such realizations brought with them a profound shock, which often resulted in an insistence on affirming contrary, feminine interests and values. These early contributions often appear flawed from the present stage of feminist theoretical development, and I shall draw attention to some of those flaws as reasons why I would not, today, wholeheartedly endorse Ruth's claims.[37] They are worthy of rearticulation, though, for this article is one of the classics of feminist philosophy which created space for the development of subsequent critiques.

There is much that is right about Ruth's contentions, but two interconnected problems make it impossible to agree completely with her: the assumptions that "male constructs" exercise a unified, univocal hegemony and that women occupy a single "unique stance." I have argued in the first section of this chapter that epistemological relativism is a strong position because it creates the possibility of raising questions about the *identity* of knowers. It opens the way for analyses of the historical, racial, social, and cultural specificity of knowers and of knowledge. Now its value would be minimal were it possible to demonstrate that cognitive activity and knowledge have been conceived in exactly the same way by all knowers since the dawn of philosophy. Precisely because it allows the interplay of common threads *and* of specific variations, relativism has a significant explanatory capacity. This capacity is tacitly denied in an account such as Ruth's, based, as it apparently is, on implicit claims about essential, eternal conceptions of femininity and masculinity, mirrored in constant interpretations of knowing and knowledge. In the face of historical, ethnographic, political and class-based evidence to the contrary, the onus would fall on Ruth, should she still wish to defend these claims, to demonstrate the constancy of the concepts.

Their assumed rigidity presents a still more serious problem. The content Ruth gives to masculinity and femininity plays directly into their essentialist, stereotypical construal in late-twentieth-century western societies. Yet there is no better reason to believe that feminine and masculine characteristics are constant across a complex society at any one time than there is to believe in their historical or cross-cultural constancy. Norms of masculinity and femininity vary across race, class, age, and ethnicity (to name only a few of the axes) within any society at any time. An acceptance of the stereotypes results in a rigidity of thinking that limits possibilities of developing nuanced analyses. In this article it creates for Ruth the troubling necessity of defining her project both *against* and *with reference to* a taken-for-granted masculine norm. No single such norm is discernible in western thought, yet when Ruth's positive recommendations in favor of different philosophical styles are sketched out by contrast with that assumed norm, their explanatory power is diminished. Ruth is right to assert that women have had "no part in defining the content of philosophical speculation, but they have had even less influence over the categories of concern and the modes of articulation."[38] The predominance of feminine and masculine stereotypes in her argument points to an unhappy implication of such early arguments for evaluative reversal: namely, that had women had such influence, their contribution would have been as monolithic as the 'masculine' one.

The broadest of Ruth's claims remains her strongest: philosophy has oppressed women in ways that feminists are still learning to understand. My point is that analyses of this oppression need to be wary lest they replicate the very structures they deplore. Much depends, in the development of feminist projects, on how women's oppression is analyzed. It is important to prevent the reactive aspects of critical response from

---

37   [Author's note] My *Metaphilosophy* article is another pertinent example. Allan Soble criticizes the essentialism of my argument in "Feminist Epistemology and Women Scientists," *Metaphilosophy* 14 (1983): pp. 291–307.

38   [Author's note] Ruth, "Methodocracy, Misogyny, and Bad Faith," p. 54. In my thinking about Ruth's article I am indebted to Jean Grimshaw's discussion in her *Philosophy and Feminist Thinking* (Minneapolis: University of Minnesota Press, 1986), pp. 53–55, 81–82.

overwhelming its creative possibilities. Ruth's analysis leans rather too heavily toward the reactive mode.

(ii) In another early, landmark article, "The Social Function of the Empiricist Conception of Mind," Sandra Harding confronts stereotypes of femininity from a different direction. Her thesis is that "the empiricist model of mind supports social hierarchy by implicitly sanctioning 'underclass' stereotypes." Emphasizing the passivity of knowers in Humean[39] empiricism, Harding contends, first, that classical empiricism can allow no place for creativity, for historical self-consciousness, or for the adoption of a critical stance. Second, she discerns a striking similarity between 'the Humean mind' and stereotypical conceptions of women's minds: "formless, passive, and peculiarly receptive to direction from outside."[40] Her intention is to show that an espousal of empiricist theory, combined with an uncritical acceptance of feminine stereotypes, legitimates manipulative and controlling treatment of women in the social world. There are striking echoes, as Harding herself notes, with the Aristotelian view of woman's lack of rational authority: a lack that, for Aristotle, likewise justifies women's inferior social position.

Present-day empiricists would no doubt contend that Harding's equation of empiricism with a 'passive' epistemology and theory of mind has little validity, given the varieties of contemporary empiricism in its transformations under the influence of philosophers such as Quine.[41] Yet even if Harding has drawn only a caricature of 'the Humean mind', her account has a heuristic value in highlighting certain tendencies of orthodox, classical empiricism. Empiricism, and its latter-day positivist offspring, could indeed serve, either as a philosophy of mind or as a theory of knowledge, to legitimate under the guise of objectivity and impartial neutrality just the kinds of social practice feminists are concerned to eradicate. The impartiality of empiricist analysis, the interchangeability of its subjects of study, work to provide rationalizations for treating people as 'cases' or 'types', rather than as active, creative cognitive agents.[42] Such rationalizations are common in positivistic social science.

More intriguing is a 'double standard' Harding discerns in classical empiricist thought. The *explicit* picture of the Humean inquirer, she maintains, is of a person who is primarily passive, receptive, and hence manipulable. Yet the very existence of Hume's own philosophy counts as evidence that he himself escapes that characterization. His intellectual activity is marked by "a critical attitude, firm purposes and a willingness to struggle to achieve them, elaborate principles of inquiry and hypotheses to be investigated, clarity of vision, precision, and facility at rational argument."[43] This description of the *implicit* Humean inquirer, Harding notes, feeds into standard gender stereotypes, in which men come across as "effective historical agents" while women are incapable of historical agency.

Harding accuses the promulgators of the classical empiricist conception of mind of false consciousness. Their own theoretical activity exempts *their* minds from the very model for which they claim universal validity: the contention that no one is a self-directed agent, everyone is a blank tablet, cannot apply to the authors themselves. Hence the empiricists presuppose a we/they structure in which 'they' indeed are as the theory describes them, but 'we', by virtue of our theoretical creativity, escape the description. In consequence, "the empiricist model of mind ... functions as a self-fulfilling *prescription* beneficial to those already in power: treat people as if they are passive and need direction from others, and they will become or remain able to be manipulated and controlled."[44] Harding

---

39   Relating to David Hume: see the notes to the selection from Hume in Chapter 4.

40   [Author's note] Sandra Harding, "The Social Function of the Empiricist Conception of Mind," *Metaphilosophy* 10 (January 1979): pp. 39, 42.

41   [Author's note] See especially Lynn Hankinson Nelson, *Who Knows: From Quine to a Feminist Empiricism* (Philadelphia: Temple University Press, 1990). Because Nelson's book was published after my manuscript was completed, I have not discussed it in this book.

42   [Author's note] I discuss this consequence of empiricist thinking more fully in Chapter 2.

43   [Author's note] Harding, "Social Function of the Empiricist Conception of Mind," pp. 43, 44.

44   [Author's note] Ibid., p. 46.

maintains that the implicit distinction between active empiricist theorist and passive ordinary inquirer maps onto the stereotypical active male/passive female distinction and acts to legitimate the social and political consequences of that stereotype in androcentered[45] power structures.

Now it is not easy to show that Harding is right either to find an implicit 'double standard' in Humean thought or to suggest that demarcations of the two 'kinds' of knower are appropriately drawn along sexual lines. Hume himself may have meant merely to distinguish a philosopher at his most sophisticated from an ordinary 'vulgar' thinker. His elitism may have been intellect- or class-related, rather than sex-related. If Harding is right, however, the Humean 'double standard' would suggest that the sex of the knower is epistemologically significant, in that it designates men alone as capable of active, creative, critical knowing—and of constructing epistemological theories. By contrast, women are capable only of receiving and shuffling information. Even if she is mistaken in her Humean attributions, then, the parallels Harding draws between the intellectual elitism that empiricism can create and sexual elitism find ample confirmation in the social world. The common relegation of women to low-status forms of employment, which differ from high-status employment partly in the kinds of knowledge, expertise, and cognitive authority they require, is just one confirming practice.[46]

What ensures Harding's paper a place in the history of feminist critiques of philosophy is less the detail of its Hume interpretation than its articulation of the political implications of metaphysical theses. In the face of challenges such as these, which have been more subtly posed both in Harding's later work and elsewhere as feminist thought has increased in sophistication, the neutrality of such theses can never be taken for granted. Should it be declared, the onus is on its declarers to demonstrate the validity of their claims. So despite the flaws in Harding's analysis, her article supports my contention that the sex of the knower is epistemologically significant. If metaphysical theories are marked by the maleness of their creators, then theories of knowledge informed by them cannot escape the marking. Whether the case can be made that both theoretical levels are thus marked, without playing into sexual stereotypes, is a difficult question, but the evidence points compellingly toward the conclusion that the sex of a philosopher informs his theory-building.

(iii) The influence of stereotypically sex-specific traits on conceptions of the proper way to do philosophy is instructively detailed in Janice Moulton's analysis of "The Adversary Method," as she perceptively names it. Moulton shows that a subtle conceptual "conflation of aggression and competence"[47] has produced a paradigm for philosophical inquiry that is modeled on adversarial confrontation between opponents. This conflation depends, above all, on an association of aggression with such positive qualities as energy, power, and ambition: qualities that count as prerequisites for success in the white, middle-class, male professional world. Moulton questions the validity of this association in its conferral of normative status on styles of behavior stereotypically described as male. Yet what is most seriously wrong with the paradigm, she argues, is not so much its maleness as its constitutive role in the production of truncated philosophical problems, inquiries, and solutions.

The adversarial method is most effective, Moulton claims, in structuring isolated disagreements about specific theses and arguments. Hence it depends for its success on the artificial isolation of such claims and arguments from the contexts that occasion their articulation. Adversarial argument aims to show that an opponent is wrong, often by attacking conclusions implicit in, or potentially consequent on, his basic or alleged premises.[48] Under the adversarial paradigm,

---

45   Male-centered.

46   [Author's note] An example of the hierarchy of cognitive relations created by such assumptions is the theme of Chapter 6.

47   [Author's note] Janice Moulton, "A Paradigm of Philosophy: The Adversary Method," in Sandra Harding and Merrill B. Hintikka, eds., *Discovering Reality* (Dordrecht: Reidel, 1983), p. 151.

48   [Author's note] I am agreeing with Moulton's association of the paradigm with maleness in using the masculine pronoun to refer to its practitioners—even though many women have learned to play the game well.

the point is to confront the most extreme opposing position, with the object of showing that one's own position is defensible even against such stark opposition. Exploration, explanation, and understanding are lesser goals. The irony, Moulton claims, is that the adversarial paradigm produces bad reasoning, because it leads philosophers to adopt the mode of reasoning best suited to defeat an opponent—she uses "counterexample reasoning" to illustrate her point[49]—as the paradigmatic model for reasoning as such. Diverse modes of reasoning which might be more appropriate to different circumstances, tend to be occluded, as does the possibility that a single problem might be amenable to more than one approach.

Moulton's analysis lends support to the contention that the sex of the knower is significant at the 'metaepistemological' level where the legitimacy of epistemological problems is established. The connection between aggressive cognitive styles and stereotypes of masculine behavior is now a commonplace of feminist thought. Moulton's demonstration that such behavior constitutes the dominant mode—the paradigm—in philosophy, which has so long claimed to stand outside 'the commonplace', is compelling. She shows that mainstream philosophy bears the marks of its androcentric derivation out of a stereotypically constructed masculinity, whatever the limitations of that construction are.

Like all paradigms, the adversarial method has a specific location in intellectual history. While it demarcates the kinds of puzzle a philosopher can legitimately consider, a recognition of its historical specificity shows that this is not how philosophy has always been done nor how it must, of necessity, be done. In according the method (interim) paradigm status, Moulton points to the historical contingency of its current hegemony. The fact that many feminist philosophers report a sense of dissonance between the supposed gender neutrality of the method and their own feminine gender[50] puts the paradigm under

serious strains. Such strains create the space and the possibilities for developing alternative methodological approaches. Whether the sex of the knower will be methodologically and/or epistemologically significant in such approaches must, for now, remain an open question.

Knowledge, Methodology, and Power

The adversarial method is but one manifestation of a complex interweaving of power and knowledge which sustains the hegemony of mainstream epistemology. Like the empiricist theory of the mind, it presents a public demeanor of neutral inquiry, engaged in the disinterested pursuit of truth. Despite its evident interest in triumphing over opponents, it would be unreasonable to condemn this disinterest as merely a pose. There is no reason to believe that practitioners whose work is informed by these methodological assumptions have ruthlessly or tyrannically adopted a theoretical stance for the express purpose of engaging in projects that thwart the intellectual pursuits of women or of other marginalized philosophers. Could such a purpose be discerned, the task of revealing the epistemological significance of the sex of the knower would be easy. Critics could simply offer such practitioners a clear demonstration of the errors of their ways and hope that, with a presumption of goodwill on their part, they would abandon the path of error for that of truth and fairness.

Taking these practitioners at their word, acknowledging the sincerity of their convictions about their neutral, objective, impartial engagement in the pursuit of truth, reveals the intricacy of this task. Certain sets of problems, by virtue of their complexity or their intrinsic appeal, often become so engrossing for researchers that they override and occlude other contenders for attention. Reasons for this suppression are often subtle and not always specifically articulable. Nor is it clear that the exclusionary process is wholly conscious. A network of sociopolitical relationships and intellectual assumptions creates an invisible system of acceptance and rejection, discourse and

49 [Author's note] Moulton, "Paradigm of Philosophy," p. 159.

50 [Author's note] See, for example, Genevieve Lloyd's observation that "the exercise of writing feminist philosophy came out of [her] experience of dissonance

between the supposed gender neutrality of philosophy and [her] gender." Lloyd, "Feminist Philosophy and the Idea of the Feminine" (manuscript, 1986), p. 22.

silence, ascendency and subjugation within and around disciplines. Implicit cultural presuppositions work with the personal idiosyncracies of intellectual authorities to keep certain issues from placing high on research agendas. Critics have to learn how to notice their absence.

In "The Discourse on Language," Michel Foucault makes the astute observation that "within its own limits, every discipline recognizes true and false propositions, but it repulses a whole teratology[51] of learning."[52] The observation captures some of the subtleties involved in attempting to understand the often imperceptible workings of hegemonic, usually masculine power in mainstream philosophy. A discipline defines itself both by what it excludes (repulses) and by what it includes. But the self-definition process removes what is excluded (repulsed) from view so that it is not straightforwardly available for assessment, criticism, and analysis. Even in accepting mainstream avowals of neutral objectivity, critics have to learn to see what is repulsed by the disciplinarily imposed limits on methodology and areas of inquiry. The task is not easy. It is much easier to seek the flaws in existing structures and practices and to work at eradicating them than it is to learn to perceive what is not there to be perceived.

Feminist philosophy simply did not exist until philosophers learned to perceive the near-total absence of women in philosophical writings from the very beginning of western philosophy, to stop assuming that 'man' could be read as a generic term. Explicit denigrations of women, which became the focus of philosophical writing in the early years of the contemporary women's movement, were more readily perceptible. The authors of derogatory views about women in classical texts clearly needed power to be able to utter their pronouncements with impunity: a power they claimed from a 'received' discourse that represented women's nature in such a way that women undoubtedly merited the negative judgments that Aristotle or Nietzsche made about them. Women are now in a position to recognize and refuse these overt manifestations of contempt.

The covert manifestations are more intransigent. Philosophers, when they have addressed the issue at all, have tended to group philosophy with science as the most gender-neutral of disciplines. But feminist critiques reveal that this alleged neutrality masks a bias in favor of institutionalizing stereotypical masculine values into the fabric of the discipline—its methods, norms, and contents. In so doing, it suppresses values, styles, problems, and concerns stereotypically associated with femininity. Thus, whether by chance or by design, it creates a hegemonic philosophical practice in which the sex of the knower is, indeed, epistemologically significant.

---

51   [Author's note] A 'teratology' is a collection of tales about marvellous and improbable creatures (such as sea monsters, or people with heads in their chests); Foucault's idea is that disciplines restrict themselves to what is familiar, and rule out or ignore the possibility of things that would be—from the perspective of the discipline—considered strange or unlikely.

52   [Author's note] Michel Foucault, "The Discourse on Language," in *The Archaeology of Knowledge*, trans. Alan Sheridan (New York: Pantheon, 1972), p. 223.

CHAPTER 3

Philosophy of Science—When, if Ever, Are Scientific Inferences Justified?

INTRODUCTION TO THE QUESTION

The philosophy of science can be thought of as being made up of two broad, intersecting streams: the epistemology of science and the metaphysics of science. The epistemology of science concerns itself with the justification, rationality, and objectivity of scientific knowledge and the so-called 'scientific method,' while the metaphysics of science examines philosophical puzzles about the reality uncovered by the various sciences. Furthermore, each of these two types of investigation can be directed at science in general or at one of the particular sciences: there are thus sub-disciplines within the philosophy of science such as 'philosophy of physics,' 'philosophy of mathematics,' 'philosophy of biology,' and 'philosophy of the social sciences.'

Many of the threads of the epistemological strand of philosophy of science can be unraveled from the following question: *What, if anything, is 'the scientific method,' and how rational is it?* Once one attempts to answer this question, a flurry of subsidiary questions arise: What is the methodological difference (if any) between science and other, non-scientific, areas of human endeavor (such as philosophy, history, or astrology)? Do all the 'real' sciences share a common methodology? If not, can we discover a single, under-lying 'unified science' which is in principle capable of encompassing all the special sciences? How *rational* are the methods of science: how much reason do they give us to accept their conclusions? How *objective* are the methods of science: how much is science influenced by its social context and the personalities of individual scientists? Are the theories produced by science ever in fact true descriptions of reality, and, in any case, is that what science should aspire to? What exactly *is* a theory, anyway (for example, is it a set of logical equations, or a kind of model, or a more informal bundle of assumptions and claims)? How adequately does science explain the natural phenomena we want explained, and what counts as a scientific explanation? And so on: these, and other similar questions, are investigated by philosophers of science.

Metaphysical questions about science can be thought of as centered on the following issue: *Are the principles and entities postulated by science actually real?* For example, many scientific theories postulate unobservable entities in order to explain the observed data. Most subatomic particles such as quarks, for instance, have never in any sense been *seen* by a scientist: rather, they are assumed to exist because their existence is the best explanation for a certain set of experimental data. In such situations, are we entitled to infer that such unobservable entities actually do exist, or should we instead treat them as instrumental fictions which are useful in generating observable predictions but which aren't literally real? (After all, plenty of unobserved entities which we now realize do not actually exist have been postulated by science in the past, such as the mythical substance of 'phlogiston' which was invoked to explain many chemical properties, or the massless 'ether' which was thought to fill the gaps between objects and serve as the medium for the transmission of light. Why should our current theories be any luckier in the hypothetical entities they invent?)

One fundamental 'unobservable' principle of science, which has historically been of great interest to philosophers of science, is the principle of *causality*. The sense in which causality is unobservable was pointed out by the philosopher David Hume in the eighteenth century: although we certainly can and do observe that events of type A are always followed by events of type B (for example, that all objects of mass m propelled with force x will always accelerate at rate y), this necessarily falls short of being able to observe *causation* itself. All we actually see is what Hume called the 'constant conjunction' of A things with B things, but we do not see the causal law which lies behind and is the reason for this conjunction: that is, we do not *see* laws of nature, but we *infer* them from regularities which we detect in nature. So it is legitimate to ask questions like the following: *Are* there really causal laws lying behind the constant conjunctions we observe—are laws of nature real? If causal laws do exist, how can we reliably tell when we've identified one—how can we tell the difference between a genuine law and a merely accidental constant conjunction? And, if causal laws exist, what is their nature—for example, are they always deterministic, or can they be probabilistic (as quantum mechanics might be taken to suggest)?

The readings in this chapter focus primarily on the epistemological aspects of the philosophy of science: what is the method of science, and how rationally justifiable is it? It is natural to begin with something like the following account of science: scientists first accumulate facts about the world by conducting careful experiments, and then use these observations to support—or 'verify'—one scientific theory rather than another. For example, one might think, by the careful observation of various chemical reactions, scientists are able to formulate and prove true general laws about the underlying chemistry. Furthermore, it is common to suppose that it is this 'experimental' method which is unique to science and the source of its special epistemological power. The first selection collected here introduces a fundamental problem for this view of scientific method, *the problem of induction*. Induction is, roughly, the process by which we infer general truths from particular observations

(for example, inferring that all copper turns green in the rain by noticing that many old copper roofs are now green). The scientific method just described rests heavily on inductive inferences to move from a finite set of experimental observations to claims about laws of nature. But the question is: is induction rational? Are inductive inferences from the particular to the general justified? David Hume argues compellingly that inductive inferences are *not* rationally justified; and if he is right, then it follows that the scientific method—at least as we have so far understood it—is not rational.

The next two readings—the authors of which are to some degree reacting to the problem of induction—introduce two different accounts of the scientific method, in an effort to improve on the simplistic 'experimental' model described above. Carl Hempel presents a mature version of the influential 'logical positivist' or 'verificationist' account of science, while Karl Popper rejects verificationism and argues instead for a 'falsificationist' view of science.

The fourth selection in this chapter, from Thomas Kuhn, introduces an important turn in late-twentieth-century philosophy away from the attempt to understand science as a rational enterprise and in favor of seeing it as a sociological phenomenon embedded in a particular historical context. Kuhn has thus been seen as launching an attack on the rationality of science. Finally the article from Helen Longino asks "Can there be a feminist science?" and if so, how different would it look from historical, supposedly 'value-free,' science?

The philosophy of science was a very active area of philosophy for a large part of the twentieth century, and there are many good books which will take you beyond the readings included in this chapter. Among them are: Brody and Grandy, eds., *Readings in the Philosophy of Science* (Prentice Hall, 1989); Alan Chalmers, *What Is This Thing Called Science?* (Hackett, 1999); Curd and Cover, eds., *Philosophy of Science: The Central Issues* (W.W. Norton, 1998); James Franklin, *What Science Knows: And How It Knows It* (Encounter Books, 2009); Donald Gillies, *Philosophy of Science in the Twentieth Century* (Blackwell, 1993); Peter Godfrey-Smith, *Theory and Reality: An Introduction to the Philosophy of Science* (University of Chicago

Press, 2003); Ian Hacking, *Representing and Intervening* (Cambridge University Press, 1983); Philip Kitcher, *The Advancement of Science* (Oxford University Press, 1993); Robert Klee, *Introduction to the Philosophy of Science: Cutting Nature at Its Seams* (Oxford University Press, 1996); James Ladyman, *Understanding Philosophy of Science* (Routledge, 2001); W.H. Newton-Smith, *The Rationality of Science* (Routledge, 1981); David Papineau, ed., *The Philosophy of Science* (Oxford University Press, 1996); Alexander Rosenberg, *The Philosophy of Science* (Routledge, 2011); Merrilee Salmon et al., *Introduction to the Philosophy of Science* (Hackett, 1999); and Bas van Fraassen, *The Scientific Image* (Oxford University Press, 1982). Useful references are *A Companion to the Philosophy of Science*, edited by W.H. Newton-Smith (Blackwell, 2001), and Psillos and Curd (eds.), *The Routledge Companion to Philosophy of Science* (Routledge, 2010).

DAVID HUME

An Enquiry Concerning Human Understanding

There is a peculiarly painful chamber inhabited solely by philosophers who have refuted Hume. These philosophers, though in Hell, have not learned wisdom. They continue to be governed by their animal propensity towards induction. But every time that they make an induction, the next instance falsifies it. This, however, happens only during the first hundred years of their damnation. After that, they learn to expect that an induction will be falsified, and therefore it is not falsified until another century of logical torment has altered their expectation. Throughout all eternity surprise continues, but each time at a higher logical level.

(Bertrand Russell)

Who Was David Hume?

David Hume has been called the most important philosopher ever to have written in English. He was born to a strict Calvinist family in Edinburgh, Scotland's capital, in 1711, and spent his youth there and in Ninewells, his family's small land-holding near the border with England. Little is known of Hume's early childhood. His father, Joseph, died when he was two, and he was educated by his mother Katherine—who never remarried—from an early age. He was a precociously intelligent and well-read child. As his mother put it, in her Scottish dialect: "Our Davie's a fine good-natured crater, but uncommon wake-minded." By the age of 16 he had begun composing his first philosophical master-work, *A Treatise of Human Nature*, on which he was to work, more or less continuously, for the next ten years.

Hume spent the years between 1723 and 1726 (i.e., between the ages of 12 and 15) studying a wide range of subjects at the University of Edinburgh but, like many students of that era, did not take a degree. His father and grandfather had both been lawyers, and his family expected him also to go into law, but, Hume later wrote, he found the law "nauseous" and discovered in himself "an unsurmountable aversion to every thing but the pursuits of philosophy and general learning."

Hume continued to read and write and, as a result of his feverish intellectual activity—motivated by his belief that he had made a major philosophical discovery—he suffered a nervous breakdown in 1734. He was forced to put philosophy aside for several months (during which time he attempted life as a businessman at

Bristol, in the employ of a Portsmouth merchant, but found that it didn't suit him) and then left Britain for France. There, in the following three years, living frugally in the countryside in Anjou (and using up all his savings), he completed most of his book.

Hume's *A Treatise of Human Nature* was published anonymously when he was 27. Hume later wrote, it "fell *dead-born from the press*, without reaching such distinction as even to excite a murmur among the zealots." Hume's career as an intellectual and man of letters seemed to have ended before it had begun, and Hume blamed not the substance of his work but its style. "I was carry'd away by the Heat of Youth & Invention to publish too precipitately. So vast an Undertaking, plan'd before I was one and twenty, & compos'd before twenty-five, must necessarily be very defective. I have repented my Haste a hundred, & a hundred times." Hume returned to Scotland to live with his mother, and began to re-cast the material of the *Treatise* into two new books, which have become philosophical classics in their own right: *An Enquiry Concerning Human Understanding* (1748), and *An Enquiry Concerning the Principles of Morals* (1751). However both these books—though more successful than the *Treatise*—were slow to become influential during Hume's own lifetime.

Needing money, Hume got his first real job at the age of 34 and spent a well-paid year as tutor to a mad nobleman (the Marquess of Annandale). In 1746 Hume accepted a position as secretary to General St. Clair's military expedition to Canada (which never reached Canada and ended, oddly enough, with a brief attack on the French coast), and for two years after that was part of a secret diplomatic and military embassy by St. Clair to the courts of Vienna and Turin. During this period Hume was twice refused academic appointments at Scottish universities—first Edinburgh, then Glasgow—because of his reputation as a religious skeptic. Shortly afterwards, between 1755 and 1757, unsuccessful attempts were made in Edinburgh to have Hume excommunicated from the Church of Scotland.

In 1752 Hume was offered the Keepership of the Advocates' Library at Edinburgh and there, poorly paid but surrounded by books, he wrote the colossal six-volume *History of England*, which (though unpopular at first) eventually became his first major literary success. At this time he also published a controversial *Natural History of Religion*.

In 1763 Hume was made secretary of the English embassy at Paris, where he found himself very much in fashion and seems to have enjoyed the experience. There he fell in love with, but failed to win the hand of, the Comtesse de Boufflers, the mistress of a prominent French noble. (Some unkindly suggest this might have been partly because at the time, when Hume was in his fifties, he had come to resemble "a fat well-fed Bernardine monk.") In 1767, back in Scotland and now a fairly wealthy man, Hume was appointed an Under-Secretary of State, a senior position in the British civil service.

By the time Hume died in 1776, of cancer of the bowel, he had become respected as one of Europe's leading men of letters and a principal architect of the Enlightenment. His death gave him the reputation of something of a secular saint, as he faced his incurable condition with cheerfulness and resignation and refused to abandon his religious skepticism. In a short autobiography, written just before he died, Hume described his own character.

I was … a man of mild dispositions, of command of temper, of an open, social, and cheerful humour, capable of attachment, but little susceptible of enmity, and of great moderation in all my passions. Even my love of literary fame, my ruling passion, never soured my temper, notwithstanding my frequent disappointments. My company was not unacceptable to the young and careless, as well as to the studious and literary; and as I took a particular pleasure in the company of modest women, I had no reason to be displeased with the reception I met from them.... I cannot say there is no vanity in making this funeral oration of myself, but I hope it is not a misplaced one; and this is a matter of fact which is easily cleared and ascertained.

What Was Hume's Overall Philosophical Project?

Hume can be called the first 'post-skeptical' modern philosopher. He was wholly convinced (by, among others, the writings of his predecessors Descartes, Locke, and Berkeley, who appear elsewhere in this volume) that no knowledge that goes beyond the mere data of our own minds has anything like secure and reliable foundations: that is, he believed, we have no certain knowledge of the inner workings of the physical world and its laws, or of God, or of absolute moral 'truth,' or even of our own 'real selves.' All we have secure knowledge of is our own mental states and their relations: our sensory impressions, our ideas, our emotions, and so on.

Despite all this, Hume's philosophical project was a positive one: he wanted to develop a new, constructive science of human nature that would provide a defensible foundation for all the sciences, including ethics, physics, and politics. Where Hume's predecessors tried in vain to argue against philosophical skepticism, Hume assumed that a certain kind of skepticism was actually true and tried to go beyond it, to say something positive about how we are to get on with our lives (including our lives as scientists and philosophers).

Much of Hume's philosophical writing, therefore, begins by showing the unstoppable power of skepticism in some domain—such as skepticism about causation or objective ethical truths—and then goes on to show how we can still talk sensibly about causation or ethics after all. The selection from *An Enquiry Concerning Human Understanding* which appears below follows this pattern.

One of the central aspects of both Hume's skeptical and his constructive philosophy is his strictly empirical methodology—a development of what was called in Hume's day 'the experimental method.' His science of human nature is based firmly on the experimental methods of the natural sciences, which emphasize the data of experience and observation, sometimes combined with mathematical or logical reasoning. Any other method of investigation—such as an appeal to 'innate intuition,' for example—is illegitimate. As Hume put it:

> If we take in our hand any volume; of divinity or school metaphysics, for instance; let us ask, *Does it contain any abstract reasoning concerning quantity or number?* No. *Does it contain any experimental reasoning concerning matter of fact and existence?* No. Commit it then to the flames: for it can contain nothing but sophistry and illusion. [This is the final paragraph of his *An Enquiry Concerning Human Understanding*.]

This assumption that all human knowledge is either a "matter of fact" or a matter of "relations of ideas"—the product of experience or of reason—is often known as 'Hume's Fork.'

What Is the Structure of This Reading?

An Enquiry Concerning Human Understanding first appeared (in 1748) under the title *Philosophical Essays Concerning Human Understanding*, and it does indeed consist of twelve somewhat loosely related philosophical essays. The underlying theme which ties the essays together is the primacy of experience and causal inference in establishing our ideas, especially such philosophically important ideas as necessity and probability, free will, and God.

Hume's argument in this reading has two parts. In the first part he argues there can be no rational justification for our expectations about those parts of the physical world we have not yet observed; in the second he presents his "skeptical solution of these doubts." First, in Section IV Part I, he introduces a distinction between relations of ideas and matters of fact. He then argues that all empirical claims which go beyond "the present testimony of our senses, or the records of our memory" are based on reasonings "founded on the relation of cause and effect." How do we come to discover relations of cause and effect? Not, Hume argues, from "reasonings *a priori*" but from experience. In Part II, Hume addresses the question: "What is the foundation of all conclusions from experience?" and, for the remainder of this part, "contents himself" with a negative answer. He argues that conclusions from experience are not "founded on reasoning, or on any process of the understanding." Part of his argument here has the following structure: Hume tries to show that all experimental arguments rely upon the assumption that nature is generally uniform—the assumption that observed regularities in nature (like the whiteness of swans or day following night) will persist from the present into the future. He then argues—very ingeniously and persuasively—that this assumption is impossible to rationally justify. His conclusion is that inductive inferences are never rationally justifiable.

Hume's constructive project, presented in Section V, has the following pattern. He begins by describing the benefits of a generally skeptical frame of mind. Then he goes on to discuss the principle that *does* cause us to leap to inductive conclusions, since we have no rational reason to do so—this psychological principle, he suggests, is "custom or habit." In Part II, Hume gives us more detail about what he thinks is really going on when we come to have beliefs about the future: he argues that *belief* is a kind of involuntary feeling, "added" to our imagination of some event. That is, we can freely *imagine* almost any future event we like, but we usually cannot make ourselves *believe* that it will happen. This "extra" feeling of belief in a future event, Hume argues, can only be generated automatically in our minds by a certain sequence of past experiences.

Some Useful Background Information

1. Hume, like John Locke (see Chapter 2), began his philosophy with a 'theory of ideas': it is useful to be aware of a few of the basics of this theory when reading this selection. For Hume, the smallest elements of thought are what he called *basic perceptions*. These can usefully be

thought of as analogous to atoms, since these basic perceptions are, in Hume's view, bound together in various ways into larger units—*complex perceptions*—according to certain fundamental psychological laws; Hume called these laws "the principle of the association of ideas." Hume thought of this system as being the counterpart of Newtonian physics: on this view, physics is the science of matter, and Humean philosophy is the science of human nature or mind. Hume himself considered this general picture, and the use he made of it, to be his greatest contribution to human thought. It is especially notable that *rationality* plays relatively little part in Hume's naturalistic picture of human nature: instead, our ideas are connected together by deterministic laws based, for example, on their similarity or their history of "constant conjunction" (that is, a history of having always appeared together in the past). Finally, for Hume, these "laws of association" may defy further explanation: we might need to treat them as basic laws—brute regularities—just as the law of gravity was for Newton.

2. Unlike Locke, Hume divides his "perceptions" into two distinct sorts: *impressions* and *ideas*. Impressions are "all our sensations, passions and emotions, as they make their first appearance in the soul," and come in two flavors: *impressions of sensation* and *impressions of reflection*. Impressions of sensation, according to Hume, appear in the mind "from unknown causes," and the reasons for their occurrence are best studied by "anatomists and natural philosophers," rather than by those, like Hume himself, interested in studying human nature. Examples of such sensations might be the visual image of a cat on the mat, or the taste of a grape-flavored Popsicle. Impressions of reflection (such as disgust, pride, or desire) arise, usually, from our perception of and reaction to our own ideas. Finally, our *ideas* are, according to Hume, "the faint images" of impressions: that is, they are copies of earlier impressions (and so, causally dependent on them: you cannot possibly have an idea of something which you haven't previously experienced). Ideas, for Hume, have

been described as "the mental tokens by which we reason," and would include, for example, our concepts of colors and shapes, of types of objects, of mathematical relationships, of historical individuals, of moral values, and so on.

3. Hume's arguments in this passage rely on two important distinctions, which it is helpful to have clear in your mind as you read. The first is the distinction which is often called 'Hume's fork' between *relations of ideas* and *matters of fact*. Relations of ideas are propositions whose truth or falsity can be discovered merely by thinking about the concepts involved, and which if true are necessarily true. For example, "a triangle has three sides" must be true since *by definition* triangles have three sides—it's just part of the concept 'triangle' that it be three-sided. In modern jargon, relations of ideas are 'analytic *a priori*' propositions. The simplest kind of relation of ideas Hume calls "intuitively certain": these propositions are just self-evidently true to anyone who understands them, such as "1 is smaller than 2."[1] Other propositions, which are also relations of ideas, may be more complex and need to be shown by some kind of 'demonstrative argument' (the proposition that 2^{16} is 65,536, for example, might not be immediately obvious, but it can be proven by a sequence of small and obvious steps).

Matters of fact, by contrast, are 'synthetic *a posteriori*' propositions—that is, only observation and experience can tell us whether they are true or false (and thus they cannot be *necessarily* true, but are only contingently true). An example might be, "sticking your finger inside a hot toaster really hurts." One of Hume's key claims is that propositions about relations of ideas never assert the existence of any non-

abstract entities (such as physical objects), while claims about matters of fact often do.

4. The second important distinction used in this reading is one between *demonstrative arguments* and *experimental arguments*. Demonstrative arguments, for Hume, are deductively valid arguments where all the premises are relations of ideas. We can know that the conclusion of a demonstrative argument is true (indeed, necessarily true) without knowing anything about the actual world—this is why Hume often calls them "reasonings *a priori*." Experimental arguments are arguments of any other kind: that is, they are either arguments which have matters of fact among their premises, or arguments which are not deductive, or (most commonly) both.

5. Finally, a word about "induction." Although Hume does not actually use the word in this reading, Section IV Part II of the *Enquiry* is usually thought of as presenting, for the first time, "the problem of induction." Induction is the modern term for the process of arriving at justified beliefs about the future on the basis of experience of the past; to put the same idea in another way, induction is the method for finding out what as-yet unobserved things are like on the basis of a sample of things we have observed. For example, we might notice that every swan we have ever seen has been white, and conclude that, very probably, the next swan we see will also be white. Furthermore, we might think, we've seen enough swans to justify concluding that probably *every* swan is white. Thus we use our experience of observing swans to draw inductive conclusions about unseen swans—generalizations about other swans in the world (such as Australian swans), and predictions about future swans as yet unhatched. This method of reasoning is extremely common. It is what (apparently) supports much of our everyday behavior, such as getting up at a certain time in the morning to go to work or school, using a kettle to make tea, relying on the morning weather forecast to help us decide what to wear, expecting the bus to come at a certain time and place, and so on. All of these

---

1 If you have already read Descartes and Locke you might notice that Hume's notion of 'intuition' is significantly different from that used by his philosophical predecessors. For example, Descartes's "I think therefore I am" would not count as 'intuitively certain' for Hume.

activities and beliefs are based on assuming that past experience is reliable evidence for expectations about the future. Science, too, is largely based on induction—physicists have only observed a tiny, infinitesimal fraction of all the electrons in the universe, for example, yet they assume that all electrons everywhere have the same charge.

We speak of "the problem of induction," because Hume has apparently shown us that we have no rational justification for induction. This would be an extremely radical conclusion if in fact it is so!

Some Common Misconceptions

1. Hume's philosophical concerns were not primarily negative or destructive: although he frequently attacks the role of reason in science and human affairs, and points out the limitations of our own experiential knowledge, he does not do so in order to leave us in a skeptical dead end. Instead, these attacks are part of his attempt to place the science of human nature upon a more reliable footing, by actually examining how we come to have the beliefs that we do.

2. Although there are differences of interpretation on this matter, it seems likely that Hume was not merely pointing out that inductive conclusions cannot be known *with certainty* to be true—that induction cannot be 100% rationally justified. For that would simply be to say that induction is not deduction, which is trivial. (It is today part of the *definition* of an inductive, as opposed to deductive, argument that its conclusion may possibly be false even if all its premises are true, and this seems to correspond reasonably well with Hume's own distinction between experimental and demonstrative methods of reasoning.) Instead, Hume is making the much more radical claim that the conclusions of inductive arguments *have no rational support at all*: they are not "founded on reasoning, or on any process of the understanding." Inductive arguments, if Hume is right, completely fail to justify their conclusions—their premises, if true, do not make their conclusions *any* more likely to be true. (Analogously, the argument "roses are red, violets are blue, therefore Brad Pitt will become President of America" is not rationally compelling since the truth of the premises—the respective colors of roses and violets—does nothing to make it more likely to be true that this particular actor will have successful political ambitions. Chapter 1 contains more information on inductive and deductive arguments.)

3. On the other hand, Hume is not arguing that induction does not actually *work*—he's not arguing that human beings are systematically *wrong* in their predictions about the future. On the contrary, he thinks that human beings are usually very successful in coming to have true beliefs about the future (that the sun will rise tomorrow, or that the next chunk of copper we mine from the earth will conduct electricity). And although it's admittedly a bit tricky to hold both that this is the case and that induction is not at all justified, it's not flat out inconsistent: it's perfectly coherent to say that some of our beliefs are true but unjustified.

How Important and Influential Is This Passage?

An influential British philosopher named C.D. Broad once called inductive reasoning "the glory of Science … [and] … the scandal of Philosophy." The scandal Broad had in mind was the failure of philosophers over the previous two hundred years (he was writing in 1952) to find a convincing answer to Hume's skeptical arguments … and this despite the wholesale (and apparently successful) reliance of the natural sciences on inductive arguments. If induction is not rationally justified, recall, then neither are most of the claims of physics, biology, chemistry, economics, and so on. Thus Hume, in effect, discovered and incisively formulated a serious new philosophical problem—the problem of induction. (H.H. Price once called Hume's discovery of this problem "one of the most important advances in the whole history of thought.") This problem has very far-reaching consequences indeed, but it is so difficult a puzzle to solve that many philosophers feel Hume has not yet been satisfactorily answered. Hume's problem of induction is still a live problem today; various answers have been proposed but no single solution has yet found widespread acceptance.

Hume's own "skeptical solution" has been much less influential than his skeptical problem: even if Hume's account in Part V is successful (which many contemporary philosophers and psychologists doubt), it will still only be a *psychological* explanation for why we believe the things we do about the future, whereas what we seem to need to defend science—and most of our everyday beliefs—is a *rational justification* for induction.

Suggestions for Critical Reflection

1. *Are* "all the objects of human reason or enquiry" divisible into exactly two piles: relations of ideas and matters of fact? What about, for example, the claim that a wall can't be simultaneously red all over and green all over: which of the two categories does this fall into? How about the statement that water is identical with H_2O?

2. Does Hume think we are being unreasonable or irrational if we continue to act as if inductive inferences are justified? Given what Hume has argued, what do you think?

3. What exactly would it mean to claim that the future resembles the past or that nature is "uniform"? Is nature uniform in *every* respect? (For example, is the sky always blue?) So what *kind* of uniformity do you think we need to look for?

4. Does the past reliability *of induction* provide evidence that future instances of induction will also be reliable? For example, on several hundred occasions in the past I inferred on the basis of previous experience that the Big Mac I was about to eat would not be poisonous, and each time I was right; do these several hundred instances of correct induction provide any evidence that induction is *generally* reliable? Why, or why not?

5. What's the difference (if any) between the psychological claim that people believe certain things about the future only out of habit, rather than because they have gone through some process of reasoning, and the claim that there is no rational justification available for our beliefs about the future? Which claim is Hume making?

6. Is it possible to formulate a skeptical problem about *deduction* that is similar to Hume's problem about induction?

7. What is the difference between believing something and merely imagining that it is true? Does Hume think that when we believe some future event will occur, as opposed to merely imagining it will occur, there is some *extra* idea present in our mind—a sort of idea of belief itself, added to the idea of the future event? Are Hume's views on the nature of belief plausible?

Suggestions for Further Reading

The following two sections of the *Enquiry* re-cast portions of Part III, Book I of the *Treatise*, so that is a good place to begin your extra reading. A critical edition of Hume's philosophical writings is currently being prepared by Oxford University Press, but in the meantime the standard editions are: *A Treatise of Human Nature* (Oxford University Press, 1978) and *Enquiries Concerning Human Understanding and Concerning the Principles of Morals* (Oxford University Press, 1975), both edited by L.A. Selby-Bigge and P.H. Nidditch.

Many good books have been written about Hume's philosophy: a handful of the best and most relevant are *Hume's Epistemology and Metaphysics* by Georges Dicker (Routledge, 1998), *Hume's Philosophy of Belief* by Antony Flew (Routledge & Kegan Paul, 1961), *Hume's Skepticism* by Robert J. Fogelin (Routledge & Kegan Paul, 1985), *David Hume* by Terence Penelhum (Purdue University Press, 1992), *Probability and Hume's Inductive Scepticism* by David Stove (Oxford University Press, 1973), and *Hume* by Barry Stroud (Routledge, 1977). Tom Beauchamp and Alexander Rosenberg defend the view that Hume is not in fact a skeptic about induction in *Hume and the Problem of Causation* (Oxford University Press, 1981).

The Cambridge Companion to Hume, edited by David Fate Norton (Cambridge University Press, 1993), is a helpful collection of specially written essays on different aspects of Hume's philosophy, which also includes Hume's short autobiography. An old, but still good, collection of critical essays on Hume is V.C. Chappell's *Hume: A Collection of Critical Essays* (Doubleday, 1966).

Some influential attempts to solve Hume's riddle of induction—apart from those encompassed by the next few readings in this text—include: P.F. Strawson in the final chapter of his book *An Introduction to Logical Theory* (Methuen, 1952); Max Black, "Inductive Support of Inductive Rules," in *Problems of Analysis* (Cornell University Press, 1954); and James Van Cleve, "Reliability, Justification, and the Problem of Induction," in *Midwest Studies in Philosophy* IX (1984). A good review article criticizing many of these attempted solutions (and tentatively suggesting another) is Wesley C. Salmon's "Unfinished Business: The Problem of Induction," *Philosophical Studies* 33 (1978).

from *An Enquiry Concerning Human Understanding*[2]

Section IV: Sceptical Doubts Concerning the Operations of the Understanding.

PART I.

All the objects of human reason or enquiry may naturally be divided into two kinds, to wit,[3] *relations of ideas*, and *matters of fact*. Of the first kind are the sciences of geometry, algebra, and arithmetic; and in short, every affirmation which is either intuitively or demonstratively certain. *That the square of the hypotenuse*[4] *is equal to the square of the two sides*, is a proposition which expresses a relation between these figures. *That three times five is equal to the half*

---

2   Hume's *An Enquiry Concerning Human Understanding* was first published in 1748. This selection is taken from the 1777 "new edition," generally considered the final version authorized by Hume. Most of the spelling, capitalization, and punctuation have been modernized.

3   "To wit" is a phrase meaning "that is to say" or "namely."

4   The hypotenuse is the side opposite the right angle of a right-angled triangle.

of thirty, expresses a relation between these numbers. Propositions of this kind are discoverable by the mere operation of thought, without dependence on what is anywhere existent in the universe. Though there never were a circle or triangle in nature, the truths demonstrated by Euclid would for ever retain their certainty and evidence.

Matters of fact, which are the second objects of human reason, are not ascertained in the same manner; nor is our evidence of their truth, however great, of a like nature with the foregoing. The contrary of every matter of fact is still possible; because it can never imply a contradiction, and is conceived by the mind with the same facility and distinctness, as if ever so conformable to reality. *That the sun will not rise to-morrow* is no less intelligible a proposition, and implies no more contradiction than the affirmation, *that it will rise*. We should in vain, therefore, attempt to demonstrate its falsehood. Were it demonstratively false, it would imply a contradiction, and could never be distinctly conceived by the mind.

It may, therefore, be a subject worthy of curiosity, to enquire what is the nature of that evidence which assures us of any real existence and matter of fact, beyond the present testimony of our senses, or the records of our memory. This part of philosophy, it is observable, has been little cultivated, either by the ancients or moderns; and therefore our doubts and errors, in the prosecution of so important an enquiry, may be the more excusable; while we march through such difficult paths without any guide or direction. They may even prove useful, by exciting curiosity, and destroying that implicit faith and security, which is the bane of all reasoning and free enquiry. The discovery of defects in the common philosophy, if any such there be, will not, I presume, be a discouragement, but rather an incitement, as is usual, to attempt something more full and satisfactory than has yet been proposed to the public.

All reasonings concerning matter of fact seem to be founded on the relation of *cause and effect*. By means of that relation alone we can go beyond the evidence of our memory and senses. If you were to ask a man, why he believes any matter of fact, which is absent; for instance, that his friend is in the country, or in France; he would give you a reason; and this reason would be some other fact; as a letter received from him, or the knowledge of his former resolutions and promises. A man finding a watch or any other machine in a desert island, would conclude that there had once been men in that island. All our reasonings concerning fact are of the same nature. And here it is constantly supposed that there is a connection between the present fact and that which is inferred from it. Were there nothing to bind them together, the inference would be entirely precarious. The hearing of an articulate voice and rational discourse in the dark assures us of the presence of some person: Why? Because these are the effects of the human make and fabric, and closely connected with it. If we anatomize[5] all the other reasonings of this nature, we shall find that they are founded on the relation of cause and effect, and that this relation is either near or remote, direct or collateral. Heat and light are collateral effects of fire, and the one effect may justly be inferred from the other.

If we would satisfy ourselves, therefore, concerning the nature of that evidence, which assures us of matters of fact, we must enquire how we arrive at the knowledge of cause and effect.

I shall venture to affirm, as a general proposition, which admits of no exception, that the knowledge of this relation is not, in any instance, attained by reasonings *a priori*;[6] but arises entirely from experience, when we find that any particular objects are constantly conjoined with each other. Let an object be presented to a man of ever so strong natural reason and abilities; if that object be entirely new to him, he will not be able, by the most accurate examination of its sensible[7] qualities, to discover any of its causes or effects. Adam,[8] though his rational faculties be supposed, at the very first, entirely perfect, could not have inferred from the fluidity and transparency of water that it would suffocate him, or from the light and warmth of fire that it would consume him. No object ever discovers,[9] by the qualities which appear to the senses, either the causes which produced it, or the effects which will arise from it; nor can our reason, unassisted by experience, ever draw any inference concerning real existence and matter of fact.

This proposition, *that causes and effects are discoverable, not by reason but by experience,* will readily be admitted with regard to such objects as we remember to have once been altogether unknown to us; since we must be conscious of the utter inability, which we then lay under, of foretelling what would arise from them. Present two smooth pieces of marble to a man who has no tincture of natural philosophy;[10] he will never discover that they will adhere together in such a manner as to require great force to separate them in a direct line, while they make so small a resistance to a lateral pressure. Such events, as bear little analogy to the common course of nature, are also readily confessed to be known only by experience; nor does any man imagine that the explosion of gunpowder, or the attraction of a loadstone,[11] could ever be discovered by arguments *a priori*. In like manner, when an effect is supposed to depend upon an intricate machinery or secret structure of parts, we make no difficulty in attributing all our knowledge of it to experience. Who will assert that he can give the ultimate reason, why milk or bread is proper nourishment for a man, not for a lion or a tiger?

But the same truth may not appear, at first sight, to have the same evidence with regard to events, which have become familiar to us from our first appearance in the world, which bear a close analogy to the whole course of nature, and which are supposed to depend on the simple qualities of objects, without any secret structure of parts. We are apt to imagine that we could discover these effects by the mere operation of our reason, without experience. We fancy, that were we brought on a sudden into this world, we could at first have inferred that one billiard-ball would com-

---

5   Closely examine.

6   Prior to experience; purely deductively.

7   "Sensible" means, here and elsewhere, able to be perceived or sensed.

8   According to the Old Testament, the first human being.

9   Here (and sometimes elsewhere) "discovers" means reveals or discloses (rather than finds out).

10   That is: no trace of knowledge of physical science.

11   A magnet (made from naturally occurring magnetic iron oxide).

municate motion to another upon impulse;[12] and that we needed not to have waited for the event, in order to pronounce with certainty concerning it. Such is the influence of custom,[13] that, where it is strongest, it not only covers our natural ignorance, but even conceals itself, and seems not to take place, merely because it is found in the highest degree.

But to convince us that all the laws of nature, and all the operations of bodies without exception, are known only by experience, the following reflections may, perhaps, suffice. Were any object presented to us, and were we required to pronounce concerning the effect, which will result from it, without consulting past observation; after what manner, I beseech you, must the mind proceed in this operation? It must invent or imagine some event, which it ascribes to the object as its effect; and it is plain that this invention must be entirely arbitrary. The mind can never possibly find the effect in the supposed cause, by the most accurate scrutiny and examination. For the effect is totally different from the cause, and consequently can never be discovered in it. Motion in the second billiard-ball is a quite distinct event from motion in the first; nor is there any thing in the one to suggest the smallest hint of the other. A stone or piece of metal raised into the air, and left without any support, immediately falls: but to consider the matter *a priori*, is there any thing we discover in this situation which can beget the idea of a downward, rather than an upward, or any other motion, in the stone or metal?

And as the first imagination or invention of a particular effect, in all natural operations, is arbitrary, where we consult not experience; so must we also esteem the supposed tie or connection between the cause and effect, which binds them together, and renders it impossible that any other effect could result from the operation of that cause. When I see, for instance, a billiard-ball moving in a straight line towards another; even suppose motion in the second ball should by accident be suggested to me, as the result of their contact or impulse; may I not conceive, that a hundred different events might as well follow from that cause? May not both these balls remain at absolute rest? May

not the first ball return in a straight line, or leap off from the second in any line or direction? All these suppositions are consistent and conceivable. Why then should we give the preference to one, which is no more consistent or conceivable than the rest? All our reasonings *a priori* will never be able to show us any foundation for this preference.

In a word, then, every effect is a distinct event from its cause. It could not, therefore, be discovered in the cause, and the first invention or conception of it, *a priori*, must be entirely arbitrary. And even after it is suggested, the conjunction of it with the cause must appear equally arbitrary; since there are always many other effects, which, to reason, must seem fully as consistent and natural. In vain, therefore, should we pretend to determine any single event, or infer any cause or effect, without the assistance of observation and experience.

Hence we may discover the reason why no philosopher,[14] who is rational and modest, has ever pretended to assign the ultimate cause of any natural operation, or to show distinctly the action of that power, which produces any single effect in the universe. It is confessed, that the utmost effort of human reason is to reduce the principles, productive of natural phenomena, to a greater simplicity, and to resolve the many particular effects into a few general causes, by means of reasonings from analogy, experience, and observation. But as to the causes of these general causes, we should in vain attempt their discovery; nor shall we ever be able to satisfy ourselves, by any particular explication of them. These ultimate springs and principles are totally shut up from human curiosity and enquiry. Elasticity, gravity, cohesion of parts, communication of motion by impulse; these are probably the ultimate causes and principles which we shall ever discover in nature; and we may esteem ourselves sufficiently happy, if, by accurate enquiry and reasoning, we can trace up the particular phenomena to, or near to, these general principles. The most perfect philosophy of the natural kind only staves off our ignorance a little longer: as perhaps the most perfect philosophy of the moral or metaphysical kind

---

12   Impact, collision.

13   Habit, repeated similar experience.

14   The word "philosopher" at this time included natural scientists.

serves only to discover larger portions of it. Thus the observation of human blindness and weakness is the result of all philosophy, and meets us at every turn, in spite of our endeavours to elude or avoid it.

Nor is geometry, when taken into the assistance of natural philosophy, ever able to remedy this defect, or lead us into the knowledge of ultimate causes, by all that accuracy of reasoning for which it is so justly celebrated. Every part of mixed mathematics[15] proceeds upon the supposition that certain laws are established by nature in her operations; and abstract reasonings are employed, either to assist experience in the discovery of these laws, or to determine their influence in particular instances, where it depends upon any precise degree of distance and quantity. Thus, it is a law of motion, discovered by experience, that the moment[16] or force of any body in motion is in the compound ratio or proportion of its solid contents[17] and its velocity; and consequently, that a small force may remove the greatest obstacle or raise the greatest weight, if, by any contrivance or machinery, we can increase the velocity of that force, so as to make it an overmatch for its antagonist.[18] Geometry assists us in the application of this law, by giving us the just dimensions of all the parts and figures which can enter into any species of machine; but still the discovery of the law itself is owing merely to experience, and all the abstract reasonings in the world could never lead us one step towards the knowledge of it. When we reason *a priori*, and consider merely any object or cause, as it appears to the mind, independent of all observation, it never could suggest to us the notion of any distinct object, such as its effect; much less, show us the inseparable and inviolable connection between them. A man must be very sagacious[19] who could discover by reasoning that crystal is the effect of heat, and ice of cold, without being previously acquainted with the operation of these qualities.

PART II.

But we have not yet attained any tolerable satisfaction with regard to the question first proposed. Each solution still gives rise to a new question as difficult as the foregoing, and leads us on to farther enquiries. When it is asked, *What is the nature of all our reasonings concerning matter of fact?* the proper answer seems to be, that they are founded on the relation of cause and effect. When again it is asked, *What is the foundation of all our reasonings and conclusions concerning that relation?* it may be replied in one word, Experience. But if we still carry on our sifting humour,[20] and ask, *What is the foundation of all conclusions from experience?* this implies a new question, which may be of more difficult solution and explication. Philosophers, that give themselves airs of superior wisdom and sufficiency,[21] have a hard task when they encounter persons of inquisitive dispositions, who push them from every corner to which they retreat, and who are sure at last to bring them to some dangerous dilemma. The best expedient to prevent this confusion, is to be modest in our pretensions; and even to discover the difficulty ourselves before it is objected to us. By this means, we may make a kind of merit of our very ignorance.

I shall content myself, in this section, with an easy task, and shall pretend[22] only to give a negative answer to the question here proposed. I say then, that, even after we have experience of the operations of cause and effect, our conclusions from that experience are *not* founded on reasoning, or any process of the

---

15 Mathematical physics (mathematics applied to the physical world).

16 Momentum.

17 Mass.

18 Here is what Hume means by this example (which comes from Newtonian physics). Imagine two bodies A and B: suppose that A has a mass of 2 and a velocity of 4 and that B has a mass of 6 and a velocity of 1. Thus the ratios of their respective masses will be 2:6 and their respective velocities 4:1. Then, A will have a higher momentum or force than B (despite only having one third the mass), since the "compound ratio" of its momentum to that of B will be 2x4 to 6x1, which is 8:6.

19 Mentally penetrating, insightful (Hume is being ironic).

20 Searching frame of mind.

21 Here "sufficiency" means ability.

22 Aim, venture.

understanding. This answer we must endeavour both to explain and to defend.

It must certainly be allowed, that nature has kept us at a great distance from all her secrets, and has afforded us only the knowledge of a few superficial qualities of objects; while she conceals from us those powers and principles on which the influence of those objects entirely depends. Our senses inform us of the colour, weight, and consistence[23] of bread; but neither sense nor reason can ever inform us of those qualities which fit it for the nourishment and support of a human body. Sight or feeling conveys an idea of the actual motion of bodies; but as to that wonderful force or power, which would carry on a moving body for ever in a continued change of place, and which bodies never lose but by communicating it to others; of this we cannot form the most distant conception. But notwithstanding this ignorance of natural powers[24] and principles, we always presume, when we see like[25] sensible qualities, that they have like secret powers, and expect that effects, similar to those which we have experienced, will follow from them. If a body of like colour and consistence with that bread, which we have formerly eat,[26] be presented to us, we make no scruple of repeating the experiment,[27] and foresee, with certainty, like nourishment and support. Now this is a process of the mind or thought, of which I would willingly know the foundation. It is allowed on all hands that there is no known connection between the sensible qualities and the secret powers; and consequently, that the mind is not led to form such a conclusion concerning their constant and regular conjunction, by any thing which it knows of their nature. As to past *experience*, it can be allowed to give *direct* and *certain* information of those precise objects only, and that precise period of time, which fell under its cognizance: But why this experience should be extended to future times, and to other objects, which for aught we know, may be only in appearance similar; this is the main question on which I would insist. The bread, which I formerly eat, nourished me; that is, a body of such sensible qualities was, at that time, endued with[28] such secret powers: but does it follow, that other bread must also nourish me at another time, and that like sensible qualities must always be attended with like secret powers? The consequence seems nowise necessary. At least, it must be acknowledged that there is here a consequence drawn by the mind; that there is a certain step taken; a process of thought, and an inference, which wants to be explained. These two propositions are far from being the same, *I have found that such an object has always been attended with such an effect*, and *I foresee, that other objects, which are, in appearance, similar, will be attended with similar effects*. I shall allow, if you please, that the one proposition may justly be inferred from the other: I know, in fact, that it always is inferred. But if you insist that the inference is made by a chain of reasoning, I desire you to produce that reasoning. The connection between these propositions is not intuitive. There is required a medium,[29] which may enable the mind to draw such an inference, if indeed it be drawn by reasoning and argument. What that medium is, I must confess, passes my comprehension; and it is incumbent on those to produce it, who assert that it really exists, and is the origin of all our conclusions concerning matter of fact.

This negative argument must certainly, in process of time, become altogether convincing, if many penetrating and able philosophers shall turn their enquiries this way and no one be ever able to discover any connecting proposition or intermediate step, which supports the understanding in this conclusion. But as the question is yet new, every reader may not trust so far to his own penetration, as to conclude, because an argument escapes his enquiry, that therefore it does not really exist. For this reason it may be requisite to venture upon a more difficult task; and enumerating all the branches of human knowledge, endeavour to show that none of them can afford such an argument.

---

23   Consistency, texture.

24   [Author's note] The word, Power, is here used in a loose and popular sense. The more accurate explication of it would give additional evidence to this argument. See Sect. 7 [not reprinted here].

25   Similar.

26   Eaten.

27   Experience.

28   Endowed with, possessed of.

29   A ground of inference; a further premise.

All reasonings may be divided into two kinds, namely, demonstrative reasoning, or that concerning relations of ideas, and moral[30] reasoning, or that concerning matter of fact and existence. That there are no demonstrative arguments in the case seems evident; since it implies no contradiction that the course of nature may change, and that an object, seemingly like those which we have experienced, may be attended with different or contrary effects. May I not clearly and distinctly conceive that a body, falling from the clouds, and which, in all other respects, resembles snow, has yet the taste of salt or feeling of fire? Is there any more intelligible proposition than to affirm, that all the trees will flourish in December and January, and decay in May and June? Now whatever is intelligible, and can be distinctly conceived, implies no contradiction, and can never be proved false by any demonstrative argument or abstract reasoning *a priori*.

If we be, therefore, engaged[31] by arguments to put trust in past experience, and make it the standard of our future judgement, these arguments must be probable only, or such as regard matter of fact and real existence according to the division above mentioned. But that there is no argument of this kind, must appear, if our explication of that species of reasoning be admitted as solid and satisfactory. We have said that all arguments concerning existence are founded on the relation of cause and effect; that our knowledge of that relation is derived entirely from experience; and that all our experimental conclusions proceed upon the supposition that the future will be conformable to the past. To endeavour, therefore, the proof of this last supposition by probable arguments, or arguments regarding existence, must be evidently going in a circle, and taking that for granted, which is the very point in question.

In reality, all arguments from experience are founded on the similarity which we discover among natural objects, and by which we are induced to expect effects similar to those which we have found to follow from such objects. And though none but a fool or madman will ever pretend to dispute the authority of experience, or to reject that great guide of human life, it may surely be allowed a philosopher to have so much curiosity at least as to examine the principle of human nature, which gives this mighty authority to experience, and makes us draw advantage from that similarity which nature has placed among different objects. From causes which, appear *similar*, we expect similar effects. This is the sum of all our experimental conclusions. Now it seems evident that, if this conclusion were formed by reason, it would be as perfect at first, and upon one instance, as after ever so long a course of experience. But the case is far otherwise. Nothing so like as eggs; yet no one, on account of this appearing similarity, expects the same taste and relish in all of them. It is only after a long course of uniform experiments in any kind, that we attain a firm reliance and security with regard to a particular event. Now where is that process of reasoning which, from one instance, draws a conclusion, so different from that which it infers from a hundred instances that are nowise different from that single one? This question I propose as much for the sake of information, as with an intention of raising difficulties. I cannot find, I cannot imagine any such reasoning. But I keep my mind still open to instruction, if any one will vouchsafe to bestow it on me.

Should it be said that, from a number of uniform experiments, we *infer* a connection between the sensible qualities and the secret powers; this, I must confess, seems the same difficulty, couched in different terms. The question still recurs, on what process of argument this *inference* is founded? Where is the medium, the interposing ideas, which join propositions so very wide of each other? It is confessed that the colour, consistence, and other sensible qualities of bread appear not, of themselves, to have any connection with the secret powers of nourishment and support. For otherwise we could infer these secret powers from the first appearance of these sensible qualities, without the aid of experience; contrary to the sentiment[32] of all philosophers, and contrary to plain

---

30 Here "moral" means inductive or having at best only a probable conclusion. (Often, however, Hume uses the phrase "moral philosophy" in a somewhat different way, to mean the study of the nature of human beings, contrasted with "natural philosophy," the study of nature.)

31 Induced, persuaded.

---

32 Opinion.

matter of fact. Here, then, is our natural state of ignorance with regard to the powers and influence of all objects. How is this remedied by experience? It only shows us a number of uniform effects, resulting from certain objects, and teaches us that those particular objects, at that particular time, were endowed with such powers and forces. When a new object, endowed with similar sensible qualities, is produced, we expect similar powers and forces, and look for a like effect. From a body of like colour and consistence with bread we expect like nourishment and support. But this surely is a step or progress of the mind, which wants to be explained. When a man says, *I have found, in all past instances, such sensible qualities conjoined with such secret powers*: and when he says, *similar sensible qualities will always be conjoined with similar secret powers*, he is not guilty of a tautology, nor are these propositions in any respect the same. You say that the one proposition is an inference from the other. But you must confess that the inference is not intuitive; neither is it demonstrative: Of what nature is it, then? To say it is experimental, is begging the question. For all inferences from experience suppose, as their foundation, that the future will resemble the past, and that similar powers will be conjoined with similar sensible qualities. If there be any suspicion that the course of nature may change, and that the past may be no rule for the future, all experience becomes useless, and can give rise to no inference or conclusion. It is impossible, therefore, that any arguments from experience can prove this resemblance of the past to the future; since all these arguments are founded on the supposition of that resemblance. Let the course of things be allowed hitherto ever so regular; that alone, without some new argument or inference, proves not that, for the future, it will continue so. In vain do you pretend to have learned the nature of bodies from your past experience. Their secret nature, and consequently all their effects and influence, may change, without any change in their sensible qualities. This happens sometimes, and with regard to some objects: why may it not happen always, and with regard to all objects? What logic, what process or argument secures you against this supposition? My practice, you say, refutes my doubts. But you mistake the purport of my question. As an agent, I am quite satisfied in the point; but

as a philosopher, who has some share of curiosity, I will not say scepticism, I want to learn the foundation of this inference. No reading, no enquiry has yet been able to remove my difficulty, or give me satisfaction in a matter of such importance. Can I do better than propose the difficulty to the public, even though, perhaps, I have small hopes of obtaining a solution? We shall at least, by this means, be sensible of our ignorance, if we do not augment our knowledge.

I must confess that a man is guilty of unpardonable arrogance who concludes, because an argument has escaped his own investigation, that therefore it does not really exist. I must also confess that, though all the learned, for several ages, should have employed themselves in fruitless search upon any subject, it may still, perhaps, be rash to conclude positively that the subject must, therefore, pass all human comprehension. Even though we examine all the sources of our knowledge, and conclude them unfit for such a subject, there may still remain a suspicion, that the enumeration is not complete, or the examination not accurate. But with regard to the present subject, there are some considerations which seem to remove all this accusation of arrogance or suspicion of mistake.

It is certain that the most ignorant and stupid peasants—nay infants, nay even brute beasts—improve by experience, and learn the qualities of natural objects, by observing the effects which result from them. When a child has felt the sensation of pain from touching the flame of a candle, he will be careful not to put his hand near any candle; but will expect a similar effect from a cause which is similar in its sensible qualities and appearance. If you assert, therefore, that the understanding of the child is led into this conclusion by any process of argument or ratiocination, I may justly require you to produce that argument; nor have you any pretence to refuse so equitable a demand. You cannot say that the argument is abstruse, and may possibly escape your enquiry; since you confess that it is obvious to the capacity of a mere infant. If you hesitate, therefore, a moment, or if, after reflection, you produce any intricate or profound argument, you, in a manner, give up the question, and confess that it is not reasoning which engages us to suppose the past resembling the future, and to expect similar effects from causes which are, to appearance, similar. This is the proposition which I intended to enforce in the present section. If I be right, I pretend not to have made any mighty discovery. And if I be wrong, I must acknowledge myself to be indeed a very backward scholar; since I cannot now discover an argument which, it seems, was perfectly familiar to me long before I was out of my cradle.

Section V: Sceptical Solution of these Doubts.

PART I.

The passion for philosophy, like that for religion, seems liable to this inconvenience, that, though it aims at the correction of our manners, and extirpation of our vices, it may only serve, by imprudent management, to foster a predominant inclination, and push the mind, with more determined resolution, towards that side which already *draws* too much,[33] by the bias and propensity of the natural temper. It is certain that, while we aspire to the magnanimous firmness of the philosophic sage, and endeavour to confine our pleasures altogether within our own minds, we may, at last, render our philosophy like that of Epictetus, and other *Stoics*,[34] only a more refined system of selfishness, and reason ourselves out of all virtue as well as social enjoyment. While we study with attention the vanity of human life, and turn all our thoughts towards the empty and transitory nature of riches and honours, we are, perhaps, all the while flattering our natural indolence, which, hating the bustle of the world, and drudgery of business, seeks a pretence of reason to give itself a full and uncontrolled indulgence. There is, however, one species of philosophy which seems little liable to this inconvenience, and that because it strikes in with no disorderly passion of the human

mind, nor can mingle itself with any natural affection or propensity; and that is the Academic or Sceptical philosophy.[35] The academics always talk of doubt and suspense of judgement, of danger in hasty determinations, of confining to very narrow bounds the enquiries of the understanding, and of renouncing all speculations which lie not within the limits of common life and practice. Nothing, therefore, can be more contrary than such a philosophy to the supine indolence of the mind, its rash arrogance, its lofty pretensions, and its superstitious credulity. Every passion is mortified by it, except the love of truth; and that passion never is, nor can be, carried to too high a degree. It is surprising, therefore, that this philosophy, which, in almost every instance, must be harmless and innocent, should be the subject of so much groundless reproach and obloquy. But, perhaps, the very circumstance which renders it so innocent is what chiefly exposes it to the public hatred and resentment. By flattering no irregular passion, it gains few partisans: by opposing so many vices and follies, it raises to itself abundance of enemies, who stigmatize it as libertine, profane, and irreligious.

Nor need we fear that this philosophy, while it endeavours to limit our enquiries to common life, should ever undermine the reasonings of common life, and carry its doubts so far as to destroy all action, as well as speculation. Nature will always maintain her rights, and prevail in the end over any abstract reasoning whatsoever. Though we should conclude, for instance, as in the foregoing section, that, in all reasonings from experience, there is a step taken by the mind which is not supported by any argument or process of the understanding; there is no danger that these reasonings, on which almost all knowledge depends, will ever be affected by such a discovery. If the mind be not engaged by argument to make this step, it must be induced by some other principle of equal weight and

---

33 Pulls too much—i.e., toward the side we already favor.

34 Epictetus (c. 55–135 CE) was a leading Stoic of the Roman era. Stoicism was a philosophical movement that flourished between roughly 300 BCE and 200 CE, and its main doctrine was that the guiding principle of nature is Reason (*logos*) and the highest virtue is to live in harmony with this rational order.

35 Hume means a kind of moderate skepticism, associated with Plato and the school he founded in Athens around 380 BCE, the Academy. This is to be contrasted with the extreme skepticism sometimes called Pyrrhonism, which seeks to suspend judgment on any question having conflicting evidence—which is to say, on nearly all questions.

authority; and that principle will preserve its influence as long as human nature remains the same. What that principle is may well be worth the pains of enquiry.

Suppose a person, though endowed with the strongest faculties of reason and reflection, to be brought on a sudden into this world; he would, indeed, immediately observe a continual succession of objects, and one event following another; but he would not be able to discover anything farther. He would not, at first, by any reasoning, be able to reach the idea of cause and effect; since the particular powers, by which all natural operations are performed, never appear to the senses; nor is it reasonable to conclude, merely because one event, in one instance, precedes another, that therefore the one is the cause, the other the effect. Their conjunction may be arbitrary and casual. There may be no reason to infer the existence of one from the appearance of the other. And in a word, such a person, without more experience, could never employ his conjecture or reasoning concerning any matter of fact, or be assured of any thing beyond what was immediately present to his memory and senses.

Suppose, again, that he has acquired more experience, and has lived so long in the world as to have observed familiar objects or events to be constantly conjoined together; what is the consequence of this experience? He immediately infers the existence of one object from the appearance of the other. Yet he has not, by all his experience, acquired any idea or knowledge of the secret power by which the one object produces the other; nor is it by any process of reasoning, he is engaged to draw this inference. But still he finds himself determined to draw it: And though he should be convinced that his understanding has no part in the operation, he would nevertheless continue in the same course of thinking. There is some other principle which determines him to form such a conclusion.

This principle is custom or habit. For wherever the repetition of any particular act or operation produces a propensity to renew the same act or operation, without being impelled by any reasoning or process of the understanding, we always say, that this propensity is the effect of *custom*. By employing that word, we pretend not to have given the ultimate reason of such a propensity. We only point out a principle of

human nature, which is universally acknowledged, and which is well known by its effects. Perhaps we can push our enquiries no farther, or pretend to give the cause of this cause; but must rest contented with it as the ultimate principle, which we can assign, of all our conclusions from experience. It is sufficient satisfaction, that we can go so far, without repining at the narrowness of our faculties because they will carry us no farther. And it is certain we here advance a very intelligible proposition at least, if not a true one, when we assert that, after the constant conjunction of two objects—heat and flame, for instance, weight and solidity—we are determined[36] by custom alone to expect the one from the appearance of the other. This hypothesis seems even the only one which explains the difficulty, why we draw, from a thousand instances, an inference which we are not able to draw from one instance, that is, in no respect, different from them. Reason is incapable of any such variation. The conclusions which it draws from considering one circle are the same which it would form upon surveying all the circles in the universe. But no man, having seen only one body move after being impelled by another, could infer that every other body will move after a like impulse. All inferences from experience, therefore, are effects of custom, not of reasoning.[37]

---

36 Caused.

37 [Author's note] Nothing is more usual than for writers, even, on *moral*, *political*, or *physical* subjects to distinguish between *reason* and *experience*, and to suppose, that these species of argumentation are entirely different from each other. The former are taken for the mere result of our intellectual faculties, which, by considering *a priori* the nature of things, and examining the effects, that must follow from their operation, establish particular principles of science and philosophy. The latter are supposed to be derived entirely from sense and observation, by which we learn what has actually resulted from the operation of particular objects, and are thence able to infer, what will, for the future, result from them. Thus, for instance, the limitations and restraints of civil government, and a legal constitution, may be defended, either from *reason*, which reflecting on the great frailty and corruption of human nature, teaches, that no man can safely be

Custom, then, is the great guide of human life. It is

trusted with unlimited authority; or from *experience* and history, which inform us of the enormous abuses, that ambition, in every age and country, has been found to make so imprudent a confidence.

The same distinction between reason and experience is maintained in all our deliberations concerning the conduct of life; while the experienced statesman, general, physician, or merchant is trusted and followed; and the unpractised novice, with whatever natural talents endowed, neglected and despised. Though it be allowed, that reason may form very plausible conjectures with regard to the consequences of such a particular conduct in such particular circumstances; it is still supposed imperfect, without the assistance of experience, which is alone able to give stability and certainty to the maxims, derived from study and reflection.

But notwithstanding that this distinction be thus universally received, both in the active and speculative scenes of life, I shall not scruple to pronounce, that it is, at bottom, erroneous, at least, superficial.

If we examine those arguments, which, in any of the sciences above mentioned, are supposed to be mere effects of reasoning and reflection, they will be found to terminate, at last, in some general principle or, conclusion, for which we can assign no reason but observation and experience. The only difference between them and those maxims, which are vulgarly esteemed the result of pure experience, is, that the former cannot be established without some process of thought, and some reflection on what we have observed, in order to distinguish its circumstances, and trace its consequences: Whereas in the latter, the experienced event is exactly and fully familiar to that which we infer as the result of any particular situation. The history of a Tiberius or a Nero makes us dread a like tyranny, were our monarchs freed from the restraints of laws and senates: but the observation of any fraud or cruelty in private life is sufficient, with the aid of a little thought, to give us the same apprehension; while it serves as an instance of the general corruption of human nature, and shows us the danger which we must incur by reposing an entire confidence in mankind. In both cases, it is experience which is ultimately the foundation of our inference and conclusion.

that principle alone which renders our experience useful to us, and makes us expect, for the future, a similar train of events with those which have appeared in the past. Without the influence of custom, we should be entirely ignorant of every matter of fact beyond what is immediately present to the memory and senses. We should never know how to adjust means to ends, or to employ our natural powers in the production of any effect. There would be an end at once of all action, as well as of the chief part of speculation.

But here it may be proper to remark, that though our conclusions from experience carry us beyond our memory and senses, and assure us of matters of fact which happened in the most distant places and most remote ages, yet some fact must always be present to the senses or memory, from which we may first proceed in drawing these conclusions. A man, who should find in a desert country the remains of pompous[38] buildings, would conclude that the country had, in ancient times, been cultivated by civilized inhabitants; but did nothing of this nature occur to him, he could never form such an inference. We learn the events of former ages from history; but then we must

There is no man so young and inexperienced, as not to have formed, from observation, many general and just maxims concerning human affairs and the conduct of life; but it must be confessed, that, when a man comes to put these in practice, he will be extremely liable to error, till time and farther experience both enlarge these maxims, and teach him their proper use and application. In every situation or incident, there are many particular and seemingly minute circumstances, which the man of greatest talent is, at first, apt to overlook, though on them the justness of his conclusions, and consequently the prudence of his conduct, entirely depend. Not to mention, that, to a young beginner, the general observations and maxims occur not always on the proper occasions, nor can be immediately applied with due calmness and distinction. The truth is, an unexperienced reasoner could be no reasoner at all, were he absolutely unexperienced; and when we assign that character to any one, we mean it only in a comparative sense, and suppose him possessed of experience, in a smaller and more imperfect degree.

38   Splendid, full of pomp.

peruse the volumes in which this instruction is contained, and thence carry up our inferences from one testimony to another, till we arrive at the eyewitnesses and spectators of these distant events. In a word, if we proceed not upon some fact, present to the memory or senses, our reasonings would be merely hypothetical; and however the particular links might be connected with each other, the whole chain of inferences would have nothing to support it, nor could we ever, by its means, arrive at the knowledge of any real existence. If I ask why you believe any particular matter of fact, which you relate, you must tell me some reason; and this reason will be some other fact, connected with it. But as you cannot proceed after this manner, *in infinitum*,[39] you must at last terminate in some fact, which is present to your memory or senses; or must allow that your belief is entirely without foundation.

What, then, is the conclusion of the whole matter? A simple one; though, it must be confessed, pretty remote from the common theories of philosophy. All belief of matter of fact or real existence is derived merely from some object, present to the memory or senses, and a customary conjunction between that and some other object. Or in other words; having found, in many instances, that any two kinds of objects—flame and heat, snow and cold—have always been conjoined together; if flame or snow be presented anew to the senses, the mind is carried by custom to expect heat or cold, and to *believe* that such a quality does exist, and will discover itself upon a nearer approach. This belief is the necessary result of placing the mind in such circumstances. It is an operation of the soul, when we are so situated, as unavoidable as to feel the passion of love, when we receive benefits; or hatred, when we meet with injuries. All these operations are a species of natural instincts, which no reasoning or process of the thought and understanding is able either to produce or to prevent.

At this point, it would be very allowable for us to stop our philosophical researches. In most questions we can never make a single step farther; and in all questions we must terminate here at last, after our most restless and curious enquiries. But still our curiosity will be pardonable, perhaps commendable, if it carry us on to still farther researches, and make us examine more accurately the nature of this *belief*, and of the *customary conjunction*, whence it is derived. By this means we may meet with some explications and analogies that will give satisfaction; at least to such as love the abstract sciences, and can be entertained with speculations, which, however accurate, may still retain a degree of doubt and uncertainty. As to readers of a different taste; the remaining part of this section is not calculated for them, and the following enquiries may well be understood, though it be neglected.

PART II.

Nothing is more free than the imagination of man; and though it cannot exceed that original stock of ideas furnished by the internal and external senses, it has unlimited power of mixing, compounding, separating, and dividing these ideas, in all the varieties of fiction and vision. It can feign[40] a train of events, with all the appearance of reality, ascribe to them a particular time and place, conceive them as existent, and paint them out to itself with every circumstance, that belongs to any historical fact, which it believes with the greatest certainty. Wherein, therefore, consists the difference between such a *fiction* and *belief*? It lies not merely in any peculiar idea, which is annexed to such a conception as commands our assent, and which is wanting[41] to every known fiction. For as the mind has authority over all its ideas, it could voluntarily annex this particular idea to any fiction, and consequently be able to believe whatever it pleases; contrary to what we find by daily experience. We can, in our conception, join the head of a man to the body of a horse; but it is not in our power to believe that such an animal has ever really existed.

It follows, therefore, that the difference between *fiction* and *belief* lies in some sentiment or feeling, which is annexed to the latter, not to the former, and which depends not on the will, nor can be commanded at pleasure. It must be excited by nature, like all other sentiments; and must arise from the particular situation, in which the mind is placed at any particular juncture. Whenever any object is presented to the

---

39   For ever, to infinity.

40   Simulate, imagine.

41   Lacking.

memory or senses, it immediately, by the force of custom, carries the imagination to conceive that object, which is usually conjoined to it; and this conception is attended with a feeling or sentiment, different from the loose reveries of the fancy. In this consists the whole nature of belief. For as there is no matter of fact which we believe so firmly that we cannot conceive the contrary, there would be no difference between the conception assented to and that which is rejected, were it not for some sentiment which distinguishes the one from the other. If I see a billiard-ball moving toward another, on a smooth table, I can easily conceive it to stop upon contact. This conception implies no contradiction; but still it feels very differently from that conception by which I represent to myself the impulse and the communication of motion from one ball to another.

Were we to attempt a *definition* of this sentiment, we should, perhaps, find it a very difficult, if not an impossible task; in the same manner as if we should endeavour to define the feeling of cold or passion of anger, to a creature who never had any experience of these sentiments. Belief is the true and proper name of this feeling; and no one is ever at a loss to know the meaning of that term; because every man is every moment conscious of the sentiment represented by it. It may not, however, be improper to attempt a *description* of this sentiment; in hopes we may, by that means, arrive at some analogies, which may afford a more perfect explication of it. I say, then, that belief is nothing but a more vivid, lively, forcible, firm, steady conception of an object, than what the imagination alone is ever able to attain. This variety of terms, which may seem so unphilosophical, is intended only to express that act of the mind, which renders realities, or what is taken for such, more present to us than fictions, causes them to weigh more in the thought, and gives them a superior influence on the passions and imagination. Provided we agree about the thing, it is needless to dispute about the terms. The imagination has the command over all its ideas, and can join and mix and vary them, in all the ways possible. It may conceive fictitious objects with all the circumstances of place and time. It may set them, in a manner, before our eyes, in their true colours, just as they might have existed. But as it is impossible that this faculty of imagination can ever, of itself, reach belief, it is evident that belief consists not in the peculiar nature or order of ideas, but in the *manner* of their conception, and in their *feeling* to the mind. I confess, that it is impossible perfectly to explain this feeling or manner of conception. We may make use of words which express something near it. But its true and proper name, as we observed before, is *belief;* which is a term that every one sufficiently understands in common life. And in philosophy, we can go no farther than assert, that *belief* is something felt by the mind, which distinguishes the ideas of the judgement from the fictions of the imagination. It gives them more weight and influence; makes them appear of greater importance; enforces them in the mind; and renders them the governing principle of our actions. I hear at present, for instance, a person's voice, with whom I am acquainted; and the sound comes as from the next room. This impression of my senses immediately conveys my thought to the person, together with all the surrounding objects. I paint them out to myself as existing at present, with the same qualities and relations, of which I formerly knew them possessed. These ideas take faster hold of my mind than ideas of an enchanted castle. They are very different to the feeling, and have a much greater influence of every kind, either to give pleasure or pain, joy or sorrow.

Let us, then, take in the whole compass of this doctrine, and allow, that the sentiment of belief is nothing but a conception more intense and steady than what attends the mere fictions of the imagination, and that this *manner* of conception arises from a customary conjunction of the object with something present to the memory or senses: I believe that it will not be difficult, upon these suppositions, to find other operations of the mind analogous to it, and to trace up these phenomena to principles still more general.

We have already observed that nature has established connections among particular ideas, and that no sooner one idea occurs to our thoughts than it introduces its correlative,[42] and carries our attention towards it, by a gentle and insensible movement. These principles of connection or association we have reduced to three, namely, *resemblance, contiguity*

---

42 The thing normally related or connected to it.

and *causation*; which are the only bonds that unite our thoughts together, and beget that regular train of reflection or discourse, which, in a greater or less degree, takes place among all mankind. Now here arises a question, on which the solution of the present difficulty will depend. Does it happen, in all these relations, that, when one of the objects is presented to the senses or memory, the mind is not only carried to the conception of the correlative, but reaches a steadier and stronger conception of it than what otherwise it would have been able to attain? This seems to be the case with that belief which arises from the relation of cause and effect. And if the case be the same with the other relations or principles of associations, this may be established as a general law, which takes place in all the operations of the mind.

We may, therefore, observe, as the first experiment to our present purpose, that, upon the appearance of the picture of an absent friend, our idea of him is evidently enlivened by the *resemblance*, and that every passion, which that idea occasions, whether of joy or sorrow, acquires new force and vigour. In producing this effect, there concur both a relation and a present impression. Where the picture bears him no resemblance, at least was not intended for[43] him, it never so much as conveys our thought to him: and where it is absent, as well as the person, though the mind may pass from the thought of the one to that of the other, it feels its idea to be rather weakened than enlivened by that transition. We take a pleasure in viewing the picture of a friend, when it is set before us; but when it is removed, rather choose to consider him directly than by reflection in an image, which is equally distant and obscure.

The ceremonies of the Roman Catholic religion may be considered as instances of the same nature. The devotees of that superstition usually plead in excuse for the mummeries,[44] with which they are upbraided, that they feel the good effect of those external motions, and postures, and actions, in enlivening their devotion and quickening their fervour, which otherwise would decay, if directed entirely to distant and immaterial objects. We shadow out the objects of our faith, say they, in sensible types and images, and render them more present to us by the immediate presence of these types, than it is possible for us to do merely by an intellectual view and contemplation. Sensible objects have always a greater influence on the fancy than any other; and this influence they readily convey to those ideas to which they are related, and which they resemble. I shall only infer from these practices, and this reasoning, that the effect of resemblance in enlivening the ideas is very common; and as in every case a resemblance and a present impression must concur, we are abundantly supplied with experiments to prove the reality of the foregoing principle.

We may add force to these experiments by others of a different kind, in considering the effects of *contiguity* as well as of *resemblance*. It is certain that distance diminishes the force of every idea, and that, upon our approach to any object; though it does not discover itself to our senses; it operates upon the mind with an influence, which imitates an immediate impression. The thinking on any object readily transports the mind to what is contiguous; but it is only the actual presence of an object, that transports it with a superior vivacity. When I am a few miles from home, whatever relates to it touches me more nearly than when I am two hundred leagues[45] distant; though even at that distance the reflecting on any thing in the neighbourhood of my friends or family naturally produces an idea of them. But as in this latter case, both the objects of the mind are ideas; notwithstanding there is an easy transition between them; that transition alone is not able to give a superior vivacity to any of the ideas, for want of some immediate impression.[46]

43 Supposed to be.
44 Silly rituals.
45 A league is roughly three miles (4.8 km).
46 [Author's note] '*Naturane nobis, inquit, datum dicam, an errore quodam, ut, cum ea loca videamus, in quibus memoria dignos viros acceperimus multim esse versatos, magis moveamur, quam siquando eorum ipsorum aut facta audiamus aut scriptum aliquod legamus? Velut ego nunc moveor. Venit enim mihi Plato in mentem, quem accepimus primum hic disputare solitum; cuius etiam illi hortuli propinqui non memoriam solum mihi afferunt, sed ipsum videntur in conspectu meo hic ponere. Hic Speusippus, hic Xenocrates, hic eius auditor Polemo; cuius ipsa illa sessio fuit, quam*

No one can doubt but causation has the same influence as the other two relations of resemblance and contiguity. Superstitious people are fond of the reliques of saints and holy men, for the same reason, that they seek after types or images, in order to enliven their devotion, and give them a more intimate and strong conception of those exemplary lives, which they desire to imitate. Now it is evident, that one of the best reliques, which a devotee could procure, would be the handywork of a saint; and if his clothes and furniture are ever to be considered in this light, it is because they were once at his disposal, and were moved and affected by him; in which respect they are to be considered as imperfect effects, and as connected with him by a shorter chain of consequences than any of those, by which we learn the reality of his existence.

Suppose, that the son of a friend, who had been long dead or absent, were presented to us; it is evident, that this object would instantly revive its correlative idea, and recall to our thoughts all past intimacies and familiarities, in more lively colours than they would otherwise have appeared to us. This is another phenomenon, which seems to prove the principle above mentioned.

We may observe, that, in these phenomena, the belief of the correlative object is always presupposed; without which the relation could have no effect. The influence of the picture supposes, that we *believe* our friend to have once existed. Contiguity to home can never excite our ideas of home, unless we *believe* that it really exists. Now I assert, that this belief, where it reaches beyond the memory or senses, is of a similar nature, and arises from similar causes, with the transition of thought and vivacity of conception here explained. When I throw a piece of dry wood into a fire, my mind is immediately carried to conceive, that it augments, not extinguishes the flame. This transition of thought from the cause to the effect proceeds not from reason. It derives its origin altogether from custom and experience. And as it first begins from an object, present to the senses, it renders the idea or conception of flame more strong and lively than any loose, floating reverie of the imagination. That idea arises immediately. The thought moves instantly towards it, and conveys to it all that force of conception, which is derived from the impression present to the senses. When a sword is levelled at my breast, does not the idea of wound and pain strike me more strongly, than when a glass of wine is presented to me, even though by accident this idea should occur after the appearance of the latter object? But what is there in this whole matter to cause such a strong conception, except only a present object and a customary transition of the idea of another object, which we have been accustomed to conjoin with the former? This is the whole operation of the mind, in all our conclusions concerning matter of fact and existence; and it is a satisfaction to find some analogies, by which it may be explained. The transition from a present object does in all cases give strength and solidity to the related idea.

Here, then, is a kind of pre-established harmony between the course of nature and the succession of our ideas; and though the powers and forces, by which the former is governed, be wholly unknown to us; yet our thoughts and conceptions have still, we find, gone

---

videmus. Equidem etiam curiam nostram, Hostiliam dico, non hanc novam, quae mihi minor esse videtur postquam est maior, solebam intuens, Scipionem, Catonem, Laelium, nostrum vero in primis avum cogitare. Tanta vis admonitionis est in locis; ut non sine causa ex his memopriae deducta sit disciplina.'—Cicero de Finibus. Lib. v. ["Should I say," he asked, "that it is natural or just an error that makes us more greatly moved when we see places where, as we have been told, famous men spent a lot of time, than we are if, at some time or another, we hear about the things which they have done, or read something written by them? I, for example, feel moved at present. For Plato comes to my mind who, we know, was the first to hold regular discussions here: that garden nearby not only brings him to memory but seems to make me see him. Here is Speusippus, here is Xenocrates, and here also is his pupil Polemo: it is the place where he used to sit that we see before us. Similarly, when I looked at our senate house (I mean the one Hostilius built and not the new building which seems to me lesser since it has been enlarged) I used to think of Scipio, Cato, and Lælius, and above all of my grandfather. Places can remind us of so much; it is not without good reason that the formal training of memory is based on them." Cicero, *On the Chief Good and Evil*, from Book V]

on in the same train with the other works of nature. Custom is that principle, by which this correspondence has been effected; so necessary to the subsistence of our species, and the regulation of our conduct, in every circumstance and occurrence of human life. Had not the presence of an object, instantly excited the idea of those objects, commonly conjoined with it, all our knowledge must have been limited to the narrow sphere of our memory and senses; and we should never have been able to adjust means to ends, or employ our natural powers, either to the producing of good, or avoiding of evil. Those, who delight in the discovery and contemplation of *final causes*,[47] have here ample subject to employ their wonder and admiration.

I shall add, for a further confirmation of the foregoing theory, that, as this operation of the mind, by which we infer like effects from like causes, and *vice*

versa, is so essential to the subsistence of all human creatures, it is not probable, that it could be trusted to the fallacious deductions of our reason, which is slow in its operations; appears not, in any degree, during the first years of infancy; and at best is, in every age and period of human life, extremely liable to error and mistake. It is more conformable to the ordinary wisdom of nature to secure so necessary an act of the mind, by some instinct or mechanical tendency, which may be infallible in its operations, may discover itself at the first appearance of life and thought, and may be independent of all the laboured deductions of the understanding. As nature has taught us the use of our limbs, without giving us the knowledge of the muscles and nerves, by which they are actuated; so has she implanted in us an instinct, which carries forward the thought in a correspondent course to that which she has established among external objects; though we are ignorant of those powers and forces, on which this regular course and succession of objects totally depends.

---

47   In this context, the purpose for the nature and arrangement of things in the universe.

CARL HEMPEL

"Scientific Inquiry: Invention and Test"

Who Was Carl Hempel?

Carl Gustav ('Peter') Hempel—probably, with Popper and Kuhn, one of the three most influential philosophers of science of the twentieth century—was born in 1905 in Orianenberg, near Berlin, Germany. After attending high school in Berlin, at eighteen he went to study mathematics and logic at the University of Göttingen with the famous mathematician David Hilbert. Although Hempel quickly fell in love with mathematical logic, he left Göttingen within the year to study at the University of Heidelberg, and then in 1924 moved back to Berlin where he studied physics with Hans Reichenbach and Max Planck, and logic with John von Neumann (all destined to become towering figures in their

fields). Reichenbach introduced him to the members of a group of intellectuals called the Berlin Circle, and in 1929 Hempel took part in the historic first congress on scientific philosophy in Prague, organized by the founders of an important twentieth-century philosophical movement called 'logical positivism.' At that conference Hempel met the philosopher of science Rudolf Carnap, and was so impressed by him that he moved to Carnap's home town of Vienna, Austria; there, he attended classes by the logical positivists Carnap, Moritz Schlick, and Friedrich Waismann and took part in meetings of the 'Vienna Circle.'

The Vienna and Berlin Circles of the 1920s and early 1930s were fairly informal, diverse, collaborative groups of "scientifically interested philosophers and philosophically interested scientists," as Hempel once put it. The members of these groups, especially the Vienna Circle, thought of themselves as decisively breaking with the past and founding a new, more effective kind of philosophical enterprise—a 'modern scientific philosophy' built on the new techniques of logical analysis and modeled on the successful empirical methods of the exact sciences. The past history of philosophy, the new 'logical empiricists' or 'logical positivists' declared, was one of fruitless strife; by contrast, in Hempel's words, "the Vienna Circle held that the purported problems of metaphysics constitute no genuine problems at all and that in an inquiry making use of an appropriately precise conceptual and linguistic apparatus, metaphysical questions could not even be formulated. They were pseudoproblems, devoid of any clear meaning."

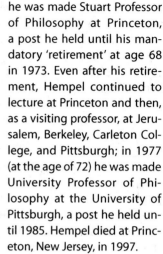

In 1934—just a week before Adolf Hitler anointed himself *Führer* of the German Third Reich—Hempel completed his PhD from the University of Berlin, with a dissertation on probability theory. In the previous year, shortly after Hitler was elected Chancellor of Germany, Hempel's supervisor Hans Reichenbach had been summarily dismissed from his Berlin chair because his father had been Jewish; Hempel himself was of pure 'Aryan' stock, but his wife Eva Ahrends had partly 'Jewish blood' and Hempel was frequently accused of the offense of "philosemitism," sympathy with the Jews. As a consequence, in 1934, Hempel fled Germany to Belgium, where he and Eva were supported by his friend and colleague Paul Oppenheim.

In 1937, because of Carnap's influence, Hempel was invited to become a Rockefeller research associate in philosophy at the University of Chicago, and Hempel officially emigrated to the United States in 1939. Between 1939 and 1948 Hempel taught at City College and Queens College in New York; during these years, Hempel's wife Eva died shortly after giving birth to a son, and Hempel married his second wife, Diane Perlow. In 1948 he moved to Yale University, and in 1955 he was made Stuart Professor of Philosophy at Princeton, a post he held until his mandatory 'retirement' at age 68 in 1973. Even after his retirement, Hempel continued to lecture at Princeton and then, as a visiting professor, at Jerusalem, Berkeley, Carleton College, and Pittsburgh; in 1977 (at the age of 72) he was made University Professor of Philosophy at the University of Pittsburgh, a post he held until 1985. Hempel died at Princeton, New Jersey, in 1997.

In a tribute to him after his death, the well-known Princeton logician Richard Jeffrey wrote of Hempel:

There was no arrogance in him; he got no thrill of pleasure from proving people wrong. His criticisms were always courteous, never triumphant. This quality was deeply rooted in his character. He was made so as to welcome opportunities for kindness, generosity, courtesy; and he gave his whole mind to such projects spontaneously, for pleasure, so that effort disappeared into zest. [His wife] Diane was another such player. (Once, in a restaurant, someone remarked on their politeness to each other, and she said, "Ah, but you should see us when we are alone together. [Pause] Then we are *really* polite.") And play it was, too. He was notably playful and incapable of stuffiness.

Hempel is commonly credited with a leading role in developing the account of scientific explanation and prediction which came to be labeled the 'Received View' by its critics in the last few decades of the twentieth century. (A more technical name for a central plank of this view is the *deductive-nomological* [D-N] or *covering law* model of scientific explanation.) According to this theory, the scientific explanation of a fact consists in the logical *deduction* of a statement that describes the fact (often called the 'explanandum'), from premises (the 'explanans') which include true scientific laws and statements of initial conditions. For example, a simple scientific explanation for why this piece of copper conducts electricity is that my bit of copper is 'covered' by a general law which says that *all* copper conducts electricity under certain circumstances. In this case, the sentence (1) "This copper conducts electricity" is a *logical consequence* of the statements (2) "All copper conducts electricity under conditions C (e.g., the copper is pure, the metal is within a certain temperature range, etc.)" and (3) "Conditions C presently hold for this bit of copper"; according to Hempel, this logical relationship is why (2) and (3) count as *explaining* (1).

Furthermore, according to Hempel, scientific *prediction* turns out to be just the flip-side of explanation. One can start from an observation, and show that a certain theory *explains* that observation because the observation is deducible from the theory; or one can start with a theory, and show that the theory *predicts* some set of observations because they are logical consequences of the theory being true. Either way, in Hempel's view, the essential logical relationship between statements of laws and statements of observations is the same.

When it comes to the issue of *confirming* which scientific laws are true and which are not (i.e., which can feature in good explanations), one of the things Hempel is best known for is formulating, in 1945, 'Hempel's paradox' (also known as the paradox of the ravens, or the paradox of confirmation). This puzzle calls into question the intuitive assumption that a general law is confirmed only by instances of that law—for example, the idea that the claim that "All ravens are black" is supported by observations of black ravens but not at all by the sighting of a blue jay. Here is the paradox. Suppose I see a white running shoe; this is an instance of the general claim that all non-black things are non-ravens (since a white shoe is neither black nor a raven). Therefore, it appears that my shoe sighting is some evidence for the claim that all non-black things are non-ravens. But "all non-black things are non-ravens" is logically equivalent to "all ravens are black." Thus it turns out that—if our intuitive understanding of induction is correct—

observations of white shoes (and blue jays, etc.) do in fact partially confirm the hypothesis that all ravens are black. But this seems absurd—it seems ridiculous to think that we could find out about birds by examining footwear; hence the paradox.

Various attempts have been made to deal with this puzzle. Hempel himself proposed that we resolve the paradox by accepting its apparently absurd conclusion: he held that *all* observations are relevant to any hypothesis, though some of them (such as sightings of white shoes) confirm it only much more weakly than others (sightings of black ravens).

What Is the Structure of This Reading?

In this reading Hempel argues that the traditional, or 'narrow inductivist,' view is incorrect, and argues that it should be replaced in our understanding of science by what he calls the 'method of hypothesis.'

Questions for Further Thought

1. "What particular sorts of data it is reasonable to collect is not determined by the problem under study, but by a tentative answer to it that the investigator entertains in the form of a conjecture or hypothesis." Do you agree? What implications would this have for the working practice of scientists?

2. According to Hempel, there can be no possible mechanical rules for generating inductive generalizations from sets of data; that is, as it is sometimes put, there is no 'logic of discovery.' What are Hempel's reasons for claiming this, and are they persuasive? Even if there are no mechanical methods for scientific discovery, might there nevertheless be some useful non-mechanical methods—and if so, what might these look like?

3. Hempel suggests that, although induction is not a useful method for generating hypotheses, it is important for assessing how well supported a theory is by the evidence. How vulnerable does this make Hempel to the kind of skepticism about induction argued for by David Hume (see the Hume reading in this chapter)?

Suggestions for Further Reading

Philosophy of Natural Science (Prentice-Hall, 1966), from which this selection is taken, is still in print and, though a short book, is considered a useful encapsulation of Hempel's philosophy of science and of the 'received view' in general; it is well worth reading. Several of Hempel's most important and influential papers are contained in *Aspects of Scientific Explanation, and Other Essays in the Philosophy of Science* (Free Press, 1965) and in the more recent anthology *The Philosophy of Carl G. Hempel: Studies in Science, Explanation, and Rationality*, edited by James Fetzer (Oxford University Press, 2000). *Selected Philosophical Essays*, edited by Richard Jeffrey (Cambridge University Press, 2000), fills this out with papers from Hempel's earlier and later philosophical phases.

Science, Explanation, and Rationality: The Philosophy of Carl G. Hempel, edited by James Fetzer (Oxford University Press, 2000), is a collection of essays about Hempel's work. Three good works of philosophy of science which address Hempel's work on explanation and confirmation are Wesley C. Salmon's *Four Decades of Scientific Explanation* (University of Minnesota Press, 1990), Israel Scheffler's *The Anatomy of Inquiry* (Hackett, 1982), and Frederick Suppe's *The Structure of Scientific Theories* (University of Illinois Press, 1979).

from "Scientific Inquiry: Invention and Test"[1]

The Role of Induction in Scientific Inquiry

We have considered some scientific investigations in which a problem was tackled by proposing tentative answers in the form of hypotheses that were then tested by deriving from them suitable test implications and checking these by observation or experiment.

But how are suitable hypotheses arrived at in the first place? It is sometimes held that they are inferred from antecedently collected data by means of a procedure called *inductive inference*, as contradistinguished

from deductive inference, from which it differs in important respects.

In a deductively valid argument, the conclusion is related to the premisses in such a way that if the premisses are true then the conclusion cannot fail to be true as well. This requirement is satisfied, for example, by any argument of the following general form:

> If *p*, then *q*.
> It is not the case that *q*.
> It is not the case that *p*.

Brief reflection shows that no matter what particular statements may stand at the places marked by the letters '*p*' and '*q*', the conclusion will certainly be true if the premisses are. In fact, our schema represents the argument form called *modus tollens*.

Another type of deductively valid inference is illustrated by this example:

> Any sodium salt, when put into the flame of a Bunsen burner,[2] turns the flame yellow.
> This piece of rock salt is a sodium salt.
> This piece of rock salt, when put into the flame of a Bunsen burner, will turn the flame yellow.

Arguments of the latter kind are often said to lead from the general (here, the premiss about all sodium salts) to the particular (a conclusion about the particular piece of rock salt). Inductive inferences, by contrast, are sometimes described as leading from premisses about particular cases to a conclusion that has the character of a general law or principle. For example, from premisses to the effect that each of the particular samples of various sodium salts that have so far been subjected to the Bunsen flame test did turn the flame yellow, inductive inference supposedly leads to the general conclusion that all sodium salts, when put into the flame of a Bunsen burner, turn the flame yellow. But in this case, the truth of the premisses obviously does *not* guarantee the truth of the conclusion; for even if it is the case that all samples

---

1   From *Philosophy of Natural Science*, 1st Edition, © 1967; pp. 10-15. Reprinted by permission of Pearson Education, Inc., Upper Saddle River, NJ.

2   A common piece of laboratory equipment that produces an adjustable gas flame.

of sodium salts examined so far did turn the Bunsen flame yellow, it remains quite possible that new kinds of sodium salt might yet be found that do not conform to this generalization. Indeed, even some kinds of sodium salt that have already been tested with positive result might conceivably fail to satisfy the generalization under special physical conditions (such as very strong magnetic fields or the like) in which they have not yet been examined. For this reason, the premises of an inductive inference are often said to imply the conclusion only with more or less high probability, whereas the premises of a deductive inference imply the conclusion with certainty.

The idea that in scientific inquiry, inductive inference from antecedently collected data leads to appropriate general principles is clearly embodied in the following account of how a scientist would ideally proceed:

> If we try to imagine how a mind of superhuman power and reach, but normal so far as the logical processes of its thought are concerned, ... would use the scientific method, the process would be as follows: First, all facts would be observed and recorded, *without selection or a priori* guess as to their relative importance. Secondly, the observed and recorded facts would be analyzed, compared, and classified, *without hypothesis or postulates* other than those necessarily involved in the logic of thought. Third, from this analysis of the facts generalizations would be inductively drawn as to the relations, classificatory or causal, between them. Fourth, further research would be deductive as well as inductive, employing inferences from previously established generalizations.[3]

This passage distinguishes four stages in an ideal scientific inquiry: (1) observation and recording of all facts, (2) analysis and classification of these facts, (3) inductive derivation of generalizations from them, and (4) further testing of the generalizations. The first two of these stages are specifically assumed not to make use of any guesses or hypotheses as to how the observed facts might be interconnected; this restriction seems to have been imposed in the belief that such preconceived ideas would introduce a bias and would jeopardize the scientific objectivity of the investigation.

But the view expressed in the quoted passage—I will call it *the narrow inductivist conception of scientific inquiry*—is untenable, for several reasons....

First, our scientific investigation as here envisaged could never get off the ground. Even its first phase could never be carried out, for a collection of *all* the facts would have to await the end of the world, so to speak; and even all the facts *up to now* cannot be collected, since there are an infinite number and variety of them. Are we to examine, for example, all the grains of sand in all the deserts and on all the beaches, and are we to record their shapes, their weights, their chemical composition, their distances from each other, their constantly changing temperature, and their equally changing distance from the center of the moon? Are we to record the floating thoughts that cross our minds in the tedious process? The shapes of the clouds overhead, the changing color of the sky? The construction and the trade name of our writing equipment? Our own life histories and those of our fellow investigators? All these, and untold other things, are, after all, among "all the facts up to now".

Perhaps, then, all that should be required in the first phase is that all the *relevant* facts be collected. But relevant to what? Though the author does not mention this, let us suppose that the inquiry is concerned with a specified *problem*. Should we not then begin by collecting all the facts—or better, all available data—relevant to that problem? This notion still makes no clear sense. Semmelweis sought to solve one specific problem, yet he collected quite different kinds of data at different stages of his inquiry.[4] And rightly so; for

---

3   [Author's note] A.B. Wolfe, "Functional Economics," in *The Trend of Economics*, ed. R.G. Tugwell (New York: Alfred A. Knopf, Inc., 1924), p. 450 (italics are quoted).

4   Hempel is referring here to a case study he described earlier: that of the Viennese doctor Ignaz Semmelweis who in the mid-nineteenth century discovered that incidences of childbed fever—a major cause of death

what particular sorts of data it is reasonable to collect is not determined by the problem under study, but by a tentative answer to it that the investigator entertains in the form of a conjecture or hypothesis. Given the conjecture that mortality from childbed fever was increased by the terrifying appearance of the priest and his attendant with the death bell, it was relevant to collect data on the consequences of having the priest change his routine; but it would have been totally irrelevant to check what would happen if doctors and students disinfected their hands before examining their patients. With respect to Semmelweis' eventual contamination hypothesis, data of the latter kind were clearly relevant, and those of the former kind totally irrelevant.

Empirical "facts" or findings, therefore, can be qualified as logically relevant or irrelevant only in reference to a given hypothesis, but not in reference to a given problem.

Suppose now that a hypothesis H has been advanced as a tentative answer to a research problem: what kinds of data would be relevant to H? Our earlier examples suggest an answer: A finding is relevant to H if either its occurrence or its nonoccurrence can be inferred from H. Take Torricelli's hypothesis, for example.[5] As we saw, Pascal[6] inferred from it that the mercury column in a barometer should grow shorter if the barometer were carried up a mountain. Therefore, any finding to the effect that this did indeed happen in a particular case is relevant to the hypotheses; but so would be the finding that the length of the mercury column had remained unchanged or that it had decreased

and then increased during the ascent, for such findings would refute Pascal's test implication and would thus disconfirm Torricelli's hypothesis. Data of the former kind may be called positively, or favorably, relevant to the hypothesis; those of the latter kind negatively, or unfavorably, relevant.

In sum, the maxim that data should be gathered without guidance by antecedent hypotheses about the connections among the facts under study is self-defeating, and it is certainly not followed in scientific inquiry. On the contrary, tentative hypotheses are needed to give direction to a scientific investigation. Such hypotheses determine, among other things, what data should be collected at a given point in a scientific investigation.

...

The second stage envisaged in our quoted passage is open to similar criticism. A set of empirical "facts" can be analyzed and classified in many different ways, most of which will be unilluminating for the purposes of a given inquiry. Semmelweis could have classified the women in the maternity wards according to criteria such as age, place of residence, marital status, dietary habits, and so forth; but information on these would have provided no clue to a patient's prospects of becoming a victim of childbed fever. What Semmelweis sought were criteria that would be significantly connected with those prospects; and for this purpose, as he eventually found, it was illuminating to single out those women who were attended by medical personnel with contaminated hands; for it was with this characteristic, or with the corresponding class of patients, that high mortality from childbed fever was associated.

Thus, if a particular way of analyzing and classifying empirical findings is to lead to an explanation of the phenomena concerned, then it must be based on hypotheses about how those phenomena are connected; without such hypotheses, analysis and classification are blind.

Our critical reflections on the first two stages of inquiry as envisaged in the quoted passage also undercut the notion that hypotheses are introduced only in the third stage, by inductive inference from antecedently collected data. But some further remarks on the subject should be added here.

---

in young mothers at that time—could be drastically reduced by disinfecting the hands of the attending doctors.

5   This is also a reference to an earlier case study. Evangelista Torricelli (1608–1647) hypothesized that the earth is surrounded by a sea of air which exerts pressure on the surface below because of its weight; thus, the higher that one is off the ground the less downward pressure the atmosphere would exert (because the less air there is above one pushing down).

6   Blaise Pascal (1623–1662) was a French mathematician and physicist.

Induction is sometimes conceived as a method that leads, by means of mechanically applicable rules, from observed facts to corresponding general principles. In this case, the rules of inductive inference would provide effective canons of scientific discovery; induction would be a mechanical procedure analogous to the familiar routine for the multiplication of integers, which leads, in a finite number of predetermined and mechanically performable steps, to the corresponding product. Actually, however, no such general and mechanical induction procedure is available at present; otherwise, the much studied problem of the causation of cancer, for example, would hardly have remained unsolved to this day. Nor can the discovery of such a procedure ever be expected. For—to mention one reason—scientific hypotheses and theories are usually couched in terms that do not occur at all in the description of the empirical findings on which they rest, and which they serve to explain. For example, theories about the atomic and subatomic structure of matter contain terms such as 'atom', 'electron', 'proton', 'neutron', 'psi-function', etc.; yet they are based on laboratory findings about the spectra of various gases, tracks in cloud and bubble chambers, quantitative aspects of chemical reactions, and so forth—all of which can be described without the use of those "theoretical terms". Induction rules of the kind here envisaged would therefore have to provide a mechanical routine for constructing, on the basis of the given data, a hypothesis or theory stated in terms of some quite novel concepts, which are nowhere used in the description of the data themselves. Surely, no general mechanical rule of procedure can be expected to achieve this. Could there be a general rule, for example, which, when applied to the data available to Galileo concerning the limited effectiveness of suction pumps, would, by a mechanical routine, produce a hypothesis based on the concept of a sea of air?

To be sure, mechanical procedures for inductively "inferring" a hypothesis on the basis of given data may be specifiable for situations of special, and relatively simple, kinds. For example, if the length of a copper rod has been measured at several different temperatures, the resulting pairs of associated values for temperature and length may be represented by points in a plane coordinate system, and a curve may be drawn through them in accordance with some particular rule of curve fitting. The curve then graphically represents a general quantitative hypothesis that expresses the length of the rod as a specific function of its temperature. But note that this hypothesis contains no novel terms; it is expressible in terms of the concepts of temperature and length, which are used also in describing the data. Moreover, the choice of "associated" values of temperature and length as data already presupposes a guiding hypothesis; namely, that with each value of the temperature, exactly one value of the length of the copper rod is associated, so that its length is indeed a function of its temperature alone. The mechanical curve-fitting routine then serves only to select a particular function as the appropriate one. This point is important; for suppose that instead of a copper rod, we examine a body of nitrogen gas enclosed in a cylindrical container with a movable piston as a lid, and that we measure its volume at several different temperatures. If we were to use this procedure in an effort to obtain from our data a *general* hypothesis representing the volume of the gas as a function of its temperature, we would fail, because the volume of a gas is a function both of its temperature and of the pressure exerted upon it, so that at the same temperature, the given gas may assume different volumes.

Thus, even in these simple cases, the mechanical procedures for the construction of a hypothesis do only part of the job, for they presuppose an antecedent, less specific hypothesis (i.e., that a certain physical variable is a function of one single other variable), which is not obtainable by the same procedure.

There are, then, no generally applicable "rules of induction", by which hypotheses or theories can be mechanically derived or inferred from empirical data. The transition from data to theory requires creative imagination. Scientific hypotheses and theories are not *derived* from observed facts, but *invented* in order to account for them. They constitute guesses at the connections that might obtain between the phenomena under study, at uniformities and patterns that might underlie their occurrence. "Happy guesses"[7] of this

---

7   [Author's note] This characterization was given already by William Whewell in his work *The Philosophy of the Inductive Sciences*, 2nd ed. (London: John W.

kind require great ingenuity, especially if they involve a radical departure from current modes of scientific thinking, as did, for example, the theory of relativity

---

Parker, 1847); II, 41. Whewell also speaks of "invention" as "part of induction" (p. 46). In the same vein, K. Popper refers to scientific hypotheses and theories as "conjectures"; see, for example, the essay "Science: Conjectures and Refutations" in his book, *Conjectures and Refutations* (New York and London: Basic Books, 1962). Indeed, A.B. Wolfe, whose narrowly inductivist conception of ideal scientific procedure was quoted earlier, stresses that "the limited human mind" has to

and quantum theory. The inventive effort required in scientific research will benefit from a thorough familiarity with current knowledge in the field. A complete novice will hardly make an important scientific discovery, for the ideas that may occur to him are likely to duplicate what has been tried before or to run afoul of well-established facts or theories of which he is not aware.

---

use "a greatly modified procedure", requiring scientific imagination and the selection of data on the basis of some "working hypothesis" (p. 450 of the essay cited [above]).

KARL POPPER

"Science: Conjectures and Refutations"

Who Was Karl Popper?

Though Popper's reputation has perhaps waned somewhat since its peak in the 1970s, he is still generally considered one among a small handful of the greatest philosophers of science of the twentieth century. In his day he found a fervent following among prominent scientists such as Peter Medawar (a Nobel Prize winner for medicine, who in 1972 called him "incomparably the greatest philosopher of science that has ever been"), neuroscientist John Eccles (another Nobel laureate, who urged his fellow scientists "to read and meditate upon Popper's writings on the philosophy of science and to adopt them as the basis of one's scientific life"), and mathematician and astronomer Hermann Bondi (who once stated, "There is no more to science than its method, and there is no more to its method that Popper has said").

Karl Raimund Popper was born in 1902 in Vienna, Austria, to Jewish parents who had converted to Protestantism. His parents were intellectual (his father's library is said to have contained 15,000 volumes)

and financially comfortable until rampant inflation in Austria after World War I reduced his family to near-poverty. In his early and middle teens Popper was a Marxist, and then—after witnessing the appalling bloodshed of a brief Communist coup in neighboring Hungary—he became an enthusiastic and active Social Democrat. Vienna after the First World War was a city bubbling over with revolutionary new movements and ideas, and, for Popper, it was a thrilling time and place to be young. As well as studying science and philosophy, Popper was involved with left-wing politics, social work with children, and also the Society for Private Concerts founded by the revolutionary atonal composer Arnold Schönberg (throughout his life, Popper had a great love of music).

During and after his education (he received his PhD in 1928), Popper worked as a schoolteacher in mathematics and physics, and occasionally as a cabinet-maker, but continued to pursue his interest in philosophy. However his ideas were then, as for most of his career, out of tune with contemporary philosophical fashions: Otto Neurath, a member of the "Vienna

Circle" of philosophers active during the 1920s and 1930s, nicknamed him "the Official Opposition" for his arguments against the then-dominant philosophy of logical positivism. In 1934 Popper published his first book, *Logik der Forschung*—a heavily edited version of a book originally twice as long—which attacked the main ideas of the logical positivists. This book was later translated into English and published as *The Logic of Scientific Discovery* (1959).

In the 1930s, the Communists and other left wing parties in Austria, Germany, and Italy failed to effectively oppose the rise to power of fascism (believing it to be the last gasp of capitalism before the inevitable Communist revolution, and so offering only a half-hearted resistance) and Popper—accurately foretelling the annexation of Austria by Nazi Germany and the onset of a second European war—fled with his wife to New Zealand. There, from 1937 until 1945, he taught philosophy at the University of Canterbury, at Christchurch. He spent this period teaching himself Greek so he could study the Greek philosophers, and writing *The Open Society and Its Enemies* (published in 1943) which, through a critique of the political theories of Plato and Marx, defends the idea of liberty and democracy against that of totalitarianism. Popper considered this to be his contribution to the war against fascism.

According to Popper, no political ideology (either on the political right or the left) can justify large-scale social engineering—it is simply impossible to formulate a demonstrably true, predictive theory of society, and so we should never act as if we alone have the key to the truth about human nature. The proper function of social institutions in an "open society"—one in which any regime can be ousted without violence—is not large-scale utopian planning but, according to Popper, piecemeal reform with the object of minimizing, as much as possible, avoidable suffering. This way, the effectiveness of each small piece of legislation can be publicly assessed, and the society can move forward collectively after learning from its mistakes.

In 1946 Popper moved to England, where he was to live until his death in 1994. Despite his growing reputation (he was knighted in 1965), Popper was never offered a position at either Oxford or Cambridge[1] and he spent the rest of his career as a professor at the London School of Economics, still out of sync with the philosophical tendencies of the day which, during those years in England, were predominantly towards "linguistic" philosophy. Popper was impatient with endless discussion about the meanings of words, and denied that exact precision of terminology was either possible or desirable in science. Popper argued that a language is an instrument and what matters is what you *do* with that instrument; philosophers who devote their lives exclusively to the analysis of language are, as Bryan Magee has put it, like carpenters who devote all their time to sharpening their tools, but never use them except on each other. Popper wrote in the preface to *The Logic of Scientific Discovery*:

> Language analysts believe that there are no genuine philosophical problems, or that the problems of philosophy, if any, are problems of linguistic usage, or of the meaning of words. I,

---

1   This may have been partly to do with his combative personality. Despite advocating risky conjectures and public refutations, by all accounts Popper was a touchy character, quick to express scorn for those who doubted his ideas. On one famous occasion, at the Moral Sciences Club in Cambridge, he almost came to blows with Ludwig Wittgenstein and—legend has it—had to be restrained by Bertrand Russell (upon which, Wittgenstein stormed out of the room).

however, believe that there is at least one problem in which all thinking men are interested. It is the problem of cosmology: *the problem of understanding the world—including ourselves, and our knowledge, as part of the world.* All science is cosmology, I believe, and for me the interest of philosophy, no less than of science, lies solely in the contributions which it has made to it.

Popper's main contribution to the philosophy of science is his proposal of a solution to the 'problem of induction,' which involves the rejection of the previously orthodox view of the scientific method and its replacement with another. The essay reprinted here, "Science: Conjectures and Refutations," is an excellent (and in itself quite influential) summary of these arguments.

What Is the Structure of This Reading?

This article is Popper's own summary of his most important work in the philosophy of science. He begins by laying out the problem which he first became interested in: the problem of the *demarcation* between science and pseudo-science (i.e., of finding a criterion for what makes something a properly scientific theory). By comparing Einstein's relativity theory (an example of science) with the psychoanalytic theories of Freud and Adler (examples of pseudo-science), Popper argues that the proper mark of a scientific theory is its *falsifiability*. In section II Popper goes on to criticize the *ad hoc* modifications of Marxism by Marx's followers that rendered the theory unfalsifiable. However, Popper then takes pains to point out that he does not consider pseudo-scientific theories—or "myths" as he calls them—to be either useless or meaningless. In section III he contrasts his falsificationism (which is a theory of demarcation and not of meaning) with the logical positivist's "verificationist" account of *meaning*, which did famously entail that all non-science is literally meaningless.

In section IV Popper begins his discussion of the problem of induction. After laying out Hume's description of the problem (see the Hume reading in this chapter), he critiques Hume's psychologistic solution to the problem and uses this critique to motivate his own alternative account: the method of trial and error,

or *conjectures and refutations*. In section V Popper suggests that this method of "trial and error" is ultimately rooted in the evolution of the human mind, and he contrasts his views with Kant's doctrine of the *synthetic a priori* (see the Kant reading in Chapter 2). Like Kant, Popper introduces a distinction between *dogmatic* and *critical* thinking, and in section VII he suggests that the scientific, critical attitude has evolved through human history from a pre-scientific dogmatism.

In section VIII Popper turns his attention to the "logic of science," and argues that it is simply a mistake to think that the scientific method is inductive: in fact, Popper asserts, real science proceeds by the method of conjecture and refutation, and scientists have in the past just misdescribed or misunderstood their own practices when they spoke of induction. Popper lays out his final solution to the problem of induction in section IX, and in the last section of the paper he responds to various reformulations of the problem. Particularly important here is his distinction between the claim that science is a *reasonable practice* for human beings to engage in, and the claim that our belief that science will eventually succeed in getting to the truth is a *rational* one: Popper supports the first claim, but unconditionally denies the second one.

Some Useful Background Information

1. Popper sought to replace the traditional inductivist view of science with a quite different account that denies induction plays any role in science at all. In order to see what Popper is reacting against, it is helpful to briefly review the traditional understanding of the scientific method. On this view (sometimes called the "Baconian" view, after Francis Bacon (1561–1626), the first philosopher to systematically lay out rules for good science) the scientist begins by making observations—by carrying out carefully controlled experiments at some outpost on the frontier between our knowledge and our ignorance. The results of these experiments are systematically recorded and shared with other workers in the field. As the body of data grows, certain regularities appear. Individual scientists formulate hypotheses which, if true,

would explain all the known facts and reveal an underlying structure explaining the regularities in the data. They then attempt to confirm their hypotheses by performing experiments which will produce supporting evidence. Eventually, after enough experiments are done, some hypothesis is verified and is added to the body of confirmed scientific theory. Science moves on to the next point on the frontier.

This process, known as the method of induction, was standardly thought to be what marked off scientific investigation from other kinds of intellectual pursuit: science, it might be said, is based on experimental *facts* (rather than, say, on claims rooted in tradition, authority, prejudice, habit, emotion, or whatever). It is this picture of science that Popper attempts to overturn, and replace with his own account of what scientists are actually up to.

2. Popper does not think that good scientific theories are good because they are true. As he once put it, "We cannot identify science with truth, for we think that both Newton's and Einstein's theories belong to science, but they cannot both be true, and they may well both be false." A formative experience for Popper as a young philosopher was the replacement of Newtonian physics—previously the crown jewel of modern science—by Einstein's theories in the early decades of the twentieth century. Newtonian physics was, in 1900, the most successful, well-confirmed, and important scientific theory ever developed, and for more than two hundred years its laws had been unfailingly corroborated by literally billions of scientific observations and, furthermore, by underpinning the most impressive advances in technology in human history. Yet, despite the huge quantity of inductive evidence apparently confirming the truth of Newtonian physics, it turned out to be false. If this quantity of evidence could not verify a theory, Popper thought, then nothing could. Nothing in science is secure; every scientific theory is open to rejection or revision; all scientific 'knowledge' is probably false, though it aspires eventually to the truth. One of Pop-

per's favorite quotations was from the early Greek philosopher Xenophanes (who lived at about 400 BCE):

The gods did not reveal, from the beginning,
All things to us, but in the course of time
Through seeking we may learn and know
   things better.
But as for certain truth, no man has known it,
Nor shall he know it, neither of the gods
Nor yet of all the things of which I speak.
For even if by chance he were to utter
The final truth, he would himself not know it:
For all is but a woven web of guesses.

3. Popper's approach to knowledge is self-consciously biological in orientation. Human beings, according to Popper, are problem-solving animals, and there is continuity between simple examples of learning by trial and error in the lower animals and the method of conjecture and refutation in human science. The human search for knowledge is ultimately rooted, for Popper, in facts about our evolutionary history.

Some Common Misconceptions

1. Though Popper claims to have "solved the problem of induction," he did not do so by showing that induction *works*. Instead, he 'solves' the problem by issuing a complete ban on induction. The conclusions of science are never positively justified: they are never established as certainly true, or even as probable. In other words, Popper's "corroboration" is not the same thing as confirmation. Conjectures are not inferences and refutations are not inductive; the failure to refute a hypothesis is *not* evidence in its favor, according to Popper.

2. Unlike the logical positivists, Popper does not dismiss pseudo-science as valueless or meaningless. Falsifiability is not, for him, a demarcation between sense and nonsense, but only between science and non-science. (For the logical positivists, verifiability was a demarcation of both kinds.) Thus, for Popper, although the

methods of science have a privileged place in the rational human pursuit of the truth, domains other than science (such as art and religion) can still have substantial value, and can even prove to be valuable starting points—though never finishing posts—in the quest for knowledge.

Suggestions for Critical Reflection

1. Popper claimed to have solved the problem of induction. Did he? If not, did he at least solve the problem of showing how the methods of science could be rational despite Hume's arguments against the rationality of induction?

2. Popper stresses the importance of ruling out *ad hoc* modifications to theories. How helpful is this advice? How easy is to tell when an adjustment to a theory is *ad hoc*, as opposed to when it is a legitimate improvement to a theory under the impact of new data? If it is not so easy, what implications (if any) does this have for Popper's account of science?

3. How plausible is Popper's suggestion that working scientists in fact adopt the method of conjecture and refutation (even though they may not realize they are doing so)? For example, do scientists deliberately pursue highly improbable claims (rather than less contentful, but more probable, hypotheses)? Do they then set out to falsify, rather than to verify, these theories? Do they abandon their theories when faced with single pieces of counter-evidence, rather than modifying their theories to accommodate this new data? If scientists do *not* in fact use the methods Popper prescribes, how much of a problem is this for Popper's philosophy of science?

4. The attempted refutation of our conjectures, according to Popper, can never positively justify those conjectures, or justify us in thinking that they are probably true. On the other hand, according to Popper, the refutation of a conjecture is a step that takes us closer to the truth. Are these two claims compatible?

5. Popper says we ought to act on—provisionally, to believe—those theories that have survived extensive testing. How is this to be distinguished from induction?

6. Popper issues a ban on induction as an irrational method of doing science; but is his own method any more rational? That is, does it give us rational reasons for preferring one theory over another? Does it give us any reason to think scientific theories are getting better and better (i.e., closer to the truth)? Can Popper consistently assert that there is growth in scientific knowledge and that science is a rational activity?

Suggestions for Further Reading

Popper published many books during his lifetime, and since his death a score more have been published based on the papers he left behind. The following six books are among his most important, and together give a fairly complete overview of his thought: *The Logic of Scientific Discovery* (Routledge, 1992), *Conjectures and Refutations: The Growth of Scientific Knowledge* (Routledge, 1989), *The Open Society and Its Enemies* (Volumes I and II, Princeton University Press, 1972/1976), *Objective Knowledge: An Evolutionary Approach* (Oxford University Press, 1972) and, co-written with John Eccles, *The Self and Its Brain* (Routledge, 1993). A two volume collection of critical essays about Popper's work, with replies from Popper, was published in 1974 by Open Court, edited by Paul A. Schilpp and called *The Philosophy of Karl Popper*. That collection also contains an extended autobiographical essay by Popper, an amended version of which was published under separate cover as *Unended Quest* (Open Court, 1982).

Bryan Magee's *Popper* (Fontana Press, 1973) is short, clear, and stimulating, if sometimes rather breathless in its adoration of Popper's work. A later, somewhat longer, introduction by Magee is his *Philosophy and the Real World: An Introduction to Karl Popper* (Open Court, 1985). Two other reliable summaries of Popper's philosophical work are Anthony O'Hear, *Popper* (Routledge & Kegan Paul, 1980) and Geoff Stokes, *Popper: Philosophy, Politics and Scientific Method* (Polity Press, 1999). Roberta Corvi's *An Introduction to the Thought of Karl Popper* (Routledge, 1996) was approved by Popper just before his death and constitutes a scholarly account of Popper's final philosophical system; however, it is written rather less accessibly than many of Popper's own writings. Finally, there is a fairly recent collection of essays about Popper's work written by prominent philosophers, edited by Anthony O'Hear: *Karl Popper: Philosophy and Problems* (Cambridge University Press, 1996).

"Science: Conjectures and Refutations"[2]

> Mr. Turnbull had predicted evil consequences, ... and was now doing the best in his power to bring about the verification of his own prophecies.
>
> (Anthony Trollope)[3]

I.

When ... ived the list of participants in this course and rea... at I had been asked to speak to philosophical colleagues I thought, after some hesitation and consultation, that you would probably prefer me to speak about those problems which interest me most, and about those developments with which I am most intimately acquainted. I therefore decided to do what I have never done before: to give you a report on my own work in the philosophy of science, since the autumn of 1919 when I first began to grapple with the problem, "*When should a theory be ranked as scientific?*" or "*Is there a criterion for the scientific character or status of a theory?*"

The problem which troubled me at the time was neither, 'When is a theory true?' nor, 'When is a theory acceptable?' My problem was different. I *wished to distinguish between science and pseudo-science*; knowing very well that science often errs, and that pseudo-science may happen to stumble on the truth.

I knew, of course, the most widely accepted answer to my problem: that science is distinguished from pseudo-science—or from 'metaphysics'—by its *empirical method*, which is essentially *inductive*, proceeding from observation or experiment. But this did not satisfy me. On the contrary, I often formulated my problem as one of distinguishing between a genuinely empirical method and a non-empirical or even a pseudo-empirical method—that is to say, a method which, although it appeals to observation and experiment, nevertheless does not come up to scientific standards. The latter method may be exemplified by astrology, with its stupendous mass of empirical evidence based on observation—on horoscopes and on biographies.

But as it was not the example of astrology which led me to my problem I should perhaps briefly describe the atmosphere in which my problem arose and the examples by which it was stimulated. After the collapse of the Austrian Empire[4] there had been a revolution in Austria: the air was full of revolutionary slogans and ideas, and new and often wild theories. Among the theories which interested me Einstein's theory of relativity was no doubt by far the most important. Three others were Marx's theory of history, Freud's psycho-analysis, and Alfred Adler's so-called 'individual psychology'.

There was a lot of popular nonsense talked about these theories, and especially about relativity (as still happens even today), but I was fortunate in those who introduced me to the study of this theory. We all—the small circle of students to which I belonged—were thrilled with the result of Eddington's eclipse observations[5] which in 1919 brought the first important

---

2   This was originally a lecture given at Peterhouse College, Cambridge, in 1953. It was first published under the title "Philosophy of Science: A Personal Report" in 1957 in *British Philosophy in Mid-Century*, edited by C.A. Mace. The copy reprinted here is taken, with permission, from Chapter 1 of *Conjectures and Refutations: The Growth of Scientific Knowledge*, fifth revised edition, London: Routledge, 1989. Copyright © University of Klagenfurt/Karl Popper Library.

3   *Phineas Finn*, Chapter XXV.

4   In 1918, with Austria-Hungary's defeat in the First World War.

5   Sir Arthur Stanley Eddington (1882–1944), during an expedition to Africa, observed the positions of stars visible around the sun during an eclipse, compared them to the positions of those same stars seen at night (when, of course, the sun is not in the same region of

confirmation of Einstein's theory of gravitation. It was a great experience for us, and one which had a lasting influence on my intellectual development.

The three other theories I have mentioned were also widely discussed among students at that time. I myself happened to come into personal contact with Alfred Adler, and even to co-operate with him in his social work among the children and young people in the working-class districts of Vienna where he had established social guidance clinics.

It was during the summer of 1919 that I began to feel more and more dissatisfied with these three theories—the Marxist theory of history, psychoanalysis, and individual psychology; and I began to feel dubious about their claims to scientific status. My problem perhaps first took the simple form, 'What is wrong with Marxism, psycho-analysis, and individual psychology? Why are they so different from physical theories, from Newton's theory, and especially from the theory of relativity?'

To make this contrast clear I should explain that few of us at the time would have said that we believed in the *truth* of Einstein's theory of gravitation. This shows that it was not my doubting the *truth* of those other three theories which bothered me, but something else. Yet neither was it that I merely felt mathematical physics to be more *exact* than the sociological or psychological type of theory. Thus what worried me was neither the problem of truth, at that stage at least, nor the problem of exactness or measurability. It was rather that I felt that these other three theories, though posing as sciences, had in fact more in common with primitive myths than with science; that they resembled astrology rather than astronomy.

I found that those of my friends who were admirers of Marx, Freud, and Adler, were impressed by a number of points common to these theories, and especially by their apparent *explanatory power*. These theories appeared to be able to explain practically everything that happened within the fields to which they referred. The study of any of them seemed to have the effect of an intellectual conversion or revelation,

opening your eyes to a new truth hidden from those not yet initiated. Once your eyes were thus opened you saw confirming instances everywhere: the world was full of *verifications* of the theory. Whatever happened always confirmed it. Thus its truth appeared manifest; and unbelievers were clearly people who did not want to see the manifest truth; who refused to see it, either because it was against their class interest, or because of their repressions which were still 'un-analysed' and crying out for treatment.

The most characteristic element in this situation seemed to me the incessant stream of confirmations, of observations which 'verified' the theories in question; and this point was constantly emphasized by their adherents. A Marxist could not open a newspaper without finding on every page confirming evidence for his interpretation of history; not only in the news, but also in its presentation—which revealed the class bias of the paper—and especially of course in what the paper did *not* say. The Freudian analysts emphasized that their theories were constantly verified by their 'clinical observations'. As for Adler, I was much impressed by a personal experience. Once, in 1919, I reported to him a case which to me did not seem particularly Adlerian, but which he found no difficulty in analysing in terms of his theory of inferiority feelings, although he had not even seen the child. Slightly shocked, I asked him how he could be so sure. 'Because of my thousandfold experience', he replied; whereupon I could not help saying: 'And with this new case, I suppose, your experience has become thousand-and-one-fold.'

What I had in mind was that his previous observations may not have been much sounder than this new one; that each in its turn had been interpreted in the light of 'previous experience', and at the same time counted as additional confirmation. What, I asked myself, did it confirm? No more than that a case could be interpreted in the light of the theory. But this meant very little, I reflected, since every conceivable case could be interpreted in the light of Adler's theory, or equally of Freud's. I may illustrate this by two very different examples of human behaviour: that of a man who pushes a child into the water with the intention of drowning it; and that of a man who sacrifices his life in an attempt to save the child. Each of these two cases can be explained with equal ease in Freudian and

---

the sky), and deduced from the shift in their positions that the light from those stars must be bent by its passage through the sun's gravitational field.

in Adlerian terms. According to Freud the first man suffered from repression (say, of some component of his Oedipus complex[6]), while the second man had achieved sublimation. According to Adler the first man suffered from feelings of inferiority (producing perhaps the need to prove to himself that he dared to commit some crime), and so did the second man (whose need was to prove to himself that he dared to rescue the child). I could not think of any human behaviour which could not be interpreted in terms of either theory. It was precisely this fact—that they always fitted, that they were always confirmed—which in the eyes of their admirers constituted the strongest argument in favour of these theories. It began to dawn on me that this apparent strength was in fact their weakness.

With Einstein's theory the situation was strikingly different. Take one typical instance—Einstein's prediction, just then confirmed by the findings of Eddington's expedition. Einstein's gravitational theory had led to the result that light must be attracted by heavy bodies (such as the sun), precisely as material bodies were attracted. As a consequence it could be calculated that light from a distant fixed star whose apparent position was close to the sun would reach the earth from such a direction that the star would seem to be slightly shifted away from the sun; or, in other words, that stars close to the sun would look as if they had moved a little away from the sun, and from one another. This is a thing which cannot normally be observed since such stars are rendered invisible in daytime by the sun's overwhelming brightness; but during an eclipse it is possible to take photographs of them. If the same constellation is photographed at night one can measure the distances on the two photographs, and check the predicted effect.

Now the impressive thing about this case is the *risk* involved in a prediction of this kind. If observation shows that the predicted effect is definitely absent, then the theory is simply refuted. The theory is *incompatible with certain possible results of observation*—in fact with results which everybody before Einstein would have expected.[7] This is quite different from the situation I have previously described, when it turned out that the theories in question were compatible with the most divergent human behaviour, so that it was practically impossible to describe any human behaviour that might not be claimed to be a verification of these theories.

These considerations led me in the winter of 1919–20 to conclusions which I may now reformulate as follows.

(1) It is easy to obtain confirmations, or verifications, for nearly every theory—if we look for confirmations.

(2) Confirmations should count only if they are the result of *risky predictions*; that is to say, if, unenlightened by the theory in question, we should have expected an event which was incompatible with the theory—an event which would have refuted the theory.

(3) Every 'good' scientific theory is a prohibition: it forbids certain things to happen. The more a theory forbids, the better it is.

(4) A theory which is not refutable by any conceivable event is non-scientific. Irrefutability is not a virtue of a theory (as people often think) but a vice.

(5) Every genuine *test* of a theory is an attempt to falsify it, or to refute it. Testability is falsifiability; but there are degrees of testability: some theories are more testable, more exposed to refutation, than others; they take, as it were, greater risks.

(6) Confirming evidence should not count *except when it is the result of a genuine test of the theory*; and this means that it can be presented as a serious but unsuccessful attempt to falsify the theory. (I now speak in such cases of 'corroborating evidence'.)

(7) Some genuinely testable theories, when found to be false, are still upheld by their admirers—for example by introducing *ad hoc*[8] some auxiliary assumption, or by re-interpreting the theory *ad hoc* in such a way that it escapes refutation. Such a procedure

---

6   According to Freud, the Oedipus complex consists in subconscious sexual desire in a child (especially a boy) for the parent of the opposite sex, usually combined with repressed hostility towards the parent of the same sex.

7   [Author's note] This is a slight oversimplification, for about half of the Einstein effect may be derived from the classical theory, provided we assume a ballistic theory of light.

8   *Ad hoc* means "for the particular situation or case at hand and for no other" (from the Latin "to this").

is always possible, but it rescues the theory from refutation only at the price of destroying, or at least lowering, its scientific status. (I later described such a rescuing operation as a *'conventionalist twist'* or a *'conventionalist stratagem'*.)

One can sum up all this by saying that *the criterion of the scientific status of a theory is its falsifiability, or refutability, or testability.*

II.

I may perhaps exemplify this with the help of the various theories so far mentioned. Einstein's theory of gravitation clearly satisfied the criterion of falsifiability. Even if our measuring instruments at the time did not allow us to pronounce on the results of the tests with complete assurance, there was clearly a possibility of refuting the theory.

Astrology did not pass the test. Astrologers were greatly impressed, and misled, by what they believed to be confirming evidence—so much so that they were quite unimpressed by any unfavourable evidence. Moreover, by making their interpretations and prophecies sufficiently vague they were able to explain away anything that might have been a refutation of the theory had the theory and the prophecies been more precise. In order to escape falsification they destroyed the testability of their theory. It is a typical soothsayer's trick to predict things so vaguely that the predictions can hardly fail: that they become irrefutable.

The Marxist theory of history, in spite of the serious efforts of some of its founders and followers, ultimately adopted this soothsaying practice. In some of its earlier formulations (for example in Marx's analysis of the character of the 'coming social revolution') their predictions were testable, and in fact falsified.[9] Yet instead of accepting the refutations the followers of Marx re-interpreted both the theory and the evidence in order to make them agree. In this way they rescued the theory from refutation; but they did so at the price of adopting a device which made it irrefutable. They thus gave a 'conventionalist twist' to the theory; and by this stratagem they destroyed its much advertised claim to scientific status.

The two psycho-analytic theories were in a different class. They were simply non-testable, irrefutable. There was no conceivable human behaviour which could contradict them. This does not mean that Freud and Adler were not seeing certain things correctly: I personally do not doubt that much of what they say is of considerable importance, and may well play its part one day in a psychological science which is testable. But it does mean that those 'clinical observations' which analysts naïvely believe confirm their theory cannot do this any more than the daily confirmations which astrologers find in their practice.[10] And as for

---

9   [Author's note] See, for example, my *Open Society and Its Enemies*, ch. 15, section iii, and notes 13–14.

10   [Author's note] 'Clinical observations', like all other observations, are *interpretations in the light of theories* (see below, sections iv ff.); and for this reason alone they are apt to seem to support those theories in the light of which they were interpreted. But real support can be obtained only from observations undertaken as tests (by 'attempted refutations'); and for this purpose *criteria of refutation* have to be laid down beforehand: it must be agreed which observable situations, if actually observed, mean that the theory is refuted. But what kind of clinical responses would refute to the satisfaction of the analyst not merely a particular analytic diagnosis but psycho-analysis itself? And have such criteria ever been discussed or agreed upon by analysts? Is there not, on the contrary, a whole family of analytic concepts, such as 'ambivalence' (I do not suggest that there is no such thing as ambivalence), which would make it difficult, if not impossible, to agree upon such criteria? Moreover, how much headway has been made in investigating the question of the extent to which the (conscious or unconscious) expectations and theories held by the analyst influence the 'clinical responses' of the patient? (To say nothing about the conscious attempts to influence the patient by proposing interpretations to him, etc.) Years ago I introduced the term *'Oedipus effect'* to describe the influence of a theory or expectation or prediction *upon the event which it predicts* or describes: it will be remembered that the causal chain leading to Oedipus' parricide was started by the oracle's prediction of this event. This is a characteristic and recurrent theme of such myths, but one which seems to have failed to attract the interest of the analysts, perhaps not accidentally. (The problem of confirmatory dreams suggested

Freud's epic of the Ego, the Super-ego, and the Id, no substantially stronger claim to scientific status can be made for it than for Homer's collected stories from Olympus.[11] These theories describe some facts, but in the manner of myths. They contain most interesting psychological suggestions, but not in a testable form.

At the same time I realized that such myths may be developed, and become testable; that historically speaking all—or very nearly all—scientific theories originate from myths, and that a myth may contain important anticipations of scientific theories. Examples are Empedocles' theory of evolution by trial and error, or Parmenides' myth of the unchanging block universe[12] in which nothing ever happens and which,

if we add another dimension,[13] becomes Einstein's block universe (in which, too, nothing ever happens, since everything is, four-dimensionally speaking, determined and laid down from the beginning). I thus felt that if a theory is found to be non-scientific, or 'metaphysical' (as we might say), it is not thereby found to be unimportant, or insignificant, or 'meaningless', or 'nonsensical'.[14] But it cannot claim to be backed by empirical evidence in the scientific sense—although it may easily be, in some genetic[15] sense, the 'result of observation'.

(There were a great many other theories of this pre-scientific or pseudo-scientific character, some of them, unfortunately, as influential as the Marxist interpretation of history; for example, the racialist interpretation of history—another of those impressive and all-explanatory theories which act upon weak minds like revelations.)

Thus the problem which I tried to solve by proposing the criterion of falsifiability was neither a problem of meaningfulness or significance, nor a problem of truth or acceptability. It was the problem of drawing a line (as well as this can be done) between the statements, or systems of statements, of the empirical sciences, and all other statements—whether they are of a religious or of a metaphysical character, or simply pseudo-scientific. Years later—it must have been in

---

by the analyst is discussed by Freud, for example in *Gesammelte Schriften*, III, 1925, where he says on p. 314: 'If anybody asserts that most of the dreams which can be utilized in an analysis … owe their origin to [the analyst's] suggestion, then no objection can be made from the point of view of analytic theory. Yet there is nothing in this fact', he surprisingly adds, 'which would detract from the reliability of our results.')

11   In Freudian theory, the *ego* is the part of the human psyche which is conscious and most directly in control of our thought and behavior, the *id* is the unconscious reservoir of primitive impulses and instincts, and the *superego* is the mostly unconscious part of our psyche which has internalized our community's moral standards and acts as a restraint on the ego. Olympus is the mythical home of many of the gods of classical Greek mythology, and Homer was a Greek epic poet whose verses often deal with the activities of the gods.

12   Empedocles of Acragas (c. 493–c. 433 BCE), a native of Sicily, was a philosopher, poet, politician, scientist and—in his own eyes—a miracle worker and a god. He believed in the immortality of the soul and is said to have committed suicide by flinging himself into the volcano Mount Etna. Parmenides of Elea, who was born about twenty years before Empedocles, was perhaps the most important Greek philosopher before Socrates. In his poem "On Nature" he wrote that a goddess had instructed him that, since nature cannot both be and not be, it must necessarily be, and he concluded from this that reality must be perfect, unchanging, motionless, and eternal.

13   The dimension of time.

14   [Author's note] The case of astrology, nowadays a typical pseudo-science, may illustrate this point. It was attacked, by Aristotelians and other rationalists, down to Newton's day, for the wrong reason—for its now accepted assertion that the planets had an 'influence' upon terrestrial ('sublunar') events. In fact Newton's theory of gravity, and especially the lunar theory of the tides, was historically speaking an offspring of astrological lore. Newton, it seems, was most reluctant to adopt a theory which came from the same stable as for example the theory that 'influenza' epidemics are due to an astral 'influence'. And Galileo, no doubt for the same reason, actually rejected the lunar theory of the tides; and his misgivings about Kepler may easily be explained by his misgivings about astrology.

15   Here "genetic" means "having to do with the origins or cause of something."

1928 or 1929—I called this first problem of mine the *'problem of demarcation'*. The criterion of falsifiability is a solution to this problem of demarcation, for it says that statements or systems of statements, in order to be ranked as scientific, must be capable of conflicting with possible, or conceivable, observations.

III.

Today I know, of course, that this *criterion of demarcation*—the criterion of testability, or falsifiability, or refutability—is far from obvious; for even now its significance is seldom realized. At that time, in 1920, it seemed to me almost trivial, although it solved for me an intellectual problem which had worried me deeply, and one which also had obvious practical consequences (for example, political ones). But I did not yet realize its full implications, or its philosophical significance. When I explained it to a fellow student of the Mathematics Department (now a distinguished mathematician in Great Britain), he suggested that I should publish it. At the time I thought this absurd; for I was convinced that my problem, since it was so important for me, must have agitated many scientists and philosophers who would surely have reached my rather obvious solution. That this was not the case I learnt from Wittgenstein's work, and from its reception; and so I published my results thirteen years later in the form of a criticism of Wittgenstein's *criterion of meaningfulness*.

Wittgenstein, as you all know, tried to show in the *Tractatus*[16] (see for example his propositions 6.53; 6.54; and 5) that all so-called philosophical or metaphysical propositions were actually non-propositions or pseudo-propositions: that they were senseless or meaningless. All genuine (or meaningful) propositions were truth functions[17] of the elementary or atomic propositions which described 'atomic facts'—i.e., facts which can in principle be ascertained by observation. In other words, meaningful propositions were fully reducible to elementary or atomic propositions which were simple statements describing possible states of affairs, and which could in principle be established or rejected by observation. If we call a statement an 'observation statement' not only if it states an actual observation but also if it states anything that *may* be observed, we shall have to say (according to the *Tractatus*, 5 and 4.52) that every genuine proposition must be a truth-function of, and therefore deducible from, observation statements. All other apparent propositions will be meaningless pseudo-propositions; in fact they will be nothing but nonsensical gibberish.

This idea was used by Wittgenstein for a characterization of science, as opposed to philosophy: We read (for example in 4.11, where natural science is taken to stand in opposition to philosophy): 'The totality of true propositions is the total natural science (or the totality of the natural sciences).' This means that the propositions which belong to science are those deducible from *true* observation statements; they are those propositions which can be *verified* by true observation statements. Could we know all true observation statements, we should also know all that may be asserted by natural science.

This amounts to a crude verifiability criterion of demarcation. To make it slightly less crude, it could be amended thus: 'The statements which may possibly fall within the province of science are those which may possibly be verified by observation statements; and these statements, again, coincide with the class of *all* genuine or meaningful statements.' For this approach, then, *verifiability, meaningfulness, and scientific character all coincide*.

---

16   Ludwig Wittgenstein (1889–1951) was one of the twentieth century's most charismatic and influential philosophers. Popper is referring to the *Tractatus Logico-Philosophicus*, published in 1921 and the only book Wittgenstein completed during his lifetime.

17   A 'truth function' is a function from the truth values of input sentences to the truth value of an output sentence. (The two possible 'truth values' are, normally, either True or False.) Thus, a compound sentence is 'truth functional' if its truth value is entirely determined by the truth values of its component sentences: for example, the sentence "A and B" is true just in case A and B both have the value 'True,' and is false otherwise. (On the other hand, many other sentences are not, at least on the face of it, truth functional in this way: for example, "A because of B" does not have its truth value determined entirely by the truth values of A and B.)

I personally was never interested in the so-called problem of meaning; on the contrary, it appeared to me a verbal problem, a typical pseudo-problem. I was interested only in the problem of demarcation, i.e., in finding a criterion of the scientific character of theories. It was just this interest which made me see at once that Wittgenstein's verifiability criterion of meaning was intended to play the part of a criterion of demarcation as well; and which made me see that, as such, it was totally inadequate, even if all misgivings about the dubious concept of meaning were set aside. For Wittgenstein's criterion of demarcation—to use my own terminology in this context—is verifiability, or deducibility from observation statements. But this criterion is too narrow (*and* too wide): it excludes from science practically everything that is, in fact, characteristic of it (while failing in effect to exclude astrology). No scientific theory can ever be deduced from observation statements, or be described as a truth-function of observation statements.

All this I pointed out on various occasions to Wittgensteinians and members of the Vienna Circle.[18] In 1931–32 I summarized my ideas in a largish book (read by several members of the Circle but never published; although part of it was incorporated in my *Logic of Scientific Discovery*); and in 1933 I published a letter to the Editor of *Erkenntnis* in which I tried to compress into two pages my ideas on the problems of demarcation and induction.[19] In this letter and elsewhere I described the problem of meaning as a pseudo-problem, in contrast to the problem of demarcation. But my contribution was classified by members of the Circle as a proposal to replace the verifiability criterion of *meaning* by a falsifiability criterion of *meaning*—which effectively made nonsense of my views.[20] My protests that I was trying to solve, not their pseudo-problem of meaning, but the problem of demarcation, were of no avail.

---

18   The Vienna Circle was a group of like-minded philosophers and scientists who met for Saturday morning seminars in Vienna from 1923 until the late 1930s. Strongly influenced by Wittgenstein's *Tractatus*, they held that the task of philosophy was not the production of new knowledge but the clarification of the basic concepts of science and ordinary language, and one of their most important goals was the unification of science under a single logical language. They spread their ideas through a series of congresses and in a journal, started in 1930, called *Erkenntnis*.

19   [Author's note] My *Logic of Scientific Discovery* (1959, 1960, 1961), here usually referred to as *L.Sc.D.*, is the translation of *Logik der Forschung* (1934), with a number of additional notes and appendices, including (on pp. 312–14) the letter to the Editor of *Erkenntnis* mentioned here in the text which was first published in *Erkenntnis*, 3, 1933, pp. 426 f. Concerning my never published book mentioned here in the text, see R. Carnap's paper 'Ueber Protokollsätze' (On Protocol-Sentences), *Erkenntnis*, 3, 1932, pp. 215–28 where he gives an outline of my theory on pp. 223–28, and accepts it. He calls my theory 'procedure B', and says (p. 224, top): 'Starting from a point of view different from Neurath's' (who developed what Carnap calls on p. 223 'procedure A'), 'Popper developed procedure B as part of his system.' And after describing in detail my theory of tests, Carnap sums up his views as follows (p. 228): 'After weighing the various arguments here discussed, it appears to me that the second language form with procedure B—that is in the form here described—is the most adequate among the forms of scientific language at present advocated ... in the ... theory of knowledge.' This paper of Carnap's contained the first published report of my theory of critical testing. (See also my critical remarks in *L.Sc.D.*, note 1 to section 29, p. 104, where the date '1933' should read '1932'; and ch. 11, below, text to note 39.)

20   [Author's note] Wittgenstein's example of a nonsensical pseudo-proposition is: 'Socrates is identical'. Obviously, 'Socrates is not identical' must also be nonsense. Thus the negation of any nonsense will be nonsense, and that of a meaningful statement will be meaningful. *But the negation of a testable (or falsifiable) statement need not be testable*, as was pointed out, first in my *L.Sc.D.*, (e.g., pp. 38 f.) and later by my critics. The confusion caused by taking testability as a criterion of *meaning* rather than of *demarcation* can easily be imagined.

My attacks upon verification had some effect, however. They soon led to complete confusion in the camp of the verificationist philosophers of sense and nonsense. The original proposal of verifiability as the criterion of meaning was at least clear, simple, and forceful. The modifications and shifts which were now introduced were the very opposite.[21] This, I should say, is now seen even by the participants. But since I am usually quoted as one of them I wish to repeat that although I created this confusion I never participated in it. Neither falsifiability nor testability were proposed by me as criteria of meaning; and although I may plead guilty to having introduced both terms into the discussion, it was not I who introduced them into the theory of meaning.

Criticism of my alleged views was widespread and highly successful. I have yet to meet a criticism of my views.[22] Meanwhile, testability is being widely accepted as a criterion of demarcation.

---

21   [Author's note] The most recent example of the way in which the history of this problem is misunderstood is A.R. White's 'Note on Meaning and Verification', *Mind*, 63, 1954, pp. 66 ff. J.L. Evans's article, *Mind*, 62, 1953, pp. 1 ff., which Mr. White criticizes, is excellent in my opinion, and unusually perceptive. Understandably enough, neither of the authors can quite reconstruct the story. (Some hints may be found in my *Open Society*, notes 46, 51 and 52 to ch. 11; and a fuller analysis in ch. 11 of the present volume.)

22   [Author's note] In *L.Sc.D.* I discussed, and replied to, some likely objections which afterwards were indeed raised, without reference to my replies. One of them is the contention that the falsification of a natural law is just as impossible as its verification. The answer is that this objection mixes two entirely different levels of analysis (like the objection that mathematical demonstrations are impossible since checking, no matter how often repeated, can never make it quite certain that we have not overlooked a mistake). On the first level, there is a logical asymmetry: one singular statement—say about the perihelion of Mercury—can formally falsify Kepler's laws; but these cannot be formally verified by any number of singular statements. The attempt to minimize this asymmetry can only lead

IV.

I have discussed the problem of demarcation in some detail because I believe that its solution is the key to most of the fundamental problems of the philosophy of science. I am going to give you later a list of some of these other problems, but only one of them—the *problem of induction*—can be discussed here at any length.

I had become interested in the problem of induction in 1923. Although this problem is very closely connected with the problem of demarcation, I did not fully appreciate the connection for about five years.

I approached the problem of induction through Hume. Hume, I felt, was perfectly right in pointing out that induction cannot be logically justified. He held that there can be no valid logical[23] arguments allowing us to establish '*that those instances, of which we have had no experience, resemble those, of which we have had experience*'. Consequently '*even after the observation of the frequent or constant conjunction of objects, we have no reason to draw any inference concerning any object beyond those of which we have had experience*'. For 'shou'd it be said that we have

---

to confusion. On another level, we may hesitate to accept any statement, even the simplest observation statement; and we may point out that every statement involves *interpretation in the light of theories*, and that it is therefore uncertain. This does not affect the fundamental asymmetry, but it is important: most dissectors of the heart before Harvey observed the wrong things—those, which they expected to see. There can never be anything like a completely safe observation, free from the dangers of misinterpretation. (This is one of the reasons why the theory of induction does not work.) The 'empirical basis' consists largely of a mixture of *theories* of lower degree of universality (of 'reproducible effects'). But the fact remains that, relative to whatever basis the investigator may accept (at his peril), he can test his theory only by trying to refute it.

23   [Author's note] Hume does not say 'logical' but 'demonstrative', a terminology which, I think, is a little misleading. The following two quotations are from the *Treatise of Human Nature*, Book I, Part III, sections vi and xii. (The italics are all Hume's.)

experience'[24]—experience teaching us that objects constantly conjoined with certain other objects continue to be so conjoined—then, Hume says, 'I wou'd renew my question, *why from this experience we form any conclusion beyond those past instances, of which we have had experience*'. This 'renew'd question' indicates that an attempt to justify the practice of induction by an appeal to experience must lead to an *infinite regress*. As a result we can say that theories can never be inferred from observation statements, or rationally justified by them.

I found Hume's refutation of inductive inference clear and conclusive. But I felt completely dissatisfied with his psychological explanation of induction in terms of custom or habit.

It has often been noticed that this explanation of Hume's is philosophically not very satisfactory. Hume, however, without doubt intended it as a *psychological* rather than a philosophical theory; for it tries to give a causal explanation of a psychological fact—*the fact that we believe in laws*, in statements asserting regularities or constantly conjoined kinds of events. Hume explains this fact by asserting that it is due to (i.e., constantly conjoined with) custom or habit. But even this reformulation of Hume's theory is unacceptable; for what I have just called a 'psychological fact' may itself be described as a custom or habit—our custom or our habit of believing in laws or regularities. It is neither surprising nor enlightening to hear that such a custom or habit can be explained as due to custom or habit, or conjoined with a custom or habit (even though a different one). Only when we remember that the words 'custom' and 'habit' are used by Hume, as they are in ordinary language, not merely to *describe* regular behaviour, but rather to *theorize about its origin* (ascribed to frequent repetition), can we reformulate his psychological theory in a more satisfactory way. Hume's theory becomes then the thesis that, like other habits, *our habit of believing in laws is the product of frequent repetition*—of the repeated observation that things of a certain kind are constantly conjoined with things of another kind.

This genetic-psychological theory is, as indicated, incorporated in ordinary language, and it is therefore hardly as revolutionary as Hume thought. It is no doubt an extremely popular psychological theory—part of 'common sense', one might say. But in spite of my love of both common sense and Hume, I felt convinced that this psychological theory was mistaken; and that it was in fact refutable on purely logical grounds.

Hume's psychology, which is the popular psychology, was mistaken, I felt, about at least three different things: (*a*) the typical result of repetition; (*b*) the genesis of habits; and especially (*c*) the character of those experiences or modes of behaviour which may be described as 'believing in a law' or 'expecting a law-like succession of events'.

(*a*) The typical result of repetition—say, of repeating a difficult passage on the piano—is that movements which at first needed attention are in the end executed without attention. We might say that the process becomes radically abbreviated, and ceases to be conscious: it becomes automatized, 'physiological'. Such a development, far from creating a conscious expectation of law-like succession, or a belief in a law, may on the contrary begin with a conscious belief and destroy it by making it superfluous. In learning to ride a bicycle we may start with the belief that we can avoid falling if we steer in the direction in which we threaten to fall, and this belief may be useful for guiding our movements. After sufficient practice we may forget the rule; in any case, we do not need it any longer. On the other hand, even if it is true that repetition may create unconscious expectations, these become conscious only if something goes wrong (we may not have heard the clock tick, but we may hear that it has stopped).

(*b*) Habits or customs do not, as a rule, *originate* in repetition. Even the habit of walking, or of speaking, or of feeding at certain hours, *begins* before repetition can play any part whatever. We may say, if we like, that they deserve to be called 'habits' or 'customs' only after repetition has played its typical part described under (*a*); but we must not say that the

24 [Author's note] This and the next quotation are from *loc. cit.*, section vi. See also Hume's *Enquiry Concerning Human Understanding*, section IV, Part II, and his *Abstract*, edited 1938 by J.M. Keynes and P. Sraffa, p. 15, and quoted in *L.Sc.D.*, new appendix *vii, text to note 6.

practices in question *originated* as the result of many repetitions.

(*c*) Belief in a law is not quite the same thing as behaviour which betrays an expectation of a law-like succession of events; but these two are sufficiently closely connected to be treated together. They may, perhaps, in exceptional cases, result from a mere repetition of sense impressions (as in the case of the stopping clock). I was prepared to concede this, but I contended that normally, and in most cases of any interest, they cannot be so explained. As Hume admits, even a single striking observation may be sufficient to create a belief or an expectation—a fact which he tries to explain as due to an inductive habit, formed as the result of a vast number of long repetitive sequences which had been experienced at an earlier period of life.[25] But this, I contended, was merely his attempt to explain away unfavourable facts which threatened his theory; an unsuccessful attempt, since these unfavourable facts could be observed in very young animals and babies—as early, indeed, as we like. 'A lighted cigarette was held near the noses of the young puppies', reports F. Bäge. 'They sniffed at it once, turned tail, and nothing would induce them to come back to the source of the smell and to sniff again. A few days later, they reacted to the mere sight of a cigarette or even of a rolled piece of white paper, by bounding away, and sneezing.'[26] If we try to explain cases like this by postulating a vast number of long repetitive sequences at a still earlier age we are not only romancing, but forgetting that in the clever puppies' short lives there must be room not only for repetition but also for a great deal of novelty, and consequently of non-repetition.

But it is not only that certain empirical facts do not support Hume; there are decisive arguments of a *purely logical* nature against his psychological theory.

The central idea of Hume's psychological theory is that of *repetition, based upon similarity* (or 'resemblance'). This idea is used in a very uncritical way. We are led to think of the water-drop that hollows the stone: of sequences of unquestionably like events slowly forcing themselves upon us, as does the tick of the clock. But we ought to realize that in a psychological theory such as Hume's, only repetition-for-us, based upon similarity-for-us, can be allowed to have any effect upon us. We must respond to situations as if they were equivalent; *take* them as similar; *interpret* them as repetitions. In this way they become for us *functionally equal*. The clever puppies, we may assume, showed by their response, their way of acting or of reacting, that they recognized or interpreted the second situation as a repetition of the first: that they expected its main element, the objectionable smell, to be present. The situation was a repetition-for-them because they responded to it by *anticipating* its similarity to the previous one.

This apparently psychological criticism has a purely logical basis which may be summed up in the following simple argument. (It happens to be the one from which I originally started my criticism.) The kind of repetition envisaged by Hume can never be perfect; the cases he has in mind cannot be cases of perfect sameness; they can only be cases of similarity. Thus *they are repetitions only from a certain point of view*. (What has the effect upon me of a repetition may not have this effect upon a spider.) But this means that, for logical reasons, there must always be a point of view—such as a system of expectations, anticipations, assumptions, or interests—*before* there can be any repetition; which point of view, consequently, cannot be merely the result of repetition. (See now also appendix *x, (1), to my *L.Sc.D.*)

We must thus replace, for the purposes of a psychological theory of the origin of our beliefs, the naïve idea of events which *are* similar by the idea of events to which we react by *interpreting* them as being similar. But if this is so (and I can see no escape from it) then Hume's psychological theory of induction leads to an infinite regress, precisely analogous to that other infinite regress which was discovered by Hume himself, and used by him to explode the logical theory of induction. For what do we wish to explain? In the example of the puppies we wish to explain behaviour which may be described as *recognizing or interpreting* a situation as a repetition of another. Clearly, we cannot hope to explain this by an appeal

---

25 [Author's note] *Treatise*, section xiii; section xv, rule 4.
26 [Author's note] F. Bäge, 'Zur Entwicklung, etc.', *Zeitschrift f. Hundeforschung*, 1933; cp. D. Katz, *Animals and Men*, ch. VI, footnote.

to earlier repetitions, once we realize that the earlier repetitions must also have been repetitions-for-them, so that precisely the same problem arises again: that of *recognizing or interpreting* a situation as a repetition of another.

To put it more concisely, similarity-for-us is the product of a response involving interpretations (which may be inadequate) and anticipations or expectations (which may never be fulfilled). It is therefore impossible to explain anticipations, or expectations, as resulting from many repetitions, as suggested by Hume. For even the first repetition-for-us must be based upon similarity-for-us, and therefore upon expectations—precisely the kind of thing we wished to explain. (Expectations must come first, *before* repetitions.)

We see that there is an infinite regress involved in Hume's psychological theory.

Hume, I felt, had never accepted the full force of his own logical analysis. Having refuted the logical idea of induction he was faced with the following problem: how do we actually obtain our knowledge, as a matter of psychological fact, if induction is a procedure which is logically invalid and rationally unjustifiable? There are two possible answers: (1) We obtain our knowledge by a non-inductive procedure. This answer would have allowed Hume to retain a form of rationalism. (2) We obtain our knowledge by repetition and induction, and therefore by a logically invalid and rationally unjustifiable procedure, so that all apparent knowledge is merely a kind of belief—belief based on habit. This answer would imply that even scientific knowledge is irrational, so that rationalism is absurd, and must be given up. (I shall not discuss here the age-old attempts, now again fashionable, to get out of the difficulty by asserting that though induction is of course logically invalid if we mean by 'logic' the same as 'deductive logic', it is not irrational by its own standards, and as inductive logic admits; as may be seen from the fact that every reasonable man applies it *as a matter of fact.* As against this, it was Hume's great achievement to break this uncritical identification of the question of fact—*quid facti?*[27]—and the question of justification

or validity—*quid juris?*[28] [See below, point (13) of the appendix to the present chapter (not reprinted here).])

It seems that Hume never seriously considered the first alternative. Having cast out the logical theory of induction by repetition he struck a bargain with common sense, meekly allowing the re-entry of induction by repetition, in the guise of a psychological fact. I proposed to turn the tables upon this theory of Hume's. Instead of explaining our propensity to expect regularities as the result of repetition, I proposed to explain repetition-for-us as the result of our propensity to expect regularities and to search for them.

Thus I was led by purely logical considerations to replace the psychological theory of induction by the following view. Without waiting, passively, for repetitions to impress or impose regularities upon us, we actively try to impose regularities upon the world. We try to discover similarities in it, and to interpret it in terms of laws invented by us. Without waiting for premises we jump to conclusions. These may have to be discarded later, should observation show that they are wrong.

This was a theory of trial and error—of *conjectures and refutations.* It made it possible to understand why our attempts to force interpretations upon the world were logically prior to the observation of similarities. Since there were logical reasons behind this procedure, I thought that it would apply in the field of science also; that scientific theories were not the digest of observations, but that they were inventions—conjectures boldly put forward for trial, to be eliminated if they clashed with observations; with observations which were rarely accidental but as a rule undertaken with the definite intention of testing a theory by obtaining, if possible, a decisive refutation.

V.

The belief that science proceeds from observation to theory is still so widely and so firmly held that my denial of it is often met with incredulity. I have even been suspected of being insincere—of denying what nobody in his senses can doubt.

But in fact the belief that we can start with pure observations alone, without anything in the nature

---

27   What is done?

28   What ought to be done?

of a theory, is absurd; as may be illustrated by the story of the man who dedicated his life to natural science, wrote down everything he could observe, and bequeathed his priceless collection of observations to the Royal Society to be used as inductive evidence. This story should show us that though beetles may profitably be collected, observations may not.

Twenty-five years ago I tried to bring home the same point to a group of physics students in Vienna by beginning a lecture with the following instructions: 'Take pencil and paper; carefully observe, and write down what you have observed!' They asked, of course, *what* I wanted them to observe. Clearly the instruction, 'Observe!' is absurd.[29] (It is not even idiomatic, unless the object of the transitive verb can be taken as understood.) Observation is always selective. It needs a chosen object, a definite task, an interest, a point of view, a problem. And its description presupposes a descriptive language, with property words; it presupposes similarity and classification, which in their turn presuppose interests, points of view, and problems. 'A hungry animal', writes Katz,[30] 'divides the environment into edible and inedible things. An animal in flight sees roads to escape and hiding places.... Generally speaking, objects change ... according to the needs of the animal.' We may add that objects can be classified, and can become similar or dissimilar, *only* in this way—by being related to needs and interests. This rule applies not only to animals but also to scientists: For the animal a point of view is provided by its needs, the task of the moment, and its expectations; for the scientist by his theoretical interests, the special problem under investigation, his conjectures and anticipations, and the theories which he accepts as a kind of background: his frame of reference, his 'horizon of expectations'.

The problem 'Which comes first, the hypothesis (*H*) or the observation (*O*)?' is soluble; as is the problem, 'Which comes first, the hen (*H*) or the egg (*O*)?'. The reply to the latter is, 'An earlier kind of egg'; to the former, 'An earlier kind of hypothesis'. It is quite true that any particular hypothesis we choose will have been preceded by observations—the observations, for example, which it is designed to explain.

But these observations, in their turn, presupposed the adoption of a frame of reference: a frame of expectations: a frame of theories. If they were significant, if they created a need for explanation and thus gave rise to the invention of a hypothesis, it was because they could not be explained within the old theoretical framework, the old horizon of expectations. There is no danger here of an infinite regress. Going back to more and more primitive theories and myths we shall in the end find unconscious, *inborn* expectations.

The theory of inborn *ideas* is absurd, I think; but every organism has inborn *reactions* or *responses*; and among them, responses adapted to impending events. These responses we may describe as 'expectations' without implying that these 'expectations' are conscious. The new-born baby 'expects', in this sense, to be fed (and, one could even argue, to be protected and loved). In view of the close relation between expectation and knowledge we may even speak in quite a reasonable sense of 'inborn knowledge'. This 'knowledge', however, is not *valid a priori*;[31] an inborn expectation, no matter how strong and specific, may be mistaken. (The newborn child may be abandoned, and starve.)

Thus we are born with expectations; with 'knowledge' which, although not *valid a priori*, is *psychologically or genetically a priori*, i.e., prior to all observational experience. One of the most important of these expectations is the expectation of finding a regularity. It is connected with an inborn propensity to look out for regularities, or with a *need* to *find* regularities, as we may see from the pleasure of the child who satisfies this need.

This 'instinctive' expectation of finding regularities, which is psychologically *a priori*, corresponds very closely to the 'law of causality' which Kant believed to be part of our mental outfit and to be *a priori* valid. One might thus be inclined to say that Kant failed to distinguish between psychologically *a priori* ways of thinking or responding and *a priori* valid beliefs. But I do not think that his mistake was quite as crude as that. For the expectation of finding

---

29   [Author's note] See section 30 of *L.Sc.D.*
30   [Author's note] Katz, *loc. cit.*

31   It is not something that can be known with certainty, even independently of any experience of the world, to be true.

regularities is not only psychologically *a priori*, but also logically *a priori*: it is logically prior to all observational experience, for it is prior to any recognition of similarities, as we have seen; and all observation involves the recognition of similarities (or dissimilarities). But in spite of being logically *a priori* in this sense the expectation is not valid *a priori*. For it may fail: we can easily construct an environment (it would be a lethal one) which, compared with our ordinary environment, is so chaotic that we completely fail to find regularities. (All natural laws could remain valid: environments of this kind have been used in the animal experiments mentioned in the next section.)

Thus Kant's reply to Hume came near to being right; for the distinction between an *a priori* valid expectation and one which is both genetically *and* logically prior to observation, but not *a priori* valid, is really somewhat subtle. But Kant proved too much. In trying to show how knowledge is possible, he proposed a theory which had the unavoidable consequence that our quest for knowledge must necessarily succeed, which is clearly mistaken. When Kant said, 'Our intellect does not draw its laws from nature but imposes its laws upon nature', he was right. But in thinking that these laws are necessarily true, or that we necessarily succeed in imposing them upon nature, he was wrong.[32] Nature very often resists quite successfully, forcing us to discard our laws as refuted; but if we live we may try again.

To sum up this logical criticism of Hume's psychology of induction we may consider the idea of building an induction machine. Placed in a simplified

---

32   [Author's note] Kant believed that Newton's dynamics was *a priori* valid. (See his *Metaphysical Foundations of Natural Science*, published between the first and the second editions of the *Critique of Pure Reason*.) But if, as he thought, we can explain the validity of Newton's theory by the fact that our intellect imposes its laws upon nature, it follows, I think, that our intellect must succeed in this; which makes it hard to understand why *a priori* knowledge such as Newton's should be so hard to come by. A somewhat fuller statement of this criticism can be found in ch. 2, especially section x, and chs. 7 and 8 of the present volume [*Conjectures and Refutations*].

'world' (for example, one of sequences of coloured counters) such a machine may through repetition 'learn', or even 'formulate', laws of succession which hold in its 'world'. If such a machine can be constructed (and I have no doubt that it can) then, it might be argued, my theory must be wrong; for if a machine is capable of performing inductions on the basis of repetition, there can be no logical reasons preventing us from doing the same.

The argument sounds convincing, but it is mistaken. In constructing an induction machine we, the architects of the machine, must decide *a priori* what constitutes its 'world'; what things are to be taken as similar or equal; and what *kind* of 'laws' we wish the machine to be able to 'discover' in its 'world'. In other words we must build into the machine a framework determining what is relevant or interesting in its world: the machine will have its 'inborn' selection principles. The problems of similarity will have been solved for it by its makers who thus have interpreted the 'world' for the machine.

VI.

Our propensity to look out for regularities, and to impose laws upon nature, leads to the psychological phenomenon of *dogmatic thinking* or, more generally, dogmatic behaviour: we expect regularities everywhere and attempt to find them even where there are none; events which do not yield to these attempts we are inclined to treat as a kind of 'background noise'; and we stick to our expectations even when they are inadequate and we ought to accept defeat. This dogmatism is to some extent necessary. It is demanded by a situation which can only be dealt with by forcing our conjectures upon the world. Moreover, this dogmatism allows us to approach a good theory in stages, by way of approximations: if we accept defeat too easily, we may prevent ourselves from finding that we were very nearly right.

It is clear that this *dogmatic attitude*, which makes us stick to our first impressions, is indicative of a strong belief; while a *critical attitude*, which is ready to modify its tenets, which admits doubt and demands tests, is indicative of a weaker belief. Now according to Hume's theory, and to the popular theory, the strength of a belief should be a product of repetition;

thus it should always grow with experience, and always be greater in less primitive persons. But dogmatic thinking, an uncontrolled wish to impose regularities, a manifest pleasure in rites and in repetition as such, are characteristic of primitives and children; and increasing experience and maturity sometimes create an attitude of caution and criticism rather than of dogmatism.

I may perhaps mention here a point of agreement with psycho-analysis. Psycho-analysts assert that neurotics and others interpret the world in accordance with a personal set pattern which is not easily given up, and which can often be traced back to early childhood. A pattern or scheme which was adopted very early in life is maintained throughout, and every new experience is interpreted in terms of it; verifying it, as it were, and contributing to its rigidity. This is a description of what I have called the dogmatic attitude, as distinct from the critical attitude, which shares with the dogmatic attitude the quick adoption of a schema of expectations—a myth, perhaps, or a conjecture or hypothesis—but which is ready to modify it, to correct it, and even to give it up. I am inclined to suggest that most neuroses may be due to a partially arrested development of the critical attitude; to an arrested rather than a natural dogmatism; to resistance to demands for the modification and adjustment of certain schematic interpretations and responses. This resistance in its turn may perhaps be explained, in some cases, as due to an injury or shock, resulting in fear and in an increased need for assurance or certainty, analogous to the way in which an injury to a limb makes us afraid to move it, so that it becomes stiff. (It might even be argued that the case of the limb is not merely analogous to the dogmatic response, but an instance of it.) The explanation of any concrete case will have to take into account the weight of the difficulties involved in making the necessary adjustments—difficulties which may be considerable, especially in a complex and changing world: we know from experiments on animals that varying degrees of neurotic behaviour may be produced at will by correspondingly varying difficulties.

I found many other links between the psychology of knowledge and psychological fields which are often considered remote from it—for example the psychology of art and music; in fact, my ideas about induction originated in a conjecture about the evolution of Western polyphony.[33] But you will be spared this story.

VII.

My logical criticism of Hume's psychological theory, and the considerations connected with it (most of which I elaborated in 1926–27, in a thesis entitled 'On Habit and Belief in Laws'[34]) may seem a little removed from the field of the philosophy of science. But the distinction between dogmatic and critical thinking, or the dogmatic and the critical attitude, brings us right back to our central problem. For the dogmatic attitude is clearly related to the tendency to *verify* our laws and schemata by seeking to apply them and to confirm them, even to the point of neglecting refutations, whereas the critical attitude is one of readiness to change them—to test them; to refute them; to *falsify* them, if possible. This suggests that we may identify the critical attitude with the scientific attitude, and the dogmatic attitude with the one which we have described as pseudo-scientific.

It further suggests that genetically speaking the pseudo-scientific attitude is more primitive than, and prior to, the scientific attitude: that it is a pre-scientific attitude. And this primitivity or priority also has its logical aspect. For the critical attitude is not so much opposed to the dogmatic attitude as super-imposed upon it: criticism must be directed against existing and influential beliefs in need of critical revision—in other words, dogmatic beliefs. A critical attitude needs for its raw material, as it were, theories or beliefs which are held more or less dogmatically.

Thus science must begin with myths, and with the criticism of myths; neither with the collection of observations, nor with the invention of experiments, but

---

33 Music with two or more independent melodic parts sounded together.

34 [Author's note] A thesis submitted under the title '*Gewohnheit and Gesetzerlebnis*' to the Institute of Education of the City of Vienna in 1927. (Unpublished.)

with the critical discussion of myths, and of magical techniques and practices. The scientific tradition is distinguished from the pre-scientific tradition in having two layers. Like the latter, it passes on its theories; but it also passes on a critical attitude towards them. The theories are passed on, not as dogmas, but rather with the challenge to discuss them and improve upon them. This tradition is Hellenic:[35] it may be traced back to Thales,[36] founder of the first *school* (I do not mean 'of the first *philosophical* school', but simply 'of the first school') which was not mainly concerned with the preservation of a dogma.[37]

The critical attitude, the tradition of free discussion of theories with the aim of discovering their weak spots so that they may be improved upon, is the attitude of reasonableness, of rationality. It makes far-reaching use of both verbal argument and observation—of observation in the interest of argument, however. The Greeks' discovery of the critical method gave rise at first to the mistaken hope that it would lead to the solution of all the great old problems; that it would establish certainty; that it would help to *prove* our theories, to *justify* them. But this hope was a residue of the dogmatic way of thinking; in fact nothing can be justified or proved (outside of mathematics and logic). The demand for rational proofs in science indicates a failure to keep distinct the broad realm of rationality and the narrow realm of rational certainty: it is an untenable, an unreasonable demand.

Nevertheless, the role of logical argument, of deductive logical reasoning, remains all-important for the critical approach; not because it allows us to prove our theories, or to infer them from observation statements, but because only by purely deductive reasoning is it possible for us to discover what our theories imply, and thus to criticize them effectively. Criticism, I said, is an attempt to find the weak spots in a theory, and these, as a rule, can be found only in the more remote logical consequences which can be derived from it. It is here that purely logical reasoning plays an important part in science.

Hume was right in stressing that our theories cannot be validly inferred from what we can know to be true—neither from observations nor from anything else. He concluded from this that our belief in them was irrational. If 'belief' means here our inability to doubt our natural laws, and the constancy of natural regularities, then Hume is again right: this kind of dogmatic belief has, one might say, a physiological rather than a rational basis. If, however, the term 'belief' is taken to cover our critical acceptance of scientific theories—a *tentative* acceptance combined with an eagerness to revise the theory if we succeed in designing a test which it cannot pass—then Hume was wrong. In such an acceptance of theories there is nothing irrational. There is not even anything irrational in relying for practical purposes upon well-tested theories, for no more rational course of action is open to us.

Assume that we have deliberately made it our task to live in this unknown world of ours; to adjust ourselves to it as well as we can; to take advantage of the opportunities we can find in it; and to explain it, if possible (we need not assume that it is), and as far as possible, with the help of laws and explanatory theories. *If we have made this our task, then there is no more rational procedure than the method of trial and error—of conjecture and refutation*: of boldly proposing theories; of trying our best to show that these are erroneous; and of accepting them tentatively if our critical efforts are unsuccessful.

From the point of view here developed all laws, all theories, remain essentially tentative, or conjectural, or hypothetical, even when we feel unable to doubt them any longer. Before a theory has been refuted we can never know in what way it may have to be modified. That the sun will always rise and set within twenty-four hours is still proverbial as a law 'established by induction beyond reasonable doubt'. It is odd that this example is still in use, though it may have served well enough in the days

---

35   Ancient Greek (from *Hellen*, a Greek).

36   Often described as the first philosopher of the Western tradition, Thales of Miletus flourished around 585 BCE. He is thought to be the first Western thinker in recorded history to attempt to give naturalistic, rather than religious, explanations for natural phenomena (such as magnetism).

37   [Author's note] Further comments on these developments may be found in chs. 4 and 5, below.

of Aristotle and Pytheas of Massalia[38]—the great traveller who for centuries was called a liar because of his tales of Thule, the land of the frozen sea and the *midnight sun.*

The method of trial and error is not, of course, simply identical with the scientific or critical approach—with the method of conjecture and refutation. The method of trial and error is applied not only by Einstein but, in a more dogmatic fashion, by the amoeba also. The difference lies not so much in the trials as in a critical and constructive attitude towards errors; errors which the scientist consciously and cautiously tries to uncover in order to refute his theories with searching arguments, including appeals to the most severe experimental tests which his theories and his ingenuity permit him to design.

The critical attitude might be described as the result of a conscious attempt to make our theories, our conjectures, suffer in our stead in the struggle for the survival of the fittest. It gives us a chance to survive the elimination of an inadequate hypothesis—when a more dogmatic attitude would eliminate it by eliminating us. (There is a touching story of an Indian community which disappeared because of its belief in the holiness of life, including that of tigers.) We thus obtain the fittest theory within our reach by the elimination of those which are less fit. (By 'fitness' I do not mean merely 'usefulness' but truth; see chapters 3 and 10, below.) I do not think that this procedure is irrational or in need of any further rational justification.

VIII.

Let us now turn from our logical criticism of the *psychology of experience* to our real problem—the problem of the *logic of science.* Although some of the things I have said may help us here, in so far as they may have eliminated certain psychological prejudices that favour induction, my treatment of the *logical problem of induction* is completely independent of this criticism, and of all psychological considerations. Provided you do not dogmatically believe in the alleged psychological fact that we make inductions, you may now forget my whole story with the exception of two logical points: my logical remarks on testability or falsifiability as the criterion of demarcation; and Hume's logical criticism of induction.

From what I have said it is obvious that there was a close link between the two problems which interested me at that time: demarcation, and induction or scientific method. It was easy to see that the method of science is criticism, i.e., attempted falsifications. Yet it took me a few years to notice that the two problems—of demarcation and of induction—were in a sense one.

Why, I asked, do so many scientists believe in induction? I found they did so because they believed natural science to be characterized by the inductive method—by a method starting from, and relying upon, long sequences of observations and experiments. They believed that the difference between genuine science and metaphysical or pseudo-scientific speculation depended solely upon whether or not the inductive method was employed. They believed (to put it in my own terminology) that only the inductive method could provide a satisfactory *criterion of demarcation.*

I recently came across an interesting formulation of this belief in a remarkable philosophical book by a great physicist—Max Born's *Natural Philosophy of Cause and Chance.*[39] He writes: 'Induction allows us to generalize a number of observations into a general rule: that night follows day and day follows night ... But while everyday life has no definite criterion for the validity of an induction, ... science has worked out a code, or rule of craft, for its application.' Born nowhere reveals the contents of this inductive code (which, as his wording shows, contains a 'definite criterion for the validity of an induction'); but he stresses that 'there is no logical argument' for its acceptance: 'it is a question of faith'; and he is therefore 'willing to call induction a metaphysical principle'. But why does he believe

---

38   Aristotle lived from 384 to 322 BCE, and Pytheas flourished around 310 BCE. Pytheas described Thule as being six days sail north of Britain, and the ancients thought of it as being at the northernmost tip of the world; the land he visited was most probably Norway.

39   [Author's note] Max Born, *Natural Philosophy of Cause and Chance*, Oxford, 1949, p. 7.

that such a code of valid inductive rules must exist? This becomes clear when he speaks of the 'vast communities of people ignorant of, or rejecting, the rule of science, among them the members of anti-vaccination societies and believers in astrology. It is useless to argue with them; I cannot compel them to accept the same criteria of valid induction in which I believe: the code of scientific rules.' This makes it quite clear that *'valid induction' was here meant to serve as a criterion of demarcation between science and pseudo-science.*

But it is obvious that this rule or craft of 'valid induction' is not even metaphysical: it simply does not exist. No rule can ever guarantee that a generalization inferred from true observations, however often repeated, is true. (Born himself does not believe in the truth of Newtonian physics, in spite of its success, although he believes that it is based on induction.) And the success of science is not based upon rules of induction, but depends upon luck, ingenuity, and the purely deductive rules of critical argument.

I may summarize some of my conclusions as follows:

(1) Induction, i.e., inference based on many observations, is a myth. It is neither a psychological fact, nor a fact of ordinary life, nor one of scientific procedure.

(2) The actual procedure of science is to operate with conjectures: to jump to conclusions—often after one single observation (as noticed for example by Hume and Born).

(3) Repeated observations and experiments function in science as *tests* of our conjectures or hypotheses, i.e., as attempted refutations.

(4) The mistaken belief in induction is fortified by the need for a criterion of demarcation which, it is traditionally but wrongly believed, only the inductive method can provide.

(5) The conception of such an inductive method, like the criterion of verifiability, implies a faulty demarcation.

(6) None of this is altered in the least if we say that induction makes theories only probable rather than certain. (See especially chapter 10, below.)

IX.

If, as I have suggested, the problem of induction is only an instance or facet of the problem of demarcation, then the solution to the problem of demarcation must provide us with a solution to the problem of induction. This is indeed the case, I believe, although it is perhaps not immediately obvious.

For a brief formulation of the problem of induction we can turn again to Born, who writes: '…no observation or experiment, however extended, can give more than a finite number of repetitions'; therefore, 'the statement of a law—B depends on A—always transcends experience. Yet this kind of statement is made everywhere and all the time, and sometimes from scanty material.'[40]

In other words, the logical problem of induction arises from (*a*) Hume's discovery (so well expressed by Born) that it is impossible to justify a law by observation or experiment, since it 'transcends experience'; (*b*) the fact that science proposes and uses laws 'everywhere and all the time'. (Like Hume, Born is struck by the 'scanty material', i.e., the few observed instances upon which the law may be based.) To this we have to add (*c*) *the principle of empiricism* which asserts that in science, only observation and experiment may decide upon the *acceptance or rejection* of scientific statements, including laws and theories.

These three principles, (*a*), (*b*), and (*c*), appear at first sight to clash; and this apparent clash constitutes the *logical problem of induction.*

Faced with this clash, Born gives up (*c*), the principle of empiricism (as Kant and many others, including Bertrand Russell, have done before him), in favour of what he calls a 'metaphysical principle'; a metaphysical principle which he does not even attempt to formulate; which he vaguely describes as a 'code or rule of craft'; and of which I have never seen any formulation which even looked promising and was not clearly untenable.

But in fact the principles (*a*) to (*c*) do not clash. We can see this the moment we realize that the acceptance by science of a law or of a theory is *tentative only*; which is to say that all laws and theories are conjec-

---

40   [Author's note] *Natural Philosophy of Cause and Chance*, p. 6.

tures, or tentative *hypotheses* (a position which I have sometimes called 'hypotheticism'); and that we may reject a law or theory on the basis of new evidence, without necessarily discarding the old evidence which originally led us to accept it.[41]

The principle of empiricism (*c*) can be fully preserved, since the fate of a theory, its acceptance or rejection, is decided by observation and experiment— by the result of tests. So long as a theory stands up to the severest tests we can design, it is accepted; if it does not, it is rejected. But it is never inferred, in any sense, from the empirical evidence. There is neither a psychological nor a logical induction. *Only the falsity of the theory can be inferred from empirical evidence, and this inference is a purely deductive one.*

Hume showed that it is not possible to infer a theory from observation statements; but this does not affect the possibility of refuting a theory by observation statements. The full appreciation of this possibility makes the relation between theories and observations perfectly clear.

This solves the problem of the alleged clash between the principles (*a*), (*b*), and (*c*), and with it Hume's problem of induction.

X.

Thus the problem of induction is solved. But nothing seems less wanted than a simple solution to an age-old philosophical problem. Wittgenstein and his school hold that genuine philosophical problems do not exist;[42] from which it clearly follows that they cannot be solved. Others among my contemporaries do believe that there are philosophical problems, and respect them; but they seem to respect them too much; they seem to believe that they are insoluble, if not taboo; and they are shocked and horrified by the claim that there is a simple, neat, and lucid, solution

to any of them. If there is a solution it must be deep, they feel, or at least complicated.

However this may be, I am still waiting for a simple, neat and lucid criticism of the solution which I published first in 1933 in my letter to the Editor of *Erkenntnis*,[43] and later in *The Logic of Scientific Discovery*.

Of course, one can invent new problems of induction, different from the one I have formulated and solved. (Its formulation was half its solution.) But I have yet to see any reformulation of the problem whose solution cannot be easily obtained from my old solution. I am now going to discuss some of these re-formulations.

One question which may be asked is this: how do we really jump from an observation statement to a theory?

Although this question appears to be psychological rather than philosophical, one can say something positive about it without invoking psychology. One can say first that the jump is not from an observation statement, but from a problem-situation, and that the theory must allow us *to explain* the observations which created the problem (that is, *to deduce* them from the theory strengthened by other accepted theories and by other observation statements, the so-called initial conditions). This leaves, of course, an immense number of possible theories, good and bad; and it thus appears that our question has not been answered.

But this makes it fairly clear that when we asked our question we had more in mind than, 'How do we jump from an observation statement to a theory?' The question we had in mind was, it now appears, 'How do we jump from an observation statement to a *good* theory?' But to this the answer is: by jumping first to *any* theory and then testing it, to find whether it is good or not; i.e., by repeatedly applying the critical method, eliminating many bad theories, and inventing many new ones. Not everybody is able to do this; but there is no other way.

Other questions have sometimes been asked. The original problem of induction, it was said, is the problem of *justifying* induction, i.e., of justifying inductive inference. If you answer this problem by

---

41 [Author's note] I do not doubt that Born and many others would agree that theories are accepted only tentatively. But the widespread belief in induction shows that the far-reaching implications of this view are rarely seen.

42 [Author's note] Wittgenstein still held this belief in 1946; see note 8 to ch. 2, below.

43 [Author's note] See note 5 [19 in this text] above.

saying that what is called an 'inductive inference' is always invalid and therefore clearly not justifiable, the following new problem must arise: how do you justify your method of trial and error? Reply: the method of trial and error is a *method of eliminating false theories* by observation statements; and the justification for this is the purely logical relationship of deducibility which allows us to assert the falsity of universal statements if we accept the truth of singular ones.

Another question sometimes asked is this: why is it reasonable to prefer non-falsified statements to falsified ones? To this question some involved answers have been produced, for example pragmatic answers. But from a pragmatic point of view the question does not arise, since false theories often serve well enough: most formulae used in engineering or navigation are known to be false, although they may be excellent approximations and easy to handle; and they are used with confidence by people who know them to be false.

The only correct answer is the straightforward one: because we search for truth (even though we can never be sure we have found it), and because the falsified theories are known or believed to be false, while the non-falsified theories may still be true. Besides, we do not prefer *every* non-falsified theory—only one which, in the light of criticism, appears to be better than its competitors: which solves our problems, which is well tested, and of which we think, or rather conjecture or hope (considering other provisionally accepted theories), that it will stand up to further tests.

It has also been said that the problem of induction is, 'Why is it *reasonable* to believe that the future will be like the past?', and that a satisfactory answer to this question should make it plain that such a belief is, in fact, reasonable. My reply is that it is reasonable to believe that the future will be very different from the past in many vitally important respects. Admittedly it is perfectly reasonable to act on the assumption that it will, in many respects, be like the past, and that well-tested laws will continue to hold (since we can have no better assumption to act upon); but it is also reasonable to believe that such a course of action will lead us at times into severe trouble, since some of the laws upon which we now heavily rely may easily prove unreliable. (Remember the midnight sun!) One might even say that to judge from past experience,

and from our general scientific knowledge, the future will *not* be like the past, in perhaps most of the ways which those have in mind who say that it will. Water will sometimes not quench thirst, and air will choke those who breathe it. An apparent way out is to say that the future will be like the past *in the sense that the laws of nature will not change*, but this is begging the question. We speak of a 'law of nature' only if we think that we have before us a regularity which does not change; and if we find that it changes then we shall not continue to call it a 'law of nature'. Of course our search for natural laws indicates that we hope to find them, and that we believe that there are natural laws; but our belief in any particular natural law cannot have a safer basis than our unsuccessful critical attempts to refute it.

I think that those who put the problem of induction in terms of the *reasonableness* of our beliefs are perfectly right if they are dissatisfied with a Humean, or post-Humean, sceptical despair of reason. We must indeed reject the view that a belief in science is as irrational as a belief in primitive magical practices—that both are a matter of accepting a 'total ideology', a convention or a tradition based on faith. But we must be cautious if we formulate our problem, with Hume, as one of the reasonableness of our *beliefs*. We should split this problem into three—our old problem of demarcation, or of how to *distinguish* between science and primitive magic; the problem of the rationality of the scientific or critical *procedure*, and of the role of observation within it; and lastly the problem of the rationality of our *acceptance* of theories for scientific and for practical purposes. To all these three problems solutions have been offered here.

One should also be careful not to confuse the problem of the reasonableness of the scientific procedure and the (tentative) acceptance of the results of this procedure—i.e., the scientific theories—with the problem of the rationality or otherwise *of the belief that this procedure will succeed*. In practice, in practical scientific research, this belief is no doubt unavoidable and reasonable, there being no better alternative. But the belief is certainly unjustifiable in a theoretical sense, as I have argued (in section V). Moreover, if we could show, on general logical grounds, that the scientific quest is likely to succeed, one could not understand why anything like success has been so rare in the long history of human endeavours to know more about our world.

Yet another way of putting the problem of induction is in terms of probability. Let t be the theory and e the evidence: we can ask for $P(t,e)$, that is to say, the probability of t, given e. The problem of induction, it is often believed, can then be put thus: construct a calculus of probability which allows us to work out for any theory t what its probability is, relative to any given empirical evidence e; and show that $P(t,e)$ increases with the accumulation of supporting evidence, and reaches high values—at any rate values greater than $\frac{1}{2}$.

In *The Logic of Scientific Discovery* I explained why I think that this approach to the problem is fundamentally mistaken.[44] To make this clear, I introduced there the distinction between *probability* and *degree of corroboration or confirmation*. (The term 'confirmation' has lately been so much used and misused that I have decided to surrender it to the verificationists and to use for my own purposes 'corroboration' only. The term 'probability' is best used in some of the many senses which satisfy the well-known calculus of probability, axiomatized, for example, by Keynes, Jeffreys,[45] and myself; but nothing of course depends on the choice of words, as long as we do not *assume*, uncritically, that degree of corroboration must also be

a probability—that is to say, that it must satisfy the calculus of probability.)[46]

I explained in my book why we are interested in theories with a *high degree of corroboration*. And I explained why it is a mistake to conclude from this that we are interested in *highly probable* theories. I pointed out that the probability of a statement (or set of statements) is always the greater the less the statement says: it is inverse to the content or the deductive power of the statement, and thus to its explanatory power. Accordingly every interesting and powerful statement must have a low probability; and *vice versa*: a statement with a high probability will be scientifically uninteresting, because it says little and has no explanatory power. Although we seek theories with a high degree of corroboration, *as scientists we do not seek highly probable theories but explanations; that is to say, powerful and improbable theories*. The opposite view—that science aims at high probability—is

---

44 [Author's note] *L.Sc.D.* (see note 5 [19 in this text] above), ch. X, especially sections 80 to 83, also section 34 ff. See also my note 'A Set of Independent Axioms for Probability', *Mind*, N.S. 47, 1938, p. 275. (This note has since been reprinted, with corrections, in the new appendix *ii of *L.Sc.D.* See also the next note but one to the present chapter.)

45 John Maynard Keynes (1883–1946) is known primarily as an economist, but he also produced an influential *Treatise on Probability* in 1921. Harold Jeffreys (1891–1989) was a professor of astronomy at Cambridge (and originated the theory that the core of the earth is liquid). His *The Theory of Probability* (1939) was the first attempt to develop a theory of scientific inference based on the ideas of Bayesian statistics.

46 [Author's note] A definition, in terms of probabilities, of $C(t,e)$, i.e., of the degree of corroboration (of a theory t relative to the evidence e) satisfying the demands indicated in my *L.Sc.D.*, sections 82 to 83, is the following:

$$C(t,e) = E(t,e) (1 + P(t)P(t,e)),$$

where $E(t,e) = (P(e,t) - P(e))/(P(e,t) + P(e))$ is a (non-additive) measure of the explanatory power of t with respect to e. Note that $C(t,e)$ is not a probability: it may have values between -1 (refutation of t by e) and $C(t,t) \leq +1$. Statements t which are lawlike and thus non-verifiable cannot even reach $C(t,e) = C(t,t)$ upon empirical evidence e. $C(t,t)$ is the *degree of corroborability* of t, and is equal to the *degree of testability* of t, or to the *content* of t. Because of the demands implied in point (6) at the end of section I above, I do not think, however, that it is possible to give a complete formalization of the idea of corroboration (or, as I previously used to say, of confirmation).

(Added 1955 to the first proofs of this paper:)

See also my note 'Degree of Confirmation', *British Journal for the Philosophy of Science*, 5, 1954, pp. 143 fl. (See also 5, pp. 334.) I have since simplified this definition as follows (*B.J.P.S.*, 1955, 5, p. 359):

$$C(t,e) = (P(e,t) - P(e))/(P(e,t) - P(e,t) + P(e))$$

For a further improvement, see *B.J.P.S.* 6, 1955, p. 56.

a characteristic development of verificationism: if you find that you cannot verify a theory, or make it certain by induction, you may turn to probability as a kind of 'Ersatz'[47] for certainty, in the hope that induction may yield at least that much.

I have discussed the two problems of demarcation and induction at some length. Yet since I set out to give you in this lecture a kind of report on the work I have done in this field I shall have to add, in the form of an *Appendix*,[48] a few words about some other problems on which I have been working, between 1934 and 1953. I was led to most of these problems by trying to think out the consequences of the solutions to the two problems of demarcation and

induction. But time does not allow me to continue my narrative, and to tell you how my new problems arose out of my old ones. Since I cannot even start a discussion of these further problems now, I shall have to confine myself to giving you a bare list of them, with a few explanatory words here and there. But even a bare list may be useful, I think. It may serve to give an idea of the fertility of the approach. It may help to illustrate what our problems look like; and it may show how many there are, and so convince you that there is no need whatever to worry over the question whether philosophical problems exist, or what philosophy is really about. So this list contains, by implication, an apology for my unwillingness to break with the old tradition of trying to solve problems with the help of rational argument, and thus for my unwillingness to participate wholeheartedly in the developments, trends, and drifts, of contemporary philosophy.

---

47 Inferior substitute (from German "replacement").

48 This Appendix is not reprinted here; it can be found in Popper's book *Conjectures and Refutations* (pages 59 to 65).

THOMAS KUHN

"Objectivity, Value Judgment, and Theory Choice"

Who Was Thomas Kuhn?

Thomas Kuhn's *The Structure of Scientific Revolutions* (first published in 1962) is the single most influential book in modern philosophy of science ... and indeed, in the opinion of some, is perhaps the most influential book published in the second half of the twentieth century.[1] In it, Kuhn presented a view of science

which seemed radically at variance with what most philosophers of science and scientists had previously supposed. Kuhn argued that most science—what he dubbed "normal science"—takes place against a background of unquestioned theoretical assumptions, which he called a *paradigm*. Typical scientists are not, contrary to popular opinion, objective, skeptical, and independent thinkers: rather, according to Kuhn, they are community-minded conservatives who accept what they have been taught by their

---

1 A report on the "most cited works of the twentieth century" issued by the Arts and Humanities Citation Index lists Lenin as the most cited author but *Structure*, by a fair margin, the most frequently mentioned book. Kuhn's book is apparently treated with reverence inside the Washington Beltway: Al Gore claimed it as

his favorite book, and both Bill Clinton and George Bush Sr. have praised its usefulness. *The Structure of Scientific Revolutions* has sold over a million copies and been translated into some twenty languages.

elders and devote their energies to solving puzzles dictated to them by their theories. Indeed, according to Kuhn, scientists habitually attempt to *ignore* research findings that threaten the existing paradigm. Occasionally, however, the pressures from anomalies—especially inexplicable experimental results—generated within that paradigm become such that a crisis occurs within the scientific community and it is necessary for a *paradigm shift* (a phrase first coined by Kuhn) to take place. These episodes in the history of science are what Kuhn called "revolutions." For example, to caricature Kuhn (who did not hold that paradigm shifts are caused entirely by the actions of single individuals), Galileo's (imagined) experiments—dropping wood and lead balls from the Leaning Tower of Pisa—caused the extinction of the Aristotelian theory that bodies fall at a speed proportional to their weight; Lavoisier's discovery of oxygen signaled the death knell for the older "phlogiston" paradigm of chemistry; Darwin's theory of natural selection overthrew ideas of a world governed by design; and Einstein's theory of relativity completely replaced Newtonian physics. Science, in other words, is "a series of peaceful interludes punctuated by intellectually violent revolutions." The old guard who worked within the previous paradigm then either undergo conversion to the new one, or simply die out and are replaced by younger scientists working in the new paradigm.

The most controversial and stimulating aspect of Kuhn's work has proved to be his claim that there can be no strictly rational reason to choose one new paradigm over another: that is, the adoption of scientific theories, according to Kuhn, is never and can never be a purely rational decision. According to the more extreme of Kuhn's adherents (though not—at least later in his career—Kuhn himself), this means that the logic and philosophy of science is to be replaced by the history and sociology of science: that is, science is best understood not as an ideally rational or logical enterprise, but as a sociological phenomenon. Furthermore, Kuhn has apparently held that successive scientific paradigms are *incommensurable*: scientists before and after a theoretical revolution essentially speak a different language and think in completely different ways, and so—since no one can think within two different paradigms at once—it is not possible for anyone to *compare* the two paradigms and see which is better. If this is the case, it seems to follow that we have no good reason to believe that the history of science is a story of progress or of the cumulative acquisition of scientific knowledge; the scientific revolutions which supplant one paradigm with another do not take us any closer to the truth about the way the world is, they simply replace one set of theoretical puzzles with a new incompatible set. The essay reprinted here, "Objectivity, Value Judgment, and Theory Choice," summarizes some of Kuhn's mature views on these topics.

Thomas Samuel Kuhn was born in Cincinnati, Ohio, in 1922, the son of an industrial engineer. He was educated in New York at a series of progressive, left-leaning schools—where, though bright, Kuhn by his own account felt anxious, isolated, and neurotic (feelings which apparently remained with him to some degree for the rest of his life)—and then in 1940 went to Harvard to take a degree in physics. His undergraduate degree completed in 1943, he joined the US army radar program as a physicist. Kuhn was assigned to work on radar profiles, first in the States and England, but was then sent to Europe in the wake of the Allied invasion—dressed in uniform so he would not be shot as a spy if captured behind enemy lines—to inspect captured German radar installations. He was present (by accident) when the victorious French general Charles de Gaulle entered Paris, and saw the German city of Hamburg after it had been flattened by Allied bombs.

After the war, Kuhn drifted into graduate work and received a PhD in physics from Harvard University in 1949. He remained at Harvard, teaching in the General Education in Science program which was aimed at giving students in the humanities and social sciences a background in natural science. However, in 1955 Kuhn was denied tenure at Harvard—on the grounds that he was insufficiently specialized in any particular academic discipline, either physics or history or philosophy—and he moved to the University of California at Berkeley, where in 1961 he became a full professor of the history of science. In 1964 Kuhn transferred to Princeton and then in 1979, after a divorce, moved again and settled at the Massachusetts Institute of Technology, where he remarried and taught until his retirement in 1991. He died in 1996.

What Is the Structure of This Reading?

Kuhn begins this paper by summarizing passages in *The Structure of Scientific Revolutions* about rational theory choice and progress in science, and claiming that his position on these matters has been seriously misunderstood by many of the book's critics. He then lays out what are sometimes known as his "five ways": five criteria, which are shared by scientists, for rational theory choice. However, he argues these five criteria are insufficient to determine the choice of one theory over another—scientists can only adopt or refuse to adopt a theory on the basis of partly *subjective* criteria. Kuhn then argues that this claim—that there is no single, shared algorithm available for theory choice in science—is a philosophically substantial finding, partly because, on Kuhn's view, there is no distinction to be made between the "contexts of discovery and justification." Furthermore, Kuhn insists, science could not properly function if there were some shared set of criteria that determined what any rational scientist must believe; instead, we should think of the five ways as *values* which influence theory choice rather than *rules* which determine it. These five shared values are more or less permanent in the history of science,

Kuhn goes on to claim, but they have no rational justification from outside of the practice of science, and furthermore they evolve and change with those practices. Finally, Kuhn addresses the sense in which the idiosyncratic factors that supplement the five ways in theory choice are 'subjective,' and reaffirms and clarifies his claim that paradigms are "incommensurable": that is, roughly, that two scientists who adopt different theories face communication barriers at least as extreme as those faced by two people who speak different languages.

Some Useful Background Information

1. A notion central to Kuhn's critique of the rationality of science is that of *incommensurability*. Two things are 'incommensurable' if they cannot be compared—if one cannot be said to be better, or truer, or more preferable than the other. For example, the number seven and the taste of apples are incommensurable: there is no scale of values on which they can both be compared. In the philosophy of science, two theories (or other linguistic systems) are said to be incommensurable if the claims of one cannot be stated in the language of the other. From this it follows also that there can be no neutral third language in which the claims of both theories can be stated and compared[2]— that is, there can be no neutral standpoint from which we can assess the theories and say that one is better than the other. And from *this*, it seems to be an inescapable conclusion that we cannot give any content to the notion that science is progressing—that scientific theories are becoming closer approximations of the truth,

---

2   Suppose there were some theoretical language—call it theory C—which is capable of stating both the claims of theory A and those of theory B; then it would follow that A and B are not incommensurable, since the statements of A could be translated into C and those C-statements in turn could be translated into the language of B, and hence the claims of A could be stated in the terms of B (and vice versa).

for example—since we cannot any longer say that a later theory is better than an earlier one.

There are various reasons why one might think that scientific theories are incommensurable. One of the most influential arguments derives from a certain theory about how theoretical terms get their *meaning*. On this view (roughly), scientific terms like "electron" or "mass" do not, as ordinary words like "cow" and "yellow" may, get their meaning from being attached as labels to observable things in the world. (After all, we cannot *see* electrons, so how can we point to them in order to label them?) Instead, terms applied to theoretical entities get their meaning entirely from their *role in the theory*: for example, the meaning of the word "mass" is, roughly, *whatever it is* that performs the function that mass does in the mathematical equations which make up the theory. If all of this is right, then it seems to follow that *if you change the theory you also change the meanings of all the theoretical terms of that theory*. For example, mass plays a different role in Newton's theory than it does in relativity theory (e.g., mass is independent of velocity in classical mechanics but for Einstein mass increases as velocity does), and hence the word "mass" must mean something different in the two theories—that is, when Einstein talks about "mass" he is using a different language than when Newton talks about it, even though the words they use happen to look and sound the same.

2. Another notion of which Kuhn made influential use and which is often appealed to in arguments for incommensurability is the idea that all observation is "theory-laden." That is, it can be argued—and in fact is generally believed by philosophers of science—that it is impossible for a scientist to make any experimental observations of the world without relying upon certain theoretical assumptions, and furthermore that these observations *are changed* by those assumptions. For example, a scientist who uses equipment—such as a microscope, radio tele-scope, or fMRI machine—to make observations must rely upon many theoretical claims about the operation of that equipment, and what she believes she is seeing will depend upon how she believes the equipment operates. More fundamentally, it is thought that even unaided observations depend for their content upon the way a scientist categorizes or conceptualizes experience. For example, seventeenth-century chemists reported having *seen* phlogiston (a mythical substance) being emitted by burning objects as flames; a modern day chemist sees much the same phenomenon and observes a violent oxidation reaction. A medieval scientist observing the dawn would have *seen* a moving sun and a static earth; today's observer is aware that she is seeing the rotation of the earth carrying the sun into view. Finally, for many scientists and engineers trained in the Aristotelian science of the Middle Ages, projectiles were apparently *observed* to behave just as they were theoretically expected to—they rose into the air in a straight line until the force of their flight was overcome by the force of their weight, and then fell straight down to the ground; nowadays, *after* Newton has changed our theoretical framework, we observe that projectiles really have a parabolic trajectory.

One of the implications of this—or at least of the most radical versions of this thesis, sometimes called the collapse of the observation-theory distinction—is, once again, a kind of incommensurability. If all observation is infected by theory, the argument goes, then there can be no neutral body of data that can be used to evaluate competing theories. The observations recorded by scientists trained in theory *A* will support that theory because they see what they expect to see; meanwhile the experiments conducted by the partisans of theory *B* will support *their* theory; since all observations are theory-laden, there are no neutral experimental results available with respect to the two theories, and so no data that can legitimately be used to falsify one or confirm the other.

Suggestions for Critical Reflection

1. Kuhn quotes himself, from the *Structure of Scientific Revolutions,* as saying: "What better criterion [for which theory it is rational to adopt] could there be than the decision of the scientific group?" Do you agree with this claim? What better criterion *could* there be? If Kuhn is right about this, could the philosophy of science be replaced by the sociology of science (i.e., by the study of how groups of scientists come to consensus)?

2. What do you think is the philosophical value of studying the history of science? How much does the *actual* behavior of scientists show us about the ideal "scientific method"? In particular, do you think Kuhn establishes that the history of science reveals that there just *is* no completely rational method available to scientists?

3. Kuhn argues that not only do scientists possess no shared set of criteria for theory choice, but that science could not *survive* if there were a rational "scientific method" for confirming or discarding theories. Do you think he is right about this?

4. What do you think Kuhn made of the theories of science represented in this chapter by readings from Hempel and Popper? In what ways do you think his own account differs from theirs?

5. Both Hempel and, especially, Popper make a firm distinction between what Kuhn calls the context of discovery and the context of justification. How successful is Kuhn in arguing that there is no such distinction? What would be the implications if this distinction were collapsed?

6. Many critics have asserted that Kuhn's account of theory choice and paradigm shifts leaves no room for the notion that science *progresses* towards a closer and closer approximation to the *truth* about reality. On the basis of Kuhn's claims in this article, do you think that this is a fair criticism?

7. One unfriendly critic of Kuhn, James Franklin, has said the following: "The basic content of Kuhn's book [*The Structure of Scientific Revolutions]* can be inferred simply by asking: what would the humanities crowd *want* said about science? Once the question is asked, the answer is obvious. Kuhn's thesis is that scientific theories are no better than ones in the humanities.... [S]cience is all theoretical talk and negotiation, which never really establishes anything" (from *The New Criterion,* June 2000). Given what Kuhn says in this article, to what degree do you think that Franklin gets Kuhn right?

Suggestions for Further Reading

The first place to pursue Kuhn's ideas is, of course, his *The Structure of Scientific Revolutions* (University of Chicago Press, 1996). His most important papers are collected in two volumes: *The Essential Tension* (University of Chicago Press, 1977) and *The Road Since Structure: Philosophical Essays, 1970–1993* (University of Chicago Press, 2000), the second of which includes a lengthy autobiographical interview. Kuhn also published two books on case studies from the history of science: *The Copernican Revolution* (Harvard University Press, 1985) and *Black-Body Theory and the Quantum Discontinuity 1894–1912* (University of Chicago Press, 1987).

Currently the most authoritative book on Kuhn's philosophy is probably Paul Hoyningen-Huene's *Reconstructing Scientific Revolutions: Thomas S. Kuhn's Philosophy of Science* (University of Chicago Press, 1993). *Thomas Kuhn* by Alexander Bird (Princeton University Press, 2001) is also helpful. A dense, stimulating, rambling, and quite controversial attack on Kuhn (both his ideas and his person) is Steve Fuller's *Thomas Kuhn: A Philosophical History for Our Times* (University of Chicago Press, 2000). *Criticism and the Growth of Knowledge,* edited by Imre Lakatos and Alan Musgrave (Cambridge University Press, 1970), is an influential collection of articles on *The Structure of Scientific Revolutions,* with a reply from Kuhn, and *World Changes: Thomas Kuhn and the Nature of Science,* edited by Paul Horwich (MIT Press, 1993), is a more recent version along much the same lines. A collection called *Paradigms and Revolutions,* edited by Gary Gutting (University of Notre Dame Press, 1979), seeks to extend Kuhn's ideas to the humanities and social sciences.

"Objectivity, Value Judgment, and Theory Choice"[3]

In the penultimate chapter of a controversial book fifteen years ago, I considered the ways scientists are brought to abandon one time-honored theory or paradigm in favor of another. Such decision problems, I wrote, "cannot be resolved by proof." To discuss their mechanism is, therefore, to talk "about techniques of persuasion, or about argument and counterargument in a situation in which there can be no proof." Under these circumstances, I continued, "lifelong resistance [to a new theory] ... is not a violation of scientific standards.... Though the historian can always find men—Priestley, for instance[4]—who were unreasonable to resist for as long as they did, he will not find a point at which resistance becomes illogical or unscientific." Statements of that sort[5] obviously raise the question of why, in the absence of binding criteria for scientific choice, both the number of solved scientific problems and the precision of individual problem solutions should increase so markedly with the passage of time. Confronting that issue, I sketched in my closing chapter a number of characteristics that scientists share by virtue of the training which licenses their membership in one or another community of specialists. In the absence of criteria able to dictate the choice of each individual, I argued, we do well to trust the collective judgment of scientists trained in this way. "What better criterion could there be," I asked rhetorically, "than the decision of the scientific group?"[6]

A number of philosophers have greeted remarks like these in a way that continues to surprise me. My views, it is said, make of theory choice "a matter for mob psychology."[7] Kuhn believes, I am told, that "the decision of a scientific group to adopt a new paradigm cannot be based on good reasons of any kind, factual or otherwise."[8] The debates surrounding such choices must, my critics claim, be for me "mere persuasive displays without deliberative substance."[9] Reports of this sort manifest total misunderstanding, and I have occasionally said as much in papers directed primarily to other ends. But those passing protestations have had negligible effect, and the misunderstandings continue to be important. I conclude that it is past time for me to describe, at greater length and with greater precision, what has been on my mind when I have uttered statements like the ones with which I just began. If I have been reluctant to do so in the past, that is largely because I have preferred to devote attention to areas in which my views diverge more sharply from those currently received than they do with respect to theory choice.

What, I ask to begin with, are the characteristics of a good scientific theory? Among a number of quite usual answers I select five, not because they are exhaustive, but because they are individually important

---

3   This paper was originally given as the Machette Lecture delivered at Furman University in South Carolina in 1973. It was first published in *The Essential Tension: Selected Studies in Scientific Tradition and Change*, by Thomas Kuhn, Chicago: University of Chicago Press, 1977, pp. 320–339. Copyright © University of Chicago 1977.

4   Joseph Priestley (1733–1804) was an English scientist and theologian who discovered oxygen in 1774, though—in accordance with the terms of the then-current theory—he thought of it as "dephlogisticated air."

5   [Author's note] *The Structure of Scientific Revolutions*, 2d ed. (Chicago, 1970), pp. 148, 151–52, 159. All the passages from which these fragments are taken appeared in the same form in the first edition, published in 1962.

6   [Author's note] Ibid., p. 170.

7   [Author's note] Imre Lakatos, "Falsification and the Methodology of Scientific Research Programmes," in I. Lakatos and A. Musgrave, eds., *Criticism and the Growth of Knowledge* (Cambridge, 1970), pp. 91–195. The quoted phrase, which appears on p. 178, is italicized in the original.

8   [Author's note] Dudley Shapere, "Meaning and Scientific Change," in R.G. Colodny, ed., *Mind and Cosmos: Essays in Contemporary Science and Philosophy*, University of Pittsburgh Series in the Philosophy of Science, vol. 3 (Pittsburgh 1966), pp. 41–85. The quotation will be found on p. 67.

9   [Author's note] Israel Scheffler, *Science and Subjectivity* (Indianapolis, 1967), p. 81.

and collectively sufficiently varied to indicate what is at stake. First, a theory should be accurate: within its domain, that is, consequences deducible from a theory should be in demonstrated agreement with the results of existing experiments and observations. Second, a theory should be consistent, not only internally or with itself, but also with other currently accepted theories applicable to related aspects of nature. Third, it should have broad scope: in particular, a theory's consequences should extend far beyond the particular observations, laws, or subtheories it was initially designed to explain. Fourth, and closely related; it should be simple, bringing order to phenomena that in its absence would be individually isolated and, as a set, confused. Fifth—a somewhat less standard item, but one of special importance to actual scientific decisions—a theory should be fruitful of new research findings: it should, that is, disclose new phenomena or unnoted relationships among those already known.[10] These five characteristics—accuracy, consistency, scope, simplicity, and fruitfulness—are all standard criteria for evaluating the adequacy of a theory. If they had not been, I would have devoted far more space to them in my book, for I agree entirely with the traditional view that they play a vital role when scientists must choose between an established theory and an upstart competitor. Together with others of much the same sort, they provide *the* shared basis for theory choice.

Nevertheless, two sorts of difficulties are regularly encountered by the men who must use these criteria in choosing, say, between Ptolemy's astronomical theory and Copernicus's,[11] between the oxygen and phlogiston theories of combustion,[12] or between Newtonian mechanics and the quantum theory.[13] Individually the criteria are imprecise: individuals may legitimately differ about their application to concrete cases. In addition, when deployed together, they repeatedly prove to conflict with one another; accuracy may, for example, dictate the choice of one theory, scope the choice of its competitor. Since these difficulties, especially the first, are also relatively familiar, I shall devote little time to their elaboration. Though my argument does demand that I illustrate them briefly, my views will begin to depart from those long current only after I have done so.

Begin with accuracy, which for present purposes I take to include not only quantitative agreement but qualitative as well. Ultimately it proves the most nearly decisive of all the criteria, partly because it is less equivocal than the others but especially because predictive and explanatory powers, which depend on it, are characteristics that scientists are particularly unwilling to give up. Unfortunately, however, theories cannot always be discriminated in terms of accuracy. Copernicus's system, for example, was not more accurate than Ptolemy's until drastically revised by Kepler[14] more than sixty years after Copernicus's

10   [Author's note] The last criterion, fruitfulness, deserves more emphasis than it has yet received. A scientist choosing between two theories ordinarily knows that his decision will have a bearing on his subsequent research career. Of course he is especially attracted by a theory that promises the concrete successes for which scientists are ordinarily rewarded.

11   Ptolemy was a second-century CE astronomer from Alexandria, in Egypt, who based his astronomical theory on the belief that all heavenly bodies revolve around a stationary earth. Nicholas Copernicus (1473–1543) was a Polish astronomer who advanced the competing theory that the earth and other planets revolve around the sun.

12   The former theory explains combustion as the violent chemical reaction of a substance with oxygen in the air around it; by contrast, the latter theory (which was current until the eighteenth century) postulated a volatile substance called phlogiston which is contained in all flammable materials and which is released as flame during combustion.

13   According to Newtonian theory, light (and other forms of what we now think of as electromagnetic energy) consisted in the mechanical motions of the particles in an all-enveloping, massless substance called "ether." Quantum theory is the modern scientific account of matter and energy; it is probabilistic rather than mechanical, and abandons the notion of a "medium" through which energy waves propagate.

14   Johannes Kepler (1571–1630), a German astronomer, is often considered the "father of modern astronomy" for his formulation of three fundamental laws of planetary motion.

death. If Kepler or someone else had not found other reasons to choose heliocentric astronomy, those improvements in accuracy would never have been made, and Copernicus's work might have been forgotten. More typically, of course, accuracy does permit discriminations, but not the sort that lead regularly to unequivocal choice. The oxygen theory, for example, was universally acknowledged to account for observed weight relations in chemical reactions, something the phlogiston theory had previously scarcely attempted to do. But the phlogiston theory, unlike its rival, could account for the metals' being much more alike than the ores from which they were formed. One theory thus matched experience better in one area, the other in another. To choose between them on the basis of accuracy, a scientist would need to decide the area in which accuracy was more significant. About that matter chemists could and did differ without violating any of the criteria outlined above, or any others yet to be suggested.

However important it may be, therefore, accuracy by itself is seldom or never a sufficient criterion for theory choice. Other criteria must function as well, but they do not eliminate problems. To illustrate I select just two—consistency and simplicity—asking how they functioned in the choice between the heliocentric and geocentric[15] systems. As astronomical theories both Ptolemy's and Copernicus's were internally consistent, but their relation to related theories in other fields was very different. The stationary central earth was an essential ingredient of received physical theory, a tight-knit body of doctrine which explained, among other things, how stones fall, how water pumps function, and why the clouds move slowly across the skies. Heliocentric astronomy, which required the earth's motion, was inconsistent with the existing scientific explanation of these and other terrestrial phenomena. The consistency criterion by itself, therefore, spoke unequivocally for geocentric tradition.

Simplicity, however, favored Copernicus, but only when evaluated in a quite special way. If, on the one hand, the two systems were compared in terms of the actual computational labor required to predict the position of a planet at a particular time, then they proved substantially equivalent. Such computations were what astronomers did, and Copernicus's system offered them no labor-saving techniques; in that sense it was not simpler than Ptolemy's. If, on the other hand, one asked about the amount of mathematical apparatus required to explain, not the detailed quantitative motions of the planets, but merely their gross qualitative features—limited elongation, retrograde motion, and the like—then, as every schoolchild knows, Copernicus required only one circle per planet, Ptolemy two.[16] In that sense the Copernican theory was the simpler, a fact vitally important to the choices made by both Kepler and Galileo and thus essential to the ultimate triumph of Copernicanism. But that sense of simplicity was not the only one available, nor even the one most natural to professional astronomers, men whose task was the actual computation of planetary position.

Because time is short and I have multiplied examples elsewhere, I shall here simply assert that these difficulties in applying standard criteria of choice are typical and that they arise no less forcefully in twentieth-century situations than in the earlier and better-known examples I have just sketched. When scientists must choose between competing theories, two men fully committed to the same list of criteria for choice may nevertheless reach different conclusions. Perhaps they interpret simplicity differently or have different convictions about the range of fields within which the consistency criterion must be met. Or perhaps they agree about these matters but differ about the relative weights to be accorded to these or to other criteria when several are deployed together. With divergences of this sort, no set of choice criteria yet proposed is of any use. One can explain, as the historian characteristically does, why particular men made particular choices at particular times. But for

---

15   "Heliocentric" means centered on the sun; "geocentric" means centered on the earth.

16   In the Ptolemaic system, celestial orbits are described by "epicycles": that is, the orbits of the sun and planets form small circles, the centers of which move around the circumference of a larger circle centered on the earth. For the Copernican system, of course, each planet's orbit is described by a single (elliptical) circle with the sun at its center.

that purpose one must go beyond the list of shared criteria to characteristics of the individuals who make the choice. One must, that is, deal with characteristics which vary from one scientist to another without thereby in the least jeopardizing their adherence to the canons that make science scientific. Though such canons do exist and should be discoverable (doubtless the criteria of choice with which I began are among them), they are not by themselves sufficient to determine the decisions of individual scientists. For that purpose the shared canons must be fleshed out in ways that differ from one individual to another.

Some of the differences I have in mind result from the individual's previous experience as a scientist. In what part of the field was he at work when confronted by the need to choose? How long had he worked there; how successful had he been; and how much of his work depended on concepts and techniques challenged by the new theory? Other factors relevant to choice lie outside the sciences. Kepler's early election of Copernicanism was due in part to his immersion in the Neoplatonic and Hermetic[17] movements of his day; German Romanticism[18] predisposed those it affected toward both recognition and acceptance of energy conservation; nineteenth-century British social thought had a similar influence on the availability

and acceptability of Darwin's concept of the struggle for existence. Still other significant differences are functions of personality. Some scientists place more premium than others on originality and are correspondingly more willing to take risks; some scientists prefer comprehensive, unified theories to precise and detailed problem solutions of apparently narrower scope. Differentiating factors like these are described by my critics as subjective and are contrasted with the shared or objective criteria from which I began. Though I shall later question that use of terms, let me for the moment accept it. My point is, then, that every individual choice between competing theories depends on a mixture of objective and subjective factors, or of shared and individual criteria. Since the latter have not ordinarily figured in the philosophy of science, my emphasis upon them has made my belief in the former hard for my critics to see.

What I have said so far is primarily simply descriptive of what goes on in the sciences at times of theory choice. As description, furthermore, it has not been challenged by my critics, who reject instead my claim that these facts of scientific life have philosophic import. Taking up that issue, I shall begin to isolate some, though I think not vast, differences of opinion. Let me begin by asking how philosophers of science can for so long have neglected the subjective elements which, they freely grant, enter regularly into the actual theory choices made by individual scientists? Why have these elements seemed to them an index only of human weakness, not at all of the nature of scientific knowledge?

One answer to that question is, of course, that few philosophers, if any, have claimed to possess either a complete or an entirely well-articulated list of criteria. For some time, therefore, they could reasonably expect that further research would eliminate residual imperfections and produce an algorithm able to dictate rational, unanimous choice. Pending that achievement, scientists would have no alternative but to supply subjectively what the best current list of objective criteria still lacked. That some of them might still do so even with a perfected list at hand would then be an index only of the inevitable imperfection of human nature.

---

17   Neoplatonism is a school of thought—originating in the third century CE, and influential in medieval and Renaissance philosophy—which fused Plato's philosophy with religious doctrines, and which sees the universe as an emanation from an omnipresent, transcendent, unchanging One. Hermeticism, which was also popular during the Renaissance, involves allegiance to the doctrines found in a collection of occult writings on magical and religious topics which were (wrongly) thought to be the texts of an ancient Egyptian priesthood.

18   Romanticism was a late eighteenth-century movement which reacted against the rationalism of the Enlightenment by embracing spontaneity, imagination, emotion, and inspiration. Among its themes was the belief that reality is ultimately spiritual, and that knowledge of nature cannot be achieved by rational and analytic means but only through a kind of intuitive absorption into the spiritual process of nature.

That sort of answer may still prove to be correct, but I think no philosopher still expects that it will. The search for algorithmic decision procedures has continued for some time and produced both powerful and illuminating results. But those results all presuppose that individual criteria of choice can be unambiguously stated and also that, if more than one proves relevant, an appropriate weight function is at hand for their joint application. Unfortunately, where the choice at issue is between scientific theories, little progress has been made toward the first of these desiderata[19] and none toward the second. Most philosophers of science would therefore, I think, now regard the sort of algorithm which has traditionally been sought as a not quite attainable ideal. I entirely agree and shall henceforth take that much for granted.

Even an ideal, however, if it is to remain credible, requires some demonstrated relevance to the situations in which it is supposed to apply. Claiming that such demonstration requires no recourse to subjective factors, my critics seem to appeal, implicitly or explicitly, to the well-known distinction between the contexts of discovery and of justification.[20] They concede, that is, that the subjective factors I invoke play a significant role in the discovery or invention of new theories, but they also insist that that inevitably intuitive process lies outside of the bounds of philosophy of science and is irrelevant to the question of scientific objectivity. Objectivity enters science, they continue, through the processes by which theories are tested, justified, or judged. Those processes do not, or at least need not, involve subjective factors at all. They can be governed by a set of (objective) criteria shared by the entire group competent to judge.

I have already argued that that position does not fit observations of scientific life and shall now assume that that much has been conceded. What is now at issue is a different point: whether or not this invocation of the distinction between contexts of discovery and of justification provides even a plausible and useful idealization. I think it does not and can best make my

point by suggesting first a likely source of its apparent cogency. I suspect that my critics have been misled by science pedagogy or what I have elsewhere called textbook science. In science teaching, theories are presented together with exemplary applications, and those applications may be viewed as evidence. But that is not their primary pedagogic function (science students are distressingly willing to receive the word from professors and texts). Doubtless *some* of them were *part* of the evidence at the time actual decisions were being made, but they represent only a fraction of the considerations relevant to the decision process. The context of pedagogy differs almost as much from the context of justification as it does from that of discovery.

Full documentation of that point would require longer argument than is appropriate here, but two aspects of the way in which philosophers ordinarily demonstrate the relevance of choice criteria are worth noting. Like the science textbooks on which they are often modelled, books and articles on the philosophy of science refer again and again to the famous crucial experiments: Foucault's pendulum,[21] which demonstrates the motion of the earth; Cavendish's demonstration of gravitational attraction;[22] or

---

19 Things lacking but needed or desired.

20 [Author's note] The least equivocal example of this position is probably the one developed in Scheffler, *Science and Subjectivity*, chap. 4.

21 This experiment was first performed in 1851 by the French physicist Jean Bernard Léon Foucault (1819–1868) in order to show that the earth spins around its axis. The oscillations of a weight swinging from a very long wire can be observed to slowly rotate (clockwise in the Northern hemisphere and anticlockwise in the Southern); however the pendulum itself must be moving in a straight line, since there is no outside force interrupting its movement; therefore, since the path of the pendulum seems to rotate with respect to the ground and yet we know that the pendulum is not rotating, it must be the *ground* which is spinning.

22 Henry Cavendish (1731–1810) used a sensitive torsion balance to measure the value of the gravitational constant G and this allowed him to estimate the mass of the Earth for the first time. Cavendish's experimental apparatus involved a light, rigid six-foot long rod, suspended from a wire, and having two small metal spheres attached to the ends of the rod. When the rod is twisted, the torsion of the wire exerts a force which is proportional to the angle of rotation of the rod, and

Fizeau's measurement of the relative speed of sound in water and air.[23] These experiments are paradigms of good reason for scientific choice; they illustrate the most effective of all the sorts of argument which could be available to a scientist uncertain which of two theories to follow; they are vehicles for the transmission of criteria of choice. But they also have another characteristic in common. By the time they were performed no scientist still needed to be convinced of the validity of the theory their outcome is now used to demonstrate. Those decisions had long since been made on the basis of significantly more equivocal evidence. The exemplary crucial experiments to which philosophers again and again refer would have been historically relevant to theory choice only if they had yielded unexpected results. Their use as illustrations provides needed economy to science pedagogy, but they scarcely illuminate the character of the choices that scientists are called upon to make.

Standard philosophical illustrations of scientific choice have another troublesome characteristic. The only arguments discussed are, as I have previously indicated, the ones favorable to the theory that, in fact, ultimately triumphed. Oxygen, we read, could explain weight relations, phlogiston could not; but nothing is said about the phlogiston theory's power or about the oxygen theory's limitations. Comparisons of Ptolemy's theory with Copernicus's proceed in the same way. Perhaps these examples should not

be given since they contrast a developed theory with one still in its infancy. But philosophers regularly use them nonetheless. If the only result of their doing so were to simplify the decision situation, one could not object. Even historians do not claim to deal with the full factual complexity of the situations they describe. But these simplifications emasculate by making choice totally unproblematic. They eliminate, that is, one essential element of the decision situation that scientists must resolve if their field is to move ahead. In those situations there are always at least some good reasons for each possible choice. Considerations relevant to the context of discovery are then relevant to justification as well; scientists who share the concerns and sensibilities of the individual who discovers a new theory are ipso facto[24] likely to appear disproportionately frequently among that theory's first supporters. That is why it has been difficult to construct algorithms for theory choice, and also why such difficulties have seemed so thoroughly worth resolving. Choices that present problems are the ones philosophers of science need to understand. Philosophically interesting decision procedures must function where, in their absence, the decision might still be in doubt.

That much I have said before, if only briefly. Recently, however, I have recognized another, subtler source for the apparent plausibility of my critics' position. To present it, I shall briefly describe a hypothetical dialogue with one of them. Both of us agree that each scientist chooses between competing theories by deploying some Bayesian algorithm[25] which permits him to compute a value for $p(T,E)$, i.e., for the probability of a theory T on the evidence

---

Cavendish carefully calibrated his instrument to determine the relationship between the angle of rotation and the amount of torsional force. He then brought two large lead spheres near the smaller spheres attached to the rod: since all masses attract, the large spheres exerted a gravitational force upon the smaller spheres and twisted the rod a measurable amount. Once the torsional force balanced the gravitational force, the rod and spheres came to rest and Cavendish was able to determine the gravitational force of attraction between the masses.

23 Armand-Hippolyte Fizeau (1819–1896) is best known for experimentally determining the speed of light, and showing that different media (such as still water, moving water, and air) can affect the speed of propagation of light and sound.

24 *Ipso facto* means "by that very fact."

25 Thomas Bayes (1702–1761) was an English clergyman who developed an influential theorem for calculating the probability of a hypothesis given a certain body of evidence. According to this theorem, in its simplest form, the probability of the hypothesis is the product of a) its prior probability (i.e., its probability before the evidence) and b) the probability of the evidence being as it is given the hypothesis, divided by the prior probability of that evidence. That is, $p(T,E) = p(T) \times (p(E,T)/p(E))$.

E available both to him and to the other members of his group at a particular period of time. "Evidence," furthermore, we both interpret broadly to include such considerations as simplicity and fruitfulness. My critic asserts, however, that there is only one such value of p, that corresponding to objective choice, and he believes that all rational members of the group must arrive at it. I assert, on the other hand, for reasons previously given, that the factors he calls objective are insufficient to determine in full any algorithm at all. For the sake of the discussion I have conceded that each individual has an algorithm and that all their algorithms have much in common. Nevertheless, I continue to hold that the algorithms of individuals are all ultimately different by virtue of the subjective considerations with which each must complete the objective criteria before any computations can be done. If my hypothetical critic is liberal, he may now grant that these subjective differences do play a role in determining the hypothetical algorithm on which each individual relies during the early stages of the competition between rival theories. But he is also likely to claim that, as evidence increases with the passage of time, the algorithms of different individuals converge to the algorithm of objective choice with which his presentation began. For him the increasing unanimity of individual choices is evidence for their increasing objectivity and thus for the elimination of subjective elements from the decision process.

So much for the dialogue, which I have, of course, contrived to disclose the non sequitur[26] underlying an apparently plausible position. What converges as the evidence changes over time need only be the values of p that individuals compute from their individual algorithms. Conceivably those algorithms themselves also become more alike with time, but the ultimate unanimity of theory choice provides no evidence whatsoever that they do so. If subjective factors are required to account for the decisions that initially divide the profession, they may still be present later when the profession agrees. Though I shall not here argue the point, consideration of the occasions on which a scientific community divides suggests that they actually do so.

My argument has so far been directed to two points. It first provided evidence that the choices scientists make between competing theories depend not only on shared criteria—those my critics call objective—but also on idiosyncratic factors dependent on individual biography and personality. The latter are, in my critics' vocabulary, subjective, and the second part of my argument has attempted to bar some likely ways of denying their philosophic import. Let me now shift to a more positive approach, returning briefly to the list of shared criteria—accuracy, simplicity, and the like—with which I began. The considerable effectiveness of such criteria does not, I now wish to suggest, depend on their being sufficiently articulated to dictate the choice of each individual who subscribes to them. Indeed, if they were articulated to that extent, a behavior mechanism fundamental to scientific advance would cease to function. What the tradition sees as eliminable imperfections in its rules of choice I take to be in part responses to the essential nature of science.

As so often, I begin with the obvious. Criteria that influence decisions without specifying what those decisions must be are familiar in many aspects of human life. Ordinarily, however, they are called not criteria or rules, but maxims, norms, or values. Consider maxims first. The individual who invokes them when choice is urgent usually finds them frustratingly vague and often also in conflict one with another. Contrast "He who hesitates is lost" with "Look before you leap," or compare "Many hands make light work" with "Too many cooks spoil the broth." Individually maxims dictate different choices, collectively none at all. Yet no one suggests that supplying children with contradictory tags like these is irrelevant to their education. Opposing maxims alter the nature of the decision to be made, highlight the essential issues it presents, and point to those remaining aspects of the decision for which each individual must take responsibility himself. Once invoked, maxims like these alter the nature of the decision process and can thus change its outcome.

Values and norms provide even clearer examples of effective guidance in the presence of conflict and equivocation. Improving the quality of life is

---

26 A *non sequitur* is something that does not follow, e.g., a conclusion that does not logically follow from the premises.

a value, and a car in every garage once followed from it as a norm. But quality of life has other aspects, and the old norm has become problematic. Or again, freedom of speech is a value, but so is preservation of life and property. In application, the two often conflict, so that judicial soul-searching, which still continues, has been required to prohibit such behavior as inciting to riot or shouting fire in a crowded theater. Difficulties like these are an appropriate source for frustration, but they rarely result in charges that values have no function or in calls for their abandonment. That response is barred to most of us by an acute consciousness that there are societies with other values and that these value differences result in other ways of life, other decisions about what may and what may not be done.

I am suggesting, of course, that the criteria of choice with which I began function not as rules, which determine choice, but as values, which influence it. Two men deeply committed to the same values may nevertheless, in particular situations, make different choices as, in fact, they do. But that difference in outcome ought not to suggest that the values scientists share are less than critically important either to their decisions or to the development of the enterprise in which they participate. Values like accuracy, consistency, and scope may prove ambiguous in application, both individually and collectively; they may, that is, be an insufficient basis for a *shared* algorithm of choice. But they do specify a great deal: what each scientist must consider in reaching a decision, what he may and may not consider relevant, and what he can legitimately be required to report as the basis for the choice he has made. Change the list, for example by adding social utility as a criterion, and some particular choices will be different, more like those one expects from an engineer. Subtract accuracy of fit to nature from the list, and the enterprise that results may not resemble science at all, but perhaps philosophy instead. Different creative disciplines are characterized, among other things, by different sets of shared values. If philosophy and engineering lie too close to the sciences, think of literature or the plastic arts. Milton's failure to set *Paradise Lost* in a Copernican universe does not indicate that he agreed with Ptolemy but that he had things other than science to do.

Recognizing that criteria of choice can function as values when incomplete as rules has, I think, a number of striking advantages. First, as I have already argued at length, it accounts in detail for aspects of scientific behavior which the tradition has seen as anomalous or even irrational. More important, it allows the standard criteria to function fully in the earliest stages of theory choice, the period when they are most needed but when, on the traditional view, they function badly or not at all. Copernicus was responding to them during the years required to convert heliocentric astronomy from a global conceptual scheme to mathematical machinery for predicting planetary position. Such predictions were what astronomers valued; in their absence, Copernicus would scarcely have been heard, something which had happened to the idea of a moving earth before. That his own version convinced very few is less important than his acknowledgment of the basis on which judgments would have to be reached if heliocentricism were to survive. Though idiosyncrasy must be invoked to explain why Kepler and Galileo were early converts to Copernicus's system, the gaps filled by their efforts to perfect it were specified by shared values alone.

That point has a corollary which may be more important still. Most newly suggested theories do not survive. Usually the difficulties that evoked them are accounted for by more traditional means. Even when this does not occur, much work, both theoretical and experimental, is ordinarily required before the new theory can display sufficient accuracy and scope to generate widespread conviction. In short, before the group accepts it, a new theory has been tested over time by the research of a number of men, some working within it, others within its traditional rival. Such a mode of development, however, *requires* a decision process which permits rational men to disagree, and such disagreement would be barred by the shared algorithm which philosophers have generally sought. If it were at hand, all conforming scientists would make the same decision at the same time. With standards for acceptance set too low, they would move from one attractive global viewpoint to another, never giving traditional theory an opportunity to supply equivalent attractions. With standards set higher, no one satisfying the criterion of rationality would be inclined to try out the new theory, to articulate it in ways which showed its fruitfulness or displayed its accuracy and scope. I doubt that science would survive the change. What from one viewpoint may seem the looseness and imperfection of choice criteria conceived as rules may, when the same criteria are seen as values, appear an indispensable means of spreading the risk which the introduction or support of novelty always entails.

Even those who have followed me this far will want to know how a value-based enterprise of the sort I have described can develop as a science does, repeatedly producing powerful new techniques for prediction and control. To that question, unfortunately, I have no answer at all, but that is only another way of saying that I make no claim to have solved the problem of induction. If science did progress by virtue of some shared and binding algorithm of choice, I would be equally at a loss to explain its success. The lacuna[27] is one I feel acutely, but its presence does not differentiate my position from the tradition.

It is, after all, no accident that my list of the values guiding scientific choice is, as nearly as makes any difference, identical with the tradition's list of rules dictating choice. Given any concrete situation to which the philosopher's rules could be applied, my values would function like his rules, producing the same choice. Any justification of induction, any explanation of why the rules worked, would apply equally to my values. Now consider a situation in which choice by shared rules proves impossible, not because the rules are wrong but because they are, as rules, intrinsically incomplete. Individuals must then still choose and be guided by the rules (now values) when they do so. For that purpose, however, each must first flesh out the rules, and each will do so in a somewhat different way even though the decision dictated by the variously completed rules may prove unanimous. If I now assume, in addition, that the group is large enough so that individual differences distribute on some normal curve, then any argument that justifies the philosopher's choice by rule should be immediately adaptable to my choice by value. A group too small, or a distribution excessively skewed by external historical pressures, would, of course, pre-

vent the argument's transfer.[28] But those are just the circumstances under which scientific progress is itself problematic. The transfer is not then to be expected.

I shall be glad if these references to a normal distribution of individual differences and to the problem of induction make my position appear very close to more traditional views. With respect to theory choice, I have never thought my departures large and have been correspondingly startled by such charges as "mob psychology," quoted at the start. It is worth noting, however, that the positions are not quite identical, and for that purpose an analogy may be helpful. Many properties of liquids and gases can be accounted for on the kinetic theory[29] by supposing that all molecules

---

27 Hole or gap.

28 [Author's note] If the group is small, it is more likely that random fluctuations will result in its members' sharing an atypical set of values and therefore making choices different from those that would be made by a larger and more representative group. External environment—intellectual, ideological, or economic—must systematically affect the value system of much larger groups, and the consequences can include difficulties in introducing the scientific enterprise to societies with inimical values or perhaps even the end of that enterprise within societies where it had once flourished. In this area, however, great caution is required. Changes in the environment where science is practiced can also have fruitful effects on research. Historians often resort, for example, to differences between national environments to explain why particular innovations were initiated and at first disproportionately pursued in particular countries, e.g., Darwinism in Britain, energy conservation in Germany. At present we know substantially nothing about the minimum requisites of the social milieux within which a sciencelike enterprise might flourish.

29 The kinetic theory is a theory of the thermodynamic behavior of matter, especially the relationships among pressure, volume, and temperature in gases. Among its central notions are that temperature depends on the kinetic energy of the rapidly moving particles of a substance, that energy and momentum are conserved in all collisions between particles, and that the average behavior of the particles in a substance can be deduced by statistical analysis.

travel at the same speed. Among such properties are the regularities known as Boyle's and Charles's law.[30] Other characteristics, most obviously evaporation, cannot be explained in so simple a way. To deal with them one must assume that molecular speeds differ, that they are distributed at random, governed by the laws of chance. What I have been suggesting here is that theory choice, too, can be explained only in part by a theory which attributes the same properties to all the scientists who must do the choosing. Essential aspects of the process generally known as verification will be understood only by recourse to the features with respect to which men may differ while still remaining scientists. The tradition takes it for granted that such features are vital to the process of discovery, which it at once and for that reason rules out of philosophical bounds. That they may have significant functions also in the philosophically central problem of justifying theory choice is what philosophers of science have to date categorically denied.

What remains to be said can be grouped in a somewhat miscellaneous epilogue. For the sake of clarity and to avoid writing a book, I have throughout this paper utilized some traditional concepts and locutions about the viability of which I have elsewhere expressed serious doubts. For those who know the work in which I have done so, I close by indicating three aspects of what I have said which would better represent my views if cast in other terms, simultaneously indicating the main directions in which such recasting should proceed. The areas I have in mind are: value invariance, subjectivity, and partial communication. If my views of scientific development are novel—a matter about which there is legitimate room for doubt—it is in areas such as these, rather than theory choice, that my main departures from tradition should be sought.

---

30   Boyle's law, formulated by Robert Boyle in 1662, is the principle that, at a constant temperature, the volume of a confined ideal gas varies inversely with its pressure. Charles's law, discovered by French scientist J.A.C. Charles in 1787, states that the volume of a fixed mass of gas held at a constant pressure varies directly with the absolute temperature.

Throughout this paper I have implicitly assumed that, whatever their initial source, the criteria or values deployed in theory choice are fixed once and for all, unaffected by their participation in transitions from one theory to another. Roughly speaking, but only very roughly, I take that to be the case. If the list of relevant values is kept short (I have mentioned five, not all independent) and if their specification is left vague, then such values as accuracy, scope, and fruitfulness are permanent attributes of science. But little knowledge of history is required to suggest that both the application of these values and, more obviously, the relative weights attached to them have varied markedly with time and also with the field of application. Furthermore, many of these variations in value have been associated with particular changes in scientific theory. Though the experience of scientists provides no philosophical justification for the values they deploy (such justification would solve the problem of induction), those values are in part learned from that experience, and they evolve with it.

The whole subject needs more study (historians have usually taken scientific values, though not scientific methods, for granted), but a few remarks will illustrate the sort of variations I have in mind. Accuracy, as a value, has with time increasingly denoted quantitative or numerical agreement, sometimes at the expense of qualitative. Before early modern times, however, accuracy in that sense was a criterion only for astronomy, the science of the celestial region. Elsewhere it was neither expected nor sought. During the seventeenth century, however, the criterion of numerical agreement was extended to mechanics, during the late eighteenth and early nineteenth centuries to chemistry and such other subjects as electricity and heat, and in this century to many parts of biology. Or think of utility, an item of value not on my initial list. It too has figured significantly in scientific development, but far more strongly and steadily for chemists than for, say, mathematicians and physicists. Or consider scope. It is still an important scientific value, but important scientific advances have repeatedly been achieved at its expense, and the weight attributed to it at times of choice has diminished correspondingly.

What may seem particularly troublesome about changes like these is, of course, that they ordinarily occur in the aftermath of a theory change. One of the objections to Lavoisier's new chemistry[31] was the roadblocks with which it confronted the achievement of what had previously been one of chemistry's traditional goals: the explanation of qualities, such as color and texture, as well as of their changes. With the acceptance of Lavoisier's theory such explanations ceased for some time to be a value for chemists; the ability to explain qualitative variation was no longer a criterion relevant to the evaluation of chemical theory. Clearly, if such value changes had occurred as rapidly or been as complete as the theory changes to which they related, then theory choice would be value choice, and neither could provide justification for the other. But, historically, value change is ordinarily a belated and largely unconscious concomitant of theory choice, and the former's magnitude is regularly smaller than the latter's. For the functions I have here ascribed to values, such relative stability provides a sufficient basis. The existence of a feedback loop through which theory change affects the values which led to that change does not make the decision process circular in any damaging sense.

About a second respect in which my resort to tradition may be misleading, I must be far more tentative. It demands the skills of an ordinary language philosopher, which I do not possess. Still no very acute ear for language is required to generate discomfort with the ways in which the terms "objectivity" and, more especially, "subjectivity" have functioned in this paper. Let me briefly suggest the respects in which I believe language has gone astray. "Subjective" is a term with several established uses: in one of these it is opposed to "objective," in another to "judgmental." When my critics describe the idiosyncratic features to which I appeal as subjective, they resort, erroneously I think, to the second of these senses. When they complain that I deprive science of objectivity, they conflate that second sense of subjective with the first.

A standard application of the term "subjective" is to matters of taste, and my critics appear to suppose that that is what I have made of theory choice. But they are missing a distinction standard since Kant when they do so. Like sensation reports, which are also subjective in the sense now at issue, matters of taste are undiscussable. Suppose that, leaving a movie theater with a friend after seeing a western, I exclaim: "How I liked that terrible potboiler!" My friend, if he disliked the film, may tell me I have low tastes, a matter about which, in these circumstances, I would readily agree. But, short of saying that I lied, he cannot disagree with my report that I liked the film or try to persuade me that what I said about my reaction was wrong. What is discussable in my remark is not my characterization of my internal state, my exemplification of taste, but rather my *judgment* that the film was a potboiler. Should my friend disagree on that point, we may argue most of the night, each comparing the film with good or great ones we have seen, each revealing, implicitly or explicitly, something about how he *judges* cinematic merit, about his aesthetic. Though one of us may, before retiring, have persuaded the other, he need not have done so to demonstrate that our difference is one of judgment, not taste.

Evaluations or choices of theory have, I think, exactly this character. Not that scientists never say merely, I like such and such a theory, or I do not. After 1926 Einstein said little more than that about his opposition to the quantum theory. But scientists may always be asked to explain their choices, to exhibit the bases for their judgments. Such judgments are eminently discussable, and the man who refuses to discuss his own cannot expect to be taken seriously. Though there are, very occasionally, leaders of scientific taste, their existence tends to prove the rule. Einstein was one of the few, and his increasing isolation from the scientific community in later life shows how very limited a role taste alone can play in

---

31   Antoine Laurent Lavoisier (1743–1794) isolated the major components of air and water, disproved the phlogiston theory by determining the role of oxygen in combustion, and organized the classification of chemical compounds upon which the modern system is based. He formulated the concept of an element as being a simple substance that cannot be broken down by any known method of chemical analysis, and he showed that although matter changes state during a chemical reaction its mass remains the same, thus leading him to propose the law of conservation of matter. Lavoisier was executed during the Reign of Terror after the French Revolution.

theory choice. Bohr,[32] unlike Einstein, did discuss the bases for his judgment, and he carried the day. If my critics introduce the term "subjective" in a sense that opposes it to judgmental—thus suggesting that I make theory choice undiscussable, a matter of taste—they have seriously mistaken my position.

Turn now to the sense in which "subjectivity" is opposed to "objectivity," and note first that it raises issues quite separate from those just discussed. Whether my taste is low or refined, my report that I liked the film is objective unless I have lied. To my judgment that the film was a potboiler, however, the objective-subjective distinction does not apply at all, at least not obviously and directly. When my critics say I deprive theory choice of objectivity, they must, therefore, have recourse to some very different sense of subjective, presumably the one in which bias and personal likes or dislikes function instead of, or in the face of, the actual facts. But that sense of subjective does not fit the process I have been describing any better than the first. Where factors dependent on individual biography or personality must be introduced to make values applicable, no standards of factuality or actuality are being set aside. Conceivably my discussion of theory choice indicates some limitations of objectivity, but not by isolating elements properly called subjective. Nor am I even quite content with the notion that what I have been displaying are limitations. Objectivity ought to be analyzable in terms of criteria like accuracy and consistency. If these criteria do not supply all the guidance that we have customarily expected of them, then it may be the meaning rather than the limits of objectivity that my argument shows.

Turn, in conclusion, to a third respect, or set of respects, in which this paper needs to be recast. I have assumed throughout that the discussions surrounding theory choice are unproblematic, that the facts appealed to in such discussions are independent of theory, and that the discussions' outcome is appropriately called a choice. Elsewhere I have challenged all three of these assumptions, arguing that communication between proponents of different theories is inevitably partial, that what each takes to be facts depends in part on the theory he espouses, and that an individual's transfer of allegiance from theory to theory is often better described as conversion than as choice. Though all these theses are problematic as well as controversial, my commitment to them is undiminished. I shall not now defend them, but must at least attempt to indicate how what I have said here can be adjusted to conform with these more central aspects of my view of scientific development.

For that purpose I resort to an analogy I have developed in other places. Proponents of different theories are, I have claimed, like native speakers of different languages. Communication between them goes on by translation, and it raises all translation's familiar difficulties. That analogy is, of course, incomplete, for the vocabulary of the two theories may be identical, and most words function in the same ways in both. But some words in the basic as well as in the theoretical vocabularies of the two theories—words like "star" and "planet," "mixture" and "compound," or "force" and "matter"—do function differently. Those differences are unexpected and will be discovered and localized, if at all, only be repeated experience of communication breakdown. Without pursuing the matter further, I simply assert the existence of significant limits to what the proponents of different theories can communicate to one another. The same limits make it difficult or, more likely, impossible for an individual to hold both theories in mind together and compare them point by point with each other and with nature. That sort of comparison is, however, the process on which the appropriateness of any word like "choice" depends.

Nevertheless, despite the incompleteness of their communication, proponents of different theories can exhibit to each other, not always easily, the concrete technical results achievable by those who practice within each theory. Little or no translation is required to apply at least some value criteria to those results. (Accuracy and fruitfulness are most immediately applicable, perhaps followed by scope. Consistency

---

32 Niels Bohr, a Danish physicist, made basic contributions to the theory of atomic structure between 1913 and 1915 and received a Nobel prize in 1922 for this work. His model of the atom made essential use of quantum theory: he suggested that electrons in an atom move in orbits, and that when an electron moves to another orbit it gives off or absorbs a quantum of radiation.

and simplicity are far more problematic.) However incomprehensible the new theory may be to the proponents of tradition, the exhibit of impressive concrete results will persuade at least a few of them that they must discover how such results are achieved. For that purpose they must learn to translate, perhaps by treating already published papers as a Rosetta stone[33] or,

---

33 The Rosetta stone is a black basalt tablet discovered in 1799 by French troops near Rosetta, a northern Egyptian town in the Nile River delta. It can be seen in the British Museum in London and bears an inscription written in three different scripts—Greek, Egyptian hieroglyphic, and Egyptian demotic. This inscription provided the key to the code of (the hitherto baffling) Egyptian hieroglyphics.

often more effective, by visiting the innovator, talking with him, watching him and his students at work. Those exposures may not result in the adoption of the theory; some advocates of the tradition may return home and attempt to adjust the old theory to produce equivalent results. But others, if the new theory is to survive, will find that at some point in the language-learning process they have ceased to translate and begun instead to speak the language like a native. No process quite like choice has occurred, but they are practicing the new theory nonetheless. Furthermore, the factors that have led them to risk the conversion they have undergone are just the ones this paper has underscored in discussing a somewhat different process, one which, following philosophical tradition, it has labelled theory choice.

HELEN LONGINO

"Can There Be a Feminist Science?"

Who Is Helen Longino?

Helen E. Longino (born 1944) has been perhaps the most influential philosopher to apply contemporary feminist approaches to epistemology and philosophy of science. As an undergraduate, she majored in literary studies, moving to logic and philosophy of science for her graduate work at Johns Hopkins University. During the 1960s and 70s, she was active in anti-war and feminist political action movements. As a faculty member at Mills College, Rice University, and University of Minnesota, she was strongly influential in establishing women's studies courses and programs. At present, she teaches in the philosophy department at Stanford University.

Some Useful Background Information

Longino's target for feminist criticism is the long-held and (for a long time) universal view that the most

important feature of good science is its *objectivity*—which was taken to mean that scientific practice, when working right, should be utterly uninfluenced by any values of the scientist, or of his culture or society—any values, that is, other than the internal scientific values of care in observation, honesty, thoroughness, and so on. The idea here was that nature itself—the external facts—should determine what's taken to be true by scientists.

Nobody thinks that real science always works this way: there are numerous high-profile examples brought to light of outright fraud, or unconscious bias, the result of what the scientist himself or the source of his funding, or the dominant culture, hopes to find. But the traditional view counts these as bad science. A very moderate feminist critique of science has, for decades, pointed out how male bias is among the factors that can make for bad science in this sense. Feminists point to scientific studies like these: a study of the causes of heart-attack which studied only males as subjects, blithely considering their conclusions to be applicable to all humans; a study of societal dynamics which looked only at traditional male activities and roles; a study of cognitive abilities that rated subjects on the basis of typically male abilities, concluding with the intellectual inferiority of women.

But this is not Longino's critique.

What Is the Structure of This Reading?

Longino begins by mentioning various sorts of feminist approaches to science that her article will not take. Her subject will instead be a feminist critique of the idea that science should be impersonal, objective, and value-free; feminists, she argues, offer an alternative that makes for better science.

After a number of preliminaries, she reveals her central argument: that confirmation in science often essentially involves background assumptions, and that these assumptions are sometimes not merely established by simple observation or common sense, but are rather tied in with "contextual values"—not mere internal rules of science, but personal, social, or cultural values.

Common Misconceptions

1. Longino does not argue that there are typically feminine characteristics that should be represented more in scientific investigations. She does not reject this view wholesale; she merely argues that this is not what she will talk about.

2. Neither does Longino argue here for a position that some readers, seeing that this is a feminist treatment of scientific practice, might expect: that the current male science gets things all wrong, and that a replacement female science would do better. She mentions that her aim is not to replace one "absolutism" by another.

Suggestions for Critical Reflection

1. Explain in your own words exactly what the difference between "contextual" and "constitutive" values in science is. Do you think that a real distinction can be made here? Do you think that

it's a good idea to try to allow input from the latter, but not from the former?

2. Longino argues that the input of "constitutive values" is sometimes inevitable. But she concludes from this that inquiry with this sort of input is "perfectly respectable." Do you think that follows?

3. Try to imagine a story about *scientifically respectable* theory-testing that includes a significant input of "contextual values." If you have studied science, you may know a bit of the real history of the field that illustrates this. What are the "contextual values" that play a part here?

4. Now try to imagine (or come up with a real example) of such testing where the input of "contextual values" made the scientific procedure unacceptable, invalid. Do you think there's a difference between instances of acceptable and unacceptable value-input science?

5. Explain how Longino uses her example of the study of the influence of sex hormones. What is the "background assumption" she thinks was at work in this study? Why does Longino think that this is connected to particular personal, cultural, or societal values? Is she right? What would have made for a better study? Do you think that a "value-free" inquiry here would have been an improvement? or that it would have been even possible?

6. A central, simple, definition of feminism sees it as a movement to counter discrimination and injustice toward women. What else might be involved in feminism as an intellectual commitment? Can you see why Longino's view of science is properly conceived of as feminist? Explain why you think it is or isn't.

7. Longino does not advocate replacement of scientifically harmful "androcentric" values by supposedly scientifically superior feminist ones. What, exactly, does she advocate?

Suggestions for Further Reading

A good place to start reading more by Longino is online: "The Social Dimensions of Scientific Knowledge," *The Stanford Encyclopedia of Philosophy (Fall 2008 Edition)*, Edward N. Zalta (ed.) <http://plato.stanford.

edu/archives/fall2008/entries/scientific-knowledge-social/>. Other articles by her are "Feminist Epistemology" *Blackwell Guide to Epistemology*, John Greco and Ernest Sosa, eds. (Blackwell, 1999), pp. 327-353; and "Cognitive and Non-Cognitive Values in Science: Rethinking the Dichotomy" *Feminism, Science, and the Philosophy of Science,* Lynn Hankinson Nelson and Jack Nelson, eds. (Kluwer, 1996), 39-58. Her books: *Science as Social Knowledge: Values and Objectivity in Scientific Inquiry* (Princeton University Press, 1990) and *The Fate of Knowledge* (Princeton University Press, 2002). She discusses examples further in Helen Longino and Ruth Doell, "Body, Bias, and Behaviour: A Comparative Analysis of Reasoning in Two Areas of Biological Science" *Signs: Journal of Women in Culture and Society* 9/2 (1983), pp. 206-227.

There has been a great deal written in the past few decades on this subject. A good place to find a variety of important short readings is in any of these anthologies: *Feminist Epistemologies*, Linda Alcoff and Elizabeth Potter, eds. (Routledge, 1993); *A Mind of One's Own: Feminist Essays on Reason and Objectivity*, Louise Antony and Charlotte Witt, eds., (Westview, 1993); *Discovering Reality: Feminist Perspectives in Epistemology, Metaphysics, Methodology and Philosophy of Science*, Sandra Harding and Merrill Hintikka, eds. (Reidel, 1983); *Engendering Rationalities*, Nancy Tuana and Sandra Morgen, eds. (SUNY Press, 2001); and *Feminism and Science*, Nancy Tuana, ed. (Indiana University Press, 1989).

"Can There Be a Feminist Science?"[1]

This paper explores a number of recent proposals regarding "feminist science" and rejects a content-based approach in favor of a process-based approach to characterizing feminist science. Philosophy of science can yield models of scientific reasoning that illuminate the interaction between cultural values and ideology and scientific inquiry. While we can use these models to expose masculine and other forms of bias, we can also use them to defend the introduction of assumptions grounded in feminist political values.

I

The question of this title conceals multiple ambiguities. Not only do the sciences consist of many distinct fields, but the term "science" can be used to refer to a method of inquiry, a historically changing collection of practices, a body of knowledge, a set of claims, a profession, a set of social groups, etc. And as the sciences are many, so are the scholarly disciplines that seek to understand them: philosophy, history, sociology, anthropology, psychology. Any answer from the perspective of some one of these disciplines will, then, of necessity, be partial. In this essay, I shall be asking about the possibility of theoretical natural science that is feminist and I shall ask from the perspective of a philosopher. Before beginning to develop my answer, however, I want to review some of the questions that could be meant, in order to arrive at the formulation I wish to address.

The question could be interpreted as factual, one to be answered by pointing to what feminists in the sciences are doing and saying: "Yes, and this is what it is." Such a response can be perceived as question-begging, however. Even such a friend of feminism as Stephen Gould dismisses the idea of a distinctively feminist or even female contribution to the sciences. In a generally positive review of Ruth Bleier's book, *Science and Gender*, Gould (1984) brushes aside her connection between women's attitudes and values and the interactionist science she calls for. Scientists (male, of course) are already proceeding with wholist[2] and interactionist[3] research programs. Why, he implied, should women or feminists have any particular, distinctive, contributions to make? There is not masculinist and feminist science, just good and

---

1   *Hypatia*, Vol. 2, No. 3, 1987, pp. 51–64.

---

2   Wholists reject the assumption, made by positivists, that observation is independent from theory, and claim that confirming or disconfirming observations cannot be specified independently of the theory they are supposed to confirm or disconfirm.

3   This is the view, taken from a theoretical position in sociology, that derives social processes—in this case, the practice of science—from human interaction.

bad science. The question of a feminist science cannot be settled by pointing, but involves a deeper, subtler investigation.

The deeper question can itself have several meanings. One set of meanings is sociological, the other conceptual. The sociological meaning proceeds as follows. We know what sorts of social conditions make misogynist science possible. The work of Margaret Rossiter (1982) on the history of women scientists in the United States and the work of Kathryn Addelson (1983) on the social structure of professional science detail the relations between a particular social structure for science and the kinds of science produced. What sorts of social conditions would make feminist science possible? This is an important question, one I am not equipped directly to investigate, although what I can investigate is, I believe, relevant to it. This is the second, conceptual, interpretation of the question: what sort of sense does it make to talk about a feminist science? Why is the question itself not an oxymoron, linking, as it does, values and ideological commitment with the idea of impersonal, objective, value-free, inquiry? This is the problem I wish to address in this essay.

The hope for a feminist theoretical natural science has concealed an ambiguity between content and practice. In the content sense the idea of a feminist science involves a number of assumptions and calls a number of visions to mind. Some theorists have written as though a feminist science is one of the theories which encode a particular world view, characterized by complexity, interaction and wholism. Such a science is said to be feminist because it is the expression and valorization[4] of a female sensibility or cognitive temperament. Alternatively, it is claimed that women have certain traits (dispositions to attend to particulars, interactive rather than individualist and controlling social attitudes and behaviors) that enable them to understand the true character of natural processes (which are complex and interactive).[5] While propo-

nents of this interactionist view see it as an improvement over most contemporary science, it has also been branded as soft—misdescribed as non-mathematical. Women in the sciences who feel they are being asked to do not better science, but inferior science, have responded angrily to this characterization of feminist science, thinking that it is simply new clothing for the old idea that women can't do science. I think that the interactionist view can be defended against this response, although that requires rescuing it from some of its proponents as well. However, I also think that the characterization of feminist science as the expression of a distinctive female cognitive temperament has other drawbacks. It first conflates feminine with feminist. While it is important to reject the traditional derogation of the virtues assigned to women, it is also important to remember that women are *constructed* to occupy positions of social subordinates. We should not uncritically embrace the feminine.

This characterization of feminist science is also a version of recently propounded notions of a 'women's standpoint' or a 'feminist standpoint' and suffers from the same suspect universalization that these ideas suffer from. If there is one such standpoint, there are many: as Maria Lugones and Elizabeth Spelman spell out in their tellingly entitled article, "Have We Got a Theory for You: Feminist Theory, Cultural Imperialism, and the Demand for 'The Woman's Voice,'" women are too diverse in our experiences to generate a single cognitive framework (Lugones and Spelman 1983). In addition, the sciences are themselves too diverse for me to think that they might be equally transformed by such a framework. To reject this concept of a feminist science, however, is not to disengage science from feminism. I want to suggest that we focus on science as practice rather than content, as process rather than product; hence, not on feminist science, but on doing science as a feminist.

The doing of science involves many practices: how one structures a laboratory (hierarchically or collectively), how one relates to other scientists (competitively or cooperatively), how and whether one engages in political struggles over affirmative action. It extends also to intellectual practices, to the activities of scientific inquiry, such as observation and reasoning. Can there be a feminist scientific inquiry?

---

4   To valorize something is to enhance its value, usually artificially, or to assign a value to it.

5   [Author's note] This seems to be suggested in Bleier (1984), Rose (1983) and in Sandra Harding's (1980) early work.

This possibility is seen to be problematic against the background of certain standard presuppositions about science. The claim that there could be a feminist science in the sense of an intellectual practice is either nonsense because oxymoronic as suggested above or the claim is interpreted to mean that established science (science as done and dominated by men) is wrong about the world. Feminist science in this latter interpretation is presented as correcting the errors of masculine, standard science and as revealing the truth that is hidden by masculine 'bad' science, as taking the sex out of science.

Both of these interpretations involve the rejection of one approach as incorrect and the embracing of the other as the way to a truer understanding of the natural world. Both trade one absolutism for another. Each is a side of the same coin, and that coin, I think, is the idea of a value-free science. This is the idea that scientific methodology guarantees the independence of scientific inquiry from values or value-related considerations. A science or a scientific research program informed by values is *ipso facto* "bad science." "Good science" is inquiry protected by methodology from values and ideology. This same idea underlies Gould's response to Bleier, so it bears closer scrutiny. In the pages that follow, I shall examine the idea of value-free science and then apply the results of that examination to the idea of feminist scientific inquiry.

II

I distinguish two kinds of values relevant to the sciences. Constitutive values, internal to the sciences, are the source of the rules determining what constitutes acceptable scientific practice or scientific method. The personal, social and cultural values, those group or individual preferences about what ought to be, I call contextual values, to indicate that they belong to the social and cultural context in which science is done (Longino 1983c). The traditional interpretation of the value-freedom of modern natural science amounts to a claim that its constitutive and contextual features are clearly distinct from and independent of one another, that contextual values play no role in the inner workings of scientific inquiry, in reasoning and observation. I shall argue that this construal of the distinction cannot be maintained.

There are several ways to develop such an argument. One scholar is fond of inviting her audience to visit any science library and peruse the titles on the shelves. Observe how subservient to social and cultural interests are the inquiries represented by the book titles alone! Her listeners would soon abandon their ideas about the value-neutrality of the sciences, she suggests. This exercise may indeed show the influence of external, contextual considerations on what research gets done/supported (i.e., on problem selection). It does not show that such considerations affect reasoning or hypothesis acceptance. The latter would require detailed investigation of particular cases or a general conceptual argument. The conceptual arguments involve developing some version of what is known in philosophy of science as the underdetermination thesis, i.e., the thesis that a theory is always underdetermined by the evidence adduced in its support, with the consequence that different or incompatible theories are supported by or at least compatible with the same body of evidence. I shall sketch a version of the argument that appeals to features of scientific inference.

One of the rocks on which the logical positivist program foundered was the distinction between theoretical and observational language. Theoretical statements contain, as fundamental descriptive terms, terms that do not occur in the description of data. Thus, hypotheses in particle physics contain terms like "electron," "pion," "muon," "electron spin," etc. The evidence for a hypothesis such as "A pion decays sequentially into a muon, then a positron" is obviously not direct observations of pions, muons and positrons, but consists largely in photographs taken in large and complex experimental apparati: accelerators, cloud chambers, bubble chambers. The photographs show all sorts of squiggly lines and spirals. Evidence for the hypotheses of particle physics is presented as statements that describe these photographs. Eventually, of course, particle physicists point to a spot on a photograph and say things like "Here a neutrino hits a neutron." Such an assertion, however, is an interpretive achievement which involves collapsing theoretical and observational moments. A skeptic would have to be supplied a complicated argument linking the elements of the photograph to traces left by particles and these to particles themselves. What counts as theory and what as data in a pragmatic sense change over time, as some ideas and experimental procedures come to be securely embedded in a particular framework and others take their place on the horizons. As the history of physics shows, however, secure embeddedness is no guarantee against overthrow.

Logical positivists and their successors hoped to model scientific inference formally. Evidence for hypotheses, data, were to be represented as logical consequences of hypotheses. When we try to map this logical structure onto the sciences, however, we find that hypotheses are, for the most part, not just generalizations of data statements. The links between data and theory, therefore, cannot be adequately represented as formal or syntactic, but are established by means of assumptions that make or imply substantive claims about the field over which one theorizes. Theories are confirmed via the confirmation of their constituent hypotheses, so the confirmation of hypotheses and theories is relative to the assumptions relied upon in asserting the evidential connection. Conformation of such assumptions, which are often unarticulated, is itself subject to similar relativization. And it is these assumptions that can be the vehicle for the involvement of considerations motivated primarily by contextual values (Longino 1979, 1983a).

The point of this extremely telescoped argument is that one can't give an a priori specification of confirmation that effectively eliminates the role of value-laden assumptions in legitimate scientific inquiry without eliminating auxiliary hypotheses (assumptions) altogether. This is not to say that all scientific reasoning involves value-related assumptions. Sometimes auxiliary assumptions will be supported by mundane inductive reasoning. But sometimes they will not be. In any given case, they may be metaphysical in character; they may be untestable with present investigative techniques; they may be rooted in contextual, value-related considerations. If, however, there is no a priori way to eliminate such assumptions from evidential reasoning generally, and, hence, no way to rule out value-laden assumptions, then there is no formal basis for arguing that an inference mediated by contextual values is thereby bad science.

A comparable point is made by some historians investigating the origins of modern science. James Jacob (1977) and Margaret Jacob (1976) have, in a series of articles and books, argued that the adoption of conceptions of matter by 17th century scientists like Robert Boyle was inextricably intertwined with political considerations. Conceptions of matter provided the foundation on which physical theories were developed and Boyle's science, regardless of his reasons for it, has been fruitful in ways that far exceed his imaginings. If the presence of contextual influences were grounds for disallowing a line of inquiry, then early modern science would not have gotten off the ground.

The conclusion of this line of argument is that constitutive values conceived as epistemological (i.e., truth-seeking) are not adequate to screen out the influence of contextual values in the very structuring of scientific knowledge. Now the ways in which contextual values do, if they do, influence this structuring and interact, if they do, with constitutive values has to be determined separately for different theories and fields of science. But this argument, if it's sound, tells us that this sort of inquiry is perfectly respectable and involves no shady assumptions or unargued intuitively based rejections of positivism. It also opens the possibility that one can make explicit value commitments and still do "good" science. The conceptual argument doesn't show that all science is value-laden (as opposed to metaphysics-laden)—that must be established on a case-by-case basis, using the tools not just of logic and philosophy but of history and sociology as well. It does show that not all science is value-free and, more importantly, that it is not necessarily in the nature of science to be value-free. If we reject that idea we're in a better position to talk about the possibilities of feminist science.

III

In earlier articles (Longino 1981, 1983b; Longino and Doell 1983), I've used similar considerations to argue that scientific objectivity has to be reconceived as a function of the communal structure of scientific inquiry rather than as a property of individual scientists. I've then used these notions about scientific methodology to show that science displaying masculine bias is not *ipso facto* improper or 'bad' science;

that the fabric of science can neither rule out the expression of bias nor legitimate it. So I've argued that both the expression of masculine bias in the sciences and feminist criticism of research exhibiting that bias are—shall we say—business as usual; that scientific inquiry should be expected to display the deep metaphysical and normative[6] commitments of the culture in which it flourishes; and finally that criticism of the deep assumptions that guide scientific reasoning about data is a proper part of science.

The argument I've just offered about the idea of a value-free science is similar in spirit to those earlier arguments. I think it makes it possible to see these questions from a slightly different angle.

There is a tradition of viewing scientific inquiry as somehow inexorable. This involves supposing that the phenomena of the natural world are fixed in determinate relations with each other, that these relations can be known and formulated in a consistent and unified way. This is not the old "unified science" idea of the logical positivists, with its privileging of physics. In its "unexplicated" or "pre-analytic" state, it is simply the idea that there is one consistent, integrated or coherent, true theoretical treatment of all natural phenomena. (The indeterminacy principle of quantum physics is restricted to our understanding of the behavior of certain particles which themselves underlie the fixities of the natural world. Stochastic[7] theories reveal fixities, but fixities among ensembles rather than fixed relations among individual objects or events.) The scientific inquirer's job is to discover those fixed relations. Just as the task of Plato's philosophers was to discover the fixed relations among forms and the task of Galileo's scientists was to discover the laws written in the language of the grand book of nature, geometry, so the scientist's task in this tradition remains the discovery of fixed relations however conceived. These ideas are part of the realist tradition in the philosophy of science.

It's no longer possible, in a century that has seen the splintering of the scientific disciplines, to give such a unified description of the objects of inquiry.

But the belief that the job is to discover fixed relations of some sort, and that the application of observation, experiment and reason leads ineluctably to unifiable, if not unified, knowledge of an independent reality, is still with us. It is evidenced most clearly in two features of scientific rhetoric: the use of the passive voice as in "it is concluded that ..." or "it has been discovered that ..." and the attribution of agency to the data, as in "the data suggest...." Such language has been criticized for the abdication of responsibility it indicates. Even more, the scientific inquirer, and we with her, become passive observers, victims of the truth. The idea of a value-free science is integral to this view of scientific inquiry. And if we reject that idea we can also reject our roles as passive onlookers, helpless to affect the course of knowledge.

Let me develop this point somewhat more concretely and autobiographically. Biologist Ruth Doell and I have been examining studies in three areas of research on the influence of sex hormones on human behavior and cognitive performance: research on the influence of pre-natal, *in utero*, exposure to higher or lower than normal levels of androgens and estrogens on so-called 'gender-role' behavior in children, influence of androgens (pre- and post-natal) on homosexuality in women, and influence of lower than normal (for men) levels of androgen at puberty on spatial abilities (Doell and Longino, forthcoming).

The studies we looked at are vulnerable to criticism of their data and their observation methodologies. They also show clear evidence of androcentric bias[8]—in the assumption that there are just two sexes and two genders (us and them), in the designation of appropriate and inappropriate behaviors for male and female children, in the caricature of lesbianism, in the assumption of male mathematical superiority. We did not find, however, that these assumptions mediated the inferences from data to theory that we found objectionable. These sexist assumptions did affect the way the data were described. What mediated the inferences from the alleged data (i.e., what functioned as auxiliary hypotheses or what provided auxiliary hypotheses) was what we called the linear model—the assumption that there is a direct one-way causal

---

6   Normative means having to do with a value—a prescribed norm.

7   Probabilistic.

8   I.e., a bias in favor of the male point of view.

relationship between pre- or post-natal hormone levels and later behavior or cognitive performance. To put it crudely, fetal gonadal hormones organize the brain at critical periods of development. The organism is thereby disposed to respond in a range of ways to a range of environmental stimuli. The assumption of unidirectional programming is supposedly supported by the finding of such a relationship in other mammals; in particular, by experiments demonstrating the dependence of sexual behaviors—mounting and lordosis[9]—on peri-natal hormone exposure and the finding of effects of sex hormones on the development of rodent brains. To bring it to bear on humans is to ignore, among other things, some important differences between human brains and those of other species. It also implies a willingness to regard humans in a particular way—to see us as produced by factors over which we have no control. Not only are we, as scientists, victims of the truth, but we are the prisoners of our physiology.[10] In the name of extending an explanatory model, human capacities for self-knowledge, self-reflection, self-determination are eliminated from any role in human action (at least in the behaviors studied).

Doell and I have therefore argued for the replacement of that linear model of the role of the brain in behavior by one of much greater complexity that includes physiological, environmental, historical and psychological elements. Such a model allows not only for the interaction of physiological and environmental factors but also for the interaction of these with a continuously self-modifying, self-representational (and self-organizing) central processing system. In contemporary neurobiology, the closest model is that being developed in the group selectionist approach to higher brain function of Gerald Edelman and other researchers (Edelman and Mountcastle 1978). We argue that a model of at least that degree of complexity is necessary to account for the human behaviors studies in the sex hormones and behavior research

and that if gonadal hormones function at all at these levels, they will probably be found at most to facilitate or inhibit neural processing in general. The strategy we take in our argument is to show that the degree of intentionality involved in the behaviors in question is greater than is presupposed by the hormonal influence researchers and to argue that this degree of intentionality implicates the higher brain processes.

To this point Ruth Doell and I agree. I want to go further and describe what we've done from the perspective of the above philosophical discussion of scientific methodology.

Abandoning my polemical mood for a more reflective one, I want to say that, in the end, commitment to one or another model is strongly influenced by values or other contextual features. The models themselves determine the relevance and interpretation of data. The linear or complex models are not in turn independently or conclusively supported by data. I doubt for instance that value-free inquiry will reveal the efficacy or inefficacy of intentional states or of physiological factors like hormone exposure in human action. I think instead that a research program in neuro-science that assumes the linear model and sex-gender dualism will show the influence of hormone exposure on gender-role behavior. And I think that a research program in neuroscience and psychology proceeding on the assumption that humans do possess the capacities for self-consciousness, self-reflection, and self-determination, and which then asks how the structure of the human brain and nervous system enables the expression of these capacities, will reveal the efficacy of intentional states (understood as very complex sorts of brain states).

While this latter assumption does not itself contain normative terms, I think that the decision to adopt it is motivated by value-laden considerations—by the desire to understand ourselves and others as self-determining (at least some of the time), that is, as capable of acting on the basis of concepts or representations of ourselves and the world in which we act. (Such representations are not necessarily correct, they are surely mediated by our cultures; all we wish to claim is that they are efficacious.) I think further that this desire on Ruth Doell's and my part is, in several ways, an aspect of our feminism. Our preference for

---

9   Arching the spine backwards or downwards, which is a sexual response in some mammals (such as cats and mice).

10   [Author's note] For a striking expression of this point of view see Witelson (1985).

a neurobiological model that allows for agency, for the efficacy of intentionality, is partly a validation of our (and everyone's) subjective experience of thought, deliberation, and choice. One of the tenets of feminist research is the valorization of subjective experience, and so our preference in this regard conforms to feminist research patterns. There is, however, a more direct way in which our feminism is expressed in this preference. Feminism is many things to many people, but it is at its core in part about the expansion of human potentiality. When feminists talk of breaking out and do break out of socially prescribed sex-roles, when feminists criticize the institutions of domination, we are thereby insisting on the capacity of humans—male and female—to act on perceptions of self and society and to act to bring about changes in self and society on the basis of those perceptions. (Not overnight and not by a mere act of will. The point is that we act.) And so our criticism of theories of the hormonal influence or determination of so-called gender-role behavior is not just a rejection of the sexist bias in the description of the phenomena—the behavior of the children studied, the sexual lives of lesbians, etc.—but of the limitations on human capacity imposed by the analytic model underlying such research.[11]

While the argument strategy we adopt against the linear model rests on a certain understanding of intention, the values motivating our adoption of that understanding remain hidden in that polemical context. Our political commitments, however, presuppose a certain understanding of human action, so that when faced with a conflict between these commitments and a particular model of brain-behavior relationships we allow the political commitments to guide the choice.

The relevance of my argument about value-free science should be becoming clear. Feminists—in and out of science—often condemn masculine bias in the sciences from the vantage point of commitment to a value-free science. Androcentric bias, once

identified, can then be seen as a violation of the rules, as "bad" science. Feminist science, by contrast, can eliminate that bias and produce better, good, more true or gender free science. From that perspective the process I've just described is anathema. But if scientific methods generated by constitutive values cannot guarantee independent from contextual values, then that approach to sexist science won't work. We cannot restrict ourselves simply to the elimination of bias, but must expand our scope to include the detection of limiting and interpretive frameworks and the finding or construction of more appropriate frameworks. We need not, indeed should not, wait for such a framework to emerge from the data. In waiting, if my argument is correct, we run the danger of working unconsciously with assumptions still laden with values from the context we seek to change. Instead of remaining passive with respect to the data and what the data suggest, we can acknowledge our ability to affect the course of knowledge and fashion or favor research programs that are consistent with the values and commitments we express in the rest of our lives. From this perspective, the idea of a value-free science is not just empty, but pernicious.

Accepting the relevance to our practice as scientists of our political commitments does not imply simple and crude impositions of those ideas onto the corner of the natural world under study. If we recognize, however, that knowledge is shaped by the assumptions, values and interests of a culture and that, within limits, one can choose one's culture, then it's clear that as scientists/theorists we have a choice. We can continue to do establishment science, comfortably wrapped in the myths of scientific rhetoric, or we can alter our intellectual allegiances. While remaining committed to an abstract goal of understanding, we can choose to whom, socially and politically, we are accountable in our pursuit of that goal. In particular we can choose between being accountable to the traditional establishment or to our political comrades.

Such accountability does not demand a radical break with the science one has learned and practiced. The development of a "new" science involves a more dialectical evolution and more continuity with established science than the familiar language of scientific revolutions implies.

---

11   [Author's note] Ideological commitments other than feminist ones may lead to the same assumptions and the variety of feminisms means that feminist commitments can lead to different and incompatible assumptions.

In focusing on accountability and choice, this conception of feminist science differs from those that proceed from the assumption of a congruence between certain models of natural processes and women's inherent modes of understanding.[12] I am arguing instead for the deliberate and active choice of an interpretive model and for the legitimacy of basing that choice on political considerations in this case. Obviously model choice is also constrained by (what we know of) reality, that is, by the data. But reality (what we know of it) is, I have already argued, inadequate to uniquely determine model choice. The feminist theorists mentioned above have focused on the relation between the content of a theory and female values or experiences, in particular on the perceived congruence between interactionist, wholist visions of nature and a form of understanding and set of values widely attributed to women. In contrast, I am suggesting that a feminist scientific practice admits political considerations as relevant constraints on reasoning, which, through their influence on reasoning and interpretation, shape content. In this specific case, those considerations in combination with the phenomena support an explanatory model that is highly interactionist, highly complex. This argument is so far, however, neutral on the issue of whether an interactionist and complex account of natural processes will always be the preferred one. If it is preferred, however, this will be because of explicitly political considerations and not because interactionism is the expression of "women's nature."

The integration of a political commitment with scientific work will be expressed differently in different fields. In some, such as the complex of research programs having a bearing on the understanding of human behavior, certain moves, such as the one described above, seem quite obvious. In others it may not be clear how to express an alternate set of values in inquiry, or what values would be appropriate. The first step, however, is to abandon the idea that scrutiny of the data yields a seamless web of knowledge. The second is to think through a particular field and try to understand just what its unstated and fundamental

assumptions are and how they influence the course of inquiry. Knowing something of the history of a field is necessary to this process, as is continued conversation with other feminists.

The feminist interventions I imagine will be local (i.e., specific to a particular area of research); they may not be exclusive (i.e., different feminist perspectives may be represented in theorizing); and they will be in some way continuous with existing scientific work. The accretion of such interventions, of science done by feminists as feminists, and by members of other disenfranchised groups, has the potential, nevertheless, ultimately to transform the character of scientific discourse.

Doing science differently requires more than just the will to do so and it would be disingenuous to pretend that our philosophies of science are the only barrier. Scientific inquiry takes place in a social, political and economic context which imposes a variety of institutional obstacles to innovation, let alone to the intellectual working out of oppositional and political commitments. The nature of university career ladders means that one's work must be recognized as meeting certain standards of quality in order that one be able to continue it. If those standards are intimately bound up with values and assumptions one rejects, incomprehension rather than conversion is likely. Success requires that we present our work in a way that satisfies those standards and it is easier to do work that looks just like work known to satisfy them than to strike out in a new direction. Another push to conformity comes from the structure of support for science. Many of the scientific ideas argued to be consistent with a feminist politics have a distinctively non-production orientation.[13] In the example discussed above, thinking of the brain as hormonally programmed makes intervention and control more likely than does thinking of it as a self-organizing complexly interactive system. The doing of science, however, requires financial support

---

12   [Author's note] Cf. note [5], above.

13   [Author's note] This is not to say that interactionist ideas may not be applied in productive contexts, but that, unlike linear causal models, they are several steps away from the manipulation of natural processes immediately suggested by the latter. See Keller (1985), especially Chapter 10.

and those who provide that support are increasingly industry and the military. As might be expected they support research projects likely to meet their needs, projects which promise even greater possibilities for intervention in and manipulation of natural processes. Our sciences are being harnessed to the making of money and the waging of war. The possibility of alternate understandings of the natural world is irrelevant to a culture driven by those interests. To do feminist science we must change the social and political context in which science is done.

So: can there be a feminist science? If this means: is it in principle possible to do science as a feminist?, the answer must be: yes. If this means: can we in practice do science as feminists?, the answer must be: not until we change present conditions.

Notes

I am grateful to the Wellesley Center for Research on Women for the Mellon Scholarship during which I worked on the ideas in this essay. I am also grateful to audiences at UC Berkeley, Northeastern University, Brandeis University and Rice University for their comments and to the anonymous reviewers for *Hypatia* for their suggestions. An earlier version appeared as Wellesley Center for Research on Women Working Paper #63.

References

Addelson, Kathryn Pine. 1983. The man of professional wisdom. In *Discovering reality*, ed. Sandra Harding and Merrill Hintikka. Dordrecht: Reidel.

Bleier, Ruth. 1984. *Science and gender*. Elmsford, NY: Pergamon.

Doell, Ruth, and Helen E. Longino. N.d. *Journal of Homosexuality*. Forthcoming.

Edelman, Gerald, and Vernon Mountcastle. 1978. *The mindful brain*. Cambridge, MA: MIT Press.

Gould, Stephen J. 1984. Review of Ruth Bleier, *Science and gender*. New York Times Book Review, VVI, 7 (August 12): 1.

Harding, Sandra. 1980. The norms of inquiry and masculine experience. In *PSA 1980*, Vol. 2, ed. Peter Asquith and Ronald Giere. East Lansing, MI: Philosophy of Science Association.

Jacob, James R. 1977. *Robert Boyle and the English Revolution, A study in social and intellectual change*. New York: Franklin.

Jacob, Margaret C. 1976. *The Newtonians and the English Revolution, 1689-1720*. Ithaca, NY: Cornell University Press.

Keller, Evelyn Fox. 1985. *Reflections on gender and science*. New Haven, CT: Yale University Press.

Longino, Helen. 1979. Evidence and hypothesis. *Philosophy of Science* 46 (1): 35-56.

———. 1981. Scientific objectivity and feminist theorizing. *Liberal Education* 67 (3): 33-41.

———. 1983a. The idea of a value free science. Paper presented to the Pacific Division of the American Philosophical Association, March 25, Berkeley, CA.

———. 1983b. Scientific objectivity and logics of science. *Inquiry* 26 (1): 85-106.

———. 1983c. Beyond "bad science." *Science, Technology and Human Values* 8 (1): 7-17.

Longino, Helen, and Ruth Doell. 1983. Body, bias and behavior. *Signs* 9 (2): 206-227.

Lugones, Maria, and Elizabeth Spelman. 1983. Have we got a theory for you! Feminist theory, cultural imperialism and the demand for "the woman's voice." *Hypatia 1*, published as a special issue of *Women's Studies International Forum* 6 (6): 573-581.

Rose, Hilary. 1983. Hand, brain, and heart: A feminist epistemology for the natural sciences. *Signs* 9 (1): 73-90.

Rossiter, Margaret. 1982. *Women scientists in America: Struggles and strategies to 1940*. Baltimore, MD: Johns Hopkins University Press.

Witelson, Sandra. 1985. An exchange on gender. *New York Review of Books* (October 24).

CHAPTER 4

Philosophy of Religion —Does God Exist?

INTRODUCTION TO THE QUESTION

The philosophy of religion is the sub-field of philosophy concerned with the rational evaluation of the truth of religious claims; in particular, the philosophy of religion deals most centrally with claims about the existence, nature and activities of God. For example, one might ask, is it coherent to say that God is absolutely all-powerful?[1] Can God be *both* all-knowing and unchanging?[2] If God is all-knowing—and so knows everything that I am going to do—then in what sense can human beings really be said to have free will? Does God exist eternally, or instead is God somehow 'outside' of time altogether? Does God listen to and answer prayers? Does God ever cause miracles to occur? Does God punish sinners, and if so then what counts as sin and how does the deity punish it? How can a deity consign souls to eternal damnation and yet still be considered benevolent? Could God command us to torture little children for fun, and if he did so would this be a moral duty? If God is inexpressibly mysterious, as some religious creeds assert,

then how does one know what one believes in if one believes in God? And so on.

The religious proposition singled out for philosophical evaluation in this chapter is something like the following: that there exists one, and exactly one, deity who is eternal, immaterial, all-powerful, all-knowing, and perfectly morally good, and who created the universe and all its inhabitants. The first five readings in this chapter introduce (and evaluate) the three main arguments in favor of the existence of such an entity and the most important argument against its existence.

One of the earliest philosophical arguments for the existence of God comes from Saint Anselm in the eleventh century, and is called the *ontological argument*. The ontological argument tries to show that God *necessarily* exists since God's existence is logically entailed by the concept of God. This argument, a version of which also appears in Descartes's *Meditations* in Chapter 2, is criticized by a monk called Gaunilo in the Anselm reading, and also in the selections in this chapter from Aquinas and Hume.

The second main type of argument for the existence of God is what is called the *cosmological argument*. Arguments of this type start from observations about the world (the 'cosmos'), such as that every event has a cause or that all natural things depend for their existence on something else, and infer from this that there must be some entity—a creator and a sustainer—which necessarily exists and upon which everything else depends for its existence. Aquinas presents three cosmological arguments, the first three of his 'Five Ways.'

---

1   Consider, for instance, this old quandary: can God make a stone so heavy that even God cannot lift it? Whichever way this question is answered, it seems that there must be at least one thing which God cannot do.

2   After all, as the world changes over time, so must the facts which God knows to be true at that time. What God knew to be true ten seconds ago will differ from what he knows to be true now, which will be different again from what will be true in ten seconds, and so on. So (it appears) God's beliefs must be constantly changing if they are to remain true, so God cannot be eternally unchanging.

Finally, the third main variety of argument for God is the so-called *teleological argument*, often known as the *argument from design*. These arguments begin from the premise that the natural world shows signs of intelligent design or purpose (the Greek for purpose is *telos*) and from this draw the conclusion that the universe must have had an intelligent designer—God. The fifth of Aquinas's arguments for God is a member of this species, and the argument from design is also presented, but then roundly criticized, by Hume.

Perhaps the most important argument *against* the existence of God is known as the *problem of evil*. This argument essentially claims that the existence of evil is incompatible with the existence of a powerful and benevolent God; since evil clearly does exist, God cannot. The problem of evil is addressed briefly by Aquinas, but turned into a serious difficulty for the existence of God by Hume in Parts X and XI of his *Dialogues Concerning Natural Religion*. Leibniz provides a classic defense of theism against the problem of evil (a 'theodicy'), but a modern philosopher, J.L. Mackie, argues that the problem of evil is logically unbeatable.

The final reading in this chapter, William James's "The Will to Believe," asks what we should do if it turns out that there *is* no rational reason to believe in God, or if there is no good evidence for God's existence be-yond the belief itself. James argues that, even if we can have no good intellectual reasons for faith, we nevertheless have the right to choose to believe in God for emotional or "passional" reasons instead.

If you want to explore this area of philosophy in more depth, there are many books available which discuss the philosophy of religion. Some of the more philosophically informed ones are: Brian Davies, *An Introduction to the Philosophy of Religion* (Oxford University Press, 2004); Anthony Flew, *God, Freedom and Immortality* (Prometheus Books, 1984); John Hick, *Arguments for the Existence of God* (Macmillan, 1970); John Hick, *Philosophy of Religion* (Prentice-Hall, 1990); Anthony Kenny, *The God of the Philosophers* (Oxford University Press, 1979); Alvin Plantinga, *God and Other Minds* (Cornell University Press, 1967); William Rowe, *Philosophy of Religion* (Wadsworth, 2006); Bertrand Russell, *Why I Am Not a Christian* (Simon and Schuster, 1957); Richard Swinburne, *The Existence of God* (Oxford University Press, 1979); and Charles Taliaferro, *An Introduction to Contemporary Philosophy of Religion* (Blackwell, 1997). Two useful reference texts are *A Companion to Philosophy of Religion*, edited by Philip Quinn and Charles Taliaferro (Blackwell, 1999), and William Wainwright (ed.), *The Oxford Handbook of Philosophy of Religion* (Oxford University Press, 2007).

ST. ANSELM OF CANTERBURY
Proslogion

Who Was St. Anselm of Canterbury?

Anselm was born in 1033 to a noble family in Aosta, Italy, but after his mother's death (when he was 23) he repudiated his inherited wealth and the political career for which his father had prepared him and took up the life of a wandering scholar. In 1060 he became a monk at the Benedictine abbey of Bec in Normandy, rose rapidly through various positions of authority, and was elected Abbot in 1078. He was highly successful as Abbot, attracting monks from all over Europe and confirming Bec in its position as one of the main centers of learning of the time; during this time he became internationally known as a leading intellectual and established himself as a spiritual counsellor to kings from Ireland to Jerusalem. In 1093, much against his will, he succeeded his old teacher Lanfranc as Archbishop of Canterbury—the head of the church in England. He died there in 1109, at the age of 76. His tenure as Archbishop was stormy in the extreme: the king of England at the time, William Rufus, "seems to have combined the virtues of an American gangster with those of a South American dictator,"[1] and was determined to make the wealthy and powerful church subservient to royal authority. Anselm, by contrast, considered himself effectively co-ruler of England on the Pope's behalf, and he resisted William's encroachments fiercely and bravely. Anselm was exiled from England twice (for a total of more than five years), but eventually reached a compromise with William's

brother and successor, Henry I, after the Pope threatened the king's excommunication.[2]

Anselm is probably the most impressive philosopher and theologian of the early Middle Ages (i.e., between about 500 and 1100 CE). His major philosophical works are *Monologion* (which means "soliloquy"), *Proslogion* (Latin for "allocution," a formal speech or address), and a series of dialogues: *On the Grammarian, On Truth,* and *On Free Will.* His most important theological writing is *Cur Deus Homo,* or "Why God Became Man." In his final, unfinished work he tried to unravel the mystery of how a soul could come into existence. When he was told that he was soon to die, he is supposed to have replied, characteristically, "If it is His will I shall gladly obey, but if He should prefer me to stay with you just long enough to solve the question of the origin of the soul which I have been turning over in my mind, I would gratefully accept the chance, for I doubt whether anybody else will solve it when I am gone."

What Was Anselm's Overall Philosophical Project?

The original title of Anselm's *Proslogion* was *Faith Seeking Understanding,* and this encapsulates Anselm's

---

1   Max Charlesworth, from his introduction to *St. Anselm's Proslogion* (Clarendon Press, 1965), p. 17.

2   To excommunicate someone is to ban them from membership in the church and so, in the Catholic tradition, to exclude them from all the sacraments such as attending mass and receiving absolution for sins. Since it was believed that this would prevent those excommunicated from entering heaven, it was considered an extremely serious punishment.

consuming theological interest: he wanted to apply the tools of reason in order to better understand some (though not all) of what he already believed on the basis of faith. In fact, Anselm is often credited with being the first major thinker in the medieval Christian tradition to place great importance on the rational justification of theology, not because faith by itself is inadequate but because rational proofs can improve our grasp of the nature of God. Anselm thought of the search for religious truth as not so much accumulating facts about God but as coming to a better personal *acquaintance* with God, as one might come to know more about a friend over time. Since we clearly cannot sit down with God over a cup of coffee and chat, this process of finding out more about God depends to a large degree on careful, rational thought about God's nature.

Anselm is best remembered for originating one of the most stimulating and controversial of the arguments for the existence of God, the so-called Ontological Argument. ("Ontological" means "concerning what exists"; in this context, the idea is that we can come to know about God's 'pure' existence, without any sensory contact with God or his effects.) The Ontological Argument, if it works, not only proves as a matter of logic that God exists but also proves that God has a certain nature—that he is wise, good, infinite, powerful, and so on. The selection from Anselm given here is his presentation of this argument from the *Proslogion*, then a critique of the argument from Gaunilo, a monk from the Abbey of Marmoutiers near Tours, and finally Anselm's response to that criticism. (Although Anselm's response to Gaunilo can be challenging reading, coming to grips with his compressed arguments is exhilarating, and important for better understanding his argument in the *Proslogion*.)

What Is the Structure of This Reading?

After a preface, in which he explains how the idea for the Ontological Argument came to him, Anselm lays out the Ontological Argument in Chapters 2 and 3 of the *Proslogion*. His argument has three parts:

(a) That something-than-which-nothing-greater-can-be-thought must really exist (Chapter 2).

(b) That furthermore it must necessarily exist: that is, it exists in such a way that it cannot be conceived by the human mind as not existing (first part of Chapter 3).

(c) That the entity described in (a) and (b) must be God (second part of Chapter 3).

In Chapter 4 Anselm responds to a possible objection to part (b) of the argument. In Chapter 5 he briefly draws some consequences about the nature of God.

In the next section Gaunilo of Marmoutiers responds "on behalf of the Fool." Gaunilo's most important objections are:

(a) That God cannot be meaningfully thought about by human beings (Paragraph 4). Anselm responds to this in parts of Replies 1, 2, 8, and 9.

(b) That even if we could think about God, thinking about things doesn't show all by itself that they exist (Paragraphs 2 and 5). Anselm deals with this in Replies 1, 2, and 6.

(c) That if the Ontological Argument establishes the existence of God it ought also to establish the existence of the "Lost Island," which is absurd (Paragraph 6). Anselm's response—which, rightly or wrongly, doesn't take the objection very seriously—is at the start of Reply 3.

(d) That that-than-which-a-greater-cannot-be-thought can be thought not to exist (Para. 7). Anselm answers in Replies 1, 3, and 9.

Some Useful Background Information

1. The Ontological Argument is an '*a priori*' argument: that is, it purports to prove the existence of God on the basis of reason alone, independently of sense experience (e.g., independently of the results of empirical science). Anselm wants to show that the *idea* of God (all by itself) proves that God must exist.

2. Anselm makes use of various distinctions that it is useful to be aware of. The first is between two kinds of existence: existence in the mind (in Latin, "in intellectu") and existence in actual reality ("in re"). Something can exist in the mind but not in reality: for example, I can imagine a gold dinosaur and this dinosaur exists only *in intellectu* but not *in re*. Or something can exist

in reality but not in anyone's mind: for example, a particular rock no one has ever seen, on the dark side of the Moon. Or something can exist in *both* the mind and reality: the Eiffel Tower, for instance, is both *in re* and *in intellectu* since it is both in Paris and in our thoughts. Finally, some unreal thing no one has ever thought of would be neither *in re* nor *in intellectu*.

3. Then there is a distinction between two ways of thinking about an idea: this is the difference between merely thinking the words that express an idea and actually thinking about the thing itself. As Anselm puts it, "in one sense a thing is thought when the word signifying it is thought; in another sense when the very object which the thing is is understood." For example, the Fool might think to himself, "God does not exist," but if he does not really know what God is, then for him only "the sound of the letters or syllables" exists *in intellectu* and not actually God himself. This is sometimes explained in terms of the meaning of words or ideas: some of the ideas you think about really are meaningful to you (such as "Paris"), but some only *seem* meaningful when all you are really doing is silently mouthing the words (such as, perhaps, "crapulous"). Notice that, on this way of talking, ideas can be meaningful for us even if we do not know *everything* about their objects. For example, I don't need to have ever visited Paris to think meaningfully about that city; similarly, Anselm held that we can think about God even though God might be unimaginably greater than any picture we can form in our minds.

4. Finally, a third distinction is raised by Gaunilo and talked about by Anselm in his reply. This is the technical distinction between *thinking* (in Latin, "cogitare") and *understanding* ("intelligere"). For Anselm and Gaunilo, to think or conceive is to entertain possibilities—it's to consider things that may not actually be true and treat them (perhaps only temporarily) as if they were. For example, although I know I currently exist I could perhaps conceive of myself as not existing; although it may turn out to be false that extraterrestrials will visit the Earth

within fifty years, I can certainly think that they will. By contrast, "understanding" is what philosophers today would call a 'success term': by definition, you cannot *understand* something to be true (or real) if it is in fact false (or unreal). Thus, according to Gaunilo, we could, strictly speaking, only understand the phrase "God exists" if in fact God does exist.

One important question we can now ask is the following: can we think meaningfully about things that are *not* possible? For example, can we think about square circles or married bachelors? According to Anselm, the answer to this question is no: we can, as it were, think the *words* "square circle," but we can't really think about the things themselves. What this means, significantly, is that for Anselm anything we can properly think about must really be possible.

Some Common Misconceptions

1. Anselm is not just claiming that we can prove something exists by simply *thinking* of it existing: he realizes that not every concept which includes the idea of existence is actually exemplified. He thinks that the concept of God (that is, that-than-which-a-greater-cannot-be-thought) is a *uniquely special* concept in this respect; God, according to Anselm, has a unique kind of reality.

2. The unwary sometimes suppose that Anselm argues in the following way: God exists in our minds (*in intellectu*); our minds exist in the world (*in re*); therefore God must also exist in the world. This, however, is not his argument. (If it were, it would merely establish that the *concept* of God exists, while Anselm wants to show that God *himself* exists. Furthermore, when Anselm says things exist *in intellectu* it's not at all clear that he literally wants to say they are *located inside our heads*; the Eiffel Tower which is the object of our thoughts is the very same one as that which is located in Paris.)

3. Anselm (perhaps contrary to what Aquinas says about him in the next reading) does not think that the existence of God is simply self-evident:

that is, he doesn't think either (a) that we all already know that God exists, or (b) that merely to say "God does not exist" is to say something obviously self-contradictory (like saying "triangles have four sides"). What he does think is that *after* hearing his argument, it becomes obvious that God must exist. Similarly, he does not claim that everyone already has the concept of God (e.g., that we are born with the knowledge of God); his claim is rather that everyone can grasp that concept if it is explained to them.

How Important and Influential Is This Passage?

Rejected as mere verbal trickery by many subsequent philosophers (including St. Thomas Aquinas, in the next selection; the influential nineteenth-century philosopher Arthur Schopenhauer called it a "charming joke"), the Ontological Argument was nevertheless popular throughout the Middle Ages, was revived by René Descartes and Gottfried Leibniz in the seventeenth and eighteenth centuries, was influentially used by G.W.F. Hegel in the nineteenth century, and is still attractive to some philosophers today. Many more contemporary philosophers think it fallacious, but it has proved frustratingly difficult to uncontroversially pin down precisely what is wrong with this 'many-faced' argument. Early in the twentieth century developments in the logic of predicates (predicates are 'describing phrases' like "… is green" or "… is taller than …") bolstered Immanuel Kant's objection that "existence is not a predicate" (see question 5 below). However, more recent developments in the logic of possibility and necessity (called modal logic) have apparently given the argument a new lease on life.

Suggestions for Critical Reflection

1. If Anselm's argument is sound, what if anything does it tell us about God (in addition to the fact that he exists)?
2. The concepts 'bachelor' or 'unicorn' do not entail that such things exist. Why does Anselm think that the concept 'God' is importantly different? Is he right? What about the concept of 'an integer between 10 and 12': do you think this concept might commit us to the existence of the number 11? Does this show that not all existence claims are empirical?
3. What do you think about Anselm's distinction between two kinds of existence (*in re* and *in intellectu*)? Do you agree that being thought about is a kind of existence?
4. Does Gaunilo's example of the "Lost Island" show that Anselm has made a mistake? If so, does it show *what* mistake (or mistakes) has been made?
5. The famous eighteenth-century German philosopher Immanuel Kant argued that the flaw in the Ontological Argument is that it mistakenly treats existence as a property. When we say that leopards are spotted we are ascribing a property (being covered in spots) to leopards; however, Kant would argue, when we say that leopards exist, we are not pointing to all the leopards and saying that they have the property of existence. Instead, we are saying something not about actual leopards but about the concept 'leopard': we are saying that something in the actual world fits that concept. If we say that Boy Scouts are honest, we might go on to talk about some Boy Scout who is *perfectly* honest—who possesses the property of honesty to perfection. However, if we say that Boy Scouts exist, it is incoherent to try to point to the perfectly existing Boy Scout. Existence, therefore, is not a property, and so (according to Kant's argument) we have no reason to believe that a being which possesses all the properties of the most perfect thing—i.e., which is that-than-which-a-greater-cannot-be-thought—must exist. What do you think of this objection to the Ontological Argument? Is it decisive?
6. Suppose we agree with Anselm (against Kant) that existence *is* a perfection. Does this mean that an actual serial killer is more perfect than a merely fictional one?
7. Another objection to the Ontological Argument is the following: we may (as human beings) be able to *think* of an absolutely perfect

being, but (contrary to Anselm's assumption) it does not follow from this that an absolutely perfect being is actually *possible*. That is, although we are unable to see what is logically impossible in the idea of a perfect being, it might nevertheless still *be* logically impossible; and since we can't rule this out, we can't show *a priori* that God exists. What do you think of this objection? If it works, what implications does it have for our knowledge of possibility?

8. Finally, a third possible objection to Anselm's Ontological Argument: Even if Anselm succeeds in showing that the being-than-which-nothing-greater-can-be-thought must be *thought of* as existing, it still doesn't follow that it actually *does* exist. To conceive of something as being a certain way, the argument goes, does not mean that it actually *is* that way, or even that one must *believe* that it is that way: for example, one can conceive of the sky as being bright green, even though it isn't. So, for God, we can and perhaps must conceive of God as existing, but it doesn't follow that God does exist (or even that we must believe that God exists). What do you think of this objection? How do you think Anselm might respond to it?

Suggestions for Further Reading

The best biography of Anselm was written by his friend and contemporary Eadmer (*The Life of St. Anselm by Eadmer*, ed. R.W. Southern, Oxford University Press, 1962). Nearly all of Anselm's writings are collected in *Anselm of Canterbury: The Major Works* (ed. Brian Davis and G.R. Evans) from Oxford University Press, 1998. M.J. Charlesworth's edition of the *Proslogion* (Clarendon Press, 1965, re-printed by the University of Notre Dame Press in 1979) contains the Latin text, a translation, and a detailed philosophical commentary. There is also *A Companion to the Study of St. Anselm* written by Jasper Hopkins (University of Minnesota Press, 1972). Two books specifically about the Ontological Argument are Jonathan Barnes, *The Ontological Argument* (Macmillan, 1972) and Charles Hartshorne, *Anselm's Discovery* (Open Court, 1965). Two useful anthologies of papers about the Onto-

logical Argument are Alvin Plantinga (ed.), *The Ontological Argument* (Doubleday, 1965) and John Hick and Arthur McGill (eds.), *The Many-Faced Argument* (Macmillan, 1967). Kant's objection to the Ontological Argument is in his *Critique of Pure Reason* (Second Division, Book II, Chapter III, Section 4), and his argument is criticized by Jerome Shaffer, "Existence, Predication and the Ontological Argument," *Mind* 71 (1962). A version of the objection that we can't know *a priori* that a perfect being exists is developed by W.L. Rowe in "The Ontological Argument and Question-Begging," *International Journal for Philosophy of Religion* 7 (1976).

Proslogion
Preface and Chapters 2–5[3]

Preface

After I had published, at the pressing entreaties of several of my brethren, a certain short tract[4] as an example of meditation on the meaning of faith from the point of view of one seeking, through silent reasoning within himself, things he knows not—reflecting that this was made up of a connected chain of many arguments, I began to wonder if perhaps it might be possible to find one single argument that for its proof required no other save itself, and that by itself would suffice to prove that God really exists, that He is the supreme good needing no other and is He whom all things have need of for their being and well-being, and also to prove whatever we believe about the Divine Being. But as often and as diligently as I turned my thoughts to this, sometimes it seemed to me that I

---

3   The *Proslogion* was written between 1077 and 1078. Gaunilo's reply was written shortly after it appeared, and Anselm's response quickly after that. The translation reprinted here, of all three works, is by M.J. Charlesworth and appears in *Anselm of Canterbury: The Major Works*, edited by Brian Davies and G.R. Evans (Oxford World's Classics, 1998). By permission of Oxford University Press.

4   The *Monologion*, probably written one year before the *Proslogion*.

had almost reached what I was seeking, sometimes it eluded my acutest thinking completely, so that finally, in desperation, I was about to give up what I was looking for as something impossible to find. However, when I had decided to put aside this idea altogether, lest by uselessly occupying my mind it might prevent other ideas with which I could make some progress, then, in spite of my unwillingness and my resistance to it, it began to force itself upon me more and more pressingly. So it was that one day when I was quite worn out with resisting its importunacy, there came to me, in the very conflict of my thoughts, what I had despaired of finding, so that I eagerly grasped the notion which in my distraction I had been rejecting.

Judging, then, that what had given me such joy to discover would afford pleasure, if it were written down, to anyone who might read it, I have written the following short tract dealing with this question as well as several others, from the point of view of one trying to raise his mind to contemplate God and seeking to understand what he believes. In my opinion, neither this tract nor the other I mentioned before deserves to be called a book or to carry its author's name, and yet I did not think they should be sent forth without some title (by which, so to speak, they might invite those into whose hands they should come, to read them); so I have given to each its title, the first being called *An Example of Meditation on the Meaning of Faith*, and the sequel *Faith in Quest of Understanding*.

However, as both of them, under these titles, had already been copied out by several readers, a number of people (above all the reverend Archbishop of Lyons, Hugh, apostolic delegate to Gaul, who commanded me by his apostolic authority) have urged me to put my name to them. For the sake of greater convenience I have named the first book *Monologion*, that is, a soliloquy; and the other *Proslogion*, that is, an allocution.

…

Chapter 2. That God truly exists

Well then, Lord, You who give understanding to faith, grant me that I may understand, as much as You see fit, that You exist as we believe You to exist, and that You are what we believe You to be. Now we believe that You are something than which nothing greater can be thought. Or can it be that a thing of such a nature does not exist, since 'the Fool has said in his heart, there is no God'?[5] But surely, when this same Fool hears what I am speaking about, namely, 'something-than-which-nothing-greater-can-be-thought', he understands what he hears, and what he understands is in his mind, even if he does not understand that it actually exists. For it is one thing for an object to exist in the mind, and another thing to understand that an object actually exists. Thus, when a painter plans beforehand what he is going to execute, he has [the picture] in his mind, but he does not yet think that it actually exists because he has not yet executed it. However, when he has actually painted it, then he both has it in his mind and understands that it exists because he has now made it. Even the Fool, then, is forced to agree that something-than-which-nothing-greater-can-be-thought exists in the mind, since he understands this when he hears it, and whatever is understood is in the mind. And surely that-than-which-a-greater-cannot-be-thought cannot exist in the mind alone. For if it exists solely in the mind, it can be thought to exist in reality also, which is greater. If then that-than-which-a-greater-cannot-be-thought exists in the mind alone, this same that-than-which-a-greater-*cannot*-be-thought is that-than-which-a-greater-*can*-be-thought. But this is obviously impossible. Therefore there is absolutely no doubt that something-than-which-a-greater-cannot-be-thought exists both in the mind and in reality.

Chapter 3. That God cannot be thought not to exist

And certainly this being so truly exists that it cannot be even thought not to exist. For something can be thought to exist that cannot be thought not to exist, and this is greater than that which can be thought not to exist. Hence, if that-than-which-a-greater-cannot-be-thought can be thought not to exist, then that-than-which-a-greater-cannot-be-thought is not the same as that-than-which-a-greater-cannot-be-thought, which is absurd. Something-than-which-a-greater-cannot-

---

5   This quotation is from the first line of Psalms 13 and 52 in the Vulgate version of the Bible, 14 and 53 in the King James version. Later citations in this reading also refer to the Vulgate.

be-thought exists so truly then, that it cannot be even thought not to exist.

And You, Lord our God, are this being. You exist so truly, Lord my God, that You cannot even be thought not to exist. And this is as it should be, for if some intelligence could think of something better than You, the creature would be above its Creator and would judge its Creator—and that is completely absurd. In fact, everything else there is, except You alone, can be thought of as not existing. You alone, then, of all things most truly exist and therefore of all things possess existence to the highest degree; for anything else does not exist as truly, and so possesses existence to a lesser degree. Why then did 'the Fool say in his heart, there is no God' when it is so evident to any rational mind that You of all things exist to the highest degree? Why indeed, unless because he was stupid and a fool?

Chapter 4. How 'the Fool said in his heart' what cannot be thought

How indeed has he 'said in his heart' what he could not think; or how could he not think what he 'said in his heart', since to 'say in one's heart' and to 'think' are the same? But if he really (indeed, since he really) both thought because he 'said in his heart' and did not 'say in his heart' because he could not think, there is not only one sense in which something is 'said in one's heart' or thought. For in one sense a thing is thought when the word signifying it is thought; in another sense when the very object which the thing is is understood. In the first sense, then, God can be thought not to exist, but not at all in the second sense. No one, indeed, understanding what God is can think that God does not exist, even though he may say these words in his heart either without any [objective] signification or with some peculiar signification. For God is that-than-which-nothing-greater-can-be-thought. Whoever really understands this understands clearly that this same being so exists that not even in thought can it not exist. Thus whoever understands that God exists in such a way cannot think of Him as not existing.

I give thanks, good Lord, I give thanks to You, since what I believed before through Your free gift I now so understand through Your illumination, that if I did not want to *believe* that You existed, I should nevertheless be unable not to *understand* it.

Chapter 5. That God is whatever it is better to be than not to be and that, existing through Himself alone, He makes all other beings from nothing

What then are You, Lord God, You than whom nothing greater can be thought? But what are You save that supreme being, existing through Yourself alone, who made everything else from nothing? For whatever is not this is less than that which can be thought of; but this cannot be thought about You. What goodness, then, could be wanting to the supreme good, through which every good exists? Thus You are just, truthful, happy, and whatever it is better to be than not to be—for it is better to be just rather than unjust, and happy rather than unhappy.

Pro Insipiente

("On Behalf of the Fool"), by Gaunilo of Marmoutiers

Paragraph 1

To one doubting whether there is, or denying that there is, something of such a nature than which nothing greater can be thought, it is said here [in the *Proslogion*] that its existence is proved, first because the very one who denies or doubts it already has it in his mind, since when he hears it spoken of he understands what is said; and further, because what he understands is necessarily such that it exists not only in the mind but also in reality. And this is proved by the fact that it is greater to exist both in the mind and in reality than in the mind alone. For if this same being exists in the mind alone, anything that existed also in reality would be greater than this being, and thus that which is greater than everything would be less than something and would not be greater than everything, which is obviously contradictory. Therefore, it is necessarily the case that that which is greater than everything, being already proved to exist in the mind, should exist not only in the mind but also in reality, since otherwise it would not be greater than everything.

Paragraph 2

But he [the Fool] can perhaps reply that this thing is said already to exist in the mind only in the sense that I understand what is said. For could I not say that all kinds of unreal things, not existing in themselves in any way at all, are equally in the mind since if anyone speaks about them I understand whatever he says? Unless perhaps it is manifest that this being is such that it can be entertained in the mind in a different way from unreal or doubtfully real things, so that I am not said to think of or have in thought what is heard, but to understand and have it in mind, in that I cannot really think of this being in any other way save by understanding it, that is to say, by grasping by certain knowledge that the thing itself actually exists. But if this is the case, first, there will be no difference between having an object in mind (taken as preceding in time), and understanding that the object actually exists (taken as following in time), as in the case of the picture which exists first in the mind of the painter and in the completed work. And thus it would be scarcely conceivable that, when this object had been spoken of and heard, it could not be thought not to exist in the same way in which God can [be thought] not to exist. For if He cannot, why put forward this whole argument against anyone denying or doubting that there is something of this kind? Finally, that it is such a thing that, as soon as it is thought of, it cannot but be certainly perceived by the mind as indubitably existing, must be proved to me by some indisputable argument and not by that proposed, namely, that it must already be in my mind when I understand what I hear. For this is in my view like [arguing that] any things doubtfully real or even unreal are capable of existing if these things are mentioned by someone whose spoken words I might understand, and, even more, that [they exist] if, though deceived about them as often happens, I should believe them [to exist]—which argument I still do not believe!

Paragraph 3

Hence, the example of the painter having the picture he is about to make already in his mind cannot support this argument. For this picture, before it is actually made, is contained in the very art of the painter and such a thing in the art of any artist is nothing but a certain part of his very understanding, since as St. Augustine says,[6] 'when the artisan is about actually to make a box he has it beforehand in his art. The box which is actually made is not a living thing, but the box which is in his art is a living thing since the soul of the artist, in which these things exist before their actual realization, is a living thing'. Now how are these things living in the living soul of the artist unless they are identical with the knowledge or understanding of the soul itself? But, apart from those things which are known to belong to the very nature of the mind itself, in the case of any truth perceived by the mind by being either heard or understood, then it cannot be doubted that this truth is one thing and that the understanding which grasps it is another. Therefore even if it were true that there was something than which nothing greater could be thought, this thing, heard and understood, would not, however, be the same as the not-yet-made picture is in the mind of the painter.

Paragraph 4

To this we may add something that has already been mentioned, namely, that upon hearing it spoken of I can so little think of or entertain in my mind this being (that which is greater than all those others that are able to be thought of, and which it is said can be none other than God Himself) in terms of an object known to me either by species or genus, as I can think of God Himself, whom indeed for this very reason I can even think does not exist. For neither do I know the reality itself, nor can I form an idea from some other things like it since, as you say yourself, it is such that nothing could be like it. For if I heard something said about a man who was completely unknown to me so that I did not even know whether he existed, I could nevertheless think about him in his very reality as a man by means of that specific or generic notion by which I know what a man is or men are. However, it could happen that, because of a falsehood on the part of the speaker, the man I thought of did not actually exist, although I thought of him nevertheless as a truly

---

6   St. Augustine, a north African bishop who lived from 354 until 430, was the most important early Christian theologian and Anselm's major intellectual influence. This quote is from his *Treatises on the Gospel of John*.

existing object—not this particular man but any man in general. It is not, then, in the way that I have this unreal thing in thought or in mind that I can have that object in my mind when I hear 'God' or 'something greater than everything' spoken of. For while I was able to think of the former in terms of a truly existing thing which was known to me, I know nothing at all of the latter save for the verbal formula, and on the basis of this alone one can scarcely or never think of any truth. For when one thinks in this way, one thinks not so much of the word itself, which is indeed a real thing (that is to say, the sound of the letters or syllables), as of the meaning of the word which is heard. However, it [that which is greater than everything] is not thought of in the way of one who knows what is meant by that expression—thought of, that is, in terms of the thing [signified] or as true in thought alone. It is rather in the way of one who does not really know this object but thinks of it in terms of an affection of his mind produced by hearing the spoken words, and who tries to imagine what the words he has heard might mean. However, it would be astonishing if he could ever [attain to] the truth of the thing. Therefore, when I hear and understand someone saying that there is something greater than everything that can be thought of, it is agreed that it is in this latter sense that it is in my mind and not in any other sense. So much for the claim that that supreme nature exists already in my mind.

Paragraph 5

That, however, [this nature] necessarily exists in reality is demonstrated to me from the fact that, unless it existed, whatever exists in reality would be greater than it and consequently it would not be that which is greater than everything that undoubtedly had already been proved to exist in the mind. To this I reply as follows: if something that cannot even be thought in the true and real sense must be said to exist in the mind, then I do not deny that this also exists in my mind in the same way. But since from this one cannot in any way conclude that it exists also in reality, I certainly do not yet concede that it actually exists, until this is proved to me by an indubitable argument. For he who claims that it actually exists because otherwise it would not be that which is greater than everything

does not consider carefully enough whom he is addressing. For I certainly do not yet admit this greater [than everything] to be any truly existing thing; indeed I doubt or even deny it. And I do not concede that it exists in a different way from that—if one ought to speak of 'existence' here—when the mind tries to imagine a completely unknown thing on the basis of the spoken words alone. How then can it be proved to me on that basis that that which is greater than everything truly exists in reality (because it is evident that it is greater than all others) if I keep on denying and also doubting that this is evident and do not admit that this greater [than everything] is either in my mind or thought, not even in the sense in which many doubtfully real and unreal things are? It must first of all be proved to me then that this same greater than everything truly exists in reality somewhere, and then only will the fact that it is greater than everything make it clear that it also subsists in itself.

Paragraph 6

For example: they say that there is in the ocean somewhere an island which, because of the difficulty (or rather the impossibility) of finding that which does not exist, some have called the 'Lost Island'. And the story goes that it is blessed with all manner of priceless riches and delights in abundance, much more even than the Happy Isles,[7] and, having no owner or inhabitant, it is superior everywhere in abundance of riches to all those other lands that men inhabit. Now, if anyone tell me that it is like this, I shall easily understand what is said, since nothing is difficult about it. But if he should then go on to say, as though it were a logical consequence of this: You cannot any more doubt that this island that is more excellent than all other lands truly exists somewhere in reality than you can doubt that it is in your mind; and since it is more excellent to exist not only in the mind alone but also in reality, therefore it must needs be that it exists. For if it did not exist, any other land existing in reality would be more excellent than it, and so this island, already conceived by you to be more

_____

7   The mythical land—often located where the sun sets in the West—where people in classical times believed the souls of heroes lived in bliss.

excellent than others, will not be more excellent. If, I say, someone wishes thus to persuade me that this island really exists beyond all doubt, I should either think that he was joking, or I should find it hard to decide which of us I ought to judge the bigger fool—I, if I agreed with him, or he, if he thought that he had proved the existence of this island with any certainty, unless he had first convinced me that its very excellence exists in my mind precisely as a thing existing truly and indubitably and not just as something unreal or doubtfully real.

Paragraph 7

Thus first of all might the Fool reply to objections. And if then someone should assert that this greater [than everything] is such that it cannot be thought not to exist (again without any other proof than that otherwise it would not be greater than everything), then he could make this same reply and say: When have I said that there truly existed some being that is 'greater than everything', such that from this it could be proved to me that this same being really existed to such a degree that it could not be thought not to exist? That is why it must first be conclusively proved by argument that there is some higher nature, namely that which is greater and better than all the things that are, so that from this we can also infer everything else which necessarily cannot be wanting to what is greater and better than everything. When, however, it is said that this supreme being cannot be *thought* not to exist, it would perhaps be better to say that it cannot be *understood* not to exist nor even to be able not to exist. For, strictly speaking, unreal things cannot be *understood*, though certainly they can be *thought* of in the same way as the Fool *thought* that God does not exist. I know with complete certainty that I exist, but I also know at the same time nevertheless that I can not-exist. And I *understand* without any doubt that that which exists to the highest degree, namely God, both exists and cannot not exist. I do not know, however, whether I can *think* of myself as not existing while I know with absolute certainty that I do exist; but if I can, why cannot [I do the same] with regard to anything else I know with the same certainty? If however I cannot, this will not be the distinguishing characteristic of God [namely, to be such that He cannot be thought not to exist].

Paragraph 8

The other parts of this tract[8] are argued so truly, so brilliantly and so splendidly, and are also of so much worth and instinct with so fragrant a perfume of devout and holy feeling, that in no way should they be rejected because of those things at the beginning (rightly intuited, but less surely argued out). Rather the latter should be demonstrated more firmly and so everything received with very great respect and praise.

Anselm's *Reply to Gaunilo*

Since it is not the Fool, against whom I spoke in my tract, who takes me up, but one who, though speaking on the Fool's behalf, is an orthodox Christian and no fool, it will suffice if I reply to the Christian.

Reply 1

You say then—you, whoever you are, who claim that the Fool can say these things—that the being than-which-a-greater-cannot-be-thought is not in the mind except as what cannot be thought of, in the true sense, at all. And [you claim], moreover, that what I say does not follow, namely, that 'that-than-which-a-greater-cannot-be-thought' exists in reality from the fact that it exists in the mind, any more than that the Lost Island most certainly exists from the fact that, when it is described in words, he who hears it described has no doubt that it exists in his mind. I reply as follows: If 'that-than-which-a-greater-cannot-be-thought' is neither understood nor thought of, and is neither in the mind nor in thought, then it is evident that *either* God is not that-than-which-a-greater-cannot-be-thought *or* is not understood nor thought of, and is not in the mind nor in thought. Now my strongest argument that this is false is to appeal to your faith and to your conscience. Therefore 'that-than-which-a-greater-cannot-be-thought' is truly understood and thought and is in the mind and in thought. For this reason, [the arguments] by which you attempt to prove the contrary are either

8 The *Proslogion* has 26 chapters, of which only chapters two to five—those which contain the ontological argument about which Gaunilo has complaints—are reprinted here.

not true, or what you believe follows from them does not in fact follow.

Moreover, you maintain that, from the fact that that-than-which-a-greater-cannot-be-thought is understood, it does not follow that it is in the mind, nor that, if it is in the mind, it therefore exists in reality. I insist, however, that simply if it can be thought it is necessary that it exists. For 'that-than-which-a-greater-cannot-be-thought' cannot be thought save as being without a beginning. But whatever can be thought as existing and does not actually exist can be thought as having a beginning of its existence. Consequently, 'that-than-which-a-greater-cannot-be-thought' cannot be thought as existing and yet not actually exist. If, therefore, it can be thought as existing, it exists of necessity.

Further: even if it can be thought of, then certainly it necessarily exists. For no one who denies or doubts that there is something-than-which-a-greater-cannot-be-thought, denies or doubts that, if this being were to exist, it would not be capable of not-existing either actually or in the mind—otherwise it would not be that-than-which-a-greater-cannot-be-thought. But, whatever can be thought as existing and does not actually exist, could, if it were to exist, possibly not exist either actually or in the mind. For this reason, if it can merely be thought, 'that-than-which-a-greater-cannot-be-thought' cannot not exist. However, let us suppose that it does not exist even though it can be thought. Now, whatever can be thought and does not actually exist would not be, if it should exist, 'that-than-which-a-greater-cannot-be-thought'. If, therefore, it were 'that-than-which-a-greater-cannot-be-thought' it would not be that-than-which-a-greater-cannot-be-thought, which is completely absurd. It is, then, false that something-than-which-a-greater-cannot-be-thought does not exist if it can merely be thought; and it is all the more false if it can be understood and be in the mind.

I will go further: It cannot be doubted that whatever does not exist in any one place or at any one time, even though it does exist in some place or at some time, can however be thought to exist at no place and at no time, just as it does not exist in some place or at some time. For what did not exist yesterday and today exists can thus, as it is understood not to have existed yesterday, be supposed not to exist at any time. And

that which does not exist here in this place, and does exist elsewhere can, in the same way as it does not exist here, be thought not to exist anywhere. Similarly with a thing some of whose particular parts do not exist in the place and at the time its other parts exist—all of its parts, and therefore the whole thing itself, can be thought to exist at no time and in no place. For even if it be said that time always exists and that the world is everywhere, the former does not, however, always exist as a whole, nor is the other as a whole everywhere; and as certain particular parts of time do not exist when other parts do exist, therefore they can be even thought not to exist at any time. Again, as certain particular parts of the world do not exist in the same place where other parts do exist, they can thus be supposed not to exist anywhere. Moreover, what is made up of parts can be broken up in thought and can possibly not exist. Thus it is that whatever does not exist as a whole at a certain place and time can be thought not to exist, even if it does actually exist. But 'that-than-which-a-greater-cannot-be-thought' cannot be thought not to exist if it does actually exist, otherwise, if it exists it is not that-than-which-a-greater-cannot-be-thought, which is absurd. In no way, then, does this being not exist as a whole in any particular place or at any particular time; but it exists as a whole at every time and in every place.

Do you not consider then that that about which we understand these things can to some extent be thought or understood, or can exist in thought or in the mind? For if it cannot, we could not understand these things about it. And if you say that, because it is not completely understood, it cannot be understood at all and cannot be in the mind, then you must say [equally] that one who cannot see the purest light of the sun directly does not see daylight, which is the same thing as the light of the sun. Surely then 'that-than-which-a-greater-cannot-be-thought' is understood and is in the mind to the extent that we understand these things about it.

Reply 2

I said, then, in the argument that you criticize, that when the Fool hears 'that-than-which-a-greater-cannot-be-thought' spoken of he understands what he hears. Obviously if it is spoken of in a known language and he does not understand it, then either he has no intelligence at all, or a completely obtuse one.

Next I said that, if it is understood it is in the mind; or does what has been proved to exist necessarily in actual reality not exist in any mind? But you will say that, even if it is in the mind, yet it does not follow that it is understood. Observe then that, from the fact that it is understood, it does follow that it is in the mind. For, just as what is thought is thought by means of a thought, and what is thought by a thought is thus, as thought, *in* thought, so also, what is understood is understood by the mind, and what is understood by the mind is thus, as understood, *in* the mind. What could be more obvious than this?

I said further that if a thing exists even in the mind alone, it can be thought to exist also in reality, which is greater. If, then, it (namely, 'that-than-which-a-greater-cannot-be-thought') exists in the mind alone, it is something than which a greater *can* be thought. What, I ask you, could be more logical? For if it exists even in the mind alone, cannot it be thought to exist also in reality? And if it can [be so thought], is it not the case that he who thinks this thinks of something greater than it, if it exists in the mind alone? What, then, could follow more logically than that, if 'that-than-which-a-greater-cannot-be-thought' exists in the mind alone, it is the same as that-than-which-a-great-er-*can*-be-thought? But surely 'that-than-which-a-greater-*can*-be-thought' is not for any mind [the same as] 'that-than-which-a-greater-*cannot*-be-thought'. Does it not follow, then, that 'that-than-which-a-greater-*cannot*-be-thought', if it exists in anyone's mind, does not exist in the mind alone? For if it exists in the mind alone, it is that-than-which-a-greater-*can*-be-thought, which is absurd.

Reply 3

You claim, however, that this is as though someone asserted that it cannot be doubted that a certain island in the ocean (which is more fertile than all other lands and which, because of the difficulty or even the impossibility of discovering what does not exist, is called the 'Lost Island') truly exists in reality since anyone easily understands it when it is described in words. Now, I truly promise that if anyone should discover for me something existing either in reality or in the mind alone—except 'that-than-which-a-greater-cannot-be-thought'—to which the logic of my argument would apply, then I shall find that Lost Island and give it, never more to be lost, to that person. It has already been clearly seen, however, that 'that-than-which-a-greater-cannot-be-thought' cannot be thought not to exist, because it exists as a matter of such certain truth. Otherwise it would not exist at all. In short, if anyone says that he thinks that this being does not exist, I reply that, when he thinks of this, either he thinks of something than which a greater cannot be thought, or he does not think of it. If he does not think of it, then he does not think that what he does not think of does not exist. If, however, he does think of it, then indeed he thinks of something which cannot be even thought not to exist. For if it could be thought not to exist, it could be thought to have a beginning and an end—but this cannot be. Thus, he who thinks of it thinks of something that cannot be thought not to exist; indeed, he who thinks of this does not think of it as not existing, otherwise he would think what cannot be thought. Therefore 'that-than-which-a-greater-cannot-be-thought' cannot be thought not to exist.

Reply 4

You say, moreover, that when it is said that this supreme reality cannot be *thought* not to exist, it would perhaps be better to say that it cannot be *understood* not to exist or even to be able not to exist. However, it must rather be said that it cannot be *thought*. For if I had said that the thing in question could not be *understood* not to exist, perhaps you yourself (who claim that we cannot understand—if this word is to be taken strictly—things that are unreal) would object that nothing that exists can be understood not to exist. For it is false [to say that] what exists does not exist, so that it is not the distinguishing characteristic of God not to be able to be understood not to exist. But, if any of those things which exist with absolute certainty can be understood not to exist, in the same way other things that certainly exist can be understood not to exist. But, if the matter is carefully considered, this objection cannot be made apropos[9] [the term] 'thought'. For even if none of those things that exist

---

9   With respect to, concerning.

can be *understood* not to exist, all however can be *thought* as not existing, save that which exists to a supreme degree. For in fact all those things (and they alone) that have a beginning or end or are made up of parts and, as I have already said, all those things that do not exist as a whole in a particular place or at a particular time can be thought as not existing. Only that being in which there is neither beginning nor end nor conjunction of parts, and that thought does not discern save as a whole in every place and at every time, cannot be thought as not existing.

Know then that you can think of yourself as not existing while yet you are absolutely sure that you exist. I am astonished that you have said that you do not know this. For we think of many things that we know to exist, as not existing; and [we think of] many things that we know not to exist, as existing—not judging that it is really as we think but imagining it to be so. We *can*, in fact, think of something as not existing while knowing that it does exist, since we can [think of] the one and know the other at the same time. And we *cannot* think of something as not existing if yet we know that it does exist, since we cannot think of it as existing and not existing at the same time. He, therefore, who distinguishes these two senses of this assertion will understand that [in one sense] nothing can be thought as not existing while yet it is known to exist, and that [in another sense] whatever exists, save that-than-which-a-greater-cannot-be-thought, can be thought of as not existing even when we know that it does exist. Thus it is that, on the one hand, it is the distinguishing characteristic of God that He cannot be thought of as not existing, and that, on the other hand, many things, the while they do exist, cannot be thought of as not existing. In what sense, however, one can say that God can be thought of as not existing I think I have adequately explained in my tract.

Reply 5

As for the other objections you make against me on behalf of the Fool, it is quite easy to meet them, even for one weak in the head, and so I considered it a waste of time to show this. But since I hear that they appear to certain readers to have some force against me, I will deal briefly with them.

First, you often reiterate that I say that that which is greater than everything exists in the mind, and that if it is in the mind, it exists also in reality, for otherwise that which is greater than everything would not be that which is greater than everything. However, nowhere in all that I have said will you find such an argument. For 'that which is greater than everything' and 'that-than-which-a-greater-cannot-be-thought' are not equivalent for the purpose of proving the real existence of the thing spoken of. Thus, if anyone should say that 'that-than-which-a-greater-cannot-be-thought' is not something that actually exists, or that it can possibly not exist, or even can be thought of as not existing, he can easily be refuted. For what does not exist can possibly not exist, and what can not exist can be thought of as not existing. However, whatever can be thought of as not existing, if it actually exists, is not that-than-which-a-greater-cannot-be-thought. But if it does not exist, indeed even if it should exist, it would not be that-than-which-a-greater-cannot-be-thought. But it cannot be asserted that 'that-than-which-a-greater-cannot-be-thought' is not, if it exists, that-than-which-a-greater-cannot-be-thought, or that, if it should exist, it would not be that-than-which-a-greater-cannot-be-thought. It is evident, then, that it neither does not exist nor can not exist or be thought of as not existing. For if it does exist in another way it is not what it is said to be, and if it should exist [in another way] it would not be [what it was said to be].

However it seems that it is not as easy to prove this in respect of what is said to be greater than everything. For it is not as evident that that which can be thought of as not existing is not that which is greater than everything, as that it is not that-than-which-a-greater-cannot-be-thought. And, in the same way, neither is it indubitable that, if there is something which is 'greater than everything', it is identical with 'that-than-which-a-greater-cannot-be-thought'; nor, if there were [such a being], that no other like it might exist—as this is certain in respect of what is said to be 'that-than-which-a-greater-cannot-be-thought'. For what if someone should say that something that is greater than everything actually exists, and yet that this same being can be thought of as not existing, and that something greater than it can be thought, even if this does not exist? In this case can it be inferred as evidently that [this being] is therefore not that which is greater than everything, as it would quite evidently be said in the other case that it is therefore not that-than-which-a-greater-cannot-be-thought? The former [inference] needs, in fact, a premiss in addition to this which is said to be 'greater than everything'; but the latter needs nothing save this utterance itself, namely, 'that-than-which-a-greater-cannot-be-thought'. Therefore, if what 'that-than-which-a-greater-cannot-be-thought' of itself proves concerning itself cannot be proved in the same way in respect of what is said to be 'greater than everything', you criticize me unjustly for having said what I did not say, since it differs so much from what I did say.

If, however, it can [be proved] by means of another argument, you should not have criticized me for having asserted what can be proved. Whether it can [be proved], however, is easily appreciated by one who understands that it can [in respect of] 'that-than-which-a-greater-cannot-be-thought'. For one cannot in any way understand 'that-than-which-a-greater-cannot-be-thought' without [understanding that it is] that which alone is greater than everything. As, therefore, 'that-than-which-a-greater-cannot-be-thought' is understood and is in the mind, and is consequently judged to exist in true reality, so also that which is greater than everything is said to be understood and to exist in the mind, and so is necessarily inferred to exist in reality itself. You see, then, how right you were to compare me with that stupid person who wished to maintain that the Lost Island existed from the sole fact that being described it was understood.

Reply 6

You object, moreover, that any unreal or doubtfully real things at all can equally be understood and exist in the mind in the same way as the being I was speaking of. I am astonished that you urge this [objection] against me, for I was concerned to prove something which was in doubt, and for me it was sufficient that I should first show that it was understood and existed in the mind *in some way or other*, leaving it to be determined subsequently whether it was in the mind alone as unreal things are, or in reality also as true things are. For, if unreal or doubtfully real things are understood and exist in the mind in the sense that,

when they are spoken of, he who hears them understands what the speaker means, nothing prevents what I have spoken of being understood and existing in the mind. But how are these [assertions] consistent, that is, when you assert that if someone speaks of unreal things you would understand whatever he says, and that, in the case of a thing which is not entertained in thought in the same way as even unreal things are, you do not say that you think of it or have it in thought upon hearing it spoken of, but rather that you understand it and have it in mind since, precisely, you cannot think of it save by understanding it, that is, knowing certainly that the thing exists in reality itself? How, I say, are both [assertions] consistent, namely that unreal things are understood, and that 'to understand' means knowing with certainty that something actually exists? You should have seen that nothing [of this applies] to me. But if unreal things are, in a sense, understood (this definition applying not to every kind of understanding but to a certain kind) then I ought not to be criticized for having said that 'that-than-which-a-greater-cannot-be-thought' is understood and is in the mind, even before it was certain that it existed in reality itself.

Reply 7

Next, you say that it can hardly be believed that when this [that-than-which-a-greater-cannot-be-thought] has been spoken of and heard, it cannot be thought not to exist, as even it can be thought that God does not exist. Now those who have attained even a little expertise in disputation and argument could reply to that on my behalf. For is it reasonable that someone should therefore deny what he understands because it is said to be [the same as] that which he denies since he does not understand it? Or if that is denied [to exist] which is understood only to some extent and is the same as what is not understood at all, is not what is in doubt more easily proved from the fact that it is in some mind than from the fact that it is in no mind at all? For this reason it cannot be believed that anyone should deny 'that-than-which-a-greater-cannot-be-thought' (which, being heard, he understands to some extent), on the ground that he denies God whose meaning he does not think of in any way at all. On the other hand, if it is denied on the ground that it is not understood completely, even so is not that which is understood in some way easier to prove than that which is not understood in any way? It was therefore not wholly without reason that, to prove against the Fool that God exists, I proposed 'that-than-which-a-greater-cannot-be-thought', since he would understand this in some way, [whereas] he would understand the former [God] in no way at all.

Reply 8

In fact, your painstaking argument that 'that-than-which-a-greater-cannot-be-thought' is not like the not-yet-realized painting in the mind of the painter is beside the point. For I did not propose [the example] of the foreknown picture because I wanted to assert that what was at issue was in the same case, but rather that so I could show that something not understood as existing exists in the mind.

Again, you say that upon hearing of 'that-than-which-a-greater-cannot-be-thought' you cannot think of it as a real object known either generically or specifically or have it in your mind, on the grounds that you neither know the thing itself nor can you form an idea of it from other things similar to it. But obviously this is not so. For since everything that is less good is similar in so far as it is good to that which is more good, it is evident to every rational mind that, mounting from the less good to the more good we can from those things than which something greater can be thought conjecture a great deal about that-than-which-a-greater-cannot-be-thought. Who, for example, cannot think of this (even if he does not believe that what he thinks of actually exists) namely, that if something that has a beginning and end is good, that which, although it has had a beginning, does not, however, have an end, is much better? And just as this latter is better than the former, so also that which has neither beginning nor end is better again than this, even if it passes always from the past through the present to the future. Again, whether something of this kind actually exists or not, that which does not lack anything at all, nor is forced to change or move, is very much better still. Cannot this be thought? Or can we think of something greater than this? Or is not this precisely to form an idea of that-than-which-a-greater-cannot-be-thought from those things than which a greater can be thought? There is, then, a way by which one can form an idea of

'that-than-which-a-greater-cannot-be-thought'. In this way, therefore, the Fool who does not accept the sacred authority [of Revelation] can easily be refuted if he denies that he can form an idea from other things of 'that-than-which-a-greater-cannot-be-thought'. But if any orthodox Christian should deny this let him remember that "the invisible things of God from the creation of the world are clearly seen through the things that have been made, even his eternal power and Godhead."[10]

Reply 9

But even if it were true that [the object] that-than-which-a-greater-cannot-be-thought cannot be thought of nor understood, it would not, however, be false that [the formula] 'that-than-which-a-greater-cannot-be-thought' could be thought of and understood. For just as nothing prevents one from saying 'ineffable'[11] although one cannot specify what is said to be ineffable; and just as one can think of the inconceivable—although one cannot think of what 'inconceivable' applies to—so also, when 'that-than-which-a-greater-cannot-be-thought' is spoken of, there is no doubt at all that what is heard can be thought of and understood even if the thing itself cannot be thought of and understood. For if someone is so witless as to say that there is not something than-which-a-greater-cannot-be-thought, yet he will not be so shameless as to say that he is not able to understand and think of what he was speaking about. Or if such a one is to be found, not only should his assertion be condemned, but he himself condemned. Whoever, then, denies that there is something than-which-a-greater-cannot-be-thought, at any rate understands and thinks of the denial he makes, and this denial cannot be understood and thought about apart from its elements. Now, one element [of the denial] is 'that-than-which-a-greater-cannot-be-thought'. Whoever, therefore, denies this understands and thinks of 'that-than-which-a-greater-cannot-be-thought'. It is evident, moreover, that in the same way one can think of and understand that which cannot not exist. And one who thinks of this

---

10   A biblical quote, from St. Paul's Epistle to the Romans (1:20).

11   "Ineffable" means unutterable or indescribable—incapable of being expressed.

thinks of something greater than one who thinks of what can not exist. When, therefore, one thinks of that-than-which-a-greater-cannot-be-thought, if one thinks of what can not exist, one does not think of that-than-which-a-greater-cannot-be-thought. Now the same thing cannot at the same time be thought of and not thought of. For this reason he who thinks of that-than-which-a-greater-cannot-be-thought does not think of something that can not exist but something that cannot not exist. Therefore what he thinks of exists necessarily, since whatever can not exist is not what he thinks of.

Reply 10

I think now that I have shown that I have proved in the above tract, not by a weak argumentation but by a sufficiently necessary one, that something-than-which-a-greater-cannot-be-thought exists in reality itself, and that this proof has not been weakened by the force of any objection. For the import of this proof is in itself of such force that what is spoken of is proved (as a necessary consequence of the fact that it is understood or thought of) both to exist in actual reality and to be itself whatever must be believed about the Divine Being. For we believe of the Divine Being whatever it can, absolutely speaking, be thought better to be than not to be. For example, it is better to be eternal than not eternal, good than not good, indeed goodness itself than not goodness-itself. However, nothing of this kind cannot but be that-than-which-a-greater-cannot-be-thought. It is, then, necessary that 'that-than-which-a-greater-cannot-be-thought' should be whatever must be believed about the Divine Nature.

I thank you for your kindness both in criticizing and praising my tract. For since you praised so fulsomely those parts that appeared to you to be worthy of acceptance, it is quite clear that you have criticized those parts that seemed to you to be weak, not from any malice but from good will.

ST. THOMAS AQUINAS
Summa Theologiae

Who Was St. Thomas Aquinas?

Saint Thomas was born in 1225 in Roccasecca in southern Italy, the son of the count of Aquino. At the age of five he was sent to be educated at the great Benedictine abbey of Monte Casino, and at 14 he went to university in Naples. His father expected him to join the respectable and wealthy Benedictine order of monks. However, when he was 19 Aquinas instead joined the recently formed Dominican order of celibate, mendicant (begging) friars. These monks had adopted a life of complete poverty and traveled Europe studying and teaching the gospel. Thomas's father was outraged, and—according to legend—he locked Aquinas in the family castle for a year and of-fered him bribes, including a beautiful prostitute, to join the Benedictines instead. Aquinas is said to have grabbed a burning brand from the fire and chased away the prostitute; his family eventually allowed him to leave and travel to Paris. He went on to study Greek and Islamic philosophy, natural science, and theology in Paris and Cologne under Albertus Magnus ("Albert the Great"), a Dominican who was famed for his vast learning. His colleagues in Cologne nicknamed Aquinas "the dumb ox," because of his reserved personality and large size; Albertus is said to have responded that Thomas's bellowing would be heard throughout the world. In 1256 Aquinas was made a regent master (professor) at the University of Paris. He taught in Paris and Naples until, on December 6, 1273, he had a deeply religious experience after which he stopped writing. "All that I have written seems to me like straw compared to what has now been revealed to me," he said. He died four months later.

Aquinas became known to later ages as the Angelic Doctor, and was canonized in 1323. In fact, starting shortly after his death, miraculous powers (such as healing the blind) were attributed to Aquinas' corpse, and the Cistercian monks who possessed the body became concerned that members of the Dominican order would steal their treasure: as a safeguard, they "exhumed the corpse of Brother Thomas from its resting place, cut off the head and placed it in a hiding place in a corner of the chapel," so that even if the body were stolen they would still have the skull. His sister was given one of his hands.

Aquinas wrote voluminously— over eight million words of closely reasoned prose, especially amazing considering he was less than 50 when he died. He is said to have committed the entire Bible to memory, and was able to dictate to six or seven secretaries at one time. (His own handwriting was so unintelligible it has been dubbed the *litera inintelligibilis*.) His two major works, both written in Latin, are *Summa contra Gentiles* and *Summa Theologiae*. The first (written between 1259 and 1264) defends Christianity against a large number of objections, without assuming in advance that Christianity is true—it was reputedly written as a handbook for missionaries seeking to convert Muslims and others to Catholicism. The second (written between 1265 and 1273) attempts to summarize Catholic doctrine in such a way that it is consistent with rational philosophy and the natural science of the day.

What Was Aquinas' Overall Philosophical Project?

Aquinas was the most important philosopher of the Middle Ages. His great achievement was that he brought together Christian theology with the in-sights of classical Greek philosophy—especially the work of Aristotle—and created a formidably systematic and powerful body of thought. Much of this system, as part of the medieval tradition called "scholasticism," became the standard intellectual world view for Christian Europe for hundreds of years: it formed the basis of European science and philosophy until the intellectual Renaissance of the sixteenth century, and still underpins much Catholic theology.[1] In 1879 Pope Leo XIII recognized the philosophical system of Aquinas as the official doctrine of the Catholic Church.

The writings of the classical philosophers like Plato and Aristotle were lost to Western Europe for centuries after the fall of the Roman empire, but they were preserved by Jewish, Byzantine, and Islamic scholars on the Eastern and Southern shores of the Mediterranean. Starting in the sixth century CE these writings, translated into Latin, trickled back into non-Arabic Europe and by the thirteenth century, when Aquinas was writing, most of the texts of Plato and Aristotle were again available to Western thinkers. In particular, in the second half of the twelfth century, Aristotle's writings on physics and metaphysics came to light. This triggered a deep intellectual conflict in Western Europe. Christian theology is ultimately based on *faith* or scriptural revelation, while the conclusions of Plato and Aristotle are supported by *reason*. When theology and philosophy disagree—and in particular, when philosophers provide us with a rationally compelling argument against a theological claim—which are we to believe? Many conservative Christian theologians at the time viewed classical philosophy as a pagan threat to

---

1   Although Aquinas' work is usually considered the keystone of scholasticism, he didn't create the tradition single-handedly. Other prominent scholastics—who did not all agree with Aquinas—were Peter Abelard (France, 1079–1142), John Duns Scotus (Scotland, c. 1266–1308), William of Occam (England, c. 1285–1349), and Jean Buridan (France, c. 1295–1358).

Christian dogma, but Aquinas was deeply impressed by the work of Aristotle—he considered him the greatest of all philosophers, often referring to him in his writings as simply "*The* Philosopher"—and set out to reconcile Aristotle's writings with Catholic doctrine. He did this, it is important to note, not because he wanted to remove any threat to Christianity from pagan science, but because he thought a lot of what Aristotle had to say was *demonstrably true*.

Aquinas' reconciliation project had two prongs. First, he tried to show whenever possible that Aristotelian thought did not conflict with Christianity but actually supported it: thus faith could be conjoined with reason—religion could be combined with science—by showing how the human powers of reason allowed us to *better understand* the revealed truths of Catholicism.

Second, Aquinas argued that when Aristotle's conclusions did conflict with revealed truth, his arguments were not rationally compelling—but that neither were there any rationally compelling arguments on the other side. For example, Aristotle argued that the universe is eternal and uncreated; Christianity holds that the universe was created a finite amount of time ago by God. Aquinas tried to show that *neither* position is provable. In situations like this, Aquinas argued, we discover that reason falls short and some truths can only be known on the basis of faith.

Together, these two kinds of argument were intended to show that there is no conflict between reason and faith and in fact, rational argument, properly carried out, can only strengthen faith, either by further supporting points of doctrine and making them comprehensible to the rational mind, or by revealing the limits of reason. Importantly, this only works when we reason rigorously and *well*. The foolish, according to Aquinas, might be led into error by arguments which are only apparently persuasive, and one important solution to this problem is not to suppress reason but to *encourage* trained, critical, rational reflection on such arguments. (Of course, this solution, Aquinas realized, was not appropriate for the poor and uneducated; the peasants should instead be urged to rely upon their faith.)

Aquinas distinguished sharply between philosophy and theology. He held that theology begins from faith in God and interprets all things as creatures of God, while philosophy moves in the other direction: it starts with the concrete objects of sense perception—such as animals, rocks, and trees—and reasons towards more general conceptions, eventually making its way to God. In our selection from *Summa Theologiae* Aquinas is doing philosophy, and so all five of the proofs for the existence of God given in the Third Article are based upon Aristotelian science—that is, each proof starts from what intellectuals in the thirteenth century thought was a properly rational understanding of ordinary objects, and shows that this scientific understanding leads us to God. Properly understood, according to Aristotle, the natural phenomena appealed to in all of the "five ways" can only be ultimately explained—even *within* a completed science—by bringing in God.

What Is the Structure of This Reading?

This reading is a good example of the medieval 'scholastic' method of doing philosophy. Aquinas begins by dividing up his subject matter—which is the knowledge of God—into a sequence of more precise questions. Question 2 of Part I of the *Summa Theologiae*, he tells us, is about God's essence, and in particular about whether God exists. He breaks down this question into three parts, and in each part—called an 'Article'—Aquinas first considers objections to his position, then lays out his view, and then answers the objections. The First Article considers whether God's existence is *self-evident*: that is, whether it is simply obvious to everyone who considers the matter that God must exist. Aquinas claims that it is not self-evident (except to the learned), and so some kind of argument will be needed to convince the unbeliever. In this section Aquinas argues against the Ontological Argument for the existence of God (see the previous section on Anselm's *Proslogion*). The Second Article discusses whether God's existence can be rationally demonstrated at all, or whether it is something that must be merely accepted on faith: Aquinas argues that God's existence can be proven. Finally, the Third Article (after considering two quite powerful objections to the existence of God) proceeds to lay out this proof; in fact, Aquinas thinks there are no fewer than *five* good arguments for the existence of God (his famous "five ways").

Some Useful Background Information

1. Some of Aquinas' terminology comes from Aristotelian logic. The basic argument form in this logic is called a 'syllogism,' and one of the most important types of syllogism is one called a 'categorical' syllogism. Such arguments, according to Aristotle, always have two premises and a conclusion and always make use of exactly three 'terms.' For example, one might argue thus: All human beings are mortal; All Canadians are human beings; Therefore, all Canadians are mortal. This has the following structure: (1) All M are P; (2) All S are M; therefore, (3) all S are P. In this argument *mortal* (P) is called the 'major term' and *Canadian* (S) is the 'minor term'—they are the predicate and subject of the conclusion, respectively. The 'middle term' is *human being* (M), and it appears in each premise but not the conclusion.

2. All five of Aquinas' arguments for the existence of God have the same basic form. They all move from some familiar empirical fact about the world to the conclusion that there must be some 'transcendent cause' upon which these facts depend. A 'transcendent cause' is a cause which transcends—lies beyond—the natural world; that is, it is a cause which is not itself *part* of the ever-changing physical universe but which *explains* the existence and nature of that universe.

3. In his first argument for the existence of God Aquinas uses the word "motion" in a somewhat technical sense. Aquinas is not just talking about a change of position but about *all* change in the physical world: the motion of the tides, the growth of a plant, the erosion of a mountain range, or someone baking a cake. Furthermore, in Aristotelian science, all motion or change is a transformation from a state of 'potentiality' to a state of 'actuality.' For example, imagine a row of dominoes standing next to each other. Each domino is *actually* standing

up, but it is *potentially* falling down. When one domino is knocked down, it bumps into the next domino in the series and converts that potentiality into actuality—it makes the domino fall down. For Aristotle and Aquinas *all* change is this kind of movement, from being only potentially X into being actually X.

One important thing to notice about the domino example is that a domino cannot be toppled by something only *potentially* falling down—the domino next to it must be *actually* falling to have any effect. In other words, mere potentiality cannot make anything happen at all—or, to put it yet another way, a domino cannot knock *itself* over. This last claim is crucial for Aquinas' argument in the First Way to work.

4. The Aristotelian notion of an 'efficient cause' plays a key role in Aquinas' Second Way. The 'efficient cause' of something, according to Aristotle, is simply the agent (the object or substance) which brings it about: for example, the 'efficient cause' of tides is the moon's gravity. It's worth noticing that, sometimes, the continuing presence of an effect requires the continuation of the cause. If the moon's gravity went away, ocean tides would also subside; if the force causing the moon to orbit the Earth disappeared, according to Aristotelian science, the moon would stop moving.[2] Thus, if God is ultimately the 'efficient cause' of, say, the movements of the tides, God must still be presently acting as that cause.

5. When Aquinas talks about 'merely possible' being in the Third Way he again does not use this phrase in quite the modern sense. For modern philosophers, something is 'merely possible' if it might not have existed—for example, the book you are holding has 'merely possible' (or contingent) being, in this modern sense, because under other circumstances it might never have

---

2   Notice that this is importantly different from modern science. Today, we know that motions like planetary orbits, once started, simply continue forever unless some force stops them—this is Newton's first law of motion.

been written at all. By contrast, many modern philosophers would agree that mathematical objects, like the number two, have necessary existence—there are no possible circumstances in which the number two could fail to exist. But this is not quite what Aquinas means by 'possible' and 'necessary': for him, something has 'merely possible' being if it is *generated* and *corruptible*. Something is generated if there was a time at which it didn't exist—a time at which it came into being. Something is corruptible if there will be a time at which it ceases to exist. Since things can't come into existence for no reason at all (according to Aquinas), all non-necessary beings must have been generated by *something else*. For example, this book was generated by me, I was generated by my parents, and so on.

6. Aquinas also distinguishes between two different sorts of necessary (i.e., eternal) being. Some entities have necessary being but were nevertheless created by something else (God). For example, suppose that angels are non-corruptible, eternal beings; nevertheless, they have this nature only because God has created them in that way, so their necessary being is derivative of the necessary being of God. God himself, by contrast, is eternal and uncreated—the necessity of his being is, so to speak, built-in, rather than derived from some other source; God is necessarily necessary.

7. In the Fifth Way, the empirical fact from which Aquinas begins is this: different kinds of things, like water and air and plants, co-operate with each other in such a way that a stable order of nature is produced and maintained. They seem to act 'for an end,' which is to say, for a particular *purpose*. For example, heat causes water to evaporate; this water then condenses as clouds and falls as rain; as it falls it nourishes plants and animals, and finally runs back into lakes and oceans where it once again evaporates; and so on. This co-operative cycle is stable and self-perpetuating, but the entities that make it up—the water, plants, and so on—do not *intend* for this to happen: they just, as a matter of fact, act in a way that preserves the system.

Some Common Misconceptions

1. Aquinas does not say that *everything* must have a cause, or that all creation involves a change in the creator. If he did say that, he would have to admit that God must himself have a cause, or that God must himself be moved. When Aquinas asserts that God is the 'first' element of a series, he means that God is importantly different than the other members of that series: God is not a changeable thing, for example, but is instead an Unmoved Mover who brings into existence even the phenomenon of change itself.

2. Although Aquinas thinks that the world in fact began a finite amount of time ago, he does not argue that the notion of an infinite time is rationally incoherent: "By faith alone do we hold, and by no demonstration can it be proved, that the world did not always exist," he says in *Summa Theologiae* (Part I, Question 46, Article 2). But this is not inconsistent with Aquinas' attempt to rationally demonstrate that there must have been a first cause. He thinks he can prove that the world must have been created by God—i.e., that God is the ultimate or underlying cause of the world—but, he argues in a treatise called *On the Eternity of the World*, no one can demonstrate that God's on-going creation of the world might not be spread over an infinitely long period of time. (Analogously, we might loosely say that the curvature of space causes gravitational effects and the curvature of space could conceivably continue for ever.) Aquinas, that is, thought of God not just as a temporally first cause of the universe, back at the beginning of time like a supernatural Big Bang, but as the most fundamental cause of everything that happens in the natural world throughout time.

3. When Aquinas says that God is a necessary being, he means (roughly) that God's existence

does not depend on the existence of anything else. He does not mean that God's existence is what modern philosophers would call "logically necessary." If God were logically necessary, then it would be impossible for God not to exist—it would be self-contradictory to assert that God does not exist, like saying that some bachelors are married. Aquinas does not think that it is self-contradictory to say that God does not exist, just that it is demonstrably false.

4. Aquinas was well aware that his Five Ways, even if they are sound, only prove the *existence* of God and, by themselves, fail to establish important positive conclusions about the nature of God (e.g., his moral goodness). In the section of the *Summa Theologiae* which comes after our selection, he goes on to give arguments about God's nature. Furthermore, Aquinas was aware he had not yet proved that there can be only one God, and he goes on to try to show—on the basis of philosophical arguments—that any entity whose necessary being is essential rather than derived must be simple, perfect, infinite, immutable, eternal, and one—i.e., if there is a God at all, there can be only one God (*Summa Theologiae* Part I, Questions 3 to 11).

5. Although Aquinas appeals to empirical facts as the premises of his arguments for God, he does not think his *conclusion* that God exists is a merely empirical hypothesis. For example, he does not think any amount of future scientific research could ever cast doubt on his arguments. Contrast that with, for example, the claim that electrons are the unseen cause of the pictures that appear on our television sets. It might be that future scientific advances could call into question our present sub-atomic theory, and so cast doubt on the existence of electrons: maybe all the phenomena we explain by talking about electrons can be better explained by talking about some other kind of invisible particle, or about some other category of thing altogether. By contrast, according to Aquinas, our proofs of the existence of God do not depend on the truth of some particular scientific

theory; they follow from the mere existence of change, causation, contingent beings, or whatever, *however* these things are ultimately explained by science.

How Important and Influential Is This Passage?

Aquinas thought that, although the existence of God is not self-evident, reason is capable of proving to the careful thinker that God exists. The "five ways" he lists in this passage include versions of many of the most important arguments for God's existence, and—as a convenient, short, and very capable outline of the main arguments—this section from Aquinas' *Summa Theologiae* has been at the center of debate about the existence of God for hundreds of years.

Suggestions for Critical Reflection

1. Do any of Aquinas' five arguments actually prove that God exists? If none of them work, does this show that God does *not* exist?

2. Do Aquinas' five arguments establish the existence of a *personal* God—of a God who resembles the Christian conception of him? Does Aquinas show that there can be only *one* God, or are his arguments compatible with the existence of numerous gods?

3. Aquinas claims that there cannot be an infinite hierarchy of causes. Is he right about this? Do you think he gives compelling arguments for his claim? We are quite familiar with infinite sequences, such as the succession of integers (... -3, -2, -1, 1, 2, 3 ...). Should Aquinas be worried about such infinite series? Why or why not?

4. Aquinas asserts that if everything were merely possible (and not necessary), then there would have to be some time in the past at which nothing at all existed. Does this follow? What might Aquinas have had in mind when he made this move?

5. For Aquinas, could anything have *both* possible and necessary being? Does this fit with your intuitions about possibility and necessity? What, if anything, is the connection between

something being eternal and it having necessary being—for example, in your view, could something necessarily exist, but only for a finite amount of time, or could something that might not have existed at all be eternal?

6. Aquinas asserts that we must have an idea of *the best*, before we can judge anything to be *better than* something else. Do you agree with this claim? Support your answer with examples.

7. To what extent do you think that Aquinas' arguments depend on specifically Aristotelian science? How much does the fact that Aristotelian science has now been discredited in favor of post-Newtonian science cast doubt on his arguments?

Suggestions for Further Reading

A standard introductory collection of Aquinas' writings is *Basic Writings of St. Thomas Aquinas*, edited by Anton Pegis (Random House, 1945). It's worth comparing the selection given here with Aquinas' other discussion of the arguments for the existence of God in *Summa contra Gentiles*, Book I, Chapters 9–14; this can be found in Aquinas' *Selected Writings*, ed. Ralph McInerny (Penguin, 1998). A useful history of philosophy of the period (including Anselm) is Frederick Copleston's *A History of Philosophy*, Volume II (Doubleday, 1950). Some good shorter books about Aquinas' thought are F.C. Copleston's *Aquinas* (Penguin, 1955), Brian Davies's *The Thought of Thomas Aquinas* (Oxford University Press, 1992), and Anthony Kenny's *Aquinas* (Oxford University Press, 1980). A book specifically about Aquinas' arguments for God is Kenny's *The Five Ways* (Routledge & Kegan Paul, 1969). Two useful collections of articles are Anthony Kenny (ed.), *Aquinas: A Collection of Critical Essays* (Anchor Doubleday, 1969) and Norman Kretzmann and Eleanor Stump (eds.), *The Cambridge Companion to Aquinas* (Cambridge University Press, 1993).

Summa Theologiae

Part I, Question 2, The Existence of God (In Three Articles)[3]

Because the chief aim of sacred doctrine is to teach the knowledge of God not only as He is in Himself, but also as He is the beginning of things and their last end, and especially of rational creatures, as is clear from what has been already said, therefore, in our endeavor to expound this science, we shall treat: (1) of God; (2) of the rational creature's movement towards God; (3) of Christ Who as man is our way to God.

In treating of God there will be a threefold division:—

For we shall consider (1) whatever concerns the divine essence. (2) Whatever concerns the distinctions of Persons. (3) Whatever concerns the procession of creatures from Him.

Concerning the divine essence, we must consider:—

(1) Whether God exists? (2) The manner of His existence, or, rather, what is *not* the manner of His existence. (3) Whatever concerns His operations—namely, His knowledge, will, power.

Concerning the first, there are three points of inquiry:—

(1) Whether the proposition *God exists* is self-evident? (2) Whether it is demonstrable? (3) Whether God exists?

First Article: Whether the existence of God is self-evident?

We proceed thus to the First Article:—

Objection 1. It seems that the existence of God is self-evident. For those things are said to be self-evident to us the knowledge of which exists naturally in us, as we can see in regard to first principles. But as

---

3   This part of the *Summa Theologiae* was written around 1265. The translation used here, by Anton C. Pegis, is taken from *Basic Writings of Saint Thomas Aquinas*, Volume I, Hackett Publishing Company, 1997; pp. 18-24. Reprinted by permission of Hackett Publishing Company, Inc. All rights reserved.

Damascene[4] says, *the knowledge of God is naturally implanted in all.* Therefore the existence of God is self-evident.

Objection 2. Further, those things are said to be self-evident which are known as soon as the terms are known, which the Philosopher[5] says is true of the first principles of demonstration. Thus, when the nature of a whole and of a part is known, it is at once recognized that every whole is greater than its part. But as soon as the signification of the name *God* is understood, it is at once seen that God exists. For by this name is signified that thing than which nothing greater can be conceived. But that which exists actually and mentally is greater than that which exists only mentally. Therefore, since as soon as the name *God* is understood it exists mentally, it also follows that it exists actually. Therefore the proposition *God exists* is self-evident.

Objection 3. Further, the existence of truth is self-evident. For whoever denies the existence of truth grants that truth does not exist: and, if truth does not exist, then the proposition *Truth does not exist* is true: and if there is anything true, there must be truth. But God is truth itself: *I am the way, the truth, and the life* (John xiv.6). Therefore *God exists* is self-evident.

On the contrary, No one can mentally admit the opposite of what is self-evident, as the Philosopher states concerning the first principles of demonstration. But the opposite of the proposition *God is* can be mentally admitted: *The fool said in his heart, There is no God* (Psalms lii.1[6]). Therefore, that God exists is not self-evident.

---

4 St. John Damascene, an eighth-century monk in Jerusalem who wrote a book called *De Fide Orthodoxa* (On the Orthodox Faith), from which this quote is taken.

5 Aristotle. This reference is to Aristotle's *Posterior Analytics.*

6 Aquinas is referring to the first line of the fifty-second psalm in the Latin "Vulgate" version of the Bible, still used by the Catholic Church. Many English translations, such as the "King James" version, number the psalms differently. The quote is found in psalms 14 and 53 in the King James.

I answer that, A thing can be self-evident in either of two ways: on the one hand, self-evident in itself, though not to us; on the other, self-evident in itself, and to us. A proposition is self-evident because the predicate is included in the essence of the subject: e.g., *Man is an animal,* for animal is contained in the essence of man. If, therefore, the essence of the predicate and subject be known to all, the proposition will be self-evident to all; as is clear with regard to the first principles of demonstration, the terms of which are certain common notions that no one is ignorant of, such as being and non-being, whole and part, and the like. If, however, there are some to whom the essence of the predicate and subject is unknown, the proposition will be self-evident in itself, but not to those who do not know the meaning of the predicate and subject of the proposition. Therefore, it happens, as Boethius[7] says, that there are some notions of the mind which are common and self-evident only to the learned, as that incorporeal substances are not in space. Therefore I say that this proposition, *God exists,* of itself is self-evident, for the predicate is the same as the subject, because God is His own existence as will be hereafter shown. Now because we do not know the essence of God, the proposition is not self-evident to us, but needs to be demonstrated by things that are more known to us, though less known in their nature—namely, by His effects.

Reply to Objection 1. To know that God exists in a general and confused way is implanted in us by nature, inasmuch as God is man's beatitude.[8] For man naturally desires happiness, and what is naturally desired by man is naturally known by him. This, however, is not to know absolutely that God exists; just as to know that someone is approaching is not the same as to know that Peter is approaching, even though it is Peter who is approaching; for there are many who imagine that man's perfect good, which is happiness, consists in riches, and others in pleasures, and others in something else.

---

7 An aristocratic Christian Roman from the early sixth century, Boethius translated Aristotle's logical writings and wrote several theological treatises.

8 Supreme blessedness or happiness.

Reply to Objection 2. Perhaps not everyone who hears this name *God* understands it to signify something than which nothing greater can be thought, seeing that some have believed God to be a body. Yet, granted that everyone understands that by this name *God* is signified something than which nothing greater can be thought, nevertheless, it does not therefore follow that he understands that what the name signifies exists actually, but only that it exists mentally. Nor can it be argued that it actually exists, unless it be admitted that there actually exists something than which nothing greater can be thought; and this precisely is not admitted by those who hold that God does not exist.

Reply to Objection 3. The existence of truth in general is self-evident, but the existence of a Primal Truth is not self-evident to us.

Second Article: Whether it can be demonstrated that God exists?

We proceed thus to the Second Article:—

Objection 1. It seems that the existence of God cannot be demonstrated. For it is an article of faith that God exists. But what is of faith cannot be demonstrated, because a demonstration produces scientific knowledge, whereas faith is of the unseen, as is clear from the Apostle[9] (Hebrews xi.1). Therefore it cannot be demonstrated that God exists.

Objection 2. Further, essence is the middle term of demonstration. But we cannot know in what God's essence consists, but solely in what it does not consist, as Damascene says. Therefore we cannot demonstrate that God exists.

Objection 3. Further, if the existence of God were demonstrated, this could only be from His effects. But His effects are not proportioned to Him, since He is infinite and His effects are finite, and between the finite and infinite there is no proportion. Therefore, since a cause cannot be demonstrated by an effect not proportioned to it, it seems that the existence of God cannot be demonstrated.

On the contrary, The Apostle says: *The invisible things of Him are clearly seen, being understood by the things that are made* (Romans i.20). But this would not be unless the existence of God could be demonstrated through the things that are made; for the first thing we must know of anything, is whether it exists.

I answer that, Demonstration can be made in two ways: One is through the cause, and is called *propter quid*, and this is to argue from what is prior absolutely. The other is through the effect, and is called a demonstration *quia*; this is to argue from what is prior relatively only to us. When an effect is better known to us than its cause, from the effect we proceed to the knowledge of the cause. And from every effect the existence of its proper cause can be demonstrated, so long as its effects are better known to us; because, since every effect depends upon its cause, if the effect exists, the cause must pre-exist. Hence the existence of God, in so far as it is not self-evident to us, can be demonstrated from those of His effects which are known to us.

Reply to Objection 1. The existence of God and other like truths about God, which can be known by natural reason, are not articles of faith, but are preambles to the articles; for faith presupposes natural knowledge, even as grace[10] presupposes nature and perfection the perfectible. Nevertheless, there is nothing to prevent a man, who cannot grasp a proof, from accepting, as a matter of faith, something which in itself is capable of being scientifically known and demonstrated.

Reply to Objection 2. When the existence of a cause is demonstrated from an effect, this effect takes the place of the definition of the cause in proving the cause's existence. This is especially the case in regard to God, because, in order to prove the existence of anything, it is necessary to accept as a middle term the meaning of the name, and not its essence, for the question of its essence follows on the question of its existence. Now the names given to God are derived

9   Aquinas means St. Paul, a Jewish Roman citizen who lived in Jerusalem in the first century CE and who became an important missionary and the most significant founder of the church after his conversion to Christianity on the road to Damascus. He is often considered to be something like the second founder of Christianity. (However, it is now thought that St. Paul probably did not in fact write the *Epistle to the Hebrews*.)

10   The unmerited favor or protection of God.

from His effects, as will be later shown. Consequently, in demonstrating the existence of God from His effects, we may take for the middle term the meaning of the name *God*.

Reply to Objection 3. From effects not proportioned to the cause no perfect knowledge of that cause can be obtained. Yet from every effect the existence of the cause can be clearly demonstrated, and so we can demonstrate the existence of God from His effects; though from them we cannot know God perfectly as He is in His essence.

Third Article: Whether God exists?

We proceed thus to the Third Article:—

Objection 1. It seems that God does not exist; because if one of two contraries[11] be infinite, the other would be altogether destroyed. But the name *God* means that He is infinite goodness. If, therefore, God existed, there would be no evil discoverable; but there is evil in the world. Therefore God does not exist.

Objection 2. Further, it is superfluous to suppose that what can be accounted for by a few principles has been produced by many. But it seems that everything we see in the world can be accounted for by other principles, supposing God did not exist. For all natural things can be reduced to one principle, which is nature; and all voluntary things can be reduced to one principle, which is human reason, or will. Therefore there is no need to suppose God's existence.

On the contrary, It is said in the person of God: *I am Who am* (Exodus iii.14).

I answer that, The existence of God can be proved in five ways.

The first and more manifest way is the argument from motion. It is certain, and evident to our senses, that in the world some things are in motion. Now whatever is moved is moved by another, for nothing can be moved except it is in potentiality to that towards which it is moved; whereas a thing moves inasmuch as it is in act. For motion is nothing else than the reduction of something from potentiality to

---

11   Contraries are properties which cannot both apply to a thing at the same time, though they can both fail to apply, e.g., being red all over and green all over, or being ugly and beautiful, or being wise and stupid.

actuality. But nothing can be reduced from potentiality to actuality, except by something in a state of actuality. Thus that which is actually hot, as fire, makes wood, which is potentially hot, to be actually hot, and thereby moves and changes it. Now it is not possible that the same thing should be at once in actuality and potentiality in the same respect, but only in different respects. For what is actually hot cannot simultaneously be potentially hot; but it is simultaneously potentially cold. It is therefore impossible that in the same respect and in the same way a thing should be both mover and moved, *i.e.*, that it should move itself. Therefore, whatever is moved must be moved by another. If that by which it is moved be itself moved, then this also must needs be moved by another, and that by another again. But this cannot go on to infinity, because then there would be no first mover, and, consequently, no other mover, seeing that subsequent movers move only inasmuch as they are moved by the first mover; as the staff moves only because it is moved by the hand. Therefore it is necessary to arrive at a first mover, moved by no other; and this everyone understands to be God.

The second way is from the nature of efficient cause. In the world of sensible things we find there is an order of efficient causes. There is no case known (neither is it, indeed, possible) in which a thing is found to be the efficient cause of itself; for so it would be prior to itself, which is impossible. Now in efficient causes it is not possible to go on to infinity, because in all efficient causes following in order, the first is the cause of the intermediate cause, and the intermediate is the cause of the ultimate cause, whether the intermediate cause be several, or one only. Now to take away the cause is to take away the effect. Therefore, if there be no first cause among efficient causes, there will be no ultimate, nor any intermediate, cause. But if in efficient causes it is possible to go on to infinity, there will be no first efficient cause, neither will there be an ultimate effect, nor any intermediate efficient causes; all of which is plainly false. Therefore it is necessary to admit a first efficient cause, to which everyone gives the name of God.

The third way is taken from possibility and necessity, and runs thus. We find in nature things that are possible to be and not to be, since they are found to be generated, and to be corrupted, and consequently, it is possible for them to be and not to be. But it is impossible for these always to exist, for that which can not-be at some time is not. Therefore, if everything can not-be, then at one time there was nothing in existence. Now if this were true, even now there would be nothing in existence, because that which does not exist begins to exist only through something already existing. Therefore, if at one time nothing was in existence, it would have been impossible for anything to have begun to exist; and thus even now nothing would be in existence—which is absurd. Therefore, not all beings are merely possible, but there must exist something the existence of which is necessary. But every necessary thing either has its necessity caused by another, or not. Now it is impossible to go on to infinity in necessary things which have their necessity caused by another, as has been already proved in regard to efficient causes. Therefore we cannot but admit the existence of some being having of itself its own necessity, and not receiving it from another but rather causing in others their necessity. This all men speak of as God.

The fourth way is taken from the gradation to be found in things. Among beings there are some more and some less good, true, noble, and the like. But *more* and *less* are predicated of different things according as they resemble in their different ways something which is the maximum, as a thing is said to be hotter according as it more nearly resembles that which is hottest; so that there is something which is truest, something best, something noblest, and, consequently, something which is most being, for those things that are greatest in truth are greatest in being, as it is written in *Metaphysics* ii.[12] Now the maximum in any genus is the cause of all in that genus, as fire, which is the maximum of heat, is the cause of all hot things, as is said in the same book. Therefore there must also be something which is to all beings the cause of their being, goodness, and every other perfection; and this we call God.

The fifth way is taken from the governance of the world. We see that things which lack knowledge, such as natural bodies, act for an end, and this is evident from their acting always, or nearly always, in the same way, so as to obtain the best result. Hence it is plain that they achieve their end, not fortuitously, but designedly. Now whatever lacks knowledge cannot move towards an end, unless it be directed by some being endowed with knowledge and intelligence; as the arrow is directed by the archer. Therefore some intelligent being exists by whom all natural things are directed to their end; and this being we call God.

Reply to Objection 1. As Augustine[13] says: *Since God is the highest good, He would not allow any evil to exist in His works, unless His omnipotence and goodness were such as to bring good even out of evil.* This is part of the infinite goodness of God, that He should allow evil to exist, and out of it produce good.

Reply to Objection 2. Since nature works for a determinate end under the direction of a higher agent, whatever is done by nature must be traced back to God as to its first cause. So likewise whatever is done voluntarily must be traced back to some higher cause other than human reason and will, since these can change and fail; for all things that are changeable and capable of defect must be traced back to an immovable and self-necessary first principle, as has been shown.

---

12   The second volume of a book by Aristotle.
13   St. Augustine, a north African bishop who lived from 354 until 430, was the most important early Christian theologian and philosopher. This quote is from his *Enchiridion* ("Handbook").

DAVID HUME

Dialogues Concerning Natural Religion

Who Was David Hume?

David Hume has been called the most important philosopher ever to have written in English. He was born to a strict Calvinist family in Edinburgh, Scotland's capital, in 1711, and spent his youth there and in Ninewells, his family's small land-holding near the border with England. Little is known of Hume's early childhood. His father, Joseph, died when he was two, and he was educated by his mother Katherine—who never re-married—from an early age. He was a precociously intelligent and well-read child,[1] and by the age of 16 he had begun composing his first philosophical master-work, *A Treatise of Human Nature*, on which he was to work, more or less continuously, for the next ten years.

Hume spent the years between 1723 and 1726 (i.e., between the ages of 12 and 15) studying a wide range of subjects at the University of Edinburgh but, like many students of that era, did not take a degree. His father and grandfather had both been lawyers, and his family expected him also to go into law, but, Hume later wrote, he found the law "nauseous" and discovered in himself "an unsurmountable aversion to every thing but the pursuits of philosophy and general learning."

Hume continued to read and write and, as a result of his feverish intellectual activity—motivated by his belief that he had made a major philosophical discovery—he suffered a nervous breakdown in 1734. He was forced to put philosophy aside for several months (during which time he attempted life as a businessman at Bristol, in the employ of a Portsmouth merchant, but found that it didn't suit him) and then left Britain for France. There, in the following three years, living frugally in the countryside in Anjou (and using up all his savings), he completed most of his book.

Hume's *A Treatise of Human Nature* was published anonymously when he was 27. Hume later wrote, it "fell *dead-born from the press*, without reaching such distinction as even to excite a murmur among the zealots." Hume's career as an intellectual and man of letters seemed to have ended before it had begun, and Hume blamed not the substance of his work but its style. "I was carry'd away by the Heat of Youth & Invention to publish too precipitately. So vast an Undertaking, plan'd before I was one and twenty, & compos'd before twenty-five, must necessarily be very defective. I have repented my Haste a hundred, & a hundred times." Hume returned to Scotland to live with his mother, and began to re-cast the material of the *Treatise* into two new books, which have become philosophical classics in their own right: *An Enquiry Concerning Human Understanding* (1748), and *An Enquiry Concerning the Principles of Morals* (1751). However both these books—though more successful than the *Treatise*—were slow to become influential during Hume's own lifetime.

---

1 As his mother put it, in her Scottish dialect: "Our Davie's a fine good-natured crater, but uncommon wake-minded."

Needing money, Hume got his first real job at the age of 34 and spent a well-paid year as tutor to a mad nobleman (the Marquess of Annandale). In 1746 Hume accepted a position as secretary to General St. Clair's military expedition to Canada (which never reached Canada and ended, oddly enough, with a brief attack on the French coast), and for two years after that was part of a secret diplomatic and military embassy by St. Clair to the courts of Vienna and Turin. During this period Hume was twice refused academic appointments at Scottish universities—first Edinburgh, then Glasgow—because of his reputation as a religious skeptic. Shortly afterwards, between 1755 and 1757, unsuccessful attempts were made in Edinburgh to have Hume excommunicated from the Church of Scotland.

In 1752 Hume was offered the Keepership of the Advocates' Library at Edinburgh and there, poorly paid but surrounded by books, he wrote the colossal six-volume *History of England*, which (though unpopular at first) eventually became his first major literary success. At this time he also published a controversial *Natural History of Religion*.

In 1763 Hume was made secretary of the English embassy at Paris, where he found himself very much in fashion and seems to have enjoyed the experience. There he fell in love with, but failed to win the hand of, the Comtesse de Boufflers, the mistress of a prominent French noble. (Some unkindly suggest this might have been partly because at the time, when Hume was in his fifties, he had come to resemble "a fat well-fed Bernardine monk.") In 1767, back in Scotland and now a fairly wealthy man, Hume was appointed an Under-Secretary of State, a senior position in the British civil service.

By the time Hume died in 1776, of cancer of the bowel, he had become respected as one of Europe's leading men of letters and a principal architect of the Enlightenment. His death gave him the reputation of something of a secular saint, as he faced his incurable condition with cheerfulness and resignation and refused to abandon his religious skepticism. In a short autobiography, written just before he died, Hume described his own character.

> I was … a man of mild dispositions, of command of temper, of an open, social, and cheerful humour, capable of attachment, but little susceptible of enmity, and of great moderation in all my passions. Even my love of literary fame, my ruling passion, never soured my temper, notwithstanding my frequent disappointments. My company was not unacceptable to the young and careless, as well as to the studious and literary; and as I took a particular pleasure in the company of modest women, I had no reason to be displeased with the reception I met from them.… I cannot say there is no vanity in making this funeral oration of myself, but I hope it is not a misplaced one; and this is a matter of fact which is easily cleared and ascertained.

What Was Hume's Overall Philosophical Project?

Hume can be called the first 'post-skeptical' modern philosopher. He was wholly convinced (by, among others, the writings of his predecessors Descartes, Locke, and Berkeley, who appear elsewhere in this volume) that no knowledge that goes beyond the mere data of our own minds has anything like secure and reliable foundations: that is, he believed, we have no certain knowledge of the inner workings of the physical world and its laws, or of God, or of absolute moral 'truth,' or even of our own 'real selves.' All we have secure knowledge of is our own mental states and their relations: our sensory impressions, our ideas, our emotions, and so on.

Despite all this, Hume's philosophical project was a positive one: he wanted to develop a new, constructive science of human nature that would provide a defensible foundation for all the sciences, including ethics, physics and politics. Where Hume's predecessors tried in vain to argue against philosophical skepticism, Hume assumed that a certain kind of skepticism was actually true and tried to go beyond it, to say something positive about how we are to get on with our lives (including our lives as scientists and philosophers).

Much of Hume's philosophical writing, therefore, begins by showing the unstoppable power of skepticism in some domain—such as skepticism about causation or objective ethical truths—and then goes on to show how we can still talk sensibly about causation or ethics after all. The selection from *An Enquiry Concerning Human Understanding* which appears in Chapter 3 follows this pattern. The structure of Hume's *Dialogues*, however, is more complex. Exactly what Hume's own religious views were remains a matter of some controversy, but a strong case can be made that Hume felt substantial conclusions about the existence and nature of God cannot be founded in experience and therefore cannot be made sense of at all. Hume may, in other words, have been unremittingly skeptical about religion.

One of the central aspects of both Hume's skeptical and his constructive philosophy is his strictly empirical methodology—a development of what was called in Hume's day 'the experimental method.' His science of human nature is based firmly on the experimental methods of the natural sciences, which emphasize the data of experience and observation, sometimes combined with mathematical or logical reasoning. Any other method of investigation—such as an appeal to 'innate intuition,' for example—is illegitimate. As Hume put it:

> If we take in our hand any volume; of divinity or school metaphysics, for instance; let us ask, *Does it contain any abstract reasoning concerning quantity or number?* No. *Does it contain any experimental reasoning concerning matter of fact and existence?* No. Commit it then to the flames: for it can contain nothing but sophistry and illusion. [This is the final paragraph of his *Enquiry Concerning Human Understanding*.]

This assumption that all human knowledge is either a "matter of fact" or a matter of "relations of ideas"—the product of experience or of reason—is often known as 'Hume's Fork.' You can find more about this in the Hume reading in Chapter 3.

This general philosophical attitude is also applied to religion. Hume's two main writings on religion are the *Dialogues Concerning Natural Religion* (which was published only after Hume's death, due to its controversial religious skepticism) and *The Natural History of Religion*. The former examines the rational basis for belief in God; the latter is a historical study of religion's origins in human nature and society: that is,

Hume studies both the *reasons* for religious belief, and the *causes* of religious belief. In the *Dialogues*, written in the 1750s, Hume raises powerful doubts about whether we could ever have good reasons for believing in God—all religion, if Hume is right, may be no more than "mere superstition." Why then is religious belief so common? In *The Natural History of Religion*, published in 1757, Hume argues that the causes of religious belief are independent of rationality and are instead based on human fear of the unpredictable and uncontrollable influences in our lives—such as the forces of nature—which we try to propitiate through worship. Furthermore, Hume suggests, religious belief is more harmful than it is beneficial. Even apart from the suffering and strife which they have historically caused, religions invent spurious sins (like suicide) which Hume argued are not really harmful, and create "frivolous merits" not grounded in any genuine good (such as attending certain ceremonies and abstaining from particular foods).

In his *Enquiry Concerning the Principles of Morals* Hume develops a secular alternative to religiously-based morality; the theory of moral life he develops there is based entirely upon an analysis of human nature and human needs and is completely independent of religion. (Hume is often thought of as the original founder of the moral doctrine called "utilitarianism.")

What Is the Structure of This Reading?

There are three speakers in this dialogue: Cleanthes, who advocates the argument from design; Demea, who defends both mysticism and, occasionally, a kind of cosmological argument; and Philo, who plays the role of a skeptical critic of both of the others. The dialogue contains twelve sections: the first, sixth, and twelfth have been omitted here.

[PART I. Introductory discussion of the relationship between religion and philosophy.]

PART II. Demea and Philo claim that the nature of God is inaccessible, since it goes beyond human experience. Cleanthes presents the argument from design (to show that experience can give results about God), but Philo objects to the argument as being weak, even for an empirical argument. Cleanthes defends the analogy between a house and the universe and Philo re-presents the design argument for Demea's benefit, but then presents several objections to it.

PART III. Cleanthes defends the argument against Philo's objections, and Demea responds.

PART IV. The three discuss the question of whether the nature of God's mind is at all similar to ours (e.g., in containing a set of ideas), and thus whether we can intelligibly speak of God as a designer. Philo suggests that to say the universe is created by a mind like ours invites us to ask what caused the ordered ideas that make up that mind (ideas don't just appear and fall into a certain pattern all by themselves, any more than matter does), and then we have an infinite regress. Cleanthes responds to this argument, and Philo replies.

PART V. Philo goes on to reconsider the principle "like effects prove like causes," and to suggest what consequences this would have for our idea of God as a cause "proportioned to the effect."

[PART VI. Philo next suggests that reasoning very like the argument from design will show that God is not the cause of the universe, but its mind or soul, and the material universe is God's body—his point is that, if this conclusion is unacceptable, something must be wrong with the arguments for both conclusions. Cleanthes responds, arguing (in part) that the universe cannot have been infinite and so cannot be God, and Philo in turn argues for its infinity.]

PART VII. Philo next objects that reasoning very like the argument from design will show that a more plausible cause for the universe is not a human-like designer, but the kind of "generation or vegetation" which we observe giving rise to plants and animals. We have no good evidence, he argues, to think that reason—thought—is the only creative power in the universe.

PART VIII. Here Philo hypothesizes that more or less random motions of matter, over an endless duration of time, would eventually produce a complex world just like ours, and once formed this world would persist for some time. Cleanthes objects that this is implausible. Philo agrees, but asserts that it is no more implausible than any other hypothesis and so "a total

suspension of judgment is here our only reasonable resource."

PART IX. Faced with the failure of the argument from design ("the argument *a posteriori*"), Demea urges a return to cosmological and ontological arguments (which he calls "the argument *a priori*"). His argument is rejected by Cleanthes.

PART X. The speakers discuss the problem of evil. Why would a good and powerful God allow pain, hardship, and misery to exist in the world? And does not the existence of evil in the world cast doubt upon our inference from the apparent design of the world to a benevolent designer?

PART XI. The three continue the discussion of the problem of evil. They examine four sources of evil, but it is suggested that at best they may establish the compatibility of evil with God and that they block any inference from a world containing evil to an infinitely good God. On the contrary, Philo suggests, the existence of evil means that we should infer an amoral origin of the universe.

[PART XII. After Demea's departure Philo completely reverses himself and admits that the argument from design does indeed show the existence of God; he claims, however, that it nevertheless tells us little about God's nature or about how human beings should behave.]

Some Useful Background Information

1. Probably, none of the three speakers in the dialogue fully and uniquely represents Hume's own views. Philo certainly comes closest to Hume's own position, but all three of the characters have philosophically important points to make. At the end of the *Dialogues* Hume offers no decisive verdict, but instead leaves his readers to grapple with the questions he raises. Furthermore, Hume's writing is often ironic, or intended to protect himself from charges of atheism: for example, claims by the various speakers that God's nature and existence is obvious to any rational thinker should be taken with a pinch of salt.

   It's important for the modern reader to understand that Hume had good reason to fear becoming known as an atheist. As recently as 1619 atheists were executed in Europe by having their tongues pulled out and then being burnt to death, and even in the eighteenth century there were stiff legal penalties in Britain for impiety: for example, in 1763, 70-year-old Peter Annet was sentenced to a year of hard labor for questioning the accounts of miracles in the Old Testament. At a minimum, a reputation for atheism could easily lead to social and professional isolation and, despite his caution, Hume himself felt some of these sorts of effects (such as twice being denied university posts).

2. In his *Dialogues* Hume is operating with certain distinctions that it is useful to be aware of. *Natural religion* (or natural theology) is religious belief that can be proven on the basis of public evidence, available to believer and unbeliever alike (such as facts about causation, or the concept of God). This is contrasted with *revealed religion* (or revelation), which is based on privileged information given only to believers (such as scripture).

   Theism is the belief in a unique, all-powerful God who created the universe, and who remains active—sustaining the universe, answering prayers, granting revelations, and so on. Typically, evidence for the existence of God the creator is thought to be part of natural religion, while claims about the continuing activity of God (often called God's "immanence" or "providence") are more often based on revelation. *Deism* is a philosophical view that accepts rational arguments for the existence of God—accepts natural theology—but is skeptical of revelation and so denies the Christian (or Judaic or Islamic) revelation of an immanent God.

   Deism was a fairly influential view during Hume's lifetime, and Hume always vigorously denied that he himself was a deist. In fact, his arguments in the *Dialogues* are much more focussed on deism than on theism, since what he is attacking is natural religion. Elsewhere in his writings, however, Hume levels a brief but seminal criticism at revealed religion, and especially at the idea that miracles can be evidence of the existence and nature of God (Section X of *An Enquiry Concerning Human Understanding*). Many modern commentators (but by no means all of them) believe that Hume was in fact some kind of 'attenuated deist': that is, he may have thought that rational argument—and especially the argument from design—did make it at least somewhat likely that God exists, but it can tell us little about God's nature.

   Anthropomorphism, by contrast, is a view which not only says that we can understand God but that we can appropriately describe God in language that draws its meaning from human activities and qualities, using such adjectives as "beautiful," "merciful," "fatherly," or "wise." ("Anthropomorphism" is from Greek words meaning "having the shape of a man.") This is a view Hume portrays Demea and Philo as rejecting.

3. Within natural religion, Hume (like other eighteenth-century thinkers) distinguishes between two types of argument, which he calls "the argument *a priori*" and "the argument *a posteriori*." The argument *a priori*, for Hume, is usually the cosmological argument for a First Cause. The argument *a posteriori* is the argument from design. See the introduction to this chapter on philosophy of religion for a little more information on these types of argument.

A Common Misconception

The *Dialogues* are deliberately written to be somewhat "literary" and philosophically ambiguous. Thus, for example, though many of the arguments he raises for and against are clear and compelling, it is not a clear-cut matter whether Hume himself would totally reject the argument from design, or tentatively endorse it, or whether he thinks the problem of evil conclusively eliminates the possibility of a morally benevolent Deity or not. It is left up to the reader to make these kinds of final judgments, on the basis of the arguments he or she has encountered in reading the *Dialogues*.

How Important and Influential Is This Passage?

In one of his last letters Hume wrote of the *Dialogues*: "Some of my Friends flatter me, that it is the best thing I ever wrote." After his death the skeptical ideas developed by Hume were gradually transmitted to the main flow of European culture (via thinkers such as Immanuel Kant, Baron d'Holbach, and the poet Percy Shelley), and by the nineteenth century Hume and others were considered to have so thoroughly overthrown the rational basis for belief in God that important religious philosophers such as Friedrich Schleiermacher (1768–1834) and Søren Kierkegaard (1813–1855) began to try to place religion less on a foundation of evidence and argument than on subjective experience and faith. Hume's own writings on religion, however, were neglected by philosophers and theologians until the 1930s (when interest in Hume was stimulated by changes in philosophical fashion, and especially the rise of a kind of radical empiricism called "logical positivism"). Since the 1960s the *Dialogues* have been widely considered the single most formidable attack on the rationality of belief in God ever mounted by a philosopher.

Suggestions for Critical Reflection

1. Do you think that Hume was an atheist, or a skeptic about God? What's the difference?
2. How close is the analogy between a machine and the universe? How about between an animal or plant and the universe? Do differences or similarities between the two things compared—e.g., between machines and the world—suggest important differences or similarities between their (alleged) designers?
3. Do you agree with Hume that "like effects prove like causes" (i.e., that similar effects demonstrate similar causes)?
4. Does the existence of order in nature *need* to be explained (or, for example, might it just be the result of random chance)? If it does require

an explanation, can it only be explained by an appeal to an intelligent Designer? If we explain the order of nature by postulating a Designer, must we then go on to explain the Designer (and then explain the explanation of that Designer, and so on)?
5. Do you think that the existence of suffering makes it impossible to believe in an omnipotent and benevolent God? Do you think that the existence of suffering makes it impossible to infer the existence of an omnipotent and benevolent God from the evidence of design that we observe in the world? Are these two different questions?
6. What do you think of Hume's claim (in Part IX) that: "Whatever we conceive as existent, we can also conceive as non-existent"? If correct, how would this principle affect *a priori* attempts to prove the existence of God?

Suggestions for Further Reading

The most complete selection of Hume's writings on religion is *David Hume: Writings on Religion*, ed. Anthony Flew (Open Court, 1992). It includes the *Dialogues*, the *Natural History of Religion*, the essays "On Suicide" and "On the Immortality of the Soul" (neither of which were published during Hume's lifetime), and some other relevant material. The editions of the *Dialogues* edited by Norman Kemp Smith (Bobbs-Merrill, 1947) and by Nelson Pike (Bobbs-Merrill, 1970), both contain valuable commentary. A well-known attack by Hume on miracles is in his *Enquiry concerning Human Understanding* (Broadview Press, 2011), and the following section, section XI, is a precursor to the arguments in the *Dialogues*.

The standard modern biography of Hume is Ernest Campbell Mossner's *The Life of David Hume*, 2nd ed., (Oxford University Press, 1980).

J.C.A. Gaskin's *Hume's Philosophy of Religion*, 2nd ed., (Macmillan, 1988) is a useful secondary text, while Keith E. Yandell's *Hume's "Inexplicable Mystery": His Views on Religion* (Temple University Press, 1990) is somewhat more critical of Hume. There is also a commentary specifically on the *Dialogues*—Stanley Tweyman, *Scepticism and Belief in Hume's Dialogues*

Concerning Natural Religion (Martinus Nijhoff, 1986)—and a book about Hume's attack on the argument from design: Hume, Newton, and the Design Argument by Robert H. Hurlbutt III, rev. ed., (University of Nebraska Press, 1985). Finally, Terence Penelhum's God and Skepticism (Reidel, 1983) is a very good general discussion of the issues Hume is thinking about.

Some useful articles are: John Bricke, "On the Interpretation of Hume's Dialogues," Religious Studies 11 (1975); Gary Doore, "The Argument from Design: Some Better Reasons for Agreeing with Hume," Religious Studies 16 (1980); J.C.A. Gaskin, "God, Hume, and Natural Belief," Philosophy 49 (1974); J. Noxon, "Hume's Agnosticism," Philosophical Review 73 (1964); Terence Penelhum, "Natural Belief and Religious Belief in Hume's Philosophy," Philosophical Quarterly 33 (1983); and Richard G. Swinburne, "The Argument from Design—A Defence," Religious Studies 11 (1972).

A significant modern attempt to revivify natural theology after Hume's critique is Richard Swinburne's The Existence of God (Clarendon Press, 1979). Finally, good places to start in thinking about how post-Humean scientific developments affect the argument from design are Richard Dawkins, The Blind Watchmaker (Longman, 1986) and John Leslie (ed.), Physical Cosmology and Philosophy (Macmillan, 1990).

from *Dialogues Concerning Natural Religion*[2]

Part II

I must own,[3] Cleanthes, said Demea, that nothing can more surprise me, than the light in which you have all along put this argument. By the whole tenor of your discourse, one would imagine that you were maintaining the being of a God, against the cavils of atheists and infidels; and were necessitated to become a champion for that fundamental principle of all religion. But

this, I hope, is not by any means a question among us. No man, no man at least of common sense, I am persuaded, ever entertained a serious doubt with regard to a truth so certain and self-evident. The question is not concerning the being, but the nature of God. This, I affirm, from the infirmities of human understanding, to be altogether incomprehensible and unknown to us. The essence of that supreme mind, his attributes, the manner of his existence, the very nature of his duration; these, and every particular which regards so divine a Being, are mysterious to men. Finite, weak, and blind creatures, we ought to humble ourselves in his august presence; and, conscious of our frailties, adore in silence his infinite perfections, which eye hath not seen, ear hath not heard, neither hath it entered into the heart of man to conceive.[4] They are covered in a deep cloud from human curiosity. It is profaneness to attempt penetrating through these sacred obscurities. And, next to the impiety of denying his existence, is the temerity[5] of prying into his nature and essence, decrees and attributes.

But lest you should think that my piety has here got the better of my philosophy, I shall support my opinion, if it needs any support, by a very great authority. I might cite all the divines,[6] almost, from the foundation of Christianity, who have ever treated of this or any other theological subject: But I shall confine myself, at present, to one equally celebrated for piety and philosophy. It is Father Malebranche,[7] who, I remember, thus expresses himself. "One ought not so much," says he, "to call God a spirit, in order to express positively what he is, as in order to signify that he is not matter. He is a Being infinitely perfect: of this we cannot doubt. But in the same manner as we ought not to imagine, even supposing him corporeal, that he is clothed with a human body, as the Anthropomorphites[8] asserted, under colour that that figure

---

2   Hume's *Dialogues* were first published, three years after Hume's death, in 1779. This is a reprint of that edition, with some modernized spelling and capitalization.

3   I must admit.

4   This is paraphrased from the Bible: 1 Corinthians 2:9.

5   Audacity or impudence, rashness.

6   Priests or theologians.

7   Malebranche was an important French philosopher and follower of Descartes; his main work was *On the Search for the Truth* (1675), and it is from this that Philo is quoting.

8   See the background information, above.

was the most perfect of any; so, neither ought we to imagine that the spirit of God has human ideas, or bears any resemblance to our spirit, under colour that we know nothing more perfect than a human mind. We ought rather to believe, that as he comprehends[9] the perfections of matter without being material … he comprehends also the perfections of created spirits without being spirit, in the manner we conceive spirit: That his true name is, He that is; or, in other words, Being without restriction, All Being, the Being infinite and universal."

After so great an authority, Demea, replied Philo, as that which you have produced, and a thousand more which you might produce, it would appear ridiculous in me to add my sentiment, or express my approbation[10] of your doctrine. But surely, where reasonable men treat these subjects, the question can never be concerning the being, but only the nature, of the Deity. The former truth, as you well observe, is unquestionable and self-evident. Nothing exists without a cause; and the original cause of this universe (whatever it be) we call God; and piously ascribe to him every species of perfection. Whoever scruples[11] this fundamental truth, deserves every punishment which can be inflicted among philosophers, to wit,[12] the greatest ridicule, contempt, and disapprobation. But as all perfection is entirely relative, we ought never to imagine that we comprehend the attributes of this divine Being, or to suppose that his perfections have any analogy or likeness to the perfections of a human creature. Wisdom, thought, design, knowledge; these we justly ascribe to him; because these words are honourable among men, and we have no other language or other conceptions by which we can express our adoration of him. But let us beware, lest we think that our ideas anywise correspond to his perfections, or that his attributes have any resemblance to these qualities among men. He is infinitely superior to our limited view and comprehension; and is more the object of worship in the temple, than of disputation in the schools.

In reality, Cleanthes, continued he, there is no need of having recourse to that affected scepticism so displeasing to you, in order to come at this determination. Our ideas reach no further than our experience. We have no experience of divine attributes and operations. I need not conclude my syllogism. You can draw the inference yourself. And it is a pleasure to me (and I hope to you too) that just reasoning and sound piety here concur in the same conclusion, and both of them establish the adorably mysterious and incomprehensible nature of the supreme Being.

Not to lose any time in circumlocutions,[13] said Cleanthes, addressing himself to Demea, much less in replying to the pious declamations of Philo; I shall briefly explain how I conceive this matter. Look round the world: contemplate the whole and every part of it: you will find it to be nothing but one great machine, subdivided into an infinite number of lesser machines, which again admit of subdivisions to a degree beyond what human senses and faculties can trace and explain. All these various machines, and even their most minute parts, are adjusted to each other with an accuracy which ravishes into admiration all men who have ever contemplated them. The curious adapting of means to ends, throughout all nature, resembles exactly, though it much exceeds, the productions of human contrivance; of human designs, thought, wisdom, and intelligence. Since, therefore, the effects resemble each other, we are led to infer, by all the rules of analogy, that the causes also resemble; and that the Author of nature is somewhat similar to the mind of man, though possessed of much larger faculties, proportioned to the grandeur of the work which he has executed. By this argument *a posteriori*, and by this argument alone, do we prove at once the existence of a Deity, and his similarity to human mind and intelligence.

I shall be so free, Cleanthes, said Demea, as to tell you, that from the beginning, I could not approve of your conclusion concerning the similarity of the Deity to men; still less can I approve of the mediums by which you endeavour to establish it. What! No demonstration of the being of God! No abstract arguments! No proofs *a priori*! Are these, which have

---

9   Includes.

10   Approval.

11   To scruple is to feel doubt or hesitation.

12   "To wit" is a phrase meaning "that is to say."

13   Unnecessarily wordy or roundabout language.

hitherto been so much insisted on by philosophers, all fallacy, all sophism?[14] Can we reach no further in this subject than experience and probability? I will not say that this is betraying the cause of a Deity: But surely, by this affected candour, you give advantages to atheists, which they never could obtain by the mere dint of argument and reasoning.

What I chiefly scruple in this subject, said Philo, is not so much that all religious arguments are by Cleanthes reduced to experience, as that they appear not to be even the most certain and irrefragable[15] of that inferior kind. That a stone will fall, that fire will burn, that the earth has solidity, we have observed a thousand and a thousand times; and when any new instance of this nature is presented, we draw without hesitation the accustomed inference. The exact similarity of the cases gives us a perfect assurance of a similar event; and a stronger evidence is never desired nor sought after. But wherever you depart, in the least, from the similarity of the cases, you diminish proportionably the evidence; and may at last bring it to a very weak analogy, which is confessedly liable to error and uncertainty. After having experienced the circulation of the blood in human creatures, we make no doubt that it takes place in Titius and Mævius:[16] but from its circulation in frogs and fishes, it is only a presumption, though a strong one, from analogy, that it takes place in men and other animals. The analogical reasoning is much weaker, when we infer the circulation of the sap in vegetables from our experience that the blood circulates in animals; and those, who hastily followed that imperfect analogy, are found, by more accurate experiments, to have been mistaken.

If we see a house, Cleanthes, we conclude, with the greatest certainty, that it had an architect or builder; because this is precisely that species of effect which we have experienced to proceed from that species of cause. But surely you will not affirm, that the universe bears such a resemblance to a house, that we can with the same certainty infer a similar cause, or that the analogy is here entire and perfect. The dissimilitude

is so striking, that the utmost you can here pretend to is a guess, a conjecture, a presumption concerning a similar cause; and how that pretension will be received in the world, I leave you to consider.

It would surely be very ill received, replied Cleanthes; and I should be deservedly blamed and detested, did I allow, that the proofs of a Deity amounted to no more than a guess or conjecture. But is the whole adjustment of means to ends in a house and in the universe so slight a resemblance? The economy of final causes?[17] The order, proportion, and arrangement of every part? Steps of a stair are plainly contrived, that human legs may use them in mounting; and this inference is certain and infallible. Human legs are also contrived for walking and mounting; and this inference, I allow, is not altogether so certain, because of the dissimilarity which you remark; but does it, therefore, deserve the name only of presumption or conjecture?

Good God! cried Demea, interrupting him, where are we? Zealous defenders of religion allow, that the proofs of a Deity fall short of perfect evidence! And you, Philo, on whose assistance I depended in proving the adorable mysteriousness of the divine nature, do you assent to all these extravagant[18] opinions of Cleanthes? For what other name can I give them? or, why spare my censure, when such principles are advanced, supported by such an authority, before so young a man as Pamphilus?[19]

You seem not to apprehend, replied Philo, that I argue with Cleanthes in his own way; and, by showing

---

14   A sophism is a clever but misleading argument.

15   Unanswerable, undeniable.

16   That is, randomly chosen, generic human beings: John or Jane Doe.

17   Hume uses the word "economy" in its now somewhat archaic sense to mean an orderly arrangement or system (of any type, not necessarily a financial system nor necessarily one characterized by frugality). "Final causes" are one of the four types of causation (material, formal, efficient, final) identified by Aristotle: final causes are, roughly, the *reasons* for things, the *purposes* that explain them. For example, the structure of a can opener can be explained in terms of its purpose: it has a sharp pointy bit, for instance, *because* it is supposed to bite into the metal top of a can.

18   Excessive, unreasonable.

19   The character who is supposed to be listening to this dialogue and later writing it down.

him the dangerous consequences of his tenets,[20] hope at last to reduce him to our opinion. But what sticks most with you, I observe, is the representation which Cleanthes has made of the argument a posteriori; and finding that that argument is likely to escape your hold and vanish into air, you think it so disguised, that you can scarcely believe it to be set in its true light. Now, however much I may dissent, in other respects, from the dangerous principles of Cleanthes, I must allow that he has fairly represented that argument; and I shall endeavour so to state the matter to you, that you will entertain no further scruples with regard to it.

Were a man to abstract from every thing which he knows or has seen, he would be altogether incapable, merely from his own ideas, to determine what kind of scene the universe must be, or to give the preference to one state or situation of things above another. For as nothing which he clearly conceives could be esteemed impossible or implying a contradiction, every chimera of his fancy would be upon an equal footing; nor could he assign any just reason why he adheres to one idea or system, and rejects the others which are equally possible.

Again; after he opens his eyes, and contemplates the world as it really is, it would be impossible for him at first to assign the cause of any one event, much less of the whole of things, or of the universe. He might set his fancy a rambling; and she might bring him in an infinite variety of reports and representations. These would all be possible; but being all equally possible, he would never of himself give a satisfactory account for his preferring one of them to the rest. Experience alone can point out to him the true cause of any phenomenon.

Now, according to this method of reasoning, Demea, it follows, (and is, indeed, tacitly allowed by Cleanthes himself,) that order, arrangement, or the adjustment of final causes, is not of itself any proof of design; but only so far as it has been experienced to proceed from that principle. For aught[21] we can know a priori, matter may contain the source or spring of order originally within itself, as well as mind does; and there is no more difficulty in conceiving, that the

several elements, from an internal unknown cause, may fall into the most exquisite arrangement, than to conceive that their ideas, in the great universal mind, from a like internal unknown cause, fall into that arrangement. The equal possibility of both these suppositions is allowed. But, by experience, we find (according to Cleanthes) that there is a difference between them. Throw several pieces of steel together, without shape or form; they will never arrange themselves so as to compose a watch: stone, and mortar, and wood, without an architect, never erect a house. But the ideas in a human mind, we see, by an unknown, inexplicable economy, arrange themselves so as to form the plan of a watch or house. Experience, therefore, proves, that there is an original principle of order in mind, not in matter. From similar effects we infer similar causes. The adjustment of means to ends is alike in the universe, as in a machine of human contrivance. The causes, therefore, must be resembling.

I was from the beginning scandalized, I must own, with this resemblance, which is asserted, between the Deity and human creatures; and must conceive it to imply such a degradation of the supreme Being as no sound theist could endure. With your assistance, therefore, Demea, I shall endeavour to defend what you justly call the adorable mysteriousness of the divine Nature, and shall refute this reasoning of Cleanthes, provided he allows that I have made a fair representation of it.

When Cleanthes had assented, Philo, after a short pause, proceeded in the following manner.

That all inferences, Cleanthes, concerning fact, are founded on experience; and that all experimental reasonings are founded on the supposition that similar causes prove similar effects, and similar effects similar causes; I shall not at present much dispute with you. But observe, I entreat you, with what extreme caution all just reasoners proceed in the transferring of experiments to similar cases. Unless the cases be exactly similar, they repose no perfect confidence in applying their past observation to any particular phenomenon. Every alteration of circumstances occasions a doubt concerning the event; and it requires new experiments to prove certainly, that the new circumstances are of no moment or importance. A change in bulk, situation, arrangement, age, disposition of the

---

20   Opinions or doctrines.
21   For all, for anything.

air, or surrounding bodies; any of these particulars may be attended with the most unexpected consequences: and unless the objects be quite familiar to us, it is the highest temerity to expect with assurance, after any of these changes, an event similar to that which before fell under our observation. The slow and deliberate steps of philosophers here, if any where, are distinguished from the precipitate march of the vulgar,[22] who, hurried on by the smallest similitude, are incapable of all discernment or consideration.

But can you think, Cleanthes, that your usual phlegm[23] and philosophy have been preserved in so wide a step as you have taken, when you compared to the universe houses, ships, furniture, machines, and, from their similarity in some circumstances, inferred a similarity in their causes? Thought, design, intelligence, such as we discover in men and other animals, is no more than one of the springs and principles of the universe, as well as heat or cold, attraction or repulsion, and a hundred others, which fall under daily observation. It is an active cause, by which some particular parts of nature, we find, produce alterations on other parts. But can a conclusion, with any propriety, be transferred from parts to the whole? Does not the great disproportion bar all comparison and inference? From observing the growth of a hair, can we learn any thing concerning the generation of a man? Would the manner of a leaf's blowing,[24] even though perfectly known, afford us any instruction concerning the vegetation of a tree?

But, allowing that we were to take the operations of one part of nature upon another, for the foundation of our judgement concerning the origin of the whole (which never can be admitted); yet why select so minute, so weak, so bounded a principle, as the reason and design of animals is found to be upon this planet? What peculiar privilege has this little agitation of the brain which we call thought, that we must thus make it the model of the whole universe? Our partiality[25]

in our own favour does indeed present it on all occasions; but sound philosophy ought carefully to guard against so natural an illusion.

So far from admitting, continued Philo, that the operations of a part can afford us any just conclusion concerning the origin of the whole, I will not allow any one part to form a rule for another part, if the latter be very remote from the former. Is there any reasonable ground to conclude, that the inhabitants of other planets possess thought, intelligence, reason, or any thing similar to these faculties in men? When nature has so extremely diversified her manner of operation in this small globe, can we imagine that she incessantly copies herself throughout so immense a universe? And if thought, as we may well suppose, be confined merely to this narrow corner, and has even there so limited a sphere of action, with what propriety can we assign it for the original cause of all things? The narrow views of a peasant, who makes his domestic economy the rule for the government of kingdoms, is in comparison a pardonable sophism.

But were we ever so much assured, that a thought and reason, resembling the human, were to be found throughout the whole universe, and were its activity elsewhere vastly greater and more commanding than it appears in this globe; yet I cannot see, why the operations of a world constituted, arranged, adjusted, can with any propriety be extended to a world which is in its embryo state, and is advancing towards that constitution and arrangement. By observation, we know somewhat of the economy, action, and nourishment of a finished animal; but we must transfer with great caution that observation to the growth of a foetus in the womb, and still more to the formation of an animalcule[26] in the loins of its male parent. Nature, we find, even from our limited experience, possesses an infinite number of springs and principles, which incessantly discover[27] themselves on every change of her position and situation. And what new and unknown principles would actuate her in so new and unknown a situation as that of the formation of a universe, we

---

22   The common people (from the Latin for "the common people," *vulgus*).

23   Calmness or coolness.

24   Blooming: i.e., growing from a bud into a fully formed leaf.

25   Bias.

---

26   A sperm cell. It was thought at the time that these were tiny animals.

27   Reveal, disclose, exhibit.

cannot, without the utmost temerity, pretend to determine.

A very small part of this great system, during a very short time, is very imperfectly discovered to us; and do we thence pronounce decisively concerning the origin of the whole?

Admirable conclusion! Stone, wood, brick, iron, brass, have not, at this time, in this minute globe of earth, an order or arrangement without human art and contrivance; therefore the universe could not originally attain its order and arrangement, without something similar to human art. But is a part of nature a rule for another part very wide of the former? Is it a rule for the whole? Is a very small part a rule for the universe? Is nature in one situation, a certain rule for nature in another situation vastly different from the former?

And can you blame me, Cleanthes, if I here imitate the prudent reserve of Simonides, who, according to the noted story,[28] being asked by Hiero, What God was? desired a day to think of it, and then two days more; and after that manner continually prolonged the term, without ever bringing in his definition or description? Could you even blame me, if I had answered at first, that I did not know, and was sensible[29] that this subject lay vastly beyond the reach of my faculties? You might cry out sceptic and railler,[30] as much as you pleased: but having found, in so many other subjects much more familiar, the imperfections and even contradictions of human reason, I never should expect any success from its feeble conjectures, in a subject so sublime, and so remote from the sphere of our observation. When two species of objects have always been observed to be conjoined together, I can infer, by custom, the existence of one wherever I see the existence of the other; and this I call an argument from experience. But how this argument can have place, where the objects, as in the present case, are single, individual, without parallel, or specific resemblance, may be difficult to explain. And will

any man tell me with a serious countenance, that an orderly universe must arise from some thought and art like the human, because we have experience of it? To ascertain this reasoning, it were requisite that we had experience of the origin of worlds; and it is not sufficient, surely, that we have seen ships and cities arise from human art and contrivance....

Philo was proceeding in this vehement manner, somewhat between jest and earnest, as it appeared to me, when he observed some signs of impatience in Cleanthes, and then immediately stopped short. What I had to suggest, said Cleanthes, is only that you would not abuse terms, or make use of popular expressions to subvert philosophical reasonings. You know, that the vulgar often distinguish reason from experience, even where the question relates only to matter of fact and existence; though it is found, where that reason is properly analysed, that it is nothing but a species of experience. To prove by experience the origin of the universe from mind, is not more contrary to common speech, than to prove the motion of the earth from the same principle. And a caviller[31] might raise all the same objections to the Copernican system,[32] which you have urged against my reasonings. Have you other earths, might he say, which you have seen to move? Have....

Yes! cried Philo, interrupting him, we have other earths. Is not the moon another earth, which we see to turn round its centre? Is not Venus another earth, where we observe the same phenomenon? Are not the revolutions of the sun also a confirmation, from analogy, of the same theory? All the planets, are they not earths, which revolve about the sun? Are not the satellites moons, which move round Jupiter and Saturn, and along with these primary planets round the sun? These analogies and resemblances, with others which I have not mentioned, are the sole proofs of the Copernican system; and to you it belongs to consider,

28   Cicero, *De Natura Deorum* ("On the Nature of the Gods").
29   Aware or conscious.
30   A "railler" is one who rails: complains vehemently or bitterly.
31   One who cavils, i.e., finds fault or makes petty criticisms.
32   The model of the solar system introduced by Polish astronomer Nicolaus Copernicus (1473–1543) in which the planets move in circular orbits around the sun (rather than orbiting the Earth, as in the older theory).

whether you have any analogies of the same kind to support your theory.

In reality, Cleanthes, continued he, the modern system of astronomy is now so much received by all inquirers, and has become so essential a part even of our earliest education, that we are not commonly very scrupulous in examining the reasons upon which it is founded. It is now become a matter of mere curiosity to study the first writers on that subject, who had the full force of prejudice to encounter, and were obliged to turn their arguments on every side in order to render them popular and convincing. But if we peruse Galileo's famous Dialogues concerning the system of the world,[33] we shall find, that that great genius, one of the sublimest that ever existed, first bent all his endeavours to prove, that there was no foundation for the distinction commonly made between elementary and celestial substances.[34] The schools,[35] proceeding from the illusions of sense, had carried this distinction very far; and had established the latter substances to be ingenerable, incorruptible, unalterable, impassable; and had assigned all the opposite qualities to the former. But Galileo, beginning with the moon, proved its similarity in every particular to the earth; its convex figure, its natural darkness when not illuminated, its density, its distinction into solid and liquid, the variations of its phases, the mutual illuminations of the earth and moon, their mutual eclipses, the inequalities of the lunar surface, &c. After many instances of this kind, with regard to all the planets, men plainly saw that these bodies became proper objects of experience; and that the similarity of their nature enabled us to extend the same arguments and phenomena from one to the other.

In this cautious proceeding of the astronomers, you may read your own condemnation, Cleanthes; or rather may see, that the subject in which you are engaged exceeds all human reason and inquiry. Can you pretend to show any such similarity between the fabric of a house, and the generation of a universe? Have you ever seen nature in any such situation as resembles the first arrangement of the elements? Have worlds ever been formed under your eye; and have you had leisure to observe the whole progress of the phenomenon, from the first appearance of order to its final consummation? If you have, then cite your experience, and deliver your theory.

Part III

How the most absurd argument, replied Cleanthes, in the hands of a man of ingenuity and invention, may acquire an air of probability! Are you not aware, Philo, that it became necessary for Copernicus and his first disciples to prove the similarity of the terrestrial and celestial matter; because several philosophers, blinded by old systems, and supported by some sensible[36] appearances, had denied this similarity? But that it is by no means necessary, that theists should prove the similarity of the works of nature to those of art; because this similarity is self-evident and undeniable? The same matter, a like form; what more is requisite to show an analogy between their causes, and to ascertain the origin of all things from a divine purpose and intention? Your objections, I must freely tell you, are no better than the abstruse[37] cavils of those philosophers who denied motion;[38] and ought to be refuted in the same manner, by illustrations, examples, and instances, rather than by serious argument and philosophy.

Suppose, therefore, that an articulate voice were heard in the clouds, much louder and more melodious than any which human art could ever reach: Suppose, that this voice were extended in the same instant over all nations, and spoke to each nation in its own language and dialect: suppose, that the words delivered not only contain a just sense and meaning,

---

33 *Dialogue Concerning the Two Chief World Systems* (1632).

34 Between the material of which earthly things are made and the stuff of which the "celestial bodies" (stars and planets) are made.

35 The medieval philosophical system called "scholasticism"—see the notes to the Aquinas reading in this chapter for more information.

36 Perceptual—appearances that can be sensed or experienced.

37 Difficult to understand, obscure.

38 For example, the Greek philosopher Zeno of Elea (born in about 490 BCE), the originator of the so-called "Zeno's paradoxes" about motion.

but convey some instruction altogether worthy of a benevolent Being, superior to mankind: Could you possibly hesitate a moment concerning the cause of this voice? And must you not instantly ascribe it to some design or purpose? Yet I cannot see but all the same objections (if they merit that appellation[39]) which lie against the system of theism, may also be produced against this inference.

Might you not say, that all conclusions concerning fact were founded on experience: that when we hear an articulate voice in the dark, and thence infer a man, it is only the resemblance of the effects which leads us to conclude that there is a like resemblance in the cause: but that this extraordinary voice, by its loudness, extent, and flexibility to all languages, bears so little analogy to any human voice, that we have no reason to suppose any analogy in their causes: and consequently, that a rational, wise, coherent speech proceeded, you know not whence, from some accidental whistling of the winds, not from any divine reason or intelligence? You see clearly your own objections in these cavils, and I hope too you see clearly, that they cannot possibly have more force in the one case than in the other.

But to bring the case still nearer the present one of the universe, I shall make two suppositions, which imply not any absurdity or impossibility. Suppose that there is a natural, universal, invariable language, common to every individual of human race; and that books are natural productions, which perpetuate themselves in the same manner with animals and vegetables, by descent and propagation.[40] Several expressions of our passions contain a universal language: all brute animals have a natural speech, which, however limited, is very intelligible to their own species. And as there are infinitely fewer parts and less contrivance in the finest composition of eloquence, than in the coarsest organised body, the propagation of an *Iliad* or *Æneid*[41] is an easier supposition than that of any plant or animal.

Suppose, therefore, that you enter into your library, thus peopled by natural volumes, containing the most refined reason and most exquisite beauty; could you possibly open one of them, and doubt, that its original cause bore the strongest analogy to mind and intelligence? When it reasons and discourses; when it expostulates, argues, and enforces its views and topics; when it applies sometimes to the pure intellect, sometimes to the affections; when it collects, disposes, and adorns every consideration suited to the subject; could you persist in asserting, that all this, at the bottom, had really no meaning; and that the first formation of this volume in the loins of its original parent proceeded not from thought and design? Your obstinacy, I know, reaches not that degree of firmness: even your sceptical play and wantonness would be abashed at so glaring an absurdity.

But if there be any difference, Philo, between this supposed case and the real one of the universe, it is all to the advantage of the latter. The anatomy of an animal affords many stronger instances of design than the perusal of Livy or Tacitus;[42] and any objection which you start in the former case, by carrying me back to so unusual and extraordinary a scene as the first formation of worlds, the same objection has place on the supposition of our vegetating library. Choose, then, your party, Philo, without ambiguity or evasion; assert either that a rational volume is no proof of a rational cause, or admit of a similar cause to all the works of nature.

Let me here observe too, continued Cleanthes, that this religious argument, instead of being weakened by that scepticism so much affected by you, rather acquires force from it, and becomes more firm and undisputed. To exclude all argument or reasoning of every kind, is either affectation or madness. The declared profession of every reasonable sceptic is only to reject abstruse, remote, and refined arguments; to adhere to common sense and the plain instincts of nature; and to assent, wherever any reasons strike him

---

39   Name.
40   By (biological) reproduction.
41   Two well-known works of classical literature, the former written by Homer and the latter by Virgil.

42   Two Roman historians. Livy (59 BCE–17 CE) wrote a 142-volume history of Rome (of which only 35 volumes survive) from its foundation to his own time, while Tacitus (55–120 CE) wrote about the period of Roman history from 14 to 96 CE.

with so full a force that he cannot, without the greatest violence, prevent it. Now the arguments for natural religion are plainly of this kind; and nothing but the most perverse, obstinate metaphysics can reject them. Consider, anatomise the eye; survey its structure and contrivance;[43] and tell me, from your own feeling, if the idea of a contriver does not immediately flow in upon you with a force like that of sensation. The most obvious conclusion, surely, is in favour of design; and it requires time, reflection, and study, to summon up those frivolous, though abstruse objections, which can support infidelity. Who can behold the male and female of each species, the correspondence of their parts and instincts, their passions, and whole course of life before and after generation, but must be sensible, that the propagation of the species is intended by nature? Millions and millions of such instances present themselves through every part of the universe; and no language can convey a more intelligible irresistible meaning, than the curious adjustment of final causes. To what degree, therefore, of blind dogmatism must one have attained, to reject such natural and such convincing arguments?

Some beauties in writing we may meet with, which seem contrary to rules, and which gain the affections, and animate the imagination, in opposition to all the precepts of criticism, and to the authority of the established masters of art. And if the argument for theism be, as you pretend, contradictory to the principles of logic; its universal, its irresistible influence proves clearly, that there may be arguments of a like irregular nature. Whatever cavils may be urged, an orderly world, as well as a coherent, articulate speech, will still be received as an incontestable proof of design and intention.

It sometimes happens, I own, that the religious arguments have not their due influence on an ignorant savage and barbarian; not because they are obscure and difficult, but because he never asks himself any question with regard to them. Whence arises the curious structure of an animal? From the copulation of its parents. And these whence? From their parents? A few removes set the objects at such a distance, that to him they are lost in darkness and confusion; nor is he

actuated by any curiosity to trace them further. But this is neither dogmatism nor scepticism, but stupidity: a state of mind very different from your sifting, inquisitive disposition, my ingenious friend. You can trace causes from effects: you can compare the most distant and remote objects: and your greatest errors proceed not from barrenness of thought and invention, but from too luxuriant a fertility, which suppresses your natural good sense, by a profusion of unnecessary scruples and objections.

Here I could observe, Hermippus,[44] that Philo was a little embarrassed and confounded: But while he hesitated in delivering an answer, luckily for him, Demea broke in upon the discourse, and saved his countenance.

Your instance, Cleanthes, said he, drawn from books and language, being familiar, has, I confess, so much more force on that account: but is there not some danger too in this very circumstance; and may it not render us presumptuous, by making us imagine we comprehend the Deity, and have some adequate idea of his nature and attributes? When I read a volume, I enter into the mind and intention of the author: I become him, in a manner, for the instant; and have an immediate feeling and conception of those ideas which revolved in his imagination while employed in that composition. But so near an approach we never surely can make to the Deity. His ways are not our ways. His attributes are perfect, but incomprehensible. And this volume of nature contains a great and inexplicable riddle, more than any intelligible discourse or reasoning.

The ancient Platonists,[45] you know, were the most religious and devout of all the pagan philosophers; yet many of them, particularly Plotinus,[46] expressly declare, that intellect or understanding is not to be ascribed to the Deity; and that our most perfect worship of him consists, not in acts of veneration, reverence, gratitude, or love; but in a certain mysterious self-

---

43 Plan or design.

44 The character to whom Pamphilus, the narrator, is supposed to be sending his written record of the dialogue.

45 Followers of the philosophy of Plato.

46 An Egyptian philosopher, founder of a movement today called Neoplatonism, who lived from 205 to 270 CE. His main work is called *The Enneads*.

annihilation, or total extinction of all our faculties. These ideas are, perhaps, too far stretched; but still it must be acknowledged, that, by representing the Deity as so intelligible and comprehensible, and so similar to a human mind, we are guilty of the grossest and most narrow partiality, and make ourselves the model of the whole universe.

All the sentiments of the human mind, gratitude, resentment, love, friendship, approbation, blame, pity, emulation, envy, have a plain reference to the state and situation of man, and are calculated for preserving the existence and promoting the activity of such a being in such circumstances. It seems, therefore, unreasonable to transfer such sentiments to a supreme existence, or to suppose him actuated by them; and the phenomena besides of the universe will not support us in such a theory. All our ideas, derived from the senses, are confessedly false and illusive; and cannot therefore be supposed to have place in a supreme intelligence: and as the ideas of internal sentiment, added to those of the external senses, compose the whole furniture of human understanding, we may conclude, that none of the materials of thought are in any respect similar in the human and in the divine intelligence. Now, as to the manner of thinking; how can we make any comparison between them, or suppose them any wise resembling? Our thought is fluctuating, uncertain, fleeting, successive, and compounded; and were we to remove these circumstances, we absolutely annihilate its essence, and it would in such a case be an abuse of terms to apply to it the name of thought or reason. At least if it appear more pious and respectful (as it really is) still to retain these terms, when we mention the supreme Being, we ought to acknowledge, that their meaning, in that case, is totally incomprehensible; and that the infirmities of our nature do not permit us to reach any ideas which in the least correspond to the ineffable sublimity of the Divine attributes.

Part IV

It seems strange to me, said Cleanthes, that you, Demea, who are so sincere in the cause of religion, should still maintain the mysterious, incomprehensible nature of the Deity, and should insist so strenuously that he has no manner of likeness or resemblance to human creatures. The Deity, I can readily allow, possesses many powers and attributes of which we can have no comprehension: But if our ideas, so far as they go, be not just, and adequate, and correspondent to his real nature, I know not what there is in this subject worth insisting on. Is the name, without any meaning, of such mighty importance? Or how do you mystics, who maintain the absolute incomprehensibility of the Deity, differ from sceptics or atheists, who assert, that the first cause of all is unknown and unintelligible? Their temerity must be very great, if, after rejecting the production by a mind, I mean a mind resembling the human (for I know of no other), they pretend to assign, with certainty, any other specific intelligible cause: and their conscience must be very scrupulous indeed, if they refuse to call the universal unknown cause a God or Deity; and to bestow on him as many sublime eulogies and unmeaning epithets as you shall please to require of them.

Who could imagine, replied Demea, that Cleanthes, the calm philosophical Cleanthes, would attempt to refute his antagonists by affixing a nickname to them; and, like the common bigots and inquisitors of the age, have recourse to invective and declamation, instead of reasoning? Or does he not perceive, that these topics are easily retorted, and that anthropomorphite is an appellation as invidious,[47] and implies as dangerous consequences, as the epithet of mystic, with which he has honoured us? In reality, Cleanthes, consider what it is you assert when you represent the Deity as similar to a human mind and understanding. What is the soul of man? A composition of various faculties, passions, sentiments, ideas; united, indeed, into one self or person, but still distinct from each other. When it reasons, the ideas, which are the parts of its discourse, arrange themselves in a certain form or order; which is not preserved entire for a moment, but immediately gives place to another arrangement. New opinions, new passions, new affections, new feelings arise, which continually diversify the mental scene, and produce in it the greatest variety and most rapid succession imaginable. How is this compatible with that perfect immutability and simplicity which all true theists ascribe to the Deity? By the same act, say they, he sees past, present, and future: His love

_____

47   Likely to arouse ill will.

and hatred, his mercy and justice, are one individual operation: He is entire in every point of space; and complete in every instant of duration. No succession, no change, no acquisition, no diminution. What he is implies not in it any shadow of distinction or diversity. And what he is this moment he ever has been, and ever will be, without any new judgement, sentiment, or operation. He stands fixed in one simple, perfect state: nor can you ever say, with any propriety, that this act of his is different from that other; or that this judgement or idea has been lately formed, and will give place, by succession, to any different judgement or idea.

I can readily allow, said Cleanthes, that those who maintain the perfect simplicity of the supreme Being, to the extent in which you have explained it, are complete mystics, and chargeable with all the consequences which I have drawn from their opinion. They are, in a word, atheists, without knowing it. For though it be allowed, that the Deity possesses attributes of which we have no comprehension, yet ought we never to ascribe to him any attributes which are absolutely incompatible with that intelligent nature essential to him. A mind, whose acts and sentiments and ideas are not distinct and successive; one, that is wholly simple, and totally immutable, is a mind which has no thought, no reason, no will, no sentiment, no love, no hatred; or, in a word, is no mind at all. It is an abuse of terms to give it that appellation; and we may as well speak of limited extension without figure, or of number without composition.[48]

Pray consider, said Philo, whom you are at present inveighing against. You are honouring with the appellation of atheist all the sound, orthodox divines, almost, who have treated of this subject; and you will at last be, yourself, found, according to your reckoning, the only sound theist in the world. But if idolaters be atheists, as, I think, may justly be asserted, and Christian theologians the same, what becomes of the argument, so much celebrated, derived from the universal consent of mankind?[49]

But because I know you are not much swayed by names and authorities, I shall endeavour to show you, a little more distinctly, the inconveniences of that anthropomorphism, which you have embraced; and shall prove, that there is no ground to suppose a plan of the world to be formed in the divine mind, consisting of distinct ideas, differently arranged, in the same manner as an architect forms in his head the plan of a house which he intends to execute.

It is not easy, I own, to see what is gained by this supposition, whether we judge of the matter by reason or by experience. We are still obliged to mount higher, in order to find the cause of this cause, which you had assigned as satisfactory and conclusive.

If reason (I mean abstract reason, derived from inquiries *a priori*) be not alike mute with regard to all questions concerning cause and effect, this sentence at least it will venture to pronounce, That a mental world, or universe of ideas, requires a cause as much as does a material world, or universe of objects; and, if similar in its arrangement, must require a similar cause. For what is there in this subject, which should occasion a different conclusion or inference? In an abstract view, they are entirely alike; and no difficulty attends the one supposition, which is not common to both of them.

Again, when we will needs force experience to pronounce some sentence, even on these subjects which lie beyond her sphere, neither can she perceive any material difference in this particular, between these two kinds of worlds; but finds them to be governed by similar principles, and to depend upon an equal variety of causes in their operations. We have specimens in miniature of both of them. Our own mind resembles the one; a vegetable or animal body the other. Let experience, therefore, judge from these samples. Nothing seems more delicate, with regard to its causes, than thought; and as these causes never operate in two persons after the same manner, so we never find two persons who think exactly alike. Nor indeed does the same person think exactly alike at any two different periods of time. A difference of age, of

---

48   Of finite extension in three dimensions without shape, or plurality without component parts.

49   This is the argument for the existence of a deity from the (presumed) fact of almost universal belief in some

sort of divinity. It appears, for example, in writings by Cicero (who lived in the first century BCE) and Sextus Empiricus (second century CE).

the disposition of his body, of weather, of food, of company, of books, of passions; any of these particulars, or others more minute, are sufficient to alter the curious machinery of thought, and communicate to it very different movements and operations. As far as we can judge, vegetables and animal bodies are not more delicate in their motions, nor depend upon a greater variety or more curious adjustment of springs and principles.

How, therefore, shall we satisfy ourselves concerning the cause of that Being whom you suppose the Author of nature, or, according to your system of anthropomorphism, the ideal world,[50] into which you trace the material? Have we not the same reason to trace that ideal world into another ideal world, or new intelligent principle? But if we stop, and go no further; why go so far? Why not stop at the material world? How can we satisfy ourselves without going on in infinitum?[51] And, after all, what satisfaction is there in that infinite progression? Let us remember the story of the Indian philosopher and his elephant.[52] It was never more applicable than to the present subject. If the material world rests upon a similar ideal world, this ideal world must rest upon some other; and so on, without end. It were better, therefore, never to look beyond the present material world. By supposing it to contain the principle of its order within itself, we really assert it to be God; and the sooner we arrive at that divine Being, so much the better. When you go one step beyond the mundane system, you only excite an inquisitive humour[53] which it is impossible ever to satisfy.

To say, that the different ideas which compose the reason of the supreme Being, fall into order of themselves, and by their own nature, is really to talk without any precise meaning. If it has a meaning, I would fain[54] know, why it is not as good sense to say, that the parts of the material world fall into order of themselves and by their own nature. Can the one opinion be intelligible, while the other is not so?

We have, indeed, experience of ideas which fall into order of themselves, and without any known cause. But, I am sure, we have a much larger experience of matter which does the same; as, in all instances of generation and vegetation,[55] where the accurate analysis of the cause exceeds all human comprehension. We have also experience of particular systems of thought and of matter which have no order; of the first in madness, of the second in corruption.[56] Why, then, should we think, that order is more essential to one than the other? And if it requires a cause in both, what do we gain by your system, in tracing the universe of objects into a similar universe of ideas? The first step which we make leads us on for ever. It were, therefore, wise in us to limit all our inquiries to the present world, without looking further. No satisfaction can ever be attained by these speculations, which so far exceed the narrow bounds of human understanding.

It was usual with the Peripatetics,[57] you know, Cleanthes, when the cause of any phenomenon was demanded, to have recourse to their faculties or occult qualities; and to say, for instance, that bread nourished by its nutritive faculty, and senna[58] purged by its purgative. But it has been discovered, that this subterfuge was nothing but the disguise of ignorance; and that these philosophers, though less ingenuous,[59] really said the same thing with the sceptics or the vulgar, who fairly confessed that they knew not the cause of these phenomena. In like manner, when it is asked, what cause produces order in the ideas of

---

50   World of ideas.

51   Forever, without limit.

52   This story, as it happens, appears in the reading from John Locke in Chapter 2. In brief, there is a myth that certain East Indian philosophers held that the world rests on the back of a giant elephant, which in turn is supported by an enormous tortoise. The problem, however, is this: What is the tortoise standing on?

53   In this context, a humour is a state of mind or disposition.

54   Willingly, gladly.

55   Animal procreation or plant growth.

56   Decay.

57   The philosophical followers of Aristotle in the third century BCE. (They were supposedly named after the *peripatos*, or covered walk, in a garden where Aristotle lectured.)

58   A laxative prepared from dried pods of the cassia tree.

59   Innocent, open.

the supreme Being; can any other reason be assigned by you, anthropomorphites, than that it is a rational faculty, and that such is the nature of the Deity? But why a similar answer will not be equally satisfactory in accounting for the order of the world, without having recourse to any such intelligent Creator as you insist on, may be difficult to determine. It is only to say, that such is the nature of material objects, and that they are all originally possessed of a faculty of order and proportion. These are only more learned and elaborate ways of confessing our ignorance; nor has the one hypothesis any real advantage above the other, except in its greater conformity to vulgar prejudices.

You have displayed this argument with great emphasis, replied Cleanthes: You seem not sensible how easy it is to answer it. Even in common life, if I assign a cause for any event, is it any objection, Philo, that I cannot assign the cause of that cause, and answer every new question which may incessantly be started? And what philosophers could possibly submit to so rigid a rule? Philosophers, who confess ultimate causes to be totally unknown; and are sensible, that the most refined principles into which they trace the phenomena, are still to them as inexplicable as these phenomena themselves are to the vulgar. The order and arrangement of nature, the curious adjustment of final causes, the plain use and intention of every part and organ; all these bespeak in the clearest language an intelligent cause or author. The heavens and the earth join in the same testimony: the whole chorus of nature raises one hymn to the praises of its Creator. You alone, or almost alone, disturb this general harmony. You start abstruse doubts, cavils, and objections: you ask me, what is the cause of this cause? I know not; I care not; that concerns not me. I have found a Deity; and here I stop my inquiry. Let those go further, who are wiser or more enterprising.

I pretend to be neither, replied Philo: And for that very reason, I should never perhaps have attempted to go so far; especially when I am sensible, that I must at last be contented to sit down with the same answer, which, without further trouble, might have satisfied me from the beginning. If I am still to remain in utter ignorance of causes, and can absolutely give an explication of nothing, I shall never esteem it any advantage to shove off for a moment a difficulty,

which, you acknowledge, must immediately, in its full force, recur upon me. Naturalists indeed very justly explain particular effects by more general causes, though these general causes themselves should remain in the end totally inexplicable; but they never surely thought it satisfactory to explain a particular effect by a particular cause, which was no more to be accounted for than the effect itself. An ideal system, arranged of itself, without a precedent design, is not a whit more explicable than a material one, which attains its order in a like manner; nor is there any more difficulty in the latter supposition than in the former.

Part V

But to show you still more inconveniences, continued Philo, in your anthropomorphism, please to take a new survey of your principles. Like effects prove like causes. This is the experimental argument; and this, you say too, is the sole theological argument. Now, it is certain, that the liker[60] the effects are which are seen, and the liker the causes which are inferred, the stronger is the argument. Every departure on either side diminishes the probability, and renders the experiment less conclusive. You cannot doubt of the principle; neither ought you to reject its consequences.

All the new discoveries in astronomy, which prove the immense grandeur and magnificence of the works of nature, are so many additional arguments for a Deity, according to the true system of theism; but, according to your hypothesis of experimental theism, they become so many objections, by removing the effect still further from all resemblance to the effects of human art and contrivance. For, if Lucretius, even following the old system of the world, could exclaim,

> Quis regere immensi summam, quis habere profundi
> Indu manu validas potis est moderanter habenas?
> Quis pariter cœlos omnes convertere? et omnes
> Ignibus ætheriis terras suffire feraces?
> Omnibus inve locis esse omni tempore præsto?[61]

---

60 The more similar.

61 Lucretius (c. 99–55 BCE) was a Roman poet whose massive poem *De Rerum Natura* ("On the Nature of Things") is the most extensive account of the atomism of the Greek philosopher Epicurus that has survived.

If Tully esteemed this reasoning so natural, as to put it into the mouth of his Epicurean: *Quibus enim oculis animi intueri potuit vester Plato fabricam illam tanti operis, qua construi a Deo atque ædificari mundum facit? quæ molitio? quæ ferramenta? qui vectes? quæ machinæ? qui ministri tanti muneris fuerunt? quemadmodum autem obedire et parere voluntati architecti aer, ignis, aqua, terra potuerunt?*[62] If this argument, I say, had any force in former ages, how much greater must it have at present, when the bounds of nature are so infinitely enlarged, and such a magnificent scene is opened to us? It is still more unreasonable to form our idea of so unlimited a cause from our experience of the narrow productions of human design and invention.

The discoveries by microscopes, as they open a new universe in miniature, are still objections, according to you, arguments, according to me. The further we push our researches of this kind, we are still led to infer the universal cause of all to be vastly different from mankind, or from any object of human experience and observation.

And what say you to the discoveries in anatomy, chemistry, botany? … These surely are no objections, replied Cleanthes; they only discover new instances of art and contrivance. It is still the image of mind reflected on us from innumerable objects. Add, a mind *like the human*, said Philo. I know of no other, replied Cleanthes, And the liker the better, insisted Philo. To be sure, said Cleanthes.

Now, Cleanthes, said Philo, with an air of alacrity and triumph, mark the consequences. *First*, by this method of reasoning, you renounce all claim to infinity in any of the attributes of the Deity. For, as the cause ought only to be proportioned to the effect, and the effect, so far as it falls under our cognisance, is not infinite; what pretensions have we, upon your suppositions, to ascribe that attribute to the divine Being? You will still insist, that, by removing him so much from all similarity to human creatures, we give in to the most arbitrary hypothesis, and at the same time weaken all proofs of his existence.

Secondly, you have no reason, on your theory, for ascribing perfection to the Deity, even in his finite capacity, or for supposing him free from every error, mistake, or incoherence, in his undertakings. There are many inexplicable difficulties in the works of nature, which, if we allow a perfect Author to be proved *a priori*, are easily solved, and become only seeming difficulties, from the narrow capacity of man, who cannot trace infinite relations. But according to your method of reasoning, these difficulties become all real; and perhaps will be insisted on, as new instances of likeness to human art and contrivance. At least, you must acknowledge, that it is impossible for us to tell, from our limited views, whether this system contains any great faults, or deserves any considerable praise, if compared to other possible, and even real systems. Could a peasant, if the *Æneid*[63] were read to him, pronounce that poem to be absolutely faultless, or even assign to it its proper rank among the produc-

---

The quotation reads:

> Who hath the power (I ask), who hath the power
> To rule the sum of the immeasurable,
> To hold with steady hand the giant reins
> Of the unfathomed deep? Who hath the power
> At once to rule a multitude of skies,
> At once to heat with fires ethereal all
> The fruitful lands of multitudes of worlds,
> To be at all times in all places near?
> (Trans. W.E. Leonard)

62 Tully is the name usually used in the eighteenth century for the Roman orator and statesman Marcus Tullius Cicero (106–43 BCE). The structure of Hume's *Dialogues* is based on Cicero's "On the Nature of the Gods." The quotation given here, taken from that work, can be translated as follows: "What power of mental vision enabled your master Plato to discern the vast and elaborate architectural process which, as he makes out, the deity adopted in building the structure of the universe? What method of engineering was employed? What tools and levers and machines? What agents carried out so vast an undertaking? And how were air, fire, water and earth enabled to obey and execute the will of the architect?"

63 An epic poem written in Latin by Virgil (70–19 BCE), describing the wanderings of the hero Aeneas for the seven years between his escape of the destruction of Troy and his settling in Italy.

tions of human wit, he, who had never seen any other production?

But were this world ever so perfect a production, it must still remain uncertain, whether all the excellences of the work can justly be ascribed to the workman. If we survey a ship, what an exalted idea must we form of the ingenuity of the carpenter who framed so complicated, useful, and beautiful a machine? And what surprise must we feel, when we find him a stupid mechanic, who imitated others, and copied an art, which, through a long succession of ages, after multiplied trials, mistakes, corrections, deliberations, and controversies, had been gradually improving? Many worlds might have been botched and bungled, throughout an eternity, ere this system was struck out; much labour lost, many fruitless trials made; and a slow, but continued improvement carried on during infinite ages in the art of world-making. In such subjects, who can determine, where the truth; nay, who can conjecture where the probability, lies; amidst a great number of hypotheses which may be proposed, and a still greater which may be imagined?

And what shadow of an argument, continued Philo, can you produce, from your hypothesis, to prove the unity of the Deity? A great number of men join in building a house or ship, in rearing a city, in framing a commonwealth; why may not several deities combine in contriving and framing a world? This is only so much greater similarity to human affairs. By sharing the work among several, we may so much further limit the attributes of each, and get rid of that extensive power and knowledge, which must be supposed in one deity, and which, according to you, can only serve to weaken the proof of his existence. And if such foolish, such vicious creatures as man, can yet often unite in framing and executing one plan, how much more those deities or dæmons,[64] whom we may suppose several degrees more perfect?

To multiply causes without necessity, is indeed contrary to true philosophy: but this principle applies not to the present case. Were one deity antecedently proved by your theory, who were possessed of every attribute requisite to the production of the universe; it would be needless, I own (though not absurd) to suppose any other deity existent. But while it is still a question, whether all these attributes are united in one subject, or dispersed among several independent beings, by what phenomena in nature can we pretend to decide the controversy? Where we see a body raised in a scale, we are sure that there is in the opposite scale, however concealed from sight, some counterpoising weight equal to it; but it is still allowed to doubt, whether that weight be an aggregate of several distinct bodies, or one uniform united mass. And if the weight requisite very much exceeds any thing which we have ever seen conjoined in any single body, the former supposition becomes still more probable and natural. An intelligent being of such vast power and capacity as is necessary to produce the universe, or, to speak in the language of ancient philosophy, so prodigious an animal exceeds all analogy, and even comprehension.

But farther, Cleanthes: men are mortal, and renew their species by generation; and this is common to all living creatures. The two great sexes of male and female, says Milton,[65] animate the world. Why must this circumstance, so universal, so essential, be excluded from those numerous and limited deities? Behold, then, the theogony[66] of ancient times brought back upon us.

And why not become a perfect anthro-pomorphite? Why not assert the deity or deities to be corporeal, and to have eyes, a nose, mouth, ears, &c.? Epicurus[67] maintained, that no man had ever seen reason but in a human figure; therefore the gods must have a human figure. And this argument, which is deservedly so much ridiculed by Cicero, becomes, according to you, solid and philosophical.

In a word, Cleanthes, a man who follows your hypothesis is able perhaps to assert, or conjecture, that the universe, sometime, arose from something like design: but beyond that position he cannot ascertain

---

64 Demigods.

65 English poet John Milton (1608–1674), best known for his epic poem "Paradise Lost."

66 An account of the genealogy of the gods: the theory of their family tree, so to speak.

67 A Greek philosopher (341–270 BCE) best known for defending an atomistic view of the world that sees it as built up entirely from an infinite number of tiny indestructible particles.

one single circumstance; and is left afterwards to fix every point of his theology by the utmost license of fancy and hypothesis. This world, for aught he knows, is very faulty and imperfect, compared to a superior standard; and was only the first rude essay[68] of some infant deity, who afterwards abandoned it, ashamed of his lame performance: it is the work only of some dependent, inferior deity; and is the object of derision to his superiors: it is the production of old age and dotage in some superannuated deity; and ever since his death, has run on at adventures,[69] from the first impulse and active force which it received from him.... You justly give signs of horror, Demea, at these strange suppositions; but these, and a thousand more of the same kind, are Cleanthes's suppositions, not mine. From the moment the attributes of the Deity are supposed finite, all these have place. And I cannot, for my part, think that so wild and unsettled a system of theology is, in any respect, preferable to none at all.

These suppositions I absolutely disown, cried Cleanthes: they strike me, however, with no horror, especially when proposed in that rambling way in which they drop from you. On the contrary, they give me pleasure, when I see, that, by the utmost indulgence of your imagination, you never get rid of the hypothesis of design in the universe, but are obliged at every turn to have recourse to it. To this concession I adhere steadily; and this I regard as a sufficient foundation for religion.

…

Part VII

But here, continued Philo, in examining the ancient system of the soul of the world, there strikes me, all on a sudden, a new idea, which, if just, must go near to subvert all your reasoning, and destroy even your first inferences, on which you repose such confidence. If the universe bears a greater likeness to animal bodies and to vegetables, than to the works of human art, it is more probable that its cause resembles the cause of the former than that of the latter, and its origin ought rather to be ascribed to generation or vegeta-

tion, than to reason or design. Your conclusion, even according to your own principles, is therefore lame and defective.

Pray open up this argument a little further, said Demea, for I do not rightly apprehend it in that concise manner in which you have expressed it.

Our friend Cleanthes, replied Philo, as you have heard, asserts, that since no question of fact can be proved otherwise than by experience, the existence of a Deity admits not of proof from any other medium. The world, says he, resembles the works of human contrivance; therefore its cause must also resemble that of the other. Here we may remark, that the operation of one very small part of nature, to wit man, upon another very small part, to wit that inanimate matter lying within his reach, is the rule by which Cleanthes judges of the origin of the whole; and he measures objects, so widely disproportioned, by the same individual standard. But to waive all objections drawn from this topic, I affirm, that there are other parts of the universe (besides the machines of human invention) which bear still a greater resemblance to the fabric of the world, and which, therefore, afford a better conjecture concerning the universal origin of this system. These parts are animals and vegetables. The world plainly resembles more an animal or a vegetable, than it does a watch or a knitting-loom. Its cause, therefore, it is more probable, resembles the cause of the former. The cause of the former is generation or vegetation. The cause, therefore, of the world, we may infer to be something similar or analogous to generation or vegetation.

But how is it conceivable, said Demea, that the world can arise from any thing similar to vegetation or generation?

Very easily, replied Philo. In like manner as a tree sheds its seed into the neighbouring fields, and produces other trees; so the great vegetable, the world, or this planetary system, produces within itself certain seeds, which, being scattered into the surrounding chaos, vegetate into new worlds. A comet, for instance, is the seed of a world; and after it has been fully ripened, by passing from sun to sun, and star to star, it is at last tossed into the unformed elements which everywhere surround this universe, and immediately sprouts up into a new system.

---

68 "Rude essay" means a rough attempt or primitive effort.

69 By chance.

Or if, for the sake of variety (for I see no other advantage), we should suppose this world to be an animal; a comet is the egg of this animal: and in like manner as an ostrich lays its egg in the sand, which, without any further care, hatches the egg, and produces a new animal; so....

I understand you, says Demea: But what wild, arbitrary suppositions are these! What *data* have you for such extraordinary conclusions? And is the slight, imaginary resemblance of the world to a vegetable or an animal sufficient to establish the same inference with regard to both? Objects, which are in general so widely different, ought they to be a standard for each other?

Right, cries Philo: This is the topic on which I have all along insisted. I have still asserted, that we have no data to establish any system of cosmogony.[70] Our experience, so imperfect in itself, and so limited both in extent and duration, can afford us no probable conjecture concerning the whole of things. But if we must needs fix on some hypothesis; by what rule, pray, ought we to determine our choice? Is there any other rule than the greater similarity of the objects compared? And does not a plant or an animal, which springs from vegetation or generation, bear a stronger resemblance to the world, than does any artificial machine, which arises from reason and design?

But what is this vegetation and generation of which you talk? said Demea. Can you explain their operations, and anatomise that fine internal structure on which they depend?

As much, at least, replied Philo, as Cleanthes can explain the operations of reason, or anatomise that internal structure on which it depends. But without any such elaborate disquisitions,[71] when I see an animal, I infer, that it sprang from generation; and that with as great certainty as you conclude a house to have been reared by design. These words, *generation, reason*, mark only certain powers and energies in nature, whose effects are known, but whose essence is incomprehensible; and one of these principles, more than the other, has no privilege for being made a standard to the whole of nature.

_____
70   The creation or origin of the universe.

71   Long explanations or speeches.

In reality, Demea, it may reasonably be expected, that the larger the views are which we take of things, the better will they conduct us in our conclusions concerning such extraordinary and such magnificent subjects. In this little corner of the world alone, there are four principles, *reason, instinct, generation, vegetation*, which are similar to each other, and are the causes of similar effects. What a number of other principles may we naturally suppose in the immense extent and variety of the universe, could we travel from planet to planet, and from system to system, in order to examine each part of this mighty fabric? Any one of these four principles above mentioned (and a hundred others which lie open to our conjecture) may afford us a theory by which to judge of the origin of the world; and it is a palpable and egregious partiality to confine our view entirely to that principle by which our own minds operate. Were this principle more intelligible on that account, such a partiality might be somewhat excusable: but reason, in its internal fabric and structure, is really as little known to us as instinct or vegetation; and, perhaps, even that vague, indeterminate word, nature, to which the vulgar refer every thing, is not at the bottom more inexplicable. The effects of these principles are all known to us from experience; but the principles themselves, and their manner of operation, are totally unknown; nor is it less intelligible, or less conformable to experience, to say, that the world arose by vegetation, from a seed shed by another world, than to say that it arose from a divine reason or contrivance, according to the sense in which Cleanthes understands it.

But methinks, said Demea, if the world had a vegetative quality, and could sow the seeds of new worlds into the infinite chaos, this power would be still an additional argument for design in its Author. For whence could arise so wonderful a faculty but from design? Or how can order spring from any thing which perceives not that order which it bestows?

You need only look around you, replied Philo, to satisfy yourself with regard to this question. A tree bestows order and organisation on that tree which springs from it, without knowing the order; an animal in the same manner on its offspring; a bird on its nest; and instances of this kind are even more frequent in the world than those of order, which arise from reason and contrivance. To say, that all this order in animals and vegetables proceeds ultimately from design, is begging the question;[72] nor can that great point be ascertained otherwise than by proving, *a priori*, both that order is, from its nature, inseparably attached to thought; and that it can never of itself, or from original unknown principles, belong to matter.

But further, Demea; this objection which you urge can never be made use of by Cleanthes, without renouncing a defence which he has already made against one of my objections. When I inquired concerning the cause of that supreme reason and intelligence into which he resolves every thing; he told me, that the impossibility of satisfying such inquiries could never be admitted as an objection in any species of philosophy. *We must stop somewhere, says he; nor is it ever within the reach of human capacity to explain ultimate causes, or show the last connections of any objects. It is sufficient, if any steps, so far as we go, are supported by experience and observation.* Now, that vegetation and generation, as well as reason, are experienced to be principles of order in nature, is undeniable. If I rest my system of cosmogony on the former, preferably to the latter, it is at my choice. The matter seems entirely arbitrary. And when Cleanthes asks me what is the cause of my great vegetative or generative faculty, I am equally entitled to ask him the cause of his great reasoning principle. These questions we have agreed to forbear on both sides; and it is chiefly his interest on the present occasion to stick to this agreement. Judging by our limited and imperfect experience, generation has some privileges above reason: for we see every day the latter arise from the former, never the former from the latter.

Compare, I beseech you, the consequences on both sides. The world, say I, resembles an animal; therefore it is an animal, therefore it arose from generation. The steps, I confess, are wide; yet there is some small appearance of analogy in each step. The world, says Cleanthes, resembles a machine; therefore it is a machine, therefore it arose from design. The steps are here equally wide, and the analogy less striking. And if he pretends to carry on my hypothesis a step further,

and to infer design or reason from the great principle of generation, on which I insist; I may, with better authority, use the same freedom to push further his hypothesis, and infer a divine generation or theogony from his principle of reason. I have at least some faint shadow of experience, which is the utmost that can ever be attained in the present subject. Reason, in innumerable instances, is observed to arise from the principle of generation, and never to arise from any other principle.

Hesiod,[73] and all the ancient mythologists, were so struck with this analogy, that they universally explained the origin of nature from an animal birth, and copulation. Plato too, so far as he is intelligible, seems to have adopted some such notion in his *Timæus*.

The Brahmins[74] assert, that the world arose from an infinite spider, who spun this whole complicated mass from his bowels, and annihilates afterwards the whole or any part of it, by absorbing it again, and resolving it into his own essence. Here is a species of cosmogony, which appears to us ridiculous; because a spider is a little contemptible animal, whose operations we are never likely to take for a model of the whole universe. But still here is a new species of analogy, even in our globe. And were there a planet wholly inhabited by spiders (which is very possible), this inference would there appear as natural and irrefragable as that which in our planet ascribes the origin of all things to design and intelligence, as explained by Cleanthes. Why an orderly system may not be spun from the belly as well as from the brain, it will be difficult for him to give a satisfactory reason.

I must confess, Philo, replied Cleanthes, that of all men living, the task which you have undertaken, of raising doubts and objections, suits you best, and seems, in a manner, natural and unavoidable to you. So great is your fertility of invention, that I am not ashamed to acknowledge myself unable, on a sudden, to solve regularly such out-of-the-way difficulties as you incessantly start upon me: though I clearly see, in general, their fallacy and error. And I question not,

---

72 Arguing in a circle; assuming what is at issue in the argument.

73 Hesiod was a Greek poet of the eighth century BCE who wrote a poem called *Theogony*, which seeks to explain natural phenomena in terms of a family of gods.

74 The priestly or intellectual caste in classical Hinduism.

but you are yourself, at present, in the same case, and have not the solution so ready as the objection: while you must be sensible, that common sense and reason are entirely against you; and that such whimsies as you have delivered, may puzzle, but never can convince us.

Part VIII

What you ascribe to the fertility of my invention, replied Philo, is entirely owing to the nature of the subject. In subjects adapted to the narrow compass of human reason, there is commonly but one determination, which carries probability or conviction with it; and to a man of sound judgement, all other suppositions, but that one, appear entirely absurd and chimerical. But in such questions as the present, a hundred contradictory views may preserve a kind of imperfect analogy; and invention has here full scope to exert itself. Without any great effort of thought, I believe that I could, in an instant, propose other systems of cosmogony, which would have some faint appearance of truth, though it is a thousand, a million to one, if either yours or any one of mine be the true system.

For instance, what if I should revive the old Epicurean hypothesis? This is commonly, and I believe justly, esteemed the most absurd system that has yet been proposed; yet I know not whether, with a few alterations, it might not be brought to bear a faint appearance of probability. Instead of supposing matter infinite, as Epicurus did, let us suppose it finite. A finite number of particles is only susceptible of finite transpositions: and it must happen, in an eternal duration, that every possible order or position must be tried an infinite number of times. This world, therefore, with all its events, even the most minute, has before been produced and destroyed, and will again be produced and destroyed, without any bounds and limitations. No one, who has a conception of the powers of infinite, in comparison of finite, will ever scruple this determination.

But this supposes, said Demea, that matter can acquire motion, without any voluntary agent or first mover.

And where is the difficulty, replied Philo, of that supposition? Every event, before experience, is equally difficult and incomprehensible; and every event, after experience, is equally easy and intelligi-ble. Motion, in many instances, from gravity, from elasticity, from electricity, begins in matter, without any known voluntary agent: and to suppose always, in these cases, an unknown voluntary agent, is mere hypothesis; and hypothesis attended with no advantages. The beginning of motion in matter itself is as conceivable *a priori* as its communication from mind and intelligence.

Besides, why may not motion have been propagated by impulse through all eternity, and the same stock of it, or nearly the same, be still upheld in the universe? As much is lost by the composition of motion, as much is gained by its resolution. And whatever the causes are, the fact is certain, that matter is, and always has been, in continual agitation, as far as human experience or tradition reaches. There is not probably, at present, in the whole universe, one particle of matter at absolute rest.

And this very consideration too, continued Philo, which we have stumbled on in the course of the argument, suggests a new hypothesis of cosmogony, that is not absolutely absurd and improbable. Is there a system, an order, an economy of things, by which matter can preserve that perpetual agitation which seems essential to it, and yet maintain a constancy in the forms which it produces? There certainly is such an economy; for this is actually the case with the present world. The continual motion of matter, therefore, in less than infinite transpositions, must produce this economy or order; and by its very nature, that order, when once established, supports itself, for many ages, if not to eternity. But wherever matter is so poised, arranged, and adjusted, as to continue in perpetual motion, and yet preserve a constancy in the forms, its situation must, of necessity, have all the same appearance of art and contrivance which we observe at present. All the parts of each form must have a relation to each other, and to the whole; and the whole itself must have a relation to the other parts of the universe; to the element in which the form subsists; to the materials with which it repairs its waste and decay; and to every other form which is hostile or friendly. A defect in any of these particulars destroys the form; and the matter of which it is composed is again set loose, and is thrown into irregular motions and fermentations, till it unite itself to some other regular form. If no such form be prepared to receive it, and if there be a great quantity of this corrupted matter in the universe, the universe itself is entirely disordered; whether it be the feeble embryo of a world in its first beginnings that is thus destroyed, or the rotten carcass of one languishing in old age and infirmity. In either case, a chaos ensues; till finite, though innumerable revolutions produce at last some forms, whose parts and organs are so adjusted as to support the forms amidst a continued succession of matter.

Suppose (for we shall endeavour to vary the expression), that matter were thrown into any position, by a blind, unguided force; it is evident that this first position must, in all probability, be the most confused and most disorderly imaginable, without any resemblance to those works of human contrivance, which, along with a symmetry of parts, discover an adjustment of means to ends, and a tendency to self-preservation. If the actuating force cease after this operation, matter must remain for ever in disorder, and continue an immense chaos, without any proportion or activity. But suppose that the actuating force, whatever it be, still continues in matter, this first position will immediately give place to a second, which will likewise in all probability be as disorderly as the first, and so on through many successions of changes and revolutions. No particular order or position ever continues a moment unaltered. The original force, still remaining in activity, gives a perpetual restlessness to matter. Every possible situation is produced, and instantly destroyed. If a glimpse or dawn of order appears for a moment, it is instantly hurried away, and confounded, by that never-ceasing force which actuates every part of matter.

Thus the universe goes on for many ages in a continued succession of chaos and disorder. But is it not possible that it may settle at last, so as not to lose its motion and active force (for that we have supposed inherent in it), yet so as to preserve an uniformity of appearance, amidst the continual motion and fluctuation of its parts? This we find to be the case with the universe at present. Every individual is perpetually changing, and every part of every individual; and yet the whole remains, in appearance, the same. May we not hope for such a position, or rather be assured of it, from the eternal revolutions of unguided matter; and

may not this account for all the appearing wisdom and contrivance which is in the universe? Let us contemplate the subject a little, and we shall find, that this adjustment, if attained by matter of a seeming stability in the forms, with a real and perpetual revolution or motion of parts, affords a plausible, if not a true solution of the difficulty.

It is in vain, therefore, to insist upon the uses of the parts in animals or vegetables, and their curious adjustment to each other. I would fain know, how an animal could subsist, unless its parts were so adjusted? Do we not find, that it immediately perishes whenever this adjustment ceases, and that its matter corrupting tries some new form? It happens indeed, that the parts of the world are so well adjusted, that some regular form immediately lays claim to this corrupted matter: and if it were not so, could the world subsist? Must it not dissolve as well as the animal, and pass through new positions and situations, till in great, but finite succession, it falls at last into the present or some such order?

It is well, replied Cleanthes, you told us, that this hypothesis was suggested on a sudden, in the course of the argument. Had you had leisure to examine it, you would soon have perceived the insuperable[75] objections to which it is exposed. No form, you say, can subsist, unless it possess those powers and organs requisite for its subsistence: some new order or economy must be tried, and so on, without intermission; till at last some order, which can support and maintain itself, is fallen upon. But according to this hypothesis, whence arise the many conveniences and advantages which men and all animals possess? Two eyes, two ears, are not absolutely necessary for the subsistence of the species. Human race might have been propagated and preserved, without horses, dogs, cows, sheep, and those innumerable fruits and products which serve to our satisfaction and enjoyment. If no camels had been created for the use of man in the sandy deserts of Africa and Arabia, would the world have been dissolved? If no lodestone[76] had been framed to give that wonderful and useful direction to the needle, would human society and the human

---

75   Impossible to overcome.

76   Magnetite: a naturally magnetic iron oxide.

kind have been immediately extinguished? Though the maxims of nature be in general very frugal, yet instances of this kind are far from being rare; and any one of them is a sufficient proof of design, and of a benevolent design, which gave rise to the order and arrangement of the universe.

At least, you may safely infer, said Philo, that the foregoing hypothesis is so far incomplete and imperfect, which I shall not scruple to allow. But can we ever reasonably expect greater success in any attempts of this nature? Or can we ever hope to erect a system of cosmogony, that will be liable to no exceptions, and will contain no circumstance repugnant to our limited and imperfect experience of the analogy of nature? Your theory itself cannot surely pretend to any such advantage, even though you have run into *anthropomorphism*, the better to preserve a conformity to common experience. Let us once more put it to trial. In all instances which we have ever seen, ideas are copied from real objects, and are ectypal,[77] not archetypal, to express myself in learned terms: You reverse this order, and give thought the precedence. In all instances which we have ever seen, thought has no influence upon matter, except where that matter is so conjoined with it as to have an equal reciprocal influence upon it. No animal can move immediately any thing but the members of its own body; and indeed, the equality of action and reaction seems to be an universal law of nature: But your theory implies a contradiction to this experience. These instances, with many more, which it were easy to collect (particularly the supposition of a mind or system of thought that is eternal, or, in other words, an animal ingenerable and immortal); these instances, I say, may teach all of us sobriety in condemning each other, and let us see, that as no system of this kind ought ever to be received from a slight analogy, so neither ought any to be rejected on account of a small incongruity. For that is an inconvenience from which we can justly pronounce no one to be exempted.

All religious systems, it is confessed, are subject to great and insuperable difficulties. Each disputant triumphs in his turn; while he carries on an offensive war, and exposes the absurdities, barbarities, and pernicious tenets of his antagonist. But all of them, on the whole, prepare a complete triumph for the sceptic; who tells them, that no system ought ever to be embraced with regard to such subjects: for this plain reason, that no absurdity ought ever to be assented to with regard to any subject. A total suspense of judgement is here our only reasonable resource. And if every attack, as is commonly observed, and no defence, among theologians, is successful; how complete must be *his* victory, who remains always, with all mankind, on the offensive, and has himself no fixed station or abiding city, which he is ever, on any occasion, obliged to defend?

Part IX

But if so many difficulties attend the argument *a posteriori*, said Demea, had we not better adhere to that simple and sublime argument *a priori*, which, by offering to us infallible demonstration, cuts off at once all doubt and difficulty? By this argument, too, we may prove the infinity of the divine attributes, which, I am afraid, can never be ascertained with certainty from any other topic. For how can an effect, which either is finite, or, for aught we know, may be so; how can such an effect, I say, prove an infinite cause? The unity too of the divine nature, it is very difficult, if not absolutely impossible, to deduce merely from contemplating the works of nature; nor will the uniformity alone of the plan, even were it allowed, give us any assurance of that attribute. Whereas the argument *a priori*....

You seem to reason, Demea, interposed Cleanthes, as if those advantages and conveniences in the abstract argument were full proofs of its solidity. But it is first proper, in my opinion, to determine what argument of this nature you choose to insist on; and we shall afterwards, from itself, better than from its useful consequences, endeavour to determine what value we ought to put upon it.

The argument, replied Demea, which I would insist on, is the common one.[78] Whatever exists must have

---

77   Of the nature of a copy rather than of a prototype.

78   Hume takes this argument primarily from Samuel Clarke's *A Discourse Concerning the Being and Attributes of God* (1705), which was very influential in its time.

a cause or reason of its existence; it being absolutely impossible for any thing to produce itself, or be the cause of its own existence. In mounting up, therefore, from effects to causes, we must either go on in tracing an infinite succession, without any ultimate cause at all; or must at last have recourse to some ultimate cause, that is *necessarily* existent: now, that the first supposition is absurd, may be thus proved. In the infinite chain or succession of causes and effects, each single effect is determined to exist by the power and efficacy of that cause which immediately preceded; but the whole eternal chain or succession, taken together, is not determined or caused by any thing; and yet it is evident that it requires a cause or reason, as much as any particular object which begins to exist in time. The question is still reasonable, why this particular succession of causes existed from eternity, and not any other succession, or no succession at all. If there be no necessarily existent being, any supposition which can be formed is equally possible; nor is there any more absurdity in nothing's having existed from eternity, than there is in that succession of causes which constitutes the universe. What was it, then, which determined something to exist rather than nothing, and bestowed being on a particular possibility, exclusive of the rest? *External* causes, there are supposed to be none. *Chance* is a word without a meaning. Was it *nothing*? But that can never produce any thing. We must, therefore, have recourse to a necessarily existent Being, who carries the *reason* of his existence in himself, and who cannot be supposed not to exist, without an express contradiction. There is, consequently, such a Being; that is, there is a Deity.

I shall not leave it to Philo, said Cleanthes, though I know that the starting[79] objections is his chief delight, to point out the weakness of this metaphysical reasoning. It seems to me so obviously ill-grounded, and at the same time of so little consequence to the cause of true piety and religion, that I shall myself venture to show the fallacy of it.

I shall begin with observing, that there is an evident absurdity in pretending to demonstrate a matter of fact, or to prove it by any arguments *a priori*. Noth-

ing is demonstrable, unless the contrary implies a contradiction. Nothing, that is distinctly conceivable, implies a contradiction. Whatever we conceive as existent, we can also conceive as non-existent. There is no being, therefore, whose non-existence implies a contradiction. Consequently there is no being, whose existence is demonstrable. I propose this argument as entirely decisive, and am willing to rest the whole controversy upon it.

It is pretended that the Deity is a necessarily existent Being; and this necessity of his existence is attempted to be explained by asserting, that if we knew his whole essence or nature, we should perceive it to be as impossible for him not to exist, as for twice two not to be four. But it is evident that this can never happen, while our faculties remain the same as at present. It will still be possible for us, at any time, to conceive the non-existence of what we formerly conceived to exist; nor can the mind ever lie under a necessity of supposing any object to remain always in being; in the same manner as we lie under a necessity of always conceiving twice two to be four. The words, therefore, *necessary existence*, have no meaning; or, which is the same thing, none that is consistent.

But further, why may not the material universe be the necessarily existent Being, according to this pretended explication of necessity? We dare not affirm that we know all the qualities of matter; and for aught we can determine, it may contain some qualities, which, were they known, would make its non-existence appear as great a contradiction as that twice two is five. I find only one argument employed to prove, that the material world is not the necessarily existent Being: and this argument is derived from the contingency both of the matter and the form of the world. "Any particle of matter," it is said, "may be *conceived* to be annihilated; and any form may be *conceived* to be altered. Such an annihilation or alteration, therefore, is not impossible."[80] But it seems a great partiality not to perceive, that the same argument extends equally to the Deity, so far as we have any conception of him; and that the mind can at least imagine him to be non-existent, or his attributes to be altered. It must be some unknown, inconceivable

---

79   A hunting metaphor: to start game (such as birds) is to startle them out of their hiding place.

80   This paraphrases an argument to be found in Clarke.

qualities, which can make his non-existence appear impossible, or his attributes unalterable: and no reason can be assigned, why these qualities may not belong to matter. As they are altogether unknown and inconceivable, they can never be proved incompatible with it.

Add to this, that in tracing an eternal succession of objects, it seems absurd to inquire for a general cause or first Author. How can any thing, that exists from eternity, have a cause, since that relation implies *a priori*ty in time, and a beginning of existence?

In such a chain, too, or succession of objects, each part is caused by that which preceded it, and causes that which succeeds it. Where then is the difficulty? But the whole, you say, wants[81] a cause. I answer, that the uniting of these parts into a whole, like the uniting of several distinct countries into one kingdom, or several distinct members into one body, is performed merely by an arbitrary act of the mind, and has no influence on the nature of things. Did I show you the particular causes of each individual in a collection of twenty particles of matter, I should think it very unreasonable, should you afterwards ask me, what was the cause of the whole twenty. This is sufficiently explained in explaining the cause of the parts.

Though the reasonings which you have urged, Cleanthes, may well excuse me, said Philo, from starting any further difficulties, yet I cannot forbear insisting still upon another topic. It is observed by arithmeticians, that the products of 9[82] compose always either 9, or some lesser product of 9, if you add together all the characters of which any of the former products is composed. Thus, of 18, 27, 36, which are products of 9, you make 9 by adding 1 to 8, 2 to 7, 3 to 6. Thus, 369 is a product also of 9; and if you add 3, 6, and 9, you make 18, a lesser product of 9. To a superficial observer, so wonderful a regularity may be admired as the effect either of chance or design: but a skilful algebraist immediately concludes it to be the work of necessity, and demonstrates, that it must for ever result from the nature of these numbers. Is it not probable, I ask, that the whole economy of the universe is conducted by a like necessity, though no human algebra can furnish a key which solves the difficulty? And instead of admiring the order of natural beings, may it not happen, that, could we penetrate into the intimate nature of bodies, we should clearly see why it was absolutely impossible they could ever admit of any other disposition? So dangerous is it to introduce this idea of necessity into the present question! And so naturally does it afford an inference directly opposite to the religious hypothesis!

But dropping all these abstractions, continued Philo, and confining ourselves to more familiar topics, I shall venture to add an observation, that the argument *a priori* has seldom been found very convincing, except to people of a metaphysical head, who have accustomed themselves to abstract reasoning, and who, finding from mathematics, that the understanding frequently leads to truth through obscurity, and, contrary to first appearances, have transferred the same habit of thinking to subjects where it ought not to have place. Other people, even of good sense and the best inclined to religion, feel always some deficiency in such arguments, though they are not perhaps able to explain distinctly where it lies; a certain proof that men ever did, and ever will derive their religion from other sources than from this species of reasoning.

Part X

It is my opinion, I own, replied Demea, that each man feels, in a manner, the truth of religion within his own breast, and, from a consciousness of his imbecility and misery, rather than from any reasoning, is led to seek protection from that Being, on whom he and all nature is dependent. So anxious or so tedious are even the best scenes of life, that futurity[83] is still the object of all our hopes and fears. We incessantly look forward, and endeavour, by prayers, adoration, and sacrifice, to appease those unknown powers, whom we find, by experience, so able to afflict and oppress us. Wretched creatures that we are! What resource for us amidst the innumerable ills of life, did not religion suggest some methods of atonement, and appease those terrors with which we are incessantly agitated and tormented?

---

81 Lacks.

82 Numbers generated by multiplying 9 together with some other number: e.g., $9 \times 1 = 9$, $9 \times 2 = 18$, etc.

83 Existence after death.

I am indeed persuaded, said Philo, that the best, and indeed the only method of bringing every one to a due sense of religion, is by just representations of the misery and wickedness of men. And for that purpose a talent of eloquence and strong imagery is more requisite than that of reasoning and argument. For is it necessary to prove what every one feels within himself? It is only necessary to make us feel it, if possible, more intimately and sensibly.

The people, indeed, replied Demea, are sufficiently convinced of this great and melancholy truth. The miseries of life; the unhappiness of man; the general corruptions of our nature; the unsatisfactory enjoyment of pleasures, riches, honours; these phrases have become almost proverbial in all languages. And who can doubt of what all men declare from their own immediate feeling and experience?

In this point, said Philo, the learned are perfectly agreed with the vulgar; and in all letters,[84] *sacred* and *profane*, the topic of human misery has been insisted on with the most pathetic[85] eloquence that sorrow and melancholy could inspire. The poets, who speak from sentiment, without a system, and whose testimony has therefore the more authority, abound in images of this nature. From Homer down to Dr. Young,[86] the whole inspired tribe have ever been sensible, that no other representation of things would suit the feeling and observation of each individual.

As to authorities, replied Demea, you need not seek them. Look round this library of Cleanthes. I shall venture to affirm, that, except authors of particular sciences, such as chemistry or botany, who have no occasion to treat of human life, there is scarce one of those innumerable writers, from whom the sense of human misery has not, in some passage or other, extorted a complaint and confession of it. At least, the chance is entirely on that side; and no one author has ever, so far as I can recollect, been so extravagant as to deny it.

There you must excuse me, said Philo: Leibniz has denied it;[87] and is perhaps the first who ventured upon so bold and paradoxical an opinion; at least, the first who made it essential to his philosophical system.

And by being the first, replied Demea, might he not have been sensible of his error? For is this a subject in which philosophers can propose to make discoveries especially in so late an age? And can any man hope by a simple denial (for the subject scarcely admits of reasoning), to bear down the united testimony of mankind, founded on sense and consciousness?

And why should man, added he, pretend to an exemption from the lot of all other animals? The whole earth, believe me, Philo, is cursed and polluted. A perpetual war is kindled amongst all living creatures. Necessity, hunger, want, stimulate the strong and courageous: fear, anxiety, terror, agitate the weak and infirm. The first entrance into life gives anguish to the new-born infant and to its wretched parent: weakness, impotence, distress, attend each stage of that life: and it is at last finished in agony and horror.

Observe too, says Philo, the curious artifices of nature, in order to embitter the life of every living being. The stronger prey upon the weaker, and keep them in perpetual terror and anxiety. The weaker too, in their turn, often prey upon the stronger, and vex and molest them without relaxation. Consider that innumerable race of insects, which either are bred on the body of each animal, or, flying about, infix their stings in him. These insects have others still less than themselves, which torment them. And thus on each hand, before and behind, above and below, every animal is surrounded with enemies, which incessantly seek his misery and destruction.

Man alone, said Demea, seems to be, in part, an exception to this rule. For by combination in society, he can easily master lions, tigers, and bears, whose greater strength and agility naturally enable them to prey upon him.

On the contrary, it is here chiefly, cried Philo, that the uniform and equal maxims of nature are most apparent. Man, it is true, can, by combination, surmount all his real enemies, and become master of the whole animal creation: but does he not immediately raise up

---

84   Literature.

85   Emotional.

86   Edward Young (1683–1765), the author of *Night Thoughts* (of which Dr. Johnson remarked "The excellence of this work is not exactness but copiousness").

---

87   In *Theodicy*: see the next reading.

to himself imaginary enemies, the dæmons of his fancy, who haunt him with superstitious terrors, and blast every enjoyment of life? His pleasure, as he imagines, becomes, in their eyes, a crime: his food and repose give them umbrage and offence: his very sleep and dreams furnish new materials to anxious fear: and even death, his refuge from every other ill, presents only the dread of endless and innumerable woes. Nor does the wolf molest more the timid flock, than superstition does the anxious breast of wretched mortals.

Besides, consider, Demea: This very society, by which we surmount those wild beasts, our natural enemies; what new enemies does it not raise to us? What woe and misery does it not occasion? Man is the greatest enemy of man. Oppression, injustice, contempt, contumely,[88] violence, sedition, war, calumny,[89] treachery, fraud; by these they mutually torment each other; and they would soon dissolve that society which they had formed, were it not for the dread of still greater ills, which must attend their separation.

But though these external insults, said Demea, from animals, from men, from all the elements, which assault us, form a frightful catalogue of woes, they are nothing in comparison of those which arise within ourselves, from the distempered condition of our mind and body. How many lie under the lingering torment of diseases? Hear the pathetic enumeration of the great poet.

> Intestine stone and ulcer, colic-pangs,
> Dæmoniac frenzy, moping melancholy,
> And moon-struck madness, pining atrophy,
> Marasmus, and wide-wasting pestilence.
> Dire was the tossing, deep the groans: Despair
> Tended the sick, busiest from couch to couch.
> And over them triumphant Death his dart
> Shook: but delay'd to strike, though oft invok'd
> With vows, as their chief good and final hope.[90]

The disorders of the mind, continued Demea, though more secret, are not perhaps less dismal and vexatious. Remorse, shame, anguish, rage, disappointment, anxiety, fear, dejection, despair; who has ever passed through life without cruel inroads from these tormentors? How many have scarcely ever felt any better sensations? Labour and poverty, so abhorred by every one, are the certain lot of the far greater number; and those few privileged persons, who enjoy ease and opulence, never reach contentment or true felicity. All the goods of life united would not make a very happy man; but all the ills united would make a wretch indeed; and any one of them almost (and who can be free from every one?) nay often the absence of one good (and who can possess all?) is sufficient to render life ineligible.[91]

Were a stranger to drop on a sudden into this world, I would show him, as a specimen of its ills, a hospital full of diseases, a prison crowded with malefactors and debtors, a field of battle strewed with carcasses, a fleet foundering in the ocean, a nation languishing under tyranny, famine, or pestilence. To turn the gay[92] side of life to him, and give him a notion of its pleasures; whither should I conduct him? To a ball, to an opera, to court? He might justly think, that I was only showing him a diversity of distress and sorrow.

There is no evading such striking instances, said Philo, but by apologies, which still further aggravate the charge. Why have all men, I ask, in all ages, complained incessantly of the miseries of life? ... They have no just reason, says one: these complaints proceed only from their discontented, repining, anxious disposition.... And can there possibly, I reply, be a more certain foundation of misery, than such a wretched temper?

But if they were really as unhappy as they pretend, says my antagonist, why do they remain in life? ... "Not satisfied with life, afraid of death."[93] This is the secret chain, say I, that holds us. We are terrified, not bribed to the continuance of our existence.

It is only a false delicacy, he may insist, which a few refined spirits indulge, and which has spread these complaints among the whole race of mankind.... And what is this delicacy, I ask, which you blame? Is it

---

88 Disgrace or insult.

89 Slander.

90 Milton, from *Paradise Lost*.

91 Unworthy of being chosen, undesirable.

92 Happy and carefree.

93 This and the following are probably references to Lucretius' Epicureanism, which includes arguments against fearing death.

any thing but a greater sensibility to all the pleasures and pains of life? And if the man of a delicate, refined temper, by being so much more alive than the rest of the world, is only so much more unhappy, what judgement must we form in general of human life?

Let men remain at rest, says our adversary, and they will be easy. They are willing artificers of their own misery.... No! reply I: an anxious languor[94] follows their repose; disappointment, vexation, trouble, their activity and ambition.

I can observe something like what you mention in some others, replied Cleanthes: but I confess I feel little or nothing of it in myself, and hope that it is not so common as you represent it.

If you feel not human misery yourself, cried Demea, I congratulate you on so happy a singularity. Others, seemingly the most prosperous, have not been ashamed to vent their complaints in the most melancholy strains. Let us attend to the great, the fortunate emperor, Charles V,[95] when, tired with human grandeur, he resigned all his extensive dominions into the hands of his son. In the last harangue which he made on that memorable occasion, he publicly avowed, *that the greatest prosperities which he had ever enjoyed, had been mixed with so many adversities, that he might truly say he had never enjoyed any satisfaction or contentment.* But did the retired life, in which he sought for shelter, afford him any greater happiness? If we may credit his son's account, his repentance commenced the very day of his resignation.

Cicero's fortune, from small beginnings, rose to the greatest lustre and renown; yet what pathetic complaints of the ills of life do his familiar letters, as well as philosophical discourses, contain? And suitably to his own experience, he introduces Cato,[96] the great, the fortunate Cato, protesting in his old age, that had he a new life in his offer, he would reject the present.

Ask yourself, ask any of your acquaintance, whether they would live over again the last ten or twenty years of their life. No! But the next twenty, they say, will be better:

And from the dregs of life, hope to receive
What the first sprightly running could not give.[97]
Thus at last they find (such is the greatness of human misery, it reconciles even contradictions), that they complain at once of the shortness of life, and of its vanity and sorrow.

And is it possible, Cleanthes, said Philo, that after all these reflections, and infinitely more, which might be suggested, you can still persevere in your anthropomorphism, and assert the moral attributes of the Deity, his justice, benevolence, mercy, and rectitude, to be of the same nature with these virtues in human creatures? His power we allow is infinite: whatever he wills is executed: but neither man nor any other animal is happy: therefore he does not will their happiness. His wisdom is infinite: He is never mistaken in choosing the means to any end: but the course of nature tends not to human or animal felicity:[98] therefore it is not established for that purpose. Through the whole compass of human knowledge, there are no inferences more certain and infallible than these. In what respect, then, do his benevolence and mercy resemble the benevolence and mercy of men?

Epicurus's old questions are yet unanswered. Is he willing to prevent evil, but not able? Then is he impotent. Is he able, but not willing? Then is he malevolent. Is he both able and willing? Whence then is evil?

You ascribe, Cleanthes (and I believe justly), a purpose and intention to nature. But what, I beseech you, is the object of that curious artifice and machinery, which she has displayed in all animals? The preservation alone of individuals, and propagation of the species. It seems enough for her purpose, if such a rank[99] be barely upheld in the universe, without any care or concern for the happiness of the members that compose it. No resource for this purpose: no machinery, in order merely to give pleasure or ease: no fund of pure joy and contentment: no indulgence, without some want or necessity accompanying it. At least, the few phenomena of this nature are overbalanced by opposite phenomena of still greater importance.

---

94   Faintness, laziness, fatigue.

95   King of Spain and Holy Roman Emperor (1519–1556).

96   A Roman statesman (234–149 BCE), known for his rigorous social and moral reforming.

97   From a play called *Aureng-zebe*, by the English dramatist and poet John Dryden (1631–1700).

98   Happiness.

99   Class, group.

Our sense of music, harmony, and indeed beauty of all kinds, gives satisfaction, without being absolutely necessary to the preservation and propagation of the species. But what racking pains, on the other hand, arise from gouts, gravels,[100] megrims,[101] toothaches, rheumatisms, where the injury to the animal machinery is either small or incurable? Mirth, laughter, play, frolic, seem gratuitous satisfactions, which have no further tendency: spleen,[102] melancholy, discontent, superstition, are pains of the same nature. How then does the divine benevolence display itself, in the sense of you anthropomorphites? None but we mystics, as you were pleased to call us, can account for this strange mixture of phenomena, by deriving it from attributes, infinitely perfect, but incomprehensible.

And have you at last, said Cleanthes smiling, betrayed your intentions, Philo? Your long agreement with Demea did indeed a little surprise me; but I find you were all the while erecting a concealed battery against me. And I must confess, that you have now fallen upon a subject worthy of your noble spirit of opposition and controversy. If you can make out the present point, and prove mankind to be unhappy or corrupted, there is an end at once of all religion. For to what purpose establish the natural attributes of the Deity, while the moral are still doubtful and uncertain?[103]

You take umbrage very easily, replied Demea, at opinions the most innocent, and the most generally received, even amongst the religious and devout themselves: and nothing can be more surprising than to find a topic like this, concerning the wickedness and misery of man, charged with no less than atheism and profaneness. Have not all pious divines and preachers, who have indulged their rhetoric on so fertile a subject; have they not easily, I say, given a solution of any difficulties which may attend it? This world is but a point in comparison of the universe; this life but a moment in comparison of eternity. The present evil

phenomena, therefore, are rectified in other regions, and in some future period of existence. And the eyes of men, being then opened to larger views of things, see the whole connection of general laws; and trace with adoration, the benevolence and rectitude of the Deity, through all the mazes and intricacies of his providence.[104]

No! Replied Cleanthes, No! These arbitrary suppositions can never be admitted, contrary to matter of fact, visible and uncontroverted. Whence can any cause be known but from its known effects? Whence can any hypothesis be proved but from the apparent phenomena? To establish one hypothesis upon another, is building entirely in the air; and the utmost we ever attain, by these conjectures and fictions, is to ascertain the bare possibility of our opinion; but never can we, upon such terms, establish its reality.

The only method of supporting divine benevolence, and it is what I willingly embrace, is to deny absolutely the misery and wickedness of man. Your representations are exaggerated; your melancholy views mostly fictitious; your inferences contrary to fact and experience. Health is more common than sickness; pleasure than pain; happiness than misery. And for one vexation which we meet with, we attain, upon computation, a hundred enjoyments.

Admitting your position, replied Philo, which yet is extremely doubtful, you must at the same time allow, that if pain be less frequent than pleasure, it is infinitely more violent and durable. One hour of it is often able to outweigh a day, a week, a month of our common insipid enjoyments; and how many days, weeks, and months, are passed by several in the most acute torments? Pleasure, scarcely in one instance, is ever able to reach ecstasy and rapture; and in no one instance can it continue for any time at its highest pitch and altitude. The spirits evaporate, the nerves relax, the fabric is disordered, and the enjoyment quickly degenerates into fatigue and uneasiness. But pain often, good God, how often! rises to torture and agony; and the longer it continues, it becomes still more genuine agony and torture. Patience is exhausted, courage languishes, melancholy seizes us,

---

100 Painful aggregations of crystals in the urinary tract, e.g., kidney stones.

101 Migraines.

102 Ill-temper.

103 Why worry about God's being the cause of the universe, or intelligent, or omnipotent, while leaving it uncertain whether God is morally good?

104 Providence is God's loving intervention in, and direction of, the world.

and nothing terminates our misery but the removal of its cause, or another event,[105] which is the sole cure of all evil, but which, from our natural folly, we regard with still greater horror and consternation.

But not to insist upon these topics, continued Philo, though most obvious, certain, and important; I must use the freedom to admonish you, Cleanthes, that you have put the controversy upon a most dangerous issue, and are unawares introducing a total scepticism into the most essential articles of natural and revealed theology. What! no method of fixing a just foundation for religion, unless we allow the happiness of human life, and maintain a continued existence even in this world, with all our present pains, infirmities, vexations, and follies, to be eligible and desirable! But this is contrary to every one's feeling and experience: it is contrary to an authority so established as nothing can subvert. No decisive proofs can ever be produced against this authority; nor is it possible for you to compute, estimate, and compare, all the pains and all the pleasures in the lives of all men and of all animals: and thus, by your resting the whole system of religion on a point, which, from its very nature, must for ever be uncertain, you tacitly confess, that that system is equally uncertain.

But allowing you what never will be believed, at least what you never possibly can prove, that animal, or at least human happiness, in this life, exceeds its misery, you have yet done nothing: for this is not, by any means, what we expect from infinite power, infinite wisdom, and infinite goodness. Why is there any misery at all in the world? Not by chance surely. From some cause then. Is it from the intention of the Deity? But he is perfectly benevolent. Is it contrary to his intention? But he is almighty. Nothing can shake the solidity of this reasoning, so short, so clear, so decisive; except we assert, that these subjects exceed all human capacity, and that our common measures of truth and falsehood are not applicable to them; a topic which I have all along insisted on, but which you have, from the beginning, rejected with scorn and indignation.

But I will be contented to retire still from this entrenchment, for I deny that you can ever force me in

it. I will allow, that pain or misery in man is compatible with infinite power and goodness in the Deity, even in your sense of these attributes: what are you advanced by all these concessions? A mere possible compatibility is not sufficient. You must prove these pure, unmixed, and uncontrollable attributes from the present mixed and confused phenomena, and from these alone. A hopeful undertaking! Were the phenomena ever so pure and unmixed, yet being finite, they would be insufficient for that purpose. How much more, where they are also so jarring and discordant!

Here, Cleanthes, I find myself at ease in my argument. Here I triumph. Formerly, when we argued concerning the natural attributes of intelligence and design, I needed all my sceptical and metaphysical subtlety to elude your grasp. In many views of the universe, and of its parts, particularly the latter, the beauty and fitness of final causes strike us with such irresistible force, that all objections appear (what I believe they really are) mere cavils and sophisms; nor can we then imagine how it was ever possible for us to repose any weight on them. But there is no view of human life, or of the condition of mankind, from which, without the greatest violence, we can infer the moral attributes, or learn that infinite benevolence, conjoined with infinite power and infinite wisdom, which we must discover by the eyes of faith alone. It is your turn now to tug the labouring oar, and to support your philosophical subtleties against the dictates of plain reason and experience.

Part XI

I scruple not to allow, said Cleanthes, that I have been apt to suspect the frequent repetition of the word *infinite*, which we meet with in all theological writers, to savour more of panegyric[106] than of philosophy; and that any purposes of reasoning, and even of religion, would be better served, were we to rest contented with more accurate and more moderate expressions. The terms, *admirable, excellent, superlatively great, wise*, and *holy*; these sufficiently fill the imaginations of men; and any thing beyond, besides that it leads into absurdities, has no influence on the affections or sentiments. Thus, in the present subject, if we abandon

---

105 Such as death.

106 A formal or elaborate speech of praise.

all human analogy, as seems your intention, Demea, I am afraid we abandon all religion, and retain no conception of the great object of our adoration. If we preserve human analogy, we must for ever find it impossible to reconcile any mixture of evil in the universe with infinite attributes; much less can we ever prove the latter from the former. But supposing the Author of nature to be finitely perfect, though far exceeding mankind, a satisfactory account may then be given of natural and moral evil,[107] and every untoward phenomenon be explained and adjusted. A less evil may then be chosen, in order to avoid a greater; inconveniences be submitted to, in order to reach a desirable end; and in a word, benevolence, regulated by wisdom, and limited by necessity, may produce just such a world as the present. You, Philo, who are so prompt at starting views, and reflections, and analogies, I would gladly hear, at length, without interruption, your opinion of this new theory; and if it deserve our attention, we may afterwards, at more leisure, reduce it into form.

My sentiments, replied Philo, are not worth being made a mystery of; and therefore, without any ceremony, I shall deliver what occurs to me with regard to the present subject. It must, I think, be allowed, that if a very limited intelligence, whom we shall suppose utterly unacquainted with the universe, were assured, that it were the production of a very good, wise, and powerful Being, however finite, he would, from his conjectures, form *beforehand* a different notion of it from what we find it to be by experience; nor would he ever imagine, merely from these attributes of the cause, of which he is informed, that the effect could be so full of vice and misery and disorder, as it appears in this life. Supposing now, that this person were brought into the world, still assured that it was the workmanship of such a sublime and benevolent Being; he might, perhaps, be surprised at the disappointment; but would never retract his former belief, if founded on any very solid argument; since such a limited intelligence must be sensible of his own blindness and ignorance, and must allow, that there may be

many solutions of those phenomena, which will for ever escape his comprehension. But supposing, which is the real case with regard to man, that this creature is not antecedently convinced of a supreme intelligence, benevolent, and powerful, but is left to gather such a belief from the appearances of things; this entirely alters the case, nor will he ever find any reason for such a conclusion. He may be fully convinced of the narrow limits of his understanding; but this will not help him in forming an inference concerning the goodness of superior powers, since he must form that inference from what he knows, not from what he is ignorant of. The more you exaggerate his weakness and ignorance, the more diffident you render him, and give him the greater suspicion that such subjects are beyond the reach of his faculties. You are obliged, therefore, to reason with him merely from the known phenomena, and to drop every arbitrary supposition or conjecture.

Did I show you a house or palace, where there was not one apartment convenient or agreeable; where the windows, doors, fires, passages, stairs, and the whole economy of the building, were the source of noise, confusion, fatigue, darkness, and the extremes of heat and cold; you would certainly blame the contrivance, without any further examination. The architect would in vain display his subtlety, and prove to you, that if this door or that window were altered, greater ills would ensue. What he says may be strictly true: the alteration of one particular, while the other parts of the building remain, may only augment the inconveniences. But still you would assert in general, that, if the architect had had skill and good intentions, he might have formed such a plan of the whole, and might have adjusted the parts in such a manner, as would have remedied all or most of these inconveniences. His ignorance, or even your own ignorance of such a plan, will never convince you of the impossibility of it. If you find any inconveniences and deformities in the building, you will always, without entering into any detail, condemn the architect.

In short, I repeat the question: Is the world, considered in general, and as it appears to us in this life, different from what a man, or such a limited being, would, *beforehand*, expect from a very powerful, wise, and benevolent Deity? It must be strange

---

107 Natural evil is badness in nature (e.g., mosquitoes, volcanoes) while moral evil is badness caused by the free actions of human beings (e.g., traffic jams, rape).

prejudice to assert the contrary. And from thence I conclude, that however consistent the world may be, allowing certain suppositions and conjectures, with the idea of such a Deity, it can never afford us an inference concerning his existence. The consistence is not absolutely denied, only the inference. Conjectures, especially where infinity is excluded from the Divine attributes, may perhaps be sufficient to prove a consistence, but can never be foundations for any inference.

There seem to be *four* circumstances, on which depend all, or the greatest part of the ills, that molest sensible creatures; and it is not impossible but all these circumstances may be necessary and unavoidable. We know so little beyond common life, or even of common life, that, with regard to the economy of a universe, there is no conjecture, however wild, which may not be just; nor any one, however plausible, which may not be erroneous. All that belongs to human understanding, in this deep ignorance and obscurity, is to be sceptical, or at least cautious, and not to admit of any hypothesis whatever, much less of any which is supported by no appearance of probability. Now, this I assert to be the case with regard to all the causes of evil, and the circumstances on which it depends. None of them appear to human reason in the least degree necessary or unavoidable; nor can we suppose them such, without the utmost license of imagination.

The *first* circumstance which introduces evil, is that contrivance or economy of the animal creation, by which pains, as well as pleasures, are employed to excite all creatures to action, and make them vigilant in the great work of self-preservation. Now pleasure alone, in its various degrees, seems to human understanding sufficient for this purpose. All animals might be constantly in a state of enjoyment: but when urged by any of the necessities of nature, such as thirst, hunger, weariness; instead of pain, they might feel a diminution of pleasure, by which they might be prompted to seek that object which is necessary to their subsistence. Men pursue pleasure as eagerly as they avoid pain; at least they might have been so constituted. It seems, therefore, plainly possible to carry on the business of life without any pain. Why then is any animal ever rendered susceptible of such a sensation? If animals can be free from it an hour,

they might enjoy a perpetual exemption from it; and it required as particular a contrivance of their organs to produce that feeling, as to endow them with sight, hearing, or any of the senses. Shall we conjecture, that such a contrivance was necessary, without any appearance of reason? And shall we build on that conjecture as on the most certain truth?

But a capacity of pain would not alone produce pain, were it not for the *second* circumstance, viz. the conducting of the world by general laws; and this seems nowise necessary to a very perfect Being. It is true, if everything were conducted by particular volitions,[108] the course of nature would be perpetually broken, and no man could employ his reason in the conduct of life. But might not other particular volitions remedy this inconvenience? In short, might not the Deity exterminate all ill, wherever it were to be found; and produce all good, without any preparation, or long progress of causes and effects?

Besides, we must consider, that, according to the present economy of the world, the course of nature, though supposed exactly regular, yet to us appears not so, and many events are uncertain, and many disappoint our expectations. Health and sickness, calm and tempest, with an infinite number of other accidents,[109] whose causes are unknown and variable, have a great influence both on the fortunes of particular persons and on the prosperity of public societies; and indeed all human life, in a manner, depends on such accidents. A being, therefore, who knows the secret springs of the universe, might easily, by particular volitions, turn all these accidents to the good of mankind, and render the whole world happy, without discovering himself in any operation. A fleet, whose purposes were salutary to society, might always meet with a fair wind. Good princes enjoy sound health and long life. Persons born to power and authority, be framed with good tempers and virtuous dispositions. A few such events as these, regularly and wisely conducted, would change the face of the world; and yet would no more seem to disturb the course of nature, or confound human conduct, than the present economy of

108 By a sequence of individual decisions (by God) for each particular case.

109 (Seemingly) random occurrences.

things, where the causes are secret, and variable, and compounded. Some small touches given to Caligula's brain in his infancy, might have converted him into a Trajan.[110] One wave, a little higher than the rest, by burying Cæsar[111] and his fortune in the bottom of the ocean, might have restored liberty to a considerable part of mankind. There may, for aught we know, be good reasons why providence interposes not in this manner; but they are unknown to us; and though the mere supposition, that such reasons exist, may be sufficient to save the conclusion concerning the Divine attributes, yet surely it can never be sufficient to *establish* that conclusion.

If every thing in the universe be conducted by general laws, and if animals be rendered susceptible of pain, it scarcely seems possible but some ill must arise in the various shocks of matter, and the various concurrence and opposition of general laws; but this ill would be very rare, were it not for the *third* circumstance, which I proposed to mention, viz. the great frugality with which all powers and faculties are distributed to every particular being. So well adjusted are the organs and capacities of all animals, and so well fitted to their preservation, that, as far as history or tradition reaches, there appears not to be any single species which has yet been extinguished in the universe. Every animal has the requisite endowments; but these endowments are bestowed with so scrupulous an economy, that any considerable diminution must entirely destroy the creature. Wherever one power is increased, there is a proportional abatement in the others. Animals which excel in swiftness are commonly defective in force. Those which possess both are either imperfect in some of their senses, or are oppressed with the most craving wants. The human species, whose chief excellency is reason and sagacity, is of all others the most necessitous, and the

most deficient in bodily advantages; without clothes, without arms, without food, without lodging, without any convenience of life, except what they owe to their own skill and industry. In short, nature seems to have formed an exact calculation of the necessities of her creatures; and, like a *rigid master*, has afforded them little more powers or endowments than what are strictly sufficient to supply those necessities. An *indulgent parent* would have bestowed a large stock, in order to guard against accidents, and secure the happiness and welfare of the creature in the most unfortunate concurrence of circumstances. Every course of life would not have been so surrounded with precipices, that the least departure from the true path, by mistake or necessity, must involve us in misery and ruin. Some reserve, some fund, would have been provided to ensure happiness; nor would the powers and the necessities have been adjusted with so rigid an economy. The Author of nature is inconceivably powerful: his force is supposed great, if not altogether inexhaustible: nor is there any reason, as far as we can judge, to make him observe this strict frugality in his dealings with his creatures. It would have been better, were his power extremely limited, to have created fewer animals, and to have endowed these with more faculties for their happiness and preservation. A builder is never esteemed prudent, who undertakes a plan beyond what his stock will enable him to finish.

In order to cure most of the ills of human life, I require not that man should have the wings of the eagle, the swiftness of the stag, the force of the ox, the arms of the lion, the scales of the crocodile or rhinoceros; much less do I demand the sagacity of an angel or cherubim. I am contented to take an increase in one single power or faculty of his soul. Let him be endowed with a greater propensity to industry and labour; a more vigorous spring and activity of mind; a more constant bent to business and application. Let the whole species possess naturally an equal diligence with that which many individuals are able to attain by habit and reflection; and the most beneficial consequences, without any allay of ill, is the immediate and necessary result of this endowment. Almost all the moral, as well as natural evils of human life, arise from idleness; and were our species, by the original constitution of their frame, exempt from this vice or

---

110 Caligula was a Roman emperor (37–41 CE), noted for his tyrannical excesses, and assassinated at the age of 29. Trajan's reign as emperor (98–117 CE) was known for its many public works.

111 Julius Cæsar (100–44 BCE), the Roman general who conquered Gaul (France) and the southern part of Britain, made himself dictator of the Roman empire in 46 BCE.

infirmity, the perfect cultivation of land, the improvement of arts and manufactures, the exact execution of every office and duty, immediately follow; and men at once may fully reach that state of society, which is so imperfectly attained by the best regulated government. But as industry is a power, and the most valuable of any, nature seems determined, suitably to her usual maxims, to bestow it on men with a very sparing hand; and rather to punish him severely for his deficiency in it, than to reward him for his attainments. She has so contrived his frame, that nothing but the most violent necessity can oblige him to labour; and she employs all his other wants to overcome, at least in part, the want of diligence, and to endow him with some share of a faculty of which she has thought fit naturally to bereave him. Here our demands may be allowed very humble, and therefore the more reasonable. If we required the endowments of superior penetration and judgement, of a more delicate taste of beauty, of a nicer sensibility to benevolence and friendship; we might be told, that we impiously pretend to break the order of nature; that we want to exalt ourselves into a higher rank of being; that the presents which we require, not being suitable to our state and condition, would only be pernicious to us. But it is hard; I dare to repeat it, it is hard, that being placed in a world so full of wants and necessities, where almost every being and element is either our foe or refuses its assistance … we should also have our own temper to struggle with, and should be deprived of that faculty which can alone fence against these multiplied evils.

The *fourth* circumstance, whence arises the misery and ill of the universe, is the inaccurate workmanship of all the springs and principles of the great machine of nature. It must be acknowledged, that there are few parts of the universe, which seem not to serve some purpose, and whose removal would not produce a visible defect and disorder in the whole. The parts hang all together; nor can one be touched without affecting the rest, in a greater or less degree. But at the same time, it must be observed, that none of these parts or principles, however useful, are so accurately adjusted, as to keep precisely within those bounds in which their utility consists; but they are, all of them, apt, on every occasion, to run into the one extreme or the other. One would imagine, that this grand production had not received the last hand of the maker; so little finished is every part, and so coarse are the strokes with which it is executed. Thus, the winds are requisite to convey the vapours along the surface of the globe, and to assist men in navigation: but how oft, rising up to tempests and hurricanes, do they become pernicious? Rains are necessary to nourish all the plants and animals of the earth: but how often are they defective? How often excessive? Heat is requisite to all life and vegetation; but is not always found in the due proportion. On the mixture and secretion of the humours and juices of the body depend the health and prosperity of the animal: but the parts perform not regularly their proper function. What more useful than all the passions of the mind, ambition, vanity, love, anger? But how oft do they break their bounds, and cause the greatest convulsions in society? There is nothing so advantageous in the universe, but what frequently becomes pernicious, by its excess or defect; nor has nature guarded, with the requisite accuracy, against all disorder or confusion. The irregularity is never perhaps so great as to destroy any species; but is often sufficient to involve the individuals in ruin and misery.

On the concurrence, then, of these *four* circumstances, does all or the greatest part of natural evil depend. Were all living creatures incapable of pain, or were the world administered by particular volitions, evil never could have found access into the universe: and were animals endowed with a large stock of powers and faculties, beyond what strict necessity requires; or were the several springs and principles of the universe so accurately framed as to preserve always the just temperament and medium; there must have been very little ill in comparison of what we feel at present. What then shall we pronounce on this occasion? Shall we say that these circumstances are not necessary, and that they might easily have been altered in the contrivance of the universe? This decision seems too presumptuous for creatures so blind and ignorant. Let us be more modest in our conclusions. Let us allow, that, if the goodness of the Deity (I mean a goodness like the human) could be established on any tolerable reasons *a priori*, these phenomena, however untoward, would not be sufficient to subvert that principle; but might easily, in some unknown manner, be reconcilable to it. But let us still assert, that as this goodness is not antecedently established, but must be inferred from the phenomena, there can be no grounds for such an inference, while there are so many ills in the universe, and while these ills might so easily have been remedied, as far as human understanding can be allowed to judge on such a subject. I am sceptic enough to allow, that the bad appearances, notwithstanding all my reasonings, may be compatible with such attributes as you suppose; but surely they can never prove these attributes. Such a conclusion cannot result from scepticism, but must arise from the phenomena, and from our confidence in the reasonings which we deduce from these phenomena.

Look round this universe. What an immense profusion of beings, animated and organised, sensible and active! You admire this prodigious variety and fecundity. But inspect a little more narrowly these living existences, the only beings worth regarding. How hostile and destructive to each other! How insufficient all of them for their own happiness! How contemptible or odious to the spectator! The whole presents nothing but the idea of a blind nature, impregnated by a great vivifying principle, and pouring forth from her lap, without discernment or parental care, her maimed and abortive children!

Here the Manichæan system[112] occurs as a proper hypothesis to solve the difficulty: and no doubt, in some respects, it is very specious,[113] and has more probability than the common hypothesis, by giving a plausible account of the strange mixture of good and ill which appears in life. But if we consider, on the other hand, the perfect uniformity and agreement of the parts of the universe, we shall not discover in it any marks of the combat of a malevolent with a benevolent Being. There is indeed an opposition of pains and pleasures in the feelings of sensible creatures: but are not all the operations of nature carried on by an opposition of principles, of hot and cold, moist and dry, light and heavy? The true conclusion is, that the original source of all things is entirely indifferent to all these principles; and has no more regard to good above ill, than to heat above cold, or to drought above moisture, or to light above heavy.

There may *four* hypotheses be framed concerning the first causes of the universe: *that* they are endowed with perfect goodness; *that* they have perfect malice; *that* they are opposite, and have both goodness and malice; *that* they have neither goodness nor malice. Mixed phenomena can never prove the two former unmixed principles; and the uniformity and steadiness of general laws seem to oppose the third. The fourth, therefore, seems by far the most probable.

What I have said concerning natural evil will apply to moral, with little or no variation; and we have no more reason to infer, that the rectitude of the supreme Being resembles human rectitude, than that his benevolence resembles the human. Nay, it will be thought, that we have still greater cause to exclude from him moral sentiments, such as we feel them; since moral evil, in the opinion of many, is much more predominant above moral good than natural evil above natural good.

But even though this should not be allowed, and though the virtue which is in mankind should be acknowledged much superior to the vice, yet so long as there is any vice at all in the universe, it will very much puzzle you anthropomorphites, how to account for it. You must assign a cause for it, without having recourse to the first cause. But as every effect must have a cause, and that cause another, you must either carry on the progression *in infinitum*, or rest on that original principle, who is the ultimate cause of all things....

Hold! Hold! cried Demea: Whither does your imagination hurry you? I joined in alliance with you, in order to prove the incomprehensible nature of the divine Being, and refute the principles of Cleanthes, who would measure every thing by human rule and standard. But I now find you running into all the topics of the greatest libertines and infidels, and betraying that holy cause which you seemingly espoused. Are you secretly, then, a more dangerous enemy than Cleanthes himself?

And are you so late in perceiving it? replied Cleanthes. Believe me, Demea, your friend Philo, from the beginning, has been amusing himself at both our expense; and it must be confessed, that the injudicious

---

112 An adaptation, by the Parthian prophet Mani (216–277 CE), who lived in what is now Iran, of the Zoroastrian belief that opposing good and evil deities (God and Satan) rule the world.

113 Having the ring of truth (but actually false).

reasoning of our vulgar theology has given him but too just a handle of ridicule. The total infirmity of human reason, the absolute incomprehensibility of the divine nature, the great and universal misery, and still greater wickedness of men; these are strange topics, surely, to be so fondly cherished by orthodox divines and doctors. In ages of stupidity and ignorance, indeed, these principles may safely be espoused; and perhaps no views of things are more proper to promote superstition, than such as encourage the blind amazement, the diffidence, and melancholy of mankind. But at present....

Blame not so much, interposed Philo, the ignorance of these reverend gentlemen. They know how to change their style with the times. Formerly it was a most popular theological topic to maintain, that human life was vanity and misery, and to exaggerate all the ills and pains which are incident to men. But of late years, divines, we find, begin to retract this position; and maintain, though still with some hesitation, that there are more goods than evils, more pleasures than pains, even in this life. When religion stood entirely upon temper and education, it was thought proper to encourage melancholy; as indeed mankind never have recourse to superior powers so readily as in that disposition. But as men have now learned to form principles, and to draw consequences, it is necessary to change the batteries,[114] and to make use of such arguments as will endure at least some scrutiny and examination. This variation is the same (and from the same causes) with that which I formerly remarked with regard to scepticism.

Thus Philo continued to the last his spirit of opposition, and his censure of established opinions. But I could observe that Demea did not at all relish the latter part of the discourse; and he took occasion soon after, on some pretence or other, to leave the company.

---

114   A military metaphor: to adjust one's fortifications or one's armaments.

GOTTFRIED LEIBNIZ
Theodicy

Who Was Gottfried Leibniz?

Gottfried Wilhelm Leibniz was born in 1646 in Leipzig (a major city in Saxony, the east-central region of what is now Germany). His father Friedrich, a professor of moral philosophy at the University of Leipzig, died when he was six, but the young Gottfried had already been infected with a love of learning. He taught himself Latin at the age of seven or eight, and he read widely in his late father's large library. He went to the University of Leipzig at the age of 14, and then at 20 moved on to the University of Altdorf near Nuremberg, graduating with degrees in law and philosophy. However, he had no intention of pursuing an academic career, and after turning down a position as professor of law at the University of Altdorf, he got employment with the Elector of Mainz[1] in 1667 as part of a project to recodify and systematize the laws of Germany.

In 1672 Leibniz was sent to Paris, the leader of a devious political embassy trying to persuade the French king Louis XIV to invade Egypt and expel the Turks (and thus weaken the French economy and turn their attention away from Germany). Leibniz never got to present this idea to the French court, but he spent four years in Paris—at that time the intellectual capital of Europe—studying mathematics and phi-

---

1   The political leader and archbishop of the region of Mainz, in Germany. Some German rulers were called "Electors" as they had the right to elect their overall ruler, the Holy Roman Emperor.

losophy and encountering, for more or less the first time, the "mechanical philosophy" of Galileo, Bacon, Descartes, Gassendi, Hobbes, and others (see the Descartes reading in Chapter 2 for more details). Intoxicated with the philosophical excitement of the time, Leibniz plunged into the new philosophy and began the development of his own philosophical and scientific system. His early work was relatively amateurish, and he was very disappointed to be refused a research position with the Paris Academy of Sciences. However, it was during this period that Leibniz independently discovered the differential calculus (the mathematics of the variation of a function with respect to changes in independent variables, a tool crucial to the development of the new Newtonian science because it allowed the formal representation of rates of change); he was later to feud bitterly and publicly with Isaac Newton over who was the first to invent it.

Leibniz returned to Germany in 1676 and became Court Councillor and Librarian to the Duke of Brunswick in Hanover, where he lived until his death in 1714. During this period he took on a wide variety of jobs—including geologist, mining engineer (unsuccessfully supervising the draining of the silver mines in the Harz mountains), diplomat, linguist, and historian—but all the while continued with his philosophical work in a series of letters, essays, and two books. He never married (though at age 50 he made a marriage proposal that he quickly thought better of). He spent months at a time without leaving his study, eating at irregular hours, falling asleep over a book at one or two in the morning and waking at seven or eight to continue his reading. He was quick to anger and resented criticism, but he was also swift to regain his good humor. In his old age he was, unfortunately, a figure of ridicule at the Court of Hanover, an irascible old fossil in a huge black wig, wearing old-fashioned, overly ornate clothes (he was also, ironically, disliked by the townspeople because it was rumored he was an atheist). When he died only one mourner attended his funeral, even though by then he was widely recognized in Europe as an important scholar and original thinker.

Leibniz was a man who sought synthesis and reconciliation between opposing points of view wherever possible. He believed, as he put it in the last year of his life, that "the majority of the philosophical sects are right in the greater part of what they affirm, but not so much in what they deny." Perhaps because his childhood years were a time of great unrest in Europe—the aftermath of the Thirty Years War between the Holy Roman Empire, France, Sweden, and Spain (1618–1648)—Leibniz was, throughout his life, interested in political and religious reconciliation; for example, he had an ambitious scheme to reunite the Catholic and Protestant churches in Germany. Part of his plan to promote peace was a project to develop an ideal, universal language, which would promote communication and understanding between divided peoples. In his physics and philosophy he generally aimed to bring together the old Aristotelian-Scholastic tradition, which he learned as a student, with the new mechanical philosophy he encountered in France.

What Was Leibniz's Overall Philosophical Project?

Leibniz the philosopher was, first and foremost, a metaphysician. Metaphysics, in this sense, can be thought of as the study of 'ultimate reality'—that is, of the essential nature of the fundamental substances that make up the world (such as, perhaps, matter and spirit). Leibniz placed a particular weight on this understanding of substance as "the key to philosophy":

he believed that his own theory of substance was "so rich, that there follow from it most of the most important truths about God, the soul, and the nature of body, which are generally either unknown or unproved."

A good way to begin to understand his account of substance is to think about the following disagreement, which Leibniz had with the influential French philosopher René Descartes, who lived in the generation just prior to Leibniz. Descartes held that matter was a substance, but he thought of it as a *single*, continuous, extended lump of stuff. For Descartes, the whole material universe is fundamentally one single thing, spread out across all of space. In other words, there is only one material substance. On the other hand, Descartes believed that there are many mental substances (though they all belong to the same *category* of substance, i.e., they are all minds): God is one (infinite, uncreated, etc.) mental substance, and each finite human mind is another. My mind is a different individual substance from your mind, for example, but according to Descartes our bodies are both part of the same substance.

It is Descartes's view of material substance with which Leibniz disagreed. He firmly rejected the notion that a single substance can 'include' a large number of separable bits, and insisted that reality must consist of a large number of discrete individual things rather than of a continuous expanse of 'stuff.' As it is sometimes put, for Leibniz "substantiality requires individuality"—i.e., substances are indivisible, complete beings which have a special kind of 'substantial unity.' The whole of material reality simply could not be a single substance, according to Leibniz, because it blatantly fails to have the right kind of unity. For example, a pile of stones or flock of sheep is not a substance since its unity (as a single heap or flock) is only *accidental*; on the other hand, a human being is a substance, according to Leibniz, because that unity is not accidental but is, so to speak, "built in" to one's personhood: it is what he called a unity *per se*, a unity "in itself."

The importance of all this for Leibniz's philosophical system is that he took very seriously the idea that reality is fundamentally made up of a collection of indivisible substances—which Leibniz calls "substantial forms"—each of which possesses substantial unity and so is complete in itself. At least by the time of his later philosophy, Leibniz held that all of reality is made up of a large collection of immaterial substances (roughly, minds or souls) which he called *monads*: the material world is an "appearance" that somehow "results" from the activities of purely immaterial minds. Furthermore, since these monads are complete in themselves, their "substantial form" encompasses their whole nature—their parts and structure, their causal powers and activities, their whole life-cycle of changing states are all derived from their substantial forms. Hence, to fully know the form of a human soul, for example, would be to know everything about its nature, according to Leibniz: one would be able to predict and understand each and every activity of that soul, throughout its entire history.

Another consequence of Leibniz's metaphysics is that it presents *physics* in an important new light. Leibniz was writing during the heyday of the "new" or "mechanical" philosophy—typified by Descartes's philosophy and Newton's physics—which sought to explain all the phenomena of the material world, not in terms of mysterious forces or essences, but solely in terms of the complex collisions between bits of matter. Leibniz was part of this "new philosophy" movement—he agreed, in general terms, with the view that physics should be thought of as the study of matter in motion. Where he disagreed with many of his contemporaries, however, was over the concept of *physical force*—over the mechanism by which motion is transferred from one body to another (or conserved in a single moving body, like a planet). This was a matter of great interest and controversy in the seventeenth century, and was a far from trivial question. If a car rear-ends another vehicle waiting in neutral at a stop light, for example, it will cause the front car to roll forward. What philosophers of Leibniz's time were puzzled by was just exactly *what* is this invisible power which is transmitted from the first car to the second, and furthermore what keeps the second car moving when it is no longer being pushed by the first? In short, the movement of three-dimensional bodies through space was thought to be well understood, but what makes the bodies move in the first place was much more mysterious.

A natural response to this problem, at the time, was to turn to God as an explanation of this mystery. One such theory was called "occasionalism," and its most famous supporter was a French philosopher called Nicolas Malebranche (1638–1715). According to occasionalism, God is the true cause of all physical motion: God watches over the world and, when one body is hit by another moving body, this is the occasion for God to step in and cause the first body to move; similarly, God is constantly acting to keep moving bodies (like the Moon) in motion—without his intervention they would immediately halt. Leibniz, however, held that this role was beneath the dignity of God. It is far more worthy of God to have produced entities capable of initiating their own movements. And Leibniz's metaphysical framework allowed him, he thought, to explain how God has done this: reality consists in substantial forms, and these forms are active in their very nature—their movement is, once again, 'built in' to the individuals in the world at the moment of their creation, so God does not have to intervene 'from the outside' to bring about natural phenomena.

Interestingly, on this view, the fundamental individuals in the world (monads) do not really *interact* with each other; rather, they each independently run through the sequence of activities 'pre-programmed' by their forms, and God has designed the world—by creating the substantial forms in a certain way—so that all these activities mesh together. Leibniz called this "the system of pre-established harmony." For example, if I see a cat in the room, this perception is *not* caused in me by the cat, according to Leibniz, but arises in me "spontaneously from [my] own nature"; meanwhile, however, God has so arranged things so that what I see corresponds to reality—that is, there really is a cat in the room.

What Is the Structure of This Reading?

This reading is broken down into eight different "objections": each objection is an argument against the traditional conception of God (that God is an infinitely good, wise, and powerful being) premised either on the presence of evil in the world or on Leibniz's own theory that this is the greatest of all possible worlds. The first objection is in the form of the traditional "problem of evil," but then there follow arguments to show that God is unjust in punishing sin, or culpable for the existence of sin, or insufficiently caring for his creation, or unfree to choose what kind of world he will create. Leibniz responds to each of these objections, trying to show that his philosophical system can answer all of them: in other words, he tries to defend the *possibility* of a God that is omniscient, omnipotent, and perfectly benevolent.

Some Useful Background Information

1. The title of Leibniz's book, *Theodicy*, is a word meaning "the vindication of God's power and goodness despite the existence of evil." That is, a theodicy is an attempt to respond to the problem of evil.

2. This reading is structured as a set of syllogisms, plus Leibniz's responses to them. A syllogism is an argument, and usually one of a particular form: it consists of two premises and a conclusion. Many of the arguments considered by Leibniz are a type of "categorical syllogism" and have the following form (known, believe it or not, by the medieval nickname "Barbara"):

    All *M* is *P*.
    All *S* is *M*.
    Therefore all *S* is *P*.

    In arguments of this form, the first line is called the "major premise" (since it includes *P*, the predicate of the conclusion) and the second line is the "minor premise" (since it includes *S*, the subject of the conclusion). "Prosyllogisms" are syllogisms which have as their conclusion one of the premises of another syllogism—that is, they are what would often be called today "sub-arguments."

3. According to Leibniz there are "two great principles" on which "our reasonings are founded." They are the "principle of contradiction" and the "principle of sufficient reason." It is the principle of contradiction "in virtue of which we judge as false anything that involves contradiction, and as true whatever is opposed or contradictory to what is false" (*Monadology*, section 31). For ex-

ample, suppose that, if some claim *P* were true, then it would follow logically that some other claim (*Q*) would have to be both true and false. To say that *Q* is both true and false is to express a contradiction: "*Q* and not-*Q*." Since (arguably) no proposition can be both true and false at the same time (i.e., no contradictions are true), this shows as a matter of logic that *P* could not possibly be true, and hence (according to Leibniz) *P* must be false or, to put the same thing another way, not-*P* must be true.

The principle of sufficient reason says "no fact could ever be true or existent … unless there were a sufficient reason why it was thus and not otherwise," as Leibniz puts it in the *Monadology*. In the case of necessary truths, they must be true because of the principle of contradiction—because their opposites must be false. In the case of contingent truths, their "sufficient reason," according to Leibniz, is "the principle of the best": that is, God could only have created the best possible world, and that is why the world is the way it is.

4. Although Leibniz probably did not invent the notion of a "possible world" (the concept can also be found in the work of his contemporary, Nicolas Malebranche, as early as 1674), he is generally thought of as the main developer of this way of talking prior to the twentieth century. The language of possible worlds is fairly straightforward, but has proved to be a powerful tool for thinking clearly and precisely about possibility, contingency, and necessity. In this way of talking, a "world" is a complete state of affairs: it is not just, say, a planet, but an entire universe, extended throughout space and time. A world is "possible" if it is logically consistent: that is, if it does not involve a contradiction. One way to think of this is to say that a possible world is a way the actual universe *might have been*. For example, the cover of this book might have been plaid, or the Vietnam War might never have taken place, or cats might have turned out to be robotic spies from outer space, or the laws of physics might have been different; and so there are possible worlds in which all these

things are the case. (The actual world, of course, is also a possible world, since it too is a way the actual world could have been!) On the other hand, there are some differences from the actual world that are *not* possible (i.e., which appear in no possible universe). For example, two plus two must always equal four, oculists must (by definition) always be eye doctors, and the sky could never be red all over and blue all over at the same time. The 'space' of possible worlds can therefore be said to be exactly the set of all the universes that are possible. According to Leibniz, God necessarily and eternally has in his mind the ideas of each of these infinitely many possible worlds, and he has chosen just one of them—the best one—to make actual through an act of creation.

5. When Leibniz says that the actual world is the best of all possible worlds, he means this in both of two different ways. First, he means that it is "metaphysically" the best possible world: God has designed it in such a way that the maximum amount of variety and richness in the natural world is produced using the simplest and most efficient possible set of natural laws. Second, he means that it is "morally" the best possible world: it has been designed with the happiness of human beings as its primary aim.

Some Common Misconceptions

1. In Voltaire's novel *Candide* (1759), Leibniz is lampooned, in the person of the character Dr. Pangloss, for his thesis that this is the best of all possible worlds: Voltaire makes it seem that Leibniz's optimism is a foolish and wickedly complacent response to the evils of our world. However, Leibniz does not deny the existence of evil: he is perfectly aware that sometimes "bad things happen to good people." Nor does Leibniz claim that the existence of evil is necessary: he thinks that God could have made a world that did not contain evil, or could have chosen not to create any world at all. What Leibniz does think is that God *could not have made any world which is better than this one*:

that is, any possible world that contains less evil than the actual world is, nevertheless, for some reason, a less good world than the actual one. Thus, precisely the amount of evil which does exist—no more and no less—is necessary for this world to be the best of all possible worlds.

2. Leibniz does not think it is incumbent upon him to prove that this actually is the best of all possible worlds. In order to counter the problem of evil, Leibniz merely has to show that the existence of evil is *consistent* with the existence of a benevolent, all-powerful God—that is, he just has to show that this *might* be the best of all possible worlds even though it contains evil. (Nevertheless, "in order to make the matter clearer," Leibniz does his best to show that "this universe must be in reality better than every other possible universe.")

3. Leibniz does not think that whatever is true is true by absolute necessity. Although this is the best of all possible worlds and the only one which God, given his nature, could have made actual, there are nevertheless a huge number of non-actual but possible worlds, that God in some sense could have created but did not.

How Important and Influential Is This Passage?

This particular passage is not an especially influential and important piece of philosophy, nor is Leibniz's *Theodicy* today thought to be a central part of his writings (although it was the only philosophical book he published during his lifetime). On the other hand, Leibniz's idea that this is the best of all possible worlds—his defense of which is summarized in this selection, but which can be found spelled out in more detail in several places in his writings—is perhaps one of the most notorious ideas in all of philosophy. The idea of possible worlds, which Leibniz developed as part of his theodicy, has also been of great influence on twentieth-century philosophy, as a useful tool for thinking about possibility and necessity. (For example, when philosophers today want to say that something is necessarily true they will often assert that it is "true in all possible worlds.")

Suggestions for Critical Reflection

1. Leibniz asserts "the best plan is not always that which seeks to avoid evil." This may be true for human beings, such as military leaders who need to risk casualties in order to win battles, but how plausible a claim is it for an omnipotent deity—for a being whose actions are not constrained by the behavior of opponents or competitors, or even by the laws of physics?

2. Where do you think human free will enters into Leibniz's picture? Is it compatible with, or even entailed by, this being the best of all possible worlds? Why do you think that Leibniz says it would be "unfitting" for God to interfere with human freedom in order to hinder sin?

3. Where does *God's* freedom fit into a theory like Leibniz's? If God could only have created the best possible world (i.e., this world), then in what sense can we say that God is free? What do you think of Leibniz's response to this problem?

4. What do you think of Leibniz's claim that "every reality purely positive or absolute is a perfection; and that imperfection comes from limitation, that is, from the privative"? Do you agree that all evil consists in the *absence* of something that could have made things better, rather than the presence of something that is positively bad?

5. It sometimes appears that Leibniz argues in the following way: this must be the best of all possible worlds because a perfect God made it, and therefore it is possible that a perfect God exists. Do you think Leibniz does make this argument, and if so, does this strike you as a good argument? If it's a bad argument, how serious a problem is this for Leibniz's theodicy?

6. Do you think that there is a "universal harmony," and if so, does it make sense of all the evil in the world? Does it make sense of it by showing that the evil is necessary for some "higher purpose," or alternatively by showing that it is not *really* evil in the first place?

Suggestions for Further Reading

Currently the only English translation of Leibniz's *Theodicy* in print is that by E.M. Huggard, published by Open Court in 1985. The three classic philosophical works by Leibniz are the *Discourse on Metaphysics* (written in 1686), the *New System of the Nature of Substances and their Communication* (published in 1695), and the *Monadology* (written in 1714). Each of these works are fairly short, and can be found collected in, for example, *G.W. Leibniz: Philosophical Texts*, translated by R.S. Woolhouse and Richard Francks (Oxford University Press, 1998). Another important work by Leibniz, his response to John Locke's *Essay Concerning Human Understanding* (see Chapter 2), is *New Essays on Human Understanding*, translated by Peter Remnant and Jonathan Bennett and published by Cambridge University Press in 1996.

Leibniz presents four arguments for the existence of God at different places in his work: an "ontological" argument (in his *Discourse on Metaphysics*, section 23, and in *New Essays on Human Understanding*, Book IV, Chapter X); a "cosmological" argument (in *Monadology*); an "argument from eternal truths" (also in *Monadology*); and an "argument from pre-established harmony" (in the *New System*, section 16).

A detailed, recent biography of Leibniz is E.J. Aiton's *Leibniz*, published by Adam Hilger in 1985. Useful books on Leibniz's philosophy as a whole include Robert Merrihew Adams's *Leibniz: Determinist, Theist, Idealist* (Oxford University Press, 1994), C.D. Broad's *Leibniz: An Introduction* (Cambridge University Press, 1975), Stuart Brown's *Leibniz* (Harvester Press, 1984), Nicholas Rescher's *Leibniz: An Introduction to his Philosophy* (University Press of America, 1979), and Bertrand Russell's *A Critical Exposition of the Philosophy of Leibniz* (Allen and Unwin, 1937). A good collection of specially-written papers on Leibniz's philosophy is *The Cambridge Companion to Leibniz*, edited by Nicholas Jolley (Cambridge University Press, 1995).

Discussion of Leibniz's response to the problem of evil can be found in the following articles: David Blumenfeld's "Is the Best Possible World Possible?" *Philosophical Review* 84 (1975); Gregory Brown, "Compossibility, Harmony, and Perfection in Leibniz," *Philosophical Review* 96 (1987); Leroy Howe, "Leibniz on Evil," *Sophia* 10 (1971); Oliver Johnson, "Human Freedom in the Best of all Possible Worlds" *Philosophical Quarterly* 4 (1954); Michael Latzer, "Leibniz's Conception of Metaphysical Evil," *Journal of the History of Ideas* 55 (1994); Lawrence Resnik, "God and the Best Possible World," *American Philosophical Quarterly* 10 (1973); and Catherine Wilson, "Leibnizian Optimism," *Journal of Philosophy* 80 (1983).

Theodicy
Abridgement of the Argument Reduced to Syllogistic Form[2]

Some intelligent persons have desired that this supplement be made, and I have the more readily yielded to their wishes as in this way I have an opportunity again to remove certain difficulties and to make some observations which were not sufficiently emphasized in the work itself.

Objection I

i.   Whoever does not choose the best is lacking in power, or in knowledge, or in goodness.

ii. God did not choose the best in creating this world.

iii. Therefore, God has been lacking in power, or in knowledge, or in goodness.

Answer

I deny the minor, that is, the second premise of this syllogism; and our opponent proves it by this:

Prosyllogism

i.   Whoever makes things in which there is evil, which could have been made without any evil, or the making of which could have been omitted, does not choose the best.

---

2   The *Theodicy* was first published in 1710. This translation from the original French was made by George M. Duncan and comes from *The Philosophical Works of Leibnitz*, published in 1890 by Tuttle, Morehouse & Taylor. I have added the numbering of the premises of the various syllogisms.

ii.   God has made a world in which there is evil, a world, I say, which could have been made without any evil, or the making of which could have been omitted altogether.

iii. Therefore, God has not chosen the best.

Answer

I grant the minor of this prosyllogism; for it must be confessed that there is evil in this world which God has made, and that it was possible to make a world without evil, or even not to create a world at all, for its creation has depended on the free will of God; but I deny the major, that is, the first of the two premises of the prosyllogism, and I might content myself with simply demanding its proof; but in order to make the matter clearer, I have wished to justify this denial by showing that the best plan is not always that which seeks to avoid evil, since it may happen that *the evil is accompanied by a greater good.* For example, a general of an army will prefer a great victory with a slight wound to a condition without wound and without victory. We have proved this more fully in the large work by making it clear, by instances taken from mathematics and elsewhere, that an imperfection in the part may be required for a greater perfection in the whole. In this I have followed the opinion of St. Augustine,[3] who has said a hundred times, that God has permitted evil in order to bring about good, that is, a greater good; and that of Thomas Aquinas (in libr. II. *sent. dist.* 32, qu. I, art. 1),[4] that the permitting of evil

tends to the good of the universe. I have shown that the ancients called Adam's fall[5] *felix culpa,* a happy sin, because it had been retrieved with immense advantage by the incarnation of the Son of God, who has given to the universe something nobler than anything that ever would have been among creatures except for it. For the sake of a clearer understanding, I have added, following many good authors, that it was in accordance with order and the general good that God allowed to certain creatures the opportunity of exercising their liberty, even when he foresaw that they would turn to evil, but which he could so well rectify; because it was not fitting that, in order to hinder sin, God should always act in an extraordinary manner. To overthrow this objection, therefore, it is sufficient to show that a world with evil might be better than a world without evil; but I have gone even farther, in the work, and have even proved that this universe must be in reality better than every other possible universe.

Objection II

i.   If there is more evil than good in intelligent creatures, then there is more evil than good in the whole work of God.

ii.   Now, there is more evil than good in intelligent creatures.

iii. Therefore, there is more evil than good in the whole work of God.

Answer

I deny the major and the minor of this conditional syllogism. As to the major, I do not admit it at all, because this pretended deduction from a part to the whole, from intelligent creatures to all creatures, supposes tacitly and without proof that creatures destitute of reason cannot enter into comparison nor into account with those which possess it. But why may it not be that the surplus of good in the non-intelligent creatures which fill the world, compensates for, and even incomparably surpasses, the surplus of evil in

---

3   Augustine, a north African bishop who lived in the early fifth century, was a highly important early Christian theologian and philosopher. Some of his influential writings on the problem of evil appear in his book *Enchiridion* (which means "handbook"); his other important works include *City of God* and the autobiographical *Confessions.*

4   Leibniz is here referring to St. Thomas Aquinas' commentary on a work called the *Sentences* by Peter Lombard (specifically, to the first article of the first question of part 32 of Book II of the commentary). Lombard was bishop of Paris between 1150 and 1152, and his *Sentences* became a standard textbook for thirteenth-century students of theology.

---

5   According to the Old Testament book of Genesis, the expulsion of Adam and Eve from the Garden of Eden for disobedience to God, and the consequent lapse of the human race into the human condition of suffering and "original sin."

the rational creatures? It is true that the value of the latter is greater; but, in compensation, the others are beyond comparison the more numerous, and it may be that the proportion of number and quantity surpasses that of value and of quality.

As to the minor, that is no more to be admitted; that is, it is not at all to be admitted that there is more evil than good in the intelligent creatures. There is no need even of granting that there is more evil than good in the human race, because it is possible, and in fact very probable, that the glory and the perfection of the blessed are incomparably greater than the misery and the imperfection of the damned, and that here the excellence of the total good in the smaller number exceeds the total evil in the greater number. The blessed approach the Divinity, by means of a Divine Mediator, as near as may suit these creatures,[6] and make such progress in good as is impossible for the damned to make in evil, approach as nearly as they may to the nature of demons. God is infinite, and the devil is limited; the good may and does go to infinity, while evil has its bounds. It is therefore possible, and is credible, that in the comparison of the blessed and the damned, the contrary of that which I have said might happen in the comparison of intelligent and non-intelligent creatures, takes place; namely, it is possible that in the comparison of the happy and the unhappy, the proportion of degree exceeds that of number, and that in the comparison of intelligent and non-intelligent creatures, the proportion of number is greater than that of value. I have the right to suppose that a thing is possible so long as its impossibility is not proved; and indeed that which I have here advanced is more than a supposition.

But in the second place, if I should admit that there is more evil than good in the human race, I have still good grounds for not admitting that there is more evil than good in all intelligent creatures. For there is an inconceivable number of genii,[7] and perhaps of other rational creatures. And an opponent could not prove that in all the City of God, composed as well of genii as of rational animals without number and of an infinity of kinds, evil exceeds good. And although in order to answer an objection, there is no need of proving that a thing is, when its mere possibility suffices; yet, in this work, I have not omitted to show that it is a consequence of the supreme perfection of the Sovereign of the universe, that the kingdom of God is the most perfect of all possible states or governments, and that consequently the little evil there is, is required for the consummation of the immense good which is found there.

Objection III

i.   If it is always impossible not to sin, it is always unjust to punish.

ii.   Now, it is always impossible not to sin; or, in other words, every sin is necessary.

iii. Therefore, it is always unjust to punish.
      The minor of this is proved thus:

First Prosyllogism

i.   All that is predetermined[8] is necessary.

ii.   Every event is predetermined.

iii. Therefore, every event (and consequently sin also) is necessary.
      Again this second minor is proved thus:

Second Prosyllogism

i.   That which is future, that which is foreseen, that which is involved in the causes, is predetermined.

ii.   Every event is such.

iii. Therefore, every event is predetermined.

Answer

I admit in a certain sense the conclusion of the second prosyllogism, which is the minor of the first; but I shall deny the major of the first prosyllogism, namely, that every thing predetermined is necessary; understanding by the necessity of sinning, for example, or by the impossibility of not sinning, or of not

---

6   Good and religious people, with the assistance of divine entities like the Virgin Mary, can become as much like God (in goodness) as is possible for mere created beings.

7   Supernatural spirits, such as the various types of angels.

8   Predetermined means "fixed in advance." See Chapter 6 for more discussion.

performing any action, the necessity with which we are here concerned, that is, that which is essential and absolute, and which destroys the morality of an action and the justice of punishments. For if anyone understood another necessity or impossibility, namely, a necessity which should be only moral, or which was only hypothetical (as will be explained shortly); it is clear that I should deny the major of the objection itself. I might content myself with this answer and demand the proof of the proposition denied; but I have again desired to explain my procedure in this work, in order to better elucidate the matter and to throw more light on the whole subject, by explaining the necessity which ought to be rejected and the determination which must take place. That *necessity* which is contrary to morality and which ought to be rejected, and which would render punishment unjust, is an insurmountable necessity which would make all opposition useless, even if we should wish with all our heart to avoid the necessary action, and should make all possible efforts to that end. Now, it is manifest that this is not applicable to voluntary actions, because we would not perform them if we did not choose to. Also their prevision[9] and predetermination are not absolute, but presuppose the will: if it is certain that we shall perform them, it is not less certain that we shall choose to perform them. These voluntary actions and their consequences will not take place no matter what we do or whether we wish them or not; but, *through* that which we shall do and through that which we shall wish to do, which leads to them. And this is involved in prevision and in predetermination, and even constitutes their ground. And the necessity of such an event is called conditional or hypothetical, or the necessity of consequence, because it supposes the will, and the other *requisites*; whereas the necessity which destroys morality and renders punishment unjust and reward useless, exists in things which will be whatever we may do or whatever we may wish to do, and, in a word, is in that which is essential; and this is what is called an absolute necessity. Thus it is to no purpose, as regards what is absolutely necessary, to make prohibitions or commands, to propose penalties or prizes, to praise or to blame; it will be none the less. On the other hand, in voluntary actions and in that which depends upon them, precepts[10] armed with power to punish and to recompense are very often of use and are included in the order of causes which make an action exist. And it is for this reason that not only cares and labours but also prayers are useful; God having had these prayers in view before he regulated things and having had that consideration for them which was proper. This is why the precept which says *ora et labora* (pray and work), holds altogether good; and not only those who (under the vain pretext of the necessity of events) pretend that the care which business demands may be neglected, but also those who reason against prayer, fall into what the ancients even then called the *lazy sophism*.[11] Thus the predetermination of events by causes is just what contributes to morality instead of destroying it, and causes incline the will, without compelling it. This is why the *determination* in question is not a necessitation—it is certain (to him who knows all) that the effect will follow this inclination; but this effect does not follow by a necessary consequence, that is, one the contrary of which implies contradiction. It is also by an internal inclination such as this that the will is determined, without there being any necessity. Suppose that one has the greatest passion in the world (a great thirst, for example), you will admit to me that the soul can find some reason for resisting it, if it were only that of showing its power. Thus, although one may never be in a perfect indifference of equilibrium and there may be always a preponderance of inclination for the side taken, it, nevertheless, never renders the resolution taken absolutely necessary.

---

9   Being seen (by God) before they happened.

10 Laws or principles.

11 The 'lazy sophism' was an argument for fatalism, proposed by the Stoic philosopher Chrysippus (280–208 BCE) and strongly criticized by the Roman poet and philosopher Cicero (106–43 BCE). It runs roughly as follows: Whatever will be, will be; Therefore nothing you can do will change things; Therefore any action to try to influence events is pointless—you might just as well do nothing.

Objection IV

i.   Whoever can prevent the sin of another and does not do so but rather contributes to it although he is well informed of it, is accessory to it.

ii. God can prevent the sin of intelligent creatures; but he does not do so, and rather contributes to it by his concurrence[12] and by the opportunities which he brings about, although he has a perfect knowledge of it.

iii. Hence, etc.

Answer

I deny the major of this syllogism. For it is possible that one could prevent sin, but ought not, because he could not do it without himself committing a sin, or (when God is in question) without performing an unreasonable action. Examples have been given and the application to God himself has been made. It is possible also that we contribute to evil and that sometimes we even open the road to it, in doing things which we are obliged to do; and, when we do our duty or (in speaking of God) when, after thorough consideration, we do that which reason demands, we are not responsible for the results, even when we foresee them. We do not desire these evils; but we are willing to permit them for the sake of a greater good which we cannot reasonably help preferring to other considerations. And this is a *consequent* will, which results from *antecedent* wills by which we will the good. I know that some persons, in speaking of the antecedent and consequent will of God, have understood by the *antecedent* that which wills that all men should be saved; and by the *consequent*, that which wills, in consequence of persistent sin, that some should be damned. But these are merely illustrations of a more general idea, and it may be said for the same reason that God, by his antecedent will, wills that men should not sin; and by his consequent or final and decreeing will (that which is always followed by its effect), he wills to permit them to sin, this permission being the result of superior reasons. And we have the right to say in general that the antecedent will of God tends to the production of good and the prevention of evil, each taken in itself and as if alone (*particulariter et secundum quid*, Thom. I, qu. 19, art. 6),[13] according to the measure of the degree of each good and of each evil; but that the divine consequent or final or total will tends toward the production of as many goods as may be put together, the combination of which becomes in this way determined, and includes also the permission of some evils and the exclusion of some goods, as the best possible plan for the universe demands. Arminius,[14] in his *Anti-perkinsus*, has very well explained that the will of God may be called consequent, not only in relation to the action of the creature considered beforehand in the divine understanding, but also in relation to other anterior[15] divine acts of will. But this consideration of the passage cited from Thomas Aquinas, and that from Scotus (I. dist. 46, qu. XI),[16] is enough to show that they make this distinction as I have done here. Nevertheless, if anyone objects to this use of terms let him substitute *deliberating* will, in place of antecedent, and final or decreeing will, in place of consequent. For I do not wish to dispute over words.

Objection V

i.   Whoever produces all that is real in a thing, is its cause.

ii. God produces all that is real in sin.

iii. Hence, God is the cause of sin.

---

12 God's maintaining things in existence by a kind of continuous divine act of will.

13 This is a reference to Part I, Question 19, article 6 of St. Thomas Aquinas' *Summa Theologiae*.

14 Jacob Arminius (1560–1609) was a Protestant Dutch theologian who rejected the doctrine of predestination—i.e., he denied that God has already decided who will be damned and who will be saved, even before they are born.

15 Earlier.

16 The Scottish philosopher and theologian John Duns (c. 1266–1308), who is usually referred to as Duns Scotus ("Duns the Scot"). The reference is to section 46 of the first part of Scotus' commentary on the *Sentences* by Peter Lombard.

Answer

I might content myself with denying the major or the minor, since the term *real* admits of interpretations which would render these propositions false. But in order to explain more clearly, I will make a distinction. *Real* signifies either that which is positive only, or, it includes also privative[17] beings: in the first case, I deny the major and admit the minor; in the second case, I do the contrary. I might have limited myself to this, but I have chosen to proceed still farther and give the reason for this distinction. I have been very glad therefore to draw attention to the fact that every reality purely positive or absolute is a perfection; and that imperfection comes from limitation, that is, from the privative: for to limit is to refuse progress, or the greatest possible progress. Now God is the cause of all perfections and consequently of all realities considered as purely positive. But limitations or privations result from the original imperfection of creatures, which limits their receptivity. And it is with them as with a loaded vessel, which the river causes to move more or less slowly according to the weight which it carries: thus its speed depends upon the river, but the retardation which limits this speed comes from the load. Thus in the *Theodicy*, we have shown how the creature, in causing sin, is a defective cause;[18] how errors and evil inclinations are born of privation; and how privation is accidentally efficient;[19] and I have

justified the opinion of St. Augustine (lib. I. *ad Simpl.* qu. 2)[20] who explains, for example, how God makes the soul obdurate,[21] not by giving it something evil, but because the effect of his good impression is limited by the soul's resistance and by the circumstances which contribute to this resistance, so that he does not give it all the good which would overcome its evil. *Nec* (inquit) *ab illo erogatur aliquid quo homo fit deterior, sed tantum quo fit melior non erogatur.*[22] But if God had wished to do more, he would have had to make either other natures for creatures or other miracles to change their natures, things which the best plan could not admit. It is as if the current of the river must be more rapid than its fall admitted or that the boats should be loaded more lightly, if it were necessary to make them move more quickly. And the original limitation or imperfection of creatures requires that even the best plan of the universe could not receive more good, and could not be exempt from certain evils, which, however, are to result in a greater good. There are certain disorders in the parts which marvellously enhance the beauty of the whole; just as certain dissonances, when properly used, render harmony more beautiful. But this depends on what has already been said in answer to the first objection.

Objection VI

i. Whoever punishes those who have done as well as it was in their power to do, is unjust.
ii. God does so.
iii. Hence, etc.

Answer

I deny the minor of this argument. And I believe that God always gives sufficient aid and grace to those

---

17 A privation is an absence, or lack, or some quality or attribute. In medieval terminology, "privation" was the name of the state in which matter was supposed to exist *before* the process of generation begins, which gives it some form or other—i.e., before the "stuff" of matter became stars, or rocks, or trees, or anything at all.

18 Caused by some defect or limitation, rather than by some "positive" quality of the creature.

19 Privation, or limitation, doesn't necessarily cause anything at all—it does not have an essential power to have effects (be 'efficient'). Instead, privation can 'accidentally' have certain effects due to the surrounding circumstances. (By analogy, a hole in the ground doesn't normally, by its nature, suck surrounding objects into it; but in certain circumstances—e.g., when combined with somebody who isn't looking where they're going—the hole can be a partial cause of an

object falling into it.)

20 A reference to question 2 of Book I of Augustine's work *To Simplicianus, On Seven Different Questions*, written in about 395 CE.

21 Stubbornly wicked.

22 "Nor (he says) is man provided by him [God] with anything by which he becomes worse, but it is only that there is not furnished that by which he becomes better."

who have a good will, that is, to those who do not reject this grace by new sin. Thus I do not admit the damnation of infants who have died without baptism or outside of the church; nor the damnation of adults who have acted according to the light which God has given them. And I believe that *if any one has followed the light which has been given him*, he will undoubtedly receive greater light when he has need of it, as the late M. Hulseman, a profound and celebrated theologian at Leipzig, has somewhere remarked; and if such a man has failed to receive it during his lifetime he will at least receive it when at the point of death.

Objection VII

i. Whoever gives only to some, and not to all, the means which produces in them effectively a good will and salutary final faith, has not sufficient goodness.
ii. God does this.
iii. Hence, etc.

Answer

I deny the major of this. It is true that God could overcome the greatest resistance of the human heart; and does it, too, sometimes, either by internal grace, or by external circumstances which have a great effect on souls; but he does not always do this. Whence comes this distinction? it may be asked, and why does his goodness seem limited? It is because, as I have already said in answering the first objection, it would not have been in order always to act in an extraordinary manner, and to reverse the connection of things. The reasons of this connection, by means of which one is placed in more favourable circumstances than another, are hidden in the depths of the wisdom of God: they depend upon the universal harmony. The best plan of the universe, which God could not fail to choose, made it so. We judge from the event itself; since God has made it, it was not possible to do better. Far from being true that this conduct is contrary to goodness, it is supreme goodness which led him to it. This objection with its solution might have been drawn from what was said in regard to the first objection; but it seemed useful to touch upon it separately.

Objection VIII

i.   Whoever cannot fail to choose the best, is not free.
ii. God cannot fail to choose the best.
iii. Hence, God is not free.

Answer

I deny the major of this argument; it is rather true liberty, and the most perfect, to be able to use one's free will for the best, and to always exercise this power, without ever being turned aside either by external force or by internal passions, the first of which causes slavery of the body, the second, slavery of the soul. There is nothing less servile, and nothing more in accordance with the highest degree of freedom, than to be always led toward the good, and always by one's own inclination, without any constraint and without any displeasure. And to object therefore that God had need of external things, is only a sophism.[23] He created them freely; but having proposed to himself an end, which is to exercise his goodness, wisdom has determined him to choose the means best fitted to attain this end. To call this a need, is to take that term in an unusual sense which frees it from all imperfection, just as when we speak of the wrath of God.

Seneca[24] has somewhere said that God commanded but once but that he obeys always, because he obeys laws which he willed to prescribe to himself: *semel jussit, semper paret*.[25] But he might better have said that God always commands and that he is always obeyed; for in willing, he always follows the inclination of his own nature, and all other things always follow his will. And as this will is always the same, it cannot be said that he obeys only that will which he formerly had. Nevertheless, although his will is always infallible and always tends toward the best, the evil, or the lesser good, which he rejects, does not

---

23 An argument which seems valid on the surface but which actually isn't.

24 A Roman playwright, philosopher, and statesman, who lived from about 5 BCE to 65 CE. He was widely known for his ethical writings, and his death by suicide was taken as a model of Stoic virtuous action.

25 "He commanded once, but obeys always."

cease to be possible in itself; otherwise the necessity of the good would be geometrical[26] (so to speak), or metaphysical, and altogether absolute; the contingency of things would be destroyed, and there would be no choice. But this sort of necessity, which does not destroy the possibility of the contrary, has this name only by analogy; it becomes effective, not by the pure essence of things, but by that which is outside of them, above them, namely, by the will of God. This necessity is called moral, because, to the sage, *necessity* and *what ought to be* are equivalent things; and when it always has its effect, as it really has in the perfect sage, that is, in God, it may be said that it is a happy necessity. The nearer creatures approach to it, the nearer they approach to perfect happiness. Also this kind of necessity is not that which we try to avoid and which destroys morality, rewards and praise. For that which it brings, does not happen whatever we may do or will, but because we will it so. And a will to which it is natural to choose well, merits praise so much the more; also it carries its reward with it, which is sovereign happiness. And as this constitution of the divine nature gives entire satisfaction to him who possesses it, it is also the best and the most desirable for the creatures who are all dependent on God. If the will of God did not have for a rule the principle of the best, it would either tend toward evil, which would be the worst; or it would be in some way indifferent to good and to evil, and would be guided by chance: but a will which would allow itself always to act by chance, would not be worth more for the government of the universe than the fortuitous concourse[27] of atoms, without there being any divinity therein. And even if God should abandon himself to chance only in some cases and in a certain way (as he would do, if he did not always work entirely for the best and if he were capable of preferring a lesser work to a greater, that is, an evil to a good, since that which prevents a greater good is an evil), he would be imperfect, as well as the object of his choice; he would not merit entire confidence; he would act without reason in such a case, and the government of the universe would be like certain games, equally divided between reason and chance. All this proves that this objection which is made against the choice of the best, perverts the notions of the free and of the necessary, and represents to us the best even as evil: which is either malicious or ridiculous.

---

26   Mathematical.

27   "Fortuitous concourse" means "coming and moving together by chance."

J.L. MACKIE
"Evil and Omnipotence"

Who Was J.L. Mackie?

John Leslie Mackie was born in Sydney, Australia, in 1917 and educated at Sydney University and Oriel College, Oxford. After serving in the Australian army during the Second World War, he taught at Sydney University from 1946 to 1954 and then at Otago University in Dunedin, New Zealand. In 1963 he moved permanently to England, and from 1967 until his death in 1981 he was a Fellow of University College, Oxford. He wrote six books and many philosophical papers, mostly on topics in metaphysics, ethics, the history of philosophy, and the philosophy of religion.

Mackie is probably best known for his 'error theory' of moral values. This holds that:

(a) There are no objective moral values.
(b) All ordinary moral judgments include a claim to objectivity, and so,
(c) All ordinary moral judgments are false.

Mackie therefore argued that morality is not discovered but is *created* by human beings. We should scrap traditional moral theory, he said, and, instead of treating moral theory as descriptive of moral facts, we should reinvent morality as a device for encouraging empathy with the points of view of others.

Mackie's work, like most Australian analytical philosophy of this century, is notable for its dislike of obfuscation and obscurantism, and for its careful attempts at clarity and precision. "Evil and Omnipotence" is well known as probably the best short modern defense of an argument called 'the problem of evil.'

it; (4) evil is due to human free will. (These responses fall naturally into two groups: 1 and 2, and 3 and 4.) Mackie argues carefully that all four of these responses to the problem of evil are fallacious.

In the course of his attack on the free-will response to the problem of evil, Mackie develops a further argument which he calls "the Paradox of Omnipotence." He argues that this paradox shows it is *logically impossible* that any (temporal) being could exist which had absolutely unlimited power.

The upshot of all this, Mackie concludes, is that God (as he is described by, say, Christianity) cannot possibly exist.

Some Useful Background Information

When Mackie talks about 'evil' in this article, he follows normal philosophical usage in this context. In everyday language the word "evil" tends to suggest an especially wicked kind of moral badness; however, the 'problem of evil,' though it certainly includes extreme ethical badness, is much broader in its scope than that. It's important to realize that, according to the argument from evil, any kind of 'sub-optimality' can be a problem for the existence of God. Therefore examples of 'evil' range along the spectrum from such mild harms as a nasty pimple, a job that does not give 100% satisfaction, or a mountain that would be just a little more beautiful if it were a slightly different shape, right up to major earthquakes, epidemics, and oil spills in the Alaskan wilderness. Moral 'evils' can be as minor as breaking a trivial promise or making a slightly cutting remark, or as serious as rape, torture, and genocide.

What Is the Structure of This Reading?

Mackie begins by introducing an argument against the existence of God (or, at least, of God as traditionally conceived) called 'the problem of evil.' He lays out its logical form (as a paradox), and tries to make clear its theological importance. He briefly discusses a kind of response to this paradox which he does think is adequate, but claims that such a response would be unacceptable to those who believe in God. Believers must thus attempt to give other solutions to the paradox, but Mackie argues that all of these attempts fail (and, he suggests, typically only seem as plausible as they do because of their vagueness and lack of clarity).

First, there are "half-hearted" responses which, Mackie says, really fail to address the problem. Then there are four more serious responses: (1) good cannot exist without evil; (2) evil is necessary as a means to good; (3) the universe is better with some evil in

A Common Misconception

Mackie is not arguing that God does not exist: he is arguing that nothing like the *theistic conception* of

God can exist. That is, although some sort of God—perhaps an extremely powerful but somehow limited being, like say the classical Greek god Zeus—can escape the problem of evil, the sort of God envisaged by the main monotheistic religions such as Christianity, Judaism, and Islam cannot possibly be real. For many if not most of the people who believe in God, this is not a trivial conclusion: if it is a sound argument, the problem of evil shows that God, if he exists at all, must be either limited in his power, or limited in his knowledge, or not entirely morally good.

Suggestions for Critical Reflection

1. Why do responses like "Evil is something to be faced and overcome, not to be merely discussed" or "God works in mysterious ways, but I have faith" fail to deal rationally with the problem of evil (if they do)?

2. What do you think goodness is? Do you think evil is merely the absence of goodness (or *vice versa*) or, can something be neither good nor evil (nor both)?

3. Is the universe better with some evil in it than it would be without any? (For example, do you think a life of successful struggle against adversity is more valuable than one of uninterrupted pleasure? If so, why?) What do you make of Mackie's arguments against this claim?

4. Could *all* evil be due to human free will? If even some of it is, should God have given us free will (if he did)? Is it coherent to think that God could have made us so that we have free will but nevertheless always choose some particular option (the best one) on every occasion?

5. Do you agree that the notion of omnipotence must have *some* limits? For example, could God have made the number two smaller than the number one, or created things that are neither rocks nor non-rocks, or made violent rape a moral duty? If even an "omnipotent" deity must be restricted in these ways, how serious a problem is this for the traditional picture of God? How much does Mackie's "paradox of omnipotence" add to these worries?

Suggestions for Further Reading

Mackie's main book on philosophy of religion is *The Miracle of Theism* (1982), where he considers and rejects the main arguments for the existence of God. His two best-known books in other areas of philosophy are *The Cement of the Universe* (Oxford University Press, 1974), which is about causation, and *Ethics: Inventing Right and Wrong* (Penguin, 1977), which develops his "error theory" of morality.

There are several recent books on the problem of evil, including Michael Peterson, *God and Evil: An Introduction to the Issues* (Westview Press, 1998), Alvin Plantinga *God, Freedom and Evil* (William B. Eerdmans, 1978), and Richard Swinburne, *Providence and the Problem of Evil* (Oxford University Press, 1998). Three useful collections of readings are Mark Larrimore (ed.), *The Problem of Evil: A Reader* (Blackwell, 2000), M.M. Adams and R.M. Adams (eds.), *The Problem of Evil* (Oxford University Press, 1990), and Michael Petersen (ed.), *The Problem of Evil: Selected Readings* (University of Notre Dame Press, 1992).

"Evil and Omnipotence"[1]

The traditional arguments for the existence of God have been fairly thoroughly criticised by philosophers. But the theologian can, if he wishes, accept this criticism. He can admit that no rational proof of God's existence is possible. And he can still retain all that is essential to his position, by holding that God's existence is known in some other, non-rational way. I think, however, that a more telling criticism can be made by way of the traditional problem of evil. Here it can be shown, not that religious beliefs lack rational support, but that they are positively irrational, that the several parts of the essential theological doctrine are inconsistent with one another, so that the theologian can maintain his position as a whole only by a much more extreme rejection of reason than in the former

---

1 This article was originally published in 1955 in the journal *Mind* (New Series, Vol. 64, Issue 254, April 1955, pp. 200–212). By permission of Oxford University Press.

case. He must now be prepared to believe, not merely what cannot be proved, but what can be *disproved* from other beliefs that he also holds.

The problem of evil, in the sense in which I shall be using the phrase, is a problem only for someone who believes that there is a God who is both omnipotent[2] and wholly good. And it is a logical problem, the problem of clarifying and reconciling a number of beliefs: it is not a scientific problem that might be solved by further observations, or a practical problem that might be solved by a decision or an action. These points are obvious; I mention them only because they are sometimes ignored by theologians, who sometimes parry a statement of the problem with such remarks as "Well, can you solve the problem yourself?" or "This is a mystery which may be revealed to us later," or "Evil is something to be faced and overcome, not to be merely discussed."

In its simplest form the problem is this: God is omnipotent; God is wholly good; and yet evil exists. There seems to be some contradiction between these three propositions, so that if any two of them were true the third would be false. But at the same time all three are essential parts of most theological positions: the theologian, it seems, at once *must* adhere and *cannot consistently* adhere to all three. (The problem does not arise only for theists,[3] but I shall discuss it in the form in which it presents itself for ordinary theism.)

However, the contradiction does not arise immediately; to show it we need some additional premises, or perhaps some quasi-logical rules connecting the terms 'good', 'evil', and 'omnipotent'. These additional principles are that good is opposed to evil, in such a way that a good thing always eliminates evil as far as it can, and that there are no limits to what an omnipotent thing can do. From these it follows that a good omnipotent thing eliminates evil completely,

and then the propositions that a good omnipotent thing exists, and that evil exists, are incompatible.

A. Adequate Solutions

Now once the problem is fully stated it is clear that it can be solved, in the sense that the problem will not arise if one gives up at least one of the propositions that constitute it. If you are prepared to say that God is not wholly good, or not quite omnipotent, or that evil does not exist, or that good is not opposed to the kind of evil that exists, or that there are limits to what an omnipotent thing can do, then the problem of evil will not arise for you.

There are, then, quite a number of adequate solutions of the problem of evil, and some of these have been adopted, or almost adopted, by various thinkers. For example, a few have been prepared to deny God's omnipotence, and rather more have been prepared to keep the term 'omnipotence' but severely to restrict its meaning, recording quite a number of things that an omnipotent being cannot do. Some have said that evil is an illusion, perhaps because they held that the whole world of temporal, changing things is an illusion, and that what we call evil belongs only to this world, or perhaps because they held that although temporal things are much as we see them, those that we call evil are not really evil. Some have said that what we call evil is merely the privation of good, that evil in a positive sense, evil that would really be opposed to good, does not exist. Many have agreed with Pope[4] that disorder is harmony not understood, and that partial evil is universal good. Whether any of these views is true is, of course, another question. But each of them gives an adequate solution of the problem of evil in the sense that if you accept it this problem does not arise for you, though you may, of course, have *other* problems to face.

---

2   "Omnipotent" means all-powerful; able to do anything at all. (Or at least anything that is not logically incoherent: God could make pigs fly, but even God, perhaps, could not make a male vixen or create a leaf that is—at the same time—both entirely green and not entirely green. This issue is discussed later in the article.)

3   For those who believe in one, powerful, benevolent God who created and watches over the universe.

4   Alexander Pope (1688–1744), an English writer best known for his mock-epic poems such as *The Rape of the Lock*. This quotation comes from Pope's *Essay on Man*, Epistle I: "All nature is but art, unknown to thee; All chance, direction, which thou canst not see; All discord, harmony, not understood; All partial evil, universal good: And, spite of pride, in erring reason's spite, One truth is clear, Whatever is, is right."

But often enough these adequate solutions are only *almost* adopted. The thinkers who restrict God's power, but keep the term 'omnipotence', may reasonably be suspected of thinking, in other contexts, that his power is really unlimited. Those who say that evil is an illusion may also be thinking, inconsistently, that this illusion is itself an evil. Those who say that "evil" is merely privation of good may also be thinking, inconsistently, that privation of good is an evil. (The fallacy here is akin to some forms of the "naturalistic fallacy" in ethics,[5] where some think, for example, that "good" is just what contributes to evolutionary progress, and that evolutionary progress is itself good.) If Pope meant what he said in the first line of his couplet, that "disorder" is only harmony not understood, the "partial evil" of the second line must, for consistency, mean "that which, taken in isolation, falsely appears to be evil", but it would more naturally mean "that which, in isolation, really is evil". The second line, in fact, hesitates between two views, that "partial evil" isn't really evil, since only the universal quality is real, and that "partial evil" is really an evil, but only a little one.

In addition, therefore, to adequate solutions, we must recognise unsatisfactory inconsistent solutions, in which there is only a half-hearted or temporary rejection of one of the propositions which together constitute the problem. In these, one of the constituent propositions is explicitly rejected, but it is covertly re-asserted or assumed elsewhere in the system.

B. Fallacious Solutions

Besides these half-hearted solutions, which explicitly reject but implicitly assert one of the constituent propositions, there are definitely fallacious solutions which explicitly maintain all the constituent propositions, but implicitly reject at least one of them in the course of the argument that explains away the problem of evil.

There are, in fact, many so-called solutions which purport to remove the contradiction without abandoning any of its constituent propositions. These must

---

5   This is the alleged fallacy of identifying an ethical concept with a "natural" (i.e., non-moral) notion, such as analyzing moral goodness as evolutionary fitness or the sensation of pleasure.

be fallacious, as we can see from the very statement of the problem, but it is not so easy to see in each case precisely where the fallacy lies. I suggest that in all cases the fallacy has the general form suggested above: in order to solve the problem one (or perhaps more) of its constituent propositions is given up, but in such a way that it appears to have been retained, and can therefore be asserted without qualification in other contexts. Sometimes there is a further complication: the supposed solution moves to and fro between, say, two of the constituent propositions, at one point asserting the first of these but covertly abandoning the second, at another point asserting the second but covertly abandoning the first. These fallacious solutions often turn upon some equivocation with the words 'good' and 'evil', or upon some vagueness about the way in which good and evil are opposed to one another, or about how much is meant by 'omnipotence'. I propose to examine some of these so-called solutions, and to exhibit their fallacies in detail. Incidentally, I shall also be considering whether an adequate solution could be reached by a minor modification of one or more of the constituent propositions, which would, however, still satisfy all the essential requirements of ordinary theism.

1. "Good cannot exist without evil" or "Evil is necessary as a counterpart to good."

It is sometimes suggested that evil is necessary as a counterpart to good, that if there were no evil there could be no good either, and that this solves the problem of evil. It is true that it points to an answer to the question "Why should there be evil?" But it does so only by qualifying some of the propositions that constitute the problem.

First, it sets a limit to what God can do, saying that God cannot create good without simultaneously creating evil, and this means either that God is not omnipotent or that there are some limits to what an omnipotent thing can do. It may be replied that these limits are always presupposed, that omnipotence has never meant the power to do what is logically impossible, and on the present view the existence of good without evil would be a logical impossibility. This interpretation of omnipotence may, indeed, be accepted as a modification of our original account which does not reject anything that is essential to theism, and I shall in general assume it in the subsequent discussion. It is, perhaps, the most common theistic view, but I think that some theists at least have maintained that God can do what is logically impossible. Many theists, at any rate, have held that logic itself is created or laid down by God, that logic is the way in which God arbitrarily chooses to think. (This is, of course, parallel to the ethical view that morally right actions are those which God arbitrarily chooses to command, and the two views encounter similar difficulties.[6]) And *this* account of logic is clearly inconsistent with the view that God is bound by logical necessities—unless it is possible for an omnipotent being to bind himself, an issue which we shall consider later, when we come to the Paradox of Omnipotence. This solution of the problem of evil cannot, therefore, be consistently adopted along with the view that logic is itself created by God.

But, secondly, this solution denies that evil is opposed to good in our original sense. If good and evil are counterparts, a good thing will not "eliminate evil as far as it can." Indeed, this view suggests that good and evil are not strictly qualities of things at all. Perhaps the suggestion is that good and evil are related in much the same way as great and small. Certainly, when the term 'great' is used relatively as a condensation of 'greater than so-and-so', and 'small' is used correspondingly, greatness and smallness are counterparts and cannot exist without each other. But in this sense greatness is not a quality, not an intrinsic feature of anything; and it would be absurd to think of a movement in favour of greatness and against smallness in this sense. Such a movement would be self-defeating, since relative greatness can be promoted only by a simultaneous promotion of relative smallness. I feel sure that no theists would be content to regard God's goodness as analogous to this—as if what he supports were not the *good* but the *better*, and as if he had the paradoxical aim that all things should be better than other things.

This point is obscured by the fact that 'great' and 'small' seem to have an absolute as well as a relative

sense. I cannot discuss here whether there is absolute magnitude or not, but if there is, there could be an absolute sense for 'great', it could mean of at least a certain size, and it would make sense to speak of all things getting bigger, of a universe that was expanding all over, and therefore it would make sense to speak of promoting greatness. But in *this* sense great and small are not logically necessary counterparts: either quality could exist without the other. There would be no logical impossibility in everything's being small or in everything's being great.

Neither in the absolute nor in the relative sense, then, of 'great' and 'small' do these terms provide an analogy of the sort that would be needed to support this solution of the problem of evil. In neither case are greatness and smallness both necessary counterparts and mutually opposed forces or possible objects for support and attack.

It may be replied that good and evil are necessary counterparts in the same way as any quality and its logical opposite: redness can occur, it is suggested, only if non-redness also occurs. But unless evil is merely the privation of good, they are not logical opposites, and some further argument would be needed to show that they are counterparts in the same way as genuine logical opposites. Let us assume that this could be given. There is still doubt of the correctness of the metaphysical principle that a quality must have a real opposite: I suggest that it is not really impossible that everything should be, say, red, that the truth is merely that if everything were red we should not notice redness, and so we should have no word 'red'; we observe and give names to qualities only if they have real opposites. If so, the principle that a term must have an opposite would belong only to our language or to our thought, and would not be an ontological principle,[7] and, correspondingly, the rule that good cannot exist without evil would not state a logical necessity of a sort that God would just have to put up with. God might have made everything good, though we should not have noticed it if he had.

But, finally, even if we concede that this is an ontological principle, it will provide a solution for the problem of evil only if one is prepared to say,

---

6   This ethical view is often called Divine Command Theory, and the usual label for its main problem is "the Euthyphro Dilemma" (from a dialogue by Plato in which the problem is first raised).

7   That is, not a principle constraining what exists.

"Evil exists, but only just enough evil to serve as the counterpart of good." I doubt whether any theist will accept this. After all, the *ontological* requirement that non-redness should occur would be satisfied even if all the universe, except for a minute speck, were red, and, if there were a corresponding requirement for evil as a counterpart to good, a minute dose of evil would presumably do. But theists are not usually willing to say, in all contexts, that all the evil that occurs is a minute and necessary dose.

2. "Evil is necessary as a means to good."

It is sometimes suggested that evil is necessary for good not as a counterpart but as a means. In its simple form this has little plausibility as a solution of the problem of evil, since it obviously implies a severe restriction of God's power. It would be a causal law that you cannot have a certain end without a certain means, so that if God has to introduce evil as a means to good, he must be subject to at least some causal laws. This certainly conflicts with what a theist normally means by omnipotence. This view of God as limited by causal laws also conflicts with the view that causal laws are themselves made by God, which is more widely held than the corresponding view about the laws of logic. This conflict would, indeed; be resolved if it were possible for an omnipotent being to bind himself, and this possibility has still to be considered. Unless a favourable answer can be given to this question, the suggestion that evil is necessary as a means to good solves the problem of evil only by denying one of its constituent propositions, either that God is omnipotent or that 'omnipotent' means what it says.

3. "The universe is better with some evil in it than it could be if there were no evil."

Much more important is a solution which at first seems to be a mere variant of the previous one, that evil may contribute to the goodness of a whole in which it is found, so that the universe as a whole is better as it is, with some evil in it, than it would be if there were no evil. This solution may be developed in either of two ways. It may be supported by an aesthetic analogy, by the fact that contrasts heighten beauty, that in a musical work, for example, there may occur discords which somehow add to the beauty of the work as a whole. Alternatively, it may be worked out in connexion with the notion of progress, that the best possible organisation of the universe will not be static, but progressive, that the gradual overcoming of evil by good is really a finer thing than would be the eternal unchallenged supremacy of good.

In either case, this solution usually starts from the assumption that the evil whose existence gives rise to the problem of evil is primarily what is called physical evil, that is to say, pain. In Hume's rather half-hearted presentation of the problem of evil, the evils that he stresses are pain and disease, and those who reply to him argue that the existence of pain and disease makes possible the existence of sympathy, benevolence, heroism, and the gradually successful struggle of doctors and reformers to overcome these evils. In fact, theists often seize the opportunity to accuse those who stress the problem of evil of taking a low, materialistic view of good and evil, equating these with pleasure and pain, and of ignoring the more spiritual goods which can arise in the struggle against evils.

But let us see exactly what is being done here. Let us call pain and misery 'first order evil' or 'evil (1)'. What contrasts with this, namely, pleasure and happiness, will be called 'first order good' or 'good (1)'. Distinct from this is 'second order good' or 'good (2)' which somehow emerges in a complex situation in which evil (1) is a necessary component—logically, not merely causally, necessary. (Exactly *how* it emerges does not matter: in the crudest version of this solution good (2) is simply the heightening of happiness by the contrast with misery, in other versions it includes sympathy with suffering, heroism in facing danger, and the gradual decrease of first order evil and increase of first order good.) It is also being assumed that second order good is more important than first order good or evil, in particular that it more than outweighs the first order evil it involves.

Now this is a particularly subtle attempt to solve the problem of evil. It defends God's goodness and omnipotence on the ground that (on a sufficiently long view) this is the best of all logically possible worlds, because it includes the important second order goods, and yet it admits that real evils, namely first order evils, exist. But does it still hold that good and evil are opposed? Not, clearly, in the sense that we set out originally: good does not tend to eliminate evil in general. Instead, we have a modified, a more complex pattern. First order good (e.g., happiness) *contrasts with* first order evil (e.g., misery): these two are opposed in a fairly mechanical way; some second order goods (e.g., benevolence) try to maximise first order good and minimise first order evil; but God's goodness is not this, it is rather the will to maximise *second* order good. We might, therefore, call God's goodness an example of a third order goodness, or good (3). While this account is different from our original one, it might well be held to be an improvement on it, to give a more accurate description of the way in which good is opposed to evil, and to be consistent with the essential theist position.

There might, however, be several objections to this solution. First, some might argue that such qualities as benevolence—and *a fortiori*[8] the third order goodness which promotes benevolence—have a merely derivative value, that they are not higher sorts of good, but merely means to good (1), that is, to happiness, so that it would be absurd for God to keep misery in existence in order to make possible the virtues of benevolence, heroism, etc. The theist who adopts the present solution must, of course, deny this, but he can do so with some plausibility, so I should not press this objection.

Secondly, it follows from this solution that God is not in our sense benevolent or sympathetic: he is not concerned to minimise evil (1), but only to promote good (2); and this might be a disturbing conclusion for some theists.

But, thirdly, the fatal objection is this. Our analysis shows clearly the possibility of the existence of a *second* order evil, an evil (2) contrasting with good (2) as evil (1) contrasts with good (1). This would include malevolence, cruelty, callousness, cowardice, and states in which good (1) is decreasing and evil (1) increasing. And just as good (2) is held to be the important kind of good, the kind that God is concerned to promote, so evil (2) will, by analogy, be the important kind of evil, the kind which God, if he were wholly good and omnipotent, would eliminate. And yet evil (2) plainly exists, and indeed most theists (in other contexts) stress its existence more than that of evil

(1). We should, therefore, state the problem of evil in terms of second order evil, and against this form of the problem the present solution is useless.

An attempt might be made to use this solution again, at a higher level, to explain the occurrence of evil (2): indeed the next main solution that we shall examine does just this, with the help of some new notions. Without any fresh notions, such a solution would have little plausibility: for example, we could hardly say that the really important good was a good (3), such as the increase of benevolence in proportion to cruelty, which logically required for its occurrence the occurrence of some second order evil. But even if evil (2) could be explained in this way, it is fairly clear that there would be third order evils contrasting with this third order good: and we should be well on the way to an infinite regress, where the solution of a problem of evil, stated in terms of evil (n), indicated the existence of an evil (n + 1), and a further problem to be solved.

4. "Evil is due to human freewill."

Perhaps the most important proposed solution of the problem of evil is that evil is not to be ascribed to God at all, but to the independent actions of human beings, supposed to have been endowed by God with freedom of the will. This solution may be combined with the preceding one: first order evil (e.g., pain) may be justified as a logically necessary component in second order good (e.g., sympathy) while second order evil (e.g., cruelty) is not *justified*, but is so ascribed to human beings that God cannot be held responsible for it. This combination evades my third criticism of the preceding solution.

The freewill solution also involves the preceding solution at a higher level. To explain why a wholly good God gave men freewill although it would lead to some important evils, it must be argued that it is better on the whole that men should act freely, and sometimes err, than that they should be innocent automata, acting rightly in a wholly determined way. Freedom, that is to say, is now treated as a third order good, and as being more valuable than second order goods (such as sympathy and heroism) would be if they were deterministically produced, and it is being assumed that second order evils, such as cruelty, are logically necessary accompaniments of freedom,

---

8   All the more, for an even stronger reason.

just as pain is a logically necessary pre-condition of sympathy.

I think that this solution is unsatisfactory primarily because of the incoherence of the notion of freedom of the will: but I cannot discuss this topic adequately here, although some of my criticisms will touch upon it.

First I should query the assumption that second order evils are logically necessary accompaniments of freedom. I should ask this: if God has made men such that in their free choices they sometimes prefer what is good and sometimes what is evil, why could he not have made men such that they always freely choose the good? If there is no logical impossibility in a man's freely choosing the good on one, or on several, occasions, there cannot be a logical impossibility in his freely choosing the good on every occasion. God was not, then, faced with a choice between making innocent automata and making beings who, in acting freely, would sometimes go wrong: there was open to him the obviously better possibility of making beings who would act freely but always go right. Clearly, his failure to avail himself of this possibility is inconsistent with his being both omnipotent and wholly good.

If it is replied that this objection is absurd, that the making of some wrong choices is logically necessary for freedom, it would seem that 'freedom' must here mean complete randomness or indeterminacy, including randomness with regard to the alternatives good and evil, in other words that men's choices and consequent actions can be "free" only if they are not determined by their characters. Only on this assumption can God escape the responsibility for men's actions; for if he made them as they are, but did not determine their wrong choices, this can only be because the wrong choices are not determined by men as they are. But then if freedom is randomness, how can it be a characteristic of *will*? And, still more, how can it be the most important good? What value or merit would there be in free choices if these were random actions which were not determined by the nature of the agent?

I conclude that to make this solution plausible two different senses of 'freedom' must be confused, one sense which will justify the view that freedom is a third order good, more valuable than other goods

would be without it, and another sense, sheer randomness, to prevent us from ascribing to God a decision to make men such that they sometimes go wrong when he might have made them such that they would always freely go right.

This criticism is sufficient to dispose of this solution. But besides this there is a fundamental difficulty in the notion of an omnipotent God creating men with free will, for if men's wills are really free this must mean that even God cannot control them, that is, that God is no longer omnipotent. It may be objected that God's gift of freedom to men does not mean that he cannot control their wills, but that he always *refrains* from controlling their wills. But why, we may ask, should God refrain from controlling evil wills? Why should he not leave men free to will rightly, but intervene when he sees them beginning to will wrongly? If God could do this, but does not, and if he is wholly good, the only explanation could be that even a wrong free act of will is not really evil, that its freedom is a value which outweighs its wrongness, so that there would be a loss of value if God took away the wrongness and the freedom together. But this is utterly opposed to what theists say about sin in other contexts. The present solution of the problem of evil, then, can be maintained only in the form that God has made men so free that he *cannot* control their wills.

This leads us to what I call the Paradox of Omnipotence: can an omnipotent being make things which he cannot subsequently control? Or, what is practically equivalent to this, can an omnipotent being make rules which then bind himself? (These are practically equivalent because any such rules could be regarded as setting certain things beyond his control, and *vice versa*.) The second of these formulations is relevant to the suggestions that we have already met, that an omnipotent God creates the rules of logic or causal laws, and is then bound by them.

It is clear that this is a paradox: the questions cannot be answered satisfactorily either in the affirmative or in the negative. If we answer "Yes", it follows that if God actually makes things which he cannot control, or makes rules which bind himself, he is not omnipotent once he has made them: there are *then* things which he cannot do. But if we answer "No", we are immediately asserting that there are things which he cannot do, that is to say that he is already not omnipotent.

It cannot be replied that the question which sets this paradox is not a proper question. It would make perfectly good sense to say that a human mechanic has made a machine which he cannot control: if there is any difficulty about the question it lies in the notion of omnipotence itself.

This, incidentally, shows that although we have approached this paradox from the free will theory, it is equally a problem for a theological determinist. No one thinks that machines have free will, yet they may well be beyond the control of their makers. The determinist might reply that anyone who makes anything determines its ways of acting, and so determines its subsequent behaviour: even the human mechanic does this by his *choice* of materials and structure for his machine, though he does not know all about either of these: the mechanic thus determines, though he may not foresee, his machine's actions. And since God is omniscient, and since his creation of things is total, he both determines and foresees the ways in which his creatures will act. We may grant this, but it is beside the point. The question is not whether God *originally* determined the future actions of his creatures, but whether he can *subsequently* control their actions, or whether he was able in his original creation to put things beyond his subsequent control. Even on determinist principles the answers "Yes" and "No" are equally irreconcilable with God's omnipotence.

Before suggesting a solution of this paradox, I would point out that there is a parallel Paradox of Sovereignty. Can a legal sovereign[9] make a law restricting its own future legislative power? For example, could the British parliament make a law forbidding any future parliament to socialise banking, and also forbidding the future repeal of this law itself? Or could the British parliament, which was legally sovereign in Australia in, say, 1899, pass a valid law, or series of laws, which made it no longer sovereign in 1933? Again, neither the affirmative nor the negative answer is really satisfactory. If we were to answer "Yes", we

should be admitting the validity of a law which, if it were actually made, would mean that parliament was, no longer sovereign. If we were to answer "No", we should be admitting that there is a law, not logically absurd, which parliament cannot validly make, that is, that parliament is not now a legal sovereign. This paradox can be solved in the following way. We should distinguish between first order laws, that is laws governing the actions of individuals and bodies other than the legislature, and second order laws, that is laws about laws, laws governing the actions of the legislature itself. Correspondingly, we should distinguish two orders of sovereignty, first order sovereignty (sovereignty (1)) which is unlimited authority to make first order laws, and second order sovereignty (sovereignty (2)) which is unlimited authority to make second order laws. If we say that parliament is sovereign we might mean that any parliament at any time has sovereignty (1), or we might mean that parliament has both sovereignty (1) and sovereignty (2) at present, but we cannot without contradiction mean both that the present parliament has sovereignty (2) and that every parliament at every time has sovereignty (1), for if the present parliament has sovereignty (2) it may use it to take away the sovereignty (1) of later parliaments. What the paradox shows is that we cannot ascribe to any continuing institution legal sovereignty in an inclusive sense.

The analogy between omnipotence and sovereignty shows that the paradox of omnipotence can be solved in a similar way. We must distinguish between first order omnipotence (omnipotence (1)), that is unlimited power to act, and second order omnipotence (omnipotence (2)), that is unlimited power to determine what powers to act things shall have. Then we could consistently say that God all the time has omnipotence (1), but if so no beings at any time have powers to act independently of God. Or we could say that God at one time had omnipotence (2), and used it to assign independent powers to act to certain things, so that God thereafter did not have omnipotence (1). But what the paradox shows is that we cannot consistently ascribe to any continuing being omnipotence in an inclusive sense.

An alternative solution of this paradox would be simply to deny that God is a continuing being, that any

---

9   To be sovereign is to exercise supreme, permanent authority.

times can be assigned to his actions at all. But on this assumption (which also has difficulties of its own) no meaning can be given to the assertion that God made men with wills so free that he could not control them. The paradox of omnipotence can be avoided by putting God outside time, but the freewill solution of the problem of evil cannot be saved in this way, and equally it remains impossible to hold that an omnipotent God *binds himself* by causal or logical laws.

Conclusion

Of the proposed solutions of the problem of evil which we have examined, none has stood up to criticism.

There may be other solutions which require examination, but this study strongly suggests that there is no valid solution of the problem which does not modify at least one of the constituent propositions in a way which would seriously affect the essential core of the theistic position.

Quite apart from the problem of evil, the paradox of omnipotence has shown that God's omnipotence must in any case be restricted in one way or another, that unqualified omnipotence cannot be ascribed to any being that continues through time. And if God and his actions are not in time, can omnipotence, or power of any sort, be meaningfully ascribed to him?

WILLIAM JAMES
"The Will to Believe"

Who Was William James?

William James was a popular essayist, one of the philosophical originators of pragmatism (often considered the first uniquely American philosophy), and one of the founders of academic psychology in America. He was born in 1842 in a New York hotel room. His family lived on a substantial inheritance from William's paternal grandfather (after whom he was named), and his father spent his time in the independent study of theology. Shortly after the birth of William's brother Henry—who was to become a famous writer, author of *The Portrait of a Lady* and *The Bostonians*—the family moved to Europe, living in London, Paris, and Windsor. There, while William was still a young boy, his father had a violent nervous breakdown and found solace in religious mysticism and the "theosophy" of Emanuel Swedenborg.[1] The family sailed back to New

York in 1847, only to return to Europe seven years later in search of a good education for the children: William was educated at a multilingual boarding school near Geneva, the Collège Impérial at Boulogne, and finally the University of Geneva.

As a young man, James was interested in science and painting. Back in Newport, Rhode Island, he embarked on a career as a painter, but quickly switched to the study of chemistry at Harvard in 1861. By then James had already begun his life-long habit of ingesting various, often hallucinogenic, chemicals (such as chloral hydrate, amyl nitrate, or mescaline) out of a scientific interest to see what effect they might have on him. After helping to care for his younger brother Wilky, badly wounded during the Civil War (during and after which the James family made attempts to help the black slaves of the

---

1 Swedenborg (1688–1772) was a Swedish scientist who came to believe that, by a special dispensation from God, his mind had been opened to "the other world" so that he could gain knowledge of it and its spiritual

inhabitants, and use this knowledge in a special interpretation of Christian scripture. He was an important influence on the artists William Blake and W.B. Yeats, as well as on the James family.

South), James entered Harvard Medical School in 1864. He took part in a scientific expedition to Brazil the following year, but was badly seasick on the trip out and suffered temporary blindness from catching a mild form of smallpox in Rio de Janeiro (he suffered from intermittent trouble with his eyes for the rest of his life). Though he decided at that point that he was "cut out for a speculative rather than an active life," he stayed with the expedition as it sailed up the Amazon. Back in Massachusetts, he continued to suffer from ill health and depression, and contemplated suicide.

He spent the period between 1867 and 1868 studying experimental psychology in Germany, and returned to Harvard to take and pass his examination for an MD but then sank into black depression, including bouts of insomnia and nervousness. He resolved never to marry for fear of passing mental illness on to his children. One of the causes of his depression in these years was his inability either to convince himself that modern science had not proved that free will was an illusion, or to resign himself to living in a deterministic, mechanical universe. Famously, in 1870, he apparently decided to shake off this particular worry and simply to decide to believe in free will *despite* all the evidence against it: he wrote in his diary, "my first act of free will shall be to believe in free will." Nevertheless, in 1872 James had a "crisis" which probably resembled that which changed his father's life 28 years earlier: "Suddenly there fell upon me without any warning, just as if it came out of the darkness, a horrible fear of my own existence.... I became a mass of quivering fear. After this the universe was changed for me altogether...."

Probably a psychological lifeline for James at this point was the offer in 1873 to teach compara-

tive anatomy and physiology at Harvard (though he hesitated over accepting it, and delayed taking up the appointment for a year due to ill health). By 1877 James was a permanent professor of physiology at Harvard, though he lectured less on physiology than on the relatively new subject of psychology under the auspices of the philosophy department. In 1878 he married Alice Gibbens; "I have found in marriage a calm and repose I never knew before." His first son, Harry, was born the following year.

In 1889 he became the first Alford Professor of Psychology at Harvard University, and the next year he finally completed his first major work, *The Principles of Psychology* (he had signed the book contract in 1878). This book, a modern-day classic, met with instant acclaim. In 1897 he published *The Will to Believe, and Other Essays in Popular Psychology* and the next year, *Human Immortality: Two Supposed Objections to the Doctrine*, then, in 1899, one of his most popular books during his own lifetime *Talks to Teachers on Psychology, and to Students on Some of Life's Ideals*. The 1902 publication of *The Varieties of Religious Experience* met with international praise and sales that substantially boosted James's income.

Throughout his life James's work was dogged by persistent health problems and nervous exhaustion, and in 1903 he tried to resign from Harvard but was persuaded to stay with a reduced teaching load. In 1906 James took a temporary appointment at Stanford University in California, but it was cut short by the great San Francisco earthquake of that year (which James witnessed, and apparently found quite exhilarating). In 1907 he finally retired from Harvard and published *Pragmatism: A New Name for Some Old Ways of Thinking*; this is arguably the most famous single work of American philosophy. That book was followed by *A Pluralistic Universe*, *The Meaning of Truth*, and the posthumous *Some Problems in Philosophy*, all of which try to develop and defend James's overall philosophical framework. James died of a chronic heart condition at his farmhouse in New Hampshire in 1910.

What Was James's Overall Philosophical Project?

James's philosophical work, including "The Will to Believe" and his other essays on religious belief, are rooted in a general metaphysical framework which James came to call "radical empiricism." Radical empiricism has three central elements, each of which has far-reaching philosophical implications.

First, there is James's emphasis on careful attention to what is "directly experienced." He thought philosophers and psychologists had generally failed to look carefully enough at what is actually delivered in experience, and to counteract this he defended what is called "the introspective method" in psychology—essentially, learning to pay close attention to the contents of one's own thought. James argued, as early as *The Principles of Psychology*, that philosophers have tended to read too much into what we experience: for example, he argued (like Hume) that there is no soul or ego or spiritual medium of thought to be seen if we actually look inside ourselves for such a thing. On the other hand, according to James, philosophers (such as Hume) have failed to notice that there is *more* to our experience than is traditionally assumed. We do not simply undergo discrete, repeatable lumps of experience, but experience a continuous stream of thought which includes transitions and relations between the more stable 'substantive' ideas; thus "we ought to say a feeling of *and*, a feeling of *if*, a feeling of *but*, and a feeling of *by*, quite as readily as we say a feeling of *blue* or a feeling of *cold*" (from *Essays in Psychology*).

Second, James rejected the traditional duality of mind and matter. Instead he postulated "a world of pure experience." Ultimately, according to James, the universe is made up not of some kind of 'stuff' but of a huge set of 'pure experiences.' Some of these experiences make up our streams of individual consciousness and, of those, some are taken by us (on the basis of their relations with other experiences) to be 'mental' and some 'physical.'

Third, James felt that he was able, on the basis of this picture of the nature of the universe, to solve the vexing problem of the *meaning of thought* (which philosophers today call "the problem of intentionality"). The problem is this: what is it about your thoughts, your sensations, or your words that makes them *about* some particular object in the external world? What is it, for example, about the word or the thought "cow" that connects it to a certain species of large, smelly mammal? According to James, the answer is relatively simple: your sensation of the cow just is the cow. The succession of pure experiences that makes up the cow, and the sequence of pure experiences that is your stream of consciousness (which is *you*) simply intersect, just as two lines can cross at a point; at that intersection is an experience that is simultaneously both thought and object of thought, mental and non-mental, you and the cow.

Our *idea* of a cow, then, is certainly *about* cows, but that 'aboutness' can now be understood in terms of the prospects for future intersections between, if you like, cow sequences and our personal autobiography. Roughly, for James, the meaning of an idea—including religious and moral ideas like *God* and *free will*—is its "cash-value" in terms of future experience. Importantly, this includes not only predictions about sensations that we might expect lie in store for us, but also the effects such an idea will have on our future behavior; how it will change *us*, and thus affect our future experience. This is the core doctrine of what James called "Pragmatism." "To attain perfect clearness in our thoughts of an object, then, we need only consider what conceivable effects of a practical kind the object may involve—what sensations we are to expect from it, and what reactions we must prepare" (*Pragmatism*).

Finally, once we know how ideas get their meaning, we can ask what it is for an idea to be *true*. For James, the answer is its "workability." Given his radical empiricism and his pragmatism, truth can't possibly consist, for James, in a kind of correspondence or matching between an idea and some sort of external reality—James has rejected that whole way of talking. For an idea to be called 'true' is not for it to have some special property or value at the moment it occurs but instead it is for it to have particularly *beneficial* effects on our future conduct and our future experiences. An idea might turn out to be true because it is especially valuable for predicting scientific events (such as eclipses, for example), or its truth might lie in the way it is spiritually ennobling to all those who believe in it.

This, then, is a sketch of James's final world-view. This over-arching philosophical structure did not come to James all at once; it was shaped and re-shaped, piece by piece, over his lifetime. Its motivation, one of James's key intellectual driving forces, was the tension that he felt between science and religion: between the cold but intelligent detachment and determinism of his 'scientific conscience,' and his attachment to the ideals of free will, morality, and an interested God. "The Will to Believe" was one of James's earlier—and, at the time and ever since, highly popular—attempts to resolve this contradiction.

What Is the Structure of This Reading?

"The Will to Believe," James announces at the outset, is to be "an essay in justification of faith." He starts out by making three distinctions between types of "options" (living or dead, forced or avoidable, momentous or trivial) and suggests that his essay is to be about options that are living, forced, and momentous—what James calls "genuine options."

James begins his discussion of this kind of option—in the second section of the paper—by immediately considering the objection that it is in some way "preposterous" to say that we could or should simply *choose* what to believe. He responds that not only can we and do we believe things on the basis of "our non-intellectual nature," but furthermore that we must and should do so—that willingness to believe is (morally and intellectually) "lawful." He tries to tie this view to the rejection of what he calls "absolutism" in science and the endorsement of "empiricism," and to the quest to "believe truth" rather than merely "avoid error."

In Section VIII James begins to present his actual arguments for the claim that "there are some op-

tions between opinions in which [our passional nature] must be regarded both as an inevitable and as a lawful determinant of our choice." He does so partly by arguing that this must be true for what he earlier called *genuine* options, and he gives as examples moral questions, issues to do with personal relationships, and—at greater length—religious faith. One of his central claims in this section is that "a rule of thinking which would absolutely prevent me from acknowledging certain kinds of truth if those truths were really there, would be an irrational rule."

Some Background Information

1. James refers to a number of people in his essay that may no longer be familiar to modern audiences. Here is a run-down of the names James drops, in the order of their appearance:
   - Leslie Stephen (1832–1904): a British writer, editor, and biographer best known as the editor of the *Dictionary of National Biography* and as Virginia Woolf's father.
   - Fridtjof Nansen (1861–1930): a Norwegian explorer, zoologist, and politician who led an Arctic expedition from 1893 to 1896.
   - Blaise Pascal (1623–1662): a French mathematician, physicist and philosopher. James is referring to the book *Pensées*, published (posthumously) in 1670.
   - Arthur Hugh Clough (1819–1861): a British poet. The quote is from a poem sometimes known as "Steadfast."
   - Thomas Henry Huxley (1825–1895): a British biologist and writer, known for championing Darwin's theory of evolution. The quotation is from "The Influence Upon Morality of a Decline in Religious Belief."
   - William Kingdon Clifford (1845–1879): a British mathematician, philosopher, and well-known agnostic who died an early death from tuberculosis. James quotes extensively from his "The Ethics of Belief," published in *Contemporary Review* 29 (1877).
   - Arthur James Balfour (1848–1930): a philosopher who went on to be British Prime Minister from 1902 to 1905 and then Foreign Secretary

(1916–1919). James is thinking of his essay "Authority and Reason," published in 1895.

- John Henry Newman (1801–1891): an English theologian who converted to Roman Catholicism in 1845 and became a cardinal in 1879.
- Johann Zöllner (1834–1882): a German astrophysicist who researched psychic phenomena and defended the existence of a "fourth dimension."
- Charles Howard Hinton (1853–1907): an English mathematician who also, independently, postulated a "fourth dimension."
- Thomas Reid (1710–1796): a Scottish philosopher and opponent of the 'skepticism' of David Hume.
- Herbert Spencer (1820–1903): an English philosopher who tried to apply the scientific theory of evolution to philosophy and ethics. He coined the phrase "the survival of the fittest."
- August Wiesmann (1834–1914): a German biologist and one of the founders of modern genetics, who defended the view that hereditary characteristics are transmitted by a germinal plasm (and so ruled out the transmission of acquired characteristics).
- Charles Secrétan (1815–1895): A (rather obscure) late nineteenth-century Swiss philosopher.

2. James's position in "The Will to Believe" is often thought to be a good example of the philosophical position called fideism. This is the thesis that religious belief is based on faith and not on either evidence or reasoning. In other words, the fundamental claims of religion cannot be established by either science or reason but nevertheless (perhaps because we should not place reason ahead of God) they should be believed to be true. Fideism comes in various flavors. Perhaps the mildest version is the view, held by St. Augustine and Pascal, that faith has to come before reason: that is, only faith can persuade us that religious doctrines are true, but once we believe, we can use our intellect to come to better understand them and to see *why* they are true and rational. The most extreme version is typified in the writings of the nineteenth-century Danish philosopher Søren Kierkegaard. Kierkegaard went so far as to say that central tenets of Christianity—e.g., that God became incarnate in the person of Jesus Christ—are actually self-contradictory, and thus irrational, so belief in them requires a "leap into faith" which cannot in any way be justified.

Some Common Misconceptions

1. James is not anti-science: he does not want to eliminate the scientific attitude in favor of a religious one, but to show that science leaves open the possibility of religious faith and that it can do so without merely ignoring religion or granting it a special sphere insulated from normal rational inquiry.
2. James does not argue that we *must* be religious but only that, even though we are reasonable and scientifically educated people, we still *can* be religious. Religious belief is, for James, a personal choice.

Suggestions for Critical Reflection

1. The American judge Oliver Wendell Holmes, a close friend, once complained that James was inclined "to turn down the lights so as to give miracle a chance," shielding religious issues from the bright light of truth and careful, scientific inquiry. Do you agree with this criticism? How do you think James responded?
2. Do you think James's position in this essay is best understood as saying religious belief is in fact rational, or that religious belief is not rational but nevertheless 'lawful'?
3. James sometimes seems to talk as if we could and should believe things on the basis of our *will*, our decision to do so, and sometimes as if it's a matter of having some beliefs based on *emotion* ("our passional nature") rather than intellect. Do you think there's a conflict between these two ways of talking? If so, which do you think James really meant?
4. W.K. Clifford begins his essay "The Ethics of Belief" with an example of a ship owner who suppresses his own doubts about the seawor-

thiness of his vessel and "putting his trust in Providence" allows the ship to sail, carrying its load of immigrants to their death at sea. Clifford argues that, though the ship owner sincerely believes in the soundness of his ship, he has *"no right to believe on such evidence as was before him"* because he did not carry out a proper investigation of the facts. This example is used to support Clifford's central theme: that beliefs must be held responsibly, or ethically, on the basis of careful and conscientious investigation. Although James takes Clifford's essay as a foil to his own position in "The Will to Believe," he never mentions this important example. What do you think of the example? If you think that Clifford makes a good point, how does this affect your view of James's arguments? Is Clifford's example relevant to the case of religious belief, either for the individual or for society as a whole?

5. Some critics of "The Will to Believe" have complained that James seems to be imagining only cases where we have no evidence at all, either for or against a particular possibility, and simply ignoring the much more common case where we are in possession of some evidence and have to weigh the balance of probabilities. Do you agree that James does this, and if so, is it a mistake on his part?

6. Another common criticism of this essay is that the religious belief James defends is highly attenuated: no more than the belief that "perfection is eternal." Do you share this reaction? Is this all that James is defending, in the end? In what way, if so, is this a "momentous" choice?

7. If you have read the Mackie selection "Evil and Omnipotence" you might want to ask yourself how James could respond to Mackie's claim that belief in a Christian/Islamic/Judaic (etc.) God is internally inconsistent and hence that no reasonable person should hold such a belief. Can James and Mackie *both* be right? If not, which of them is (if either)?

Suggestions for Further Reading

The standard edition of William James's works is published (in seventeen volumes) by Harvard University Press. Central works include *The Will to Believe* (1979), *Pragmatism* (1975), *The Meaning of Truth* (1975), *Essays in Radical Empiricism* (1976), and *Varieties of Religious Experience* (1985). Biographies of James include the early standard by one of his friends, Ralph Barton Perry, *The Thought and Character of William James* (Little, Brown, 1935); a good more recent one is by Gerald E. Myers, *William James: His Life and Thought* (Yale University Press, 1986).

Other relevant books on James's philosophy include *William James* by Graham Bird (Routledge & Kegan Paul, 1986), *William James and Phenomenology* by James Edie (Indiana University Press, 1987), *William James's Philosophy* by Marcus Peter Ford (University of Massachusetts Press, 1982), *Metaphysics, Experience and Religion in William James's Thought* by David Lamberth (Cambridge University Press, 1999), *James's Will-to-Believe Doctrine: A Heretical View* by James Wernham (University of Toronto Press, 1987), and *The Radical Empiricism of William James* by John Wild (Doubleday, 1989).

There is a *Cambridge Companion to William James* edited by Ruth Anna Putnam (Cambridge University Press, 1997). Three useful articles are: Richard Gale, "William James and the Ethics of Belief," *American Philosophical Quarterly* 17 (1980), Van A. Harvey, "The Ethics of Belief Reconsidered," *Journal of Religion* 59 (1979), and Kauber and Hare, "The Right and Duty to Will to Believe," *Canadian Journal of Philosophy* 4 (1974).

"The Will to Believe"[2]

In the recently published *Life* by Leslie Stephen of his brother, Fitz-James, there is an account of a school to

---

2   This essay was an address to the Philosophical Clubs of Yale and Brown Universities, and was first published in the *New World*, June 1896. This reprint is based on the text in *The Will to Believe, and Other Essays in Popular Philosophy* published by Longmans, Green

which the latter went when he was a boy. The teacher, a certain Mr. Guest, used to converse with his pupils in this wise: "Gurney, what is the difference between justification and sanctification?—Stephen, prove the omnipotence of God!" etc. In the midst of our Harvard freethinking and indifference we are prone to imagine that here at your good old orthodox College conversation continues to be somewhat upon this order; and to show you that we at Harvard have not lost all interest in these vital subjects, I have brought with me to-night something like a sermon on justification by faith to read to you,—I mean an essay in justification *of* faith, a defence of our right to adopt a believing attitude in religious matters, in spite of the fact that our merely logical intellect may not have been coerced. "The Will to Believe," accordingly, is the title of my paper.

I have long defended to my own students the lawfulness of voluntarily adopted faith; but as soon as they have got well imbued with the logical spirit, they have as a rule refused to admit my contention to be lawful philosophically, even though in point of fact they were personally all the time chock-full of some faith or other themselves. I am all the while, however, so profoundly convinced that my own position is correct, that your invitation has seemed to me a good occasion to make my statements more clear. Perhaps your minds will be more open than those with which I have hitherto had to deal. I will be as little technical as I can, though I must begin by setting up some technical distinctions that will help us in the end.

I.

Let us give the name of *hypothesis* to anything that may be proposed to our belief; and just as the electricians speak of live and dead wires, let us speak of any hypothesis as either *live* or *dead*. A live hypothesis is one which appeals as a real possibility to him to whom it is proposed. If I ask you to believe in the Mahdi,[3] the notion makes no electric connection with your nature,—it refuses to scintillate with any credibility at all. As an hypothesis it is completely dead. To an

Arab, however (even if he be not one of the Mahdi's followers), the hypothesis is among the mind's possibilities: it is alive. This shows that deadness and liveness in an hypothesis are not intrinsic properties, but relations to the individual thinker. They are measured by his willingness to act. The maximum of liveness in an hypothesis, means willingness to act irrevocably. Practically, that means belief; but there is some believing tendency wherever there is willingness to act at all.

Next, let us call the decision between two hypotheses an *option*. Options may be of several kinds. They may be—1, *living* or *dead*; 2, *forced* or *avoidable*; 3, *momentous* or *trivial*; and for our purposes we may call an option a *genuine* option when it is of the forced, living, and momentous kind.

1.   A living option is one in which both hypotheses are live ones. If I say to you: "Be a theosophist[4] or be a Mohammedan,"[5] it is probably a dead option, because for you neither hypothesis is likely to be alive. But if I say: "Be an agnostic or be a Christian," it is otherwise: trained as you are, each hypothesis makes some appeal, however small, to your belief.

2.   Next, if I say to you: "Choose between going out with your umbrella or without it," I do not offer you a genuine option, for it is not forced. You can easily avoid it by not going out at all. Similarly, if I say, "Either love me or hate me," "Either call my theory true or call it false," your option is avoidable. You may remain indifferent to me, neither loving nor hating, and you may decline to offer any judgment as to my theory. But if I say, "Either accept this truth or go without it," I put on you a forced option, for there is no standing place outside of the alternative. Every dilemma based on a complete logical disjunction, with no possibility of not choosing, is an option of this forced kind.

& Co. in 1897.

3   In Islam, a messianic leader who, it is believed, will appear shortly before the end of the world to establish a reign of righteousness.

4   A member of a religious sect, the Theosophical Society, founded in New York in 1875, which incorporates aspects of Buddhism and Brahmanism.

5   A Muslim.

3. Finally, if I were Dr. Nansen and proposed to you to join my North Pole expedition, your option would be momentous; for this would probably be your only similar opportunity, and your choice now would either exclude you from the North Pole sort of immortality altogether or put at least the chance of it into your hands. He who refuses to embrace a unique opportunity loses the prize as surely as if he tried and failed. *Per contra*,[6] the option is trivial when the opportunity is not unique, when the stake is insignificant, or when the decision is reversible if it later prove unwise. Such trivial options abound in the scientific life. A chemist finds an hypothesis live enough to spend a year in its verification: he believes in it to that extent. But if his experiments prove inconclusive either way, he is quit for his loss of time,[7] no vital harm being done.

It will facilitate our discussion if we keep all these distinctions well in mind.

II.

The next matter to consider is the actual psychology of human opinion. When we look at certain facts, it seems as if our passional and volitional nature lay at the root of all our convictions. When we look at others, it seems as if they could do nothing when the intellect had once said its say. Let us take the latter facts up first.

Does it not seem preposterous on the very face of it to talk of our opinions being modifiable at will? Can our will either help or hinder our intellect in its perceptions of truth? Can we, by just willing it, believe that Abraham Lincoln's existence is a myth, and that the portraits of him in McClure's Magazine[8] are all of some one else? Can we, by any effort of our will, or by any strength of wish that it were true, believe ourselves well and about when we are roaring with rheumatism in bed, or feel certain that the sum of the two one-dollar bills in our pocket must be a hundred dollars? We can say any of these things, but we are absolutely impotent to believe them; and of just such things is the whole fabric of the truths that we do believe in made up,—matters of fact, immediate or remote, as Hume said,[9] and relations between ideas, which are either there or not there for us if we see them so, and which if not there cannot be put there by any action of our own.

In Pascal's *Thoughts* there is a celebrated passage known in literature as Pascal's wager. In it he tries to force us into Christianity by reasoning as if our concern with truth resembled our concern with the stakes in a game of chance. Translated freely his words are these: You must either believe or not believe that God is—which will you do? Your human reason cannot say. A game is going on between you and the nature of things which at the day of judgment will bring out either heads or tails. Weigh what your gains and your losses would be if you should stake all you have on heads, or God's existence: if you win in such case, you gain eternal beatitude;[10] if you lose, you lose nothing at all. If there were an infinity of chances, and only one for God in this wager, still you ought to stake your all on God; for though you surely risk a finite loss by this procedure, any finite loss is reasonable, even a certain one is reasonable, if there is but the possibility of infinite gain. Go, then, and take holy water, and have masses said; belief will come and stupefy your scruples,—*Cela vous fera croire et vous abêtira.*[11] Why should you not? At bottom, what have you to lose?

You probably feel that when religious faith expresses itself thus, in the language of the gaming table,[12] it is put to its last trumps. Surely Pascal's own personal belief in masses and holy water had far other springs; and this celebrated page of his is but an argument for others, a last desperate snatch at a weapon against the hardness of the unbelieving heart. We feel that a faith in masses and holy water adopted

---

6   "On the other hand."

7   That is, free to stop with no penalty except for the loss of his time.

8   An influential American muckraking periodical, founded in 1893.

9   See the Hume selections in this chapter and in Chapter 3.

10 Blessedness or happiness.

11 "That will make you believe and will stupefy you."

12 Near to death, in desperate straits.

wilfully after such a mechanical calculation—would lack the inner soul of faith's reality; and if we were ourselves in the place of the Deity, we should probably take particular pleasure in cutting off believers of this pattern from their infinite reward. It is evident that unless there be some pre-existing tendency to believe in masses and holy water, the option offered to the will by Pascal is not a living option. Certainly no Turk ever took to masses and holy water on its account; and even to us Protestants these means of salvation seem such foregone impossibilities that Pascal's logic, invoked for them specifically, leaves us unmoved. As well might the Mahdi write to us, saying, "I am the Expected One whom God has created in his effulgence. You shall be infinitely happy if you confess me; otherwise you shall be cut off from the light of the sun. Weigh, then, your infinite gain if I am genuine against your finite sacrifice if I am not!" His logic would be that of Pascal; but he would vainly use it on us, for the hypothesis he offers us is dead. No tendency to act on it exists in us to any degree.

The talk of believing by our volition seems, then, from one point of view, simply silly. From another point of view it is worse than silly, it is vile. When one turns to the magnificent edifice of the physical sciences, and sees how it was reared; what thousands of disinterested moral lives of men lie buried in its mere foundations; what patience and postponement, what choking down of preference, what submission to the icy laws of outer fact are wrought into its very stones and mortar; how absolutely impersonal it stands in its vast augustness,—then how besotted and contemptible seems every little sentimentalist who comes blowing his voluntary smoke-wreaths, and pretending to decide things from out of his private dream! Can we wonder if those bred in the rugged and manly school of science should feel like spewing such subjectivism out of their mouths? The whole system of loyalties which grow up in the schools of science go dead against its toleration; so that it is only natural that those who have caught the scientific fever should pass over to the opposite extreme, and write sometimes as if the incorruptibly truthful intellect ought positively to prefer bitterness and unacceptableness to the heart in its cup.

It fortifies my soul to know

That, though I perish, Truth is so—

sings Clough, while Huxley exclaims: "My only consolation lies in the reflection that, however bad our posterity may become, so far as they hold by the plain rule of not pretending to believe what they have no reason to believe, because it may be to their advantage so to pretend [the word 'pretend' is surely here redundant], they will not have reached the lowest depth of immorality." And that delicious *enfant terrible*[13] Clifford writes: "Belief is desecrated when given to unproved and unquestioned statements for the solace and private pleasure of the believer.... Whoso would deserve well of his fellows in this matter will guard the purity of his belief with a very fanaticism of jealous care, lest at any time it should rest on an unworthy object, and catch a stain which can never be wiped away.... If [a] belief has been accepted on insufficient evidence [even though the belief be true, as Clifford on the same page explains] the pleasure is a stolen one.... It is sinful because it is stolen in defiance of our duty to mankind. That duty is to guard ourselves from such beliefs as from a pestilence which may shortly master our own body and then spread to the rest of the town.... It is wrong always, everywhere, and for every one, to believe anything upon insufficient evidence."

III.

All this strikes one as healthy, even when expressed, as by Clifford, with somewhat too much of robustious pathos in the voice. Free-will and simple wishing do seem, in the matter of our credences, to be only fifth wheels to the coach. Yet if any one should thereupon assume that intellectual insight is what remains after wish and will and sentimental preference have taken wing, or that pure reason is what then settles our opinions, he would fly quite as directly in the teeth of the facts.

It is only our already dead hypotheses that our willing nature is unable to bring to life again. But what has made them dead for us is for the most part a previous action of our willing nature of an antagonistic kind.

---

13   'Bad boy'—a person whose behavior or ideas shock or embarrass those with more conventional attitudes.

When I say 'willing nature,' I do not mean only such deliberate volitions as may have set up habits of belief that we cannot now escape from,—I mean all such factors of belief as fear and hope, prejudice and passion, imitation and partisanship, the circumpressure of our caste and set. As a matter of fact we find ourselves believing, we hardly know how or why. Mr. Balfour gives the name of 'authority' to all those influences, born of the intellectual climate, that make hypotheses possible or impossible for us, alive or dead. Here in this room, we all of us believe in molecules and the conservation of energy, in democracy and necessary progress, in Protestant Christianity and the duty of fighting for 'the doctrine of the immortal Monroe,'[14] all for no reasons worthy of the name. We see into these matters with no more inner clearness, and probably with much less, than any disbeliever in them might possess. His unconventionality would probably have some grounds to show for its conclusions; but for us, not insight, but the *prestige* of the opinions, is what makes the spark shoot from them and light up our sleeping magazines[15] of faith. Our reason is quite satisfied, in nine hundred and ninety-nine cases out of every thousand of us, if it can find a few arguments that will do to recite in case our credulity is criticized by someone else. Our faith is faith in someone else's faith, and in the greatest matters this is most the case. Our belief in truth itself, for instance, that there is a truth, and that our minds and it are made for each other,—what is it but a passionate affirmation of desire, in which our social system backs us up? We want to have a truth; we want to believe that our experiments and studies and discussions must put us in a continually better and better position towards it; and on this line we agree to fight out our thinking lives.

But if a pyrrhonistic sceptic[16] asks us *how we know* all this, can our logic find a reply? No! certainly it cannot. It is just one volition against another,—we willing to go in for life upon a trust or assumption which he, for his part, does not care to make.[17]

As a rule we disbelieve all facts and theories for which we have no use. Clifford's cosmic emotions find no use for Christian feelings. Huxley belabors the bishops because there is no use for sacerdotalism[18] in his scheme of life. Newman, on the contrary, goes over to Romanism, and finds all sorts of reasons good for staying there, because a priestly system is for him an organic need and delight. Why do so few 'scientists' even look at the evidence for telepathy, so called? Because they think, as a leading biologist, now dead, once said to me, that even if such a thing were true, scientists ought to band together to keep it suppressed and concealed. It would undo the uniformity of Nature and all sorts of other things without which scientists cannot carry on their pursuits. But if this very man had been shown something which as a scientist he might *do* with telepathy, he might not only have examined the evidence, but even have found it good enough. This very law which the logicians would impose upon us—if I may give the name of logicians to those who would rule out our willing nature here—is based on nothing but their own natural wish to exclude all elements for which they, in their professional quality of logicians, can find no use.

Evidently, then, our non-intellectual nature does influence our convictions. There are passional tendencies and volitions which run before and others which come after belief, and it is only the latter that are too late for the fair; and they are not too late when the previous passional work has been already in their own direction. Pascal's argument, instead of being powerless, then seems a regular clincher, and is the last stroke needed to make our faith in masses and holy water complete. The state of things is evidently far from simple; and pure insight and logic, whatever

---

14   This is the "Monroe Doctrine," set out by American President James Monroe in 1823, which states that while the US would not interfere with existing European colonies in the Western hemisphere, it would regard additional attempts by European powers to establish new colonies or otherwise interfere in the Americas as acts of aggression. (James himself disliked what he thought of as US threat tactics, which had been recently displayed in a dispute with the British over Venezuela.)

15   A storehouse of explosive ammunition.

16   A radical sceptic, one who is determined to withhold assent from almost all beliefs.

17   [Author's note] Compare the admirable page 310 in S.H. Hodgson's *Time and Space*, London, 1865.

18   The institution of the priesthood.

they might do ideally, are not the only things that really do produce our creeds.

IV.

Our next duty, having recognized this mixed-up state of affairs, is to ask whether it be simply reprehensible and pathological, or whether, on the contrary, we must treat it as a normal element in making up our minds. The thesis I defend is, briefly stated, this: *Our passional nature not only lawfully may, but must, decide an option between propositions, whenever it is a genuine option that cannot by its nature be decided on intellectual grounds; for to say, under such circumstances, "Do not decide, but leave the question open," is itself a passional decision,—just like deciding yes or no,—and is attended with the same risk of losing the truth.* The thesis thus abstractly expressed will, I trust, soon become quite clear. But I must first indulge in a bit more of preliminary work.

V.

It will be observed that for the purposes of this discussion we are on 'dogmatic' ground,—ground, I mean, which leaves systematic philosophical scepticism altogether out of account. The postulate that there is truth, and that it is the destiny of our minds to attain it, we are deliberately resolving to make, though the sceptic will not make it. We part company with him, therefore, absolutely, at this point. But the faith that truth exists, and that our minds can find it, may be held in two ways. We may talk of the *empiricist* way and of the *absolutist* way of believing in truth. The absolutists in this matter say that we not only can attain to knowing truth, but we can *know* when we have attained to knowing it; while the empiricists think that although we may attain it, we cannot infallibly know when. To *know* is one thing, and to know for certain *that* we know is another. One may hold to the first being possible without the second; hence the empiricists and the absolutists, although neither of them is a sceptic in the usual philosophic sense of the term, show very different degrees of dogmatism in their lives.

If we look at the history of opinions, we see that the empiricist tendency has largely prevailed in science, while in philosophy the absolutist tendency has

had everything its own way. The characteristic sort of happiness, indeed, which philosophies yield has mainly consisted in the conviction felt by each successive school or system that by it bottom-certitude had been attained. "Other philosophies are collections of opinions, mostly false; *my* philosophy gives standing-ground forever,"—who does not recognize in this the key-note of every system worthy of the name? A system, to be a system at all, must come as a *closed* system, reversible in this or that detail, perchance, but in its essential features never!

Scholastic orthodoxy,[19] to which one must always go when one wishes to find perfectly clear statement, has beautifully elaborated this absolutist conviction in a doctrine which it calls that of 'objective evidence.' If, for example, I am unable to doubt that I now exist before you, that two is less than three, or that if all men are mortal then I am mortal too, it is because these things illumine my intellect irresistibly. The final ground of this objective evidence possessed by certain propositions is the *adæquatio intellectus nostri cum rê.*[20] The certitude it brings involves an *aptitudinem ad extorquendum certum assensum*[21] on the part of the truth envisaged, and on the side of the subject a *quietem in cognitione,*[22] when once the object is mentally received, that leaves no possibility of doubt behind; and in the whole transaction nothing operates but the *entitas ipsa*[23] of the object and the *entitas ipsa* of the mind. We slouchy modern thinkers dislike to talk in Latin,—indeed, we dislike to talk in set terms at all; but at bottom our own state of mind is very much like this whenever we uncritically abandon ourselves: You believe in objective evidence, and I do. Of some things we feel that we are certain: we know, and we know that we do know. There is something that gives a click

---

19 The dominant philosophy of the Middle Ages, combining remnants of ancient Greek philosophy (especially Aristotle) with Christian theology.

20 "Perfect correspondence of our understanding with the thing."

21 "The aptitude or tendency to force a certain agreement."

22 "Repose in knowledge," i.e., passive acceptance of knowledge.

23 "Being itself," real being.

inside of us, a bell that strikes twelve, when the hands of our mental clock have swept the dial and meet over the meridian hour.[24] The greatest empiricists among us are only empiricists on reflection: when left to their instincts, they dogmatize like infallible popes. When the Cliffords tell us how sinful it is to be Christians on such 'insufficient evidence,' insufficiency is really the last thing they have in mind. For them the evidence is absolutely sufficient, only it makes the other way. They believe so completely in an anti-Christian order of the universe that there is no living option: Christianity is a dead hypothesis from the start.

VI.

But now, since we are all such absolutists by instinct, what in our quality of students of philosophy ought we to do about the fact? Shall we espouse and endorse it? Or shall we treat it as a weakness of our nature from which we must free ourselves, if we can?

I sincerely believe that the latter course is the only one we can follow as reflective men. Objective evidence and certitude are doubtless very fine ideals to play with, but where on this moonlit and dream-visited planet are they found? I am, therefore, myself a complete empiricist so far as my theory of human knowledge goes. I live, to be sure, by the practical faith that we must go on experiencing and thinking over our experience, for only thus can our opinions grow more true; but to hold any one of them—I absolutely do not care which—as if it never could be reinterpretable or corrigible,[25] I believe to be a tremendously mistaken attitude, and I think that the whole history of philosophy will bear me out. There is but one indefectibly certain truth, and that is the truth that pyrrhonistic scepticism itself leaves standing,—the truth that the present phenomenon of consciousness exists. That, however, is the bare starting-point of knowledge, the mere admission of a stuff to be philosophized about. The various philosophies are but so many attempts at expressing what this stuff really is. And if we repair to our libraries what disagreement do we discover! Where is a certainly true answer found?

Apart from abstract propositions of comparison (such as two and two are the same as four), propositions which tell us nothing by themselves about concrete reality, we find no proposition ever regarded by any one as evidently certain that has not either been called a falsehood, or at least had its truth sincerely questioned by some one else. The transcending of the axioms of geometry, not in play but in earnest, by certain of our contemporaries (as Zöllner and Charles H. Hinton), and the rejection of the whole Aristotelian logic by the Hegelians, are striking instances in point.

No concrete test of what is really true has ever been agreed upon. Some make the criterion external to the moment of perception, putting it either in revelation, the *consensus gentium*,[26] the instincts of the heart, or the systematized experience of the race. Others make the perceptive moment its own test,—Descartes, for instance, with his clear and distinct ideas guaranteed by the veracity of God; Reid with his 'common-sense'; and Kant with his forms of synthetic judgment *a priori*.[27] The inconceivability of the opposite; the capacity to be verified by sense; the possession of complete organic unity or self-relation, realized when a thing is its own other,—are standards which, in turn, have been used. The much lauded objective evidence is never triumphantly there; it is a mere aspiration or *Grenzbegriff*,[28] marking the infinitely remote ideal of our thinking life. To claim that certain truths now possess it, is simply to say that when you think them true and they *are* true, then their evidence is objective, otherwise it is not. But practically one's conviction that the evidence one goes by is of the real objective brand, is only one more subjective opinion added to the lot. For what a contradictory array of opinions have objective evidence and absolute certitude been claimed! The world is rational through and through,—its existence is an ultimate brute fact; there is a personal God,—a personal God is inconceivable; there is an extra-mental physical world immediately known,—the mind can

---

24 Noon—i.e., the hour when the sun is at its meridian, its highest point in the sky.

25 Correctable.

26 "Public consensus."

27 See Chapter 2 for relevant selections from Descartes and Kant.

28 From Kant's *Critique of Pure Reason*, this literally means a concept at the edge or limit of our understanding; it is often translated "limiting concept."

only know its own ideas; a moral imperative exists,—obligation is only the resultant of desires; a permanent spiritual principle is in every one,—there are only shifting states of mind; there is an endless chain of causes,—there is an absolute first cause; an eternal necessity,—a freedom; a purpose,—no purpose; a primal One,—a primal Many; a universal continuity,—an essential discontinuity in things; an infinity,—no infinity. There is this,—there is that; there is indeed nothing which some one has not thought absolutely true, while his neighbor deemed it absolutely false; and not an absolutist among them seems ever to have considered that the trouble may all the time be essential, and that the intellect, even with truth directly in its grasp, may have no infallible signal for knowing whether it be truth or no. When, indeed, one remembers that the most striking practical application to life of the doctrine of objective certitude has been the conscientious labors of the Holy Office of the Inquisition,[29] one feels less tempted than ever to lend the doctrine a respectful ear.

But please observe, now, that when as empiricists we give up the doctrine of objective certitude, we do not thereby give up the quest or hope of truth itself. We still pin our faith on its existence, and still believe that we gain an ever better position towards it by systematically continuing to roll up experiences and think. Our great difference from the scholastic lies in the way we face. The strength of his system lies in the principles, the origin, the *terminus a quo*[30] of his thought; for us the strength is in the outcome, the upshot, the *terminus ad quem*.[31] Not where it comes from but what it leads to is to decide. It matters not to an empiricist from what quarter an hypothesis may come to him: he may have acquired it by fair means or by foul; passion may have whispered or accident suggested it; but if the total drift of thinking continues to confirm it, that is what he means by its being true.

_____

29 A tribunal formerly held in the Roman Catholic Church and directed at the forceful suppression of heresy; its best known variant is the notorious Spanish Inquisition of the late fifteenth century.

30 "The point from which it comes."

31 "The point to which it goes."

VII.

One more point, small but important, and our preliminaries are done. There are two ways of looking at our duty in the matter of opinion,—ways entirely different, and yet ways about whose difference the theory of knowledge seems hitherto to have shown very little concern. *We must know the truth*; and *we must avoid error*,—these are our first and great commandments as would-be knowers; but they are not two ways of stating an identical commandment, they are two separable laws. Although it may indeed happen that when we believe the truth *A*, we escape as an incidental consequence from believing the falsehood *B*, it hardly ever happens that by merely disbelieving *B* we necessarily believe *A*. We may in escaping *B* fall into believing other falsehoods, *C* or *D*, just as bad as *B*; or we may escape *B* by not believing anything at all not even *A*.

Believe truth! Shun error—these, we see, are two materially different laws; and by choosing between them we may end by coloring differently our whole intellectual life. We may regard the chase for truth as paramount, and the avoidance of error as secondary; or we may, on the other hand, treat the avoidance of error as more imperative, and let truth take its chance. Clifford, in the instructive passage which I have quoted, exhorts us to the latter course. Believe nothing, he tells us, keep your mind in suspense forever, rather than by closing it on insufficient evidence incur the awful risk of believing lies. You, on the other hand, may think that the risk of being in error is a very small matter when compared with the blessings of real knowledge, and be ready to be duped many times in your investigation rather than postpone indefinitely the chance of guessing true. I myself find it impossible to go with Clifford. We must remember that these feelings of our duty about either truth or error are in any case only expressions of our passional life. Biologically considered, our minds are as ready to grind out falsehood as veracity, and he who says, "Better go without belief forever than believe a lie!" merely shows his own preponderant private horror of becoming a dupe. He may be critical of many of his desires and fears, but this fear he slavishly obeys. He cannot imagine any one questioning its binding force. For my own part, I have also a horror of being duped; but I can believe that worse things than being duped may happen to a man in this world: so Clifford's exhortation has to my ears a thoroughly fantastic sound. It is like a general informing his soldiers that it is better to keep out of battle forever than to risk a single wound. Not so are victories either over enemies or over nature gained. Our errors are surely not such awfully solemn things. In a world where we are so certain to incur them in spite of all our caution, a certain lightness of heart seems healthier than this excessive nervousness on their behalf. At any rate, it seems the fittest thing for the empiricist philosopher.

VIII.

And now, after all this introduction, let us go straight at our question. I have said, and now repeat it, that not only as a matter of fact do we find our passional nature influencing us in our opinions, but that there are some options between opinions in which this influence must be regarded both as an inevitable and as a lawful determinant of our choice.

I fear here that some of you my hearers will begin to scent danger, and lend an inhospitable ear. Two first steps of passion you have indeed had to admit as necessary,—we must think so as to avoid dupery, and we must think so as to gain truth; but the surest path to those ideal consummations, you will probably consider, is from now onwards to take no further passional step.

Well, of course, I agree as far as the facts will allow. Wherever the option between losing truth and gaining it is not momentous, we can throw the chance of *gaining truth* away, and at any rate save ourselves from any chance of *believing falsehood*, by not making up our minds at all till objective evidence has come. In scientific questions, this is almost always the case; and even in human affairs in general, the need of acting is seldom so urgent that a false belief to act on is better than no belief at all. Law courts, indeed, have to decide on the best evidence attainable for the moment, because a judge's duty is to make law as well as to ascertain it, and (as a learned judge once said to me) few cases are worth spending much time over: the great thing is to have them decided on *any* acceptable principle, and got out of the way. But in our dealings with objective nature we obviously are

recorders, not makers, of the truth; and decisions for the mere sake of deciding promptly and getting on to the next business would be wholly out of place. Throughout the breadth of physical nature facts are what they are quite independently of us, and seldom is there any such hurry about them that the risks of being duped by believing a premature theory need be faced. The questions here are always trivial options, the hypotheses are hardly living (at any rate not living for us spectators), the choice between believing truth or falsehood is seldom forced. The attitude of sceptical balance is therefore the absolutely wise one if we would escape mistakes. What difference, indeed, does it make to most of us whether we have or have not a theory of the Röntgen rays,[32] whether we believe or not in mind-stuff, or have a conviction about the causality of conscious states? It makes no difference. Such options are not forced on us. On every account it is better not to make them, but still keep weighing reasons *pro et contra*[33] with an indifferent hand.

I speak, of course, here of the purely judging mind. For purposes of discovery such indifference is to be less highly recommended, and science would be far less advanced than she is if the passionate desires of individuals to get their own faiths confirmed had been kept out of the game. See for example the sagacity which Spencer and Weismann now display. On the other hand, if you want an absolute duffer in an investigation, you must, after all, take the man who has no interest whatever in its results: he is the warranted incapable, the positive fool. The most useful investigator, because the most sensitive observer, is always he whose eager interest in one side of the question is balanced by an equally keen nervousness lest he become deceived.[34] Science has organized this nervousness into a regular *technique*, her so-called method of verification; and she has fallen so deeply in love with the method that one may even say she has ceased to care for truth by itself at all. It is only truth

---

32 Named for the German physicist who discovered them, these are today called X-rays.

33 "For and against."

34 [Author's note] Compare Wilfrid Ward's Essay, "The Wish to Believe," in his *Witnesses to the Unseen*, Macmillan & Co., 1893.

as technically verified that interests her. The truth of truths might come in merely affirmative form, and she would decline to touch it. Such truth as that, she might repeat with Clifford, would be stolen in defiance of her duty to mankind. Human passions, however, are stronger than technical rules. "Le coeur a ses raisons," as Pascal says, "que la raison ne connaît pas;"[35] and however indifferent to all but the bare rules of the game the umpire, the abstract intellect, may be, the concrete players who furnish him the materials to judge of are usually, each one of them, in love with some pet 'live hypothesis' of his own. Let us agree, however, that wherever there is no forced option, the dispassionately judicial intellect with no pet hypothesis, saving us, as it does, from dupery at any rate, ought to be our ideal.

The question next arises: Are there not somewhere forced options in our speculative questions, and can we (as men who may be interested at least as much in positively gaining truth as in merely escaping dupery) always wait with impunity till the coercive evidence shall have arrived? It seems *a priori* improbable that the truth should be so nicely adjusted to our needs and powers as that. In the great boarding-house of nature, the cakes and the butter and the syrup seldom come out so even and leave the plates so clean. Indeed, we should view them with scientific suspicion if they did.

IX.

Moral questions immediately present themselves as questions whose solution cannot wait for sensible proof. A moral question is a question not of what sensibly exists, but of what is good, or would be good if it did exist. Science can tell us what exists; but to compare the *worths*, both of what exists and of what does not exist, we must consult not science, but what Pascal calls our heart. Science herself consults her heart when she lays it down that the infinite ascertainment of fact and correction of false belief are the supreme goods for man. Challenge the statement, and science can only repeat it oracularly,[36] or else prove it by

showing that such ascertainment and correction bring man all sorts of other goods which man's heart in turn declares. The question of having moral beliefs at all or not having them is decided by our will. Are our moral preferences true or false, or are they only odd biological phenomena, making things good or bad for *us*, but in themselves indifferent? How can your pure intellect decide? If your heart does not *want* a world of moral reality, your head will assuredly never make you believe in one. Mephistophelian[37] scepticism, indeed, will satisfy the head's play-instincts much better than any rigorous idealism can. Some men (even at the student age) are so naturally cool-hearted that the moralistic hypothesis never has for them any pungent life, and in their supercilious presence the hot young moralist always feels strangely ill at ease. The appearance of knowingness is on their side, of *naïveté*, and gullibility on his. Yet, in the inarticulate heart of him, he clings to it that he is not a dupe, and that there is a realm in which (as Emerson says) all their wit and intellectual superiority is no better than the cunning of a fox.[38] Moral scepticism can no more be refuted or proved by logic than intellectual scepticism can. When we stick to it that there *is* truth (be it of either kind), we do so with our whole nature, and resolve to stand or fall by the results. The sceptic with his whole nature adopts the doubting attitude; but which of us is the wiser, Omniscience only knows.

Turn now from these wide questions of good to a certain class of questions of fact, questions concerning personal relations, states of mind between one man and another. *Do you like me or not?*—for example. Whether you do or not depends, in countless instances, on whether I meet you half-way, am willing to assume that you must like me, and show you trust and expectation. The previous faith on my part in your liking's existence is in such cases what makes your liking come. But if I stand aloof, and refuse to budge an inch until I have objective evidence, until

---

35 "The heart has its reasons which reason knows nothing of."

36 In the manner of an oracle: solemnly and enigmatically, but without giving reasons.

37 Mephistopheles is the devil to whom, according to a sixteenth-century German legend, Faust sold his soul: something is "Mephistophelian," therefore, if it is fiendish and tricky.

38 A reference to the poet Ralph Waldo Emerson's essay "The Sovereignty of Ethics" (1884).

you shall have done something apt, as the absolutists say, *ad extorquendum assensum meum*,[39] ten to one your liking never comes. How many women's hearts are vanquished by the mere sanguine insistence of some man that they *must* love him! he will not consent to the hypothesis that they cannot. The desire for a certain kind of truth here brings about that special truth's existence; and so it is in innumerable cases of other sorts. Who gains promotions, boons, appointments, but the man in whose life they are seen to play the part of live hypotheses, who discounts them, sacrifices other things for their sake before they have come, and takes risks for them in advance? His faith acts on the powers above him as a claim, and creates its own verification.

A social organism of any sort whatever, large or small, is what it is because each member proceeds to his own duty with a trust that the other members will simultaneously do theirs. Wherever a desired result is achieved by the co-operation of many independent persons, its existence as a fact is a pure consequence of the precursive faith in one another of those immediately concerned. A government, an army, a commercial system, a ship, a college, an athletic team, all exist on this condition, without which not only is nothing achieved, but nothing is even attempted. A whole train of passengers (individually brave enough) will be looted by a few highwaymen, simply because the latter can count on one another, while each passenger fears that if he makes a movement of resistance, he will be shot before any one else backs him up. If we believed that the whole car-full would rise at once with us, we should each severally rise, and train-robbing would never even be attempted. There are, then, cases where a fact cannot come at all unless a preliminary faith exists in its coming. *And where faith in a fact can help create the fact*, that would be an insane logic which should say that faith running ahead of scientific evidence is the 'lowest kind of immorality' into which a thinking being can fall. Yet such is the logic by which our scientific absolutists pretend to regulate our lives!

X.

In truths dependent on our personal action, then, faith based on desire is certainly a lawful and possibly an indispensable thing.

But now, it will be said, these are all childish human cases, and have nothing to do with great cosmical matters, like the question of religious faith. Let us then pass on to that. Religions differ so much in their accidents[40] that in discussing the religious question we must make it very generic and broad. What then do we now mean by the religious hypothesis? Science says things are; morality says some things are better than other things; and religion says essentially two things.

First, she says that the best things are the more eternal things, the overlapping things, the things in the universe that throw the last stone, so to speak, and say the final word. "Perfection is eternal,"—this phrase of Charles Secrétan seems a good way of putting this first affirmation of religion, an affirmation which obviously cannot yet be verified scientifically at all.

The second affirmation of religion is that we are better off even now if we believe her first affirmation to be true.

Now, let us consider what the logical elements of this situation are *in case the religious hypothesis in both its branches be really true.* (Of course, we must admit that possibility at the outset. If we are to discuss the question at all, it must involve a living option. If for any of you religion be a hypothesis that cannot, by any living possibility be true, then you need go no farther. I speak to the 'saving remnant' alone.) So proceeding, we see, first, that religion offers itself as a *momentous* option. We are supposed to gain, even now, by our belief, and to lose by our non-belief, a certain vital good. Secondly, religion is a *forced* option, so far as that good goes. We cannot escape the issue by remaining sceptical and waiting for more light, because, although we do avoid error in that way *if religion be untrue*, we lose the good, *if it be true*, just as certainly as if we positively chose to disbelieve. It is as if a man should hesitate indefinitely to ask a certain woman to marry him because he was not perfectly sure that she would prove an angel after he brought her home. Would he not cut himself off from that

---

39   "To force my unqualified assent."

40   Non-essential properties or attributes.

particular angel-possibility as decisively as if he went and married some one else? Scepticism, then, is not avoidance of option; it is option of a certain particular kind of risk. *Better risk loss of truth than chance of error*,—that is your faith-vetoer's exact position. He is actively playing his stake as much as the believer is; he is backing the field against the religious hypothesis, just as the believer is backing the religious hypothesis against the field. To preach scepticism to us as a duty until 'sufficient evidence' for religion be found, is tantamount therefore to telling us, when in presence of the religious hypothesis, that to yield to our fear of its being error is wiser and better than to yield to our hope that it may be true. It is not intellect against all passions, then; it is only intellect with one passion laying down its law. And by what, forsooth, is the supreme wisdom of this passion warranted? Dupery for dupery, what proof is there that dupery through hope is so much worse than dupery through fear? I, for one, can see no proof; and I simply refuse obedience to the scientist's command to imitate his kind of option, in a case where my own stake is important enough to give me the right to choose my own form of risk. If religion be true and the evidence for it be still insufficient, I do not wish, by putting your extinguisher upon my nature (which feels to me as if it had after all some business in this matter), to forfeit my sole chance in life of getting upon the winning side,—that chance depending, of course, on my willingness to run the risk of acting as if my passional need of taking the world religiously might be prophetic and right.

All this is on the supposition that it really may be prophetic and right, and that, even to us who are discussing the matter, religion is a live hypothesis which may be true. Now, to most of us religion comes in a still further way that makes a veto on our active faith even more illogical. The more perfect and more eternal aspect of the universe is represented in our religions as having personal form. The universe is no longer a mere *It* to us, but a *Thou*, if we are religious; and any relation that may be possible from person to person might be possible here. For instance, although in one sense we are passive portions of the universe, in another we show a curious autonomy, as if we were small active centres on our own account. We feel, too, as if the appeal of religion to us were made to our own active good-will, as if evidence might be forever withheld from us unless we met the hypothesis half-way. To take a trivial illustration: just as a man who in a company of gentlemen made no advances, asked a warrant for every concession, and believed no one's word without proof, would cut himself off by such churlishness from all the social rewards that a more trusting spirit would earn—so here, one who should shut himself up in snarling logicality and try to make the gods extort his recognition willy-nilly, or not get it at all, might cut himself off forever from his only opportunity of making the gods' acquaintance. This feeling, forced on us we know not whence, that by obstinately believing that there are gods (although not to do so would be so easy both for our logic and our life) we are doing the universe the deepest service we can, seems part of the living essence of the religious hypothesis. If the hypothesis *were* true in all its parts, including this one, then pure intellectualism, with its veto on our making willing advances, would be an absurdity; and some participation of our sympathetic nature would be logically required. I, therefore, for one, cannot see my way to accepting the agnostic rules for truth-seeking, or wilfully agree to keep my willing nature out of the game. I cannot do so for this plain reason, that *a rule of thinking which would absolutely prevent me from acknowledging certain kinds of truth if those kinds of truth were really there, would be an irrational rule*. That for me is the long and short of the formal logic of the situation, no matter what the kinds of truth might materially be.

I confess I do not see how this logic can be escaped. But sad experience makes me fear that some of you may still shrink from radically saying with me, *in abstracto*,[41] that we have the right to believe at our own risk any hypothesis that is live enough to tempt our will. I suspect, however, that if this is so, it is because you have got away from the abstract logical point of view altogether, and are thinking (perhaps without realizing it) of some particular religious hypothesis which for you is dead. The freedom to 'believe what we will' you apply to the case of some patent superstition; and the faith you think of is the faith defined by the schoolboy when he said, "Faith

----

41   "In the abstract."

is when you believe something that you know ain't true." I can only repeat that this is misapprehension. *In concreto*,[42] the freedom to believe can only cover living options which the intellect of the individual cannot by itself resolve; and living options never seem absurdities to him who has them to consider. When I look at the religious question as it really puts itself to concrete men, and when I think of all the possibilities which both practically and theoretically it involves, then this command that we shall put a stopper on our heart, instincts, and courage, and *wait*—acting of course meanwhile more or less as if religion were *not* true[43]—till doomsday, or till such time as our intellect and senses working together may have raked in evidence enough,—this command, I say, seems to me the queerest idol ever manufactured in the philosophic cave. Were we scholastic absolutists, there might be more excuse. If we had an infallible intellect with its objective certitudes, we might feel ourselves disloyal to such a perfect organ of knowledge in not trusting to it exclusively, in not waiting for its releasing word. But if we are empiricists, if we believe that no bell in us tolls to let us know for certain when truth is in our grasp, then it seems a piece of idle fantasticality to preach so solemnly our duty of waiting for the bell. Indeed we *may* wait if we will,—I hope you do not think that I am denying that,—but if we do so, we do so at our peril as much as if we believed. In either case we *act*, taking our life in our hands. No one of us ought to issue vetoes to the other, nor should we bandy words of abuse. We ought, on the contrary, delicately and profoundly to respect one another's mental freedom: then only shall we bring about the intellectual republic; then only shall we have that spirit of inner tolerance without which all our outer tolerance is soulless, and which is empiricism's glory; then only shall we live and let live, in speculative as well as in practical things.

I began by a reference to Fitz-James Stephen; let me end by a quotation from him. "What do you think of yourself? What do you think of the world? ... These are questions with which all must deal as it seems good to them. They are riddles of the Sphinx, and in some way or other we must deal with them.... In all important transactions of life we have to take a leap in the dark.... If we decide to leave the riddles unanswered, that is a choice; if we waver in our answer, that, too, is a choice: but whatever choice we make, we make it at our peril. If a man chooses to turn his back altogether on God and the future, no one can prevent him; no one can show beyond reasonable doubt that he is mistaken. If a man thinks otherwise and acts as he thinks, I do not see that any one can prove that he is mistaken. Each must act as he thinks best; and if he is wrong, so much the worse for him. We stand on a mountain pass in the midst of whirling snow and blinding mist, through which we get glimpses now and then of paths which may be deceptive. If we stand still we shall be frozen to death. If we take the wrong road we shall be dashed to pieces. We do not certainly know whether there is any right one. What must we do? 'Be strong and of a good courage.' Act for the best, hope for the best, and take what comes.... If death ends all, we cannot meet death better."[44]

---

42 "In concrete (or actual) cases."

43 [Author's note] Since belief is measured by action, he who forbids us to believe religion to be true, necessarily also forbids us to act as we should if we did believe it to be true. The whole defence of religious faith hinges upon action. If the action required or inspired by the religious hypothesis is in no way different from that dictated by the naturalistic hypothesis, then religious faith is a pure superfluity, better pruned away, and controversy about its legitimacy is a piece of idle trifling, unworthy of serious minds. I myself believe, of course, that the religious hypothesis gives to the world an expression which specifically determines our reactions, and makes them in a large part unlike what they might be on a purely naturalistic scheme of belief.

44 [Author's note] *Liberty, Equality, Fraternity*, p. 353, 2nd edition. London, 1874.

CHAPTER 5

Philosophy of Mind—What Is the Place of Mind in the Physical World?

INTRODUCTION TO THE QUESTION

The philosophy of mind has three main parts: the philosophy of psychology, philosophical psychology, and the metaphysics of mental phenomena. The philosophy of psychology (which can also be thought of as a branch of the philosophy of science) consists in the critical evaluation of the claims and methodologies of cognitive science. For example, in the first half of the twentieth century philosophers were involved with assessing the claims made by psychoanalytic theory (such as that of Sigmund Freud) and of psychological behaviorism, which controversially held that the only theoretical goals of psychology are the prediction and control of human behavior. More recently, philosophers have played a role in creating and critiquing psychological models which are based on analogies between the human mind and computer programs. For example, philosophers of mind examine the question of whether Artificial Intelligence is really possible (and how we would know if we found it), and whether the kind of information processing which is performed by the brain more resembles a familiar 'computational' type or a variety of more diffuse 'neural net' processing.

Philosophical psychology, by contrast, does not examine the science of psychology but instead engages in analysis of our ordinary, commonsensical concepts of the mental. It deals with such conceptual questions as the difference between deliberate action and mere behavior, the nature of memory and of perception, the notion of rationality, the concept of personal identity, and so on.

Finally, the metaphysics of the mind has to do with coming to understand the inherent nature of mental phenomena. The questions asked in this area are really at the heart of the philosophy of mind, and the four most important of them are the following:

1) What is the relationship between mind and brain? Of course, everyone knows that our minds and brains are closely connected: when certain things happen in our brains (perhaps caused by the ingestion of hallucinogenic chemicals) certain corresponding things happen in our minds. But what is the nature of this connection? Is the mind *nothing but* the physical brain (so that the brain chemicals *just are* the hallucinations, so to speak), or is it something distinct from the brain, either because it is made of some different metaphysical 'stuff' (such as soul-stuff) or because it belongs to a different level or category of being (as a software program belongs to a different metaphysical category than the hard drive on which it is stored).

2) What explains the fact that some of our mental states are directed at the world: how do some of our mental states come to be *meaningful*? The words on this page are meaningful because we use them as signs—when we learn to read, what we are learning is how to connect certain squiggles on the page with meaningful ideas. It is a much harder problem, however, to understand how bits of our mind or brain can become signs, all by themselves, even though there is no one inside the head to 'read' them and give them meaning.

3) What explains the fact that some of our mental states have a certain qualitative *feel*? Put another way, where does *consciousness* come from? For example, the sensation of being tickled, or the smell of cook-

ing onions, both have a distinctive feel to them: there is 'something it is like' for you to be tickled. However, if you think about it, this is a very unusual and quite puzzling fact; after all, for the vast majority of physical objects in the world, if you tickle them they don't feel a thing. So what makes *minds* special and unique in this respect? How do minds come to have a 'light on inside'—to be centers of consciousness and feeling in an unconscious, unfeeling universe? This is manifestly puzzling if you think of the mind as being nothing more than the three-and-a-bit-pound physico-chemical blob inside our skulls, but it turns out to be an extremely difficult problem for any theory of the mind. (In fact, arguably, it is the most difficult and pressing problem in all of philosophy.)

4) How do our mental states interact causally with the physical world? In particular, if our thoughts obey the laws of rationality instead of brute causality, then how can the workings of our mind be part of, or related to, the natural world? When I believe that this pesto sauce contains pine nuts, and I know that I am allergic to pine nuts and that if I eat any I will swell up like a balloon, and I don't want to swell up like a balloon, then it is (apparently) for this *reason* that I refuse to eat the pesto: my behavior is to be explained by the logical, rational connections between my beliefs and desires. The laws of physics, by contrast, are not rational laws. If a bullet ricochets off a lamppost and hits an innocent bystander during a bank robbery, it does not do so because it *ought* to bounce that way (nor does it do a bad thing because it has bounced *irrationally* or illogically)—its path is merely a physical consequence of the way it glanced off the metal of the lamppost. So, the laws of thought are rational and the laws of nature are arational: the problem is, then, how can thought be part of nature (be *both* rational and arational)? And if it is *not* part of nature, then how can it make things happen in the physical world (and vice versa)?

It is worth noting that, today, all of these questions are asked against the background of a default position called *physicalism*. Generally, in the sciences, we assume that the real world is nothing more than the physical world: that all the things which exist are physical (roughly, made of either matter or energy) and obey exclusively physical laws (i.e.,

those described by fundamental physics). In most domains—such as chemistry, biology, or geology—this methodological assumption has proved fruitful; however, in psychology the question is much more vexed. In fact, the mind seems to be the last holdout of the non-physical in the natural world. How can the feeling of pain or the taste of honey be made of either matter or energy? How can falling in love or choosing to become a politician be subject to the laws of physics? If the study of the human mind is ever to be integrated within the rest of (scientific) human knowledge, these phenomena will need to be accounted for in a physicalist framework: the big question is, can this be done, and how?

The issue in the philosophy of mind which is focussed on in this chapter is the mind-body problem: what is the relationship between the mind and the brain? The traditional mind-body theory—the dominant story until about the middle of the twentieth century—is called *substance dualism*: on this view, mind and body are two completely different entities made up of two quite different substances, spirit, and matter. The classic source for this view is Descartes's *Meditations*, which appears in Chapter 2; Gilbert Ryle introduces the theory in this chapter, and then subjects it to a fairly devastating critique, calling it the 'dogma of the ghost in the machine.' The next main mind-body theory to appear, dualism's successor, was called *behaviorism*: this theory holds that the mind is neither brain nor spirit, but instead consists in dispositions to behave in certain ways. Ryle is usually thought of as the primary philosophical practitioner and originator of this approach; all the rest of the readings in this chapter contain elements of a critique of behaviorism.

A natural approach to mental phenomena from a 'scientific' point of view is to attempt to reduce them to brain events. This tactic is called *mind-brain identity theory*. An important criticism of this theory can be found in the Putnam piece, which instead puts forward a theory called *functionalism*. The essential idea behind functionalism is that the mind is best thought of as a sort of abstract information-processing device (rather like a computer program), and a mental state is really a kind of complex input-output relation between sensory stimuli and (internal and external) behavior. Functionalism is attacked in the following two readings, especially the one by John Searle.

In recent years there has been a resurgence of interest in dualism—not the substance dualism of Descartes, however, but a variant called *property dualism*. This theory agrees that there is nothing in our skulls over and above the brain, but asserts that brains have special non-physical properties which are responsible for the existence of meaning and consciousness. Some of the motivations for a view like this are presented by Thomas Nagel in his article "What Is It Like to Be a Bat?", and further arguments in favor of property dualism are advanced in the readings by Frank Jackson and David Chalmers.

The philosophy of mind has been a particularly active field for the past thirty years or so, and there is any number of good books available which will take you further into these fascinating questions. Some of the best are: David Armstrong, *The Mind-Body Problem* (Westview, 1999); David Braddon-Mitchell and Frank Jackson, *Philosophy of Mind and Cognition* (Blackwell, 2006); Keith Campbell, *Body and Mind* (University of Notre Dame Press, 1984); David Chalm-ers, *The Conscious Mind* (Oxford University Press, 1996); Paul Churchland, *Matter and Consciousness* (MIT Press, 1988); Tim Crane, *The Mechanical Mind* (Routledge, 2003); Daniel Dennett, *Consciousness Explained* (Little, Brown, 1991); Fred Dretske, *Naturalizing the Mind* (MIT Press, 1995); Owen Flanagan, *The Science of the Mind* (MIT Press, 1991); Jerry Fodor, *Psychosemantics* (MIT Press, 1989); Howard Gardner, *The Mind's New Science* (Basic Books, 1985); John Heil, *Philosophy of Mind* (Routledge, 2004); Ted Honderich, *Mind and Brain* (Oxford University Press, 1990); Jaegwon Kim, *Philosophy of Mind* (Westview, 2005); Colin McGinn, *The Character of Mind* (Oxford University Press, 1982); John Searle, *The Rediscovery of the Mind* (MIT Press, 1992); and Peter Smith and O.R. Jones, *The Philosophy of Mind* (Cambridge University Press, 1986). A good reference work on the philosophy of mind is *A Companion to the Philosophy of Mind*, edited by Samuel Guttenplan (Blackwell, 1996); there is also *The Oxford Handbook of Philosophy of Mind*, edited by Brian P. McLaughlin and Ansgar Beckermann (Oxford University Press, 2009), and *A Companion to Cognitive Science*, edited by William Bechtel and George Graham (Blackwell, 1999).

GILBERT RYLE

The Concept of Mind

Who Was Gilbert Ryle?

Gilbert Ryle, who died in 1976, was one of the most influential figures in British philosophy in the 1950s and 1960s—he is often credited with a large part in reviving philosophy in Britain after the Second World War and with making Oxford University, for a period, the world center of philosophical activity. He was Waynflete Professor of Metaphysical Philosophy at Oxford from 1945 to 1968, and editor of the pre-eminent British journal of philosophy at the time, *Mind*, between 1948 and 1971.

Ryle was born in 1900 in the seaside town of Brighton, in the south of England. His father was a doctor who had a strong interest in philosophy and astronomy; he was in fact one of the founders of the Aristotelian Society, perhaps Britain's most important philosophical society for most of the twentieth century. In 1919 Ryle went to Queen's College, Oxford, to study Classics, but the subject that made the most impression on him was logic, which, he later wrote, unlike Classics, "felt to me like a grown-up subject, in which there were still unsolved problems." He also spent a great deal of time rowing, and captained the Queen's College Boat Club. In 1923 he gained a first-class honors degree in "Greats" (classical studies and philosophy) and in 1924 got *another* first-class undergraduate degree in "Modern Greats" (Philosophy, Politics, and Economics). In the same year he became a lecturer at Christ Church College.

Early in his career, in the 1930s, Ryle became preoccupied with the question of what philosophy itself is: what, if anything, is its special method and subject matter? It is not, he felt, merely the scholarly study of old texts, it's not just science without the experiments,[1] nor is it *simply* the examination of the meanings of words. His view, in the end, was that philosophy consists in the analysis of certain kinds of meaning*less* expressions—with showing how certain combinations of ordinary words make no sense, and so resolving the problems created by these special kinds of nonsense. For example, "Florence hates the thought of going to hospital" is a grammatically misleading sentence, Ryle would say, since it appears to have the same form as "Florence hates Henry," which erroneously suggests that "the thought of going to hospital," like "Henry," is an expression which refers to an individual thing. This creates the apparent philosophical puzzle of trying to explain what kind of thing a thought is, and how they can be "of" one thing rather than another ... whereas Ryle would have us *dissolve* the problem by

refusing to be trapped by surface grammar and insisting that talk of thoughts as "things" in this way is just *nonsense* created by our loose ways of speaking. Two early articles by Ryle which explore his view of the philosophical method are "Systematically Misleading Expressions" (1932) and "Categories" (1938); both can be found in the second volume of his *Collected Papers*.

Ryle's philosophical method should not be seen as entirely negative. It can be thought of as the attempt to map out the "logical geography" of the problems he considers. That is, he tries to expose the mistaken conceptual maps of other philosophers, and replace them with a new chart giving the correct locations of our ordinary concepts. *The Concept of Mind*, Ryle's first and best-known book and a modern classic of philosophy, applies this method to Cartesian dualism. As he once put it, Ryle was looking around for "some notorious and large-size Gordian Knot" upon which to "exhibit a sustained piece of analytical hatchet-work," and he happened to settle upon our set of traditional—and in his view mistaken—assumptions about the nature of mind. His hatchet-work was immensely successful: partly because of the influence of *The Concept of Mind*, it is today almost (but not entirely) impossible to find a professional philosopher of mind who will admit to believing in the traditional dualism of Descartes (which makes mind and body separate substances).

With the coming of the Second World War in 1939, Ryle volunteered for military service and was commissioned in the Welsh Guards, where he was involved in intelligence work. Immediately after the war Ryle was elected to the Waynflete chair of philosophy at Oxford, and when *The Concept of Mind* came out four years later Ryle was immediately established as a leading British philosopher. Representative book reviews by his peers said, "this is probably one of the two or three most important and original works of

---

1 Ryle was quite candid about his general ignorance of science and psychology, but he did not feel this harmed his philosophy.

general philosophy which have been published in English in the last twenty years" and "it stands head and shoulders above its contemporaries."

During the next thirty years in which Ryle taught at Oxford and edited *Mind*, then perhaps the world's leading philosophical journal, he had a substantial impact on the growth and flourishing of the subject of philosophy in the second half of the twentieth century. Many of his students (such as A.J. Ayer, J.J.C. Smart, and Daniel Dennett) went on to become well-known philosophers; he was a constant presence at philosophical conferences all over the world (but especially the main British annual conference, the Joint Session of the Mind and Aristotelian Societies); and his editorship of *Mind* favored a new style of short, focussed, analytical papers, and was deliberately encouraging to younger philosophers and philosophers from outside of Britain. Ryle retired from his Oxford chair in 1968, but remained philosophically active until his death in 1976.

What Is the Structure of This Reading?

"Descartes's Myth" is the first chapter of *The Concept of Mind*, which contains ten chapters in all. The functions of this first chapter are (a) to lay out Ryle's target, Cartesian dualism, in preparation for Ryle's attack; (b) to describe generally the kind of logical error that dualism makes (a "category mistake"); and (c) to speculate about the historical origins of this mistake. The rest of the book consists, more or less, of a sequence of chapters each of which consider different aspects of mental life—such as intelligence, the will, emotion, sensation, imagination, and self-knowledge—and try to expose the absurdities of the traditional Cartesian "logical geography" of these notions. In place of these faulty conceptual maps, Ryle argues for an account of the mind that generally treats mental states simply as dispositions or tendencies to behave in certain ways rather than others. Intelligence, for example, according to Ryle should not be seen as something *additional* to behavior (a kind of ghostly mechanism which plans our behavior by judging possible actions according to a set of internally stored rules) but as itself a *kind* of behavior—a disposition to regularly perform task *X* well, in a variety of different contexts.

Some Useful Background Information

Ryle is often described as rejecting traditional dualism and replacing it with a new philosophical theory of the mind called *behaviorism*. Behaviorism, which was founded by the American psychologist John B. Watson in 1913 (and explained at length in his 1925 book *Behaviorism*), was originally intended to be an experimental method for psychology. Watson's view was that psychology ought to be a strictly empirical and 'respectable' science; it therefore should not rely on the solitary introspective examination of one's own private mental states, but instead should restrict its data to objective, repeatable facts about "what an organism does and says." The business of psychology, then, should be the construction of psychological laws describing correlations between stimuli and reactions; psychology is best seen, not as the study of consciousness, but as the explanation and prediction of behavior. This form of behaviorism is usually called *methodological* (or *scientific*) *behaviorism*, and it is important to notice that it need not actually *deny* the existence of internal mental states but just says that the science of behavior can avoid talking about them.[2]

In the hands of the philosophers, behaviorism became not just a psychological method but a *theory* of the nature of mental states. In its purest form, this is the view that statements about mental phenomena can be completely analyzed in terms of (or reduced to, or translated into) statements about behavior and dispositions to behave. To have a mind *just is* to behave in a certain way. For example, to say that Othello is feeling jealous is, according to behaviorism, to say no more and no less than that he is behaving in a way characteristic of jealousy, or that he would behave in that way given suitable provocation. According to this theory, there are no internal "mental states" *in addition to* the patterns of human behavior. It is this kind of behaviorism—often called *logical* (or *analytic*) *behaviorism*—which is usually attributed to Gilbert

---

2   Although many behaviorists, such as Watson and B.F. Skinner, do in fact seem to have flirted with the notion that the mind can be eliminated—that it is just a kind of fiction designed to explain the complex movements of human bodies.

Ryle (even though he himself, somewhat unconvincingly, denied that he was a behaviorist): indeed, *The Concept of Mind* is frequently cited as the central text of logical behaviorism.

Today, few if any philosophers are logical behaviorists. It is generally accepted that no analysis of the behavior corresponding to any particular belief or desire is possible, since what someone is disposed to do depends not only on a single belief but, in a potentially infinite variety of ways, on a whole system of connected beliefs. For example, the belief that a glass is half full of water will be associated with different behaviors depending on what else one believes about water (e.g., believing that it is a lethal acid), what one desires (e.g., whether or not you are thirsty), what one believes about the current perceptual conditions (e.g., thinking you are dreaming), and so on. There just is no single behavioral analysis of what it is to believe the glass is half full, and so that belief can't just *be* a set of behaviors.

Another major sticking point for behaviorism has been the worry that the behaviorist cannot treat mental states as being the *causes* of behavior since, for them, mentality just *is* a particular pattern of behavior. For example, a behaviorist cannot correctly say that someone winces because they feel pain, or is a crackerjack Scrabble player because they have a large vocabulary, since wincing and playing Scrabble well are *part* of what it is to feel pain or have a large vocabulary, rather than *effects* of those things.

Other forms of philosophical behaviorism live on today however in, for example, the following three modern theories:.

1. *Analytical functionalism* is the view that the meanings of mental terms can be analyzed in terms of their role in our commonsense theory of behavior, "folk psychology." This view was held by, for example, David Lewis.
2. *Eliminative behaviorism* is a theory, associated with W.V. Quine, which denies any reality to internal mental states and talks only of overt behavior.
3. A theory developed by Donald Davidson, sometimes called *interpretivism*, holds that an "ideal interpreter" can have as complete and infallible access as is possible to the mental life of another

person (because, for Davidson, to have a certain belief *just is* to be the kind of organism an ideal interpreter would attribute that belief to).

A Common Misconception

It is important to realize that the Ryle selection presented here, though itself a seminal piece of philosophy, is only a small part of a larger work. In this chapter, Ryle does not attempt to present all of his arguments against the doctrine of the ghost in the machine, nor does he explicitly describe his alternative behaviorist theory. Much of the power of Ryle's diagnosis comes from its initial plausibility, rather than from a battery of overt arguments. On the other hand, Ryle does make a couple of arguments, and it is also possible to see the seeds of other lines of argument being planted in this reading.

Suggestions for Critical Reflection

1. Ryle's central conceptual tool in his critique of the doctrine of the ghost in the machine is the notion of a *category mistake*. How clear is this notion? Is it precise enough to do the job Ryle wants it to do?
2. Do you think that what Ryle describes as the "official doctrine" is now defunct? Should it be? Does Ryle persuade you that it is absurd?
3. A big part of Ryle's assault on the ghost in the machine is his attack on the "causal hypothesis." How radical would it be if we abandoned this view of the mind as "para-mechanical"? What consequences would this have for our understanding of the mind and human action?
4. On the basis of the evidence available in this reading, how behavioristic do you think Ryle is? How much does what he has to say about what the mind is *not* tell us about what he thinks the mind *is*?
5. Ryle once said, "science talks about the world, while philosophy talks about talk about the world." How much, if at all, does his admitted ignorance of psychology and neuroscience harm Ryle's arguments about the nature of the mind? What does your answer to this question suggest about the nature of philosophy?

Suggestions for Further Reading

I recommend reading the rest of Ryle's *The Concept of Mind* (issued in various editions, including one from the University of Chicago Press and one from Penguin). His second book, *Dilemmas* (Cambridge University Press, 1954), continues to apply Ryle's philosophical method, and most of his papers are collected in two volumes originally published by Hutchinson in 1971. The two best secondary sources on Ryle's work are *Gilbert Ryle: An Introduction to his Philosophy*, by William Lyons (Harvester Press, 1980), and *Ryle: A Collection of Critical Essays*, edited by O.P. Wood and G.W. Pitcher (Doubleday, 1970).

A modern case for Cartesian dualism has been ably put by John Foster in *The Immaterial Self* (Routledge, 1991). The best source for methodological behaviorism is probably B.F. Skinner's book *Science and Human Behavior* (Macmillan, 1953); he also presented his vision of a utopian society run according to proper behaviorist principles in the novel *Walden Two* (Macmillan, 1948). A short yet rigorous presentation of logical behaviorism is Carl Hempel's "The Logical Analysis of Psychology," which can be found in *Readings in Philosophy of Psychology*, Volume 1, edited by Ned Block (Harvard University Press, 1980). P.T. Geach's book *Mental Acts* (Routledge & Kegan Paul, 1957) is sometimes considered to be the decisive refutation of classical logical behaviorism, while methodological behaviorism is effectively savaged in Noam Chomsky's review of Skinner's *Verbal Behavior* in the journal *Language* 35 (1959).

The Concept of Mind

Chapter 1: Descartes's Myth[3]

(1) The Official Doctrine

There is a doctrine about the nature and place of minds which is so prevalent among theorists and even among laymen that it deserves to be described as the official theory. Most philosophers, psychologists and religious teachers subscribe, with minor reservations, to its main articles and, although they admit certain theoretical difficulties in it, they tend to assume that these can be overcome without serious modifications being made to the architecture of the theory. It will be argued here that the central principles of the doctrine are unsound and conflict with the whole body of what we know about minds when we are not speculating about them.

The official doctrine, which hails chiefly from Descartes,[4] is something like this. With the doubtful exceptions of idiots[5] and infants in arms every human being has both a body and a mind. Some would prefer to say that every human being is both a body and a mind. His body and his mind are ordinarily harnessed together, but after the death of the body his mind may continue to exist and function.

Human bodies are in space and are subject to the mechanical laws which govern all other bodies in space. Bodily processes and states can be inspected by external observers. So a man's bodily life is as much a public affair as are the lives of animals and reptiles and even as the careers of trees, crystals and planets.

But minds are not in space, nor are their operations subject to mechanical laws. The workings of one mind are not witnessable by other observers; its career is private. Only I can take direct cognisance of the states and processes of my own mind. A person therefore lives through two collateral histories, one consisting of what happens in and to his body, the other consisting of what happens in and to his mind. The first is public, the second private. The events in the first history are events in the physical world, those in the second are events in the mental world.

---

3   This is the first chapter of Ryle's book *The Concept of Mind*, copyright © 1984 London: Routledge and Chicago: The University of Chicago Press. Reproduced by permission of Taylor & Francis Books UK and with

permission of the Principal, Fellows, and Scholars of Hertford College in the University of Oxford.

4   See Descartes's *Meditations on First Philosophy*, especially the Second and Sixth Meditations.

5   The term "idiot" here comes from out-of-date clinical terminology where it means someone so mentally deficient as to be permanently incapable of rational conduct; it was often defined as having a "mental age" below three years.

It has been disputed whether a person does or can directly monitor all or only some of the episodes of his own private history; but, according to the official doctrine, of at least some of these episodes he has direct and unchallengeable cognisance. In consciousness, self-consciousness and introspection he is directly and authentically apprised of the present states and operations of his mind. He may have great or small uncertainties about concurrent and adjacent episodes in the physical world, but he can have none about at least part of what is momentarily occupying his mind.

It is customary to express this bifurcation of his two lives and of his two worlds by saying that the things and events which belong to the physical world, including his own body, are external, while the workings of his own mind are internal. This antithesis of outer and inner is of course meant to be construed as a metaphor, since minds, not being in space, could not be described as being spatially inside anything else, or as having things going on spatially inside themselves. But relapses from this good intention are common and theorists are found speculating how stimuli, the physical sources of which are yards or miles outside a person's skin, can generate mental responses inside his skull, or how decisions framed inside his cranium can set going movements of his extremities.

Even when 'inner' and 'outer' are construed as metaphors, the problem how a person's mind and body influence one another is notoriously charged with theoretical difficulties. What the mind wills, the legs, arms and the tongue execute; what affects the ear and the eye has something to do with what the mind perceives; grimaces and smiles betray the mind's moods and bodily castigations[6] lead, it is hoped, to moral improvement. But the actual transactions between the episodes of the private history and those of the public history remain mysterious, since by definition they can belong to neither series. They could not be reported among the happenings described in a person's autobiography of his inner life, but nor could they be reported among those described in someone else's biography of that person's overt career. They can be inspected neither by introspection nor by laboratory experiment. They are theoretical shuttlecocks which are forever being bandied from the physiologist back to the psychologist and from the psychologist back to the physiologist.

Underlying this partly metaphorical representation of the bifurcation of a person's two lives there is a seemingly more profound and philosophical assumption. It is assumed that there are two different kinds of existence or status. What exists or happens may have the status of physical existence, or it may have the status of mental existence. Somewhat as the faces of coins are either heads or tails, or somewhat as living creatures are either male or female, so, it is supposed, some existing is physical existing, other existing is mental existing. It is a necessary feature of what has physical existence that it is in space and time; it is a necessary feature of what has mental existence that is in time but not in space. What has physical existence is composed of matter, or else is a function of matter; what has mental existence consists of consciousness, or else is a function of consciousness.

There is thus a polar opposition between mind and matter, an opposition which is often brought out as follows. Material objects are situated in a common field, known as 'space', and what happens to one body in one part of space is mechanically connected with what happens to other bodies in other parts of space. But mental happenings occur in insulated fields, known as 'minds', and there is, apart maybe from telepathy, no direct causal connexion between what happens in one mind and what happens in another. Only through the medium of the public physical world can the mind of one person make a difference to the mind of another. The mind is its own place and in his inner life each of us lives the life of a ghostly Robinson Crusoe. People can see, hear and jolt one another's bodies, but they are irremediably blind and deaf to the workings of one another's minds and inoperative upon them.

What sort of knowledge can be secured of the workings of a mind? On the one side, according to the official theory, a person has direct knowledge of the best imaginable kind of the workings of his own mind. Mental states and processes are (or are normally) conscious states and processes, and the consciousness which irradiates them can engender no illusions and leaves the door open for no doubts. A person's

---

6   "Castigation" means "severe punishment."

present thinkings, feelings and willings, his perceivings, rememberings and imaginings are intrinsically 'phosphorescent'; their existence and their nature are inevitably betrayed to their owner. The inner life is a stream of consciousness of such a sort that it would be absurd to suggest that the mind whose life is that stream might be unaware of what is passing down it.

True, the evidence adduced recently by Freud[7] seems to show that there exist channels tributary to this stream, which run hidden from their owner. People are actuated[8] by impulses the existence of which they vigorously disavow; some of their thoughts differ from the thoughts which they acknowledge; and some of the actions which they think they will to perform they do not really will. They are thoroughly gulled[9] by some of their own hypocrisies and they successfully ignore facts about their mental lives which on the official theory ought to be patent to them. Holders of the official theory tend, however, to maintain that anyhow in normal circumstances a person must be directly and authentically seized of the present state and workings of his own mind.

Besides being currently supplied with these alleged immediate data of consciousness, a person is also generally supposed to be able to exercise from time to time a special kind of perception, namely inner perception, or introspection. He can take a (non-optical) 'look' at what is passing in his mind. Not only can he view and scrutinize a flower through his sense of sight and listen to and discriminate the notes of a bell through his sense of hearing; he can also reflectively or introspectively watch, without any bodily organ of sense, the current episodes of his inner life. This self-observation is also commonly supposed to be immune from illusion, confusion or doubt. A mind's reports of its own affairs have a certainty superior to the best that is possessed by its reports of matters in the physical world. Sense-perceptions can, but consciousness and introspection cannot, be mistaken or confused.

On the other side, one person has no direct access of any sort to the events of the inner life of another. He cannot do better than make problematic inferences from the observed behaviour of the other person's body to the states of mind which, by analogy from his own conduct, he supposes to be signalized by that behaviour. Direct access to the workings of a mind is the privilege of that mind itself; in default of such privileged access, the workings of one mind are inevitably occult[10] to everyone else. For the supposed arguments from bodily movements similar to their own to mental workings similar to their own would lack any possibility of observational corroboration. Not unnaturally, therefore, an adherent of the official theory finds it difficult to resist this consequence of his premisses, that he has no good reason to believe that there do exist minds other than his own. Even if he prefers to believe that to other human bodies there are harnessed minds not unlike his own, he cannot claim to be able to discover their individual characteristics, or the particular things that they undergo and do. Absolute solitude is on this showing the ineluctable destiny of the soul. Only our bodies can meet.

As a necessary corollary of this general scheme there is implicitly prescribed a special way of construing our ordinary concepts of mental powers and operations. The verbs, nouns and adjectives, with which in ordinary life we describe the wits, characters and higher-grade performances of the people with whom we have to do, are required to be construed as signifying special episodes in their secret histories, or else as signifying tendencies for such episodes to occur. When someone is described as knowing, believing or guessing something, as hoping, dreading, intending or shirking something, as designing thus or being

---

7   Sigmund Freud (1856–1939) was, of course, an Austrian psychologist and the main founder of psychoanalysis. One of his main ideas was that the motives for human action are far more numerous and complex than is commonly thought, and that our most basic and constant motives—which result from various significant experiences throughout our life, and particularly in early childhood—are unconscious in the sense that it is difficult for us to acknowledge them and so we "repress" them.

8   Caused to act.

9   Tricked or fooled.

10   Ryle does not literally mean "supernatural," but hidden from human view or beyond the normal range of human knowledge. (The word comes from the Latin for "secret" or "covered over.")

amused at that, these verbs are supposed to denote the occurrence of specific modifications in his (to us) occult stream of consciousness. Only his own privileged access to this stream in direct awareness and introspection could provide authentic testimony that these mental-conduct verbs were correctly or incorrectly applied. The onlooker, be he teacher, critic, biographer or friend, can never assure himself that his comments have any vestige of truth. Yet it was just because we do in fact all know how to make such comments, make them with general correctness and correct them when they turn out to be confused or mistaken, that philosophers found it necessary to construct their theories of the nature and place of minds. Finding mental-conduct concepts being regularly and effectively used, they properly sought to fix their logical geography. But the logical geography officially recommended would entail that there could be no regular or effective use of these mental-conduct concepts in our descriptions of, and prescriptions for, other people's minds.

(2) The Absurdity of the Official Doctrine

Such in outline is the official theory. I shall often speak of it, with deliberate abusiveness, as 'the dogma of the Ghost in the Machine'. I hope to prove that it is entirely false, and false not in detail but in principle. It is not merely an assemblage of particular mistakes. It is one big mistake and a mistake of a special kind. It is, namely, a category-mistake. It represents the facts of mental life as if they belonged to one logical type or category (or range of types or categories), when they actually belong to another. The dogma is therefore a philosopher's myth. In attempting to explode the myth I shall probably be taken to be denying well-known facts about the mental life of human beings, and my plea that I aim at doing nothing more than rectify the logic of mental-conduct concepts will probably be disallowed as mere subterfuge.

I must first indicate what is meant by the phrase 'Category-mistake'. This I do in a series of illustrations.

A foreigner visiting Oxford or Cambridge[11] for the first time is shown a number of colleges, libraries, playing fields, museums, scientific departments and administrative offices. He then asks 'But where is the University? I have seen where the members of the Colleges live, where the Registrar works, where the scientists experiment and the rest. But I have not yet seen the University in which reside and work the members of your University.' It has then to be explained to him that the University is not another collateral institution, some ulterior counterpart to the colleges, laboratories and offices which he has seen. The University is just the way in which all that he has already seen is organized. When they are seen and when their coordination is understood, the University has been seen. His mistake lay in his innocent assumption that it was correct to speak of Christ Church, the Bodleian Library, the Ashmolean Museum[12] *and* the University, to speak, that is, as if 'the University' stood for an extra member of the class of which these other units are members. He was mistakenly allocating the University to the same category as that to which the other institutions belong.

The same mistake would be made by a child witnessing the march-past of a division, who, having had pointed out to him such and such battalions, batteries, squadrons, etc., asked when the division was going to appear. He would be supposing that a division was a counterpart to the units already seen, partly similar to them and partly unlike them. He would be shown his mistake by being told that in watching the battalions, batteries and squadrons marching past he had been watching the division matching past. The march past was not a parade of battalions, batteries, squadrons *and* a division; it was a parade of the battalions, batteries and squadrons *of* a division.

---

11   Oxford and Cambridge, unlike most modern universities, are not single, unified institutions but consist of collections of 30 or 40 independent colleges and their facilities, plus a few general university buildings used by all the colleges, such as the Examination Schools at Oxford. One consequence of this is that neither Oxford nor Cambridge have a campus or even a central "University" building, but are spread out in various buildings across their respective towns.

12   Christ Church College, the Bodleian, and the Ashmolean are all institutions at Oxford.

One more illustration. A foreigner watching his first game of cricket learns what are the functions of the bowlers, the batsmen, the fielders, the umpires and the scorers. He then says 'But there is no one left on the field to contribute the famous element of team-spirit. I see who does the bowling, the batting and the wicket-keeping, but I do not see whose role it is to exercise *esprit de corps*.' Once more, it would have to be explained that he was looking for the wrong type of thing. Team-spirit is not another cricketing-operation supplementary to all of the other special tasks. It is, roughly, the keenness with which each of the special tasks is performed, and performing a task keenly is not performing two tasks. Certainly exhibiting team spirit is not the same thing as bowling or catching, but nor is it a third thing such that we can say that the bowler first bowls *and* then exhibits team-spirit or that a fielder is at a given moment *either* catching *or* displaying *esprit de corps*.

These illustrations of category-mistakes have a common feature which must be noticed. The mistakes were made by people who did not know how to wield the concepts *University*, *division* and *team-spirit*. Their puzzles arose from inability to use certain items in the English vocabulary.

The theoretically interesting category-mistakes are those made by people who are perfectly competent to apply concepts, at least in the situations with which they are familiar, but are still liable in their abstract thinking to allocate those concepts to logical types to which they do not belong. An instance of a mistake of this sort would be the following story. A student of politics has learned the main differences between the British, the French, and the American Constitutions, and has learned also the differences and connexions between the Cabinet, Parliament, the various Ministries, the Judicature and the Church of England. But he still became embarrassed when asked questions about the connexions between the Church of England, the Home Office and the British Constitution. For while the Church and the Home Office are institutions, the British Constitution is not another institution in the same sense of that noun. So inter-institutional relations which can be asserted or denied to hold between the Church and the Home Office cannot be asserted or denied to hold between either of them and the British Constitution. 'The British Constitution' is not a term of the same logical type as 'the Home Office' and 'the Church of England'. In a partially similar way, John Doe may be a relative, a friend, an enemy or a stranger to Richard Roe; but he cannot be any of these things to the Average Taxpayer. He knows how to talk sense in certain sorts of discussions about the Average Taxpayer, but he is baffled to say why he could not come across him in the street as he can come across Richard Roe.

It is pertinent to our main subject to notice that, so long as the student of politics continues to think of the British Constitution as a counterpart to the other institutions, he will tend to describe it as a mysteriously occult institution, and so long as John Doe continues to think of the Average Taxpayer as a fellow-citizen, he will tend to think of him as an elusive insubstantial man, a ghost who is everywhere yet nowhere.

My destructive purpose is to show that a family of radical category-mistakes is the source of the double-life theory. The representation of a person as a ghost mysteriously ensconced in a machine derives from this argument. Because, as is true, a person's thinking, feeling and purposive doing cannot be described solely in the idioms of physics, chemistry and physiology, therefore they must be described in counterpart idioms. As the human body is a complex organized unit, so the human mind must be another complex organized unit, though one made of a different sort of stuff and with a different sort of structure. Or, again, as the human body, like any other parcel of matter, is a field of causes and effects, so the mind must be another field of causes and effects, though not (Heaven be praised) mechanical causes and effects.

(3) The Origin of the Category-Mistake

One of the chief intellectual origins of what I have yet to prove to be the Cartesian category-mistake seems to be this. When Galileo showed that his methods of scientific discovery were competent to provide a mechanical theory which should cover every occupant of space, Descartes found in himself two conflicting motives. As a man of scientific genius he could not but endorse the claims of mechanics, yet as a religious and moral man he could not accept, as Hobbes accepted, the discouraging rider to those claims, namely that human nature differs only in degree of complexity from clockwork. The mental could not be just a variety of the mechanical.

He and subsequent philosophers naturally but erroneously availed themselves of the following escape-route. Since mental-conduct words are not to be construed as signifying the occurrence of mechanical processes, they must be construed as signifying the occurrence of non-mechanical processes; since mechanical laws explain movements in space as the effects of other movements in space, other laws must explain some of the non-spatial workings of minds as the effects of other non-spatial workings of minds. The difference between the human behaviours which we describe as intelligent and those which we describe as unintelligent must be a difference in their causation; so, while some movements of human tongues and limbs are the effects of mechanical causes, others must be the effects of non-mechanical causes, i.e., some issue from movements of particles of matter, others from workings of the mind.

The differences between the physical and the mental were thus represented as differences inside the common framework of the categories of 'thing', 'stuff', 'attribute', 'state', 'process', 'change', 'cause' and 'effect'. Minds are things, but different sorts of things from bodies; mental processes are causes and effects, but different sorts of causes and effects from bodily movements. And so on. Somewhat as the foreigner expected the University to be an extra edifice, rather like a college but also considerably different, so the repudiators of mechanism represented minds as extra centres of causal processes, rather like machines but also considerably different from them. Their theory was a paramechanical hypothesis.

That this assumption was at the heart of the doctrine is shown by the fact that there was from the beginning felt to be a major theoretical difficulty in explaining how minds can influence and be influenced by bodies. How can a mental process, such as willing, cause spatial movements like the movements of the tongue? How can a physical change in the optic nerve

have among its effects a mind's perception of a flash of light? This notorious crux[13] by itself shows the logical mould into which Descartes pressed his theory of the mind. It was the self-same mould into which he and Galileo set their mechanics. Still unwittingly adhering to the grammar of mechanics, he tried to avert disaster by describing minds in what was merely an obverse[14] vocabulary. The workings of minds had to be described by the mere negatives of the specific descriptions given to bodies; they are not in space, they are not motions, they are not modifications of matter, they are not accessible to public observation. Minds are not bits of clockwork, they are just bits of not-clockwork.

As thus represented, minds are not merely ghosts harnessed to machines, they are themselves just spectral machines. Though the human body is an engine, it is not quite an ordinary engine, since some of its workings are governed by another engine inside it—this interior governor-engine being one of a very special sort. It is invisible, inaudible and it has no size or weight. It cannot be taken to bits and the laws it obeys are not those known to ordinary engineers. Nothing is known of how it governs the bodily engine.

A second major crux points the same moral. Since, according to the doctrine, minds belong to the same category as bodies and since bodies are rigidly governed by mechanical laws, it seemed to many theorists to follow that minds must be similarly governed by rigid non-mechanical laws. The physical world is a deterministic system, so the mental world must be a deterministic system. Bodies cannot help the modifications that they undergo, so minds cannot help pursuing the careers fixed for them. *Responsibility*, *choice*, *merit* and *demerit* are therefore inapplicable concepts—unless the compromise solution is adopted of saying that the laws governing mental processes, unlike those governing physical processes, have the

---

13   The crux of a question is its most basic, critical, or deeply puzzling feature. (This term probably comes from the Medieval Latin phrase *crux interpretum*, or "torment of interpreters.")

14   A thing's obverse is its complement or counterpart: e.g., the obverse of black is white, and the obverse of front is back.

congenial attribute of being only rather rigid. The problem of the Freedom of the Will was the problem how to reconcile the hypothesis that minds are to be described in terms drawn from the categories of mechanics with the knowledge that higher-grade human conduct is not of a piece with the behaviour of machines.

It is an historical curiosity that it was not noticed that the entire argument was broken-backed. Theorists correctly assumed that any sane man could already recognize the differences between, say, rational and non-rational utterances or between purposive and automatic behaviour. Else there would have been nothing requiring to be salved from mechanism. Yet the explanation given presupposed that one person could in principle never recognize the difference between the rational and the irrational utterances issuing from other human bodies, since he could never get access to the postulated immaterial causes of some of their utterances. Save for the doubtful exception of himself, he could never tell the difference between a man and a Robot. It would have to be conceded, for example, that, for all that we can tell, the inner lives of persons who are classed as idiots or lunatics are as rational as those of anyone else. Perhaps only their overt behaviour is disappointing; that is to say, perhaps 'idiots' are not really idiotic, or 'lunatics' lunatic. Perhaps, too, some of those who are classed as sane are really idiots. According to the theory, external observers could never know how the overt behaviour of others is correlated with their mental powers and processes and so they could never know or even plausibly conjecture whether their applications of mental-conduct concepts to these other people were correct or incorrect. It would then be hazardous or impossible for a man to claim sanity or logical consistency even for himself, since he would be debarred from comparing his own performances with those of others. In short, our characterizations of persons and their performances as intelligent, prudent and virtuous or as stupid, hypocritical and cowardly could never have been made, so the problem of providing a special causal hypothesis to serve as the basis of such diagnoses would never have arisen. The question, 'How do persons differ from machines?' arose

just because everyone already knew how to apply mental-conduct concepts before the new causal hypothesis was introduced. This causal hypothesis could not therefore be the source of the criteria used in those applications. Nor, of course, has the causal hypothesis in any degree improved our handling of those criteria. We still distinguish good from bad arithmetic, politic[15] from impolitic conduct and fertile from infertile imaginations in the ways in which Descartes himself distinguished them before and after he speculated how the applicability of these criteria was compatible with the principle of mechanical causation.

He had mistaken the logic of his problem. Instead of asking by what criteria intelligent behaviour is actually distinguished from non-intelligent behaviour, he asked 'Given that the principle of mechanical causation does not tell us the difference, what other causal principle will tell it us?' He realized that the problem was not one of mechanics and assumed that it must therefore be one of some counterpart to mechanics. Not unnaturally psychology is often cast for just this role.

When two terms belong to the same category, it is proper to construct conjunctive[16] propositions embodying them. Thus a purchaser may say that he bought a left-hand glove and a right-hand glove, but not that he bought a left-hand glove, a right-hand glove and a pair of gloves. 'She came home in a flood of tears and a sedan-chair'[17] is a well known joke based on the absurdity of conjoining terms of different types. It would have been equally ridiculous to construct the disjunction. 'She came home either in a flood of tears or else in a sedan-chair.' Now the dogma of the Ghost in the Machine does just this. It maintains that there exist both bodies and minds; that there occur physical

---

15 Judicious, careful.

16 A conjunction is an 'and' statement (e.g., "It's 2 AM and you're past curfew"); a disjunction is an 'or' sentence (e.g., "Either he's drunk or very nervous.").

17 A sedan chair is an enclosed chair carried on horizontal poles on the shoulders of two or four porters. This form of transport was common in Europe in the seventeenth and eighteenth centuries and can still sometimes be seen in India and parts of the Far East.

processes and mental processes; that there are mechanical causes of corporeal movements and mental
causes of corporeal movements. I shall argue that
these and other analogous conjunctions are absurd;
but, it must be noticed, the argument will not show
that either of the illegitimately conjoined propositions
is absurd in itself. I am not, for example, denying that
there occur mental processes. Doing long division is
a mental process and so is making a joke. But I am
saying that the phrase 'there occur mental processes'
does not mean the same sort of thing as 'there occur
physical processes', and, therefore, that it makes no
sense to conjoin or disjoin the two.

If my argument is successful, there will follow
some interesting consequences. First, the hallowed
contrast between Mind and Matter will be dissipated, but dissipated not by either of the equally
hallowed absorptions of Mind by Matter or of Matter by Mind, but in quite a different way. For the
seeming contrast of the two will be shown to be as
illegitimate as would be the contrast of 'she came
home in a flood of tears' and 'she came home in a
sedan-chair'. The belief that there is a polar opposition between Mind and Matter is the belief that they
are terms of the same logical type.

It will also follow that both Idealism and Materialism are answers to an improper question. The
'reduction' of the material world to mental states
and processes, as well as the 'reduction' of mental
states and processes to physical states and processes,
presupposes the legitimacy of the disjunction 'Either
there exist minds or there exist bodies (but not both)'.
It would be like saying, 'Either she bought a left-hand
and right-hand glove or she bought a pair of gloves
(but not both)'.

It is perfectly proper to say, in one logical tone of
voice, that there exist minds, and to say, in another
logical tone of voice, that there exist bodies. But these
expressions do not indicate two different species of
existence, for 'existence' is not a generic word like
'coloured' or 'sexed'. They indicate two different
senses of 'exist', somewhat as 'rising' has different
senses in 'the tide is rising', 'hopes are rising', and
'the average age of death is rising'. A man would be
thought to be making a poor joke who said that three
things are now rising, namely the tide, hopes and

the average age of death. It would be just as good or
bad a joke to say that there exist prime numbers and
Wednesdays and public opinions and navies; or that
there exist both minds and bodies. In the succeeding
chapters I try to prove that the official theory does rest
on a batch of category-mistakes by showing that logically absurd corollaries follow from it. The exhibition
of these absurdities will have the constructive effect
of bringing out part of the correct logic of mental-
conduct concepts.

(4) Historical Note

It would not be true to say that the official theory
derives solely from Descartes's theories, or even
from a more widespread anxiety about the implications of seventeenth-century mechanics. Scholastic and Reformation theology[18] had schooled
the intellects of the scientists as well as of the
laymen, philosophers and clerics of that age. Stoic-
Augustinian[19] theories of the will were embedded in
the Calvinist[20] doctrines of sin and grace; Platonic
and Aristotelian theories of the intellect shaped the
orthodox doctrines of the immortality of the soul.
Descartes was reformulating already prevalent

18   Scholasticism was the educational tradition of the
     medieval universities and a system of thought which
     brought together Catholic doctrine with elements of
     classical Greek philosophy. The Reformation was a
     sixteenth-century movement to reform the Roman
     Catholic church which resulted in the establishment
     of the Protestant churches.

19   Stoicism is an ancient philosophical system (founded
     by Zeno of Citium in about 300 BCE) which held,
     among other things, that the virtuous will should be
     brought into harmony with *logos*—the rational nature
     of things, or God. It had a great influence on early
     Christian thinkers, including Saint Augustine (354–430
     CE) who defended the view that humans have free
     control of their will and so are responsible for their
     own sin.

20   Calvinism is the theology of John Calvin (1509–1564)
     and his followers. One of its central doctrines is that
     human actions are predetermined by God and that we
     are all sinners, but that God has bestowed his grace on
     some believers, allowing them to be redeemed by faith.

theological doctrines of the soul in the new syntax of Galileo. The theologian's privacy of conscience became the philosopher's privacy of consciousness, and what had been the bogy of Predestination reappeared as the bogy of Determinism.[21]

---

21 Predestination is the view that God has already decided, at the beginning of time, for every soul whether it will be saved or damned. (The theological problem then is: what use are faith or good works, if our fate is already sealed?) Determinism is the thesis that all events or situations are determined or fixed by prior events or states of affairs: for example, the current situation of a physical particle might be said to be wholly determined by all its previous positions and interactions with other particles. (See Chapter 6.)

It would also not be true to say that the two-worlds myth did no theoretical good. Myths often do a lot of theoretical good, while they are still new. One benefit bestowed by the para-mechanical myth was that it partly superannuated the then prevalent para-political myth. Minds and their Faculties had previously been described by analogies with political superiors and political subordinates. The idioms used were those of ruling, obeying, collaborating and rebelling. They survived and still survive in many ethical and some epistemological discussions. As, in physics, the new myth of occult Forces was a scientific improvement on the old myth of Final Causes, so, in anthropological and psychological theory, the new myth of hidden operations, impulses and agencies was an improvement on the old myth of dictations, deferences and disobediences.

HILARY PUTNAM
"The Nature of Mental States"

Who Is Hilary Putnam?

Hilary W. Putnam is one of the most important American philosophers since World War II and is today a sort of "elder statesman" for North American philosophy. He was born in Chicago in 1926, the son of a well-known author and translator named Samuel Putnam, and his parents lived in France until he was 8, when they moved to Philadelphia. Putnam did his undergraduate degree at the University of Pennsylvania and his PhD, completed in 1951, at the University of California at Los Angeles, where he worked with the eminent philosophers of science Hans Reichenbach and Rudolph Carnap. Putnam taught for a few years at Northwestern University, Princeton, and the Massachusetts Institute of Technology before mov-

ing to Harvard University in 1965, where he is now a Professor Emeritus after retiring in 2000. He is married to Ruth Anna Putnam, who is also a well-known philosopher.

In the 1960s, Putnam was known for his fierce criticism of the US role in the Vietnam War (1954–1975). In 1963, at MIT, he organized one of the first faculty-student committees against the war, and at Harvard he led various campus protests and taught courses on Marxism. He became the official faculty advisor to the Students for a Democratic Society—at that time the main anti-Vietnam-War organization at Harvard—and later joined the "Progressive Labor" faction, which endorsed, in Putnam's words, an "idiosyncratic version of Marxism-Leninism." Though he later abandoned Marxism, Putnam has never ceased to believe that philosophers have a social and political responsibility as well as an academic one.[1]

Putnam began his professional career working in logic and the philosophy of mathematics and science, and since then has done important, often ground-breaking work in the philosophy of mind, the philosophy of language, metaphysics, American pragmatism, and even ethics and politics. John Passmore, a historian of philosophy, has remarked that trying to describe the essence of Putnam's philosophy is like trying to "capture the wind with a fishing net." This is true partly because of the great range of his philosophical writings, but also because Putnam is notorious for changing his position several times on key philosophical issues. A good example of this is the article reprinted here: in "The Nature of Mental States," Putnam founded the theory of mind called functionalism, which is today the most widely held and influential theory of mind. Putnam himself, however, has publicly changed his mind about functionalism and has leveled a battery of arguments against his own theory in his 1988 book *Representation and Reality*.

Putnam's main contributions to philosophy, apart from functionalism, are the following. In the late 1950s and early 1960s Putnam, under the influence of a philosopher named W.V. Quine, published a series of devastating articles attacking the then-dominant school of philosophy, headed by his former teachers at UCLA, called logical positivism. (In particular, he attacked positivist doctrines about the "verifiability theory of meaning," the "analytic-synthetic distinction,"

and the sharp distinction between mathematics and empirical science.)

In the 1970s, together with a philosopher called Saul Kripke, Putnam revolutionized the philosophy of language by developing a new theory of meaning, often called "semantic externalism." The central insight of this theory is that the meanings of words cannot be completely accounted for in terms of what is inside the heads of their users. In other words, we do not give our words meaning simply by *intending* to use them in a particular way, or by somehow "linking" them to a *concept* or a description of what they mean—instead, language gets its meaning from its role in a *community* of speakers and, especially, by its referential connections to the *world*. In Putnam's most famous example, the word "water" gets its meaning not from ideas in the minds of its user, but by the causal connection between our use of the word and the actual stuff—H_2O—we use it about.

To illustrate this, Putnam tells a now-famous science fiction story where he imagines a planet called Twin Earth that is molecule-for-molecule identical with ours, except for one difference: on that planet, what we call "water" is not H_2O but is made of some other chemical compound, XYZ. When Oscar on Earth and Twin Oscar on Twin Earth say the words "water is wet," they will be in the same psychological state (since they are molecule-for-molecule identical), but according to Putnam they nevertheless mean *different* things by their utterances: Oscar means that water is wet, whereas Twin Oscar means that twin water is wet. Since nothing about the speakers is different but only their environment, this shows, as Putnam puts it, that "meanings just ain't in the head." Putnam's most influential presentation of these views is in his article "The Meaning of 'Meaning'" (1975).

Finally, Putnam's most radical change of mind, which earned him the nickname "renegade Putnam" in some quarters, was sprung on the philosophical

---

1   Biographical details about Hilary Putnam were taken from Lance P. Hickey, "Hilary Putnam," in volume 279, *American Philosophers, 1950–2000*, of the *Dictionary of Literary Biography* (Thomson Gale, 2003), pp. 226–237.

community during his presidential address to the American Philosophical Society in 1976. Up to that time, Putnam had been a leading advocate of "scientific realism": the view that the entities postulated by true scientific theories (such as electrons and black holes) really exist, independently of the theories that describe them. In 1976 he more or less reversed his position, and denied that there is any such thing as theory-independent truth; there is no such thing as an "absolute" perspective from which the "real truth" about reality can be seen. According to Putnam's new "internal realism" (which has close affinities both with Immanuel Kant and with American pragmatism—see the notes to William James in Chapter 4) there is nothing more to truth than what would be rationally accepted after "sufficient" (scientific) inquiry. His books *The Many Faces of Realism* (1986) and *Realism with a Human Face* (1987) pursue this line of thought, but his most famous attack on "metaphysical realism," his so-called brain-in-a-vat argument, appears in *Reason, Truth and History* (1982).

Putnam's approach to philosophy can perhaps be summed up by a quote from the German poet Rainer Maria Rilke that Putnam placed at the front of one of his books:

> Be patient toward all that is unsolved in your heart and try to love the *questions themselves* like locked rooms and like books that are written in a very foreign tongue.... *Live* the questions now. Perhaps you will then gradually, without noticing it, live along some distant day into the answer.

What Is the Structure of This Reading?

Putnam's question in this paper is "Is pain a brain state?" and his answer to that question is that it is not, but for novel and important reasons. He begins by considering the nature of identity questions—that is, of questions which ask whether some thing *A* is identical with (the same thing as) *B*. The point of this section is to argue that the mind-brain identity theory is not an *analytic* claim, and thus is neither analytically true nor analytically false: the claim that pain is a brain state should not be thought of as an analysis of the

concepts of "pain" and "brain state" (in the same way as "an oculist is an eye doctor" is an analytic claim) but instead as a claim about those *properties* (like the claim that temperature is mean molecular kinetic energy). This means that it cannot be, as many philosophers at the time argued, just a logical mistake to hold that the mind is identical with the brain. So, Putnam is claiming, if identity theory is false it must be false "on empirical and methodological grounds." However, he then argues, it *is* false.

He tries to show that the identity theory is false—that pains are not brain states—by advancing a competing account and showing that it is empirically and methodologically a better theory. Thus, in section II of the paper, he describes his proposal, which has come to be called the theory of *functionalism* (because it identifies mental states with *functions* from inputs to outputs). Then, in section III, he contrasts functionalism with identity theory and argues that it is, empirically, a more adequate theory. Of particular importance in this section is Putnam's argument that the mind-brain identity theory is unlikely to be true. This argument, today called the "multiple realization" thesis, has had an influence out of all proportion with its apparent simplicity. In section IV Putnam contrasts functionalism with behaviorism, and argues that functionalism has all the virtues of behaviorism without its fatal shortcomings. Finally, Putnam closes the article by describing some of the methodological advantages of functionalism as a scientific theory of the mind.

Some Useful Background Information

In his description of functionalism, Putnam relies heavily on the notion of a "Turing Machine." A Turing Machine is an abstract computing device named after the British logician and mathematician who came up with the idea in 1936, Alan Turing. It operates on an indefinitely long tape divided into squares which it "rolls" along, scanning the square which is directly below it. Each square may contain a symbol from a finite alphabet, and when the machine reads a symbol (or detects the absence of a symbol) it is triggered to perform an action: the symbol on the tape can therefore be thought of as the *input* to the machine.

In addition to reading these inputs, a Turing Machine is also capable of occupying any of a finite number of internal states. What action the machine will perform on any particular occasion is determined by these two things: the input, and the machine's current internal state. A Turing Machine can be programmed to perform two types of actions. It can change its internal state. Or it can produce some "output": it can move one square to the left or right, or it can erase what is on the input square, or it can write a symbol on the square.

Here is an example of a program for a Turing Machine (which starts in state S_1) telling it to count to three.

	q_0	q_1
S_1	$q_1 S_1$	LS_2
S_2	$q_1 S_2$	LS_3
S_3	$q_1 S_3$	H

All the possible internal states for our very simple machine are listed on the left and the possible inputs (symbols on the tape) are in the top row. The other cells describe what actions the machine will take for every combination of input and internal state. Suppose the machine starts in internal state S_1. Then, if it looks at the square below it and sees a blank—input q_0—it will produce output q_1 (i.e., write the symbol "1" on the tape) and stay in internal state S_1. On the other hand, if it had seen a 1 already written on the square, it would produce output L (i.e., move one square to the left) and go into internal state S_2. In state S_2, seeing a blank square, it would write 1 and stay in S_2; while detecting a 1 already written would cause it to move to the left without writing anything and to change its internal state to S_3; and so on. Following this program, as long as it is started in state S_1, the Turing Machine will produce a line of exactly three 1s and then halt its operation (output H).

A table of the type written above, which lays out the program for a Turing Machine, is called a Machine Table (or, sometimes, a State Table). It's important for Putnam's paper that the inputs q_0 and q_1 in the Machine Table need not be a blank square and a square with "1" written on it, but could be the symbols 0 and

1, or the symbols ↑ and ↓, or a picture of an elephant and a picture of a donkey—any input at all which plays the same role in the system as q_0, counts as q_0. Something similar is true of the internal states S_1, S_2, and S_3. This is what Putnam means when he says that the states and inputs can be specified only "implicitly," i.e., only by describing their role in the program.

Some Common Misconceptions

1. Some people find it initially puzzling to see why functionalism is supposed to be so different from mind-brain identity theory. After all, functionalism is a sort of identity theory—it says that mental states *are identical with* functional states—and functional states are often thought of as just rather abstract physical states. For instance, common examples of functional properties include being a mousetrap and being a computer program. Mousetraps and computers are obviously physical objects, with physical properties, so *why not* talk about, say, a computer-program–hard-drive identity theory and, similarly, mind-brain identities, even if functionalism is true?

   Actually there may well be some philosophical substance to this puzzle (see Jaegwon Kim, "Multiple Realization and the Metaphysics of Reduction," *Philosophy and Phenomenological Research* 52 [1992], if you're interested), but you need to take care not to get involved in a "type-token" confusion: just because each *token* of a property (i.e., each individual instance of the property) is physical, it does not follow that the property is itself physical—that it is a physical *type*. For example, even though it might seem likely that the actual instances, or tokens of some computer program, each happen to be identical with some physical configuration of some hard drive or other, it seems very implausible to say that *every* possible instance of that program *must* be a magnetic trace on a plastic disk, never mind that each installation of the program creates *exactly the same type* of physical pattern on the drive (consider, for example, the fact that the low-level "machine language" operations of the program might be quite different in the Windows version, the Macintosh version, the UNIX version, and so on). In short, if these kinds of "multiple realizability" considerations are persuasive, functional types are not physical types even though the objects which actually have those functions may all be entirely physical. And the claim that "pains are identical with brain states" is a claim about types rather than tokens: that is, it doesn't just say that some particular pain (say, the pain of my twisted ankle last Tuesday) is identical with some particular brain state (also mine, last Tuesday)—it is the much more ambitious theoretical claim that *all* pains are brain states of a particular sort. (For this reason mind-brain identity theory is often called "type-type physicalism.")

2. When considering the functional description of a human mind, it is tempting to think of the internal states S_i as being the functional specifications of our internal mental states. For example, if you believe that the garden needs watering (i.e., you are in state S_1) then a given input— the sight of rain clouds, say—will produce one sort of output: perhaps a pleased smile. On the other hand if you are in state S_2, hoping to have a barbecue in an hour, then the output might be different. This way of thinking of Turing Machine functionalism is not entirely wrong, but needs one important qualification: at least in the version of functionalism that Putnam describes in his 1967 paper, the state S_1 is *not* a belief and the state S_2 is *not* a desire. Rather, S_1 is the *Total State* of the organism at that particular time; it might in some sense "include" the belief that the garden needs watering, but it isn't itself that belief. For example, a second later you will probably still believe the garden needs watering, but you will no longer be in S_1 (since your *Total State* will be different), but perhaps in state S_3; in fact, plausibly, you will *never* in your lifetime occupy the same internal Total State twice. This means that, as Putnam has put it in another article, "*no* psychological state in any customary sense can be a Turing Machine state" ("Philosophy and Our Mental Life" [1973]).

Suggestions for Critical Reflection

1. Putnam chooses *pain* for his example of a mental state which can be identified with a functional state, and one might gauge his success in this by asking two slightly different questions. First, how successful is he in showing that *the state which is the cause of pain behavior* (and so of our ascriptions of pain to others, and so on) is a functional state, rather than a physical state or a behavioral disposition? Second, how successful is he in showing that *our personal experience of pain* is an experience of a functional state? That is, is it plausible that "what it is like to feel pain" (to use an expression from Thomas Nagel—see his paper in this chapter) can be captured by a functional analysis? If it cannot be, does this matter? Is this a serious problem for functionalism as a theory of the mind?

2. Putnam does not, in this article, talk about cognitive mental states like beliefs and desires. One of the main features of such mental states is that they are *meaningful* (or, in the technical vocabulary, "intentional"); beliefs and perceptions, for example, are standardly understood as *representing* the world as being a certain way, and as such they can be either true or false. Do you think that what makes a mental state *meaningful* could be cashed out in a functionalist way? If so, how do you think this might go? If not, how serious a set-back would this be for functionalism?

3. Putnam gives a functional analysis, spelled out in four conditions, of what it is *for an organism to be in pain*. Is this the same thing as a functional account of what it is for an internal state of the organism to be *a pain state*? If not, how would you functionally specify a pain state— i.e., identify a bit of the brain as having the function of being pain? Can it be done at all using a theory based on the Turing Machine model? If not, is this a problem—does it make the theory less plausible?

4. Does Putnam successfully show that the mind-brain identity theory is almost certainly empirically false?

Suggestions for Further Reading

Putnam's most important papers outlining his functionalism appear in the second volume of his collected papers, *Mind, Language and Reality* (Cambridge University Press, 1975). (This book also contains some of his most important papers on semantic externalism, including "The Meaning of 'Meaning.'") Conversely, Putnam's main attack on functionalism is in *Representation and Reality* (MIT Press, 1988), especially chapter 5: "Why Functionalism Didn't Work." Among the other important books by Putnam are *Reason, Truth and History* (Cambridge University Press, 1981), *Realism and Reason* (Cambridge University Press, 1983), *The Many Faces of Realism* (Open Court, 1987), *Realism With a Human Face* (Harvard University Press, 1990), *Renewing Philosophy* (Harvard University Press, 1992), and *Words and Life* (Harvard University Press, 1994). There is a special issue of the journal *Philosophical Topics* devoted to Putnam's work (Vol. 20, 1992), and a collection of papers edited by Peter Clark and Bob Hale called *Reading Putnam* (Blackwell, 1994).

The literature on functionalism is very large indeed, but it tends to be scattered in the journals and, since the 1970s, fractured among the different species of functionalism which have emerged (machine functionalism or computationalism, teleological functionalism, homuncular functionalism, biosemantics, and so forth). Probably the best starting point is with the papers collected in Part Three of *Readings in Philosophy of Psychology*, Volume One, edited by Ned Block (Harvard University Press, 1980). Especially useful are Block's introduction to the section on functionalism and his classic paper "Troubles with Functionalism." Also, any good introductory text or collection of readings on the philosophy of mind will include a section or more on functionalism (for example Jaegwon Kim's book *Philosophy of Mind* [Westview Press, 1996] and the reader edited by William G. Lycan, *Mind and Cognition*, from Blackwell, second edition, 1999).

"The Nature of Mental States"[2]

The typical concerns of the Philosopher of Mind might be represented by three questions: (1) How do we know that other people have pains? (2) Are pains brain states? (3) What is the analysis of the concept *pain*? I do not wish to discuss questions (1) and (3) in this paper. I shall say something about question (2).[3]

I. Identity Questions

"Is pain a brain state?" (Or, "Is the property of having a pain at time *t* a brain state?")[4] It is impossible to discuss this question sensibly without saying something about the peculiar rules which have grown up in the course of the development of "analytical philosophy"—rules which, far from leading to an end to all conceptual confusions, themselves represent considerable conceptual confusion. These rules—which are, of course, implicit rather than explicit in the practice of most analytical philosophers—are (1) that a statement of the form "being *A* is being *B*" (e.g., "being in pain is being in a certain brain state") can be *correct* only if it follows, in some sense, from the meaning of the terms *A* and *B*; and (2) that a statement

---

2   This paper was written for a 1965 conference at Oberlin College and first published (under the title "Psychological Predicates") in the proceedings of that conference, *Art, Mind, and Religion*, edited by W.H. Capitan and D.D. Merrill (University of Pittsburgh Press, © 1967). It is reprinted by permission of the University of Pittsburgh Press.

3   [Author's note] I have discussed these and related topics in the following papers: "Minds and Machines," in *Dimensions of Mind*, ed. Sidney Hook, New York, 1960, pp. 148–179; "Brains and Behavior," in *Analytical Psychology, second series*, ed. Ronald Butler, Oxford, 1965, pp. 1–20; and "The Mental Life of Some Machines," to appear in a volume edited by Hector Neri Castaneda, Detroit.

4   [Author's note] In this paper I wish to avoid the vexed question of the relation between *pains* and *pain states*. I only remark in passing that one common argument *against* identification of these two—viz., that a pain can be in one's arm but a state (of the organism) cannot be in one's arm—is easily seen to be fallacious.

of the form "being A is being B" can be philosophically *informative* only if it is in some sense reductive (e.g., "being in pain is having a certain unpleasant sensation" is not philosophically informative; "being in pain is having a certain behavior disposition" is, if true, philosophically informative). These rules are excellent rules if we still believe that the program of reductive analysis[5] (in the style of the 1930's) can be carried out; if we don't, then they turn analytical philosophy into a mug's game, at least so far as "is" questions are concerned.

In this paper I shall use the term "property" as a blanket term for such things as being in pain, being in a particular brain state, having a particular behavior disposition, and also for magnitudes such as temperature, etc—i.e., for things which can naturally be represented by one-or-more-place predicates or functors.[6] I shall use the term "concept" for things which can be identified with synonymy-classes[7] of

expressions. Thus the concept *temperature* can be identified (I maintain) with the synonymy-class of the word "temperature."[8] (This is like saying that the number 2 can be identified with the class of all pairs. This is quite a different statement from the peculiar statement that 2 *is* the class of all pairs. I do not maintain that concepts *are* synonymy-classes, whatever that might mean, but that they can be identified with synonymy classes, for the purpose of formalization of the relevant discourse.)

The question "What is the concept *temperature*?" is a very "funny" one. One might take it to mean "What is temperature? Please take my question as a conceptual one." In that case an answer might be (pretend for a moment 'heat' and 'temperature' are synonyms) "temperature is heat," or even "the concept of temperature is the same concept as the concept of heat." Or one might take it to mean "What are *concepts*, really? For example, what is 'the concept of temperature'?"

---

5   Reductive analysis is the attempt to show that some concept, belief, or theory can be broken down into component parts and that those component elements belong to some more basic category than the thing being analyzed. Examples of the kind of reductive analysis Putnam has in mind here are the attempt to analyze statements about physical objects into sets of reports about sensations (sense-data), and the project of analyzing statements about mental states into sets of statements about actual and possible behavior.

6   A one-place predicate (or "propositional function" or "functor") is simply an incomplete (or "open") sentence which includes a space left open for some referring expression or other. For example, "___ is green" is a one-place predicate, and it can be turned into a (true or false) complete sentence by filling the gap with a name or a description, as in "Polly the Parrot is green," "grass is green," "this cheese is green" or "the Gobi desert is green." "___ is taller than ___" is a two-place predicate, "___ is further south of ___ than ___" is a three-place predicate, and so on.

7   A synonymy-class is a set of all the linguistic expressions which are synonymous with each other. What exactly it is to be "synonymous" turns out to be a philosophically tricky question, but the basic idea is that two bits of language are synonymous if they have

the same meaning. For example, the following words {rain, rainfall, shower, precipitation, heavy drizzle, light downpour, Scotch mist, *precipitación, précipitations, Niederschlag, pioggia,* ...} form (roughly) a synonymy-class.

8   [Author's note] There are some well-known remarks by Alonzo Church on this topic. Those remarks do not bear (as might at first be supposed) on the identification of concepts with synonymy-classes as such, but rather support the view that (in formal semantics) it is necessary to retain Frege's distinction between the normal and the "oblique" use of expressions. That is, even if we say that the concept of temperature *is* the synonymy-class of the word 'temperature,' we must not thereby be led into the error of supposing that 'the concept of temperature' is synonymous with 'the synonymy-class of the word "temperature"'— for then 'the concept of temperature' and 'der Begriff der Temperatur' would not be synonymous, which they are. Rather, we must say that 'the concept of temperature' *refers to* the synonymy-class of the word 'temperature' (on this particular reconstruction); but that class is *identified* not as "the synonymy-class to which such-and-such a word belongs," but in another way (e.g., as the synonymy-class whose members have such-and-such a characteristic use).

In that case heaven knows what an "answer" would be. (Perhaps it would be the statement that concepts *can be identified with* synonymy-classes.)

Of course, the question "What is the property temperature?" is also "funny." And one way of interpreting it is to take it as a question about the concept of temperature. But this is not the way a physicist would take it.

The effect of saying that the property P_1 can be identical with the property P_2 only if the terms P_1, P_2 are in some suitable sense "synonyms" is, to all intents and purposes, to collapse the two notions of "property" and "concept" into a single notion. The view that concepts (intensions[9]) *are* the same as properties has been explicitly advocated by Carnap[10] (e.g., in *Meaning and Necessity*). This seems an unfortunate view, since "temperature is mean molecular kinetic energy" appears to be a perfectly good example of a true statement of identity of properties, whereas "the concept of temperature is the same concept as the concept of mean molecular kinetic energy" is simply false.

Many philosophers believe that the statement "pain is a brain state" violates some rules or norms of English. But the arguments offered are hardly convincing. For example, if the fact that I can know that I am in pain without knowing that I am in brain state S shows that pain cannot be brain state S, then, by exactly the same argument, the fact that I can know that the stove is hot without knowing that the mean molecular kinetic energy is high (or even that molecules exist) shows that it is *false* that temperature is mean molecular kinetic energy, physics to the contrary. In fact, all that immediately follows from the fact that I can know that I am in pain without knowing that I am in brain state S is that the concept of pain is not the same concept as the concept of being in brain state S. But either pain, or the state of being in pain, or some pain, or some pain state, might still be brain state S. After all, the concept of temperature is not the same concept as the concept of mean molecular kinetic energy. But temperature is mean molecular kinetic energy.

Some philosophers maintain that both 'pain is a brain state' and 'pain states are brain states' are unintelligible. The answer is to explain to these philosophers, as well as we can, given the vagueness of all scientific methodology, what sorts of considerations lead one to make an empirical reduction (i.e., to say such things as "water is H_2O," "light is electromagnetic radiation," "temperature is mean molecular kinetic energy"). If, without giving reasons, he still maintains in the face of such examples that one cannot imagine parallel circumstances for the use of 'pains are brain states' (or, perhaps, 'pain states are brain states') one has grounds to regard him as perverse.

Some philosophers maintain that "P_1 is P_2" is something that can be true, when the 'is' involved is the 'is' of empirical reduction, only when the properties P_1 and P_2 are (a) associated with a spatio-temporal region; and (b) the region is one and the same in both cases. Thus "temperature is mean molecular kinetic energy" is an admissible empirical reduction, since the temperature and the molecular energy are associated with the same space-time region, but "having a pain in my arm is being in a brain state" is not, since the spatial regions involved are different.

This argument does not appear very strong. Surely no one is going to be deterred from saying that mirror images are light reflected from an object and then from the surface of a mirror by the fact that an image

---

9   This is a technical term for, roughly, the meaning of a term or predicate; it is contrasted with a term's *extension*, which is the set of things of which it is true. For example, the intension of the word "marsupial" is, let's suppose, something like what you would discover in a dictionary if you looked the word up. The extension of "marsupial," by contrast, is not any kind of concept or definition but is a large number of non-placental mammals, many but not all of them living in Australasia, including wallabies, wombats, bandicoots, and opossums.

10   Rudolf Carnap (1891–1970), one of the most important analytic philosophers of the first half of the twentieth century, was born in Germany but left Europe in the 1930s to live and work for the rest of his life in America (first at Chicago, then at UCLA). His work is perhaps the most classic example of the "reductive analysis in the style of the 1930s" which Putnam alludes to above, especially his 1928 book *Der logische Aufbau der Welt* ("The Logical Structure of the World"). *Meaning and Necessity*, an important book about formal semantics, was published in 1947.

can be "located" three feet *behind* the mirror! (Moreover, one can always find *some* common property of the reductions one is willing to allow—e.g., temperature is mean molecular kinetic energy—which is not a property of some one identification one wishes to disallow. This is not very impressive unless one has an argument to show that the very purposes of such identification depend upon the common property in question.)

Again, other philosophers have contended that all the predictions that can be derived from the conjunction of neurophysiological laws with such statements as "pain states are such-and-such brain states" can equally well be derived from the conjunction of the same neurophysiological laws with "being in pain is correlated with such-and-such brain states," and hence (sic)![11] there can be no methodological grounds for saying that pains (or pain states) *are* brain states, as opposed to saying that they are *correlated* (invariantly) with brain states. This argument, too, would show that light is only correlated with electromagnetic radiation. The mistake is in ignoring the fact that, although the theories in question may indeed lead to the same predictions, they open and exclude different *questions*. "Light is invariantly correlated with electromagnetic radiation" would leave open the questions "What is the light then, if it isn't the same as the electromagnetic radiation?" and "What makes the light accompany the electromagnetic radiation?"—questions which are excluded by saying that the light *is* the electromagnetic radiation. Similarly, the purpose of saying that pains are brain states is precisely to exclude from empirical meaningfulness the questions "What is the pain, then, if it isn't the same as the brain state?" and "What makes the pain accompany the brain state?" If there are grounds to suggest that these questions represent, so to speak, the wrong way to look at the matter, then those grounds are grounds for a theoretical identification of pains with brain states.

_____

11   *Sic* is the Latin word meaning "so," or "thus," and is used like this after a quotation or paraphrase to mean something like "they really did say this—I'm not making this up, but quoting them exactly!"

If all arguments to the contrary are unconvincing, shall we then conclude that it is meaningful (and perhaps true) to say either that pains are brain states or that pain states are brain states?

(1)   It is perfectly meaningful (violates no "rule of English," involves no "extension of usage") to say "pains are brain states."

(2)   It is not meaningful (involves a "changing of meaning" or "an extension of usage," etc.) to say "pains are brain states."

My own position is not expressed by either (1) or (2). It seems to me that the notions "change of meaning" and "extension of usage" are simply so ill-defined that one cannot in fact say *either* (1) or (2). I see no reason to believe that either the linguist, or the man-on-the-street, or the philosopher possesses today a notion of "change of meaning" applicable to such cases as the one we have been discussing. The *job* for which the notion of change of meaning was developed in the history of the language was just a *much* cruder job than this one.

But, if we don't assert either (1) or (2)—in other words, if we regard the "change of meaning" issue as a pseudo-issue in this case—then how are we to discuss the question with which we started? "Is pain a brain state?"

The answer is to allow statements of the form "pain is *A*," where 'pain' and '*A*' are in no sense synonyms, and to see whether any such statement can be found which might be acceptable on empirical and methodological grounds. This is what we shall now proceed to do.

II. Is Pain a Brain State?

We shall discuss "Is pain a brain state?," then. And we have agreed to waive the "change of meaning" issue.

Since I am discussing not what the concept of pain comes to, but what pain is, in a sense of 'is' which requires empirical theory-construction (or, at least, empirical speculation), I shall not apologize for advancing an empirical hypothesis. Indeed, my strategy will be to argue that pain is *not* a brain state, not on *a priori* grounds, but on the grounds that another hypothesis is more plausible. The detailed development and verification of my hypothesis would be just as Utopian a task as the detailed development and verification of the brain state hypothesis. But the putting-forward, not of detailed and scientifically "finished" hypotheses, but of schemata for hypotheses, has long been a function of philosophy. I shall, in short, argue that pain is not a brain state, in the sense of a physical-chemical state of the brain (or even the whole nervous system), but another *kind* of state entirely. I propose the hypothesis that pain, or the state of being in pain, is a functional state of a whole organism.

To explain this it is necessary to introduce some technical notions. In previous papers I have explained the notion of a Turing Machine and discussed the use of this notion as a model for an organism. The notion of a Probabilistic Automaton is defined similarly to a Turing Machine, except that the transitions between "states" are allowed to be with various probabilities rather than being "deterministic." (Of course, a Turing Machine is simply a special kind of Probabilistic Automaton, one with transition probabilities 0, 1.) I shall assume the notion of a Probabilistic Automaton has been generalized to allow for "sensory inputs" and "motor outputs"—that is, the Machine Table specifies, for every possible combination of a "state" and a complete set of "sensory inputs," an "instruction" which determines the probability of the next "state," and also the probabilities of the "motor outputs." (This replaces the idea of the Machine as printing on a tape.) I shall also assume that the physical realization of the sense organs responsible for the various inputs, and of the motor organs, is specified, but that the "states" and the "inputs" themselves are, as usual, specified only "implicitly"—i.e., by the set of transition probabilities given by the Machine Table.

Since an empirically given system can simultaneously be a "physical realization" of many different Probabilistic Automata, I introduce the notion of a *Description* of a system. A Description of S where S is a system, is any true statement to the effect that S possesses distinct states $S_1, S_2, ..., S_n$ which are related to one another and to the motor outputs and sensory inputs by the transition probabilities given in such-and-such a Machine Table. The Machine Table mentioned in the Description will then be called the Functional Organization of S relative to that Description, and the S_i such that S is in state S_i at a given time will be called the Total State of S (at that time) relative to that De-

scription. It should be noted that knowing the Total State of a system relative to a Description involves knowing a good deal about how the system is likely to "behave," given various combinations of sensory inputs, but does not involve knowing the physical realization of the S_i as, e.g., physical-chemical states of the brain. The S_i, to repeat, are specified only *implicitly* by the Description—i.e., specified *only* by the set of transition probabilities given in the Machine Table.

The hypothesis that "being in pain is a functional state of the organism" may now be spelled out more exactly as follows:

(1)   All organisms capable of feeling pain are Probabilistic Automata.

(2)   Every organism capable of feeling pain possesses at least one Description of a certain kind (i.e., being capable of feeling pain is possessing an appropriate kind of Functional Organization).

(3)   No organism capable of feeling pain possesses a decomposition into parts which separately possess Descriptions of the kind referred to in (2).

(4)   For every Description of the kind referred to in (2), there exists a subset of the sensory inputs such that an organism with that Description is in pain when and only when some of its sensory inputs are in that subset.

This hypothesis is admittedly vague, though surely no vaguer than the brain-state hypothesis in its present form. For example, one would like to know more about the kind of Functional Organization that an organism must have to be capable of feeling pain, and more about the marks that distinguish the subset of the sensory inputs referred to in (4). With respect to the first question, one can probably say that the Functional Organization must include something that resembles a "preference function," or at least a preference partial ordering, and something that resembles an "inductive logic" (i.e., the Machine must be able to "learn from experience"). (The meaning of these conditions, for Automata models, is discussed in my paper "The Mental Life of Some Machines.") In addition, it seems natural to require that the Machine possess "pain sensors," i.e., sensory organs which normally signal damage to the Machine's body, or dangerous temperatures, pressures, etc., which transmit a special subset of the inputs, the subset referred to in (4). Finally, and with respect to the second question, we would want to require at least that the inputs in the distinguished subset have a high disvalue on the Machine's preference function or ordering (further conditions are discussed in "The Mental Life of Some Machines"). The purpose of condition (3) is to rule out such "organisms" (if they can count as such) as swarms of bees as single pain-feelers. The condition (1) is, obviously, redundant, and is only introduced for expository reasons. (It is, in fact, empty, since everything is a Probabilistic Automaton under *some* Description.)

I contend, in passing, that this hypothesis, in spite of its admitted vagueness, is far *less* vague than the "physical-chemical state" hypothesis is today, and far more susceptible to investigation of both a mathematical and an empirical kind. Indeed, to investigate this hypothesis is just to attempt to produce "mechanical" models of organisms—and isn't this, in a sense, just what psychology is about? The difficult step, of course, will be to pass from models of *specific* organisms to a *normal form* for the psychological description of organisms—for this is what is required to make (2) and (4) precise. But this too seems to be an inevitable part of the program of psychology.

I shall now compare the hypothesis just advanced with (a) the hypothesis that pain is a brain state, and (b) the hypothesis that pain is a behavior disposition.

III. Functional State Versus Brain State

It may, perhaps, be asked if I am not somewhat unfair in taking the brain-state theorist to be talking about *physico-chemical* states of the brain. But (a) these are the only sorts of states ever mentioned by brain-state theorists. (b) The brain-state theorist usually mentions (with a certain pride, slightly reminiscent of the Village Atheist) the incompatibility of his hypothesis with all forms of dualism and mentalism.[12] This is

natural if physical-chemical states of the brain are what is at issue. However, functional states of whole systems are something quite different. In particular, the functional-state hypothesis is *not* incompatible with dualism! Although it goes without saying that the hypothesis is "mechanistic" in its inspiration, it is a slightly remarkable fact that a system consisting of a body and a "soul," if such things there be, can perfectly well be a Probabilistic Automaton. (c) One argument advanced by Smart is that the brain-state theory assumes only "physical" properties, and Smart finds "non-physical" properties unintelligible. The Total States and the "inputs" defined above are, of course, neither mental nor physical *per se*, and I cannot imagine a functionalist advancing this argument. (d) If the brain-state theorist does mean (or at least allow) states other than physical-chemical states, then his hypothesis is completely empty, at least until he specifies *what* sort of "states" he *does* mean.

Taking the brain-state hypothesis in this way, then, what reasons are there to prefer the functional-state hypothesis over the brain-state hypothesis? Consider what the brain-state theorist has to do to make good his claims. He has to specify a physical-chemical state such that *any* organism (not just a mammal) is in pain if and only if (a) it possesses a brain of a suitable physical-chemical structure; and (b) its brain is in that physical-chemical state. This means that the physical-chemical state in question must be a possible state of a mammalian brain, a reptilian brain, a mollusc's brain (octopuses are mollusca, and certainly feel pain), etc. At the same time, it must *not* be a possible (physically possible) state of the brain of any physically possible creature that cannot feel pain. Even if such a state can be found, it must be nomologically certain[13] that it will also be a state of the brain of any extra-terrestrial life that may be found that will be capable of feeling pain before we can even entertain the supposition that it may *be* pain.

It is not altogether impossible that such a state will be found. Even though octopus and mammal are examples of parallel (rather than sequential) evolution, for example, virtually identical structures (physically speaking) have evolved in the eye of the octopus and

---

12 Mentalism is the view that the causation of human behavior cannot be satisfactorily explained in purely non-mental terms but only by appealing to such psychological entities as beliefs, desires, thoughts, hopes, feelings, and so on.

---

13 Physically necessary, required by the laws of physics.

in the eye of the mammal, notwithstanding the fact that this organ has evolved from different kinds of cells in the two cases. Thus it is at least possible that parallel evolution, all over the universe, might *always* lead to *one and the same* physical "correlate" of pain. But this is certainly an ambitious hypothesis.

Finally, the hypothesis becomes still more ambitious when we realize that the brain state theorist is not just saying that *pain* is a brain state; he is of course, concerned to maintain that *every* psychological state is a brain state. Thus if we can find even one psychological predicate which can clearly be applied to both a mammal and an octopus (say "hungry"), but whose physical-chemical "correlate" is different in the two cases, the brain-state theory has collapsed. It seems to me overwhelmingly probable that we can do this. Granted, in such a case the brain-state theorist can save himself by *ad hoc* assumptions[14] (e.g., defining

---

14 An *ad hoc* assumption is one introduced for no other reason than to defeat a particular objection (rather than for reasons found within the theory itself). Since one can defend even the most ridiculous theory by continually inventing new *ad hoc* assumptions to meet every new refutation, *ad hoc* assumptions are generally thought to be worthless in science. (For example, imagine a scientific law which says that balls of a particular mass will roll down slopes of a particular incline at some particular velocity. Now, suppose that empirical tests show that these types of balls on those types of slope actually travel downhill at a slower velocity. The theory could be defended in various ways, some *ad hoc* and some not. A non-*ad hoc* response would be to point out that the sloping surfaces used in the experiments had surfaces which exerted friction on the rolling balls, and once this is factored in the theory always gives the right answer. Examples of *ad hoc* responses, by contrast, would be to assume that the theory is true but, in the case of these particular experiments, the observers were sleepy and measured badly, or that little invisible demons got in the way of the balls and slowed them down, and so on. It's not that these assumptions wouldn't preserve the theory against refutation; it's that we have no independent reason to believe the assumptions true *except* that they would prevent the theory from being refuted.)

the disjunction of two states to be a single "physical-chemical state"), but this does not have to be taken seriously.

Turning now to the considerations *for* the functional-state theory, let us begin with the fact that we identify organisms as in pain, or hungry, or angry, or in heat, etc., on the basis of their *behavior*. But it is a truism that similarities in the behavior of two systems are at least a reason to suspect similarities in the functional organization of the two systems, and a much *weaker* reason to suspect similarities in the actual physical details. Moreover, we expect the various psychological states—at least the basic ones, such as hunger, thirst, aggression, etc.—to have more or less similar "transition probabilities" (within wide and ill-defined limits, to be sure) with each other and with behavior in the case of different species, because this is an artifact of the way in which we identify these states. Thus, we would not count an animal as *thirsty* if its "unsatiated" behavior did not seem to be directed toward drinking and was not followed by "satiation for liquid." Thus any animal that we count as capable of these various states will at least *seem* to have a certain rough kind of functional organization. And, as already remarked, if the program of finding psychological laws that are not species-specific—i.e., of finding a normal form for psychological theories of different species—ever succeeds, then it will bring in its wake a delineation of the kind of functional organization that is necessary and sufficient for a given psychological state, as well as a precise definition of the notion "psychological state." In contrast, the brain-state theorist has to hope for the eventual development of neurophysiological laws that are species-independent, which seems much less reasonable than the hope that psychological laws (of a sufficiently general kind) may be species-independent, or, still weaker, that a species-independent *form* can be found in which psychological laws can be written.

IV. Functional State Versus Behavior Disposition

The theory that being in pain is neither a brain state nor a functional state but a behavior disposition has one apparent advantage: it appears to agree with the way in which we verify that organisms are in pain. We do not in practice know anything about the brain state of an animal when we say that it is in pain; and we possess little if any knowledge of its functional organization, except in a crude intuitive way. In fact, however, this "advantage" is no advantage at all: for, although statements about how we verify that x is A may have a good deal to do with what the concept of being A comes to, they have precious little to do with what the property A *is*. To argue on the ground just mentioned that pain is neither a brain state nor a functional state is like arguing that heat is not mean molecular kinetic energy from the fact that ordinary people do not (they think) ascertain the mean molecular kinetic energy of something when they verify that it is hot or cold. It is not necessary that they should; what is necessary is that the marks that they take as indications of heat should in fact be explained by the mean molecular kinetic energy. And, similarly, it is necessary to our hypothesis that the marks that are taken as behavioral indications of pain should be explained by the fact that the organism is in a functional state of the appropriate kind, but not that speakers should *know* that this is so.

The difficulties with "behavior disposition" accounts are so well known that I shall do little more than recall them here. The difficulty—it appears to be more than "difficulty," in fact—of specifying the required behavior disposition except as "the disposition of X to behave as if X were in *pain*," is the chief one, of course. In contrast, we *can* specify the functional state with which we propose to identify pain, at least roughly, without using the notion of pain. Namely, the functional state we have in mind is the state of receiving sensory inputs which play a certain role in the Functional Organization of the organism. This role is characterized, at least partially, by the fact that the sense organs responsible for the inputs in question are organs whose function is to detect damage to the body, or dangerous extremes of temperature, pressure, etc., and by the fact that the "inputs" themselves, whatever their physical realization, represent a condition that the organism assigns a high disvalue to. As I stressed in "The Mental Life of Some Machines," this does *not* mean that the Machine will always *avoid* be-

ing in the condition in question ("pain"); it only means that the condition will be avoided unless not avoiding it is necessary to the attainment of some more highly valued goal. Since the behavior of the Machine (in this case, an organism) will depend not merely on the sensory inputs, but also on the Total State (i.e., on other values, beliefs, etc.), it seems hopeless to make any general statement about how an organism in such a condition *must* behave; but this does not mean that we must abandon hope of characterizing the condition. Indeed, we have just characterized it.[15]

Not only does the behavior-disposition theory seem hopelessly vague; if the "behavior" referred to is peripheral behavior, and the relevant stimuli are peripheral stimuli (e.g., we do not say anything about what the organism will do if its brain is operated upon), then the theory seems clearly false. For example, two animals with all motor nerves cut will have the same actual and potential "behavior" (viz., none to speak of); but if one has cut pain fibers and the other has uncut pain fibers, then one will feel pain and the other won't. Again, if one person has cut pain fibers, and another suppresses all pain responses deliberately due to some strong compulsion, then the actual and potential peripheral behavior may be the same, but one will feel pain and the other won't. (Some philosophers maintain that this last case is conceptually impossible, but the only evidence for this appears to be that *they* can't, or don't want to, conceive of it.)[16] If instead of pain, we take some sensation the "bodily expression" of which is easier to suppress—say,

---

15 [Author's note] In "The Mental Life of Some Machines" a further, and somewhat independent, characteristic of pain inputs is discussed in terms of Automata models—namely the spontaneity of the inclination to withdraw the injured part, etc. This raises the question, which is discussed in that paper, of giving a functional analysis of the notion of a spontaneous inclination. Of course, still further characteristics come readily to mind—for example, that feelings of pain are (or seem to be) *located* in the parts of the body.

16 [Author's note] C.f. the discussion of "super-spartans" in "Brains and Behavior."

a slight coolness in one's left little finger—the case becomes even clearer.

Finally, even if there *were* some behavior disposition invariantly correlated with pain (species-independently!), and specifiable without using the term 'pain,' it would still be more plausible to identify being in pain with some state whose presence *explains* this behavior disposition—the brain state or functional state—than with the behavior disposition itself. Such considerations of plausibility may be somewhat subjective; but if other things were equal (of course, they aren't) why shouldn't we allow considerations of plausibility to play the deciding role?

V. Methodological Considerations

So far we have considered only what might be called the "empirical" reasons for saying that being in pain is a functional state, rather than a brain state or a behavior disposition; viz., that it seems more likely that the functional state we described is invariantly "correlated" with pain, species-independently, than that there is either a physical-chemical state of the brain (must an organism have a *brain* to feel pain? perhaps some ganglia will do) or a behavior disposition so correlated. If this is correct, then it follows that the identification we proposed is at least a candidate for consideration. What of methodological considerations?

The methodological considerations are roughly similar in all cases of reduction, so no surprises need be expected here. First, identification of psychological states with functional states means that the laws of psychology can be derived from statements of the form "such-and-such organisms have such-and-such Descriptions" together with the identification statements ("being in pain is such-and-such a functional state," etc.). Secondly, the presence of the functional state (i.e., of inputs which play the role we have described in the Functional Organization of the organism) is not merely "correlated with" but actually explains the pain behavior on the part of the organism. Thirdly, the identification serves to exclude questions which (if a naturalistic view is correct) represent an altogether wrong way of looking at the matter, e.g., "What *is* pain if it isn't either the brain state or the functional state?" and "What causes the pain to be always accompanied by this sort of functional state?" In short, the identification is to be tentatively accepted as a theory which leads to both fruitful predictions and to fruitful *questions*, and which serves to discourage fruitless and empirically senseless questions, where by 'empirically senseless' I mean "senseless" not merely from the standpoint of verification, but from the standpoint of what there in fact *is*.

JOHN R. SEARLE
"Minds, Brains and Programs"

Who Is John R. Searle?

John Rogers Searle was born in Denver, Colorado in 1932, the son of an electrical engineer and a doctor. He began his undergraduate work in 1949 at the University of Wisconsin, but in 1952 he went to Oxford University as a Rhodes Scholar and completed a BA in Politics, Philosophy, and Economics there. In 1959 he received his doctorate at Oxford, influenced especially by P.F. Strawson and the famous philosopher of language J.L. Austin. Between 1957 and 1959 he was a lecturer at Christ Church College, Oxford, but he has spent the rest of his career teaching at the University of California, Berkeley.

Searle's early work was devoted to the elaboration and improvement of Austin's theory of "speech acts," and most of his later work has derived in some way from the philosophical theory he developed at this time. A speech act is an action performed by saying (or writing, etc.) something. For example, one might make a promise or a threat, insult somebody and hurt their feelings, assert that something is true or false, ask a question, and so on. Searle holds that all human linguistic communication consists in the performance of speech acts, which he sees as forms of human behavior governed by particular rules. Nearly all the philosophical problems to do with language and meaning, according to Searle, are to be solved by examining these rules (e.g., the rules of promising or of describing). Much of Searle's work in the philosophy of language is encapsulated in his books *Speech Acts* (1969) and *Expression and Meaning* (1979).

This interest in the theory of meaning led to Searle's subsequent career in the philosophy of mind, where his work has had three themes: first, his development of a theory of "intentionality"; second his attack on computationalism and strong AI; and third his attempt to formulate a "naturalized" theory of consciousness.

In his book *Intentionality* (1983), Searle tries to provide a general theory of intentionality (i.e., 'aboutness' or 'representationality'—see the background information below) using a fairly small number of explanatory concepts. For example, he formulated and applied the notions of the "direction of fit" of a mental state (which can be world-to-mind, mind-to-world, or null) and its "direction of causation" (which can be mind-to-world or world-to-mind). Searle does not, however, think that intentionality can be *reduced* to (or analyzed into) these kinds of notions—his view is that intentionality is an irreducible feature of the world, one that can be described or explained but not eliminated.

Searle's most famous attack on strong AI is the extremely controversial article reprinted here.

His work on consciousness appears mainly in the books *The Rediscovery of Mind* (1992) and *The Mystery of Consciousness* (1997). Searle's theory of consciousness has two main features which, independently, are not that unusual, but which Searle is almost alone in holding at the same time. First, his thesis of "ontological subjectivity" insists that consciousness is an irreducibly first-person, subjective phenomenon which, in principle, cannot be fully explained by a third-person, neurological theory. Nevertheless, he *also* defends "biological naturalism," which holds that consciousness is an entirely natural, biological phenomenon; according to Searle, brain processes "cause" conscious states (in much the same way as the molecular structure of water "causes" it to be liquid at room temperature, or gravity "causes" a thrown baseball to come back down), and therefore, he concludes, conscious states *just are* features of the neurobiological substrate. (As Searle put it once, "I think that this is one of those rare questions in philosophy where you can have your cake and eat it too.") Searle argues that most of contemporary cognitive science and philosophy of mind is inadequate because most mental phenomena cannot be understood without a proper understanding of consciousness, and this in turn, he argues, cannot be attained without paying attention to our subjective, phenomenological *experience* of consciousness.

What Is the Structure of This Reading?

Searle begins by describing his target, what he calls "strong Artificial Intelligence," in essence the claim that a suitably adequate AI computer program would not be merely a *simulation* of intelligent thought—it really would *be* thought, and any machine running such a program would be a thinking creature.[1] Searle denies this and (after describing a particular candidate computer program as a concrete target) he presents his argument against it: what is usually called his "Chinese room" thought experiment. He realizes that this argument will not seem persuasive to many workers in cognitive science, so he tries to forestall objections by answering six he has encountered previously from audiences at Berkeley, MIT, Stanford, and Yale: the systems reply, the robot reply, the brain simulator reply, the combination reply, the other minds reply, and the many mansions reply.

Searle then returns to an underlying question, which he had briefly raised earlier: if the Chinese room does not understand, but a human language-user does, what exactly *explains* this different between them? After some comments on this question, he moves on to "state some of the general philosophical points implicit in the [Chinese room] argument," which he does in question-and-answer form, ending by speculating why many, if not most, cognitive scientists are so attracted to the computational model he attacks.

Some Useful Background Information

1. Searle's "Minds, Brains and Programs" is often described as an attack on the form of functionalism called computationalism. Computationalism is the hypothesis that the mind is, quite literally, a computer program (and the brain is the machine which runs it). According to the classical computationalist picture ("classical" in this case meaning dating back to the 1970s), mental representations such as beliefs are symbol structures encoded in the brain, and mental processes—such as playing chess or planning the perfect date—are the manipulations of these representations in accordance with symbolic algorithms; that is, thinking precisely *is* the performance of "computations," in just the same sense as a laptop performs computations. The difference between a human mind and, say, a database program is purely one of complexity and computational power; it is not, according to this theory, a difference in kind.

2. 'Intentionality' is often used as a technical term in philosophy. Sometimes philosophers use "intentional" in the everyday sense, to mean something which is done on purpose, but frequently they use it to mean instead *something which is about* ("directed at," "represents," "of") *something else*. Thus, for example, a sentence, a thought, an action, a sculpture, or a map can be intentional (or "have intentionality") while a person, a star, or a house usually are not. The term was coined in the Middle Ages, and comes from the Latin verb *intendo*, which means "to point at." It was revived in the late nineteenth century by a German philosopher and psychologist called Franz Brentano, who claimed that intentionality was "the mark of the mental"—that is, he held that all mental states are intentional and no physical states are. Nowadays, however, most philosophers think that while many mental states are intentional (such as a fear of snakes) others are not (such as a vague, undirected feeling of anxiety).

   For Searle, it is important that intentionality comes in two different flavors: intrinsic and derived. Some entities, such as thoughts, are *intrinsically* intentional, according to Searle: they have their 'aboutness,' so to speak, objectively built in to them. On the other hand, the intentionality of many other entities is *derived*: they are not about things or for things all by them-

---

1   Thus, its intelligence would be "artificial" in the sense that it was not created in the normal biological way (as in "artificial insemination") but *not* artificial in the sense of being "not really" intelligent (as in "artificial sugar").

selves, but only when they are *interpreted* that way by an observer. For example, a five dollar bill is a meaningless piece of paper unless it is part of a system of conventional exchange created by thinking beings. The sequence of symbols e-l-e-p-h-a-n-t, and the sound you make by sounding out the word, don't by themselves have any magical, objective connection to the largest land mammal—they are just the signs we *use* in English to refer to elephants (and we could just as easily have chosen to use the symbol-strings "heelpant" or "peltahen" instead). Shaking someone's hand is a physical action which we interpret as a friendly gesture, but which in another society might be treated as a mortal insult. And so on. A key point for Searle is that nothing can have derived intentionality unless something else has intrinsic intentionality: that is, only creatures with *minds* can project meaningfulness into the surrounding universe.

3. Searle's argument in this article depends heavily on the distinction between syntax and semantics. The syntax of a language consists of the rules which govern the grammatical formation of sentences in that language (e.g., the rules which say it's OK in English to utter "The cat is on the mat" but not "Cat the mat is on"). In a *formalized* language, such as the various languages of logic, the syntax also includes what are called "transformation rules": these rules specify how one set of strings of symbols can legitimately be turned into another set of symbol-strings. (For example the formula expressing "if P then Q" can be turned into one expressing "not-P or Q.") These logical rules are usually set up so that if the input sentences are all true, the output sentences will all be true as well. However, it is important to notice that the rules themselves pay no attention to the truth or the meaning of the sentences they deal with—they simply take an input of a particular shape or *form*, and produce an output of another form. This is exactly why logic is called "formal" logic—because it deals with the *shapes* of symbol-strings, not directly with their meaning. As Searle puts it, syntactical rules operate on "uninterpreted formal symbols": on strings of symbols which could mean almost anything at all, or nothing at all. (For example, "(P & Q)" could mean "The corn is high and your Mamma's good looking," or "Hitler and Stalin were not nice men," or "1 + 1 = 3 and 2^3 is 7," or we might not even *know* what it means if the letters remain uninterpreted.)

So where does the meaning come from? The meaning of the symbols in a language is provided by its semantics (a system for specifying what any grammatical sentence of the language *means* and whether or not it is *true*). In a natural language like English the semantics is extremely complicated to specify; but in most formalized languages the semantics is much simpler, consisting of an *interpretation* of the meaning and/or the truth value of all the most elementary building blocks of the language.

4. Finally, another motto of Searle's which deserves explanation is the slogan "everything is a digital computer." This is, in some circles, quite a controversial claim, though there is a widely accepted assumption somewhat similar to this thesis. The widely accepted claim is called the Church-Turing thesis, dates back to 1936, and says that *any* effective mathematical method can be computed on a "Universal Turing Machine." What that means is that any finite computation (no matter how large or complex) can, in principle, be run on any physical system capable of a few very simple operations. These operations are, basically, just moving between a finite number of different internal states, and perhaps "writing" and "erasing" at least two symbols in a large enough workspace. (See the notes to the Putnam selection in this chapter for more details on Turing Machines.) From this it follows that a large number of physical systems that we would not ordinarily think of as computers are nevertheless capable of running computations—they could be *used* as computers: notorious examples include the infinite roll of toilet paper and pile of small stones alluded to by Searle, or the population of Belgium all linked together by two-way radios and fol-

lowing certain simple instructions, or a hive of trained bees shifting position on cue and using eggs and honey as symbols.

The even more radical, and more controversial, claim which Searle wants to make is that any, even remotely complex, hunk of matter can be described as if it *already* is running a computer program and (according to Searle) since there is nothing more to being a computer than being describable in this way, *everything* already *is* a computer. The basic idea here is that anything (even a rock) can be correctly described as passing through a finite sequence of different internal states (e.g., different states of radioactive decay). Therefore, we can always write a program which will describe the transformation of each state into the next, and which will also interpret some aspects of the physical system, at a particular time, as "outputs"—i.e., we can draw up a Machine Table (see the notes on Putnam) to describe the actual behavior of the system over time. The rock is following the instructions laid down in the Machine Table, the Machine Table is a computer program; this means that the system is literally *running* whatever program the Machine Table describes. Thus, rocks are computers—indeed, everything is a computer. Even more strangely, it has been argued (in the appendix to Hilary Putnam's book *Representation and Reality*, for example) that we could interpret the inner states of our rock in any way we choose in order to construct whatever Machine Table we desire. For example, we could interpret the rock as running a program for speaking fluent Chinese.

Some Common Misconceptions

1. Some people reading this article for the first time think Searle is arguing that no computer program could exactly replicate the linguistic behavior of a fluent speaker of Chinese. However this is not correct: by contrast, Searle is actually willing to *assume* without argument that such a program *could* be written, and it is just this program which he imagines running in the Chinese room (i.e., from the outside, the Chinese room *does* appear to speak Chinese). Furthermore, Searle thinks that Chinese people could also be correctly described as running a language-speaking program, and so whatever program can be read from the brains of sinophones is one which is capable of producing Chinese-language behavior.

2. Despite framing the target of his attack as "strong AI," Searle doesn't in fact argue that computers do not, or could never, really think. He is making the slightly (but importantly) different case that thought is not essentially *just* computation. In other words, according to Searle, computers might well someday be able to really think—but, if they do think, it will not be *because* they are computers but for some other reason.

Suggestions for Critical Reflection

1. Searle uses the Chinese room thought experiment to argue against strong AI. If he is successful in defeating strong AI, do you think *any* form of functionalism could survive? (And, of course, *is* he successful?) What theories of the mind, if any, (e.g., dualism, behaviorism, identity theory) would be left standing by Searle's argument?

2. What do you think of the various responses to his argument which Searle considers and rejects? Are any of them more plausible than Searle gives them credit for? Can you think of any plausible response which Searle has not already considered?

3. Searle is quite ready to admit that *from the outside* the Chinese room really looks like it speaks Chinese. How far does his argument depend upon his insistence that we take a view "from the inside," a so-called "first-person" perspective? Is this methodological maxim legitimate or is it a mistake?

4. What would it be like to look at the details of a physical system which does understand (such as the human brain) and "see the understand-

ing"? Does the fact that we don't "see" the intentionality in the Chinese room cut any philosophical ice?

5. The cognitive scientist Douglas Hofstadter spoke for many in the cognitive science community when he said that Searle's article is more like a "religious diatribe against AI, masquerading as a serious scientific argument" than a serious objection to functionalism or computationalism. What do you think? Is this response warranted, or is it just an expression of the desire to hang onto strong AI at all costs?

6. What is the importance of the distinction between intrinsic and derived intentionality for this argument? (E.g., can you re-state the argument using this distinction, and if so does it make it any stronger and clearer?) Is this distinction a sensible one?

7. Searle argues that computer programs do not have an intrinsic semantics, but at the time he wrote this article he assumed that they do have an objective syntax. Is this right? Or does the claim that "everything is a digital computer" suggest that computer programs don't have an intrinsic syntax either? If computer syntax is also derived rather than intrinsic, does this make Searle's argument stronger or weaker (or neither)?

Suggestions for Further Reading

The journal *Behavioral and Brain Sciences*, where Searle's article originally appeared, is an innovative journal which publishes, in addition to "target articles," extensive "peer commentaries" (dozens of short pieces, often by well-established experts in the relevant field) which raise criticisms of the article, and then a response by the author. The first place to read more about Searle's Chinese room, therefore, is in *Behavioral and Brain Sciences*, Volume 3, Issue 3 (September 1980). Especially notable are the comments by Fodor and Dennett and Searle's response "Intrinsic Intentionality." *Scientific American* 262 (January 1990) also includes a skirmish over the Chinese room between Searle and Paul and Patricia Churchland.

Searle re-presents his Chinese room argument in various places, including *Minds, Brains, and Science* (Harvard University Press, 1984), *The Rediscovery of the Mind* (MIT Press, 1992), and *The Mystery of Consciousness* (New York Review, 1997). One of Searle's latest books, in which he tries to draw together the various threads of his thought, is *Mind, Language and Society: Philosophy in the Real World* (Basic Books, 1998). There is a collection of essays about Searle called *John Searle and His Critics*, edited by Ernest Lepore and Robert van Gulick (Blackwell, 1991), and a book describing his philosophy, *John Searle*, by Nick Fotion (Princeton University Press, 2000).

"Minds, Brains and Programs"[2]

What psychological and philosophical significance should we attach to recent efforts at computer simulations of human cognitive capacities? In answering this question, I find it useful to distinguish what I will call 'strong' AI from 'weak' or 'cautious' AI (Artificial Intelligence). According to weak AI, the principal value of the computer in the study of the mind is that it gives us a very powerful tool. For example, it enables us to formulate and test hypotheses in a more rigorous and precise fashion. But according to strong AI, the computer is not merely a tool in the study of the mind; rather, the appropriately programmed computer really *is* a mind, in the sense that computers given the right programs can be literally said to understand and have other cognitive states. In strong AI, because the programmed computer has cognitive states, the programs are not mere tools that enable us to test psychological explanations; rather, the programs are themselves the explanations.

I have no objection to the claims of weak AI, at least as far as this article is concerned. My discussion here will be directed at the claims I have defined as those of strong AI, specifically the claim that the appropriately programmed computer literally has cognitive states and that the programs thereby explain human cogni-

---

2   This article was first published in *Behavioral and Brain Sciences*, Volume 3, Issue 3 (September 1980), pp. 417–424.

tion. When I hereafter refer to AI, I have in mind the strong version, as expressed by these two claims.

I will consider the work of Roger Schank and his colleagues at Yale (Schank and Abelson 1977), because I am more familiar with it than I am with any other similar claims, and because it provides a very clear example of the sort of work I wish to examine. But nothing that follows depends upon the details of Schank's programs. The same arguments would apply to Winograd's SHRDLU (Winograd 1973), Weizenbaum's ELIZA (Weizenbaum 1965),[3] and indeed any Turing machine[4] simulation of human mental phenomena.

Very briefly, and leaving out the various details, one can describe Schank's program as follows: the aim of the program is to simulate the human ability to understand stories. It is characteristic of human beings' story-understanding capacity that they can answer questions about the story even though the information that they give was never explicitly stated in the story. Thus, for example, suppose you are given the following story: 'A man went into a restaurant and ordered a hamburger. When the hamburger arrived it was burned to a crisp, and the man stormed out of the restaurant angrily, without paying for the hamburger or leaving a tip.' Now, if you are asked 'Did the man

eat the hamburger?' you will presumably answer, 'No, he did not.' Similarly, if you are given the following story: 'A man went into a restaurant and ordered a hamburger; when the hamburger came he was very pleased with it; and as he left the restaurant he gave the waitress a large tip before paying his bill,' and you are asked the question, 'Did the man eat the hamburger?', you will presumably answer, 'Yes, he ate the hamburger.' Now Schank's machines can similarly answer questions about restaurants in this fashion. To do this, they have a 'representation' of the sort of information that human beings have about restaurants, which enables them to answer such questions as those above, given these sorts of stories. When the machine is given the story and then asked the question, the machine will print out answers of the sort that we would expect human beings to give if told similar stories. Partisans of strong AI claim that in this question and answer sequence the machine is not only simulating a human ability but also

1. that the machine can literally be said to *understand* the story and provide the answers to questions, and

2. that what the machine and its program do *explain* the human ability to understand the story and answer questions about it.

Both claims seem to me to be totally unsupported by Schank's[5] work, as I will attempt to show in what follows.

One way to test any theory of the mind is to ask oneself what it would be like if my mind actually worked on the principles that the theory says all minds work on. Let us apply this test to the Schank program with the following *Gedankenexperiment*.[6] Suppose

---

3   SHRDLU was a program which manipulated virtual blocks in a simulated space and answered questions about them. ELIZA was a program (versions of it can still be found and played with on the Internet) which appears to carry on a conversation with a human interlocutor: that is, if you ask it questions, it will respond to you (in a manner rather like a psychotherapist) and ask you questions in return. Interestingly, Terry Winograd has now repudiated his earlier research project (typified by SHRDLU) and, like Searle, denies that human intelligence can be understood in terms of the computational manipulation of representations. Joseph Weizenbaum, too, has said publicly and forcefully that he thinks people were over-impressed by ELIZA's human-like performance, and that computers can have no real intelligence since they do not understand the symbols they are using.

4   See the notes to the reading by Hilary Putnam in this chapter for more information on Turing Machines.

5   [Author's note] I am not, of course, saying that Schank himself is committed to these claims.

6   This is German for "thought experiment." A thought experiment is a controlled exercise of the imagination in which a test case is carefully constructed to see if it is coherent, or whether it is compatible with some proposed theory. Thought experiments are used by philosophers, but also by theoretical physicists (Galileo and Einstein, for example, made extensive use of them). The idea is to try to find out what is and is not *possibly* true (an *empirical* experiment tries to find out what is actually true).

that I'm locked in a room and given a large batch of Chinese writing. Suppose furthermore (as is indeed the case) that I know no Chinese, either written or spoken, and that I'm not even confident that I could recognize Chinese writing as Chinese writing distinct from, say, Japanese writing or meaningless squiggles. To me, Chinese writing is just so many meaningless squiggles. Now suppose further that after this first batch of Chinese writing I am given a second batch of Chinese script together with a set of rules for correlating the second batch with the first batch. The rules are in English, and I understand these rules as well as any other native speaker of English. They enable me to correlate one set of formal symbols with another set of formal symbols, and all that 'formal' means here is that I can identify the symbols entirely by their shapes. Now suppose also that I am given a third batch of Chinese symbols together with some instructions, again in English, that enable me to correlate elements of this third batch with the first two batches, and these rules instruct me how to give back certain Chinese symbols with certain sorts of shapes in response to certain sorts of shapes given to me in the third batch. Unknown to me, the people who are giving me all these symbols call the first batch 'a script,' they call the second batch a 'story,' and they call the third batch 'questions.' Furthermore, they call the symbols I give them back in response to the third batch 'answers to the questions,' and the set of rules in English that they gave me, they call 'the program.' Now just to complicate the story a little, imagine that these people also give me stories in English, which I understand, and they then ask me questions in English about these stories, and I give them back answers in English. Suppose also that after a while I get so good at following the instructions for manipulating the Chinese symbols and the programmers get so good at writing the programs that from the external point of view—that is, from the point of view of somebody outside the room in which I am locked—my answers to the questions are absolutely indistinguishable from those of native Chinese speakers. Nobody just looking at my answers can tell that I don't speak a word of Chinese. Let us also suppose that my answers to the English questions are, as they no doubt would be, indistinguishable from those of other native English speakers, for the simple reason

that I am a native English speaker. From the external point of view—from the point of view of somebody reading my 'answers'—the answers to the Chinese questions and the English questions are equally good. But in the Chinese case, unlike the English case, I produce the answers by manipulating uninterpreted formal symbols. As far as the Chinese is concerned, I simply behave like a computer; I perform computational operations on formally specified elements. For the purposes of the Chinese, I am simply an instantiation of the computer program.

Now the claims made by strong AI are that the programmed computer understands the stories and that the program in some sense explains human understanding. But we are now in a position to examine these claims in light of our thought-experiment.

1. As regards the first claim, it seems to me quite obvious in the example that I do not understand a word of the Chinese stories. I have inputs and outputs that are indistinguishable from those of the native Chinese speaker, and I can have any formal program you like, but I still understand nothing. For the same reasons, Schank's computer understands nothing of any stories, whether in Chinese, English or whatever, since in the Chinese case the computer is me, and in cases where the computer is not me, the computer has nothing more than I have in the case where I understand nothing.

2. As regards the second claim, that the program explains human understanding, we can see that the computer and its program do not provide sufficient conditions of understanding since the computer and the program are functioning, and there is no understanding. But does it even provide a necessary condition or a significant contribution to understanding? One of the claims made by the supporters of strong AI is that when I understand a story in English, what I am doing is exactly the same—or perhaps more of the same—as what I was doing in manipulating the Chinese symbols. It is simply more formal symbol-manipulation that distinguishes the case in English, where I do understand, from the case in Chinese, where I don't. I have not demonstrated that this claim is false, but it would certainly appear an incredible claim in the example. Such plausibility as the claim has derives from the supposition that we can

construct a program that will have the same inputs and outputs as native speakers, and in addition we assume that speakers have some level of description where they are also instantiations of a program. On the basis of these two assumptions we assume that even if Schank's program isn't the whole story about understanding, it may be part of the story. Well, I suppose that is an empirical possibility, but not the slightest reason has so far been given to believe that it is true, since what is suggested—though certainly not demonstrated—by the example is that the computer program is simply irrelevant to my understanding of the story. In the Chinese case I have everything that artificial intelligence can put into me by way of a program, and I understand nothing; in the English case I understand everything, and there is so far no reason at all to suppose that my understanding has anything to do with computer programs, that is, with computational operations on purely formally specified elements. As long as the program is defined in terms of computational operations on purely formally defined elements, what the example suggests is that these by themselves have no interesting connection with understanding. They are certainly not sufficient conditions, and not the slightest reason has been given to suppose that they are necessary conditions or even that they make a significant contribution to understanding. Notice that the force of the argument is not simply that different machines can have the same input and output while operating on different formal principles—that is not the point at all. Rather, whatever purely formal principles you put into the computer, they will not be sufficient for understanding, since a human will be able to follow the formal principles without understanding anything. No reason whatever has been offered to suppose that such principles are necessary or even contributory, since no reason has been given to suppose that when I understand English I am operating with any formal program at all.

Well, then, what is it that I have in the case of the English sentences that I do not have in the case of the Chinese sentences? The obvious answer is that I know what the former mean, while I haven't the faintest idea what the latter mean. But in what does this consist and why couldn't we give it to a machine, whatever it is?

I will return to this question later, but first I want to continue with the example.

I have had the occasions to present this example to several workers in artificial intelligence, and, interestingly, they do not seem to agree on what the proper reply to it is. I get a surprising variety of replies, and in what follows I will consider the most common of these (specified along with their geographic origins).

But I first want to block some common misunderstandings about 'understanding': in many of these discussions one finds a lot of fancy footwork about the word 'understanding.' My critics point out that there are many different degrees of understanding; that 'understanding' is not a simple two-place predicate;[7] that there are even different kinds and levels of understanding, and often the law of excluded middle[8] doesn't even apply in a straightforward way to statements of the form 'x understands y'; that in many cases it is a matter for decision and not a simple matter of fact whether x understands y; and so on. To all of these points I want to say: of course, of course. But they have nothing to do with the points at issue. There are clear cases in which 'understanding' literally applies and clear cases in which it does not apply; and these two sorts of cases are all I need for this argument.[9] I understand stories in English; to a lesser degree I can understand stories in French; to a still lesser degree, stories in German; and in Chinese,

7 A two-place predicate is (roughly) a "describing phrase" which is used to describe two things at once: for example "___ is to the left of ___" or "___ and ___ are sisters" or "___ understands ___."

8 This is the logical principle which, when it applies, says that for any proposition p, either p or not-p: that is, there is nothing 'intermediate' between something being so and something not being so. (Incidentally, this should not be confused with the claim that, for any proposition p, p is either true or false: this principle, called the principle of bivalence, is logically different and has somewhat different implications.)

9 [Author's note] Also, 'understanding' implies both the possession of mental (intentional) states and the truth (validity, success) of these states. For the purposes of this discussion we are concerned only with the possession of the states.

not at all. My car and my adding machine, on the other hand, understand nothing: they are not in that line of business. We often attribute 'understanding' and other cognitive predicates by metaphor and analogy to cars, adding machines, and other artifacts, but nothing is proved by such attributions. We say, 'The door *knows* when to open because of its photoelectric cell,' 'The adding machine *knows how* (*understands how*, is *able*) to do addition and subtraction but not division,' and 'The thermostat *perceives* changes in the temperature.' The reason we make these attributions is quite interesting, and it has to do with the fact that in artifacts we extend our own intentionality,[10] our tools are extensions of our purposes, and so we find it natural to make metaphorical attributions of intentionality to them; but I take it no philosophical ice is cut by such examples. The sense in which an automatic door 'understands instructions' from its photoelectric cell is not at all the sense in which I understand English. If the sense in which Schank's programmed computers understand stories is supposed to be the metaphorical sense in which the door understands, and not the sense in which I understand English, the issue would not be worth discussing. But Newell and Simon (1963) write that the kind of cognition they claim for computers is exactly the same as for human beings. I like the straightforwardness of this claim, and it is the sort of claim I will be considering. I will argue that in the literal sense the programmed computer understands what the car and the adding machine understand, namely, exactly nothing. The computer understanding is not just (like my understanding of German) partial or incomplete; it is zero.

Now to the replies:

1. The Systems Reply (Berkeley)

'While it is true that the individual person who is locked in the room does not understand the story, the fact is that he is merely part of a whole system, and

the system does understand the story. The person has a large ledger in front of him in which are written the rules, he has a lot of scratch paper and pencils for doing calculations, he has "data banks" of sets of Chinese symbols. Now, understanding is not being ascribed to the mere individual; rather it is being ascribed to this whole system of which he is a part.'

My response to the systems theory is quite simple: let the individual internalize all of these elements of the system. He memorizes the rules in the ledger and the data banks of Chinese symbols, and he does all the calculations in his head. The individual then incorporates the entire system. There isn't anything at all to the system that he does not encompass. We can even get rid of the room and suppose he works outdoors. All the same, he understands nothing of the Chinese, and *a fortiori*[11] neither does the system, because there isn't anything in the system that isn't in him. If he doesn't understand, then there is no way the system could understand because the system is just a part of him.

Actually I feel somewhat embarrassed to give even this answer to the systems theory because the theory seems to me so unplausible to start with. The idea is that while a person doesn't understand Chinese, somehow the *conjunction* of that person and bits of paper might understand Chinese. It is not easy for me to imagine how someone who was not in the grip of an ideology would find the idea at all plausible. Still, I think many people who are committed to the ideology of strong AI will in the end be inclined to say something very much like this; so let us pursue it a bit further. According to one version of this view, while the man in the internalized systems example doesn't understand Chinese in the sense that a native Chinese speaker does (because, for example, he doesn't know that the story refers to restaurants and hamburgers, etc.), still 'the man as a formal symbol-manipulation system' *really does understand Chinese.* The subsystem of the man that is the formal symbol-manipulation system for Chinese should not be confused with the subsystem for English.

So there are really two subsystems in the man; one understands English, the other Chinese, and 'it's just that the two systems have little to do with each other.'

---

10 [Author's note] Intentionality is by definition that feature of certain mental states by which they are directed at or about objects and states of affairs in the world. Thus, beliefs, desires, and intentions are intentional states; undirected forms of anxiety and depression are not. For further discussion see Searle (1979b).

11 Even more conclusively.

But, I want to reply, not only do they have little to do with each other, they are not even remotely alike. The subsystem that understands English (assuming we allow ourselves to talk in this jargon of 'subsystems' for a moment) knows that the stories are about restaurants and eating hamburgers, he knows that he is being asked questions about restaurants and that he is answering questions as best he can by making various inferences from the content of the story, and so on. But the Chinese system knows none of this. Whereas the English system knows that 'hamburgers' refers to hamburgers, the Chinese subsystem knows only that 'squiggle squiggle' is followed by 'squoggle squoggle.' All he knows is that various formal symbols are being introduced at one end and manipulated according to rules written in English, and other symbols are going out at the other end. The whole point of the original example was to argue that such symbol manipulation by itself couldn't be sufficient for understanding Chinese in any literal sense because the man could write 'squoggle squoggle' after 'squiggle squiggle' without understanding anything in Chinese. And it doesn't meet that argument to postulate subsystems within the man, because the subsystems are no better off than the man was in the first place; they still don't have anything even remotely like what the English-speaking man (or subsystem) has. Indeed, in the case as described, the Chinese subsystem is simply a part of the English subsystem, a part that engages in meaningless symbol manipulation according to rules in English.

Let us ask ourselves what is supposed to motivate the systems reply in the first place; that is, what *independent* grounds are there supposed to be for saying that the agent must have a subsystem within him that literally understands stories in Chinese? As far as I can tell the only grounds are that in the example I have the same input and output as native Chinese speakers and a program that goes from one to the other. But the whole point of the examples has been to try to show that that couldn't be sufficient for understanding, in the sense in which I understand stories in English, because a person, and hence the set of systems that go to make up a person, could have the right combination of input, output, and program and still not understand anything in the relevant literal sense in which I understand English. The only motivation for saying there

must be a subsystem in me that understands Chinese is that I have a program and I pass the Turing-test;[12] I can fool native Chinese speakers. But precisely one of the points at issue is the adequacy of the Turing-test. The example shows that there could be two 'systems,' both of which pass the Turing-test, but only one of which understands; and it is no argument against this point to say that since they both pass the Turing-test they must both understand, since this claim fails to meet the argument that the system in me that understands English has a great deal more than the system that merely processes Chinese. In short, the systems reply simply begs the question by insisting without argument that the system must understand Chinese.

Furthermore, the systems reply would appear to lead to consequences that are independently absurd. If we are to conclude that there must be cognition in me on the grounds that I have a certain sort of input and output and a program in between, then it looks like all sorts of noncognitive subsystems are going to turn out to be cognitive. For example, there is a level of description at which my stomach does information-processing, and it instantiates any number of computer-programs, but I take it we do not want to say that it has any understanding (cf. Pylyshyn 1980). But if we accept the systems reply, then it is hard to see how we avoid saying that stomach, heart, liver, and so on, are all understanding subsystems, since there is no principled way to distinguish the motivation for saying the Chinese subsystem understands from saying that the stomach understands. It is, by the way, not an answer to this point to say that the Chinese system has information as input and output and the stomach has food and food products as input and output, since from the point of view of the agent, from my point

---

12   The Turing test was proposed by the British mathematician Alan Turing in 1950 as a way of determining whether a computer can think. Basically, a person and a computer—whose respective identities are kept hidden during the test—are both asked a series of questions, and are allowed to say anything they like in answer to those questions in order to persuade their interrogator that they are a human being. If the tester cannot tell the difference between them, then the computer passes the test.

of view, there is no information in either the food or the Chinese—the Chinese is just so many meaningless squiggles. The information in the Chinese case is solely in the eyes of the programmers and the interpreters, and there is nothing to prevent them from treating the input and output of my digestive organs as information if they so desire.

This last point bears on some independent problems in strong AI, and it is worth digressing for a moment to explain it. If strong AI is to be a branch of psychology, then it must be able to distinguish those systems that are genuinely mental from those that are not. It must be able to distinguish the principles on which the mind works from those on which non-mental systems work; otherwise it will offer us no explanations of what is specifically mental about the mental. And the mental–non-mental distinction cannot be just in the eye of the beholder but it must be intrinsic to the systems; otherwise it would be up to any beholder to treat people as non-mental and, for example, hurricanes as mental if he likes. But quite often in the AI literature the distinction is blurred in ways that would in the long run prove disastrous to the claim that AI is a cognitive enquiry. McCarthy, for example, writes, 'Machines as simple as thermostats can be said to have beliefs, and having beliefs seems to be a characteristic of most machines capable of problem solving performances' (McCarthy 1979). Anyone who thinks strong AI has a chance as a theory of the mind ought to ponder the implications of that remark. We are asked to accept it as a discovery of strong AI that the hunk of metal on the wall that we use to regulate the temperature has beliefs in exactly the same sense that we, our spouses, and our children have beliefs, and furthermore that 'most' of the other machines in the room—telephone, tape recorder, adding machine, electric light switch—also have beliefs in this literal sense. It is not the aim of this article to argue against McCarthy's point, so I will simply assert the following without argument. The study of the mind starts with such facts as that humans have belief, while thermostats, telephones, and adding machines don't. If you get a theory that denies this point you have produced a counter-example to the theory and the theory is false. One gets the impression that people in AI who write this sort of thing think they

can get away with it because they don't really take it seriously, and they don't think anyone else will either. I propose for a moment at least, to take it seriously. Think hard for one minute about what would be necessary to establish that that hunk of metal on the wall over there had real beliefs, beliefs with direction of fit, propositional content, and conditions of satisfaction; beliefs that had the possibility of being strong beliefs or weak beliefs; nervous, anxious, or secure beliefs; dogmatic, rational, or superstitious beliefs; blind faiths or hesitant cognitions; any kind of beliefs. The thermostat is not a candidate. Neither is stomach, liver, adding machine, or telephone. However, since we are taking the idea seriously, notice that its truth would be fatal to strong AI's claim to be a science of the mind. For now the mind is everywhere. What we wanted to know is what distinguishes the mind from thermostats and livers. And if McCarthy were right, strong AI wouldn't have a hope of telling us that.

2. The Robot Reply (Yale)

'Suppose we wrote a different kind of program from Schank's program. Suppose we put a computer inside a robot, and this computer would not just take in formal symbols as input and give out formal symbols as output, but rather would actually operate the robot in such a way that the robot does something very much like perceiving, walking, moving about, hammering nails, eating, drinking—anything you like. The robot would, for example, have a television camera attached to it that enabled it to "see," it would have arms and legs that enabled it to "act," and all of this would be controlled by its computer "brain." Such a robot would, unlike Schank's computer, have genuine understanding and other mental states.'

The first thing to notice about the robot reply is that it tacitly concedes that cognition is not solely a matter of formal symbol-manipulation, since this reply adds a set of causal relations with the outside world (cf. Fodor 1980). But the answer to the robot reply is that the addition of such 'perceptual' and 'motor' capacities adds nothing by way of understanding, in particular, or intentionality, in general, to Schank's original program. To see this, notice that the same thought-experiment applies to the robot case. Suppose that instead of the computer inside the robot, you put me inside the room and, as in the original Chinese case, you give me more Chinese symbols with more instructions in English for matching Chinese symbols to Chinese symbols and feeding back Chinese symbols to the outside. Suppose, unknown to me, some of the Chinese symbols that come to me come from a television camera attached to the robot and other Chinese symbols that I am giving out serve to make the motors inside the robot move the robot's legs or arms. It is important to emphasize that all I am doing is manipulating formal symbols: I know none of these other facts. I am receiving 'information' from the robot's 'perceptual' apparatus, and I am giving out 'instructions' to its motor apparatus without knowing either of these facts. I am the robot's homunculus,[13] but unlike the traditional homunculus, I don't know what's going on. I don't understand anything except the rules for symbol manipulation. Now in this case I want to say that the robot has no intentional states at all; it is simply moving about as a result of its electrical wiring and its program. And furthermore, by instantiating the program I have no intentional states of the relevant type. All I do is follow instructions about manipulating formal symbols.

3. The Brain Simulator Reply (Berkeley and MIT)

'Suppose we design a program that doesn't represent information that we have about the world, such as the information in Schank's scripts, but simulates the actual sequence of neuron firings at the synapses of the brain of a native Chinese speaker when he under-

---

13   Literally "little man." The idea behind the (mythical) homuncular theory is that our actions are to be explained by little men in our head, who perform various mental functions such as seeing, hearing, planning, instructing the limbs to move, and so on. Even if the notion of a "little man" is not taken too literally, this general form of psychological theory is often accused of committing the "homunculus fallacy": explaining visual perception by postulating an internal device which "scans" or "views" mental images displayed on a sort of inner screen, for example, is actually to explain nothing at all, since the inner device "sees" the internal images and this *seeing* is precisely what we wanted to explain in the first place.

stands stories in Chinese and gives answers to them. The machine takes in Chinese stories and questions about them as input, it simulates the formal structure of actual Chinese brains in processing these stories, and it gives out Chinese answers as outputs. We can even imagine that the machine operates, not with a single serial program, but with a whole set of programs operating in parallel, in the manner that actual human brains presumably operate when they process natural language. Now surely in such a case we would have to say that the machine understood the stories; and if we refuse to say that, wouldn't we also have to deny that native Chinese speakers understood the stories? At the level of the synapses, what would or could be different about the program of the computer and the program of the Chinese brain?'

Before countering this reply I want to digress to note that it is an odd reply for any partisan of artificial intelligence (or functionalism, etc.) to make: I thought the whole idea of strong AI is that we don't need to know how the brain works to know how the mind works. The basic hypothesis, or so I had supposed, was that there is a level of mental operations consisting of computational processes over formal elements that constitute the essence of the mental and can be realized in all sorts of different brain processes, in the same way that any computer program can be realized in different computer hardwares: on the assumptions of strong AI, the mind is to the brain as the program is to the hardware, and thus we can understand the mind without doing neurophysiology. If we had to know how the brain worked to do AI, we wouldn't bother with AI. However, even getting this close to the operation of the brain is still not sufficient to produce understanding. To see this, imagine that instead of a monolingual man in a room shuffling symbols we have the man operate an elaborate set of water pipes with valves connecting them. When the man receives the Chinese symbols, he looks up in the program, written in English, which valves he has to turn on and off. Each water connection corresponds to a synapse in the Chinese brain, and the whole system is rigged up so that after all the right firings, that is after turning on all the right faucets, the Chinese answers pop out at the output end of the series of pipes.

Now where is the understanding in this system? It takes Chinese as input, it simulates the formal structure of the synapses of the Chinese brain, and it gives Chinese as output. But the man certainly doesn't understand Chinese, and neither do the water pipes, and if we are tempted to adopt what I think is the absurd view that somehow the *conjunction* of man *and* water pipes understands, remember that in principle the man can internalize the formal structure of the water pipes and do all the 'neuron firings' in his imagination. The problem with the brain simulator is that it is simulating the wrong things about the brain. As long as it simulates only the formal structure of the sequence of neuron firings at the synapses, it won't have simulated what matters about the brain, namely its causal properties, its ability to produce intentional states. And that the formal properties are not sufficient for the causal properties is shown by the water pipe example: we can have all the formal properties carved off from the relevant neurobiological causal properties.

4. The Combination Reply (Berkeley and Stanford)

'While each of the previous three replies might not be completely convincing by itself as a refutation of the Chinese room counter-example, if you take all three together they are collectively much more convincing and even decisive. Imagine a robot with a brain-shaped computer lodged in its cranial cavity, imagine the computer programmed with all the synapses of a human brain, imagine the whole behaviour of the robot is undistinguishable from human behaviour, and now think of the whole thing as a unified system and not just as a computer with inputs and outputs. Surely in such a case we would have to ascribe intentionality to the system.'

I entirely agree that in such a case we would find it rational and indeed irresistible to accept the hypothesis that the robot had intentionality, as long as we knew nothing more about it. Indeed, besides appearance and behaviour, the other elements of the combination are really irrelevant. If we could build a robot whose behaviour was indistinguishable over a large range from human behaviour, we would attribute intentionality to it, pending some reason not to. We wouldn't need to know in advance that its computer brain was a formal analogue of the human brain.

But I really don't see that this is any help to the claims of strong AI; and here's why: According to

strong AI, instantiating a formal program with the right input and output is a sufficient condition of, indeed is constitutive of, intentionality. As Newell (1979) puts it, the essence of the mental is the operation of a physical-symbol system. But the attributions of intentionality that we make to the robot in this example have nothing to do with formal programs. They are simply based on the assumption that if the robot looks and behaves sufficiently like us, then we would suppose, until proven otherwise, that it must have mental states like ours that cause and are expressed by its behaviour and it must have an inner mechanism capable of producing such mental states. If we knew independently how to account for its behaviour without such assumptions we would not attribute intentionality to it, especially if we knew it had a formal program. And this is precisely the point of my earlier reply to objection 2.

Suppose we knew that the robot's behaviour was entirely accounted for by the fact that a man inside it was receiving uninterpreted formal symbols from the robot's sensory receptors and sending out uninterpreted formal symbols to its motor mechanisms, and the man was doing this symbol manipulation in accordance with a bunch of rules. Furthermore, suppose the man knows none of these facts about the robot, all he knows is which operations to perform on which meaningless symbols. In such a case we would regard the robot as an ingenious mechanical dummy. The hypothesis that the dummy has a mind would now be unwarranted and unnecessary, for there is now no longer any reason to ascribe intentionality to the robot or to the system of which it is a part (except of course for the man's intentionality in manipulating the symbols). The formal symbol manipulations go on, the input and output are correctly matched, but the only real locus of intentionality is the man, and he doesn't know any of the relevant intentional states; he doesn't, for example, *see* what comes into the robot's eyes, he doesn't *intend* to move the robot's arm, and he doesn't *understand* any of the remarks made to or by the robot. Nor, for the reasons stated earlier, does the system of which man and robot are a part.

To see this point, contrast this case with cases in which we find it completely natural to ascribe intentionality to members of certain other primate species such as apes and monkeys and to domestic animals such as dogs. The reasons we find it natural are, roughly, two: we can't make sense of the animal's behaviour without the ascription of intentionality, and we can see that the beasts are made of similar stuff to ourselves—that is an eye, that a nose, this is its skin, and so on. Given the coherence of the animal's behaviour and the assumption of the same causal stuff underlying it, we assume both that the animal must have mental states underlying its behaviour, and that the mental states must be produced by mechanisms made out of the stuff that is like our stuff. We would certainly make similar assumptions about the robot unless we had some reason not to, but as soon as we knew that the behaviour was the result of a formal program, and that the actual causal properties of the physical substance were irrelevant we would abandon the assumption of intentionality. (See Multiple authors 1978.)

There are two other responses to my example that come up frequently (and so are worth discussing) but really miss the point.

5. The Other Minds Reply (Yale)

'How do you know that other people understand Chinese or anything else? Only by their behaviour. Now the computer can pass the behavioural tests as well as they can (in principle), so if you are going to attribute cognition to other people you must in principle also attribute it to computers.'

This objection really is only worth a short reply. The problem in this discussion is not about how I know that other people have cognitive states, but rather what it is that I am attributing to them when I attribute cognitive states to them. The thrust of the argument is that it couldn't be just computational processes and their output because the computational processes and their output can exist without the cognitive state. It is no answer to this argument to feign anesthesia. In 'cognitive sciences'[14] one presupposes

the reality and knowability of the mental in the same way that in physical sciences one has to presuppose the reality and knowability of physical objects.

6. The Many Mansions Reply (Berkeley)

'Your whole argument presupposes that AI is only about analogue and digital computers. But that just happens to be the present state of technology. Whatever these causal processes are that you say are essential for intentionality (assuming you are right), eventually we will be able to build devices that have these causal processes, and that will be artificial intelligence. So your arguments are in no way directed at the ability of artificial intelligence to produce and explain cognition.'

I really have no objection to this reply save to say that it in effect trivializes the project of strong AI by redefining it as whatever artificially produces and explains cognition. The interest of the original claim made on behalf of artificial intelligence is that it was a precise, well-defined thesis: mental processes are computational processes over formally defined elements. I have been concerned to challenge that thesis. If the claim is redefined so that it is no longer that thesis, my objections no longer apply because there is no longer a testable hypothesis for them to apply to.

Let us now return to the question I promised I would try to answer: granted that in my original example I understand the English and I do not understand the Chinese, and granted therefore that the machine doesn't understand either English or Chinese, still there must be something about me that makes it the case that I understand English and a corresponding something lacking in me makes it the case that I fail to understand Chinese. Now why couldn't we give those somethings, whatever they are, to a machine?

I see no reason in principle why we couldn't give a machine the capacity to understand English or Chinese, since in an important sense our bodies with our brains are precisely such machines. But I do see very strong arguments for saying that we could not give

14 Cognitive science is an interdisciplinary research program, dating back to about 1956, which includes psychologists, computer scientists, neuroscientists, philosophers, linguists, and anthropologists. It is devoted to the study and modeling of intelligent activity in humans and other, natural and artificial, organisms, and was founded on the assumption that thought can

fruitfully be seen as a kind of information-processing: that is, the mind is an instrument which takes in data from the environment, processes it, and produces behavior as output.

such a thing to a machine where the operation of the machine is defined solely in terms of computational processes over formally defined elements; that is, where the operation of the machine is defined as an instantiation of a computer program. It is not because I am the instantiation of a computer program that I am able to understand English and have other forms of intentionality (I am, I suppose, the instantiation of any number of computer programs), but as far as we know it is because I am a certain sort of organism with a certain biological (i.e., chemical and physical) structure, and this structure, under certain conditions, is causally capable of producing perception, action, understanding, learning, and other intentional phenomena. And part of the point of the present argument is that only something that had those causal powers could have that intentionality. Perhaps other physical and chemical processes could produce exactly these effects; perhaps, for example, Martians also have intentionality but their brains are made of different stuff. That is an empirical question, rather like the question whether photosynthesis can be done by something with a chemistry different from that of chlorophyll.

But the main point of the present argument is that no purely formal model will ever be sufficient by itself for intentionality because the formal properties are not by themselves constitutive of intentionality, and they have by themselves no causal power except the power, when instantiated, to produce the next stage of the formalism when the machine is running. And any other causal properties that particular realizations of the formal model have, are irrelevant to the formal model because we can always put the same formal model in a different realization where those causal properties are obviously absent. Even if, by some miracle, Chinese speakers exactly realize Schank's program, we can put the same program in English speakers, water pipes, or computers, none of which understand Chinese, the program notwithstanding.

What matters about brain operations is not the formal shadow cast by the sequence of synapses but rather the actual properties of the sequences. All the arguments for the strong version of artificial intelligence that I have seen insist on drawing an outline around the shadows cast by cognition and then claiming that the shadows are the real thing.

By way of concluding I want to try to state some of the general philosophical points implicit in the argument. For clarity I will try to do it in a question and answer fashion, and I begin with that old chestnut of a question:

'Could a machine think?'

The answer is, obviously, yes. We are precisely such machines.

'Yes, but could an artifact, a man-made machine, think?'

Assuming it is possible to produce artificially a machine with a nervous system, neurons with axons and dendrites, and all the rest of it, sufficiently like ours, again the answer to the question seems to be obviously, yes. If you can exactly duplicate the causes, you could duplicate the effects. And indeed it might be possible to produce consciousness, intentionality, and all the rest of it using some other sorts of chemical principles than those that human beings use. It is, as I said, an empirical question.

'OK, but could a digital computer think?'

If by 'digital computer' we mean anything at all that has a level of description where it can correctly be described as the instantiation of a computer program, then again the answer is, of course, yes, since we are the instantiations of any number of computer programs, and we can think.

'But could something think, understand, and so on *solely* in virtue of being a computer with the right sort of program? Could instantiating a program, the right program of course, by itself be a sufficient condition of understanding?'

This I think is the right question to ask, though it is usually confused with one or more of the earlier questions, and the answer to it is no.

'Why not?'

Because the formal symbol-manipulations by themselves don't have any intentionality; they are quite meaningless; they aren't even *symbol* manipulations, since the symbols don't symbolize anything. In the linguistic jargon, they have only a syntax but no semantics. Such intentionality as computers appear to have is solely in the minds of those who program them and those who use them, those who send in the input and those who interpret the output.

The aim of the Chinese room example was to try to show this by showing that as soon as we put something into the system that really does have intentionality (a man), and we program him with the formal program, you can see that the formal program carries no additional intentionality. It adds nothing, for example, to a man's ability to understand Chinese.

Precisely that feature of AI that seemed so appealing—the distinction between the program and the realization—proves fatal to the claim that simulation could be duplication. The distinction between the program and its realization in the hardware seems to be parallel to the distinction between the level of mental operations and the level of brain operations. And if we could describe the level of mental operations as a formal program, then it seems we could describe what was essential about the mind without doing either introspective psychology or neurophysiology of the brain. But the equation, 'mind is to brain as program is to hardware' breaks down at several points, among them the following three:

First, the distinction between program and realization has the consequence that the same program could have all sorts of crazy realizations that had no form of intentionality. Weizenbaum (1976: ch. 2), for example, shows in detail how to construct a computer using a roll of toilet paper and a pile of small stones. Similarly, the Chinese story-understanding program can be programmed into a sequence of water pipes, a set of wind machines, or a monolingual English speaker, none of which thereby acquires an understanding of Chinese. Stones, toilet paper, wind, and water pipes are the wrong kind of stuff to have intentionality in the first place—only something that has the same causal powers as brains can have intentionality—and though the English speaker has the right kind of stuff for intentionality you can easily see that he doesn't get any extra intentionality by memorizing the program, since memorizing it won't teach him Chinese.

Second, the program is purely formal, but the intentional states are not in that way formal. They are defined in terms of their content, not their form. The belief that it is raining, for example, is not defined as a certain formal shape, but as a certain mental content with conditions of satisfaction, a direction of fit (see Searle 1979a), and the like. Indeed the belief as such hasn't even got a formal shape in this syntactic sense, since one and the same belief can be given an indefinite number of different syntactic expressions in different linguistic systems.

Third, as I mentioned before, mental states and events are literally a product of the operation of the brain, but the program is not in that way a product of the computer.

'Well if programs are in no way constitutive of mental processes, why have so many people believed the converse? That at least needs some explanation.'

I don't really know the answer to that one. The idea that computer simulations could be the real thing ought to have seemed suspicious in the first place because the computer isn't confined to simulating mental operations, by any means. No one supposes that computer simulations of a five-alarm fire will burn the neighbourhood down or that a computer simulation of a rainstorm will leave us all drenched. Why on earth would anyone suppose that a computer simulation of understanding actually understood anything? It is sometimes said that it would be frightfully hard to get computers to feel pain or fall in love, but love and pain are neither harder nor easier than cognition or anything else. For simulation, all you need is the right input and output and program in the middle that transforms the former into the latter. That is all the computer has for anything it does. To confuse simulation with duplication is the same mistake, whether it is pain, love, cognition, fires, or rainstorms.

Still, there are several reasons why AI must have seemed—and to many people perhaps still does seem—in some way to reproduce and thereby explain mental phenomena, and I believe we will not succeed in removing these illusions until we have fully exposed the reasons that give rise to them.

First, and perhaps most important, is a confusion about the notion of 'information-processing': many people in cognitive science believe that the human brain, with its mind, does something called 'information processing,' and analogously the computer with its program does information-processing; but fires and rainstorms, on the other hand, don't do information-processing at all. Thus, though the computer can simulate the formal features of any process whatever, it stands in a special relation to the mind and brain because when the computer is properly programmed, ideally with the same program as the brain, the information-processing is identical in the two cases, and this information-processing is really the essence of the mental. But the trouble with this argument is that it rests on an ambiguity in the notion of 'information.' In the sense in which people 'process information' when they reflect, say, on problems in arithmetic or when they read and answer questions about stories, the programmed computer does not do 'information-processing.' Rather, what it does is manipulate formal symbols. The fact that the programmer and the interpreter of the computer output use the symbols to stand for objects in the world is totally beyond the scope of the computer. The computer, to repeat, has a syntax but no semantics. Thus, if you type into the computer '2 plus 2 equals?' it will type out '4.' But it has no idea that '4' means 4 or that it means anything at all. And the point is not that it lacks some second-order information about the interpretation of its first-order symbols, but rather that its first-order symbols don't have any interpretations as far as the computer is concerned. All the computer has is more symbols. The introduction of the notion of 'information-processing' therefore produces a dilemma: either we construe the notion of 'information processing' in such a way that it implies intentionality as part of the process or we don't. If the former, then the programmed computer does not do information-processing, it only manipulates formal symbols. If the latter, then, though the computer does information-processing, it is only doing so in the sense in which adding machines, typewriters, stomachs, thermostats, rainstorms, and hurricanes do information-processing; namely, they have a level of description at which we can describe them as taking information in at one end, transforming it, and producing information as output. But in this case it is up to outside observers to interpret the input and output as information in the ordinary sense. And no similarity is established between the computer and the brain in terms of any similarity of information processing.

Second, in much of AI there is a residual behaviourism or operationalism.[15] Since appropriately pro-

grammed computers can have input-output patterns similar to those of human beings, we are tempted to postulate mental states in the computer similar to human mental states. But once we see that it is both conceptually and empirically possible for a system to have human capacities in some realm without having any intentionality at all, we should be able to overcome this impulse. My desk adding machine has calculating capacities, but no intentionality, and in this paper I have tried to show that a system could have input and output capabilities that duplicated those of a native Chinese speaker and still not understand Chinese, regardless of how it was programmed. The Turing test is typical of the tradition in being unashamedly behaviouristic and operationalistic, and I believe that if AI workers totally repudiated behaviourism and operationalism much of the confusion between simulation and duplication would be eliminated.

Third, this residual operationalism is joined to a residual form of dualism; indeed strong AI only makes sense given the dualistic assumption that, where the mind is concerned, the brain doesn't matter. In strong AI (and in functionalism, as well) what matters are programs, and programs are independent of their realization in machines; indeed, as far as AI is concerned, the same program could be realized by an electronic machine, a Cartesian mental substance, or a Hegelian world spirit.[16] The single most surprising discovery that I have made in discussing these issues

---

15 Operationalism is the view, formulated by the physicist P.W. Bridgman in 1927, that a word or concept should be *defined* by the operation we carry out to find out whether the word or concept applies. For example, on this view, the concept 'having a length of one meter'

amounts to saying that something of that length will fit exactly against a standard meter stick (which in turn will fit exactly against the distance traveled by light in a vacuum in 1/299,792,458 of a second). Similarly, for the operationalist, to say that someone is hungry is just to say that they will eat if given the chance, claim to be hungry if asked, and so on.

16 G.W.F. Hegel (1770–1831), an extremely influential German philosopher, held that natural entities embody thoughts—mind is embedded in the very structure of the universe—and the passage of human history is a gradual revealing of the categories embedded in nature. In the process, what Hegel called "absolute spirit" (the spirit of the world, or God) ascends to "freedom" and "self-consciousness."

is that many AI workers are quite shocked by my idea that actual human mental phenomena might be dependent on actual physical-chemical properties of actual human brains. But if you think about it a minute you can see that I should not have been surprised; for unless you accept some form of dualism, the strong AI project hasn't got a chance. The project is to reproduce and explain the mental by designing programs, but unless the mind is not only conceptually but empirically independent of the brain you couldn't carry out the project, for the program is completely independent of any realization. Unless you believe that the mind is separable from the brain both conceptually and empirically—dualism in a strong form—you cannot hope to reproduce the mental by writing and running programs since programs must be independent of brains or any other particular forms of instantiation. If mental operations consist in computational operations on formal symbols, then it follows that they have no interesting connection with the brain; the only connection would be that the brain just happens to be one of the indefinitely many types of machines capable of instantiating the program. This form of dualism is not the traditional Cartesian variety that claims there are two sorts of substances, but it is Cartesian in the sense that it insists that what is specifically mental about the mind has no intrinsic connection with the actual properties of the brain. This underlying dualism is masked from us by the fact that AI literature contains frequent fulminations against 'dualism'; what the authors seem to be unaware of is that their position presupposes a strong version of dualism.

'Could a machine think?' My own view is that only a machine could think, and indeed only very special kinds of machines, namely brains and machines that had the same causal powers as brains. And that is the main reason strong AI has had little to tell us about thinking, since it has nothing to tell us about machines. By its own definition, it is about programs, and programs are not machines. Whatever else intentionality is, it is a biological phenomenon, and it is as likely to be as causally dependent on the specific biochemistry of its origins as lactation, photosynthesis, or any other biological phenomena. No one would suppose that we could produce milk and sugar by running a computer simulation of the formal sequences in lactation and photosynthesis, but where the mind is concerned many people are willing to believe in such a miracle because of a deep and abiding dualism: the mind they suppose is a matter of formal processes and is independent of quite specific material causes in the way that milk and sugar are not.

In defence of this dualism the hope is often expressed that the brain is a digital computer (early computers, by the way, were often called 'electronic brains'). But that is no help. Of course the brain is a digital computer. Since everything is a digital computer, brains are too. The point is that the brain's causal capacity to produce intentionality cannot consist in its instantiating a computer program, since for any program you like it is possible for something to instantiate that program and still not have any mental states. Whatever it is that the brain does to produce intentionality, it cannot consist in instantiating a program since no program, by itself, is sufficient for intentionality.[17]

References

Fodor, J.A. (1980). 'Methodological Solipsism Considered as a Research Strategy in Cognitive Psychology.' *Behavioral and Brain Sciences* 3: 63–110.

McCarthy, J. (1979). 'Ascribing Mental Qualities to Machines.' In M. Ringle (ed.), *Philosophical Perspectives in Artificial Intelligence*, pp. 161–95. Atlantic Highlands, NJ: Humanities Press.

[Multiple authors] (1978). 'Cognition and Consciousness in Non-Human Species.' *Behavioral and Brain Sciences* 1 (4): entire issue.

Newell, A. (1979). 'Physical Symbol Systems.' Lecture at the La Jolla Conference on Cognitive Science. Later published in *Cognitive Science* 4 (1980): 135–83.

---

17   [Author's note] I am indebted to a rather large number of people for discussion of these matters, and for their patient attempts to overcome my ignorance of artificial intelligence. I would especially like to thank Ned Bock, Hubert Dreyfus, John Haugeland, Roger Schank, Robert Wilensky, and Terry Winograd.

Newell, A. and Simon, H.A. (1963). 'GPS—A Program that Simulates Human Thought.' In E.A. Feigenbaum and J.A. Feldman (eds.), *Computers and Thought*, pp. 279–96. New York: McGraw-Hill.

Pylyshyn, Z.W. (1980). 'Computation and Cognition: Issues in the Foundation of Cognitive Science.' *Behavioral and Brain Sciences* 3: 111–32.

Schank, R.C. and Abelson, R.P. (1977). *Scripts, Plans, Goals, and Understanding*. Hillsdale, NJ: Erlbaum.

Searle, J.R. (1979a). 'Intentionality and the Use of Language.' In A. Margolit (ed.), *Meaning and Use*. Dordrecht: Reidel.

Searle, J.R. (1979b). 'What Is an Intentional State?' *Mind* 88: 74–92.

Weizenbaum, J. (1965). 'ELIZA—A Computer Program for the Study of Natural Language Communication Between Man and Machine.' *Commun. ACM* 9: 36–45.

Weizenbaum, J. (1976). *Computer Power and Human Reason*. San Francisco: W.H. Freeman.

Winograd, T. (1973). 'A Procedural Model of Language Understanding.' In R.C. Schank and K.M. Colby (eds.), *Computer Models of Thought and Language*, pp.152–86. San Francisco: W.H. Freeman.

THOMAS NAGEL
"What Is It Like to Be a Bat?"

Who Is Thomas Nagel?

Thomas Nagel, an important American philosopher, is currently a Professor of Law and Philosophy at New York University. Born in 1937, Nagel was educated at Cornell (BA), Corpus Christi College, Oxford (BPhil), and Harvard (PhD, completed in 1963). After working at Berkeley and Princeton, he moved to New York University in 1980.

Throughout his career a main theme of Nagel's philosophical writing has been the difficulty of reconciling two fundamentally different points of view: our first-person, subjective, personal point of view, and the impartial, third-person, objective perspective.[1]

The first-person perspective is typically thought of as being more partial than the third-person—partial both in the sense of being constrained by local horizons, and of being infected with personal concerns and biases. (For example, from *my* point of view it is right and natural to eat with a knife and fork, but this seems natural to me only because of the place and manner of my upbringing: speaking objectively, forks are no more nor less 'natural' than chopsticks or fingers.) As a result, subjective impressions are often thought of as being less reliable or 'true' than objective claims, and the first-person perspective tends to be treated as something to be avoided in serious knowledge-gathering enterprises such as science or good journalism. Nagel's guiding philosophical question is this: *could* we completely understand the universe from the third-person point of view—that is, is the subjective completely reducible to (or eliminable in favor of) the objective? As he puts it in one of his books, he wants to know "how to combine the perspective of a particular person inside the world with

---

1   "First-person" and "third-person" are terms taken from grammatical categories: "I am hungry," is a first-person sentence as it's about the speaker; "She/he/it is hungry," is a third-person sentence, as it's about a third party. ("You are hungry," would be an example of a second-person sentence.)

an objective view of that same world, the person and his viewpoint included."

The short version of Nagel's response to this problem is the following:

1. The subjective perspective is ineliminable in various highly important ways, and a refusal to notice this can lead to philosophical errors. "Appearance and perspective are essential parts of what there is." Our objectivity is limited by the fact that we cannot leave our own viewpoints entirely behind.

2. However, objectivity is also to be valued and fostered as a crucial method of coming to understand aspects of the world as it is in itself. It is important that we struggle to transcend our local horizons and try to get a better view of our place in the universe.

Most of Nagel's books trace these themes, in one way or another. *The View From Nowhere*, his best-known book, published in 1986, is explicitly about the relation between the subjective and the objective. His first book, *The Possibility of Altruism*, dealt with the conflict between personal and impersonal reasons for individual action, and one of his later books, *Equality and Partiality*, examines the issue of reconciling individual claims with those of a group. Nagel's latest book, *The Last Word*, defends the objectivity and importance of rationality against a kind of "anything goes" subjectivism which Nagel opposes. "What Is It Like to Be a Bat?" is probably Nagel's most famous and influential article. In it he applies his theme to the philosophy of mind, and contends that all current third-person theories of the mind (such as identity-theory, behaviorism, or functionalism) are radically incomplete since they fail to capture "what it is like to be" conscious, and this subjective character of experience, Nagel suggests, is a central aspect of mentality.

In the preface to his book *Mortal Questions*, Nagel describes his view of philosophy, and it is worth repeating here:

I believe one should trust problems over solutions, intuition over arguments, and pluralistic discord over systematic harmony. Simplicity and elegance are never reasons to think that a philosophical theory is true: on the contrary, they are usually grounds for thinking it false. Given a knockdown argument for an intuitively unacceptable conclusion, one should assume there is probably something wrong with the argument that one cannot detect—though it is always possible that the source of the intuition has been misidentified.... Often the problem has to be reformulated because an adequate answer to the original formulation fails to make the *sense* of the problem disappear.... Superficiality is as hard to avoid in philosophy as it is anywhere else. It is too easy to reach solutions that fail to do justice to the difficulty of the problems. All one can do is try to maintain a desire for answers, a tolerance for long periods without any, an unwillingness to brush aside unexplained intuitions, and an adherence to reasonable standards of clear expression and cogent argument.

What Is the Structure of This Reading?

Nagel begins by saying that the problem of reducing the mental to the physical—of completely describing and explaining our mental life in physical, non-psychological terms—is uniquely difficult because of the nature of conscious experience, and he goes on to explain this by discussing the relation between subjective and objective facts, using bats as an example. After an aside, where he discusses the relation between facts and conceptual schemes for representing those facts, Nagel proceeds to argue that subjective facts about consciousness make the mind-body problem intractable. One of his central claims is that the reduction of experience to neurophysiology (i.e., the physiology of the brain and nervous system) is importantly different from standard cases of reduction (e.g., the reduction of heat to mean molecular motion). Nagel then discusses what philosophical moral should be drawn from all this—what implications it has, for example, for the claim that mental states are identical with brain states. He closes by suggesting that we pursue a solution to the problem he has raised by trying to develop an "objective phenomenology" of the mental.

Some Useful Background Information

Nagel is reacting against attempts in the 1960s and early 1970s to *reduce* the mental to the physical—that is, to show that, properly understood, mental phenomena are nothing more than physical phenomena. There are two central varieties of reduction, sometimes called "ontological reduction" and "theory reduction." Ontological reduction consists in showing that objects (or properties or events) of the first type are identical with—or "realized by"—objects (properties, events) of the second: for example, it might be that genes are identical with DNA molecules, or that lightning is nothing but a kind of electrical discharge, or that the color purple is just reflected light of a particular wavelength. Theory reduction consists in showing that all the statements of one higher-level theory can be translated into (or otherwise deduced from) statements of another more fundamental theory: for example (roughly speaking), the Mendelian laws of genetics are entailed by molecular biology, and our commonsense "theory" of temperature can be translated into the kinetic theory of matter.

Nagel's anti-reductive claim is, therefore, that any optimism we might feel, that mental entities such as beliefs and emotions can be shown to be identical with neurological or functional states, or that

psychological theories can someday be translated into some non-psychological language, is seriously misguided.

Some Common Misconceptions

1. It is sometimes thought Nagel argues that physicalism is false: that is, that the mental involves something *extra* over and above the physical. (This would make Nagel some kind of dualist.) However, Nagel does not claim this: instead, he argues that *existing* physicalist theories of the mental (behaviorism, identity theory, functionalism) must be wrong, and he suggests that, although physicalism may be true—or even demonstrably true—it will be very hard for us to understand *how* it can be true. That is, he worries about the difficulty of giving any kind of objective theory of the mind.

2. There are various kinds of "subjectivity," and it has sometimes puzzled people exactly which kind Nagel is worrying about (perhaps because Nagel himself does not distinguish between some of them). One variety of non-objectivity that Nagel is clear he is *not* endorsing, however, is a particular kind of privacy of the mental. Some philosophers (such as Descartes) have held that consciousness is radically private in the sense that we have a special kind of access to our own mental states which, in principle, we cannot have to physical states. If this were true, then I could look as hard as I liked at your brain (which is a physical object) and *never* see any of your mental states; it would mean that the only access to consciousness must necessarily be from the first person, and thus that science would be forever excluded from studying and describing it. It is easy to see how this view might be confused with the one Nagel develops in this article, but nevertheless it is importantly different. For example, Nagel actually *denies* that we could never come to know anything at all about other people's consciousness, and even asserts that we can be corrected by other people when we make mistakes about what we ourselves are feeling (i.e., we are not

"incorrigible"). For Nagel, the problem is not some metaphysical difference of access to the mental and physical, but a problem about reconciling subjective and objective categories. Other versions of "subjectivity" which may (or may not) be in play in this article include:

- having a particular point of view or perspective;
- being phenomenal or experiential (i.e., feeling a certain way);
- having a sense of oneself as being a subject—as being a creature that, for example, undergoes sensations, forms intentions to do things, and controls its own actions;
- being infallibly known or present to one's awareness (like the kind of raging toothache which is impossible to ignore and which one couldn't possibly be mistaken about).

Suggestions for Critical Reflection

1. Many commentators suggest (as hinted above) that Nagel collapses together two or three different kinds of subjectivity that would be better kept separate. Do you agree with this criticism? If so, how much of a problem (if any) does this cause for Nagel's arguments?

2. Do you think Nagel makes a good case for the claim that the reduction of, say, pain to some objectively-describable physical state is a very different ball game than the reduction of, for example, heat or liquidity to microphysical properties? If he's right about this, what philosophical implications are there (if any)?

3. Do you agree that there must be some facts—some things which are true—which could never be known by any human being, no matter how smart or well-informed?

4. Given Nagel's arguments, do you think that physicalism could possibly be true? That is, does Nagel leave open the possibility that everything that exists is, at bottom, physical (e.g., composed out of matter and energy)?

5. What do you think of Nagel's proposal for an "objective phenomenology"? What might such a theory look like? Is it even possible? Does

Nagel *really* hold open the possibility of an objective description of the subjective character of experience?

Suggestions for Further Reading

Nagel's main works are *The Possibility of Altruism* (Oxford University Press, 1970), *The View From Nowhere* (Oxford University Press, 1986), *The Last Word* (Oxford, 1997), and the collection of papers *Mortal Questions* (Cambridge University Press, 1979), which includes "What Is It Like to Be a Bat?" "Brain Bisection and the Unity of Consciousness," another of Nagel's influential papers on the philosophy of mind, also appears in this volume. He has also written a popular short introduction to philosophy, *What Does It All Mean?* (Oxford University Press, 1987). Nagel's views on the subjectivity of consciousness are discussed in many works: two useful discussions to start with are found in Daniel Dennett's *Consciousness Explained* (Little, Brown, 1991) and John Searle's *The Rediscovery of Mind* (MIT Press, 1992). Dennett argues Nagel is wrong; Searle says he is right, but that it doesn't matter.

"What Is It Like to Be a Bat?"[2]

Consciousness is what makes the mind-body problem really intractable. Perhaps that is why current discussions of the problem give it little attention or get it obviously wrong. The recent wave of reductionist euphoria has produced several analyses of mental phenomena and mental concepts designed to explain the possibility of some variety of materialism, psychophysical identification, or reduction.[3] But the

---

2   This article was first published in 1974 in *The Philosophical Review* (Volume 83, Issue 4, October 1974, pp. 435–450). Published by Duke University Press.

3   [Author's note] Examples are J.J.C. Smart, *Philosophy and Scientific Realism* (London, 1963); David K. Lewis, "An Argument for the Identity Theory," *Journal of Philosophy*, LXIII (1966), reprinted with addenda in David M. Rosenthal, *Materialism & the Mind-Body Problem* (Englewood Cliffs, N.J., 1971);

problems dealt with are those common to this type of reduction and other types, and what makes the mind-body problem unique, and unlike the water-H$_2$O problem or the Turing machine-IBM machine problem[4] or the lightning-electrical discharge problem or the gene-DNA problem or the oak tree-hydrocarbon problem, is ignored.

Every reductionist has his favorite analogy from modern science. It is most unlikely that any of these unrelated examples of successful reduction will shed light on the relation of mind to brain. But philosophers share the general human weakness for explanations of what is incomprehensible in terms suited for what is familiar and well understood, though entirely different. This has led to the acceptance of implausible accounts of the mental largely because they would permit familiar kinds of reduction. I shall try to

---

Hilary Putnam, "Psychological Predicates" in Capitan and Merrill, *Art, Mind, & Religion* (Pittsburgh, 1967), reprinted in Rosenthal, *op. cit.*, as "The Nature of Mental States"; D.M. Armstrong, *A Materialist Theory of the Mind* (London, 1968); D.C. Dennett, *Content and Consciousness* (London, 1969). I have expressed earlier doubts in "Armstrong on the Mind," *Philosophical Review*, LXXIX (1970), 394–403; "Brain Bisection and the Unity of Consciousness," *Synthèse*, 22 (1971); and a review of Dennett, *Journal of Philosophy*, LXIX (1972). See also Saul Kripke, "Naming and Necessity" in Davidson and Harman, *Semantics of Natural Language* (Dordrecht, 1972), esp. pp. 334–342; and M.T. Thornton, "Ostensive Terms and Materialism," *The Monist*, 56 (1972).

4   By "IBM machine" Nagel simply means a computer. A Turing machine is an idealized computing device (thought up by the British mathematician Alan Turing in 1936) which consists in nothing more than a (potentially infinite) paper tape divided into squares, and a read-write head which moves left or right one square at a time and can write or erase the symbol "1" on the tape. Turing argued that any effective mathematical method or "algorithm"—and thus any computer program whatever, such as say Microsoft Word for Macintosh—can in principle be run on a Turing machine. See the notes to the Putnam reading in this chapter for more information.

explain why the usual examples do not help us to understand the relation between mind and body—why, indeed, we have at present no conception of what an explanation of the physical nature of a mental phenomenon would be. Without consciousness the mind-body problem would be much less interesting. With consciousness it seems hopeless. The most important and characteristic feature of conscious mental phenomena is very poorly understood. Most reductionist theories do not even try to explain it. And careful examination will show that no currently available concept of reduction is applicable to it. Perhaps a new theoretical form can be devised for the purpose, but such a solution, if it exists, lies in the distant intellectual future.

Conscious experience is a widespread phenomenon. It occurs at many levels of animal life, though we cannot be sure of its presence in the simpler organisms, and it is very difficult to say in general what provides evidence of it. (Some extremists have been prepared to deny it even of mammals other than man.) No doubt it occurs in countless forms totally unimaginable to us, on other planets in other solar systems throughout the universe. But no matter how the form may vary, the fact that an organism has conscious experience *at all* means, basically, that there is something it is like to *be* that organism. There may be further implications about the form of the experience; there may even (though I doubt it) be implications about the behavior of the organism. But fundamentally an organism has conscious mental states if and only if there is something that it is like to *be* that organism—something it is like *for* the organism.

We may call this the subjective character of experience. It is not captured by any of the familiar, recently devised reductive analyses of the mental, for all of them are logically compatible with its absence. It is not analyzable in terms of any explanatory system of functional states, or intentional states,[5] since these could be ascribed to

---

5   A functional state is characterized by its causal role (rather than by, say, what it is made of). *Being a can opener* is a functional property since anything which takes a certain kind of input—closed cans—and pro-

robots or automata that behaved like people though they experienced nothing.[6] It is not analyzable in terms of the causal role of experiences in relation to typical human behavior—for similar reasons.[7] I do not deny that conscious mental states and events cause behavior, nor that they may be given functional characterizations. I deny only that this kind of thing exhausts their analysis. Any reductionist program has to be based on an analysis of what is to be reduced. If the analysis leaves something out, the problem will be falsely posed. It is useless to base the defense of materialism on any analysis of mental phenomena that fails to deal explicitly with their subjective character. For there is no reason to suppose that a reduction which seems plausible when no attempt is made to account for consciousness can be extended to include consciousness. Without some idea, therefore, of what the subjective character of experience is, we cannot know what is required of a physicalist theory.

While an account of the physical basis of mind must explain many things, this appears to be the most difficult. It is impossible to exclude the phenomenological[8] features of experience from a reduction in the same way that one excludes the phenomenal features of an ordinary substance from a physical or chemical reduction of it—namely, by explaining them as effects on the minds of human observers.[9] If physicalism is to be defended, the phenomenological features must themselves be given a physical account. But when we examine their subjective character it seems that such a result is impossible. The reason is that every subjective phenomenon is essentially connected with a single point of view, and it seems inevitable that an objective, physical theory will abandon that point of view.

Let me first try to state the issue somewhat more fully than by referring to the relation between the subjective and the objective, or between the *pour-soi* and the *en-soi*.[10] This is far from easy. Facts about what it is like to be an *X* are very peculiar, so peculiar that some may be inclined to doubt their reality, or the significance of claims about them. To illustrate the connection between subjectivity and a point of view, and to make evident the importance of subjective features, it will help to explore the matter in relation to an example that brings out clearly the divergence between the two types of conception, subjective and objective.

I assume we all believe that bats have experience. After all, they are mammals, and there is no more doubt that they have experience than that mice or pigeons or whales have experience. I have chosen bats

---

duces a certain kind of output—cans neatly opened at one end—is a can opener. (By contrast, *being a piece of gold* is usually considered a physical but not a functional property: it has to do with what the lump is made of, rather than what it does.)

An intentional state is one which has what philosophers call "intentionality," a technical term for 'aboutness' or, roughly, meaningfulness. Thus an intentional state is one which is about something else (such as the state of a register in a computer's CPU, as compared with, say, the position of a randomly chosen pebble on a beach). See the notes to the Searle reading in this chapter for more information on intentionality.

6   [Author's note] Perhaps there could not actually be such robots. Perhaps anything complex enough to behave like a person would have experiences. But that, if true, is a fact which cannot be discovered merely by analyzing the concept of experience.

7   [Author's note] It is not equivalent to that about which we are incorrigible, both because we are not incorrigible about experience and because experience is present in animals lacking language and thought, who have no beliefs at all about their experiences.

8   "Phenomenological" means having to do with phenomenology, and phenomenology is the description of the features of our lived conscious experience (as opposed to the features of what it is experience *of*). So, for example, the phenomenology of our perception of trees does not concern itself with actual trees and their relations to perceivers, but instead examines what it *feels* like to see a tree—what kind of picture we have in our head, if you like.

9   [Author's note] Cf. Richard Rorty, "Mind-Body Identity, Privacy, and Categories," *The Review of Metaphysics*, XIX (1965), esp. 37–38.

10 *Pour-soi* means "for itself" and *en-soi* means "in itself." In this context, the phrase refers to the contrast between consciousness and mere thing-hood.

instead of wasps or flounders because if one travels too far down the phylogenetic tree,[11] people gradually shed their faith that there is experience there at all. Bats, although more closely related to us than those other species, nevertheless present a range of activity and a sensory apparatus so different from ours that the problem I want to pose is exceptionally vivid (though it certainly could be raised with other species). Even without the benefit of philosophical reflection, anyone who has spent some time in an enclosed space with an excited bat knows what it is to encounter a fundamentally *alien* form of life.

I have said that the essence of the belief that bats have experience is that there is something that it is like to be a bat. Now we know that most bats (the microchiroptera, to be precise) perceive the external world primarily by sonar, or echolocation, detecting the reflections, from objects within range, of their own rapid, subtly modulated, high-frequency shrieks. Their brains are designed to correlate the outgoing impulses with the subsequent echoes, and the information thus acquired enables bats to make precise discriminations of distance, size, shape, motion, and texture comparable to those we make by vision. But bat sonar, though clearly a form of perception, is not similar in its operation to any sense that we possess, and there is no reason to suppose that it is subjectively like anything we can experience or imagine. This appears to create difficulties for the notion of what it is like to be a bat. We must consider whether any method will permit us to extrapolate to the inner life of the bat from our own case,[12] and if not, what alternative methods there may be for understanding the notion.

Our own experience provides the basic material for our imagination, whose range is therefore limited. It will not help to try to imagine that one has webbing on one's arms, which enables one to fly around at dusk and dawn catching insects in one's mouth; that one has very poor vision, and perceives the surrounding world by a system of reflected high-frequency sound signals; and that one spends the day hanging upside down by one's feet in an attic. In so far as I can imagine this (which is not very far), it tells me only what it would be like for *me* to behave as a bat behaves. But that is not the question. I want to know what it is like for a *bat* to be a bat. Yet if I try to imagine this, I am restricted to the resources of my own mind, and those resources are inadequate to the task. I cannot perform it either by imagining additions to my present experience, or by imagining segments gradually subtracted from it, or by imagining some combination of additions, subtractions, and modifications.

To the extent that I could look and behave like a wasp or a bat without changing my fundamental structure, my experiences would not be anything like the experiences of those animals. On the other hand, it is doubtful that any meaning can be attached to the supposition that I should possess the internal neurophysiological constitution of a bat. Even if I could by gradual degrees be transformed into a bat, nothing in my present constitution enables me to imagine what the experiences of such a future stage of myself thus metamorphosed would be like. The best evidence would come from the experiences of bats, if we only knew what they were like.

So if extrapolation from our own case is involved in the idea of what it is like to be a bat, the extrapolation must be incompletable. We cannot form more than a schematic conception of what it is like. For example, we may ascribe general *types* of experience on the basis of the animal's structure and behavior. Thus we describe bat sonar as a form of three-dimensional forward perception; we believe that bats feel some versions of pain, fear, hunger, and lust, and that they have other, more familiar types of perception besides sonar. But we believe that these experiences also have in each case a specific subjective character, which it is beyond our ability to conceive. And if there is conscious life elsewhere in the universe, it is likely that some of it will not be describable even in the most general experiential terms available to us.[13] (The

---

11   (Roughly) the scale of evolutionary development.

12   [Author's note] By "our own case" I do not mean just "my own case," but rather the mentalistic ideas that we apply unproblematically to ourselves and other human beings.

13   [Author's note] Therefore the analogical form of the English expression "what it is *like*" is misleading. It does not mean "what (in our experience) it *resembles*," but rather "how it is for the subject himself."

problem is not confined to exotic cases, however, for it exists between one person and another. The subjective character of the experience of a person deaf and blind from birth is not accessible to me, for example, nor presumably is mine to him. This does not prevent us each from believing that the other's experience has such a subjective character.)

If anyone is inclined to deny that we can believe in the existence of facts like this whose exact nature we cannot possibly conceive, he should reflect that in contemplating the bats we are in much the same position that intelligent bats or Martians[14] would occupy if they tried to form a conception of what it was like to be us. The structure of their own minds might make it impossible for them to succeed, but we know they would be wrong to conclude that there is not anything precise that it is like to be us: that only certain general types of mental state could be ascribed to us (perhaps perception and appetite would be concepts common to us both; perhaps not). We know they would be wrong to draw such a skeptical conclusion because we know what it is like to be us. And we know that while it includes an enormous amount of variation and complexity, and while we do not possess the vocabulary to describe it adequately, its subjective character is highly specific, and in some respects describable in terms that can be understood only by creatures like us. The fact that we cannot expect ever to accommodate in our language a detailed description of Martian or bat phenomenology should not lead us to dismiss as meaningless the claim that bats and Martians have experiences fully comparable in richness of detail to our own. It would be fine if someone were to develop concepts and a theory that enabled us to think about those things; but such an understanding may be permanently denied to us by the limits of our nature. And to deny the reality or logical significance of what we can never describe or understand is the crudest form of cognitive dissonance.

This brings us to the edge of a topic that requires much more discussion than I can give it here: namely, the relation between facts on the one hand and conceptual schemes or systems of representation on the other. My realism about the subjective domain in all its forms implies a belief in the existence of facts beyond the reach of human concepts. Certainly it is possible for a human being to believe that there are facts which humans never *will* possess the requisite concepts to represent or comprehend. Indeed, it would be foolish to doubt this, given the finiteness of humanity's expectations. After all, there would have been transfinite numbers even if everyone had been wiped out by the Black Death before Cantor[15] discovered them. But one might also believe that there are facts which *could* not ever be represented or comprehended by human beings, even if the species lasted forever—simply because our structure does not permit us to operate with concepts of the requisite type. This impossibility might even be observed by other beings, but it is not clear that the existence of such beings, or the possibility of their existence, is a precondition of the significance of the hypothesis that there are humanly inaccessible facts. (After all, the nature of beings with access to humanly inaccessible facts is presumably itself a humanly inaccessible fact.) Reflection on what it is like to be a bat seems to lead us, therefore, to the conclusion that there are facts that do not consist in the truth of propositions expressible in a human language. We can be compelled to recognize the existence of such facts without being able to state or comprehend them.

I shall not pursue this subject, however. Its bearing on the topic before us (namely, the mind-body problem) is that it enables us to make a general observation about the subjective character of experience. Whatever may be the status of facts about what it is like to be a human being, or a bat, or a Martian, these appear to be facts that embody a particular point of view.

---

14   [Author's note] Any intelligent extraterrestrial beings totally different from us.

15   Georg Cantor (1845–1918) was a German mathematician. His theory of transfinite numbers is a mathematical theory of infinity which introduces a sequence of infinite cardinal numbers (called 'aleph-numbers,' and written $\aleph_0$, $\aleph_1$, $\aleph_2$ ...) of increasing size. That is, intuitively, Cantor formalized the fact that some infinities are bigger than others.

I am not adverting here to the alleged privacy of experience to its possessor. The point of view in question is not one accessible only to a single individual. Rather it is a *type*. It is often possible to take up a point of view other than one's own, so the comprehension of such facts is not limited to one's own case. There is a sense in which phenomenological facts are perfectly objective: one person can know or say of another what the quality of the other's experience is. They are subjective, however, in the sense that even this objective ascription of experience is possible only for someone sufficiently similar to the object of ascription to be able to adopt his point of view—to understand the ascription in the first person as well as in the third, so to speak. The more different from oneself the other experiencer is, the less success one can expect with this enterprise. In our own case we occupy the relevant point of view, but we will have as much difficulty understanding our own experience properly if we approach it from another point of view as we would if we tried to understand the experience of another species without taking up *its* point of view.[16]

---

16   [Author's note] It may be easier than I suppose to transcend inter-species barriers with the aid of the imagination. For example, blind people are able to detect objects near them by a form of sonar, using vocal clicks or taps of a cane. Perhaps if one knew what that was like, one could by extension imagine roughly what it was like to possess the much more refined sonar of a bat. The distance between oneself and other persons and other species can fall anywhere on a continuum. Even for other persons the understanding of what it is like to be them is only partial, and when one moves to species very different from oneself, a lesser degree of partial understanding may still be available. The imagination is remarkably flexible. My point, however, is not that we cannot *know* what it is like to be a bat. I am not raising that epistemological problem. My point is rather that even to form a *conception* of what it is like to be a bat (and a fortiori to know what it is like to be a bat) one must take up the bat's point of view. If one can take it up roughly, or partially, then one's conception

This bears directly on the mind-body problem. For if the facts of experience—facts about what it is like *for* the experiencing organism—are accessible only from one point of view, then it is a mystery how the true character of experiences could be revealed in the physical operation of that organism. The latter is a domain of objective facts *par excellence*[17]—the kind that can be observed and understood from many points of view and by individuals with differing perceptual systems. There are no comparable imaginative obstacles to the acquisition of knowledge about bat neurophysiology by human scientists, and intelligent bats or Martians might learn more about the human brain than we ever will.

This is not by itself an argument against reduction. A Martian scientist with no understanding of visual perception could understand the rainbow, or lightning, or clouds as physical phenomena, though he would never be able to understand the human concepts of rainbow, lightning, or cloud, or the place these things occupy in our phenomenal world. The objective nature of the things picked out by these concepts could be apprehended by him because, although the concepts themselves are connected with a particular point of view and a particular visual phenomenology, the things apprehended from that point of view are not: they are observable from the point of view but external to it; hence they can be comprehended from other points of view also, either by the same organisms or by others. Lightning has an objective character that is not exhausted by its visual appearance, and this can be investigated by a Martian without vision. To be precise, it has a *more* objective character than is revealed in its visual appearance. In speaking of the move from subjective to objective characterization, I wish to remain noncommittal about the existence of an end point, the completely objective intrinsic nature of the thing, which one might or might not be able to reach. It may be more accurate to think of objectivity as a direction in which the understanding can travel. And in understanding a phenomenon like

---

will also be rough or partial. Or so it seems in our present state of understanding.

17   French for "being the best example of its kind."

lightning, it is legitimate to go as far away as one can from a strictly human viewpoint.[18]

In the case of experience, on the other hand, the connection with a particular point of view seems much closer. It is difficult to understand what could be meant by the *objective* character of an experience, apart from the particular point of view from which its subject apprehends it. After all, what would be left of what it was like to be a bat if one removed the viewpoint of the bat? But if experience does not have, in addition to its subjective character, an objective nature that can be apprehended from many different points of view, then how can it be supposed that a Martian investigating my brain might be observing physical processes which were my mental processes (as he might observe physical processes which were bolts of lightning), only from a different point of view? How, for that matter, could a human physiologist observe them from another point of view?[19]

We appear to be faced with a general difficulty about psychophysical reduction. In other areas the process of reduction is a move in the direction of greater objectivity, toward a more accurate view of the real nature of things. This is accomplished by reducing our dependence on individual or species-specific points of view toward the object of investigation. We describe it not in terms of the impressions it makes on our senses, but in terms of its more general effects and of properties detectable by means other than the human senses. The less it depends on a specifically

18   [Author's note] The problem I am going to raise can therefore be posed even if the distinction between more subjective and more objective descriptions or viewpoints can itself be made only within a larger human point of view. I do not accept this kind of conceptual relativism, but it need not be refuted to make the point that psychophysical reduction cannot be accommodated by the subjective-to-objective model familiar from other cases.

19   [Author's note] The problem is not just that when I look at the "Mona Lisa," my visual experience has a certain quality, no trace of which is to be found by someone looking into my brain. For even if he did observe there a tiny image of the "Mona Lisa," he would have no reason to identify it with the experience.

human viewpoint, the more objective is our description. It is possible to follow this path because although the concepts and ideas we employ in thinking about the external world are initially applied from a point of view that involves our perceptual apparatus, they are used by us to refer to things beyond themselves—toward which we *have* the phenomenal point of view. Therefore we can abandon it in favor of another, and still be thinking about the same things.

Experience itself, however, does not seem to fit the pattern. The idea of moving from appearance to reality seems to make no sense here. What is the analogue in this case to pursuing a more objective understanding of the same phenomena by abandoning the initial subjective viewpoint toward them in favor of another that is more objective but concerns the same thing? Certainly it *appears* unlikely that we will get closer to the real nature of human experience by leaving behind the particularity of our human point of view and striving for a description in terms accessible to beings that could not imagine what it was like to be us. If the subjective character of experience is fully comprehensible only from one point of view, then any shift to greater objectivity—that is, less attachment to a specific viewpoint—does not take us nearer to the real nature of the phenomenon: it takes us farther away from it.

In a sense, the seeds of this objection to the reducibility of experience are already detectable in successful cases of reduction; for in discovering sound to be, in reality, a wave phenomenon in air or other media, we leave behind one viewpoint to take up another, and the auditory, human or animal viewpoint that we leave behind remains unreduced. Members of radically different species may both understand the same physical events in objective terms, and this does not require that they understand the phenomenal forms in which those events appear to the senses of members of the other species. Thus it is a condition of their referring to a common reality that their more particular viewpoints are not part of the common reality that they both apprehend. The reduction can succeed only if the species-specific viewpoint is omitted from what is to be reduced.

But while we are right to leave this point of view aside in seeking a fuller understanding of the external world, we cannot ignore it permanently, since it is the essence of the internal world, and not merely a point of view on it. Most of the neobehaviorism of recent philosophical psychology results from the effort to substitute an objective concept of mind for the real thing, in order to have nothing left over which cannot be reduced. If we acknowledge that a physical theory of mind must account for the subjective character of experience, we must admit that no presently available conception gives us a clue how this could be done. The problem is unique. If mental processes are indeed physical processes, then there is something it is like, intrinsically,[20] to undergo certain physical processes.

---

20 [Author's note] The relation would therefore not be a contingent one, like that of a cause and its distinct effect. It would be necessarily true that a certain physical state felt a certain way. Saul Kripke (*op. cit.*) argues that causal behaviorist and related analyses of the mental fail because they construe, e.g., "pain" as a merely contingent name of pains. The subjective character of an experience ("its immediate phenomenological quality" Kripke calls it [p. 340]) is the essential property left out by such analyses, and the one in virtue of which it is, necessarily, the experience it is. My view is closely related to his. Like Kripke, I find the hypothesis that a certain brain state should *necessarily* have a certain subjective character incomprehensible without further explanation. No such explanation emerges from theories which view the mind-brain relation as contingent, but perhaps there are other alternatives, not yet discovered.

A theory that explained how the mind-brain relation was necessary would still leave us with Kripke's problem of explaining why it nevertheless appears contingent. That difficulty seems to me surmountable, in the following way. We may imagine something by representing it to ourselves either perceptually, sympathetically, or symbolically. I shall not try to say how symbolic imagination works, but part of what happens in the other two cases is this. To imagine something perceptually, we put ourselves in a conscious state resembling the state we would be in if we perceived it. To imagine something sympathetically, we put ourselves in a conscious state resembling the thing itself. (This method can be used only to imagine mental events and states—our own or another's.) When we try to imagine

What it is for such a thing to be the case remains a mystery.

What moral should be drawn from these reflections, and what should be done next? It would be a mistake to conclude that physicalism must be false. Nothing is proved by the inadequacy of physicalist hypotheses that assume a faulty objective analysis of mind. It would be truer to say that physicalism is a position we cannot understand because we do not at present have any conception of how it might be true. Perhaps it will be thought unreasonable to require such a conception as a condition of understanding. After all, it might be said, the meaning of physicalism is clear enough: mental states are states of the body; mental events are physical events. We do not know *which* physical states and events they are, but that should not prevent us from understanding the hypothesis. What could be clearer than the words "is" and "are"?

But I believe it is precisely this apparent clarity of the word "is" that is deceptive. Usually, when we are told that *X* is *Y* we know *how* it is supposed to be true, but that depends on a conceptual or theoretical background and is not conveyed by the "is" alone. We know how both "*X*" and "*Y*" refer, and the kinds

---

a mental state occurring without its associated brain state, we first sympathetically imagine the occurrence of the mental state: that is, we put ourselves into a state that resembles it mentally. At the same time, we attempt to perceptually imagine the non-occurrence of the associated physical state, by putting ourselves into another state unconnected with the first: one resembling that which we would be in if we perceived the nonoccurrence of the physical state. Where the imagination of physical features is perceptual and the imagination of mental features is sympathetic, it appears to us that we can imagine any experience occurring without its associated brain state, and vice versa. The relation between them will appear contingent even if it is necessary, because of the independence of the disparate types of imagination.

(Solipsism, incidentally, results if one misinterprets sympathetic imagination as if it worked like perceptual imagination: it then seems impossible to imagine any experience that is not one's own.)

of things to which they refer, and we have a rough idea how the two referential paths[21] might converge on a single thing, be it an object, a person, a process, an event, or whatever. But when the two terms of the identification are very disparate it may not be so clear how it could be true. We may not have even a rough idea of how the two referential paths could converge, or what kind of things they might converge on, and a theoretical framework may have to be supplied to enable us to understand this. Without the framework, an air of mysticism surrounds the identification.

This explains the magical flavor of popular presentations of fundamental scientific discoveries, given out as propositions to which one must subscribe without really understanding them. For example, people are now told at an early age that all matter is really energy. But despite the fact that they know what "is" means, most of them never form a conception of what makes this claim true, because they lack the theoretical background.

At the present time the status of physicalism is similar to that which the hypothesis that matter is energy would have had if uttered by a pre-Socratic philosopher.[22] We do not have the beginnings of a conception of how it might be true. In order to understand the hypothesis that a mental event is a physical event, we require more than an understanding of the word "is." The idea of how a mental and a physical term might refer to the same thing is lacking, and the usual analogies with theoretical identification in other fields fail to supply it. They fail because if we construe the reference of mental terms to physical events on the usual model, we either get a reappearance of separate subjective events as the effects through which mental reference to physical events is secured, or else we get

a false account of how mental terms refer (for example, a causal behaviorist[23] one).

Strangely enough, we may have evidence for the truth of something we cannot really understand. Suppose a caterpillar is locked in a sterile safe by someone unfamiliar with insect metamorphosis, and weeks later the safe is reopened, revealing a butterfly. If the person knows that the safe has been shut the whole time, he has reason to believe that the butterfly is or was once the caterpillar, without having any idea in what sense this might be so. (One possibility is that the caterpillar contained a tiny winged parasite that devoured it and grew into the butterfly.)

It is conceivable that we are in such a position with regard to physicalism. Donald Davidson has argued that if mental events have physical causes and effects, they must have physical descriptions. He holds that we have reason to believe this even though we do not—and in fact *could* not—have a general psychophysical theory.[24] His argument applies to intentional mental events, but I think we also have some reason to believe that sensations are physical processes, without being in a position to understand how. Davidson's position is that certain physical events have irreducibly mental properties, and perhaps some view describable in this way is correct. But nothing of which we can now form a conception corresponds to it; nor have we any idea what a theory would be like that enabled us to conceive of it.[25]

Very little work has been done on the basic question (from which mention of the brain can be entirely omitted) whether any sense can be made of experiences' having an objective character at all. Does it

---

21 By "referential paths" Nagel means something like the various ways in which we fix the reference of our words to a certain thing (e.g., by personal acquaintance or by a description in a text book). For example, I have at least two "referential paths" to the stuff picked out by the word *water*: it is the liquid which comes out of the tap in my kitchen, and it is the substance which has the molecular composition H_2O.

22 A philosopher who lived before or around the time of Socrates (a Greek philosopher who died in 399 BCE).

23 Nagel presumably means the idea that our mental states are defined as whatever physically causes certain characteristic patterns of behavior (e.g., the word "pain" refers to the cause of pain behavior).

24 [Author's note] See "Mental Events" in Foster and Swanson, *Experience and Theory* (Amherst, 1970); though I don't understand the argument against psychophysical laws.

25 [Author's note] Similar remarks apply to my paper "Physicalism," *Philosophical Review* LXXIV (1965), 339–356, reprinted with postscript in John O'Connor, *Modern Materialism* (New York, 1969).

make sense, in other words, to ask what my experiences are *really* like, as opposed to how they appear to me? We cannot genuinely understand the hypothesis that their nature is captured in a physical description unless we understand the more fundamental idea that they *have* an objective nature (or that objective processes can have a subjective nature).[26]

I should like to close with a speculative proposal. It may be possible to approach the gap between subjective and objective from another direction. Setting aside temporarily the relation between the mind and the brain, we can pursue a more objective understanding of the mental in its own right. At present we are completely unequipped to think about the subjective character of experience without relying on the imagination—without taking up the point of view of the experiential subject. This should be regarded as a challenge to form new concepts and devise a new method—an objective phenomenology not dependent on empathy or the imagination. Though presumably it would not capture everything, its goal would be to describe, at least in part, the subjective character of experiences in a form comprehensible to beings incapable of having those experiences.

We would have to develop such a phenomenology to describe the sonar experiences of bats; but it would also be possible to begin with humans. One might try, for example, to develop concepts that could be used to explain to a person blind from birth what it was like to see. One would reach a blank wall eventually, but it should be possible to devise a method of expressing in objective terms much more than we can at present, and with much greater precision. The loose intermodal[27] analogies—for example, "Red is like the sound of a trumpet"—which crop up in discussions of this subject are of little use. That should be clear to anyone who has both heard a trumpet and seen red. But structural features of perception might be more accessible to objective description, even though something would be left out. And concepts alternative to those we learn in the first person may enable us to arrive at a kind of understanding even of our own experience which is denied us by the very ease of description and lack of distance that subjective concepts afford.

Apart from its own interest, a phenomenology that is in this sense objective may permit questions about the physical[28] basis of experience to assume a more intelligible form. Aspects of subjective experience that admitted this kind of objective description might be better candidates for objective explanations of a more familiar sort. But whether or not this guess is correct, it seems unlikely that any physical theory of mind can be contemplated until more thought has been given to the general problem of subjective and objective. Otherwise we cannot even pose the mind-body problem without sidestepping it.[29]

---

26 [Author's note] This question also lies at the heart of the problem of other minds, whose close connection with the mind-body problem is often overlooked. If one understood how subjective experience could have an objective nature, one would understand the existence of subjects other than oneself.

27 Crossing between modes of sensation, such as sight and touch.

28 [Author's note] I have not defined the term "physical." Obviously it does not apply just to what can be described by the concepts of contemporary physics, since we expect further developments. Some may think there is nothing to prevent mental phenomena from eventually being recognized as physical in their own right. But whatever else may be said of the physical, it has to be objective. So if our idea of the physical ever expands to include mental phenomena, it will have to assign them an objective character—whether or not this is done by analyzing them in terms of other phenomena already regarded as physical. It seems to me more likely, however, that mental-physical relations will eventually be expressed in a theory whose fundamental terms cannot be placed clearly in either category.

29 [Author's note] I have read versions of this paper to a number of audiences, and am indebted to many people for their comments.

FRANK JACKSON

"Epiphenomenal Qualia" and "What Mary Didn't Know"

Who Is Frank Jackson?

Frank Cameron Jackson was born in Australia in 1943. He studied mathematics and philosophy at the University of Melbourne and received his PhD in philosophy from La Trobe University. His main appointments have been in Australia: at the University of Adelaide, Monash University, and the Australian National University. He has also had numerous visiting appointments, at (among other places) Harvard, Princeton, Oxford, and Cambridge. He is the author of many books and articles; his research covers philosophical logic, cognitive science, epistemology and metaphysics, and meta-ethics, but has concentrated mainly on the philosophy of mind. His example of Mary the brain scientist is extremely well-known and widely discussed;

his somewhat less famous yet still influential example is Fred the tomato sorter. Both were introduced in his article "Epiphenomenal Qualia," (1982); his later article "What Mary Didn't Know" (1986) deals with Mary's case in more detail. Both articles are excerpted below. In these articles Jackson, like Chalmers, defends dualism about mind and body on the basis of the impossibility of providing a physical explanation of experience. It should be noted, however, that in articles published in 1995 and later, Jackson recanted his earlier dualism.

What Is the Structure of These Articles?

After some introductory remarks, Jackson introduces the case of Fred, who consistently sorts ripe tomatoes by means of an apparent color-difference nobody else can see. Jackson uses this thought-experiment to show that there would be something about Fred that we don't know and couldn't know, despite all the knowledge one could wish about his discrimination-behavior and physiology: what these new colors are to Fred, as he experiences them. Because there's something left out when the whole physical story is spelled out to us, it follows, argues Jackson, that the physical story leaves something out.

Jackson then introduces his second famous example: Mary, a super brain-scientist, who knows all there is to know about the physical story of how we perceive, process, and recognize colors, but who has never seen color. Jackson suggests that when Mary sees colors for the first time she learns something new, something that all that physical knowledge did not provide her with. Again, the physical information is shown to be incomplete.

Jackson, like Chalmers in the next reading, is willing to grant that the causes for external behavior and internal mental and physical events are all purely physical. Thus, the whole story explaining Fred's discriminations among tomatoes would be given in terms of physical events involving reflected light from the tomatoes, and in Fred's eyes and brain. What Mary knows would, similarly, give us all the information needed to fit into the causal explanation of behavior based on color perception, and of results of such perception. Experience—what's missing from the physical story—then, according to both philosophers, has no causal influence over anything in Fred or Mary or us. Experience, is caused (in this case) by physical neural stimulation, but has no physical effects. For both philosophers, the character of experience is entirely an *epiphenomenon* of the physical situation. (An epiphenomenon in a system is something caused by the system, but without effects. The noise your car makes when it's running, for example, is caused by the physical events in your car, but has no effect on them; it's an epiphenomenon.)

Jackson considers three objections to an epiphenomenal theory of mind: (i) It seems obvious that qualia are causes. (ii) If qualia have no effects, having them is not conducive to fitness; so why did they evolve? And (iii) if qualia have no behavioral effects, how could we have evidence that other minds have them? Jackson responds to each of these objections, and finally reacts to the criticism that qualia "*do* nothing, they *explain* nothing, they serve merely to soothe the intuitions of dualists, and it is left a total mystery how they fit into the world view of science. In short we do not and cannot understand the how and why of them." His retort is that all this may be true, but that it is overly optimistic to think that the human mind can understand everything.

The selection from "What Mary Didn't Know" is entitled "Three Clarifications"; they are in fact three responses to objections to Jackson's Mary argument in the earlier paper. The first interprets Jackson's claim about Mary to be what Mary can't imagine (as, for example, in the Nagel article printed earlier, there appears to be the claim that we can't imagine what it's like to be a bat). But Jackson replies that his point is about limits of knowledge, not of imagination. The second responds to an objection to the Knowledge Argument that antedates Jackson's paper: that the fact that someone knows that X is there, but doesn't know that Y is there, doesn't show that X is not in fact Y. We'll have more to say about this matter below, in the Suggestions for Critical Reflection section. The third points out that Mary's lack of knowledge when in her cell is about others, not about herself.

Some Useful Background Information

Jackson, in our readings, defends epiphenomenalism about the mental, the position that certain mental events—experiences of qualia—are caused by physical (presumably neural) events, but that these mental events have no effects of any kind on physical events in one's nervous system, or in one's behavior. Chalmers, one of whose papers is reprinted below, does not claim to be an epiphenomenalist, but it has seemed clear to commentators on his work that this is a consequence of his position.

Epiphenomenalism about mind has a long philosophical history. It came into its own with the growth of modern science, beginning in the Renaissance; it gradually seemed more and more likely that physical events of every sort had physical causes only. Descartes (the most influential historical substance dualist) ran into a good deal of criticism because he held that mental events could cause physical ones. By the twentieth century, the most common response to this difficulty was to deny dualism: to hold that mental events actually were physical ones, so could be causes (and effects) of other physical events. But epiphenomenalists attempted to maintain dualism while accepting the idea that mental could not cause physical, by denying that mental events could be causes.

A very influential mid-twentieth-century argument against epiphenomenalism about mind (and about dualism in general) was due to Herbert Feigl. If physical events caused mental ones, he argued, there would presumably be scientific laws connecting them; but such laws would be, in his words, "nomological danglers." ("Nomological" means *having to do with scientific laws*.) These are, Feigl argued, at least very suspect, in that they cannot be accounted for, being outside of the scope of, science. They "dangle" from the web of scientific theory and its laws.[1]

---

1 Feigl's essay "The 'Mental' and the 'Physical'" first appeared in Volume II of *Minnesota Studies in the Philosophy of Science: Concepts, Theories, and the Mind-Body Problem*, edited by Herbert Feigl, Michael Scriven, and Grover Maxwell and published

Suggestions for Critical Reflection

1. Anti-epiphenomenalists claim that it's just obvious that our thoughts and feelings have causal influence on our other thoughts and feelings, and on our actions. Does Jackson give an adequate rebuttal to this idea?

2. Consider this objection; is it right?

   If Mary knows everything physical there is to know about colors and color-perception, then she'd know what it's like to experience red things, even though while locked in her cell she'd never done that. To argue that there's something she doesn't know is simply to beg the question.

3. Consider this objection; is it right?

   What Mary gets when she emerges from her room is not new knowledge of some sort of fact. It's new "acquaintance-knowledge"— a new way of experiencing something that may have been (in Mary's case, *would* have been) otherwise experienced earlier.

4. Consider this objection; is it right?

   The difference between Fred and us is that he has color-discrimination abilities which are more finely tuned than ours. It's a difference in know-how, not knowing-that, and this difference in know-how, Jackson agrees, might totally be accounted for by a story about Fred's physical perceptual and neural system.

5. As mentioned above, Jackson now has changed his mind about the knowledge argument. Here's his account of what went wrong with his knowledge argument:

Intensionalism means that no amount of tub-thumping assertion by dualists (including by me in the past) that the *redness* of seeing red cannot be accommodated in the austere physicalist picture carries any weight. That striking feature is a feature of how things are being represented to be, and if, as claimed by the tub thumpers, it is transparently a feature that has no place in the physicalist picture, what follows is that physicalists should deny that anything has that striking feature. And this is no argument against physicalism. Physicalists can allow that people are sometimes in states that represent that things have a non-physical property. Examples are people who believe that there are fairies. What physicalists must deny is that such properties are instantiated.[2]

See if you can explain what he means here in your own terms: what might it be to deny that there is any such thing as "the *redness* of seeing red"? By contrast, how does Jackson try to deal with the intensionality of knowledge in "What Mary Didn't Know"? Who do you think is right, the earlier or the later Jackson?

Suggestions for Further Reading

Excellent detailed surveys of the state of the art regarding epiphenomenalism and the Knowledge Argument are both online in the *Stanford Encyclopedia of Philosophy*: "Epiphenomenalism" by William Robinson, <http://plato.stanford.edu/entries/epiphenomenalism/> and "Qualia—The Knowledge Argument" by Martine Nida-Rümelin <http://plato.stanford.edu/entries/qualia-knowledge/>. The best place to look for articles about Mary is a collection by noted philosophers devoted entirely to the Mary argument: *There's Something about Mary,* Peter Ludlow, Yujin Nagasawa, and Daniel Stoljar (eds.), Cambridge, MA: MIT Press, 2004.

---

by the University of Minnesota Press in 1958. It was republished in 1967 as a book with a new Postscript, a preface to the Postscript, and an additional bibliography; and it appears online at http://www.ditext.com/feigl/mp/mp.html. J.J.C. Smart used the objectionable nature of nomological danglers to argue for his version of the physicalist identity theory in his equally influential paper, "Sensations and Brain Processes" (*The Philosophical Review*, Vol. 68 Issue 2 (1959): 141-156).

---

2 "Mind and Illusion" in *Minds and Persons: Royal Institute of Philosophy Supplement* 53, edited by A. O'Hear (Cambridge: Cambridge University Press, 2003). Online at http://consc.net/neh/papers/jackson.htm.

from "Epiphenomenal Qualia"[3]

It is undeniable that the physical, chemical and biological sciences have provided a great deal of information about the world we live in and about ourselves. I will use the label 'physical information' for this kind of information, and also for information that automatically comes along with it. For example, if a medical scientist tells me enough about the processes that go on in my nervous system, and about how they relate to happenings in the world around me, to what has happened in the past and is likely to happen in the future, to what happens to other similar and dissimilar organisms, and the like, he or she tells me—if I am clever enough to fit it together appropriately—about what is often called the functional role of those states in me (and in organisms in general in similar cases). This information, and its kin, I also label 'physical'.

I do not mean these sketchy remarks to constitute a definition of 'physical information', and of the correlative notions of physical property, process, and so on, but to indicate what I have in mind here. It is well known that there are problems with giving a precise definition of these notions, and so of the thesis of Physicalism that all (correct) information is physical information. But—unlike some—I take the question of definition to cut across the central problems I want to discuss in this paper.

I am what is sometimes known as a "qualia freak".[4] I think that there are certain features of the bodily sensations especially, but also of certain perceptual experiences, which no amount of purely physical information includes. Tell me everything physical there is to tell about what is going on in a living brain, the kind of states, their functional role, their relation to what goes on at other times and in other brains, and so on and so forth, and be I as clever as can be in fitting it all together, you won't have told me about the hurtfulness of pains, the itchiness of itches, the pangs of jealousy, or about the characteristic experience of tasting a lemon, smelling a rose, hearing a loud noise or seeing the sky.

There are many qualia freaks, and some of them say that their rejection of Physicalism is an unargued intuition. I think that they are being unfair to themselves. They have the following argument. Nothing you could tell of a physical sort captures the smell of a rose, for instance. Therefore, Physicalism is false. By our lights this is a perfectly good argument. It is obviously not to the point to question its validity, and the premise is intuitively obviously true both to them and to me.

I must, however, admit that it is weak from a polemical point of view. There are, unfortunately for us, many who do not find the premise intuitively obvious. The task then is to present an argument whose premises are obvious to all, or at least to as many as possible. This I try to do in §I with what I will call "the Knowledge argument". In §II I contrast the Knowledge argument with the Modal argument and in §III with the "What is it like to be" argument. In §IV I tackle the question of the causal role of qualia. The major factor in stopping people from admitting qualia is the belief that they would have to be given a causal role with respect to the physical world and especially the brain; and it is hard to do this without sounding like someone who believes in fairies. I seek in §IV to turn this objection by arguing that the view that qualia are epiphenomenal[5] is a perfectly possible one.

I. The Knowledge Argument for Qualia

People vary considerably in their ability to discriminate colours. Suppose that in an experiment to catalogue this variation Fred is discovered. Fred has better colour vision than anyone else on record; he makes

---

3   From *The Philosophical Quarterly* Volume 32, Number 127, April 1982; pp. 127–130 and pp. 133–136. Reproduced by permission of Wiley-Blackwell Inc.

4   Qualia (pronounced KWAH-lee-a; singular *quale* [KWAH-lay]) are subjective qualities of conscious experience, for example, pains, tastes, the visual experience of colors.

5   An epiphenomenon (plural *epiphenomena*) is something caused by some system of events, but having no effects in that system. An example is the sound made by a running car: it's caused by vibrations at various places in the car, but it has no effect on the car. An epiphenomenalist about mind holds that mental events are epiphenomena—physically caused, but having no mental or physical effect.

every discrimination that anyone has ever made, and moreover he makes one that we cannot even begin to make. Show him a batch of ripe tomatoes and he sorts them into two roughly equal groups and does so with complete consistency. That is, if you blindfold him, shuffle the tomatoes up, and then remove the blindfold and ask him to sort them out again, he sorts them into exactly the same two groups.

We ask Fred how he does it. He explains that all ripe tomatoes do not look the same colour to him, and in fact that this is true of a great many objects that we classify together as red. He sees two colours where we see one, and he has in consequence developed for his own use two words 'red$_1$' and 'red$_2$' to mark the difference. Perhaps he tells us that he has often tried to teach the difference between red$_1$ and red$_2$ to his friends but has got nowhere and has concluded that the rest of the world is red$_1$- red$_2$ colourblind—or perhaps he has had partial success with his children, it doesn't matter. In any case he explains to us that it would be quite wrong to think that because 'red' appears in both 'red$_1$' and 'red$_2$' that the two colours are shades of the one colour. He only uses the common term 'red' to fit more easily into our restricted usage. To him red$_1$ and red$_2$ are as different from each other and all the other colours as yellow is from blue. And his discriminatory behaviour bears this out: he sorts red$_1$ from red$_2$ tomatoes with the greatest of ease in a wide variety of viewing circumstances. Moreover, an investigation of the physiological basis of Fred's exceptional ability reveals that Fred's optical system is able to separate out two groups of wave-lengths in the red spectrum as sharply as we are able to sort out yellow from blue.

I think that we should admit that Fred can see, really see, at least one more colour than we can; red$_1$ is a different colour from red$_2$. We are to Fred as a totally red-green colour-blind person is to us. H.G. Wells' story "The Country of the Blind" is about a sighted person in a totally blind community.[6] This person never manages to convince them that he can see, that he has an extra sense. They ridicule this sense as quite inconceivable, and treat his capacity to avoid falling

into ditches, to win fights and so on as precisely that capacity and nothing more. We would be making their mistake if we refused to allow that Fred can see one more colour than we can.

What kind of experience does Fred have when he sees red$_1$ and red$_2$? What is the new colour or colours like? We would dearly like to know but do not; and it seems that no amount of physical information about Fred's brain and optical system tells us. We find out perhaps that Fred's cones respond differentially to certain light waves in the red section of the spectrum that make no difference to ours (or perhaps he has an extra cone) and that this leads in Fred to a wider range of those brain states responsible for visual discriminatory behaviour. But none of this tells us what we really want to know about his colour experience. There is something about it we don't know. But we know, we may suppose, everything about Fred's body, his behaviour and dispositions to behaviour and about his internal physiology, and everything about his history and relation to others that can be given in physical accounts of persons. We have all the physical information. Therefore, knowing all this is *not* knowing everything about Fred. It follows that Physicalism leaves something out.

To reinforce this conclusion, imagine that as a result of our investigations into the internal workings of Fred we find out how to make everyone's physiology like Fred's in the relevant respects; or perhaps Fred donates his body to science and on his death we are able to transplant his optical system into someone else—again the fine detail doesn't matter. The important point is that such a happening would create enormous interest. People would say, "At last we will know what it is like to see the extra colour, at last we will know how Fred has differed from us in the way he has struggled to tell us about for so long". Then it cannot be that we knew all along all about Fred. But *ex hypothesi* we did know all along everything about Fred that features in the physicalist scheme; hence the physicalist scheme leaves something out.

Put it this way. *After* the operation, we will know *more* about Fred and especially about his colour experiences. But beforehand we had all the physical information we could desire about his body and brain, and indeed everything that has ever featured

_____

6   [Author's note] H.G. Wells, *The Country of the Blind and Other Stories* (London, n.d.).

in physicalist accounts of mind and consciousness. Hence there is more to know than all that. Hence Physicalism is incomplete.

Fred and the new colour(s) are of course essentially rhetorical devices. The same point can be made with normal people and familiar colours. Mary is a brilliant scientist who is, for whatever reason, forced to investigate the world from a black and white room *via* a black and white television monitor. She specialises in the neurophysiology of vision and acquires, let us suppose, all the physical information there is to obtain about what goes on when we see ripe tomatoes, or the sky, and use terms like 'red', 'blue', and so on. She discovers, for example, just which wave-length combinations from the sky stimulate the retina, and exactly how this produces *via* the central nervous system the contraction of the vocal chords and expulsion of air from the lungs that results in the uttering of the sentence 'The sky is blue'. (It can hardly be denied that it is in principle possible to obtain all this physical information from black and white television, otherwise the Open University[7] would *of necessity* need to use colour television.)

What will happen when Mary is released from her black and white room or is given a colour television monitor? Will she *learn* anything or not? It seems just obvious that she will learn something about the world and our visual experience of it. But then it is inescapable that her previous knowledge was incomplete. But she had *all* the physical information. *Ergo* there is more to have than that, and Physicalism is false.

Clearly the same style of Knowledge argument could be deployed for taste, hearing, the bodily sensations and generally speaking for the various mental states which are said to have (as it is variously put) raw feels, phenomenal features or qualia. The conclusion in each case is that the qualia are left out of the physicalist story. And the polemical strength of the Knowledge argument is that it is so hard to deny the central claim that one can have all the physical information without having all the information there is to have.

...

---

7   A British university offering distance education, partly through broadcast lectures.

IV. The Bogey of Epiphenomenalism

Is there any really *good* reason for refusing to countenance the idea that qualia are causally impotent with respect to the physical world? I will argue for the answer no, but in doing this I will say nothing about two views associated with the classical epiphenomenalist position. The first is that mental *states* are inefficacious with respect to the physical world. All I will be concerned to defend is that it is possible to hold that certain *properties* of certain mental states, namely those I've called qualia, are such that their possession or absence makes no difference to the physical world. The second is that the mental is *totally* causally inefficacious. For all I will say it may be that you have to hold that the instantiation of *qualia* makes a difference to *other mental states* though not to anything physical. Indeed general considerations to do with how you could come to be aware of the instantiation of qualia suggest such a position.

Three reasons are standardly given for holding that a quale like the hurtfulness of a pain must be causally efficacious in the physical world, and so, for instance, that its instantiation must sometimes make a difference to what happens in the brain. None, I will argue, has any real force....

(i) It is supposed to be just obvious that the hurtfulness of pain is partly responsible for the subject seeking to avoid pain, saying 'It hurts' and so on. But, to reverse Hume, anything can fail to cause anything. No matter how often B follows A, and no matter how initially obvious the causality of the connection seems, the hypothesis that A causes B can be overturned by an over-arching theory which shows the two as distinct effects of a common underlying causal process.

To the untutored the image on the screen of Lee Marvin's fist moving from left to right immediately followed by the image of John Wayne's head moving in the same general direction looks as causal as anything. And of course throughout countless Westerns images similar to the first are followed by images similar to the second. All this counts for precisely nothing when we know the over-arching theory concerning how the relevant images are both effects of an underlying causal process involving the projector and the film. The epiphenomenalist can say exactly the same about the connection between, for example, hurtfulness and behaviour. It is simply a consequence of the fact that certain happenings in the brain cause both.

(ii) The second objection relates to Darwin's Theory of Evolution. According to natural selection the traits that evolve over time are those conducive to physical survival. We may assume that qualia evolved over time—we have them, the earliest forms of life do not—and so we should expect qualia to be conducive to survival. The objection is that they could hardly help us to survive if they do nothing to the physical world.

The appeal of this argument is undeniable, but there is a good reply to it. Polar bears have particularly thick, warm coats. The Theory of Evolution explains this (we suppose) by pointing out that having a thick, warm coat is conducive to survival in the Arctic. But having a thick coat goes along with having a heavy coat, and having a heavy coat is *not* conducive to survival. It slows the animal down.

Does this mean that we have refuted Darwin because we have found an evolved trait—having a heavy coat—which is not conducive to survival? Clearly not. Having a heavy coat is an unavoidable concomitant of having a warm coat (in the context, modern insulation was not available), and the advantages for survival of having a warm coat outweighed the disadvantages of having a heavy one. The point is that all we can extract from Darwin's theory is that we should expect any evolved characteristic to be either conducive to survival *or* a by-product of one that is so conducive. The epiphenomenalist holds that qualia fall into the latter category. They are a by-product of certain brain processes that are highly conducive to survival.

(iii) The third objection is based on a point about how we come to know about other minds. We know about other minds by knowing about other behaviour, at least in part. The nature of the inference is a matter of some controversy, but it is not a matter of controversy that it proceeds from behaviour. That is why we think that stones do not feel and dogs do feel. But, runs the objection, how can a person's behaviour provide any reason for believing he has qualia like mine, or indeed any qualia at all, unless this behaviour can be regarded as the *outcome* of the

qualia. Man Friday's footprint was evidence of Man Friday because footprints are causal outcomes of feet attached to people. And an epiphenomenalist cannot regard behaviour, or indeed anything physical, as an outcome of qualia.

But consider my reading in *The Times* that Spurs[8] won. This provides excellent evidence that *The Telegraph* has also reported that Spurs won, despite the fact that (I trust) *The Telegraph* does not get the results from *The Times*. They each send their own reporters to the game. *The Telegraph*'s report is in no sense an outcome of *The Times*', but the latter provides good evidence for the former nevertheless.

The reasoning involved can be reconstructed thus. I read in *The Times* that Spurs won. This gives me reason to think that Spurs won because I know that Spurs' winning is the most likely candidate to be what caused the report in *The Times*. But I also know that Spurs' winning would have had many effects, including almost certainly a report in *The Telegraph*.

I am arguing from one effect back to its cause and out again to another effect. The fact that neither effect causes the other is irrelevant. Now the epiphenomenalist allows that qualia are effects of what goes on in the brain. Qualia cause nothing physical but are caused by something physical. Hence the epiphenomenalist can argue from the behaviour of others to the qualia of others by arguing from the behaviour of others back to its causes in the brains of others and out again to their qualia.

You may well feel for one reason or another that this is a more dubious chain of reasoning than its model in the case of newspaper reports. You are right. The problem of other minds is a major philosophical problem, the problem of other newspaper reports is not. But there is no special problem of Epiphenomenalism as opposed to, say, Interactionism here.

There is a very understandable response to the three replies I have just made. "All right, there is no knockdown refutation of the existence of epiphenomenal qualia. But the fact remains that they are an excrescence. They *do* nothing, they *explain* nothing, they serve merely to soothe the intuitions of dualists, and it is left a total mystery how they fit into the

_____

8   The London soccer team Tottenham Hotspur.

world view of science. In short we do not and cannot understand the how and why of them."

This is perfectly true; but is no objection to qualia, for it rests on an overly optimistic view of the human animal, and its powers. We are the products of Evolution. We understand and sense what we need to understand and sense in order to survive. Epiphenomenal qualia are totally irrelevant to survival. At no stage of our evolution did natural selection favour those who could make sense of how they are caused and the laws governing them, or in fact why they exist at all. And that is why we can't.

It is not sufficiently appreciated that Physicalism is an extremely optimistic view of our powers. If it is true, we have, in very broad outline admittedly, a grasp of our place in the scheme of things. Certain matters of sheer complexity defeat us—there are an awful lot of neurons—but in principle we have it all. But consider the antecedent probability that everything in the Universe be of a kind that is relevant in some way or other to the survival of *homo sapiens*. It is very low surely. But then one must admit that it is very likely that there is a part of the whole scheme of things, maybe a big part, which no amount of evolution will ever bring us near to knowledge about or understanding. For the simple reason that such knowledge and understanding is irrelevant to survival.

Physicalists typically emphasise that we are a part of nature on their view, which is fair enough. But if we are a part of nature, we are as nature has left us after however many years of evolution it is, and each step in that evolutionary progression has been a matter of chance constrained just by the need to preserve or increase survival value. The wonder is that we understand as much as we do, and there is no wonder that there should be matters which fall quite outside our comprehension. Perhaps exactly how epiphenomenal qualia fit into the scheme of things is one such.

This may seem an unduly pessimistic view of our capacity to articulate a truly comprehensive picture of our world and our place in it. But suppose we discovered living on the bottom of the deepest oceans a sort of sea slug which manifested intelligence. Perhaps survival in the conditions required rational powers. Despite their intelligence, these sea slugs have only a very restricted conception of the world by comparison with ours, the explanation for this being the nature of their immediate environment. Nevertheless they have developed sciences which work surprisingly well in these restricted terms. They also have philosophers, called slugists. Some call themselves tough-minded slugists, others confess to being soft-minded slugists.

The tough-minded slugists hold that the restricted terms (or ones pretty like them which may be introduced as their sciences progress) suffice in principle to describe everything without remainder. These tough-minded slugists admit in moments of weakness to a feeling that their theory leaves something out. They resist this feeling and their opponents, the soft-minded slugists, by pointing out—absolutely correctly—that no slugist has ever succeeded in spelling out how this mysterious residue fits into the highly successful view that their sciences have and are developing of how their world works.

Our sea slugs don't exist, but they might. And there might also exist super beings which stand to us as we stand to the sea slugs. We cannot adopt the perspective of these super beings, because we are not them, but the possibility of such a perspective is, I think, an antidote to excessive optimism.

from "What Mary Didn't Know"[9]

...

I. Three Clarifications

The knowledge argument does not rest on the dubious claim that logically you cannot imagine what sensing red is like unless you have sensed red. Powers of imagination are not to the point. The contention about Mary is not that, despite her fantastic grasp of neurophysiology and everything else physical, she *could not imagine* what it is like to sense red; it is that, as a matter of fact, she *would not know*. But if physicalism is true, she would know; and no great powers of imagination would be called for. Imagination is a faculty that those who *lack* knowledge need to fall back on.

---

9   From *The Journal of Philosophy* 83 (May 1986), pp. 291–295 (excerpt).

Secondly, the intensionality of knowledge[10] is not to the point. The argument does not rest on assuming falsely that, if S knows that a is F and if $a = b$, then S knows that b is F. It is concerned with the nature of Mary's total body of knowledge before she is released: is it complete, or do some facts escape it? What is to the point is that S may know that a is F and *know* that $a = b$, yet arguably not know that b is F, by virtue of not being sufficiently logically alert to follow the consequences through. If Mary's lack of knowledge were at all like this, there would be no threat to physicalism in it. But it is very hard to believe that her lack of knowledge could be remedied merely by her explicitly following through enough logical consequences of her vast physical knowledge. Endowing her with great logical acumen and persistence is not in itself enough to fill in the gaps in her knowledge. On being let out, she will not say "I could have worked all this out before by making some more purely logical inferences."

Thirdly, the knowledge Mary lacked which is of particular point for the knowledge argument against physicalism is *knowledge about the experiences of others*, not about her own. When she is let out, she has new experiences, color experiences she has never had before. It is not, therefore, an objection to physicalism that she learns *something* on being let out. Before she was let out, she could not have known facts about her experience of red, for there were no such facts to know. That physicalist and nonphysicalist alike can agree on. After she is let out, things change; and physicalism can happily admit that she learns this; after all, some physical things will change, for instance, her brain states and their functional roles. The trouble for physicalism is that, after Mary sees her first ripe tomato, she will realize how impoverished her conception of the mental life of *others* has been *all along*. She will realize that there was, all the time she was carrying out her laborious investigations into the neurophysiologies of others and into the functional roles of their internal states, something about these people she was quite unaware of. All along their experiences (or many of them, those got from tomatoes, the sky, ...) had a feature conspicuous to them but until now hidden from her (in fact, not in logic). But she knew all the physical facts about them all along; hence, what she did not know until her release is not a physical fact about their experiences. But it is a fact about them. That is the trouble for physicalism....

---

10   To say that knowledge is intensional is to say that one might know something when it is expressed in one way but not know *the same thing* when it is expressed another way. For example, I might know that Snoop Dogg is a rap musician but deny any knowledge of Calvin Cordozar Broadus, Jr. Yet they're the same person.

DAVID CHALMERS
"The Puzzle of Conscious Experience"

Who Is David Chalmers?

David Chalmers was born in Australia in 1966. His undergraduate degree, at the University of Adelaide, concentrated in mathematics and computer science, and he went to the University of Oxford to do graduate work in mathematics, but then, his interest in the philosophy of mind having become dominant, he switched to Indiana University, working in Douglas Hofstadter's Center for Research on Concepts and Cognition there. After his PhD in 1993, he had a two-year post-doctoral fellowship at Washington University in St. Louis, then taught at UC Santa Cruz, and then at the University of Arizona. He moved to the Australia National University in August 2004, and is also part-time at New York University. He looks and dresses like a rock star.

What Is Chalmers's Overall Philosophical Project?

Chalmers may be the best-known of the group of contemporary philosophers of mind known (mostly by their philosophical opponents) as Mysterians: those who claim that the central feature of the mental is conscious experience, and that this feature must forever remain a mystery to physical science (though Chalmers himself, in the article we include here, claims he is not a Mysterian). Famously he distinguished what he called the "easy problem" and the "hard problem" for a science of mind. The former—not really easy, but at least doable—was to give a scientific account of mental functions, such as sensory discriminations. The latter—not merely hard, but rather, he argued, impossible—was to give a physical account of the experiences that were the constituents of our conscious minds.

The view that consciousness must elude physical scientific treatment is not a new one. It was a gener-

ally held view among philosophers of mind for centuries; usually this was a consequence of their substance dualism: their view that mind and matter were two completely different kinds of stuff. But, with the advance of science, explaining more and more of what had previously seemed inexplicable, Mysterianism gradually became more and more rare. In the twentieth century, however, it had a rebirth in various forms, in the view that although everything in the universe might turn out to be constructed of physical matter obeying physical laws, it would not follow that physical laws could explain mental goings-on. (See the section below, Some Useful Background Information, for brief descriptions of these positions.) Importantly, however, these positions shared the view that, notwithstanding the impossibility of explanation of the mental by physicalist science, mental events might each be identical to physical events, and that the basic tenet of physicalism, that everything that exists is physical, could still be true.

Chalmers, however, has placed himself in a small minority of philosophers of mind by arguing that physicalism is false, and that the properties that constitute conscious experience may be fundamentally non-physical properties.

What Is the Structure of This Reading?

Chalmers begins with a distinction he thinks is fundamental to the philosophy of mind: between the functions carried out by the mental faculties, of gathering information from sensation, directing muscular activity, and so on, on the one hand, and the experiences of conscious life—of our impressions of shapes and colors, our feelings of pain and pleasure, our emotions and thoughts: in sum, our mental life—on the other. He's willing to grant that neuroscience could give a physicalist explanation of all of the former phenomena; his argument is that science can never begin to explain our mental life, to answer questions like: Why do we have *that* experience when we eat strawberries? Why are there any experiences at all? The first job of explanation he calls the "easy problem"—not meaning that it's easy to do, but rather just that science knows how to approach it, and it's scientifically doable; the second he calls the "hard problem"—not meaning that it's simply more difficult, but rather that it's really impossible for physicalist science.

His first section refers to the case of Mary the brain scientist. This is a famous example due to Frank Jackson, and is the subject of the previous reading in this chapter. Chalmers next goes on to consider some work by neuropsychologists and philosophers on the subject of consciousness; his claim is that almost all of this (properly) addresses part of the 'easy' problem, leaving the 'hard' problem untouched.

He then suggests that the right way of approaching the 'hard' problem would be to abandon the idea that only physical entities and properties and events are the ground-floor basis for explanation, and to accept mental items as basic, or "irreducible," as well. Then science can correlate mental types with physical (presumably neurological) types, with the ultimate goal of producing psychophysical laws—laws relating the two basic types of events. This sort of "theory of everything" could solve the 'hard' problem, because it includes the mental as basic, instead of trying to explain it in terms of the physical. He finishes by suggesting that such a theory might centrally involve the concept of information.

Some Useful Background Information

As science made enormous progress during the nineteenth and early twentieth centuries, a growing number of philosophers came to believe that the physical, scientific categories that had been deployed so successfully in explaining events elsewhere would someday have equal success in dealing with the mental; equally, more and more philosophers came to think that a unified view of reality was the correct one: a view that took there to be one sort of physical stuff that everything was made of.

These two ideas, however, were separable. While (probably) most philosophers remained physicalist, believing that everything was ultimately constructed out of the same sort of matter, basically obeying the same sorts of laws, doubts grew during the second half of the twentieth century that physical explanation for mental events would be possible—that is, that there was, for example, a kind of brain event that happened every time anyone thought about dinner, that *constituted* thinking about dinner.

The most common theory denying the explainability of the mental by the physical came from the functionalists, who typically held that mental events were classified functionally—that is, by their typical causes and effects—and instances of a single mental type (e.g., wishing you had a hamburger now) might be realized by any of a possibly infinite number of different physical types of event. We can imagine, for example, that a Martian, whose brain was built on entirely different principles from ours, might also yearn for a hamburger, but this yearning might be identical in his case to a totally different physical brain event than in you. If there could not be a physical type corresponding, in an exceptionless way, to any mental type, then there could not be mental-physical bridge laws, and thus no physical explanation of the mental. (Most functionalists are, however, physicalists—believing that each particular mental event really is a physical event. See the selection by Hilary Putnam in this chapter.)

Other arguments to the same conclusion relied on the basically normative character of mental ascriptions; the idea here is that whenever we assign beliefs and desires to others, we assume their rationality (otherwise their behavior might be correlated with any beliefs and desires whatever). Rationality is essentially an evaluative notion, thus having no place in physical sciences like neurophysiology. Thus mental categories must cut up phenomena differently from physical ones; and again exceptionless "bridge" laws linking the two would be impossible. (Again, philosophers who accept this argument are generally physicalists.)

Chalmers, by contrast, accepts the idea that there are relations between the mental and the physical that can be described in terms of scientific laws. He denies, however, that these can be completely physical laws: they would have to describe correlations between the physical and the irreducibly mental.

Suggestions for Critical Reflection

1. Chalmers (but not in the reading we have) gives an argument for his position based on the premise that it's possible (though not actual) that zombies exist. Zombies (in the sense philosophers of mind speak of them) are organisms physically just like us, inside and out, behaving in the same ways we do; the only difference is that they have no consciousness. See if you can fill in the rest of the argument: what is the conclusion we're supposed to draw from the possibility of zombies? How is that conclusion supposed to follow?

2. Valerie Gray Hardcastle suggests we

   consider the following exchange. A water-mysterian wonders why water has this peculiar property [being wet]. She inquires and you give an explanation of the molecular composition of water and a brief story about the connection between micro-chemical properties and macro-phenomena. Ah, she says … I am convinced that you have properly correlated water with its underlying molecular composition. I also have no reason to doubt that your story about the macro-effects of chemical properties to be wrong. But I still am not satisfied, for you have left off in your explanation what I find most puzzling. Why *is* water H_2O? Why couldn't it be XYZ? Why couldn't it have some other radically different chemical story behind it? I can imagine a possible world in which water has all the macro-properties that it has now, but is not composed of H_2O … What *can* one say? I think nothing. Water-mysterians are antecedently convinced of the mysteriousness of water and no amount of scientific data is going to change that perspective. Either you already believe that science is going to give you a correct identity statement, or you don't and you think that there is always going to be something left over, the wateriness of water.[1]

   What analogy is Hardcastle drawing with Chalmers's position? The suggestion here is that consciousness-mysterianism is just as baseless as water-mysterianism, but that there are no arguments that could convince either mysterian that their positions are wrong. Do you agree?

3. Hardcastle points out that both materialists and dualists accept some facts as "brute facts"—unexplainable features of the universe, just the way it is; but she remarks that "it seems highly unlikely that some relatively chauvinistic *biological* fact should ever be brute." If this is to be a criticism of Chalmers, what's the "relatively chauvinistic biological fact" in his view? (What does "chauvinistic" mean in this context?) See if you can explain why Hardcastle thinks that this view is "highly unlikely."

4. There's something discreditable about being a Mysterian. What do you suppose it is? Why does Chalmers claim he's not a Mysterian? Do you think he sufficiently rebuts the charge of discreditable Mysterianism?

---

1   "The Why of Consciousness: A Non-issue for Materialists." *Journal of Consciousness Studies*, 3, No. 1, 1996, pp. 7–13.

5. What is Chalmers's "principle of organizational invariance"? What are its implications, if it's true? (Is it true?)

6. At the end of the reading Chalmers raises the prospect of 'panpsychism': the view that everything (or at least everything that 'processes information,' including certainly thermostats and All Wheel Drive traction systems, and possibly even natural processes such as convection) is conscious. How palatable is this notion? If we must reject it, what problems might this cause for Chalmers?

Suggestions for Further Reading

The definitive statement of Chalmers's ideas is found in his book, *The Conscious Mind: In Search of a Fundamental Theory* (Oxford: Oxford University Press, 1996). *Explaining Consciousness: The Hard Problem*, edited by Jonathan Shear (MIT Press, 1997), is a collection of articles responding to Chalmers. These articles, and others by and responding to Chalmers, are in various issues of the *Journal of Consciousness Studies*.

"The Puzzle of Conscious Experience"[2]

Conscious experience is at once the most familiar thing in the world and the most mysterious. There is nothing we know about more directly than consciousness, but it is extraordinarily hard to reconcile it with everything else we know. Why does it exist? What does it do? How could it possibly arise from neural processes in the brain? These questions are among the most intriguing in all of science.

From an objective viewpoint, the brain is relatively comprehensible. When you look at this page, there is a whir of processing: photons strike your retina, electrical signals are passed up your optic nerve and between different areas of your brain,

and eventually you might respond with a smile, a perplexed frown or a remark. But there is also a subjective aspect. When you look at the page, you are conscious of it, directly experiencing the images and words as part of your private, mental life. You have vivid impressions of the colors and shapes of the images. At the same time, you may be feeling some emotions and forming some thoughts. Together such experiences make up consciousness: the subjective, inner life of the mind.

For many years, consciousness was shunned by researchers studying the brain and the mind. The prevailing view was that science, which depends on objectivity, could not accommodate something as subjective as consciousness. The behaviorist movement in psychology, dominant earlier in this century, concentrated on external behavior and disallowed any talk of internal mental processes. Later, the rise of cognitive science focused attention on processes inside the head. Still, consciousness remained off-limits, fit only for late-night discussion over drinks.

Over the past several years, however, an increasing number of neuroscientists, psychologists and philosophers have been rejecting the idea that consciousness cannot be studied and are attempting to delve into its secrets. As might be expected of a field so new, there is a tangle of diverse and conflicting theories, often using basic concepts in incompatible ways. To help unsnarl the tangle, philosophical reasoning is vital.

The myriad views within the field range from reductionist theories, according to which consciousness can be explained by the standard methods of neuroscience and psychology, to the position of the so-called mysterians, who say we will never understand consciousness at all. I believe that on close analysis both of these views can be seen to be mistaken and that the truth lies somewhere in the middle.

Against reductionism I will argue that the tools of neuroscience cannot provide a full account of conscious experience, although they have much to offer. Against mysterianism I will hold that consciousness might be explained by a new kind of theory. The full details of such a theory are still out of reach, but careful reasoning and some educated inferences can

---

2   This article was published in *Scientific American* in December 1995. It was reprinted, slightly updated, in 2002 in the Scientific American Special Edition *The Hidden Mind* (Volume 12, Issue 1), pp. 90–100.

reveal something of its general nature. For example, it will probably involve new fundamental laws, and the concept of information may play a central role. These faint glimmerings suggest that a theory of consciousness may have startling consequences for our view of the universe and of ourselves.

The Hard Problem

Researchers use the word "consciousness" in many different ways. To clarify the issues, we first have to separate the problems that are often clustered together under the name. For this purpose, I find it useful to distinguish between the "easy problems" and the "hard problem" of consciousness. The easy problems are by no means trivial—they are actually as challenging as most in psychology and biology—but it is with the hard problem that the central mystery lies.

The easy problems of consciousness include the following: How can a human subject discriminate sensory stimuli and react to them appropriately? How does the brain integrate information from many different sources and use this information to control behavior? How is it that subjects can verbalize their internal states? Although all these questions are associated with consciousness, they all concern the objective mechanisms of the cognitive system. Consequently, we have every reason to expect that continued work in cognitive psychology and neuroscience will answer them.

The hard problem, in contrast, is the question of how physical processes in the brain give rise to subjective experience. This puzzle involves the inner aspect of thought and perception: the way things feel for the subject. When we see, for example, we experience visual sensations, such as that of vivid blue. Or think of the ineffable sound of a distant oboe, the agony of an intense pain, the sparkle of happiness or the meditative quality of a moment lost in thought. All are part of what I call consciousness. It is these phenomena that pose the real mystery of the mind.

To illustrate the distinction, consider a thought experiment devised by the Australian philosopher Frank Jackson. Suppose that Mary, a neuroscientist in the 23rd century, is the world's leading expert on the brain processes responsible for color vision. But Mary has lived her whole life in a black-and-white room and has never seen any other colors. She knows everything there is to know about physical processes in the brain—its biology, structure and function. This understanding enables her to grasp all there is to know about the easy problems: how the brain discriminates stimuli, integrates information and produces verbal reports. From her knowledge of color vision, she knows how color names correspond with wave-lengths on the light spectrum. But there is still something crucial about color vision that Mary does not know: what it is like to experience a color such as red. It follows that there are facts about conscious experience that cannot be deduced from physical facts about the functioning of the brain.

Indeed, nobody knows why these physical processes are accompanied by conscious experience at all. Why is it that when our brains process light of a certain wavelength, we have an experience of deep purple? Why do we have any experience at all? Could not an unconscious automaton have performed the same tasks just as well? These are questions that we would like a theory of consciousness to answer.

Is Neuroscience Enough?

I am not denying that consciousness arises from the brain. We know, for example, that the subjective experience of vision is closely linked to processes in the visual cortex. It is the link itself that perplexes, however. Remarkably, subjective experience seems to emerge from a physical process. But we have no idea how or why this is.

Given the flurry of recent work on consciousness in neuroscience and psychology, one might think this mystery is starting to be cleared up. On closer examination, however, it turns out that almost all the current work addresses only the easy problems of consciousness. The confidence of the reductionist view comes from the progress on the easy problems, but none of this makes any difference where the hard problem is concerned.

Consider the hypothesis put forward by neurobiologists Francis Crick of the Salk Institute for Biological Studies in San Diego and Christof Koch of the California Institute of Technology. They suggest that consciousness may arise from certain oscillations in the cerebral cortex, which become synchronized as neurons fire 40 times per second. Crick and Koch believe the phenomenon might explain how different attributes of a single perceived object (its color and shape, for example), which are processed in different parts of the brain, are merged into a coherent whole. In this theory, two pieces of information become bound together precisely when they are represented by synchronized neural firings.

The hypothesis could conceivably elucidate one of the easy problems about how information is integrated in the brain. But why should synchronized oscillations give rise to a visual experience, no matter how much integration is taking place? This question involves the hard problem, about which the theory has nothing to offer. Indeed, Crick and Koch are agnostic about whether the hard problem can be solved by science at all.

The same kind of critique could be applied to almost all the recent work on consciousness. In his 1991 book *Consciousness Explained*, philosopher Daniel C. Dennett laid out a sophisticated theory of how numerous independent processes in the brain combine to produce a coherent response to a perceived event. The theory might do much to explain how we produce verbal reports on our internal states, but it tells us very little about why there should be a subjective experience behind these reports. Like other reductionist theories, Dennett's is a theory of the easy problems.

The critical common trait among these easy problems is that they all concern how a cognitive or behavioral function is performed. All are ultimately questions about how the brain carries out some task— how it discriminates stimuli, integrates information, produces reports and so on. Once neurobiology specifies appropriate neural mechanisms, showing how the functions are performed, the easy problems are solved.

The hard problem of consciousness, in contrast, goes beyond problems about how functions are performed. Even if every behavioral and cognitive function related to consciousness were explained, there would still remain a further mystery: Why is the performance of these functions accompanied by conscious experience? It is this additional conundrum that makes the hard problem hard.

The Explanatory Gap

Some have suggested that to solve the hard problem, we need to bring in new tools of physical explanation: nonlinear dynamics, say, or new discoveries in neuroscience, or quantum mechanics. But these ideas suffer from exactly the same difficulty. Consider a proposal from Stuart R. Hameroff of the University of Arizona and Roger Penrose of the University of Oxford. They hold that consciousness arises from quantum-physical processes taking place in microtubules, which are protein structures inside neurons. It is possible (if not likely) that such a hypothesis will lead to an explanation of how the brain makes decisions or even how it proves mathematical theorems, as Hameroff and Penrose suggest. But even if it does, the theory is silent about how these processes might give rise to conscious experience. Indeed, the same problem arises with any theory of consciousness based only on physical processing.

The trouble is that physical theories are best suited to explaining why systems have a certain physical structure and how they perform various functions. Most problems in science have this form; to explain life, for example, we need to describe how a physical system can reproduce, adapt and metabolize. But consciousness is a different sort of problem entirely, as it goes beyond the scientific explanation of structure and function.

Of course, neuroscience is not irrelevant to the study of consciousness. For one, it may be able to reveal the nature of the neural correlate of consciousness—the brain processes most directly associated with conscious experience. It may even give a detailed correspondence between specific processes in the brain and related components of experience. But until we know why these processes give rise to conscious experience at all, we will not have crossed what philosopher Joseph Levine has called the explanatory gap between physical processes and consciousness. Making that leap will demand a new kind of theory.

In searching for an alternative, a key observation is that not all entities in science are explained in terms of more basic entities. In physics, for example, space-time, mass and charge (among other things) are regarded as fundamental features of the world, as they are not reducible to anything simpler. Despite this irreducibility, detailed and useful theories relate these entities to one another in terms of fundamental laws. Together these features and laws explain a great variety of complex and subtle phenomena.

A True Theory of Everything

It is widely believed that physics provides a complete catalogue of the universe's fundamental features and laws. As physicist Steven Weinberg puts it in his 1992 book *Dreams of a Final Theory*, the goal of physics is a "theory of everything" from which all there is to know about the universe can be derived. But Weinberg concedes that there is a problem with consciousness. Despite the power of physical theory, the existence of consciousness does not seem to be derivable from physical laws. He defends physics by arguing that it might eventually explain what he calls the objective correlates of consciousness (that is, the neural correlates), but of course to do this is not to explain consciousness itself. If the existence of consciousness cannot be derived from physical laws, a theory of physics is not a true theory of everything. So a final theory must contain an additional fundamental component.

Toward this end, I propose that conscious experience be considered a fundamental feature, irreducible to anything more basic. The idea may seem strange at first, but consistency seems to demand it. In the 19th century it turned out that electromagnetic phenomena could not be explained in terms of previously known principles. As a consequence, scientists introduced electromagnetic charge as a new fundamental entity and studied the associated fundamental laws. Similar reasoning should be applied to consciousness. If existing fundamental theories cannot encompass it, then something new is required.

Where there is a fundamental property, there are fundamental laws. In this case, the laws must relate experience to elements of physical theory. These laws will almost certainly not interfere with those of the physical world; it seems that the latter form a closed system in their own right. Rather the laws will serve as a bridge, specifying how experience depends on underlying physical processes. It is this bridge that will cross the explanatory gap.

Thus, a complete theory will have two components: physical laws, telling us about the behavior of physical systems from the infinitesimal to the cosmological, and what we might call psychophysical laws, telling us how some of those systems are associated with conscious experience. These two components will constitute a true theory of everything.

Supposing for the moment that they exist, how might we uncover such psychophysical laws? The greatest hindrance in this pursuit will be a lack of data. As I have described it, consciousness is subjective, so there is no direct way to monitor it in others. But this difficulty is an obstacle, not a dead end. For a start, each one of us has access to our own experiences, a rich trove that can be used to formulate theories. We can also plausibly rely on indirect information, such as subjects' descriptions of their experiences. Philosophical arguments and thought experiments also have a role to play. Such methods have limitations, but they give us more than enough to get started.

These theories will not be conclusively testable, so they will inevitably be more speculative than those of more conventional scientific disciplines. Nevertheless, there is no reason they should not be strongly constrained to account accurately for our own first-person experiences, as well as the evidence from subjects' reports. If we find a theory that fits the data better than any other theory of equal simplicity, we will have good reason to accept it. Right now we do not have even a single theory that fits the data, so worries about testability are premature.

We might start by looking for high-level bridging laws, connecting physical processes to experience at an everyday level. The basic contour of such a law might be gleaned from the observation that when we are conscious of something, we are generally able to act on it and speak about it—which are objective, physical functions. Conversely, when some information is directly available for action and speech, it is generally conscious. Thus, consciousness correlates well with what we might call "awareness": the process by which information in the brain is made globally available to motor processes such as speech and bodily action.

Objective Awareness

The notion may seem trivial. But as defined here, awareness is objective and physical, whereas consciousness is not. Some refinements to the definition of awareness are needed, in order to extend the concept to animals and infants, which cannot speak. But at least in familiar cases, it is possible to see the rough outlines of a psychophysical law: where there is awareness, there is consciousness, and vice versa.

To take this line of reasoning a step further, consider the structure present in the conscious experience. The experience of a field of vision, for example, is a constantly changing mosaic of colors, shapes and patterns and as such has a detailed geometric structure. The fact that we can describe this structure, reach out in the direction of many of its components and perform other actions that depend on it suggests that the structure corresponds directly to that of the information made available in the brain through the neural processes of objective awareness.

Similarly, our experiences of color have an intrinsic three-dimensional structure that is mirrored in the structure of information processes in the brain's visual cortex. This structure is illustrated in the color wheels and charts used by artists. Colors are arranged in a systematic pattern—red to green on one axis, blue to yellow on another, and black to white on a third. Colors that are close to one another on a color wheel are experienced as similar. It is extremely likely that they also correspond to similar perceptual representations in the brain, as one part of a system of complex three-dimensional coding among neurons that is not yet fully understood. We can recast the underlying concept as a principle of structural coherence: the structure of conscious experience is mirrored by the structure of information in awareness, and vice versa.

Another candidate for a psychophysical law is a principle of organizational invariance. It holds that physical systems with the same abstract organization will give rise to the same kind of conscious experience, no matter what they are made of. For example, if the precise interactions between our neurons could be duplicated with silicon chips, the same conscious experience would arise. The idea is somewhat controversial, but I believe it is strongly supported by thought experiments describing the gradual replacement of neurons by silicon chips. The remarkable implication is that consciousness might someday be achieved in machines.

Theory of Consciousness

The ultimate goal of a theory of consciousness is a simple and elegant set of fundamental laws, analogous to the fundamental laws of physics. The principles described above are unlikely to be fundamental, however. Rather they seem to be high-level psychophysical laws, analogous to macroscopic principles in physics such as those of thermodynamics or kinematics. What might the underlying fundamental laws be? No one really knows, but I don't mind speculating.

I suggest that the primary psychophysical laws may centrally involve the concept of information. The abstract notion of information, as put forward in the 1940s by Claude E. Shannon of the Massachusetts Institute of Technology, is that of a set of separate states with a basic structure of similarities and differences between them. We can think of a 10-bit binary code as an information state, for example. Such information states can be embodied in the physical world. This happens whenever they correspond to physical states (voltages, say) and when differences between them can be transmitted along some pathway, such as a telephone line.

We can also find information embodied in conscious experience. The pattern of color patches in a visual field, for example, can be seen as analogous to that of the pixels covering a display screen. Intriguingly, it turns out that we find the same information states embedded in conscious experience and in underlying physical processes in the brain. The three-dimensional encoding of color spaces, for example, suggests that the information state in a color experience corresponds directly to an information state in the brain. Thus, we might even regard the two states as distinct aspects of a single information state, which is simultaneously embodied in both physical processing and conscious experience.

Aspects of Information

A natural hypothesis ensues. Perhaps information, or at least some information, has two basic aspects: a physical one and an experiential one. This hypothesis has the status of a fundamental principle that might underlie the relation between physical processes and experience. Wherever we find conscious experience, it exists as one aspect of an information state, the other aspect of which is embedded in a physical process in the brain. This proposal needs to be fleshed out to make a satisfying theory. But it fits nicely with the principles mentioned earlier—systems with the same organization will embody the same information, for example—and it could explain numerous features of our conscious experience.

The idea is at least compatible with several others, such as physicist John A. Wheeler's suggestion that information is fundamental to the physics of the universe. The laws of physics might ultimately be cast in informational terms, in which case we would have a satisfying congruence between the constructs in both physical and psychophysical laws. It may even be that a theory of physics and a theory of consciousness could eventually be consolidated into a single grander theory of information.

A potential problem is posed by the ubiquity of information. Even a thermostat embodies some information, for example, but is it conscious? There are at least two possible responses. First, we could constrain the fundamental laws so that only some

information has an experiential aspect, perhaps depending on how it is physically processed. Second, we might bite the bullet and allow that all information has an experiential aspect—where there is complex information processing, there is complex experience, and where there is simple information processing, there is simple experience. If this is so, then even a thermostat might have experiences, although they would be much simpler than even a basic color experience, and there would certainly be no accompanying emotions or thoughts. This seems odd at first, but if experience is truly fundamental, we might expect it to be widespread. In any case, the choice between these alternatives should depend on which can be integrated into the most powerful theory.

Of course, such ideas may be all wrong. On the other hand, they might evolve into a more powerful proposal that predicts the precise structure of our conscious experience from physical processes in our brains. If this project succeeds, we will have good reason to accept the theory. If it fails, other avenues will be pursued, and alternative fundamental theories may be developed. In this way, we may one day resolve the greatest mystery of the mind.

CHAPTER 6

Freedom and Determinism— Do We Have Free Will?

INTRODUCTION TO THE QUESTION

The problem of free will is traditionally considered to be an issue of metaphysics. Metaphysics is the philosophical study of the most fundamental categories of existence. It deals with questions about reality which lie beyond or behind those capable of being tackled by the methods of empirical science (typically because they address phenomena that are taken as unquestioned *givens* by science).[1] Central topics in metaphysics include, therefore, the nature of space and time, the nature of causation, the real nature of substance (such as matter), and the nature of possibility and necessity. Other metaphysical questions address very basic questions about *existence*. Why is there something rather than nothing? Does the 'external world' exist independently of our minds, or is it in some sense constituted by our perceptions of it? Is the world fundamentally a collection of *events*, or of *states of affairs*, or what? Do abstract objects (such as numbers, propositions, or moral values) actually in some sense *exist*, over and above the concrete spatio-temporal furniture of the world? Do *properties* exist over and above the individual objects which possess them: is there such a thing as redness, for example, *in addition to* all the particular red things in the world? (This is known by philosophers as 'the problem of universals,' and is harder to answer than it may at first seem: after all, if there is nothing to redness over and above all the red things, then how can we explain what *makes* a red thing red—how can we talk about what all the red things *have in common*?)

Even everyday individual objects such as trees, boats and human beings can generate metaphysical puzzles. In particular, there are deep problems about the *identity* of particular objects: What makes this boat an individual thing (rather than, say, a collection of things)? What makes it the *same* boat as the one that existed yesterday or will exist tomorrow? What properties are *necessary* for something to be the thing it is, and which are merely 'accidental'? And, for people, what is it that gives me my *personal identity*? (E.g., is it my body? my history? my memories? my consciousness?)

Finally, a perennial topic in metaphysics, oddly enough, is whether metaphysics is even possible. After all, metaphysics explicitly tries to go beyond the possible reach of empirical knowledge—it tries to think about phenomena which in principle cannot be addressed by the methods of any conceivable empiri-

---

1   The word 'metaphysics' originally comes from the Greek phrase *ta meta ta physika*, meaning 'what comes after physics,' but this etymology is really only an accident of history. When the works of Aristotle were collected together in the first century BCE, his books on 'first philosophy'—the fundamental categories of reality, such as being, substance, causality, and so on—were placed by his editors *after* his books on physics, and so were known as "the books after the books on physics."

One popular sense of 'metaphysics,' which connects it to the study of supernatural, occult, or mystical phenomena (such as ghosts, messages from the afterlife, ley lines, and what-have-you), is strictly *non*-philosophical, insofar as most of these phenomena are questionable on both scientific and philosophical (and commonsensical) grounds.

cal science, phenomena which go beyond (or lie behind) any possible human experience. It is a serious philosophical question whether such an endeavor is at all fruitful, or whether 'metaphysics' is a sphere where no real knowledge can ever be gained—a realm where we are doomed to endless futile speculation, or even to uttering claims which are, strictly speaking, *meaningless* because they have no connection to any possible human experience.

Six good general introductions to metaphysics, all of which go by the title *Metaphysics*, are those by Bruce Aune (University of Minnesota Press, 1985), D.W. Hamlyn (Cambridge University Press, 1984), Michael J. Loux (Routledge, 2006), John Post (Paragon House, 1991), Richard Taylor (Prentice Hall, 1991), and Peter Van Inwagen (Westview Press, 2008). Of these, Loux is my favorite and Taylor is the shortest. There is also *A Survey of Metaphysics* by E.J. Lowe (Oxford University Press, 2002). Two very good anthologies of contemporary papers in metaphysics are Kim and Sosa (eds.), *Metaphysics: An Anthology* (Blackwell, 1999) and Laurence and Macdonald (eds.), *Contemporary Readings in the Foundations of Metaphysics* (Blackwell, 1998). Kim and Sosa (eds.), *A Companion to Metaphysics* (Blackwell, 2009), is a fine work of reference.

The particular metaphysical topic which is addressed in this chapter is the problem of free will. This problem is generated by the following argument:

(i)   All human behavior is determined: that is, the state of the world at a particular time (e.g., the moment of your birth) entirely fixes what the state of the world will be at every moment into the future (e.g., now), and that includes fixing what actions you will ever perform.

(ii) If determinism is true, then human beings are (in at least one important sense) not free to choose their actions—we could not have done otherwise than we did, and so we do not possess genuine free will.

(iii) Therefore human beings do not have free will (and, furthermore, may lack moral responsibility for their actions, lead lives that have no meaning, and so on).

This is a straightforwardly valid argument. The problem, of course, is that both of the premises (i) and (ii) are highly plausible (or at least, can be made to seem

so with a certain amount of argumentation), and yet the conclusion is, we hope and believe, *false*: we feel like free agents, able to choose to do one thing rather than another; we believe that people often have moral (and other kinds of) responsibility for their action; we think that people can guide their own destinies in a meaningful way. The philosophical problem, therefore, is to say what if anything is wrong with the argument, and since the argument is valid the only way to criticize it is to call into question the truth of the premises. This means there are exactly three main philosophical positions on the problem of free will:

The first position, usually called *hard determinism* or just *determinism*, is the view that the argument is sound: that is, both of the premises are true and hence freedom (and moral responsibility and so on) is a mere illusion. This stance is represented here by the reading from Paul Rée. The second position, usually called *libertarianism* (or *metaphysical libertarianism*), accepts premise (ii) but argues that the first premise is false—that is, libertarians agree that determinism is incompatible with freedom, but argue that we have free will because *indeterminism* is true. This tactic is represented in this chapter by a reading from C.A. Campbell (a classic statement of libertarianism) .

The third and by far the most popular philosophical approach to free will is known as *soft determinism* or *compatibilism*. Compatibilists typically accept premise (i), determinism, but deny premise (ii): that is, they deny that the truth of determinism implies that we lack at least one important variety of freedom. Instead, they argue in a variety of ways that determinism is compatible with all the types of freedom worth wanting: that we can be *both* free and determined. A classic compatibilist account from A.J. Ayer is reprinted here. Finally, there is an influential discussion by Bernard Williams and Thomas Nagel of "moral luck"— the degree to, and complex ways in which, matters of chance and determination interact with the question of moral responsibility.

There are many decent collections of articles on the problem of free will, including Gerald Dworkin (ed.), *Determinism, Free Will, and Moral Responsibility* (Prentice Hall, 1970); John Martin Fischer (ed.), *Moral Responsibility* (Cornell University Press, 1986); Robert

Kane (ed.), *Free Will* (Blackwell, 2009) and *The Oxford Handbook of Free Will* (Oxford University Press, 2005); Timothy O'Connor (ed.), *Agents, Causes, and Events* (Oxford University Press, 1995); and Gary Watson (ed.), *Free Will* (Oxford University Press, 2003). Useful and fairly accessible single-author discussions of the problem of free will include Daniel Dennett, *Elbow Room* (MIT Press, 1985); Ted Honderich, *How Free Are You?* (Oxford University Press, 1993); Robert Kane, *A Contemporary Introduction to Free Will* (Oxford University Press, 2005); Graham McFee, *Free Will* (McGill-Queen's University Press, 2000); Daniel John O'Connor, *Free Will* (Macmillan, 1971); Timothy O'Connor, *Persons and Causes* (Oxford University Press, 2000); and Jennifer Trusted, *Free Will and Responsibility* (Oxford University Press, 1984).

Finally, here are a few recent influential books on free will which are not cited in the Further Reading sections elsewhere in the chapter: Richard Double, *The Non-Reality of Free Will* (Oxford University Press, 1991); John Martin Fischer, *The Metaphysics of Free Will* (Blackwell, 1996); Ted Honderich, *A Theory of Determinism* (two volumes, Oxford University Press, 1988); Murphy and Brown (eds.), *Did My Neurons Make Me Do It?: Philosophical and Neurobiological Perspectives on Moral Responsibility and Free Will* (Oxford University Press, 2009); Derk Pereboom, *Living Without Free Will* (Cambridge University Press, 2001); Galen Strawson, *Freedom and Belief* (Oxford University Press, 1986); Peter Van Inwagen, *An Essay on Free Will* (Oxford University Press, 1983); and Daniel Wegner, *The Illusion of Conscious Will* (MIT Press, 2005).

PAUL RÉE

The Illusion of Free Will

Who Was Paul Rée?

Paul Rée, a German philosopher and psychologist, is best remembered for his association with Friedrich Nietzsche and for his uncompromising moral relativism and atheism. Born in 1849, Rée was the son of a wealthy Prussian landowner. In his early twenties he fought in the Franco-Prussian war of 1870–71, in which Prussian troops advanced into France and decisively defeated the French army at Sedan (a town near the Belgian border). The outcome was the fall of the French Second Empire and the establishment of a new, united German Empire—the first Reich—under its first chancellor, Prince Otto Leopold von Bismarck. On his return from the war, wounded, Rée went to Switzerland to recuperate and, abandoning the law studies he had begun before the war, devoted himself to the study of philosophy and psychology. In 1875 he received a doctorate in philosophy from the University of Halle (a city in central Germany), and

also published a book of psychological aphorisms, *Psychologische Beobachtungen*.

In 1873 Rée had met the famous German philosopher Friedrich Nietzsche in Basel, and after the publication of Rée's *Psychological Observations* Nietzsche wrote him a letter complimenting the work. As a result, the two struck up a close friendship—which Nietzsche's biographer, Walter Kaufmann, has called "among the best things which ever happened to Nietzsche"—that lasted about seven years. However, Rée was ethnically Jewish (though not a religious practitioner), and several of Nietzsche's anti-Semitic friends and Nietzsche's unpleasant sister resented his influence on Nietzsche. In 1882, after Nietzsche bitterly broke off his relationship with the tempestuous and bewitching Lou Salomé, to whom Rée had originally introduced him, Rée's friendship with the famous philosopher came to an end, and they never spoke again. Later, Rée was to dismiss Nietzsche's ethical writings as "a mixture of insanity and nonsense."

In 1877 Rée published *Ursprung der moralischen Empfindungen* (The Origin of the Moral Sentiments). In this book, strongly influenced by Charles Darwin and David Hume, Rée argued that there are no universally true moral principles, and that what is regarded as morally right or wrong, in any given society, is a function of its needs and cultural conditions. *The Illusion of Free Will*, in which Rée advocates abandoning notions of moral responsibility in practical as well as philosophical life, was published in 1885, when Rée was 36. In the same year, he published *Die Entstehung des Gewissens* (The Origin of Conscience) and in the process of writing this book he became concerned about his own lack of knowledge of the natural sciences. The next year Rée enrolled at the University of Munich to study medicine. After obtaining his MD, Rée returned to his family estate in Stibbe, West Prussia. There he practiced medicine, charging no fees, and when his own medical knowledge fell short in particular cases, paid all the hospital expenses for the peasants and laborers who were his patients.

For the last ten years of his life, Rée led an isolated, ascetic existence living at Stibbe with his brother, and spent much of his time working on a major book which would encapsulate all his philosophical reflections. Rée told a friend that when it was finished he would give up philosophy, but that since he could not live without doing philosophy, there would be nothing left for him but to die. This is more or less what happened: in 1900, when his book was almost completed, Rée, a passionate mountain climber, returned to live in Switzerland and fell to his death from the icy ridge of a Swiss mountain in 1901. His book, *Philosophie*, was published posthumously in 1903

Lou von Salomé, Paul Rée, and Friedrich Nietzsche. In the studio of Jules Bonnet, Luzern 1882.

and, to this day, has been almost completely ignored. In this work, Rée roundly condemned metaphysics as a system of "fairy tales" and "lies," and argued that religions "are true neither in the literal nor in an allegorical sense—they are untrue in every sense. Religion issues from a marriage of error and fear."

What Is the Structure of This Reading?

This selection contains most of Chapters 1 and 2 of Paul Rée's 1885 book *Die Illusion der Willensfreiheit* (The Illusion of Free Will). The final (third) chapter of the book, which is not reprinted here, contains a detailed critique of Immanuel Kant's views on free will. Rée begins by defining freedom of the will as the ability to act as "an absolute beginning"—i.e., a thought or action is free, according to Rée, just in the case where it is not the necessary result of prior causes. Rée then goes on to argue that *no* event is uncaused, and thus that there can be no such thing as free will. To show this, he first examines the example of an act of decision in a donkey and then extends similar considerations to human beings. He insists that even actions performed solely from a sense of duty are not genuinely free, and he argues that one must be careful to distinguish between correct and incorrect senses of the claim "I can do what I want." Finally, he diagnoses our mistaken belief in free will as being the result of ignorance of the causes of our own actions. Because we do not see how our actions are caused, we fallaciously assume that they are not caused.

In section 5, which marks the start of Chapter 2 of his book, Rée explores the implications for morality of the truth of determinism. He argues that if all our actions are necessary effects of prior causes, then we cannot be held morally responsible for them: we cannot legitimately be praised or blamed for our actions. The true philosopher, Rée hints, will try to rid herself of the bad habit of assigning moral responsibility. On the other hand, we certainly do *prefer* some actions (and some types of people) over others, and this is legitimate; but our preferences themselves are to be explained as causal effects of our genetic inheritance and social upbringing.

Some Useful Background Information

There is a useful and commonly made philosophical distinction which is helpful for understanding Rée's position on free will: the contrast between necessary and sufficient conditions. A is a *necessary* condition for B if B could not have occurred (or been true) without A—that is, if there would be no B unless A. For example, being connected to a power supply is a necessary condition for a bulb to light up (the bulb could not light unless connected to a source of electricity). On the other hand, A is a *sufficient* condition for B if the occurrence (or truth) of A is *sufficient* for the occurrence (or truth) of B—that is, if B happens every time A does. Being connected in the right way to a properly functioning circuit with an adequate source of power, under normal physical circumstances, with the power switch in the "on" position is, altogether, a sufficient circumstance for a bulb to light.

It follows from this that if A is a sufficient condition for B, then if A occurs B must *necessarily* occur as well.[1] (On the other hand, if A is merely a necessary condition for B, the occurrence of A only tells us that B *may* happen, but not that it actually will.)

---

1   This claim is a bit more complicated than it seems, however, because of the various flavors which necessity can come in: for example, the fact that B always follows A in the actual world perhaps means that B is a 'physically necessary' consequence of A, but it need not follow that B follows from A by *logical* necessity.

Suggestions for Critical Reflection

1. "To say that the will is not free means that it is subject to the law of causality." Is this right? Or could the will somehow be *both* free and subject to causal laws?
2. Rée admits that "man has the ability to free himself from being dominated by his drives." Does this undermine his claim that determinism is incompatible with moral responsibility?
3. Rée suggests that anyone who comes to properly grasp the truth of determinism will immediately abandon any belief in moral responsibility (though perhaps will be unable to shake off the habit of making moral judgments). Is this claim plausible? How strong are his reasons for making it?
4. Here are two claims:
    a) Some event A will occur *whenever* its sufficient cause is present.
    b) Some event A will occur *only* when its sufficient cause is present.

    Do these two claims say different things (i.e., could one be true when the other one is false)? Does Rée clearly differentiate between the two of them? How might the difference between the two claims cause problems for Rée's argument?
5. "Observation teaches us that for every act of will, some causes were the determining factors." Is this true and, if so, is it sufficient to establish determinism?
6. One of the consequences of Rée's determinism, he suggests, is that people can *only* do what they want to do—that is, according to Rée, it is impossible to deliberately do something that you do not want to do. Does this seem right to you? Does it actually follow from the thesis of determinism?
7. Is it *fair* to prefer some people over others, to seek the company of the former, and to shun the latter, if they are not responsible for their character traits? For example, is it okay to dislike depressed people if it's not their fault they are depressed? Is the question of 'fairness' even appropriate, if human beings have no free will?

Suggestions for Further Reading

The Rée reading and much of the information reprinted here about him comes from the third edition of *A Modern Introduction to Philosophy*, edited by Paul Edwards and Arthur Pap (Free Press, 1973). As far as I am aware, no more of Rée's writings have yet been published in English. One of the best-known "determinists" of the century before Rée was Paul-Henri Thiry, the Baron d'Holbach (1723–1789). His most important book is *The System of Nature* (1770, reissued by Clinamen Press, 2000), in which he defended an unflinching atheistic materialism; however, unlike Rée, d'Holbach took pains to argue that determinism is compatible with altruism and moral virtue. Another precursor was the French mathematician Pierre-Simon de Laplace (1749–1827), famous for formulating the idea that a superhuman intelligence, capable of knowing the entire state of the universe at a given moment, could compute exactly how everything in the universe would evolve, down to the minutest detail, for the rest of time. (Such a being is now usually known as "Laplace's demon.") A rigorous intellectual biography of Laplace, with information about his demon, is Charles Coulston Gillespie's *Pierre Simon Laplace, 1749–1827* (Princeton University Press, 2000).

Two particularly notorious twentieth-century determinist tracts are Clarence Darrow's, *Crime, Its Cause and Treatment* (Crowell, 1922) and B.F. Skinner's, *Beyond Freedom and Dignity* (Knopf, 1971). Probably the best recent book on the scientific basis for determinism is John Earman's *A Primer on Determinism* (Kluwer, 1986), and a useful recent exploration of its philosophical consequences is Roy Weatherford's *The Implications of Determinism* (Routledge, 1991).

The Illusion of Free Will
Chapters 1 and 2 [2]

1. Nothing Happens without a Cause

… To say that the will is not free means that it is subject to the law of causality. Every act of will is in fact preceded by a sufficient cause. Without such a cause the act of will cannot occur; and, if the sufficient cause is present, the act of will must occur.

To say that the will is free would mean that it is not subject to the law of causality. In that case every act of will would be an absolute beginning [a first cause] and not a link [in a chain of events]: it would not be the effect of preceding causes.

The reflections that follow may serve to clarify what is meant by saying that the will is not free.… Every object—a stone, an animal, a human being—can pass from its present state to another one. The stone that now lies in front of me may, in the next moment, fly through the air, or it may disintegrate into dust or roll along the ground. If, however, one of these *possible* states is to be *realized*, its sufficient cause must first be present. The stone will fly through the air if it is tossed. It will roll if a force acts upon it. It will disintegrate into dust, given that some object hits and crushes it.

It is helpful to use the terms "potential" and "actual" in this connection. At any moment there are innumerably many potential states. At a given time, however, only *one* can become actual, namely, the one that is triggered by its sufficient cause.

The situation is no different in the case of an animal. The donkey that now stands motionless between two piles of hay may, in the next moment, turn to the left or to the right, or he may jump into the air or put his head between his legs. But here, too, the sufficient

---

2   Paul Rée's *Die Illusion der Willensfreiheit* was first published in Berlin in 1885. This selection was translated by Stefan Bauer-Mengelberg and edited by Paul Edwards and Arthur Pap (who also supplied the section headings) in 1973. It is reprinted here with the kind permission of Dr. Tim Madigan, Literary Executor to Paul Edwards.

cause must first be present if of the *possible* modes of behavior one is to be *realized*.

Let us analyze one of these modes of behavior. We shall assume that the donkey has turned toward the bundle on his right. This turning presupposes that certain muscles were contracted. The cause of this muscular contraction is the excitation of the nerves that lead to them. The cause of this excitation of the nerves is a state of the brain. It was in a state of decision. But how did the brain come to be in that condition? Let us trace the states of the donkey back a little farther.

A few moments before he turned, his brain was not yet so constituted as to yield the sufficient cause for the excitation of the nerves in question and for the contraction of the muscles; for otherwise the movement would have occurred. The donkey had not yet "decided" to turn. If he then moved at some subsequent time, his brain must in the meantime have become so constituted as to bring about the excitation of the nerves and the movement of the muscles. Hence the brain underwent some change. To what causes is this change to be attributed? To the effectiveness of an impression that acts as an external stimulus, or to a sensation that arose internally; for example, the sensation of hunger and the idea of the bundle on the right, by jointly affecting the brain, change the way in which it is constituted so that it now yields the sufficient cause for the excitation of the nerves and the contraction of the muscles. The donkey now "wants" to turn to the right; he now turns to the right.

Hence, just as the position and constitution of the stone, on the one hand and the strength and direction of the force that acts upon it, on the other, necessarily determine the kind and length of its flight, so the movement of the donkey—his turning to the bundle on the right—is no less necessarily the result of the way in which the donkey's brain and the stimulus are constituted at a given moment. That the donkey turned toward this particular bundle was determined by something trivial. If the bundle that the donkey did not choose had been positioned just a bit differently, or if it had smelled different, or if the subjective factor—the donkey's sense of smell or his visual organs—had developed in a somewhat different way, then, so we may assume, the donkey would have turned to the left.

But the cause was not complete there, and that is why the effect could not occur, while with respect to the other side, where the cause was complete, the effect could not fail to appear.

For the donkey, consequently, just as for the stone, there are innumerably many *potential* states at any moment; he may walk or run or jump, or move to the left, to the right, or straight ahead. But only the one whose sufficient cause is present can ever become *actual*.

At the same time, there is a difference between the donkey and the stone in that the donkey moves because he wants to move, while the stone moves because it is moved. We do not deny this difference. There are, after all, a good many other differences between the donkey and the stone. We do not by any means intend to prove that this dissimilarity does not exist. We do not assert that the donkey is a stone, but only that the donkey's every movement and act of will has causes just as the motion of the stone does. The donkey moves because he wants to move. But that he wants to move at a given moment, and in this particular direction, is causally determined.

Could it be that there was no sufficient cause for the donkey's wanting to turn around—that he simply wanted to turn around? His act of will would then be an absolute beginning. An assumption of that kind is contradicted by experience and the universal validity of the law of causality. By experience, since observation teaches us that for every act of will some causes were the determining factors. By the universal validity of the law of causality, since, after all, nothing happens anywhere in the world without a sufficient cause. Why, then, of all things should a donkey's act of will come into being without a cause? Besides, the state of willing, the one that immediately precedes the excitation of the motor nerves, is no different in principle from other states—that of indifference, of lassitude, or of weariness. Would anyone believe that all of these states exist without a cause? And if one does not believe that, why should just the state of willing be thought to occur without a sufficient cause?

It is easy to explain why it seems to us that the motion of the stone is necessary while the donkey's act of will is not. The causes that move the stone are, after all, external and visible. But the causes of the donkey's act of will are internal and invisible; between us and the locus of their effectiveness lies the skull of the donkey. Let us consider this difference somewhat more closely. The stone lies before us as it is constituted. We can also see the force acting upon it, and from these two factors, the constitution of the stone and the force, there results, likewise visible, the rolling of the stone. The case of the donkey is different. The state of his brain is hidden from our view. And, while the bundle of hay is visible, its effectiveness is not. It is an internal process. The bundle does not come into visible contact with the brain but acts at a distance. Hence the subjective and the objective factor—the brain and the impact that the bundle has upon it—are invisible.

Let us suppose that we could depict the donkey's soul in high relief, taking account of and making visible all those states, attitudes, and feelings that characterize it before the donkey turns. Suppose further that we could see how an image detaches itself from the bundle of hay and, describing a visible path through the air, intrudes upon the donkey's brain and how it produces a change there in consequence of which certain nerves and muscles move. Suppose, finally, that we could repeat this experiment arbitrarily often, that, if we returned the donkey's soul into the state preceding his turning and let exactly the same impression act upon it, we should always observe the very same result. Then we would regard the donkey's turning to the right as necessary. We would come to realize that the brain, constituted as it was at that moment, had to react to such an impression in precisely that way.

In the absence of this experiment it seems as though the donkey's act of will were not causally determined. We just do not see its being causally determined and consequently believe that no such determination takes place. The act of will, it is said, is the cause of the turning, but it is not itself determined; it is said to be an absolute beginning.

The opinion that the donkey's act of will is not causally determined is held not only by the outsider; the donkey himself, had he the gift of reflection, would share it. The causes of his act of will would elude him, too, since in part they do not become conscious at all and in part pass through consciousness fleetingly, with the speed of lightning. If, for example, what tipped the scales was that he was closer by a hair's breadth to the bundle on the right, or that it smelled a shade better, how should the donkey notice something so trivial, something that so totally fails to force itself upon his consciousness?

In *one* sense, of course, the donkey is right in thinking "I could have turned to the left." His state at the moment, his position relative to the bundle, or its constitution need merely have been somewhat different, and he really would have turned to the left. The statement "I could have acted otherwise" is, accordingly, true in this sense: turning to the left is one of the movements possible for me (in contrast, for example, to the movement of flying); it lies within the realm of my possibilities.

We arrive at the same result if we take the law of inertia as our point of departure. It reads: every object strives to remain in its present state. Expressed negatively this becomes: without a sufficient cause no object can pass from its present state to another one. The stone will lie forever just as it is lying now; it will not undergo the slightest change if no causes—such as the weather or a force—act upon it to bring about a change. The donkey's brain will remain in the same state unchanged for all eternity if no causes—the feeling of hunger or fatigue, say, or external impressions—bring about a change.

If we reflect upon the entire life of the donkey *sub specie necessitatis*,[3] we arrive at the following result. The donkey came into the world with certain properties of mind and body, his genetic inheritance. Since the day of his birth, impressions—of the companions with whom he frolicked or worked, his feed, the climate—have acted upon these properties. These two factors, his inborn constitution and the way in which it was formed through the impressions of later life, are the cause of all of his sensations, ideas, and moods, and of all of his movements, even the most trivial

---

3   Latin for "under the aspect of necessity"—that is, seen from the standpoint of necessity. (This expression is modeled on philosopher Baruch Spinoza's coinage *sub specie aeternitatis*, "under the aspect of eternity," which Spinoza uses in his *Ethics* (1677) to characterize the highest form of knowledge as that in which the world is seen from the standpoint of timelessness or eternity.)

ones. If, for example, he cocks his left ear and not the right one, that is determined by causes whose historical development could be traced back ad infinitum;[4] and likewise when he stands, vacillating,[5] between the two bundles. And when action, the act of feeding, takes the place of vacillation, that, too, is determined: the idea of the one bundle now acts upon the donkey's mind, when it has become receptive to the idea of that particular sheaf, in such a way as to produce actions.

2. Human Beings and the Law of Causality

Let us now leave the realm of animals and proceed to consider man. Everything is the same here. Man's every feeling is a necessary result. Suppose, for example, that I am stirred by a feeling of pity at this moment. To what causes is it to be attributed? Let us go back as far as possible. An infinite amount of time has elapsed up to this moment. Time was never empty; objects have filled it from all eternity. These objects ... have continually undergone change. All of these changes were governed by the law of causality; not one of them took place without a sufficient cause.

We need not consider what else may have characterized these changes. Only their *formal* aspect, only this *one* point is of concern to us: no change occurred without a cause.

At some time in the course of this development, by virtue of some causes, organic matter was formed, and finally man. Perhaps the organic world developed as Darwin described it. Be that as it may, it was in any case due to causes that I was born on a particular day, with particular properties of body, of spirit, and of heart. Impressions then acted upon this constitution; I had particular governesses, teachers, and playmates. Teaching and example in part had an effect and in part were lost upon me; the former, when my inborn constitution made me receptive to them, when I had an affinity for them. And that is how it has come to be, through the operation of [a chain of] causes, that I am stirred by a feeling of pity at this moment. The course of the world would have had to be somewhat different if my feelings were to be different now.

It is of no consequence for the present investigation whether the inborn capacity for pity, for taking pleasure in another's pain, or for courage remains constant throughout life or whether teaching, example, and activity serve to change it. In any case the pity or pleasure in another's pain, the courage or cowardice, that a certain person feels or exhibits at a given moment is a necessary result, whether these traits are inborn—an inheritance from his ancestors—or were developed in the course of his own life.

Likewise every intention, indeed, every thought that ever passes through the brain, the silliest as well as the most brilliant, the true as well as the false, exists of necessity. In that sense there is no freedom of thought. It is necessary that I sit in this place at this moment, that I hold my pen in my hand in a particular way, and that I write that every thought is necessary; and if the reader should perchance be of the opinion that this is not the case, i.e., if he should believe that thoughts may not be viewed as effects, then he holds this false opinion of necessity also.

Just as sensations and thoughts are necessary, so, too, is action. It is, after all, nothing other than their externalization, their objective embodiment. Action is born of sensations and thoughts. So long as the sensations are not sufficiently strong, action cannot occur, and when the sensations and thoughts are constituted so as to yield the sufficient cause for it, then it must occur; then the appropriate nerves and muscles are set to work. Let us illustrate this by means of an action that is judged differently at different levels of civilization, namely, murder.[6] Munzinger,[7] for example, says that among the Bogos[8] the murderer, the terror

---

4   Without limit, forever.

5   Swaying indecisively between one course of action and another.

---

6   The German word Rée used here was *Raubmord*, a compound noun denoting a combination of murder and robbery (with overtones of pillage and rape).

7   Werner Munzinger (1832–1875) was a Swiss linguist and explorer. He spent many years traveling in Eritrea, Abyssinia, and the Sudan, three countries in northeast Africa south of Egypt (Abyssinia is now known as Ethiopia).

8   The Bogos were a tribe living in the highlands of northern Abyssinia and southern Eritrea. Munzinger described the customs of the Bogos in his 1859 book *Über die Sitten und das Recht der Bogos*.

of the neighborhood, who never tires of blood and murder, is a man of respect. Whoever has been raised with such views will not be deterred from murder either by external or by internal obstacles. Neither the police nor his conscience forbids him to commit it. On the contrary, it is his habit to praise murder; his parents and his gods stimulate him to commit it, and his companions encourage him by their example. And so it comes to be that, if there is a favorable opportunity, he does the deed. But is this not terribly trivial? After all, everyone knows that an act of murder is due to *motives*! True, but almost no one (except perhaps a philosopher) knows that an act of murder, and indeed every action, has a *cause*. Motives are a part of the cause. But to admit that there are motives for an action is not yet to recognize that it is causally determined, or to see clearly that the action is determined by thoughts and sensations—which in turn are effects—just as the rolling of a ball is determined by a force. But it is this point, and only this one, to which we must pay heed.

Let us now consider the act of murder from the same point of view in the case of civilized peoples. Someone raised at a higher level of civilization has learned from childhood on to disapprove of murder and to regard it as deserving punishment. God, his parents, and his teachers—in short, all who constitute an authority for him—condemn acts of this kind. It is, moreover, inconsistent with his character, which has been formed in an era of peace. Lastly, too, fear of punishment will deter him. Can murder prosper on such soil? Not easily. Fear, pity, the habit of condemning murder—all these are just so many bulwarks that block the path to such an action. Nevertheless need, passion, or various seductive influences will perhaps remove one after another of these bulwarks. Let us consider the cause of an act of murder more closely. First it is necessary to distinguish between two components, the subjective and the objective, in the total cause. The *subjective* part of the cause consists of the state of the murderer at the moment of the deed. To this we must assign all ideas that he had at the time, the conscious as well as the unconscious ones, his sensations, the temperature of his blood, the state of his stomach, of his liver—of each and every one of his bodily organs. The *objective* component consists

of the appearance of the victim, the locality in which the deed took place, and the way it was illuminated. The act of murder was necessarily consummated at that moment because these impressions acted upon a human being constituted in that particular way at the time. "Necessarily" means just that the act of murder is an effect; the state of the murderer and the impressions acting upon it are its cause. If the cause had not been complete, the effect could not have occurred. If, for example, the murderer had felt even a trifle more pity at that moment, if his idea of God or of the consequences that his deed would have here on earth had been somewhat more distinct, or if the moon had been a little brighter, so that more light would have fallen upon the victim's face and his pleading eyes—then, perhaps, the cause of the act of murder would not have become complete, and in consequence the act would not have taken place.

Thus for man, as for animal and stone, there are at any moment innumerably many *potential* states. The murderer might, at the moment when he committed the murder, have climbed a tree instead or stood on his head. If, however, instead of the murder one of these actions were to have become *actual*, then its sufficient cause would have had to be present. He would have climbed a tree if he had had the intention of hiding, or of acting as a lookout, that is to say, if at that moment he had had other ideas and sensations. But this could have been the case only if the events that took place in the world had been somewhat different [stretching back in time] ad infinitum.

3. Determinism and Will-Power

But I can, after all, break through the network of thoughts, sensations, and impressions that surrounds me by resolutely saying "I will not commit murder!" No doubt. We must, however, not lose sight of the fact that a resolute "I will" or "I will not" is also, wherever it appears, a necessary result; it does not by any means exist without a cause. Let us return to our examples. Although the Bogo really has reasons only to commit murder, it is nevertheless possible for a resolute "I will not commit murder" to assert itself. But is it conceivable that this "I will not" should occur without a sufficient cause? Fear, pity, or some other feeling, which in turn is an effect, overcomes him and gives rise to this "I will not" before the cause of the murder has yet become complete. Perhaps Christian missionaries have had an influence upon him; hence the idea of a deity that will visit retribution on him for murder comes before his soul, and that is how the "I will not" comes to be. It is easier to detect the causes of the resolute "I will not commit murder" in someone raised at a higher level of civilization; fear, principles, or the thought of God in most cases produce it in time.

A resolute will can be characteristic of a man. No matter how violently jealousy, greed, or some other passion rages within him, he does not want to succumb to it; he does not succumb to it. The analogue of this constitution is a ball that, no matter how violent a force acts upon it, does not budge from its place. A billiard cue will labor in vain to shake the earth. The earth victoriously resists the cue's thrusts with its mass. Likewise man resists the thrusts of greed and jealousy with the mass of his principles. A man of that kind, accordingly, is free—from being dominated by his drives. Does this contradict determinism? By no means. A man free from passion is still subject to the law of causality. He is necessarily free. It is just that the word "free" has different meanings. It may be correctly predicated of man in every sense except a single one: he is not free from the law of causality. Let us trace the causes of his freedom from the tyranny of the passions.

Let us suppose that his steadfastness of will was not inherited, or, if so, merely as a disposition. Teaching, example, and, above all, the force of circumstances developed it in him. From early childhood on he found himself in situations in which he had to control himself if he did not want to perish. Just as someone standing at the edge of an abyss can banish dizziness by thinking "If I become dizzy, then I will plunge," so thinking "If I yield to my excitation—indeed, if I so much as betray it[9]—I will perish" has led him to control of his drives.

It is often thought that those who deny that the will is free want to deny that man has the ability to free himself from being dominated by his drives. However, one can imagine man's power to resist passions to be

as great as one wants, even infinitely great; that is to say, a man may possibly resist even the most violent passion: his love of God or his principles have still more power over him than the passion. The question whether even the most resolute act of will is an effect is entirely independent of this.

But is being subject to the law of causality not the weak side of the strong? By no means. Is a lion weak if he can tear a tiger apart? Is a hurricane weak if it can uproot trees? And yet the power by means of which the lion dismembers and the storm uproots is an effect, and not an absolute beginning. By having causes, by being an effect, strength is not diminished.

Just as resolute willing is to be considered an effect, so is irresolute willing. A vacillating man is characterized by the fact that he alternately wants something and then doesn't want it. To say that someone contemplating murder is still vacillating means that at one time the desire for possessions, greed, and jealousy predominate—then he wants to commit murder, at another time fear of the consequences, the thought of God, or pity overcomes him, and then he does not want to commit murder. In the decisive moment, when his victim is before him, everything depends upon which feeling has the upper hand. If at that moment passion predominates, then he wants to commit murder; and then he commits murder.

We see that, from whatever point of view we look at willing, it always appears as a necessary result, as a link [in a chain of events], and never as an absolute beginning.

But can we not prove by means of an experiment that willing is an absolute beginning? I lift my arm because I *want* to lift it.... Here my *wanting* to lift my arm is the cause of the lifting, but this wanting, we are told, is not itself causally determined; rather, it is an absolute beginning. I simply want to lift my arm, and that is that. We are deceiving ourselves. This act of will, too, has causes; my intention to demonstrate by means of an experiment that my will is free gives rise to my wanting to lift my arm. But how did this intention come to be? Through a conversation, or through reflecting on the freedom of the will. Thus the thought "I want to demonstrate my freedom" has the effect that I want to lift my arm. There is a gap in

---

9   Reveal it, let it show.

this chain. Granted that my intention to demonstrate that my will is free stands in some relation to my wanting to lift my arm, why do I not demonstrate my freedom by means of some other movement? Why is it *just my arm* that I want to lift? This specific act of will on my part has not yet been causally explained. Does it perhaps not have causes? Is it an uncaused act of will? Let us note first that someone who wishes to demonstrate that his will is free will usually really extend or lift his arm, and in particular his right arm. He neither tears his hair nor wiggles his belly. This can be explained as follows. Of all of the parts of the body that are subject to our voluntary control, there is none that we move more frequently than the right arm. If, now, we wish to demonstrate our freedom by means of some movement, we will automatically make that one to which we are most accustomed.... Thus we first have a conversation about or reflection on the freedom of the will; this leads to the intention of demonstrating our freedom; this intention arises in an organism with certain [physiological] habits [such as that of readily lifting the right arm], and as a result we want to lift (and then lift) the right arm.

I remember once discussing the freedom of the will with a left-handed man. He asserted "My will is free; I can do what I want." In order to demonstrate this he extended his *left* arm.

It is easy to see, now, what the situation is with regard to the assertion "I can do what I want." In one sense it is indeed correct; in another, however, it is wrong. The *correct* sense is to regard willing as a cause and action as an effect. For example, I can kill my rival if I want to kill him. I can walk to the left if I want to walk to the left. The causes are *wanting* to kill and *wanting* to walk; the effects are killing and walking. In some way every action must be preceded by the act of willing it, whether we are aware of it or not. According to this view, in fact, I can do *only* what I want to do, and only if I want to do it. The *wrong* sense is to regard willing *merely* as a cause, and not at the same time as the effect of something else. But, like everything else, it is cause *as well as effect*. An absolutely initial act of will does not exist. Willing stands in the middle: it brings about killing and walking to the left; it is the effect of thoughts and sensations (which in turn are effects).

4. Ignorance of the Causation of Our Actions

Hence our volition (with respect to some action) is always causally determined. But it seems to be free (of causes); it seems to be an absolute beginning. To what is this appearance due?

We do not perceive the causes by which our volition is determined, and that is why we believe that it is not causally determined at all.

How often do we do something while "lost in thought"! We pay no attention to what we are doing, let alone to the causes from which it springs. While we are thinking, we support our head with our hand. While we are conversing, we twist a piece of paper in our hand. If we then reflect on our behavior—stimulated perhaps by a conversation about the freedom of the will—and if we are quite incapable of finding a sufficient cause for it, then we believe that there was no sufficient cause for it at all, that, consequently, we could have proceeded differently at that moment, e.g., supporting our head with the left hand instead of the right....

To adduce yet another example: suppose that there are two eggs on the table. I take one of them. Why not the other one? Perhaps the one I took was a bit closer to me, or some other trivial matter, which would be very difficult to discover and is of the kind that almost never enters our consciousness, tipped the scales. If I now look back but do not see why I took *that* particular egg, then I come to think that I could just as well have taken the other.

Let us replace "I could have taken the other egg" by other statements containing the expression "I could have." For example, I could, when I took the egg, have chopped off my fingers instead, or I could have jumped at my neighbor's throat. Why do we never adduce such statements ... but always those contemplating an action close to the one that we really carried out? Because at the moment when I took the egg, chopping off my fingers and murder were far from my mind. From this point of view the two aspects of our subject matter—the fact that acts of will are necessary and that they appear not to be necessary—can be perceived especially clearly. *In fact* taking the other egg was at that moment just as impossible as chopping off a finger. For, whether a nuance of a sensation or a whole army of sensations and thoughts is lacking in the complete cause obviously does not matter; the effect cannot occur so long as the cause is incomplete. But it *seems* as though it would have been possible to take the other egg at that moment; if something almost happened, we think that it could have happened.

While in the case of unimportant matters we perhaps do not notice the causes of our act of will and therefore think that it has no causes, the situation is quite different—it will be objected—in the case of important matters. We did not, after all, marry one girl rather than another while "lost in thought." We did not close the sale of our house while "lost in thought." Rather, everyone sees that motives determined such decisions. In spite of this, however, we think "I could have acted differently." What is the source of this error?

In the case of unimportant matters we do not notice the cause of our action at all; in the case of important ones we perceive it, but not adequately. We do, to be sure, see the separate parts of the cause, but the special relation in which they stood to one another at the moment of the action eludes us.

Let us first consider another example from the realm of animals. A vixen vacillated whether to sneak into the chicken coop, to hunt for mice, or to return to her young in her den. At last she sneaked into the chicken coop. Why? Because she wanted to. But why did she want to? Because this act of will on her part resulted from the relation in which her hunger, her fear of the watchdog, her maternal instinct, and her other thoughts, sensations, and impressions stood to one another at that time. But a vixen with the gift of reflection would, were she to look back upon her action, say "I could have willed differently." For, although she realizes that hunger influenced her act of will, the *degree* of hunger on the one hand, and of fear and maternal instinct on the other, present at the moment of the action elude her. Having become a different animal since the time of the action, perhaps because of it, she thinks—by way of a kind of optical illusion—that she was that other animal already then. It is the same in the case of man. Suppose, for example, that someone has slain his rival out of jealousy. What does he himself, and what do others, perceive with respect to this action? We see that on the one hand jealousy, the desire for possessions, hatred, and

rage were present in him, and on the other fear of punishment, pity, and the thought of God. We do not, however, see the particular relation in which hatred and pity, and rage and fear of punishment, stood to one another at the moment of the deed. If we could see this, keep it fixed, and recreate it experimentally, then everyone would regard this action as an effect, as a necessary result.

Let us now, with the aid of our imagination, suppose that the sensations and thoughts of the murderer at the moment of the deed were spread out before us, clearly visible as if on a map. From this reflection we shall learn that *in fact* we are lacking such an overview, and that this lack is the reason why we do not ascribe a cause (or "necessity") to the action.

The kaleidoscopically changing sensations, thoughts, and impressions would, in order for their relation to one another to become apparent, have to be returned to the state in which they were at the moment of the deed, and then made rigid, as if they were being nailed to their place. But beyond that, the thoughts and sensations would have to be spatially extended and endowed with a colored surface; a stronger sensation would have to be represented by a bigger lump. A clearer thought would have to wear, say, a bright red color, a less clear one a gray coloration. Jealousy and rage, as well as pity and the thought of God, would have to be plastically exhibited[10] for us in this way. We would, further, have to see how the sight of the victim acts upon these structures of thoughts and sensations, and how there arises from these two factors first the desire to commit murder and then the act of murder itself.

Moreover, we would have to be able to repeat the process, perhaps as follows: we return the murderer to the state of mind that he had some years before the act of murder; we equip his mind with precisely the same thoughts and sensations, and his body with the same constitution. Then we let the very same impressions act upon them; we bring him into contact with the same people, let him read the same books, nourish him with the same food, and, finally, we will place the murdered person, after having called him back to life, before the murderer with the very same

---

10   Modeled in three dimensions.

facial expression, in the same illumination and at the same distance. Then, as soon as the parts of the cause have been completely assembled, we would always see that the very same effect occurs, namely, wanting to commit, and then committing, murder.

Finally, too, we would have to vary the experiment, in the manner of the chemists; we would have to be able now to weaken a sensation, now to strengthen it, and to observe the result that this produces.

If these conditions were fulfilled, if we could experimentally recreate the process and also vary it, if we were to see its components and, above all, their relation to one another with plastic clarity before us—on the one hand, the *degree* of jealousy and of rage present at the moment; on the other, the *degree* of fear of punishment and of pity—then we would acknowledge that wanting to commit murder and committing murder are necessary results. But as it is we merely see that, on the one hand, jealousy and related feelings, and, on the other, pity and the idea of God, were present in the murderer. But, since we do not see the particular relation in which the sensations and thoughts stood to one another at the moment of the deed, we simply think that the *one* side could have produced acts of will and actions as well as the *other*, that the murderer could, at the moment when he wanted to commit and did commit murder, just as well have willed and acted differently, say compassionately.

It is the same if we ourselves are the person who acts. We, too, think "I could have willed differently." Let us illustrate this by yet another example. Yesterday afternoon at 6:03 o'clock I sold my house. Why? Because I wished to do so. But why did I wish to do so? Because my intention to change my place of residence, and other circumstances, caused my act of will. But was I compelled to will? Could I not have postponed the sale or forgone it altogether? It seems so to me, because I do not see the particular relation in which my thoughts, sensations, and impressions stood to one another yesterday afternoon at 6:03 o'clock.

Thus: we do not see the sufficient cause (either not at all, in the case of unimportant matters; or inadequately, in the case of important ones); consequently it does not exist for us; consequently we think that our volition and our actions were not causally determined at all, that we could just as well have willed and acted differently. No one would say "I could have willed differently" if he could see his act of will and its causes displayed plastically before him, in an experiment permitting repetition.

But who are the mistaken "we" of whom we are speaking here? Patently the author does not consider himself to be one of them. Does he, then, set himself, along with a few fellow philosophers, apart from the rest of mankind, regarding them as ignorant of the truth? Well, it really is not the case that mankind has always concerned itself with the problem of the freedom of the will and only a small part arrived at the result that the will is not free; rather, in precivilized ages no one, and in civilized ages almost no one, concerned himself with this problem. But of the few who did address themselves to this question, as the history of philosophy teaches us, almost all recognized that there is no freedom of the will. The others became victims of the illusion described above, without ever coming to grips with the problem in its general form (is the will subject to the law of causality or not?) ....

5. Determinism Is Inconsistent with Judgments of Moral Responsibility

We hold ourselves and others responsible without taking into account the problem of the freedom of the will.

Experience shows that, if someone has lied or murdered, he is told that he has acted reprehensibly and deserves punishment. Whether his action is uncaused or whether, like the other processes in nature, it is subject to the law of causality—how would people come to raise such questions in the ordinary course of their lives? Or has anyone ever heard of a case in which people talking about an act of murder, a lie, or an act of self-sacrifice discussed these actions in terms of the freedom of the will? It is the same if we ourselves are the person who acted. We say to ourselves "Oh, if only I had not done this! Oh, if only I had acted differently!" or "I have acted laudably, as one should act." At best a philosopher here or there chances upon the question whether our actions are causally determined or not, certainly not the rest of mankind.

Suppose, however, that someone's attention is directed to the fact that the will is not free. At first it will be very difficult to make this plausible to him. His volition is suspended from threads that are too nearly invisible, and that is why he comes to think that it is not causally determined at all. At last, however—so we shall assume—he does come to recognize that actions are effects, that their causes are thoughts and impressions, that these must likewise be viewed as effects, and so on. How will he then judge these actions? Will he continue to maintain that murder is to be punished by *reprisal* and that benevolent actions are to be considered *meritorious*? By no means. Rather, the first conclusion that he will—validly— draw from his newly acquired insight is that we cannot hold anyone responsible. "*Tout comprendre c'est tout pardonner*";[11] no one can be made to answer for an *effect*.

In order to illustrate this important truth, that whoever considers intentions to be effects will cease to assign merit or blame for them, let us resume discussion of the examples above. From early childhood on the Bogo … has learned to praise murder. The praiseworthiness of such an action already penetrated the consciousness of the child as a secondary meaning of the word "murder," and afterward it was confirmed by every impression: his gods and his fellow men praise murder. In consequence he involuntarily judges acts of murder to be praiseworthy, no matter whether it was he himself or someone else who committed them. Let us assume, now, that a philosopher had succeeded in persuading the Bogos that the act of murder and the intention to practice cruelty are causally determined. Then their judgment would undergo an essential modification.

To conceive of actions and intentions as causally determined, after all, means the following. We go back in the history of the individual, say to his birth, and investigate which of his characteristics are inborn and to what causes they are due.[12] Then, ever guided by the law of causality, we trace the development or transformation of these properties; we see how impressions, teachings, and examples come to him

and, if his inborn constitution has an affinity for them, are taken up and transformed by it, otherwise passing by without leaving a trace. Finally we recognize that the keystone, the necessary result of this course of development, is the desire to commit murder and the act of murder.

A Bogo who looks upon murder and the intention to practice cruelty in this way—that is, as an effect—will say that it is impossible to regard them as meritorious.

But will he now look upon these actions with apathy, devoid of all feeling? By no means. He will still consider them to be pleasant or unpleasant, agreeable or disagreeable.

When the action is directed against himself, he will perceive it as pleasant or as unpleasant; the prospect of being murdered is unpleasant for everyone, whether he considers the action to be causally determined or uncaused.

Similarly our liking or dislike for the character of a human being will persist even if we regard it as the result of causes. To say that I find someone agreeable means that I am drawn to him; I like him. Of a landscape, too, one says that it is agreeable, and, just as this liking cannot be diminished even if we consider the trees, meadows, and hills to be the result of causes, so our liking for the character of a human being is not diminished if we regard it *sub specie necessitatis*. Hence to the Bogo who has come to see that murder is causally determined it is still agreeable or disagreeable. Usually he will consider it to be agreeable. He will say that it warms the cockles of his heart to observe such an action; it accords with his wild temperament, as yet untouched by civilization. Therefore he will, in view of the necessity, suspend only the specifically moral practice of regarding it as meritorious. But his liking may become love, and even esteem and reverence. It will be objected, however, that "I revere a mode of behavior" entails "I consider it meritorious for a person to behave in that way," and similarly for esteem. To be sure, the words "reverence" and "esteem" *frequently* have this meaning, and *to the extent that they do* a determinist would cease using them. But all words that denote human feelings have not only one, but several meanings. They have, if I may express it in that way, a harem of meanings,

---

11   "To understand all is to forgive all" (old French saying).

12   [Author's note] An investigation as detailed as that is, of course, never possible in practice.

and they couple now with this one, now with that one. So, if I "revere" someone, it means also that I esteem him, that he impresses me, and that I wish to be like him…. Reverence and esteem in *this* sense can coexist with determinism.

Hence the Bogo who conceives of the intention to practice cruelty and the act of murder as effects can nevertheless consider them to be agreeable or disagreeable, and in a certain sense he can also have esteem and reverence for them, but he will not regard them as meritorious.

Let us now consider the act of murder at high levels of civilization. Civilization, as it progressed, stigmatized murder and threatened penalties for it on earth and in heaven. This censure already penetrates the consciousness of the child as a secondary meaning of the word "murder" and afterward is confirmed through every impression. All the people whom one knows, all the books that one reads, the state with its institutions, pulpit and stage always use "murder" in a censorious sense. That is how it comes to be that we involuntarily declare an act of murder to be blameworthy, be it that others or that we ourselves, driven by passion, committed it. Whether the action was determined by causes or uncaused—that question is raised neither by the person who acted nor by the uninvolved observers. But *if* it is raised, if someone considers the act of murder *sub specie necessitatis*, then he ceases to regard it as blameworthy. He will then no longer want to see punishment in the proper sense—suffering as retribution—meted out for it, but merely punishment as a safety measure.[13] The feelings of liking and dislike, however, will continue to exist even then. On the whole, someone raised at a high level of civilization will have a feeling of dislike for acts of murder; he will not feel drawn to whoever commits it; he will not like him. For such an act does not accord with his temperament, which was formed as he was engaged in non-violent occupations. In spite of the recognition that the action was necessary, this dislike can at times grow to revulsion, and even to contempt—given that the latter notion is stripped of the specifically moral elements that it contains (the

attribution of blame). It will then mean something like this: I do not want to be like that person.

The situation is the same in the case of benevolent actions and those performed out of a sense of duty; we cease to regard them as meritorious if we consider them to be effects. Let us look more closely at actions performed out of a sense of duty. To say that someone acts out of a sense of duty means that he performs an action, perhaps contrary to his inclinations, because his conscience commands him to do it. But how does conscience come to issue such commandments? As follows: with some actions (and intentions) there is linked for us from early childhood on a categorical "thou shalt do (or have) them"; for example, "you *should* help everyone as much as possible." If someone then makes this habitual judgment into the guiding principle of his behavior, if he helps a person because his conscience commands "thou *shalt* help thy fellow man," then he is acting "out of a sense of duty".… If we want to consider such an action from the point of view of eternity and necessity, we shall have to proceed as follows: we investigate (1) the constitution of the child who receives the teaching "thou shalt help," (2) the constitution of those who give it to him. The child absorbing this doctrine has some inborn constitution of nerves, of blood, of imagination, and of reason. The commandment "thou shalt help" is impressed upon this substance with some degree of insistence; the deity, heaven, hell, approval of his fellow men and of his own conscience—these ideas are presented to him, depending upon his teachers, as being more or less majestic and inspiring. And the child transforms them with greater or lesser intensity, depending upon his receptivity. The ultimate constitution of a man, the preponderance within him of the sense of duty over his own desires, is in any case a necessary result, a product of his inborn constitution and the impressions received. To someone who contemplates this, such a temperament may, to be sure, still seem agreeable (perhaps because he himself is or would like to be similarly constituted), but no one can regard as *meritorious* behavior that he conceives to be an *effect*.

But what if we ourselves are the person who acted? Then the circumstances are analogous; then, too, liking and dislike remain, while the attribution of merit or blame (the "pangs of conscience") disappears.

---

13   [Author's note] Punishments are causes that prevent the repetition of the action punished.

Our own action, too, can remain agreeable or become disagreeable for us after it has occurred. It is agreeable if the disposition from which we acted persists after the action; it will become disagreeable if we change our frame of mind. Suppose, for example, that we have acted vengefully and are still in the same mood; then the act of revenge is still agreeable, whether we conceive it to be an effect or not. If, however, a feeling of pity takes the place of our desire for revenge, then we come to dislike our action; we cannot stand our earlier self—the less so, the more pronounced our feeling of pity is. The reflection that the action is an effect in no way affects this feeling of dislike, perhaps of disgust, or even of revulsion for ourselves. We say to ourselves that the desire for revenge was, to be sure, necessarily stronger than the ideas and impressions that stood in its way, hence the action took place necessarily, too; but now it happens that pity is necessarily present, and, along with it, regrets that we acted as we did....

6. Can We Abandon Judgments of Moral Responsibility?

But is it really possible to shake off feelings of guilt so easily? Do they disappear, like a spook, when the magic word *effect* is pronounced? Is the situation with respect to this feeling not quite like that with regard to dislike? It was, to be sure, necessary that I took revenge, but now I necessarily feel dislike for my own action, along with guilt. I can no more prevent the onset of the one feeling than of the other. But if the feeling of guilt asserts itself in spite of the recognition that actions are effects, should we not suspect that our holding others responsible, too, will persist in spite of this insight? Did we commit an error somewhere? Is it that responsibility and necessity do not exclude each other? The situation is as follows. The reason why we assign moral praise to some actions and moral censure to others has already been mentioned repeatedly. Censure already penetrates the consciousness of the child as a secondary meaning of the words "murder," "theft," "vengefulness," and "pleasure in another's pain," and praise as a secondary meaning of the words "benevolence" and "mercy." That is why censure seems to him to be a constituent part of murder, and praise, of benevolence. At a later point

in his life, perhaps in his twentieth year, the insight comes to him from somewhere that all actions are effects and therefore cannot earn merit or blame. What can this poor little insight accomplish against the accumulated habits of a lifetime of judging? The habit of mind of assigning blame for actions like murder makes it very difficult to think of them without this judgment. It is all very well for reason to tell us that we may not assign blame for such actions, since they are effects—our habit of judging, which has become a feeling, will see to it that it is done anyway. But—let habit confront habit! Suppose that, whenever someone involuntarily wants to assign blame or merit for an action, he ascends to the point of view of eternity and necessity. He then regards the action as the necessary result of [a chain of events stretching back into] the infinite past. Through that way of looking at things the *instinctive* association between the action and the judgment will be severed, if not the first time, then perhaps by the thousandth. Such a man will shed the habit of assigning blame or merit for any action whatsoever.

In fact, of course, human beings almost never behave like that; this way of looking at things is completely foreign to them. Furthermore, human beings determine their actions by considering whether they will make them happy or unhappy; but shedding the habit of making judgments [of moral responsibility] would hardly increase their happiness....

The situation with respect to a person's character is no different from that with respect to his individual actions. *Customarily* one assigns blame or merit, whether to himself or to others, for a single action: a single act of cheating or of giving offense. But *sometimes* we go back from the action to its source, to a person's character. In reality, of course, character, in its broadest as well as its smallest traits, is just as necessary as an individual action; it is the product of [a chain of events stretching back into] the infinite past, be it that it was inherited in its entirety or that it was formed in part during the individual's lifetime. But with regard to character, too, hardly anyone adopts this point of view. Just as in the case of particular actions, character is regarded neither as free nor as necessary; that is to say, people do not raise the question at all whether the law of causality is applicable also to actions and character. Hence one assigns blame and merit for character as for actions, though they are effects; for one does not see that they are effects. If one sees this, if one regards character *sub specie necessitatis*, then he ceases to assign blame or merit for it. Liking and dislike, on the other hand, nevertheless persist even then: a character closely related to mine will garner my liking, my love, and perhaps even, in the sense mentioned above, my esteem and reverence—whether I conceive of it as an effect or not.

Hence we assign blame or merit for character and actions out of the habit of judging, without concerning ourselves with the question whether they are causally determined or not. We cease to assign blame or merit for character and actions as soon as we recognize that they are causally determined (if we ignore the remnants of our habits).

Let us recapitulate: the character, the intentions, and the actions of every human being are effects, and it is impossible to assign blame or merit for effects.

C.A. CAMPBELL

On Selfhood and Godhood

Who Was C.A. Campbell?

Charles Arthur Campbell (known to his friends as Arthur) was born in Scotland in 1897 and died there in 1974. He served with the Tenth Border Regiment during the First World War but was invalided out in 1917: his injuries put an end to what might have been a successful athletic career and left him plagued with intermittently serious health problems for the rest of his life. After attending university at Glasgow and at Balliol College, Oxford, he lectured in the moral philosophy department of Glasgow University. From 1932 to 1938 he was professor of philosophy at the University of North Wales, Bangor, and then returned to Glasgow where he was appointed to the chair of Logic and Rhetoric, a position which he held until retirement in 1961.

Campbell's main publications were *Scepticism and Construction* (1931), *Moral Intuition and the Principle of Self-Realisation* (1948), *On Selfhood and Godhood* (1957), and *In Defence of Free Will* (1967). *On Selfhood and Godhood* has been called (by the philosopher H.D. Lewis) "one of the most impressive defences of theism ever attempted."

It's fair to say that, for much of his career, Campbell was considered rather old fashioned and out of step with the spirit of the philosophical times. As Campbell writes in the preface to *On Selfhood and Godhood*,

Readers of this book will not be long in discovering my inability to do obeisance to the twin gods of so much recent British philosophy—linguisticism and empiricism.... Perhaps it was a little naïve of the older generation of contemporary British philosophers to be so taken aback by [the] apparently total absence [of readiness to re-examine their first principles] in logical positivists and later heralds of a new dawn. Perhaps also, however, it was pardonable that philosophers whose reflections upon the premises of latter-day empiricism and of linguisticism left them profoundly sceptical of their validity should have been disquieted, incensed, or infuriated—according to temperament—by the practice that prevailed in most modernist quarters of automatically dismissing as worthless all writings which did not conform to modernist preconceptions (on the assumption, apparently, that their authors could only be philosophic Rip Van Winkles talking in their sleep).... The more tranquil and judicial assessment of gains and losses which is now practicable, and of which there are some instructive examples already in being, must surely be welcomed by all who do not think it priggish to believe that philosophy is neither a word-game, nor a social accomplishment, nor a gladiatorial exhibition, but, quite simply, the rational pursuit of such truth as is attainable by human minds about the general character of the universe in which we find ourselves.

H.D. Lewis described Campbell as "a peculiarly sharp controversialist, [but] he was also totally devoid of rancour or bitterness."

The lecture reprinted here is a classic statement of one important version of the *libertarian* position on free will: that, although most events are causally determined, some human actions—those we do, not from personal inclination, but from moral duty—are not determined by anything except moral law. That is, we are free because, if we choose to, we can do what we *ought* to do as opposed to what we *want* to do.

What Is the Structure of This Reading?

Campbell begins his lecture by stressing the importance of carefully and precisely formulating the problem of free will, before we can see what would count as a solution to it. He defines the kind of freedom at issue: a freedom belonging to "inner acts," of which the self is the sole author, and which are such that the agent, categorically, could have acted otherwise. On the other hand, it is not necessary that these acts be morally good ones; if we are free, then we are free to choose to behave immorally. Having defined the kind of free will he is concerned with, Campbell goes on to discuss (from section 5 onwards) whether such freedom exists in reality. He defends the view that it *is* real, though its area of functioning is limited to moral decisions made in response to situations of moral temptation. He argues by:

a) Claiming we have "phenomenological" evidence for the existence of this kind of free will—that we know from our own experience that we sometimes act out of duty, against our own inclinations;

b) Arguing that if this result conflicts with *theoretical* reasons for doubting free will, it is not necessarily the phenomenological—practical—side that must concede defeat; and

c) Rejecting what he considers the two main theoretical objections to the existence of genuinely free will: the claim that our free will is inconsistent with facts about human predictability; and the claim that the free-will doctrine is unintelligible, since it apparently disconnects 'our' actions from our selves.

Some Useful Background Information

1. Campbell rejected what he calls a "naturalistic" study of the human mind: i.e., he rejected the assumption that the human mind is just one among all the other objects in the natural world, and that it is fully open to study and explanation using the methods of the natural sciences. His main objection to naturalizing the mind is captured by the following quotation (from Lecture III of *On Selfhood and Godhood*):

The naturalistic standpoint, the standpoint proper to, and indeed alone possible for, the study of physical objects, is the standpoint of the external observer. But that standpoint is bound to be inadequate to the study of that which is something not merely for an external observer, but also *for itself*. It will not afford us even a glimpse of this latter aspect of the thing's being; and in the degree that this latter aspect is important to the thing's being, any account which abstracts from it is bound to result in travesty.... Accordingly it seems to me clear that the naturalistic approach to the study of the mind, abstracting wholly from the standpoint of the experiencing subject, which can alone throw light upon what the mind is for itself, is in principle hopelessly incapable of revealing to us mental experience as it really is, and as, in our less doctrinaire moments, we all believe it to be.

2. Although Campbell does not say so explicitly, when he defines the problem of free will in this selection he sets it up as an "incompatibilist" thesis. He argues that the existence of (the right kind of) free will is *incompatible* with the claim that all of our actions are causally determined.

Suggestions for Critical Reflection

1. How accurate is Campbell's characterization of the free-will problem? Are actions genuinely free *only* if they are inner acts for which the agent is solely responsible and which are such that the agent could (categorically) have chosen not to do them?

2. Does Campbell have to admit that most of our choices or actions are *not* free? That is, do we exercise free will, on his account, when we do what we want—when we do things without exerting any "moral effort"? If not, is this a serious blow to his account of free will?

3. How much legitimate evidence for freedom of the will comes from the fact that we *feel* free? After all, don't people sometimes sincerely, but falsely, believe they are acting freely (e.g., when they are under the influence of hypnotism, or suffering from a brain disorder)?

4. Campbell passes lightly over "criticisms based upon the universality of causal law as a supposed postulate of science." Is he right to do so? Campbell tacitly appeals to the probabilistic mathematics of quantum mechanics to suggest that even scientists are uncertain about the universality of causality. Does this help his case? Is there an important difference between quantum randomness and the kind of freedom Campbell wants to defend?

5. "A free will is *ex hypothesi* the sort of thing of which the request for an *explanation* is absurd." Do you agree?

6. Campbell argues that, from the "inner standpoint" it is clear we sometimes do things that go against our own character: roughly, we do things we really do not want to do. But is this really true? Or is the internal conflict we sometimes feel really a conflict between different things we *do* want to do—such as visiting our sick mother in hospital or going skiing—and our inner struggles just a matter of finding out what we want to do *most*?

Suggestions for Further Reading

The two books in which C.A. Campbell paid most attention to the problem of free will are *On Selfhood and Godhood* (George Allen & Unwin, 1957) and *In Defence of Free Will* (George Allen & Unwin, 1967). One of his articles, which is frequently anthologized, is "Is 'Free Will' a Pseudo-Problem?" *Mind* 60 (1951). In this article Campbell criticizes compatibilist accounts of free will. Ideas similar to those expressed by Campbell can be found in the writings of the eighteenth-century Scottish "common sense" philosopher Thomas Reid. See his *Essays on the Active Powers of the Human Mind* (1788, reprinted by MIT Press, 1969).

Articles that defend or are generally sympathetic to Campbell's line include Keith Lehrer's "Can We Know That We Have Free Will by Introspection?" *Journal of Philosophy* 57 (1960); "The Moral and Religious Philosophy of C.A. Campbell" by H.P. Owen, *Religious Studies* 3 (1967); and Betty Powell's "Uncharacteristic Actions," *Mind* 68 (1959). Three articles which attack Campbell's views are Phillip Gosselin "C.A. Campbell's Effort of Will Argument" *Religious Studies* 13 (1977); J.J.C. Smart, "Free-Will, Praise and Blame," *Mind* 70 (1961); and Edward Walter, "Is Libertarianism Logically Coherent?" *Philosophy and Phenomenological Research* 38 (1978). A good discussion of the evidence for freedom from introspection is Douglas Browning's "The Feeling of Freedom," *Review of Metaphysics* 18 (1964).

On Selfhood and Godhood

Lecture IX, "Has the Self Free Will?"[1]

1.

… It is something of a truism that in philosophic enquiry the exact formulation of a problem often takes one a long way on the road to its solution. In the case of the Free Will problem I think there is a rather special need of careful formulation. For there are many sorts of human freedom; and it can easily happen that one wastes a great deal of labour in proving or disproving a freedom which has almost nothing to do with the freedom which is at issue in the traditional problem of Free Will. The abortiveness of so much of the argument for and against Free Will in contemporary philosophical literature seems to me due in the main to insufficient pains being taken over the preliminary definition of the problem. There is, indeed, one outstanding exception, Professor Broad's[2] brilliant inaugural lecture entitled, 'Determinism, Indeterminism, and Libertarianism,'[3] in which forty-three pages are devoted to setting out the problem, as against seven to its solution! I confess that the solution does not seem to myself to follow upon the formulation quite as easily as all that:[4] but Professor Broad's

eminent example fortifies me in my decision to give here what may seem at first sight a disproportionate amount of time to the business of determining the essential characteristics of the kind of freedom with which the traditional problem is concerned.

Fortunately we can at least make a beginning with a certain amount of confidence. It is not seriously disputable that the kind of freedom in question is the freedom which is commonly recognised to be in some sense a precondition of moral responsibility. Clearly, it is on account of this integral connection with moral responsibility that such exceptional importance has always been felt to attach to the Free Will problem. But in what precise sense is free will a precondition of moral responsibility, and thus a postulate of the moral life in general? This is an exceedingly troublesome question; but until we have satisfied ourselves about the answer to it, we are not in a position to state, let alone decide, the question whether 'Free Will' in its traditional, ethical, significance is a reality.

Our first business, then, is to ask, exactly what kind of freedom is it which is required for moral responsibility? And as to method of procedure in this inquiry, there seems to me to be no real choice. I know of only one method that carries with it any hope of success; viz.[5] the critical comparison of those acts for which, on due reflection, we deem it proper to attribute moral praise or blame to the agents, with those acts for which, on due reflection, we deem such judgments to be improper. The ultimate touchstone, as I see it, can only be our moral consciousness as it manifests itself in our more critical and considered moral judgments. The 'linguistic' approach by way of the analysis of moral *sentences* seems to me, despite its present popularity, to be an almost infallible method for reaching wrong results in the moral field; but I must reserve what I have to say about this.

2.

The first point to note is that the freedom at issue (as indeed the very name 'Free *Will* Problem' indicates) pertains primarily not to overt acts but to inner acts. The nature of things has decreed that, save in the case of one's self, it is only overt acts which one can direct-

---

1   This selection is taken from Chapter IX of *On Selfhood and Godhood* (pages 158–179), London: HarperCollins Publishers Ltd. (Originally published by George Allen & Unwin, 1957.) Copyright © C.A. Campbell, 1957. Reprinted by permission of Taylor & Francis Books UK. The book is based on the Gifford Lectures which Campbell gave at the University of St. Andrews, in Scotland, between 1953 and 1955.

2   C.D. Broad was the well-respected professor of moral philosophy at Cambridge from 1933 to 1953. Broad's typical method was a detailed and careful elaboration of all the possible answers to a particular philosophical question, and then a tentative suggestion as to which of them was most plausible.

3   [Author's note] Reprinted in *Ethics and the History of Philosophy, Selected Essays*.

4   [Author's note] I have explained the grounds for my dissent from Broad's final conclusion on pp. 27 ff. of *In Defence of Free Will* (Jackson Son & Co., 1938).

5   Namely, that is (from the Latin *videlicet*).

ly observe. But a very little reflection serves to show that in our moral judgments upon others their overt acts are regarded as significant only insofar as they are the expression of inner acts. We do not consider the acts of a robot to be morally responsible acts; nor do we consider the acts of a man to be so save in so far as they are distinguishable from those of a robot by reflecting an inner life of choice. Similarly, from the other side, if we are satisfied (as we may on occasion be, at least in the case of ourselves) that a person has definitely elected to follow a course which he believes to be wrong, but has been prevented by external circumstances from translating his inner choice into an overt act, we still regard him as morally blameworthy. Moral freedom, then, pertains to *inner* acts.

The next point seems at first sight equally obvious and uncontroversial; but, as we shall see, it has awkward implications if we are in real earnest with it (as almost nobody is). It is the simple point that the act must be one of which the person judged can be regarded as the *sole* author. It seems plain enough that if there are any *other* determinants of the act, external to the self, to that extent the act is not an act which the *self* determines, and to that extent not an act for which the self can be held morally responsible. The self is only part-author of the act, and his moral responsibility can logically extend only to those elements within the act (assuming for the moment that these can be isolated) of which he is the *sole* author.

The awkward implications of this apparent truism will be readily appreciated. For, if we are mindful of the influences exerted by heredity and environment, we may well feel some doubt whether there is any act of will at all of which one can truly say that the self is sole author, sole determinant. No man has a voice in determining the raw material of impulses and capacities that constitute his hereditary endowment, and no man has more than a very partial control of the material and social environment in which he is destined to live his life. Yet it would be manifestly absurd to deny that these two factors do constantly and profoundly affect the nature of a man's choices. That this is so we all of us recognise in our moral judgments when we 'make allowances,' as we say, for a bad heredity or a vicious environment, and acknowledge in the victim of them a diminished moral

responsibility for evil courses. Evidently we do *try*, in our moral judgments, however crudely, to praise or blame a man only in respect of that of which we can regard him as *wholly* the author. And evidently we do recognise that, for a man to be the author of an act in the full sense required for moral responsibility, it is not enough merely that he 'wills' or 'chooses' the act: since even the most unfortunate victim of heredity or environment does, as a rule, 'will' what he does. It is significant, however, that the ordinary man, though well enough aware of the influence upon choices of heredity and environment, does not feel obliged thereby to give up his assumption that moral predicates *are* somehow applicable. Plainly he still believes that there is *something* for which a man is morally responsible, something of which we can fairly say that he is the sole author. *What is this something?* To that question commonsense is not ready with an explicit answer—though an answer is, I think, implicit in the line which its moral judgments take. I shall do what I can to give an explicit answer later in this lecture. Meantime it must suffice to observe that, if we are to be true to the deliverances of our moral consciousness, it is very difficult to deny that *sole* authorship is a necessary condition of the morally responsible act.

Thirdly we come to a point over which much recent controversy has raged. We may approach it by raising the following question. Granted an act of which the agent is sole author, does this 'sole authorship' suffice to make the act a morally free act? We may be inclined to think that it does, until we contemplate the possibility that an act of which the agent is sole author might conceivably occur as a necessary expression of the agent's nature; the way in which, e.g., some philosophers have supposed the Divine act of creation to occur. This consideration excites a legitimate doubt; for it is far from easy to see how a person can be regarded as a proper subject for moral praise or blame in respect of an act which he *cannot help* performing—even if it be his own 'nature' which necessitates it. Must we not recognise it as a condition of the morally free act that the agent 'could have acted otherwise' than he in fact did? It is true, indeed, that we sometimes praise or blame a man for an act about which we are prepared to say, in the light of our knowledge of his established character, that he 'could no other.' But I think that a little reflection shows that in such cases we are not praising or blaming the man strictly for what he does *now* (or at any rate we ought not to be), but rather for those past acts of his which have generated the firm habit of mind from which his *present* act follows 'necessarily.' In other words, our praise and blame, so far as justified, are really retrospective, being directed not to the agent *qua*[6] performing *this* act, but to the agent *qua* performing those past acts which have built up his present character, and in respect to which we presume that he *could* have acted otherwise, that there really *were* open possibilities before him. These cases, therefore, seem to me to constitute no valid exception to what I must take to be the rule, viz. that a man can be morally praised or blamed for an act only if he could have acted otherwise.

Now philosophers today are fairly well agreed that it is a postulate[7] of the morally responsible act that the agent 'could have acted otherwise' in *some* sense of that phrase. But sharp differences of opinion have arisen over the way in which the phrase ought to be interpreted. There is a strong disposition to water down its apparent meaning by insisting that it is not (as a postulate of moral responsibility) to be understood as a straightforward categorical proposition, but rather as a disguised hypothetical proposition.[8] All that we really require to be assured of, in order to justify our holding X morally responsible for an act, is, we are told, that X could have acted otherwise *if* he had *chosen* otherwise (Moore, Stevenson[9]); or perhaps that X could have acted otherwise *if* he had had a different character, or *if* he had been placed in different circumstances.

I think it is easy to understand, and even, in a measure, to sympathise with, the motives which induce

6   *Qua* means "as being," "in the capacity of."

7   A presupposition or basic principle.

8   A categorical proposition asserts that something is true; a hypothetical proposition says only that something is true *if* something else is. It's the difference between, for example, "Billy is a good boy" and "Billy is a good boy if someone is watching."

9   G.E. Moore (1873–1958) and C.L. Stevenson (1908–1979). Both philosophers are known for their (widely divergent) moral theories.

philosophers to offer these counter-interpretations. It is not just the fact that 'X could have acted otherwise,' as a bald categorical statement, is incompatible with the universal sway of causal law—though this is, to some philosophers, a serious stone of stumbling. The more widespread objection is that it at least looks as though it were incompatible with that causal continuity of an agent's character with his conduct which is implied when we believe (surely with justice) that we can often tell the sort of thing a man will do from our knowledge of the sort of man he is.

We shall have to make our accounts with that particular difficulty later. At this stage I wish merely to show that neither of the hypothetical propositions suggested—and I think the same could be shown for *any* hypothetical alternative—is an acceptable substitute for the categorical proposition 'X could have acted otherwise' as the presupposition of moral responsibility.

Let us look first at the earlier suggestion—'X could have acted otherwise *if* he had chosen otherwise.' Now clearly there are a great many acts with regard to which we are entirely satisfied that the agent is thus situated. We are often perfectly sure that—for this is all it amounts to—if X had chosen otherwise, the circumstances presented no external obstacle to the translation of that choice into action. For example, we often have no doubt at all that X, who in point of fact told a lie, could have told the truth *if* he had so chosen. But does our confidence on this score allay all legitimate doubts about whether X is really blameworthy? Does it entail that X is free in the sense required for moral responsibility? Surely not. The obvious question immediately arises: 'But *could* X have *chosen* otherwise than he did?' It is doubt about the true answer to *that* question which leads most people to doubt the reality of moral responsibility. Yet on this crucial question the hypothetical proposition which is offered as a sufficient statement of the condition justifying the ascription of moral responsibility gives us no information whatsoever.

Indeed this hypothetical substitute for the categorical 'X could have acted otherwise' seems to me to lack all plausibility unless one contrives to forget why it is, after all, that we ever come to feel fundamental doubts about man's moral responsibility. Such doubts are born, surely, when one becomes aware of certain reputable world-views in religion or philosophy, or of certain reputable scientific beliefs, which in their several ways imply that man's actions are necessitated, and thus could not be otherwise than they in fact are. But clearly a doubt so based is not even touched by the recognition that a man could very often act otherwise *if* he so chose. That proposition is entirely compatible with the necessitarian theories which generate our doubt: indeed it is this very compatibility that has recommended it to some philosophers, who are reluctant to give up either moral responsibility or Determinism. The proposition which we *must* be able to affirm if moral praise or blame of X is to be justified is the categorical proposition that X could have acted otherwise because—not if—he could have chosen otherwise; or, since it is essentially the inner side of the act that matters, the proposition simply that X could have chosen otherwise.

For the second of the alternative formulae suggested we cannot spare more than a few moments. But its inability to meet the demands it is required to meet is almost transparent. 'X could have acted otherwise,' as a statement of a precondition of X's moral responsibility, really means (we are told) 'X could have acted otherwise *if* he were differently constituted, or *if* he had been placed in different circumstances.' It seems a sufficient reply to this to point out that the person whose moral responsibility is at issue is X; a specific individual, in a specific set of circumstances. It is totally irrelevant to X's moral responsibility that we should be able to say that some person differently constituted from X, or X in a different set of circumstances, could have done something different from what X did.

3.

Let me, then, briefly sum up the answer at which we have arrived to our question about the kind of freedom required to justify moral responsibility. It is that a man can be said to exercise free will in a morally significant sense only in so far as his chosen act is one of which he is the sole cause or author, and only if—in the straightforward, categorical sense of the phrase—he 'could have chosen otherwise.'

I confess that this answer is in some ways a disconcerting one; disconcerting, because most of us,

however objective we are in the actual conduct of our thinking, would *like* to be able to believe that moral responsibility is real: whereas the freedom required for moral responsibility, on the analysis we have given, is certainly far more difficult to establish than the freedom required on the analyses we found ourselves obliged to reject. If, e.g., moral freedom entails only that I could have acted otherwise *if* I had chosen otherwise, there is no real 'problem' about it at all. I am 'free' in the normal case where there is no external obstacle to prevent my translating the alternative choice into action, and not free in other cases. Still less is there a problem if all that moral freedom entails is that I could have acted otherwise *if* I had been a differently constituted person, or been in different circumstances. Clearly I am *always* free in *this* sense of freedom. But, as I have argued, these so-called 'freedoms' fail to give us the pre-conditions of moral responsibility, and hence leave the freedom of the traditional free-will problem, the freedom that people are really concerned about, precisely where it was.

4.

Another interpretation of freedom which I am bound to reject on the same general ground, i.e., that it is just not the kind of freedom that is relevant to moral responsibility[10], is the old idealist[10] view which identifies the *free* will with the *rational* will; the rational will in its turn being identified with the will which wills the moral law in whole-hearted, single-minded obedience to it. This view is still worth at least a passing mention, if only because it has recently been resurrected in an interesting work by Professor A.E. Teale.[11] Moreover, I cannot but feel a certain nostalgic tenderness for a view in which I myself was (so to speak) philosophically cradled. The almost apostolic fervour with which my revered nursing-mother, the late Sir Henry Jones, was wont to impart it to his charges, and, hardly less, his ill-concealed scorn for

---

10   By "idealist" here, Campbell means the view that reality is, in some sense, fundamentally mental or spiritual in nature. He is thinking mainly of Immanuel Kant's "transcendental idealism."

11   [Author's note] *Kantian Ethics*.

ignoble natures (like my own) which still hankered after a free will in the old 'vulgar' sense, are vividly recalled for me in Professor Teale's stirring pages.

The true interpretation of free will, according to Professor Teale, the interpretation to which Kant, despite occasional back-slidings, adhered in his better moments, is that 'the will is free in the degree that it is informed and disciplined by the moral principle.'[12]

Now this is a perfectly intelligible sense of the word 'free'—or at any rate it can be made so with a little explanatory comment which Professor Teale well supplies but for which there is here no space. But clearly it is a very different sort of freedom from that which is at issue in the traditional problem of free will. This idealist 'freedom' sponsored by Teale belongs, on his own showing, only to the self in respect of its *good* willing. The freedom with which the traditional problem is concerned, inasmuch as it is the freedom presupposed by moral responsibility, must belong to the self in respect of its *bad*, no less than its *good*, willing. It is, in fact, the freedom to decide between genuinely open alternatives of good and bad willing.

Professor Teale, of course, is not unaware that the freedom he favours differs from freedom as traditionally understood. He recognises the traditional concept under its Kantian title of 'elective' freedom. But he leaves the reader in no kind of doubt about his disbelief in both the reality and the value of this elective freedom to do, or forbear from doing, one's duty.

The question of the reality of elective freedom I shall be dealing with shortly; and it will occupy us to the end of the lecture. At the moment I am concerned only with its value, and with the rival view that all that matters for the moral life is the 'rational' freedom which a man has in the degree that his will is 'informed and disciplined by the moral principle.' I confess that to myself the verdict on the rival view seems plain and inescapable. No amount of verbal ingenuity or argumentative convolutions can obscure the fact that it is in flat contradiction to the implications of moral responsibility. The point at issue is really perfectly straightforward. If, as this idealist theory maintains, my acting in defiance of what I deem to be my duty is not a 'free' act in *any* sense, let alone in

the sense that 'I could have acted otherwise,' then I cannot be morally blameworthy, and that is all there is to it. Nor, for that matter, is the idealist entitled to say that I am morally praiseworthy if I act dutifully; for although that act is a 'free' act in the idealist sense, it is on his own avowal not free in the sense that 'I could have acted otherwise.'

It seems to me idle, therefore, to pretend that if one has to give up freedom in the traditional elective sense one is not giving up anything important. What we are giving up is, quite simply, the reality of the moral life. I recognise that to a certain type of religious nature (as well as, by an odd meeting of extremes, to a certain type of secular nature) that does not appear to matter so very much; but, for myself, I still think it sufficiently important to make it well worthwhile enquiring seriously into the possibility that the elective freedom upon which it rests may be real after all.

5.

That brings me to the second, and more constructive, part of this lecture. From now on I shall be considering whether it is reasonable to believe that man does in fact possess a free will of the kind specified in the first part of the lecture. If so, just how and where within the complex fabric of the volitional[13] life are we to locate it?—for although free will must presumably belong (if anywhere) to the volitional side of human experience, it is pretty clear from the way in which we have been forced to define it that it does not pertain simply to volition as such; not even to all volitions that are commonly dignified with the name of 'choices.' It has been, I think, one of the more serious impediments to profitable discussion of the Free Will problem that Libertarians and Determinists alike have so often failed to appreciate the comparatively narrow area within which the free will that is necessary to 'save' morality is required to operate. It goes without saying that this failure has been gravely prejudicial to the case for Libertarianism. I attach a good deal of importance, therefore, to the problem of locating free will correctly within the volitional orbit.

---

12   [Author's note] *Op. cit.*, p. 261.

13   "Volitional" means concerned with volitions, which are exercises of the will; consciously doing one thing rather than another.

Its solution forestalls and annuls, I believe, some of the more tiresome clichés of Determinist criticism.

We saw earlier that Common Sense's practice of 'making allowances' in its moral judgments for the influence of heredity and environment indicates Common Sense's conviction, both that a just moral judgment must discount determinants of choice over which the agent has no control, and also (since it still accepts moral judgments as legitimate) that *something* of moral relevance survives which can be regarded as genuinely self-originated. We are now to try to discover what this 'something' is. And I think we may still usefully take Common Sense as our guide. Suppose one asks the ordinary intelligent citizen *why* he deems it proper to make allowances for X, whose heredity and/or environment are unfortunate. He will tend to reply, I think, in some such terms as these: that X has more and stronger temptations to deviate from what is right than Y or Z, who are normally circumstanced, so that he must put forth a *stronger moral effort* if he is to achieve the same level of external conduct. The intended implication seems to be that X is just as morally praiseworthy as Y or Z *if* he exerts an equivalent moral effort, even though he may not thereby achieve an equal success in conforming his will to the 'concrete' demands of duty. And this implies, again, Common Sense's belief that *in moral effort* we have something for which a man is responsible *without qualification*, something that is not affected by heredity and environment but depends *solely* upon the self itself.

Now in my opinion Common Sense has here, in principle, hit upon the one and only defensible answer. Here, and here alone, so far as I can see, in the act of deciding whether to put forth or withhold the moral effort required to resist temptation and rise to duty, is to be found an act which is free in the sense required for moral responsibility; an act of which the self is sole author, and of which it is true to say that 'it could be' (or, after the event, 'could have been') 'otherwise.' Such is the thesis which we shall now try to establish.

6.

The species of argument appropriate to the establishment of a thesis of this sort should fall, I think, into two phases. First, there should be a consideration of the evidence of the moral agent's own inner experience. What *is* the act of moral decision, and what does it imply, from the standpoint of the actual participant? Since there is no way of knowing the act of moral decision—or for that matter any other form of activity—except by actual participation in it, the evidence of the subject, or agent, is on an issue of this kind of palmary[14] importance. It can hardly, however, be taken as in itself conclusive. For even if that evidence should be overwhelmingly to the effect that moral decision does have the characteristics required by moral freedom, the question is bound to be raised—and in view of considerations from other quarters pointing in a contrary direction is *rightly* raised—Can we *trust* the evidence of inner experience? That brings us to what will be the second phase of the argument. We shall have to go on to show, if we are to make good our case, that the extraneous[15] considerations so often supposed to be fatal to the belief in moral freedom are in fact innocuous to it.

In the light of what was said in the last lecture[16] about the self's experience of moral decision as a *creative* activity, we may perhaps be absolved from developing the first phase of the argument at any great length. The appeal is throughout to one's own experience in the actual taking of the moral decision in the situation of moral temptation. 'Is it possible,' we must ask, 'for anyone so circumstanced to *dis*believe that he could be deciding otherwise?' The answer is surely not in doubt. When we decide to exert moral effort to resist a temptation, we feel quite certain that we *could* withhold the effort; just as, if we decide to withhold the effort and yield to our desires, we feel quite certain that we *could* exert it—otherwise we should not blame ourselves afterwards for having succumbed. It may be, indeed, that this conviction is mere self-delusion. But that is not at the moment our concern. It is enough at present to establish that the act of deciding to exert or to withhold moral effort, as we know it from the inside in actual moral living, belongs to the category of acts which 'could have been otherwise.'

---

14   Great, outstanding.
15   External, coming from outside.
16   "Self-Activity and Its Modes."

Mutatis mutandis,[17] the same reply is forthcoming if we ask, 'Is it possible for the moral agent in the taking of his decision to *dis*believe that he is the *sole* author of that decision?' Clearly he cannot disbelieve that it is *he* who takes the decision. That, however, is not in itself sufficient to enable him, on reflection, to regard himself as *solely* responsible for the act. For his 'character' as so far formed might conceivably be a factor in determining it, and no one can suppose that the constitution of his 'character' is uninfluenced by circumstances of heredity and environment with which *he* has nothing to do. But as we pointed out in the last lecture, the very essence of the moral decision as it is experienced is that it is a decision whether or not to *combat* our strongest desire, and our strongest desire *is* the expression in the situation of our character as so far formed. Now clearly our character cannot be a factor in determining the decision whether or not to *oppose* our character. I think we are entitled to say, therefore, that the act of moral decision is one in which the self is for itself not merely 'author' but 'sole author.'

7.

We may pass on, then, to the second phase of our constructive argument; and this will demand more elaborate treatment. Even if a moral agent *qua* making a moral decision in the situation of 'temptation' cannot help believing that he has free will in the sense at issue—a moral freedom between real alternatives, between genuinely open possibilities—are there, nevertheless, objections to a freedom of this kind so cogent that we are bound to distrust the evidence of 'inner experience'?

I begin by drawing attention to a simple point whose significance tends, I think, to be underestimated. If the phenomenological analysis we have offered is substantially correct, no one while functioning as a moral agent can help believing that he enjoys free will. Theoretically he may be completely convinced by Determinist arguments, but when actually confronted with a personal situation of conflict between duty and desire he is quite certain that it lies with him

here and now whether or not he will rise to duty. It follows that if Determinists could produce convincing theoretical arguments against a free will of this kind, the awkward predicament would ensue that man has to deny as a theoretical being what he has to assert as a practical being. Now I think the Determinist ought to be a good deal more worried about this than he usually is. He seems to imagine that a strong case on general theoretical grounds is enough to prove that the 'practical' belief in free will, even if inescapable for us as practical beings, is mere illusion. But in fact it proves nothing of the sort. There is no reason whatever why a belief that we find ourselves obliged to hold *qua* practical beings should be required to give way before a belief which we find ourselves obliged to hold *qua* theoretical beings; or, for that matter, *vice versa*. All that the theoretical arguments of Determinism can prove, unless they are reinforced by a refutation of the phenomenological analysis that supports Libertarianism, is that there is a radical conflict between the theoretical and the practical sides of man's nature, an antinomy[18] at the very heart of the self. And this is a state of affairs with which no one can easily rest satisfied. I think therefore that the Determinist ought to concern himself a great deal more than he does with phenomenological analysis, in order to show, if he can, that the assurance of free will is not really an inexpugnable[19] element in man's practical consciousness. There is just as much obligation upon him, convinced though he may be of the soundness of his theoretical arguments, to expose the errors of the Libertarian's phenomenological analysis, as there is upon us, convinced though we may be of the soundness of the Libertarian's phenomenological analysis, to expose the errors of the Determinist's theoretical arguments.

8.

However, we must at once begin the discharge of our own obligation. The rest of this lecture will be devoted to trying to show that the arguments which seem to carry the most weight with Determinists are, to say the least of it, very far from compulsive.

---

17   With appropriate alterations. The Latin means "things having been changed that need to be changed."

18   Contradiction, paradox.

19   Impossible to put aside or overcome.

Fortunately, a good many of the arguments which at an earlier time in the history of philosophy would have been strongly urged against us make almost no appeal to the bulk of philosophers today, and we may here pass them by. That applies to any criticism of 'open possibilities' based on a metaphysical theory about the nature of the universe as a whole. Nobody today *has* a metaphysical theory about the nature of the universe as a whole! It applies also, with almost equal force, to criticisms based upon the universality of causal law as a supposed postulate of science. There have always been, in my opinion, sound philosophic reasons for doubting the validity, as distinct from the convenience, of the causal postulate in its universal form, but at the present time, when scientists themselves are deeply divided about the need for postulating causality even within their own special field, we shall do better to concentrate our attention upon criticisms which are more confidently advanced. I propose to ignore also, on different grounds, the type of criticism of free will that is sometimes advanced from the side of religion, based upon religious postulates of Divine Omnipotence and Omniscience.[20] So far as I can see, a postulate of human freedom is every bit as necessary to meet certain religious demands (e.g., to make sense of the 'conviction of sin'), as postulates of Divine Omniscience and Omnipotence are to meet certain other religious demands. If so, then it can hardly be argued that religious experience as such tells more strongly against than for the position we are defending; and we may be satisfied, in the present context, to leave the matter there. It will be more profitable to discuss certain arguments which contemporary philosophers do think important, and which recur with a somewhat monotonous regularity in the literature of anti-Libertarianism.

These arguments can, I think, be reduced in principle to no more than two: first, the argument from 'predictability'; second, the argument from the alleged meaninglessness of an act supposed to be the self's act and yet not an expression of the self's character. Contemporary criticism of free will seems to me to consist almost exclusively of variations on these two themes. I shall deal with each in turn.

9.

On the first we touched in passing at an earlier stage. Surely it is beyond question (the critic urges) that when we know a person intimately we can foretell with a high degree of accuracy how he will respond to at least a large number of practical situations. One feels safe in predicting that one's dog-loving friend will not use his boot to repel the little mongrel that comes yapping at his heels; or again that one's wife will not pass with incurious eyes (or indeed pass at all) the new hat shop in the city. So to behave would not be (as we say) 'in character.' But, so the criticism runs, you with your doctrine of 'genuinely open possibilities,' of a free will by which the self can diverge from its own character, remove all rational basis from such prediction. You require us to make the absurd supposition that the success of countless predictions of the sort in the past has been mere matter of chance. If you *really* believed in your theory, you would not be surprised if tomorrow your friend with the notorious horror of strong drink should suddenly exhibit a passion for whisky and soda, or if your friend whose taste for reading has hitherto been satisfied with the sporting columns of the newspapers should be discovered on a fine Saturday afternoon poring over the works of Hegel. But of course you *would* be surprised. Social life would be sheer chaos if there were not well-grounded social expectations; and social life is not sheer chaos. Your theory is hopelessly wrecked upon obvious facts.

Now whether or not this criticism holds good against some versions of Libertarian theory I need not here discuss. It is sufficient if I can make it clear that against the version advanced in this lecture, according to which free will is localised in a relatively narrow field of operation, the criticism has no relevance whatsoever.

Let us remind ourselves briefly of the setting within which, on our view, free will functions. There is X, the course which we believe we ought to follow, and Y, the course towards which we feel our desire is strongest. The freedom which we ascribe to the agent is the freedom to put forth or refrain from putting forth the

---

20   Roughly, that God can do anything (omnipotence) and knows everything (omniscience).

moral effort required to resist the pressure of desire and do what he thinks he ought to do.

But then there is surely an immense range of practical situations—covering by far the greater part of life—in which there is no question of a conflict within the self between what he most desires to do and what he thinks he ought to do? Indeed such conflict is a comparatively rare phenomenon for the majority of men. Yet over that whole vast range there is nothing whatever in our version of Libertarianism to prevent our agreeing that character determines conduct. In the absence, real or supposed, of any 'moral' issue, what a man chooses will be simply that course which, after such reflection as seems called for, he deems most likely to bring him what he most strongly desires; and that is the same as to say the course to which his present character inclines him.

Over by far the greater area of human choices, then, our theory offers no more barrier to successful prediction on the basis of character than any other theory. For where there is no clash of strongest desire with duty, the free will we are defending has no business. There is just nothing for it to do.

But what about the situations—rare enough though they may be—in which there is this clash and in which free will does therefore operate? Does our theory entail that there, at any rate, as the critic seems to suppose, 'anything may happen'?

Not by any manner of means. In the first place, and by the very nature of the case, the range of the agent's possible choices is bounded by what he thinks he ought to do on the one hand, and what he most strongly desires on the other. The freedom claimed for him is a freedom of decision to make or withhold the effort required to do what he thinks he ought to do. There is no question of a freedom to act in some 'wild' fashion, out of all relation to his characteristic beliefs and desires. This so-called 'freedom of caprice,' so often charged against the Libertarian, is, to put it bluntly, a sheer figment of the critic's imagination, with no *habitat*[21] in serious Libertarian theory. Even in situations where free will does come into play it is perfectly possible, on a view like ours, given the ap-

propriate knowledge of a man's character, to predict within certain limits how he will respond.

But 'probable' prediction in such situations can, I think, go further than this. It is obvious that where desire and duty are at odds, the felt 'gap' (as it were) between the two may vary enormously in breadth in different cases. The moderate drinker and the chronic tippler may each want another glass, and each deem it his duty to abstain, but the felt gap between desire and duty in the case of the former is trivial beside the great gulf which is felt to separate them in the case of the latter. Hence it will take a far harder moral effort for the tippler than for the moderate drinker to achieve the same external result of abstention. So much is matter of common agreement. And we are entitled, I think, to take it into account in prediction, on the simple principle that the harder the moral effort required to resist desire the less likely it is to occur. Thus in the example taken, most people would predict that the tippler will very probably succumb to his desires, whereas there is a reasonable likelihood that the moderate drinker will make the comparatively slight effort needed to resist them. So long as the prediction does not pretend to more than a measure of probability, there is nothing in our theory which would disallow it.

I claim, therefore, that the view of free will I have been putting forward is consistent with predictability of conduct on the basis of character over a very wide field indeed. And I make the further claim that that field will cover all the situations in life concerning which there is any empirical evidence that successful prediction is possible.

10.

Let us pass on to consider the second main line of criticism. This is, I think, much the more illuminating of the two, if only because it compels the Libertarian to make explicit certain concepts which are indispensable to him, but which, being desperately hard to state clearly, are apt not to be stated at all. The critic's fundamental point might be stated somewhat as follows:

'Free will as you describe it is completely unintelligible. On your own showing no *reason* can be given, because there just *is* no reason, why a man decides to exert rather than to withhold moral effort, or *vice*

---

21   Dwelling place.

458 FREEDOM AND DETERMINISM

versa. But such an act—or more properly, such an 'occurrence'—it is nonsense to speak of as an act of a *self*. If there is nothing in the self's character to which it is, even in principle, in any way traceable, the self has nothing to do with it. Your so-called 'freedom,' therefore, so far from supporting the self's moral responsibility, destroys it as surely as the crudest Determinism could do.'

If we are to discuss this criticism usefully, it is important, I think, to begin by getting clear about two different senses of the word 'intelligible.'

If, in the first place, we mean by an 'intelligible' act one whose occurrence is in principle capable of being inferred, since it follows necessarily from something (though we may not know in fact from what), then it is certainly true that the Libertarian's free will is unintelligible. But that is only saying, is it not, that the Libertarian's 'free' act is not an act which follows necessarily from something! This can hardly rank as a *criticism* of Libertarianism. It is just a description of it. That there can be nothing unintelligible in *this* sense is precisely what the Determinist has got to *prove*.

Yet it is surprising how often the critic of Libertarianism involves himself in this circular mode of argument. Repeatedly it is urged against the Libertarian, with a great air of triumph, that on his view he can't say *why* I now decide to rise to duty, or now decide to follow my strongest desire in defiance of duty. Of course he can't. If he could he wouldn't *be* a Libertarian. To 'account for' a 'free' act is a contradiction in terms. A free will is *ex hypothesi*[22] the sort of thing of which the request for an *explanation* is absurd. The assumption that an explanation must be in principle possible for the act of moral decision deserves to rank as a classic example of the ancient fallacy of 'begging the question.'[23]

But the critic usually has in mind another sense of the word 'unintelligible.' He is apt to take it for granted that an act which is unintelligible in the *above* sense (as the morally free act of the Libertarian undoubtedly is) is unintelligible in the *further* sense that we can attach no meaning to it. And this is an altogether more serious matter. If it could really be shown that the Libertarian's 'free will' were unintelligible in this sense of being meaningless, that, for myself at any rate, would be the end of the affair. Libertarianism would have been conclusively refuted.

But it seems to me manifest that this can *not* be shown. The critic has allowed himself, I submit, to become the victim of a widely accepted but fundamentally vicious[24] assumption. He has assumed that whatever is meaningful must exhibit its meaningfulness to those who view it from the standpoint of external observation. Now if one chooses thus to limit one's self to the rôle of external observer, it is, I think, perfectly true that one can attach no meaning to an act which is the act of something we call a 'self' and yet follows from nothing in that self's character. But then *why should we* so limit ourselves, when what is under consideration is a subjective activity? For the apprehension of subjective acts there is *another* standpoint available, that of *inner experience*, of the practical consciousness in its actual functioning. If our free will should turn out to be something to which we can attach a meaning from *this* standpoint, no more is required. And no more ought to be expected. For I must repeat that only from the inner standpoint of living experience *could* anything of the nature of 'activity' be directly grasped. Observation from without is in the nature of the case impotent to apprehend the active *qua* active. We can from without observe sequences of states. If into these we read activity (as we sometimes do), this can only be on the basis of what we discern in ourselves from the inner standpoint. It follows that if anyone insists upon taking his criterion of the meaningful simply from the standpoint of external observation, he is really deciding in advance of the evidence that the notion of activity, and *a fortiori*[25] the notion of a free will, is 'meaningless.' He looks for the free act through a medium which is in the nature of the case incapable of revealing it, and then, because inevitably he doesn't find it, he declares that it doesn't exist!

But if, as we surely ought in this context, we adopt the inner standpoint, then (I am suggesting) things appear in a totally different light. From the inner

---

22 On this (libertarian) hypothesis, given this assumption.
23 Assuming as true that which needs to be proved.
24 Faulty, defective.
25 Even more so.

standpoint, it seems to me plain, there is no difficulty whatever in attaching meaning to an act which is the self's act and which nevertheless does not follow from the self's character. So much I claim has been established by the phenomenological analysis, in this and the previous lecture, of the act of moral decision in face of moral temptation. It is thrown into particularly clear relief where the moral decision is to make the moral effort required to rise to duty. For the very function of moral effort, as it appears to the agent engaged in the act, is to enable the self to act against the line of least resistance, against the line to which his character as so far formed most strongly inclines him. But if the self is thus conscious here of *combating* his formed character, he surely cannot possibly suppose that the act, although his own act, *issues from* his formed character? I submit, therefore, that the self knows very well indeed—from the inner standpoint—what is meant by an act which is the *self*'s act and which nevertheless does not follow from the self's *character*.

What this implies—and it seems to me to be an implication of cardinal importance for any theory of the self that aims at being more than superficial—is that the nature of the self is for itself something more than just its character as so far formed. The 'nature' of the self and what we commonly call the 'character' of the self are by no means the same thing, and it is utterly vital that they should not be confused. The 'nature' of the self comprehends, but is not without remainder reducible to, its 'character'; it must, if we are to be true to the testimony of our experience of it, be taken as including *also* the authentic creative power of fashioning and refashioning 'character.'

The misguided, and as a rule quite uncritical, belittlement, of the evidence offered by inner experience has, I am convinced, been responsible for more bad argument by the opponents of Free Will than has any other single factor. How often, for example, do we find the Determinist critic saying, in effect, '*Either* the act follows necessarily upon precedent states, *or* it is a mere matter of chance and accordingly of no moral significance.' The disjunction is invalid for it does not exhaust the possible alternatives. It seems to the critic to do so only because he *will* limit himself to the standpoint which is proper, and indeed alone possible, in

dealing with the physical world, the standpoint of the external observer. If only he would allow himself to assume the standpoint which is not merely proper for, but necessary to, the apprehension of subjective activity, the inner standpoint of the practical consciousness in its actual functioning, he would find himself obliged to recognise the falsity of his disjunction. Reflection upon the act of moral decision as apprehended from the inner standpoint would force him to recognise a *third* possibility, as remote from chance as from necessity, that, namely, of *creative activity*, in which (as I have ventured to express it) nothing determines the act save the agent's doing of it.

11.

There we must leave the matter. But as this lecture has been, I know, somewhat densely packed, it may be helpful if I conclude by reminding you, in bald summary, of the main things I have been trying to say. Let me set them out in so many successive theses.

1. The freedom which is at issue in the traditional Free Will problem is the freedom which is presupposed in moral responsibility.

2. Critical reflection upon carefully considered attributions of moral responsibility reveals that the only freedom that will do is a freedom which pertains to inner acts of choice, and that these acts must be acts (*a*) of which the self is *sole* author, and (*b*) which the self could have performed otherwise.

3. From phenomenological analysis of the situation of moral temptation we find that the self as engaged in this situation is inescapably convinced that it possesses a freedom of precisely the specified kind, located in the decision to exert or withhold the moral effort needed to rise to duty where the pressure of its desiring nature is felt to urge it in a contrary direction.

Passing to the question of the *reality* of this moral freedom which the moral agent believes himself to possess, we argued:

4. Of the two types of Determinist criticism which seem to have most influence today, that based on the predictability of much human behaviour fails to touch a Libertarianism which confines the area of free will as above indicated. Libertarianism so understood is compatible with all the predictability that the empirical facts warrant. And:

5. The second main type of criticism, which alleges the 'meaninglessness' of an act which is the self's act and which is yet not determined by the self's character, is based on a failure to appreciate that the standpoint of inner experience is not only legitimate but indispensable where what is at issue is the reality and nature of a subjective activity. The creative act of moral decision is inevitably meaningless to the mere external observer; but from the inner standpoint it is as real, and as significant, as anything in human experience.[26]

---

26   [Author's note] An earlier, but not in substance dissimilar, version of my views on the Free Will problem has been criticised at length in Mr. Nowell-Smith's *Ethics*. A detailed reply to these criticisms will be found in Appendix B [of Part One of *On Selfhood and Godhood*].

A.J. AYER
"Freedom and Necessity"

Who Was A.J. Ayer?

Sir Alfred Jules Ayer (1910–1989), known to all his friends as Freddie, was born into a wealthy European-origin family in London. He attended the pre-eminent English private school Eton, then went on scholarship to Oxford. He served as an officer in a British espionage and sabotage unit during World War II, then taught at University College London and at Oxford.

When only 24, Ayer wrote *Language, Truth, and Logic*, the book that made his name. In it, he briefly, simply, and persuasively to many, argued for logical positivism, a form of radical empiricism that had been developed largely by the group of philosophers called the Vienna Circle, whose ideas Ayer had picked up while studying with them in Austria. Logical positivism dominated Anglophone philosophy for decades; while objections (especially to Ayer's rather simplified version) came thick and fast, everyone was at least aware of it as a philosophical force to be reckoned with.

While *Language, Truth, and Logic* was by far his best-seller, Ayer wrote a good deal of other important work, especially in epistemology. While his work is not now generally included in lists of all-time philosophical landmarks, he was considered, in terms of influence if not of originality, second only to Bertrand Russell among the English philosophers of his day.

Ayer was extraordinarily well-known by the British public. He wrote and spoke on all sorts of popular issues, all over the media. In those days, TV networks programed witty intellectual chatter, and Ayer was a master at this. He loved his celebrity, and hobnobbed with the famous and influential.

What Is the Structure of This Reading?

The problem Ayer will talk about, clearly set out in the first few paragraphs of his article, is how free action—action for which one is morally responsible—is possible, given the assumption that all human action, like everything else in the world, is determined by causes, and, given the causes, could not have been otherwise.

Ayer points out that the alternative to an action's being determined by causes appears to be that it is totally random; and that would certainly not be the sort of action for which we could count someone as morally responsible. He admits that libertarians often deny that total randomness is the non-determination they argue is a pre-requisite for freedom and responsibility; but he asks, then, what do they argue for? If what they're thinking of as what one is responsible for is action in accord with one's character, then that seems to be wholly compatible with universal causality: one's character itself may well be entirely determined by antecedent causes.

He then reveals his main positive argument: that freedom (thus responsibility) is incompatible with *constraint*, not with causal determination. One is constrained when one's choice over actions is not operative: for example, if one were hypnotized, or if someone held a gun at one's head, or if one had a compelling psychological influence over what one did.

He concludes by attempting to explain and defuse the tendency many philosophers have of counting causal determination as constraining. A constrained action, he argues, is one that you'll do whatever you decide, if anything. But free actions, on his understanding, are those in which your decision is operative: they would not have occurred had you not decided to do them. Your decision, for a determinist, is itself causally determined; but that's not relevant. The fact that the causal chain behind the action includes your decision is what makes it a "free" action, an action for which you're responsible.

Suggestions for Critical Reflection

1. Consider the following case. An ingenious physiologist has hooked up wires to your brain; by pushing buttons, he can cause you to have a variety of "volitions"; these are what Ayer would presumably count as decisions to act, so he would count your resulting actions as free. But it is feminist to claim that in this case you would be entirely unfree—merely the physiologist's puppet. Which position is right? Where does the other position go wrong?

2. You've been called to act as a witness for the prosecution in a criminal trial, and friends of the accused tell you that all of your family will be in great danger if you testify honestly. You decide that all you can do is to lie to the court, and say you can't remember anything. This is ordinarily an immoral act, but is it under the circumstances? Are you constrained to act as you did? (Compare Ayer's example of someone's holding a gun to your head.) If this is genuine constraint, then does that mean you're not morally responsible for lying?

3. Fatalism is the position that something will happen in the future *no matter what*. In the last few paragraphs, Ayer attempts to distinguish determinism from fatalism, and to argue that it is the second, not the first, that is incompatible with responsibility and freedom. Try to explain his argument, in your own terms. Some philosophers think that determinism and fatalism are the same thing. Why do you think they would say this? Who is right?

Suggestions for Further Reading

There are really two independent positions here: *determinism* (the thesis that all events, including human actions and decisions, are determined by antecedent causes) and *compatibilism* (the thesis that freedom and responsibility are compatible with determinism). A classic essay on both, and their connection, is "Of Liberty and Necessity" by David Hume; this is a section of Hume's great work, *An Enquiry Concerning Human Understanding*, available online and in many anthologies and editions. Hume's influence is certainly apparent in Ayer. An excellent and very thorough survey of compatibilist positions and arguments, with a thorough bibliography, is online: McKenna, Michael, "Compatibilism", *The Stanford Encyclopedia of Philosophy (Winter 2009 Edition)*, Edward N. Zalta (ed.), <http://plato.stanford.edu/archives/win2009/entries/compatibilism/>. *The Stanford Encyclopedia* does a similarly good job on determinism: Hoefer, Carl, "Causal Determinism", *The Stanford Encyclopedia of Philosophy (Spring 2010 Edition)*, Edward N. Zalta (ed.), <http://plato.stanford.edu/archives/spr2010/entries/determinism-causal/>. A very interesting and accessible work on freedom, modifying the compatibilist view considerably, is Harry Frankfurt's article "Freedom of the Will and the Concept of the Person." This was originally published in *Journal of Philosophy*, LXVII, No. 1 (Jan. 1971), but it's also widely anthologized. Another one is Daniel Dennet's book *Elbow Room: The Varieties of Free Will Worth Wanting* (Bradford, 1984).

"Freedom and Necessity"[1]

When I am said to have done something of my own free will it is implied that I could have acted otherwise; and it is only when it is believed that I could have acted otherwise that I am held to be morally responsible for what I have done. For a man is not thought to be morally responsible for an action that it was not in his power to avoid. But if human behaviour is entirely governed by causal laws, it is not clear how any action that is done could ever have been avoided. It may be said of the agent that he would have acted otherwise if the causes of his action had been different, but they being what they were, it seems to follow that he was bound to act as he did. Now it is commonly assumed both that men are capable of acting freely, in the sense that is required to make them morally responsible, and that human behaviour is entirely governed by causal laws: and it is the apparent conflict between these two assumptions that gives rise to the philosophical problem of the freedom of the will.

Confronted with this problem, many people will be inclined to agree with Dr. Johnson: 'Sir, we *know*

our will is free, and *there's* an end on't.'[2] But, while this does very well for those who accept Dr. Johnson's premiss, it would hardly convince anyone who denied the freedom of the will. Certainly, if we do know that our wills are free, it follows that they are so. But the logical reply to this might be that since our wills are not free, it follows that no one can know that they are: so that if anyone claims, like Dr. Johnson, to know that they are, he must be mistaken. What is evident, indeed, is that people often believe themselves to be acting freely; and it is to this 'feeling' of freedom that some philosophers appeal when they wish, in the supposed interests of morality, to prove that not all human action is causally determined. But if these philosophers are right in their assumption that a man cannot be acting freely if his action is causally determined, then the fact that someone feels free to do, or not to do, a certain action does not prove that he really is so. It may prove that the agent does not himself know what it is that makes him act in one way rather than another: but from the fact that a man is unaware of the causes of his action, it does not follow that no such causes exist.

So much may be allowed to the determinist; but his belief that all human actions are subservient to causal laws still remains to be justified. If, indeed, it is necessary that every event should have a cause, then the rule must apply to human behaviour as much as to anything else. But why should it be supposed that every event must have a cause? The contrary is not unthinkable. Nor is the law of universal causation a necessary presupposition of scientific thought. The scientist may try to discover causal laws, and in many cases he succeeds; but sometimes he has to be content with statistical laws, and sometimes he comes upon events which, in the present state of his knowledge, he is not able to subsume under any law at all. In the case of these events he assumes that if he knew more he would be able to discover some law, whether causal or statistical, which would enable him to account for them. And this assumption cannot be disproved. For

---

1   This paper first appeared in *Polemic* No. 5 in 1946; it is reprinted from Ayer's *Philosophical Essays*, published in New York by St. Martin's Press, 1969. Reproduced with permission of Palgrave Macmillan.

2   Samuel Johnson (1709–1784) was a prominent English essayist and the compiler of the first great *Dictionary of the English Language*; he is quoted in James Boswell's *Life of Johnson* (1769: AETAT, 60).

however far he may have carried his investigation, it is always open to him to carry it further; and it is always conceivable that if he carried it further he would discover the connection which had hitherto escaped him. Nevertheless, it is also conceivable that the events with which he is concerned are not systematically connected with any others: so that the reason why he does not discover the sort of laws that he requires is simply that they do not obtain.

Now in the case of human conduct the search for explanations has not in fact been altogether fruitless. Certain scientific laws have been established; and with the help of these laws we do make a number of successful predictions about the ways in which different people will behave. But these predictions do not always cover every detail. We may be able to predict that in certain circumstances a particular man will be angry, without being able to prescribe the precise form that the expression of his anger will take. We may be reasonably sure that he will shout, but not sure how loud his shout will be, or exactly what words he will use. And it is only a small proportion of human actions that we are able to forecast even so precisely as this. But that, it may be said, is because we have not carried our investigations very far. The science of psychology is still in its infancy and, as it is developed, not only will more human actions be explained, but the explanations will go into greater detail. The ideal of complete explanation may never in fact be attained: but it is theoretically attainable. Well, this may be so: and certainly it is impossible to show *a priori* that it is not so: but equally it cannot be shown that it is. This will not, however, discourage the scientist who, in the field of human behaviour, as elsewhere, will continue to formulate theories and test them by the facts. And in this he is justified. For since he has no reason *a priori* to admit that there is a limit to what he can discover, the fact that he also cannot be sure that there is no limit does not make it unreasonable for him to devise theories, nor, having devised them, to try constantly to improve them.

But now suppose it to be claimed that, so far as men's actions are concerned, there is a limit: and that this limit is set by the fact of human freedom. An obvious objection is that in many cases in which a person feels himself to be free to do, or not to do, a certain action, we are even now able to explain, in causal terms, why it is that he acts as he does. But it might be argued that even if men are sometimes mistaken in believing that they act freely, it does not follow that they are always so mistaken. For it is not always the case that when a man believes that he has acted freely we are in fact able to account for his action in causal terms. A determinist would say that we should be able to account for it if we had more knowledge of the circumstances, and had been able to discover the appropriate natural laws. But until those discoveries have been made, this remains only a pious hope. And may it not be true that, in some cases at least, the reason why we can give no causal explanation is that no causal explanation is available; and that this is because the agent's choice was literally free, as he himself felt it to be?

The answer is that this may indeed be true, inasmuch as it is open to anyone to hold that no explanation is possible until some explanation is actually found. But even so it does not give the moralist what he wants. For he is anxious to show that men are capable of acting freely in order to infer that they can be morally responsible for what they do. But if it is a matter of pure chance that a man should act in one way rather than another, he may be free but he can hardly be responsible. And indeed when a man's actions seem to us quite unpredictable, when, as we say, there is no knowing what he will do, we do not look upon him as a moral agent. We look upon him rather as a lunatic.

To this it may be objected that we are not dealing fairly with the moralist. For when he makes it a condition of my being morally responsible that I should act freely, he does not wish to imply that it is purely a matter of chance that I act as I do. What he wishes to imply is that my actions are the result of my own free choice: and it is because they are the result of my own free choice that I am held to be morally responsible for them.

But now we must ask how it is that I come to make my choice. Either it is an accident that I choose to act as I do or it is not. If it is an accident, then it is merely a matter of chance that I did not choose otherwise; and if it is merely a matter of chance that I did not choose otherwise, it is surely irrational to hold me morally responsible for choosing as I did. But if it is not an accident that I choose to do one thing rather than another, then presumably there is some causal explanation of my choice: and in that case we are led back to determinism.

Again, the objection may be raised that we are not doing justice to the moralist's case. His view is not that it is a matter of chance that I choose to act as I do, but rather that my choice depends upon my character. Nevertheless he holds that I can still be free in the sense that he requires; for it is I who am responsible for my character. But in what way am I responsible for my character? Only, surely, in the sense that there is a causal connection between what I do now and what I have done in the past. It is only this that justifies the statement that I have made myself what I am: and even so this is an over-simplification, since it takes no account of the external influences to which I have been subjected. But, ignoring the external influences, let us assume that it is in fact the case that I have made myself what I am. Then it is still legitimate to ask how it is that I have come to make myself one sort of person rather than another. And if it be answered that it is a matter of my strength of will, we can put the same question in another form by asking how it is that my will has the strength that it has and not some other degree of strength. Once more, either it is an accident or it is not. If it is an accident, then by the same argument as before, I am not morally responsible, and if it is not an accident we are led back to determinism.

Furthermore, to say that my actions proceed from my character or, more colloquially, that I act in character, is to say that my behaviour is consistent and to that extent predictable: and since it is, above all, for the actions that I perform in character that I am held to be morally responsible, it looks as if the admission of moral responsibility, so far from being incompatible with determinism, tends rather to presuppose it. But how can this be so if it is a necessary condition of moral responsibility that the person who is held responsible should have acted freely? It seems that if we are to retain this idea of moral responsibility, we must either show that men can be held responsible for actions which they do not do freely, or else find some

way of reconciling determinism with the freedom of the will.

It is no doubt with the object of effecting this reconciliation that some philosophers[3] have defined freedom as the consciousness of necessity. And by so doing they are able to say not only that a man can be acting freely when his action is causally determined, but even that his action must be causally determined for it to be possible for him to be acting freely. Nevertheless this definition has the serious disadvantage that it gives to the word 'freedom' a meaning quite different from any that it ordinarily bears. It is indeed obvious that if we are allowed to give the word 'freedom' any meaning that we please, we can find a meaning that will reconcile it with determinism: but this is no more a solution of our present problem than the fact that the word 'horse' could be arbitrarily used to mean what is ordinarily meant by 'sparrow' is a proof that horses have wings. For suppose that I am compelled by another person to do something 'against my will'. In that case, as the word 'freedom' is ordinarily used, I should not be said to be acting freely: and the fact that I am fully aware of the constraint to which I am subjected makes no difference to the matter. I do not become free by becoming conscious that I am not. It may, indeed, be possible to show that my being aware that my action is causally determined is not incompatible with my acting freely: but it by no means follows that it is in this that my freedom consists. Moreover, I suspect that one of the reasons why people are inclined to define freedom as the consciousness of necessity is that they think that if one is conscious of necessity one may somehow be able to master it. But this is a fallacy. It is like someone's saying that he wishes he could see into the future, because if he did he would know what calamities lay in wait for him and so would be able to avoid them. But if he avoids the calamities then they don't lie in the future and it is not true that he foresees them. And similarly if I am able to master necessity, in the sense of escaping the operation of a necessary law, then the law in question is not necessary. And if the law is not necessary, then

---

3   Karl Marx is a prominent example of a philosopher who makes this claim.

neither my freedom nor anything else can consist in my knowing that it is.

Let it be granted, then, that when we speak of reconciling freedom with determinism we are using the word 'freedom' in an ordinary sense. It still remains for us to make this usage clear: and perhaps the best way to make it clear is to show what it is that freedom, in this sense, is contrasted with. Now we began with the assumption that freedom is contrasted with causality: so that a man cannot be said to be acting freely if his action is causally determined. But this assumption has led us into difficulties and I now wish to suggest that it is mistaken. For it is not, I think, causality that freedom is to be contrasted with, but constraint. And while it is true that being constrained to do an action entails being caused to do it, I shall try to show that the converse does not hold. I shall try to show that from the fact that my action is causally determined it does not necessarily follow that I am constrained to do it: and this is equivalent to saying that it does not necessarily follow that I am not free.

If I am constrained, I do not act freely. But in what circumstances can I legitimately be said to be constrained? An obvious instance is the case in which I am compelled by another person to do what he wants. In a case of this sort the compulsion need not be such as to deprive one of the power of choice. It is not required that the other person should have hypnotized me, or that he should make it physically impossible for me to go against his will. It is enough that he should induce me to do what he wants by making it clear to me that, if I do not, he will bring about some situation that I regard as even more undesirable than the consequences of the action that he wishes me to do. Thus, if the man points a pistol at my head I may still choose to disobey him: but this does not prevent its being true that if I do fall in with his wishes he can legitimately be said to have compelled me. And if the circumstances are such that no reasonable person would be expected to choose the other alternative, then the action that I am made to do is not one for which I am held to be morally responsible.

A similar, but still somewhat different, case is that in which another person has obtained an habitual ascendancy over me. Where this is so, there may be no question of my being induced to act as the other person wishes by being confronted with a still more disagreeable alternative: for if I am sufficiently under his influence this special stimulus will not be necessary. Nevertheless I do not act freely, for the reason that I have been deprived of the power of choice. And this means that I have acquired so strong a habit of obedience that I no longer go through any process of deciding whether or not to do what the other person wants. About other matters I may still deliberate; but as regards the fulfilment of this other person's wishes, my own deliberations have ceased to be a causal factor in my behaviour. And it is in this sense that I may be said to be constrained. It is not, however, necessary that such constraint should take the form of subservience to another person. A kleptomaniac is not a free agent, in respect of his stealing, because he does not go through any process of deciding whether or not to steal. Or rather, if he does go through such a process, it is irrelevant to his behaviour. Whatever he resolved to do, he would steal all the same. And it is this that distinguishes him from the ordinary thief.

But now it may be asked whether there is any essential difference between these cases and those in which the agent is commonly thought to be free. No doubt the ordinary thief does go through a process of deciding whether or not to steal, and no doubt it does affect his behaviour. If he resolved to refrain from stealing, he could carry his resolution out. But if it be allowed that his making or not making this resolution is causally determined, then how can he be any more free than the kleptomaniac? It may be true that unlike the kleptomaniac he could refrain from stealing if he chose: but if there is a cause, or set of causes, which necessitate his choosing as he does, how can he be said to have the power of choice? Again, it may be true that no one now compels me to get up and walk across the room: but if my doing so can be causally explained in terms of my history or my environment, or whatever it may be, then how am I any more free than if some other person had compelled me? I do not have the feeling of constraint that I have when a pistol is manifestly pointed at my head; but the chains of causation by which I am bound are no less effective for being invisible.

The answer to this is that the cases I have mentioned as examples of constraint do differ from the others: and they differ just in the ways that I have tried to bring out. If I suffered from a compulsion neurosis, so that I got up and walked across the room, whether I wanted to or not, or if I did so because somebody else compelled me, then I should not be acting freely. But if I do it now, I shall be acting freely, just because these conditions do not obtain; and the fact that my action may nevertheless have a cause is, from this point of view, irrelevant. For it is not when my action has any cause at all, but only when it has a special sort of cause, that it is reckoned not to be free.

But here it may be objected that, even if this distinction corresponds to ordinary usage, it is still very irrational. For why should we distinguish, with regard to a person's freedom, between the operations of one sort of cause and those of another? Do not all causes equally necessitate? And is it not therefore arbitrary to say that a person is free when he is necessitated in one fashion but not when he is necessitated in another?

That all causes equally necessitate is indeed a tautology, if the word 'necessitate' is taken merely as equivalent to 'cause': but if, as the objection requires, it is taken as equivalent to 'constrain' or 'compel', then I do not think that this proposition is true. For all that is needed for one event to be the cause of another is that, in the given circumstances, the event which is said to be the effect would not have occurred if it had not been for the occurrence of the event which is said to be the cause, or *vice versa*, according as causes are interpreted as necessary, or sufficient, conditions: and this fact is usually deducible from some causal law which states that whenever an event of the one kind occurs then, given suitable conditions, an event of the other kind will occur in a certain temporal or spatio-temporal relationship to it. In short, there is an invariable concomitance[4] between the two classes of events; but there is no compulsion, in any but a metaphorical sense. Suppose, for example, that a psycho-analyst is able to account for some aspect of my behaviour by referring it to some lesion[5] that I suffered in my childhood. In that case, it may be said that my childhood experience, together with certain other events, necessitates my behaving as I do. But all that this involves is that it is found to be true in gen-

eral that when people have had certain experiences as children, they subsequently behave in certain specifiable ways; and my case is just another instance of this general law. It is in this way indeed that my behaviour is explained. But from the fact that my behaviour is capable of being explained, in the sense that it can be subsumed under some natural law, it does not follow that I am acting under constraint.

If this is correct, to say that I could have acted otherwise is to say, first, that I should have acted otherwise if I had so chosen; secondly, that my action was voluntary in the sense in which the actions, say, of the kleptomaniac are not; and thirdly, that nobody compelled me to choose as I did: and these three conditions may very well be fulfilled. When they are fulfilled, I may be said to have acted freely. But this is not to say that it was a matter of chance that I acted as I did, or, in other words, that my action could not be explained. And that my actions should be capable of being explained is all that is required by the postulate of determinism.

If more than this seems to be required it is, I think, because the use of the very word 'determinism' is in some degree misleading. For it tends to suggest that one event is somehow in the power of another, whereas the truth is merely that they are factually correlated. And the same applies to the use, in this context, of the word 'necessity' and even of the word 'cause' itself. Moreover, there are various reasons for this. One is the tendency to confuse causal with logical necessitation, and so to infer mistakenly that the effect is contained in the cause. Another is the uncritical use of a concept of force which is derived from primitive experiences of pushing and striking. A third is the survival of an animistic conception of causality, in which all causal relationships are modelled on the example of one person's exercising authority over another. As a result we tend to form an imaginative picture of an unhappy effect trying vainly to escape from the clutches of an overmastering cause. But, I repeat, the fact is simply that when an event of one type occurs, an event of another type occurs also, in a certain temporal or spatio-temporal relation to the first. The rest is only metaphor. And it is because of the metaphor, and not because of the fact, that we come to think that there is an antithesis between causality and freedom.

---

4   Co-occurrence or co-existence.

5   Abnormal or damaged brain tissue; an injury.

Nevertheless, it may be said, if the postulate of determinism is valid, then the future can be explained in terms of the past: and this means that if one knew enough about the past one would be able to predict the future. But in that case what will happen in the future is already decided. And how then can I be said to be free? What is going to happen is going to happen and nothing that I do can prevent it. If the determinist is right, I am the helpless prisoner of fate.

But what is meant by saying that the future course of events is already decided? If the implication is that some person has arranged it, then the proposition is false. But if all that is meant is that it is possible, in principle, to deduce it from a set of particular facts about the past, together with the appropriate general laws, then, even if this is true, it does not in the least entail that I am the helpless prisoner of fate. It does not even entail that my actions make no difference to the future: for they are causes as well as effects; so that if they were different their consequences would be different also. What it does entail is that my behaviour can be predicted: but to say that my behaviour can be predicted is not to say that I am acting under constraint. It is indeed true that I cannot escape my destiny if this is taken to mean no more than that I shall do what I shall do. But this is a tautology, just as it is a tautology that what is going to happen is going to happen. And such tautologies as these prove nothing whatsoever about the freedom of the will.

BERNARD WILLIAMS AND THOMAS NAGEL
"Moral Luck"

Who Was Bernard Williams?

His obituary in the [London] *Times*, June 14, 2003, called Sir Bernard Williams "the most brilliant and most important British moral philosopher of his time," remarking, however, that his work "effortlessly spanned the entire discipline of philosophy." Williams, born in 1929, turned to philosophy during his Oxford education, and following his military service, taught at Oxford, then at University College London, Bedford College (also part of the University of London), and, from 1967 until 1988, Cambridge. Unhappy with Thatcherite educational policy, he moved to UC Berkeley, but returned in 1990 to Oxford. He was knighted in 1999 and died in 2003.

What Was Williams's Overall Philosophical Project?

Williams is known, in moral philosophy, as a critic of both utilitarianism and Kantianism. His contribution to the book *Utilitarianism, For and Against*, argued that the utilitarian framework was wrong in its basic approach because (among other faults) it ignored individuals' connections to those nearer to them. His criticism of Kantianism, seen in his article here, is that it purifies ethics of all contingent matters such as your circumstances and the consequences of your actions. The emotional aspects of morality, he argued contrary to Kant, must be integrated into a full understanding of ethics.

In a remembrance of Williams published in the *Boston Review* (Oct/Nov 2003), the influential political philosopher Martha Nussbaum wrote that, according to Williams,

> Utilitarianism and Kantianism ... simplified the moral life in ways that he found egregious, failing to understand, or even actively denying, the heterogeneity of values, the sometimes tragic collisions between one thing we care

for and another. They also underestimated the importance of personal attachments and projects in the ethical life and, in a related way, neglected the valuable role emotions play in good choice.

His work on political theory and on personal identity has also been very important.

For information on Thomas Nagel and his overall project, please see the notes on Nagel's "What Is It Like to Be a Bat?" in Chapter 5.

What Is the Structure of These Readings?

I.

Williams begins his article by mentioning the old philosophical tradition which argues for the central value of internal tranquility immune from contingent "luck"—from how the external world happens to turn out. The more modern correlate of this, he points out, is the Kantian tradition which chooses a life of morally correct action as the most important thing, but equally sees this as independent of luck. For Kantians, a morally good action is one that arises from the right intentions, however its effects turn out. It is Williams's intention in this article, to show that this view is false.

If moral considerations were the most important thing—the only intrinsically important thing—then moral regret would be the most basic form of regret; and if morality was "unconditioned"—independent of worldly eventualities—moral regret should not depend on how things turned out. But Williams claims that the most basic kind of regret we have in fact is partly determined by outside events—things beyond our control. Thus his overall point: this sort of unconditioned morality could not be the only thing of basic importance in our lives.

To demonstrate the "conditioned" nature of basic regret, Williams considers the life of 'Gauguin' (loosely based on the French artist of that name), who left his job, family, and country to live in the South Seas and pursue his painting. Whether he can justify this radical choice to himself, in the long run, can be determined only retrospectively, once he knows how it turns out. He will find it justified (or else regret it), in the pro-

found way that one judges the justifiability of one's own most basic decisions, depending on whether he eventually takes himself to realize what he thought were his gifts as a painter.

Williams distinguishes this sort of justification from, on the one hand, Kantian moral justification, which can be done in advance: it depends supposedly only on the good will and its intentions based on moral principle; it has nothing to do with how one's actions turn out. And he also distinguishes it, on the other hand, from utilitarian moral justification, which would consider whether, all in all, the world as a whole was better off as the result of Gauguin's actions and their consequences. This sort of justification considers merely whether it is better or worse that it happened, not whether the person who did it can consider himself a success or a failure.

This particular kind of regret, Williams argues, is appropriate only when failure is "intrinsic to the project itself." Thus, if Gauguin failed in his plans because of an accidental injury, he would not have been unjustified in his earlier decision, and would not regret it in that way. Williams discusses Anna Karenina's disastrous affair, for which she left her family, as a clearer case of intrinsic failure of a project: in Williams's words, "her hopes were not just negated, but refuted, by what happened."

Williams goes on to distinguish this kind of "agent-regret" from other sorts of regret at bad luck in various ways, including the fact that one can express the former by gestures of reparation to those harmed.

His overall point here is that this sort of action is shown to be justified or unjustified by events out of one's control—by good or bad luck—and that the values expressed here are deep and important; Kant's narrower conception of morality is, he indicates, certainly not what he conceives it to be: the only basic value there is.

II.

Nagel begins his response to Williams by accusing him of sidestepping the question: ignoring *moral* luck altogether, he instead describes cases involving values that have nothing to do with morality, though luck may certainly play a part there. He reminds us that the problem raised by moral luck arises because, on the one hand, there is a plausible general principle that people cannot be assessed, be praised or blamed, because of events beyond their control; but on the other, most of our assessments are in fact based on things not in the agents' control.

Nagel distinguishes several ways in which assessments are "disturbingly subject to luck": those involving *constitutive luck* (the kind of person the agent is—his inclinations, capacities, and temperament); involving *one's circumstances* (the kinds of situation one happens to find oneself in); and involving the *causes and effects* of one's actions.

He says that Williams's cases (involving effects) do not show *moral* luck: the agents' regret is not a matter of moral assessment at all. In moral cases, one can make assessment of actions in advance, for oneself or others, but often this will be a hypothetical judgment, depending on outcome. The truck driver who negligently fails to check his brakes is morally more to blame if he kills a child who runs into the road than if he luckily completes his trip without incident—even though whether a child runs into his path or not is not something within his control.

Nagel, in other words, does admit that our ordinary *moral* judgments do take account of events beyond agents' control; this is problematic. It's clearly irrational to hold someone morally responsible for what he has no control over.

One response to this problem is to "pare down each act to the morally essential core," for example, by judging merely the pure will and intentions of the agent, and ignoring consequences. Similarly, one might ignore "constitutive" differences by paring away the antecedent kind of person the agent is, considering only the person's immediate will. But this shrinks the area of genuine agency "down to an extensionless point": when all external factors are removed, it seems nothing is left.

Nagel then leaves us with what he calls a "paradox"—a problem with no solution. Moral judgment must exclude luck, but this leaves us with a mysterious inner self we have no grasp of. The problem is, it seems, the result of an irreconcilable conflict between the inner view we have of ourselves as responsible agents, and the external view that "forces itself on us when we see how everything we do belongs to a world that we have not created."

Some Useful Background Information

1. The famous passage from Kant in which he presents his view that the only morally relevant thing is a good will which is totally independent of effects, appears in his *Foundations of the Metaphysics of Morals*. Here is the passage, from Part I:

> The good will is not good because of what it effects or accomplishes or because of its competence to achieve some intended end; it is good only because of its willing (i.e., it is good in itself).... Even if it should happen that, by a particularly unfortunate fate or by the niggardly provision of a step-motherly nature, this will should be wholly lacking in power to accomplish its purpose, and even if the greatest effort should not avail it to achieve anything of its end, and if there remained only the good will—not as a mere wish, but as the summoning of all means in our power—it would sparkle like a jewel all by itself, as something that had its full worth in itself. Usefulness or fruitlessness can neither diminish nor augment this worth.

2. Nagel remarks on the connection between the issue of moral luck and the long-standing debate about free will and moral responsibility. This issue is discussed in depth in the other readings in this chapter, but we'll here briefly indicate how our current topic hooks up with the free-will debate.

Libertarians hold that one can be morally responsible only for actions that are uncaused; and they believe that the will is capable of uncaused action. Thus they would accept the Kantian view that antecedent events have no causal relevance to morally significant acts of the will; so that category of "moral luck" (Nagel's third) would be empty. Determinists, however, believe that the will, like all other natural phenomena, is caused. Some determinists, as a result, reject moral responsibility altogether—and this corresponds to Nagel's point that the realm of morally relevant action seems to dwindle and disappear from the external viewpoint, as causes (and other things beyond one's control) are discovered. Other determinists are compatibilists, holding that the fact that one's decisions and actions have causes does not imply that one is not morally responsible for them. Nagel mentions the corresponding possibility of compatibilism in the moral-luck debate: one might hold, and Williams actually seems to, that moral responsibility is not compromised by the existence of "moral luck"—factors in the action under consideration that are outside one's power.

Suggestions for Critical Reflection

1. What situation does Williams take to be an example that shows that we have "deep and persistent reasons to be grateful" that morality is not universally respected? What's his reasoning here?

2. Why does Williams think that the sort of justification he's thinking about could not be provided in advance?

3. What is, according to Williams, the wrong sort of question utilitarians would ask about the Gauguin case?

4. What is the difference Williams draws between extrinsic and intrinsic luck? Which one does he think "relates to unjustification"? Explain.

5. What is the difference, for Williams, between the cases of Gauguin and Anna Karenina?

6. Explain what Williams means when he says that "real supremacy of the moral would imply its ubiquity.... If it were to be genuinely unconditioned, there would have to be nothing to condition it." What does he think is wrong with the idea that the moral is thus supreme?

7. Why does Nagel deny that Williams's two examples, Gauguin and Anna Karenina, are cases of *moral* luck?

8. What is the "condition of control" Nagel speaks about? He admits that there are numerous highly plausible counterexamples to this condition. Why does he not conclude that this condition is false? Explain his reasoning in the paragraphs following "What rules out this escape...."

9. Nagel's argument (contra Williams) is that one can give a moral evaluation of one's acts in advance—but a *hypothetical* evaluation. Explain his point.

10. Explain what Nagel means when he says that "The area of genuine agency, and therefore of legitimate judgment, seems to shrink under this scrutiny to an extensionless point." Under what scrutiny? Why does this scrutiny "shrink" these areas?

11. Explain what Nagel means when he says that "The problem arises ... because the self ... is threatened with dissolution by the absorption of its acts and impulses into the class of events." Why does the "acknowledgement that we are parts of the world" leave us with "no one to be"?

Suggestions for Further Reading

Williams's major work including this article and others more or less related is *Moral Luck* (Cambridge University Press, 1981). He has also written a postscript to this article, printed in *Moral Luck*, D. Statman, ed. (State University of New York Press, 1993).

For Nagel's major works, see Suggestions for Further Reading in the introduction to his article in Chapter 5 of this book.

An important anthology of articles on the topic is D. Statman (ed.), *Moral Luck* (State University of New York Press, 1993).

Two excellent online surveys of the problem, each including an extensive bibliography, are: A. Latus, 2001, "Moral Luck," *The Internet Encyclopedia of Philosophy*, J. Feiser (ed.) <http://www.iep.utm.edu/moralluc/> and Dana K. Nelkin, "Moral Luck", *The Stanford Encyclopedia of Philosophy (Fall 2008 Edition)*, Edward N. Zalta (ed.), <http://plato.stanford.edu/archives/fall2008/entries/moral-luck/>.

"Moral Luck"[1]

I—B.A.O. Williams

There has been a strain of philosophical thought which has identified the end of life as happiness, happiness as reflective tranquillity, and tranquillity as the product of self-sufficiency—for what is not in the domain of the self is not in its control, and so is subject to luck and the contingent enemies of tranquillity. The most extreme versions of this outlook in the Western tradition are certain doctrines of classical antiquity; though it is a notable fact about them that while the good man, the sage, was immune to the impact of incident luck, it was a matter of what may be called constitutive luck[2] that one was a sage, or capable of becoming one: for the many and vulgar this was not (on the prevailing view) an available course.

The idea that one's whole life can in some such way be rendered immune to luck has perhaps rarely prevailed since (it did not prevail, for instance, in mainstream Christianity), but its place has been taken by the still powerfully influential idea that there is one basic form of value, moral value, which is immune to luck and—in the crucial term of the idea's most rigorous exponent[3]—"unconditioned". Both the disposition to correct moral judgment, and the objects of such judgment, are on this view free from external contingency, for both are, in their related ways, the product of the unconditioned will. Anything which is the product of happy or unhappy contingency is no proper object of moral assessment, and no proper determinant of it either. Just as in the realm of character it is motive, not style, or powers, or endowment, that counts, so in action, it is not changes actually effected in the world, but intention. With these considerations

there is supposed to disappear even that constitutive luck which the ancient sages were happy to benefit from; the capacity for moral agency is supposedly present to any rational agent whatever, to anyone for whom the question can even present itself. The successful moral life, removed from considerations of birth, lucky upbringing, or indeed of the incomprehensible Grace of a non-Pelagian[4] God, is presented as a career open not merely to the talents, but to a talent which all rational beings necessarily possess in the same degree. Such a conception has an ultimate form of justice at its heart, and that is its allure. Kantianism is only superficially repulsive[5]—despite appearances, it offers an inducement, solace to a sense of the world's unfairness.

Any conception of "moral luck", on this view, is radically incoherent, and the fact that the phrase indeed sounds strange may express a fit, not unexpected, between that view and some of our implicit conceptions of morality. But the view is false. Morality itself cannot be rendered immune to luck: most basically, the dispositions of morality, however far back they are placed in the area of intention and motive, are as "conditioned" as anything else. This, the matter of what I have called "constitutive" luck, I shall leave entirely on one side. But there is a further issue. Even if moral value had been radically unconditioned by luck, it would not have been enough merely to exhibit it as one kind of value among others. Little would be affirmed unless moral values possessed some special,

1 From *Proceedings of the Aristotelian Society, Supplementary Volume.* Volume 50, 1976; pp. 115–135 and pp. 137–151. Reprinted by courtesy of the Editor of the Aristotelian Society: © 1976.

2 This concerns what Nagel calls, below, "the kind of person you are, where this is not just a question of what you deliberately do, but of your inclinations, capacities, and temperament."

3 Immanuel Kant (1724–1804).

4 Pelagianism, an early version of Christianity based on the thought of the (possibly British) monk Pelagius (354–c. 420), taught that humans were completely free to do good or evil, and were completely responsible for their own actions and salvation. The mainstream church had this view declared heretical, believing instead that humans were evil by nature, because of original sin, and could achieve goodness and salvation only through the unearned grace of God.

5 Williams does, however, find Kant's view repulsive (if only superficially) in the sense that it repels rather than attracts, due to its insistence that the only source for morality is abstract duty, and that desires other than to do one's duty are irrelevant, as are considerations of the values of happiness or pleasure.

indeed supreme, kind of dignity or importance: the thought that there is a kind of value which is, unlike others, accessible to all rational agents, offers little encouragement if that kind of value is merely a last resort, the doss-house[6] of the spirit. Rather, it must have a claim on one's most fundamental concerns as a rational agent, and in one's recognition of that, one is supposed to grasp, not only morality's immunity to luck, but one's own partial immunity to luck through morality.

It has notoriously not been easy for Kantianism to make clear what the recognition consists in.[7] But one consequence of it, at least, would be something very widely held: that anyone who is genuinely open to moral considerations must regard moral regret for his actions as the most basic form of regret there is, and (connectedly), in so far as he is rational, will not let his most basic regrets be determined by other than what he was fully responsible for, what lay within his voluntary control. In this way, though his life may be subject to luck, at the most basic level of his self-assessment as a rational agent, he will not be.

It is in this area of regret, justification, and the retrospective view of one's own actions, that I shall raise my questions. Some views of regret which I shall

question (roughly that the most profound aspects of first-personal[8] regret must attach to voluntary actions) are implied by this conception of morality, but may well not imply it, or indeed any specific view of morality, as opposed to certain conceptions of rationality. In so far as that is so, the discussion will have broader implications for the self's exposure to luck, though the examples centrally in question do essentially involve considerations of morality.

I shall use the notion of "luck" generously, undefinedly, but, I think, comprehensibly. (I hope it will be clear that when I say of something that it is a matter of luck, this is not meant to carry any implication that it is uncaused.) My procedure in general will be to invite reflection about how to think and feel about some rather less usual situations, in the light of an appeal to how we—many people—tend to think and feel about other more usual situations, not in terms of substantive moral opinions or "intuitions" but in terms of the experience of those kinds of situation. There is no suggestion that it is impossible for human beings to lack these feelings and experiences. In the case of the less usual there is only the claim that the thoughts and experiences I consider are possible, coherent, and intelligible, and that there is no ground for condemning them as irrational. In the case of the more usual, there are suggestions, with the outline of a reason for them, that unless we were to be merely confused or unreflective, life without these experiences would involve a much vaster reconstruction of our sentiments and our views of ourselves than may be supposed: supposed, in particular, by those philosophers who discuss these matters as though our experience of our own agency and the sense of our regrets not only could be tidied up to accord with a very simple image of rationality, but already had been.

Let us take first an outline example of the creative artist who turns away from definite and pressing human claims on him in order to live a life in which, as he supposes, he can pursue his art. Without feeling that we are limited by any historical facts, let us call

---

6   A very cheap boarding-house, or a shelter provided by a municipality or charity—minimal accommodation for those who can get nothing better.

7   [Author's note] The question centres on the rôle of the Categorical Imperative. On the major issue here, I agree with what I take to be the substance of Philippa Foot's position ("Morality as a System of Hypothetical Imperatives", *Phil. Rev.* 1972; and her reply to Frankena, *Philosophy* 1975), but not at all with her way of putting it. In so far as there is a clear distinction between categorical and hypothetical imperatives, and in so far as morality consists of imperatives, it consists of categorical imperatives. The point is that the fact that an imperative is (in this sense) categorical provides no reason at all for obeying it. Nor need Kant think it does: the authority of the Categorical Imperative is supposed (mysteriously enough) to derive not just from its being (in this sense) categorical, but from its being categorical and self-addressed by the agent as a rational being.

8   The "first person" in grammar is the person speaking—"I." So first-personal regret is regret about one's own actions, not about someone else's.

him *Gauguin*.[9] Gauguin might have been a man who was not at all interested in the claims on him, and simply preferred to live another life, and from that life, and perhaps from that preference, his best paintings came. That sort of case, in which the claims of others simply have no hold on the agent, is not what concerns us now: though it serves to remind us of something related to the present concerns, that while we are sometimes guided by the notion that it would be the best of worlds in which morality were universally respected and all men were of a disposition to affirm it, we have in fact deep and persistent reasons to be grateful that that is not the world we have.

We are interested here in a narrower phenomenon, more intimate to moral thought itself. Let us take, rather, a Gauguin who is concerned about these claims and what is involved in their being neglected (we may suppose this to be grim), and that he nevertheless, in the face of that, opts for the other life. This other life he might perhaps not see very determinately under the category of realising his gifts as a painter: but to make consideration simpler, let us add that he does see it determinately in that light—it is as a life which will enable him really to be a painter that he opts for it. It will then be more clear what will count for him as eventual success in his project: at least some possible outcomes will be clear examples of success (which of course is not meant to be equivalent to recognition), however many others may be unclear.

Whether he will succeed cannot, in the nature of the case, be foreseen; we are not dealing here with the removal of an external obstacle to something which, once that is removed, will fairly predictably go through. Gauguin, in our story, is putting a great deal on a possibility which has not unequivocally declared itself. I want to explore and uphold the claim that it is possible that in such a situation the only thing that will justify his choice will be success itself. If he fails—and we shall come shortly to what, more precisely, failure may be—then he did the wrong thing, not just in the sense in which that platitudinously follows, but in the sense that having done the wrong thing in those circumstances he has no basis for the thought that he was justified in acting as he did; while if he succeeds, he does have a basis for that thought. This notion of justification, which I shall try to make clearer, is not one by which, if he succeeds, he will necessarily be able to justify himself *to others*. The reproaches of others he may never have an answer to, in the sense of having a right that they accept or even listen to what he has to say; but if he fails, he will not even have anything to say.

The justification, if there is to be one, will be essentially retrospective. Gauguin could not do something which is often thought to be essential to rationality and to the notion of justification itself, which is to apply the justifying considerations at the time of the choice and in advance of knowing whether one was right (in the sense of its coming out right). How this can be in general, will form a major part of the discussion. First, however, we should consider a more limited question, whether there could be a moral justification in advance. A moral theorist, recognizing that some value attached to the success of Gauguin's project and hence possibly to his choice, might try to accommodate that choice within a framework of moral rules, by forming a subsidiary rule which could, before the outcome, justify that choice. What could that rule be? It could not be that one is morally justified in deciding to neglect other claims if one is a great creative artist: apart from basic doubts about its moral content, that saving clause begs the question which at the relevant time one is in no position to answer. On the other hand, ".... if one is convinced that one is a great creative artist" will serve to make obstinacy and fatuous self-delusion conditions of justification; while "... if one is reasonably convinced that one is a great creative artist" is, if anything, worse. What is reasonable conviction supposed to be in such a case? Should Gauguin consult professors of art? The absurdity of such riders surely expresses an absurdity in the whole enterprise of trying to find a place for such cases within the rules.

If there cannot be a moral justification which is accessible in advance, then, according to the conception of morality which purges it of luck, there cannot

---

9   Williams's choice of this name for his hypothetical agent is an allusion to the French post-impressionist painter Paul Gauguin (1848–1903), who left his wife and family, and job as a stockbroker, to live among the natives in tropical islands and paint.

be a moral justification at all. Whether there could in *any* sense be a moral justification of the Gauguin-type decision is not a question I shall try to resolve here. There are other issues that need discussion first, and I suspect that when they have been discussed, that will turn out to be a question of diminishing interest. But there is one point that needs to be mentioned. One consequence of finding a moral justification (a motive, perhaps for trying to find one) might be thought to be that those who suffer from the decision would then have no justified, or at least correct, ground of reproach. There is no reason to think that we want that result. But there is also no obvious reason to think that it would be a consequence: one needs some very strong assumption about the nature of ethical consistency in order to deliver it.

Utilitarian formulations are not going to contribute any more to understanding these situations than do formulations in terms of rules. They can offer the thought "it is better (worse) that he did it", where the force of that is, approximately, "it is better (worse) that it happened", but this in itself does not help to a characterization of the agent's decision or its possible justification, and Utilitarianism has no special materials of its own to help in that. It has its own well-known problems, too, in spelling out the content of the "better"—on standard doctrine, Gauguin's decision would seem to have been a better thing, the more popular a painter he eventually became. But more interesting than that class of difficulty is the point that the Utilitarian perspective, not uniquely but clearly, will fail to attach importance to something which is actually important for these thoughts, the question of what "failure" may relevantly be. From the perspective of consequences, the goods or benefits for the sake of which Gauguin's choice was made either materialize in some degree, or do not materialize. But it matters considerably to the thoughts we are considering, in what way the project fails to come off, if it fails. If Gauguin sustains some injury on the way to Tahiti which prevents his ever painting again, that certainly means that his decision (supposing it now to be irreversible) was for nothing, and indeed there is nothing in the outcome to set against the other people's loss. But that train of events does not provoke the thought in question, that after all he was wrong and unjusti-

fied: he does not, and never will, know whether he was wrong. What would prove him wrong in his project would not just be that it failed, but that he failed.

This distinction shows that while Gauguin's justification is in some ways a matter of luck, it is not equally a matter of all kinds of luck. It matters how intrinsic the cause of failure is to the project itself. The occurrence of an injury is, relative to these undertakings at least, luck of the most external and incident kind. Irreducibly, luck of this kind affects whether he will be justified or not, since if it strikes, he will not be justified. But it is too external for it to unjustify him, something which only his failure as a painter can do: yet still that is, at another level, luck, the luck of being able to be as he hoped he might be. It might be wondered whether that is luck at all, or, if so, whether it may not be luck of that constitutive kind which affects everything and which we have already left on one side. But it is more than that. It is not merely luck that he is such a man, but luck relative to the deliberations that went into his decision, that he turns out to be such a man: he might (epistemically) not have been.[10] That is what sets the problem.

In some cases, though perhaps not in Gauguin's, success in such decisions might be thought not to be a matter of epistemic luck relative to the decision: there might be grounds for saying that the person who was prepared to take the decision, and was in fact right, actually knew that he would succeed, however subjectively uncertain he may have been. But even if this is right for some cases, it does not help with the problems of retrospective justification. For the concept of knowledge here is itself applied restrospectively, and while there is nothing necessarily wrong with that, it does not enable the agent at the time of his decision to make any distinctions he could not already make. As one might say, even if it did turn out in such a case that the agent did know, it was still luck, relative to the considerations available to him at the time and at the level at which he made his decision, that he should turn out to have known.

---

10   That is, given what we currently know, he might not have been. A claim is epistemically possible if it may be true, for all we know.

Some luck, in a decision of Gauguin's kind, is extrinsic to his project, some intrinsic; both are necessary for success, and hence for actual justification, but only the latter relates to unjustification. If we now broaden the range of cases slightly, we shall be able to see more clearly the notion of intrinsic luck. In Gauguin's case the nature of the project is such that two distinctions do, roughly, coincide: the distinction between luck intrinsic to the project, and luck extrinsic to it, and another distinction between what is, and what is not, determined by him and by what he is. The intrinsic luck in Gauguin's case concentrates itself on virtually the one question of whether he is a genuinely gifted painter who can succeed in doing genuinely valuable work. Not all the conditions of the project's coming off lie in him, obviously, since others' actions and refrainings provide many necessary conditions of its coming off—and that is an important locus of extrinsic luck. But the conditions of its coming off which are relevant to unjustification, the locus of intrinsic luck, largely lie in him—which is not to say, of course, that they depend on his will, though some may. This rough coincidence of two distinctions is a feature of this case. But in others, the locus of intrinsic luck (intrinsic, that is to say, to the project) may lie partly outside the agent, and this is an important, and indeed the more typical, case.

Consider an almost equally schematized account of another example, that of Anna Karenina.[11] Anna remains conscious in her life with Vronsky of the cost exacted from others, above all her son. She could have lived with that consciousness, we may suppose, if things had gone better; and relative to her state of understanding when she left Karenin, they could have gone better. As it turns out, the social situation and her own state of mind are such that the relationship with Vronsky has to carry too much weight, and the more obvious that becomes, the more it has to carry; and that I take that to be a truth not only about society but about her and Vronsky, a truth which, however inevitable Tolstoy ultimately makes it seem, could, relative to her earlier thoughts, have been otherwise. It is, in the present terms, a matter of intrinsic luck, and a failure in the heart of her project. But its locus is not by any means entirely in her, for it also lies in him.

It would have been an intrinsic failure, also, if Vronsky had actually committed suicide. But it would not have been that, but rather an extrinsic misfortune, if Vronsky had been accidentally killed: though her project would have been at an end, it would not have failed as it does fail. This difference illustrates precisely the thoughts we are concerned with. For if Anna had then committed suicide, her thought might essentially have been something like: "there is nothing more for me". But I take it that as things are, her thought in killing herself is not just that, but relates inescapably also to the past and to what she has done. What she did she now finds insupportable, because she could have been justified only by the life she hoped for, and those hopes were not just negated, but refuted, by what happened.

It is these thoughts that I want to explore and to place in a structure which will make their sense plainer. The discussion is not in the first place directed to what we or others might say or think of these agents (though it has implications for that), but on what they can be expected coherently to think about themselves. A notion we shall be bound to use in describing their state of mind is *regret*, and there are certain things that need, first, to be said about this notion.

The constitutive thought of regret in general is something like "how much better if it had been otherwise", and the feeling can in principle apply to anything of which one can form some conception of how it might have been otherwise, together with consciousness of how things would then have been better. In this general sense of regret, what are regretted are states of affairs, and they can be regretted, in principle, by anyone who knows of them. But there is a particularly important species of regret, which I shall call "agent-regret", which a person can feel only towards his own past actions (or, at most, actions in which he regards himself as a participant). In this case, the supposed possible difference is that one might have acted otherwise, and the focus of the regret is

---

11   She is the central character in the great 1878 novel bearing her name, by the Russian author Leo Tolstoy (1828–1910). The moral and psychological depth of this novel is of course not done justice by this plot summary: Anna abandons a loveless marriage for a doomed affair with the handsome Count Vronsky.

on that possibility, the thought being formed in part by first-personal conceptions of how one might have acted otherwise. "Agent-regret" is not distinguished from regret in general solely or simply in virtue of its subject-matter. There can be cases of regret directed to one's own past actions which are not cases of agent-regret, because the past action is regarded purely externally, as one might regard anyone else's action. Agent-regret requires not merely a first-personal subject-matter, nor yet merely a particular kind of psychological content, but also a particular kind of expression, something which I hope will become a little clearer in what follows.

The sentiment of agent-regret is by no means restricted to *voluntary* agency. It can extend far beyond what one intentionally did to almost anything for which one was causally responsible in virtue of something one intentionally did. Yet even at deeply accidental or non-voluntary levels of agency, sentiments of agent-regret are different from regret in general, such as might be felt by a spectator, and are acknowledged in our practice as being different. The lorry driver[12] who, through no fault of his, runs over a child, will feel differently from any spectator, even a spectator next to him in the cab, except perhaps to the extent that the spectator takes on the thought that he might have prevented it, an agent's thought. Doubtless, and rightly, people will try, in comforting him, to move the driver from this state of feeling, move him indeed from where he is to something more like the place of a spectator; but it is important that this is seen as something that should need to be done, and indeed some doubt would be felt about a driver who too blandly or readily moved to that position. We feel sorry for the driver, but that sentiment co-exists with, indeed presupposes, that there is something special about his relation to this happening, something which cannot merely be eliminated by the consideration that it was not his fault. It may be still more so in cases where agency is fuller than in such an accident, though still involuntary through ignorance.

The differences between agent-regret and any felt by a spectator come out not just in thoughts and im-

_____
12   British for truck driver.

ages that enter into the sentiment, but in differences of expression. The lorry driver may act in some way which he hopes will constitute or at least symbolise some kind of recompense or restitution, and this will be an expression of his agent-regret. But the willingness to give compensation, even the recognition that one should give it, does not necessarily express agent-regret, and the preparedness to compensate can present itself at very different levels of significance in these connexions. We may recognize the need to pay compensation for damage we involuntarily cause, and yet this recognition be of an external kind, accompanied only by regret of a general kind, or by no regret at all. The general structure of these situations may merely be that it would be unfair for the sufferer to bear the cost if there is an alternative, and there is an alternative to be found in the agent whose intentional activities produced the damage as a side-effect. This area of compensation can be seen as part of the general regulation of boundary effects between agents' activities.

In such cases, the relevant consciousness of having done the harmful thing is basically that of its having happened as a consequence of one's acts, together with the thought that the cost of its happening can in the circumstances fairly be allocated to one's account. A test of whether that is an agent's state of mind in acknowledging that he should compensate is offered by the question whether from his point of view insurance cover would do at least as well. Imagine the premiums already paid (by someone else, we might add, if that helps to clarify the test): then if knowledge that the victim received insurance payments would settle any unease the agent feels, then it is for him an external case. It is an obvious and welcome consequence of this test that whether an agent can acceptably regard a given case externally is a function not only of his relations to it, but of what sort of case it is—besides the question of whether he should compensate rather than the insurance company, there is the question whether it is the sort of loss that can be compensated at all by insurance. If it is not, an agent conscious that he was unintentionally responsible for it might still feel that he should do something, not necessarily because he could actually compensate where insurance money could not, but because (if he is lucky) his actions might have some reparative significance other than compensation.

In other cases, again, there is no room for any appropriate action at all. Then only the desire to make reparation remains, with the painful consciousness that nothing can be done about it; some other action, perhaps less directed to the victims, may come to express this. What degree of such feeling is appropriate, and what attempts at reparative action or substitutes for it, are questions for particular cases, and that there is room in the area for irrational and self-punitive excess, no one is likely to deny. But equally it would be a kind of insanity never to experience sentiments of this kind towards anyone, and it would be an insane concept of rationality which insisted that a rational person never would. To insist on such a conception of rationality, moreover, would, apart from other kinds of absurdity, suggest a large falsehood: that we might, if we conducted ourselves clear-headedly enough, entirely detach ourselves from the unintentional aspects of our actions, relegating their costs to, so to speak, the insurance fund, and yet still retain our identity and character as agents. One's history as an agent is a web in which anything that is the product of the will is surrounded and held up and partly formed by things that are not, in such a way that reflection can go only in one of two directions: either in the direction of saying that responsible agency is a fairly superficial concept, which has a limited use in harmonizing what happens, or else that it is not a superficial concept, but that it cannot ultimately be purified—if one attaches importance to the sense of what one is in terms of what one has done and what in the world one is responsible for, one must accept much that makes its claim on that sense solely in virtue of its being actual.[13]

13 [Author's note] That acceptance is central to tragedy, something which presses the question of how we want to think about these things. When Oedipus says "I did not do it" (Sophocles *OC* 539) he speaks as one whose exile proclaims that he did do it, and to persons who treat him as quite special because he did. Could we have, and do we want, a concept of agency by which what Oedipus said would be simply true, and by which he would be seeing things rightly if for him it

The cases we are concerned with are, of course, cases of voluntary agency, but they share something with the involuntary cases just mentioned, for the "luck" of the agents relates to those elements which are essential to the outcome but lie outside their control, and what we are discussing is in this way a very drastic example of determination by the actual, the determination of the agent's judgment on his decision by what, beyond his will, actually occurs. Besides that, the discussion of agent-regret about the involuntary also helps us to get away from a dichotomy which is often relied on in these matters, expressed in such terms as *regret* and *remorse*, where "regret" is identified in effect as the regret of a spectator, while "remorse" is what we have called "agent-regret", but under the restriction that it applies only to the voluntary. The fact that we have agent-regret about the involuntary, and would not readily recognize a life without it (though we may think we might), shows already that there is something wrong with this dichotomy: such regret is neither mere spectator's regret, nor (by this definition) remorse.

There is a difference between agent-regret as we have so far discussed it, and the agents' feelings in the present cases. As we elicited it from the non-voluntary examples, agent-regret involved a wish on the agent's part that he had not done it: he deeply wishes that he had made that change which, had he known it, was in his power and which would have altered the outcome. But Gauguin or Anna Karenina, as we have represented them, wish they had acted otherwise only if they are unsuccessful. (At least, that wish attends their unsuccess under the simplifying assumption that their subsequent thoughts and feelings are still essentially formed by the projects we have ascribed to them. This is an oversimplification, since evidently they might form new projects in the course of unsuccess itself; though Anna did not. I shall sustain the assumption in what follows.) Whatever feelings these agents had after their decision, but before the declaration of their success or failure, lacked the fully-developed wish to

was straight off as though he had no part in it? (These questions have little to do with how the law should be: punishment and public amends are a different matter.)

have acted otherwise—that wish comes only when failure is declared.

Regret necessarily involves a wish that things had been otherwise, for instance that one had not had to act as one did. But it does not necessarily involve the wish, all things taken together, that one had acted otherwise. An example of this, largely independent of the present issues, is offered by the cases of conflict between two courses of action each of which is morally required, where either course of action, even if it is judged to be for the best, leaves regrets—which are, in our present terms, agent-regrets about something voluntarily done.[14] We should not entirely assimilate agent-regret and the wish, all things taken together, to have acted otherwise. We must now look at some connexions of these to each other, and to certain ideas of justification. This will add the last element to our attempt to characterize our cases.

It will be helpful to contrast our cases with more straightforward cases of practical deliberation and the types of retrospective reflexion appropriate to them. We may take first the simplest cases of pure egoistic deliberation, where not only is the agent's attention confined to egoistic projects, but moral critics would agree that it is legitimately so confined. Here, in one sense the agent does not have to justify his deliberative processes, since there is no one he is answerable to; but it is usually supposed that there is some sense in which even such an agent's deliberative processes can be justified or unjustified—the sense, that is, in which his decision can be reasonable or unreasonable relative to his situation, whatever its actual outcome. Considerations bearing on this include at least the consistency of his thoughts, the rational assessment of probabilities, and the optimal ordering of actions in time.[15]

While the language of justification is used in this connexion, it is less clear than is usually assumed what its content is, and, in particular, what the point

is of an agent's being retrospectively concerned with the rationality of his decision, and not just with its success. How are we to understand the retrospective thought of one who comes to see a mismatch between his deliberations and the outcome? If he deliberates badly, and as a result of this his projects go wrong, it is easy to see *in that case* how his regret at the outcome appropriately attaches itself to his deliberations. But if he deliberates well, and things go wrong; particularly if, as sometimes happens, they would have gone better if he had deliberated worse; what is the consciousness that he was "justified" supposed to do for the disposition of his undoubted regret about how things actually turned out? His thought that he was justified seems to carry with it something like this: while he is sorry that things turned out as they did, and, in a sense corresponding to that, he wishes he had acted otherwise, at the same time he does not wish he had acted otherwise, for he stands by the processes of rational deliberation which led to what he did. Similarly with the converse phenomenon, where having made and too late discovered some mistake of deliberation, the agent is by luck successful, and indeed would have been less successful if he had done anything else. Here his gladness that he acted as he did (his lack of a wish to have acted otherwise) operates at a level at which it is compatible with such feelings as self-reproach or retrospective alarm at having acted as he did.

These observations are truisms, but it remains obscure what their real content is. Little is effected by talk of self-reproach or regret at all, still less of co-existent regret and contentment, unless some expression, at least, of such sentiments can be identified. Certainly it is not to be identified in this case with any disposition to compensate other persons, for none is affected. Connected with that, criticism by other persons would be on a different basis from criticism offered where they had a grievance, as in a case where an agent risks goods of which he is a trustee, through deliberative error or (interestingly) merely through the choice of a high-risk strategy to which he would be perfectly entitled if he were acting solely in his own interests. The trustee is not entitled to gamble with the infants' money even if any profits will certainly go to the infants, and success itself will not remove, or start

---

14   [Author's note] For some discussion of this see "Ethical Consistency", in *Problems of the Self* (Cambridge 1973), pp. 166–186.

15   [Author's note] A useful outline of such considerations is in D.A.J. Richards, *A Theory of Reasons for Action* (Oxford 1971), ch. 3.

to remove, that objection. That sort of criticism is of course not appropriate in the purely egoistic case; and in fact there is no reason to think that criticism by others is more than a consequential consideration in the egoistic case, derived from others' recommendation of the virtues of rational prudence, which need to be explained first.

Granted that there is no issue of compensation to others in the purely egoistic case, the form of expression of regret seems necessarily to be, as Richards has said,[16] the agent's resolutions for his future deliberations. Regrets about his deliberations express themselves as resolves, at least, to think better next time; satisfaction with the deliberation, however disappointing the particular outcome, expresses itself in this, that he finds nothing to be *learned* from the case, and is sure that he will have no better chance of success (at a given level of payoff) next time by changing his procedures. If this is right, then the notions of regret or lack of regret at the past level of deliberative excellence make sense only in the context of a policy or disposition of rational deliberation applied to an on-going class of cases.

This is a modest enough conception—it is important to see how modest it is. It implies a class of cases sufficiently similar for deliberative practices to be translated from one to another of them; it does not imply that these cases are all conjointly the subject of deliberative reasoning. I may make a reasoned choice between alternatives of a certain kind today, and, having seen how it turns out, resolve to deal rather differently with the next choice of that kind; but I need not either engage in or resolve to engage in any deliberative reasoning which weighs the options of more than one such occasion together.[17]

In so far as the outcomes of different such situations affect one another, there is indeed pressure to say that rational deliberation should in principle consider them together. But, further, if one knew enough, any choice would be seen to affect all later ones; so it has seemed to some that the ideal limit of this process is something which is a far more ambitious extension of the modest notion of an ongoing disposition to rational deliberation: this is the model of rational deliberation as directed to a *life-plan*, in Rawls' sense, which treats all times of one's life as of equal concern to one.[18] The theorists of this picture agree that as a matter of fact ignorance and other factors do usually make it rational to discount over remoteness in time,[19] but these are subsequent considerations brought to a model which is that of one's life as a rectangle, so to speak, presented all at once and to be optimally filled in. This model is presented not only as embodying the ideal fulfilment of a rational urge to harmonize all one's projects. It is also supposed to provide a special grounding for the idea that a more fundamental form of regret is directed to deliberative error than to mere mistake. The regret takes the form of self-reproach, and the idea is that we protect ourselves against reproaches from our future self if we act with deliberative rationality: "nothing can protect us from the ambiguities and limitations of our knowledge, or guarantee that we find the best alternative open to us. Acting with deliberative rationality can only ensure that our conduct is above reproach, and that we are responsible to ourselves as one person over time."[20] These strains come together in Rawls' advocacy of "... the guiding principle that a rational individual is always to act so that he need never blame himself no matter how things finally transpire."[21]

Rawls seems to regard this injunction as, in a sense, formal, and as not determining how risky or conservative a strategy the agent should adopt; but

---

16   [Author's note] *Op. cit*. pp. 70–71, and *cf*. ch. 13.

17   [Author's note] The notion of treating cases together, as opposed to treating them separately but in the light of experience, applies not only to deliberation which yields in advance a conjunctive resolution of a number of cases, but also to deliberation which yields hypothetical conclusions to the effect that a later case will receive a certain treatment if an earlier case turns out in a certain way: as in a staking system.

18   [Author's note] John Rawls, *A Theory of Justice* (Oxford, 1972), esp. ch VII; Thomas Nagel, *The Possibility of Altruism* (Oxford, 1970).

19   That is, to treat events or situations further away in time as less important than those closer in time.

20   [Author's note] Rawls, pp. 422–423.

21   [Author's note] p. 422.

it is worth remarking that if any grounding for self-reproach about deliberative error is to be found in the notion of the recriminations of one's later self, the injunction will in fact have to be taken in a more materially cautious sense. For the grounding relies on an analogy with the responsibility to other persons: I am a trustee for my own future. If this has any force at all, it is hard to see why it does not extend to my being required, like any other trustee, to adopt a cautious strategy with the entrusted goods—which are, in this case, almost everything I have.

However that may be, the model that gives rise to the injunction is false. Apart from other difficulties,[22] it implicitly ignores the obvious fact that what one does and the sort of life one leads condition one's later desires and judgments: the standpoint of that retrospective judge who will be my later self will be the product of my earlier choices. So there is no set of preferences both fixed and relevant, relative to which the various fillings of my life-space can be compared; if the fillings are to be evaluated by reference to what I variously, in them, want, the relevant preferences are not fixed, while if they are to be evaluated by what I now (for instance) want, this will give a fixed set of preferences, but one which is not necessarily relevant. The recourse from this within the life-space model is to assume (as Utilitarianism does) that there is some currency of satisfactions, in terms of which it is possible to compare quite neutrally the value of one set of preferences together with their fulfilments, as against a quite different set of preferences together with their fulfilments. But there is no reason to suppose that there is any such currency, nor (still less) that the idea of practical rationality should implicitly presuppose it.

If there is no such currency, then we can only to a limited extent abstract from the projects and preferences we actually have, and cannot in principle gain a standpoint from which the alternative fillings of our life-rectangle could be compared without prejudice. The perspective of deliberative choice on one's life is constitutively *from here*. Correspondingly the perspective of assessment with greater knowledge is necessarily *from there*, and not only can I not guarantee how factually it will then be, but I cannot ultimately guarantee from what standpoint of assessment my major and most fundamental regrets will be.

For many decisions which are part of the agent's ongoing activity (the "normal science",[23] so to speak, of the moral life) we can see why it is that the presence or absence of regrets is more basically conditioned by the retrospective view of the deliberative processes, than by the particular outcomes. Oneself and one's viewpoint are more basically identified with the dispositions of rational deliberation, applicable to an ongoing series of decisions, than they are with the particular projects which succeed or fail on those occasions. But there are certain other decisions, as on the cases we are considering, which are not like this. There is indeed some room for the presence and subsequent assessment of deliberative rationality: the agents in our cases might well not be taken as seriously as they would otherwise if they did not, to the limited extent which the situation permits, take as rational thought as they can about the realities of their situation. But this is not the aspect under which they will primarily look back on it, nor is it as a contribution to a series of deliberative situations that it will have its importance for them; though they will learn from it, it will not be in that way. In these cases, the project in the interests of which the decision is made is one with which the agent is identified in such a way that if it succeeds, his standpoint of assessment will be from a life which then derives an important part of its significance for him from that very fact; while if he fails, it can, necessarily, have no such significance in his life. If he succeeds, it cannot be that while welcoming the outcome he more basically regrets the decision; while if he fails, his standpoint

---

22   [Author's note] It ignores also the very basic fact that the size of the rectangle is up to me: I have said something about this in "Persons, Character and Morality", in Amélie Rorty, ed., *The Identity of Persons*, (California UP, forthcoming).

23   This term was brought into philosophical currency by Thomas Kuhn, in his book, *The Structure of Scientific Revolutions*. He uses it to describe the sort of science carried on within stable accepted "paradigms" for basic theory and procedures, without attempt to challenge these underlying assumptions. Scientific revolution challenges and replaces them.

will be of one for whom the ground project of the decision has proved worthless, and this (under the simplifying assumption that other adequate projects are not generated in the process) must leave him with the most basic regrets. So if he fails, his most basic regrets will attach to his decision, and if he succeeds, they cannot. That is the sense in which his decision can be justified, for him, by success.

On this account, it is clear that the type of decisions we are concerned with is not merely very risky ones, or even very risky ones with a substantial outcome. The outcome has to be substantial in a special way—in a way which importantly conditions the agent's sense of what is significant in his life, and hence his standpoint of retrospective assessment. It follows from this that they are, indeed, risky, and in a way which helps to explain the importance for such projects of the difference between extrinsic and intrinsic failure. With an intrinsic failure, the project which generated the decision is revealed as an empty thing, incapable of grounding the agent's life. With extrinsic failure, it is not so revealed, and while he must acknowledge that it has failed, nevertheless it has not been discredited, and may, perhaps in the form of some new aspiration, contribute to making sense of what is left. In his retrospective thought, and its allocation of basic regret, he cannot in the fullest sense identify with his decision, and so does not find himself justified; but he is not totally alienated from it either, cannot just see it as a disastrous error, and so does not find himself unjustified.

This structure of retrospective understanding can occur without the concern introduced by the interests of others, which is central to our cases; but that concern is likely to be present in such decisions, and certainly it contributes importantly to their nature when it is present. The risks taken by our agents are taken in part with others' goods. The risks are taken also with their own, which increases our respect for them. But for themselves, they have a chance of winning, while the others do not; worse off than those served by the gambling trustee, the others' loss is settled from the start. There is no ground, whatever happens, for demanding that they drop their resentment. If they are eventually going to feel better towards him, it will not be through having re-

ceived an answer to their complaints—nor, far from it, need it be because the agent is successful. They are not recompensed by the agent's success—or only if they are prepared to be.

But what about the rest of us? Here, for the first time, it is worth mentioning a difference between our cases, that if Gauguin's project succeeds, it could yield a good for the world as Anna's success could not. There is no reason why those who suffer from Gauguin's decision should be impressed by this fact, and there are several reasons (one of which we touched on earlier, in the matter of moral justification) why Gauguin should not. Nor should we be overimpressed by the difference, in considering what can be learned from such cases. But eventually the spectator has to consider the fact that he has reason to be glad that Gauguin succeeded, and hence that he tried. At the very least, this may stand as an emblem for cases in which we are glad. Perhaps fewer of us than is pretended care about the existence of Gauguin's paintings, but we are supposed to care, which gives an opportunity for reflection to start out and work towards the cases where we really care, where we salute the project. The fact is that if we believe in any other values at all, then it is likely that at some point we shall have reason to be glad that moral values (taken here in the simple sense of a concern for others' rights and interests) have been treated as one value among others, and not as unquestionably supreme. Real supremacy of the moral would imply its ubiquity. Like Spinoza's substance, if it were to be genuinely unconditioned,[24] there would have to be nothing to condition it.

There is a public dimension of appreciation for such cases: how Gauguin stands with us (taking him emblematically as one whose project is saluted); whether we are, taking it all together, glad that he did it; depends on his success. That question, moreover, whether we are, taking it all together, glad, is the

---

24 What is unconditioned is without limits or restrictions from, or influenced or brought about by, anything else. Spinoza argues that since unconditioned substance must be infinite, include all attributes, etc., it (= God) must encompass everything: there *can't be* anything else.

question we should take seriously. The various dichotomies which can be brought in to break up that question—such as moral v. non-moral, or agent v. act, or act v. outcome—often only help to evade the basic and connected questions of what one really wants the world to be like and what human dispositions are involved in its being like that.

These questions for the spectator we will leave; they would arise, as we noticed at the beginning, even if the agent had no concern for others' interests at all. But assuming (as we have throughout) that he has such a concern, then for him success makes a special kind of difference. It runs against the widely held view mentioned before, that moral regret is ultimate, and ultimate regret is immune to luck. If he fails, above all if he intrinsically fails, nothing is left except the cost to others for which (we are supposing) he in any case feels regret. In success, it must be dishonest or confused of him to regard that regret as his most basic feeling about the situation; if it were, he would at the most basic level wish that he had acted otherwise. In failure, that regret can consistently be part of his most basic feelings about what he has done. This is one way—only one of many—in which an agent's moral view of his life can depend on luck.

II—T. Nagel

Williams sidesteps the fascinating question raised in his paper.[25] He does not defend the possibility of moral luck against Kantian doubts, but instead redescribes the case which seems to be his strongest candidate in terms which have nothing to do with moral judgment. Gauguin's talent as a painter may be a matter of luck, but it does not, according to Williams, warrant the retrospective judgment that his desertion of his family is morally acceptable. In fact, it does not warrant any judgment about his prior decision that pretends to objective validity for everyone, or even to timeless validity for him. According to Williams, the effect of the fortunate outcome on Gauguin's attitude to his earlier choice will be merely to make him not regret, at the most basic level, having made it. He will not regret it because it has resulted in a success which

forms the centre of his life. This attitude can hardly be called a judgment at all, let alone a moral judgment. Williams says Gauguin cannot use it to justify himself to others. It does not even imply the truth of an hypothetical judgment made in advance, of the form "If I leave my family and become a great painter, I will be justified by success; if I don't become a great painter, the act will be unforgivable." And if the rest of us are glad that Gauguin left his family, Williams says that this is because we do not always give priority to moral values.

The importance of luck in human life is no surprise, even in respect of those matters about which we feel most deeply glad or regretful. It is the place of luck in ethics that is puzzling. Williams misdescribes his result in the closing paragraph of the paper: he has argued not that an agent's moral view of his life can depend on luck but that ultimate regret is not immune to luck because ultimate regret need not be moral. This is consonant with his tendency, here and in other recent writings,[26] to reject the impersonal claims of morality in favour of more personal desires and projects. Even if Williams has successfully explained away the appearance of moral luck in the case of Gauguin, however, the explanation applies only to a narrow range of phenomena and leaves most of the area untouched. Williams acknowledges that he has dealt with only one type of case, but I do not believe these cases can be treated in isolation from the larger problem.

Why is there a problem? Not because morality seems too basic to be subject to luck. Some very important non-moral assessments of people deal with what is not their fault. We deplore madness or leprosy in ourselves and others, we rejoice in beauty or talent, but these, though very basic, are not moral judgments. If we ask ourselves why, the natural explanation is that these attributes are not the responsibility of their possessors, they are merely good or back luck. Prior to reflection it is intuitively plausible that people cannot be morally assessed for what is not their fault, or

---

25   [Author's note] "Moral Luck", *Aristotelian Society Supplementary Volume* 1976.

26   [Author's note] "Egoism and Altruism", in *Problems of the Self* (Cambridge, 1973); "Persons, Character, and Morality", in A. Rorty, ed., *The Identities of Persons* (Berkeley, Calif., forthcoming).

for what is due to factors beyond their control. This proposition uses an unanalysed concept of moral assessment that is presumably logically independent of the idea of control—otherwise the problem could not arise. Such a judgment is different from the evaluation of something as a good or bad thing, or state of affairs. The latter may be present in addition to moral judgment, but when we blame someone for his actions we are not merely saying it is bad that they happened, or bad that he exists: we are judging *him*, saying he is bad, which is different from his being a bad thing. This kind of judgment takes only a certain kind of object. Without being able to explain exactly why, we feel that the appropriateness of moral assessment is easily undermined by the discovery that the act or attribute, no matter how good or bad, is not under the person's control. While other evaluations remain, this one seems to lose its footing.

However, if the condition of control is consistently applied, it threatens to erode most of the moral assessments we find it natural to make. For in various ways, to be discovered, the things for which people are morally judged are not under their control, or are determined to some extent by what is beyond their control. And when the seemingly natural requirement of fault or responsibility is applied in light of these facts, it leaves few pre-reflective moral judgments intact.

Why not conclude, then, that the condition of control is false—that it is an initially plausible hypothesis refuted by clear counter-examples? One could in that case look instead for a more refined condition which picked out the *kinds* of lack of control that really undermine certain moral judgments, without yielding the unacceptable conclusion derived from the broader condition, that most or all ordinary moral judgments are illegitimate.

What rules out this escape is that we are dealing not with a theoretical conjecture but with a philosophical problem. The condition of control does not suggest itself merely as a generalization from certain clear cases. It seems correct in the further cases to which it is extended beyond the original set. When we undermine moral assessment by considering new ways in which control is absent, we are not just discovering what *would* follow given the general hypothesis, but

are actually being persuaded that in itself the absence of control is relevant in these cases too. The erosion of moral judgment emerges not as the absurd consequence of an over-simple theory, but as a natural consequence of the ordinary idea of moral assessment, when it is applied in view of a more complete and precise account of the facts. It would therefore be a *mistake* to argue from the unacceptability of the conclusions to the need for a different account of the conditions of moral responsibility. The view that moral luck is paradoxical is not a mistake, ethical or logical, but a perception of one of the ways in which the intuitively acceptable conditions of moral judgment threaten to undermine it all.

It resembles the situation in another area of philosophy, the theory of knowledge. There too conditions which seem perfectly natural, and which grow out of the ordinary procedures for challenging and defending claims to knowledge, threaten to undermine all such claims if consistently applied.[27] Most sceptical arguments have this quality: they do not depend on the imposition of arbitrarily stringent standards of knowledge, arrived at by misunderstanding, but appear to grow inevitably from the consistent application of ordinary standards.[28] There is a substantive parallel as well, for epistemological scepticism arises from consideration of the respects in which our beliefs and their relation to reality depend on factors beyond our control. External and internal causes produce our beliefs. We may subject these processes to scrutiny in an effort to avoid error, but our conclusions at this next level also result, in part, from influences which we do not control directly. The same will be true no matter how far we carry the investigation. Our beliefs are always, ultimately, due to factors outside our control, and the impossibility of encompassing those factors without being at the mercy of others leads us to doubt

---

27   Nagel is thinking of a family of familiar problems, e.g., how to justify your belief that you really do perceive an external world (and are not dreaming, or hallucinating, or being fed false experience by a computer wired into your brain). See Chapter 2.

28   [Author's note] See Thompson Clarke, "The Legacy of Skepticism", *Journal of Philosophy* LXIX (1972), pp. 754–769.

whether we know anything. It looks as though, if any of our beliefs are true, it is pure biological luck rather than knowledge.

Moral luck is like this because while there are various respects in which the natural objects of moral assessment are out of our control or influenced by what is out of our control, we cannot reflect on these facts without losing our grip on the judgments.

There are roughly four ways in which the natural objects of moral assessment are disturbingly subject to luck. One is the phenomenon of constitutive luck mentioned by Williams at the beginning of his paper—the kind of person you are, where this is not just a question of what you deliberately do, but of your inclinations, capacities, and temperament. Another category is luck in one's circumstances—the kind of problems and situations one faces. The other two have to do with the causes and effects of action. Williams' discussion is confined to the last category, but all of them present a common problem. They are all opposed by the idea that one cannot be more culpable or estimable for anything than one is for that fraction of it which is under one's control. It seems irrational to take or dispense credit or blame for matters over which a person has no control, or for their influence on results over which he has partial control. Such things may create the conditions for action, but action can be judged only to the extent that it goes beyond these conditions and does not just result from them.

Let us first consider luck, good and bad, in the way things turn out—the type of case Williams examines. We may note that the category includes a range of examples, from the truck driver who accidentally runs over a child to Gauguin and beyond. The driver, if he is entirely without fault, will feel terrible about his rôle in the event, but will not have to reproach himself. Therefore this example of what Williams calls agent-regret is not yet a case of *moral* bad luck. However, if the driver was guilty of even a minor degree of negligence—failing to have his brakes checked recently, for example—then if that negligence contributes to the death of the child, he will not merely feel terrible. He will blame himself for its death. And what makes this an example of moral luck is that he would have to blame himself only slightly for the negligence itself if no situation arose which

required him to brake suddenly and violently to avoid hitting a child. Yet the *negligence* is the same in both cases, and the driver has no control over whether a child will run into his path.

The same is true at higher levels of negligence. If someone has had too much to drink and his car swerves on to the sidewalk, he can count himself morally lucky if there are no pedestrians in its path. If there were, he would be to blame for their deaths, and would probably be prosecuted for manslaughter. But if he hurts no one, although his recklessness is exactly the same, he is guilty of a far less serious legal offence and will certainly reproach himself and be reproached by others much less severely. To take another legal example, the penalty for attempted murder is less than that for successful murder—however similar the intentions and motives of the assailant may be in the two cases. His degree of culpability can depend, it would seem, on whether the victim happened to be wearing a bullet-proof vest, or whether a bird flew into the path of the bullet—matters beyond his control.

Finally, there are cases of decision under uncertainty—common in public and in private life. Anna Karenina goes off with Vronsky, Gauguin leaves his family, Chamberlain signs the Munich agreement,[29] the Decembrists persuade the troops under their command to revolt against the Czar,[30] the American colonies declare their independence from Britain, you introduce two people in an attempt at match-making. It is tempting in all such cases to feel that some decision must be possible, in the light of what is known at the time, which will make reproach unsuitable no mat-

---

29   Neville Chamberlain, British Prime Minister, signed an agreement with Hitler in Munich in 1938 yielding the Sudetenland (a portion of Czechoslovakia) to Germany in exchange for Hitler's promise that this would end Germany's expansion. Chamberlain famously announced "peace for our time"; but Hitler's promise was soon broken, and Chamberlain has ever since been blamed for useless appeasement with tragic results.

30   The Decembrists were imperial Russian army officers who led a failed revolt against Nicholas I's assumption of the throne in 1825 (because they were loyal to his older brother, Constantine, who should constitutionally have been the next czar rather than Nicholas).

ter how things turn out. But, as Williams says, this is not true; when someone acts in such ways he takes his life, or his moral position, into his hands, because how things turn out determines what he has done. It is possible *also* to assess the decision from the point of view of what could be known at the time, but this is not the end of the story. If the Decembrists had succeeded in overthrowing Nicholas I in 1825 and establishing a constitutional regime, they would be heroes. As it is, not only did they fail and pay for it, but they bore some responsibility for the terrible punishments meted out to the troops who had been persuaded to follow them. If the American Revolution had been a bloody failure resulting in greater repression, then Jefferson, Franklin and Washington would still have made a noble attempt, and might not even have regretted it on their way to the scaffold, but they would also have had to blame themselves for what they had helped to bring on their compatriots. (Perhaps peaceful efforts at reform would eventually have succeeded.) If Hitler had not overrun Europe and exterminated millions, but instead had died of a heart attack after occupying the Sudetenland, Chamberlain's action at Munich would still have utterly betrayed the Czechs, but it would not be the great moral disaster that has made his name a household word.[31]

In many cases of difficult choice the outcome cannot be foreseen with certainty. One kind of assessment of the choice is possible in advance, but another kind must await the outcome, because the outcome determines what has been done. The same degree of culpability or estimability in intention, motive, or concern is compatible with a wide range of judgments, positive or negative, depending on what happened beyond the point of decision. The *mens rea*[32] which could have existed in the absence of any consequences does not exhaust the grounds of moral judgment.

31   [Author's note] For a fascinating but morally repellent discussion of the topic of justification by history, see Maurice Merleau-Ponty, *Humanism and Terror* (Beacon Press, Boston: 1969).

32   Latin: *guilty mind.* One is usually not considered guilty of a criminal act without this: the understanding of what one's actions would or might involve, thus the intentionality of the action.

I have said that Williams does not defend the view that these are instances of moral luck. The fact that Gauguin will or will not feel basic regret over his decision is a separate matter, and does nothing to explain the influence of actual results on culpability or esteem in those unquestionably ethical cases ranging from negligence through political choice. In such cases one can say *in advance* how the moral verdict will depend on the results. If one negligently leaves the bath running with the baby in it, one will realize, as one bounds up the stairs toward the bathroom, that if the baby has drowned one has done something awful, whereas if it has not one has merely been careless. Someone who launches a violent revolution against an authoritarian regime knows that if he fails he will be responsible for much suffering that is in vain, but if he succeeds he will be justified by the outcome. I don't mean that any action can be retroactively justified by history. Certain things are so bad in themselves, or so risky, that no results can make them all right. Nevertheless, when moral judgment does depend on the outcome, it is objective and timeless and not dependent on a change of standpoint produced by success or failure. The judgment after the fact follows from an hypothetical judgment that can be made beforehand, and it can be made as easily by someone else as by the agent.

From the point of view which makes responsibility dependent on control, all this seems absurd. How is it possible to be more or less culpable depending on whether a child gets into the path of one's car, or a bird into the path of one's bullet? Perhaps it is true that what is done depends on more than the agent's state of mind or intention. The problem then is, why is it not irrational to base moral assessment on what people do, in this broad sense? It amounts to holding them responsible for the contributions of fate as well as for their own—provided they have made some contribution to begin with. If we look at cases of negligence or attempt, the pattern seems to be that overall culpability corresponds to the product of mental or intentional fault and the seriousness of the outcome. Cases of decision under uncertainty are less easily explained in this way, for it seems that the overall judgment can even shift from positive to negative depending on the outcome. But here too it seems rational to subtract the effects of occurrences subsequent to the choice, that were merely possible at the time, and concentrate moral assessment on the actual decision in light of the probabilities. If the object of moral judgment is the *person*, then to hold him accountable for what he has done in the broader sense is akin to strict liability,[33] which may have its legal uses but seems irrational as a moral position.

The result of such a line of thought is to pare down each act to its morally essential core, an inner act of pure will assessed by motive and intention. Adam Smith advocates such a position in *The Theory of Moral Sentiments*, but notes that it runs contrary to our actual judgments.

> But how well soever we may seem to be persuaded of the truth of this equitable maxim, when we consider it after this manner, in abstract, yet when we come to particular cases, the actual consequences which happen to proceed from any action, have a very great effect upon our sentiments concerning its merit or demerit, and almost always either enhance or diminish our sense of both. Scarce, in any one instance, perhaps, will our sentiments be found, after examination, to be entirely regulated by this rule, which we all acknowledge ought entirely to regulate them.[34]

Joel Feinberg points out further that restricting the domain of moral responsibility to the inner world will not immunize it to luck. Factors beyond the agent's control, like a coughing fit, can interfere with his decisions as surely as they can with the path of a bullet from his gun.[35]

---

33 This legal term refers to the responsibility to compensate for the damages inflicted by one's actions, even though the damage was unintentional or unforeseen or unforeseeable, and even though the actions were reasonable and not negligent. This is the kind of responsibility relevant to a civil suit, not a criminal trial.

34 [Author's note] Part II, Section III, Introduction, paragraph 5 [1759].

35 [Author's note] "Problematic Responsibility in Law and Morals", in Joel Feinberg, *Doing and Deserving* (Princeton, 1970).

Nevertheless the tendency to cut down the scope of moral assessment is pervasive, and does not limit itself to the influence of effects. It attempts to isolate the will from the other direction, so to speak, by separating out what Williams calls constitutive luck. Let us consider that next.

Kant was particularly insistent on the moral irrelevance of qualities of temperament and personality that are not under the control of the will. Such qualities as sympathy or coldness might provide the background against which obedience to moral requirements is more or less difficult, but they could not be objects of moral assessment themselves, and might well interfere with confident assessment of its proper object—the determination of the will by the motive of duty. This rules out moral judgment of many of the virtues and vices, which are states of character that influence choice but are certainly not exhausted by dispositions to act deliberately in certain ways. A person may be greedy, envious, cowardly, cold, ungenerous, unkind, vain, or conceited, but *behave* perfectly by a monumental effort of will. To possess these vices is to be unable to help having certain feelings under certain circumstances, and to have strong spontaneous impulses to act badly. Even if one controls the impulses, one still has the vice. An envious person hates the greater success of others. He can be morally condemned as envious even if he congratulates them cordially and does nothing to denigrate or spoil their success. Conceit, likewise, need not be displayed. It is fully present in someone who cannot help dwelling with secret satisfaction on the superiority of his own achievements, talents, beauty, intelligence, or virtue. To some extent such a quality may be the product of earlier choices; to some extent it may be amenable to change by current actions. But it is largely a matter of constitutive bad fortune. Yet people are morally condemned for such qualities, and esteemed for others equally beyond control of the will: they are assessed for what they are *like*.

To Kant this seems incoherent because virtue is enjoined on everyone and therefore must be in principle possible for everyone. It may be easier for some than for others, but it must be possible to achieve it by making the right choices, against whatever temperamental background.[36] One may want to have a generous spirit, or regret not having one, but it makes no sense to condemn oneself or anyone else for a quality which is not within the control of the will. Condemnation implies that you shouldn't be like that, not that it's unfortunate that you are.

Nevertheless, Kant's conclusion remains intuitively unacceptable. We may be persuaded that these moral judgments are irrational, but they reappear involuntarily as soon as the argument is over. This is the pattern throughout the subject.

The third category to consider is luck in one's circumstances, and I shall mention it briefly. The things we are called upon to do, the moral tests we face, are importantly determined by factors beyond our control. It may be true of someone that in a dangerous situation he would behave in a cowardly or heroic fashion, but if the situation never arises, he will never have the chance to distinguish or disgrace himself in this way, and his moral record will be different.[37]

A conspicuous example of this is political. Ordinary citizens of Nazi Germany had an opportunity to behave heroically by opposing the regime. They also had an opportunity to behave badly, and most of them are culpable for having failed this test. But it is a test to which the citizens of other countries were not subjected, with the result that even if they, or some of them, would have behaved as badly as the Germans in like circumstances, they simply didn't and therefore are not similarly culpable. Here again one is morally at the mercy of fate, and it may seem irrational upon reflection, but our ordinary moral attitudes would be unrecognizable without it. We judge people for what they actually do or fail to do, not just for what they would have done if circumstances had been different.[38]

This form of moral determination by the actual is also paradoxical, but we can begin to see how deep in the concept of responsibility the paradox is embedded. A person can be morally responsible only for what he does; but what he does results from a great deal that he does not do; therefore he is not morally responsible for what he is and is not responsible for. (This is not a contradiction, but it is a paradox.)

It should be obvious that there is a connection between these problems about responsibility and

---

36 [Author's note] "... if nature has put little sympathy in the heart of a man, and if he, though an honest man, is by temperament cold and indifferent to the sufferings of others, perhaps because he is provided with special gifts of patience and fortitude and expects or even requires that others should have the same—and such a man would certainly not be the meanest product of nature—would not he find in himself a source from which to give himself a far higher worth than he could have got by having a good-natured temperament?" *Foundations of the Metaphysics of Morals*, Akademie edition p. 398.

37 [Author's note] *Cf.* Thomas Gray, "Elegy Written in a Country Churchyard":

"Some mute inglorious Milton here may rest,
Some Cromwell, guiltless of his country's blood."

An unusual example of circumstantial moral luck is provided by the kind of moral dilemma with which someone can be faced through no fault of his own, but which leaves him with nothing to do which is not wrong. See T. Nagel, "War and Massacre", *Philosophy and Public Affairs* Vol. 1 No. 2 (Winter 1972); and B. Williams, "Ethical Consistency", *PASS* XXXIX (1965), also in *Problems of the Self.*

38 [Author's note] Circumstantial luck can extend to aspects of the situation other than individual behaviour. For example, during the Vietnam War even US citizens who had opposed their country's actions vigorously from the start often felt compromised by its crimes. Here they were not even responsible; there was probably nothing they could do to stop what was happening, so the feeling of being implicated may seem unintelligible. But it is nearly impossible to view the crimes of one's own country in the same way that one views the crimes of another country, no matter how equal one's lack of power to stop them in the two cases. One is a citizen of one of them, and has a connexion with its actions (even if only through taxes that cannot be withheld)—that one does not have with the other's. This makes it possible to be ashamed of one's country, and to feel a victim of moral bad luck that one was an American in the 'sixties.

control and an even more familiar problem, that of freedom of the will. That is the last type of moral luck I want to take up, though I can do no more within the scope of this paper than indicate its connection with the other types.

If one cannot be responsible for consequences of one's acts due to factors beyond one's control, or for antecedents of one's acts that are properties of temperament not subject to one's will, or for the circumstances that pose one's moral choices, then how can one be responsible even for the stripped-down acts of the will itself, if *they* are the product of antecedent circumstances outside of the will's control?

The area of genuine agency, and therefore of legitimate moral judgment, seems to shrink under this scrutiny to an extensionless point. Everything seems to result from the combined influence of factors, antecedent and posterior to action, that are not within the agent's control. Since he cannot be responsible for them, he cannot be responsible for their results—thought it may remain possible to take up the aesthetic or other evaluative analogues of the moral attitudes that are thus displaced.

It is also possible, of course, to brazen it out and refuse to accept the results, which indeed seem unacceptable as soon as we stop thinking about the arguments. Admittedly, if certain surrounding circumstances had been different, then no unfortunate consequences would have followed from a wicked intention, and no seriously culpable act would have been performed; but since the circumstances were *not* different, and the agent *in fact* succeeded in perpetrating a particularly cruel murder, *that* is what he did, and that is what he is responsible for. Similarly, we may admit that if certain antecedent circumstances had been different, the agent would never have developed into the sort of person who would do such a thing; but since he *did* develop (as the inevitable result of those antecedent circumstances) into the sort of swine he is, and into the person who committed such a murder, *that* is what he is blameable for. In both cases one is responsible for what one actually does—even if what one actually does depends in important ways on what is not within one's control.

This compatibilist account[39] of our moral judgments would leave room for the ordinary conditions of responsibility—the absence of coercion, ignorance, or involuntary movement—as part of the determination of what someone has done—but it is understood not to exclude the influence of a great deal that he has not done.[40] It is essentially what Williams means when he says, above,

> One's history as an agent is a web in which anything that is the product of the will is surrounded and held up and partly formed by things that are not, in such a way that reflection can go only in one of two directions: either in the direction of saying that responsible agency is a fairly superficial concept, which has a limited use in harmonizing what happens, or else that it is not a superficial concept, but that it cannot ultimately be purified—if one attaches importance to the sense of what one is in terms of what one has done and what in the world one is responsible for, one must accept much that makes its claim on that sense solely in virtue of its being actual.

The only thing wrong with this solution is its failure to explain how sceptical problems arise. For they arise not from the imposition of an arbitrary external requirement, but from the nature of moral judgment itself. Something in the ordinary idea of what someone does must explain how it can seem necessary to

---

39   Compatibilism is the position that moral responsibility for one's actions is compatible with the fact that those actions are ultimately causally determined by facts outside one's control—provided that those actions are caused by one's decisions (even though those decisions themselves are determined by external causes).

40   [Author's note] The corresponding position in epistemology would be that knowledge consists of true beliefs formed in certain ways, and that it does not require all aspects of the process to be under the knower's control, actually or potentially. Both the correctness of these beliefs and the process by which they are arrived at would therefore be importantly subject to luck. The Nobel Prize is not awarded to people who turn out to be wrong, no matter how brilliant their reasoning.

subtract from it anything that merely happens—even though the ultimate consequence of such subtraction is that nothing remains. And something in the ordinary idea of knowledge must explain why it seems to be undermined by any influences on belief not within the control of the subject—so that knowledge seems impossible without an impossible foundation in autonomous reason. But let us leave epistemology aside and concentrate on action, character, and moral assessment.

The problem arises, I believe, because the self which acts and is the object of moral judgment is threatened with dissolution by the absorption of its acts and impulses into the class of events. Moral judgment of a person is judgment not of what happens to him, but of him. It does not say merely that a certain event or state of affairs is fortunate or unfortunate or even terrible. It is not an evaluation of a state of the world, or of an individual as part of the world. We are not thinking just that it would be better if he were different, or didn't exist, or hadn't done some of the things he has done. We are judging *him*, rather than his existence or characteristics. The effect of concentrating on the influence of what is not under his control is to make this responsible self seem to disappear, swallowed up by the order of mere events.

What, however, do we have in mind that a person must be to be the object of these moral attitudes? While the concept of agency is easily undermined, it is very difficult to give it a positive characterization. That is familiar from the literature on Free Will.

I believe that in a sense the problem has no solution, because something in the idea of agency is incompatible with actions being events, or people being things. But as the external determinants of what someone has done are gradually exposed, in their effect on consequences, character, and choice itself, it becomes gradually clear that actions are events and people things. Eventually nothing remains which can be ascribed to the responsible self, and we are left with nothing but a portion of the larger sequence of events, which can be deplored or celebrated, but not blamed or praised.

Though I cannot define the idea of the active self that is thus undermined, it is possible to say something about its sources. Williams is right to point out the important difference between agent-regret and regret about misfortunes from which one is detached, but he does not emphasise the corresponding distinction in our attitudes toward others, which comes from the extension to them of external agent-centred evaluations corresponding to the agent-regret that they can feel about themselves. This causes him to miss the truly moral character of such judgments, which can be made not only by the agent himself, though they involve the agent's point of view.

There is a close connexion between our feelings about ourselves and our feelings about others. Guilt and indignation, shame and contempt, pride and admiration are internal and external sides of the same moral attitudes. We are unable to view ourselves simply as portions of the world, and from inside we have a rough idea of the boundary between what is us and what is not, what we do and what happens to us, what is our personality and what is an accidental handicap. We apply the same essentially internal conception of the self to others. About ourselves we feel pride, shame, guilt, remorse—and what Williams calls agent-regret. We do not regard our actions and our characters merely as fortunate or unfortunate episodes—though they may also be that. We cannot *simply* take an external evaluative view of ourselves—of what we most essentially are and what we do. And this remains true even when we have seen that we are not responsible for our own existence, or our nature, or the choices we have to make, or the circumstances that give our acts the consequences they have. Those acts remain ours and we remain ourselves, despite the persuasiveness of the reasons that seem to argue us out of existence.

It is this internal view that we extend to others in moral judgment—when we judge *them* rather than their desirability or utility. We extend to others the refusal to limit ourselves to external evaluation, and we accord to them selves like our own. But in both cases this comes up against the brutal inclusion of humans and everything about them in a world from which they cannot be separated and of which they are nothing but contents. The external view forces itself on us at the same time that we resist it. One way this occurs is through the gradual erosion of what we do by the subtraction of what happens.[41]

The inclusion of consequences in the conception of what we have done is an acknowledgement that we are parts of the world, but the paradoxical character of moral luck which emerges from this acknowledgement shows that we are unable to operate with such a view, for it leaves us with no one to be. The same thing is revealed in the appearance that determinism obliterates responsibility. Once we see an aspect of what we or someone else does as something that happens, we lose our grip on the idea that it has been done and that we can judge the doer and not just the happening. This explains why the absence of determinism is no more hospitable to the concept of agency than its presence is—a point that has been noticed often. Either way the act is viewed externally, as part of the course of events.

The problem of moral luck cannot be understood without an account of the internal conception of agency and its special connection with the moral attitudes as opposed to other types of value. I do not have such an account. The degree to which the problem has a solution can be determined only by seeing whether in some degree the incompatibility between this conception and the various ways in which we do not control what we do is only apparent. I have nothing to offer on that topic either. But it is not enough to say merely that our basic moral attitudes toward ourselves and others are determined by what is actual; for they are also threatened by the sources of that actuality, and by the external view of action which forces itself on us when we see how everything we do belongs to a world that we have not created.

---

41   [Author's note] See P.F. Strawson's discussion of the conflict between the objective attitude and personal reaction attitudes in "Freedom and Resentment", *Proceedings of the British Academy*, 1962, reprinted in Strawson, ed., *Studies in the Philosophy of Thought and Action* (London, O.U.P., 1968), and in Strawson, *Freedom and Resentment and Other Essays* (London, Methuen, 1974).

APPENDIX 1

Philosophical Puzzles and Paradoxes

INTRODUCTION

Paradoxes and puzzles have played an important role in philosophy since the beginning of philosophical thought. They make us question our beliefs and presuppositions—often very basic ones. They don't always make us reject what we had taken for granted, but they do always subject it to scrutiny from a new and fascinating direction.

A paradox is an argument that appears to derive an absurd or obviously false conclusion by entirely valid reasoning from clearly acceptable premises. Sometimes philosophers argue that a premise is, despite appearances, actually false, or that the reasoning is actually invalid. Sometimes they argue that the premises and reasoning are fine, but the conclusion is true. Sometimes philosophers simply don't know what to do about a paradox. Any of these reactions is surprising, and may be of deep philosophical importance.

Puzzles are questions that seem like they ought to have a satisfying answer—but apparently do not. Philosophical reactions here include arguments for an (unobvious) solution, claims that there's something wrong with the unanswerable question in the first place, or just puzzlement. Again, any of these reactions is surprising and can be instructive.

The puzzles and paradoxes presented here are almost all very well-known and widely discussed in the philosophical literature. We'll often include a brief indication of how, in general, philosophers have reacted. We have not included very much discussion of philosophical reactions, or bibliographies, but you won't have any trouble finding these on the Internet. We have also little to say about philosophical implications. What we aim at here is to give you enough of an introduction to each puzzle or paradox to stimulate your own philosophical intelligence—to get you to think about these brain-twisters on your own—and

we're confident you'll often find this engaging, enlightening, and fun.

BARBER PARADOX

Imagine a town in which there's a (male) barber who shaves all the men who don't shave themselves, and only those men. Does he shave himself? The answer can't be yes—because he doesn't shave men who shave themselves. The answer can't be no—because he does shave all the men who don't shave themselves. This paradox is resolved by concluding that there can't be a town with a barber who is the way we're trying to imagine.

BERTRAND'S BOX PARADOX

Imagine three boxes, each containing two drawers. In one box, both drawers contain a gold coin. (Call this box GG.) In another box, both drawers contain a silver coin. (Call this box SS.) In the third box, one drawer has a gold coin, the other has a silver. (Call this box GS.) You pick a box at random, open one drawer, and find a gold coin. What's the probability the other drawer in that box contains a silver coin? (Stop now and try to answer.)

Here's how most people reason. You've got a gold coin, so that means that the box you picked isn't SS. It's equally likely—50%—to be GG or GS. So the likelihood that the other coin is silver is 50%.

But that's wrong. What you've got might be (1) drawer G of GS; (2) drawer G1 of GG; (3) drawer G2 of GG. The probability of each of these is equal:

33%. So the probability the other drawer has a silver coin is the probability of outcome (1): 33%.

BLACKMAIL PARADOX

It's neither illegal nor immoral to ask somebody for money. It's neither illegal nor immoral to threaten to expose somebody's theft. But it's both illegal and immoral to ask somebody for money, threatening that if you don't get the money, you'll expose their theft.

This is a paradox only if you accept the principle that if it's not illegal (or immoral) to do X, and it's not illegal (or immoral) to do Y, then it's not illegal (immoral) to do X and Y. But that's clearly a false principle. There are plenty of counter-examples. It's not illegal (or immoral) for example to drink, or to drive, but it is illegal to drink-and-drive (and probably immoral too, because of the increased risk of a damaging accident).

What is illegal (and immoral) in the blackmail case is not merely doing both actions—I might threaten to expose your theft, and also, unconnectedly, ask you for money—but to do both with a particular connection between them. What connection? What's the general principle here?

BURIDAN'S ASS

Imagine an ass (come on now, we mean a donkey) who is very hungry and very thirsty, and is placed equidistant between equal quantities of hay and water. If we assume that the ass is determined to choose by a variety of factors (more hungry or thirsty?; which hunger/thirst remover is nearer?; which is larger?), since all these are equal, nothing would cause the ass to go to one or the other; so it would stay stuck in the middle and starve to death.

Some philosophers argue that because this could never happen, decisions (even from an ass) cannot be fully determined in this fashion: there must be an arbitrary—free—element that's at least capable of resolving ties. (This free element is supposedly of primary importance in human decisions.) Others argue, however, that this sort of paralysis between equally attractive options could happen, but rarely does because such perfect equality is so uncommon.

THE CIRCLE THAT'S A STRAIGHT LINE

As the radius of a circle gets larger and larger, the curvature of the circle gets less and less. A circle with infinite radius would thus be a straight line!

Sometimes it's said that we should accept this odd result, and that it's just one of the odd things that happen when infinite magnitudes are imagined. (See, for example, the St. Petersburg Paradox, below.) Others point out that this would be true only if space is Euclidian—which it isn't, in fact.

CURRY'S PARADOX

Consider this sentence, which we'll call 'S':

If S is true, then Santa Claus exists.

Is S true? Well, suppose for the moment it is. Now we have the antecedent of the true conditional statement S, so the consequent follows: Santa Claus exists. When we assume S is true we derive Santa Claus exists, and this is the standard way to prove the truth of a conditional statement. So we've just proven If S is true then Santa Claus exists. But this is Statement S; so it follows that Santa Claus exists.

What's wrong here is not a matter of whether you're a Santa-believer or not. It's that this kind of reasoning can be used to prove any arbitrary proposition. What has gone wrong? Briefly, we can see the problem here as one of many odd consequences of allowing self-referential statements. (Statement S mentions itself.) See also, among others, Grelling's Paradox and The Liar Paradox.

DETERRENCE PARADOX

Think back to when the cold war between the US and the USSR was raging. Both countries had hundreds of nuclear warheads aimed at each other's cities. Each warned the other that the other's first strike would result in massive retaliation, in which hundreds of cities would be devastated and millions of innocent civilians killed and injured.

The aim here on both sides was preventing war, and in hindsight it seems we can say it was an astoundingly successful strategy. It's hard to find any other instances in history in which a face-off between powerful armed enemies did not result in major war.

But there are other moral considerations to raise here besides the morally laudable aim of preventing war. When one side threatens retaliation, it is announcing its intention to commit an absolutely horrible act. Is an intention to commit a hugely immoral act under certain circumstances itself immoral, even though—thankfully—those circumstances never come about?

Imagine that back then accidentally or on purpose the USSR bombed one or more US cities. Then what? The US would have had to choose whether to go forward with its threatened massive and unspeakably horrible retaliation on the USSR. That would have been in itself hugely immoral—it would have made things much worse than they already were, and would have been completely without any possible good effect. (At that point, nobody would have been deterred from anything.) If the US government had had any shred of morality left at that point, it would not have retaliated.

But surely the Soviet planners knew that the US people would have been thinking this way, and in fact would not have retaliated. (And vice versa: the US planners knew this about the Soviets.) If so, everyone would have known that all the threats of retaliation were empty.

To give retaliation-threats some force, in a situation like this, there would have to be some mechanism that unleashed retaliation automatically, no matter what the attacked side wanted to do then. (This is the "Doomsday Machine" imagined in the great movie *Doctor Strangelove*.) But then, having suffered a first strike from side B, horrible, useless, immoral retaliation would be unavoidable, whatever side A did—and they set it up to be this way!

GRELLING'S PARADOX

A couple of definitions:

- an adjective is homological if it describes itself.
- an adjective is heterological if it doesn't.

The adjective 'short' is homological because it's short. The adjective 'German' is heterological: it's not German—it's English.

Now consider the adjective 'heterological'. Which category does it go into? Is it heterological? If it is, then it doesn't describe itself; but if 'heterological' doesn't describe it, then it isn't heterological. So if it is heterological, then it isn't.

Is it then homological? If it is, then it does describe itself, but if 'heterological' describes itself, then it isn't homological. So if it is homological, then it isn't.

Either way, we get a self-contradiction. Another paradox resulting from self-reference; this one was formulated in 1908 by German mathematician Kurt Grelling. (See Russell's Paradox, below, which is analogous.)

GRUE (GOODMAN'S NEW RIDDLE OF INDUCTION)

Definitions:

- Time T is midnight on New Year's Eve at the end of the year 2020.
- X is grue provided that (a) it's T or earlier, and X is green; or (b) it's later than T, and X is blue.
- X is bleen provided that (a) it's T or earlier, and X is blue; or (b) it's later than T, and X is green.

All the emeralds we've seen so far have been green, so (because it's not yet T), they've also been grue. Ordinary scientific reasoning predicts the future on the basis of past observation, so we predict that after T, emeralds will still be green. But this sort of reasoning also predicts that after T emeralds will still be grue. But after T, something that's still green won't be grue any longer—it will have turned bleen overnight! It order to stay grue, it would have to turn blue.

A common reaction to this problem is to try to explain why 'grue' and 'bleen' are illegitimate properties to do science with. But what's wrong with them? The way we have defined them, they seem unlike regular color properties, in that their definitions include mention of time. Scientists who wanted to see whether things stayed grue around time T would have to keep checking their watches. But note that this is just a matter of the way we've been putting things. We could just as well have taken 'grue' and 'bleen' as the real color properties, and defined 'blue' and 'green' in terms of these, plus time T. (See if you can produce these definitions.) And a grue/bleen perceiving scientist would look at an emerald at time T, and might say, without consulting a watch, 'Yep, it stayed grue okay!' or 'Jeez! It suddenly turned bleen!'

HARMING THE DEAD

Imagine your best friend gives you a shirt which you hate, but you wear occasionally when you see her, so as not to insult. If she knew you hated it, she'd be upset, and you don't want that. But now your friend has died. You still think very kindly of her memory, but is it okay to throw away that awful shirt now? The answer seems to be yes. After all, the only morally relevant thing here is that you not hurt her feelings. That would be harming her. But after death, people can't be harmed.

But now consider other things that might be done to "harm the dead." Suppose you maliciously do what you can to destroy the good reputation of someone now dead. A lot of people think that there's something wrong with this. But what? Sometimes it's thought that the morality of actions regarding others isn't all a

matter of helping or harming them, because this never applies to the dead. So what other moral considerations are relevant for "dealing with" dead people? and why?

HERACLITUS' PARADOX

The paradox associated with this ancient Greek philosopher is the claim that you can't step into the same river twice. Why not? Because at every instant, the water that makes up this section of the river (or the river as a whole, for that matter), changes.

What this shows, of course, is that identical water is not the basis for the same river. What then is? Note that the same sort of question might be raised with regard to the "same" anything, which (almost) always changes, to some small or large degree, over time.

HOTEL INFINITY

(HILBERT'S HOTEL)

David Hilbert was a pioneer in the mathematical treatment of infinity. He illustrated one way that notion introduces strange results by asking us to imagine a hotel with an infinite number of rooms, all completely booked for the night. A traveler arrives, asking for a room—a request that would be denied by an ordinary completely-booked hotel—but in Hilbert's Hotel, matters are easily solved: the guests in room 1 are asked to move to room 2, while those in room 2, move to room 3, and those in 3 to room 4, and so on. This leaves room 1 empty for the arrivals.

HYPOTHETICAL DESIRE

PARADOX

If you're right-handed, you'd probably assent to this:

If I have to lose an arm, I want to lose my left arm.

Now imagine that, unfortunately, the antecedent of this conditional (hypothetical statement) becomes true: you have to lose one arm. Given the truth of the conditional, it follows by very elementary logic that you want to lose your left arm. But wait! That's hardly true. You don't want to lose either arm! Is this a counter-example to the very basic logical principle called modus ponens: If P then Q; P; therefore Q?

Instead of rejecting modus ponens, it has been suggested, we might understand that original proposition not as "If P then I want X," but rather, "I want: (If P then X)." From P and the latter, X does not follow. But now we need a logic to distinguish hypothetical desires from desires for hypotheticals.

LIAR PARADOX
(EPIMENIDES' PARADOX)

Suppose Fred says, "I'm lying right now." Is he telling the truth? Well, telling the truth isn't lying, so he isn't lying. But what he says is that he is lying, so if he's telling the truth he is lying. On the other hand, if he's not telling the truth, then ... well the same kind of self-negating puzzle emerges. Turns out both the assumption that Fred's statement is true and that it's false both imply self-contradictions.

There are many versions of this sort of paradox. Another one frequently seen is the Postcard Paradox: on one side of a postcard, it says, "What's written on the other side is false." On the other side, it says, "What's written on the other side is true." See if you can work out how there isn't any way to assign truth and falsity here.

And another variant is this book title:

> There Are Two Errors in the
> the Title of this Book

The Liar Paradox is one of the most basic and oldest versions of a self-referential paradox. It's sometimes called the Epimenides Paradox, after the ancient Cretan philosopher who wrote that all Cretans (probably intending to exclude himself) were liars. There has been a great deal written ever since in the attempt to try to cope with self-reference. One major tack has been to try to find a way in principle to rule out self-reference (without making arbitrary restrictions).

LOTTERY PARADOX

Imagine a lottery that will randomly draw one winning ticket from a million tickets. It's unreasonable to believe that the ticket you hold—number 439,664—will win, and you believe it won't win. But it's also unreasonable to believe that number 439,665 will win, and to believe that 439,666 will win, and so on, for every one of the million tickets. So for each of the tickets, you completely reasonably believe it won't win. But you also believe, completely reasonably again, that one of the million will win. So your set of a million and one completely reasonable beliefs is inconsistent.

One sort of reply points out that ground-floor inconsistency of belief requires a belief that P and a belief that not-P; but that's not what we have here, unless we believe a principle of agglomeration: that if you believe Q and you believe R, then you do (or should) believe (Q and R). Some sort of principle of this type is very attractive, but perhaps needs to yield here.

MONTY HALL PARADOX

Loosely based on the TV gameshow of which Monty Hall was the emcee, the question is this:

You're presented with three doors, and told that one hides a valuable car, the other two each a worthless goat. You pick a door at random. Then Monty, the emcee, knowing what's behind the other two, picks one that hides a goat, and opens it, revealing the contents. Now he asks you: do you want to stick to your door or switch to the contents of the remaining closed door?

This widely-publicized problem got wrong answers from a huge variety of people including many mathematicians. They reasoned: you've picked (say) Door A: Door C is opened to reveal a goat. Now it's 50/50 whether the car is behind your door or behind door B. If there's any advantage to sticking to door A (e.g., you're offered $100 to stay put) you should do so; but otherwise there's no reason to stay put or switch.

The correct (but widely disbelieved) answer is this: there's 1/3 probability that Door A, the one you picked first, has the car, thus 2/3 that the car is behind one of Door B or Door C. Monty knows what's back there, and he picks one of (or the only) door hiding a goat (say Door C) and opens it. But there's still a 2/3 chance that a door you haven't picked—only Door B now—has the car; and a 1/3 chance that Door A has it. So you'll double your chances by switching.

(See also the related Bertrand's Box Paradox, above.)

MORAL LUCK

Fred and Barney are both at a party at Wilma's house, and both of them are drinking way more than they should, given that each will be driving himself home. When the booze runs out and Wilma kicks both of them out, they each get in their cars, and attempt to drive to their homes. They're barely capable of steering effectively, and both frequently swerve onto the wrong side of the road. Fred is stopped by the police half-way home, and is charged (and eventually convicted) of driving under the influence. He pays a large fine, and has his license suspended for a year. Barney is unlucky, however: while driving on the opposite side of the road, his car collides head-on with one coming the other way, killing its driver. Barney is convicted of second-degree murder, and is sentenced to a very long jail term.

What Fred and Barney did was significantly similar. Both drank far too much at the party, given that they intended to drive themselves home. Both drove themselves, at great risk, despite knowing that they had drunk too much. Both were swerving all over the road. The difference was merely a matter of luck: Fred didn't crash into anything, and the property and persons of others were unharmed, but unluckily for Barney, an oncoming car just happened to be there just where he swerved off of his side of the road.

Everyone feels that Barney's more to blame than Fred is, and that his much more severe legal punishment was entirely justified. But the difference between his case and Fred's was entirely out of either's control: one was comparatively lucky, the other wasn't. How can we distribute moral blame and judicial punishment differently on the basis of this sort of luck (or un-luck)? But we do it all the time.

NEWCOMB'S PARADOX

Imagine a really smart computer, able to predict people's responses almost perfectly having been fed information about their personality and background. This computer presents you with a choice involving two boxes, Box A and Box B. You can choose to take either the contents of Box B alone, or else what's in Box A plus what's in Box B. In Box A there is $10,000, and it's transparent, so you can see the big pile of $100 notes sitting inside. The contents of Box B, you're told, however, depends on the computer's prediction of what you're going to do. If it has predicted that you'll take Box B alone, it has already put $1 million in Box B. If it has predicted that you'll take Box A plus Box B, it has put nothing into Box B. Should you take what's in Box B alone, or what's in both boxes? There are two lines of reasoning that attempt to answer this question.

(1) At the time you must decide, the computer has already set up what's in Box B—maybe nothing or maybe $1 million. Anyway, your decision won't cause a change in what's in there. You can take whatever's in Box B alone, or else that plus the $10,000 in Box A. Maybe there's a million in Box B, maybe nothing; either way, you'd get $10,000 more by taking both boxes, so do it.

(2) The computer, remember, is almost always right in its predictions. That means that if you take both boxes, it almost certainly has predicted that, and put nothing in Box B, and you'll get $10,000. But if you take just Box B, it almost certainly has predicted that, and put $1 million in Box B, so you'll get a million. Go with the probabilities. Take just Box B.

This interesting problem has resulted in a lot of response. Reactions are divided between advocating strategy (1) and advocating strategy (2), and there are interesting implications for decision theory about which strategy might be the right one.

OMNISCIENCE PROOF OF GOD'S EXISTENCE

God is often conceived of as omniscient—that is, all-knowing. That means that He knows everything that's the case. Maybe we'd like to express that fact this way:

> For all propositions P (P is true if and only if God knows that P).

The trouble is that this seems to presuppose the existence of God, so atheists wouldn't accept it. Let's reformulate it more neutrally:

> For all propositions P (P is true if and only if, if God existed, God would know that P).

That sounds unexceptionable. Now, if that's true for all propositions, it's true in particular for the proposition, God exists. So we can infer:

> 'God exists' is true if and only if, if God existed, God would know that he exists.

Consider the second part of that sentence:

> if God existed, God would know that he exists.

Nobody, it seems—atheist or believer—could deny this. After all, if anybody exists, he'd know that he exists, right?

But when you have a true sentence made of two parts connected by 'if and only if', and when one of those parts is true, it follows that the other is true. So from the truth of the second part of that sentence, we can validly infer the truth of the first part:

> 'God exists' is true.

Or, putting the same thing more briefly,

> God exists.

The reason there has to be something wrong in this reasoning is not that there isn't any God. The reason is that we appear to be pulling a proof of God's existence out of thin air—something atheists and believers alike should be suspicious of. What, exactly, has gone wrong here?

THE PREFACE

If you find out that what you say or believe is inconsistent, you shouldn't rationally continue to say or believe that: you should try to fix it, right? It's irrational to allow to stand what you know is an inconsistent set of statements one makes or beliefs one has, right? Wrong and wrong. Here's why.

Often one finds in the preface of a book the modest statement that the book surely contains errors, but that these are the fault of the author, not of the numerous people thanked for help in writing the book.

Now consider the set of sentences consisting of everything stated in book B, including the statement in its preface, "There's at least one error in here." It's logically impossible that this whole set is true. Here's why. If the preface-statement is true, then there's at least one false statement elsewhere in the set. But if the preface is false, then again the whole set isn't true. That set is what logicians call a logically inconsistent set: one such that it's logically impossible that everything in it is true.

Never mind about books and their prefaces. Everyone who is a clear thinker and who doesn't have inappropriately and ridiculously inflated views about his own omniscience knows that some of his many beliefs—one hopes not many, but some anyway—must be false. This is a rational thing to believe. Rational, but rendering one's whole belief set logically inconsistent.

PRISONER'S DILEMMA

You and your buddy are arrested for a major crime; the police know you both did it, but have evidence only good enough for convictions on a rather trivial charge. So they put you two in separate cells, and offer you a deal: your sentence will depend on whether or not you confess, implicating yourself and the other guy, and on what your buddy does when offered the same deal. The following chart summarizes how this works, specifies the years in jail you will serve under all four eventualities.

	He confesses	He stays silent
You confess	7 years	1 year
You stay silent	10 years	3 years

The best outcome for you is confession—if he stays silent. But he's offered the same deal, so his best deal is confession, while you stay silent. And if both of you confess, you'll both be badly off.

It seems that what's best for both of you would be to both keep quiet; you'd each get your second-best possible outcome, but you'd both avoid other possible disasters. If there were a way of making an enforceable and effective deal that both of you would keep silent, this would be good. But there isn't.

Under the circumstances, then, it seems that the most rational thing for you to do is to confess. Whatever he does, you'll come out better than if you stayed silent. This, however, is the most rational choice for the other guy as well. So if both of you do what's rational, both will get seven years in jail—next to the worst of the four possibilities. It seems that there's something irrational about doing what's most rational.

This little story can be taken as a simplified model for a wide range of social situations: competition vs. cooperation between individuals, and between nations. Psychologists and social and ethical philosophers have had a lot to say about it.

PROTAGORAS' PARADOX

The famous ancient Greek philosopher Protagoras taught law to Euathlus, with the agreement that Euathlus would pay Protagoras tuition fees if he won his first case; but if he lost, he wouldn't have to pay. Euathlus finishes his education, sets himself up as a lawyer, but for some reason takes on no cases. Finally, Protagoras gets fed up, and sues Euathlus for the money.

Protagoras points out that he's suing for the fees, so if he wins, Euathlus would have to pay, and if he loses, Euathlus wouldn't have to. But Euathlus reminds the court of the contract for payment: if he wins his first case, he pays the tuition; if he loses he doesn't. And this, of course, is his first case.

So who is right?

(Also called The Lawyer, Euathlus, the Paradox of the Court.)

THE QUESTION PARADOX

An angel visits the Annual Meetings of the American Philosophical Association, and tells the philosophers there that they will be given the gift of asking God exactly one question, and that God in His omniscience will answer it.

There is a good deal of debate about what is the one question to ask. "What is the meaning of life?" is ruled out as too vague, and as very likely to have an unsatisfying answer. "How do you best remove red wine stains from a light-colored carpet?" is a question whose answer many philosophers have an interest in, but in the end it's thought too trivial for such a great opportunity. There's some enthusiasm for asking "What is the most important question we could ask, and what is its answer?" but there's a worry this might be counted as two questions. A logician suggests they avoid this potential difficulty by converting this to one question: "What is the ordered pair consisting of (a) the most important question that could be asked and (b) the answer to that question?"

The angel appears, is asked this question, and five minutes later returns with God's answer: "The most important question you could ask is 'What is the ordered pair consisting of (a) the most important question that could be asked and (b) the answer to that question?' and the answer to that question is what I'm saying now."

RAVEN PARADOX

This famous paradox challenges two seemingly obvious assumptions: (1) that scientific generalizations are confirmed by observation of instances of them (e.g., that 'All ravens are black' is confirmed a little every time an additional black raven is observed); and (2) that if some observation O confirms generalization G, and G is logically equivalent to H, then O must also confirm H (because, after all, when two statements are logically equivalent, they say the same thing—anything that makes one true (or false) does the same to the other).

G: All non-black things are non-ravens is logically equivalent to H: All ravens are black. The observation of a yellow pencil confirms G, but it surely does not seem to confirm H. (Otherwise H would be confirmed by the uncountable number of observations of non-black non-ravens everyone makes all the time.)

Maybe, on the other hand, you might want to insist that that pencil does confirm (to an extremely tiny degree) the raven generalization. Or else, you might want to explore the idea that scientific confirmation is not at all merely a simple matter of observations of instances of a generalization.

RUSSELL'S PARADOX

Think of a class in the technical sense involved here as a collection of things that share a common attribute. Some classes are not members of themselves: the class of poodles, for example, is not itself a poodle.

Call these classes non-self-inclusive. Some classes are members of themselves: examples are the class of non-poodles (which is itself not a poodle), or the class of things with more than five members, which itself has more than five members. Call these classes self-inclusive.

Now consider the class of non–self-inclusive classes. It contains poodles, planets, and so on, but is it a member of itself? Try two answers:

> YES: but since it's the class of non–self-inclusive classes, if it's a member of itself, then it's non–self-inclusive, so it doesn't include itself.

> NO: but if it's not in there, it must be in the class of self-inclusive classes; so it does include itself.

Bertrand Russell discovered this paradox in 1901, and shortly thereafter told the great logician Frege about it. Frege realized that this paradox showed that two very basic axioms used in his book on formal logic, about to be published, were inconsistent. There has been a great deal of consideration about the implications of Russell's Paradox ever since. (See Grelling's Paradox, above, which is analogous.)

RUSSELL'S PROOF OF GOD'S EXISTENCE

The next time you're driving around, take a look at the first license plate number you see: it's EJR 036 (or whatever). What are the odds against seeing exactly that license plate number, out of all the possible ones, just then? They're minuscule, one out of several million or more. It's a miracle! God must exist.

This "proof" was cooked up by Bertrand Russell, who was a well-known atheist and of course had his tongue firmly planted in his cheek. Of course this goes no way toward proving God's existence. But the interesting question it raises is: why exactly is seeing that license plate not a hugely unlikely—almost miraculous—event?

SAYING WHAT YOU MEAN

Can you say, "Gloob! Gloob! Gloob!" but mean, It's snowing in Tibet? No? Why not?

SHIP OF THESEUS

According to ancient Greek legend, Theseus kept repairing the ship of which he was captain while at sea, replacing, one at a time, old rotten planks with new sound ones. When this process was complete, there was not a single bit of the ship that was there at the start of the voyage. Is the ship Theseus returned in the same one as the one he started out in? If yes, then how come? If no, then what happened to the old one?

In the seventeenth century, Thomas Hobbes added a wrinkle to this story by imagining further that Theseus kept all the old rotten lumber, and eventually a (pretty useless) ship was constructed out of this. At that point there are two ships: the one made of new, sound lumber, and the one made of rotten old planks. Which is the one Theseus began his voyage in?

SIMPSON'S PARADOX

In basketball, you get two points for a basket shot from closer in, 3 points from further out. The following table lists successes/attempts at 2- and 3-point shots made during a season by two players, Wilt Jordan and Michael Chamberlain:

	Jordan	Chamberlain
2 pt	200 / 400: 50%	440 / 950: 46.3%
3 pt	80 / 320: 25%	30 / 190: 15.8%

As you can see, Jordan's average is better at scoring on attempted 2-point shots and 3-point shots. That implies that Jordan is better at making shots altogether, right? Wrong. Here are the totals:

Jordan	Chamberlain
280 / 720: 38.9%	470 / 1140: 41.2%

Check the arithmetic yourself: there's no trick here. This sort of counterintuitive result is quite common in statistics. It was brought to wide attention by a mathematician named E.H. Simpson.

SORITES PARADOX

A person 7 feet high is definitely tall. Subtract a ¼ inch from this, and consider a person 6 feet 11¾ inches high: that person is definitely tall too. Now imagine a series of subtractions, each of ¼ inch; is there a height H in this series such that a person of height H is tall, but a person of height (H–¼") is not tall? It seems not. If you think there is, try to specify that height, and see if you can get anyone to agree with you. But if there is no such H, then we can keep subtracting ¼", and still have the height of a tall person; so reach the obviously false conclusion that a person 3 feet high is tall. What has gone wrong here?

There are practical (mis)applications of this fallacious reasoning. Someone considering one more little sip of beer before driving home can believe correctly that one more little sip won't make any difference in his driving ability. But this is true of each little sip in a series in which, at some point, the drinker has become completely disabled.

A lot of thought has been given to how to rethink matters to locate and fix the mistake in reasoning of this sort.

'Sorites', pronounced so-RIGHT-eez, is Greek for heap (another traditional name for this paradox); a very early version imagined starting with one grain of sand—clearly not a heap—and reasoning that adding one additional grain never transformed a non-heap into a heap. Another traditional example reasons that removal of just one hair from a head cannot transform a non-bald head into a bald one.

THE SPECIOUS PRESENT

Your third birthday party does not exist—now. Nothing in the past exists. Neither does anything in the future. All that exists is the present.

Now consider apparently present facts: the cat is on the mat, Cleveland is in Ohio, Jupiter is the largest planet. Each of these has a time span, with a past and (we'd expect) a future component. But the past and future components, as we've seen, don't exist. Well, what about the present component? How long does that last? If it has any non-zero duration, then part of it is non-existent, in the past or in the future. Anything that's completely present must have a zero duration. But here's the problem: something that lasts for zero time is nothing at all. So the supposedly zero-duration present doesn't exist either. It apparently follows that nothing exists.

Obviously this reasoning is mistaken. But it's no easy job to figure out exactly where. In the process of considering this, in any case, we can get clearer on some things we would never otherwise consider, some basic presuppositions about duration and existence.

ST. PETERSBURG PARADOX

When you're playing a game of chance, a fair bet is the amount of money you should pay to play, expecting to come out even in the long run. (Of course, casinos never offer a fair bet in this sense—they need to make a profit on you.)

You calculate a fair bet by summing the products of multiplying the probability of each outcome times the payoff given that outcome. Imagine a coin flip that would pay you $1 for heads, $2 for tails. Each outcome has a probability of .5, so the fair bet is $(.5 \times \$1) + (.5 \times \$2)$. This equals $1.50.

Now consider the St. Petersburg Game. You flip a fair coin counting the number of flips till it comes up tails, when the game ends. Call the number of flips in a finished game n; the payoff is then $\$2^n$. (A run of three heads then a tails would thus have $n = 4$, and a payoff of $16.)

What's the fair bet for St. Petersburg? The probability that $n = 1$ is 1/2; its payoff is $2. The probability that $n = 2$ is 1/4; its payoff is $4. The probability that $n = 3$ is 1/8; its payoff is $8. And so on. You can see where this is going. The sum of $(1/2 \times 2) + (1/4 \times \$4) + (1/8 \times \$8)$ and so on equals $1 + $1 + $1 + $1 and so on. The fair bet is an infinite amount of money! In other words, any finite amount you pay to play each game will be smaller than your eventual winnings, if you play long enough.

Of course, you'd probably run out of money to bet before you had an enormous win; or the casino would close, or you'd die. This is not a practical plan. But it does, probability theorists think, raise important theoretical questions about the ideas taken for granted in thinking about fair bets on chance events.

THE THOMSON LAMP

This is an imaginary light-fixture. You push a button to turn it on, and in ½ of a minute, it turns itself off; then after another ¼ of a minute, it turns back on again, then after another ⅛ of a minute, it turns back off, and so on. Imagine (contrary, perhaps, to the laws of physics) that it can do this switching an infinite number of times. It doesn't take a great deal of mathematical skill to sum this series, and determine that the whole series will finish exactly one minute after you start it. The question is: at the end of this minute, will the lamp be on or off? (or, bizarrely, neither or both?)

This kind of peculiar event has been treated extensively in the literature, where it's sometimes called a supertask.

THE TIME AND THE PLACE OF A MURDER

On December 2, 2002, Bob is visiting a tourist attraction, the Four Corners Monument, located at the only point in the US where four states come together and you can stand with one foot overlapping all four states (should that sound exciting to you). Bob notices his enemy Bart standing nearby, pulls out his gun, and shoots Bart in the foot. Police apprehend Bob, and Bart is taken to hospital, and eventually dies of his wound.

Bob is guilty of murder, but where did it take place? Bob was standing in Arizona when he shot Bart, but about eighteen inches of his right arm, with the gun in hand, extended east into New Mexico. Bart was standing north of Bob, in Utah, but his foot, when it was shot, was slightly over the state line, and was in Colorado. Did the murder take place where Bob was? And was that in Arizona or New Mexico (or both)? Or did it take place where Bart was? And was that in Utah or Colorado (or both)? Or maybe the murder took place in all four states?

Bart's medical condition deteriorated despite treatment, and he died in hospital in early January. This raises questions about timing. Did the murder take place when Bart was shot, in December, or when he died, the following January? Or maybe it was a spread-out event, taking about a month to happen? Imagine you're the police officer at the press conference in December, following Bob's apprehension. You're asked, "Was that murder?" What's the answer: "Not yet!" because Bart was still alive? But when he dies in January, does that retroactively transform the shooting, done the previous month, into murder? Or was it murder all along, though given Bart's survival through December, nobody knew it yet?

How these questions are answered may have practical bearing: the location questions if the laws regarding murder are different in each of the four states; the timing question if there's a change in law to take place on January 1. A court may have to decide these answers. Notice however that there don't seem to be any facts that could be discovered that would determine the right answers. We already know all the relevant facts, and they don't add up to any answers. Would the answers to these questions then be a matter of totally arbitrary decision?

TIME TRAVEL

The main paradox involved here involves the question about whether a time traveler could change the past. For example, could you, on Tuesday, go back to Monday, and move that coffee cup away from the edge of the table, so that it didn't get knocked off and break? This is hard to understand. We start by supposing that it's Tuesday, and the coffee cup did break on Monday. Then, supposedly, you go back and prevent this; but then does it happen that on Tuesday that the coffee cup didn't break earlier? Do those pieces of coffee-cup in the trash suddenly disappear? Or were they never there in the first place?

This sort of science-fiction story is familiar: Fred goes back 60 years, finds his grandfather aged 15, and tries to kill him. If Fred succeeds, then he wouldn't have been born, but then who went back in time and killed grandpa? Some philosophers argue that this doesn't show that time travel is inherently self-contradictory, but rather that no matter what else you accomplish when going back in time, you won't kill your grandfather when he was a teenager, because—simply put—it didn't happen!

TRAGEDY OF THE COMMONS

A commons is a piece of land in the center of a town which traditionally was publicly owned and reserved for shared use. Sometimes all the livestock owners in the town were allowed to graze their animals on this land. When grazed by too many animals, however, the grass could not grow back, and the land was ruined for this use.

The problem here is that it's clearly to each individual herder's self-interest to graze as many animals as he could on the commons. It would be highly unlikely that putting just his few animals there would overload an otherwise sustainable grass crop; if the land was already overloaded by general use, and the grass crop was headed for extinction, it would still be to each herder's interest to get as much as he could out of it, before it became useless.

The generalized problem illustrated here is that in many situations, when individuals act in their own undoubted rational self-interest, a shared general resource will ultimately be depleted, contrary to anyone's interest. What's at issue here is very much like the problem raised, above, by the Prisoner's Dilemma.

TREASURE-HUNTER PARADOX

Years ago, the CBC interviewed a historian who was researching treasure-hunting in Nova Scotia, where the numerous islands and hidden coves gave pirates an ideal place to bury their treasure. Of the many attempts to find buried treasure, a few had actually found it; the historian reported that a very large proportion of successful diggers had deepened holes made by previous searchers. The earlier searches had stopped just short of success. So the interviewer asked the historian what advice to give future treasure-hunters, on the basis of this information. The historian hesitated for a moment, then replied that he guessed that they should dig a little deeper than they do.

TRISTRAM SHANDY

This is the name of the hero of the novel bearing his name. In the novel, he has undertaken to write his autobiography, but he writes so slowly that he takes a year to cover only one day of his life. That means, as time goes on, he'll fall more and more behind. Bertrand Russell, however, pointed out in an influential study of infinity, that paradoxically if Shandy would live for an infinite length of time, despite falling further and further behind at any moment, he'd nevertheless be able to finish his work. One of the many paradoxes of infinity.

TROLLEY PROBLEM

You're standing next to trolley tracks, and see an out-of-control trolley fast approaching. Five people are tied to the tracks farther down, and would die when the trolley gets there; but you can throw a switch which would steer the trolley instead on to another track where only one person would die.

Some philosophers react to this story (introduced by Philippa Foot and widely discussed) that one is not morally permitted to throw the switch, because that would amount to killing the one person on the alternate track; one must, then, accept the (nevertheless horrible) outcome of the death of the five, because that's not the result of your wrongdoing. Killing is wrong; allowing to die is under some circumstances permitted.

Other philosophers, however, have the strong reaction that all that's relevant here is that you have the choice of five dying, or just one; so you must throw the switch: they deny that the difference between acting and refraining from acting has any moral significance.

TWO ENVELOPES PARADOX

You're presented with two sealed envelopes, a red and a blue one, and told that one contains twice the amount of money as the other; but you can't tell which is which. You pick the red one, at random. But before opening it, you're offered the option of swapping it for the blue one. Should you take that option?

At first glance, it seems that it's a matter of indifference whether you swap or not. But consider this reasoning: Call the amount of money in the red envelope (whatever that is) M. It's 50% probable that the blue envelope contains $\frac{1}{2} \times M$, and 50% probable it contains $2 \times M$. So it's equiprobable that swapping would increase your payoff by M, or decrease it by $\frac{1}{2}$ M. Swapping is a good bet. It's probably advantageous for you to swap.

Now, imagine that the reasoning convinces you, and you agree to swap, and exchange envelopes. Now you hold the blue envelope. But now you're offered the option of swapping again, back to the red one. You reason this way: Call the amount of money in the blue envelope (whatever that is) N. It's 50% probable that the red envelope contains ½ × N, and 50% probable it contains 2 × N. So it's equiprobable that swapping would increase your payoff by N, or decrease it by ½ N. Swapping is a good bet. It's probably advantageous for you to swap. So you swap again.

But it's clear that something has gone wrong here. It's impossible that this could go on and on, with your reasoning telling you that every time that each swap adds to your advantage. That can't be. Okay, it's clear that somewhere there's a mistake in your reasoning: but where?

There's a variant of the Two-Envelopes Paradox called the Two-Wallet Game. Here's how this works. You and a friend are drinking in a bar, and he suggests this game. You both put your wallets on the table, and whoever's wallet has less money in it gets the money that's in the other's wallet. (Neither of you has any idea of how much is in the others' wallet, or in your own.)

You reason: Call the amount of money in my wallet (whatever it is) A, and call the amount of money in Buddy's wallet B. It's equally likely that A is less than B, or more. So there's a 50% probability that A is more than B, and I'd lose A. But it's 50% probability that I'd win B—if B was larger than A. So if I won, what I'd win is more than what I'd lose if I lost. The game is favorable to me.

Buddy, of course, is reasoning the same way. It can't be that this game is favorable to both players. Both of you have made a mistake, and maybe you have the feeling that it's the same sort of mistake that showed up in the reasoning about the envelope switch.

UNEXPECTED (SURPRISE) HANGING (OR EXAM) PARADOX

On Friday, your algebra teacher announces that there will be a surprise quiz during one of the classes next week—'surprise' meaning that you won't be able to figure out when it will take place before the class starts in which it is given.

You reason: there are classes on Monday, Wednesday, and Friday. If the test were on Friday, we'd know that in advance—after class on Wednesday—because there was no test on Monday or Wednesday, and it had to be on one of those three days. So a Friday quiz wouldn't be a surprise. It can't be on Friday.

So it must be on Monday or Wednesday. But if it were on Wednesday, we'd know that in advance—after class on Monday; as we've already figured out, so since it wasn't on Monday, it would have to be on Wednesday. So a Wednesday quiz wouldn't be a surprise. It can't be on Wednesday.

So it must be on Monday, the only remaining possibility. But we can figure that out—know already that it has to be Monday. But that wouldn't be a surprise then.

So a surprise quiz under these conditions is impossible.

This is a very perplexing paradox because it's perfectly clear that there can be a surprise quiz, and so there has to be an error in the reasoning above. But philosophers have had some trouble finding a persuasive account of what has gone wrong.

Does this addition to the story help you figure out what's wrong? Having done all the reasoning above, you show up in Monday's algebra class, and the teacher hands out the quiz. "But!" you object, "But! But!" The teacher says, "Surprise!!"

(A nastier version of the same story involves the surprise timing of the hanging of a condemned man.)

UNINTERESTING NUMBERS

Consider what we'll call interesting numbers—positive integers with special facts or associations attached to them. 1 is surely an interesting number: it's the number of gods believed in by many religions, the smallest prime number, etc. 2 is also interesting: it's the smallest even number. 3 is the number of blind mice, of little pigs, of bears Goldilocks met, etc. 4 is the July date celebrated as the US national holiday. 5 is the number of fingers on one hand. Probably you can think of something that sets apart 6, 7, 8, 9, 10, and more, and makes them interesting. What then is the smallest uninteresting number? Hard to say, but let's suppose that it's 2,693, a number associated with no facts whatsoever. Oh but wait: there is something that makes this number stand out: it's the smallest uninteresting number, so it's interesting after all. (A contradiction?) Okay, anyway, let's keep looking. How about 2,694 then? If that's the smallest uninteresting number, that's an interesting fact about it. And so on, as high as you care to go. So we've proven that every number is interesting, right?

What's foolish about this reasoning?

VOTER'S PARADOX (1)

In the most common sort of election, the candidate wins who receives more votes than the others; and there are special procedures in the regulations concerning ties.

Voters often want to see their candidate get a large number of votes, win or lose, but we'll ignore this for our purposes, and consider only what's by far the chief motivation for voting: you want your candidate to win. Regarding this motivation, your vote can make a difference if, without it, your candidate would be tied for first place, or if your vote creates a tie.

Now, consider the chances of either of these happening in an election with more than a handful of voters. A statistics professor estimates that a tied congressional election might be expected to occur in the US once approximately every 400 years. It is overwhelmingly unlikely that your vote will make a difference in this and in almost every other sort of election.

So why vote? Your chances of being hit by lightning on the way to the polling station are probably greater than the chance of making a difference.

VOTER'S PARADOX (2)

Confusingly sometimes known by the same name as the one just considered, this one shows that under certain circumstances, voting is not a way to produce a rational general will out of individual preferences.

Consider this simple case: There are three candidates for a position, A, B, and C, and three voters, 1, 2, and 3. The three voters each have preferences among the candidates, in this order:

voter 1: prefers A to B, and B to C

voter 2: prefers B to C, and C to A

voter 3: prefers C to A, and A to B

A simple vote in which each voted for his/her preferred candidate would result in a tie: one vote for each of A, B, and C, and no decision.

Let's try a series of votes to see in general what preferences the voters have when considering only two of the three. Vote first on A and B: 1 and 3 prefer A to B; only 2 disagrees. Good so far. Now let's compare B and C: 1 and 2 prefer B to C.

So now we have majority votes preferring A to B, and B to C. Does that mean that the general will is best served by ranking them in the order A, B, C, giving the victory to A, with C coming in third? To make sure, let's compare A and C: 2 and 3 both prefer A to C. Whoops.

ZENO'S PARADOXES

Zeno of Elea was a fifth-century BCE Greek philosopher who is now known for having created a number of paradoxes involving motion, plurality, and change. Nine of these are known today, on the basis of quotation or discussion by other philosophers; we'll briefly look at the three best-known of them.

On the surface, Zeno's paradoxes seem like silly denials of the obvious, but really they are, in Russell's words, "immeasurably subtle and profound" explorations of problems involved in our presuppositions about time, space, motion, and so on.

Achilles and the Tortoise is the most famous of Zeno's paradoxes. Suppose speedy Achilles is in a race with a tortoise. Achilles can run much faster than the tortoise, so the latter is given a head start, beginning farther down the track than Achilles. The race begins, and Achilles very soon runs to the place the tortoise started from; but by then the tortoise has run (or waddled) on to a point a little further on. So then Achilles continues running till he gets to this second point, but by then the tortoise has gone on to a third point. And so on. No matter how many times Achilles catches up to where the tortoise just left, he hasn't caught up with him. Conclusion: he can never catch up.

This conclusion is obviously false, and modern mathematics (given the figures for the speed of each, and the head-start distance) can tell us exactly when Achilles will catch up—and pass—the tortoise. But then what has gone bad in this reasoning? This is a hard question to answer. (Note, by the way, the connection between this item and what's discussed above in the Thomson Lamp section.)

The Racecourse is closely related to the first Achilles paradox. Here Zeno concentrates simply on Achilles' run down the racecourse, ignoring the tortoise. Can Achilles reach the end of the course? To do so, he must first reach the half-way point; then, having gotten there, he must travel half of the remaining portion, arriving at the point ¾ of the way down the field; then he must again cover half the remaining distance, arriving at the ⅞ point; and so on and so on. There's an endless series of smaller and smaller runs he must make, and at the end of each run in the series there's still some distance to go. So he can never get to the end of the field. (This paradox is also often called The Dichotomy.)

The Arrow. Consider an arrow flying through the air. At any one moment—a dimensionless point in time, with zero duration—it's in exactly one well-defined space, which is not moving. At another moment, it's in another motionless space, not moving. There isn't any moment during its flight when this is not true. So how can it be moving?

Philosophical Lexicon

INTRODUCTION

Philosophy, having been around the longest of any academic discipline, has accumulated what may be the longest list of technical jargon terms. These are useful shorthand for philosophers already familiar with these words, but they can provide stumbling-blocks for students. We've included here a rather minimal dictionary of the more common philosophical terms, including some that occur in the readings in this volume, and others that don't.

This is a revised and severely shortened version of a much more inclusive philosophical lexicon: *The Philosopher's Dictionary*, by Robert M. Martin (Broadview Press).

LEXICON

abstract / concrete entities / ideas Abstract entities are supposed not to be locatable in space or time, not perceptible, without causes or effects, necessarily existing. Putative examples are properties, universals, sets, geometrical figures, and numbers. Something is, by contrast, concrete when it is particular and spatially and temporally locatable—perhaps material. There's a long history of philosophical argument about the reality of certain abstracta. Clearly some of them aren't real, for example, the average American family, with its 2.6 children. Reification is mistakenly taking something to be real that's merely abstract; this sort of reasoning is known as the fallacy of misplaced concreteness.

There's a good deal of historical debate about whether we can even have abstract ideas at all. We experience only particulars, so abstract ideas were a problem for the classical empiricists, who thought that every idea was a copy of an experience. Plato and others argued that we must have innate abstract ideas, not originating with sensation, in order to be able to classify the particulars.

act / agent moralities Some moral philosophers think that the basic sort of thing ethics evaluates is the worth of actions people do (act morality); others think that what's basic to moral theory is the worth of the person who acts (agent morality). Kant argued that good actions were those done by people with the right sort of motives, so his ethical theory is one species of agent morality; another species is virtue ethics. The utilitarians held that the basic kind of ethical reasoning evaluates actions (via their consequences), whatever the motives or moral worth of the people who do them, so their ethics is a variety of act morality.

action at a distance The effect that one thing can have on another that it is not touching and to which it is not connected by something in-between. Gravitation is an example. Some philosophers and scientists—e.g., Leibniz—thought that this was impossible. One way they tried to explain gravitation is to suppose that bodies that gravitationally attract each other are connected by some intervening invisible thing that fills the space between them and transfers the gravitational force.

action theory The branch of philosophy that considers questions about action. Examples of these are: What differentiates an action from other movements? Can there be actions that are refrainings from acting? Where does an action end and its consequences begin? What sort of explanation is suitable for actions?

Moral questions (about, for example, acts / omissions) and the questions of free will and responsibility are sometimes included in action theory.

acts / omissions An act is doing something, by contrast with an omission (or refraining), which is merely failing to do something. Some philosophers think that there can be a moral difference between these even when they have the same motives and outcome.

a fortiori (Latin: "from what is stronger") Means 'with even stronger reason', 'even more so'. "You owe thanks to someone who lets you use his car for a day. So a fortiori, you should really be grateful to Fred, who let you have his car for a whole month."

agent An agent is one who can perform a genuine intentional action, and who is thus morally responsible for what he/she does. This excludes people, for example, who are unable to perceive relevant facts, or who can't reason about consequences.

agent / event causation Often it is thought that causes and effects must be events. But if our actions are caused by other events, then how can we be responsible for them? It's sometimes argued that the cause of an action is not an event but rather the agent who did it.

agnosticism is in general the position that one does not, maybe cannot, know the truth or falsity of statements in some area—that there is insufficient reason to believe either. This term is used most frequently regarding religion, to contrast with theism and atheism (which are confident that we know that God does / doesn't exist).

alienation Estrangement, separation. Hegel discussed the possibility of human estrangement from the natural world. The existentialists thought that our alienation from nature and from each other was an important and inevitable part of the human condition. In Marx, 'alienation' means the separation from the products of our labor (as employees, we don't own what we produce) as well as from society and from ourselves.

altruism 1. Generosity. 2. The philosophical position that one ought to act for the benefit of others; contrast with egoism.

analogy / disanalogy An analogy is a similarity of two things. Reasoning from (or by) analogy—'analogical argument'—concludes that because two things share one or more characteristics, they share another; e.g., that because others show external behavior similar to one's own, others must have a similar internal life. A disanalogy is a difference between compared things; disanalogies between things reduce the strength of an argument from analogy.

analysis Some things are capable of being understood in terms of their component parts; analysis takes them apart into their simpler elements. Some twentieth century anglophone philosophers took analysis of concepts to be the job of philosophy. What is to be analyzed is called the analysandum, and what provides the analysis is called the analysans.

analytic / synthetic Kant called a judgment analytic when the "predicate was contained in the subject"; thus, for example, the judgment that all bachelors are unmarried is analytic because the subject ('bachelors') "contains" the predicate ('unmarried'). Later philosophers preferred to make this distinction in terms of sentences and meanings: a sentence is analytic when the meaning of the subject of that sentence contains the meaning of the predicate: 'unmarried' is part of the definition of 'bachelor'. So an analytic sentence is one that is true merely because of the meanings of the words. 'It's snowing or it's not snowing' is true merely because of the meaning of the words 'or' and 'not', so perhaps we should count this as analytic too. But since the relevant words in this case are "logical" words, this sentence is more particularly known as a logical truth. A synthetic truth is a sentence that is true, but not merely because of the meaning of the words. 'Pigs don't fly' is true partially because of the meaning of the words, of course: if 'pigs' meant 'woodpeckers', then that sentence would be false. But since the definition of 'pig' tells us nothing about flying, this sentence is not true merely because of the meaning of the words. One can speak also about analytically false sentences, for example, 'There exists a married bachelor'. Analytic sentences are necessarily true, and may (sometimes) be known a priori; but Kant argued that there are also synthetic a priori statements. Quine argued that the analytic / synthetic distinction is not a good one, because one cannot distinguish between matters of meaning of the words of a sentence and matters of fact.

ancient philosophy Ancient philosophy began in primitive form, we suppose, in prehistory; the earliest Western philosopher of whose work we have a historical account is Thales (c. 580 BCE). The end of this period is often marked by the beginning of medieval philosophy, with the work of Augustine (about 400 CE).

antecedent conditions The events or states of affairs that come before a given event and that cause it, or are necessary or sufficient (See necessary / sufficient conditions) for it to happen.

a priori / a posteriori Two different ways in which something might be known to be true (or false). It can be known a priori if it can be known before—that is, or independently of—sense-experience of the fact in question. It can be known a posteriori if it can be known after—that is, on the basis of—sense-experience of the fact. One can know that all bachelors are unmarried a priori; one doesn't need to observe even one bachelor to know this is true. In this case (but perhaps not in all cases) a priori knowledge is possible because what's known is a conceptual truth or because the sentence that expresses this truth is analytic or logically true. Kant argued that certain a priori truths (for example, that every event has a cause) were not conceptual or analytic.

argument An argument in ordinary talk is a debate, especially a heated one. But in philosophical usage, an argument is one or more statements (called 'premises'; singular 'premise' or 'premiss') advanced in order to support another statement (the conclusion). Thus philosophers need not get angry when they argue. Premises actually support a conclusion only when there is the appropriate sort of logical connection between the premises and the conclusion. In deductive arguments, the conclusion must be true given the truth of the premises; in an inductive argument, the truth of the premises makes the conclusion more probable. Any deductive argument in which the premises really do have the appropriate logical connection with the conclusion is called a 'valid' argument; in invalid arguments, this connection is lacking. A valid argument may, however, fail to support its conclusion because one or more of its premises is false—for example: All pigs fly. All flying things are lighter than air. Therefore all pigs are lighter than air. This argument is valid, but it fails to convince because both of its premises are false. An argument with at least one false premise is called 'unsound'; a sound argument is a valid argument all of whose premises are true. A sound argument provides a proof of its conclusion (though in logic it's often said that a proof is provided merely when the argument is valid).

argument from illusion / hallucination The argument (against naïve realisms) that the existence of perceptual illusions and hallucinations shows that we really directly perceive only sense-data and not an independent world.

artificial intelligence An area of study in computer science and psychology that involves building (or imagining) machines, or programming computers, to mimic certain complex intelligent human activities. The creation of a program that can play chess at a high level is one of its successes. Artificial intelligence might shed light on what human mentality is like, and its successes and failures enter into arguments about materialism.

artificial / natural language A natural language is one used by some actual group of people, that has developed on its own, culturally and historically. An artificial language is one developed for some purpose—examples are computer languages and symbolic logic.

association of ideas One thought produces another: when you think about shoes, maybe this drags along the thought of socks. Associationism was the view that this sort of thing is at the core of our mental life, and that its laws constitute a scientific cognitive psychology.

atheism Atheists believe that God doesn't exist, and (sometimes) that religious practice is foolish, or that the morality fostered by religion is wrong. Because atheism has been so unpopular, atheistic philosophers have sometimes disguised their views. Lucretius and Hume were probably atheists. Russell was open about his atheism, and got into trouble for it. Not every religion includes the belief in God—Buddhism, for example, is sometimes said to be an atheistic religion. Atheism contrasts with theism, the view that God does exist, and with agnosticism, the view that there isn't any good reason to believe either that God exists or that He doesn't.

atomism The view that things are composed of elementary basic parts. From ancient times onward physics was often atomistic (though what's now called an 'atom' is no longer regarded as a basic component—contemporary physicists think that much smaller parts might be basic).

automata These are (arguably) mindless devices that imitate the intelligent and goal-directed actions of people—robots, for example. Descartes thought that animals were automata—merely physical "mechanisms" without mind.

autonomy / heteronomy Autonomy is self-governance—the ability or right to determine one's own actions and beliefs. Some ethical theories see the respect for autonomy as a central ethical principle. Heteronomy is its opposite: dependence on others.

average / total utilitarianism Utilitarianism needs to specify how to understand the greatest good for the greatest number of people. Is the measure of the worth of a society the average utility of its members, or the total utility?

axiom / postulate / posit An axiom is a statement regarded as obviously true, used as a starting point for deriving other statements. An axiomatic theory is one that is based on axioms. Non-axiomatic theories don't have such basic statements. 'Postulate' (as a noun) is often used to mean the same thing, though sometimes it refers only to such statements within a particular theory, while axioms are basic and obvious statements common to many theories (for example, the basic laws of logic). The verb 'to postulate' means the act of postulation—assumption, often of the existence of something, for theoretical purposes. A posit is an assumption, especially some thing assumed to exist; to posit something is to assume it.

basic statement The truth or falsity of some statements is determined by appeal to some others (by means of logic or scientific method, for example), but some philosophers think that there must be a starting point: basic statements. Whether there are basic statements, what they are, and why they are acceptable, are all controversial questions.

behaviorism Early in the twentieth century, many psychologists decided that introspection was not a good basis for the science of the mind; instead they advocated reliance on subjects' external, observable behavior. Methodological (psychological) behaviorism is the view that only external behavior should be investigated by science. Metaphysical or analytical behaviorism is the philosophical view that public behavior is all there is—that this is what we're talking about when we refer to mental events or characteristics in others, and even in ourselves. This is a form of materialism.

best of all possible worlds A phrase associated with Leibniz, who believed that God, being perfectly good, knowing, and powerful, could not have created anything less than perfect; thus this world (despite how it sometimes appears) is the best of all possible worlds.

bioethics The ethics involved in various sorts of biology-related activities, mostly centering on medical matters, where subjects for debate include, for example, abortion, genetic control, euthanasia, and in vitro fertilization.

biting the bullet What philosophers are said to do when they choose to accept the unlikely counterintuitive consequences of their position, rather than taking them as counterexamples. The phrase supposedly arose because biting down on something would help with the pain of surgery without anaesthetic.

bodily interchange This is what would happen if the same person existed at one time in one body and at another time in another body, for example, through reincarnation, or through a variety of science-fiction techniques such as brain or memory transplant. The topic is important in religious contexts and in thought experiments about personal identity.

bourgeoisie / proletariat Names of the two social /economic classes important in Marx's analysis. The former is the capitalist class—employers, financiers, landlords, etc., though more generally now the bourgeoisie is taken to include middle class wage earners as well. The latter is the working class.

bundle theory In general, the view of classical empiricists who argued that things are nothing more than bundles of properties, and that there is no need to think of substrata (underlying substance). The phrase most often refers to Hume's bundle theory of personal identity: we don't perceive a continuing self, so our self-idea must refer to an introspectible continuously changing "bundle" of different mental events.

burden of proof When there is a disagreement, it's sometimes the case that one side has the burden of proof, that is, it is expected to prove its case, and if it can't, the other wins by default. It may be the side with the position that is surprising, or unorthodox, or that runs counter to other well-accepted beliefs.

calculus An abstract system of symbols, aimed at calculating something. One can call each symbol-system of symbolic logic a 'calculus': for example, the sentential and quantifier calculi. The system for calculating probabilities is called the 'probability calculus'. Some philosophers think of the various sciences as interpreted calculi; a calculus is interpreted (given a "valuation") when its symbols are given meaning by relating them to things in the real world; uninterpreted, it is just a bunch of symbols with syntax but no semantics. 'The calculus' names a branch of mathematics independently developed by Leibniz and Newton during the late seventeenth century.

casuistry The determination of right and wrong by reasoning involving general principles applied to particular cases. Because religious casuists sometimes reasoned in overly complex ways to silly conclusions, this word has come to have disparaging overtones.

categorical / hypothetical imperative Kant's distinction. An imperative is a command. 'Categorical' means absolute—not dependent on particular aims or circumstances; 'hypothetical' means relative to, depending on, particular aims or circumstances. Thus, 'Tell the truth' is a categorical imperative, but 'If it is to everyone's benefit, tell the truth' and 'If you want others to trust you, tell the truth' are hypothetical imperatives. Kant argued that hypothetical imperatives could give useful practical advice, but do not express the standards of morality, which are expressed only by categorical imperatives. He argued further that there is one command central to all morality—the categorical imperative: Act in a way such that the general rule behind your action could consistently be willed to be a universal law. He argued that this was equivalent to saying that others should be treated as ends, never as means only.

category mistake A claim that's absurd because it makes an ascription completely inappropriate to the category of the object in question. To claim that the number 7 is faster than the number 8 is to assert this kind of absurdity. Gilbert Ryle introduced this term arguing that the standard Cartesian view of mind/body dualism committed this kind of mistake.

causal theories A variety of theories that make the notion of cause basic in some way. The causal theory of knowledge proposes, as a condition of 'P knows that x', that P's belief be causally connected in some appropriate way to the fact that x. The causal theory of perception points out that a "blue sensation" is one normally caused by a blue thing, and tries to avoid sense-data by explaining that what is happening when there is no blue thing there is that the sensation is one that would have been caused by a blue thing, were the situation normal. Functionalism is a causal theory of mind. The causal theory of meaning / reference makes the meaning / reference of terms a matter of the causal connections their uses have with the external world.

causation The relation that holds between a cause and its effect. Also called 'causality'. Long-standing philosophical problems are concerned with the nature of cause, and how we find out about it. Hume skeptically argued that we perceive no "power" in causal connections, and that when we say that x causes y, we're only saying that things of x-sort regularly precede things of y-sort. Critics object that this fails to distinguish between causal connections and mere accidental but universal regularities.

cause-of-itself (Latin: causa sui) Narrowly, a thing that causes itself to exist (or to be the way it is). God is commonly thought to be the only thing that is capable of this. But because causes are supposed to precede their effects, a cause-of-itself would (problematically) have to precede its own existence. Thinking of cause in an older way, as explanation, perhaps avoids this difficulty, but has its own problems: how can something provide the explanation for its own existence?

certainty A belief is called 'certain' in ordinary talk when it is believed very strongly, or when one is unable to think, or even imagine, that it might be false. Philosophers often don't want to rely on a subjective and psychological test for certainty, and demand proof that some belief really is beyond rational doubt. Some philosophers think that all our knowledge must have a certain foundation. 'Moral certainty' means sufficiently warranted to justify action; 'metaphysical certainty' means warranted not merely by fallible perception of particulars, but rather by some presumably more reliable reasoning about all being; 'logical certainty' is the extremely strong warrant we get for a proposition which is in some sense a truth of logic.

ceteris paribus (Latin: "other things being equal") This is used in comparing two things while assuming they differ only in the one characteristic under consideration. For example, it could be said that, ceteris paribus, a simple theory is better than a complicated one; though if everything else is not equal—if, for example, the simpler theory has fewer true predictions—then it might not be better.

circular reasoning / definition A definition is (viciously) circular (and thus useless) when the term to be defined, or a version of it, occurs in the definition; for example, the definition of 'free action' as 'action that is freely done'. (Viciously) circular reasoning defends some statement by assuming the truth of that statement; e.g.: "Why do you think what the Bible says is true?" "Because the Bible is the Word of God." "How do you know that it is the Word of God?" "Because it says so in the Bible, and everything there is true." Some philosophers argue that not all circles are vicious, and that some sorts of circular reasoning are acceptable—"virtuously circular"—for example, when the circle is wide enough. A dictionary, for example, must be circular, defining words in terms of other words; but this is okay. Circular reasoning is also known as 'begging the question'. Careless speakers sometimes think that this means 'raising the question'; it doesn't. Begging the question is sometimes called by its Latin name, 'petitio principii'.

cognitive / emotive meaning The former is what a sentence states—what makes it true or false. The latter is its "expressive" content—the speaker's feelings that it communicates, rather than any beliefs. Some theories of ethical statements hold that they have emotive, but no cognitive, meaning.

cognition The operations of the mind; sometimes particularly believing and awareness; sometimes, more particularly, the mental process by which we get knowledge.

cognitive science A recently-developed discipline combining philosophers, psychologists, and computer scientists, devoted to providing theories of cognition.

cognitivism / noncognitivism Cognitivism is the position that something can be known. Ethical cognitivism is the view that ethical statements are statements about (supposed) facts and thus are true or false, and might be known to be true or false. This is opposed to the noncognitivist position that ethical statements are not knowable. A species of ethical noncognitivism is emotivism, which argues that ethical statements are expressions of approval or disapproval (like 'Hooray for that!'), or invitations to action (like 'Please do that!') and are thus neither true nor false, and not knowable.

coherence / incoherence A set of beliefs or sentences is coherent when it fits together in a logical way—that is, when everything in the set is consistent, or when the items in it confirm others in it. A set in which one item would be false, or probably false, given the truth of others is not coherent (is incoherent).

collectively / distributively What applies to a group collectively applies to it as a whole only, i.e., not to its individual members (not distributively). The atoms that constitute a pig collectively, but not distributively, outweigh a fly.

collective responsibility The controversial idea that a group or nation or culture can bear responsibility as a whole for bad acts: for example, the whole German nation for Nazi atrocities.

commensurability / incommensurability Different things are commensurable when they can be measured on the same scale. Utilitarians sometimes assume that different people's different pleasures are commensurable on a common scale of utiles; but it has been argued that there's no way to make sensible quantity comparisons. Another example of supposed incommensurability is in the comparison of science and religion: some philosophers think that it's foolish to criticize religious statements using the criteria of scientific adequacy.

common sense 1. Until the eighteenth century or so, this term named the supposed mental faculty which combined input from different senses to give us a unified idea of an external object, combining, for example, the smell, taste, look and feel of a peach. 2. More recently, it has come to mean the mental faculty which all people are supposed to possess "in common," for knowledge of basic everyday truths. This is sometimes taken to answer skeptical doubts about the obvious truths that there exists an external world, other minds, etc. The eighteenth-century Scottish "common sense philosophers" relied heavily on this notion as a vindication of ordinary views and a refutation of skepticism.

communitarianism Advocates the position in social philosophy that the rights of individuals are not basic—that groups, or society as a whole, can have rights that are not constituted by or based on the individual rights of the members of those groups, and that these group rights may override claims to individual rights. Fascism is a rather extreme example of communitarianism. Communitarianism is a form of holism in social theory; the contrast is with individualism.

compatibilism Any philosophical position that claims that two things are compatible (they can both exist at once), most referring to the view that free will and determinism are compatible—that is, that people's actions are (sometimes) free even though they are fully causally determined. Compatibilists argue that we're not free when we're acting under compulsion (that is, forced to act), but that this is a different thing from the action's being determined or caused.

compulsion An action is said to be done under compulsion (also known as 'constraint' or 'coercion') when it is "forced" by internal or external circumstances, and thus the doer of that action can't be held morally responsible for doing it. If you steal something, for example, because someone is forcing you to do it at gunpoint, or because you are a kleptomaniac, that doesn't make your action any better, but it does mean that you're not to blame. Compatibilists about free will argue that compulsion makes one unfree and not responsible, but that ordinary actions are causally determined but not compelled in this sense.

concept May refer to the ability to categorize things; thus to say that someone has the concept of duck is to say that that person can sort things correctly into ducks and non-ducks. A concept is sometimes distinguished from a percept, which is a particular mental item had while sensing a particular thing. A concept, then, may be thought to be a generalization or abstraction from one or many percepts. Thus a percept is sometimes considered a particular idea, and a concept a general or abstract idea.

conceptual scheme The most general framework of someone's view of the world—a structured system of concepts that divide that person's world into kinds of things. It has sometimes been supposed that two people's conceptual schemes might differ so much that one would never be able to understand or translate what the other said.

conceptual truth A statement that is true merely because of the nature of the concepts that make it up. The fact that all bachelors are unmarried is a conceptual truth, because the concept of being a bachelor involves being unmarried. Compare: snow is white is not a conceptual truth, because being white, despite being true of snow, is not part of the concept of snow. We can imagine, consistent with our concept of snow, that snow is always green. (Substitute 'word' for 'concept' in this definition, and it turns into the definition of 'analytic truth'.)

confirmation / disconfirmation / verification / falsification Confirmation is the collection of evidence for a statement. Because there might be some evidence for a false statement, a statement might be confirmed though false. Collecting evidence that a statement is false is called 'disconfirmation'. 'Verification' means 'confirmation' and 'falsification' means 'disconfirmation', though one tends to speak of a statement as having been verified (or falsified) only if the statement is really true (or false), and has been shown to be so by the evidence. Confirmation theory is the attempt to give a general account of what counts as confirmation.

conscience This is the sense of right and wrong that is sometimes supposed to be a way of knowing moral facts, perhaps through a reliable internal "voice" or moral sense-perception, or a faculty of moral intuition.

consciousness 1. The state that we are in when awake: mental events are going on. 2. Awareness of something. (You aren't usually conscious of the position of your tongue.) 3. = mind (though it might be that the mind exists even while we are asleep or not aware of anything). The fact that we are conscious is supposed by some to distinguish people from machines and other non-living things, and perhaps from (at least the lower) animals.

consequentialism The position that people's actions are right or wrong because of their consequences (their results). This sort of ethical theory also called 'teleological', is contrasted with deontological theories—those that hold that results of actions are morally irrelevant. Thus, for example, a deontologist might think that lying is always wrong just in itself, whereas a consequentialist might think that lying is morally permissible in those circumstances in which the lie results in good consequences overall.

consistency A set of statements is consistent if it is logically possible that all the statements in that set are true. It is inconsistent if this is not possible—if one statement contradicts another, or if a contradiction results from reasoning from the set. The set consisting of this one statement 'It's raining and it's not raining' is inconsistent, because this statement is self-contradictory.

contingency To say that a statement is contingent is to say that it is neither necessary nor impossible. Metaphysical contingency is contrasted with what must be true or false; logical contingency is contrasted with logical truth / falsity.

contra-causal freedom It's sometime argued that a free action—one we're responsible for—could only be one that is not caused by previous events. Libertarians believe that some of our actions are free because contra-causal.

contradiction / contrary Two statements are contradictories when the truth of one logically requires the falsity of the other, and the falsity of one requires the truth of the other—in other words, when it is impossible that both are true, and it is impossible that both are false. 'It's raining' and 'It's not raining' are contradictory: exactly one of them must be true. Two statements are contraries when it is impossible that they are both true, though they might both be false. 'No pigs fly' and 'All pigs fly' are contraries, not contradictories. It is logically impossible that both of them are true, though they both might be false (were it the case that some, but not all, pigs fly). One can also call a self-contradiction a 'contradiction'.

cosmological argument for God's existence Given that every natural event has a cause, an apparently unacceptable infinite chain of past events would follow—unless there were an initial uncaused (supernatural) cause, identified with God. A very commonly encountered argument, with versions dating back at least to Plato. It's also commonly known as the first-cause argument.

counterexample An example intended to show that some general claim is false. Reasoning by counterexample is frequently a useful philosophical tactic for arguing against some position. (Also called 'counterinstance'.)

counterfactual A counterfactual (also called a 'counterfactual conditional' or a 'contrary-to-fact conditional') is a conditional statement whose antecedent is false. The subjunctive is used in English counterfactuals: 'If Fred were here, you wouldn't be doing that'. (This is properly said only when Fred isn't here.) One important and controversial area in modern logic is concerned with the truth-conditions for counterfactuals. A powerful and widely accepted way of understanding counterfactuals uses the notion of possible worlds: a counterfactual is true when the consequent is true in the nearest possible world (i.e., a world as much as possible like ours) in which the antecedent is true.

covering law A general law applying to a particular instance. The covering law theory (or "model") of explanation (also called the 'Deductive-Nomological' or 'D-N' theory) says that a particular event is explained by providing one or more covering laws that, together with particular facts, imply the event. For example, we can explain why a piece of metal rusted by appealing to the covering law that iron rusts when exposed to air and moisture, and the facts that the metal is iron, and was exposed to air and moisture.

criterion A test or standard for the presence of a property, or for the applicability of a word, or for the truth or falsity of a proposition. This word is singular; its plural is 'criteria'.

crucial experiment This is an experiment whose outcome would provide a central or conclusive test for the truth or falsity of some position or scientific hypothesis. Sometimes called, in Latin, 'experimentum crucis'.

decision theory The largely mathematical theory of decision-making. Generally includes some way of evaluating desirability of outcomes and their probabilities when not certain.

deconstructionism A skeptical and frequently anti-intellectual postmodern movement which seeks to interpret texts and the positions held in them by "deconstructing" them—showing their incoherence, the hidden and often contradictory presuppositions, prejudices, motives, and political aims behind them.

de dicto / de re (Latin: "about what's said" / "about a thing") A de re belief is a belief considered with respect to the actual thing that it's about. Thus, if someone mistakenly thinks that the moving thing in the sky he's looking at is a satellite, whereas it's actually a meteor, then he has the de re belief that a meteor is moving in the sky—more clearly: about that meteor, he believes it's moving in the sky above him. But he has the de dicto belief that a satellite is moving in the sky above him. Philosophers speak also of a distinction between de dicto and de re necessity. It is de re necessary of the number of planets that it is larger than five (because nine is necessarily larger than five); but it is de dicto contingent, because there might have been only three planets.

deduction / induction 1. In an outdated way of speaking, deduction is reasoning from the general to the particular, and induction is reasoning from the particular to the general. 2. Nowadays, this distinction between kinds of reasoning is made as follows: correct ("valid") deductive reasoning is reasoning of the sort that if the premises are true, the conclusion must be true; whereas correct inductive reasoning supports the conclusion by showing only that it's more probably true. Examples:

Deduction: No pigs fly; Porky is a pig; therefore, Porky doesn't fly.
Induction: Porky, Petunia, and all the other pigs observed in a wide variety of circumstances don't fly; therefore no pigs fly.

These examples in fact fit definition 1; but here are examples of deduction according to definition 2 that do not fit definition 1:

No pigs fly; therefore all pigs are non-flying things.
Porky doesn't fly; Porky is a pig; therefore not all pigs fly.

A common form of induction works by enumeration: as support for the conclusion that all A's are B's, one lists many examples of A's that are B's.

defeasible Means 'defeatible', in the sense of 'capable of being overruled'. A driver's license confers a defeasible right to drive, for example, because under certain circumstances (e.g., when he is drunk) the holder of a valid license would nevertheless not be allowed to drive. A defeasible proposition is one that can be overturned by future evidence.

definiens / definiendum A definiendum (Latin: "to be defined") is a word or phrase to be defined, and the definition is the definiens (Latin: "defining thing").

degrees of perfection argument for God's existence One of many different forms of this argument: Comparative terms describe degrees of approximation to superlative terms. Nothing would count as falling short of the superlative unless the superlative thing existed. Ordinary things are less than perfect, so there must be something completely perfect; and what is completely perfect is God. Objection: Comparative terms do not imply the existence of a superlative instance. For example, the existence of people who are more or less stupid does not imply that someone exists who is maximally, completely, perfectly stupid.

deism A form of religious belief especially popular during the Enlightenment. Deists practice "natural religion"—that is, they rely on reason, distrusting faith, revelation, and the institutional churches. They believe that God produced the universe with its laws of nature, but then left it alone to operate solely by these laws. Deism seems incompatible with some aspects of conventional religion, for example, with the notion of a loving God, or with the practice of prayer.

denotation / connotation The denotation or reference of a word is what that word refers to—the thing in the world that it "names." The connotation or sense of a word is, by contrast, its meaning. Synonymous with 'extension / intension'. A word can have connotation but no denotation: 'unicorn' has meaning but no reference. Note that the philosophical use of 'connotation' is different from the ordinary one, in which it refers not to what a word means, but to more or less distant associations it has; for example, the word 'roses' may carry the connotation of romance to many people. A connotative definition is one that gives the characteristics shared by all and only the objects to which the term refers; often a definition by genus / species. A denotative definition defines by identifying the denotation—for example, by pointing out or listing several things to which the word applies.

deontic Means 'having to do with obligation'. Deontic logic is that branch of modal logic dealing with connections of sentences saying what one ought to do, must do, is permitted to do, etc.

derivation A method for proving deductive validity, in which one moves from premises to succeeding steps using accepted rules of inference, eventuating at the conclusion. There are other methods of proof; for example, in sentential logic, the truth table.

determinism The view that every event is necessitated by previous causes, so that given its causes, each event must have existed in the form it does. There is some debate about how (and whether) this view can be justified. The view that at least some events are not fully caused is called 'indeterminism'. Determinism is often taken to be a presupposition of science; Kant thought it was necessary; but quantum physics says that it is false. One of the main areas of concern about determinism arises when it is considered in connection with free will.

deterrence A motive for punishment: that threatening punishment can prevent future occurrences of undesirable acts. (Other competing theories of punishment attempt to justify it as retribution or rehabilitation.) So one may try to justify jailing criminals by claiming that the threat of similar jailing will discourage them and others from future crime. One may even successfully deter crime by framing the innocent. Deterrence as a national defence policy attempts to prevent other nations' aggression by threatening them with massive (perhaps nuclear) retaliation. The moral status of deterrence is controversial. Preventing war is of course a good thing, but is threatening deterrence justified when it involves the willingness to go through with really horrible retaliation?

dialectic Sometimes this word refers to a style of philosophical discourse most famously due to Plato, involving dialogue: claims, counterclaims, and logical argument. (A contrasting style is rhetoric.) In Kant, dialectical reasoning fallaciously attributes external existence to objects internal to our minds. In Hegel, Marx, and other Continental philosophers, the Dialectic is the interplay of contradictory forces supposed to be a central principle of metaphysical and social existence and change.

divine command theory The ethical theory which explains morality as what is commanded by God. It is often argued that this has things backwards: God commands it because it is right, not vice versa.

double effect The doctrine of double effect holds that, although it is always wrong to use a bad means to a good end, one may act to bring about a good result when also knowingly bringing about bad results, under the following conditions: 1) The bad result is not caused by the good result—both are caused by the action (thus 'double effect'); (2) there's no way of getting the good result without the bad; 3) the good result is so good that it's worth accepting the bad one.

For example, a dentist is allowed to drill, and thus cause some pain (the bad result) for the sake of dental improvements (the good result), since these conditions hold—most notably (1): the pain doesn't cause the improvement; both are results of the drilling.

This principle is associated with Catholic morality, and has been applied most frequently in contexts of medical ethics. It is disputed by some philosophers, who sometimes argue that the distinction between double effect and bad means / good end is artificial and not morally relevant.

doxastic Means 'pertaining to belief', as in 'doxastic state', 'doxastic principle' (for justifying beliefs).

dualism Dualists hold that there are two sorts of things that exist, neither of which can be understood in terms of the other—often, in particular, mental and physical. Other sorts of dualism distinguish the visible and invisible, the actual and the possible, God and the universe, etc. The contrast here is with monism.

egalitarianism The view that people are equal—that they are entitled to equal rights and treatment in society, or to equal possessions or satisfactions.

egoism, ethical / psychological Psychological egoism is the position that people in fact act only in their own interests. It's sometimes argued that even the most generous act is done for the doer's own satisfaction; but this might simply be a way of saying that even the most generous act is motivated—something nobody would deny. Ethical egoism is the position that I (or people in general) ought to act only in my (their) own interests.

emotivism A position in meta-ethics that holds that ethical utterances are to be understood not as statements of fact that are either true or false, but rather as expressions of approval or disapproval, and invitations to the listener to have the same reactions and to act accordingly. Thus emotivists emphasize the "emotive meaning" of ethical utterances, denying that they have cognitive meaning. Emotivists can nevertheless agree that evaluative utterances have some "descriptive content": when I say this is a good apple, I express my approval, but also describe it as having certain characteristics on which my approval rests: that it is, for example, not worm-infested.

empirical This means having to do with sense-experience and experiment. Empirical knowledge is knowledge we get through experience of the world; thus it is a posteriori. An empirical concept is one that is not innate; it can be developed only through experience.

empiricism The position (usually contrasted with rationalism) that all our concepts and substantive knowledge come from sense experience. Empiricists deny that there are innate concepts. While they grant that certain kinds of trivial knowledge (of conceptual, analytic, and logical truths) can be gained by reason alone, independently of experience, they deny the existence of the synthetic a priori.

end in itself 1. Something sought for its own sake; an intrinsic good. 2. Someone is seen as an end in him / herself when that person's aims are seen as having value just because they are that person's aims. Treating people as ends in themselves is respecting their aims, and refraining from thinking of, or using, that person merely as a means to your aims.

ends / means A long-standing controversy in ethics is whether one might be permitted to use bad means to a good end: does the end justify the means? For example, is it permitted to lie to someone if everyone will be better off in the long run as a result? Extreme opponents of consequentialism sometimes hold that no action that is bad in itself is ever permitted no matter how good the consequences. Notice that this means that telling a little lie would not be justified even if it would prevent the destruction of the earth. A more moderate view merely warns against actions which are so bad in themselves that the good consequences do not overwhelm this badness.

Enlightenment The Enlightenment was a cultural and philosophical movement of the seventeenth and eighteenth centuries whose chief features were a belief in rationality and scientific method, and a tendency to reject conventional religion and other traditions. The Age of Enlightenment is also known as the 'Age of Reason'.

enthymeme An argument with some steps left unstated but understood. All pigs are sloppy eaters, so Porky is a sloppy eater is an enthymeme, leaving unsaid Porky is a pig.

epiphenomenalism A variety of dualism in which mental events are just "by-products" of physical ones: physical events cause mental ones, but not vice versa. Analogy: the noise your car makes is caused by the mechanical goings-on inside, but it has no effect on them.

epistemic Having to do with knowledge. Epistemic logic is that branch of modal logic dealing with relations between sentences involving 'knows', 'believes', etc.

epistemology Theory of knowledge: one of the main branches of philosophy. Among the central questions studied here are: What is the difference between knowledge and mere belief? Is all (or any) knowledge based on sense-perception? How, in general, are our knowledge-claims justified?

essence / accident The essential characteristics of something are the ones that it must have in order to be what it is, or the kind of thing it is. It is essential, for example, for a tree to be a plant—if something was not a plant, it could not be a tree. By contrast, a tree that in fact is thirty-three meters high could still be a tree if it weren't that height; thus this characteristic is accidental. (Note that 'accident' and 'accidental' don't have their ordinary meanings in this philosophical use.) Some philosophers think that the essence / accident distinction does not concern the real characteristics of something, but is only a consequence of the words we apply to them: being a plant is said to be an essential characteristic of a tree only because it's part of the definition of 'tree'. But essentialist philosophers believe in real, objective essences.

ethics The general philosophical study of what makes things good or bad, right or wrong. Often the following areas of study are distinguished within ethics: (1) Descriptive ethics: the discovery of what ethical views particular societies in fact have; and speculative anthropological theorizing about the origin and function of these views; (2) Normative ethics: theorizing about what the basic principles are that might serve systematically to distinguish right from wrong. (3) Applied ethics: the normative ethics of particular areas or disciplines: medical ethics, business ethics, computer ethics ... . (4) Meta-ethics: the study of the meaning of moral language and the possibility of ethical knowledge.

'Morality' and 'ethics' (and 'moral' and 'ethical') are usually used as synonyms, though 'ethics' is more frequently generally used as the name of the philosophical study of these matters. Philosophers usually avoid the tendency in ordinary talk to restrict the word 'ethics' to an official code of acceptable behavior in some area (as in 'professional ethics').

ethnocentric Someone is ethnocentric who regards the views or characteristics of his / her own race or culture as the only correct or important ones. Other "-centric" words have arisen by analogy: eurocentric, logocentric, phallocentric for example.

euthanasia Mercy killing, the intentional bringing-about or hastening the death of someone, presumably for his own good, when his life is judged not to be worth continuing, typically when that person is suffering from an untreatable, fatal illness causing horrible unavoidable pain or suffering. Voluntary euthanasia is done at the expressed wish of that person; this wish is not expressed in the case of involuntary euthanasia (for example, when the person has mentally deteriorated beyond the point of being able to express, or perhaps even to have, coherent wishes). Passive euthanasia involves refraining from providing life-prolonging treatment to someone suffering from a fatal condition; active euthanasia is killing, for example, by administering a fatal injection. Ethical opinion is deeply divided concerning euthanasia. Some who argue in favor of its permissibility would accept it only when voluntary, and/or only when passive.

expected utility / value The expected utility (or expected value) of an action is calculated by multiplying the utility (or value) of each possible result of that action by its probability, and adding up the results. For example, consider this betting game: you get $10 if a random draw from a deck of cards is a spade; and you pay $4 if it's any other suit. Assuming the utility of each dollar is 1, to calculate the expected utility of this game we add: [.25 (probability of a spade) x 10 (the utility if it's a spade)] + [.75

(the probability of a non-spade) x -4 (the utility of a non-spade)]. Since (.25 x 10) + (.75 x -4) = 2.5 - 3 = -.5, the game thus has an expected utility of -.5, so you'll average 50 cents loss per play in the long run. One (controversial) theory for rational decision-making advocates maximizing expected utility, so you should not play this game. (But if you enjoy gambling, this has to be figured in too, and might make it worthwhile.)

explanans / explanandum An explanandum (Latin: "to be explained") is something that is being explained: what does the explaining is the explanans (Latin: "explaining thing").

explanation An explanation answers the question 'Why?' and provides understanding; sometimes it also provides us with the abilities to control, and to predict (and retrodict) the world. This is fairly vague, and philosophers have tried to provide theories of explanation—to give a general account of how explanations work, and what makes some good and some bad. One important account is the covering law model. One (but only one) sort of explanation is causal: we explain something by saying what its causes are. Sometimes, instead, we explain by telling what something is made of, or by giving reasons for human actions, as in some explanations in history.

externalism / internalism A variety of related doctrines. Meta-ethical externalism holds that the fact that something is good does not by itself automatically supply the motivation for someone to do it; in addition, motivation ("external" to the mere belief about goodness) must be supplied; internalism is the view that the judgment that something is good itself guarantees or includes the motivation to do it. As a theory of mind, externalism is the view that to specify the "content" of a belief one must refer to the external facts or objects that the belief is about.

fallacy An argument of a type that may seem correct but in fact is not. (Thus, not just any mistaken argument should be called 'fallacious'.) Formal fallacies are mistakes in reasoning that

spring from mistakes in logical form; their persuasiveness springs from their similarity, on first glance, to valid forms. Informal fallacies spring instead from ambiguities in meaning or grammar, or from psychological tendencies to be convinced by reasons that are not good reasons.

fatalism The position that our futures are inevitable, whatever we do—that events are "fated" to happen. It's important to distinguish this from determinism, which claims merely that our futures are determined. A determinist who is not a fatalist thinks that our futures are not inevitable—they depend on what we do.

feminism The name of various philosophical—especially ethical, social, and political—theories and social movements that see elements of our society as unjust to and exploitative of women. Feminists often advocate equality under the law and equal economic status for women; but many go further, arguing in favor of preferential treatment for women to counteract past injustices. Sometimes they find male bias and male patterns of thought in many areas of our personal, social, and intellectual lives. Recent developments are feminist theories of the self, of knowledge, and of science.

formal In philosophy this means pertaining to structure (as opposed to content); or rigorous and rule-governed.

foundationalism The position that there is a particular sort of statement (sometimes thought to be indubitable) from which all other statements comprising a system of belief should be derived. There are foundationalist theories of knowledge, of ethics, etc.

free will To say that we have free will (or freedom) is to say that our decisions and actions are sometimes entirely (or at least partially) "up to us"—not forced or determined by anything internal or external to us. We can then either do or not do—we have alternatives. It seems that this is necessary for responsibility for our actions. But if determinism is true, then our actions and "decisions" are determined by previous causes, themselves determined by still earlier causes, and ultimately whatever we decide or do is determined by events that happened a long time ago, and that are not up to us. Thus, it seems that determinism is incompatible with free will. There are three main responses to this apparent problem: (1) Hard determinists accept determinism, which they take to rule out free will. (2) Libertarians accept free will. They think that this means determinism is false, at least for some human events. Both libertarianism and hard determinism are incompatibilist; that is, they hold that the freedom of an act is incompatible with its being determined. (3) Soft determinists are compatibilists, in that they attack the reasoning above, and argue that our actions might be determined, but also free in some sense—that a determined action might nevertheless be up to the doer, and one that the doer is morally responsible for—when it's determined but not compelled.

functional A functional definition defines by giving the typical use of the kind of thing, or its typical cause-and-effect relations with other things; a functional explanation explains something by its function, for example, telling what use the pancreas is in the body, or a social ritual in a particular society. A functional kind is defined by causes and effects (and not, for example, by shape or physical make-up). Functionalism centrally argues that a kind of thing is a functional kind. In philosophy of mind, functionalists argue that mental kinds are functional kinds.

generalization A statement about a group of things, or about everything in a particular category (contrasted with a 'particular statement / proposition'); or the process of reasoning that arrives at one of these. Inductive logic studies the principles of deriving them from particular instances; the rule in deductive logic for deriving one is called universal generalization. An ethical generalization is a rule everyone should follow; Kant argued that the right action was the one whose maxim could be generalized.

general will What is desired by, or desirable for, society as a whole; sometimes taken to be the appropriate justification for government policy. This notion can be problematic when it is taken to mean something other than what's revealed by majority vote or unanimity.

hedonism The advocacy of pleasure as the basic good; philosophical hedonists often distinguish between the "higher" (sometimes = mental or spiritual) and the "lower" pleasures (the merely sensual), making the former more important. Psychological hedonism claims that people in fact seek only pleasure; ethical hedonism claims that people ought to seek pleasure (or only pleasure).

holism / individualism In philosophical use, holism involves the claim that certain sorts of things are more than merely the sum of their parts—that they can be understood only by examining them as a whole; contrasted with individualism. In social science and history, for example, holists argue that one can't explain events on the basis of individual people's actions, because these get their significance only in a society. Semantic holism insists that words and sentences get their meaning only through their relationships with all other words and sentences. Holism about living things refuses to see them merely as the sum of their non-living parts. Methodological individualism is the method in sociology of investigating social facts by discovering facts about individual people. Individualism in ethics emphasizes individual rights and freedoms, contrasting with communitarianism.

hypothesis A tentative suggestion that may be merely a guess or a hunch, or may be based on some sort of reasoning; in any case it needs further evidence to be rationally acceptable as true. Some philosophers think that all scientific enquiry begins with hypotheses.

idea / impression An "idea" is, in general, any thought or perception in the mind. Platonic forms are sometimes called 'ideas'. In Hume, ideas are the faint imprint left on the mind by impressions, which are the mental events one has as the immediate result of, and while, using one's senses (= sense-data); ideas may be called up later in the absence of sensation. Empiricists believe that all ideas are copies of impressions.

idealism In the philosophical sense of this word, it's the view that only minds and their contents really or basically exist. Its competitors are materialism and dualism.

ideal observer theory A theory of ethics that attempts to explain what is really good as what would be chosen by an ideal observer—that is, someone who would have all the relevant information, and who would not be misled by particular interests or biases.

identity 1. Your identity is what you are—what's important about you, or what makes you different from everyone else. 2. Two different things might be said to be 'identical' when they are exactly alike in some characteristics; this is sometimes called qualitative identity. 3. Object a and object b are said to be (strictly or numerically or quantitatively) identical when a and b are in fact the same thing—when 'a' and 'b' are two different names or ways of referring to exactly the same object. 4. Identity (over time) is the relation between something at one time and that same thing at another time: they are said to be two temporal stages (or time-slices) of the same continuing thing.

identity theory of mind The view that each mental state is really a physical state, probably of the brain. Often identity theorists believe in addition in the type-identity of mental and physical states.

illusion / hallucination / delusion Illusions and hallucinations are "false" perceptual experiences—ones that lead, or could lead, to mistakes about what is out there. A hallucination is the apparent perception of something that does not exist at all (as in dreaming, mirages, drug-induced states). An illusion is the incorrect perception of something that does exist. A delusion is a perception that actually results in a false belief; illusions and hallucinations can delude, but often do not. The argument from illusion draws epistemological conclusions from the existence of these things.

imagination Sometimes philosophers have used this word to refer to the faculty of having images—mental pictures.

immaterialism 1. The view that some things exist that are not material: that are not made of ordinary physical stuff, but of mental or spiritual—immaterial stuff instead. This is the denial of materialism. The most extreme form of immaterialism is the view that no material things exist: this is idealism. 2. The view that objects are merely collections of qualities, without a substratum to hold them together. If one thinks of qualities as essentially mental perceptions, then this is a species of immaterialism in sense 1.

immediate / mediate In its more technical philosophical sense 'immediate' means 'without mediation'—that is, 'directly'. In this sense, for example, philosophers ask whether external things are sensed immediately, or mediated by the sensing of internal images. An immediate inference is one performed in one step, needing only a single use of only one rule, for example, when Q is inferred from (P and Q).

immorality / amorality The first means 'contrary to morality'; the second, 'without morality'. Someone who knows about moral rules but intentionally disobeys them or rejects them is immoral; someone who doesn't know or think about morality is amoral. Amorality is typical of small children; immorality of adults.

incorrigibility / corrigibility 'Corrigibility' means 'correctibility'. Something is incorrigible when it is impossible to correct it, or when it is guaranteed correct. Some philosophers have thought that our beliefs about our own mental states are incorrigible. For example, if you sincerely believe that you are now feeling a pain, how could you be wrong?

indubitability / dubitability 'Dubitable' means 'doubtable'. Dubitable statements are not just ones we are psychologically capable of doubting, but ones about which even highly fanciful and unlikely doubts might be raised, doubts that no one in his/her right mind would seriously have. Thus Descartes thought that because our senses might be fooled, information from them was dubitable. He then went on to try to discover what sort of belief was really indubitable: about which it could be proven that no doubt can be raised.

inference / implication / entailment 1. Implication (also known as entailment) is a logical relation that holds between two statements when the second follows deductively from the first. The first is then said to 'imply' (or 'entail') the second. Be careful not to confuse these with 'inference', which is something that people do, when they reason from one statement to another. A rule of inference is an acceptable procedure for reasoning from one set of statements of a particular form to another statement. 2. Sometimes a sentence 'implies' what it doesn't literally state. For example, if I said "Fred is now not robbing banks," I imply that at one time he was robbing banks. This is sometimes called conversational or contextual implicature, or pragmatic implication, to distinguish it from logical implicature.

infinite regress A sequence (of definition, explanation, justification, cause, etc.) that must continue backwards endlessly. For example, if every event must have a cause, then a present event must be caused by some past event; and this event by another still earlier, and so on infinitely. Sometimes the fact that reasoning leads to an infinite regress shows that it is faulty. One then calls it a vicious regress.

informal / formal logic The latter is that kind of logic that relies heavily on symbols and rigorous procedures much like those in mathematics; it concentrates on reasoning that is correct because of syntax. Only a small fraction of the ordinary sorts of reasoning we do can be explained this way, and there is a vast scope for informal logic, which analyzes good and bad arguments semantically, and relies less heavily on symbols and mathematics-style procedures.

informed consent Agreement based on sufficient knowledge of relevant information; relevant especially to medical ethics. It's widely agreed that informed consent by the patient is necessary for all medical procedures, but problems arise here: how much information is enough? What should be done when the patient is unable to understand the information or to make a rational choice?

innateness A belief, concept, or characteristic is innate when it is inborn—when it doesn't come from experience or education—though experience may be thought necessary to make conscious or actualize something that is given innately. An argument for the innateness of something is that experience is not sufficient to produce it in us.

in principle Contrasted with 'in fact' or 'in practice'. Philosophers talk about things we can do in principle, meaning that we could do them if we had the time or technology, or if other merely practical difficulties did not stand in the way. For example, we can verify the statement 'There is a red pebble lying on the north pole of Mars' in principle, though at the moment we can't test this by observation. In principle, we can count to one trillion, because we know the rules for doing it, though in fact we lack the patience and wouldn't live long enough anyway.

intentionality Sometimes this refers to what's true of things done on purpose—intentionally. But in contemporary usage in philosophy of mind, it usually refers to aboutness—the power of referring to or meaning real or imagined external objects. It's sometimes argued that this is a necessary, unique, and essential characteristic of mental states.

interactionism A form of mind / body dualism. It holds that mind and body can interact—that is, that mental events can cause physical events (e.g., when your decision to touch something causes your physical hand movement) and that physical events can cause mental events (e.g., when a physical stimulation to your body causes a mental feeling of pain). A standard objection to this commonsense position is that it's hard to see how this sort of causal interaction could take place, since the mental and the physical work according to their own laws: how could an electrical impulse in a (physical) nerve cell cause a non-physical pain in a mind?

intrinsic / inherent / instrumental / extrinsic Something has intrinsic value when it is valuable for its own sake and not merely as a means to something else. Pleasure, for example, is intrinsically valuable. Something by contrast has instrumental value when it is valuable as a means to some other end. The value of money is primarily instrumental. An intrinsic or inherent or natural right is one people have permanently or essentially, because of the very nature of a person. An extrinsic right is one people have only temporarily, or one they don't have unless they are granted it.

introspection The capacity for finding things out about oneself by "looking inward"—by direct awareness of one's own mental states. You might find out that you have a headache, for example, by introspection. This is contrasted with the way someone else might find this out, by observing your outward behavior—your groaning, holding your head, etc. Sometimes called 'reflection'.

intuition A belief that comes immediately, without reasoning, argument, evidence; before analysis (thus 'preanalytic'). Some philosophers think that certain intuitions are the reliable, rational basis for knowledge of certain sorts. Some beliefs that arise immediately when we perceive are the basis of our knowledge of the outside world (though perceptual intuitions are not always reliable). Our ethical intuitions are sometimes taken to be the basis and the test of ethical theories. Intuitionism is any theory that holds that intuition is a valid source of knowledge.

is / ought problem Clearly what is is sometimes different from what ought to be; but can one infer the latter from the former? Some philosophers hold that you can't: no matter how detailed an account you have of how things are, they don't imply how things ought to be. But

ethical naturalists and other objectivists typically claim that they do, because ethical facts are facts too. The supposed is / ought gap is also known as the fact-value gap.

lawlike statements Statements which have the logical form of laws whether they are true or not. Part of the philosophy of science is the attempt to specify the logic of lawlike statements.

law of the indiscernibility of identicals The supposed law of metaphysics (associated with Leibniz, thus also called 'Leibniz's law') that says that if x and y are identical—that is, if x is y—then x and y are indiscernible (share all the same properties). Distinguish this from its reverse, the law of the identity of indiscernibles: if x and y are indiscernible, then they are identical. Imagine two things that are alike in every detail: they even occupy the same space at the same time. Why then think of them as two? Wouldn't there really be only one thing?

libertarianism 1. The position that some of our actions are free in the sense of not being caused. 2. The political position that people have a strong right to political liberty. Thus libertarians tend to object to restrictive laws, taxes, the welfare state, and state economic control. A more specific variety of (traditional) liberalism, though nowadays this position tends to be espoused by some of those who are called 'conservatives'.

logic Loosely speaking, logic is the process of correct reasoning, and something is logical when it makes sense. Philosophers often reserve this word for reasoning norms covered by various particular theories of inference, justification, and proof. Traditional logic was fairly narrowly restricted, concentrating on the syllogism. Nowadays, symbolic deductive and inductive logics cover a much wider area, but far from the totality of reasoning.

logical form The form of a sentence is its general structure, ignoring the particular content it has. For example, If it's Tuesday, then I'm late for class and If Peru is in Asia, then Porky is a frog have the same overall logical form (if P then Q). The sort of logic that works by exhibiting, often in symbolic notation, the logical form of sentences is called 'formal logic'.

logical positivism A school of philosophy (also known as "logical empiricism"), subscribed to by many twentieth-century English-speaking philosophers. Impressed by empiricism and by the success and rigor of science, the logical positivists advocated that philosophers avoid speculation about matters only science and experience could settle; if a sentence was not scientifically verifiable or a matter of logical truth or conceptual truth, it was nonsense and should be discarded (the verifiability criterion). Ethical statements were thought not verifiable, so without literal meaning: they were sometimes thought merely to be expressions of feelings of approval or disapproval.

logical truth / falsity A sentence is logically true (or false) when it is true (or false) merely because of its logical structure. Examples: All ducks are ducks. Either it's raining or it's not raining. These should be distinguished from analytic truths / falsehoods, which are true / false merely because of the meaning of their words: for example, All fathers are male. Logical truths / falsehoods are also called logically necessary / impossible sentences, but these should also be distinguished from (metaphysically) necessary truths / falsehoods (see necessary / contingent truth): those that must be true or false. 'Tautology' is sometimes used as a synonym for 'logical truth', though in ordinary talk a tautology is something that says the same thing twice. Thus, It's raining and it's raining is a tautology in the ordinary sense, though not in the philosophers' sense (since it might be false). Sentences that are neither logically true nor logically false— that are merely true or false—are said to be logically contingent (or logically indeterminate).

materialism As a philosophical term, this refers to the position that all that exists is physical. (Synonym: physicalism.) Materialists about mind sometimes argue that apparently non-physical things like the soul or mind or thoughts are actually material things. Central-state materialists identify mental events with physical events central in the body (i.e., in the nervous system). Eliminative materialists, however, think that categorizing things as mental is altogether a mistake (like believing in ghosts).

matter of fact / relation of ideas Hume's distinction. He seems to have meant that a matter of fact is a contingent state of affairs, to be discovered a posteriori; a relation of ideas is a conceptual or analytic or logical truth, which can be known a priori.

medieval philosophy The dividing lines between ancient, medieval, and modern philosophy are rough, but it's often said that medieval philosophy starts with Augustine (c. 400), and ends just before Descartes (c. 1600).

meta- This prefix often means 'beyond', or 'about', so thinking about meta-x is (sometimes) thinking about the structure or nature of x. Examples of its use are 'meta-language' and 'meta-ethics'; it is used differently, however, in 'metaphysics'.

metaphysics One of the main branches of philosophy, having to do with the ultimate components of reality, the types of things that exist, the nature of causation, change, time, God, free will.

mind-body problem What is the relation between mental and physical events? Is one sort of event reducible to the other? Are mental events merely a sort of bodily event? Or are they distinct? If so, how are they connected?

modal statements are (roughly speaking) the ones that are not straightforward assertions, and have complexities involved in the logic of their relations (studied in modal logic), their confirmation, etc. The basic kind of modal statements are those affirming necessity and possibility; but also considered in this category are belief, tense, moral, counterfactual, causal, and lawlike statements.

modern philosophy The borderline between medieval philosophy and modern philosophy is rough, but it is usually said that Descartes was the first modern philosopher (around 1600). The era of modern philosophy can be said to extend through the present, though it's often taken to end around the beginning of the nineteenth century, or later with the advent of postmodernism.

monism A monistic metaphysics is the belief that there is one basic kind of thing in existence. Monists about mind deny dualism (belief in two irreducible substances, mind and matter). Nowadays most monists are materialists, but historically, many were idealists (believing that this one kind of stuff was basically mental).

monotheism / polytheism / pantheism Monotheism is the belief in one (and only one) God. Polytheism is the belief in many gods. Pantheism is the belief that God somehow exists in everything, or that everything is God.

moral argument for God's existence One version of this argument: There is a real objective difference between right and wrong, but the only way to make sense of this is to think of it as arising from a divine moral order. So the existence of morality shows that God exists.

moral realism The view that there are real, objective, knowable moral facts.

moral sense theory The idea that we have a way of "sensing" the objective moral properties, on the analogy of the way we can sense the property of redness using our eyes. Moral sensation would clearly be a very different kind of sensation, however; what is the sense organ involved? Is it at all reliable?

mutatis mutandis (Latin: "having changed the things that were to be changed") Philosophers say things like "This case is, mutatis mutandis, like the other," meaning that the two cases are alike except for certain details—that one can derive one case from the other by making the appropriate substitutions or changes.

mutually exclusive / jointly exhaustive Mutually exclusive sets do not overlap each other in membership. For example, each of these sets: mammals, birds, fish, reptiles, amphibians, is exclusive of the others, since nothing belongs to more than one of them. The list is jointly exhaustive of vertebrates, since every vertebrate is included in these categories. It is mutually exclusive and jointly exhaustive because every vertebrate is included in exactly one of these categories.

mystical experience argument for God's existence The existence and nature of the mystical experiences some people have are sometimes taken to show God's existence. One criticism of this argument is that even though having this experience sometimes provides a compelling motivation for belief, it's not reliable evidence.

mysticism A variety of religious practice that relies on direct experience which is often taken to be a union with God or with the divine ground of all being. The content of these experiences is often taken to be ineffable, but we are told that they produce enlightenment or bliss. Mystics often advocate exercises or rituals designed to induce the abnormal psychological states in which these experiences occur.

naïve realism What's supposed to be the ordinary view about perception: that it (usually) reveals external objects to us directly, the way they really are. The implication is that this "naïve" view is overturned by philosophical sophistication. Also called common-sense realism or direct realism.

naturalism This term names the view that everything is a natural entity, and thus to be studied by the usual methods of natural science. Naturalistic or "naturalizing" theories in philosophy try to apply ordinary scientific categories and methods to philosophical problems. Philosophers have proposed naturalized epistemology, philosophy of mind, and ethics.

natural kind Some philosophers think that some of the ways we divide the world into kinds correspond to the way nature really is divided—they "cut nature at the joints." Classically, a natural kind is a kind that things belong to necessarily: thus, human being is a natural kind because Fred is necessarily human; but living within fifty miles of the Empire State Building is not: Fred might move further away; or, if he doesn't he might have. Some contemporary thinkers hold that natural kinds are the ones that support certain modal implications needed in science; but others argue that there are no natural kinds—all kinds are artificial human creations.

natural law There are several philosophically relevant senses of this phrase: 1. A law of nature—i.e., a formulation of a regularity found in the natural world, the sort of thing science discovers. 2. A principle of proper human action or conduct, taken to be God-given, or to be a consequence of "human nature"—our structure or function. In this sense, there are "natural law" theories in ethics and in political philosophy. 3. The view that the validity of the laws of a legal system depends on their coherence with God-given or otherwise objective morality.

necessary / contingent truth A necessary truth is one that could not possibly be false; a contingent truth could be false but isn't, just as a matter of fact. Some philosophers think that the necessity or contingency of some fact is a metaphysical matter—is a matter of the way the external world is—but others hold that this difference is merely a matter of the way we think or talk about the world—that a truth taken to be necessary is merely a conceptual or logical or analytic truth. A necessary truth is also called a necessity, a contingent truth a contingency, and a necessary falsehood an impossibility.

necessary / sufficient condition x is a sufficient condition for y when: if x is true, then y must also be true—that x can't exist without y. This is the same as saying: x can't be without y. x is a necessary condition for y when: if y is true, then x must also be true. In other words, y can't be without x. If you can't have either without the other, then x and y are both necessary and sufficient for each other.

nomic Means 'having to do with law'. A nomic regularity is distinguished from a mere (accidental) regularity or coincidence, in that the first represents a law of nature. One way this difference is explained is by saying that a nomic regularity supports counterfactuals: it's not only the case that all A's are B's, but it's also the case that if something were an A, it would be a B. (Synonym: nomological.)

norm / normative A norm is a standard. 'Normative' means prescribing a norm. When somebody says, "We think abortion is wrong," that statement may be descriptive—informing you what a group's views are, or normative—morally condemning abortion.

obligation Generally, something one morally must do, a synonym for 'duty'. What one must do is perhaps not all there is to morality. Some good things are supererogatory—above and beyond the call of duty—great if you do them, but nobody would blame you if you didn't.

omni- Many (not all) religious thinkers take God to be omnibenevolent—totally, perfectly good; omnipotent—all-powerful, able to do anything; omnipresent—everywhere at once, or influential in everything; and omniscient—all-knowing.

ontological argument for God's existence A variety of arguments that rely on the concept of God to prove His existence. In the best-known version it is supposed that part of the concept of God is that He is perfect: since something would not be perfect if it did not exist, it follows that God exists.

ontology The philosophical study of existence or being. Typical questions are: What basic sorts of things exist? What are the basic things out of which others are composed, and the basic relations between things?

operational definition Defines by giving an account of the procedures or measurements used to apply the word. For example, one might describe weighing procedures and outcomes to define 'weight'.

operationalism / instrumentalism Operationalism is the view that scientific concepts should have operational definitions, and that any terms not definable in this way should be eliminated from science as meaningless. Instrumentalists are operationalists who are explicitly anti-realists about theoretical entities. They say that electrons, for example, don't really exist; electron-talk is about nothing but what's observable.

ordinary language philosophy A branch of twentieth-century philosophy that held that philosophical problems arose because of confusions about, or complexities in, ordinary language, and might be solved (or dissolved) by attention to the subtleties of actual talk.

overdetermination An event is overdetermined when two or more events have happened, each of which is individually a sufficient condition for it. Thus someone's death is overdetermined when he is given a fatal dose of poison and then shot through the heart.

parallelism Because of the difficulties in interactionism some philosophers were led to the belief that mind and body events don't cause each other, but just run along independently; they are coordinated, however, perhaps inexplicably, or maybe because God sets them up in advance (occasionalism) to run in parallel, like two clocks set in advance to chime the hour simultaneously.

Pascal's wager is Blaise Pascal's famous argument for belief in God: Belief in God might result in infinite benefit—eternal salvation—if He exists, while we risk only a little—wasting some time, and foregoing some pleasures forbidden to believers—if He doesn't. Conversely, disbelief might result in infinite harm—eternal damnation—if He exists, or could provide a tiny benefit if we were right. So even if there isn't any evidence one way or the other, it's a very good bet to believe.

paternalism Paternalistic action provides for what is taken to be someone's good, without giving that person responsibility for determining his/her own aims or actions. It arises from a sort of benevolence plus lack of trust in people's ability to decide what's to their own benefit or to act for their own real long-range good. Some critics of paternalism argue that the only way to determine someone's good is to see what that person chooses. Some argue that respect for individual autonomy means that we shouldn't interfere even when someone is

choosing badly. This issue arises most importantly in political theory and medical ethics, since governments and physicians often act paternalistically.

patriarchy Societal and familial institutions are patriarchal when they systematically embody male dominance over women: when they arrange things so that men hold power and women do not. Feminists emphasize the widespread incidence of patriarchal institutions in historical and contemporary families and societies.

perception In its broadest use, this means any sort of mental awareness, but it's more often used to refer to the awareness we get when using the senses.

person Philosophers sometimes use this word in such a way that persons do not necessarily coincide with living human organisms. The idea here is that a person is anything that has special rights (for example, the right to life, or to self-determination) or special dignity or worth. Sometimes it's held that some humans (e.g., those in a permanent coma) are not persons in this sense, or that some higher animals are.

personal identity 1. What makes you you. Is it your body, your mind, your personality, your memories, or something else? 2. What makes this person now the same person as that one, earlier. Is it a continuing body, or mind, or personality, or that this later stage remembers the experiences that happened to the earlier one?

phenomenalism Phenomenalists believe (on the basis, for example, of the argument from illusion) that all we're ever aware of is appearances or sense-data, the mental events we have when using our senses. Accepting the empiricist rule that we're entitled to believe in only what's given by our senses, they deny the existence of external objects independent of perception. Ordinary "objects" like tables and chairs are thus thought to be collections of these appearances—actual and perhaps possible ones.

phenomena / noumena Philosophers sometimes use 'phenomenon' in the ordinary sense, referring merely to something that happens, but often it's used in a more technical way, referring to a way things seem to us—to something as we perceive it. Noumena are, by contrast, things-in-themselves—things as they really are. These are unavailable to the senses, but perhaps rationally comprehensible; though Kant argued that they are unknowable.

pluralism Pluralist theories argue for a multiplicity of basic kinds. To be a pluralist about value is to believe that there are many incompatible, but equally valid, value systems.

positivism The philosophy associated with Auguste Comte, which holds that scientific knowledge is the only valid kind of knowledge, and that anything else is idle speculation. Sometimes this term is loosely used to refer to logical positivism, which is a twentieth-century outgrowth of more general nineteenth-century positivism.

possible worlds This world—the collection of all facts—is the actual world. The set of possible worlds includes the actual world plus non-actual worlds—ones in which one or more things are not as they actually are, but might have been.

postmodernism Various late twentieth-century movements, in general characterized by a rejection of foundationalism, an interest in textual interpretation and deconstruction, antagonism to analytic philosophy, rejection of the goals of the Enlightenment, tendency to perspectivism, denial of the applicability of the concepts of reality, objectivity, truth.

poststructuralism A postmodern view, thought of as a successor to structuralism. Holds in general that the meaning of words is their relation to other words (in a "text"), not their relation to reality; that human activity is not lawlike, but understood through its relations to power and the unconscious.

pragmatism A largely American school of philosophers who emphasized the relevance of the practical application of things, their connections to our lives, our activities and values, demanding instrumental definitions of philosophically relevant terms, and urged that we

judge beliefs on the basis of their benefit to the believer.

pre-Socratics The ancient Greek philosophers before Socrates, that is, of the sixth and fifth centuries BCE. Their thought is the earliest recorded Western philosophy.

presupposition A necessary condition for the truth of a statement, assumed beforehand by the speaker, but not itself stated. The speaker of 'The present king of France is bald' assumes that there is a present king of France. Because there isn't, the statement is not true, but is it false, or rather inappropriate and lacking a truth value?

prima facie (Latin: "at first appearance") Based on the first impression: what would be true, or seem to be true in general, before we have additional information about a particular case. Prima facie duties are what we're in general obliged to do, but that might not turn out to be obligatory in particular cases. Prima facie evidence can be overridden by contrary considerations.

primary / secondary qualities Locke (and others) argued that some characteristics we perceive are really as perceived in external objects (the primary qualities), whereas others (the secondary qualities) don't exist as perceived in the real world, but are just powers of external objects to produce ideas in us which don't resemble what's out there. Something's dimensions are supposed to be primary, but its color secondary.

privileged access Supposedly a special way you alone can find out about the contents of your mind. Other people need to infer what's in your mind from your external behavior, but you can discover your mental states directly.

problem of evil A problem for religious believers: God is supposed to be all-powerful, benevolent, and all-knowing. Evil is what is bad for us, so God must eliminate all evil. But there clearly is evil. So a God with all of these features does not exist.

problem of induction Everyone believes that the basic regularities we have observed in the past will continue into the future; this principle is called the principle of induction or the principle of the uniformity of nature. Note however that it would be circular to justify this principle by our past experience. How then to justify it?

problem of other minds If only your mind and its contents can be "perceived" directly only by you, this raises the problem of what ground (if any) you have for thinking that anyone else has a mind, and is not, for example, just a body with external appearance and behavior much like yours.

proposition This term has been used in a confusing variety of ways. Sometimes it means merely a sentence or a statement. Perhaps the most common modern use is the one in which a proposition is what is expressed by a (declarative) sentence: an English sentence and its French translation express the same proposition, and so do Seymour is Marvin's father and Marvin's male parent is Seymour.

propositional attitudes These are our mental states which are, so to speak, directed at propositions. For example, toward the proposition It will snow on Christmas, one can have the propositional attitude of wishing (I wish that it would snow on Christmas), believing, fearing, and so on. Compare these with mental states which are not directed at propositions: feeling happy, enjoying an ice cream, remembering Mama.

punishment Must punishment be unpleasant? Then a judicial sentence of not-unpleasant corrective therapy wouldn't be punishment. Must punishment be given in response to a previous bad act? Then a jail sentence given to an innocent person, either by mistake or to set an example for future wrongdoers, wouldn't count as punishment.

A continuing philosophical problem is the attempt to justify the existence of punishment. The deterrence and rehabilitation theories claim punishments are justified when they have good effects: for example, the prevention of future bad acts through the deterrent threat of punishment to others, or the reform of the wrongdoer. Retributivists claim that such uses of punishment are immoral, and that punishment is justified for wrongdoers merely because wrongdoing demands it—because it's justice—or a restoration of the moral order—to inflict punishment on wrongdoers.

pure reason 1. Pure reason is often taken to be reason working on its own, as contrasted with practical reason which connects facts with desires and yields conclusions about what we ought to do. 2. Pure reason is sometimes spoken of in contrast to empirical reason; thus it's a priori reasoning, supposedly independent of what we get from the senses.

qua (Latin: "as") Means considered as (such and such). Usage example: "He is investigating hip hop qua social phenomenon, not qua music."

qualia 1. = characteristics (old-fashioned use). 2. = sense-data. 3. The characteristics of sensations (of sense-data), distinguished from characteristics of things sensed; for example, the flavor of an apple, as tasted, or the feel of a headache. The existence of qualia is sometimes supposed to be a problem for functionalism.

quality / attribute / property These words are synonyms. They each mean a characteristic of something. Some philosophers argue that a thing cannot be composed entirely of qualities; there must be something else, the thing itself, which these are qualities of, in which these qualities are said to "inhere".

rationalism Broadly, any philosophical position which makes reasoning or rationality extra-important. More particularly the view, contrasted with empiricism, that reason alone, unaided by sense experience, is capable of reliable and substantive knowledge; rationalists also tend to believe in innate ideas. Sometimes by "the rationalists" one means the modern continental rationalists, notably Descartes, Leibniz, and Spinoza.

rational self-interest Acting from self-interest is seeking one's own benefit. Some philosophers have sometimes argued that sometimes one can achieve this only by fulfilling some interests of others too; so they argue that rational self-interest often involves more than narrow selfishness.

realism / antirealism Realists hold views (in a variety of philosophical areas) that some sort of entity has external existence, independent of the mind; anti-realists think that that sort of entity is only a product of our thought.

reasons / causes You sometimes have reasons for doing something, but is this to be understood causally? That is, does that mean that there is a special sort of cause for your action? One reason to think that reasons are not causes is that talk about reasons often mentions the future, but a cause of x must occur before x does.

recursive Something (for example, a definition or a function) is recursive when it is to be applied over and over again to its own previous product. For example, one can define 'integer' by saying that 0 is an integer, and if x is an integer, then x + 1 is an integer. Thus, applying the second part of this definition to the first, 1 is an integer, applying the second part to this result, 2 is an integer, and so on.

reduction To reduce some notion is to define (or analyze) it in terms of others, and thus to eliminate it from the list of basic entities in the field under discussion. Reductionism about some notion is the idea that that notion can be reduced—can be given a reductive analysis.

reflective equilibrium A goal sometimes thought to guide the construction of theories. A theory is in reflective equilibrium when the basic general principles of the theory square with the particular facts the theory is supposed to explain. We start with beliefs about particulars, and construct some general principles to explain these. Alterations might then be made in other beliefs about particulars when they conflict with the principles, or in the principles when they conflict with beliefs about particulars.

reification The mistaken way of thinking about some abstract notion as if it were a real thing.

relational / intrinsic properties A property is intrinsic if things have that property in themselves, rather than in relation to other things. Thus being 100 meters tall is an intrinsic property, but being the tallest building in town is a relational property, because this is relative to the heights of other buildings in town.

relativism / absolutism Relativists argue that when certain views vary among individual people and among cultures (cultural relativism) there is no universal truth: there is instead, only "true for me (or us); false for you (or them)". This contrasts with absolutism (sometimes called objectivism): the position that there is an objectively right view. The most common relativist views concern morality (ethical relativism).

Renaissance The period (fourteenth through sixteenth century) characterized by the diminution of the authority of the Church in favor of a new humanism, and the rapid growth of science.

representationalism Theories that hold that mental contents—thoughts, perceptions, etc.—represent reality. If these representations are the only thing directly available to the mind, how do we know that the external world is actually being represented—and what it is really like?

retrocausation "Backward" causation, in which the effect occurs before the cause. The possibility of retrocausation is debatable.

retrodiction Means 'prediction backwards'—"prediction" of the past. A historian might retrodict, for example, on the basis of certain historical documents, that a battle took place centuries ago at a certain location. This retrodiction can be confirmed by present evidence, for example, by artifacts of war dug up at that site.

rights You are said to have a right to do or have something when it is thought that nobody should be allowed to keep you from it. Thus, we can speak of a right to property, or to vote, or to life. Having a right to do something doesn't mean you must or even ought to do it, but merely that you're allowed to do it if you want. Utilitarians might be able to justify according certain rights, but usually rights-theorists insist that a right is independent of utility:

that someone morally can exercise a genuine right even if it is contrary to the general welfare. An inalienable right is a right that one cannot give up or get rid of. A civil right is a right that is (or ought to be) guaranteed and enforced by government. Conventional rights are rights produced or guaranteed by society (by government or agreement, or just by custom). Natural rights, on the other hand, are rights we are supposed to have just because we are human (perhaps because they are God-given).

rigid designator A rigid designator is a term that refers to the same thing in every other possible world in which it exists. It's often thought that proper names are rigid designators, but definite descriptions aren't—they're non-rigid.

self-consciousness In philosophical use, this may mean the sort of knowledge one has of one's self that one gets by adopting the perspective that others might have of one; or else the sort of self-awareness one gets by introspection.

self-contradiction A statement is self-contradictory when it asserts and denies the same thing (It's raining and it's not raining), or when it's logically false. An inconsistent set is self-contradictory. Sometimes (more loosely) a statement that is analytically false is called a self-contradiction.

semantics / syntax / pragmatics These terms name aspects of language and the study of these aspects. Semantics is that part of language which has to do with meaning and reference. Syntax has to do with grammar or logical form. Syntax, then, can tell you whether a sentence is formed correctly (for example, 'Is the on but but' is not formed correctly), but cannot tell you what a correctly formed sentence means, or what conditions would make it true. Pragmatics concerns the relations between bits of language and their uses by language-users.

sense-data The data of the senses—what they give us: the internal event or picture or representation we get when perceiving external objects—or sometimes, as when we dream or hallucinate, even in their absence. A straight stick half under water looks bent; we then have

a bent sense-datum, the same sort of internal picture we would have if we saw a bent stick out of water. The argument from illusion is supposed to show that all we really directly (immediately) perceive are sense-data, and that we only infer external objects from these.

simple / complex ideas A complex idea is one that can be analyzed into simpler ideas. Brother, for example, names a complex idea that is "composed" of the ideas of male and sibling; but green perhaps names a simple idea.

skepticism The view that knowledge in some area is not possible. The Skeptics were a group of (skeptical!) Greek philosophers. Skeptics often don't really doubt the truth of the belief about which they are skeptical: their central claim is that we don't have justification for that belief.

slippery slope A form of moral reasoning in which it is argued that some act or practice is undesirable not because it's bad in itself, but because its acceptance will or might lead to a series of other acts that differ from each other in small ways, and eventuate in something clearly bad. It might be argued, for example, that a city's allowing street vendors on one corner isn't in itself bad, but this might gradually lead to more and more permissiveness, resulting eventually in the clogging of city sidewalks by all sorts of undesirables.

social contract A way of justifying the legitimacy of a ruler or government, or the restrictions imposed by government or by moral rules, on the basis of an agreement (whether explicit or tacit or merely hypothetical) of the people involved. It is supposed that people agree (or would agree) to these restrictions because of the resulting long-range benefits to everyone. This agreement is called a 'social contract'. Thinking about this social contract is usually intended (by contractarians) to provide not an actual history of the origin of these rules, but rather a justification of their existence and of their binding force.

solipsism The position that the self is the only thing that can be known, or, more extremely, that one's own mind is the only thing that exists in the universe. Nobody sane ever believed this latter view, but it is philosophically interesting to try to refute it.

state of nature The condition of human societies—typically but not invariably thought to be unpleasant—before the invention of governmental or conventional rules regulating conduct, typically held to justify such invention.

Stoicism The views of the Stoics, an ancient Greek and Roman school. They held that virtue is the highest good, and stressed control of the passions and indifference to pleasure and pain (thus the ordinary use of 'stoic').

straw man Straw man argument or reasoning (or "setting up a straw man") is a bad form of reasoning in which one argues against some position by producing and refuting a false and stupid version of that position.

structuralism Wide-ranging and controversial largely French twentieth-century philosophical school of thought. Its central idea is that cultural phenomena should be understood as manifesting unchanging and universal abstract structures or forms; their meaning can be understood only when these forms are revealed.

subjective / objective Whether something is objective—a feature of the real external mind-independent world, or subjective—in our minds only—is a perennial and pervasive topic in all areas of philosophy. Examples: ethical subjectivism, for example, holds that our ethical "judgments" reflect our own feelings only, not facts about externals. Aesthetic subjectivism puts beauty (and other aesthetic properties) in the eye of the beholder.

substance Any basic, independently existing entity or subject; the stuff of which things are made. Thought sometimes to be unavailable to our senses, but conceptually necessary as that which "underlies" or "supports" characteristics we can sense, and as that which is responsible for things existing through time despite changes in characteristics. Dualists believe there are two substances: (1) physical (material, corporeal, or extended substance), making up physical things, that to which material qualities (size and shape, weight or mass, etc.) apply; (2) mental (immaterial or incorporeal), what mental or spiritual things are made of, and to which characteristics such as thinking, feeling, desiring apply.

supervenience Things of kind A supervene on things of kind B (the 'supervenience base') when the presence or absence of things of kind A is completely determined by the presence or absence of things of kind B; there can be no difference of sort A without a difference in sort B (though there may be differences in B without differences in A). A clear example is the supervenience of the biological on the microphysical: things have biological properties in virtue of their microphysical properties, and there can be no biological difference without a microphysical difference. It is sometimes thought that ethical properties, and mental properties, supervene on the physical.

tabula rasa (Latin: "blank slate") The term is associated with Locke; he and others opposed to innateness think that at birth our minds have no concepts or beliefs in them—they are "blank slates" that will get things "written" on them only after, and by, sense experience.

teleological argument for God's existence Arguments based on the apparent goal-directedness of things in nature. A common version: Living things are adapted to their environment—they are built in complex and clever ways to function well in their surroundings. This could not have happened merely by the random and mechanical processes of nature. They must have been constructed this way, with their functions in mind, by a creator much more clever and powerful than humans; thus they are evidence for God's existence. The usual reply to this argument is that Darwinian evolutionary theory provides a scientific account of how these things arose merely by the mechanical processes of nature, so one need not posit something unseen and supernatural to account for them.

teleology The study of aims, purposes, or functions. Much ancient philosophical and scientific thought saw teleology as a central principle of things, and a very important basis for explanation. Teleology is much less important in contemporary thought, but philosophers are still interested in what teleology remains (for example, scientific talk about what the pancreas is for, or about the function of individual species in the ecosystem). Teleological ethics sees the aim of actions—good results—as the basic concept, from which the notions of right action and good person can be derived.

theism Belief in the existence of at least one god; often, however, more narrowly monotheism—the belief in just one God. The contrast here is with atheism.

theory Scientists and philosophers do not mean "just a guess" by the word theory. A theory here is a system of interrelated statements designed to explain a variety of phenomena. Sometimes a theory is distinguished from a law or set of laws insofar as a theory postulates the existence of unseen theoretical entities.

thought experiment A state of affairs or story we are asked to imagine to raise a philosophical question, or to illustrate or test some philosophical point. For example, imagine that the brains of two people were interchanged; what you would then say about the location of the two might have implications for the principles of personal identity. (Sometimes encountered in its German translation, *Gedankenexperiment*.)

transcendental The most general philosophical usage of this term applies to any idea or system that goes beyond some supposed limit. The word is most often encountered, however, in connection with transcendental idealism, the name of Kant's system; he produced transcendental arguments that were supposed to show truths beyond the evidence of our senses, as necessary presuppositions of any rational experience or thought.

twin-earth An imaginary planet almost exactly like our Earth, commonly referred to in philosophical thought-experiments. Suppose, for example, that rivers and oceans on twin-earth are filled with XYZ, not H_2O, though the two are (except by chemists) indistinguishable. Then when on twin-earth Twin-John asks for "water" in his scotch, does this mean the same as in English?

type / token Two different things that are both of a certain sort are said to be two tokens of one type. Thus, in the sentence 'The cat is on the mat' there are six word tokens, but only five word types. Token physicalism is the view that each particular mental event is identical with (the same thing as) a particular physical event (e.g., a brain event). Type physicalism (sometimes known as the type-type identity theory) adds that each kind of mental event is also a kind of physical event. Functionalists tend to be token physicalists but not type physicalists. Identity theorists tend to be type physicalists. Anomalous monism admits token identity, but denies type identity.

underdetermination Something is underdetermined by a set of conditions if these conditions don't determine how (or that) it will exist. Thus, the striking of a match underdetermines its lighting because it's not sufficient. Language behavior underdetermines a translation manual when different equally adequate translation manuals can be constructed for that behavior. Scientific theory is underdetermined by empirical evidence when two rival hypotheses are both consistent with all the evidence.

universalizability True of a particular action when it can be universalized—that is, when the rule behind it can consistently or reasonably be conceived of as a universal law (one that could apply to everyone). The test of consistent rational universalizability is roughly what Kant thought to be the test of ethically right action. The test of practical universalizability (not Kant's test) is perhaps what we apply when we think morally about some action by evaluating the consequences if everyone were to do that sort of thing.

universals These are "abstract" things—beauty, courage, redness, etc. The problem of universals is whether these exist in the external world. Thus, one may be a realist or anti-realist about universals. Plato's theory of forms is an early and well-known realism about universals; the empiricists are associated with anti-realism. Nominalism is a variety of anti-realism that claims that only particulars exist, and that such abstractions are merely the result of the way we talk.

utilitarianism Utilitarians think that the moral worth of any action can be measured by the extent to which it provides valued results—usually pleasure or happiness—to the greatest number of people. Thus, their general moral principle is the principle of utility, also known as the 'greatest happiness principle': "Act so as to produce the greatest happiness for the greatest number of people." Act utilitarians hold that moral thinking evaluates each act, in context, separately; rule utilitarians argue that morality is concerned with general rules for action, and that a particular action is right if it is permitted or recommended by a moral code whose acceptance in the agent's society would maximize utility, even if that act in particular does not.

utility In utilitarianism, this means the quantity of value or desirability something has. Often it is thought that the utility of something can be given a number (the quantity of "utiles" it possesses), and utilities can be compared or added.

vacuous Means 'empty'. In logic, the statement All A's are B's is understood to be equivalent to For all x, if x is an A then x is a B. Suppose there aren't any A's at all. Then it's always false that any x is an A: but this makes the conditional, if x is an A then x is a B true. It follows, then, that if there aren't any A's, all statements of the form All A's are B's are true. So, for example, because there aren't any unicorns, the statement All unicorns are mammals is true, and so is All unicorns are non-mammals. This strange kind of truth is called vacuous truth.

vagueness In a technical logician's sense, a term is vague whose application involves borderline cases: thus, 'tall' is vague, because there are some people who are clearly tall, some clearly not tall, and some who are in a borderline area, and are not clearly tall or not tall.

verifiability A statement is verifiable when there exist (at least in principle) procedures that would show that it is true or false. 'In principle' is added here because there do not need to be procedures actually available now or ever, as long as we can imagine what they are. So, for example, the statement There is a planet on a star seven million light years from here is unverifiable given our current (and perhaps future) technology, but because we can imagine what would be evidence for its truth or falsity, it is verifiable in principle.

virtue Moral excellence or uprightness; the state of character of a morally worthwhile person. The virtues are those character traits that make for a good person. Some philosophers think that virtue, not good states of affairs or right action, is the central notion in ethics: thus virtue ethics.

zombies These are, of course, the walking dead of horror movies, starring also in the problem of absent qualia which haunts functionalism. In this thought experiment, we are to imagine that zombies show normal stimulus-response connections, but no qualia—no consciousness. The functionalist would have to grant them mentality; this is supposed to show what's wrong with functionalism.

IMAGE CREDITS

Line drawing portraits by Rose McNeil:

A.J. Ayer
Carl Hempel
Thomas Kuhn
J.L. Mackie
Karl Popper
Gilbert Ryle

Author images contributed by their respective authors:

David Chalmers
Lorraine Code
Edmund Gettier
Frank Jackson
Thomas Nagel
Hilary Putnam

ACKNOWLEDGMENTS

The publisher has made every attempt to locate the authors of the copyrighted material or their heirs and assigns, and would be grateful for information that would allow correction of any errors or omissions in subsequent editions of the work.

Anselm of Canterbury, St. From *Anselm of Canterbury: The Major Works*, translated by M.J. Charlesworth and edited by Brian Davies and G.R. Evans, (Oxford World's Classics, 1998). Reprinted with the permission of Oxford University Press.

Aquinas, St. Thomas. "Summa Theologiae," Part I, Question 2: "The Existence of God (in Three Articles)," from *Basic Writings of Saint Thomas Aquinas*, Volume I, translated by Anton C. Pegis. Copyright © 1945 by Random House, Inc.; renewed 1973. Reprinted 1997 by Hackett Publishing Company, Inc. Reprinted by permission of Hackett Publishing Company, Inc. All rights reserved.

Ayer, A.J. "Freedom and Necessity," from *Philosophical Essays*, published 1963. Copyright © 1954, Macmillan and Company Ltd. Reprinted with the permission of Palgrave Macmillan.

Berkeley, George. *Three Dialogues Between Hylas and Philonous*, 3rd ed. (revised), 1734.

Campbell, C.A. From Chapter IX, "Has the Self Free Will?" from *On Selfhood and Godhood*. London: HarperCollins Publishers Ltd., pp. 158-179. Originally published by George Allen & Unwin, 1957. Copyright © C.A. Campbell, 1957. Reproduced by permission of Taylor & Francis.

Chalmers, David. "The Puzzle of Conscious Experience," in *Scientific American*, December 1995. Reprinted with the permission of David Chalmers.

Code, Lorraine. "Is the Sex of the Knower Epistemologically Significant?" from *What Can She Know? Feminist Theory and the Construction of Knowledge.*

Copyright © 1991 by Cornell University. Used by permission of the publisher, Cornell University Press.

Descartes, René. Excerpt from *Meditations on First Philosophy*, 1641. Translated by Ian Johnston.

Gettier, Edmund. "Is Justified True Belief Knowledge?" in *Analysis* 23 (June 1963): 121-123. Reprinted with the permission of Oxford University Press, via Copyright Clearance Center.

Hempel, Carl G. "Scientific Inquiry: Invention and Test," from *Philosophy of Natural Science*, 1st ed., © 1967. Reprinted by permission of Pearson Education, Inc., Upper Saddle River, NJ.

Hume, David. *Dialogues Concerning Natural Religion.* 1779.

Hume, David. *Enquiry Concerning Human Understanding.* 1748; 1777.

Jackson, Frank. "Epiphenomenal Qualia," in *Philosophical Quarterly* 32 (1982): 127-130 and 133-136, copyright © 1982. Reproduced with the permission of Blackwell Publishing Ltd.

Jackson, Frank. "What Mary Didn't Know," in *Journal of Philosophy* 83 (May 1986): 291-295. Reprinted by permission of the *Journal of Philosophy* and Frank Jackson.

James, William. "The Will to Believe." From *The Will to Believe, and Other Essays in Popular Philosophy.* Longmans, Green & Co., 1897, pp. 1-31.

Kant, Immanuel. Introduction from *The Critique of Pure Reason*, translated by Norman Kemp Smith;

published 1991. Copyright © 1929, Macmillan and Company Ltd. Reprinted with the permission of Palgrave Macmillan.

Kuhn, Thomas. "Objectivity, Value Judgment and Theory Choice," from *The Essential Tension: Selected Studies in Scientific Tradition and Change.* Copyright © 1977 by the University of Chicago. Reprinted with the permission of the University of Chicago Press.

Leibniz, Gottfried. "Theodicy: Abridgement of the Argument Reduced to Syllogistic Form," from *The Philosophical Works of Leibnitz,* translated by George M. Duncan. Tuttle, Morehouse & Taylor, 1890.

Locke, John. *An Essay Concerning Human Understanding* was first published in 1690. The excerpts given here are from the 6th ed. of 1710.

Longino, Helen. "Can There Be a Feminist Science?" in *Hypatia* Volume 2, Issue 3 (1987): 51-64. Reprinted with the permission of *Hypatia,* via Copyright Clearance Center.

Mackie, J.L. "Evil and Omnipotence," in *Mind* Volume 64, Issue 254 (April 1955): 200-212. Reprinted with the permission of Oxford University Press via Copyright Clearance Center.

Nagel, Thomas. "What Is It Like to Be a Bat?" in *The Philosophical Review,* Volume 83, Issue 4 (October 1974): 435-450. Published by Duke University Press.

Popper, Karl. "Science: Conjectures and Refutations," from *Conjectures and Refutations: The Growth of Scientific Knowledge,* 5th ed., Routledge 1989. Copyright © University of Klagenfurt, Karl Popper Library. Reprinted by permission of the University of Klagenfurt, Karl Popper Library.

Putnam, Hilary. "The Nature of Mental States," originally published as "Psychological Predicates" by Hilary Putnam, in *Art, Mind, and Religion,* edited by W.H. Capitan and D.D. Merrill, copyright © 1967. Reprinted by permission of the University of Pittsburgh Press.

Rée, Paul. "Determinism and the Illusion of Moral Responsibility," from *The Illusion of Free Will/Die Illusion der Willensfreiheit,* Berlin, 1885. Translated by Stefan Bauer-Mengelberg; edited by Paul Edwards and Arthur Pap, 1973. Reprinted with the kind permission of Dr. Tim Madigan, Literary Executor to Paul Edwards.

Russell, Bertrand. Chapters 1-3 of *The Problems of Philosophy.* The Home University Library Series, Williams and Norgate, 1912. Reprinted with the permission of Oxford University Press.

Ryle, Gilbert. "Descartes' Myth," from *The Concept of Mind,* copyright © 1984, London: Routledge and Chicago: The University of Chicago Press. Reproduced by permission of Taylor and Francis, and with permission of the Principal, Fellows, and Scholars of Hertford College in the University of Oxford.

Searle, John R. "Minds, Brains, and Programs," in *Behavioral and Brain Sciences,* Volume 3, Issue 3 (September 1980): 417-424. Reprinted with the permission of Cambridge University Press via Copyright Clearance Center.

Williams, B.A.O. and Thomas Nagel. "Moral Luck," in *Proceedings of the Aristotelian Society,* Supplementary Volumes. Volume 50, 1976; pp. 115-135 and pp. 137-151. Reprinted by courtesy of the Editor of the Aristotelian Society: © 1976.

SOURCES FOR QUOTATIONS

CHAPTER 1

Plato, *Apology*. In Plato *Complete Works*, ed. John M. Cooper (Indianapolis: Hackett, 1997) this quote appears on page 33.

Immanuel Kant, "An Answer to the Question: What Is Enlightenment?" In Kant, *Practical Philosophy*, ed. Mary J. Gregor (Cambridge: Cambridge University Press, 1996) this quote appears on page 17.

Bertrand Russell, *The Problems of Philosophy* (Oxford: Oxford University Press, 1912), 93–94.

CHAPTER 2

Descartes

René Descartes, *Discourse on the Method*, Part 1. In *The Philosophical Writings of Descartes*, ed. Cottingham, Stoothoff and Murdoch (Cambridge: Cambridge University Press, 1985) the quote is in Volume I, page 115.

René Descartes, *Rules for the Direction of the Mind*, Rule Four. In *The Philosophical Writings of Descartes*, *ibid.*, the quote is in Volume I, page 19.

René Descartes, *Principles of Philosophy*, Part 64. In *The Philosophical Writings of Descartes*, *ibid.*, the quote is in Volume I, page 247.

René Descartes, *Principles of Philosophy*, Part 51. In *The Philosophical Writings of Descartes*, *ibid.*, the quote is in Volume I, page 210.

Bernard Williams, "Introduction" to Descartes's *Meditations on First Philosophy*, trans. John Cottingham (Cambridge: Cambridge University Press, 1996), vii.

John Cottingham, *The Cambridge Companion to Descartes*, ed. John Cottingham (Cambridge: Cambridge University Press, 1992), 1.

David Hume, *An Enquiry Concerning Human Understanding*, ed. Selby-Bigge and Nidditch (Oxford: Clarendon Press, 1975), 153.

Elizabeth Anscombe, "The First Person," in S. Guttenplan (ed.) *Mind and Language: Wolfson College Lectures 1974* (Oxford: Oxford University Press, 1975), 45–65.

Locke

P.H. Nidditch, "Introduction" to *An Essay Concerning Human Understanding* (Oxford: Oxford University Press, 1975), vii.

Kant

Immanuel Kant, *Critique of Practical Reason*, ed. Mary Gregor (Cambridge: Cambridge University Press, 1997), 133.

Immanuel Kant, *Critique of Pure Reason*, ed. Norman Kemp Smith (New York: Palgrave, 192), 24–25.

Russell

Bertrand Russell, *Autobiography* (London: George Allen & Unwin, 1967), Volume I, 145.

CHAPTER 3

Hume

Bertrand Russell, "The Metaphysician's Nightmare" in *Nightmares of Eminent Persons* (London: Simon & Schuster, 1955).

Hempel

Richard Jeffrey, "Preface," to Hempel's *Selected Philosophical Essays*, ed. Jeffrey (Cambridge: Cambridge University Press, 2000), ix.

Popper

Peter Medawar, BBC Radio 3, 28 July 1972.

John Eccles, *Facing Reality* (New York: Springer-Verlag, 1970).

CHAPTER 4

Anselm

Max Charlesworth, "Introduction" to *St. Anselm's Proslogion* (Oxford: Clarendon Press, 1965), 17.

Eadmer, *The Life of St. Anselm*, ed. R.W. Southern (Oxford: Clarendon Press, 1962), 142.

Hume

David Hume, "The Life of David Hume, Esq. Written by Himself," reprinted in *The Cambridge Companion to Hume*, ed. David Fate Norton (Cambridge: Cambridge University Press, 1993), 351, 352, 356.

David Hume, *An Enquiry Concerning Human Understanding*, ed. Selby-Bigge and Nidditch (Oxford: Clarendon Press, 1975), 165.

David Hume, letter of 8th June 1776, which can be found in *The Letters of David Hume*, ed. J.Y.T. Greig (Oxford: Clarendon Press, 1935).

Leibniz

Gottfried Leibniz, letter to Remond of 10th January 1714, which can be found in *Die philosophischen Schriften von Gottfried Wilhelm Leibniz*, ed. C.I. Gerhardt (Berlin), Volume III, 60.

Gottfried Leibniz, letter to Bourget of 22nd March 1714, which can be found in *Die philosophischen Schriften von Gottfried Wilhelm Leibniz*, ed. C.I. Gerhardt (Berlin), Volume III, 567.

Gottfried Leibniz, *Reflections on the Advancement of True Metaphysics and Particularly on the Nature of Substance Explained by Force* (1694), section 4.

James

William James, "Diary" for April 30th, 1870, in *The Letters of William James*, ed. Henry James, Jr. (Boston: Atlantic Monthly Press, 1920), Volume I, 147–148.

William James, *The Varieties of Religious Experience* (1902), Lectures VI and VII. In *William James, The Essential Writings*, ed. Bruce Wilshire (Albany: State University of New York Press, 1984) the quote is on page 232.

William James, *Pragmatism*. In the Harvard edition (Cambridge, MA: Harvard University Press, 1975) the quote is on page 29.

CHAPTER 5

Nagel

Thomas Nagel, *The View from Nowhere* (Oxford: Oxford University Press, 1986), 3.

CHAPTER 6

Rée

Walter Kaufmann, *Nietzsche: Philosopher, Psychologist, Antichrist* (Princeton: Princeton University Press, 1978), 48.

Campbell

H.D. Lewis, "Obituary of C.A. Campbell," *The (London) Times* March 19, 1974.

from the publisher

A name never says it all, but the word "broadview" expresses a good deal of the philosophy behind our company. We are open to a broad range of academic approaches and political viewpoints. We pay attention to the broad impact book publishing and book printing has in the wider world; we began using recycled stock more than a decade ago, and for some years now we have used 100% recycled paper for most titles. As a Canadian-based company we naturally publish a number of titles with a Canadian emphasis, but our publishing program overall is internationally oriented and broad-ranging. Our individual titles often appeal to a broad readership too; many are of interest as much to general readers as to academics and students.

Founded in 1985, Broadview remains a fully independent company owned by its shareholders—not an imprint or subsidiary of a larger multinational.

If you would like to find out more about Broadview and about the books we publish, please visit us at **www.broadviewpress.com**. And if you'd like to place an order through the site, we'd like to show our appreciation by extending a special discount to you: by entering the code below you will receive a 20% discount on purchases made through the Broadview website.

Discount code: **broadview20%**

Thank you for choosing Broadview.

Please note: this offer applies only to sales of
bound books within the United States or Canada.

LIST
of products used:

1,819 lb(s) of Rolland Opaque50
50% post-consumer

RESULTS
Based on the Cascades products you selected
compared to products in the industry made with
100% virgin fiber, your savings are:

 8 trees

 6,308 gal. US of water
68 days of water consumption

 1,597 lbs of waste
15 waste containers

 4,890 lbs CO2
9,272 miles driven

 24 MMBTU
117,277 60W light bulbs for one
hour

 15 lbs NOX
emissions of one truck during 21
days